44th Edition

Warman's®

Antiques & Collectibles
2011 Price Guide

Mark F. Moran

Published by

700 East State Street • Iola, WI 54990-0001
715-445-2214 • 888-457-2873
www.krausebooks.com

Our toll-free number to place an order or obtain
a free catalog is (800) 258-0929.

ISSN 1076-1985

ISBN-13: 978-1-4402-0408-1

ISBN-10: 1-4402-0408-X

Designed by Wendy Wendt

Edited by Mark F. Moran

Printed in China

ON THE COVER, CLOCKWISE FROM UPPER LEFT:

Johann Frankenberger (Austrian, 1807-1874), Portrait of Beauty Cutting Grapes, 1846, oil on canvas, signed lower left, 39 1/2" x 32". $5,000 — Photo courtesy Quinn's Auction Galleries, Falls Church, Va.; *www.QuinnsAuction.com*

Tiffany Studios Footed Candy Dish. With applied gold iridescent border on opaque blue body and foot. Scratched in "59" on the underside. 6" diameter. Multiple chips to foot rim, some scratches on interior. $60 — Photo courtesy James D. Julia Auctioneers, Fairfield, Maine; *www.JuliaAuctions.com*

Gilbert Rohde, mirrored glass and chrome-plated metal table clock, model no. 4708, manufactured by Herman Miller Modern Electric Clocks, circa 1939. 6 3/8" x 6 1/8" x 3". $1,000+ — Photo courtesy Heritage Auction Galleries, Dallas; *www.HA.com*

Carette, circa 1911, clockwork hand-painted tin luxury limo has beveled glass windows, nickel lamps, fully opening doors, embossed upholstered seating, roof rack and full running boards, 16" long. $39,100 — Photo courtesy Bertoia Auctions, Vineland, N.J.; *www.BertoiaAuctions.com*

Contents

WARMAN'S IDENTIFICATION AND PRICE GUIDES

American & European Art Pottery Guide
Carnival Glass
Children's Books
Civil War Collectibles
Civil War Weapons
Coca-Cola® Collectibles
Coins and Paper Money
Cookie Jars
Costume Jewelry Figurals
Depression Glass
Dolls: Antique to Modern
Duck Decoys
English & Continental Pottery & Porcelain
Fenton Glass
Fiesta
Flea Market Price Guide
Gas Station Collectibles
Hull Pottery
Jewelry
John Deere Collectibles
Little Golden Books®
Majolica
McCoy Pottery
Modernism Furniture and Accessories
North American Indian Artifacts
Political Collectibles
Red Wing Pottery
Rookwood Pottery
Roseville Pottery
Sporting Collectibles
Sterling Silver Flatware
Vietnam War Collectibles
Vintage Jewelry
Vintage Quilts
Weller Pottery
World War II Collectibles

WARMAN'S COMPANIONS

Carnival Glass
Collectible Dolls
Collectible Fishing Lures
Depression Glass
Fenton Glass
Fiesta
Hallmark Keepsake Ornaments
Hot Wheels
McCoy Pottery
PEZ®
Roseville Pottery
U.S. Coins & Currency
Watches
World Coins & Currency

WARMAN'S FIELD GUIDES

Action Figures
Antique Jewelry
Barbie Doll
Bean Plush
Bottles
Buttons
Coca-Cola®
Depression Glass
Disney Collectibles
Dolls
Farm Toys
Precious Moments®
Fishing Lures
G.I. Joe
Hot Wheels
Kitschy Kitchen Collectibles
Lionel Train 1945-1969
Lunch Boxes
Matchbox
Pepsi
Star Wars
Tools
Transformers
U.S. Coins & Currency
U.S. Stamps
Vintage Guitars
Watches
Zippo Lighters

Introduction

WELCOME TO THE NEW WARMAN'S GUIDE FOR 2011

The 44th edition of Warman's Antiques & Collectibles Price Guide is better than ever, and continues our efforts to bring a fresh, 21st-century perspective to the collecting world.

Our list of auction houses features more than 70 businesses from coast to coast, covering hundreds of collecting categories. The number of consulting experts in various fields has also grown, and we have included new sections on both established and emerging collecting areas.

An important returning feature is a focus on the "Future of the Markets," advising collectors on the best places to invest:

Author Kathy Flood charts the future of jewelry categories. By her own admission, Flood "is a journalist who fell in love with jewelry while having her hair cut, when the salon's latest Vogue fell open on her lap to a page of Christmas tree brooches by Bulgari, Cartier and Mme. Belperron. Since then, her interests in jewelry have branched out: She collects more widely, owns several Internet jewelry shops and has written about bijoux for newspapers and magazines across the country." She is the author of *Warman's Costume Jewelry Figurals* and is at work on the fourth edition of *Warman's Jewelry,* whose editor she blames for her increasingly upmarket taste in gems.

Kathy Flood

Catherine Saunders-Watson

Catherine Saunders-Watson writes of the outlook for the antique-toy market, and interviews auctioneer Dan Morphy on the topic of mechanical banks. Saunders-Watson is president and CEO of The Saunders-Watson Group, a boutique public relations firm specializing in the antiques, auction and fine-art sector. Her 25 year background in antiques and fine art has included serving as co-publisher of *Style Century Magazine,* editor of *Antique Trader,* national editor of *AntiqueWeek,* and as antiques columnist with the Times of London Group newspapers. In her latest venture in electronic media, she serves as editor-in-chief of *AuctionCentralNews.com* and *ToyCollectorMagazine.com.*

Dan Morphy

Our section on vintage clothing and couture has been expanded, and features prices realized and images from Leslie Hindman Auctioneers of Chicago, plus an overview of the market by Caroline Ashleigh, owner of Birmingham, Mich.-based Caroline Ashleigh Associates LLC. Ashleigh has also contributed to our section on western memorabilia. She is a graduate of New York University in Appraisal Studies in Fine and Decorative Arts and is a board-certified senior member of the Appraisers Association of America. Ashleigh is an internationally known appraiser and regularly appears on the PBS program *Antiques Roadshow.* Caroline Ashleigh Associates conducts fully catalogued online auctions. Visit *www.appraiseyourart.com or www.auctionyourart.com.*

Caroline Ashleigh

In our last edition, Noah Fleisher, media and public relations liaison for Heritage Auction Galleries in Dallas and former editor of Antique Trader magazine, helped us to create a section on Modernism. He's back again with chapters on space memorabilia and illustrator art. Fleisher has also written extensively for New England Antiques Journal, Northeast Journal of Antiques and Art and all their online components in the recent years.

Noah Fleisher

Eli Wilner, assisted by his gallery director, Suzanne Smeaton, guides readers through the intricacies of antique framing. Wilner is the founder and CEO of Eli Wilner & Co., a New York City art gallery that specializes in American and European frames from the 17th through mid-20th Century. He is a leading frame dealer, restorer and collector, as well as an acknowledged and published authority on the art of framing. His book, *Antique American Frames: Identification and Price Guide,* written with Mervyn Kaufman, was first published by Avon in 1995.

Eli Wilner

Brent Frankenhoff provided great new insights on comic books. Frankenhoff is the editor of *Comics Buyer's Guide.* He has collected comics for 40 years and has built a collection that spans more than seven decades.

We have expanded our chapter on the creations of Tiffany, which includes an introduction written by Reyne Haines, a specialist in 20th-century decorative arts. Haines, owner of Reyne Gallery in Cincinnati, is a regular appraiser on PBS' *Antiques Roadshow.* She is the author of *The Art of Glass: The Collection from the Dayton Art Institute* and has contributed to numerous books and articles on collecting. Haines is also the co-owner and founder of *www.JustGlass.com.* Her current project is the book, *Fine Vintage Watches,* for Krause Publications.

Brent Frankenhoff

You will find hundreds of new, detailed color photos in the 44th edition of Warman's, and expanded information with each image, as well. Every new photo caption will include not only the name of the contributing auction house, but also its location and its Web address.

The Warman's Advantage

The Warman's Advantage manifests itself in several important ways in the 2011 edition. As we reviewed past volumes, we wanted to make this book as easy to use as possible. To that end, we've consolidated and reorganized how we present several key categories. Our new mantra is, "What is it first?"

For instance, an antique clock may also have an advertising component, an ethnic element (like black memorabilia), reflect a specific design theme (like Art Deco) and be made of cast iron. But first and foremost, it's a clock, and that's where you'll find it listed, even though there are other collecting areas involved.

There are a few categories that remain iconic in the collecting world. Coca-Cola collectibles cross many interests, as do folk art, Oriental antiques and Tiffany designs, to name just a few. These still have their own broad sections.

In addition to space memorabilia and western/cowboy collectibles, newly expanded sections include jewelry, tribal arts, lighting, Tiffany, photography and art glass. We are also continuing to highlight sections on paperback books, salt- and peppershakers, and objects associated with the Vietnam War.

Prices

The prices in this book have been established using the results of auction sales all across the country, and by tapping the resources of knowledgeable dealers and collectors. These values reflect not only current collector trends, but also the wider economy. The adage that "an antique (or collectible) is worth what someone will pay for it" still holds. A price guide measures value, but it also captures a moment in time, and sometimes that moment can pass very quickly.

Beginners should follow the same advice that all seasoned collectors have learned: Make mistakes and learn from them; talk with other collectors and dealers; find reputable resources (including books and Web sites), and learn to invest wisely, buying the best examples you can afford.

Words of Thanks

This 44th edition of the Warman's guide is the best we've ever published. Dozens of auction houses have generously shared their resources, but a few deserve special recognition: Andrew Truman, assisted by Lisa Oakes and Lisa Warren, at James D. Julia Auctioneers, Fairfield, Maine; Anthony Barnes at Rago Arts and Auction Center, Lambertville, N.J.; Anne Trodella at Skinner Inc., Boston; Heritage Auction Galleries, Dallas; Morphy Auctions, Denver, Pa.; Bertoia Auctions, Vineland, N.J.; and Abigail Rutherford at Leslie Hindman Auctioneers, Chicago.

Read All About It

There are many fine publications that collectors and dealers may consult about antiques and collectibles in general. Space does not permit listing all of the national and regional publications in the antiques and collectibles field; this is a sampling:

- *Antique Trader*, published by Krause Publications, 700 E. State St., Iola, WI, 54990 – *www.antiquetrader.com*
- *Antique & The Arts Weekly*, 5 Church Hill Road, Newton, CT 06470 – *www.antiquesandthearts.com*
- *AntiqueWeek*, P.O. Box 90, Knightstown, IN 46148 – *www.antiqueweek.com*
- *Maine Antique Digest*, P.O. Box 358, Waldoboro, ME 04572 – *www.maineantiquedigest.com*
- *New England Antiques Journal*, 24 Water St., Palmer, MA 01069 – *www.antiquesjournal.com*
- *The Journal of Antiques and Collectibles*, P.O. Box 950, Sturbridge, MA 01566 – *www.journalofantiques.com*
- *Southeastern Antiquing & Collecting* magazine, P.O. Box 510, Acworth, GA 30101 – *www.go-star.com/antiquing*

Let us know what you think

We're always eager to hear what you think about this book and how we can improve it. Contact:

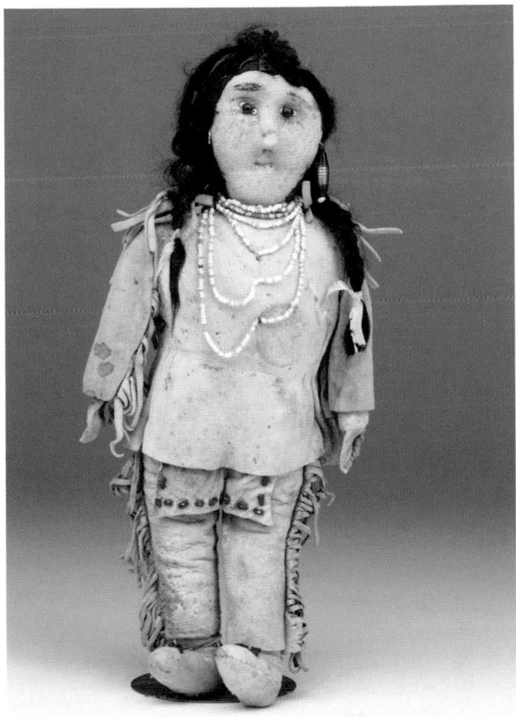

Photo courtesy Rago Arts and Auction Center, Lambertville, N.J.; www.RagoArts.com

Sioux Doll, Midwest: Cloth body with pressed and stitched leather face accented with glass bead eyes, earrings and necklace and attached human hair, clothed in elk hide garments, late 19th - early 20th century. Fair condition overall with light stains and lost to hair. 12". **$600**

Mark F. Moran
Senior Editor, Antiques & Collectibles Books
Krause Publications
700 E. State St.
Iola, WI 54990-0001
715-445-2214, Ext. 13461
Mark.Moran@fwmedia.com

Visit an antique show

One of the best ways to really enjoy the world of antiques and collectibles is to take the time to really explore an antiques show. Some areas, like Manchester, N.H., turn into antique meccas for a few days each summer when dealers and collectors come for both specialized and general antiques shows, plus auctions.

Here are a few of our favorites:

Brimfield, Mass., shows, held three times a year in May, July and September, *www.brimfield.com.*

Photo courtesy Heritage Auction Galleries, Dallas; www.HA.com

U.S. Flag Carried on the Moon by Neil Armstrong, affixed to a 12" x 14" wooden shield plaque, flag is 6" x 3 3/4" and an Apollo 11 patch, covered in clear plastic. The 5" x 3" metallic plaque affixed certifies that "This flag was carried on the moon by/ astronaut Neil Armstrong/ on July 20, 1969/ and presented to/ Joe D. Garino Jr./ by/ The Apollo 11 Astronauts." As Armstrong set foot on the lunar surface, he carried this flag. Accompanied by a signed certificate of authentication from Garino verifying its provenance. **$56,763**

Round Top, Texas, antique shows, held spring and fall, *www.roundtop.com/antique1.htm*

Antiques Week in and around Manchester, N.H., held every August.

Palmer/Wirfs Antique & Collectible Shows, including the Portland, Ore., Expos, *www.palmer-wirfs.com*

The Original Miami Beach Antique Show, *www.dmgantiqueshows.com*

Merchandise Mart International Antiques Fair, Chicago, *www.merchandisemart.com/chicagoantiques*

High Noon Western Americana Show & Auction, Phoenix, *www.highnoon.com*

Ask an expert

Many contributors have proved invaluable in sharing their expertise during the compilation of the 44th edition of the Warman's guide. For more information on their collecting specialties, call or visit their Web sites.

Caroline Ashleigh
Caroline Ashleigh Associates LLC
1000 S. Old Woodward, Suite 105
Birmingham, MI 48009-6734
248-792-2929
www.auctionyourart.com
Vintage Clothing, Couture and Accessories, Textiles, Western Wear

Al Bagdade
The Country Peasants
1325 N. State Parkway, Apt 15A
Chicago, IL 60610
312-397-1321
Quimper

Dudley Browne
James D. Julia, Inc.
P.O. Box 830
Fairfield, ME 04937
207-453-7125
www.juliaauctions.net
E-mail: dbrowne@jamesdjulia.com
Glass & Lamps

Tim Chambers
Missouri Plain Folk
501 Hunter Ave
Sikeston, MO 63801-2115
573-471-6949
E-mail: plainfolk@charter.net
Folk Art

Wes Dillon and Bill Taylor
James D. Julia, Inc.
P.O. Box 830
Fairfield, ME 04937
207-453-7125
www.juliaauctions.net
E-mail: wdillon@jamesdjulia.com
btaylor@jamesdjulia.com
Firearms

Noah Fleisher
E-mail: noah.fleisher@yahoo.com
Modernism

Bill Gage
James D. Julia, Inc.
P.O. Box 830
Fairfield, ME 04937
207-453-7125
www.juliaauctions.net

E-mail: antiques@jamesdjulia.com
Antiques & Fine Art

Reyne Haines
Reyne Gallery
17 E. Eighth St.
Cincinnati, OH 45202
513-504-8159
www.reyne.com
E-mail: reyne@reyne.com
Tiffany, 20th Century Decorative Arts

Ted Hake
Hake's Americana & Collectibles Auctions
P.O. Box 1444
York, PA 17405
717-848-1333
E-mail: auction@hakes.com
Disneyana, Political

Mark B. Ledenbach
P.O. Box 2421
Orangevale, CA 95662
www.HalloweenCollector.com
Halloween Items

Mary P. Manion
Landmarks Gallery & Restoration Studio
231 N. 76th St.
Milwaukee, WI 53213
800-352-8892
www.landmarksgallery.com
Fine Art & Restoration

Mark F. Moran
Senior Editor, Antiques & Collectibles Books
Krause Publications
700 E. State St.
Iola, WI 54990-0001
715-445-2214, Ext. 13461
Mark.Moran@fwmedia.com
Folk Art, Fine Art, Americana

Suzanne Perrault
Perrault Rago Gallery
333 N. Main St.
Lambertville, NJ 08530
609-397-1802
www.ragoarts.com
E-mail: suzanne@ragoarts.com
Ceramics

David Rago
Rago Arts and Auction Center
333 N. Main St.
Lambertville, NJ 08530
609-397-9374
www.ragoarts.com
Art Pottery, Arts & Crafts

Dennis Raleigh Antiques & Folk Art
P.O. Box 745
Wiscasset, ME 04578
207-882-7821
3327 Cones Ct.
Midland, MI 48640
989-631-2603
www.dennisraleighantiques.com
E-mail: dgraleigh@verizon.net
Decoys, Silhouettes, Portrait Miniatures

Henry A. Taron
Tradewinds Antiques
P.O. Box 249
Manchester-By-The-Sea, MA 01944-0249
(978) 526-4085
www.tradewindsantiques.com
Canes

Photo courtesy Mosby & Co. Auction, Frederick, Md.; www.mosbyauctions.com

Large 9" prewar Japanese celluloid Betty Boop with fur stole. **$2,805**

Photo courtesy Leslie Hindman Auctioneers, Chicago; www.LeslieHindman.com

Ring, 18k yellow gold, lapis lazuli and green enamel, David Webb, the fluted design decorated with green enamel with a carved lapis lazuli frog set on top. Stamp: DAVID WEBB 18K. 15.10 dwts. **$2,928**

Andrew Truman
James D. Julia, Inc.
P.O. Box 830
Fairfield, ME 04937
207-453-7125
www.juliaauctions.net
E-mail: atruman@jamesdjulia.com
Toys, Dolls & Advertising

Auction Houses

A&S Antique Auction Co.
900 East Loop 340
Waco, TX 76716
254-799-6044
www.asauctions.com
Full service, western memorabilia, firearms

Sanford Alderfer Auction & Appraisal
501 Fairgrounds Road
Hatfield, PA 19440
215-393-3000
www.alderferauction.com
Full service

All Out Auctions & Delivery Inc.
5015 Babcock St.
Palm Bay, Fl 32905.
321-984-8484
www.alloutauctions.com
Full service

American Bottle Auctions
2523 J St. Suite 203
Sacramento, CA 95816
800-806-7722
www.americanbottle.com
Antique bottles, jars

American Pottery Auction
Waasdorp Inc.
P. O. Box 434
Clarence, NY 14031
716-759-2361
www.antiques-stoneware.com
Stoneware, redware

American Sampler
P.O. 371
Barnesville, Md. 20838
301-972-6250
www.castirononline
Cast-iron bookends, doorstops

Americana Auctions
Glen Rairigh
P.O. Box 337
Sunfield, MI 48890
800-919-1950
www.americanaauctions.com
Full service

Antiques and Estate Auctioneers
44777 St. Route 18 E.
Wellington, OH 44090
440-647-4007
Fax: 440-647-4006
www.estateauctioneers.com
Full service

Auctions Neapolitan
1100 First Ave. S.
Naples, FL 34102
239-262-7333
www.auctionsneapolitan.com
Full service

Belhorn Auction Services LLC
P.O. Box 20211
Columbus, Ohio 43220

614-921-9441
www.belhorn.com
Full service, American art pottery

Bertoia Auctions
2141 DeMarco Drive
Vineland, NJ 08360
856-692-1881
www.bertoiaauctions.com
Toys, banks, holiday, doorstops

Brunk Auctions
P.O. Box 2135
Asheville, NC 28802
828-254-6846
www.brunkauctions.com
Full service

Caroline Ashleigh Associates LLC
1000 S. Old Woodward, Suite 105
Birmingham, MI 48009-6734
248-792-2929
www.auctionyourart.com
Full service, vintage clothing, couture and accessories, textiles, western wear

Clars Auction Gallery
5644 Telegraph Ave.
Oakland, CA 94609
888-339-7600
www.clars.com
Full service

Cowan's
6270 Este Ave.
Cincinnati, OH 45232
513-871-1670
www.cowanauctions.com
Full service, historic Americana, Native American objects

Craftsman Auctions
109 Main St.
Putnam, CT 06260
800-448-7828
www.craftsman-auctions.com
Arts & Crafts furniture and accessories

Cyr Auction Co.
P.O. Box 1238
Gray, ME 04039
207-657-5253
www.cyrauction.com
Full service

Dotta Auction Co. Inc.
Nazareth Auction Center
330 W. Moorestown Road (Route 512)
Nazareth, Pa. 18064
610-759-7389 or 610-433-7555
www.dottaauction.com
Full service

Early Auction Co. LLC.
123 Main St.
Milford, OH 45150
513-831-4833
www.earlyauctionco.com
Art glass

Elder's Antiques
901 Tamiami Trail (US 41) S.
Nokomis, FL 34275
941-488-1005
www.eldersantiques.com
Full service

Photo courtesy Skinner Inc., Boston; www.SkinnerInc.com

Sign, Painted Wood, "Fresh Eggs", American, early 20th century, double-sided rectangular panel, 7 3/4" x 24". Normal wear with some paint losses, stains, surface grime. **$830**

Greg Martin Auctions
660 Third St., Suite 100
San Francisco, CA 94107
800-509-1988
www.gregmartinauctions.com
Firearms, edged weapons, armor, Native American objects

Grey Flannel
8 Moniebogue Lane
Westhampton Beach, NY 11978
631-288-7800
www.greyflannel.com
Sports jerseys, memorabilia

Guyette & Schmidt Inc.
P.O. Box 1170
24718 Beverly Road
St. Michaels, MD 21663
410-745-0485
www.guyetteandschmidt.com
Antique decoys

Hake's Americana & Collectibles Auctions
P.O. Box 1444
York, PA 17405
717-848-1333
www.hakes.com
Character collectibles, pop culture

Heritage Auctions Inc.
3500 Maple Ave., 17th Floor
Dallas, TX 75219-3941
800-872-6467
www.ha.com
Full service, coins, pop culture

iGavel Inc.
229 E. 120th St.
New York, NY 10035
866-iGavel6 or 212-289-5588
auction.igavel.com
Online auction, arts, antiques and collectibles

Ivey-Selkirk
7447 Forsyth Blvd.
Saint Louis, MO 63105
314-726-5515
www.iveyselkirk.com
Full service

Photo courtesy Antiques and Estate Auctioneers, Wellington, Ohio; www.EstateAuctioneers.com

Large Flow Blue Mug. Brush-stroke decorated with tulips, buds and leaves. Shows some wear and crazing. **$153**

Jackson's International Auctioneers and Appraisers
2229 Lincoln St.
Cedar Falls, Iowa 50613
319-277-2256
www.jacksonsauction.com
Full service, religious and Russian objects, postcards

James D. Julia Inc.
P.O. Box 830
Fairfield, ME 04937
207-453-7125
www.juliaauctions.net
Full service, toys, glass, lighting, firearms

Jeffrey S. Evans & Associates
P.O. Box 2638
Harrisonburg, VA 22801-2638
540-434-3939
www.jeffreysevans.com
Full service, glass, lighting, Americana

John Moran Auctioneers Inc.
735 W. Woodbury Road
Altadena, CA 91001
626-793-1833
www.johnmoran.com
Full service, California art

Leigh Keno Auctions
127 E. 69th St.
New York, NY 10021
212-734-2381
www.kenoauctions.com
Fine antiques, decorative arts

Lang's Sporting Collectibles
663 Pleasant Valley Road
Waterville, NY 13480
315-841-4623
www.langsauction.com
Antique fishing tackle and memorabilia

Leslie Hindman Auctioneers
1338 W. Lake St.
Chicago, Il 60607
312-280-1212
www.lesliehindman.com
Full service

McMasters Harris Auction Co.
5855 John Glenn Hwy
P.O. Box 1755
Cambridge, OH 43725
740-432-7400
www.mcmastersharris.com
Dolls and accessories

Michael Ivankovich Auction Co.
P.O. Box 1536
Doylestown, PA 18901
215-345-6094
www.wnutting.com
Wallace Nutting objects

Leland Little Auctions & Estate Sales Ltd.
246 S. Nash St.
Hillsborough, NC 27278
919-644-1243
www.llauctions.com
Full Service

Litchfield County Auctions Inc.
425 Bantam Road (Route 202)
Litchfield, CT 06759
860-567-4661
212-724-0156
www.litchfieldcountyauctions.com
Full service

Mark Mattox Auctioneer & Real Estate Broker Inc.
3740 Maysville Road
Carlisle, KY 40311
859-289-5720
www.mattoxrealestate.com
Full service

Morphy Auctions
2000 N. Reading Road
Denver, PA 17517
717-335-3435
www.morphyauctions.com
Toys, banks, advertising, pop culture

Mosby & Co. Auctions
905 West 7th St., #228
Frederick, MD 21701
301-304-0352
www.mosbyauctions.com
Mail, phone, Internet sales

New Orleans Auction Galleries Inc.
801 Magazine St.
New Orleans, LA 70130
800-501-0277
www.neworleansauction.com
Full service, Victorian

Photo courtesy James D. Julia Auctioneers, Fairfield, Maine; www.JuliaAuctions.com

Fenton Red Karnak Vase. Rich red, slightly iridescent body with an applied cobalt blue foot. The iridescence on the vase shows flashes of gold and blue. 5 3/4" t. **$1,150**

Noel Barrett Vintage Toys @ Auction
P.O. Box 300
Carversville, PA 18913
215-297 5109
www.noelbarrett.com
Toys, banks, holiday, advertising

Old Town Auctions
P.O. Box 91
Boonsboro, MD 21713
240-291-0114
301-416-2854
www.oldtownauctions.com
Toys, Advertising, Americana; no Internet sales

Old Toy Soldier Auctions USA
P.O. Box 13324
Pittsburgh, PA 15243
Ray Haradin
412-343-8733
800-349-8009
www.oldtoysoldierauctions.com

Old World Auctions
2155 W. Hwy 89A, Suite 206
Sedona, AZ 86336
800-664-7757
www.oldworldauctions.com
Maps, documents

Past Tyme Pleasures
39 California Ave., Suite 105
Pleasanton, CA 94566
925-484-6442
www.pasttyme1.com
Internet catalog auctions

Philip Weiss Auctions
1 Neil Court
Oceanside, NY 11572
516-594-0731
www.prwauctions.com
Full service, comic art

Pook & Pook Inc.
463 East Lancaster Ave.
Downingtown, PA 19335
610-629-0695
www.pookandpook.com
Full service, Americana

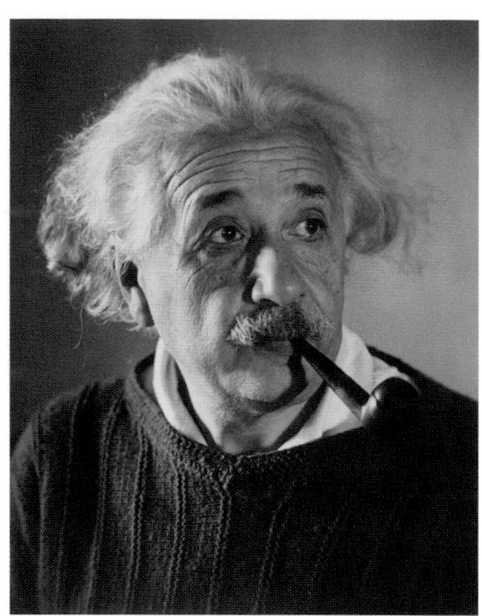

Photo courtesy Rago Arts and Auction Center, Lambertville, N.J.; www.RagoArts.com

Roman Vishniac (Russian, 1897-1990) Albert Einstein in Princeton, circa 1941; gelatin silver print; Signed, titled and inscribed; 13 1/2" x 10 3/4" (sheet). **$1,200**

Professional Appraisers & Liquidators LLC
16 Lemington Court
Homosassa, FL 34446
800-542-3877
www.charliefudge.com
Full Service

Quinn's Auction Galleries & Waverly Rare Books
431 N. Maple Ave.
Falls Church, VA 22046
703-532-5632
www.quinnsauction.com
www.waverlyauctions.com
Full service, rare books and prints

Rago Arts and Auction Center
333 N. Main St.
Lambertville, NJ 08530
609-397-9374
www.ragoarts.com
Arts & Crafts, modernism, fine art

Red Baron's Antiques Inc.
6450 Roswell Road
Atlanta, GA 30328
404-252-3770

www.redbaronsantiques.com
Full service, Victorian, architectural objects

Rich Penn Auctions
P.O. Box 1355
Waterloo, IA 50704
319-291-6688
www.richpennauctions.com
Advertising and country-store objects

Richard D. Hatch & Associates
913 Upward Road
Flat Rock, NC 28731
828-696-3440
www.richardhatchauctions.com
Full service

Robert Edward Auctions LLC
P.O. Box 7256
Watchung, NJ 07069
908-226-9900
www.robertedwardauctions.com
Baseball, sports memorabilia

Rock Island Auction Co.
4507 49th Ave.
Moline, IL 61265-7578
800-238-8022
www.rockislandauction.com
Firearms, edged weapons and accessories

St. Charles Gallery Inc.
1330 St. Charles Ave.
New Orleans, LA 70130
504-586-8733
www.stcharlesgallery.com
Full service, Victorian

Samuel T. Freeman & Co.
1808 Chestnut St.
Philadelphia, PA 19103
215-563-9275
www.freemansauction.com
Full service, Americana

Seeck Auctions
P.O. Box 377
Mason City, IA 50402
641-424-1116
www.seeckauction.com
Full service, carnival glass

Photo courtesy Leslie Hindman Auctioneers, Chicago; www.LeslieHindman.com

Ear clips, Christian Lacroix, with bows and rhinestones. Stamped: Christian Lacroix. **$48**

Skinner Inc.
357 Main St.
Bolton, MA 01740
978-779-6241
www.skinnerinc.com
Full service, Americana

Sloans and Kenyon
7034 Wisconsin Ave.
Chevy Chase, MD 20815
301-634-2344
www.sloansandkenyon.com
Full service

Slotin Folk Art
Folk Fest Inc.
5619 Ridgetop Drive
Gainesville, GA 30504
770-532-1115
www.slotinfolkart.com
Naïve and outsider art

Stanton's Auctioneers & Realtors
144 S. Main St.
P.O. Box 146
Vermontville, MI 49096
517-726 0181
www.stantons-auctions.com
Full service, phonographs

Strawser Auctions
P.O. Box 332, 200 N. Main
Wolcottville, IN 46795
260-854-2859
www.strawserauctions.com
Full service, majolica, Fiesta ware

Susanin's Auctions
900 S. Clinton
Chicago, IL 60607
312-832-9800
www.susanins.com
Full service

Swann Galleries Inc.
104 E. 25th St.
New York, NY 10010
212-254-4710
www.swanngalleries.com
Rare books, prints, photographs, posters

Theriault's
P.O. Box 151
Annapolis, MD 21404
800-638-0422
www.theriaults.com
Dolls and accessories

Tom Harris Auction Center
203 S. 18th Ave.
Marshalltown, IA 50158
641-754-4890
www.tomharrisauctions.com
Full service, clocks, watches

Tradewinds Antiques
P.O. Box 249
Manchester-By-The-Sea, MA 01944-0249
978-526-4085
www.tradewindsantiques.com
Canes

Treadway Gallery
2029 Madison Road
Cincinnati, OH 45208
513-321-6742
John Toomey Gallery
818 North Blvd.
Oak Park, IL 60301
708-383-5234

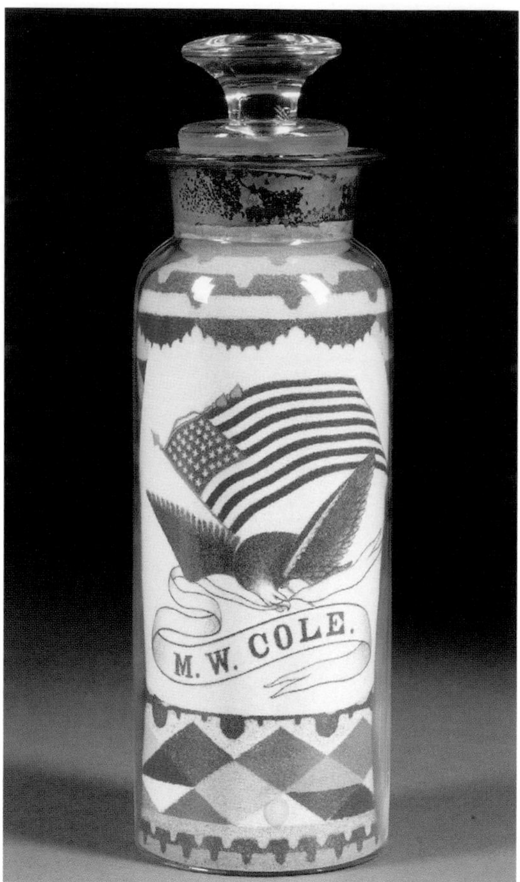

Photo courtesy Skinner Inc., Boston; www.SkinnerInc.com

Sand Picture in a Glass Bottle with American Eagle, Flag, and Urn of Flowers, Andrew Clemens, McGregor, Iowa, circa 1885, multicolored sand arranged in a glass bottle, one side of the bottle portraying an American eagle in flight, an American flag, and a banner reading "M.W. COLE," the reverse depicting a flower-filled urn, both designs flanked by several multicolored and shaped borders, 9 3/4" h. Note: Andrew Clemens was born in Dubuque, Iowa, in 1857. At the age of five he became deaf and mute after an illness. He earned his livelihood by painstakingly arranging colored sand to make pictures in glass bottles. The sand came from the naturally colored sandstone in the Pictured Rocks area of Iowa. He worked in McGregor, and for a short time he made and exhibited his work at South Side Museum, a dime museum in Chicago, Ill. He died in 1894 at the age of 37. **$7,110**

www.treadwaygallery.com
Arts & Crafts, modernism, fine art

Victorian Casino Antiques
5585 S. Valley View Blvd., Suite 1
Las Vegas, NV 89118
702-382-2466
www.vcaauction.com
Coin-ops, gambling

Advertising

ADVERTISING

Commercial messages and displays have been found in the ruins of ancient Arabia. Egyptians used papyrus to create sales messages and wall posters, while lost-and-found advertising was common in ancient Greece and Rome. As printing developed in the 15th and 16th centuries, advertising expanded to include handbills. In the 17th century, advertisements started to appear in weekly newspapers in England.

Also see Coca-Cola, Posters, Toys.

Ashtray, plates, Moxie, lot of six items, sandwich plates feature Moxie girl logo and ashtray features pointing Frank Archer. Plates, 8 1/4" d. Ashtray, 5 1/2" d. Plates: three good to very good while other three have some spider cracks. Ashtray has some cigarette staining. .... **$201 all**

Calendar, Firestone Tires, 1935, deco image on textured paper from the Rome, N.Y., Tire and Battery Service, 20 3/4" w x 42" h; original metal hanging strip and full date pad. Two small punctures to field but otherwise very good condition with strong bright colors. **$288**

Calendar, Hercules Powder Co., 1916, four-page calendar with cover illustration of ring-neck pheasant. Other images include farm scene, black-breasted plovers and a gold miner; 11 1/2" w x 27 1/2" h; retains original metal hanging strip, subtle edge tears. **$1,725**

Calendar, Lykens Brewing Co., 1912, springtime illustration by Arthur J. Elsley of mother and daughter with their faithful St. Bernard companion; 17" w x 23 1/4" h in frame. **$172**

Calendar, S.S. Patterson, 1904, stone lithographed image of reclining damsel with her beer from this Dillon, Mont., distributor of Val Blatz Brewing Co.'s Milwaukee Beer; 16" w x 24" h in frame; small circular surface cut at bottom margin, possibly a minor repair. One or two tiny edge tears. **$632**

Calendar, Peters Cartridge Co., 1909, hunting dog illustration by A. Muss-Arnolt titled, The First Lesson-Steady; 13 3/4" w x 27 1/4" h; soft roll creases; retains top and bottom metal bands; December date sheet only. **$2,415**

Containers, Planter's Peanuts, lot of six includes five glass peanut jars and one 10-pound peanut tin for Pennant-brand salted peanuts. Two "octagon jars" with lids; two "fishbowl" jars with lids, one with most of its original label; one square jar with lid. Good to very good condition, a few lids and necks of jars show light chips and nibbles. **$201**

Photo courtesy James D. Julia Auctioneers, Fairfield, Maine; www.JuliaAuctions.com

Calendar, Dubuque Malting Co., 1902, scarce, colorful calendar from this Iowa brewer promoting their line of Banquet Beer, 17" w x 22 3/4" h in frame; top and bottom margins have been replaced; professional restoration to bottom right corner; repaired horizontal tear through entire image just above trademark logo; two pages of calendar date sheets in-painted. **$1,035**

Photo courtesy James D. Julia Auctioneers, Fairfield, Maine; www.JuliaAuctions.com

Calendar, Bowler Bros. Ltd. Brewing Co., 1900, scarce stone lithograph depicting a bathing-suit-attired young beauty at the shore, Image 13 3/4" w x 22 3/4" h in frame; areas of professional restoration and in-painting, particularly along several horizontal creases and to the blue water background. **$1,020**

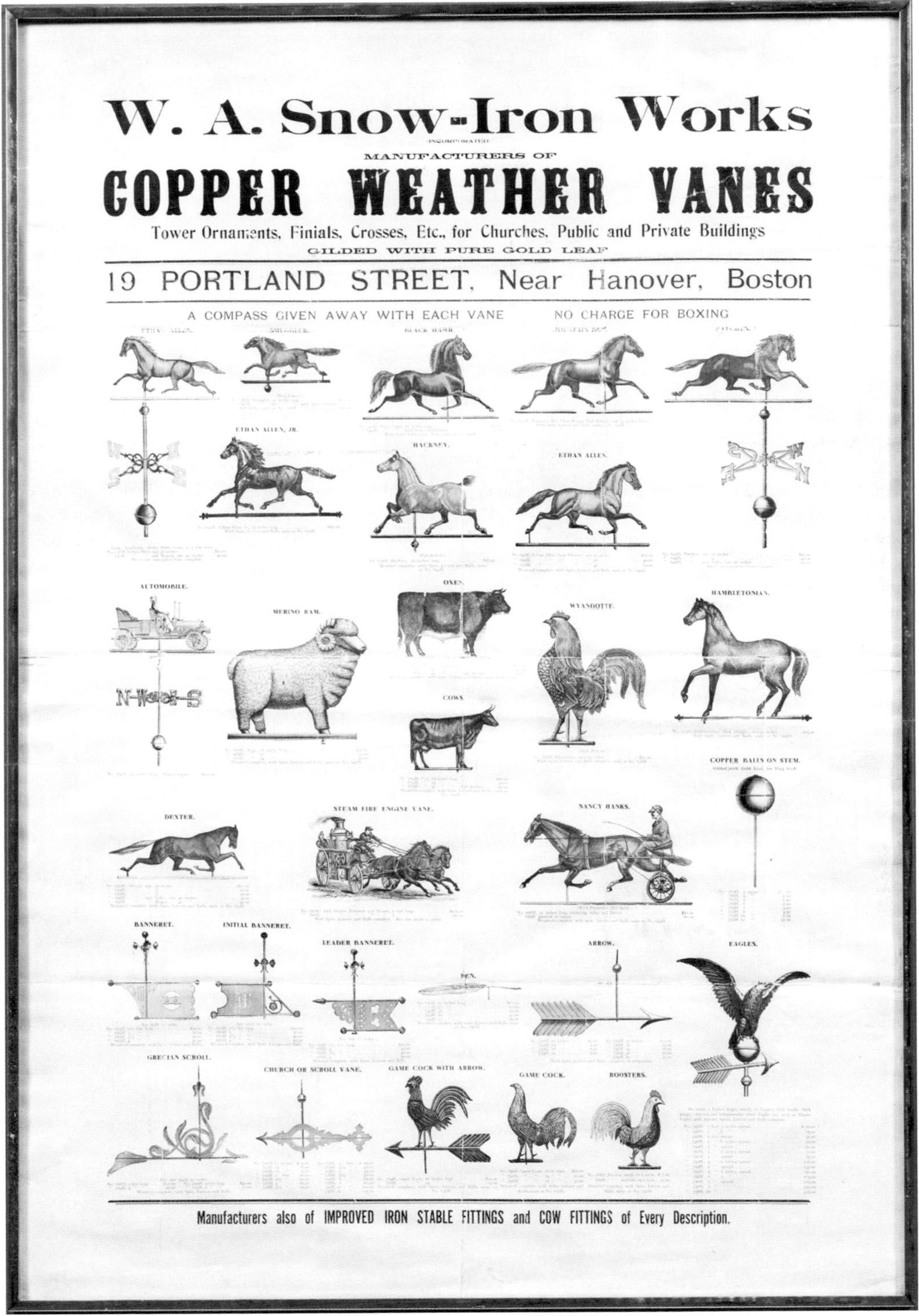

Photo courtesy Skinner Inc., Boston; www.SkinnerInc.com

Broadside, "W.A. Snow Iron Works" Weather Vanes, Boston, late 19th century, black-printed broadside depicting a selection of the weathervanes offered by the maker, (creases), 35" x 24 1/2", in a contemporary aluminum frame.
$385

Photo courtesy Skinner Inc., Boston; www.SkinnerInc.com

Signs, Pair of Painted Turned Wooden Barber Poles, American, 19th century, including wall mounts, (old repaint, paint losses), each 30" l. **$1,541 pair**

Photo courtesy James D. Julia Auctioneers, Fairfield, Maine; www.JuliaAuctions.com

Calendar, Prospect Brewing Co., 1893, a seldom-seen advertisement from this Philadelphia brewer. Small colorful vignettes flank the calendar dates and commemorate a variety of national holidays, 18 1/2" w x 28" h in frame; horizontal fold crease four inches from the top; vertical scuff at top center. **$4,370**

Photo courtesy James D. Julia Auctioneers, Fairfield, Maine; www.JuliaAuctions.com

Calendar, Weisbrod & Hess Brewing Co., 1907, elusive calendar from this Philadelphia brewer, with a variety of vignettes showing outdoor activities in the surrounding Pennsylvania countryside. Lower portion of calendar has illustrations of their Rheingold and Shakespeare brews, 19" w x 28" h in frame; some flattened paper creases across top; small area of paper loss to the "S" in Shakespeare; minor in-painting at bottom. **$1,380**

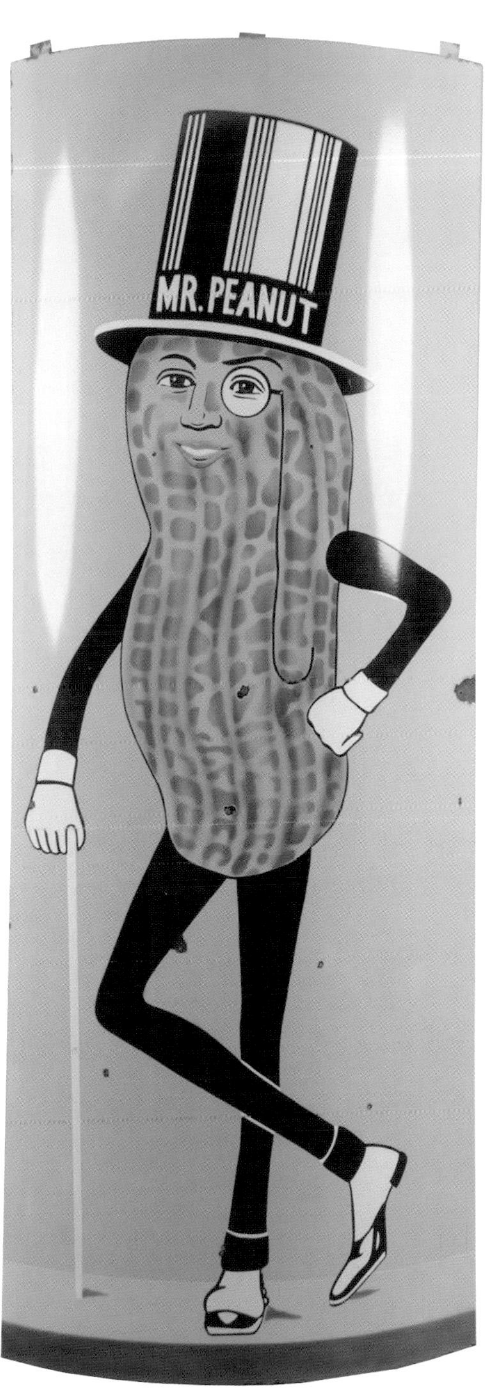

Photo courtesy Morphy Auctions, Denver, Pa.; www.MorphyAuctions.com

Planters porcelain half-moon-shape Mr. Peanut advertising sign made in the 1930s-40s. **$16,100**

Photo courtesy James D. Julia Auctioneers, Fairfield, Maine; www.JuliaAuctions.com

Calendar, Firestone Tires, 1935, deco image on textured paper from the Rome, N.Y., Tire and Battery Service, 20 3/4" w x 42" h; original metal hanging strip and full date pad. Two small punctures to field but otherwise very good condition with strong bright colors. **$288**

Photo courtesy James D. Julia Auctioneers, Fairfield, Maine; www.JuliaAuctions.com

Calendar, Peters Cartridge Co., 1909, hunting dog illustration by A. Muss-Arnolt titled, The First Lesson-Steady; 13 3/4" w x 27 1/4" h; soft roll creases; retains top and bottom metal bands; December date sheet only. **$2,415**

Opening page:

Photo courtesy Skinner Inc., Boston; www.SkinnerInc.com

Sign, Polychrome Painted Pine "Dr. Whitcher" Trade Sign with Indian Figures, American, late 19th century, rectangular pine panel with applied molding, one side painted with the figure of a Native American man wearing a feathered headdress standing with bow and arrows in one hand, and a leafy branch in the other, in a river valley landscape; the reverse showing a Native American woman standing in a landscape with shrubs and trees, both with black painted lettering below, overall 25 1/4" h, 19" w. Scattered paint losses, age cracks, one is 16" l going through male figure, a couple ring stains, the other side with female is somewhat dark and faded. **$17,775**

Photo courtesy Morphy Auctions, Denver, Pa.; www.MorphyAuctions.com

Pre-1900 reverse-on-glass oval corner sign advertising Yuengling's brewery of Pottsville, Pa. **$6,600**

Photo courtesy James D. Julia Auctioneers, Fairfield, Maine; www.JuliaAuctions.com

Calendar, Lykens Brewing Co., 1912, springtime illustration by Arthur J. Elsley of mother and daughter with their faithful St. Bernard companion; 17" w x 23 1/4" h in frame. **$172**

Dispenser, Hires, ceramic, classic hourglass-shaped soda fountain dispenser, complete with pump and Hires ceramic insert, 14" h. Light discoloration to bottom of dispenser, small stress crack to exterior. **$420**

Dispenser, Kola Mint keg/syrup dispenser with original crate, thick wooden barrel keg with copper rings, painted with red and white lettering stating "Demonstrating Dept., Williamsport Penna." Lid with porcelain knob. Barrel has plaque that reads "U.C. Water Cooler, Union Cooperage Co., St. Louis". Rests on separate round wooden base on four bent steel legs. Original wooden crate with similar lettering style "K-M-Co., Williamsport PA 2" with hinged side handles. Interior has partial paper label on inner lid showing contents. Barrel only, 19" h. Crate with various chips and scratches. **$920**

Dispenser, Liberty Root Beer, ceramic, lettering to two sides with the logo "Try a Stein-It's Fine". Includes correct style pump with "Root Beer" ceramic insert, 13 3/4" h. **$3,450**

Display, Baker Chocolate, thick cardboard die-cut window advertisement featuring the Baker Chocolate girl with tray of goodies approaching a group of Revolutionary War-era nobles enjoying Baker's hot chocolate. Large banner at top reads, "The Mills of Walter Baker & Co. Ltd. 52 Highest awards." Shown with vignettes around perimeter of various Baker products. Center section is open suggesting that this was a window display to have presentation behind; 38 1/4" w x 28" h. Some restoration to top section and showing some edge wear and crease at top corner, overall very good. **$345**

Photo courtesy Hake's Americana & Collectibles, York, Pa; www.Hakes.com

Display, Baranger Honeymoon Rocket, motion display, with original shipping crate, working, minor age wear, minor paint wear to base, 19" h, 20" w, 14" deep. **$12,100**

Photo courtesy Green Valley Auctions, Mt. Crawford, Va., www.GreenValleyAuctions.com

Display, American carved and painted wood and painted wrought iron figure of a hackney, viceroy and driver, the horse features a braided mane and is fitted with harness, the driver is outfitted in a suit and top hat with a red lap robe covering his legs, the cart features an iron chassis and shafts, a "W" is carved on each side. A note indicates that this was part of a St. Louis tack shop window display. Second quarter 20th century; 22 1/2" h, 47" l, excellent condition, minor repairs to driver, reins detached. **$12,100**

Photo courtesy Hake's Americana & Collectibles, York, Pa; www.Hakes.com

Display dolls (theatrical size), Mickey Mouse and Minnie Mouse, giant display-model dolls, made by Charlotte Clark, early 1930s, 44" h Mickey and 48" h Minnie (smaller dolls shown for comparison). **$151,534 pair**

Photo courtesy Heritage Auction Galleries, Dallas; www.HA.com

Walt Disney Vintage Advertisement/Club Membership Group (Disney, circa 1930s). Seven pieces of advertising and club membership ephemera. It includes a certificate to join the Mickey Mouse Globe-Trotters club, printed in red and black ink; a certificate to join the Mickey Mouse Good Teeth Brigade, printed in red and black ink, with a small 1/3" tear on the upper right corner; a full-color handbill, encouraging kids to "Be a ringmaster of your own Walt Disney Pinocchio Circus"; a die-cut Ringmaster top hat for the Pinocchio Circus, printed in black and red; a die-cut wall hanger/certificate to join the Mickey Mouse Globe-Trotters Club, printed in full-color; and two different die-cut cardboard ads for the free Mickey Mouse Scrap Book, both printed in full-color. **$262 all**

Photo courtesy James D. Julia Auctioneers, Fairfield, Maine; www.JuliaAuctions.com

Display, Lone Star Beer, chalkware, reclining armadillo wrapped around a bottle of Lone Star Beer; 12" w x 11 1/2" h x 6" deep. Good to very good condition with a few tiny chips to base. **$402**

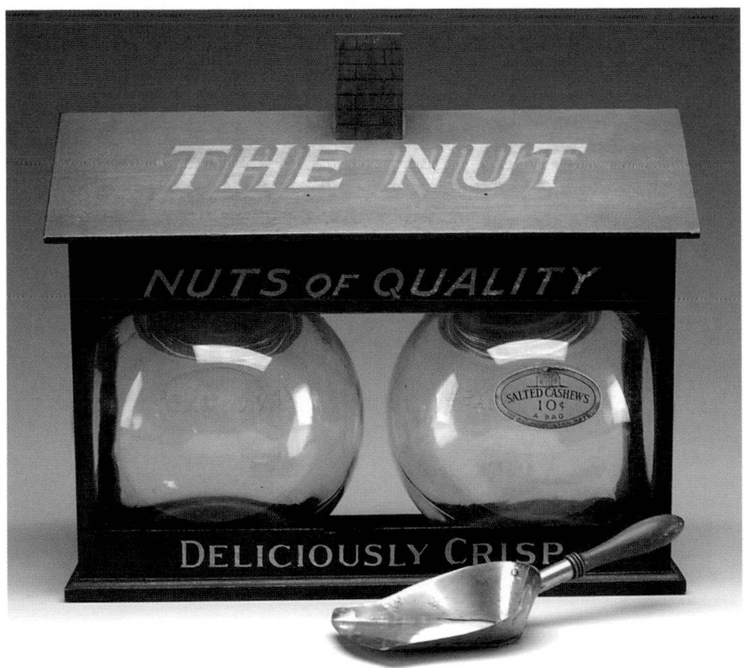

Photo courtesy James D. Julia Auctioneers, Fairfield, Maine; www.JuliaAuctions.com

Display, Nut House, uncommon mahogany figural countertop display complete with two embossed glass jars and scoop. The roof and sides of the house retain their original gilt lettering; 18" w, 16" h x 8" deep. Very good to excellent condition, backside of the house reveals two wood chips, one at the roof and one at the lower edge of one side. **$480**

Photo courtesy Morphy Auctions, Denver, Pa.; www.MorphyAuctions.com

Dispenser, Crawford's Cherry-Fizz, circa 1920s, ceramic with original ball pump. Light soiling and minor wear. No chips or cracks. **$10,350**

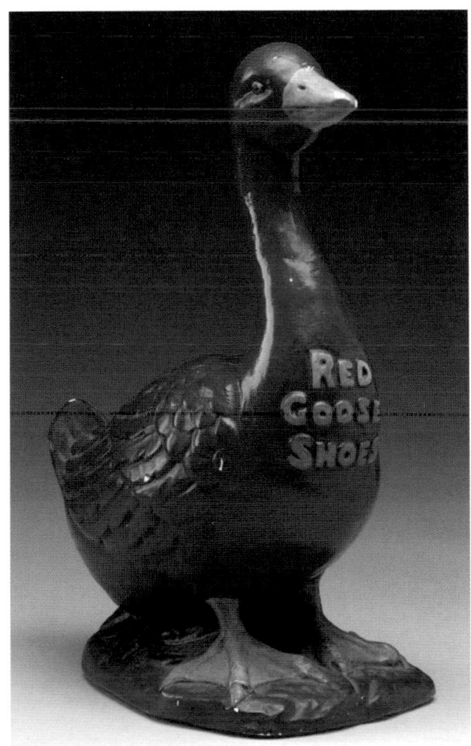

Photo courtesy James D. Julia Auctioneers, Fairfield, Maine; www.JuliaAuctions.com

Figure, Red Goose Shoes, plaster, figure on a green base was a counter decoration. Has raised lettering on the chest reading "Red Goose Shoes." Approximately 11 1/4" h. Generally, very good condition. A few scattered paint chips over the surface; retains almost all of its paint. **$115**

Photo courtesy Morphy Auctions, Denver, Pa.; www.MorphyAuctions.com

Fan pull or hanging sign, Hires Root Beer, circa 1900, cardboard lithograph, two-sided, depicts an early version of the Ugly Kid holding a mug feeding a living planet Earth. Minor bend, minor edge wear, and a few mildew spots on back. One small closed crack, 11" x 10". **$52,000**

Display, Bear Brand Hosiery, papier-mâché, countertop store advertisement featuring Papa Bear, Momma Bear and Baby Bear; 18 1/2" h. Spots of wear to base but otherwise very good condition. **$1,035**

Display, Buster Brown Shoes, chalkware, uncommon countertop display featuring Buster Brown and his dog, Tighe, for the "Tread Straight" line of shoes; 16 1/2" h. Generally good condition; several chips to base and Buster's hat; paint loss to base, shoe sign and Buster's leg. **$460**

Display, Crawford Cigars, wood, countertop display is hand lettered on all four sides "Smoke the Crawford 5 cent Cigar." It appears this display originally had smoke pumped through a tube located in the back to a pipe that extends up from the top, possibly having held at one time a cigar or figural smoking head; 20 1/2" w, 28" h x 12" deep. Appears to be all original surfaces; a few chips to wooden base. **$805**

Display, Crystal Rock Beer, chalkware, from the Cleveland and Sandusky Brewing Co. of a bartender wearing a Crystal Rock apron pouring a mug of brew; 10" w x 13 1/2" h x 7" deep. A few surface nicks and a few fine age lines, but otherwise very good condition. **$575**

Display, Edison Mazda Lamps light bulbs, with the colorful "Get Together" front panel illustration by Maxfield Parrish. Features twelve porcelain sockets radiating around a figural light-bulb shaped counter top display. Each socket has an individual on/off switch, which collectively held a variety of Edison Mazda-GE light bulbs; 15 3/4" w x 23 1/2" h. Good to very good condition; front panel shows areas of discoloration but the Parrish graphics remain unaffected with the exception of a few fine scratches. Back base panel has some loss of color; one porcelain socket and switch have old break, original cord is frayed and has not been tested. **$2,300**

Display, Indian brave seated cross-legged, holding pennant – Quoddy Moccasins – on pole, painted wood, red painted 20" square base, 30" h overall, minor paint loss, crazing to surface on back and chest; braided hair possibly repaired. **$977**

Displays, "Amos" and "Andy" Pepsodent Toothpaste, cardboard, die cut featuring the popular radio personalities of Amos and Andy promoting Pepsodent Toothpaste. Copyright 1930. Andy 22" w x 61" h, Amos 21" w x 54" h. Fair to good condition; some cardboard and paper loss, staining, creases and edge tears. .... **$460 pair**

Displays, Ritz Ice Cream Cone, composition, pair, feature bathing boy and girl clutching colossal ice cream cones standing atop stylized Art Deco bases, which read "Ice Cream with a Facchino Cone;" 22" h. Bathing girl figure shows some cracking to the base, which doesn't effect its stability, otherwise both figures in good to very good condition. **$1,035**

Fan, Lucky Strike, Frank Sinatra appears on this tobacco leaf fan given to audience members during the 1950-1959 telecast of "Your Hit Parade" show, sponsored by Lucky Strike. Lot includes two glossy photos; 7 1/2" w x 13" h in frame. Good condition; repair to paper tear at top; cellophane tape left side; slight paper loss right side. **$690**

Lithograph, Frank Abbott, colorful image of buckskin-clad Indian maiden for this Chicago retailer of lumber, bank and office fittings. Paul B. King illustration printed on textured paper. Image size, 16 1/4" w x 20 1/4" h. Near excellent with bright strong colors. **$604**

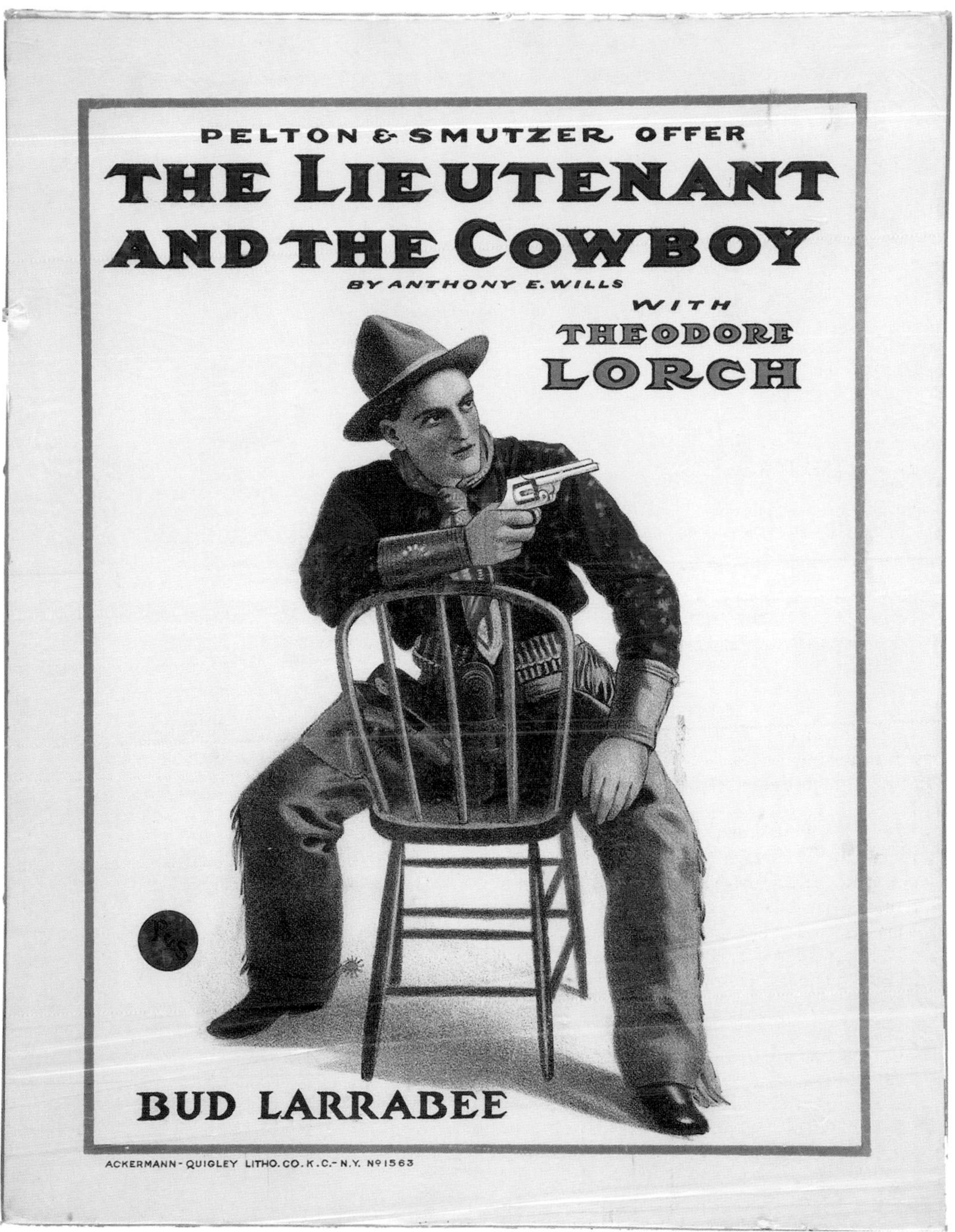

Photo courtesy Heritage Auction Galleries, Dallas; www.HA.com

Multicolor Lithograph of Cowboy with Pistol, circa 1910s-1920, depicts a cowboy sitting in chair with chaps, spurs, kerchief, gauntlets and revolver. A stage advertising poster. Measures approx. 11" x 14". **$179**

Photo courtesy Old Town Auctions LLC, Boonsboro, Md.; www.OldTownAuctions.com

Panel truck, Harley-Davidson 1934 Ford panel truck with old "wings" logo on both sides, purportedly used by a Harley dealer in the early 1950s as a delivery vehicle, running, flathead V-8, one of about 800 built. **$15,950**

Photo courtesy James D. Julia Auctioneers, Fairfield, Maine; www.JuliaAuctions.com

Sign, Campbell's Soups, tin, the Holy Grail of all advertising signs, rarely seen and seldom ever appearing on the auction block. When Campbell's introduced this sign to their selected retail accounts, it created such a public controversy by using an image of the American Flag for commercial self-promotion that most of the signs were quickly withdrawn and destroyed. Lithographed by the Standard Adv. Co., Coshocton, Ohio; 39 1/4" l x 27 1/4" h. Overall fair to good condition. Perimeter edges exhibit bending, nail holes, scuffs and scratches. Field of sign shows multiple nail holes and two 1/2" diameter holes, cause unknown. Bottom left corner of the "flag" and the word "Just" show some corrosion with a build up of some tar-like substance. **$18,400**

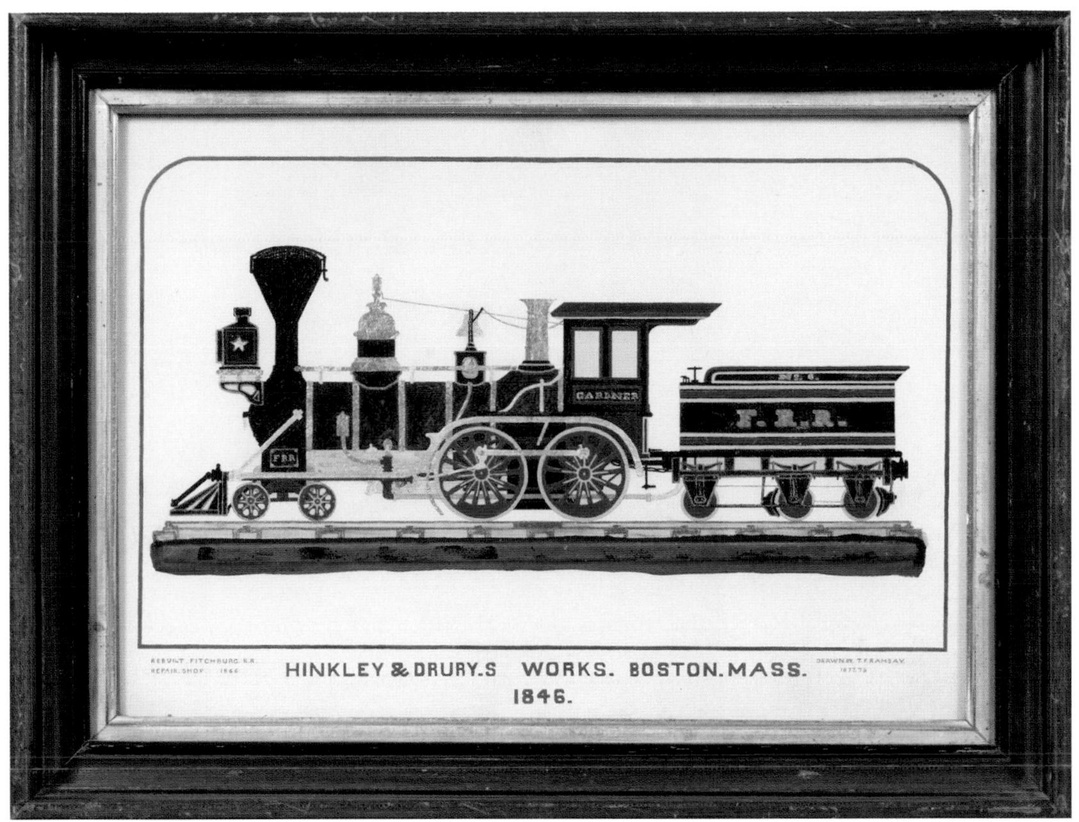

Photo courtesy Skinner Inc., Boston; www.SkinnerInc.com

Sign, T.F. Ramsay (American, 19th Century), Hinkley & Drury's Works Boston Mass. 1846. Fitchburg Railroad Locomotive. Signed and dated 1877-78 l.r., identified below. Pigment with applied gilt foil paper accents and wood rail on academy board, 12" x 17", in a period molded wood frame with gilt liner. Some subtle surface grime and stray marks. Note: Holmes Hinkley and Gardner P. Drury built stationary engines and began building locomotives 1840. According to inscriptions, the locomotive was built in 1846, and later rebuilt at the Fitchburg Railroad repair shop in 1866. **$711**

Lithograph, Phoenix Brewing Co., springtime farmyard illustration from this Rice Lake, Wis., brewer. Image 14 1/4" w x 18 3/4" h in frame. Good to very good condition with some light surface scuffs. Staple marks would indicate this was probably used as a calendar. **$862**

Lithograph, Sweet Home Soap, little girl with roses, copyright 1895. Lithograph appears to be in original ornate frame. Image size, 13 1/2" w x 27 1/2" h. Water stain along bottom edge; a few areas of discoloration from original wood backing boards; light soiling overall to white background. **$345**

Lithograph, Yardley's Old English Lavender, on textured paper laid down on cardboard of colorful English street peddlers with their baskets of lavender. The textured surface and lithographic quality of this advertisement lend it the look of an oil painting. Image size, 27 1/2" w x 21 1/2" h. Very good condition with some light surface scuffs. **$805**

Plaque, Goodyear Tires Zeppelin, brass, manufactured by the Medallic-Art Co., N.Y., and given to tire dealers of distinction to commemorate ten years of working relationships; 12" w x 17" h. Very good condition. **$345**

Pocket mirror, Garrett's Rye, celluloid, mirror featuring a semi-nude Diana the Huntress standing in a landscape with her bow. The caption, "Garrett's XXXX Baker Rye, Oldest Rye in Baltimore." Approximately 2 3/4" l. A small blister spot on celluloid surface by Diana's wrist; otherwise, very good condition. Retains original mirror. **$345**

Pocket mirror, Pepsi-Cola, celluloid, features a Lillian Russell-type figure holding a glass of Pepsi-Cola at a soda fountain. Above, "The Pepsi-Cola Girl 5¢;" 2 3/4" l. Celluloid generally in good condition. The mirror on the reverse side broken. **$575**

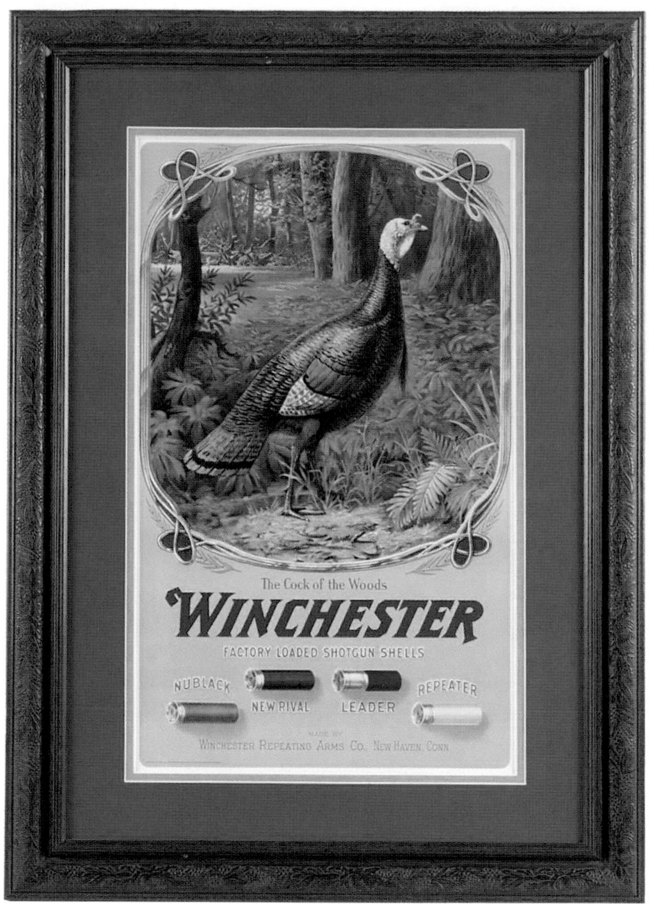

Photo courtesy Morphy Auctions, Denver, Pa.; www.MorphyAuctions.com

Framed paper Winchester Cartridges sign featuring wild turkey. **$10,350**

Photo courtesy Morphy Auctions, Denver, Pa.; www.MorphyAuctions.com

Sign, Alaska Fur Co., double sided with detailed carving, original finish, circa 1890. Manufactured by the City Sign Co. Comes with mounting bracket, 55" l x 53" h. **$79,000**

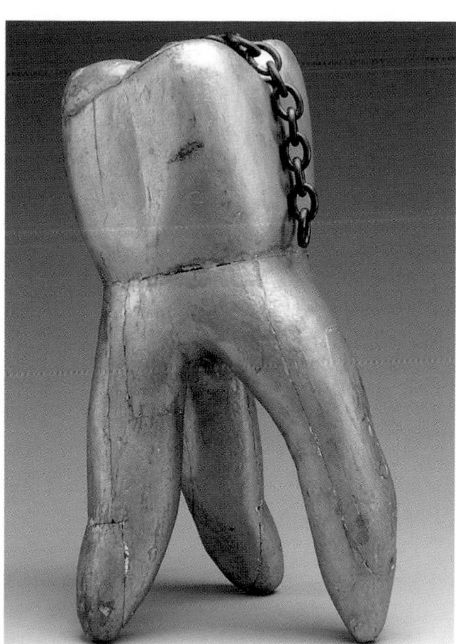

Photo courtesy James D. Julia Auctioneers, Fairfield, Maine; www.JuliaAuctions.com

Sign, dentist tooth, carved wood with chain, which likely was displayed outside the dentist's office; 9" w x 15 1/2" h. Good to very good condition, appears to have multiple layers of gilt paint. **$2,243**

Sign, The Berengaria Steamship, tin, illustration of this triple-stack passenger steamer entering New York City harbor with the Statue of Liberty in the background. Original illustration by A.F. Bishop, 1924; 39 1/2" w x 29 1/2" h. Sign nailed to wood stretchers at perimeter edge and in center; light scattered scuffs, stains, scratches. **$480**

Sign, Brown's Shoes, tin, early embossed advertisement with graphic pointing finger from the company that introduced the Buster Brown brand in 1904. Image 19 1/2" w x 11 1/2" h, in wood frame. Fair condition, several nail holes, creasing, margin tear and surface discoloration. **$57**

Sign, Canada Dry Spur, cardboard, aviatrix leaning against her airplane taking time out for a refreshing Spur; 27" w x 44" h. Fair to good condition; horizontal crease with some cellophane tape; multiple staple holes across top and bottom. **$115**

Sign, Carter's Ink Bottle/Mucilage, tin, rare embossed sign, circa 1870s with stereotyped black youth attempting to extricate a fashionably attired gent stuck to a crate of Carter's Mucilage, captioned "The Great Stickist." Image size 13 1/4" w x 9 1/4" h. Strong graphic appeal and rarity offsets some of its condition drawbacks, which include nail holes at corners, light surface pitting and loss of pigment bottom right corner. **$3,738**

Sign, Chicago, Rock Island & Pacific reverse-on-glass, train panorama of engine tender and five cars, painted and highlighted with slices of mother-of-pearl. This 1902 version showing the Rocky Mountain Limited train with the Colorado Rockies in the background; 89" l x 14" h. Overall very good to excellent condition. Some spots of discoloration to background of cars and tender. **$9,775**

Sign, Chiclets Gum, tin, die cut, fox character, one of a set of six animals produced by Chiclets Gum circa 1916. Includes tin easel back for counter display; 7" w x 10" h. Good to very good condition. Matte surface with some soiling and wear. **$402**

Sign, Clark's Mile-End Spool Cotton, cardboard with profile view of portly man in red striped pants and blue coat carrying a sample of Clark's thread, all on black background. Bottom reads, "Thos. Russell & Co., Sole Agents." In old, possibly original, frame; 28 1/2" h x 22" w. Some in-painting, predominantly to oval logo in top left corner, but also various spots to the background. Some light warping, overall good. **$230**

Sign, Cleveland and Sandusky Brewing Co., tin, oval advertisement featuring a raised simulated wood-grain frame, depicting a satisfied consumer. Lithographed by the H.D. Beach Co., Coshocton, Ohio, circa 1902; 22 1/4" w x 28 1/2" h. Generally good condition with some light wear; nail hole at top; and some spotting and yellowing to original surface finish. **$258**

Sign, Clossman Hardware Company, tin, circa late 1920s to early 1930s, embossed with open touring car and bi-plane graphics from this Zanesville, Ohio, company. Lithographed V. Crystal Adv. Co., Zanesville; 27 3/4" w x 19 3/4" h. Has a vertical crease with some paint loss just to the back of the touring car; a few other light soft creases with paint chips; otherwise in good to very good condition. **$403**

Sign, Cooks Beer, tin on cardboard, southern plantation scene with black waiter and maid promoting Cooks Goldblume beer for this Evansville, Ind., brewer; 21" w x 13" h. Good to very good condition; some light surface pitting, a few soft perimeter bends and a vertical scratch to waiter's leg. Retains original brass chain hanger. **$287**

Photo courtesy Skinner Inc., Boston, www.SkinnerInc.com

Sign, Father Time, painted cast iron and tin, American, late 19th century, double sided sign, (dial repainted), 29" h, 25" w. **$829**

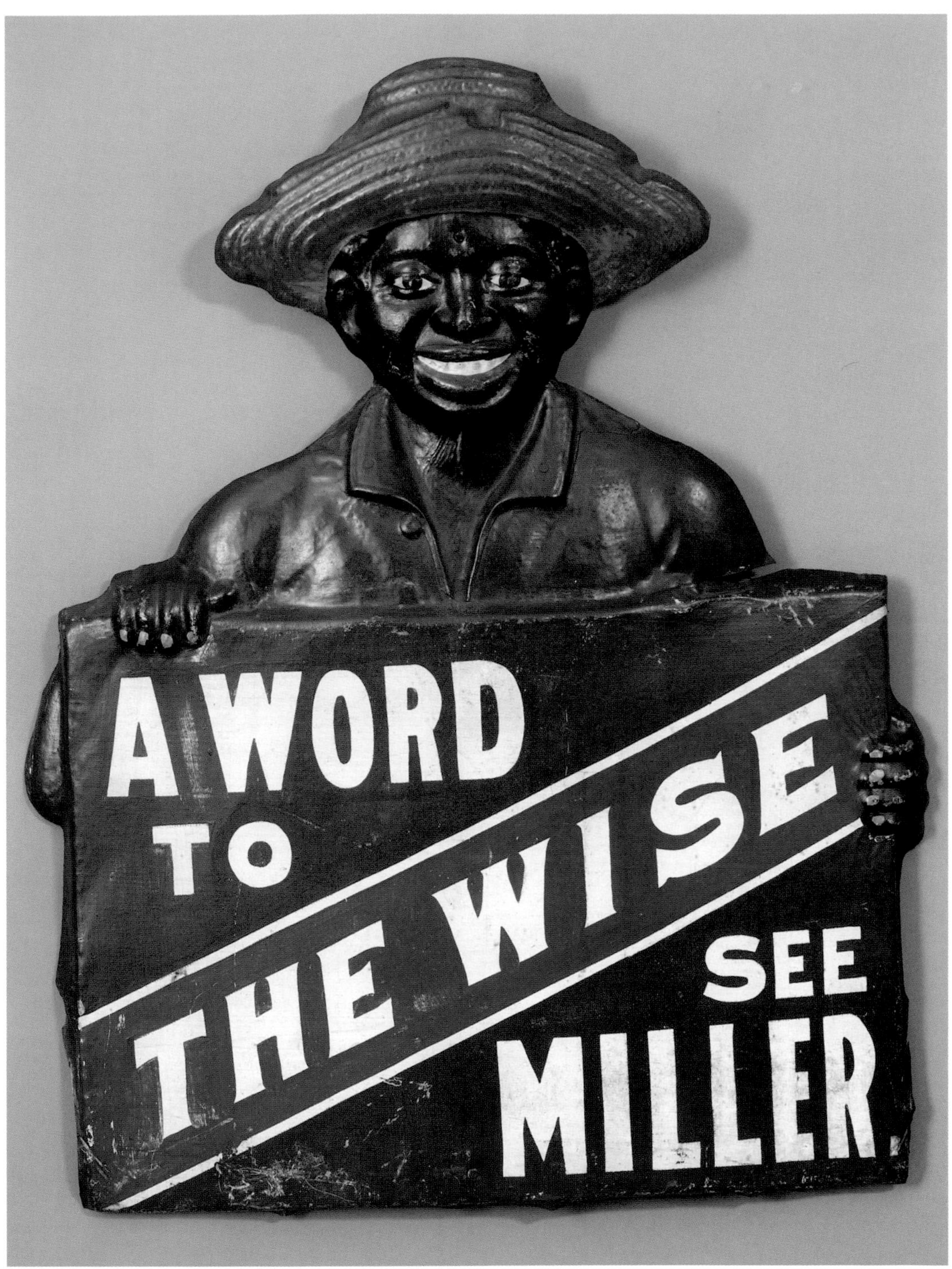

Photo courtesy Skinner Inc., Boston, www.SkinnerInc.com

Sign, figural, painted molded tin, American, late 19th/early 20th century, depicting a figure of a black man holding a sign inscribed, "A Word to the Wise/See Miller," scattered small paint losses, possible line of retouch on lower portion of shirt, 33 3/4", 27" w. **$2,251**

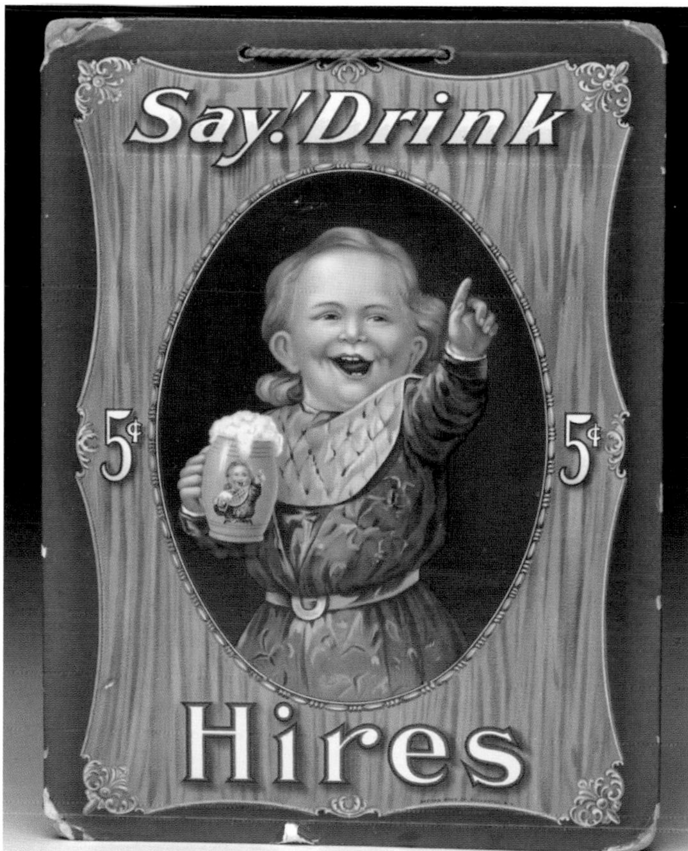

Photo courtesy James D. Julia Auctioneers, Fairfield, Maine; www.JuliaAuctions.com

Sign, Hire's Root Beer, celluloid over cardboard, with original manufacturer's label on reverse. Features an illustration of the Hires Root Beer boy and mug. Lithographed by Bastian Bros. Co., Rochester, N.Y.; 6" w x 8" h. Edge wear concentrated at corners with a few chips along edges, otherwise very good condition. **$3,162**

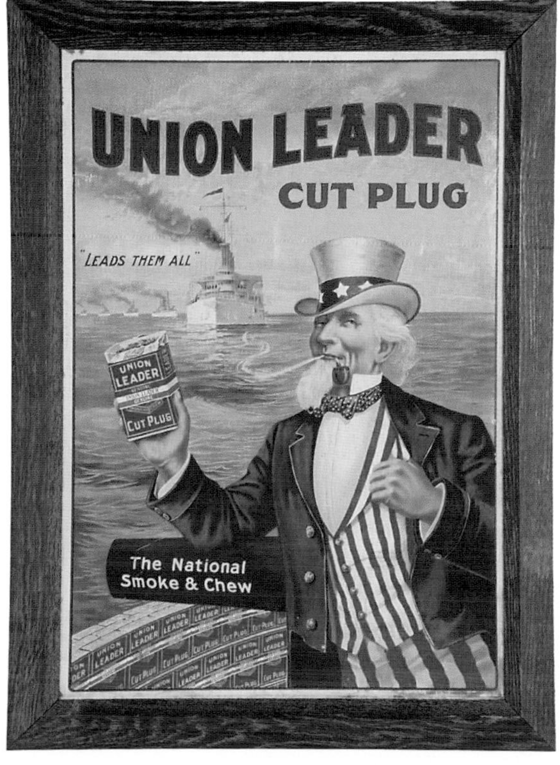

Photo courtesy Morphy Auctions, Denver, Pa.; www.MorphyAuctions.com

Oak-framed cardboard Union Leader Cut Plug Tobacco sign issued in 1899. **$4,600**

Photo courtesy James D. Julia Auctioneers, Fairfield, Maine; www.JuliaAuctions.com

Sign, Home Run Cigarettes, cardboard, stone-lithographed advertisement with baseball illustration. Copyright 1909 by the American Tobacco Co. Image 11 1/2" w x 17 1/2" h. Very good condition; outer white border has a couple chips, but only one at the bottom actually extends slightly into the printed image. **$5,750**

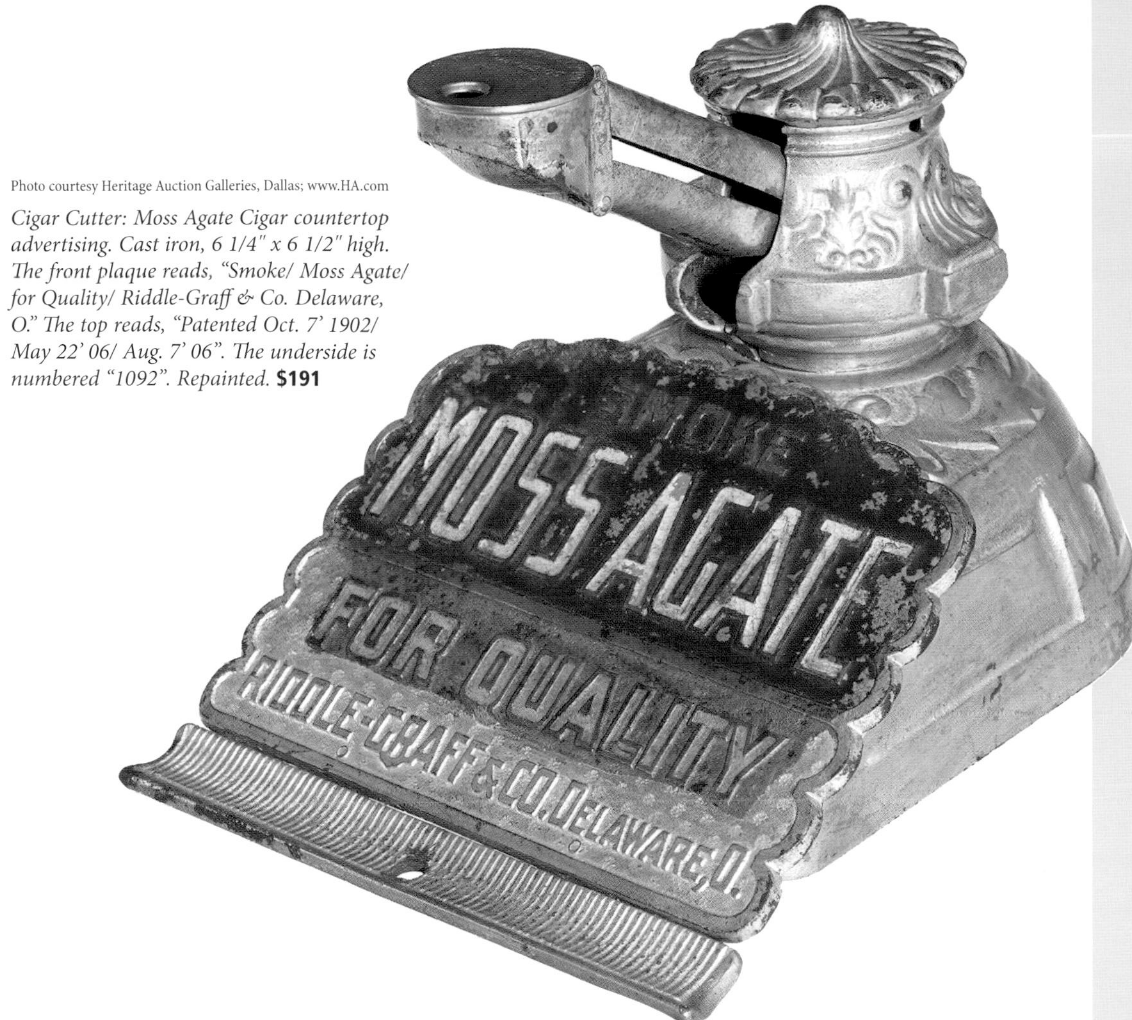

Photo courtesy Heritage Auction Galleries, Dallas; www.HA.com

Cigar Cutter: Moss Agate Cigar countertop advertising. Cast iron, 6 1/4" x 6 1/2" high. The front plaque reads, "Smoke/ Moss Agate/ for Quality/ Riddle-Graff & Co. Delaware, O." The top reads, "Patented Oct. 7' 1902/ May 22' 06/ Aug. 7' 06". The underside is numbered "1092". Repainted. **$191**

Sign, Dutch Baby, porcelain, convex advertisement for Dutch Baby Condensed Milk with tin can illustration of Holland countryside with windmill; 35 1/2" w x 24" h. Good to very good condition with some perimeter edge chips and two areas of fine surface stress cracks. **$1,093**

Sign, Ericsson Steamship, tin, self-framed illustration of the steamship Lord Baltimore leaving the dock with a full accompaniment of passengers, which emphasizes their speedy "20 Knot Day Boat" service between Philadelphia and Baltimore. Lithographed by Meek Co., Coshocton, Ohio, after the painting by H.C. Greaves; 33" w x 23" h. Sign has had professional paint restoration. Displays good to very good with some light surface discoloration, paint chips and light spotting. **$2,875**

Sign, Fleet Bros. Department Store, tin, flat die-cut tin advertisement for a Florida department store depicting a portly gent in red, white, and black encouraging the viewer to "Visit the Big Store First." Mounted to newer wooden backing with similar cut for support; 48" h x 18" w. Overall weather-related chipping and wear. **$210**

Sign, Fry's Chocolate, porcelain, English candy manufacturer with humorous images of a young boy in various stages of anticipation of a Fry's chocolate treat, circa 1910; 30" w x 22" h. Large chip to top middle mounting hole, otherwise only minor chips to perimeter edge. Some very light spotting to white background, otherwise very good condition. **$1,680**

Sign, H.P. Hood & Sons Ice Cream, porcelain, colorful version of this truck sign, with illustration of dairy cow in a summer pasture. Manufactured by the Ingram-Rich Co., Beaver Falls, Pa., circa 1934; 30" d. Good condition; chips to mounting holes and several in field; some light iron stains to the blue sky; some scattered light surface scuffs; some waviness to perimeter edge. **$3,738**

Photo courtesy Old Town Auctions LLC, Boonsboro, Md.; www.OldTownAuctions.com

Sign, Moxie, self-framed tin, featuring the company's mascot horse in a convertible, scarce size and design, some light edge wear and marks to mounting holes, 36 3/8" x 12 3/8". **$4,675**

Sign, Hire's Root Beer, cardboard, embossed with image of bottle on one side and root-beer syrup box on the other; 11" w x 7" h. A few spots of light soiling, otherwise very good condition. **$2,875**

Sign, Hood's Ice Cream, tin, two embossed advertisements back-to-back in their original steel sidewalk sign holder. Overall 20 1/2" w x 33 1/2" h. Sign is good to very good condition; holder good with weathered surface. **$660**

Sign, Iver Johnson Revolver, tin, Double-sided, die cut captioned, "Hammer the Hammer" with graphics to match; 15 3/4" w x 11 3/4" h. Two minor soft bends to bottom, otherwise near excellent condition with original surface gloss. **$5,750**

Sign, J.B. Lewis Shoemaker, tin, illustration of shoemaker at work in his shop to promote this Boston shoe manufacturer. Image size 13 1/4" w x 19 1/4" h. Generally good condition; a few filled nail holes, in-painted "S" to work apron dent, overall soiling and wear, and what appears to be a clear coat that has left some spotting. **$477**

Sign, J.G. Goodwin Slippers, wood, curved, hand-carved sign with original sand paint and gilt highlights, circa late 1800s; 17 1/4" w x 30" h. Very good to excellent condition with nice surface patina. **$230**

Sign, Kool Cigarettes, NRA, illustration of penguin smoking a cigarette for this circa-WWII advertisement from the Brown & Williamson Co.; 17 1/2" w x 11 3/4" h. Good to very good condition. **$201**

Sign, Lakeside Club Bouquet Whiskey, vitrolite, lithograph on milk glass of a Victorian couple sampling a round or two from the Wm. Drueke Co., Grand Rapids, Mich.; 20" w x 17" h. Loss of coloring to portions of litho; chip bottom left corner. ... **$460**

Sign, Maumee Brewing Co., cardboard, illustration of Colonialists enjoying the ale, porter and brown stout from this Toledo, Ohio, brewery. Image 13 3/4" w x 17 1/4" h in vintage frame. Repaired break bottom right with in-painting; repair to top right corner; some chips to image at top margin. **$517**

Sign, Pepsi-Cola, tin, die-cut bottle form, circa 1941, embossed; 12" w x 44 1/2" h. Very good condition with some scattered light black paint overspray. **$360**

Sign, pointing finger, tin, with contemporary plywood reinforcement. Age uncertain; 46" w x 19" h. Fair to good condition. **$230**

Sign, Procter & Gamble's Soaps reverse-on-glass, elaborate lettering highlighted with foil and mother-of-pearl flank this Cincinnati company's trademark logo of the Man in the Moon. Manufactured by the Meuttmann Co., Cincinnati. Image size: 29 1/2" l x 21 1/2" h. Good to very good condition with several areas of paint lifting and loss, notably to the black background surrounding the stars and some of the letters where what appears to be ground mother-of-pearl has been lost. **$1,668**

Sign, Schlitz Brewing Co., tin, fanciful characterization of a gent with the embodiment of the Schlitz trademark logo. Background is realistically lithographed to imitate quarter-sawn oak. Chas. W. Shonk Litho., Chicago. Image 13" w x 19" h in vintage frame. Very good condition with a few soft bends to top and bottom edges. **$1,495**

Sign, Sen-Sen Mints, cardboard, illustration of fashionably attired lady singing on stage with background of chrysanthemums to promote this maker's line of throat and breath lozenges; 12" w x 48" h. Generally good condition; water stain to lady's dress; in-painting at top left margin; surface scuffs and a few small punctures. **$518**

Sign, Sherwin Williams Paints, porcelain, larger version of the die-cut "Cover the Earth" trademark logo; 35 1/2" w x 63" h. Good condition, with some fading and oxidation in places. **$210**

Sign, Sun Oil Co. "two-fisted," tin, die cut, unusual embossed sign to promote their gasoline's performance. Copyright 1932; 39" w x 16" h. Fair condition; several rust spots, pitting, and color loss. Sign reverse features contemporary wood support bracket. **$920**

Photo courtesy James D. Julia Auctioneers, Fairfield, Maine; www.JuliaAuctions.com

Sign, Old Diamond Wedding Rye, reverse on glass, gilt lettering against a blue background. Advertisement from Aug. Baetzhold distributor Buffalo, N.Y. Image 25 1/2" w x 15 1/2" h in period frame. Some lifting to blue background, otherwise good condition. **$258**

Sign, Sweet-Orr Overalls, curved corner advertisement created using both printed lithography and traditional ground-glass firings. Illustration of men engaged in a tug-of-war with a pair of this maker's overalls as testimony to their durability; 18" w x 14" h. Very good condition with only a few small edge chips and nibbles. Retains original corner mounting bracket. **$1,610**

Sign, Thixton, Millett & Co. Distillers, tin, Louisville, Ky., featuring a rustic log cabin whiskey distillery with a buckskin clad "Daniel Boone" character guarding the door. Copyrighted 1904 by Thixton, Millett & Co. Lithographed by Hafusermann Co., N.Y.; 22 1/4" l x 14" h. Very good condition with scattered spots of surface pitting, some of which are difficult to see except upon close inspection. **$1,265**

Sign and tray, Carnation Gum advertisements, includes square tin sign with raised simulated wood grain frame with an illustration of the Carnation Girl. Also includes tip tray with gum package and carnation graphics. Lower left is marked, "Copyright 1906 by the American Art Works, Coshocton, Ohio;" sign measures 13 3/4" square; tip tray 4 1/4" d. Frame of sign appears professionally restored while the field appears to have one small spot of in-painting; tip tray generally good. .... **$805 pair**

String holder, Moxie Soda, traditional bent-wire bottom attached to upper milk-glass panel that advertises "Drink Moxie-Clean-Safe" on one side; 8" w x 26" h. Good to very good condition. **$360**

Thermometer, Moxie, tin, version with Frank Archer image at the bottom and a Moxie bottle at the top. Complete with working thermometer tube and wood holder; 9 3/4" w x 25 1/2" h. Very good condition with scattered scuffs and some minor dents to bottom edge. **$1,020**

Tray, City Brewing Co., pre-Prohibition tray from this Toledo, Ohio, brewer for their Preferred Stock beer featuring the Carnation Girl illustration; 13" d. Very good to excellent condition with a dry, very finely crazed surface finish. .. **$316**

Tray, Eagle Brewing Co., circa 1908, captioned "Good Morning" lithographed by The Meek Co. for this Waterbury, Conn., brewer. 13 1/4" square. Good to very good condition with some professional in-painting concentrated around raised perimeter rim. **$345**

Tray, Evans & Giehl Brewing Co., illustration of thoroughbred filly and her colt used to promote this Rome, N.Y., brewer's line of pure ales; 13 1/4" square. Some professional restoration and in-painting especially to the sky. **$840**

Tray, Finlay Brewing Co., pre-Prohibition tray with young woman holding aloft a bottle of this Toledo, Ohio, brewer's Salvator beer; 12" d. Good, overall matte surface with some crazing to the paint. **$316**

Tray, Moerlein Brewing Co., pre-Prohibition tray from this Cincinnati brewer lithographed by the Chas. W. Shonk Co., Litho, Chicago; 12" d. A few spots of light flaking, otherwise good condition. **$270**

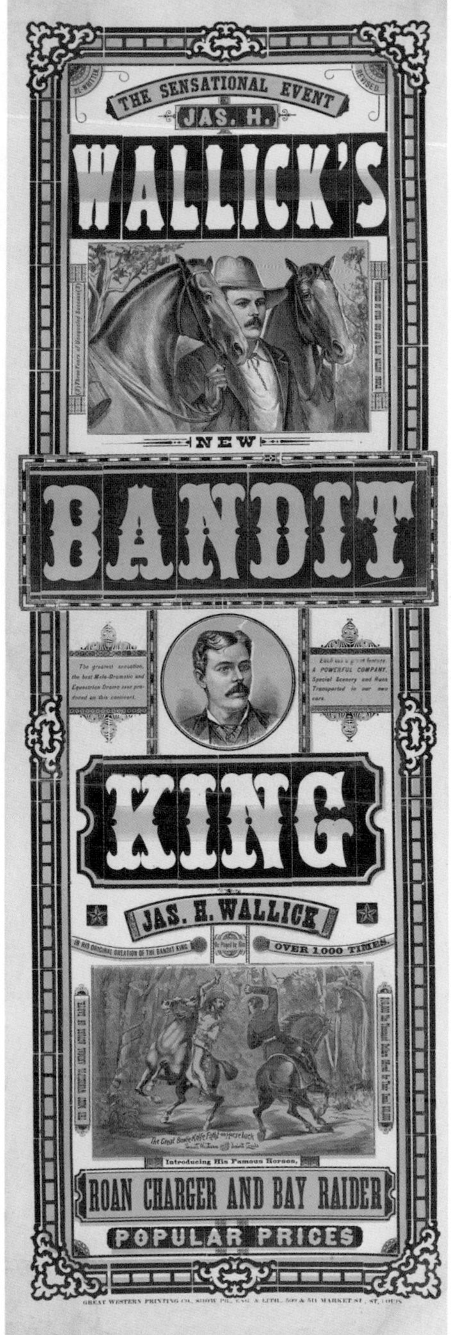

Photo courtesy Heritage Auction Galleries, Dallas; www.HA.com

Nineteenth-Century Lithographic Poster for The Bandit King, a Melodrama, Circa 1886, 14" x 42 1/4" mounted on a larger board. Printed by the Great Western Printing Co., Show PR., Eng. & Litho., 509 & 511 Market Street, St. Louis. The Bandit King was one of the most profitable melodramas of the day. The poster calls this a popularization of the life of Jessie James. The author, producer, manager, and star of the Bandit King, James H. Hallick, shared the billing with his horse actors, "Raider" and "Charger". Professionally restored and repaired. **$1,912**

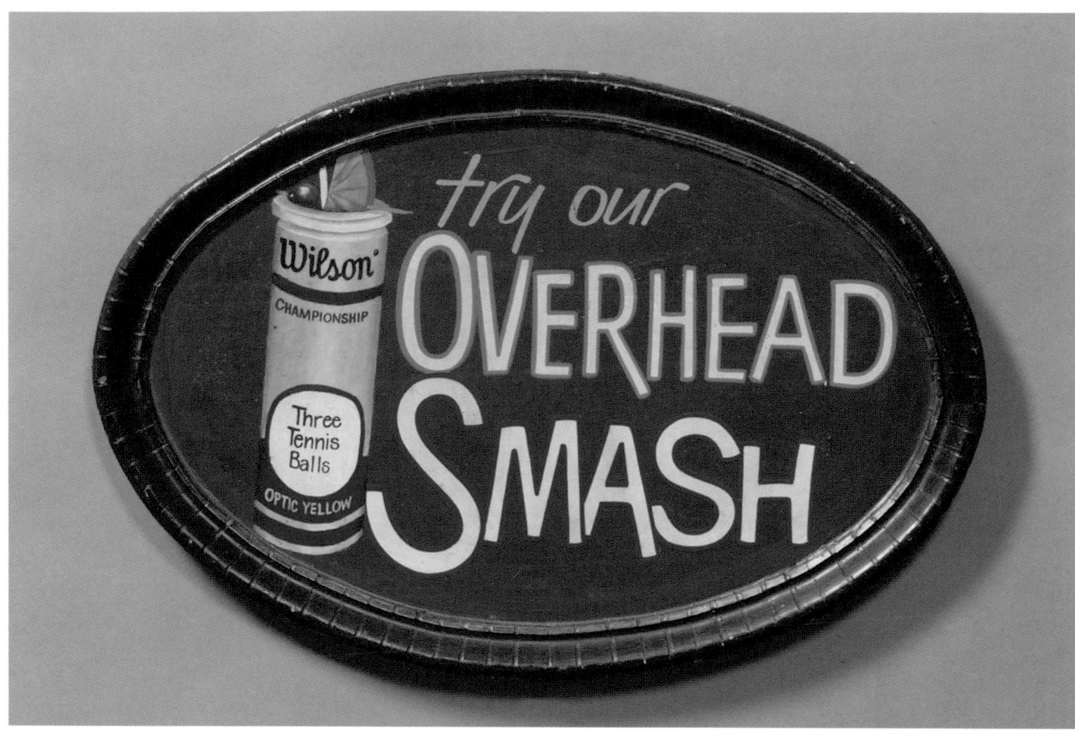

Photo courtesy Skinner Inc., Boston; www.SkinnerInc.com

Sign, Polychrome Painted Oval Country Club Drink, American, mid-20th century, oval wood panel with applied molding depicting a tennis ball canister topped with fruit and a straw with painted lettering "try our Overhead Smash," 16" x 23 1/4". **$296**

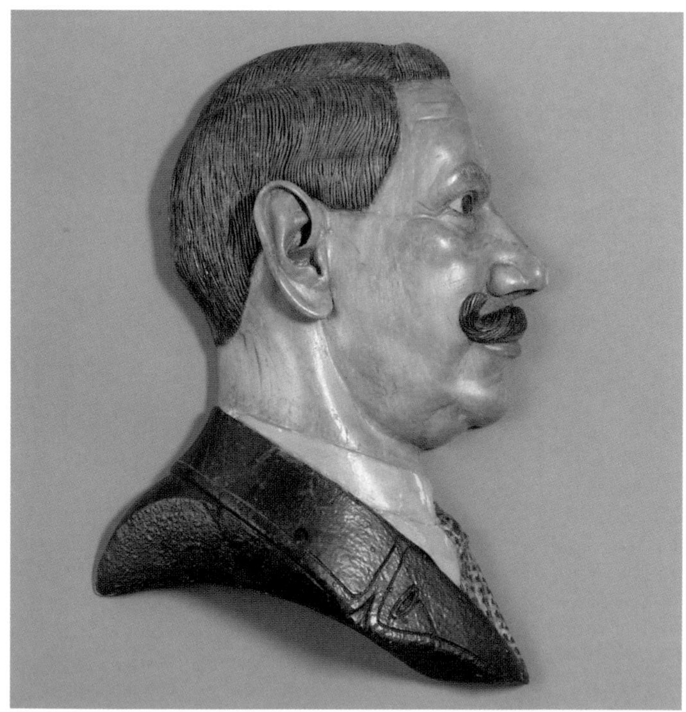

Photo courtesy Skinner Inc., Boston; www.SkinnerInc.com

Sign, Relief Carved and Painted Gent's Head, American, late 19th/early 20th century, 14" x 9 3/4". Possible repair to ear or else it is the original attachment. **$1,500+**

Photo courtesy Skinner Inc., Boston; www.SkinnerInc.com

Sign, Painted Wood, "Fresh Eggs", American, early 20th century, double-sided rectangular panel, 7 3/4" x 24". Normal wear with some paint losses, stains, surface grime. **$830**

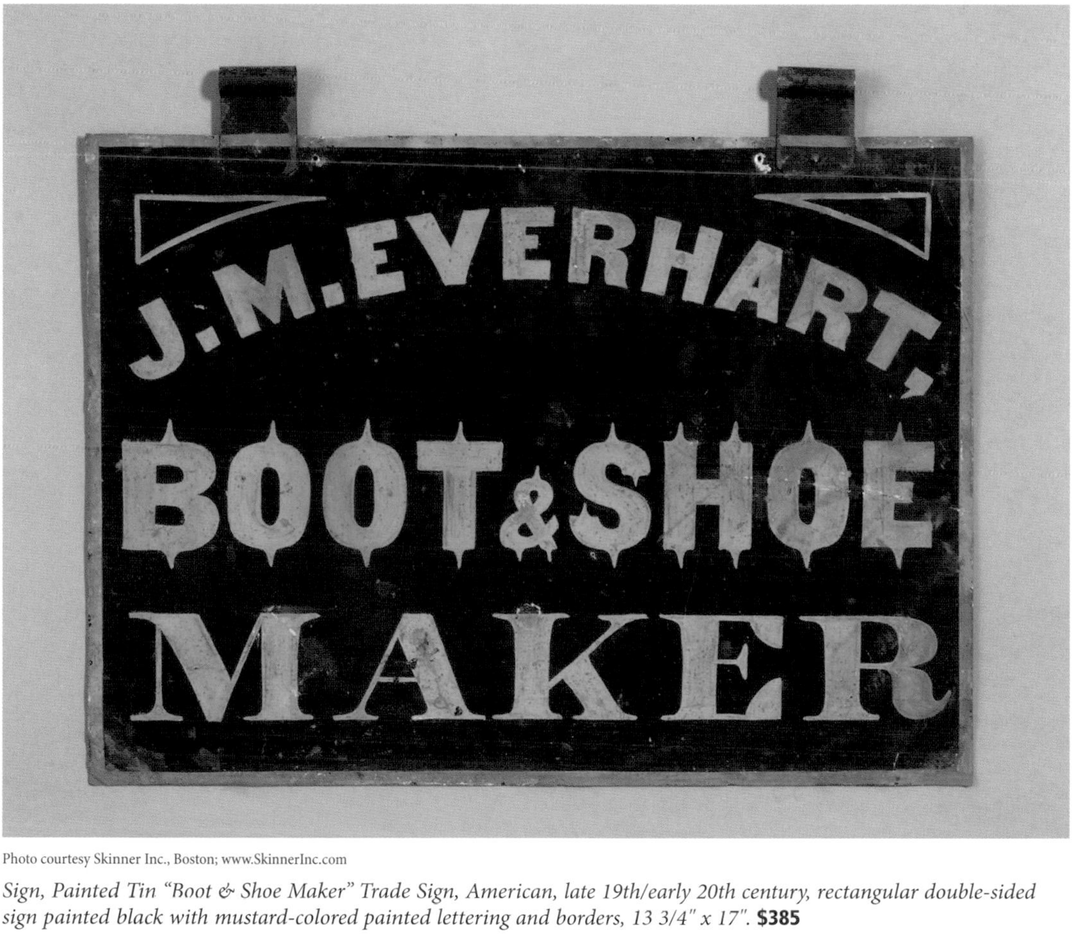

Photo courtesy Skinner Inc., Boston; www.SkinnerInc.com

Sign, Painted Tin "Boot & Shoe Maker" Trade Sign, American, late 19th/early 20th century, rectangular double-sided sign painted black with mustard-colored painted lettering and borders, 13 3/4" x 17". **$385**

ARCHITECTURAL ELEMENTS

Architectural elements, many of which are handcrafted, are those items that have been removed or salvaged from buildings, ships or gardens.

Beginning about 1840, decorative building styles began to feature carved wood and stone, stained glass, and ornate ironwork. At the same time, builders and manufacturers also began to use fancy doorknobs, doorplates, hinges, bells, window locks, shutter pulls and other decorative hardware as finishing touches on new homes and commercial buildings.

Hardware was primarily produced from bronze, brass and iron, and doorknobs also were made from clear, colored and cut glass. Highly ornate hardware began appearing in the late 1860s and remained popular through the early 1900s. Figural pieces that featured animals, birds and heroic or mythological images were popular, as were ornate and graphic designs that complimented the many architectural styles that emerged in the late 19th century.

Photo courtesy Heritage Auction Galleries, Dallas; www.HA.com

Pair of Spanish Colonial-Style Carved and Partially Painted Wood Architectural Panels, 20th century, pine, 95 1/2" x 24" each, rectangular panel in three sections, the lower most with radiating scroll and fluted carving centering quatrefoil medallion; the center most with radiating fluted carving centering painted panels, one of the Madonna and Child, the other of Christ and a Child, above stylized floral motifs and winged head; the top most with full relief figures, of of the Madonna and Child, the other of St. Luke. **$600 pair**

Photo courtesy Heritage Auction Galleries, Dallas; www.HA.com

Pair of Renaissance Revival-Style Stained-Glass Windows, Continental, 19th century, iron, leading, glass, 105" x 24 1/4" each. Hand-painted, bottle-green ground glass, each panel with arched top center reserve of soldier in Renaissance-style costume, surrounded by pendant, cartouche, scroll and floral motifs; within iron frames; minor buckling, rusting to iron. **$3,585 pair**

Art

FUTURE OF THE MARKET: ART

Find a niche with staying power

By Mary P. Manion

Acting Director, Landmarks Gallery and Restoration Studio, Milwaukee

The cable television cliché about 500 channels with nothing on is almost – but not entirely – true. Most of us have discovered a handful of channels that reflect our tastes and echo our interests. It's a long way from a nation of three networks where virtually everyone was exposed to the same programming.

Enter the world of niche audiences, where the masses count for little if a small, devoted coterie can be secured. The phenomenon has always been with us, especially for high-end products, but has been democratized with the spread of cable, satellite dishes and the Internet.

Likewise, the art market has never been without niche collectors, whether of Southwestern art, wildlife prints or Byzantine icons. But in recent years, niche collecting has been accentuated by the trend in art toward no real trend at all. There are no longer any over-arching movements, no Abstract Expressionism or Pop Art, to capture the public's imagination. The "shock of the new," as critic Robert Hughes memorably described Modern Art, is no longer especially shocking or even relevant to many art buyers. The last new artist everyone was talking about, Andy Warhol, made his mark more than 40 years ago and has been dead for two decades.

Everything in art is a niche nowadays, but some niches will have greater staying power than others. Many contemporary artists from the 1990s and later have fulfilled Warhol's prophesy about the diminishing shelf life of celebrity. After enjoying their 15 minutes of fame in the galleries of Manhattan and the pages of Art Forum, they have often been supplanted by new faces. In this environment, the most obvious future indicator for market prices points to the work of stellar artists that has only increased in value over time, whether an El Greco, a Van Gogh or a Hopper. But despite the proliferation of wealth and prestige collecting in rising societies such as China, Russia, India and the Persian Gulf states, this is a game relatively few can play.

In any event, collectors of Hudson River School, folk art and 20th-century Modernism are themselves niches in a world where no one group of taste makers can legislate for everyone else. In these well-explored peaks of the art market, prices will continue to climb into the stratosphere. In recent years auction results for naturalist and Hudson River School painter Martin Johnson Heade (1819-1904) have reached new levels. Unless the global economy sinks into depression, there is every likelihood that artworks by renowned figures in these areas will gain in value.

Below these peaks stretch vast continents of collectible artwork; some well explored, others less so. Some are still on the frontier of the art market, where unknown artists await discovery and bargains can be found. Many of these genres are islands unto themselves. Fanciers of John James Audubon avian prints have little to say to aficionados of Montague Dawson nautical paintings. Devotees of the Harlem Renaissance seldom cross paths with collectors of black-and-white fashion photography. It makes little difference. There is value to be found and investments to be made in most of these areas.

One of the most familiar niche markets involves art produced during the Great Depression by the Works Progress Administration (WPA). The federal program launched by the Roosevelt Administration provided employment for artists by commissioning them to paint murals and produce other artworks for schools, courthouses and other public buildings. Many of the paintings were idealized depictions of America at a time when American values were being tested. Many of the artists who worked for the WPA were involved with various forms of social realism, including the Midwest Regionalism of Grant Wood (1891-1942) and Thomas Hart Benton (1889-1975). As with other genres, Midwest Regionalism nurtured many obscure but talented artists along with a handful of familiar figures. The work of the lesser-knowns can still sometimes be found in local antique or resale stores; the value of even the unknowns has seen modest growth.

Like the Midwest Regionalists, the California Plein Air Impressionist and scene painters of the 1930s-1950s continue to captivate collectors with their representations of the beauty of a particular landscape during a time when the countryside was abundant and relatively untouched by development and environmental pollution. Big names in the genre – such as Edgar Payne (1882-1947) and Alson Skinner Clark (1876-1949) – command big prices. Many galleries in the Southwest feature fine art from this era and have Web sites providing histories of the artists, as well as online purchasing of inventory.

The Harlem Renaissance refers to an African-American cultural movement that flourished in 1920s New York. It is historically important as an early turning point where black Americans began to represent themselves and their lives, endowing their experience with dignity. Painters such as Aaron Douglas (1898-1979) and Jacob Lawrence (1917-2000) command interest beyond collectors of black heritage on the strength of their artistry and have gradually produced gains at the auction block. Imitators of the genre can be found at estate sales and antique shops throughout the country. If a painting from the 1920s through mid-century bears the signature of a black artist, chances are the style was influenced by the Harlem Renaissance.

The advent of photography in the 19th century resulted in a new mode of expression. Of course, many photographs were intended as documents, not artworks, freezing families and public events in time; others were composed and rendered with the intention of being taken seriously as art. The line between art and commerce in photography was often blurry, especially in the areas of portraiture and fashion photography. From Margaret Bourke White (1904-1971) to Henri Cartier Bresson (1908-2004), the market for fine-art photography continues to grow among collectors. Ansel Adams (1902-1984), environmentalist and photographer, was instrumental in calling attention to the natural beauty of the landscape and the preservation of nature. His black-and-white photos are often highly detailed studies of trees, mountain peaks and desert ground, executed with a contrasting palette in which every nuance of black and gray is exquisitely composed against the stark, white sky. His influence can be seen in many works of many contemporary photographers who believe in the conservation of nature. As the world recognizes the importance of "going green," this niche market has a growing interest for many environmentalists.

The first edition of Audubon's portfolio, Birds of America, has enjoyed a niche in fine art collecting since the day they were produced. When the print production began in 1827, the enormous project yielded 456 hand-colored prints of different species in editions of 100 prints each, published on a subscription basis. Reproductions of the series have been printed since his death in 1851, making the original series all the more attractive to the collector.

Audubon wasn't the only visual exponent of Americana. The frontier legend of the American West was indelibly stamped by painters of the 19th and early 20th centuries, who captured the folklore, history and culture of this vast expanse of territory. Frederic Remington (1861-1909) was an American sculptor and painter who rendered cowboys and Indians in bronze. Edward Curtis (1868-1952) turned the new medium of photography on the Western landscape, artfully rendering the vanishing culture of the Plains Indians. Examples of his work perform well at auction, although his photos can still be found in antique shops and estate sales by the astute collector.

Some niche venues have broader range. Works on paper, such as etchings and mezzotints, can be collected not only for individual artists, but according to subject, aesthetic appeal or historical significance. Many collectors of works on paper have a keen interest in history and collect antique pictures that record a period of historical interest. They can be a window onto the past, preserving a simple moment from a different era.

In many respects, the future of collecting will focus on genres or artists that have attracted devoted followings under the radar of the media and in more modest price ranges. Often, scarcity will drive the market upward, as well as speculation by investors who are looking to turn over artwork for profit the way they might sell real estate. Everyone knows that the market price of a Rothko or a Rembrandt can only continue to climb because so few are available for sale. Likewise, if on a smaller scale, the same will hold true for Meiji Era Japanese woodblock prints, 18th-century Persian miniatures and other pieces of fine art that may never reach the heights of the market, but will continue to gain value as demand rises and supply in private hands diminishes.

Also see Folk Art, Oriental Objects, Photographs, Tiffany.

Photo courtesy Heritage Auction Galleries, Dallas; www.HA.com

Arthur Dove (American 1880-1946), Continuity, 1939, tempera and encaustic on canvas, 6" x 8", signed lower center: Dove. Titled Continuity on exhibition label attached to stretcher. **$131,450**

Artists, A to Z

Charles Partridge Adams, (American, 1858-1942), San Juan Mountains, large oil on canvas, scene shows partially snow covered peaks reflecting a pink sunset, a crescent moon is seen under a blue sky and shadows are cast on the mountains backside. Signed on reverse of canvas and titled on the stretcher. Housed in a gesso decorated period fame, which is "as is", 36" x 29", craquelure with surface dirt. **$10,925**

Carol Anthony, (American, b. 1943) Late Beach in Newport, 1979; Cray-Pas and enamel on paper (framed); Signed, dated and titled; 22" x 30" (sheet). **$1,440**

Milton Clark Avery, attributed (American, 1885-1965), The Purple Sofa, oil on canvas, scene shows two women seated facing each other on a purple sofa. One wears blue, the other brown. Signed bottom right, "Milton Avery 1951". Housed in what appears to be its original gilt wood frame, 18" x 25 3/4". **$6,000**

Joseph Barrett, (American, b. 1935) Early Morning; Oil on canvas (artist-made frame); Signed and titled; 30" x 32", 39" x 37" (frame). **$7,200**

Walter Emerson Baum, (American, 1884-1956) Autumn Forest Scene, 1908; Oil on board (framed); Signed and dated; 18 1/8" x 12 1/8". **$3,000**

Walter Emerson Baum, (American, 1884-1956) Bucks County Winter Scene; Oil on canvas (framed); Signed; 32" x 40". **$9,000**

Walter Emerson Baum, (American, 1884-1956) Bucks County Road, 1946; Oil on board (framed); Signed, dated and titled; 16" x 20". **$5,100**

Reynolds Beal, (American, 1867-1951), The Circus is in Town, pastel on paper, summer scene shows a multi-tent circus with wagon set up for business. Several figures are seen around tents and flags fly off the big top. Pencil signed lower right. Housed in a modern carved and gilt double frame with glass, 8 1/2" x 11 1/2" (sight). **$2,990**

Reynolds Beal, (American, 1867-1951), Sparks Circus, mixed media, scene shows a number of circus workers and participants outside a big top flying two American flags. A large crowd is seen along with an elephant and figure on horseback. Signed lower right, dated "1931" and titled. Housed in a gesso decorated modern frame with double matte, 14 1/2" x 16 1/4" (sight). **$4,312**

Romare Bearden, (American, 1914-1988) Slave Ship, 1977; Screen print, in colors (framed); Signed and numbered 101/144; 30 1/2" x 20" (sight). **$2,160**

Robert Beck, (American, b. 1950) Untitled; Oil on board (framed); Signed; 15 3/4" x 23 3/4". **$1,140**

Thomas Hart Benton, (American, 1889-1975) Study for The Crane, circa 1915-20; Pencil on paper (both sides, framed); 7 3/8" x 6 1/4" (sight). **$600**

Johann Berthelsen, (American, 1883-1972) Plaza Hotel, New York; Oil on canvas (framed); Signed and titled; 16" x 12". **$9,000**

Carrie Horton Blackman, (American, 1856-1935), Nasturtiums Still Life, oil on canvas glued to cardboard,

Photo courtesy Heritage Auction Galleries, Dallas; www.HA.com

William Herbert Dunton (American, 1878-1936), The Badger Hole (The Spill), 1906, oil on canvas 28" x 19", signed lower right: W. Herbert Dunton / '06.
$143,400

Photo courtesy James D. Julia Auctioneers, Fairfield, Maine; www.JuliaAuctions.com

Johann Berthelsen, (American, 1883-1972), Times Square, New York City, oil on board, winter street scene shows the intersection at Times Square. Several pedestrians cross in front of stopped cars. Signed lower right. Housed in a partial gilt French-style frame, 20" x 14". **$18,400**

scene shows colorful flowers in a rose-colored pitcher. Two flowers are seen on tabletop. Signed lower right. Housed in a period carved wood gold frame, 17 3/4" x 13 3/4". Inconsistent varnish. **$900**

Susan M. Blubaugh, (American, b. 1952) The House Across the Creek; Oil on linen (framed); Signed; 20" x 24". **$1,140**

Oscar Florianus Bluemner, (American, 1867-1938) Two works of art: View on the Harlem River, New York, Sept. 17, 1914; Black crayon on paper (framed); Signed, dated and titled; 5" x 6 3/4" (sheet); Harlem River, New York, Oct. 18, 1914; Ink and wash on paper (framed); Titled and dated; 5" x 6 3/4" (sheet). .... **$1,200 pair**

Rosalie (Rosa) Bonheur, (American, 1822-1899), Comanche Red River, water-colored pencil sketch of an Indian brave standing, holding a shield, bow and arrows in one hand and a spear in the other. Pencil titled above figure. Signed lower right "Rosa B-" and dated lower left "1876". Housed in a gilt frame with watercolor highlighted matte, 9" x 5 1/2" (sight). Some wrinkling to paper. **$5,750**

Bruce Braithwaite, (American, b. 1950) Taxi Driver, New York City; Oil on canvas (framed); Signed and titled; 24" x 32". **$3,600**

Carl W. Brandien, (American, 1886-1965) Edge of Grand Canyon; Oil on canvas (framed); Signed and titled; 24" x 30". **$1,200**

Albert Thompson Bricher, (American, 1837-1908), Rocks and Seaweed, watercolor, coastline scene of a beach at low tide with seaweed-covered rocks and pine-covered bluff. Signed lower left with conjoined first initials "A. T. Bricher". Housed in a dark-stained molded wood period frame, 10" x 20", top edge with some loss, generally good. Some toning. **$4,600**

Alfred Thompson Bricher, (American, 1837-1908), Rock-Strewn Beach, watercolor on paper, shows a beach with large and small rocks, small waves with sailboat nearby and one in distance. A grass-covered sand dune is seen at the end of a beach. Signed lower right with conjoined "AT Bricher 35". Housed in a gilt reeded-edge frame with white matte. Deeley Gallery, Manchester Village, Vt., label affixed to reverse, 10 1/4" x 26 1/2". **$6,325**

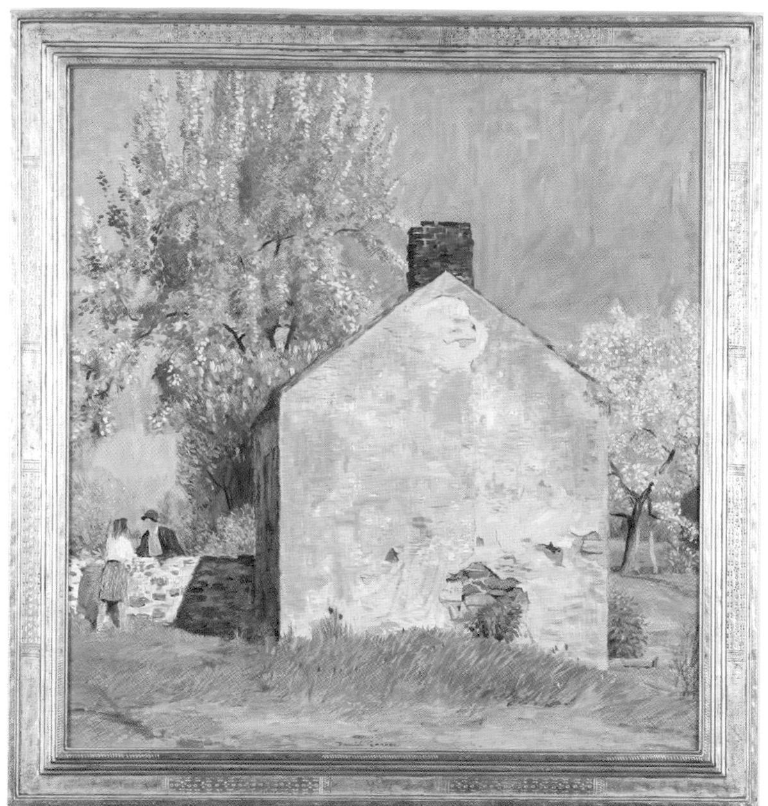

Photo courtesy Sanford Alderfer Auction & Appraisal, Hatfield, Pa.; www.AlderferAuction.com

Daniel Garber (American, 1880-1958), May Day, completed 1941, oil on canvas, 30" x 28", signed lower center, "Daniel Garber". In a Ben Badura frame. Exhibited: Woodmere, 1942. Included in the Daniel Garber catalog raisonne (2006), written by Lance Humphries, published by Hollis Taggart Galleries, Vollume II, page 268, plate 765. **$207,000**

Photo courtesy Sanford Alderfer Auction & Appraisal, Hatfield, Pa.; www.AlderferAuction.com

Walter Emerson Baum, (American, 1884-1956), winter scene of village with snow falling, oil on canvas, signed lower right, 25" x 30". **$31,625**

Photo courtesy James D. Julia Auctioneers, Fairfield, Maine; www.JuliaAuctions.com

Reynolds Beal, (American, 1867-1951), Downey Bros. Circus, Elephants and Appaloosa, mixed media, scene shows a wide view of a circus with three large tents flying American flags, two large elephants with riders, a man on horse and other performers. Signed lower left, dated "1934" and inscribed "Downey Bros. Circus". Housed in a carved and gilt double frame with white matte, 14 1/4" x 17 3/4" (sight). **$2,640**

Photo courtesy Sanford Alderfer Auction & Appraisal, Hatfield, Pa.; www.AlderferAuction.com

George W. Sotter (American, 1879 1953), Winter Hillside, oil on canvas, 22" x 26", signed lower right, "G.W. Sotter". **$172,500**

John Bunyan Bristol, (American, 1826-1909), Ausable Lake, New York, oil on canvas, scene shows a small sailboat on calm water with mountain background and green tree shoreline in foreground. Lifting clouds and mist blanket some of the mountain view. Signed lower right "J B Bristol". Housed in a modern gilt molded wood frame, 18" x 30"; five small patches to reverse with corresponding in-painting, visible stretcher lines. **$6,900**

Harrison Bird Brown, (American, 1831-1915), Coastal Landscape, oil on canvas, scene shows waves crashing upon steep cliffs having grass-covered tops. Signed bottom right "H.B 1874". Housed in a gesso decorated gilt frame, 9" x 15". **$2,530**

Everett Lloyd Bryant, (American, 1864-1945) Untitled; Oil on wood panel; Signed; 40" x 48". **$3,360**

Maude Drein Bryant, (American, 1880-1946) Trees and Evergreens; Oil on canvas board (framed); With artist's studio stamp; 12" x 16". **$1,920**

Emile Bulcke, (Belgian, 1875-1963), The Flute Player, large oil on canvas, woodland pond scene shows a child playing a flute only draped in a blue cloth sitting on a grassy bank next to a pond filled with lilies. Housed in its original decorated wood frame having an artist name plaque and dated "1926". Painting is unsigned, 34" x 44". Some in-painting. **$2,400**

David Davidovich Burliuk, (Ukranian, 1882-1967) Untitled; Mixed media on panel (framed); Signed; 6 3/4" x 8 1/4". **$3,900**

Howard Russell Butler, (American, 1856-1934) Untitled; Oil on canvas (framed); Signed; 31" x 39". **$2,040**

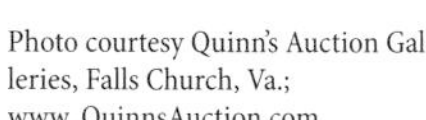
Photo courtesy Quinn's Auction Galleries, Falls Church, Va.; www. QuinnsAuction.com

Bert Geer Phillips (American, 1868-1956), Voices of the Woods, 35" x 48" (framed) oil on canvas by noted Taos school painter. Woolsey Brothers frame. Originally purchased from artist in 1911 by Iowa Senator James Henry Trewin.
$300,000+

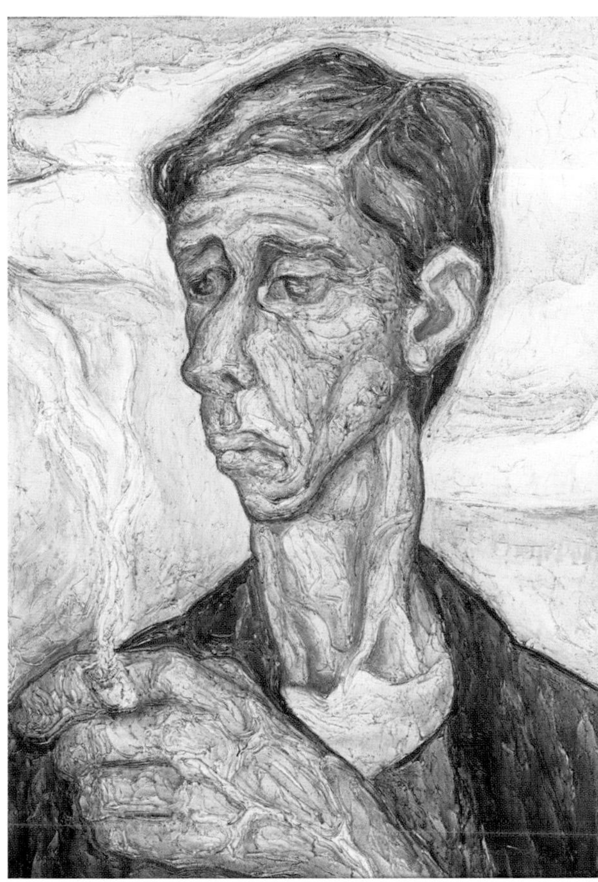

Photo courtesy Rago Arts and Auction Center, Lambertville, N.J.; www.RagoArts.com

Oswaldo Guayasamin, (Ecuadorian, 1919-1999) Hombre Fumando, 1941; Oil on board (framed); Signed, dated and titled; 26 1/4" x 19" (sight). **$39,000**

Ranulph Bye, (American, 1916-2003) A Farm in New Jersey, Everittstown, Feb. 3, 1999; Watercolor on paper (framed); Signed; 12 3/4" x 20 1/4" (sight). **$1,200**

Kenneth L. Callahan, (American, 1905-1986) Untitled, 1926; Gouache on paper (framed); Signed and dated; 19" x 23 1/2" (sight). **$4,200**

Kenneth L. Callahan, (American, 1905-1986) Fiery Night, 1955; Tempera and ink on Bristol Board (framed); Signed and dated; 23 1/4" x 31 1/8". **$3,900**

Laurence A. Campbell, (American, b. 1940) Broadway near Union Square; Oil on Masonite (framed); Signed and titled; 16" x 12". **$16,800**

Sir David Young Cameron, (United Kingdom 1865-1945), Luxor, Egypt, watercolor and graphite, scene shows the ruins with large pillars and grand entrance. Watercolor highlights to background, buildings and sky. Pencil signed bottom right. Housed in modern gilt frame with a double matte with lined highlights and artist name. Original label from Jas. McClure & Son, Glasgow, with artist name and title, dated "16/10/28". 16 1/2" x 9" (sight). **$632**

Mary Helen Carlisle, (American, 1869-1925), Water Garden at Newton, Tipperary, oil on canvas mounted on wood panel, scene shows a colorful garden landscape with water, trees, flowers and Greek-style building with columns. Initialed bottom right. Also having partial labels and a full title label. Housed in wide gilt frame with inner liner. This artist is best known for her pastel and oil paintings of

Photo courtesy John Moran Auctioneers Inc., Altadena, Calif.; www.JohnMoran.com

Nicolai Fechin, (Russian-American, 1881-1955), The Wood Engraver, this image won the 1924 Thomas R. Proctor Award for Portraiture at the National Academy of Design. **$1,092,500**

Photo courtesy James D. Julia Auctioneers, Fairfield, Maine; www.JuliaAuctions.com

Abbott Fuller Graves, (American, 1859-1936), Nature's Color Pallet, oil on canvas still life shows a variety of colorful flowers in a tiered arrangement against a mottled background. Flowers include red, pink and white zinnias, blue lupines, yellow and white wildflowers. All with different shades of green leaves. Signed lower right "Abbott Graves". Housed in its original gilt frame liner, 30" x 15", professionally cleaned, some light craquelure. **$31,625**

famous gardens in the United States and Great Britain, 32" x 24". **$2,300**

Constance Cochrane, (American, 1888-1962) Iris; Oil on board (framed); Signed; 8" x 10". **$1,080**

Fern Isabel Kuns Coppedge, (American, 1883-1951) Untitled; Oil on board (framed); Signed; 12" x 15 3/4" (sight). **$7,800**

Fern Isabel Kuns Coppedge, (American, 1883-1951) Harbor Afternoon; Oil on canvas (framed); Signed; 16" x 16". **$28,800**

Stark Davis, (American, 1885-1950) Untitled; Oil on canvas (framed); Signed; 34" x 34". **$3,240**

Mauritz Frederik De Haas, (American, 1832-1895), Hudson Under the Moonlight, large oil on canvas, scene shows a large paddle-wheel steamer plying a waterway while a small boat with three men net fish. A ferry landing with several sailboats is seen on right side with buildings and dock. Mountains are seen on right side. Signed lower left "MFH de Haas N.A." Housed in a wide gilt frame, 27 1/2" x 41". **$34,500**

Franklin Benjamin DeHaven, (American, 1856-1934) Waterfall; Oil on canvas (framed); Signed; 40" x 32". **$1,560**

Franklin Benjamin DeHaven, (American, 1856-1934) Rural Farm Scene; Oil on board (framed); Signed; 18" x 24". **$1,080**

James Denmark, (American, b. 1936) Friends Walking, 1972; Collage (framed); Signed; 15 3/4" x 11 1/2" (sight). **$4,800**

James Denmark, (American, b. 1936) Bread eaters, 1972; Collage (framed); Signed; 12" x 10" (sight). **$4,800**

James Denmark, (American, b. 1936) Reclining Woman, 1972; Collage (framed); Signed; 10 1/2" x 14 3/8" (sight). **$3,900**

Thomas Colman Dibdin, (British, 1810-1893), Abbeville, watercolor street scene shows a large cathedral in background with busy street in foreground. Storefronts line both sides. People ride in carriages on a dirt street. Titled and signed lower left with date "1877". Housed in a modern burl-type frame with white matte, 21 1/4" x 14 1/2" (sight). **$575**

Arthur Vidal Diehl, (American, 1870-1929) Untitled, 1922; Oil on board (framed); Signed, dated and inscribed; 4 7/8" x 10 3/4". **$3,120**

Walt Disney Studios, limited-edition framed animation art, Villainous Portraits, COA affixed verso, 16" h x 30" w. **$100**

Mstislav Valerianovich Dobujinsky, (Russian, 1875-1957), Monument to Peter the Great in St. Petersburg, Russia, lithograph, heightened by china white, blue green and pale red applied by the artist. The scene shows E.M. Falconet sculpture of man on rearing horse on rock plinth. Pencil signed bottom right and dated "22" in the print. Note: Accompanying lot is a copy of the artist obituary and small memorial exhibition pamphlet. Housed in a modern silver frame with white matte, 9 1/2" x 14 1/4" (sight). **$1,380**

David Y. Ellinger, (American, 1913-2003), framed theorem, basket of fruit with bird perched on grape cluster to right, signed "D.V.E." lower right below basket, oil on velvet, 10 3/4" x 13 3/4" (sight); red and black painted frame. **$3,450**

Frank F. English, (American, 1854-1922) Untitled; Watercolor on paper (framed); Signed; 19 3/4" x 28 1/8" (sheet). **$2,280**

Gary Thomas Erbe, (American, b. 1944) 76 Special, 1975; Oil on canvas (framed); Signed and dated; 8" x 15"; Exhibitions: "Gary T. Erbe: 25 Years in Retrospect," The Butler Institute of American Art, Youngstown, Ohio, Jan. 21 - March 5. .... **$24,000**

Philip Howard Evergood, (American, 1901-1973), Flowers by the Lake, oil on canvas scene shows a young blonde girl in

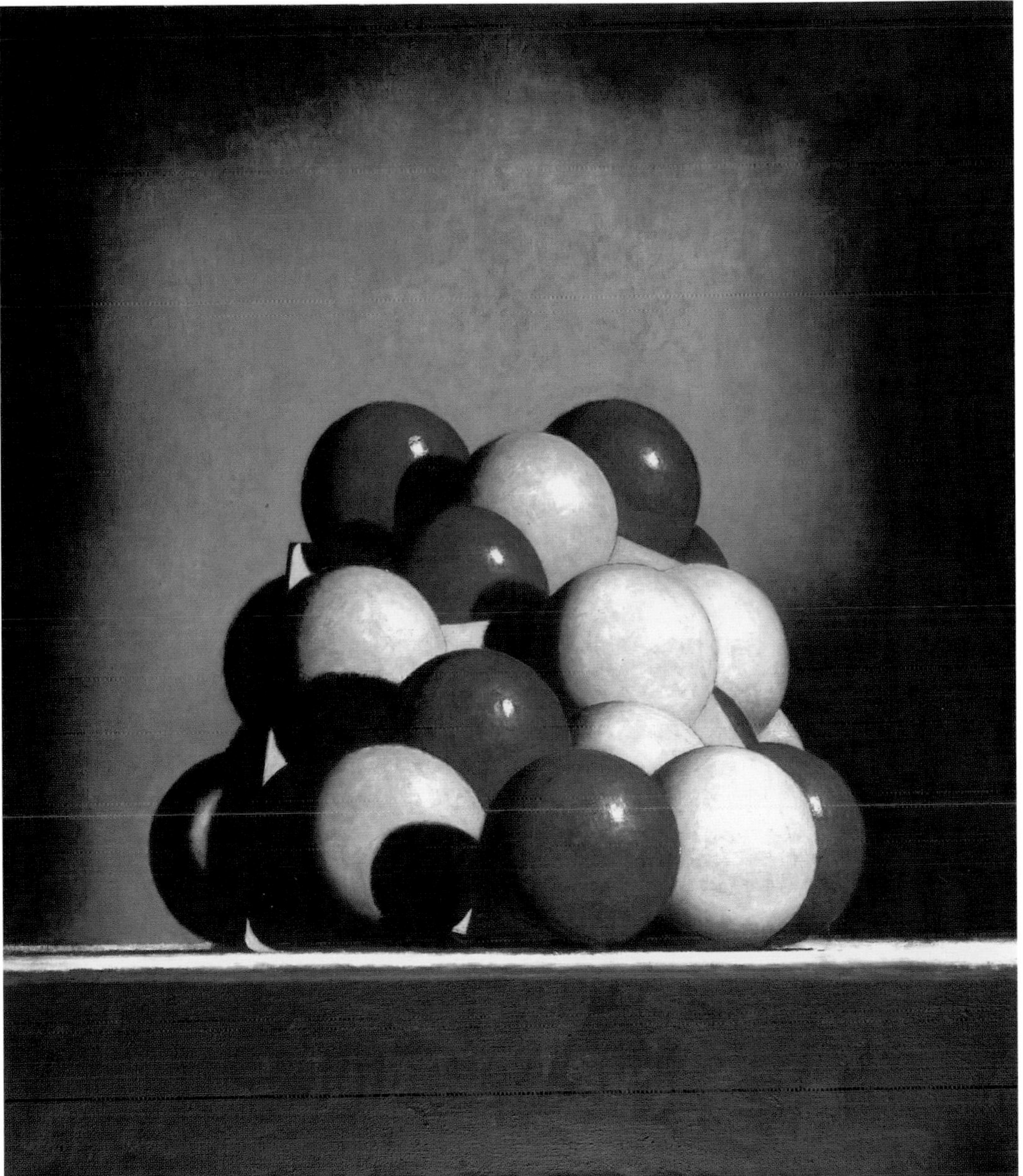

Photo courtesy Rago Arts and Auction Center, Lambertville, N.J.; www.RagoArts.com

John Stuart Gibson, (American, b. 1958) Arrangement in Blue and White, 1990; Oil on canvas (framed); Signed, dated and titled; 47" x 42". **$4,200**

yellow bikini at the top of a stairway holding an earthenware bulbous vase full of red poppies. The red poppies with green stems fill half of the painting and partly obscure the scene behind her, which includes several large boats on water, one of which is going through a railroad bridge, which has rotated to allow it through. A lighthouse is seen next to multi-storied house and the open ocean is beyond. Signed lower left "Philip Evergood" and dated "55". Housed in a period partial gilt molded wood frame with linen liner. There are three labels, one from the Wadsworth Atheneum, Hartford Conn., with artist, title and owner as Whitney Museum of American Art. The other label of Terry Dintenfass, Inc., New York; and a third label which is only a fragment, 48 1/2" x 30", very good condition, some craquelure. There are several small white-painted sections that fluoresce under UV light, which appear to be the same white in other areas. **$201,250**

Henry Lawrence Faulkner, (American, 1924-1981) Untitled; Oil on board (framed); Signed; 7" x 5". **$1,920**

John Fery, (Austrian/American, 1859-1934) Untitled; Oil on canvas; Signed; 36" x 72". **$12,000**

Photo courtesy James D. Julia Auctioneers, Fairfield, Maine; www.JuliaAuctions.com

George Inness Jr., (American, 1854-1926), After the Storm, oil on canvas, panoramic scene shows a valley landscape with cultivated fields and a village nestled on the valley floor. Hills are seen in the background, partially obscured by dark rain clouds, and a rainbow is present. Two travelers follow a hay wagon in the foreground. Signed "G Inness 18_8". Housed in an antique gilt frame, 14" x 20". Relined, restored with in-painting. **$2,990**

Photo courtesy Rago Arts and Auction Center, Lambertville, N.J.; www.RagoArts.com

Walt Francis Kuhn, (American, 1877-1949) Apples, 1933; Oil on canvas (Newcomb-Macklin frame); Signed and dated; 13" x 22", 22 1/4" x 31" (frame); Exhibition: Walt Kuhn Memorial Exhibition, Cincinnati Art Museum, Cincinnati, 1960 (label on verso). **$9,600**

Photo courtesy John Moran Auctioneers Inc., Altadena, Calif.; www.JohnMoran.com

William Joseph McCloskey, (American, 1859-1941), Florida Oranges, signed and dated oil on canvas of his best-known subject of oranges with paper wrappers. **$546,250**

Washington F. Friend, (Canadian, 1820-1886) A View of Cheltenham, Pennsylvania, historical watercolor panoramic view on bluff above a large river. The oval watercolor shows the river full of large three-mast sailing vessels along busy wharfs dotted with large buildings. A man and woman sit on the river's edge in the foreground looking out over this view. The city with large buildings, one having a dome, others with spires and on the left hand hill there appears to be a large fort with flag. Mountains are seen in the background. Along the wharf are two white river side-wheel boats. Signed lower left "W F Friend". Housed in what appears to be its original gilt frame with oval cutout gilt matte. Old label attached to back

Photo courtesy Heritage Auction Galleries, Dallas; www.HA.com

American Artist (20th Century), Cupid, oil on canvas, 20" x 16 1/2", unsigned. **$926**

with location, 13" x 21 3/4" sight. Some toning, generally in good condition. **$3,450**

Charles Arthur Fries, (American, 1854-1940) Untitled; Oil on un-stretched canvas (framed); Signed; 5" x 4 1/8". **$1,800**

Henry Martin Gasser, (American, 1909-1981) Farm Road; Watercolor on paper mounted on illustration board (framed); Signed; 7 1/2" x 10" (sight). **$480**

Henry Martin Gasser, (American, 1909-1981) Untitled, 1950s; Watercolor on paper laid on palette (framed); Signed; 11 1/4" x 15 1/2" (sight, irregular). **$1,920**

Gertrude Gazelle Gardner, (American, 1878-1975), New England Harbor Scene, oil on canvas scene shows a schooner moored in a calm harbor with building on tall posts and grass-lined shore. Beyond is a hillside with many buildings. Possibly a Maine setting. Signed lower left. Housed in a carved and gesso decorated gilt frame, 16" x 20", very good condition. **$960**

Jane Gilday, (American, 20th century) On a Lane in Kingwood; Oil on board (artist-made frame); Signed and titled; 25" x 25", 29" x 29" (with frame). **$2,520**

Jeff Gola, (American, 20th century) The Johnson Ferry House; Egg Tempera on board (framed); Signed and titled; 18" x 19 3/4". **$2,640**

John R. Grabach, (American, 1886-1981) Untitled, 1950s; Oil on palette (framed); Signed; 11 1/2" x 15 3/4" (sight, irregular); Literature: Katlan, Alexander, "The Palette Reveals the Artist," American Art Review, Volume XVI, Number 5, September - October 2004 (illustrated). **$1,800**

Charles C. Gruppe, (American, 1928-), Winter Solitude, large oil on canvas, scene shows snow-covered water surrounded by low hills and trees. A fence-lined road leads to the frozen water. Signed lower right "C Gruppe". Housed in a modern aluminum frame, 48" x 32". **$1,150**

Charles P. Gruppe, (American, 1860-1940), Fishing Boat, oil on canvas, seascape shows two fishing boats passing each other under gray skies. Signed lower right "C.P. Gruppe". Elliot Galleries label affixed to reverse. Housed in its original gesso decorated gilt frame, 8" x 10". Frame with losses. **$1,840**

David Hahn, (American, 20th century) Winter Landscape, Erwinna; Acrylic on canvas (framed); Signed and titled; 30" x 40". **$1,560**

Lilian Westcott Hale, (American, 1881-1963) Portrait of Miss Anita Potts (Mrs. Edward Boit); Charcoal on paper (framed); Signed and titled; 20 1/4" x 13 3/4" (sight). **$6,000**

Helen Hamilton, (American, 1889-1970) Looking Out to Sea; Oil on canvas (framed); 20" x 22"; Exhibition: "Helen Hamilton (1889-1970): An American Post-Impressionist," Westmoreland Museum of Art, Greensburg, Pa., July 6 – Aug. 31, 1986. .... **$3,600**

Frederick William Harer, (American, 1879-1947) View Across the Delaware; Oil on board (framed); Signed; 10" x 14". **$1,320**

Glenn D. Harren, (American, b. 1952) Sienna Grass; Oil on Masonite (framed); Signed and titled; 18" x 24". **$660**

Judy Henn, (American, 20th century) She's Never Been Simple; Acrylic on board (framed); Signed; 15 1/2" x 19 1/4" (sight). **$420**

Photo courtesy Heritage Auction Galleries, Dallas; www.HA.com

Walter Whitehead (American, 1874-1936), Encore, Cream of Wheat ad illustration, 1908, oil on canvas, 31 1/4" x 20", signed with a monogram lower right. Many of the Cream of Wheat paintings traveled across the U.S. in a series of landmark museum exhibitions presented by Nabisco's historian and archivist, David Stivers. **$3,585**

Hilaire Hiler, (French/American, 1898-1966) Backyard, 1927; Oil on canvas board (framed); Signed, dated and titled with studio stamp; 18" x 15". **$5,100**

John William Hill, (American, 1812-1879) Untitled; Watercolor on paper; Signed; 4 3/4" x 7 1/4" (sheet). **$3,120**

Margo Hoff, (American, mid-20th Century), Balcony View New York City, oil on canvas, view of city looking across a wide street with cars and tree-lined water. A white pigeon in foreground is seen on a fancy wrought-iron railing. Signed lower left "M. Hoff". Housed in a partially painted blue molded wood frame, 30" x 15". **$1,150**

Harry Horn, (American, 1901-1982) Untitled; Oil on board (framed); Signed; 7 1/2" x 9 3/8" (sight). **$600**

Josef Israels, (Dutch, 1824-1911), Preparing the Meal, oil on canvas interior scene shows a young mother with infant seated at a table with a man and woman peeling vegetables. Another woman pours coffee while a cat watches the infant. A window is on left side, cascading light on the scene. Signed lower left. Housed in a modern gesso decorated frame, 22 1/4" x 26 1/4". Several old patches to reverse, in-painting, stretcher lines. **$13,200**

William Jachwak, (American, b. 1954) Bucks County Spring; Oil on canvas (framed); Signed; 20" x 24". **$1,800**

Don F. Kaiser, (American, b. 1958) Winter Daybreak; Oil on canvas (framed); Signed and titled; 20" x 24". **$1,140**

Max Kuehne, (American, 1880-1968) Looking Up from the River, New Hope, Pennsylvania; Watercolor and graphite on paper (framed); With estate stamp; 14 1/2" x 18 1/2" (sight). **$1,200**

Walt Francis Kuhn, (American, 1877-1949), Parade, watercolor, scene shows a parading horse with man dressed in fancy uniform. Signed lower right and dated "41". Titled bottom left of a hand-line highlighted matte, which is housed in a modern frame with wide white matte, 7" x 8" (sight). **$1,955**

Andreas Christian G. Lapine, (Russian/Canadian, 1866-1952) Birches and Poplars; Oil on canvas board (framed); Signed; 16" x 20". **$3,000**

William Langson Lathrop, (American, 1859-1938) North Shore, Long Island; Oil on canvas (framed); Signed; 10" x 13". **$7,200**

William Langson Lathrop, (American, 1859-1938) Evening; Charcoal and watercolor on paper (framed); Signed; 8 1/8" x 10 7/8" (sight). **$1,560**

Ernest Lawson, (American, 1873-1939), Autumn Landscape, pastel with fall colors shows a line of trees in front of a body of water with rolling hills. Signed lower right "E. Lawson." Housed in a gilt replacement frame, 14 3/4" x 20 3/4". One corner chipped. Mounted on light cardboard. **$9,200**

Sadie H. Lowes, (American, 1870-?), Winter in Chicago, oil on panel, shows heavy snow that has fallen on a residential area with tall building in background. Signed lower right "Lowes". Housed in a stepped gilt wood carved frame, 24" x 18 1/4". Minor in-painting. **$920**

Harry Leith-Ross, (American, 1886-1973) New Hope, Pa.; Watercolor on paper (framed); Signed; 20 1/4" x 28 3/4" (sight). **$12,000**

Thomas Corwin Lindsay, (American, 1838-1907) Untitled; Oil on canvas (framed); Signed; 18" x 22". **$1,800**

Raoul Maucherat de Longpre, (French, 1855-1911) Lilacs; Watercolor and gouache on paper (framed); Signed; 27" x 19 1/4" (sight). **$2,880**

George Benjamin Luks, (American, 1867 1933), Memorial Library, watercolor, scene shows a column-front library with figures on stairs. The library sits on a small grassy knoll surrounded by trees. Signed lower left. Housed in a modern gilt wood frame with white matte, 15 1/2" x 19 1/4" (sight). **$9,200**

Rene Magritte, (Belgian, 1898-1967), Vignette Sketches, pencil and watercolor, small sketches on a folded hotel card bearing an engraving of the hotel on one quarter of it with the other three quarters having a variety of sketches, some of which are in black watercolor. Most have a title and most are of single objects. Signed lower left "Magritte". Housed in a modern frame with black and gold matte which has

Photo courtesy Sanford Alderfer Auction & Appraisal, Hatfield, Pa.; www.AlderferAuction.com

George W. Sotter, (American, 1879-1953), The Valley of the Delaware, hillside view of the Delaware River, oil on canvas, 22" x 26", signed lower left, Sotter; complemented by a signed gilt floral-carved Ben Badura frame, minor loss to frame, sight: 21 1/2" x 25 1/2", width: 2 1/2", painting titled verso. **$97,750**

Photo courtesy Skinner Inc., Boston, www.SkinnerInc.com

William Matthew Prior, (American, (1806-1873), portrait of a young boy, circa 1852, oil on canvas, the child seated wearing a red dress bordered in white, holding a white rose with a whip laid across his legs. Signed and inscribed on reverse, "Wm. M. Prior East Boston Trenton Street./Kingly Express," 26" x 20", unframed. Good condition, minor retouch. **$112,575**

the backside matted also with viewing glass, 3 1/2" x 8 1/4" (sight). **$6,325**

Thomas Rathbone Manley, (American, 1853-1938) South Beach, Nantucket; Oil on wood panel (framed); Signed and titled; 10 1/2" x 13 3/4". **$3,120**

John Marin, (American, 1870-1953), Lobsterman's Pier, Port Clyde, Maine, watercolor scene shows harbor with buildings, docks and boats. A green forested shoreline. Signed bottom right "Marin '23". A typed piece of paper on the back indicates, "This watercolor scene painted by John Marin at Port Clyde, Maine, in June of 1923 and given to Dock Attendant Avery Bullock in appreciation, for his Yeoman's work." Housed in what appears to be its original oak frame, 11 1/4" x 15 1/2" (sight), all over even toning, scratch to upper left, otherwise very good condition. **$2,300**

Pat Martin, (American, b. 1934) Terrace View; Oil and collage on wood panel (framed); Signed and titled; 16" x 16". **$840**

Harry McChesney, hand-carved and painted Canada goose, black and white neck and head, glass eyes, brown feathers with white tips. Original business card taped to bottom with artist name, 13 1/2" h x 27" l. **$201**

Joseph Meierhans, (Swiss/American, 1890-1980) Untitled; Oil on Masonite (artist-made frame); Signed; 31 3/4" x 27 7/8", 35" x 30 7/8" (frame). **$4,500**

Willard Leroy Metcalf, (American, 1858-1925), Pastel Impressions, oil on canvas, scene shows a stream curving through flat grassy area towards woods that have a lavender hue. Artist monogrammed with a capital "M" in circle bottom right. Housed in a modern gilt molded wood frame, 14 3/4" x 19 1/2". **$14,375**

Henri Moreau, (Belgian, 1869-1943) Indian Scout; Oil on wood panel (framed); Signed; 14" x 30". **$720**

Lucille (Mrs. H.M. Dingley Jr.) Mudgett, (American, 1911-), Still Life with Flowers in Blue Vase, oil on canvas board, shows a blue glass pedestal vase having colorful wildflower arrangement. Next to the vase is a brass figural lighter. Signed lower right. Housed in a wide gilt molded wood frame, 30" x 20". Discolored varnish, in need of cleaning. **$345**

H. Murray, (British, 19th/20th century), Stuck in the Snow, watercolor shows a stagecoach laden with passengers and luggage, stuck in a snowdrift. A man from a nearby house walks with shovel to help. The sign indicates they are between London and Brighton. Signed lower left, "H. Murray". In a decorative gilt frame with a watercolor highlighted matte, 11 1/4" x 17". **$480**

Lowell Blair Nesbitt, (American, 1933-1993) Violet Iris, 1982; Oil on canvas (framed); Signed, dated and titled; 70" x 70". **$3,240**

Lloyd Raymond Ney, (American, 1893-1965) Untitled, 1946; Mixed media on paper; Signed and dated; 11 1/2" x 15 1/2". **$1,200**

Anthony Oberman, (Dutch, 1781-1845), Still Life with Flowers, Bird and Butterfly, unframed oil on canvas, flowers including roses and chrysanthemums, and blue, white and purple wild flowers. Lion-decorated pedestal urn rests upon a tabletop, which has one flower and a finch-type bird which looks up at a butterfly. At the right edge of table is signature of the artist "A. Oberman," 32 1/2" x 22 1/4", relined with several layers of restoration and masking varnish. **$14,950**

Fried Pal, (American/Hungarian 1893-1976), Nude with Red Shawl, pastel on paper, three-quarter portrait of a nude woman with a red drape over lower part of body. Arm rests on a linen-covered table and her eyes are closed. Signed lower left. Housed in a white-highlighted carved wood frame with white matte and anti-glare glass, 22" x 18". **$1,080**

Petro Pavesi, (Italian, early 20th century), Cardinals Visit with the Pope, interior watercolor shows two cardinals having tea with the pope. Library setting has a fancy interior with bookshelves and hung tapestry. Chairs and table rest on a Caucasian Oriental rug. Signed lower left "P. Pavesi 1901". Housed in a gesso decorated period frame with gold liner, 17 1/4" x 12 3/4" (sight). **$460**

Photo courtesy Slotin Auction, Buford, Ga.; www.SlotinFolkArt.com

Bill Traylor, Blue Cat, circa 1939-1942. Not signed. Show-card color on cardboard, 7" x 11". **$42,550**

Photo courtesy Morphy Auctions, Denver, Pa.; www.MorphyAuctions.com

Guy Carleton Wiggins, (American, 1883-1962), The Public Library, oil on canvas, active scene of Manhattan in the snow, with the focal point being the New York Public Library, with its well-known lion statues. Depiction includes seven American Flags, pedestrians with umbrellas, a bus and taxicabs. Snow is blowing at an angle, and awnings are visibly out. Signed lower right. Guy Carleton Wiggins was born in Lyme, Conn., and was educated there at his father's (Carleton Wiggins, seldom used his given name, John) art school. Before he settled on a career as a painter, the younger Wiggins worked with the Foreign Service. He would paint local scenes wherever he was posted. After taking an early retirement from the job, Wiggins entered the Art Students League in New York, followed by a course of study in the artists colony of Old Lyme. Wiggins is best known for his Impressionistic paintings of New York in the snow, as well as for his renderings of Connecticut landscapes, 29 1/2" x 23 1/4" (framed). **$17,250**

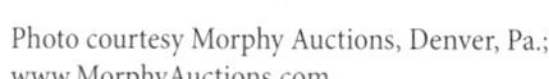

Photo courtesy Morphy Auctions, Denver, Pa.; www.MorphyAuctions.com

Guy Carleton Wiggins, (American, 1883-1962), 5th Avenue and 2nd Street, oil on canvas, signed Guy Wiggins. N.A. Manhattan snow scene features pedestrians walking with umbrellas, city traffic, a row of apartment buildings and two American Flags, 15 1/2" x 11 1/2" (framed). **$23,000**

Elizabeth Vaughan Okie Paxton, (American, 1877-1971), Copper jug with Apples, oil on canvas scene of a table top still life shows a large copper-handled jug on a white tablecloth with green cup and saucer and three apples. Signed upper right. Housed in its original period carved and gilt Arts & Crafts frame. Title in pencil on back of stretcher, 20" square, very good condition. **$4,600**

William McGregor Paxton, (American, 1869-1941), Portrait of a Woman, oil on canvas, half portrait of a woman in a red dress. She looks off to the right against a green and black background. Signed lower right "Paxton". Housed in a gilt wood frame, 20" x 16". **$920**

Margaretta Angelica Peale, attributed (American, 1795-1882), Fruit on a Plate, oil on canvas, still life shows a pear, apple, banana and grapes on a gold-trimmed white plate. Unsigned. Housed in a period gesso decorated gilt frame, 7" x 9". Some in-painting. **$2,880**

Charles Rollo Peters, (American, 1862-1928), Yerba Buena, a nocturne scene depicting San Francisco Bay, with an original note from the artist, ... **$40,250**

Jane Peterson, (American, 1876-1965), Gloucester Harbor, oil on board harbor scene shows a green schooner tied up to dock with other rowboats beside. Hillside beyond with many houses under a white and blue sky. Signed lower right "Jane Peterson". Housed in a period molded wood frame with a Marshall Field & Co. label, 20" x 23". Surface dirt, very good condition. **$8,625**

Photo courtesy Sanford Alderfer Auction & Appraisal, Hatfield, Pa.; www.AlderferAuction.com

Edward Willis Redfield (American, 1869-1965), Snow Scene, Center Bridge, Pa., oil on canvas, 22 1/2" x 25 1/2", signed lower right, "E.W. Redfield", with original bill of sale and Grand Central gallery label, in a Newcomb Macklin frame.
$163,800

Josef Pilters, (German, 1877-1957) Untitled; Oil on canvas (framed); Signed; 22 1/4" x 17 3/4". **$1,800**

Lucien Pissaro, (French, 1863-1944), Summer Fields, watercolor, landscape shows tall grassy field with trees and walkway. Monogrammed "LP" in a circle and dated "1930" in lower right. Housed in a modern wood frame with linen and wood matte, 4 1/2" x 6 1/2" (sight). **$1,495**

Henry Clarence Pitz, (American, 1895-1976) Untitled; Ink and pencil on paper (framed); Signed; 11 1/2" x 10 1/2" (sight). **$480**

Ace Powell, (American, 1912-1978) Untitled; Oil on canvas (framed); Signed; 8" x 14". **$1,200**

George Thompson Pritchard, (American, 1878-1962) Untitled; Oil on canvas (framed); Signed; 21" x 25". **$4,200**

Edward Willis Redfield, (American, 1869-1965) Untitled; Oil on board (framed); 9 1/4" x 12 1/4". **$10,800**

Frank Knox Morton Rehn, (American, 1848-1914) Untitled; Oil on canvas (framed); Signed; 25" x 30". **$4,200**

Louis Leon Ribak, (American, 1902-1979) Untitled; Oil on canvas (framed); Signed; 14" x 40". **$1,320**

Henry R. Rittenberg, (American, 1879-1969) Portrait of Jonas Lie, President of the National Academy; Oil on canvas (framed); Signed; 56" x 36". **$1,440**

Diego Rivera, (Mexican, 1886-1957), Femme Nue, pen and ink drawing, of a nude female with hand held up and finger pointing. Signed lower right. Housed in a modern gilt frame with blue matte and inner gold liner. Accompanying the drawing is a catalog entry from the sale at auction of the Hemingway Collection by Kruse Auctioneers, Oct. 29, 1978. This study was probably done in Italy, 1920-1921, 7 1/2" x 5" (sight). **$3,738**

Guy Rose, (American, 1867-1925), California Coastline, oil on board, scene shows an ocean bay surrounded by mountains under colorful sky. Signed lower right. Housed in a deep walnut Victorian frame with gilt liner, 4 1/2" x 6 1/2" (sight). **$3,105**

Charles Rosen, (American, 1878-1950) Brick Yard; Oil on board (framed); Signed and titled; 16 1/2" x 24". **$5,100**

Ernest David Roth, (German/American, 1879-1964) Swiss Village by a Lake Shore; Watercolor on paper (framed); Signed; 18 1/2" x 25" (sight). **$600**

Tadeusz Rybkowski, (Polish, 1848-1926), Crimean Scene of Two Soldiers with Troika, oil on panel, depicting a wounded Crimean soldier in a straw-lined litter drawn by a horse with Troika, another soldier tends to him in the snow. Signed lower left, "TAD. RYBKOWSKI, 1877," In original Eastlake-style frame with gilt gesso design and black and gilt decorated liner. Retains old paper label on reverse, 6 1/2" x 4 1/2". **$3,450**

John Schwab, (American, b. 1982) Untitled; Acrylic on canvas (framed); Signed; 35 3/4" x 47 1/2". **$480**

James Seymour, (in the manner of, British, 1702-1752), The Prince of Wales at Newmarket, 1797, large 19th-century oil on canvas panoramic scene shows the Prince of Wales in an elegant carriage pulled by six white horses in the center of a large field and slight hill. There are many horses and riders galloping and being led. Other spectators are seen in a carriage and on foot, with the English hillside in the background under a blue and cloudy sky. Unsigned and by an accomplished hand. Housed in a modern gilt molded wood frame with title plaque, 23 1/2" x 49 1/2", some in-painting, relined. **$5,400**

Ben Shahn, (American, 1898-1969), City Tenements, oil on masonite, scene shows inner-city buildings with narrow alley. Signed lower right, also signed on reverse. Housed in a carved molded wood frame, 22 1/4" x 15 1/4". Some old chipping and loss. **$2,875**

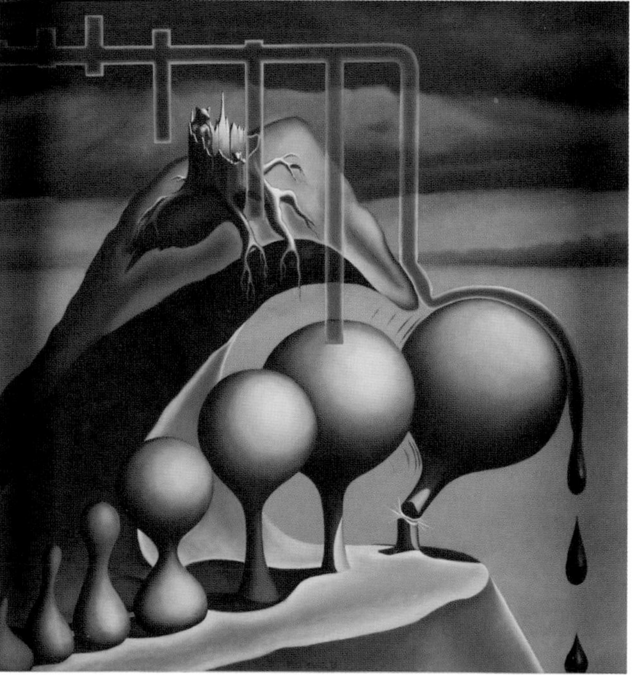

Photo courtesy Rago Arts and Auction Center, Lambertville, N.J.; www.RagoArts.com

Franz Jozef Ponstingl, (American, 1927-2004) Pollution, 1984, 1965; Oil on board (framed); Signed, dated and titled; 22" x 21". **$1,320**

Photo courtesy Clars Auction Gallery, Oakland, Calif.; www.Clars.com

Yellow Submarine (1968), framed animation celluloid depicting the four Beatles following two Apple Bonkers, 10" h x 12" w sight. **$1,600**

Dorothea Sharp, (British, 1874-1955), Study for 'Vivi at Play,' 1926, oil on canvas interior scene shows a young blonde-haired girl in green dress holding doll in one arm and walking stick in other. A ball sits on rag runner, doorway in background. Titled at bottom center "Vivi," bottom right dated with artist cipher and signed "Dorothea Sharp". Back of canvas has title, date and artist name. Housed in a gilt oak frame, 22" x 18 1/2". **$15,525**

Joseph Henry Sharp, (American, 1859-1953) Untitled, 1896; Oil on wood panel (framed); Signed and dated; 7" x 12 1/2". **$8,400**

David Sharpe, (American, b. 1936) Reclining Nude, 1983; Oil on canvas; Signed and dated; 36" x 48". **$840**

Christopher High Shearer, (American, 1840-1926) Untitled; Oil on canvas (framed); Signed; 22" x 36". **$2,160**

Paul Signac, (French, 1863-1935), Barfleur, ink and watercolor scene shows several boats at low tide in a harbor with large buildings. Lower left is titled and dated "32," signed bottom right. Housed in a gesso decorated gilt frame with linen matte and gold liner, 8 1/4" x 11" (sight). **$18,400**

Henry Bayley Snell, (American, 1858-1943) Untitled; Watercolor on paper (framed); Signed; 8 7/8" x 11 7/8", (sight). **$1,440**

George W. Sotter, (American, 1879-1953) Fish Window, New Jersey State Museum, Trenton, N.J.; Watercolor on illustration board (framed); Signed and titled; 38" x 25" (sight). **$4,500**

George W. Sotter, (American, 1879-1953) Untitled, 1946; Oil on Masonite (framed); Signed and dated; 22" x 26". **$144,000**

Moses Soyer, (Russian/American, 1899-1974) Dancer Resting; Oil on canvas (framed); Signed and titled; 16" x 12". **$3,600**

Raphael Soyer, (American, 1899-1987), Out of Work and Keeping Warm, watercolor, outdoor scene shows five black men seated and standing around a trash can fire. Several bottles of wine are seen at their feet and there is a building with trees in the background. Signed upper left, "R. Soyer," 7 3/4" x 8 1/4". **$632**

Marion Williams Steele, (American, 1912-2001), Sunset-Gloucester Harbor, oil on canvas scene shows a colorful sky reflecting in harbor water. Two figures work on a two-mast schooner next to dock with building. Other boats dot the docksides surrounding the harbor. Housed in a period carved gold frame; 25" x 30", very good condition. **$3,680**

William Lester Stevens, (American, 1888-1969) Untitled; Oil on canvas (framed); Signed; 20 1/4" x 24 1/4". **$3,120**

Seth W. Steward, (American, 1844-1927), Squaw Mtn from East of Greenville, Moosehead Lake, Maine, 1897, oil on board landscape shows early fall scene, cows, pasture and house in foreground with lake and mountains under a colorful sky. Signed lower left "S. W. Steward 97," housed in a gesso decorated gilt frame. Titled and initialed on reverse, 11 1/2" x 17 1/2", very good condition. **$2,875**

Harry P. Sutton Jr., (American 1897-1984), By the Light of the Window, oil on canvas, interior scene shows a woman sitting on a windowsill, which is bathed with outside light, a chair stands beside her. Window shade is partially down. Signed lower right "Sutton". Housed in a modern gilt molded wood frame with Guido Frame Studio label, 20" x 16". **$11,500**

Anthony Thieme, (American, 1888-1954), Back Beach, Rockport, Ma., large oil on canvas scene shows a dirt road winding along the northern section of Rockport Harbor alongside Back Beach with two figures under a tree, rocky shoreline with the town on a peninsula beyond. A sailboat exits the harbor area on a blue ocean. Along the dirt road are houses with a solitary figure in red. Scene is framed with large trees and light blue sky. Housed in a fine carved gilt custom frame with a Guido Frame Studio label. Several labels are attached to reverse including an exhibit label from the Lynn (Mass.) Museum & Historical Society. The back has title and artist number "1508," 30" x 36", very good condition. **$54,625**

George Thompson, (American, 20th century) Looking Across to New Hope; Oil on linen laid on board (framed); Signed; 12" x 24". **$720**

Mike Trovato, (American, 20th century) Reflections along the Canal, Lambertville, N.J.; Oil on canvas (framed); Signed; 40" x 30". **$720**

Martha C. Walter, (American, 1875-1976), Ellis Island, oil on masonite, Scene shows immigrants crowded in a interior of a building. Signed lower left. Housed in an antique gold frame, 10 1/2" x 14". **$6,727**

Mary E. Loring Warner, (American, 1860-?), Woodland Pool, oil on canvas laid on board, scene shows a stream with small waterfall cascading into a pool. Sunlight shines in the background, trees reflect on water. Signed lower right "M E Loring" (her maiden name). Housed in an Art Nouveau-style wide period frame, 12 1/2" x 18 1/4". Spot in-painting, generally very good. **$1,265**

Gustave Weigand, (American, 1872-1957) Summer Landscape at Twilight; Oil on canvas laid on Masonite (framed); Signed; 24 1/4" x 36". **$1,080**

Mary L. Weiss, (American, early 20th Century), Hollyhocks, large oil on canvas, floral scene shows a large group of colorful white, red and pink hollyhocks. Signed lower right "Mary L. Weiss". Housed in its original gilt and gesso decorated frame, 30" x 28". **$4,140**

Daniel F. Wentworth, (American, 1850-1934), Spring Time, large oil on canvas landscape shows five cows under a blossoming apple tree. Farmhouse is seen in distance and three of the cows look toward viewer. Signed lower left "DF Wentworth". Housed in an antique gesso decorated frame. Title on back of canvas, 24" x 36", good condition, some surface dirt with in-painting. **$5,175**

Constantin Aleksandrovich Westchiloff, (Russian, 1877-1945), The Street Merchant, oil on board, scene shows a merchant next to a small tent of wares with nearby white stucco buildings. A small burro carrying produce is tied to a tree all under a blue sky. Signed "C. Westchiloff" on bottom right. Unframed, 10 1/2" x 8 1/2". Some roughness at very edge of corners. **$1,150**

Marie Christine Westfeldt Reid, (American, 20th century) Untitled (Brulatour Courtyard, New Orleans); Oil on board (framed); Signed; 8" x 10". **$900**

Philip Richardson Whitney, (American, 1878-1960) Old Bridge in Winter, 1940; Oil on canvas (framed); Signed and dated; 25 1/4" x 30 1/4". **$7,200**

(John) Carleton Wiggins, (American, 1848-1932), A Holstein Cow, oil on canvas, cow is prominent in a grassy field leading to a wood's edge. Seen under a gray and white cloudy sky. Signed lower left. Also signed and titled on reverse of canvas. Housed in a gilt molded wood antique frame, 25" x 30". One old patch to reverse with corresponding in-painting. **$2,012**

Christopher G. Willett, (American, b. 1958) Untitled; Oil on canvas board (framed); Signed; 16" x 20". **$1,320**

Anna Woodward, (American, early 20th century) Two Ladies Having Tea; Oil on board (framed); Signed; 15 1/4" x 12 1/4" (sight). **$720**

Yellow Submarine (1968), framed animation celluloid depicting John Lennon and three of the Blue Meanies, 11" h x 15" w sight. **$900**

Josef Zenk, (American, 1904-2000) Yonkers, 1931; Watercolor on paper (framed); Signed; 9 1/2" x 6 3/4" (sight). **$660**

Photo courtesy Rago Arts and Auction Center, Lambertville, N.J.; www.RagoArts.com

Orrin Augustine White, (American, 1883-1969) Untitled; Oil on canvas (framed); Signed; 20" x 24". **$7,200**

FUTURE OF THE MARKET: ANTIQUE FRAMING

By Eli Wilner

Eli Wilner & Co., New York

When I started collecting and studying period frames in earnest in the early 1980's, they were still being discarded with the daily trash. Learning about the frames then was an uphill struggle with little information readily available. Today, nearly 25 years later, there is a growing body of scholarship available: books, videos, exhibition catalogs and essays.

Values noted are "current retail replacement values," or what a person can expect to pay if seeking such flames for artworks at a dealer in frames. As is true in most areas, the factors of condition, rarity and size are of key importance. A word about the market for period frames: it is important to recognize that it is an illiquid market—not one where auctions regularly take place and allow a wider value to be established. The wide margin between what a dealer will pay when purchasing frames for their inventory and what the frames may ultimately retail for is influenced by several factors unique to frames.

First: the frame size. There was little standardization in painting sizes during the 19th century, so few frames fit without alteration. Sensitive and competent alteration of period frames is a costly and labor-intensive process than must be executed properly for frame value to be maintained.

Second: Due in part to this size issue and also because of historically appropriate framing (the attempt to marry artworks with frames of the same period) a fine frame may languish in inventory for many years simply because the right confluence of factors hasn't occurred to allow the frame to be selected. (Indeed, some of our most spectacular frames have been in our inventory since I started the gallery.)

Third: There are nearly always restoration costs in order to put the frame in suitable condition.

Fourth: The market in fine period frames is inextricably entwined with the art market. The extraordinary prices achieved in frames correlates to the value of the paintings they can surround. If a client has just spent $200,000 or $300,000 on the Hudson River landscape of their dreams, it is not that far-fetched to understand that they are willing to pay as little as 10% of the cost of the painting on a fine period frame that will best complement and contain their prize. This cannot he emphasized enough. When assessing any period frame, you must look not only at what artwork it may be on at present, but also its inherent quality as a frame of its period, and the quality of artwork it may be able to surround.

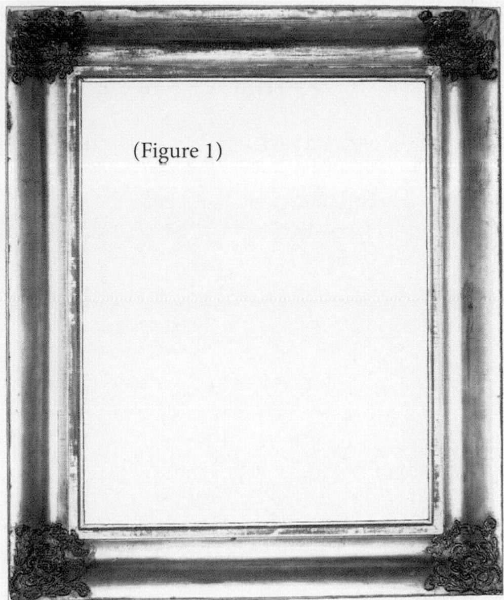

(Figure 1)

The style of American frames can be closely associated with trends in art, architecture, design and decorative trends, and as the swing of a pendulum, styles tended to shift from simple to elaborate and back again. In the early years of the 19th century when the simple elegance of Duncan Phyfe furniture reigned supreme, the primary sort of art being made was portraiture. For the simple dignified images produced, frames of simple cove moldings were made. If any ornament was used it was often a simple twist ornament in the cove and shells or leaves for corner embellishments. Other motifs from the Empire style — wreaths, palmettes and urns — occasionally appeared.

(Figure 2)

As the century progressed painting moved toward landscape, the celebration of what was seen as divinity expressed through the untamed American wilderness. Ornaments on frames of the 1850's reflected elements in the compositions: naturalistic forms such as vines, flowers and berries proliferated. The simple rectangles of earlier years softened and frames frequently had softly projecting corners and centers, and oval openings. These features echoed the popular Belter furniture created during the Rococo Revival period.

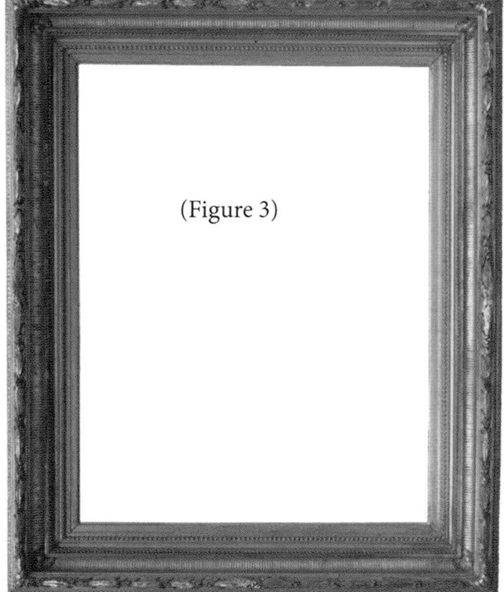

(Figure 3)

During the 1860's the pendulum swung back to a simpler style with the Renaissance Revival and the delight in neoclassical ornament. Soft undulant forms were replaced by the fluted cove design. The fluted cove was widely used and along with the laurel leaf and berry motif at the top edge, this form became the quintessential frame style for Hudson River landscapes.

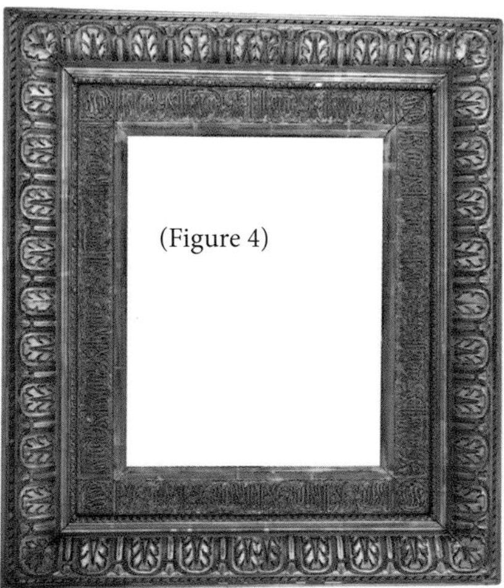

(Figure 4)

In the 1870's painting styles grew to include genre scenes and depictions of the exotic locales of the Near East. Geometric motifs that echoed furniture and architecture in the artworks were employed. Moorish and Islamic pattern and calligraphy were used to embellish frames that enclosed scenes such as the interior of a mosque.

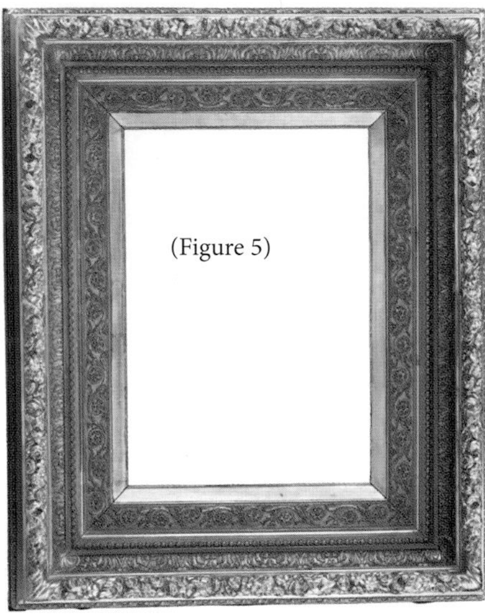

(Figure 5)

The 1880's signaled the height of Victorian eclecticism: There was no such thing as "too much of a good thing." During this time, frames were elaborately composed of many different patterns of ornament at once.

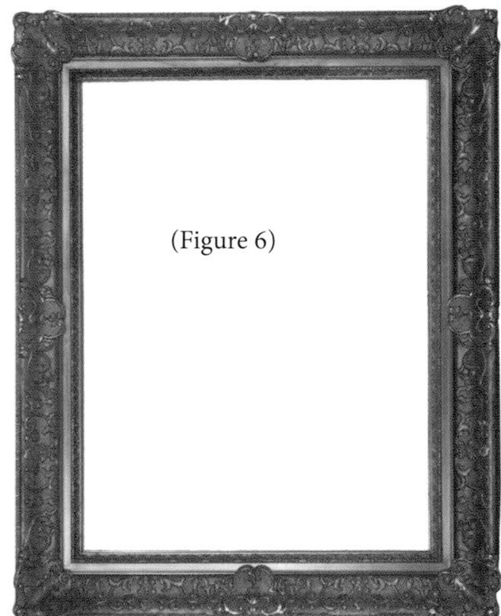

(Figure 6)

The French Barbizon style of frame (itself a design based on 17th century Louis XIII frames) gained popularity and was widely reinterpreted in America. This was also a time of widespread industrialization and frame manufacture was no exception. Machines were made that allowed pattern to be stamped onto lengths of molding that could he chopped and joined, and silver leaf was widely used as an alternative to gold at less expense.

(Figure 7)

One of the results of this mass-manufacture was that ornament on frames was not carefully applied to resolve in a pleasing way. Patterns were joined together with jarring effect with little or no attention to form (Figure 7). Corner leaves that were made to mask the crude miters were made of pewter or lead and nailed on.

(Figure 8)

Eastlake-style frames also became popular with myriad variations available. The central characteristic that defines an American Eastlake-style frame is the incised design that usually appears at the corners. Painted surfaces emulating precious stone and black lacquer were popular surface treatments (Figure 8). Most of these frames were mass-produced to surround tintypes, the "everyman's portraiture" of the day, and this is why most of these frames are found in small formats and can still be found in antique shop and flea markets today.

(Figure 9)

The turn of the 19th to the 20th century saw the creation of some of America's most unique and elegant frame designs, especially those by Stanford White. Though White was an architect, his skill as a master of decorative interiors is legend, and his love of the Italian Renaissance informed his creations. White's list of friends reads like a

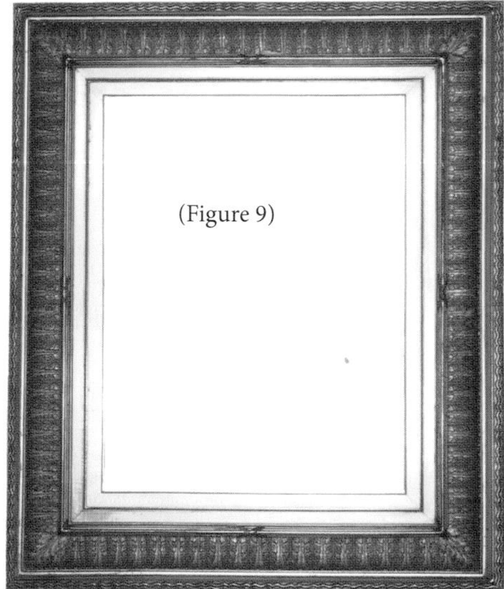

veritable Who's Who of American artists of the day: Augustus Saint-Gaudens, Thomas Wilmer Dewing, Dwight Tryon, George DeForest Brush and Abbott Thayer to name a few. It was White who used the tabernacle-style frame to such dramatic effect, often adding many of his own stylistic embellishments.

(Figure 10)

Due to White's untimely death in 1906 these frames are exceedingly rare. Some of White's designs were acquired by the Newcomb-Macklin Co. after his death and produced posthumously. These vary greatly in quality and must be taken case by case. Many of these posthumous frames are gilded with metal leaf rather than the superior gold leaf that White would have specified.

(Figure 11)

As American Impressionism took hold and artists were experimenting with new styles of brushwork and a new palette of color, a new style of frame for this new art was born. It is appropriate that this was introduced by an artist.

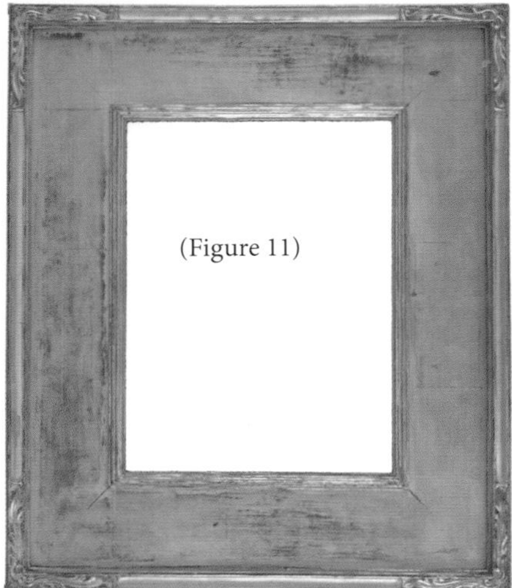
(Figure 11)

Hermann Dudley Murphy lived and worked in Boston and was greatly influenced by James McNeill Whistler, who was himself a frame reformer. Upon Murphy's return from his travels in Europe, he purchased the necessary materials and taught himself to carve and gild. In doing so, he began to create frames based on the Venetian cassetta-style frame, a profile characterized by a broad flat panel and raised inner and outer edges. Murphy's designs and those that followed are now widely referred to as American Impressionist-style frames.

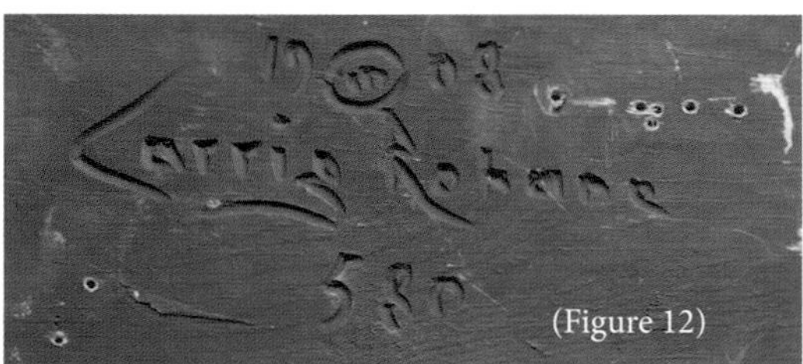
(Figure 12)

(Figure 12)

In addition, after each frame was made, Murphy inscribed it, signaling that this, too, was an artwork worthy of a signature and a date.

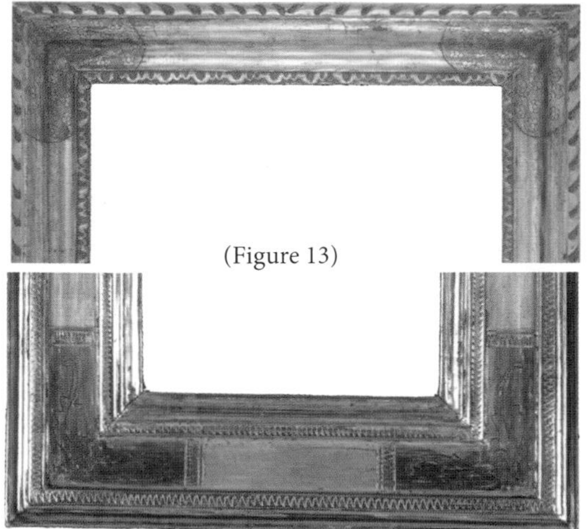
(Figure 13)

(Figure 13)

Signed frames are always highly prized even when the maker is unknown. There were other makers who signed their frames, such as Charles Prendergast and Frederick Harer (Figure 13). During this period there was also a heightened interest in the tonalities of the gilded surface and many frames were finished in silver, various shades of gold leaf and the much more coppery-colored metal leaf to better complement the artworks they enclosed.

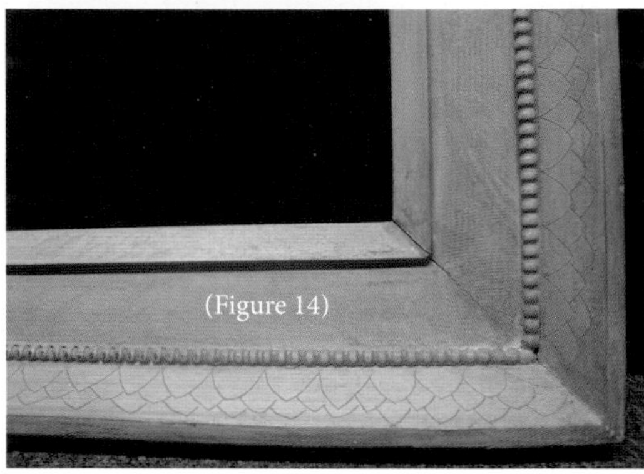
(Figure 14)

(Figure 14)

With the conclusion of World War I, the coming depression and an increasingly technologically oriented society, art changed again. In frames, gilding gave way to painted and manipulated surface treatments. American Modernist painters such as Arthur Dove created simple wood frames with copper accents. John Marin took mass-produced flames and made them his own by drawing, painting and carving on them. Though at first glance these frames appear crude, they are often integral to the overall artwork and create a dynamic presentation where the hand of the artist is powerfully present.

Key points to keep in mind when acquiring frames that are likely to increase in value are the same as in many fields (age, style, size, rarity). A frame in good condition with its original gilded surface is most desirable. It should also be of a style that is well suited to fine art. Frame values increase as they are paired with exceptional artworks. Lastly, if a frame has been altered, the alteration should be nearly impossible to detect. A clumsy alteration can destroy a great frame.

As frame studies advance and the market continues to evolve, I hope that we'll all continue to take a deeper look at the art of the frame.

For more information, contact Eli Wilner & Co., 1525 York Ave., New York, NY, 10028, *www.eliwilner.com.*

Prints

Nathaniel Currier

American Field Sports-Retrieving, by N. Currier, in large color folio showing hunter with two retrievers. Print after a painting by A.F. Tait and lithographed by N. Currier, N.Y., 1857. Image, 18" x 26". Print exhibits toning/foxing with some reverse burning with show-through and glue residue near matt opening. Puncture at left side. **$70**

The Pursuit by N. Currier, in large color folio showing man on horseback chasing an Indian with spear on horseback. Print after a painting by A.F. Tait and lithographed by N. Currier, N.Y., 1856. Image, 24" x 31". Print exhibits toning/foxing with some reverse burning with show-through. **$750**

Currier & Ives

American Farmyard - Evening, colored large folio lithograph shows a farmyard filled with livestock with the farmhouse beyond a white picket fence, dated 1857. Housed in a Victorian deep walnut frame with gold liner. Image, 19" x 25 1/2". Very good condition. Not examined out of frame. **$1,150**

Four Civil War Brown Water Navy lithographs, C&I, titles include; Bombardment and Capture of Fort Henry, Tenn.; Admiral Porter's Fleet Running the Rebel Blockade of the Mississippi at Vicksburg, April 16th 1863; Brilliant Naval Victory on the Mississippi River, Near Fort Wright, May 10th 1862; Bombardment of "Island Number Ten" in the Mississippi River. .... **$920 set**

Four Civil War medium-folio lithographs, C&I, titles include: The Battle of Antietam, MD. Sept. 17th 1862; The Night After The Battle; Capture of Roanoke Island, Feby. 8th 1862; Surrender of Fort Hudson, LA. July 8th 1863. All 16" x 12" (unframed) 12 1/2" x 7 3/4" (sight). .... **$1,380 set**

Four Civil War medium-folio lithographs, C&I, titles include: General Stoneman's Great Cavalry Raid, may, 1863; Battle of Chancellorsville, Va. May, 3rd 1863; The Storming of Fort Doneldson, Tenn. Feby. 15th 1862; The Battle of Pittsburg, Tenn. April 7th 1862. All 16" x 12" (unframed) 12 1/2" x 7 3/4" (sight). .... **$805 set**

Four Civil War medium-folio lithographs, C&I, titles include: Battle of Fredericksburg, VA. Dec. 13th 1862; Battle of Williamsburg VA. May 5th 1862; The Battle of Fair Oaks, Va. May 31st 1862; Genl. Shields at the Battle of Winchester, Va. 1862. All 16" x 12" (unframed) 12 1/2" x 7 3/4" (sight). .... **$805 set**

The Great East River Bridge. To Connect the Cities of New York & Brooklyn, 1872, small folio lithograph with hand coloring on paper, sheet size 11 3/8" x 14 7/8", unframed. Margins of 1 1/4" or more, two repaired tears, creases, minor toning. **$592**

Photo courtesy Skinner Inc., Boston, www.SkinnerInc.com

Central Park in Winter, undated, small folio lithograph with hand coloring on paper, sheet size 9 7/8" x 13 7/8", in a contemporary bird's-eye maple veneer frame. Margins of 5/8" or more, 1/2" old repaired tear left center through the letter "N" in title, minor toning, hinged at the top with old tape. **$2,725**

Photos courtesy Heritage Auction Galleries, Dallas; www.HA.com

Currier & Ives, Above: Series No. 13, "The Darktown Fire Brigade - Investigating a Smoke." Below: Series No. 11, "The Darktown Fire Brigade - All on their Mettle." Color lithography, circa 1889, 18 1/4" x 14". The partnership of lithographers Nathaniel Currier and James Merritt Ives began in 1857. Minor chipping. **$478 each**

Photo courtesy Heritage Auction Galleries, Dallas; www.HA.com

Nathaniel Currier, "Death Of Tecumseh. Battle Of The Thames Oct 5th 1813." Hand-Colored Lithograph, 1841. Early Currier engraving depicts Colonel Richard M. Johnson killing the Shawnee Chief Tecumseh. By J.L. McGee and published by N. Currier, New York, 1841. Measures approximately 9" x 12". The Battle of the Thames was a decisive War of 1812 victory for a future president, William Henry Harrison, who commanded the American Army as well as a future vice president, Richard Mentor Johnson, who led the volunteer cavalry and fired the fatal shot at Tecumseh, whose death led to the crumbling of the Indian coalition. This lithograph depicts that death scene. **$448**

Prints, A to Z

Karel Appel, (Dutch, 1921-2006), Cat Suite, color serigraph shows a colorful cat against a black background. Pencil signed and numbered "55/125" lower right. A certificate of authenticity from Genesis Galleries affixed to reverse. Housed in a metal frame with double matte (frame with tape marks), 23 1/2" x 30 1/2" (sight). **$300**

Frank Weston Benson, (American, 1862-1951), In Dropping Flight, drypoint on paper, scene shows four ducks landing in clear water. Pencil signed lower left, 1926 edition of 134, housed in a hinged matte, 10 3/4" x 13 3/4" (plate). **$1,725**

Thomas Hart Benton, (American, 1889-1975), Island Hay, limited-edition signed original lithograph, showing several men with scythes haying a field with barn in background. Pencil signed bottom right "Benton". Housed in a modern molded wood frame with beige matte, 10 1/2" x 13" (sight). Light toning to edges, very good condition. **$3,680**

Georges Braque, (French, 1882-1963) Gelinotte, 1960; Lithograph in colors (framed); Signed and numbered HC (aside from the edition of 75); 15" x 19" (sight); Printer: Mourlot, Paris; Publisher: Maeght, Paris; Literature: Vallier 149. .... **$1,920**

Bernard Buffet, (French, 1928-1999) New York I; Lithograph in colors (framed); Signed and numbered 141/150; 28 1/4" x 19 3/4" (sight). **$2,760**

Paul Cadmus, (American, 1904-1999), Waiting for Rehearsal, limited-edition etching, shows three dancers outside a doorway rehearsing for the New York City Ballet. Signed lower right. Titled and numbered "53/175". Housed in a modern silver black-edged frame with wide white matte, 11 3/4" x 8 1/2" (sight). **$1,560**

Roland H. Clark, (American, 1874-1957), A Memory, drypoint on paper, scene shows a flock of ducks coming into a marshy area. Signed in pencil lower right and titled in the print, 1928 from an edition of 75. Housed in a hinged matte. Along with a book, To Keep a Tryst with the Dawn: An Appreciation of Roland Clark by John T. Ordman, limited edition numbered 1006 and signed, 16" x 12 3/4" (plate). Slight overall toning. **$977**

Salvador Dali, (Spanish, 1904-1989) Untitled, signed limited-edition color lithograph, depicts a man's head and torso against green tree background. Protruding from the man's mouth are human legs and an object protrudes from his head. Numbered "128/150". Signed bottom right. Housed in a gilt frame with wide matte and inner gold liner. Also pen signed on back with cutout for viewing, 11 3/4" x 8 1/4" (sight). **$540**

Salvador Dali, (Spanish, 1904-1989) The Twelve Signs of the Zodiac, 1967; Thirteen lithographs in colors on Arches wove paper with remnants of the original linen-covered portfolio; Each signed and numbered 113/250; 28 3/4" x 20 1/2" (sheet) each; Printer: Fernand Mourlot, Paris, October 1967; Publisher: Leon Amiel, New York and Paris, 1968. .... **$7,200 set**

Herbert Thomas Dicksee, (British, 1862-1942), Leopard Cubs at Play and Danger, pair of large etchings, both pencil signed "Herbert Dicksee". 1) Scene shows two leopards on a fallen tree trunk with two butterflies in grasses. Below image "Copyright 1907 by Frost & Reed, Bristol, England in the United States of America." Above is "Published at 8 Clare Street, Bristol by Frost & Reed Printsellers of Bristol, Clifton & London May 1st 1907 Berlin Stiefbold & Co., No. 25, Markgrafemstrasse, Copyright Registered." Housed in its period oak frame with thick white matte. 2) Scene shows a lion and lioness with her cubs in amongst a cleared area with grass. Above image "Copyright 1905 by Mess'rs Arthur Tooth & Sons 586 Hay Market, London 14 Boulevard Des Capucineo Paris 299 Fifth Avenue, New York & Mess'rs Stiefbold & Co., Berlin." Housed in a flat oak frame with thick matte. 1) Image, 19 1/2" x 26 1/2". 2) Image, 16" x 27 1/2". 1) Image is very good; the border has foxing, matte with stains. 2) Image is very good with foxing to borders. .... **$1,035 pair**

Photo courtesy James D. Julia Auctioneers, Fairfield, Maine; www.JuliaAuctions.com

John Steuart Curry (American 1897-1946), John Brown, pencil-signed lithograph, shows John Brown in a wild demeanor with a tornado behind him and a sword on his side. Pencil signed bottom right and having an Associated American Artist label affixed to the reverse. Housed in simple ivory frame with white matte, 15 1/2" x 11 1/2" (sight). Some toning at edges. **$4,600**

Arthur Wesley Dow, (American, 1857-1922), color woodblock print of illustrated poem by Everett S. Hubbard, Rain in May. Matted and framed, 7 1/2" x 6" sight. **$1,200**

Arthur Wesley Dow, (American, 1857-1922), four woodblock prints, Little Venice, 5 1/2" x 3"; Seashore Landscape, sheet, 6 1/2" x 9"; Lily, colored drawing from Ipswich prints series F, 5 1/2" x 4"; and Emerson House Greeting Cards, 3 3/4" x 3". All matted and framed, last two marked. .... **$3,600 set**

Arthur Wesley Dow, (American, 1857-1922), color woodblock print, The Lost Boat. Matted and framed, unsigned, 5 3/4" x 4" image. **$4,200**

Erte, (Romain de Tirtoff, Russian, 1892-1990), The Zodiac Suite, 1982, 12 serigraphs in original portfolio. Each signed,

titled and numbered 341/350, 25 1/2" x 20" (sheet) each. Tristar Publishing Ltd., New York. **$2,040**

Daniel Garber, (American, 1880-1958) Fisherman's Hut; Etching (framed); Signed and titled; 8 1/4" x 10" (sight). **$1,680**

William Henry Johnson, (American, 1901-1970) Bazaars Behind Church of Our Savior, Oslo, Norway; Woodcut in colors; Signed; 14 1/2" x 15 3/4" (sheet). **$7,800**

Rockwell Kent, (American, 1882-1971), Sacco & Vanzetti, pencil-signed engraving shows two heads on a pole with crosses in the background. Housed in silver gilt molded wood frame and double matte, 5" x 3" (sight). Light signature and minor foxing. **$300**

Henri Matisse, (French, 1869-1954) Etudes pour Saint Dominique, 1950-1951; Lithograph on Chine applique (framed); Signed and numbered 154/200; 10 3/8" x 7 3/8" (sight); Literature: Duthuit, 658. .... **$2,880**

George Loftus Noyes, (American, 1864-1954) Untitled; Monotype (framed); Signed; 3 3/4" x 4 1/2" (sight). **$720**

Our Heroes and Our Flags, copyright 1896 by Southern Lithograph Co. Print features central vignette of full standing portraits of Generals Lee, Jackson and Beauregard, surrounded by 17 small vignettes of other generals and Confederate flags. Print measures 24" x 18" and is framed. **$115**

Pablo Picasso, after (Spanish, 1881-1973) Musicien, Danseur, Chevre et Oiseau, 1959; Lithograph on Arches (framed); Signed and numbered 90/200; 27 1/2" x 21" (sheet). **$2,400**

Fairfield Porter, (American, 1907-1975) Interior with Christmas Tree, 1971; Lithograph in colors (framed); Signed; 26 1/2" x 21" (sight). **$1,020**

Aiden Lassell Ripley, (American, 1896-1969), Ruffled Grouse in Winter, unframed etching shows two grouse in a sunlit snow-covered scene. Pencil titled and signed. Accompanying the lot is the book Sporting Etchings by A. Lassell Ripley. This etching is illustrated on page 90. Image 11" x 9 1/4". Very good condition. **$1,380**

Rufino Tamayo, (Mexican 1899-1991), Watermelon Man, silkscreen (?), scene shows a man seated at a table eating a section of watermelon with pieces on the table and a piece resting on a stand behind him, watermelon seeds scattered around. Bright colors on masonite. Housed in a painted

Photo courtesy Rago Arts and Auction Center, Lambertville, N.J.; www.RagoArts.com

Gustave Baumann, (American, 1881-1971), color woodblock print, Fox River Farmyard, 1908. Soiled paper, dime-sized stain to lower margin. Matted. Pencil-signed and dated, 6 3/4" x 8 3/4" image. **$1,320**

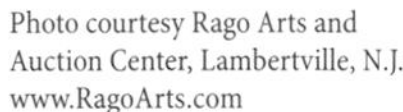

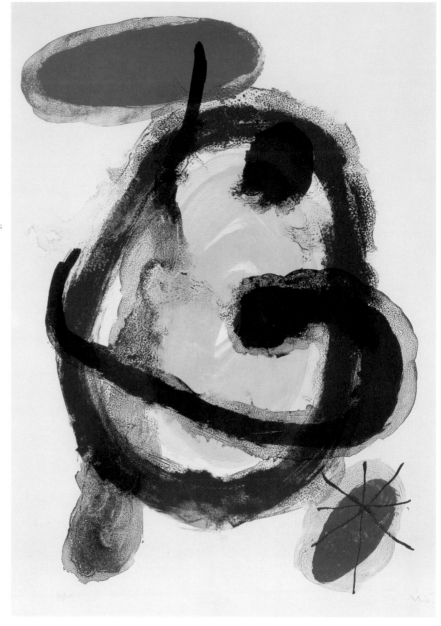

Photo courtesy Rago Arts and Auction Center, Lambertville, N.J.; www.RagoArts.com

Joan Miro, (Spanish, 1893-1983) Untitled; Lithograph in colors (framed); Signed and numbered 20/100; 26 3/4" x 18 3/4" (sight); Printer/ Publisher: Maeght, Paris; Literature: Mourlot 295. **$2,760**

molded wood frame. Signed lower left "Tamayo 40", 28" x 22". One small scrape below watermelon. **$920**

Rembrandt Harmenszoon Van Rijn, (Dutch, 1606-1669), Joseph's Coat Brought to Jacob, 1633, 18th-century impression), etching (framed), signed in the plate, 4 3/8" x 3 3/8" (sheet). **$2,280**

Stow Wengenroth, (American, 1906-1978), The Church, lithograph on paper, scene shows the side view of the front of a Wiscasset Maine church in October, 1947. Pencil signed and numbered "Ed/60". Housed in a silver gilt frame with white matte, 15 1/2" x 11 1/4" (image). **$780**

James Abbott McNeill Whistler, (American, 1834-1903), Billingsgate, 1859, etching on tan woven paper (framed). Signed, 5 5/8" x 8 7/8" (sheet). **$480**

The Worship of Bacchus, large framed colored engraving, after a painting housed in the National Gallery; printed by R. Holdgate and published June 20, 1864, by Wilhelm Tweedie, London. Figures outlined on the steel plate by George Cruikshank, and the engraving finished by Charles Mottram. Scene showing a monument surrounded by hundreds of people in a chaotic scene with vignettes. Housed in an antique molded wood frame with gold liner and glass; 28 1/2" x 44 1/2". Toned with slight fading, otherwise good condition. **$300**

Statuary

Also see *Oriental Objects.*

Jean de Bologne (after), Mercury Riding the North Wind, bronze, on round marble base, 16" h. **$250**

Eugene Bormel, (19th century), bronze sculpture of winged goddess with flowers and a basket, on a marble socle, 1897. Cast in two separate pieces and joined at the hip. Signed "Bormel 1897", 16 5/8" h. **$480**

Victor David Brenner, (American, 1871-1924) Abraham Lincoln, 1809-1865, 1907; Bronze; Signed and dated "COPYRIGHT 1907 BY V.D. BRENNER" and titled "ABRAHAM LINCOLN / 1809 1865"; 9 1/2" x 7 1/8". **$2,040**

Bronze casting, of battling rams on a rocky perch on marble base, 9" h x 13" l. **$175**

Continental bronzes, Ovide Yencesse (French, 1869-1947) bronze plaque of a mother and child reading, framed, signed upper right O. Yencesse; and Ernest Sanglan (French, 19th-20th century) two-handled vase with sleeping satyr, signed on side E. Sanglan with foundry seal and #7537 on base. Vase: 7 1/4". .... **$900 pair**

William Couper, (American, 1853-1942) Untitled; Marble (with base); Signed; 20" high, 24" with base. **$2,400**

Jose De Creeft, (French/American, 1884-1982) Head of a Baby, circa 1935; Pear wood; Signed; 11" x 12 1/2" x 10 1/2". **$5,400**

Edmond Drappier, (French, 19th-20th century), bronze statue of a bull, on wooden base. Signed E. Drappier, 10" x 16" x 9". **$2,040**

Emmanuel Fremiet, (French, 1824-1910), bronze figurine of a dog, signed E. Fremiet; together with a bronze horse on a rectangular base, by unknown maker, broken tail, slightly rubbed patina and one ear bent forward, 19th century, taller: 9 1/4". .... **$840 pair**

Emil Fuchs, (Austrian/American, 1866-1929) The First Lesson, 1913; Bronze; Signed and dated; From an edition of two; 20 3/4" x 13 3/4", 22 1/2" high (with base). **$6,600**

Adrien Étienne Gaudez, (French, 1845-1902), "Etoile du Matin," bronze statue with base. Signed "A. GAUDEZ H.C" and titled "ETOILE/DU MATIN", 21 3/4" h, 22 3/4" w (with base). **$1,800**

Photo courtesy Rago Arts and Auction Center, Lambertville, N.J.; www.RagoArts.com

Alfred Barye (French 1839-1882), bronze animalier statue of a rooster on round base. Signed Barye, 13" h. **$1,920**

Photo courtesy Rago Arts and Auction Center, Lambertville, N.J.; www.RagoArts.com

Austrian bronze, horse-drawn coach on green marble base, 20th century, stamped "Made in Austria," circled AT monogram. 9 1/2" x 28 3/4" x 7 1/2". Reportedly one of only two made, commissioned by the Winmill family of Warrenton, Va. A copy of the book, "Gone Away with the Winmills" (1877) by Virginia Winmill Livingstone Armstrong, accompanies bronze. **$4,800**

Eugen Gauss, (American, 1905-1988) OLC Salome, 1945; Cast stone composite; Signed and dated; 18 3/4" h. **$1,320**

Maurice Glickman, (American, 1906-1981) Untitled; Cast terra cotta; Signed; 16 3/4". **$960**

Belle Campbell Harriss, (American, 20th century) Dougie, My Grandson, 1931; Bronze; Signed and dated "BELLE C. HARRISS -" 31", 14" with base. **$1,560**

Anna Vaughn Hyatt Huntington, (American, 1876-1973) Charging Mountain Goats; Bronze; Signed "Anna V. Hyatt" with foundry mark "GORHAM CO. FOUNDERS"; 7 1/4" h. **$9,000**

Boris Lovet-Lorski, (Lithuanian/American, 1894-1973) Untitled, 1963; Slate (incised on both sides); Signed and dated; 13 1/4" x 7" x 5/8", 17 3/4" h (with base). **$2,640**

Paul Howard Manship, (American, 1885-1966) Virgo, August 23 - September 23 (Zodiac Series Ashtray), 1946; Bronze; Signed and dated "PAUL MANSHIP (C) 1946 and titled "VIRGO / AUGUST.23..SEPTEMBER.23."; 6" d. **$1,440**

P.J. Mene, (French, 1810-1877), bronze sculpture of a horse standing by a makeshift fence, freestanding on black marble base. Signed on base P.J. Mene, Susse Freres & Co. foundry mark. With base: 14" x 19" x 8 1/2". **$4,800**

Jules Moigniez, Patinated bronze sculpture of an owl preparing to land, signed (after), 33" h x 24" w. **$325**

Louis-Auguste Moreau, (French, 1855-1919), "David," bronze sculpture, signed "L. Moreau," 29" h. **$3,240**

Mathurin Moreau, (French, 1822-1912), "Echo," bronze sculpture, signed "Math Moreau / Hors. Concours" and stamped "MEDAILLE HONNEUR", 26 3/4" h. **$3,000**

Alexander Phimister Proctor, (American, 1860-1950) Princeton Tiger, 1912; Bronze; Signed and dated "A.P. PROCTOR 1912," titled "PRINCETON TIGER" with foundry mark "GORHAM CO FOUNDERS / 0454#97"; 4" x 9" x 2 1/4". **$3,900**

Alexander Phimister Proctor, after (American, 1860-1950) The Buckaroo, 1915 (posthumously cast); Bronze; Signed "A.P.PROCTOR", dated "c 1915" with foundry mark "ROMAN BRONZE WORKS N-Y-"; 26 1/2" h. **$6,000**

Pierre-Auguste Renoir, (French, 1841-1919), Profil de Coco, plaque, framed bronze, signed "Renoir" lower left, inscribed "H.C. IV" on lower edge, A. Valsuani foundry mark stamped lower center, plaque: approximately 8" diameter, overall (oval frame): 27" h x 22 1/2" w. **$950**

Robert H. Rockwell, (American, 1885-1973) A Woodland Tragedy; Bronze; Signed "R. H. ROCKWELL", titled "A WOODLAND TRAGEDY" with foundry mark "Roman Bronze Works N-Y-"; 11" x 22" x 9". **$7,800**

Jean Jules Salmson, (French, 1823-1902), bronze sculpture of a woman in the Oriental style, a jar in her hand. Drilled for lamp, with small repair on back of neck. Marked Salmson, 21" h. **$2,640**

Vaclaw Bernard (Victor) Szczeblewski, (Polish, 19th century), bronze sculpture, "Boy Whisting," on marble base, 1889. Signed and dated. With base: 9" h. **$780**

Charles Valton, (French 1851-1918), bronze statue of a mastiff with sign 'Passez au Large.' Signed C.H. Valton, 18 1/4" h. **$2,640**

Photo courtesy Rago Arts and Auction Center, Lambertville, N.J.; www.RagoArts.com

Henry Étienne Dumaige, (French, 1830-1888), untitled (Young Couple), gilt bronze statue on rotating gilt bronze base. Provenance: Signed "Henr. Dumaige" and with foundry mark "E. Colin", 22" h, 25" w (with base). **$4,200**

Vienna bronzes, cold painted: two bird figurines, late 19th/early 20th century, both marked on underside of tail, one with Geschutzt 1801, the other initialed FB with illegible writing, taller: 3 1/2". .... **$900 pair**

Bessie Onahotema Potter Vonnoh, (American, 1872-1955) Girl Dancing, 1899; Bronze; Signed, dated and titled "Girl Dancing / B[4]essie O Potter / Sculptor / copyrighted 1899", with foundry mark "THE HENRY-BONNARD BRONZE CO / FOUNDERS.N-Y.1899"; 14" h. **$54,000**

Philip H. Wolfrom, (American, 1870-1904) Head of a Lioness, 1896-1899; Bronze; Signed "P.H. Wolfrom" with foundry mark "ROMAN BRONZE WORKS N-Y-"; 13 5/8" x 8 7/8" x 10". **$4,200**

William Zorach, (American, 1887-1966) Mother and Child, circa 1942; Hard plaster; Signed and inscribed "Limited Edition / Robinson Galleries Inc. / New York"; 15" h. **$1,200**

Photo courtesy Rago Arts and Auction Center, Lambertville, N.J.; www.RagoArts.com

Dog group, bronze, two hunting dogs (dachshunds) on a red marble plinth, 19th century, each stamped with numbers and Geschutzt, 2 1/2" x 4 1/2". **$480**

Photo courtesy Rago Arts and Auction Center, Lambertville, N.J.; www.RagoArts.com

R. Clark, cowboy bronze, figure on horseback leading two horses and covered wagon, the packhorses with a deer, antlers and supplies, 20th century, signed R. Clark. 32" x 13". **$1,440**

Photo courtesy Slotin Auction, Buford, Ga.; www.SlotinFolkArt.com

Woolsey, Clarence. Blue Face Bunny. Bottle-cap construction on wood. Excellent condition. 39" h x 19" w. **$9,775**

Photo courtesy Rago Arts and Auction Center, Lambertville, N.J.; www.RagoArts.com

Enoch Henryck (Enrico) Glicenstein, (Polish/American, 1870-1942) Bust of Jimmy Walker, City Hall, June 14, 1929; Bronze; Signed, dated and titled "Enrico Glicenstein City Hall / June 14 1929". **$1,920**

Photo courtesy Rago Arts and Auction Center, Lambertville, N.J.; www.RagoArts.com

Henry Schonbauer (American, b. 1895), bronze sculpture, "The Stone Roller," 1936. Signed and dated, with accompanying paperwork, 18 1/4" x 30" x 10 1/2".
$11,400

Photo courtesy Rago Arts and Auction Center, Lambertville, N.J.; www.RagoArts.com

Polygnotus G. Vagis, (Greek/American, 1894-1965) Aviation, March 6, 1919; Painted plaster; Signed and dated; 18" x 19 3/4" x 8 3/4".
$3,120

ILLUSTRATION ART: THE "REAL ART OF AMERICA"

By Noah Fleisher

The late collector Charles Martignette – who died in early 2008 and left behind what is arguably the finest collection of illustration art ever assembled – once wrote of the form he loved so much: " … American illustration art was the real art of America."

It's hard to disagree with his assessment.

Spend a bit of time with the classic, bold imagery of American illustration art (roughly 1880-1960, give or take a decade on either side) and you'll quickly be won over. The men and women who populate the genre were among the greatest artistic talent of their day. From the early days of American illustration with Howard Pyle and the Brandywine luminaries, through its Golden Age with the likes of Norman Rockwell and J.C. Leyendecker, and into Mid-Century America with its iconic Gil Elvgren calendar girls and Alberto Vargas' Esquire gatefolds and Playboy drawings, they were simply plying their trades in an effort to make a living doing what they loved.

Noah Fleisher

This was no gilded age of great art patrons. It was a time of national growth and expansion, of the industrial revolution and World Wars, and without a mass media to instantly relay the everyday images of American lives, as we have today, Illustration Art became the default medium through which distilled – and often idealized – imagery spread. It was the advent of easily reproducible photography in the 1950s and 1960s that ultimately heralded the end of widespread illustration use.

There is barely enough room in these few pages to simply touch on the most basic aspects of Illustration Art, let alone effectively convey its full depth and meaning to the development of American pop culture and how the American people ultimately viewed themselves.

Photo courtesy Heritage Auction Galleries, Dallas; www.HA.com

Gil Elvgren (American 1914 - 1980), Fascination, 1952. Oil on canvas, 30" x 24", signed right-center. Reproduced as figure 360 in Gil Elvgren All His Glamorous American Pin-Ups by Charles G. Martignette and Louis K. Meisel, Taschen Books, 1996. **$262,900**

Photo courtesy Heritage Auction Galleries, Dallas; www.HA.com

Norman Rockwell (American 1894-1978), Two Old Men and Dog: Hunting, Brown & Bigelow: Four Seasons Calendar, Autumn, 1950. Oil on masonite, 24" x 22", signed lower left. **$274,850**

If what you see in the pages that follow stirs the collector in you to do more, then you will have a long and satisfying journey of erudition and collecting ahead of you as you ply the ocean that is Illustration Art. If you simply like to look at great art that resolutely puts on no airs, then you'll have an equally satisfying side trip into some amazingly diverse art.

Three Types of Illustration Art

Pin-up and Glamour

This artwork was routinely done for calendars, cards and men's magazines. They present a decidedly romanticized view of the female form, one where a lady's modesty is usually compromised, whether by design or surprise. What is so powerful about the work is the range of innocence to sophistication across subjects, artists and time periods. There is always something more going on than you might think at first, so a deeper look is recommended.

The most popular examples of American Illustration Art you will see in the mainstream these days are bound to be Pin-up and Glamour, and those examples are likely to be by Gil Elvgren, maybe Alberto Vargas and occasionally a few other names: Earl Moran, Al Buell, Haddon Sundblom, George Petty and Enoch Bolles, to name a few.

Gillette "Gil" Elvgren is the king of the form. Make no mistake: no American artist of the 1930s, 1940s and 1950s so captured the male imagination like Elvgren did with his girls on Brown & Bigelow calendars. The best examples of his work bring upwards of $250,000 today and his popularity only continues to grow as pieces of his greatest work make their way back into the collecting population with the disbursement at auction of Martignette's estate over the course of the next three years.

Mainstream Illustration

Four words: The Saturday Evening Post. There is almost no American alive who has not seen one of the iconic covers of this venerable publication, and it is the epitome of what "mainstream" illustration is. If you think of most any Norman Rockwell painting you'll have a prime example. Joseph Christian (J.C.) Leyendecker almost single-handedly defined American male style of the post-World War I era with his highly stylized and sharply painted Kuppenheimer Clothing ads. Other contemporaries – think John Clymer, N.C. Wyeth, Amos Sewell, Dean Cornwell, James Montgomery Flagg and Howard Chandler Christy – were the most famous, and prosperous, of this form.

These artists painted "everyday" life in America, and their simple homespun scenes conveyed the enthusiasm and straightforwardness of the emerging post-Industrial Revolutionary world order, with America leading the way.

Before photography, before movies and television, there was only illustration to punctuate books, stories and magazines. As such, the diversity of subjects in this subset ranges from the aforementioned wholesome Mid-American scene to chaotic cityscapes, the Wild West, pirates on the high seas, historical and most anything you can think of in between. In sum, the possibilities for collecting are only limited by your passion and your bank account. The top pieces go for hundreds of thousands, if not millions of dollars, though a determined collector can still get decent examples for as little as a few hundred dollars, sometimes even less. With a few thousand to spend, the possibilities are greatly expanded.

Pulps, Pulp-like Fiction and Paperbacks

This subset is perhaps the most under-appreciated though easily the most fascinating aspect of this rapidly changing market. The publications that many of these paintings and drawings were done for were, literally, meant to be read once and thrown away; the paper upon which they were printed was the cheapest possible, as often was the content. It was not until at least a half-century later for the greatest artists of the genre that their original artwork started getting the attention it so richly deserves.

If the stories were mostly trashy, the art was strictly top notch, and holds up quite well today. Even with subjects that today are more kitschy than menacing, there is a wonderful noir irony that speaks to the American love of being entertained. Whether it's square-jawed toughs getting knocked out by trench-coated detectives, scenes of World War II battles, or sci-fi images of other-world battles of life and death, there is wonderful drama and movement present, and collectors respond viscerally to the work.

Unlike Mainstream and Pin-up Illustration, there is no one single name that dominates Pulp, Pulp-like Fiction and Paperback art. Names like Margaret Brundage, Norman Saunders, Hugh Joseph Ward, James Avati, Mort Künstler and Frank R. Paul have logged the highest prices, but there is still a great and affordable plethora of quality artists whose work can be had at good prices with just a little research and a healthy bit of patience.

Noah Fleisher, media and public relations liaison for Heritage Auction Galleries in Dallas and former editor of Antique Trader, has also written extensively for New England Antiques Journal, Northeast Journal of Antiques and Art and their online components in the recent years.

Photo courtesy Hertiage Auction Galleries, Dallas; www.HA.com

George Rozen (American 1895 - 1974), The Creeping Death, The Shadow Magazine pulp cover, Jan. 15, 1933. Oil on canvas, 30" x 21", signed lower left. This early Shadow Magazine cover, The Creeping Death, was the 22nd cover printed, and this masterwork hails from within two years of the pulp magazine's debut. **$47,800**

Photo courtesy Hertiage Auction Galleries, Dallas; www.HA.com

N.C. Wyeth (American 1882-1945), Mrs. Van Anden Sings, A Story of the North Country, Scribner's Magazine illustration, June 1913. Oil on canvas, 25" x 34", signed lower left. Caption: "We all listened breathless even after the last chord of it had ceased to throb." A Scribner's Magazine publication label is affixed to the back of this piece. **$107,550**

Photo courtesy Hertiage Auction Galleries, Dallas; www.HA.com

Dean Cornwell (American, 1892-1960), Captain Blood Inspecting the Treasure Chest Jewels, Cosmopolitan illustration, July 1930. Oil on canvas, 26" x 52", initialed lower right. Originally a two-page illustration for Rafael Sabatini's story, "Ransom -- Captain Blood". From the Estate of Charles Martignette. **$53,775**

Photo courtesy Hertiage Auction Galleries, Dallas; www.HA.com

Alberto Vargas (American, 1896-1982), Esquire calendar girl, December 1946. Watercolor on board, 28" x 22", not signed. From the Estate of Charles Martignette. **$53,775**

Photo courtesy Hertiage Auction Galleries, Dallas; www.HA.com

Enoch Bolles (American, 1883-1976), Slipping Beauty, Film Fun Magazine cover, February 1935. Oil on canvas, 25" x 20", not signed. Reproduced as figure 76 in The Great American Pin-Up by Charles G. Martignette and Louis K. Meisel. From the Estate of Charles Martignette. **$65,725**

Photo courtesy Hertiage Auction Galleries, Dallas; www.HA.com

Earl Moran (American 1893-1984), Blonde Dancer, pinup drawing. Pastel on board, 26" x 18", signed lower right.
$33,460

Photo courtesy Hertiage Auction Galleries, Dallas; www.HA.com

Vaughan Alden Bass (American, 20th Century), Watch the Birdie. Oil on canvas, 28" x 22", signed lower right. Reproduced as figure 757 in The Great American Pin-Up by Charles G. Martignette and Louis K. Meisel. From the Estate of Charles Martignette. **$13,145**

Photo courtesy Hertiage Auction Galleries, Dallas; www.HA.com

Jessie Willcox Smith (American 1863-1935), The Then Lover. Mixed-media on board, 21 1/2" x 15 1/2", signed lower right. **$89,625**

Photo courtesy Hertiage Auction Galleries, Dallas; www.HA.com

Maurice Sendak (American b. 1928), Wild Things Backdrop Landscape. Ink and watercolor on paper, 15 1/2" x 35 1/2", signed lower right. **$75,687**

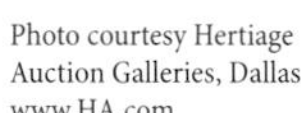

Photo courtesy Hertiage Auction Galleries, Dallas; www.HA.com

Amos Sewell (American, 1901-1983), Kids Playing Cowboy, Saturday Evening Post cover, March 11, 1950. Gouache on board, 33" x 22 1/2", signed lower left. From the Estate of Charles Martignette. **$41,825**

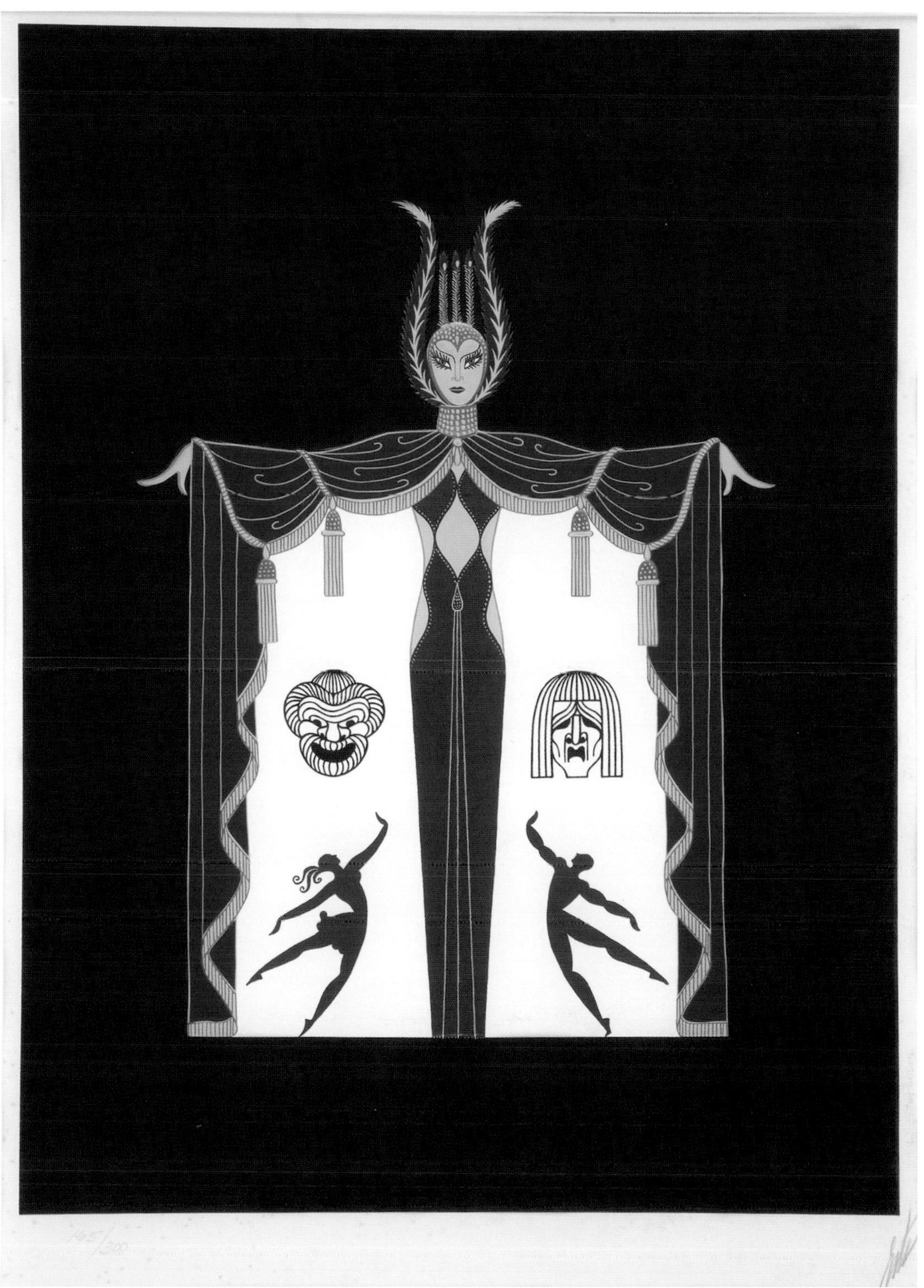

Photo courtesy Hertiage Auction Galleries, Dallas; www.HA.com

Erte (Romain De Tirtoff) (French 1892-1990), 1978. Silk Screen Print, 17 1/2" x 13", signed lower right, edition: 165/300, published by Circle Fine Arts Corp. **$286**

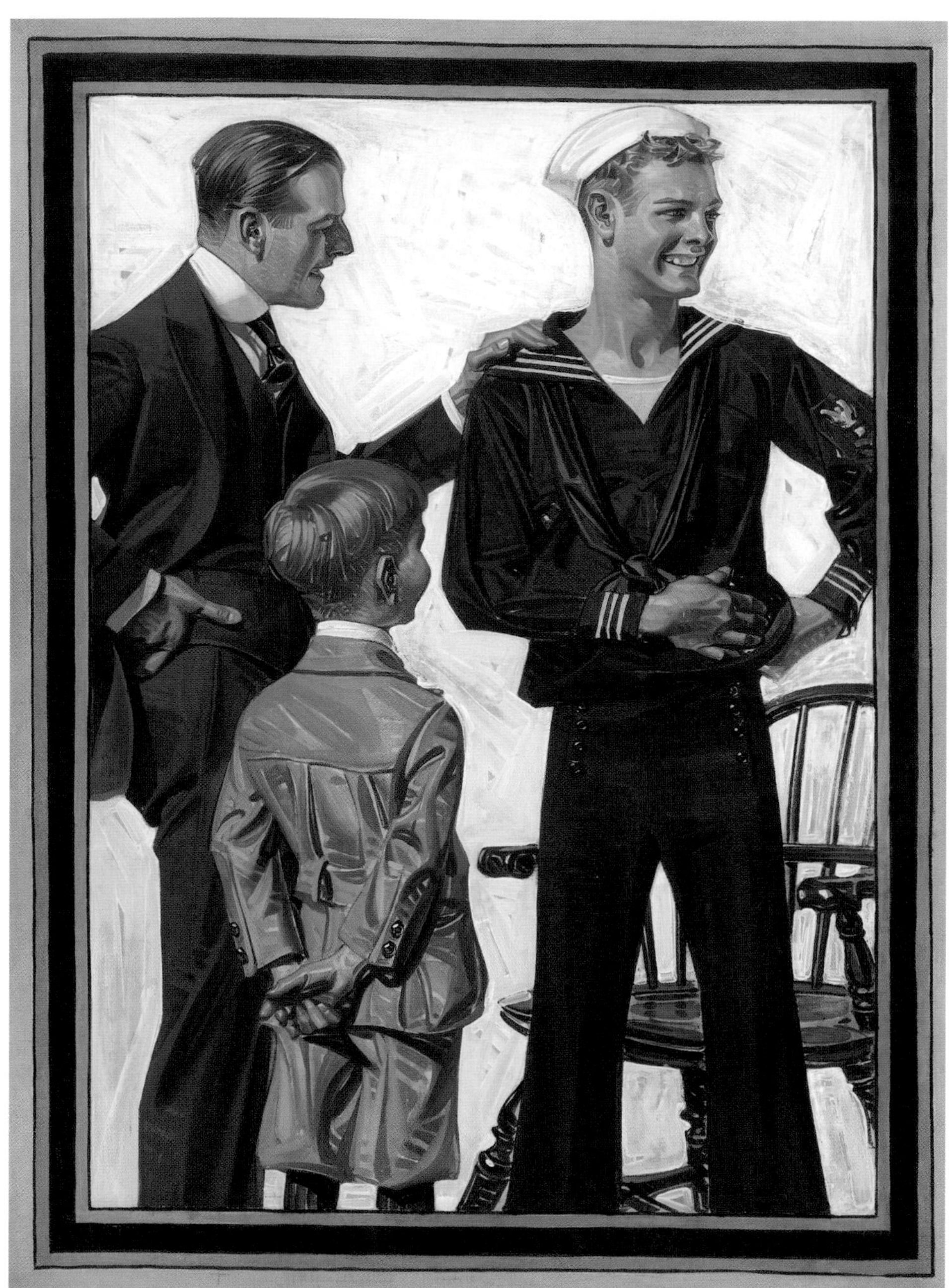

Photos courtesy Hertiage Auction Galleries, Dallas; www.HA.com

Joseph Christian Leyendecker (American, 1874-1951), A Proud WW I Sailor's New Uniform, House of Kuppenheimer ad diptych, 1917. Oil on canvas, 29" x 46", not signed.

Photos courtesy Hertiage Auction Galleries, Dallas; www.HA.com

This illustration is one of the most reproduced images of J. C. Leyendecker's career. From the Estate of Charles Martignette. **$155,350**

Photos courtesy Hertiage Auction Galleries, Dallas; www.HA.com

Above: Michael Whelan (American b. 1950), Fighting Man of Mars, paperback cover, 1979. Acrylic on board, 21" x 27", signed with a monograph lower right and used on the cover of Edgar Rice Burroughs' novel, Fighting Man of Mars, the seventh of Burroughs' Mars novels, Del Rey, 1979. **$20,315**

Right: Margaret Brundage (American, 1900-1976), The Altar of Melek, Weird Tales cover, September 1932. Pastel on paper, 20" x 17 1/2", signed lower right. This was the first Margaret Brundage cover published on Weird Tales. **$50,787**

AUTOGRAPHS

Autographs appear on an amazing array of objects: letters, photographs, books, cards, clothing, etc. Most collectors focus on a particular person, country or category, like movie stars, musicians or athletes.
Also see Sports Memorabilia.

Photo courtesy Heritage Auction Galleries, Dallas; www.HA.com

Hank Aaron, single-signed baseball. **$95**

By His Excellency
Samuel Adams, Esquire,
Governor and Commander in Chief of the
COMMONWEALTH OF MASSACHUSETTS.

To Mark Fernald Gentleman Greeting

YOU being appointed Captain of a Company of Cavalry in the First Brigade, Sixth Division of the Militia of this Commonwealth. By Virtue of the Power vested in me, I do by these Presents, (reposing special Trust and Confidence in your Ability, Courage and good Conduct) COMMISSION you accordingly :— You are, therefore, carefully and diligently to discharge the Duty of Captain in Leading, Ordering and Exercising said [illegible] in Arms, both inferior Officers and Soldiers ; and to keep them in good Order and Discipline : And they are hereby commanded to obey you as their Captain And you are yourself to observe and follow such Orders and Instructions, as you shall from Time to Time receive from me, or your superior Officers.

GIVEN under my Hand, and the Seal of the said Commonwealth, the [illegible] Day of June in the Year of our LORD, 1796 and in the [illegible] Year of the Independence of the United States of AMERICA.

John Avery

Photo courtesy Swann Auction Galleries, New York; www.SwannGalleries.com

Samuel Adams, 1796, partly printed document signed as Governor of Massachusetts, appointing Mark Fernald "captain of a Company of Cavalry in the First Brigade, Sixth." Countersigned by Secretary John Avery. Approximately 9" x 14 1/2"; diagonal tear lower right (not affecting text), docketed on verso, paper seal intact. **$2,280**

Woody Allen, 5" x 6" headshot postcard, signed in black ink. **$59**

"All in the Family", signatures from co-stars Sally Struthers, Rob Reiner, Carroll O'Connor and Jean Stapleton, matted with a 5" x 6" color photo of the cast. **$215**

Louis Armstrong, white silk handkerchief signed in black ink, matted and framed along with a color 12" x 12" photo of Armstrong to an overall size of 17" x 21". **$717**

Fred Astaire and Ginger Rogers, vintage promotional photo. **$298**

Pearl Bailey, 1990, pictorial greeting card: "You stand so majestic – you invite the world to look up past you to the heavens. '100 years old –' amazing – your youth overpowers your age, I love you." (Marking the 100th anniversary of the Eiffel Tower.) **$360**

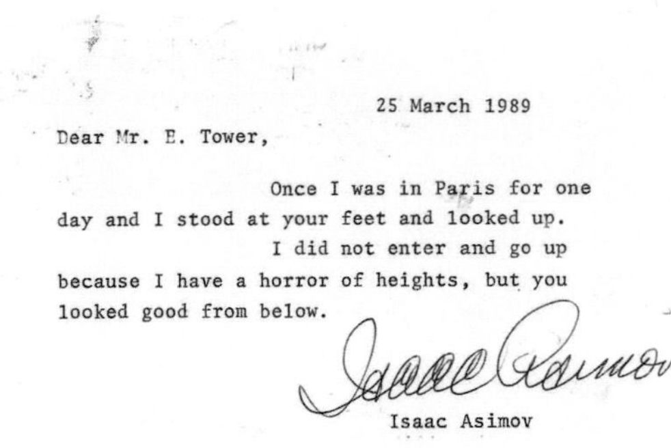

25 March 1989

Dear Mr. E. Tower,

Once I was in Paris for one day and I stood at your feet and looked up.

I did not enter and go up because I have a horror of heights, but you looked good from below.

Isaac Asimov

Isaac Asimov

Photo courtesy Swann Auction Galleries, New York; www.SwannGalleries.com

Isaac Asimov, 1989, typed note on a card: "Dear Mr. E. Tower, Once I was in Paris for one day and I stood at your feet and looked up. I did not enter and go up because I have a horror of heights, but you looked good from below." (Marking the 100th anniversary of the Eiffel Tower.) **$660**

Photos courtesy Heritage Auction Galleries, Dallas; www.HA.com

Myrna Loy signed photo, B&W 11" x 14", inscribed "To B.D. Burnes/Cordially," and signed by Loy in black fountain ink, with mild toning, light wear to the edges, and a crease to the top left corner. **$507**

Leonard Bernstein, (1918-1990), photograph showing him sitting behind a music stand at the New York Philharmonic Young People's Concert in 1964. Signed in the image. Approximately 9" x 7"; some dings, staining at right edge. **$330**

Napoleon Bonaparte, 1814, letter, written as the Continental powers march toward Paris, to the Duke of Feltre, in French, ordering the deployment of two troop divisions and requesting to be informed about their prompt arrival, as "[t]he fate of the capital may depend on it." One page, folds, tiny holes in lower left (not affecting signature). **$6,000**

James Brown, B&W 8" x 10" photo, circa 1992, in blue ballpoint. **$149**

James Cagney, photo from the 1931 movie, "The Public Enemy." **$107**

Johnny Cash and June Carter Cash, 22-page tour book from the mid-'70s, full of color photos, signed on the inside front cover in black ballpoint. Some mild wear and moderate spine stress. **$179**

James Fenimore Cooper, 1841, letter to the Boston publisher George Roberts, rejecting the idea of writing a novel because, "It would not tally with my notions to publish a novel in the way you mention," and offering other projects. One full page, small tear in left margin, closed tear in right margin repaired, folds. **$2,040**

Dallas Cowboys, 1992 Super Bowl Champions helmet, including Troy Aikman, Emmitt Smith, Michael Irvin, Jerry Jones, Dave Wannstedt, Daryl Johnston, Bill Bates, Jay Novacek and many more. **$1,075**

Bobby Darin, signed contract, 1967. Initialed and signed in blue ink with his real name, Bob Cassotto. Overall age toning and smudging of the ink in a couple spots, while the signature reads clearly. **$155**

James Dean, (1931-1955), photograph, bust portrait in jacket and t-shirt, signed in the image. Approximately 10" x 8"; minor handling, circa 1955. .... **$6,240**

Cecil B. DeMille, signed contract, dated Nov. 22, 1950, negotiating the use of cinematographer and visual effects designer Gordon Jennings for the 1952 drama, "The Greatest Show on Earth," signed by in blue ink. Minimal edge wear and mild discoloration. **$239**

Frederick Douglass, 1891, letter written as Minister and American Consul in Haiti, to a Mr. Halford, asking for a bigger portrait of President Harrison. In full: "I have a very excellent picture of President Harrison, but it is too small for the size of the U.S. Legation at this place. I want our American sea captains to see a good picture of our President. Could you cause one to be sent to me? I would be much obliged to you. My fervent best wishes of the season;" 1 1/2 pages, written on the first and third pages of a single folded sheet. **$4,320**

Clint Eastwood, poster for "Unforgiven" (1992) in gold ink. The poster has an overall size of 28" x 40". **$567**

Edward, Duke of Windsor, 1922, letter signed, "Edward P.," as Prince of Wales, to Lord Richard: "Thank you very much for your kind present; it was very nice of you to think of me on my birthday. I hope you are keeping well." One page, St. James' Palace stationery; horizontal fold, minor soiling. **$210**

Albert Einstein, 1934, typed letter to Charles D. Hart, in German, thanking him for an invitation to a Stokowski concert and declining due to his obligations. One-half page, usual folds; notes in pencil in another hand in lower left on recto, two holes punched in left margin. **$2,280**

Photo courtesy Heritage Auction Galleries, Dallas; www.HA.com

Ray Bolger, vintage promotional photo from "The Wizard of Oz." **$298**

Photo courtesy Swann Auction Galleries, New York; www.SwannGalleries.com

Enrico Caruso, 1911, photograph, showing him standing, arms crossed, in costume as Pagliacci. Signed in the image. Approximately 9" x 5" (image). **$1,800**

Photo courtesy Swann Auction Galleries, New York; www.SwannGalleries.com

Dwight D. Eisenhower and Douglas MacArthur, photograph signed by both, silver print image by Thomas Shafer showing the two generals side by side in a car during Eisenhower's visit to Tokyo in May 1946. Approximately 8" x 10"; minor creases and dings, marginal chips, photographer's stamp on verso. **$36,000** *(Eisenhower and MacArthur's enmity toward each other is well documented, making this image an exceptional association piece. Shafer was a combat photographer during World War II and spent most of the war in the Pacific Theater. He made some 18 troop landings with the 1st Cavalry division, and took many of the widely distributed photos of MacArthur wading ashore on his "I have returned" landing in the Philippines. After the Japanese surrender, Shafer spent time in Japan and took the first close-up photos of Emperor Hirohito and became essentially MacArthur's personal photographer. In May 1946, Eisenhower was Army Chief of Staff and MacArthur the head of the U.S. occupation of Japan. Ike was in Tokyo on an inspection trip visiting U.S. troops stationed in the Far East. In the photograph, the two generals are seated in MacArthur's official Cadillac limousine. It appeared in newspapers on June 2, 1946, but Shafer personally had the two generals sign the photograph in his presence while Ike was still in Tokyo.)*

"Messieurs Tichnor & Fields": "Please send to the 'Union Club' a copy of 'Emerson's Works' entirely bound in calf, with my compliments, & charge them to the account of your obed't serv't." One page, small numerals written in ink in top left on recto, horizontal folds. **$1,200**

Gerald Ford, 1976, his signature as President, and date, added to a typed letter signed by Susan Ford, which offers thanks for a letter and responds to a photograph request. One page, White House stationery; horizontal fold thorough GRF signature; matted and framed. Not examined out of frame. **$120**

Aretha Franklin, signed contract for "Shindig" television appearances, 1965. A 15" x 9" matted display, accompanied by an image of Franklin. Minor age-toning to contract. **$107**

Robert Fulton, 1813, affidavit excusing himself from appearing at the arbitration of a patent dispute with John Sullivan, and appointing John Devereux Delacy to act on his behalf. Additionally Signed by DeWitt Clinton as Mayor of New York, affirming Delacy's power of attorney. Two pages, with integral blank; damp stained, separations at folds repaired, docketed on terminal page. **$2,880**

(The dispute concerned Fulton's request for a patent for towing boats by steam and warping them over rapids. Despite the competency of Delacy, Fulton's personal secretary, and the legal assistance of Elihu Whitney, arbitration at Hartford found in favor of Sullivan and denied the patent.)

George and Ira Gershwin, framed, ex-Kaye Ballard collection. **$657**

Ulysses S. Grant, 1867, partly printed letter signed as Secretary of War ad interim, to Miles W. Keogh, informing him of the president's appointing him Lieutenant Colonel by brevet for his service at the Battle of Dallas, Ga. One page, with integral blank; horizontal folds. **$2,040**

Horace Greeley, 1862, letter to Thomas A. Hillbanse (?), opining that Thomas I. Sawyer, whose two sons were "enlisted as privates at the first tidings of the attack on Sumter," should have been appointed Lieutenant, and requesting that he contact Mr. Sawyer about whether there had been a mistake. One full page, Daily Tribune stationery; small closed tear at right edge repaired, minor soiling, vertical fold. **$270**

Hank Greenberg, 8" x 10" black and white photo. **$537**

John Hancock, 1783, letter with initials, a retained draft of a letter to George Washington, praising him for his virtues and past service on the occasion of his retiring to his Mount Vernon plantation: "May you long live, my dear General, and long have the joy to see the increasing splendor and prosperity of a rising nation aided by your councils and defended by your sword." Two pages, with integral blank; folds, minor foxing, minor soiling on terminal page, docketed on the terminal page. **$78,000**

Ernest Hemingway, (1899-1961), book, The Sun Also Rises (1927), inscribed on the front blank, to Donald R. Williams. Publisher's cloth, some chipping at spine ends, spine label chipped at edges and darkened; front blank (signature page) nearly completely separated at gutter. Later printing. **$2,880**

Patrick Henry, 1777, letter signed as Governor of Virginia, to Colonel Evan Shelby, requesting him to "order Capt. Joseph Martin, agent in the Cherokee Nation, to be supply'd with provisions for himself & his servants among that people." With a two-line autograph postscript signed with initials. One page, folds, minor soiling, docketed on verso. **$5,760**

Sir Edmund Hillary, (1919-2008), drawing in ink on a card, image of a man atop a mountain, followed by a Sherpa. ...**$850**

Buddy Holly and the Crickets, twice-autographed British Tour souvenir program, also been signed by Holly on the interior pages along with Des O'Connor (supporting act). With mild overall wear and bent lower left rear corner. **$5,078**

Langston Hughes, 1944, book, Shakespeare in Harlem (1942), inscribed, and dated on the front free endpaper, to "Libby Holman with happy good wishes from Langston Hughes." Publisher's cloth, chipping at spine ends; pages evenly toned; dust jacket, front inside panel separated at fold, chipped at all edges. First edition. **$425**

Washington Irving, 1857, letter to later critic, William Alfred Jones, thanking him for sending a copy of a book which is "in a department of literature very much to my taste, and in which you have proved yourself a master," and saying of him that "your worthy father was one of the first to applaud and encourage my early attempts at authorship ..." Two and 1/2 pages, written on a single folded sheet; minor soiling. **$1,020**

Reggie Jackson, "563 HR" single-signed baseball. **$89**

Lyndon B. Johnson, (1908-1973), photograph inscribed, "[t]o George Ball with high regard," image of LBJ, Ball and another man seated beside someone speaking at the presidential podium. Approximately 11" x 14"; minor fading to signature, mounted; matted and framed. **$390**

Kaleleonalani, Queen Consort of the Hawaiian Islands, signature, 1862. One page, approximately 5 1/2" x 3 1/2", personal stationery, bold signature. **$720**
(Kaleleonalani [1836-1885] was Queen to King Kamehameha IV of Hawaii between 1856 and 1863. For a short period after the death of her son, she went by the name "Kaleleokalani," a name that is reflected in the signature.)

Robert Kennedy, 1960, book, inscribed first-edition copy of The Enemy Within, "For Deda with love, Bobby, XX OO XX," on the front free endpaper. Publisher's cloth, back strip faded, lacks the dust jacket. **$720**

Photo courtesy Swann Auction Galleries, New York; www.SwannGalleries.com

Theodore Geisel (Dr. Seuss) (1904-1991), book, If I Ran the Zoo (1950), inscribed with a small original drawing, on the verso of the front free endpaper, "For Susan West! With best wishes - Dr. Seuss." Publisher's pictorial boards, covers worn, back strip replaced by tape; lacking rear free endpaper. **$900**

Photos courtesy Heritage Auction Galleries, Dallas; www.HA.com

John Wayne signed yearbook, copy of the Glendale, Calif., Union High School 1924 Stylus yearbook autographed by junior class vice president John Wayne using his birth name, Marion Morrison. The yearbook is signed by Wayne in black ink on pages 121 (junior class intro page), and his football team photo can be found on page 159; with a fair amount of soiling and appreciable edge wear to the covers, pages in very good condition. **$1,314**

reading, they will reflect, and feel the duties we owe to that race of men.
I wish that was the only blot in our moral history, and that no other race
had higher charges to bring against us. I am not apt to despair; yet I see not
how we are to disengage ourselves from that deplorable entanglement, we have
the wolf by the ears and feel the danger of either holding or letting him loose.
I shall not live to see it but those who come after us will be wiser than we are,
for light is spreading and man improving. to that advancement I look, and to
the dispensations of an all-wise and all-powerful providence to devise the
means of effecting what is right. I pray you to accept assurances of my high
and respectful consideration.

Mrs Sigourney. Th: Jefferson

Photo courtesy Swann Auction Galleries, New York; www.SwannGalleries.com

Thomas Jefferson, 1824, signed letter written in the hand of his granddaughter, Virginia, to the poet Lydia H. Sigourney, thanking her for her letter and for her notice of the part he played in the Revolution, agreeing with her views regarding the advocacy of "Indian rights," and expressing the wish that these wrongs were "the only blot in our moral history, and that no other race had higher charges to bring against us." One and 1/2 pages, with integral address leaf, detached; addressed in his hand and with franking signature. Small hole at fold of address leaf with loss to "J" of signature, seal tear, and minor soiling; docketed. **$48,000**

Rudyard Kipling, (1865-1936), letter to Gabriel Hanotaux, apologizing for being unable to meet the day before, arranging a meeting for the next day, and thanking Hanotaux "for all your kindness in suggesting to us so charming a retreat as we have found here." One and 1/2 pages, written on recto and verso of a single sheet; horizontal fold. Circa 1926. .... **$390**

Marquis de Lafayette, Gilbert Du Motier, 1823, letter to an unnamed recipient ("mon cher ami"), in French, following up on a mission and delivery of paperwork by Mechin, and writing "I was forced to leave for Lagrange immediately after the funeral of M. Savoie-Rollin, who is so justly missed; I will return to Paris Saturday morning for four or five hours and will use this chance to see my two colleagues." One page, remnants of prior mounting in left margin recto. **$900**

John Lennon, twice-inscribed photo, color 8" x 10", signed "John Lennon to Bill" on the front in blue ball point, and features the following inscription on the reverse in black ink: "Dear Bill, A lot of water under the bridge, and over the wall! A sad story, love, John." Slight wear. **$3,585**

Charles Lindbergh, 1930, First Flight airmail cover, mounted in front of a Lindbergh print titled "The Lone Eagle". The cover postmarked from Grand Central Station, New York, April 25, 1930, a green 20-cent airmail stamp with a First Flight stamp commemorating the first direct Caribbean flight and the seven-day flight from New York to Buenos Aires. The cover is signed upper left "CA Lindbergh, Dec. 1934". Housed in a modern gilt molded wood frame with double matte, 14 3/4" x 19" (sight). Print shows some folds but generally very good, the cover has a dog-ear fold through first part of signature, otherwise good. **$360**

Charles Lindbergh, (1902-1974), photo by Underwood & Underwood, shows a young Lindbergh with flight cap and goggles. Signed on side "CA Lindbergh", 6 1/4" x 4 1/2". Margin shows frame toning, otherwise very good. **$862**

Henry Wadsworth Longfellow, 1855, quotation, five lines from his poem, Excelsior: "The shades of night were

Photo courtesy Swann Auction Galleries, New York; www.SwannGalleries.com

Rev. Martin Luther King Jr. (1929-1968), photograph inscribed, "[t]o Mrs. Libby Shanker with great respect & admiration, Martin Luther King Jr.," image by Faingold of MLK standing behind a chair. Signed in the image, approximately 7 1/2" x 9 1/2"; signature in blue ink against a dark background, some dings; matted and in a silver frame engraved with the words, "Libby with my love, Clifton [Webb]." **$3,120**

Photo courtesy Heritage Auction Galleries, Dallas; www.HA.com

B.B. King, black six-string Epiphone Junior electric guitar signed on the body, with wall-mountable metal carrying case with a Plexiglas viewing window on one side. **$597**

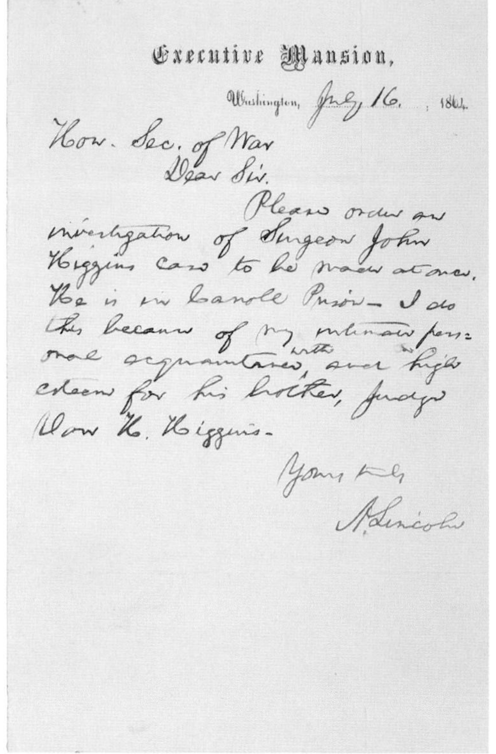

Executive Mansion,
Washington, July 16, 1864.
Hon. Sec. of War
Dear Sir.
Please order an investigation of Surgeon John Higgins case to be made at once. He is in Carroll Prison – I do this because of my intimate personal acquaintance with and high esteem for his brother, Judge Van H. Higgins.
Yours truly
A. Lincoln

Photo courtesy Swann Auction Galleries, New York; www.SwannGalleries.com

Abraham Lincoln, 1864, letter to Secretary of War Edwin M. Stanton, requesting that an investigation be made into the case of a friend's brother in Carroll Prison. One page, Executive Mansion stationery; vertical fold through "A" of signature, mounted along top edge verso to a larger sheet, recent owner's gift inscription in ink on verso, minor soiling. **$22,800**
("Please order an investigation of Surgeon John Higgins case to be made at once. He is in Carroll Prison – I do this because of my intimate personal acquaintance with and high esteem for his brother, Judge Van H. Higgins.")

Photos courtesy Heritage Auction Galleries, Dallas; www.HA.com

James Dean signed yearbook. This copy of the 1948 Black and Gold yearbook for Fairmount (Ind.) High School features a Junior class photo of Dean. The book is signed "Jim Dean" in blue ink under his basketball photo in the Sports section, and is in overall good condition with moderate wear to the cover, which has detached from the the contents of the book. Presented in a framed display box. **$1,673**

falling fast / As through an Alpine village passed / A youth, who bore, 'mid snow and ice, / A banner with the strange device / Excelsior!" Approximately 4 1/2" x 6 3/4" 1; stained at edges on verso from prior mounting, mounted to bottom is a strip of paper on which is written in HL's hand, "With W. Longfellow's compliments." **$570**

Douglas MacArthur, (1880-1964), book, Reminiscences, McGraw-Hill, photographic illustrations, with publisher's slipcase. First limited edition, number 204 of 1750 copies signed by MacArthur. **$600**

Groucho Marx, childhood photograph, signed "This is the way I looked as a kid." **$956**

James A. Michener, 1990, typed note on a card [in all capitals]: "I have said many times that a nation or a city is fortunate if it has some architectural feature which represents it to the world. No symbol is more universally known and loved that [sic] the Eiffel tower. It sets the

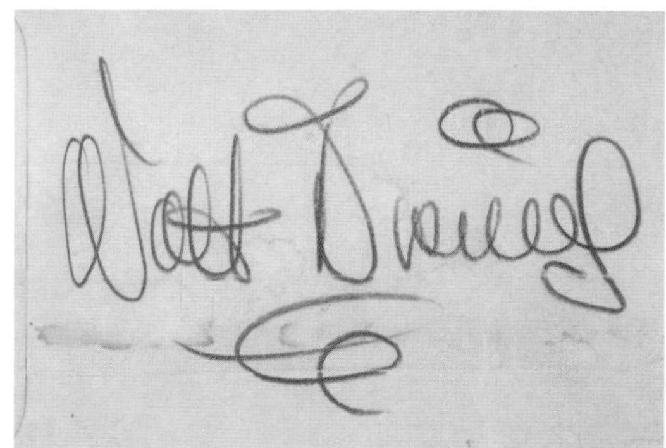

Photos courtesy Heritage Auction Galleries, Dallas; www.HA.com

Walt Disney autographed envelope, 3 1/4" x 5 1/2", signed in large script on one side, with some mild stains that do not overtly affect the signature. **$1,135**

standard that others strive to equal. My salute!!!!" (Marking the 100th anniversary of the Eiffel Tower.) **$240**

James Monroe, 1821, letter signed as President, to an unnamed recipient ("Dear Sir"), sending $350 "with great pleasure." One-half page, folds. **$2,280**
("I send you with great pleasure a check for $350 to which I will add more if at all material to you. The payment of this sum is extended with no inconvenience to me. Very sensible of your kindness be assured of my constant & sincere friendship.")

Franklin D. Roosevelt, (1882-1945), signature as President, on a White House card. Approximately 2 3/4" x 4 1/4"; partially mounted; framed, circa 1933-45. .... **$960**

Theodore Roosevelt, 1893, book, Wilderness Hunter, publisher's cloth; covers stained, spine soiled and darkened; front blanks nearly loose. One of 200 numbered copies, signed by Roosevelt. **$2,160**

Jonas Salk, (1914-1995), inscribed copy of The Survival of the Wisest (1973). Signed on the front free endpaper. Publisher's cloth; dust jacket. **$270**

William H. Seward, 1839, letter, as Governor of New York, to Peter B. Porter, responding to a letter recommending that Mr. Bird be considered for the office of Canal Commissioner and remarking that he "shall have great pleasure in making known your wishes on the subject to our common friends in the legislature ..." One page, with integral address leaf; folds, docket and postal stamp on terminal page. **$270**

James Stewart, 2" x 2" photo, inscribed, "To Michael, Jimmy Stewart." Two small sets of staple holes and a bit of tape on the top left corner. **$143**

Leo Tolstoy, 1903, letter in Russian, to Pyotr Petrovich Nikolaev, in which the master advises a fellow writer on his manuscript. Three pages, written on the first and third page

Photo courtesy Swann Auction Galleries, New York; www.SwannGalleries.com

Eleanor Roosevelt (1884-1962), photograph inscribed, to "Roberta dear, with my love, Eleanor Roosevelt," an image by Harris & Ewing showing her seated in a gown, signed in the image. Approximately 9 1/2" x 6 1/2"; minor soiling; matted, circa 1930s. **$780**

Photos courtesy Heritage Auction Galleries, Dallas, www.HA.com

Mary Astor and Dolores Del Rio signed photos, B&W 11" x 14" inscribed and signed portraits includes Del Rio in black ink and Astor in blue, with mild toning, curling, and corner wear, and tack holes to the corners of the Del Rio photo. **$334 pair**

Photos courtesy Heritage Auction Galleries, Dallas; www.HA.com

Charlie Chaplin signed photo. A vintage B&W 8" x 10" photo of the iconic silent era comedian, inscribed "With compliments to B.D. Burns", signed, and dated 1929 by Chaplin in black fountain ink, with some toning and mild edge wear. **$717**

of a folded sheet and the first page of another folded sheet, Japan paper; folds. **$14,400**

John Travolta, "Saturday Night Fever" soundtrack LP (1977). **$155**

Harry S. Truman, 1943, letter, signed as senator, to William B. Welling, responding to a note involving the proposal of a Committee on the Progress of the War: "... I don't think tactics and strategy has any place in the United States Senate." One page, U.S. Senate stationery; horizontal folds. **$960**

Kurt Vonnegut, (1922-2007), ink drawing, signed twice, self-portrait on a card with a note: "Why should it make me so happy every time I see it? That's crazy." **$480**

Artemas Ward, July 9, 1776, letter to Ebenezer Hancock, Deputy Paymaster General of the Army of the United States, requesting him to "Pay to Col John Glover eight hundred & eighty pounds three shillings, equal to two thousand nine hundred & thirty three dollars . . . it being for one month's pay of the Regiment of Foot in the service of the United Colonies ..." Countersigned by Glover, acknowledging receipt of the money. Written on verso is Colonel Glover's itemized list of his regiment and their monthly wages, which is additionally signed and dated by Glover: "Camp in Beverly, July 7, 1776." One page, folds, minor bleed-through. **$2,880**

(Ward [1727-1800] was commissioned as general and commander-in-chief of the Massachusetts troops in 1775 and resigned in 1776 when his rank was reduced to major-general upon Washington's being given supreme command.)

George Washington, (1732-1799), undated letter signed with initials, to Mr. [James?] Madison, in full: "At as early an hour this evening as you can make it convenient I should be glad to see you. Y's Sincerely & affect'y." One-half page, with integral address leaf; minor soiling, small edge tears, remnants of prior soiling along left edge of terminal page, staining and offsetting from seal in corners of each page. **$7,200**

Daniel Webster, (1752-1852), undated letter, to Dr. Parsons, thanking him for his "kind advice & attendance, which I feel to have been highly instrumental in relieving me from an indisposition which threatened to be serious." One page, with integral address leaf; closed separation at fold just below signature repaired, toned, damp staining and repairs on terminal page. **$300**

Chuck Yeager, (1923-), letter with a drawing. **$330**

("Dear Miss Tower, Happy birthday! The first time I saw you, you were 55 years old and I was 21. You looked like this [the drawing] because I was in the cockpit of a P-51 Mustang at 3000 meters above you. The date was Feb 13, 1944, my 21st birthday! Things were very hostile in the sky above you that day. Later I learned to like you very much. I hope that we have many more birthdays.")

Photo courtesy Greg Martin Auctions, San Francisco; www.GregMartinAuctions.com

Badge (suspension), multicolor gold and blue enamel, for Buck Garrett (1871-1929), Chief of Police, Ardmore, Indian Territory. **$36,800**

BADGES AND MEDALS

Badges and medals have been used for centuries to designate rank or official duties, to commemorate events and public observances, and even to mark the duties of slaves. Also see Political and Vietnam Collectibles.

42nd Pa. Buck Tails, Co. A "ladder" badge, German silver, four-part with braided brass tassel, each bar stamped with recessed area painted black, top bar/pin-back reads "Co. A., 42, Penn. Buck Tails," 2" x 5". **$862**

(The Buck Tails got their name by wearing the tail of a deer on their headgear.)

Army of the Potomac, 5th Corps badge, German silver, border engraved around the outline of a Maltese cross with sunburst in the center. **$632**

Black Hawk War, pin-back bronze and silk badge, undated, alternating red and black silk stripes with gold lettering, mint condition with the original storage envelope and backing with St. Louis Button Co. logo; 5" l. **$2,415**

(The short-lived Black Hawk War fought during the spring and summer of 1832 forcibly ejected the last native tribes, the Sauk and Fox, from the old Northwest Territory. It ushered in an era of active Indian removal. Roughly 4,000 Illinois militia and regulars commanded by Winfield Scott were marshaled to defeat Black Hawk and all were later accorded the status of "veterans.")

Photo courtesy Heritage Auction Galleries, Dallas; www.HA.com

1813 Charleston Porter Slave Hire Badge. Number 300. A nearly flat octagonal tag with a hole at the top for suspension, approximately 2" x 2". John Joseph LaFar, a prominent Charleston silversmith, manufactured it; a very light "LAFAR" hallmark is punched on the back. The elements on the front are as follows (top to bottom): "CHARLESTON" in a crescent-shaped bar punch; "1813" bar punched; "PORTER" in a rectangular punch; "No" in a square punch (faint) followed by an incuse, and a hand-engraved "300". This is the last year in which numbers were engraved. From 1814 on, numbers were individually punched. The badge has been repaired where crimped above the word "PORTER" and at an elliptical area to the left of the "P". **$2,031**

Brotherhood of Locomotive Engineers medals (six), including 1st, 2nd, 3rd, chief engineer and chaplain, housed in case with gilt title "Easton (Pa.), Div. No 259". Medals made by the Webb C. Ball Watch Co. of Cleveland, feature a locomotive motif, each 3" x 2". .... **$228 all**

Eagle Scout medal, cased, 3" x 1 1/2"; reverse of bar marked "Sterling." Interior of case marked "Eagle Scout Badge Awarded by the Boy Scouts of America." Housed in Art Deco-style case measuring 4" x 2", early 20th century. **$69**

GAR badge and medal from 15th Iowa, in German silver, two-part with arrow-form pin-back with "War 1861-5" with shield-shaped hanger reading "Wm. Makinster./Co. A/15 Iowa/Vol. Inf.," 2" x 2", plus a typical cast-bronze and silk three-part GAR medal, 1 1/2" x 4 3/4", and enameled brass shoulder bar with black enameled ground and applied sterling silver Bird Colonel spread-winged eagle, 1 1/2" l. .... **$690 both**

GAR presentation past officer's badge, fancy jeweler-made enameled and gold-plated pattern, 1887 five-pointed GAR star with T-bar clasp suspended from a silver eagle rank strap, engraved on reverse, "Presented to/ J.F. Crichton/ Julius White Post/740/1900" with flag ribbon edged in faded light blue indicating past post commander. With original folding leatherette case gold stenciled, "Chas. H. Pfeil/182 State Street/Chicago, Ill" with push-button closure. **$373**

Grant's Tomb dedication badge, New York, April 27, 1897, for Pennsylvania Legislature member, in red, white and blue silk, with attached U.S. flag and aluminum alloy medal, made by the Shaw Co. of Philadelphia. **$144**

Police badge, presentation, solid gold jeweler-made, six-pointed star pin-back, with enamel decoration and gemstone center, Chicago Police Post No. 207 American Legion, reverse marked "Solid Gold" and engraved "Presented to National Commander American Legion Raymond J. Kelly by Chicago Police Post No. 207 Feb. 11, 1940," with original black leather case, tested 10K. **$300**

Photo courtesy Greg Martin Auctions, San Francisco; www.GregMartinAuctions.com

Badge (presentation), 19th century, engraved gold, made for Benjamin Franklin Rogers, Chief of Police, Stockton, Calif. **$36,800**

Photo courtesy Heritage Auction Galleries, Dallas; www.HA.com

Identification Badge of a Pennsylvanian Wounded at Gettysburg. Suspension badge with stamped battle honors belonged to an enlisted man who was wounded twice in battle before being captured and dying from the effects of prison life. The commercially produced, gray metal identification badge features a raised profile of Maj. Gen. Kearney in the shield at the top. Suspended from it by way of two rotating links is a 1 1/4" circular disk on which is stamped "Wm McCUTCHEON/ Co. B/ 105 REG/P V/ BROOKVILLE Pa" On the reverse is a raised leaf design with "WAR OF 1861" at the top. Under this, and filling the remaining space on the back, have been stamped "Yorktown/ Williamsburg/ Fair Oaks/ 7 Days/ Before Richmond/ Malvern Hill/ Bull Run/ Chantilly/ Fredericksburg/ Chancellorsville." **$4,182**

Quaker's pin-back badge, coin silver, shield-shaped with engraved heart and S/F and motto at top, "One Heart One Way," 0.8" x 1". **$180**

Washington Monument dedication badge, Philadelphia, May 15, 1897, for Pennsylvania Legislature member, in red, white and blue silk with bronze medal, made by the Shaw Co. of Philadelphia. **$60**

Twelve law enforcement badges, including a Sheriff Oakland County, Mich.; Dearborn County; Deputy Sheriff Wayne County; 1981 Official Inauguration badge for D.C. Police; Captain's Police; Official CTS; Deputy Sheriff Wayne County; Department of Police Edgewater PK; Special Detective Atlantic City, N.J.; Conservation Officer State of Michigan; Serg't Of Police M.C. RR; and Sheriffs Assn. badge. .... **$460 all**

Four 18th and 19th century European silver badges, all have inscriptions in German. Oldest is oval-shaped 4" x 3" inscribed "Der Schutzen Campagne Zu Osterberg zu Ehren," dated 1752. Second-oldest is star-shaped 4 1/2" x 3" with inscription "W. Stengel" and dated 1839. Third-oldest is star shaped 3 1/2" with 13 points (14th is missing) and dated 1871. Fourth-oldest is octagonal 1 1/2" and inscribed "Leht Konig," 1875. .... **$431 all**

Grouping of Civil War veterans/reunion ribbons (23), includes nine reunion ribbons for the 3rd Pennsylvania Heavy Artillery, seven ribbons from the Juniata County Veteran's Association, with the balance being military related; with two Civil War belt plates. .... **$575 all**

Photo courtesy Heritage Auction Galleries, Dallas; www.HA.com

Silver Civil War Provost Guard Badge with Intriguing ID. 1 3/4" diameter riband engraved with buckle at the bottom, inscribed "D. D. Bulman Provost Guard". The pierced star in the center is inscribed with the date 1864. T-bar pinback. The back of the badge also exhibits hand-inscribed Masonic symbols. Untouched patina, the pin and closure loop are missing, but the T-bar base for the pin is intact. **$1,673**

FUTURE OF THE MARKET: MECHANICAL BANKS

By Catherine Saunders-Watson

Within the entire realm of antique collecting, there is no category that can truthfully be described as "bulletproof," but mechanical banks come very close to it. Whether the bulls or the bears are in charge on Wall Street at any given time, history has shown that bank collectors pay them little mind and remain active throughout the ups and downs.

"They might slow down the pace at which they collect – maybe buying three good banks a year as opposed to five or six – but they don't stop collecting," said Dan Morphy, co-founder of Morphy Auctions and author of the book The Official Price Guide to Mechanical Banks.

Morphy cited a recent example in which a "very well-known collection" changed hands discreetly for several million dollars, seemingly oblivious to the worst economic recession America has experienced in 80 years. And even after the 9/11 tragedies brought American business to a standstill, Morphy said, a collection of mechanical banks was sold privately for $1.4 million.

"To some degree, mechanical banks are their own independent micro-economy," Morphy said. "They're not entirely immune to the whims of the financial markets, but they can really take a punch and stay on their feet better than any other type of antique I can think of.

"At the moment, the market for mechanical banks is as strong as it has ever been," he observed. "Even though we've all heard that the decision to buy antiques should never be based on the hope of one day making a profit, the type of person who is chasing banks right now is looking at it as an investment as much as a hobby. For that reason, today's mechanical bank collector is much more inclined to put his or her money into an example they think is going to be a sound investment. They're making their own rules."

Morphy believes the main catalyst that drives the mechanical-bank market and keeps the values buoyant in challenging times is the American legacy and social significance associated with many banks. "They do cross over as toys, but they're looked at with a different eye because there's a strong historical and folk-art side to them. Many of these banks are surviving witnesses to the most important events and social movements of the past century and a half. Some, which have a racially stereotypical theme, are tangible reminders of the injustices of a past era."

By far, the most valuable and sought-after banks are those made of cast iron or painted lead. Generally, American collectors prefer American-made examples, with some of the better-known manufacturers being J. & E. Stevens, Shepard Hardware and Kyser & Rex. The most desirable subjects in cast-iron banks are those that represent an aspect of history, a Biblical theme, baseball, or an occupation, e.g., the Dentist bank, the Mason bank, etc.

European collectors are more attracted to lithographed-tin banks, and rarities in this classification, such as those made in the 1930s by Saalheimer & Strauss, can fetch a substantial price. A circa-1928 tin Mickey Mouse Accordion Player bank by the German manufacturer sold at Morphy's in 2007 for $48,875.

Morphy has handled his fair share of high-end banks, including those offered at the record-smashing $7.7 million auction in October 2007 of the Stephen and Marilyn Steckbeck Collection. Now widely acknowledged as the highest-grossing toy auction ever held, the 492-lot sale surpassed the previously held record by a margin of more than $2.5 million. The result was reported to the Guinness Book of World Records.

Dan Morphy

The Steckbecks built their collection over a 53-year period and took a very proactive approach in adding to it. Steve Steckbeck had pickers scouring several states on his behalf, and as his collection grew and he became more familiar with the better-quality banks, he made the natural transition that many bank collectors make as they grow more seasoned: he started to focus on acquiring only the rarest examples in the best possible condition. Steve and Marilyn's circa-1910 North Pole bank was one of the finest known (it sold for $149,500); and their turn of the century Kenton Hardware Mama Katzenjammer bank in superior, near-mint-plus condition, had actually been a manufacturer's showroom sample. It sold for $74,750. Almost every bank auctioned in that now-legendary sale had some sort of blue-chip provenance.

Mechanicals and money have always had a symbiotic connection, and not just the obvious one to be drawn from the fact that moneyboxes were created as storehouses for children's savings. They've always been viewed from an investment angle, even if it was just a few canny collectors who recognized the potential decades ago when the hobby was still in its formative years. The Steckbeck banks, for example, were featured over the years in a number of business and investment publications, including Forbes, Money and Wealth.

The Steckbecks' unrelenting efforts at networking, buying and selling resulted in a collection that contained spectacular examples from early collections of now-historic stature, e.g., those of financier Edwin Mosler, F.H. Griffith, Walter P. Chrysler and Andrew Emerine.

At the auction of the Steckbeck collection, successful bidders wrote checks that could have paid off many people's mortgages: $414,000 for a late-1880s Jonah and the Whale/Jonah Emerges bank, $287,500 for a circa-1886

Mikado bank depicting an illusionist conducting a shell game, and $195,500 for a Roller Skating bank with a clever mechanism that propelled its skating figures.

The biggest buzz in the gallery was over the "politically incorrect" banks that had captured the attention of a CBS Sunday Morning film crew from New York. None of the crewmembers had ever seen 19th-century mechanical banks with cruel, racially stereotypical depictions of African-Americans and Chinese immigrant workers. In the end, the CBS producer, realizing how historically significant the banks were, chose to develop the entire segment around the valuable black-theme banks, later adding commentary – pro and con – from African-American historians.

Of the top 10 banks in the sale, two exhibited a black theme: the rare 1880s-vintage Charles A. Bailey painted-lead "Darky Fisherman," which sold for $287,500; and the circa-1888 J. & E. Stevens cast-iron "Darky and Watermelon," which reached $195,500. Another unbelievable indictment of our society 130 years ago was Charles A. Bailey's circa-1888 painted-lead "Chinaman in Boat" bank, which earned $103,500.

"By displaying banks of this type, collectors are not condoning the message that is inherent in them," said Morphy. "They are displaying a fragment of history that cannot be changed. Banks of this type are absolutely at the top of the most-wanted list with collectors who buy with investment in mind."

It's not just the old-timers who are collecting mechanical banks. Many new collectors are getting into the hobby, and a fair number of them are in their 20s. "We're definitely seeing new faces coming into the fold, and some are collectors of other types of antiques who've become interested in banks," Morphy said. "I just sold two banks for five figures to a buyer who got into it only a year ago."

While rarities can run into the hundreds of thousands of dollars, as confirmed by prices realized in the Steckbeck sale, there are many banks available in the $300 to $800 price range and probably more than 100 different models available in the under-$1,000 range. They may not be in pristine condition, but they are a good starting point and can always be upgraded.

An example would be the Darktown Battery bank, which merges the desirable themes of baseball and black Americana. If perfect, such a bank would run in the thousands of dollars, but a collector can acquire a perfectly acceptable example of this bank for around $500. It might have imperfections or issues with its paint or surface, or it might have been restored at some point in its life, but it's still very presentable and is a fine entry-level acquisition.

The key for beginners is to do as much research as possibly before diving in and making that first purchase. Because there are fakes and cleverly repaired banks out there, Morphy advises novices to "go to auctions, and hook up with someone trustworthy – a dealer who will be honest with you and steer you in the right direction." He cautions that the Internet is "a horrible way to buy – and I don't mean bidding in an auction online that is produced by a reputable auction house that knows and understands banks. That's just fine because you know whom you're dealing with and can ask questions. I mean buying 'blindly' from people you don't know who either intentionally or unintentionally might misrepresent a bank's authenticity and condition. Nine times out of 10, you're asking for trouble doing it that way." Morphy said it's better to pay an expert to advise you on whether or not to buy a particular bank that to buy on good faith alone.

An excellent way for potential bank collectors/investors to get started in the hobby is by joining the Mechanical Bank Collectors of America.

"I personally would sponsor anyone who wants to join that club; that's how important I think it is," Morphy said. The club holds an annual convention featuring informative seminars on a host of educational and practical topics, such as how to black-light banks to detect repairs. The group also maintains an excellent Web site whose members-only area contains a treasure trove of archival information, including articles written as far back as the 1930s. Membership in the MBCA is quite possibly the best investment any potential mechanical-bank collector will ever make. *www.mechanicalbanks.org.*

Photo courtesy Morphy Auctions, Denver, Pa.; www.MorphyAuctions.com

J. & E. Stevens, around 1907, the Clown, Harlequin and Columbine bank features an intricate action involving all three figures. As the columbine (harlequin's mistress in the Italian commedia dell'arte) dancer spins, the coin is deposited, ex-Stephen and Marilyn Steckbeck collection.
$103,500

Reproduction Alert. Reproductions, fakes and forgeries exist for many banks. Forgeries of some mechanical banks were made as early as 1937, so age alone is not a guarantee of authenticity.

Photo courtesy Morphy Auctions, Denver, Pa.; www.MorphyAuctions.com

J. & E. Stevens, circa 1901, the Magician bank performs a trick in which the coin placed on the table disappears beneath the top hat. This example was accompanied by its factory box, ex-Stephen and Marilyn Steckbeck collection. **$25,875**

Photo courtesy Morphy Auctions, Denver, Pa.; www.MorphyAuctions.com

Kyser & Rex, Mikado, circa 1886, the cast-iron bank's complex interior mechanism enables the character to perform a "shell game" illusion, ex-Stephen and Marilyn Steckbeck collection. **$287,500**

Photo courtesy Morphy Auctions, Denver, Pa.; www.MorphyAuctions.com

Kyser & Rex, Merry-Go-Round, late 1880s, when the handle is turned, bells chime, the figures revolve, and the attendant raises the stick and gathers in any coins deposited on the stand, ex-Stephen and Marilyn Steckbeck collection. **$172,500**

Photo courtesy James D. Julia Auctioneers, Fairfield, Maine; www.JuliaAuctions.com

Kyser & Rex, Boy Stealing Watermelon Bank, when lever is pressed, dog appears from the doghouse. Boy is slinking through the garden in an attempt to steal the watermelon and raises his right hand. While along the fence, a boy runs off with another watermelon in hand. Probably in the 1880s, it was considered a very comical bank, 5" h x 6 1/2" l. Bank is missing spring and trap. Needs cleaning. **$6,325**

Photo courtesy James D. Julia Auctioneers, Fairfield, Maine; www.JuliaAuctions.com

Shepherd Hardware, Mason Bank with original box; the mason, constructing a wall of brick, is being assisted by the hod carrier, who has the coin contained within the hod. Upon depressing the lever, the hod tips forward depositing the coin into the wall as the mason raises his trowel to even out the cement on the bricks. (Typical of most mechanical and steel banks, they depicted various nationalities of their time. This bank features two Irishmen.); 7 1/2" h x 7 1/4" l. Near excellent condition and would be greatly enhanced by a cleaning. Original box is lacking slide lid. **$13,225**

Kyser & Rex, Zoo Bank, push gorilla's face and shutters open to reveal a bear and a lion. Coin is deposited into bank, 4 1/2" h x 4" w. Trap is missing but bank is in near-excellent condition. **$1,840**

Mechanical Novelty Works, Initiating Bank 2nd Degree, press lever and man riding goat springs forward and deposits coin in frog's mouth. This is a fairly rare bank, 7" h x 7 1/2" l. The bank was over-painted gold at some point. **$2,300**

Shepard Hardware, Stump Speaker and Uncle Sam banks, Uncle Sam throws coin in satchel and Stump Speaker drops coin in carpetbag, 11 1/2" h x 4 7/8" w x 10" h x 5" w. Stump Speaker has a replaced coin trap; otherwise both banks are in good to very good condition. .... **$2,300 pair**

Photo courtesy Morphy Auctions, Denver, Pa.; www.MorphyAuctions.com

Kyser & Rex, Roller Skating, 1880s, bank is comprised of a rink and skaters that glide around the perimeter when a coin is deposited, man turns as if to present a wreath to the little girl, ex-Stephen and Marilyn Steckbeck collection. **$195,500**

Photo courtesy Morphy Auctions, Denver, Pa.; www.MorphyAuctions.com

Stevens, Germania Exchange, 1880s, when a coin is placed on the goat's tail and the faucet on the beer keg is turned, the goat deposits the money and presents a glass of beer to the depositor, ex-Stephen and Marilyn Steckbeck collection. **$149,500**

Photo courtesy Morphy Auctions, Denver, Pa.; www.MorphyAuctions.com

Stevens, North Pole, circa 1910, when a coin is placed in the slot and pressed forward, it causes an American Flag to pop up at the top, ex-Stephen and Marilyn Steckbeck collection. **$149,500**

Stevens, Chief Big Moon Bank with red base; Chief sits by tepee holding a fish in hand. When lever is pressed, frog springs from under pond and the chief pulls back the fish and coin is deposited in bank. This also is the rare version of the bank with a red and yellow base; 6" h x 10" l. Colors are bright and bank is in excellent condition with some minor scratches and chipping. **$3,910**

Photo courtesy James D. Julia Auctioneers, Fairfield, Maine; www.JuliaAuctions.com

Stevens, Girl Skipping Rope Bank, when the clockwork mechanism is wound, the girl gracefully skips rope while at the same time her head sways from left to right and her feet swing back and forth in a very realistic manner. Some of the collectors of these banks take pride in how many revolutions of swinging their bank can accomplish, 8 1/4" h x 8" l. Appears all original with even wear throughout bank. Overall very good condition. **$13,225**

Photo courtesy Morphy Auctions, Denver, Pa.; www.MorphyAuctions.com

Chronometer, cast-iron mechanical bank in original condition. **$20,700**

Photo courtesy Morphy Auctions, Denver, Pa.; www.MorphyAuctions.com

Stevens, Jonah and the Whale/Jonah Emerges, late 1880s, pull back the knob located behind the whale's tail to lock it into position. Place a coin in the small slot shaped like a boat next to the whale's tail and press the lever. The coin falls into the bank as the whale opens his mouth and Jonah emerges. The whale's tail flips up during the action, all original and one of the finest known examples of its type, ex-Stephen and Marilyn Steckbeck collection. **$414,000**

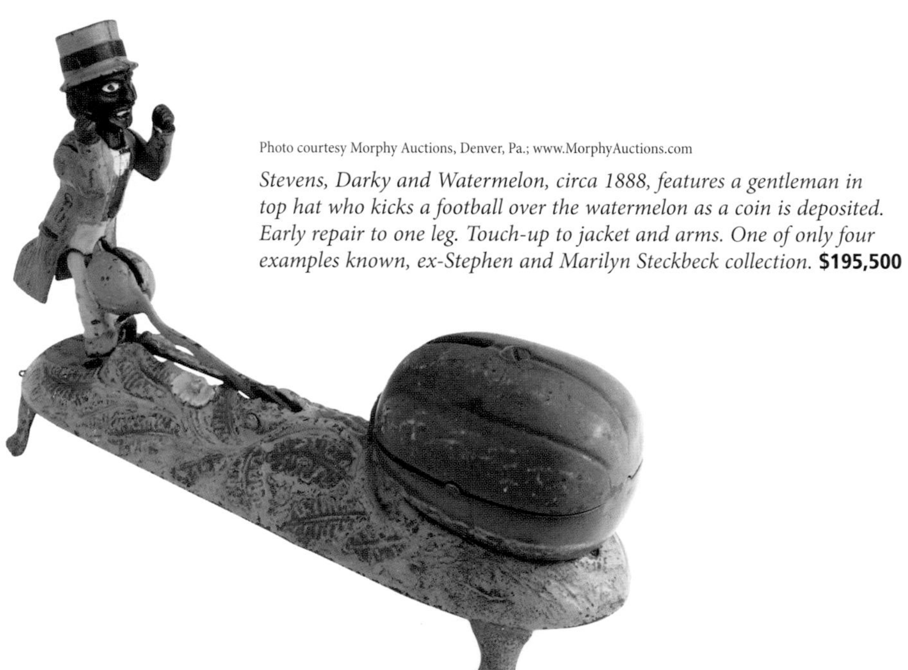

Photo courtesy Morphy Auctions, Denver, Pa.; www.MorphyAuctions.com

Stevens, Darky and Watermelon, circa 1888, features a gentleman in top hat who kicks a football over the watermelon as a coin is deposited. Early repair to one leg. Touch-up to jacket and arms. One of only four examples known, ex-Stephen and Marilyn Steckbeck collection. **$195,500**

Stevens, Eagle & Eaglets Bank, glass-eyed eagle on rocky outcropping feeds eaglets and deposits coin in bank, 6" h x 7" w. Uniform wear throughout, overall good to very good. **$720**

Stevens, I Always Did 'Spise a Mule Bank, place coin in the black jockey's mouth and when lever is pressed, mule bucks jockey over, hitting his head on log and depositing coin, 8" h x 10" l. Very good overall condition. Replaced trap. **$517**

Stevens, Magic Bank, painted red, white and blue. When door is opened, cashier appears with tray in hand. Place coin on tray, press lever. Door closes and the coin is deposited in bank; 5 1/2" h x 4 1/2" l. Bank has very strong paint, needs a good cleaning but otherwise is in near-excellent condition. **$4,370**

Photo courtesy Bertoia Auctions, Vineland, N.J.; www.BertoiaAuctions.com

Smith & Egge, late 19th-century Boston State House, in the small version at 5 1/8". **$12,650**

Photo courtesy Morphy Auctions, Denver, Pa.; www.MorphyAuctions.com

Barrel-shaped man with outstretched arms. **$1,100**

BANKS, STILL

Banks with no mechanical action are known as still banks. The first still banks were made of wood or pottery. Redware and stoneware banks, made by America's early potters, are prized possessions of today's collectors.

Still banks reached a golden age with the arrival of the cast-iron bank. Leading makers include Arcade Mfg. Co., J. Chein & Co., Hubley, J. & E. Stevens, and A.C. Williams. The banks often were ornately painted to enhance their appeal. Still bank were often used as a form of advertising.

The tin lithograph bank reached its zenith from 1930 to 1955. The tin bank was an important premium, whether a Pabst Blue Ribbon beer can bank or a Gerber's Orange Juice bank. Most tin advertising banks resembled the packaging of the product.

Many of the early glass candy containers also converted to a bank after the candy was eaten. Thousands of varieties of still banks were made, and hundreds of new varieties appear on the market each year.

Photo courtesy Morphy Auctions, Denver, Pa.; www.MorphyAuctions.com

Kyser & Rex painted cast-iron still bank depicting an apple on a branch. **$3,200**

BASKETS

Today's collectors often focus on baskets made of splint, rye straw or willow. Emphasis is placed on handmade examples. Nails or staples, wide splints that are thin and evenly cut, or a wire bail handle may denote factory construction, which can date back to the mid-19th century.

Baskets are collected by (a) type—berry, egg or field; (b) region—Nantucket or Shaker; and (c) composition—splint, rye or willow.

Also see Native American.

Nantucket basket, woven cane, early 20th century, cane losses, 5 5/8" h, 7 1/4" d. **$1,292**

Shaker pine and ash picnic basket, red-stained, New Lebanon, N.Y., mid- to late 19th century, pine sides and bottom on rectangular form with two hinged lids, upright ash handle, imperfections, 13" h, 10 3/4" w, 18 1/4" l. . **$440**

Shaker woven splint basket, found in Shirley, Mass., 19th century, round basket over square base with four runners, carved handles and double-wrapped rim, 15 3/4" h, 21" d. **$763**

Shaker woven splint hamper basket, possibly Canterbury, N.H., second half 19th century, deep oblong form with carved upright handle, two lids hinged at the center with copper wires, few minor breaks and losses, 16 1/2" h, 9 3/4" w, 15 5/8" l. **$293**

Woven splint basket, with carved wooden handles, large. **$235**

Woven splint basket, with handholds, deep rectangular. **$88**

Woven splint basket, American, 19th century, oval rim on rectangular base with carved wooden handles, base corner breaks, 13 3/4" h, 23" w, 25" l. **$176**

Woven splint feather basket, American, late 19th century, painted green with conforming cover, (loss to lashing on basket rim), 13 1/2" h. **$940**

Woven splint ribbed basket, American, 19th century, with entwined bentwood handle, 14 1/2" h, 15" w, 25" l. **$176**

Photo courtesy Sanford Alderfer Auction & Appraisal, Hatfield, Pa.; www.AlderferAuction.com

Buttocks basket with fixed handle, fine-weave splint oak, 11" h, 14 1/2" w. **$2,300**

Photo courtesy Skinner Inc., Boston; www.SkinnerInc.com

Woven splint basket, American, 19th century, round with square bottom with carved wooden swing handle, painted sea-foam green, 5 3/8" h to rim, 8 3/4" d. **$558**

Photo courtesy Skinner Inc., Boston; www.SkinnerInc.com

Nantucket basket, John Kittla Jr., 1961, cylindrical form, cover centered with a carved ivory floral medallion, the base inscribed "Nantucket Light Ship Basket 1961 by John Kittla Jr.," (break on latch), 7 3/4" h. **$503**

Photo courtesy Skinner Inc., Boston; www.SkinnerInc.com

Nantucket basket, woven rattan, American, circa 1950, wooden bottom with pyrographic inscriptions, "Frances B. Smith/F.H. Dewey III" and "Nantucket Lightship P.B. + B.S. Heywood 1-28-50.", 13 1/2" to top of handle, 11 1/8" d. **$881**

COMIC BOOKS

By Brent Frankenhoff

Shortly after comics first appeared in newspapers of the 1890s, they were reprinted in book format and often used as promotional giveaways by manufacturers, movie theaters and candy and stationery stores. The first modern-format comic was issued in 1933.

The magic date in comic collecting is June 1938, when DC issued *Action Comics* No. 1, marking the first appearance of Superman. Thus began the Golden Age of comics, which lasted until the early 1950s and witnessed the birth of the major comic-book publishers, titles and characters.

In 1954, Fredric Wertham wrote *Seduction of the Innocent*, a book that pointed a guilt-laden finger at the comics industry for corrupting youth, causing juvenile delinquency and undermining American values. Many publishers were forced out of business, while others established the Comics Code to assure parents that their comics were in compliance with morality and decency standards established by the Code Authority.

The Silver Age of comics, mid-1950s through the end of the 1960s, saw the revival of many of the characters from the Golden Age in new comic formats. The era began with *Showcase* No. 4 in October 1956, which marked the origin and first appearance of the Silver-Age Flash.

While the 1970s might be perceived as a low point for the genre, it was a gestation period for the revival in popularity for comics in the early 1980s. The late 1970s also marked the rise of the comic-book shop and non-returnable comics sales to those shops (previously, most comics had been sold on a fully returnable basis on newsstands), which also fueled the 1980s renaissance.

The boom time continued in the mid- and late 1980s and on into the early 1990s, when overspeculation in a number of "events," including such stories as "The Death of Superman" led to a large collapse in prices for many of those comics. Even today, it's difficult to realize cover price for most comic books from that era.

It took the better part of a decade, but, with the success of comics-related movies in the 2000s, interest in comics has been growing for the past several years, as movie studios and TV production companies look at comics for interesting properties to develop in other media.

In the list that follows, we'll give both the highest auction price realized to date by Heritage Comic Auctions (unless otherwise noted, those values are for copies professionally graded on a 10-point scale by Certified Guaranty Company (CGC) and sealed in a plastic holder) and the current value of a Near Mint (abbreviated NM) unsealed copy. "Near Mint" is one of the grading descriptions for comics collectors and describes a nearly perfect copy. Bends, rips, tears, smudges, and other damage or defects will reduce the grade and the price.

In addition, the Heritage price is also for copies that are not from a pedigreed collection, a factor which often lends additional impetus to the prices realized.

Reproduction Alert. Publishers frequently reprint popular stories, even complete books, so the buyer must pay strict attention to the title, not just the portion printed in oversized letters on the front cover. If there is any doubt, look inside at the fine print on the bottom of the inside cover or first page. The correct title will be printed there in capital letters. Also pay attention to the dimensions of the comic book. Reprints often differ in size from the original.

Brent Frankenhoff

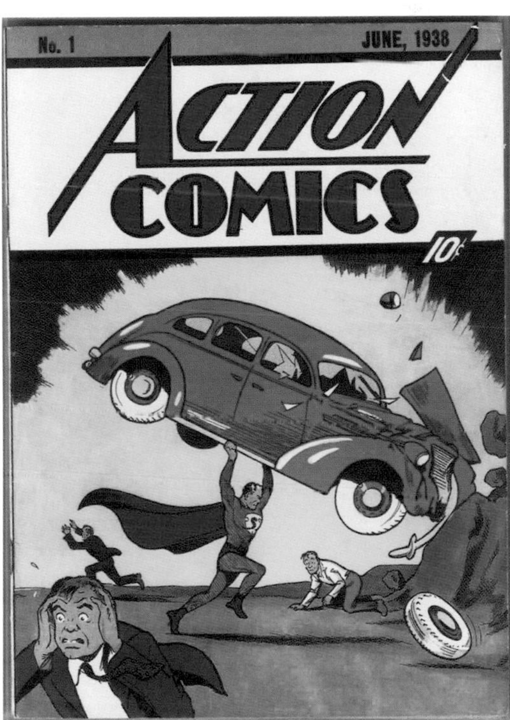

Photo courtesy Heritage Auction Galleries, Dallas; www.HA.com

Action Comics #1 (DC, 1938): The first appearance of Superman. While a $1 million bounty has been offered for a Near Mint copy (currently valued at $330,000) of the comic book that started the Golden Age of comics, no one has yet stepped forward to claim the prize and it's doubtful anyone ever will. The highest price realized to date by Heritage was $120,750 for a CGC-graded copy in Fine- (5.5 on a 10-point scale) in 2003.

Photo courtesy Heritage Auction Galleries, Dallas; www.HA.com

Amazing Spider-Man #583 (Marvel, 2009). One of the most sought-after books in 2009, this salute to the inauguration of President Barack Obama caught the public's eye and sent Marvel back to press six times, with each printing having some slight variation, making it collectible as well. Heritage has not sold any copies to date, but dozens of copies are available on eBay, with many lots offering bundled sets of the multiple printings. A copy of the first printing by itself, graded 9.8 (Near Mint/Mint) by CGC sold for $125 in late July. The current Near Mint price for an unsealed copy is $25 with the later printings at lower prices.

Photo courtesy Heritage Auction Galleries, Dallas; www.HA.com

Captain America Comics #1 (Timely, 1941). The origin and first appearance of Captain America and Bucky. With the 2007 death of Captain America (he got better in 2009), interest in all things Cap increased. Heritage's highest sale to date was $95,600 for a copy CGC-graded 8.5 (Very Fine+) in 2009. The current Near Mint price for an unsealed copy is $80,000.

Photo courtesy Heritage Auction Galleries, Dallas; www.HA.com

Batman #1 (DC, 1940). The first appearances of The Joker and Catwoman. While prices for most Batman-related comics rose in 1989 with the first Batman movie, they leveled off again in the late 1990s. The relaunch of the movie franchise with Batman Begins and The Dark Knight did little to drive prices upward, although some slight sales spikes were noted. The highest Heritage price to date was $98,587.50 for a CGC-graded copy in 7.0 (Fine/Very Fine) in 2009. The current Near Mint value for an unsealed copy is $80,000.

Photo courtesy Heritage Auction Galleries, Dallas; www.HA.com

Captain Marvel Adventures (#1) (Fawcett, 1941). This is the only issue of the title to have Jack Kirby art, and it was drawn on the "night shift" at the time Kirby was working on Captain America by day. This first issue's cover art is by C. C. Beck. **$10,755**

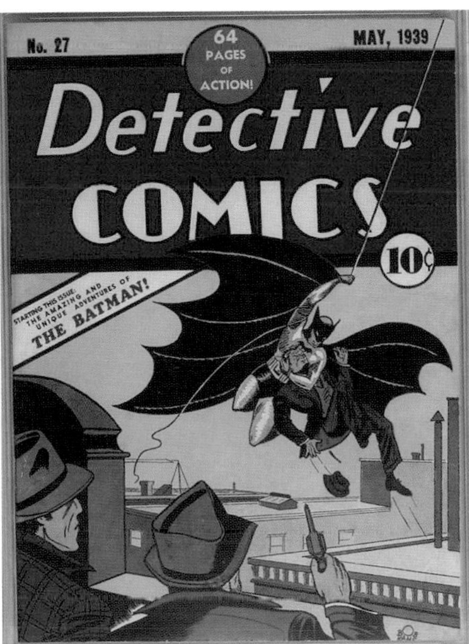

Photo courtesy Heritage Auction Galleries, Dallas; www.HA.com

Detective Comics #27 (DC, 1939). Batman's first appearance. Within a year, the grim avenger would acquire a kid sidekick with the addition of Robin to the mythos and would also acquire his own self-titled series. Strangely enough, a low-grade copy is Heritage's highest sale to date and it came from an original owner collection in 2009. The copy, graded 1.5 (Fair/Good) sold for $83,650 and received the low grade due to a split spine that had occurred with age. An unsealed copy in Near Mint (something more than likely impossible to find) is valued at **$250,000.**

Photo courtesy Heritage Auction Galleries, Dallas; www.HA.com

DC 100-Page Super Spectacular #5 (DC, 1971). These squarebound comics, mainly consisting of super-hero reprints from the 40s, 50s, and 60s, are fondly remembered by fans and are still a great value. The trick is to find copies in high grade as the format required stapling the pages together and then gluing the cover to the square spine, leading to numerous possible defects and easily detachable covers. This issue was the one romance-related issue in the series. Heritage's highest sale to date was in 2006 for a copy graded 9.2 (Near Mint-) for **$1,553.** *An unsealed Near Mint copy is valued at $200.*

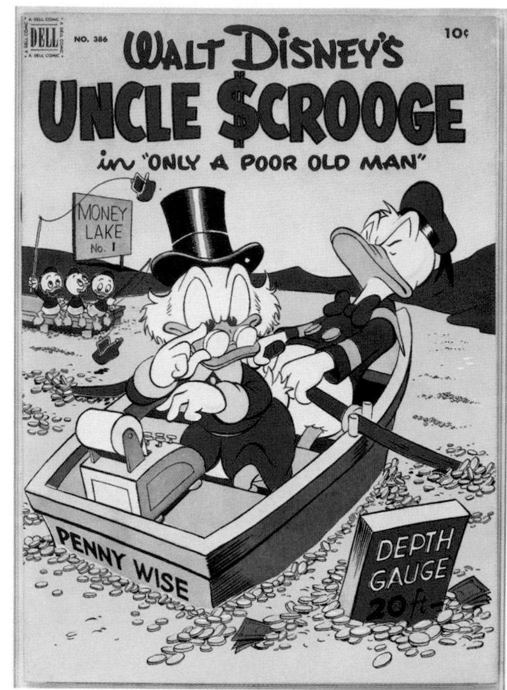

Photo courtesy Heritage Auction Galleries, Dallas; www.HA.com

Four Color (2nd series) #386 (Dell, 1952). What the heck is this strange Dell comic book with a high number on the cover? It's one of the oddities of Dell's publishing program, when it produced "tryout" issues of various series before committing to an ongoing series. Heritage's highest sale to date was for a 9.4 (NM) copy in 2007 for **$28,680.** *An unsealed Near Mint copy is valued at $1,100.*

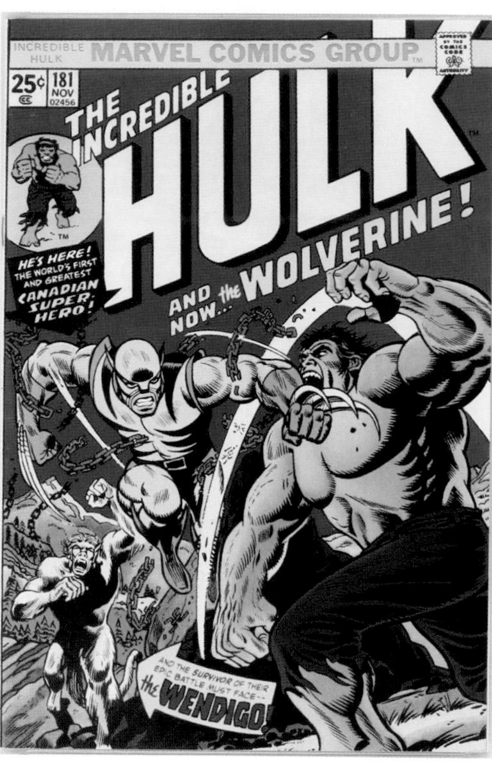

Photo courtesy Heritage Auction Galleries, Dallas; www.HA.com

Incredible Hulk #181 (Marvel, 1974). One of the "Holy Grails" for collectors of 1970s comics, this issue introduced Wolverine to the Marvel Universe. Heritage's highest sale to date was in 2009 for a copy graded 9.8 (Near Mint/ Mint) for **$26,290.** Compare that to the current unsealed Near Mint price of $900.

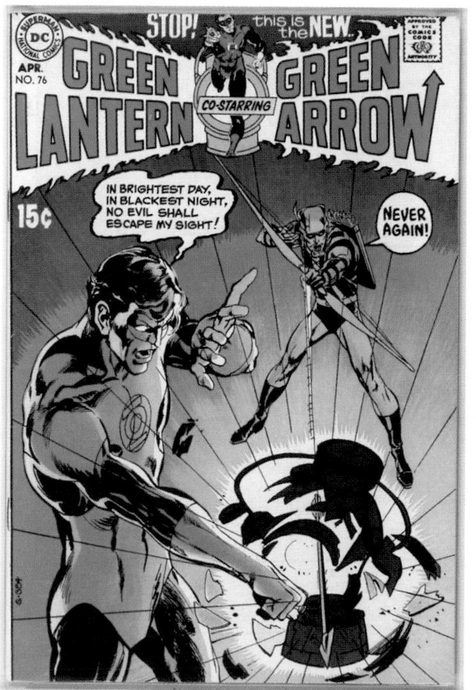

Photo courtesy Heritage Auction Galleries, Dallas; www.HA.com

Green Lantern (2nd series) #76 (DC, 1970). Writer Denny O'Neil and artist Neal Adams sent spacefaring super-hero Green Lantern and down-on-his-luck super-hero Green Arrow on a journey of discovery across contemporary America in a series of well-received and fondly remembered stories. Heritage's highest sale to date was in 2007 for a copy graded 9.4 (Near Mint) for **$8,365.** *An unsealed Near Mint copy is valued at $350.*

Photo courtesy Heritage Auction Galleries, Dallas; www.HA.com

Showcase #4 (DC, 1956). The revival of The Flash in 1956 is considered by most collectors to mark the start of The Silver Age of comics. Heritage's highest sale to date was in 2009 with a record-setting price of **$179,250** *for a copy graded 9.6 (Near Mint+). An unsealed Near Mint copy is valued at $30,000.*

Photo courtesy Heritage Auction Galleries, Dallas; www.HA.com

Superman #1 (DC, 1939). The first DC hero to receive his own self-titled series, The Man of Steel continues to entertain readers more than 70 years after his debut. Heritage's highest sale to date was in 2004 for a copy graded 4.5 (Very Good+) for **$47,150.** *An unsealed Near Mint copy is valued at $175,000.*

Photo courtesy Heritage Auction Galleries, Dallas; www.HA.com

Justice League of America #1 (DC, 1960). JLA #1 has been a tough book to find in high grade. Heritage's highest sale to date for this issue was in 2008 for a 9.8 (Near Mint/Mint) copy, which sold for **$35,850.** *An unsealed Near Mint copy is valued at $3,000.*

Photo courtesy Heritage Auction Galleries, Dallas; www.HA.com

X-Men #1 (Marvel, 1963). Origin and first appearance of the X-Men (the Angel, the Beast, Cyclops, Iceman and Marvel Girl). First appearances of Professor X and Magneto. Jack Kirby cover and art. **$2,151**

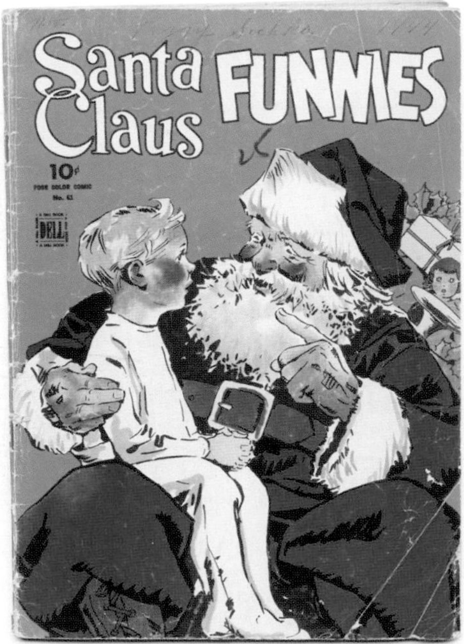

Afterthought: In the entire history of comics, millions of comic books have reached readers of all ages. Few are worth the premiums commanded by the "key" issues shown here. Many more are in the condition shown above, which is considered "Fair" on the comics grading scale, and many of those can be purchased for the price of a current comic book today.

Photo courtesy Heritage Auction Galleries, Dallas; www.HA.com

Wonder Woman (2nd series) #1 (DC, 1987). As part of its revamp of its main characters in 1986 and 1987, DC relaunched the Amazon warrior's series with the first 30-odd issues written and illustrated by George Pérez. Heritage's highest sale to date was in 2008 for a 9.8 (Near Mint/Mint) copy realizing **$79.** *An unsealed Near Mint copy is valued at $5.*

BOOKS, PAPERBACKS

The first mass-market, pocket-sized, paperback book printed in the U.S. was an edition of Pearl Buck's *The Good Earth*, produced by Pocket Books in late 1938, sold in New York City.

At first, paperbacks consisted entirely of reprints, but publishers soon began publishing original works. Genre categories began to emerge, and mass-market book covers reflected those categories. Mass-market paperbacks had an impact on slick magazines (slicks) and pulp magazines. The market for cheap magazines diminished when buyers went to cheap books instead. Authors also turned from magazines and began writing for the paperback market. Many pulp magazine cover artists were hired by paperback publishers to entice readers with their alluring artwork. Several well-known authors were published in paperback, including Arthur Miller and John Steinbeck, and some, like Dashiell Hammett, were published as paperback originals.

For more information and details on condition grades (values here are in three grades: good, very good and fine), consult *Antique Trader Collectible Paperbacks Price Guide* by Gary Lovisi, or visit *www.gryphonbooks.com*. Books in this year's edition of the guide come from Lovisi's *Dames, Dolls & Delinquents — A Collector's Guide to Sexy Pulp Fiction Paperbacks.*

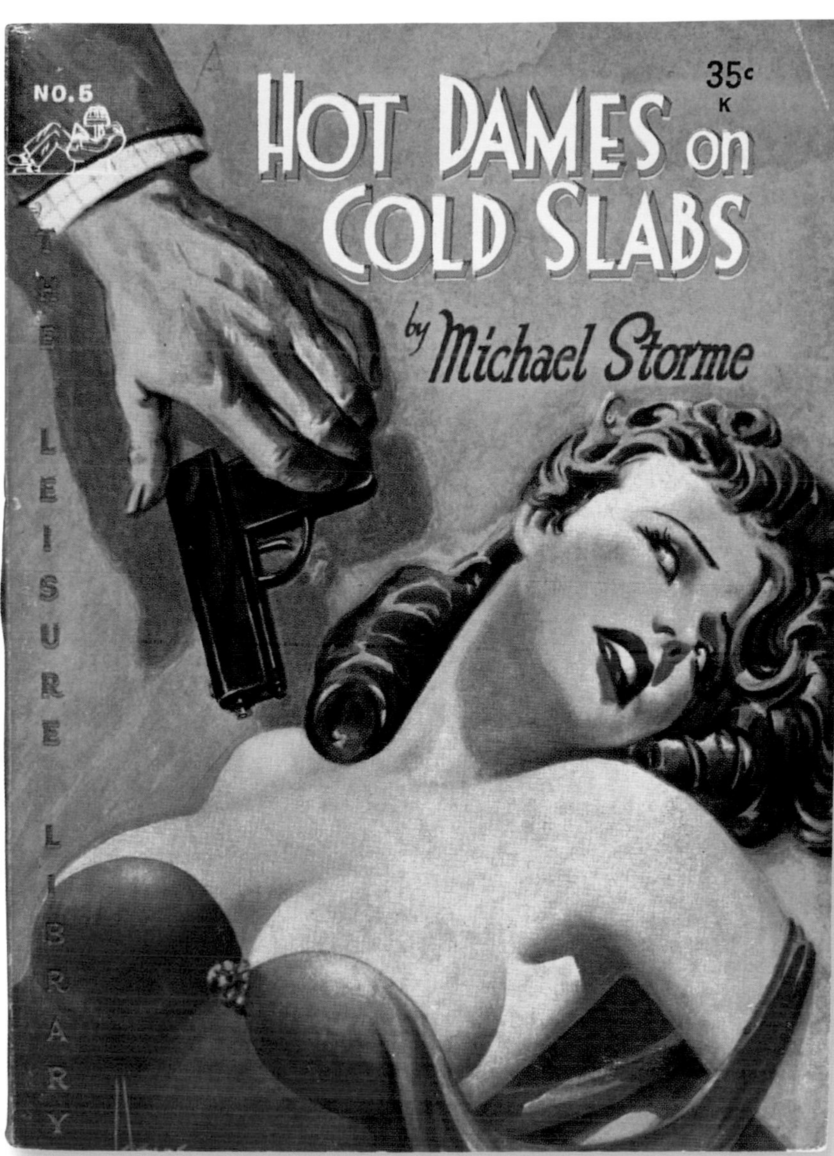

Hot Dames on Cold Slabs by Michael Storme. Cover art by Reginald Heade. The Leisure Library #5, 1952, digest-size paperback. One of the most evocative of hard-boiled titles.
$14-$35-$100

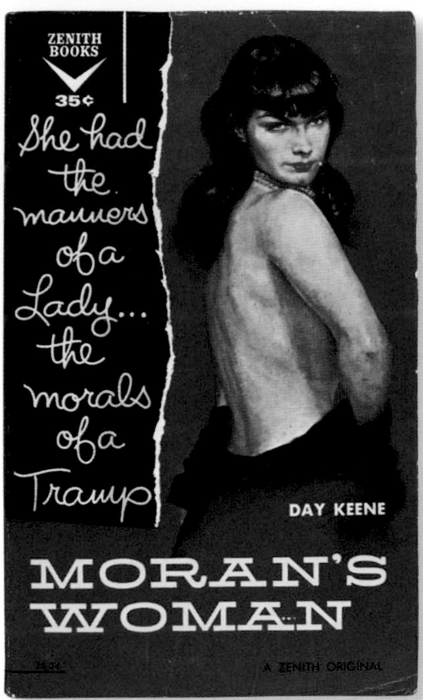

Moran's Woman by Day Keene. Cover art by Jack Faragasso. Zenith Book #ZB-24, 1959. Cover art shows pin-up model Bettie Page. **$15-$50-$145**

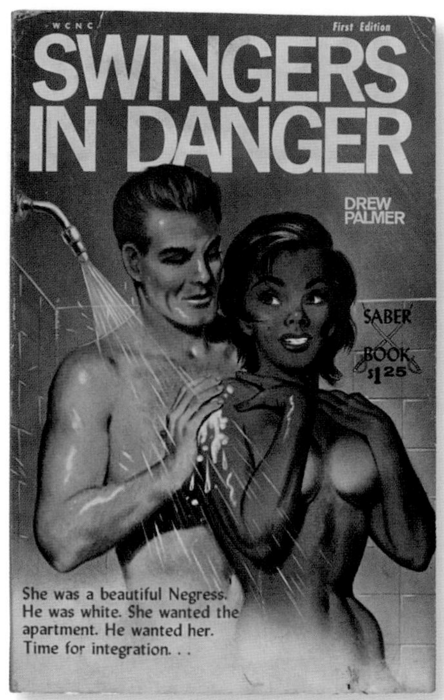

Swingers in Danger by Drew Palmer. Cover art probably by Bill Edwards. Saber Book #SA-135, 1968. **$10-$25-$65.**

This Woman is Death by Michael Storme. Cover art by Reginald Heade. Leisure Library #23, 1955, digest-size paperback. **$10-$30-$90**

Champagne and Choppers! by Bart Carson. Cover art by J. Pollack. Hamilton & Co, circa 1950, British digest-size paperback. Gangster crime novel; a "chopper" is slang for a Thompson machine gun! **$20-$65-$125**

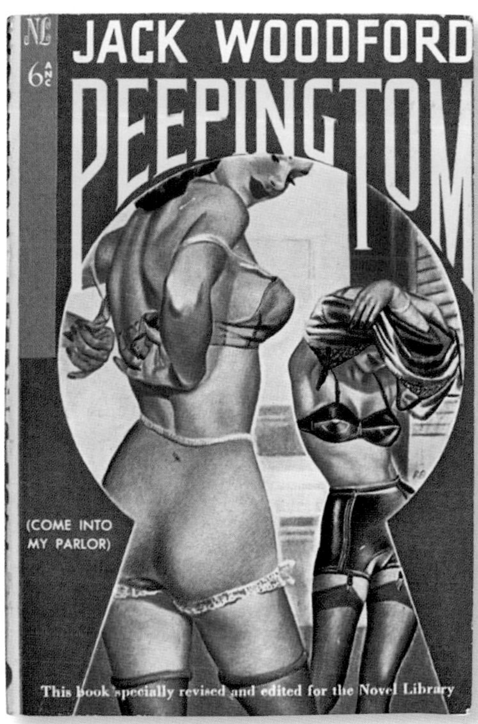

Peeping Tom by Jack Woodford. Cover art by "R.B." Novel Library #6, 1948. This is one of the most evocative vintage paperback covers. **$15-$60-$125**

I Spit On Your Grave by Griff. Cover art by Ray Theobald. Modern Fiction, circa 1951, British digest-size paperback. **$20-$75-$150**

Naked on Roller Skates by Maxwell Bodenheim. Cover artist unknown. Novel Library #46, 1950. Art and title evoke a charming innocence about nudity and sexuality. **$12-$55-$145**

Bad Sue by Norman Bligh. Cover artist unknown. Quarter Book #79, 1951, digest-size paperback. **$12-$65-$135**

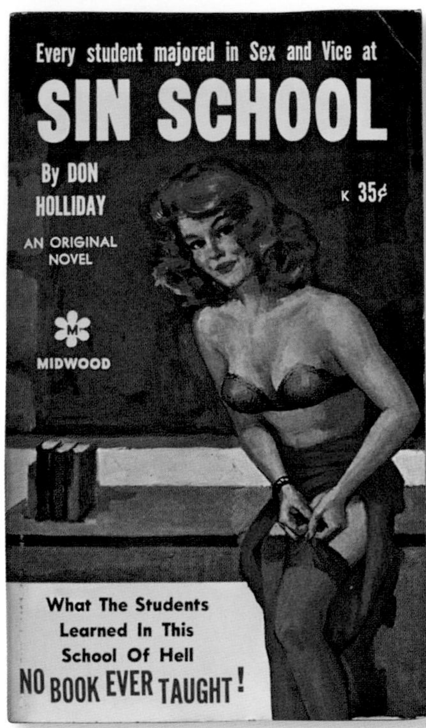

Sin School by Don Holliday. Cover artist unknown. Midwood Book #25, 1959. **$10-$22-$60**

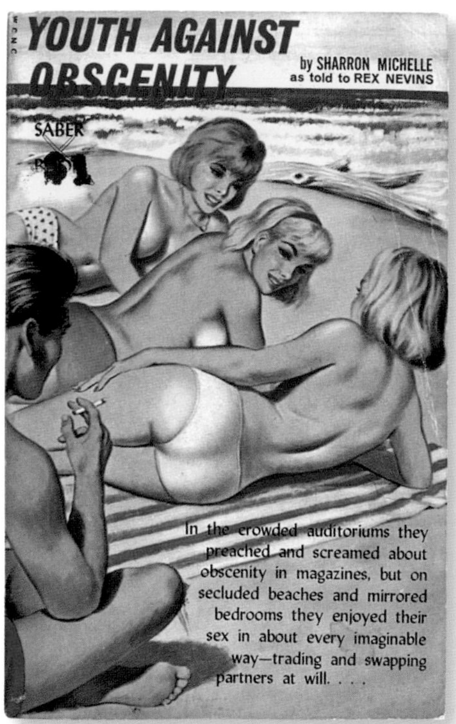

Youth Against Obscenity by Sharron Michelle. Cover artist unknown. Saber Book #SA-106, 1966. **$8-$18-$45**

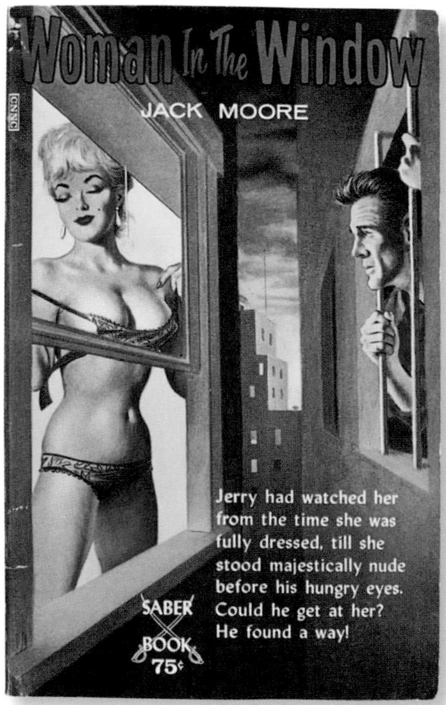

Woman in The Window by Jack Moore. Cover art by Bill Edwards. Saber Book #SA-89, 1965. **$8-$20-$45**

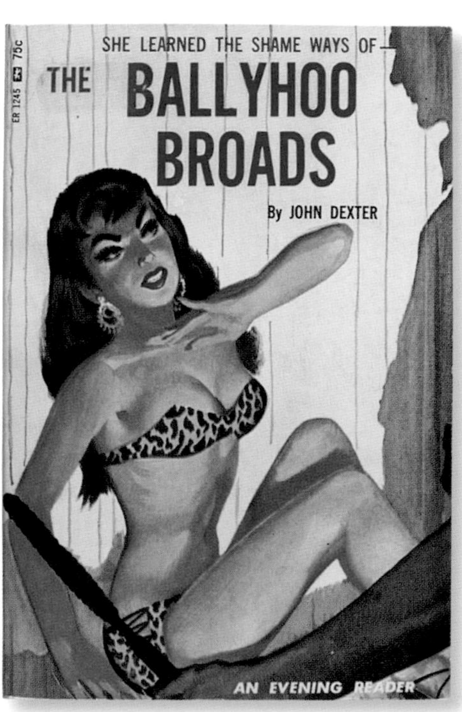

The Ballyhoo Broads by John Dexter. Cover artist unknown. Evening Reader #ER1245, 1966. **$5-$16-$35**

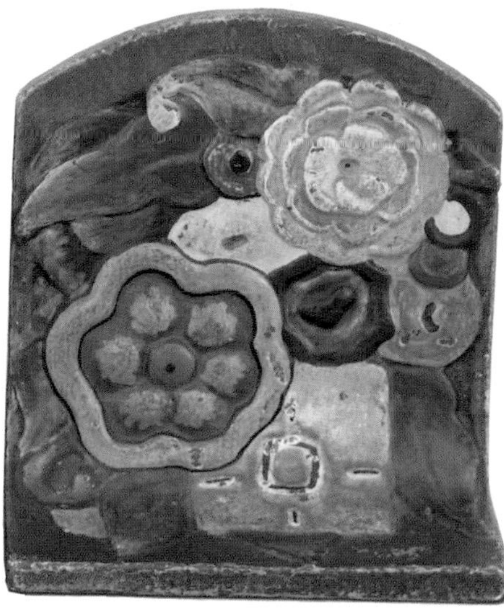

Art Deco Flowers, 4 3/4" x 4 3/8". Numbered "32". **$100-$200**

BOOKENDS

This section on cast-iron bookends comes courtesy of John C. and Nancy Smith, owners of American Sampler, P.O. 371, Barnesville, Md. 20838; 301-972-6250. Their Web site is *www.castirononline*. The Smiths are also the authors of *The Doorstop Book — An Encyclopedia of Doorstop Collecting* (Schiffer, 2006).

Accordion Player, 6" x 4 1/2". Made by Hubley, cat. #497. Full-figure. .... **$200-$250**

Alamo, 4 1/4" x 6 1/2". Signed, "50th Anniversary, 1878-1928, Alamo Iron Works, San Antonio, Tex." .... **$200-$300**

Amish Girl and Boy, 5 1/4" x 3 7/8". Made by John Wright. Background farm scene. .... **$50-$100**

Sitting Amish Boy and Girl, 4" x 4". Made by Wilton Products. .... **$200-$300**

Angelus (After Millet's Painting), 4 3/4" x 5". Signed on front of base, "Angelus". .... **$50-$100**

Art Deco Drape Woman, 6" x 5 1/4". Made by Hubley and numbered "73". .... **$100-$200**

Art Deco Nude Woman with Swan, 3 7/8" x 7 1/2". The swan's wings form a V. .... **$100-$200**

Art Deco Swaying Nude Woman, 4 1/2" x 6 3/4". Numbered "202". .... **$75-$150**

Art Deco "The Storm", 5 7/8" x 3 7/8". Made by Connecticut Foundry. Signed and dated, "The Storm, Copyright 1928". .... **$150-$250**

Art Deco Ballerina, 7 1/4" x 5". .... **$100-$200**

Art Deco Nude Woman Inside of Wreath, 5" x 4 1/2". Numbered "53". .... **$75-$150**

Art Deco Woman with Arched Back, 5 1/2" x 4 3/8". Numbered "154". .... **$75-$150**

Art Deco Woman with Drape, 6" x 4 3/4". Made by Creations. Marked "Copr. 130, C. Co., #217". .... **$75-$150**

Art Deco Swaying Nude Woman, 4 1/2" x 6 3/4". Numbered "202". .... **$75-$150**

Beaver with an O, 5" x 51/4". Logo for Oregon Sate. .... **$400-$500**

Bedouin, 5 3/4" x 5 1/4". Made by Hubley, cat. #418. Full-figure. .... **$200-$250**

Boston Terrier, 5 1/4" x 4 7/8". Signed "B&H" (Bradley and Hubbard). .... **$200-$300**

Boston Terrier on Base, 5" x 5 1/2". Made by Hubley, cat. #361. Full-figure. .... **$300-$400**

Boy & Girl Riding Rocking Horses, 5 1/2" x 5". Made by cjo (Judd Co.) and numbered "9690". .... **$500-$700**

Buccaneer, 5 3/4" x 4". Made by Hubley, cat. #420. Full-figure. .... **$100-$200**

Buffalo, 5 3/8" x 6 7/8". Signed, "Verona, Pat. Pend." .... **$200-$300**

Canadian Mounted Police, 6 3/8" x 4". Numbered "730". .... **$250-$350**

Cardinal (bird), 5 1/4" x 3". Made by Albany Fdry. Co. .... **$100-$200**

Children on Gate, 5 1/4" x 3 7/8". Made by Hubley. Numbered and artist signed, "© G.G.D. (Grace Drayton), #209, #210". .... **$300-$500**

Church and Coach, 5 1/2" x 4 1/8". Signed, "B&H" (Bradley and Hubbard). .... **$200-$300**

Clown, 6 1/4" x 3". Made by Hubley, cat. #32. .... **$500-$700**

Conestoga Covered Wagon with Horses, 3 5/8" x 6 1/2". Signed and numbered, "Hubley, 378". .... **$100-$200**

Conestoga Covered Wagon with Oxen, 2 7/8" x 6 1/8". Signed, dated and numbered, "Arion Hardware Co., copyright 1931, #1849". .... **$50-$150**

Conestoga Covered Wagon with Oxen, 6 1/8" x 6 1/4". Signed, "Cincinnati Artistic, Patent Appld. For". Marked on front of base, "Trecking West". **$100-$200**

Crowing Fantail Rooster, 6" x 5". Made by Creations Co. **$100-$200**

Cottage in Woods, 5 1/2" x 5". Made by Hubley and numbered "292". **$100-$200**

Cowboy, 6 1/2" x 5". Made by Hubley, cat. #495. Full-figure. **$200-$300**

Cowboy on Bucking Horse, 7 1/8" x 5 1/8". Signed, "Bronze Mfg." **$250-$350**

Cowboy on Bucking Horse, 5 7/8" x 4 1/4". Signed and numbered, "© AC, 136". **$250-$350**

Cowboys Roping Steer, 4 3/4" x 5 1/8". Made by Hubley. **$100-$200**

Crane in the Bullrushes, 6 1/2" x 5". Made by Hubley, cat. #413. **$200-$300**

Dachshund, 4" x 8". Made by Hubley and numbered "355". **$500-$700**

Begging Scottie, 4" x 2 1/2". Signed, "Spencer, Guilford, Conn." **$200-$300**

Docile Jocelyn, the Donkey, 4 1/2" x 5". Made by Hubley, cat. #492. Full-figure. **$200-$250**

Doe, 5 3/4" x 4 1/4". Made by Hubley and numbered "399". **$300-$400**

Doe and Fawn, 4 1/2" x 5 1/2". Made by Hubley, cat. #494. Full-figure. **$150-$250**

Dog with Cat on Fence, 5 3/4" x 4 3/4". Made by Wilton Products. **$150-$250**

Dolly and Bobby with Puppy, 4 7/8" x 4 1/8". Made by Hubley. Signed and numbered, "Made in USA, 498". **$150-$250**

Eagle on Rocks with Spread Wings, 2 1/2" x 5". Made by Littco Products. Full-figure. **$75-$150**

Elephant, 4 3/4" x 5 1/4". Made by Creations Co. **$50-$100**

Elephant, 5 1/4" x 6 1/2". Signed, "Verona, Pat. Pend." **$150-$250**

Elephant, 5 5/8" x 6 1/2". Signed "B&H" (Bradley and Hubbard). **$300-$400**

Embossed Mixed Flowers in Basket, 5 5/8" x 4 7/8". Signed "B&H" (Bradley and Hubbard). **$150-$250**

Embossed Mixed Flowers in Urn, 3 7/8" x 5 1/2". Signed "B&H" (Bradley and Hubbard). **$100-$200**

End of the Trail, 6" x 5 1/4". Made by Hubley, cat. #372. Full-figure. **$250-$350**

English Tudor-Style Cottage, 5 3/4" x 4 1/2". **$100-$200**

Football Player, 5 1/2" x 6". Made by Hubley and numbered "416". **$300-$400**

Fireplace, 5 5/8" x 5 3/4". Made by National Foundry and numbered "147". **$75-$150**

Fish, 5 1/4" x 5". Made by Hubley, cat. #448. Full-figure. **$200-$250**

Fish, 6 1/2" x 4 1/2". Made by Littco Products. Full-figure. **$75-$150**

Gazelle, 6 1/2" x 5". Made by Hubley and numbered "410". **$150-$250**

German Shepherd on Base, 5 1/4" x 6". Made by Hubley, cat. #364. Full-figure. **$200-$300**

Bird on Branch, 4" x 4 7/8". Marked "Luca License". **$100-$200**

Ibex, 4 7/8" x 5". Made by Hubley and numbered "417". **$200-$300**

Girl Holding Dress, 5" x 4 3/4". Signed, "Albany Fdry. Co., 150". .... **$50-$150**

Hide and Seek, 6" x 5 3/4". Little girl playing hide and seek. .... **$200-$300**

Horse at Dutch Door, 4 3/4" x 3 1/4". Made by Hubley and numbered "2". .... **$150-$250**

Horse Head, 4 1/2" x 4". Made by Hubley. Belgian draft horse against brick wall surrounded by horseshoe. .... **$200-$300**

Hunter and Dog, 6 1/4" x 5". Made by Hubley, cat. #423. Full-figure. **$400-500**

Indian Brave on Horseback, 6" x 6". Made by Hubley. .... **$300-$500**

Indian Chief, 5" x 4 3/8". Made by Creations Co. .... **$75-$150**

Indian Planting Seeds, 3 3/8" x 4 1/2". .... **$100-$200**

Illinois Indian, 4 1/8" x 4 1/2". Signed and dated, "Shop Laboratorie – LaForce Bailey Sculpture, 1923". Mascot for University Illinois. .... **$100-$200**

John Alden & Priscilla, 7" x 2 3/8". Made by John Wright. Each signed, one "John Alden" and other "Priscilla". .... **$75-$150**

Kissing Dutch Boy and Girl, 4 3/4" x 4". Made by Hubley and numbered "332". .... **$100-$200**

Kneeling Kissing Asian Couple, 4 5/8" x 4 5/8". .... **$75-$150**

Lamb, 6 1/4" x 4 1/2". Made by Hubley, cat. #496. Full-figure. .... **$100-$200**

Laying Down Dromedary, 4 1/2" x 6 1/2". Made by Hubley, cat. #358. Full-figure. .... **$250-$350**

Lazy Pedro, 6 1/2" x 3". Made by Hubley, cat. #493. Full-figure. .... **$150-$250**

Lincoln Cabin, 3 7/8" x 4 7/8". Signed and numbered, "cjo (Judd Co.), 8678". .... **$100-$200**

Lion, 5 1/2" x 5". Signed, "Bronze Met, Copyright 1926". .... **$50-$150**

Man in Chair, 5 1/4" x 4 3/8". Signed, "B&H" (Bradley and Hubbard). .... **$300-$400**

Mixed Flowers in Hanging Basket, 7 3/4" x 6 3/8". Signed and numbered, "Albany Fdry. Co., 137". .... **$75-$150**

Mixed Flowers in Splint Basket, 5 5/8" x 3 1/2". Signed and numbered "Jersey, 30". .... **$75-$150**

Mount Vernon, 4" x 6 3/8". Made by Albany Fdry. Co. .... **$150-$250**

Owl, 5 1/8" x 6 1/2". Made by cjo (Judd Co.) and numbered "9729". .... **$150-$250**

Owl Perched Under Arch, 6" x 5 1/8". Signed "B&H" (Bradley and Hubbard). .... **$200-$300**

Parrot on Stump, 6 1/2" x 3 1/4". Signed, dated and numbered, "Albany Fdry. Co., 1922, #80". .... **$100-$200**

Owl on Branch, 5 1/2" x 3 1/2". Made by cjo (Judd Co.) and numbered "9890". **$150-$250**

Peacock, 6 1/8" x 4 1/2". Signed, "B&H" (Bradley and Hubbard). .... **$200-$300**

Pekingese, 5" x 5 1/4". Made by Hubley and numbered "366". .... **$400-$500**

Penguin, 5 3/4" x 3 3/8". Full-figure standing on square base. .... **$400-$500**

Pointer, 4" x 8". Made by Hubley and numbered "303". .... **$200-$300**

Pointer, 4 1/2" x 5 1/4". Made by Creations Co. ..... **$75-$150**

Pointer Bottle Opener, 5 1/4" x 3 7/8". Made by John Wright. .... **$100-$200**

Polar Bear, 3 1/2" x 6". Made by Hubley, cat. #370. Full-figure. .... **$300-$400**

Polo Player, 5 3/8" x 4 1/4". Made by Littco Products. .... **$100-$200**

Puppies in Barrel, 7" x 7 3/8". Made by Wilton Products. .... **$200-$300**

Quail, 5 1/2" x 5 3/4". Made by Hubley and numbered "461". Fred Everett designer. .... **$300-$500**

Raggedy Ann & Andy, 5 1/2" x 4". Signed "Copyright P.F. Volland Co., 1931". .... **$700-$1,000**

Sailboat, 5 3/4" x 5 1/2". Made by Hubley. Signed, "Made in USA". .... **$200-$300**

Scottie by Rose Fence, 6 3/4" x 4 1/2". Made by Hubley and numbered "430". .... **$200-$300**

Scottie by Lattice Fence, 6 3/8" x 4 3/4". Signed, "Kenco, Littlestown, PA., No. 20, Scotty". .... **$200-$300**

Scottie Leaning on Picket Fence, 6 1/4" x 4 1/4". .... **$100-$200**

Setter, 4 3/8" x 5 1/8". Signed "B&H" (Bradley and Hubbard). .... **$100-$200**

Setter, 5 1/4" x 6 1/4". Made by Hubley and numbered "281". .... **$250-$350**

Setter on Base, 5" x 8". Made by Hubley, cat. #363. Full-figure. .... **$200-$300**

Shakespeare's House, 4 5/8" x 5 3/4". Numbered "262". Marked on front of base, "Shakespeare's House, Stratford of Avon". .... **$50-$100**

Parakeet Love Birds, 6" x 4 3/8". **$200-$300**

Sheik, 6 1/4" x 4 1/2". Made by Hubley, cat. #421. Full-figure. .... **$200-$250**

Ship, 4" x 4". Made by Albany Fdry. Co. .... **$50-$100**

Ship, 4 1/4" x 4 3/4". Signed, "Pirate Galleon, copyright". .... **$100-$200**

Ship, 5" x 5 1/4". Numbered "90620". .... **$75-$150**

Ship, 5 5/8" x 5 1/8". Signed, "English Galleon, Copr. 1928", with "Connecticut Fdry" logo. .... **$75-$150**

Ship Old Ironsides, 4" x 5 3/8". Signed "B&H" (Bradley and Hubbard). .... **$200-$300**

Sir Galahad, 5 7/8" x 4 3/8". Marked on front of base, "Sir Galahad". .... **$50-$100**

Sitting Boston Terrier Pup, 4 1/2" x 6". Made by Hubley, cat. #392. Full-figure. .... **$200-$300**

Sitting Cat, 6" x 4 3/4". Made by Creations Co. .... **$50-$100**

Sitting Scotty, 5" x 6". Made by Hubley, cat. #391. Full-figure. .... **$200-$250**

Sitting Sealyham, 4 1/2" x 6 1/2". Made by Hubley, cat. #426. Full-figure. .... **$200-$300**

Great Dane, 6 1/4" x 6 3/4". Made by Hubley and numbered "354". **$300-$500**

Zebra, 4 3/4" x 6". Made by Hubley and numbered "2419". **$700-$1,000**

Sitting Wirehaired Fox Terrier, 4 3/4" x 6". Made by Hubley, cat. #390. Full-figure. .... **$200-$300**

Spread Winged Duck, 7" x 5 1/2". Made by Littco Products. Full-figure. .... **$75-$150**

Spirit of St. Louis Airplane, 4 7/8" x 4 3/4". Marked on front of base, "Spirit of St. Louis". .... **$200-$300**

Stage Coach with Horses, 4" x 7". Made by Hubley and numbered "379". .... **$100-$200**

Standing Boston Terrier Pup, 4 1/2" x 6". Made by Hubley, cat. #409. Full-figure. .... **$200-$300**

Standing Cocker Spaniel, 4 1/2" x 6 3/4". Made by Hubley, cat. #427. Full-figure. .... **$200-$300**

Standing Scottie, 4 3/8" x 5 3/8". Signed, "Spencer, Guilford, Conn." .... **$100-$200**

Standing Scotty, 5" x 6 1/2". Made by Hubley, cat. #408. Full-figure. .... **$200-$250**

Standing Sealyham, 4 3/4" x 5 1/8". Made by Hubley and numbered "52". .... **$300-$500**

Standing Wirehaired Fox Terrier, 5" x 6 1/2". Made by Hubley, cat. #407. Full-figure. .... **$200-$300**

St. Joseph's Parrish, 7 7/8" x 5". "Commemorating the 100th Anniversary of St. Joseph Parrish 1835-1935". .... **$300-$400**

The Thinker, 5" x 4 3/8". Made by Creations Co. .... **$50-$100**

The Whipper-in or Steeplechase, 5" x 4 3/4". Made by Hubley and numbered "415". .... **$250-$350**

Three Daisies with Bow, 5" x 3 1/2". .... **$200-$300**

Three Kittens in Basket, 4 5/8" x 5 5/8". Made by Wilton Products. .... **$150-$250**

Three Kittens on Book, 4 5/8" x 5 5/8". Signed "B&H" (Bradley and Hubbard). .... **$250-$350**

Three Singing Dog, 4 3/4" x 5". Made by Wilton Products. .... **$200-$300**

Totem Pole, 6" x 3". .... **$300-$500**

Water Lilies, 4 1/8" x 7 1/2". Signed and numbered, "Albany Fdry. Co., 52". .... **$150-$250**

Wirehaired Terrier, 5 1/8" x 5 1/2". Signed, "Spencer, Guilford, Conn." .... **$200-$300**

Wirehaired Terrier, 5 1/4" x 5 3/8". Made by Hubley and numbered "294". .... **$75-$150**

Wirehaired Terrier, 5 3/8" x 3 7/8". Signed "B&H" (Bradley and Hubbard). **$200-300**

Wirehaired Terrier, 5 5/8" x 5 1/2". Made by Hubley and numbered "351". .... **$200-$300**

Wirehaired Terrier on Base, 4 1/2" x 4 3/8". Made by Hubley, cat. #162. Full-figure. .... **$300-$400**

Wirehaired Terrier & Scottie, 4 3/4" x 5 3/8". Made by Hubley and numbered "263". .... **$200-$300**

Wolfhound, 6 5/8" x 3 5/8". Signed, "Spencer, Guilford, Conn." .... **$300-$500**

Sitting Kitten on Book, 4 7/8" x 3 3/4". Signed "B&H" (Bradley and Hubbard). **$300-$500**

CANES AND WALKING STICKS

Canes and walking sticks have existed through the ages, first as staffs or symbols of authority. They evolved into a fashion accessory that might incorporate carved ivory, precious metals, jewels, porcelain and enamel.

Canes have also been a favorite form of expression for folk artists, with intricate pictorial carving on shafts and handles.

Another category of interest to collectors features gadget canes or "system sticks" that contain hidden objects, from weapons to drinking flasks, telescopes, compasses and even musical instruments.

Agate and tortoiseshell with jewels, brown agate handle is 3 1/4" high and 1" at its widest. It is encased in four long gilded silver strands with dozens of turquoise and garnet stones set in raised bezels. There is a fancy 1" gilded silver collar on a slender tortoiseshell-veneer shaft that ends with a 1 1/4" brass and iron ferrule. It comes in original leather-covered case with brass fittings and gold velvet lining. The overall length is 37 1/4" and there is a small gap of normal age shrinkage just above the ferrule. Possibly French, circa 1880. .... **$2,300**

Art glass with garnets, one-piece blown glass handle is 2 1/4" high with a gold-decorated flat knob top that is 1 1/8" in diameter. A 1/8" rose-cut garnet is at its center and there are several other tiny garnets in various locations. The handle has a central core of deep cobalt blue. The stem is octagonal-shaped and highlighted with bright gold areas that have tiny raised decoration. There is a 2/3" decorated gilded collar on a stepped partridgewood shaft with a 7/8" brass ferrule. The overall length is 34 1/3". A few of the tiny are garnets missing. Possibly continental, circa 1895. .... **$1,955**

Ball and hand, elephant ivory handle is 2 1/3" high and 1 1/2" at its widest. It is carved in the form of a hand clutching a ball. There are four ring separators, two of ebony. With 3/4" ivory ferrule. The overall length is 34 3/4". Possibly Anglo-Indian, circa 1890. .... **$431**

Battle of Gettysburg Memorial, made from a single piece of hickory, it has an "L" handle that is 4 3/4" to the side and 1 1/2" thick. The butt end of the handle is inscribed in ink: "Round Top" (probably where the wood was cut), "Gettysburg July 63", and "made Aug. 94". The entire cane is highlighted with poker-burned dots and lines under the finish. Extending down the shaft are inked images and identification of most of the Union units that fought at the Battle. There is a house marked "Mead's Headq'ters" above another marked "Lee's Headquarters". Created in fine detail, are monuments to, and identification of, 27 units that participated in the Battle, with where they fought identified on some of the images. A sampling of them includes the "8th Penn. Cavalry", "93rd. N.Y., Wolf Hill", "10th N.Y. Battery, Peach Orchard", "73rd Penn., Cemetery Hill", etc. It is signed at the base: "C.N. Sneads, Artist, Gettysburg". The piece ends with a 7/8" white metal ferrule. The overall length is 34 3/4". (The cane belonged to Rufus K. Hamlin, who fought with the Maine 12th Infantry and was the cousin of Hannibal Hamlin, prominent Maine politician and vice president under Lincoln.) **$2,990**

Photo courtesy Heritage Auction Galleries, Dallas; www.HA.com

Pistol Cane with Carved Wood Monkey Head Handle. The mechanism is an unusual variety of rim-fire pistol. The breech opens to the left side by pulling a spring-loaded hammer/lever. A cartridge is locked in place. The hammer is released by pushing a firing button on the right side. It appears that the pistol uses a 9mm rim-fire shot cartridge. The handle is a realistically carved monkey with a sterling collar. Originally the handle/pistol was disengaged by pushing a steel release button. The shaft included is a damaged replacement. One glass eye is missing. **$1,434**

Photo courtesy Tradewinds Antiques & Auctions, Manchester-by-the-Sea, Mass.; www.TradewindsAntiques.com

Cat with animated mouth, painted wood and burl handle is 5" high and 2" at its widest. It depicts a white, brown and black domestic cat with yellow glass eyes. When a lever at its throat is engaged, the cat's mouth opens to reveal a pink interior. Upon release, it snaps shut on a strong spring. There is a 3/4" silver collar on a malacca shaft with a 1" horn ferrule. The overall length is 33 1/2". Possibly Black Forest, circa 1900. **$1,150**

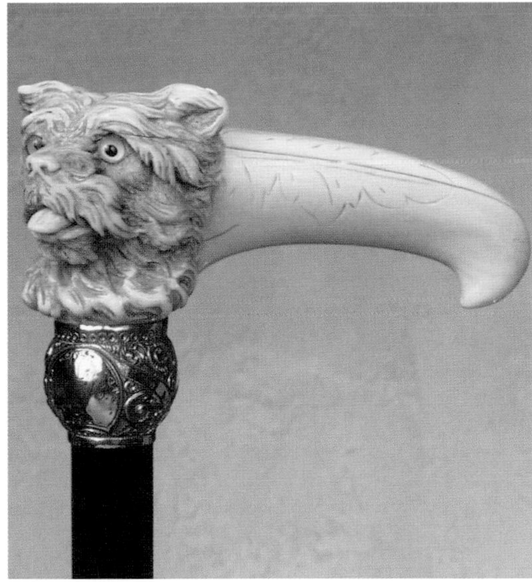

Photo courtesy Tradewinds Antiques & Auctions, Manchester-by-the-Sea, Mass.; www.TradewindsAntiques.com

Dog motif, substantial elephant ivory "L" handle is 2 1/8" high and 5" to the side. It is incised with two long leaves and is carved at the shaft end with the shaggy head of a terrier with yellow glass eyes and tongue protruding. There is a 1 1/8" blown-out gold-filled collar that is decorated and initialed "C.G.H." The shaft is ebony with a 1" replaced brass ferrule. The overall length is 35 3/4". Possibly American, circa 1880. **$3,450**

Bears motif, elephant ivory handle is 11 3/4" long and 1" at its widest. It depicts a chain of seven full-bodied bears standing on each other's backs. Signed in red characters by the maker. There is a 1/3" silver collar on a black enameled hardwood shaft and a 3/4" burnished brass ferrule. The overall length is 37". Possibly English with an imported handle, circa 1895. .... **$632**

Beer or wine measure, elephant ivory handle is 2" high and 1 1/3" in diameter. The top is inlaid with a 1" gilt disc with an image of a stag with an arrow through its neck, presumably the logo of the maker. The cap unscrews and reveals the underside of the gilt disc that is marked "Enfield-Birmingham", probably the locations of the purveyor. A 36" long, round wooden measure can be withdrawn from the shaft. It is calibrated in inches as well as in markings to gauge the amount of the beer or wine that might remain in a cask. There is a 1/4" brass collar on a malacca shaft that ends with a 3 3/4" burnished brass and iron ferrule. The overall length is 37 1/4". It is English, circa 1850. .... **$1,380**

Bird motif, elephant ivory handle is 5 3/4" high and 1 3/4" at its widest. It depicts a stylized tropical bird with a long curved beak and 1/3" round abalone discs at the shoulders of its wings. Two carved feet are at the base. The shaft is dark-stained tropical wood with a crisscross pattern of incised carving that extends for 13". The cane ends with a 1" brass ferrule. The overall length is 35 1/2". Possibly South Pacific in origin and was made in about the mid-20th century. **$115**

Black man, mahogany handle is 3 1/4" high and 2 3/4" at its widest. It depicts the head of a black man with amber glass eyes and detailed features. There is a 1/3" lined brass collar on a dark palmwood shaft with round ivory eyelets and a 7/8" brass ferrule. The overall length is 35 3/4". Possibly Continental, circa 1880. .... **$316**

Boar's tusk, handle measures about 6 1/2" along the arc and is 1" at its widest point. It has mottled brown staining and is carved with decorative grooves. There is a 1 1/2" silver collar rimmed with two hammered rings and marked "Sterling". The shaft may be cherry with a 1 1/2" horn ferrule. The overall length is 36 1/4". American, circa 1895. .... **$230**

Cigar cutter and match safe, "L" silver handle is 2 1/8" high and 3 3/4" to the side. At the end, there is a cap that covers a spring-loaded device with a thin rod at its center. When a cigar was pushed downward on it, a hole was created that made a channel for smoking. At the shoulder of the handle, a lid provided access to a chamber for holding matches and the underside of the lid is scored as a striker. The stem of the handle is inscribed: "Willie Lewellen Palmer, 20th Hussars" and there is a registration number, the name and address of the Regent Street purveyor, as well as London hallmarks for 1902. The shaft is stepped partridgewood with a 3/4" worn brass ferrule. The overall length is 36". **$805**

Dagger cane, hardwood shaft is carved to simulate bamboo and it has a short knob top that is 7/8" high and 7/8" in diameter. Five and one quarter inches down the shaft there is a 2/3" silver collar London hallmarked for 1910. At that point the dagger can be withdrawn. It is 14" long, ends in a sharp point, and has a squared configuration. The cane ends with a 1 1/2" worn brass and iron ferrule. The overall length is 34 1/4", with some cosmetic repair to an age crack in the shaft. **$345**

Dog motif, elephant ivory "L" handle is 1 1/2" high and 4 1/4" long. It depicts a detailed greyhound with amber glass eyes. There is a 1/2" silver collar fashioned as a belt and buckle. The shaft is rosewood with a 7/8" replaced brass ferrule. The overall length is 33", with minor roughness on the ear tips. Probably English, circa 1880. .... **$805**

Dog motif, ivory and silver, walrus ivory "L" handle is 2 1/2" high and 3 3/4" to the side. It is overlaid with reticulated silver so the ivory shows through, and there are owner's initials on the end-cap. The silver is elaborately engraved with scrolls and the underside is scored for secure gripping. On the stem portion, a 3/4" silver face of a terrier is fashioned in high relief. The shaft is tan bamboo with a 3/4" worn brass ferrule. The overall length is 34 1/4" and the condition is very good. By style and appearance, the piece is undoubtedly American, circa 1870. ..... **$1,150**

Photo courtesy Tradewinds Antiques & Auctions, Manchester-by-the-Sea, Mass.; www.TradewindsAntiques.com

Elephant on a horn ball, elephant ivory handle is 3 1/8" high and 2 1/8" at its widest. It depicts a baby elephant with pale yellow glass eyes, struggling to hold its footing on a large horn ball that is resting on an ivory pedestal. There is a 2/3" smooth silver collar on an exotic snakewood shaft with a 1 1/2" white metal and iron ferrule. The overall length is 38 1/2". Possibly American, circa 1900, an unusual interpretation of the circus theme. **$3,450**

Eagle motif, elephant ivory "L" handle is 1 3/4" high and 4" to the side. It depicts a fierce looking eagle head with brown glass eyes. There is a 1/2" coin silver collar on a full-bark malacca shaft with a 7/8" burnished brass and iron ferrule. The overall length is 35". Probably American, circa 1870. .... **$4,830**

Eagle motif, German Art Deco, silver "L" handle is 2 3/4" high and 5" long. It is fashioned with lines and acute edges to give it a classic Art Deco flavor. It depicts an eagle with yellow glass eyes. It is marked "800" and "Geschutz" the mark meaning "registered" in Germany and Austria. The shaft is stepped partridgewood with a 1" worn brass and iron ferrule. The overall length is 34 1/2", with light denting of the bird's beak. It is circa 1920. .... **$2,645**

Eating tools, silver collar, initialed "F.S.", is 1" high and 1 3/4" in diameter. It can be removed to reveal two compartments, one holding two ivory and pewter serving spoons, and the other two silver open salts. The compartments are designed to accept their contents in a tight fit. The shaft is thick hardwood with lacquered ring of whipping for decoration. About 11" down the shaft the cane opens again at a silver fitting to reveal eating implements placed in their own compartments. At the center is an ebony-handled carving knife, ringed by two sets of ivory and silver chopsticks, a pair of tools with twin tines, a metal knife sharpener, and a long pointed ivory device of unknown purpose. The cane ends with a 3 3/4" long metal ferrule. The overall length is 37". Possibly Chinese, circa 1900, exported to England. **$3,737**

English piqué and enamel, mid-17th century, elephant ivory cylindrical handle is 3 3/4" high and 1" in diameter. It is decorated in silver hollow dots, string inlay, and red and

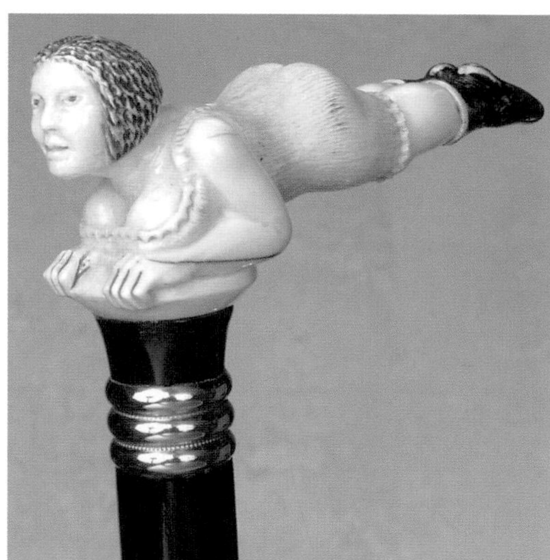

Photo courtesy Tradewinds Antiques & Auctions, Manchester-by-the-Sea, Mass.; www.TradewindsAntiques.com

Female acrobat, walrus ivory "L" handle is 1 3/4" high and 4 3/4" to the side. It depicts a detailed performing acrobat. She is fully stretched out and is holding onto the edge of a stand. She has short brown hair, black boots and is wearing a short, form fitting costume with a revealing décolletage. There is a 2/3" ringed silver collar on a black hardwood shaft with a 1" horn ferrule. The overall length is 36". Possibly French, circa 1880. **$1,150** green enamel highlights. The top is decorated with a 3/4" circle rimmed with piqué. Around a solid smaller circle at the center is silver string inlay that identifies the maker, John Pointer. The sides are decorated with rings of piqué as well as lines of tiny spherules of green and red enamel that frame eight panels. The panels have birds, animals and flowers done in string inlay with enamel highlights. There is a 1/3" silver collar that is scalloped and punch-decorated in the style of the handle. The shaft is Malacca and terminates with a 4 1/2" brass ferrule with a rusty iron tip. The overall length is 37 7/8" and the general condition is very good with most of the piqué and string inlay still intact. **$29,900**

English ivory piqué pomander, elephant ivory handle is 3 1/2" high and 1 1/3" in diameter. It has a lid that is decorated with a small central circle of piqué and eight star-shaped holes, as well as "R.C." for the owner and "92", (1692), in a frame of pique. The lid unscrews to reveal a shallow receptacle that was designed to hold a bit of wool or cloth that was soaked with healing herbs and potions that the user could sniff through the holes to ward off illness. The handle is pierced with eyelets for a cord, and it has a raised central ring. It is elaborately decorated with piqué in flowers and scrolls. There is a 1" silver collar with line decoration on a shaft of malacca with a 1 3/4" brass and iron ferrule. The overall length is 36 1/3". **$6,325**

Fire screen/sunshade, plain silver handle is 1 3/4" high and 1 1/4" in diameter. There are worn hallmarks, perhaps French. The handle unscrews at its mid-point to reveal a 3/4" upright ivory knob in an acorn shape. By gently lifting the knob, a 6 3/4" pleated, round, stiff-linen screen emerges from a cardboard storage tube to which it is attached. It is painted with purple flowers and green leaves with brown stems. The screen is in good condition. The shaft is dark bamboo with a 1" white metal and iron ferrule. The overall length is 36" and the condition is very good with some wear to the silver at the lower half of the handle. It is circa 1870. Fire screen/sunshades were used by women to protect their complexions from the heat of open fireplaces, and also from the sun. **$2,300**

Folk art, polychrome, made from a single piece of hardwood, it has a thin 1" tin disc affixed with a nail as a protector at the top. It has a crazed, painted finish. There is a brown and red eagle, a long brown snake, a bathing beauty in a modest red suit, a black sailboat with three masts, a red cricket, a red, green and brown bulls-eye, another bather in green and red, a brown and red rooster, a brown and red airplane with open cockpit and pilot, a brown and green star, a boat with red keel, a dirigible, and a brown fox. The piece ends with a 2/3" brass homemade pipe ferrule. The overall length is 34". American, circa 1915, found in the Midwest. **$575**

Frog motif, stained elephant ivory handle is 3 1/4" high and 2" at its widest. It depicts a greenish frog with brown glass eyes sitting on the 1/2" silver collar at the top of the cane. The shaft is tan bamboo with a 7/8" replaced brass ferrule. The overall length is 36 1/3". Probably English, circa 1890. .... **$2,415**

GAR veteran's cane, by Edwin H. Smith. Fashioned from a single piece of basswood, it has a burnished bronze octagonal handle that is 1" high and 1 1/8" in diameter. It is carved for its entire length in raised relief. Below the handle is an American flag around which is inscribed: "In God We Trust" and "We Will Stand By The Flag". There are numerous GAR corps badges around a long encircling ribbon that says: "To William J. Copeland from Edwin H. Smith, National Soldiers Home, Va.". A 1 1/2" white metal and iron ferrule completes the piece. The overall length is 34 3/4". It is circa 1885. (The carver, Edwin H. Smith, was a disabled veteran who served as a private in the N.Y. 72nd Infantry. He was wounded and discharged for disability in 1863. William J. Copeland was a private in the N.Y. 123rd Infantry and was discharged in 1865. Smith carved canes for comrades at several of the Soldiers Homes.) **$1,725**

Photo courtesy Tradewinds Antiques & Auctions, Manchester-by-the-Sea, Mass.; www.TradewindsAntiques.com

Hare motif, elephant ivory "L" handle is 4 1/2" to the side and 1 1/4" at its widest. It depicts a detailed long-eared hare with brown glass eyes. There is a 1 1/2" smooth sterling collar Chester hallmarked for 1862. The shaft is malacca with a 1 1/2" burnished brass and iron ferrule. The overall length is 34". **$690**

Gargoyle, Art Nouveau, silver "L" handle is 3" high and 4 1/2" to the side. It depicts a gargoyle with the head of a wild cat, long wings, a scaly snake's body, and claws of a raptor. There are French hallmarks as well as those of a maker. The shaft is ebony with a 1" worn brass and iron ferrule. The overall length is 37 1/4", with some wear to the shaft's finish. It is circa 1900. .... **$1,150**

Gun cane, 19th century, smoothbore, .36 caliber, 28 3/4" steel barrel, threaded at breech. Brass mount to horn handle. **$1,092**

Gun cane, Remington dog head, "L" handle is 2 1/3" high and 3 1/4" long. It depicts the Remington gutta-percha large hound head. It has the model number "539" near the base of the handle. There is a 1/3" lined nickel collar and the gun unscrews 7" down the shaft so that a .32 caliber rim-fire cartridge could be inserted. It is cocked with a straight pull that allows a notched gun sight to pop up. A round trigger under the handle fires the piece and all mechanics are in working order. The shaft is covered in gutta-percha that is all intact except for a small semi-circular chip near the opening. Some of the Remington marks on the surface of the gutta-percha above the opening are faint and barely visible using a strong glass. However, the patent date "Feb. 9, 1858" is visible as is "N.Y." from the Remington address in Ilion. The piece ends with a 1 3/4" hollow nickel ferrule. The overall length is 35 1/4". Circa 1860s. **$9,200**

Gun cane, Remington percussion, semi-crook gutta-percha handle is about 4" long and 1" thick. Below it is a 1/3" lined nickel collar. The remainder of the shaft is gutta-percha veneer. The piece unscrews 4 1/4" down the shaft so it could be loaded. It cocks with a pull that allows a notched sight to pop up, and so that a percussion cap could be placed on the hollow nib. After closing it was fired by a round trigger below the handle that caused a hammer to strike the percussion cap. All mechanics are working. There is a 2" hollow steel ferrule that is marked: "T.E.. Thomas, patent Feb. 9, 1858, Remington & Sons, Ilion, N.Y." and the registration number "12" which means it was the 12th number of this model made. Since the percussion type was the first gun cane made by Remington, this piece would be one of the earliest examples. The overall length is 34 1/2". **$5,462**

Hunting motif, made of a single piece of elephant ivory, the pistol-grip handle is 8" high and 2 1/2" to the side. It is carved on the stem portion in high relief. Depicted is a hound with a calling horn on a cord around its neck. There is also a flintlock rifle and powder horn, a dagger in a sheath, and a game bag hung on a tree branch. Finally, there is the head of a majestic elk sporting a large antler rack. At the base of the handle there is an etched and inked ducal crown along with owner's initials above a carved ivory belt and buckle. The overall length is 34 3/4" with an almost imperceptible tiny chip on the side of the hound's nose. It is continental, circa 1850. .... **$4,312**

Andrew Jackson, presentation cane, gold and hickory, solid gold knob, tested to be at least 18k, is 1 1/3" high and 1" in diameter. Inscribed on top is "Andrew Jackson to Silas E. Burrows, June 12th, 1832". The sides of the handle have two decorated raised rings. The shaft is crooked, natural hickory with fancy gold eyelets and a 5 1/4" burnished brass and rusted iron ferrule. The overall length is 38 1/4" and the condition is very good with some minor loss of bark above the ferrule. (Jackson and Burrows are linked in U.S. history to the creation of a monument for Mary Ball Washington, George Washington's mother. When her grave was in jeopardy of being moved, Burrows wrote the mayor of Fredericksburg, Va., protesting the removal and offered to pay for a monument to be erected at her chosen site. In 1833, Jackson laid the cornerstone for the Burrows Monument. Because the date on the cane is 1832, the year before the dedication ceremony, it is believed that it was a gift from Jackson to thank Burrows. Burrows, the stonemason and the contractor all died before the monument could be completed, leaving the project in disarray. It was not completed until Grover Cleveland's administration in 1894.) **$9,200**

Jade ball, handle is 1 1/2" diameter and it rests on a silver "crown" mount. The mount has eight points that cradle the stone that is moss green with mottled white shading. The silver is engraved with a cloverleaf maker's mark. The heavy shaft is exotic snakewood. It terminates with a 7/8" replaced brass ferrule. The overall length is 36 1/4" and the condition is very good with a small area of surface roughness near the top of the jade ball. Possibly continental, circa 1900. .... **$1,150**

Jolly monk, handle is 3" high and 2" at its widest. It depicts a smiling monk with his face carved in elephant ivory and wearing a carved wood cloak. There is a 1 1/4" decorated silver collar on a full-bark malacca shaft with a 1" replaced brass ferrule. The overall length is 37 1/2". Possibly English, circa 1880. .... **$1,955**

Monkeys clinging to a tree, handle made of elephant ivory over snakewood is 2 1/2" high and 2" at its widest. It depicts a pair of long-tailed monkeys with arms, legs and tails intertwined on the side of a tree, with an ivory umbrella of palm fronds at the top. The monkeys have dark-brown glass eyes. There is a 1 1/3" gilt silver collar decorated with "C" scrolls and a shield cartouche. The shaft is dark exotic wood with a 1" white metal and iron ferrule. The overall length is 37". Probably English, circa 1905. .... **$1,495**

Franklin Murphy, Governor of New Jersey, elephant ivory handle is 1 1/2" high and 4 2/3" long. It is relief-carved with classical scrolls and is accented with 15 small, beaded silver bars. It has a fancy end cap that is initialed "F.M." for Franklin Murphy. There is 7/8" silver collar that matches the end cap. It is inscribed with Murphy's Newark, N.J., address and is also marked: "Gorham Mfg. Co., Sterling". The shaft is exotic coromandel that ends with a 1 1/2" white metal and iron ferrule. The overall length is 36 3/4". It is circa 1890. (Franklin Murphy [1846-1920] served in the Union Army during the Civil War, fighting at Antietam, Chancellorsville, Gettysburg and the Atlanta Campaign. He then was active in commerce and New Jersey politics and eventually became governor.) **$1,840**

Photo courtesy Tradewinds Antiques & Auctions, Manchester-by-the-Sea, Mass.; www.TradewindsAntiques.com

Man with a long hat, porcelain handle is 2 1/4" high, 4 1/2" long and 1 3/4" at its widest. It depicts a fashionable man with a very long black hat. There are blue maker's marks in the porcelain on the back of his neck. There is a 1/2" silver collar on a black hardwood shaft with a 1" replaced brass ferrule. The overall length is 34 3/4". Possibly Italian, circa 1880. **$2,300**

Nautical cane with fist, whale ivory handle is 2 1/2" h and 1 1/2" w. It depicts a detailed clenched fist with a hole for a carrying cord. The lower portion of the handle is octagonal-carved and blends into the thick palm wood shaft, also octagonal-carved for 11 1/2", and then a smooth taper. (Such configuration was in vogue in cane construction from about 1840 to about 1860.) A 1/3" old hand-made brass ferrule completes the piece. The overall length is 33 3/4". Probably American, circa 1850. .... **$3,680**

Nude maiden, German Art Nouveau, silver crook handle measures about 7 1/2" l and is 1 1/3" at its widest. It depicts a nude maiden astride a fish among other swimming fish, cattails and reeds. It is inscribed on a ring at the base: "Geschuz" (registered) and "900", for the silver purity, and there are worn maker's marks. It is mounted on a shaft of macassar ebony with a 1 1/3" black horn ferrule. The overall length is 36 1/4". Circa 1900. .... **$1,380**

Odd Fellows, made of a single piece of elephant ivory, the knob handle is 3 7/8" h and 1 2/3" in d. The top is inlaid with a 3/4" silver disc that is engraved with Odd Fellows symbols including the three-link chain and the heart in hand. There is a 3/4" coin silver collar that is inscribed: "John Morrill, Nashua N.H." and "Feb. 5, 1844". The shaft is rosewood with round silver eyelets and a 3 1/3" brass and iron ferrule. The overall length is 34 2/3", with age lines at the top of the ivory knob. (John Merrill was a blacksmith and a founding member of the Grand Lodge of Odd Fellows established in Nashua on Sept. 11, 1843.) **$431**

Pike with a trout, elephant ivory "L" handle is 1 1/2" h and 4" to the side. It depicts a full-bodied pike grasping its prey, a small trout, in its jaws. Each fish has yellow glass eyes. There is a 1 1/2" gold-filled collar fashioned as a buckle on a honey-toned malacca shaft with a 1" burnished brass and iron ferrule. The overall length is 36". Probably American, circa 1890. .... **$805**

Pistol grip, damascene handle is 3" high and 1 1/2" at its widest. It is decorated in two colors of gold with several differently styled panels that feature the distinctive flying dragon seen on pieces made in Toledo, Spain. The shaft is snakewood. It terminates with a 1" brass and iron ferrule. The overall length is 35 3/4". It is circa 1900. .... **$3,220**

Pitch pipe, ivory and silver handle is 2 1/2" long and 3/4" thick. It is made with eight blowing holes that are marked with various major and minor keys, (A, D, G, F, etc.) There are vent holes on the underside to expel the air, and it is in working order. There is a 1 2/3" silver collar on a fine snakewood shaft with a 1" brass ferrule. The overall length is 34" and the condition is very good. Possibly English, circa 1900. .... **$1,725**

Pool cue, textured silver knob handle is 1 1/2" high and 1 1/4" in diameter. It unscrews from a rosewood shaft in order to withdraw the long maple end of a cue stick. After removing the 7/8" brass ferrule, the maple end can be screwed into the shaft to form a real working cue. The ferrule can be screwed into the silver handle for safe-keeping, and when the handle is re-attached to the rosewood shaft, the 58" cue is ready to have a fresh cue tip affixed to the ivory top for use. The overall length when a cane is 34", with minor dents in the silver handle and some surface cracks in the rosewood. Possibly English, circa 1900. .... **$977**

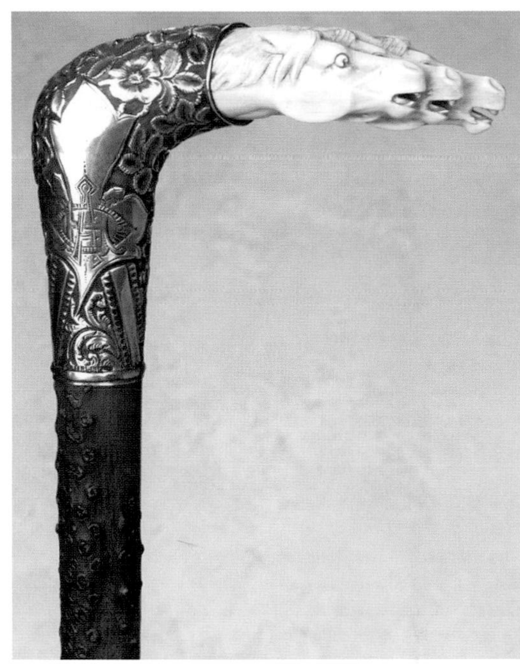

Photo courtesy Tradewinds Antiques & Auctions, Manchester-by-the-Sea, Mass.; www.TradewindsAntiques.com

Racing horses, ivory and silver, elephant ivory and silver "L" handle is 3 1/3" high and 4 1/4" to the side. Three racing horses are carved nose to nose in a racing motif and are rendered in fine detail. The silver portion of the handle is chased in flowers and leaves and there is an unusually fashioned cartouche with owner's initials, "A.H." It is also marked "Sterling." The shaft is scarred medlar with a 1 1/2" white metal and iron ferrule. (Medlar is a flowering shrub whose branches were scarred with a special tool while still growing. When harvested, it has an unusual texture.) The overall length is 34 1/4" and the condition is very good. It is American, circa 1895. **$1,495**

Rock crystal, enamel and silver with an amethyst stone, cylindrical handle is 3 1/2" high and 3/4" in diameter. The top is fully inlaid with a faceted amethyst set into a guilloche-turned silver mount with blue enamel rings as highlights. The long tapered rock crystal stem is surmounted with a double festoon of silver laurel roping. A 1/2" silver mount at the base has matching blue enamel showing through the reticulated silver, and there are continental hallmarks. The shaft is natural applewood with a 1 2/3" white metal and iron ferrule. The overall length is 36". It is circa 1900. .... **$1,495**

Roman Empress, large elephant ivory handle is 4 3/4" high and 2 1/4" at its widest. It depicts the bust of a Roman lady, perhaps Pompeia, the wife of Julius Caesar, upon a plinth, adorned in regal finery. The shaft is honey-toned malacca with a 1 1/4" horn ferrule. It is staff length at 41 1/4", with a fine creamy patina. Possibly Continental, circa 1860. .... **$7,475**

Sailor's whimsy nautical cane, whale ivory handle is 1 3/4" high and 1 1/3" in diameter. The round top is done in melon configuration with concentric grooves meeting at the center. There is another 2 1/2" of octagonal-carved whale ivory that joins the whalebone shaft that is carved as follows: There are two chambers with concave posts that measure a total of 5 1/4". Within each separate chamber is a freely moving whalebone ball that rolls up and down as the cane is tilted. (This type of whimsy is often seen in wood "ball and chamber" canes.) The carving continues down the shaft with an area of tiny diamond configuration, then fluting with lines, and finally, rope-twist above a short tapered base. It never had a ferrule. The overall length is 33 1/4" and the condition is very good. It is quite straight indicating that it came from the center of the panbone. Possibly American, circa 1850. .... **$21,850**

Shakespeare motif, elephant ivory handle is 3 1/4" high and 1 1/4" at its widest. It depicts a detailed bust of William Shakespeare on a fancy base. There is a 1" textured silver collar on a Macassar ebony shaft with a 1 2/3" white metal and iron ferrule. The overall length is 37 1/2" and the condition is very good. It is English, circa 1880. .... **$690**

Shibayama, Japanese ivory, one-piece elephant ivory handle is 8" long and 7/8" in diameter. It is inlaid in the Shibayama manner with various colored hard stones and mother-of-pearl, as well as having inked etching. It depicts a multicolored bird perched in a trailing floral vine. All of the inlay is intact. It is signed in an oval cartouche by the Japanese artist. There is a 3/4" sterling collar inscribed, "Nina," and there are London hallmarks for 1913. The shaft is figured snakewood with a 7/8" burnished brass and iron ferrule. The overall length is 37 1/4" and the condition is excellent. **$1,150**

Shibayama insects, elephant ivory "L" handle is 1 1/4" high and 3 3/4" long. It is scored on the underside for a better grip and there are eight different insects randomly inlaid in the Japanese Shibayama manner. They are fashioned with various polished hardstones, mother-of-pearl and abalone, with each insect having etched legs and antennae. It is signed by the maker. There is a 1" silver collar with a presentation done in initials. The shaft is malacca with a 3/4" ivory ferrule. The overall length is 33". Probably fashioned in England with an imported handle, circa 1890. .... **$3,220**

Silver and turquoise enamel, cylindrical silver handle is 3" high and 7/8" in diameter. Inlaid on top is a 3/4" turquoise colored guilloche-worked enamel disc rimmed with a thin vermeil ring, and another of white enamel. Below the top is a ring of silver acanthus leaves, a white enamel ring, and then the long turquoise enamel body, also worked in guilloche. Another white enamel ring as well as one of silver acanthus leaves completes the decoration on the handle. The base is marked "925" and there are hallmarks, perhaps Irish. The shaft is dark brown hardwood with a 1" horn ferrule. The overall length is 36". First half of the 20th century. **$1,725**

Snake and frog, folk art made from a single piece of wood, perhaps red oak, it has a black-painted round knob handle that is 1" high and 1 1/3" in diameter. The top is inlaid with a round disc and six teardrops of mother of pearl. There are pale blue beads inlaid around the sides. Below the handle, a green and black frog is wrapped around the shaft, above a thick black ring. Below the ring is a long, menacing snake painted black and green. The snake has a forked tongue of copper protruding out of its red mouth as well as mother-of-pearl eyes. Its long body encircles the shaft all the way down. A 2" gilded metal homemade ferrule completes the piece. The overall length is 36". Possibly American, circa 1900. .... **$488**

Stallion motif, elephant ivory handle is 1 1/2" high and 3 3/4" long. It depicts a detailed stallion with brown glass eyes, mouth agape, veins protruding and a flowing mane. There is a decorated sterling collar initialed "F.H.B." in script with Birmingham hallmark for 1913. The shaft is honey-toned malacca with a 1" replaced brass ferrule. The overall length is 35 3/4". **$862**

"Sunday Stick" golf driver, elephant ivory handle measures about 3" long and is 1 1/2" at its widest point. It is fashioned as a golf driver complete with a simulated foot and a simulated weight on the side opposite the club-face, much like the construction of an early club. It is inscribed with "special". There is a 2/3" brass collar on a dark bamboo shaft with a 7/8" replaced brass ferrule. The overall length is 35". It is English, circa 1900. (Canes fashioned as golf clubs were sometimes called "Sunday Sticks" because some avid golfers liked to stroll on the golf course sporting their club canes on Sundays when playing was not allowed.) **$517**

Sword cane, ivory and malacca, elephant ivory knob handle is 2" high and 1 1/3" in diameter. There is a 1/3" silver collar on a malacca shaft with silver oval eyelets followed by a 2/3" silver band. At that point a 15 1/2" triangular short sword can be withdrawn from a tight and well-hidden juncture. A

Photo courtesy Tradewinds Antiques & Auctions, Manchester-by-the-Sea, Mass.; www.TradewindsAntiques.com

Rose quartz and crystal, rose quartz handle is 2" high and 1 1/4" in diameter. One large and two smaller rock-crystal rings span the handle. The quartz is pale pink with the internal crystalline fissures for which this stone is noted. The shaft is ebony and it never had a ferrule. The overall length is 37". Probably American, circa 1890. **$1,725**

5 1/4" burnished brass and iron ferrule completes the piece. It has numerous dings and a slight bend from two centuries of age and use. The overall length is 36". American, circa 1790. .... **$1,150**

Sword cane, 1826, stag horn and gold, straight stag-horn handle is 3 1/2" high and 1 1/2" at its widest. There is a square solid gold cartouche on top that is engraved with a Masonic square and compass. There is a 7/8" solid gold collar inscribed: "Presented to Br. Edw'd Arents by Morton Lodge No. 108 as a testimony of esteem, N.Y. Aug. 17th, AL5826 (Masonic method of dating for 1826)". The shaft is dark bamboo with gold oval eyelets ending with a 2 2/3" brass ferrule. At the second step of the bamboo, the sword withdraws from a well-hidden juncture. It is 27 1/2" long, in early concave "small sword" configuration, with 12" of engraving. The overall length is 36". **$1,150**

Sword cane, with quillons, silver knob handle is 1 1/8" high and 1 1/4" in diameter. It has a round cartouche on top that contains an applied silver ducal crown. The body of the handle is also engraved in a floral pattern. Six inches down the malacca shaft there is a 1/3" silver band at which point the blade can be withdrawn with a straight pull from a tight fitting. As it is withdrawn, two brass spring-driven quillons (hand guards) snap into place. The 23 1/3" steel blade is diamond-shaped and comes to a sharp point. The cane ends with a 1 1/4" worn metal ferrule. The overall length is 36". Possibly continental, circa 1885. .... **$1,610**

Thousand Faces motif, sterling knob handle is 2" high and 1" in diameter. It is London hallmarked for 1895 and "J.H." for the English maker. It is fashioned "a la japonais" with 14 round smiling faces in raised repousse. The shaft is malacca with a 1 1/8" burnished brass and iron ferrule. The overall length is 36". **$1,035**

Webb cameo glass, ball handle is 1 1/2" in diameter. It is fashioned with off-white clematis leaves, vines and flowers on a deep blue background that has a lightly glossed finish. It is beautifully crafted resembling a cameo, hence the name. (English cameo glass was produced primarily by Thomas Webb, the inventor of this glassmaking technique in which a design was etched onto the surface of blown glass with white acid.) There is a 1/3" gold collar on a malacca shaft with a 1 1/2" old brass and iron ferrule. The overall length is 35 1/2". English, circa 1895. .... **$2,185**

Whale ivory and whalebone, with mother of pearl, single whale tooth handle is 3 1/2" h and 1 1/3" in d at the flat knob top. It is line decorated and inlaid with a large 1" MOP disc on top. There is a 1/4" baleen separator on a whalebone shaft that is octagonal-carved for 13" followed by 1" of angled lines, then twist-carved for the remaining 16 3/4". It never had a ferrule. The overall length is 34 1/2". It is American and undoubtedly sailor-made, circa 1860. .... **$3,737**

Whale ivory and whalebone, with elaborate inlay, constructed of two pieces, the whale ivory handle measures about 5" along the arc and is 2" wide at the foot end. There is a 2/3" oval inlay of exotic wood set into the foot and two ring spacers set off the parts of the handle. Going down the shaft there is 6 1/2" of elaborate inlay done in whale ivory and exotic wood. The decoration includes rings, squares, spherules and triangles. The remainder of the shaft is a smooth taper ending in a 2/3" brass ferrule. The overall length is 34". Possibly English, circa 1860. .... **$8,625**

FOLK ART CANES

Cane with thick-soled shoe-form handle, and burnt-carved geometric design, circa 1930. .... **$150**

Cane with crook handle, and carved shaft with oval openings, original crazed varnished surface, circa 1910. .... **$90**

Basswood cane with knob handle, and large snake wrapped around shaft, circa 1940. .... **$60**

Walnut cane with squared knob handle, and faceted shaft, with pyramidal points and shallow-carved geometric design, circa 1910. .... **$100**

Cane with high-top shoe-form handle, (natural fissures) and spot-burned shaft, rubber tip, circa 1920. .... **$150**

Natural-bark walking stick with carved stars, arrow and "W.J.BRYAN," dated 1896, original varnished surface. **$100**

Walking stick with notch-carved and reeded shaft, original varnished surface, metal ferrule, circa 1900. .... **$80**

Natural-bark walking stick with double-ring collar, deeply carved with types of wood-working tools, Masonic and Odd fellow emblems, cutlery, pistol, kitchen utensils, man playing fiddle and man dancing near tree, oaken bucket and coffee pot, fish, lobster, turtle, man facing off against large animal (lion, dog?), boot, jug, barrel, mermaid, sad iron, lady's leg, cat (?), bootjack, stylized tree, large pitcher, pipe, broom and wrapped snake, circa 1890. .... **$500**

Walking stick with orange Bakelite steering-wheel knob handle, large brass collar marked "WENCK," faceted shaft with original varnished surface, circa 1930s. **$100**

Natural-form cane with snake handle, paint detailed, brass cap ferrule (shotgun shell?), circa 1920. .... **$150**

Elegant rosewood walking stock with knob handle, spiral shaft and strong two-tone wood grain, circa 1910. .... **$200**

German regimental pipe cane, with elk-horn knob, ivory screw top, tulip-form, cow-horn decoration, ebony block with regimental insignia, turned sections, natural-bark shaft with heavy varnish, bone tip with screw stopper, disassembles, all original, circa 1890. .... **$300**

Walking stick with egg-shaped handle, faceted shaft of cherry and maple arranged in contrasting bands, metal ferrule, heavy original varnished surface, 1930s. **$120**

Oversize walking stick with knobbed L-handle, heavy varnish, found in Iowa, circa 1940s. **$50**

Large walking stick with primitive clenched-fist handle, square tapering shaft with beveled corners, painted black, circa 1920. .... **$200**

Cane with stylized horse-head handle, Scandinavian influence but made in U.S., worn varnished surface, circa 1940. .... **$150**

Chicago World's fair cane, with barrel dandle and attached wooden beer glass, paper spiral-decorated shaft, original tassel, missing spigot, metal ferrule. **$120**

Natural-bark handle walking stick, with carved decoration and double-snake-wrapped shaft, circa 1910. .... **$80**

Walnut cane, with shaft composed of tapering wooden disks on metal rod, metal ferrule, circa 1920. .... **$90**

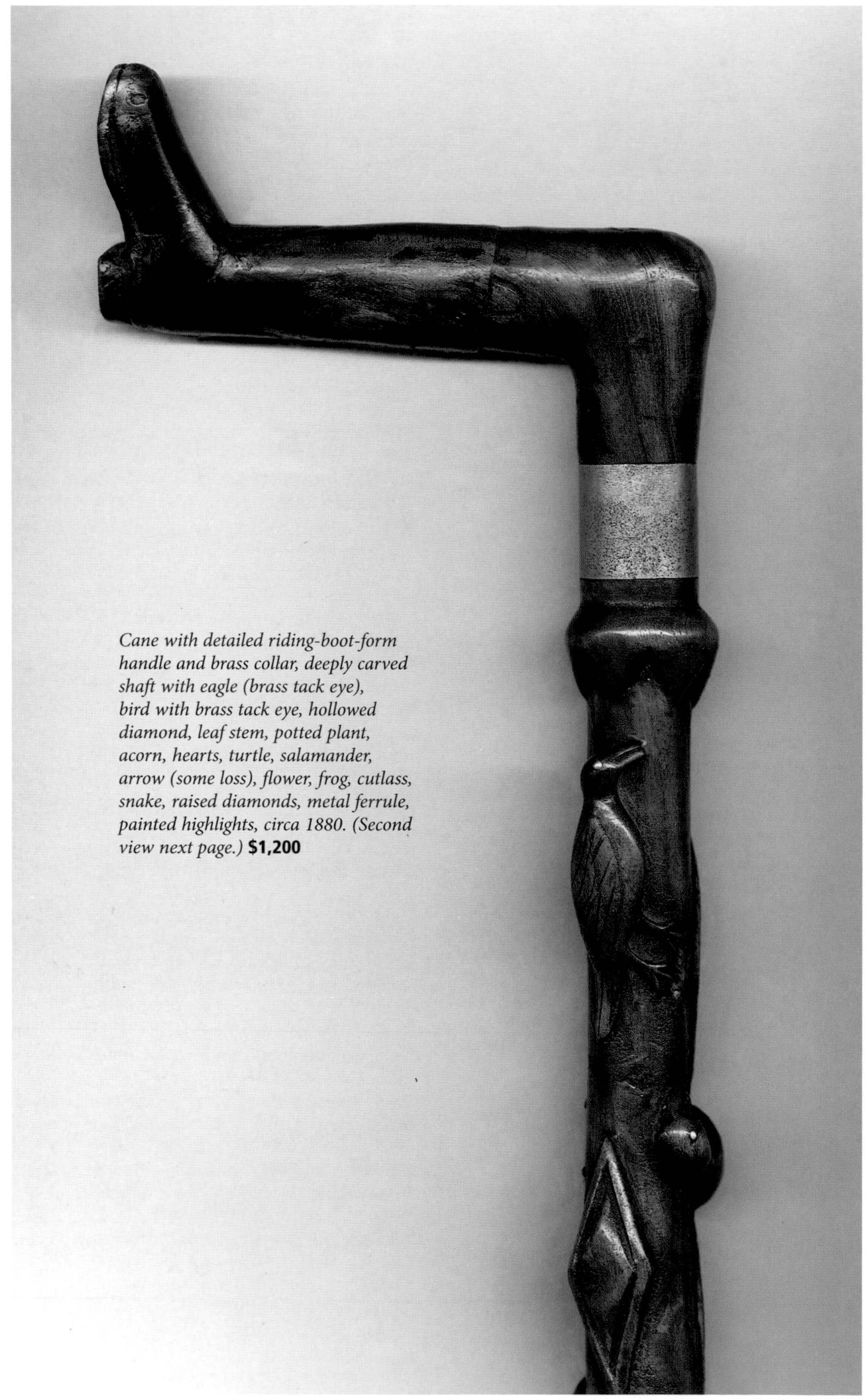

Cane with detailed riding-boot-form handle and brass collar, deeply carved shaft with eagle (brass tack eye), bird with brass tack eye, hollowed diamond, leaf stem, potted plant, acorn, hearts, turtle, salamander, arrow (some loss), flower, frog, cutlass, snake, raised diamonds, metal ferrule, painted highlights, circa 1880. (Second view next page.) **$1,200**

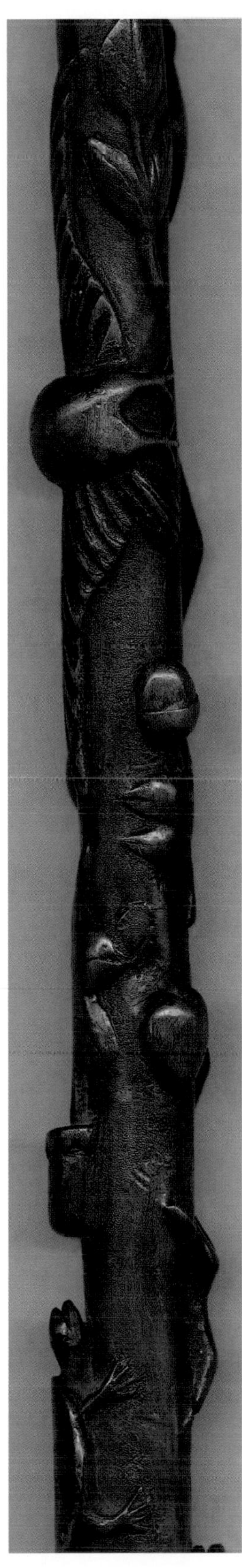

Heavy walking stick, with shaft decorated with eagle holding snake, shield, burnt-carved and crosshatched decoration, probably Mexican, circa 1900. .... **$75**

Walking stick with natural-bark handle, shaft with deeply carved and painted stern-faced Indian brave with feathers, black shaft with shallow-carved geometric and leaf designs and tepee, possibly Penobscot, circa 1930. .... **$300**

Cedar walking stick with knob handle and flaring form, with carved recessed panel with conjoined initials "WLD," original varnished surface, circa 1930s. **$80**

Natural-bark cane, with detailed-carved eagle-head handle, shaft with deeply carved stylized leaf forms, metal ferrule, original varnished surface, circa 1910. .... **$120**

Slender cane with finely carved handle, in the form of a leg with bare foot, metal ferrule, original varnished surface, circa 1920. .... **$100**

Cane with bentwood handle, notch-carved shaft, original varnished surface, circa 1910. .... **$90**

Briarwood cane with bentwood handle, double-snake-wrapped shaft, painted decoration, metal ferrule, circa 1920. .... **$120**

Slender cane with finely carved handle, in the form of a bearded and helmeted soldier, one glass eye missing, circa 1900. .... **$80**

Natural-bark walking stick, with shaft shallow-carved in geometric patterns, hearts and arrows, circa 1910. .... **$100**

Round tapering walking stick, with shaft carved in raised letters, "PETER ROSTAD – GHS – '31," remnants of varnish. **$80**

Walking stick with worn natural-bark handle, shaft carved with bird, high-top shoes, running deer, wrapped snake, running horse, skull and crossed bones, star, flower, butterfly, leaves, original stained and varnished surface, circa 1900. .... **$300**

Walking stick, with handle primitively carved in the form of a human face, circa 1910. .... **$120**

Walking stick, with stylized wrapped snake with glass eyes, spot burned, metal ferrule, original varnished surface, circa 1920. .... **$90**

Souvenir cane, brightly painted and crudely carved with Indian and snake, probably Mexican in origin, circa 1950s. **$30**

Natural-wood cane with entwined branches, shallow-carved on shaft, "FLUME" and "1900," probably from Vermont. **$200**

Glass cane in red, with spiral bands in yellow and white, circa 1930s. **$200**

Glass can in pale green, with applied black highlights, circa 1910. .... **$150**

Ceramics

CERAMICS, AMERICAN

Also see Tiffany, Redware, Stoneware.

Arequipa

Arequipa Sanatorium operated in Marin County north of San Francisco, treating tuberculosis patients from 1911-1918. The facility's art directors included Frederick Rhead, Albert Solon and Fred Wilde.

Batchelder and Brown

Ernest Allan Batchelder founded the Batchelder Tile Co. in Pasadena, Calif., in 1909. He took on Frederick L. Brown as his partner, renaming the pottery Batchelder and Brown in 1912. The firm closed in 1932.

Batchelder, triptych of an ox cart caravan with blue engobe. A few small chips to edges, some grout on back. No visible mark. 8" x 18" each. **$5,100**

Burley, and Burley Winter

Several generations of the Burley and Winter families operated potteries in and around the Ohio communities of Crooksville, Zanesville and Mt. Sterling from the early 19th to the early 20th centuries.

Photo courtesy Belhorn Auction Services LLC, Columbus, Ohio; www.Belhorn.com

Burley Winter, floor vase with Grecian women and green over brick red glazes. Marked 'Burley Winter, Crooksville, O.' Mint. 17" h x 10 1/2" w. **$575**

Photo courtesy Rago Arts and Auction Center, Lambertville, N.J.; www.RagoArts.com

Arequipa flaring bowl by Frederick Rhead, its interior decorated in squeezebag with clusters of stylized trees in front of dark mountains and white clouds. (One of only a few Arequipa landscapes known). Ink mark with Arequipa California 269. 2 1/4" x 6 1/4" d. **$20,400**

Photo courtesy Rago Arts and Auction Center, Lambertville, N.J.; www.RagoArts.com

Batchelder and Brown early and large triptych of pumpkin field. (Featured in the exposition, "California Tile: The Golden Era 1910-1940," The California Heritage Museum, Santa Monica, 2001.) A few small edge chips. Stamped BATCHELDER PASADENA. 19 1/2" x 63". **$10,800**

Rose Cabat

Rose Cabat, born 1914, New York, is a Tucson, Ariz.-based potter known for her "feelies" — small, narrow-necked porcelain pots with soft glazes that feel feathery to the touch.

Photo courtesy Belhorn Auction Services LLC, Columbus, Ohio; www.Belhorn.com

Rose Cabat "Feelie" in turquoise with color streaking down the sides. Marked 841 Cabat 48. Mint. 3 3/4" h x 1 5/8" w. **$500**

Photo courtesy Belhorn Auction Services LLC, Columbus, Ohio; www.Belhorn.com

Rose Cabat fig "Feelie" with shades of lime green and tan. Marked Cabat 12 43. Mint. 3 1/8" h x 2" w. **$575**

Photo courtesy Belhorn Auction Services LLC, Columbus, Ohio; www.Belhorn.com

Rose Cabat "Feelie" with rare performance trial glaze. Marked 84T Cabat 28N. Mint. 2 1/2" h x 2 1/4" w. **$700**

Camark

Camark Art Tile and Pottery Co. operated in Camden, Ark., from 1926 until the mid-1970s. Art director John Lessell created many of the firm's distinctive glazes.

Camark, Blue Crackle Bright folded-rim vase in deep cobalt blue with gold crackle effect. Marked with die impressed Arkansas stamp. 7 1/8" h x 7 3/8" w. **$700**

Photo courtesy Belhorn Auction Services LLC, Columbus, Ohio; www.Belhorn.com

Camark, Ivory Crackle Matte vase. Marked with a gold Arkansas ink stamp over an impressed mark. Mint. 10 3/8" h x 5 1/4" w. **$525**

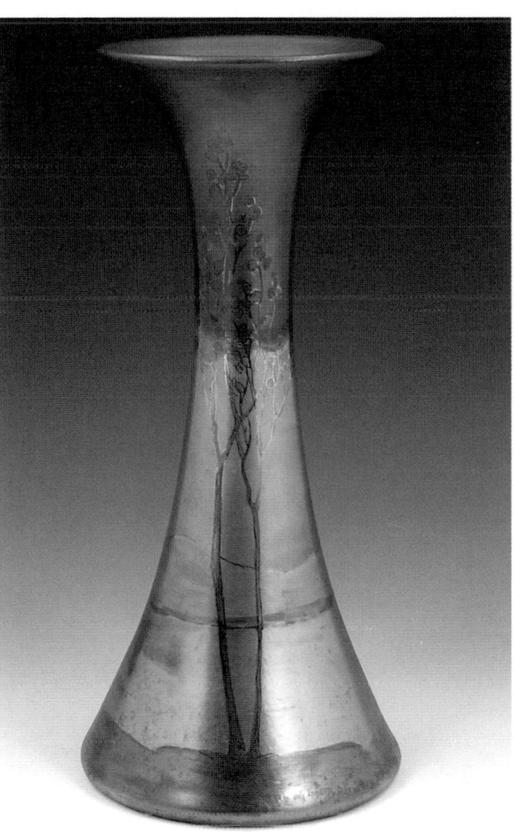

Photo courtesy Belhorn Auction Services LLC, Columbus, Ohio; www.Belhorn.com

Camark Lessell, tapered trumpet vase with scene of trees on a lake with deep red upper sky and golden iridescent tones. Marked Lessell. 10" h. **$1,100**

Photo courtesy Belhorn Auction Services LLC, Columbus, Ohio; www.Belhorn.com

Camark, Jeanne vase with a plethora of iridescent flowers on a black background with gold trim. 9 3/8" h x 4 3/4" w. **$800**

Photo courtesy Belhorn Auction Services LLC, Columbus, Ohio; www.Belhorn.com

Camark Lessell (LeCamark), vase with scene of trees on a lake with deep red upper sky and golden iridescent tones. Marked Le-Camark. 6" h. **$675**

Photo courtesy Belhorn Auction Services LLC, Columbus, Ohio; www.Belhorn.com

Camark Lessell (LeCamark), vase with scene of palm trees on a shore, mountains in the far background and the sun behind a cloud. Decorated in iridescent gold and bronze tones. Marked Le-Camark. 9 7/8" h x 5" w. **$925**

Photo courtesy Rago Arts and Auction Center, Lambertville, N.J.; www.RagoArts.com

Clewell Pottery Co. (Canton, Ohio, 1902-1940, 1951-1965) tall copper-clad vase, modeled around a stylized Arts & Crafts landscape, rare. Fine original patina. A few splits to copper. Pottery body stamped X2. 13 1/2" x 4". **$3,900**

Clewell Pottery Co., (Canton, Ohio, 1902-1940, 1951-1965) copper-clad vase with a good verdigris patina. Incised Clewell 351-2-9. 7" x 3 3/4". **$1,320**

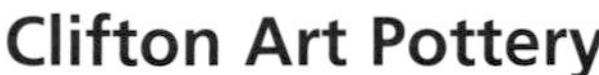

Clifton Art Pottery

CLIFTON

The Clifton Art Pottery, Newark, N.J., was established by William A. Long, once associated with Lonhuda Pottery, and Fred Tschirner, a chemist.

Production consisted of two major lines: Crystal Patina, which resembled true porcelain with a subdued crystal-like glaze, and Indian Ware or Western Influence, an adaptation of the American Indians' unglazed and decorated pottery with a high-glazed black interior. Other lines included Robin's-Egg Blue and Tirrube. Robin's-Egg Blue is a variation of the Crystal Patina line, but in blue-green instead of straw-colored hues and with a less-prominent crushed-crystal effect in the glaze. Tirrube, which is often artist signed, features brightly colored, slip-decorated flowers on a terra-cotta ground.

Marks are incised or impressed. Early pieces may be dated and impressed with a shape number. Indian wares are identified by tribes.

Photo courtesy Rago Arts and Auction Center, Lambertville, N.J.; www.RagoArts.com

Clifton, vases (two) in matte green glaze, one embossed with poppies. Both marked, poppy vase hand-incised Clifton First Fire October 1905. 5 1/2" and 6 1/2". **$1,200 pair**

Common Ground, (Madison, Wis.), tile, contemporary, calla lily design, held in an Arts & Crafts-style frame, marked, signed by Eric Olson, #262, 8" sq. **$75**

Photo courtesy Belhorn Auction Services LLC, Columbus, Ohio; www.Belhorn.com

J.B. Cole, Seagrove, N.C., vase with ring handles attributed to Waymon Cole with chrome red treatment. Unmarked. Excellent condition. 16 1/2" h x 16" w. **$675**

Photo courtesy Belhorn Auction Services LLC, Columbus, Ohio; www.Belhorn.com

Cowan, Elephant bookends in Oriental Red by Margaret Postgate. Marked with die-impressed circular Cowan mark and COWAN in die-impressed letters. Mint and uncrazed. 7 3/8" h. **$1,000 pair**

Cowan Pottery

R. Guy Cowan was born in 1884 in East Liverpool, Ohio, and educated at the New York State School of Ceramics at Alfred. He founded the Cowan Pottery Studio in Lakewood, Ohio (a suburb of Cleveland) in 1912. The firm closed in 1931.

Photo courtesy Belhorn Auction Services LLC, Columbus, Ohio; www.Belhorn.com

Cowan, Art Deco figurine titled, "Introspection." Finish in black semi-matte glaze. Designed by A. Drexler Jacobson, the piece is marked with die-impressed circular Cowan mark and the artist's monogram on the plinth. Mint and uncrazed. 8 3/8" h. **$1,600**

Photo courtesy Belhorn Auction Services LLC, Columbus, Ohio; www.Belhorn.com

Cowan, Kneeling Nude flower figure in Original Ivory attributed to Walter Sinz. Unmarked. Mint and uncrazed. 6" h. **$800**

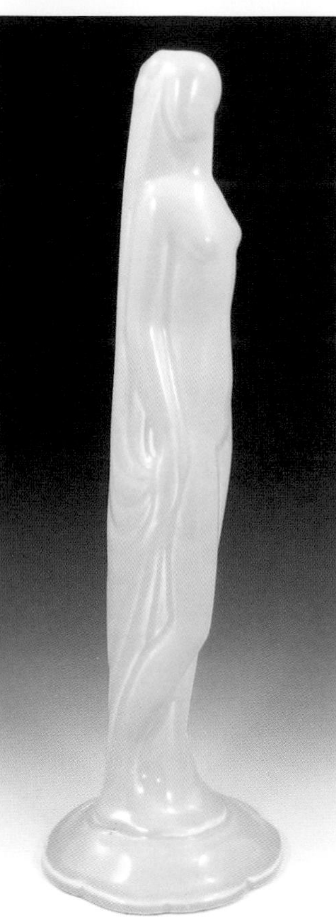

Photo courtesy Belhorn Auction Services LLC, Columbus, Ohio; www.Belhorn.com

Cowan, Lorelei lamp base in April Green by Wayland Gregory. Marked COWAN in die-impressed letters. There is a tight 1" stress line to the base. 16 3/4" h. **$875**

Photo courtesy Belhorn Auction Services LLC, Columbus, Ohio; www.Belhorn.com

Cowan, F-9 Pan flower figure in Special Ivory. Marked with die-impressed circular Cowan mark and COWAN in die-impressed letters and F9 in crayon. Mint. 9 3/8" h. **$325**

Photo courtesy Belhorn Auction Services LLC, Columbus, Ohio; www.Belhorn.com

Cowan, Hunting Set, Standing Gentleman in Shadow White. Marked COWAN in die-impressed letters. Mint. 7 3/4" h. **$350**

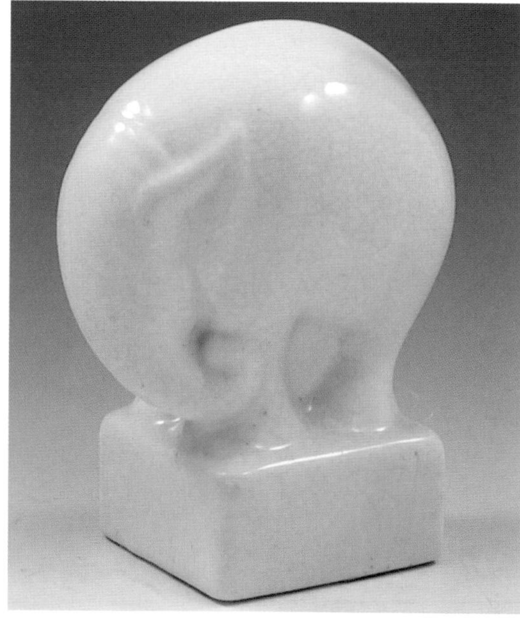

Photo courtesy Belhorn Auction Services LLC, Columbus, Ohio; www.Belhorn.com

Cowan, D-3 elephant paperweight designed by Margaret Postgate (circa 1930) in ivory semi-gloss glaze. Marked with die-impressed circular Cowan mark and COWAN in die-impressed letters. Mint. 4 3/8" h x 3 1/2" w. **$300**

Photo courtesy Belhorn Auction Services LLC, Columbus, Ohio; www.Belhorn.com

Cowan, V-99 handled vase in Lemon yellow designed by Viktor Schreckengost. Marked twice with die-impressed circular Cowan mark and V99 in black crayon. 6" h. **$375**

Photo courtesy Belhorn Auction Services LLC, Columbus, Ohio; www.Belhorn.com

Cowan, V-99 vase by Viktor Schreckengost in Egyptian Blue. Marked with die-impressed circular Cowan mark and V99 in black crayon. Mint. 5" h x 7" w. **$300**

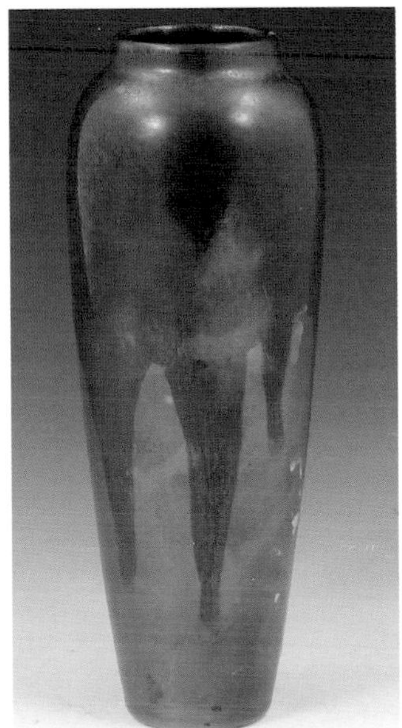

Photo courtesy Belhorn Auction Services LLC, Columbus, Ohio; www.Belhorn.com

Cowan, #552 vase with Mulberry over Copper flambe. Marked Cowan Pottery 552 in block letters. 7 1/2" h. **$240**

Photo courtesy Belhorn Auction Services LLC, Columbus, Ohio; www.Belhorn.com

Cowan, V-853-A Modernist or Stepped Parfait vase in April Green. Marked with die-impressed circular Cowan mark. Mint. 5 7/8" h x 4 5/8" w. **$450**

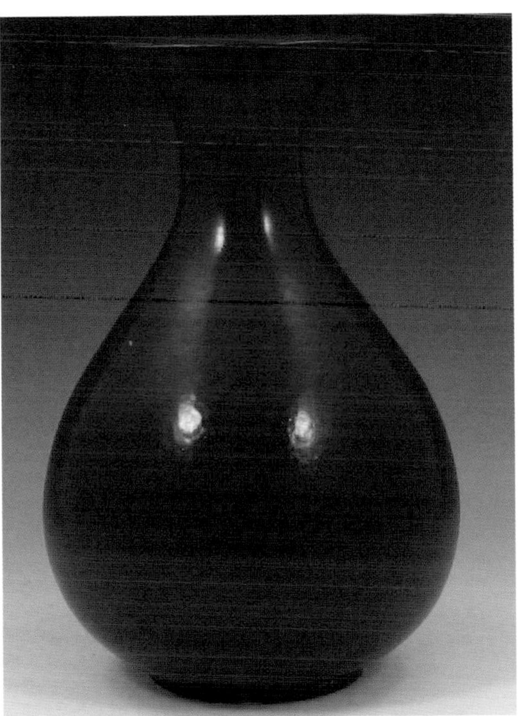

Photo courtesy Belhorn Auction Services LLC, Columbus, Ohio; www.Belhorn.com

Cowan, V-932 vase in uncommon Feu Rouge glaze. Marked with die-impressed circular Cowan mark and COWAN in die-impressed letters. Mint and uncrazed. 8" h. **$290**

Photo courtesy Belhorn Auction Services LLC, Columbus, Ohio; www.Belhorn.com

Cowan, #933 vase in Feu Rouge. Marked with die-impressed circular Cowan mark and 933 in black crayon. Mint. 5 1/2" h. **$230**

Photo courtesy Belhorn Auction Services LLC, Columbus, Ohio; www.Belhorn.com

R. Guy Cowan, mustard pot, rare and early, with sterling silver lid by Horace E. Potter and an ivory finial. The spoon is also ivory and marked "FRANCE." Incised with RGC monogram and signed R.G. Cowan. Mint. 4 1/4" h x 2 7/8" w. **$3,000**

Photo courtesy Belhorn Auction Services LLC, Columbus, Ohio; www.Belhorn.com

Cowan, vase with unusual matrix glaze of purple and yellow. Marked with die-impressed circular Cowan mark. Also marked with illegible shape notation and 881X/Purple. Mint and uncrazed. 6 1/2" h x 4 3/4" w. **$525**

Photo courtesy Rago Arts and Auction Center, Lambertville, N.J.; www.RagoArts.com

Albert Cusick exceptional and tall vase, probably done at the Craven Art Pottery, East Liverpool, Ohio, completely decorated in squeeze bag with a large scenic band flanked by curvilinear flowers and tulips in polychrome. Cusick's work of this caliber is extremely rare. Incised Cusick on side. 14 1/2" x 5". **$9,000**

Dedham Pottery

Alexander W. Robertson established a pottery in Chelsea, Mass., in about 1866. After his brother, Hugh Cornwall Robertson, joined him in 1868, the firm was called A. W. & H. C. Robertson. Their father, James Robertson, joined his sons in 1872, and the name Chelsea Keramic Art Works Robertson and Sons was used.

The pottery's initial products were simple flower and bean pots, but the firm quickly expanded its output to include a wide variety of artistic pottery. It produced a fine red-ware body used in classical forms, some with black backgrounds imitating ancient Greek and Apulian (an Iron and Bronze Age Greek colony) works. It experimented with under-glaze slip decoration on vases. The Chelsea Keramic Art Works also produced high-glazed vases, pitchers and plaques with a buff clay body, with either sculpted or molded applied decoration.

James Robertson died in 1880 and Alexander moved to California in 1884, leaving Hugh alone in Chelsea, where his experiments eventually yielded an imitation of the Chinese Ming-era blood-red glaze. Hugh's vases with that glaze were marked with an impressed "CKAW." Creating these red-glazed vases was expensive, and even though they received critical acclaim, the company declared bankruptcy in 1889.

Recapitalized by a circle of Boston art patrons in 1891, Hugh started the Chelsea Pottery U.S., which produced gray crackle-glazed dinnerware with cobalt-blue decorations, the rabbit pattern being the most popular.

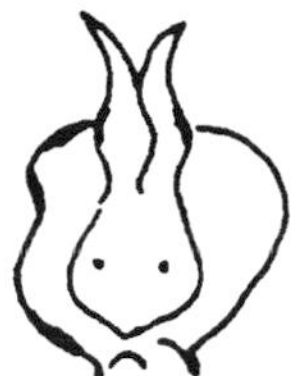

The business moved to new facilities in Dedham, Mass., and began production in 1896 under the name Dedham Pottery. Hugh's son and grandson operated the business until it closed in 1943, by which time between 50 and 80 patterns had been produced.

The following marks help determine the approximate age of items:

- "Chelsea Keramic Art Works Robertson and Sons," impressed, 1874-1880.
- "CKAW," impressed, 1875-1889.
- "CPUS," impressed in a cloverleaf, 1891-1895.
- Foreshortened rabbit only, impressed, 1894-1896.
- Conventional rabbit with "Dedham Pottery" in square blue-stamped mark along with one impressed foreshortened rabbit, 1896-1928.
- Blue rabbit stamped mark, "reg. stamp" beneath, along with two impressed foreshortened rabbit marks, 1929-1943

Photo courtesy James D. Julia Auctioneers, Fairfield, Maine; www.JuliaAuctions.com

Dedham Pottery "Polar Bear" Pattern Plate. Painted in dark blue with a border of polar bears on ice floes against a band of water. Stamped "Dedham Pottery" rabbit mark in underglaze blue. 9 3/4" diameter.
$690

Photo courtesy James D. Julia Auctioneers, Fairfield, Maine; www.JuliaAuctions.com

Dedham Pottery Tri-Color "Rabbit" Pattern Plate. Painted in medium to dark blue with a border of crouching rabbits alternating with rare raised green decorated foliage. Impressed with "CPUS" mark (Chelsea Pottery US, circa 1881-1895). 8 5/8" diameter. **$8,190**

Dedham Pottery, "Elephant" Child's Mug And "Night And Morning" Pitcher. The 3 1/2" high child's mug in Elephant pattern, stamped with "DEDHAM POTTERY" blue rabbit mark. The 5" pitcher in Night and Morning pattern, stamped with "DEDHAM POTTERY/REGISTERED" blue rabbit mark. Mug with old professional repair to handle. Pitcher with flake on top edge near spout. .... **$468 pair**

Dedham Pottery, "Horse Chestnut" Pattern Steak Platter And Three Other Pieces. The first, a 14" oval platter in Horse Chestnut pattern. The second, a #1 Grape pattern 9" bowl. The third, an 8 1/2" Chick pattern plate. The fourth, a 5 1/2" Chick pattern bowl. All with the "DEDHAM POTTERY" rabbit mark in blue. The platter with some minor bubbling, all with normal crackle. .... **$3,335 all**

Six Dedham Pottery Butter Plates. Consisting of two Duck plates, one Horse Chestnut plate, one Iris plate, one Magnolia plate, and one Pond Lily plate. Four with impressed rabbit marks, and all with "DEDHAM POTTERY" rabbit marks in under-glaze blue. Average diameter 6". Iris plate with worn glazing and minor discoloration, the Pond Lily with rim chips, glazing loss, and wear. **$300 all**

Photo courtesy James D. Julia Auctioneers, Fairfield, Maine; www.JuliaAuctions.com

Photo courtesy James D. Julia Auctioneers, Fairfield, Maine; www.JuliaAuctions.com

Dedham Pottery "Elephant And Baby" Pattern Plate. Painted in dark blue with a border of elephants walking with single calf following. Two impressed rabbit marks, also stamped "DEDHAM POTTERY REGISTERED" rabbit mark in under-glaze blue. 8 1/2" diameter. Flake in foot rim. **$805**

Photo courtesy James D. Julia Auctioneers, Fairfield, Maine; www.JuliaAuctions.com

Dedham Pottery "Turtles" Pattern Plate. Painted in dark blue, the border with five pairs of turtles. Stamped "DEDHAM POTTERY" rabbit mark. 8 3/8" diameter. With 1/8" rim imperfection under glaze, small area of craquelure on underside of plate base. **$575**

Photo courtesy James D. Julia Auctioneers, Fairfield, Maine; www.JuliaAuctions.com

Unusual Dedham Pottery "Crested Duck" Pattern Plate. In medium blue, the border decorated with swimming ducks with crested heads in repeat, among rolling waves and water lilies. With impressed rabbit mark and the word "Dry" in under-glaze blue. 8 1/2" diameter. Minor foot rim flake. **$230**

Photo courtesy James D. Julia Auctioneers, Fairfield, Maine; www.JuliaAuctions.com

Dedham Pottery Pitcher, Eggcup And Creamer. Including a No. 14-size Rabbit pattern pitcher (6 1/2" h.) in the design of a No. 2 (with single blue line above rabbit band), a single eggcup in Elephant and Baby pattern (2 1/2" h.), and a Style of 1850 pattern pitcher with fluted shaped sides and leaf-tip handle (5" h.). Nominal glazing defects. **$1,404 all**

Photo courtesy James D. Julia Auctioneers, Fairfield, Maine; www.JuliaAuctions.com

Two Dedham Pottery "No. 2" Sugar Bowls. The first in Elephant And Baby pattern, the second in Elephant pattern. Each with lid and decorated with a dark blue border of striding elephants. Both with "DEDHAM POTTERY REGISTERED" rabbit mark in under-glaze blue. Each 3 1/2" overall h. x 4 1/4" diameter. **$1,380 both**

Photo courtesy James D. Julia Auctioneers, Fairfield, Maine; www.JuliaAuctions.com

Dedham Pottery "Elephant And Baby" Pattern Bowl. The No. 5 bowl with border painted in dark blue decorated with striding elephants and calf following, stamped with "DEDHAM POTTERY" rabbit mark in under-glaze blue. 5 1/4" diameter. Foot rim flake and glazing imperfections. **$690**

Photo courtesy James D. Julia Auctioneers, Fairfield, Maine; www.JuliaAuctions.com

Collection Of Dedham Pottery Cups And Saucers. Each cup-and-saucer set decorated in the following patterns: Elephant, Swan, Azalea, Magnolia, Duck, Iris, together with a Rabbit pattern demitasse set. All marked with "DEDHAM POTTERY" rabbit mark in under-glaze blue. Average c/s diameters 4" and 6" respectively. Demitasse set 2" and 4". **$1,035 all**

Lonhuda

Lonhuda Pottery Co. of Steubenville, Ohio, was organized in 1892 by William Long, with investors W.H. Hunter and Alfred Day. "Lonhuda" combines the first two letters of the partners' last names.

Denver Denaura/Lonhuda, baluster vase modeled and incised with daffodils, covered in vellum matte green glaze, rare form. 1 1/2" tight hairline from rim. Stamped indigo arrow mark, Denaura 85 18?, incised Lonhuda. 8 1/2" x 5". **$3,000**

Photo courtesy Belhorn Auction Services LLC, Columbus, Ohio; www.Belhorn.com

Ephraim Faience Pottery, (Deerfield, Wis.), #817 Dragonfly vase in matte green. Retired 12/31/02 with an edition of 301 pieces. Marked with circular 2000 Ephraim mark and Kevin Hicks' impressed name. Mint. 12" h. **$625**

Photo courtesy Belhorn Auction Services LLC, Columbus, Ohio; www.Belhorn.com

Ephraim Faience Pottery, (Deerfield, Wis.), #318 Underwater Crab vase in dark green matte and tan. One of 61 made. 9 1/2" w x 4 1/2" h. **$450**

Fiesta

The Homer Laughlin China Co. introduced Fiesta, dinnerware in January 1936 at the Pottery and Glass Show in Pittsburgh. Frederick Rhead designed the pattern; Arthur Kraft and Bill Bensford molded it. Dr. A.V. Bleininger and H.W. Thiemecke developed the glazes.

The original five colors were red, dark blue, light green (with a trace of blue), brilliant yellow and ivory. A vigorous marketing campaign took place between 1939 and 1943. In mid-1937, turquoise was added. Red was removed in 1943 because some of the chemicals used to produce it were essential to the war effort; it did not reappear until 1959. In 1951, light green, dark blue and ivory were retired and forest green, rose, chartreuse and gray were added to the line. Other color changes took place in the late 1950s, including the addition of "medium green."

Fiesta, was redesigned in 1969 and discontinued about 1972. In 1986, Homer Laughlin reintroduced Fiesta. The new china body shrinks more than the old semi-vitreous and ironstone pieces, thus making the new pieces slightly smaller than the earlier pieces. The modern colors are also different in tone or hue, e.g., the cobalt blue is darker than the old blue.

Homer Laughlin has continued to introduce new colors in the popular Fiesta, pattern. It's important for collectors to understand when different colors were made.

All Fiesta, listings and images in this edition come courtesy of Strawser Auction Group, Wolcottville, Ind., *www.strawserauctions.com,* facilitated by Artfact, *www.artfact.com.*

Fiesta, #1 mixing bowl lid, light green. **$190**
Fiesta, #1 mixing bowl, red. **$100**
Fiesta, #1 mixing bowl, yellow, inside rings, rim nick. **$50**
Fiesta, #2 mixing bowl lid, yellow, glaze nick. **$150**
Fiesta, #2 mixing bowl, cobalt, inside rings, rim nicks and wear to bottom. **$10**
Fiesta, #2 mixing bowl, light green, inside rings. **$50**
Fiesta, #3 mixing bowl lid, red, glaze nick. **$140**
Fiesta, #3 mixing bowl, cobalt. **$80**
Fiesta, #3 mixing bowl, light green. **$25**
Fiesta, #3 mixing bowl, yellow. **$55**
Fiesta, #4 mixing bowl lid, light green. **$250**
Fiesta, #4 mixing bowl, ivory. **$35**
Fiesta, #5 mixing bowl, turquoise. **$35**
Fiesta, #5 mixing bowl, yellow. **$40**
Fiesta, #6 mixing bowl, red, inside rings. **$90**
Fiesta, #6 mixing bowl, turquoise, glaze imperfection to bottom. **$45**
Fiesta, #7 mixing bowl, cobalt, inside rings, minor scratches to bottom. **$140**
Fiesta, #7 mixing bowl, red, wear to bottom, rim nicks. . **$70**

Color Guide		
Color Name	Color palette	Years of Production
Red	Reddish-orange	1936-43, 1959-72
Blue	Cobalt blue	1936-51
Ivory	Creamy yellow-white	1936-51
Yellow	Golden yellow	1936-69
Green	Light green	1936-51
Turquoise	Sky blue	1937-69
Rose	Dark dusky rose	1951-59
Chartreuse	Yellow-green	1951-59
Forest green	Dark hunter green	1951-59
Gray	Light gray	1951-59
Medium green	Deep bright green	1959-69
Antique gold	Dark butterscotch	1969-72
Turf green	Olive green	1969-72
Cobalt blue	Very dark blue, almost black	1986-
Rose	Bubblegum pink	1986-
White	Pearly white	1986-
Black	High gloss black	1986-
Apricot	Peach-beige	1986-98
Turquoise	Greenish-blue	1988-
Yellow	Pale yellow	1987-2002
Periwinkle blue	Pastel gray-blue	1989-
Sea mist green	Pastel light green	1991-
Lilac	Pastel violet	1993-95
Persimmon	Coral	1995-
Sapphire (Bloomingdale's exclusive)	Blue	1996-97
Chartreuse	More yellow than green	1997-99
Pearl gray	Similar to vintage gray, more transparent	1999-2001
Juniper green	Dark blue-green	1999-2001
Cinnabar	Brown-maroon	2000-
Sunflower	Muted yellow	2001-
Plum	Rich purple	2002-
Shamrock	Grassy green	2002-
Tangerine	Soft orange	2003-
Scarlet	Deep red	2004 -
Peacock	Rich light blue	2005 -
Heather	Muted burgundy	2006 - 2009
Evergreen	Dark green	2007 -
Ivory	Ivory	2008 -
Chocolate	Dark brown	2008 -
Lemongrass	Sage green	2009
Marigold (75th Anniversary)	Rich yellow 2008-2009	

Fiesta, #7 mixing bowl, turquoise. **$200**

Fiesta, 10 1/2" compartment plate group: cobalt, yellow, two turquoise, red and forest green, each with minor wear. **$25 all**

Fiesta, 10 1/2" compartment plate, chartreuse. **$10**

Fiesta, 10 1/2" compartment plate, gray. **$10**

Fiesta, 10 1/2" compartment plate, ivory. **$5**

Fiesta, 10 1/2" compartment plate, light green. **$20**

Fiesta, 10 1/2" compartment plate, rose. **$10**

Fiesta, 10 1/2" compartment plate, yellow. **$10**

Fiesta, 10" flower vase, ivory. **$350**

Fiesta, 10" flower vase, light green. **$170**

Fiesta, 10" flower vase, red. **$375**

Fiesta, 10" flower vase, turquoise. **$225**

Fiesta, 10" plate group, all 11 colors: medium green, gray, rose, forest green, chartreuse, red, cobalt, ivory, turquoise, light green and yellow. **$65 all**

Fiesta, 10" plate group: eight medium green, two with glaze misses. **$160 all**

Fiesta, 10" plate group: six chartreuse. **$40 all**

Fiesta, 10" plate group: six cobalt. **$15 all**

Fiesta, 10" plate group: six forest green. **$40 all**

Fiesta, 10" plate group: six gray. **$15 all**

Fiesta, 10" plate group: six ivory. **$15 all**

Fiesta, 10" plate group: six light green. **$15 all**

Fiesta, 10" plate group: six red. **$60 all**

Fiesta, 10" plate group: six rose. **$35 all**

Fiesta, 10" plate group: six turquoise. **$25 all**

Fiesta, 10" plate group: six yellow. **$10 all**

Fiesta, 11 3/4" fruit bowl, light green, rim nick. **$65**

Fiesta, 11 3/4" fruit bowl, red. **$100**

Fiesta, 12" compartment plate red and cobalt, minor nick to red. **$15**

Fiesta, 12" compartment plate, light green. **$20**

Fiesta, 12" compartment plate, yellow. **$15**

Fiesta, 12" comport, ivory. **$55**

Fiesta, 12" comport, red. **$95**

Fiesta, 12" comport, turquoise. **$50**

Fiesta, 12" flower vase, ivory. **$400**

Fiesta, 12" flower vase, turquoise. **$350**

Fiesta, bud vase with smoked brown/burnt glaze, unusual glaze. **$650**

Fiesta, carafe in experimental rose ebony color, no lid, chip to base, extremely rare. **$1,050**

Fiesta, 13" chop plate group, all six original colors, red, cobalt, ivory, turquoise, light green and yellow. **$35 all**

Fiesta, 13" chop plate, chartreuse. **$25**

Fiesta, 13" chop plate, forest green. **$10**

Fiesta, 13" chop plate, gray. **$5**

Fiesta, 13" chop plate, ivory. **$10**

Fiesta, 13" chop plate, medium green. **$110**

Fiesta, 13" chop plate, red. **$15**

Fiesta, 13" chop plate, rose. **$30**

Fiesta, 15" chop plate, chartreuse. **$10**

Fiesta, 15" chop plate, cobalt. **$10**

Fiesta, 15" chop plate, forest green. **$10**

Fiesta, 15" chop plate, gray. **$15**

Fiesta, 15" chop plate, ivory. **$10**

Fiesta, 15" chop plate, light green. **$5**

Fiesta, 15" chop plate, red. **$20**

Fiesta, 15" chop plate, rose. **$25**

Fiesta, 15" chop plate, turquoise and light green. **$20**

Fiesta, 15" chop plate, turquoise. **$35**

Fiesta, 15" chop plate, yellow. **$5**

Fiesta, 1955 green 10" calendar plate. **$15**

Fiesta, 1955 ivory 10" calendar plate. **$5**

Fiesta, 4 3/4" fruit bowl group, 10 colors: forest green, rose gray, chartreuse, red, cobalt, ivory, turquoise, light green and yellow. **$50 all**

Fiesta, 4 3/4" fruit bowl group, four turquoise. **$5 all**

Fiesta, 4 3/4" fruit bowl group, four yellow. **$5 all**

Fiesta, 4 3/4" fruit bowl group: ivory, turquoise, yellow, two gray, forest green, cobalt, chartreuse and rose. **$25 all**

Fiesta, 4 3/4" fruit bowl group: rose, two ivory, two yellow, light green and turquoise. **$20 all**

Fiesta, 4 3/4" fruit bowl, medium green. **$180**

Fiesta, 5 1/2" fruit bowl group: medium green, rose, forest green, chartreuse, red, two cobalt, ivory, turquoise, light green and yellow. **$80 all**

Fiesta, 5 1/2" fruit group: three yellow, turquoise, forest green and ivory. **$25 all**

Fiesta, 5 1/2" fruit, cobalt, "Lazarus 1851-1938 87th Anniversary." **$80**

Fiesta, 6" dessert bowl group, 50's colors: chartreuse, gray, rose, forest green, rim nick to forest green. **$35 all**

Fiesta, 10" plate group: five medium green. **$100 all**

Fiesta, 6" dessert bowl group: red, cobalt, turquoise, light green and yellow. **$50 all**
Fiesta, 6" dessert bowl, medium green. **160**
Fiesta, 6" dessert bowl, rose. **$15**
Fiesta, 7" plate group, all 11 colors, medium green, chartreuse, forest green, gray, rose, red, cobalt, ivory, turquoise, light green and yellow. **$50 all**
Fiesta, 7" plate group: six chartreuse. **$25 all**
Fiesta, 7" plate group: six cobalt. **$25 all**
Fiesta, 7" plate group: six forest green. **$25 all**
Fiesta, 7" plate group: six ivory. **$15 all**
Fiesta, 7" plate group: six light green. **$15 all**
Fiesta, 7" plate group: six medium green. **$45 all**
Fiesta, 7" plate group: six red. **$30 all**
Fiesta, 7" plate group: six rose. **$10 all**
Fiesta, 7" plate group: six turquoise. **$10 all**
Fiesta, 7" plate group: six yellow. **$10 all**
Fiesta, 8 1/2" nappy bowl group, original six colors: red, cobalt, ivory, turquoise, light green and yellow. **$35 all**
Fiesta, 8 1/2" nappy bowl group: chartreuse, forest green and rose. **$20 all**

Fiesta, covered onion soup bowl, turquoise, rare. **$2,700**

Fiesta, 8 1/2" nappy bowl group: red, ivory, turquoise, yellow and light green. **$15 all**
Fiesta, 8 1/2" nappy bowl, ivory. **$5**
Fiesta, 8 1/2" nappy bowl, medium green. **$30**
Fiesta, 8 1/2" nappy bowl, rose. **$5**
Fiesta, 8" flower vase, ivory. **$170**
Fiesta, 8" flower vase, light green. **$130**
Fiesta, 8" flower vase, red. **$250**
Fiesta, 8" flower vase, turquoise, hairline. **$35**
Fiesta, 8" flower vase, yellow. **$140**
Fiesta, 9 1/2" nappy bowl, cobalt. **$40**
Fiesta, 9 1/2" nappy bowl, ivory. **$35**
Fiesta, 9 1/2" nappy bowl, light green. **$35**
Fiesta, 9 1/2" nappy bowl, red. **$30**
Fiesta, 9 1/2" nappy bowl, turquoise. **$15**
Fiesta, 9 1/2" nappy bowl, yellow. **$35**
Fiesta, 9" plate group: eight yellow. **$10 all**
Fiesta, 9" plate group: seven cobalt. **$5 all**
Fiesta, 9" trial plate in rare experimental caramel color, numbered #3431 on back. **$375**
Fiesta, ashtray, "Roosevelt Hotel in Pittsburgh, PA", red. **$90**
Fiesta, ashtray, chartreuse. **$30**
Fiesta, ashtray, cobalt. **$15**
Fiesta, ashtray, forest green. **$30**
Fiesta, ashtray, gray. **$10**
Fiesta, ashtray, ivory. **$25**
Fiesta, ashtray, light green and turquoise. **$30**
Fiesta, ashtray, light green and yellow. **$25**
Fiesta, ashtray, light green. **$10**
Fiesta, ashtray, medium green. **$130**
Fiesta, bud vase, cobalt. **$60**
Fiesta, bud vase, ivory. **$30**
Fiesta, bud vase, light green. **$25**
Fiesta, bud vase, red. **$25**
Fiesta, bud vase, turquoise. **$15**
Fiesta, bud vase, yellow. **$65**
Fiesta, bulb candle holder with experimental gold glaze over light green, rare. **$120**
Fiesta, bulb candle holders, yellow. **$40 pair**
Fiesta, bulb candleholders, cobalt, nick to one. **$35 pair**

Fiesta, bulb candleholders, ivory. **$35 pair**
Fiesta, bulb candleholders, light green. **$40 pair**
Fiesta, bulb candleholders, three, red. **$65 all**
Fiesta, bulb candleholders, turquoise. **$35 pair**
Fiesta, carafe base, ivory. **$45**
Fiesta, carafe lid, turquoise, very minor nick to tip. **$20**
Fiesta, carafe, cobalt. **$100**
Fiesta, carafe, red. **$95**
Fiesta, carafe, turquoise. **$120**
Fiesta, casserole lid, forest green. **$55**
Fiesta, casserole lid, ivory. **$20**
Fiesta, casserole lid, medium green. **$60**
Fiesta, casserole lid, turquoise. **$5**
Fiesta, casserole lid, yellow. **$20**
Fiesta, casserole, gray. **$80**
Fiesta, casserole, medium green, rim chip to lid. **$225**
Fiesta, casserole, medium green, very minor rim glaze nick to base rim. **$325**
Fiesta, casserole, rose, rim glaze nick to base. **$25**
Fiesta, casserole, turquoise. **$25**
Fiesta, casserole, yellow. **$70**
Fiesta, coffee pot, cobalt, repair to finial. **$20**
Fiesta, coffee pot, cobalt. **$70**
Fiesta, coffee pot, ivory. **$85**
Fiesta, coffee pot, red. **$100**
Fiesta, coffee pot, turquoise, nick to finial. **$15**
Fiesta, coffee pot, yellow, nick to finial. **$30**
Fiesta, comport, light green. **$50**
Fiesta, comport, red. **$50**
Fiesta, covered onion soup bowl, cobalt, minor glaze nick to base handle. **$150**
Fiesta, covered onion soup bowl, ivory. **$200**
Fiesta, covered onion soup bowl, light green. **$200**
Fiesta, covered onion soup bowl, red, minor glaze nick to base handle. **$275**
Fiesta, covered onion soup bowl, yellow. **$200**
Fiesta, cream and sugar, chartreuse. **$40 both**
Fiesta, cream and sugar, gray. **$15 both**
Fiesta, cream and sugar, hairline to creamer, gray. **$5 both**
Fiesta, cream and sugar, medium green. **$150 both**
Fiesta, cream and sugar, minor nick to finial of sugar lid, medium green. **$60 both**

Fiesta, marmalade, red. **$160**

Fiesta, mustard, yellow. **$130**

Fiesta, cream and sugar, nick to lid finial, forest green. **$5 both**
Fiesta, cream and sugar, red. **$5 both**
Fiesta, cream and sugar, rose. **$10 both**
Fiesta, cream and sugar, turquoise. **$10 both**
Fiesta, cream soup group, original six colors: red, cobalt, ivory, turquoise, light green and yellow. **$180 all**
Fiesta, cream soup with metal handle, chartreuse. **$45**
Fiesta, cream soup with metal handle, rose. **$60**
Fiesta, cream soup, turquoise. **$10**
Fiesta, cup/saucer group, all 11 colors, medium green, gray, rose, forest green, chartreuse, red, cobalt, ivory, yellow, turquoise, and light green. **$45 all**
Fiesta, deep plate group, 50's colors: chartreuse, rose, gray and forest green. **$45 all**
Fiesta, deep plate group, original six colors: red, cobalt, ivory, turquoise, light green and yellow. **$80 all**
Fiesta, deep plate, medium green. **$25**
Fiesta, demitasse coffee pot lid, yellow. **$60**
Fiesta, demitasse coffee pot, ivory. **$200**
Fiesta, demitasse coffee pot, yellow. **$150**
Fiesta, demitasse cup/saucer, chartreuse. **$140**
Fiesta, demitasse cup/saucer, cobalt. **$50**
Fiesta, demitasse cup/saucer, forest green. **$140**
Fiesta, demitasse cup/saucer, gray. **$150**
Fiesta, demitasse cup/saucer, ivory. **$50**
Fiesta, demitasse cup/saucer, light green. **$30**
Fiesta, demitasse cup/saucer, red. **$45**
Fiesta, demitasse cup/saucer, rose. **$160**
Fiesta, demitasse cup/saucer, turquoise. **$40**
Fiesta, demitasse cup/saucer, yellow. **$45**
Fiesta, demitasse saucer, chartreuse, hairline. **$10**
Fiesta, demitasse saucer, forest green. **$55**
Fiesta, disk juice pitcher, celadon green. **$85**
Fiesta, disk juice pitcher, red. **$325**
Fiesta, disk juice pitcher, yellow. **$5**
Fiesta, disk water pitcher, chartreuse. **$35**
Fiesta, disk water pitcher, cobalt. **$30**
Fiesta, disk water pitcher, ivory. **$35**
Fiesta, disk water pitcher, light green. **$35**
Fiesta, disk water pitcher, minor nick, forest green. **$10**
Fiesta, disk water pitcher, red, minor nick. **$25**
Fiesta, disk water pitcher, turquoise. **$25**

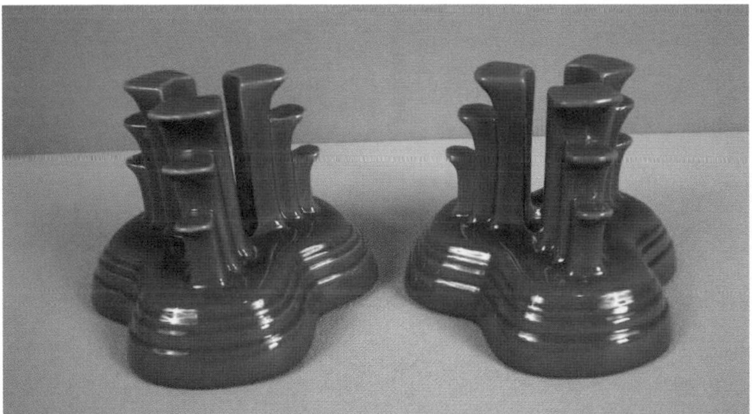

Fiesta, tripod candleholders, red. **$225 pair**

Fiesta, eggcup group, original six colors: red, cobalt, ivory, turquoise, light green and yellow, nick to cobalt. .... **$100 all**

Fiesta, eggcup with experimental silver over light green glaze, rim flake, rare. **$50**

Fiesta, eggcup, chartreuse. **$45**

Fiesta, eggcup, cobalt. **$25**

Fiesta, eggcup, forest green. **$45**

Fiesta, eggcup, gray. **$50**

Fiesta, eggcup, rose. **$35**

Fiesta, figure-8 tray, turquoise. **$50**

Fiesta, French casserole, yellow. **$100**

Fiesta, footed salad bowl, red. **$300**

Fiesta, footed salad bowl, yellow. **$120**

Fiesta, go-along wood snack tray with fish toothpick holder. **$15**

Fiesta/Harlequin, teapot lid, turquoise. **$25**

Fiesta, ice-lip pitcher, cobalt. **$60**

Fiesta, ice-lip pitcher, light green. **$50**

Fiesta, ice-lip pitcher, yellow. **$45**

Fiesta, individual cream and sugar with cobalt figure-8 tray. .... **$55 set**

Fiesta, individual creamer, red. **$85**

Fiesta, individual salad bowl, medium green. **$25**

Fiesta, individual salad bowl, red. **$35**

Fiesta, individual salad bowl, turquoise. **$25**

Fiesta, medium teapot, medium green. **$600**

Fiesta, individual salad bowl, yellow. **$30**

Fiesta, ivory trial plate numbered #2779 on back. **$200**

Fiesta, juice tumbler group - original six colors: red, cobalt ivory, turquoise, light green and yellow. .... **$40 all**

Fiesta, juice tumbler group: red, cobalt, ivory, light green, yellow and rose. .... **$45 all**

Fiesta, juice tumbler, yellow. **$15**

Fiesta, Kitchen Kraft cake server, cobalt with label. **$80**

Fiesta, Kitchen Kraft covered jug, red, hairline to base. .. **$30**

Fiesta, Kitchen Kraft covered jug, yellow, rim repair to lid and nick to base. **$25**

Fiesta, Kitchen Kraft fork, light green. **$30**

Fiesta, Kitchen Kraft fork, light green. **$40**

Fiesta, Kitchen Kraft individual casserole, cobalt. **$40**

Fiesta, Kitchen Kraft individual casserole, light green. ... **$50**

Fiesta, Kitchen Kraft individual casserole, red. **$30**

Fiesta, Kitchen Kraft individual casserole, yellow. **$45**

Fiesta, Kitchen Kraft large and small casserole lids, red. .... **$10 pair**

Fiesta, Kitchen Kraft large covered jar lid, yellow. **$10**

Fiesta, Kitchen Kraft large covered jar, red. **$90**

Fiesta, Kitchen Kraft large covered jar, yellow. **$90**

Fiesta, Kitchen Kraft medium covered jar lid, red. **$40**

Fiesta, Kitchen Kraft Mexicana Oven Serve large mixing bowl, glaze imperfection in bottom of bowl. **$40**

Fiesta, Kitchen Kraft mixing bowls, small red, medium cobalt, minor nick to red. .... **$40 both**

Fiesta, Kitchen Kraft Oven Serve white small covered jar. **$80**

Fiesta, Kitchen Kraft range shakers, red. **$60**

Fiesta, Kitchen Kraft range shakers, yellow. **$45**

Fiesta, Kitchen Kraft red cake lifter and yellow cake plate. .... **$50 both**

Fiesta, Kitchen Kraft small covered jar, yellow. **$85**

Fiesta, Kitchen Kraft spoon, red. **$45**

Fiesta, Kitchen Kraft stacking set with red lid and one unit, light green and cobalt stacking units, minor nicks to each unit, lid in good condition. .... **$100 set**

Fiesta, Kitchen Kraft stacking units with red lid and one unit, yellow and light green stacking units, nick to yellow. .... **$140 all**

Fiesta, Kitchen Kraft stacking units, yellow and light green, nick to green. **$20**

Fiesta, large teapot lid, red. **$20**

Fiesta, large teapot, ivory. **$35**
Fiesta, large teapot, light green. **$50**
Fiesta, large teapot, red. **$80**
Fiesta, large teapot, turquoise. **$40**
Fiesta, light green eggcup, "Lazarus 1851-1940 89th Anniversary." **$40**
Fiesta, light green water tumbler, "Lazarus 1851-1941 90th Anniversary." **$40**
Fiesta, marmalade, light green, rim nick to base. **$55**
Fiesta, marmalade, turquoise. **$100**
Fiesta, marmalade, yellow. **$110**
Fiesta, medium green plate group: 10", 9" and 7". .... **$50 all**
Fiesta, medium green trial 6" plate, numbered #20834 on back. **$200**
Fiesta, medium teapot lid, chartreuse. **$30**
Fiesta, medium teapot lid, forest green. **$35**
Fiesta, medium teapot lid, red. **$35**
Fiesta, medium teapot, chartreuse. **$70**
Fiesta, medium teapot, cobalt. **$60**
Fiesta, medium teapot, forest green. **$60**
Fiesta, medium teapot, gray. **$55**
Fiesta, medium teapot, ivory. **$50**
Fiesta, medium teapot, light green. **$45**
Fiesta, medium teapot, rose. **$50**
Fiesta, medium teapot, turquoise. **$40**
Fiesta, medium teapot, yellow. **$40**
Fiesta, Mexicana contemporary spoon and cake server. .... **$50 both**
Fiesta, Mexicana group: platter, two fruit bowls, cup/saucer, sauce boat and 6" plate. .... **$75 all**
Fiesta, mug group, 50's colors: forest green, chartreuse, rose and gray. .... **$25 all**
Fiesta, mug group, original six colors: red, cobalt, ivory, turquoise, light green and yellow. .... **$45 all**
Fiesta, mug, medium green. **$55**
Fiesta, mustard, light green. **$75**
Fiesta, mustard, red, minor rim nick to lid. **$55**
Fiesta, mustard, turquoise. **$95**
Fiesta, platter group, 50's colors, chartreuse, forest green, gray and rose. .... **$25 all**
Fiesta, platter group, six original colors, red, cobalt, ivory, turquoise, light green and yellow. .... **$35 all**
Fiesta, platter, ivory. **$5**

Fiesta, syrup pitcher, turquoise. **$130**

Fiesta, Kitchen Kraft medium covered jar, red with label. **$130**

Fiesta, relish tray, complete all six colors: turquoise tray, yellow center and red, cobalt, ivory and light green sides. **$250**

Fiesta, platter, medium green. $50
Fiesta, platter, yellow. $5
Fiesta, Promotional casserole with yellow pie plate, cobalt casserole base and red lid. $80
Fiesta, red cream soup bowl with odd finish to handles. $30
Fiesta, red syrup tea container with cork and label, very rare. $300
Fiesta, relish tray center insert, cobalt. $25
Fiesta, relish tray center insert, turquoise. $25
Fiesta, relish tray center insert, yellow. $30
Fiesta, relish tray, complete all turquoise. $160
Fiesta, relish tray, complete all yellow. $200
Fiesta, relish tray, complete: red tray and one side, turquoise center, ivory, light green and cobalt sides. $170
Fiesta, salt/pepper, ivory. $5
Fiesta, salt/pepper, medium green. $45
Fiesta, salt/pepper, red and cobalt. $15
Fiesta, salt/pepper, red. $10
Fiesta, salt/pepper, yellow and ivory. $15
Fiesta, sauce boat, chartreuse. $25
Fiesta, sauce boat, cobalt. $35
Fiesta, sauce boat, forest green. $15
Fiesta, sauce boat, gray. $15
Fiesta, sauce boat, ivory. $15
Fiesta, sauce boat, light green. $30
Fiesta, sauce boat, red. $20
Fiesta, sauce boat, rose. $15
Fiesta, sauce boat, turquoise. $10
Fiesta, sauce boat, yellow. $20
Fiesta, stick-handle creamer, cobalt. $40
Fiesta, stick-handle creamer, light green. $20
Fiesta, stick-handle creamer, red. $25
Fiesta, stick-handle creamer, yellow. $25
Fiesta, sugar base in experimental "Lava Red" color with normal red lid, rare. $55
Fiesta, sugar lid, chartreuse. $20
Fiesta, sugar lid, ivory. $10

Fiesta, 12" flower vase, cobalt. **$400**

Fiesta, demitasse coffee pot, ivory with blue stripes, extremely rare. **$6,500**

Fiesta, sugar lid, medium green. $20
Fiesta, sugar lid, turquoise. $20
Fiesta, sugar with experimental silver over cobalt blue, rare. $140
Fiesta, sweets comport, cobalt. $50
Fiesta, sweets comport, ivory, marked HLC. $50
Fiesta, sweets comport, light green. $50
Fiesta, sweets comport, red, marked HLC. $60
Fiesta, sweets comport, red. $55
Fiesta, sweets comport, turquoise. $50
Fiesta, sweets comport, yellow, marked HLC. $45
Fiesta, syrup pitcher, cobalt. $140
Fiesta, syrup pitcher, ivory. $150
Fiesta, syrup pitcher, light green. $140
Fiesta, syrup pitcher, red. $170
Fiesta, syrup pitcher, yellow. $150
Fiesta, tidbit tray, three-tier: gray, chartreuse and rose. $45
Fiesta, tidbit tray, two-tier: turquoise and light green. $10
Fiesta, tripod candleholders, cobalt. $170 pair
Fiesta, tripod candleholders, ivory, nick to one. $190 pair
Fiesta, tripod candleholders, yellow. $170 pair
Fiesta, turquoise saucers (two) in original package. $30 pair
Fiesta, two-pint jug, chartreuse. $45
Fiesta, two-pint jug, forest green, nick to spout. $30
Fiesta, two-pint jug, ivory. $20
Fiesta, two-pint jug, red. $35
Fiesta, two-pint jug, rose. $35
Fiesta, two-pint jug, turquoise. $35
Fiesta, two-pint jug, yellow. $15
Fiesta, unlisted salad bowl, yellow. $70
Fiesta, water tumbler group, original six colors: red, cobalt, ivory, turquoise, light green and yellow. $55 all
Fiesta, water tumblers, turquoise and ivory. $25 both
Fiesta, World's Fair American Potter George Washington and Martha Washington jugs. $110 pair
Fiesta, yellow salt and pepper, employee invention, "Poor Ernie" and "Mac" under glaze. $100

Fiesta, Post 86 sapphire pyramid candle holder, rare trail piece, one of few known to exist. **$600**

Fiesta, Post 86 white 1986 experimental marmalade, rare. **$700**

Post 86

Fiesta, Post 86 2003 Conference Giveaway in baseball theme: teapot and 2 covered sugars, teapot is 1 of 40. .... **$100 all**

Fiesta, Post 86 chartreuse beverage set with dancing girl, NIB. **$35**

Fiesta, Post 86 chartreuse four-piece place setting with dinner plate, salad plate, mug and bowl, NIB. .... **$35 all**

Fiesta, Post 86 chartreuse medium vase, Millennium vase and bud vase, NIB. .... **$60 all**

Fiesta, Post 86 chartreuse wall plate clock, NIB. **$55**

Fiesta, Post 86 child's first tea set: teapot, two plates, two cups/saucers and cream/sugar, NIB. .... **$45 set**

Fiesta, Post 86 juniper set of five four-piece place settings with dinner and salad plates, mug and soup bowl. ... **$60 all**

Fiesta, Post 86 lilac beverage set. **65**

Fiesta, Post 86 lilac disc water pitcher. **$40**

Fiesta, Post 86 lilac teapot. **$50**

Fiesta, Post 86 pearl gray group: Millennium vase, eight napkin rings, two beverage sets, six chili bowls, AD cup/saucer, two mugs, pyramid candle holder, bread tray, 30 pieces. .... **$85 all**

Fiesta, Post 86 periwinkle disk water pitcher with Scottie dogs advertising Black and White Scotch. **$35**

Fiesta, Post 86 sapphire beverage set and serving tray. .... **$55 all**

Fiesta, Post 86 sapphire hostess tray, very rare, one of 12 known. **$350**

Fiesta, Post 86 turquoise salad bowl and three-piece utensil set. **$55**

Fiesta, Post 86 white Christmas group: two three-piece place settings, two salad plates and two bulb candleholders. .... **$60 all**

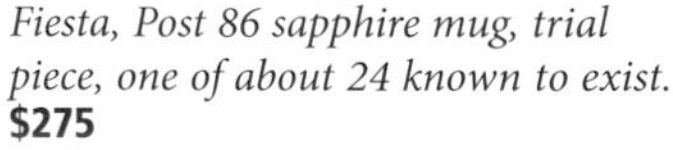

Fiesta, Post 86 sapphire mug, trial piece, one of about 24 known to exist. **$275**

Photo courtesy Rago Arts and Auction Center, Lambertville, N.J.; www.RagoArts.com

Susan Frackelton, (1848-1932), rare stoneware vase carved in a foliate and heraldic pattern and covered in green and indigo matte glazes, 1879. Dedicated to her husband and incised around the rim CUM. GRANO. SALIS. AD1879 (Translation: "With a grain of salt," which, according to family history, is a play on words, remarking both on the use of salt in the glaze, as well as a gentle dig at her husband, Richard Goodrich Frackelton, who apparently disapproved of her profession, and to whom this was a gift.) Incised on bottom SF No 2 6/3/79 For RGF. 7" x 5 1/4". **$18,000**

Photo courtesy Belhorn Auction Services LLC, Columbus, Ohio; www.Belhorn.com

Fraunfelter, vase with hand decorated flowers on a shimmering silver-gray background by John Lessell. Signed Lessell at the base and marked Fraunfelter USA 93. Mint. 6 1/4" h. **$500**
(Fraunfelter China Co., Indiana and Ohio, 1923-1939.)

Fulper Pottery Co.

The firm that became Fulper Pottery Co. of Flemington, N.J., originally made stoneware pottery and utilitarian wares beginning in the early 1800s. Fulper made art pottery from about 1909 to 1935.

The company's earliest artware was called the Vase-Kraft line (1910-1915). Its middle period (1915-1925) included some of the earlier shapes, but they also incorporated Oriental forms. Their glazing at this time was less consistent but more diverse. The last period (1925-1935) was characterized by Art Deco forms.

FULPER in a rectangle is known as the "ink mark" and dates from 1910-1915. The second mark, as shown, dates from 1915-1925; it was incised or in black ink. The final mark, FULPER, die-stamped, dates from about 1925 to 1935.

Photo courtesy Belhorn Auction Services LLC, Columbus, Ohio; www.Belhorn.com

Fulper, vase, in green over rose flambe glaze with ring handles. Marked with vertical oval Fulper ink stamp. Mint. 12 3/4" h. **$450**

Photo courtesy Rago Arts and Auction Center, Lambertville, N.J.; www.RagoArts.com

Galloway, (Philadelphia, early 20th century), pair of large oil jars covered in a fine mottled blue-purple and amber. Some glaze chips. Unmarked. 23 1/2" x 16". **$1,440 pair**

Photo courtesy Rago Arts and Auction Center, Lambertville, N.J.; www.RagoArts.com

Grueby tile incised and modeled with polar bear on iceberg, rare. Small chip to one corner and flake to back. Stamped GRUEBY BOSTON. 5 1/2" x 7". **$11,400**

Grueby, Cuenca-style tile depicting St. George Slaying the Dragon in rich matte colors, extremely rare. Artist signed. 8" sq. **$10,800**
(This Spanish style of pottery is named for Cuenca, Ecuador.)

Grueby, tile with stylized tree on blue ground, rare. Small chip to corner, light abrasion to surface. Stamped GRUEBY BOSTON M.B. 6" sq. **$5,400**

Grueby, two-tile frieze decorated in Cuenca style, with a procession of horses. Restoration to corners. Mounted in new Arts & Crafts frame. Each tile 6" sq. **$7,200**
(This Spanish style of pottery is named for Cuenca, Ecuador.)

Grueby, frieze of three red clay tiles decorated in Cuenca style, with ivory water lilies and light green lily pads on dark green water. A few flakes to edges. Stamped GRUEBY BOSTON. 6" sq. ea. **$2,400**

Grueby, unusual and large squat bulbous vase by Wilhelmina Post, completely cut back with stylized alternating razor clam leaves, under an exceptional matte green glaze. Impressed pottery mark/WP. 7 1/2" x 8". **$8,400**

Grueby, vase by Wilhelmina Post with three full-height leaves alternating with yellow buds. Restoration to a couple of rim chips. Circular stamp WP. 8 1/2" x 5". **$6,600**

Grueby, vase with full-height tooled and applied leaves covered in a frothy matte green glaze. Touch-ups to tips of three leaves. Circular stamp. 8" x 4 1/2". **$2,280**

Grueby, large melon-shaped vase by Ruth Erickson with full-height leaves alternating with yellow buds, covered in fine leathery matte green glaze. Circular pottery stamp RE 36. 11" x 7 3/4". **$22,800**

Hampshire Pottery Co.

In 1871, James S. Taft founded the Hampshire Pottery Co. in Keene, N.H. Production began with redware and stoneware, followed by majolica in 1879.

Until World War I, the factory made an extensive line of utilitarian and artware, including souvenir items. After the war, the firm resumed operations, but made only hotel dinnerware and tiles. The company was dissolved in 1923.

Photo courtesy Rago Arts and Auction Center, Lambertville, N.J.; www.RagoArts.com

Hampshire, vases (two) in fine blue and green frothy glazes. Both marked, 5 1/2" and 8 1/2". **$1,140 pair**

Hull Pottery Co.

In 1905, Addis E. Hull purchased the Acme Pottery Co. of Crooksville, Ohio. In 1917, the A.E. Hull Pottery Co. began making art pottery, novelties, stoneware and kitchenware, later including the famous Little Red Riding Hood line. Most items had a matte finish, with shades of pink and blue or brown predominating.

After a flood and fire in 1950, the factory reopened in 1952 as the Hull Pottery Co. New pieces, mostly with a glossy finish, were produced. The firm closed in 1985.

Pre-1950 vases are marked "Hull USA" or "Hull Art USA" on the bottom. Many also retain their paper labels. Post-1950 pieces are marked "Hull" in large script or "HULL" in block letters.

Each pattern has a distinctive letter or number, e.g., Wildflower has a "W" and a number; Water Lily, "L" and number; Poppy, numbers in the 600s; Orchid, in the 300s. Early stoneware pieces are marked with an "H."

Photo courtesy Belhorn Auction Services LLC, Columbus, Ohio; www.Belhorn.com

Hull, experimental Blossom Flite T3 pitcher in green with yellow and pink flower and gold swirl. Unmarked. Mint. 8 3/4" h. **$500**

Photo courtesy Belhorn Auction Services LLC, Columbus, Ohio; www.Belhorn.com

Hull, Bow Knot basket in pink and blue. Marked USA Hull Art B-29-12". Mint. 11 3/4" h x 11" w. **$950**

Photo courtesy Belhorn Auction Services LLC, Columbus, Ohio; www.Belhorn.com

Hull, Bow Knot basket in pink and blue. Marked Hull Art USA B-12-10 1/2. 11 1/4" h. **$350**

Photo courtesy Belhorn Auction Services LLC, Columbus, Ohio; www.Belhorn.com

Hull, Bow Knot pitcher in blue and turquoise. Marked Hull Art USA B-15-13 1/2". 14" h. **$375**

Photo courtesy Belhorn Auction Services LLC, Columbus, Ohio; www.Belhorn.com

Hull, Bow Knot vase in blue and turquoise with partial original label. Marked Hull Art USA B-4-6 1/2". Mint. 6 5/8" h. **$130**

Photo courtesy Belhorn Auction Services LLC, Columbus, Ohio; www.Belhorn.com

Hull, Continental #55 Basket in Mountain Blue. Marked Hull USA 55. Mint. 12 3/8" h. **$325**

Photo courtesy Belhorn Auction Services LLC, Columbus, Ohio; www.Belhorn.com

Hull, Corky Pig bank in blue and pink with gold trim. Marked Pat Pend Corky Pig Copyright USA 1957 HPCo. 7 1/2" long x 5" h. **$230**

Photo courtesy Belhorn Auction Services LLC, Columbus, Ohio; www.Belhorn.com

Hull, Corky Pig bank in gray. Marked Pat. Pend. Corky Pig HPCo Copyright 1957 USA. 6 3/4" long x 5" h. **$650**

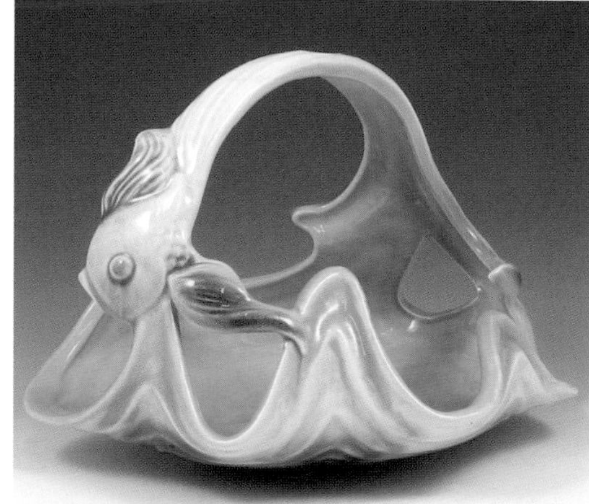

Photo courtesy Belhorn Auction Services LLC, Columbus, Ohio; www.Belhorn.com

Hull, Ebb Tide E-5 fish basket in pink and turquoise. Unmarked. Mint. 6 5/8" h x 9 1/8" w. **$550**

Photo courtesy Belhorn Auction Services LLC, Columbus, Ohio; www.Belhorn.com

Hull, Gingerbread Man cookie jar in sand. Marked Hull Copyright Crooksville, Ohio Oven Proof USA. 11 3/4" h. **$500**

Photo courtesy Belhorn Auction Services LLC, Columbus, Ohio; www.Belhorn.com

Hull, House & Garden chicken covered casserole in gray in the original box. Marked Hull Oven Proof USA. Mint. 10" long x 9 3/4" h. **$400**

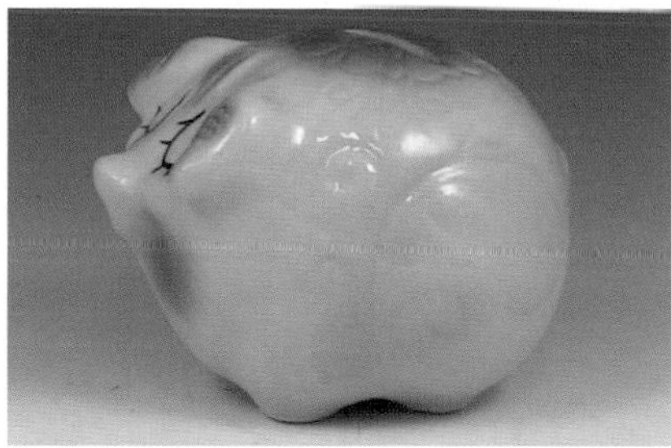

Photo courtesy Belhorn Auction Services LLC, Columbus, Ohio; www.Belhorn.com

Hull, Hull Pottery Association commemorative piece from 1996, a small Corky Pig bank. Marked Copyright USA HP 58 on the base and H.P.C. 96 on the "rear." Mint. 3 1/4" h x 4 1/2" l. **$300**

Photo courtesy Belhorn Auction Services LLC, Columbus, Ohio; www.Belhorn.com

Hull. Hull Pottery Association Commemorative Gingerbread Man bank from 1999 in gray. Marked Hull Pottery Association Commemorative 1999. Mint and uncrazed. 9 3/8" h x 7 1/2" w. **$200**

Photo courtesy Belhorn Auction Services LLC, Columbus, Ohio; www.Belhorn.com

Hull, Little Red Riding Hood Baby Feeding Dish, exceptionally rare. Unmarked. 8" w x 4 3/4" h. **$1,400**

Photo courtesy Belhorn Auction Services LLC, Columbus, Ohio; www.Belhorn.com

Hull, Magnolia Matte tea set in pink and blue with original label on the teapot's lid. All marked. All mint. 3 1/8" to 5 3/4" h. **$250 set**

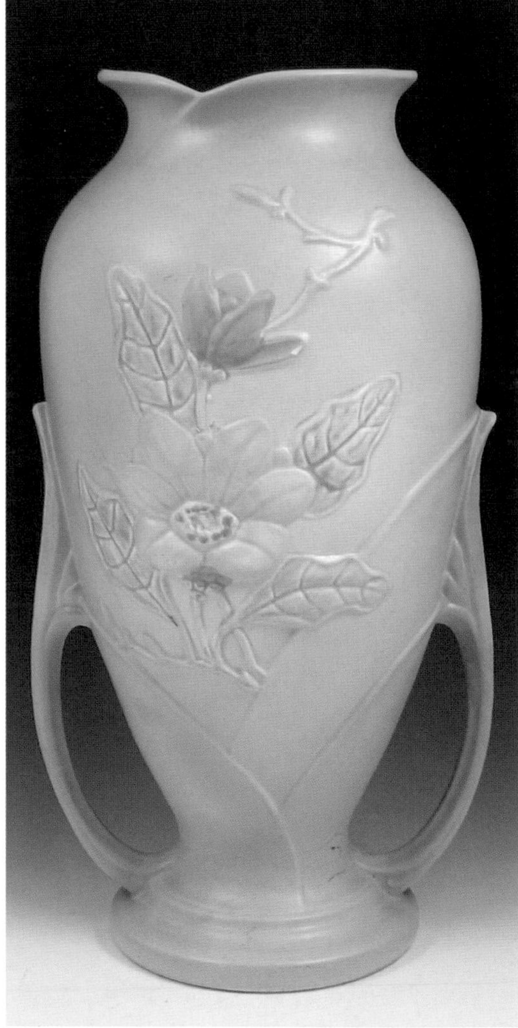

Photo courtesy Belhorn Auction Services LLC, Columbus, Ohio; www.Belhorn.com

Hull, Magnolia Matte 16-15" floor vase in pink and blue. Marked Hull Art USA 16-15". Mint. 15 1/4" h. **$240**

Photo courtesy Belhorn Auction Services LLC, Columbus, Ohio; www.Belhorn.com

Hull, early novelty donkey planter. Marked with original Hull Sample 1 1/2" label with Style No. 953 Donkey, yellow, Large. 7 1/8" h. **$375**

Photo courtesy Belhorn Auction Services LLC, Columbus, Ohio; www.Belhorn.com

Hull, unusually colored llama planter in white and green high gloss. Unmarked. Mint. 11 3/4" long x 10 3/4" h. **$210**

Photo courtesy Belhorn Auction Services LLC, Columbus, Ohio; www.Belhorn.com

Hull, early novelty #936 monkey scratching his head. Unmarked. Mint with the exception of some loss to the cold-painted decoration. 5 3/4" h. **$275**

Photo courtesy Belhorn Auction Services LLC, Columbus, Ohio; www.Belhorn.com

Hull, Tropicana vase with female Caribbean musician. Marked Hull USA 54. Mint and uncrazed. 12 1/4" h. **$700**

Photo courtesy Belhorn Auction Services LLC, Columbus, Ohio; www.Belhorn.com

Hull, Water Lily ewer in pink and turquoise. Marked Hull Art USA L-17-13 1/2. Mint with a factory kiln flaw to the handle. 14 1/8" h. **$250**

Photo courtesy Belhorn Auction Services LLC, Columbus, Ohio; www.Belhorn.com

Hull, Tropicana vase with Caribbean man holding a spear for fishing. Marked Hull USA 56. Mint and uncrazed. 12 5/8" h. **$700**

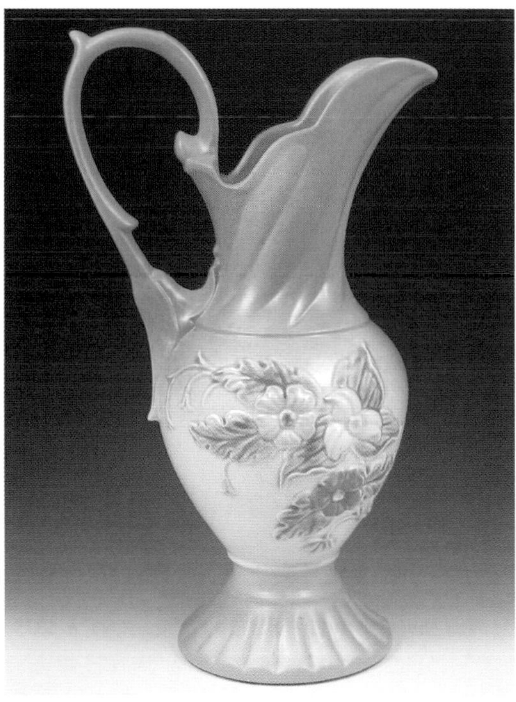

Photo courtesy Belhorn Auction Services LLC, Columbus, Ohio; www.Belhorn.com

Hull, Wildflower pitcher in pink and blue. Marked Hull Art USA W-19-13 1/2". Mint. 13 5/8" h. **$275**

Photo courtesy Rago Arts and Auction Center, Lambertville, N.J.; www.RagoArts.com

J. & J.G. Low, plastic sketch by Arthur Osborne, "Spring Time," covered in amber glaze and mounted in new frame. Incised AO, back covered. Sight: 10" x 5". **$1,080**

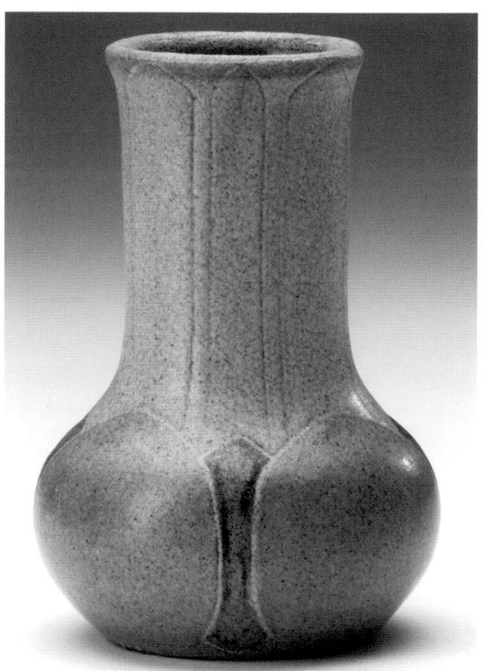

Photo courtesy Rago Arts and Auction Center, Lambertville, N.J.; www.RagoArts.com

Marblehead early bulbous vase by Arthur Baggs incised with a stylized design in blue-grays and pale yellow. Small glaze flake to rim. Incised M with seagull, AB. 4 3/4" x 3 1/4". **$45,000**

Marblehead

This hand-thrown pottery was first made in 1905 as part of a therapeutic program introduced by Dr. J. Hall for the patients confined to a sanitarium located in Marblehead, Mass. In 1916, production was removed from the hospital to another site. The factory continued under the directorship of Arthur E. Baggs until it closed in 1936.

Most pieces found today are glazed with a smooth, porous, even finish in a single color. The most desirable pieces have a conventional design with one or more subordinate colors.

Marblehead, ovoid vase by Hannah Tutt incised with brown oak leaves and acorns on a mustard ground. Stamped ship mark, HT. 7" x 4". **$3,900**

Marblehead, tapered vase incised and painted with stylized green leaves on a speckled rich brown ground. Stamped ship mark. 6" x 4 1/4". **$3,900**

Marblehead, vase carved by Hannah Tutt with crouching panthers and stylized trees on matte olive green ground. (Strong color and modeling). Very short, very tight line to rim, almost impossible to see. Stamped ship mark/HT. 6 3/4" x 5". **$15,600**

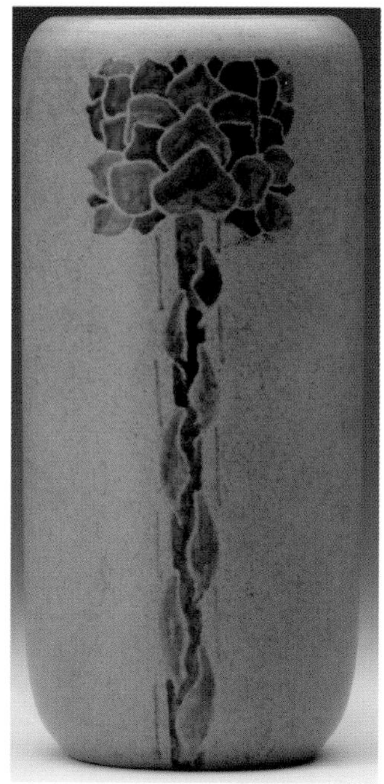

Photo courtesy Rago Arts and Auction Center, Lambertville, N.J.; www.RagoArts.com

Marblehead tall and unusual vase designed by Arthur Baggs with incised and surface-painted blue flower stalks on a pebble gray ground. Impressed ship mark, incised AEB cipher. 8 1/2" x 4". **$6,000**

Marblehead, squat bulbous vase with a repeating design of yellow and blue flowers on green and brown foliage against a gray ground. Impressed ship mark. 3 1/2" x 5". **$3,240**

Marblehead, cabinet vase incised with yellow blossoms and brown leaves. Stamped ship mark. 3 1/2" x 3". **$1,440**

Marblehead, early and exceptional geometric-decorated vase with deep brown incised decoration repeating against a rich pea green ground. (Probably done within the first several years of Marblehead's production, the quality typical of this period). Pinhead-sized fleck inside rim. Impressed ship mark, incised N T. 5" x 4 3/4". **$13,200**

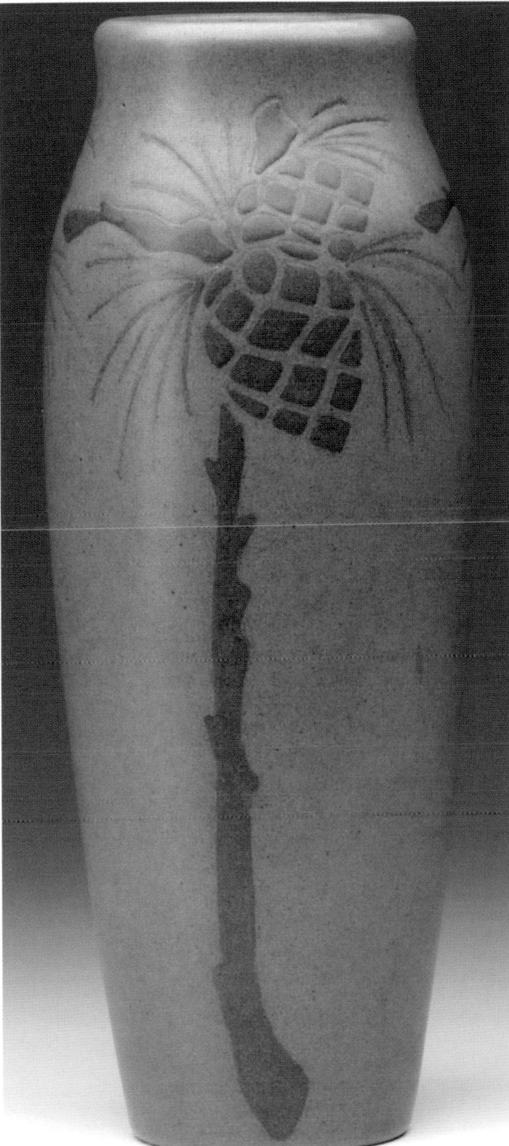

Photo courtesy Rago Arts and Auction Center, Lambertville, N.J.; www.RagoArts.com

Marblehead tall vase by Arthur Baggs, tooled and surface painted with brown pine boughs on green speckled ground. (Perhaps the only surviving example of this form without post-manufacturing flaws). Restoration to two kiln kisses. Ship mark AB. 12" x 4 1/2". **$8,400**

MCCOY POTTERY

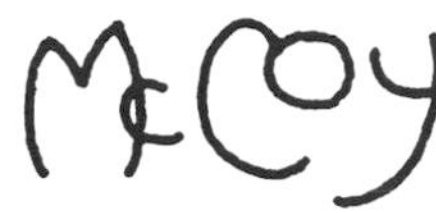

The J. W. McCoy Pottery Co. was established in Roseville, Ohio, in September 1899. The early McCoy company produced both stoneware and some art pottery lines, including Rosewood. In October 1911, three potteries merged, creating the Brush-McCoy Pottery Co. This firm continued to produce the original McCoy lines and added several new art lines. Much of the early pottery is not marked.

In 1910, Nelson McCoy and his father, J. W. McCoy, founded the Nelson McCoy Sanitary Stoneware Co. In 1925, the McCoy family sold their interest in the Brush-McCoy Pottery Co. and started to expand and improve the Nelson McCoy Co. The new company produced stoneware, earthenware specialties, and artware.

Marks: The Nelson McCoy Co. made most of the pottery marked "McCoy."

Vesta line vase, 1962, McCoy mark, 8 1/2" h. **$15-$20**

Two Disc vases in glossy cobalt blue and burgundy, 1940s, also found in yellow and white, USA mark, 6 3/4" h. **$40-$50 each**

Three Leaves and Berries fan vases, commonly found in aqua, pink, white and yellow; cobalt blue is hard to find, and the under-glaze decorated example at left is very rare; late 1930s or early '40s, McCoy USA or unmarked, 6" h, from left: **$75-$100; $50-$60; $30-$40.** Beware of reproductions, which are lighter, have soft mold details, and thinner glazes.

Phial vase in dusty pink, mid-1980s, Designer Accents with USA and 44 mark, 12" w. **$5-$10**

J.W. McCoy Olympia vase, with rare cream-drip glaze overflow, early 1900s, marked 28, 5 1/4" h. **$80-$90**

Sand Dollar vase in matte white, stoneware, 1940s, unmarked, also found in pastel colors, and brown and green, **$100-$125, depending on color.**

Scandia Line floor vase, 1970s, McCoy LCC mark, 14 1/2" h, **$25-$35**

Tall Scroll vase in matte green (often found in glossy tan-brown), late 1940s, USA mark, 14" h, **$50-$700**

From left: Grape vase in gold trim, 1950s, McCoy USA mark, also found with brown and green glazes, 9" h, **$40-$50.**
Sunburst gold vase, 1950s, faint McCoy USA mark, 6" h, **$30-$40**

From left: Tassel vase in glossy raspberry, 1930s, stoneware, unmarked, 8" h, **$25-$35.**
Flower pot with cold-paint decoration, 1940s, shield mark 10, 6" h, **$35-$45**

Photo courtesy Rago Arts and Auction Center, Lambertville, N.J.; www.RagoArts.com

Merrimac (Newburyport, Mass., 1902-1908) cabinet vase with applied rows of leaves under a fine feathered semi-matte green glaze, 1903. A couple of small glaze flakes. Incised E.Q. 1903. 2 3/4" x 4". **$1,920**

Merrimac, (Newburyport, Mass., 1902-1908) jardinière carved and embossed with lotus leaves under a feathered microcrystalline matte green glaze. Abrasion to high points, some glaze flakes. Incised EB. 5 1/4" x 8 1/2". **$3,000**

Newcomb College

The Sophie Newcomb Memorial College, an adjunct of Tulane University in New Orleans, was originated as a school to train local women in the decorative arts. While metalworking, painting and embroidery were among the classes taught, the production of handcrafted art pottery remains its most popular and collectible pursuit.

Pottery was made by the Newcomb women for nearly 50 years, with earlier work being the rarest and most valuable. This is characterized by glossy finishes and broad, flat-painted and modeled designs. More common, though still quite valuable, are the matte-glaze pieces, often depicting bayou scenes and native flora. All bear the impressed NC mark.

Newcomb College, bowl, decorated with an incised band of animal figures, dark blue at rim and foot, cream interior, base with stamped "N within C" cipher, incised "MWS" for Mary Williamson Summey, decorator; impressed "JM" cipher for Joseph Fortune Meyer, potter; painted "DQ-44" for 1910, and impressed "B" for clay body. First quarter 20th century. 2" h, 5 1/2" d. **$8,250**

Newcomb College, tall vase carved by A.F. Simpson with a moonlit landscape of Spanish moss and live oak trees, 1927. Marked NC/AFS/JM/150QC32. 10 1/2" x 4 1/2". **$10,800**

Photo courtesy Rago Arts and Auction Center, Lambertville, N.J.; www.RagoArts.com

Newcomb College, transitional chocolate set by Ora Reams, complete with six cups and saucers, carved with yellow daisies. Small chip to edge of two saucers, tight opposing lines to one cup. Chocolate pot marked NC/JM/B/ORA REAMS 1913/FH2. Pot: 10 1/2" x 6". **$15,600**

Photo courtesy Belhorn Auction Services LLC, Columbus, Ohio; www.Belhorn.com

Newcomb College, moss and moon vase, large, by Sadie Irvine from 1931. Marked TB66 with the artist's mark. 9 3/4" h x 6 1/2" w. **$3,700**

Newcomb College, tall and early vase carved by Marie Ross with light blue blossoms and rich blue-green leaves, 1903. Very short, very tight line to rim. Stamped NC/S11/JM/Ross. 9 1/4" x 6". **$7,200**

Newcomb College, transitional vase carved by Cynthia Littlejohn with stylized trees, 1913. Marked NC/JM/B/231/CL13/FX16. 7" x 5 1/2". **$6,000**

Newcomb College, early and exceptional high-glaze vase by S. Massegale, brightly decorated as a stylized sunflower blossom in yellow, blue, and green on a cream ground, circa 1900. Marked NC/Massegale/P. 4 1/2" x 5". **$5,100**

Newcomb College, vase crisply carved in the Espanol pattern by A.F. Simpson, 1929. Marked NC/RM77/77/JH/AFS. 7" x 3 1/2". **$6,600**

Newcomb College, exceptional, early bulbous vase by Marie De Hoa LeBlanc with deeply incised jonquil blossoms in cream, yellow, and green on an alternating dark, medium, and light blue ground, 1909. Invisible repair to very small rim chip. Marked NC/JM/Q/DD52/MHLB. 6 1/2" x 7 1/2". **$13,200**

Photo courtesy Rago Arts and Auction Center, Lambertville, N.J.; www.RagoArts.com

Newcomb College bulbous vase by Corinna Luria with ring handles in a stylized geometric design. (Rare form). Bruise to rim, firing line to shoulder. Marked NC/C.L./KD18/192. 6" x 5". **$3,240**

Photo courtesy Belhorn Auction Services LLC, Columbus, Ohio; www.Belhorn.com

Nicodemus, matching pair of handled vases in mottled green and brown semi-gloss glaze. Both marked Nicodemus. Mint. 7 1/2" h x 6" w. **$350 pair**
(Chester Nicodemus, 1901-1990, Ohio teacher and potter.)

George Ohr, teapot covered in cobalt blue glaze. Restoration to 4" chip and touch-up to finial. Script signature. 5" x 9". **$4,800**

George Ohr, sculptural vessel of marbleized clay. Script signature. 4" x 6". **$12,000**

George Ohr, flaring vase covered in a fine raspberry, green, and gunmetal mottled glaze. Minute fleck to rim. Script signature. 3 1/2" x 5 1/2". **$3,480**

George Ohr, goblet covered in a fine purple, green, and brown mottled glaze. Tiny glazed hole to side. Script signature. 3 3/4" x 3 1/2". **$3,900**

George Ohr, squat vessel with deep in-body twist, covered in indigo and plum speckled glaze. G.E.OHR Biloxi, Miss. 4" x 4 1/2". **$5,700**

George Ohr, bulbous vase with deep in-body twist covered in brown speckled glaze, with black sponged-on pattern. G. E. OHR, Biloxi, Miss. 5 1/4" x 3 1/2". **$4,500**

George Ohr, tapering vessel with deep in-body twist at rim, covered in emerald green and black gunmetal glaze. GEO.E. OHR, BILOXI MISS. 3 1/2" x 4". **$3,900**

Photo courtesy Rago Arts and Auction Center, Lambertville, N.J.; www.RagoArts.com

George Ohr Joe Jefferson mug, its incised motto entirely covered with raspberry, green, white, and indigo sponged-on glaze, 1896. Stamped G.E.OHR Biloxi, Miss. Incised 3-18-96. 4 1/2" x 4 1/2". **$5,700**

Photo courtesy Rago Arts and Auction Center, Lambertville, N.J.; www.RagoArts.com

George Ohr vase with pinched top, covered in green speckled mustard glaze. Stamped GO. E. OHR BILOXI, MISS. 4" x 4 1/2". **$6,600**

George Ohr, vessel with ribbed body and pinched floriform rim, covered in dark brown mottled glaze. G.E.OHR, Biloxi, Miss. 3 1/2" x 4". **$3,120**

Overbeck Pottery

Four Overbeck sisters – Margaret, Hannah, Elizabeth and Mary Frances – established the Overbeck Pottery in their Cambridge City, Ind., home in 1911. Production ended with the death of Mary Frances in 1955.

Photo courtesy Rago Arts and Auction Center, Lambertville, N.J.; www.RagoArts.com

Overbeck, bulbous vase excised with panels of stylized birds in green and brown. Incised OBK E F. 4 3/4" x 5 1/4". **$5,700**

Photo courtesy Rago Arts and Auction Center, Lambertville, N.J.; www.RagoArts.com

Overbeck vase incised with stylized figures of children amidst red hollyhock blossoms, on a matte mustard ground. (An important piece, pictured in The Chronicle of Overbeck Pottery by Kathleen Postle, 1978, plate XXVIII.) Restoration to rim chip. Incised OBK F with paper label possibly covering E. 10 1/2" x 7". **$72,000**

Overbeck, large barrel-shaped vase excised with stylized birds and blossoms in matte mustard glaze on a rich chocolate brown ground. Incised OBK E F. 9 1/4" x 6". **$15,600**

Overbeck, squat vessel excised with elephants and birds in russet against a pale orange ground. Incised OBK, E F. 3 1/2" x 5 1/2". **$10,200**

Owens Pottery

J.B. Owens began making pottery in 1885 near Roseville, Ohio. In 1891, he built a plant in Zanesville and in 1897, began producing art pottery. After 1907, most of the firm's production centered on tiles.

Owens Pottery, employing many of the same artists and designs as its two cross-town rivals, Roseville and Weller, can appear similar to that of its competitors, e.g., Utopian (brown glaze), Lotus (light glaze) and Aqua Verde (green glaze).

Photo courtesy Rago Arts and Auction Center, Lambertville, N.J.; www.RagoArts.com

Owens, large tile decorated in Cuenca style, with a cottage in a bucolic landscape. Framed. Unmarked. 11 1/2" x 17 1/2". **$4,200**
(This Spanish style of pottery is named for Cuenca, Ecuador.)

Photo courtesy Belhorn Auction Services LLC, Columbus, Ohio; www.Belhorn.com

Owens, matte blue Utopian jardiniere with slip-decorated tulips in white, unmarked. Mint. 7 5/8" h x 9 3/4" w. **$300**

Photo courtesy Belhorn Auction Services LLC, Columbus, Ohio; www.Belhorn.com

Owens, Utopian portrait vase by Mary F. Stevens. Well-executed portrait of Native American Indian Jack Red Cloud of the Ogallala Sioux (titled and signed on back of vase). Marked J.B. Owens Utopian 1010 8. Mint. 10 3/8" h x 5" w. **$4,500**

Photo courtesy Belhorn Auction Services LLC, Columbus, Ohio; www.Belhorn.com

Owens, Utopian standard-glaze handled vase with clover decoration signed MS by the artist. Marked J.B. Owens Utopian 953. Excellent condition. 4 7/8" h. **$160**

Photo courtesy Belhorn Auction Services LLC, Columbus, Ohio; www.Belhorn.com

Pennsbury, Bluebird. Marked #103 Blue Bird Pennsbury Pottery K. Mint and uncrazed. 3 1/2" h. **$190**
(Pennsbury Pottery, Morrisville, Pa., 1950-1971.)

Photo courtesy Rago Arts and Auction Center, Lambertville, N.J.; www.RagoArts.com

Peters & Reed, Landsun vase finely decorated with a farm scene and cottage. Short under-glaze line to rim. Unmarked. 7 1/2" x 4". **$600**

There were a few techniques used exclusively at Owens. These included Red Flame ware (slip decoration under a high red glaze) and Mission (over-glaze, slip decorations in mineral colors) depicting Spanish Missions. Other specialties included Opalesce (semi-gloss designs in luster gold and orange) and Coralene (small beads affixed to the surface of the decorated vases).

Peters & Reed

J.D. Peters and Adam Reed founded their pottery in South Zanesville, Ohio, in 1900. Common flowerpots, jardiniéres and cooking wares comprised the majority of their early output. Occasionally, art pottery was attempted, but it was not until 1912 that their Moss Aztec line was introduced and widely accepted. Other art wares include Chromal, Landsun, Montene, Pereco and Persian.

Peters retired in 1921 and Reed changed the name of the firm to Zane Pottery Co.

Marked pieces of Peters & Reed Pottery are not known.

Peters & Reed, Landsun vase decorated with tree-lined hills. Minor grinding around base. Unmarked. 9 1/2" x 3 3/4". **$480**

Peters & Reed, Moss Aztec jardinière and pedestal set decorated with bands of poppies. A few minor nicks and abrasions to edges. Unmarked. 30" x 15" overall. **$960**

Photo courtesy Belhorn Auction Services LLC, Columbus, Ohio; www.Belhorn.com

Pigeon Forge, Kingfisher by Douglas Ferguson. Signed by the artist. Mint. 9 3/4" h. **$350**

Providential Tile Works, Trenton, N.J., tiles, pair, with pendant portraits, head of bearded man, head of classical woman, teal glaze, both Design C, 6" x 6"; framed; 1896 wedding gift. .... **$360 pair**

Providential Tile Works, Trenton, N.J., tiles, two pair, with pendant portraits, head of lady wearing net cap and head of lady wearing plain cap, mottled brown and green glaze, 6" x 6"; framed. Lady and gentleman, greenish brown glaze, 6" x 6"; framed. .... **$373 all**

RED WING POTTERY

The Red Wing pottery category includes several potteries from Red Wing, Minn. In 1868, David Hallem started Red Wing Stoneware Co., the first pottery with stoneware as its primary product. The Minnesota Stoneware Co. started in 1883. The North Star Stoneware Co. was in business from 1892 to 1896.

The Red Wing Stoneware Co. and the Minnesota Stoneware Co. merged in 1892. The new company, the Red Wing Union Stoneware Co., made stoneware until 1920 when it introduced a pottery line that it continued until the 1940s. In 1936, the name was changed to Red Wing Potteries, Inc. During the 1930s, this firm introduced several popular patterns of hand-painted dinnerware, which

Red Wing, "Woman with Two Tubes," double bud vase No. 1175, designed by Charles Murphy, 1942, 10 1/2" h. **$700+**

Country Garden dinner plate, 1953, from the Anniversary line, 11" diameter. **$10+**

Crazy Rhythm covered casserole, 1955, part of the Futura line, 11 1/2" wide, impressed mark, "Red Wing USA." **$25+**

Desert water pitcher, left, No. 252, 1952, part of the Fancy Free line, 10" tall, ink-stamped, "Red Wing Hand Painted." **$50+**

Caprice beverage server, 1952, part of the Fancy Free line, 10 1/2" tall, ink-stamped, "Red Wing Hand Painted." **$60+**

Coffee "Dripolators", two styles, late 1930s; left, 7 1/2" tall, impressed mark, "Red Wing"; right, No. 255, 6 3/4" tall, unmarked. **$40+ each**

Photo courtesy Rago Arts and Auction Center, Lambertville, N.J.; www.RagoArts.com

Rhead/Santa Barbara, footed bottle-shaped vase, hand modeled by Frederick Rhead with an applied lizard, glazed green against a pale yellow body. Potter at the wheel stamp. 7 1/2" x 3 3/4". **$22,800**

Photo courtesy Rago Arts and Auction Center, Lambertville, N.J.; www.RagoArts.com

Adelaide Alsop Robineau, (1865-1929) porcelain kylyx bowl-form with a cafe-au-lait exterior with full-blown blue crystals, black handles, and a rose-to-brown interior. Very short and tight line to rim, restoration to small chip at rim. Unmarked. 3 1/2" x 8". **$1,680**

Rockingham, glazed pottery cat figure, American, late 19th century, unobtrusive repaired cracks on base, 13 3/4" h. ..**$474**

were distributed through department stores, mail-order catalogs, and gift-stamp centers. Dinnerware production declined in the 1950s and was replaced with hotel and restaurant china in the early 1960s. The plant closed in 1967.

Marks: Red Wing Stoneware Co. was the first firm to mark pieces with a red wing stamped under the glaze. The North Star Stoneware Co. used a raised star and the words "Red Wing" as its mark.

Rookwood

Maria Longworth Nichols Storer of Cincinnati founded Rookwood Pottery in 1880. The name of the pottery came from her family estate, Rookwood, named for the crows that inhabited the grounds.

Though the Rookwood pottery filed for bankruptcy in 1941, it was soon reorganized under new management. Efforts at maintaining the pottery proved futile, and it was sold in 1956 and again in 1959. The pottery was moved to Starkville, Miss., in conjunction with the Herschede Clock Co. It finally ceased operating in 1967.

There are five elements to the Rookwood marking system: the clay or body mark, the size mark, the decorator mark, the date mark and the factory mark. The best way to date Rookwood art pottery is from factory marks.

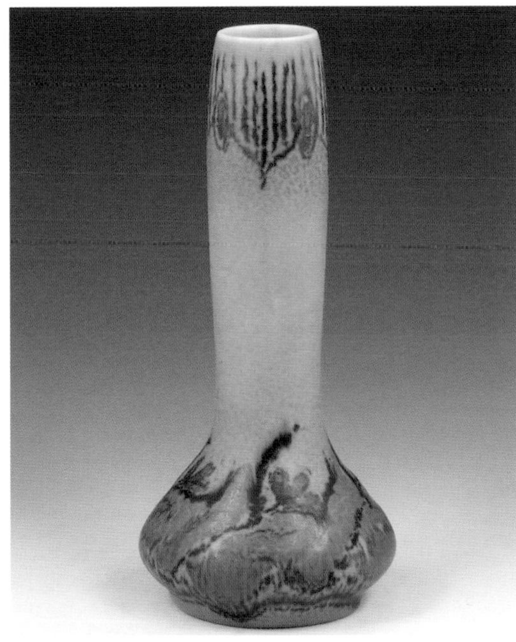

Photo courtesy Belhorn Auction Services LLC, Columbus, Ohio; www.Belhorn.com

Rookwood, vase from 1922 decorated by Louise Abel. Double Vellum example with mottling to the glaze and color. Marked with Rookwood logo, XXII, the shape number 2308 and the artist's incised mark. Mint. 7" h. **$675**

Photo courtesy Belhorn Auction Services LLC, Columbus, Ohio; www.Belhorn.com

Rookwood, 1923 matte glaze vase by Katherine Jones. Decorated with red berries and green leaves on a red and pink mottled background. Marked with Rookwood logo, XXIII, 919E and the artist's mark. Mint and uncrazed. 4 1/8" h. **$750**

Photo courtesy of Treadway Toomey Galleries, Cincinnati and Oak Park, Ill.; www.treadwaygallery.com

Rookwood, plaque, covered in a Vellum glaze with painted landscape, executed by Fred Rothenbusch in 1904, held in an Arts and Crafts oak frame; plaque 14 1/2" w x 9 1/2" h; overall 20" w x 15" h. **$10,000**

From 1880 to 1882, the factory mark was the name "Rookwood" incised or painted on the base. Between 1881 and 1886, the firm name, address and year appeared in an oval. Beginning in 1886, the impressed "RP" monogram appeared and a flame mark was added for each year until 1900. After 1900, Roman numerals, indicating the last two digits of the year of production, were added at the bottom of the "RP" flame mark.

Photo courtesy Belhorn Auction Services LLC, Columbus, Ohio; www.Belhorn.com

Rookwood, vase from 1939 with Art Deco motif and blue-green matte crystalline glaze. Marked with Rookwood logo, XXXIX and the shape number 6462. Mint. 5 1/8" h. **$300**

Rookwood, experimental Iris Glaze crescent-shaped vase by Ed Diers with a purple iris, covered in a silvered modeled iris, 1900. Tight 2" hairline from rim. Flame mark/T1236/ED/W. 4 1/2" x 4". **$7,200**

Rookwood, Jewel Porcelain faceted vase painted by Elizabeth Barrett with large clematis blossoms, 1944. Two small burst bubbles to rim. Flame mark/XLIV/6864/artist's cipher. 7 1/2" x 5 1/2". **$1,200**

Rookwood, Jewel Porcelain vase finely painted by Arthur Conant with large chrysanthemums on a deep blue ground, 1918. Flame mark/XVIII/999C/P/artist's cipher. 8 3/4" x 6 3/4". **$10,800**

Rookwood, Jewel Porcelain barrel-shaped vase painted by Lorinda Epply with amber fish on a butter-yellow ground, 1930. Uncrazed. Flame mark/XXX/6203C/LE. 8" x 6 1/4". **$4,500**

Rookwood, Jewel Porcelain vase by Kataro Shirayamadani with an all-over, chintz-like pattern of cherry blossoms on a raspberry pink ground, 1922. Uncrazed, superficial glaze fleck to rim. Flame mark/XXII/589F/artist's Japanese cipher. 7 1/2" x 3". **$4,200**

Rookwood, Jewel Porcelain vase by Kataro Shirayamadani with white and orange blossoms and green leaves against a shaded peach to gray ground, 1919. Uncrazed. Flame mark/XIX/1929/Japanese cipher. 5" x 7". **$1,920**

Rookwood, large Jewel Porcelain bulbous vase painted by Sara Sax with birds and magnolias on a rich blue and black ground, 1917. Uncrazed. Flame mark/XVII/2272/P/artist's cipher. 12 1/4" x 7 1/2". **$4,500**

Rookwood, Later Mat/Mat Moderne squat vessel by William Hentschel with sprigs in brown and indigo on

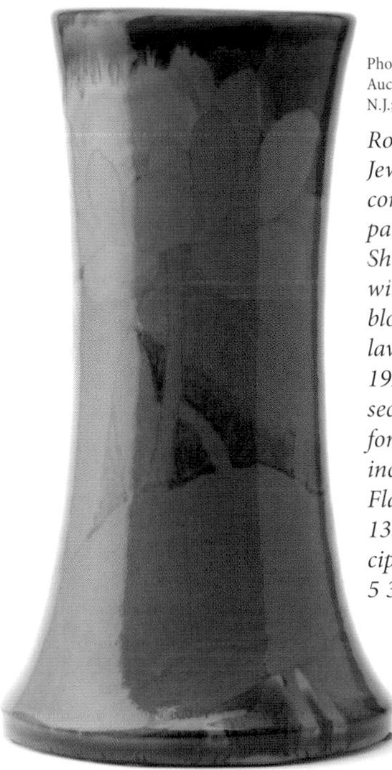

Photo courtesy Rago Arts and Auction Center, Lambertville, N.J.; www.RagoArts.com

Rookwood, tall Jewel Porcelain corseted vase painted by Kataro Shirayamadani with pink lotus blossoms and lavender leaves, 1924. Uncrazed, seconded mark for glazing inconsistencies. Flame mark/XXIV/1358C/Japanese cipher/X. 10 1/2" x 5 3/4". **$2,040**

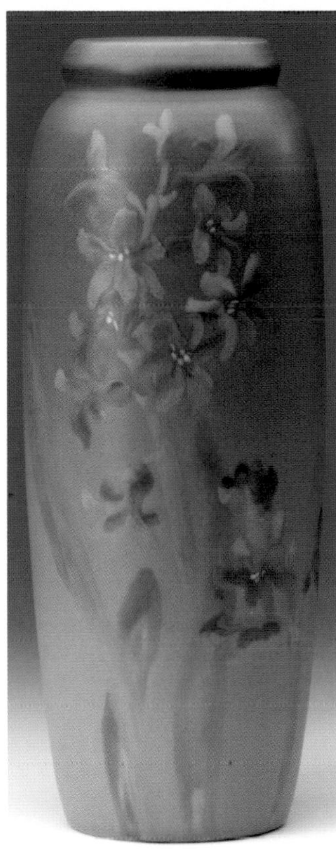

Photo courtesy Rago Arts and Auction Center, Lambertville, N.J.; www.RagoArts.com

Rookwood, tall Painted Mat vase executed by A.R. Valentien with purple orchids on green ground, 1901. Flame mark/I/188VZ/A.R.VALENTIEN. 12 1/4" x 4 1/2". **$7,800**

Photo courtesy Morphy Auctions, Denver, Pa.; www.MorphyAuctions.com

Rookwood, vase with hand-painted image of Sioux chief Black Bird, 13" h. **$15,500**

ivory ground, 1931. Flame mark/XXXI/6199F/WEH. 4" x 4 1/2". **$840**

Rookwood, Later Mat/Mat Moderne squat vessel William Hentschel with beige leaves on a yellow ground, 1931. Flame mark/XXXI/1110F/WEH. 3 3/4" x 5 1/4". **$1,320**

Rookwood, Scenic Vellum vase by Sallie Coyne with lake landscape, 1921. Flame mark/XXI/2067/V/artist's cipher. 7 3/4" x 3 1/2". **$1,920**

Rookwood, Scenic Vellum vase by Sallie Coyne with a full moon over a lake landscape, 1913. Overall crazing. Flame mark/XIII/2064/V/artist's cipher. 7 1/2" x 3 1/2". **$1,320**

Rookwood, Scenic Vellum vase by Sallie Coyne with lake landscape, 1920. Minimal crazing. Flame mark/XX/808/V/artist's cipher. 8" x 3 1/2". **$2,040**

Rookwood, Scenic Vellum by Sallie Coyne with a banded moonlit lake landscape, 1908. Flame mark/VIII/1657/SEC/V/C. 8" x 4 1/4". **$2,400**

Rookwood, Scenic Vellum vase by Ed Diers with a misty landscape, 1909. Some peppering to upper half. Flame mark/IX/1658D/V/ED. 9 3/4" x 4 3/4". **$1,440**

Rookwood, Scenic Vellum vase by Ed Diers with a lake landscape, 1919. Flame mark/XIX/1369D/V/ED. 9 1/4" x 5 1/4". **$2,040**

Rookwood, Scenic Vellum plaque by Fred Rothenbusch with a snow-covered alpine landscape, 1913. In original frame. 1/3" glaze flake to edge. Flame mark/XIII/V/FR. Plaque: 8 1/2" x 10 3/4". **$5,400**

Photo courtesy Rago Arts and Auction Center, Lambertville, N.J.; www.RagoArts.com

Rookwood tall Scenic Vellum vase by Lorinda Epply with a lake landscape in deep and vivid colors, 1916. Light peppering. Flame mark/XVI/977/V/LE. 11" x 5 1/2". **$2,520**

Photo courtesy Rago Arts and Auction Center, Lambertville, N.J.; www.RagoArts.com

Rookwood, Sung Plum vase by Sara Sax with fleshy poppies on raspberry ground, 1927. (The crispness of the piece suggests some hand tooling by Sax). Flame mark/XXVII/6006/artist's cipher. 12" x 7". **$20,400**

Photo courtesy Rago Arts and Auction Center, Lambertville, N.J.; www.RagoArts.com

Rookwood, Later Mat/Mat Moderne squat vessel by William Hentschel with beige leaves on a caramel ground, 1931. (Seconded mark for no apparent reason.) Flame mark/XXXI/6199F/WEH/X. 4" x 4 3/4". **$1,440**

Photo courtesy Belhorn Auction Services LLC, Columbus, Ohio; www.Belhorn.com

Rookwood, Vellum vase with a banded scene of bamboo by Lorinda Epply from 1908. Marked with Rookwood logo, VIII, the shape number 1124E, V (twice) and the artist's incised initials. Mint. 7" h x 3 1/8" w. **$1,200**

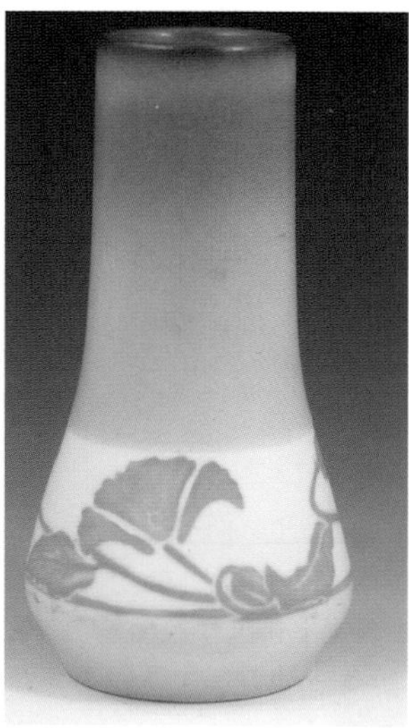

Photo courtesy Belhorn Auction Services LLC, Columbus, Ohio; www.Belhorn.com

Rookwood, vase with Vellum Glaze and stylized floral decoration by Elizabeth Lincoln from 1908. Marked with Rookwood logo, VIII, the shape number 1278E, V for Vellum Glaze (twice) and the artist's mark. Mint. 7 3/8" h x 3 5/8" w. **$600**

Rookwood, Scenic Vellum vase by Fred Rothenbusch with lake landscape, 1921. Flame mark/XXI/614E/V/FR. 8 3/4" x 4". **$2,520**

Rookwood, large terra cotta garden urn and stand decorated in the Italian Renaissance style with blue engobe. A few small chips commensurate with age, largest 2". Stamped 3041Y RP. Overall: 43" x 26". **$3,900**

Rookwood, Vellum vase painted by Carl Schmidt with two large dragonflies, 1904. Seconded mark for peppering. Flame mark/IV/915D/artist's cipher/X. 7" x 5 1/2". **$9,000**

Roseville

In the late 1880s, a group of investors purchased the J.B. Owens Pottery in Roseville, Ohio, and made utilitarian stoneware items. In 1892, the firm was incorporated and joined by George F. Young, who became general manager. Four generations of the Young family controlled Roseville until the early 1950s.

A series of acquisitions began: Midland Pottery of Roseville in 1898, Clark Stoneware Plant in Zanesville (formerly used by Peters and Reed), and Muskingum Stoneware (Mosaic Tile Co.) in Zanesville. In 1898, the offices also moved from Roseville to Zanesville.

In 1900, Roseville introduced Rozane, an art pottery. Rozane became a trade name to cover a large series of lines. The art lines were made in limited amounts after 1919.

The success of Roseville depended on its commercial lines, first developed by John J. Herald and Frederick Rhead in the first decades of the 1900s. In 1918, Frank

Photo courtesy Belhorn Auction Services LLC, Columbus, Ohio; www.Belhorn.com

Roseville, Blackberry 569-5" volcano vase. Marked 596 in red grease pencil and with partial foil label. Mint. 5 1/4" h x 4 1/4" w. **$250**

Photo courtesy Belhorn Auction Services LLC, Columbus, Ohio; www.Belhorn.com

Roseville, Blue Falline candleholders 1092-3 1/2". Both marked 1092 in red grease pencil and with original foil label. Mint. 4 1/4" h. **$575 Pair**

Photo courtesy Rago Arts and Auction Center, Lambertville, N.J.; www.RagoArts.com

Roseville, bulbous Baneda-style (introduced 1932) factory lamp base decorated with band of yellow flowers and leaves on a green to blue ground. Unmarked. 10". **$960**

Photo courtesy Rago Arts and Auction Center, Lambertville, N.J.; www.RagoArts.com

Roseville, Blue Falline two-handled vase with stepped neck. Foil label. 7 1/4" x 6 1/2". **$1,320**

Ferrell became art director and developed more than 80 lines of pottery.

In the 1940s, a series of high-gloss glazes were tried in an attempt to revive certain lines. In 1952, Raymor dinnerware was produced. None of these changes brought economic success and in November 1954, Roseville was bought by the Mosaic Tile Co.

Photo courtesy Belhorn Auction Services LLC, Columbus, Ohio; www.Belhorn.com

Roseville, Blue Falline 642-6" vase with large, looping handles in blue. Unmarked. Mint. 6 1/8" h x 6 3/8" w. **$725**

Photo courtesy Belhorn Auction Services LLC, Columbus, Ohio; www.Belhorn.com

Roseville, Columbine basket in blue. Marked Roseville USA 366-8". Mint. 8" h x 8 1/4" w. **$200**

Photo courtesy Rago Arts and Auction Center, Lambertville, N.J.; www.RagoArts.com

Roseville, Crystalis massive vase with tall neck over squat base, covered in a fine golden crystalline glaze. Post-factory drill hole to bottom. Unmarked. 25" x 13 1/2". **$4,200**

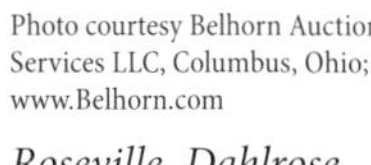

Photo courtesy Belhorn Auction Services LLC, Columbus, Ohio; www.Belhorn.com

Roseville, Dahlrose 1069-3" candleholders (pair). Unmarked. Mint. 3 1/2" h x 5 1/2" w. **$200 pair**

Photo courtesy Belhorn Auction Services LLC, Columbus, Ohio; www.Belhorn.com

Roseville, Decorated Matte 468-7" jardiniere, signed in slip by the artist near the base. Marked only with an impressed 8. 8 3/4" w x 6 1/8" h. **$725**

Photo courtesy Rago Arts and Auction Center, Lambertville, N.J.; www.RagoArts.com

Roseville, Della Robbia gourd-shaped vase with penguins and trees in celadon on blue-gray. Restoration to chips on rim and base. Rozane medallion and marked EL. 8 1/4" x 4 1/2". **$2,760**

Roseville, Aztec vase decorated in squeeze bag with swags and blossoms on blue-gray ground. A few minor flecks to decoration. Unmarked. 11 1/4" x 4 3/4". **$390**

Roseville, Blackberry jardinière and pedestal set. Unmarked. 28 1/2" x 13 1/2". **$2,760**

Roseville, Crystalis massive vase covered in frothy matte mustard glaze. Post-factory drill hole to bottom. Unmarked. 29" x 12". **$2,400**

Roseville, Della Robbia (Rozane) early and rare vase carved with concentric rings of incised daisies on a blue ground. Two chips to rim, some glaze nicks. Rozane Ware medallion, marked MF. 8 1/2" x 6 1/2". **$11,400**

Roseville, Della Robbia bottle-shaped vase carved with peach-colored gardenias on a blue-gray ground, with

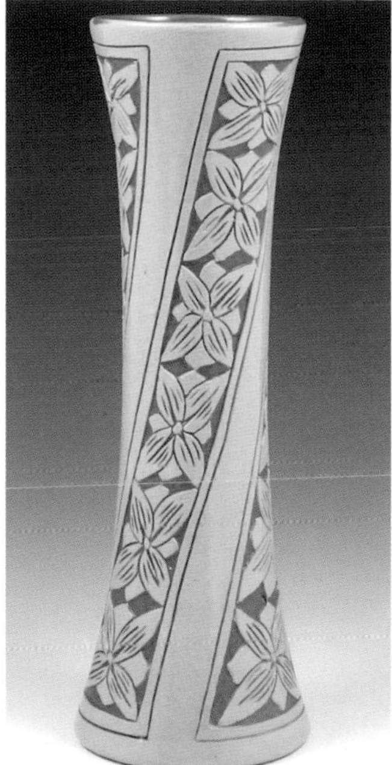

Photo courtesy Belhorn Auction Services LLC, Columbus, Ohio, www.Belhorn.com

Roseville, Della Robbia 9-10 1/4" vase in two colors with hand carved flowers. 10" h x 3 3/8" w. **$1,400**

Photo courtesy Belhorn Auction Services LLC, Columbus, Ohio; www.Belhorn.com

Roseville, Early Velmoss matte green Arts & Crafts jardiniere. Very fine glaze and form. Unmarked. Mint. 15" w x 10" h. **$1,650**

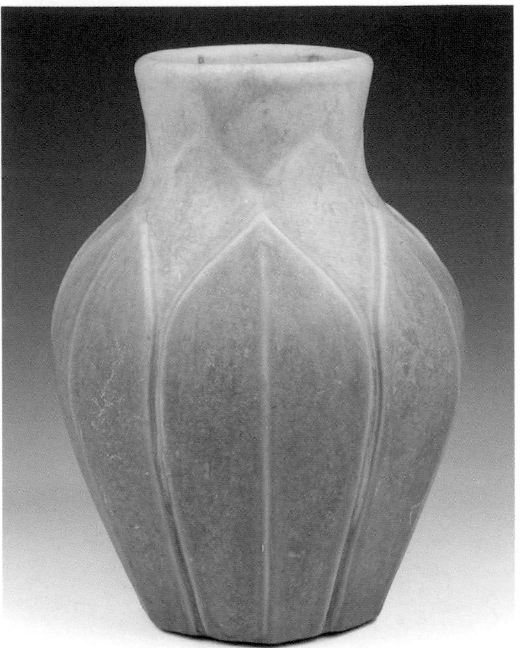

Photo courtesy Belhorn Auction Services LLC, Columbus, Ohio; www.Belhorn.com

Roseville, Early Velmoss 130-8" vase in matte green and mustard yellow with strong Arts & Crafts motif. Unmarked. Mint. 7 7/8" h. **$525**

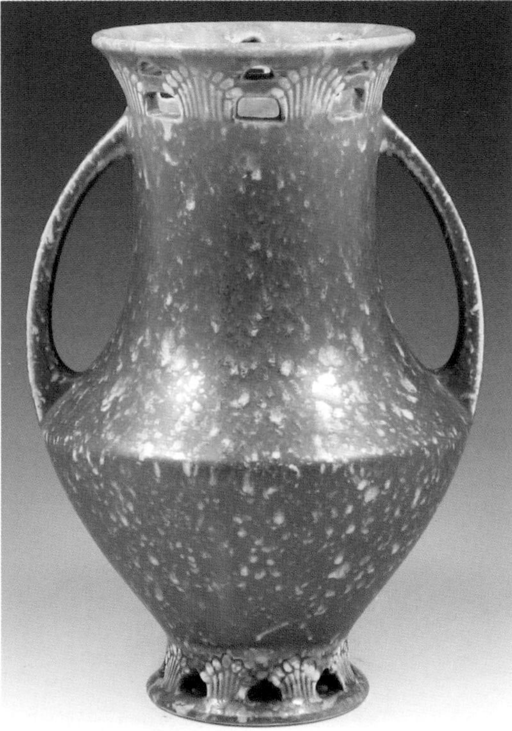

Photo courtesy Belhorn Auction Services LLC, Columbus, Ohio; www.Belhorn.com

Roseville, Ferella handled 510-9" vase, red. Unmarked. Mint. 9 1/4" h. **$1,150**

reticulated rim. Rozane Ware medallion and marked W.M. (to both side and bottom). 10" x 6 3/4". **$6,000**

Roseville, Della Robbia exceptional vase excised with lavender tulips and blue and green leaves on celadon ground. Light peppering on blossoms, missing lid. Marked G. 7 3/4" x 7". **$6,600**

Photo courtesy Belhorn Auction Services LLC, Columbus, Ohio; www.Belhorn.com

Roseville, Freesia basket in green. Marked Roseville USA 391-8". Mint. 8 1/4" h x 8 5/8" w. **$275**

Photo courtesy Rago Arts and Auction Center, Lambertville, N.J.; www.RagoArts.com

Roseville, Fuchsia jardinière and pedestal set, green. 3" bruise and faint spider lines to base of jard. Faint impressed mark to jard. 32" x 16". **$960**

Roseville, Della Robbia exceptional and tall vase with blossoms in apricot, yellow, and blue on a celadon ground. Restoration to base and rim. 15 3/4" x 4 1/2". **$21,600**

Roseville, Egypto rare four-sided vase embossed with medallions, covered in frothy matte green glaze. Professional restoration to a few small chips at base. Rozane Ware Egypto medallion. 12 1/2" x 3 1/2". **$1,080**

Roseville, Early Lily planter with insert, decorated in squeeze bag with yellow and black water lilies on a green ground. A few flecks overall, 1/4" bruise to rim of liner, dark crazing to rim of planter (lines do not go through). Unmarked. 8 3/4" x 11". **$300**

Roseville, Fuchsia vase, brown, 904-15". Restoration to 3" area at rim. Impressed mark. **$360**

Roseville, Fudjiyama twisted, four-sided vase finely decorated with deep blue poppies, and designs in tan, blue and green around rim and body. A few extremely minor areas of wear on body, excellent condition overall. Rozane Ware seal. 9 1/2" x 3 1/2". **$2,280**

Roseville, Futura four-footed, four-sided vase with floral pattern on burgundy ground. Small glazed-over chip to inner foot. Unmarked. 9" x 5". **$1,140**

Photo courtesy Belhorn Auction Services LLC, Columbus, Ohio; www.Belhorn.com

Roseville, Futura 435-10" Elephant Leg vase. Unmarked. Mint. 10" h x 7 1/2" w. **$1,450**

Photo courtesy Rago Arts and Auction Center, Lambertville, N.J.; www.RagoArts.com

Roseville, Imperial II triple wall pocket covered in a frothy orange and green glaze. Unmarked. 6 1/2" x 8 1/4". **$600**

Photo courtesy Belhorn Auction Services LLC, Columbus, Ohio; www.Belhorn.com

Roseville, Pauleo floor vase with hand-decorated band of strawberries, leaves, blossom and branches on a golden-orange luster background. Marked 312 in slip. Mint. 16 7/8" h. **$875**

Photo courtesy Belhorn Auction Services LLC, Columbus, Ohio; www.Belhorn.com

Roseville, Luffa 687-8" vase in brown and green. Unmarked. Mint. 8 1/4" h x 5 7/8" w. **$250**

Photo courtesy Belhorn Auction Services LLC, Columbus, Ohio; www.Belhorn.com

Roseville, Pine Cone vase, brown. Marked Roseville 838-6". Mint. 6 1/4" h x 5" w. **$140**

Photo courtesy Belhorn Auction Services LLC, Columbus, Ohio; www.Belhorn.com

Roseville, Pauleo vase with metallic luster glaze tones of red, copper and gold, unmarked. 18 7/8" h. **$1,050**

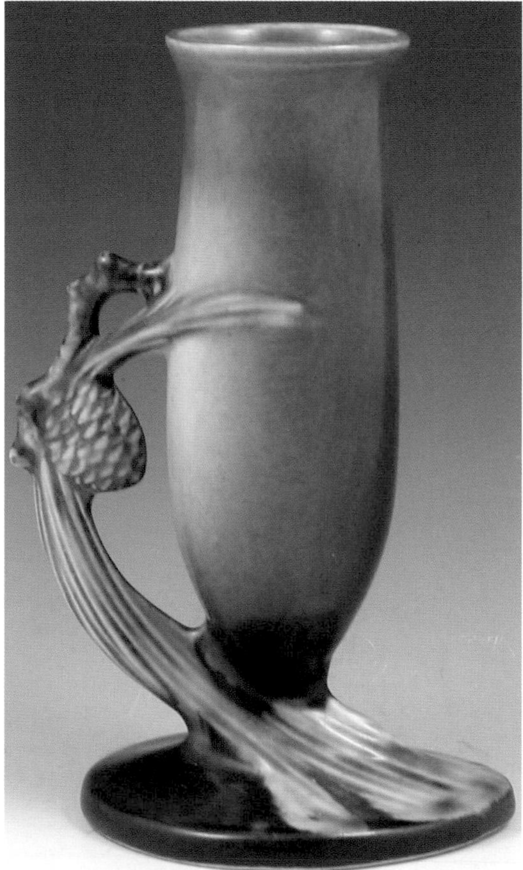

Photo courtesy Belhorn Auction Services LLC, Columbus, Ohio; www.Belhorn.com

Roseville, Pine Cone bud vase in blue. Marked Roseville 112-7. Mint. 7 5/8" h. **$120**

Photo courtesy Belhorn Auction Services LLC, Columbus, Ohio; www.Belhorn.com

Roseville, Rosecraft Black 316-10" vase with handles. Unmarked. Mint and uncrazed. 10 3/8" h x 5 3/4" w. **$230**

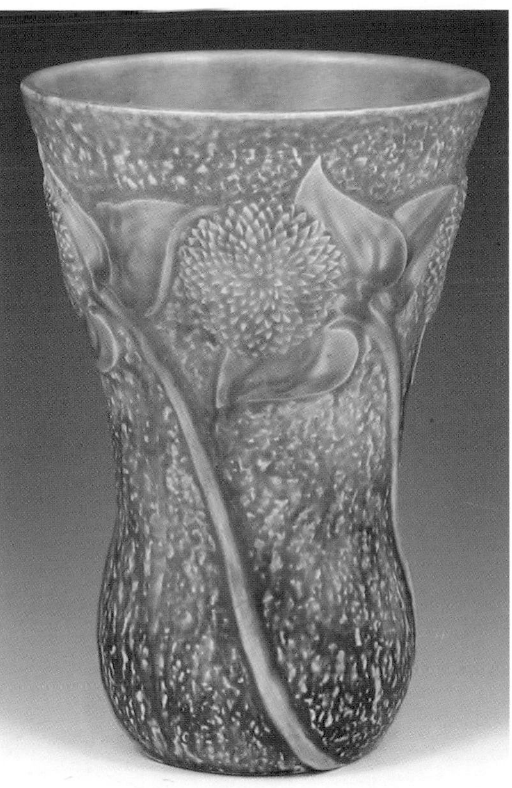

Photo courtesy Belhorn Auction Services LLC, Columbus, Ohio; www.Belhorn.com

Roseville, Sunflower 487-7" flaring vase. Marked 487 in red grease pen. Mint. 7 1/4" h x 5" w. **$525**

Photo courtesy Belhorn Auction Services LLC, Columbus, Ohio; www.Belhorn.com

Roseville, Savona vase in light blue high glaze. Partially marked 372 in red crayon. Mint. 6" h x 5" w. **$275**

Photo courtesy Belhorn Auction Services LLC, Columbus, Ohio; www.Belhorn.com

Roseville, Sunflower 485-6" vase. Marked with original black paper label. Mint. 6 1/8" h x 5" w. **$450**

Roseville, Imperial II ovoid vase covered in a rich, mottled blue and yellow glaze over a ribbed body. Restoration to two drill holes, one on side and one on bottom. Foil label. 11 1/4" x 6 1/2". **$840**

Roseville, Mostique jardinière and pedestal set. A few small nicks overall. Unmarked. 28 1/4" x 14". **$1,320**

Photo courtesy Belhorn Auction Services LLC, Columbus, Ohio; www.Belhorn.com

Roseville, Thornapple rose bowl in blue. Marked Roseville 305-8". Mint. 10 1/2" w x 6 1/4" h. **$100**

Photo courtesy Belhorn Auction Services LLC, Columbus, Ohio; www.Belhorn.com

Roseville, Wincraft oak and acorn ewer in blue, uncommon. Marked Roseville USA 218-18". Mint. 18 3/4" h. **$525**

Photo courtesy Belhorn Auction Services LLC, Columbus, Ohio; www.Belhorn.com

Roseville, Topeo 245-6" rose bowl in matte blue, green and pink pastel tones. Marked with original foil label, 7 1/2" w x 6" h. **$300**

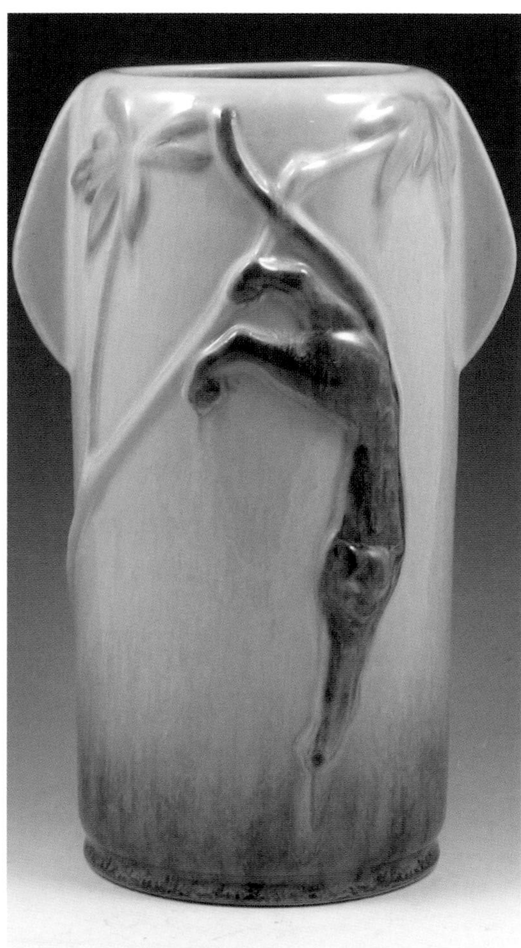

Photo courtesy Belhorn Auction Services LLC, Columbus, Ohio; www.Belhorn.com

Roseville, Wincraft panther vase in blue. Marked Roseville USA 290-11". Mint. 10 1/2" h x 6 3/4" w. **$500**

Roseville, Pauleo vase covered in a dark black and green mottled glaze. Post-factory drill hole to bottom. Unmarked. 2 1" x 1 1". **$2,040**

Roseville, Pine Cone massive urn, brown, 912-15". Impressed mark. 15 1/4" x 1 1". **$1,440**

Roseville, Pink Foxglove jardinière and pedestal set, 659-10". Tight line to rim of jard. Raised marks. **$570**

Roseville, Russco-type (introduced 1934) factory lamp base covered in a mottled orange to green glaze. Unmarked. 10 1/2". **$480**

Roseville, Russco-type (introduced 1934) factory lamp base covered in a mottled orange to yellow glaze. Unmarked. 10 1/2" x 4". **$480**

Roseville, spherical factory lamp base decorated with yellow, purple, and blue flowers with green leaves, on a mottled orange ground. Unmarked. 8 1/2" x 7 1/2". **$960**

Roseville, Windsor large squat vessel, brown. Good color. Professional restoration to small chip under each handle. Remnant of foil label. 7" x 9 1/2". **$780**

Roseville, Wisteria bulbous vase, blue. Foil label. 7" x 8 1/2". **$840**

Photo courtesy Rago Arts and Auction Center, Lambertville, N.J.; www.RagoArts.com

Saturday Evening Girls, cereal bowl decorated in "Cuerda Seca" technique with a band of hens and chicks around "ELIZA" in yellow and white, 1909. Light wear around rim. Signed F.L. 241-4-09. SEG in vessel. 1 3/4" x 6". **$1,140**

(Cuerda Seca literally means "dry string." A wax outline is drawn on the pottery and glaze is applied with a syringe. During the firing process, the glaze beads up against the wax barrier creating subtle flooded areas. Sometimes the outline is done with black wax and serves as a black outline in the design.)

Saturday Evening Girls, Paul Revere Pottery

Paul Revere Pottery, Boston, was an outgrowth of a club known as the Saturday Evening Girls. The S.E.G. was composed of young female immigrants who met on Saturday nights to read and participate in craft projects, such as ceramics.

Regular pottery production began in 1908, and the name "Paul Revere" was adopted because the pottery was located near the Old North Church. In 1915, the firm moved to Brighton, Mass. Known as the "Bowl Shop," the pottery grew steadily. In spite of popular acceptance and technical advancements, the pottery required continual subsidies. It finally closed in 1942.

Items produced range from plain and decorated vases to tableware to illustrated tiles. Many decorated wares were incised and glazed either in an Art Nouveau matte finish or an occasional high glaze.

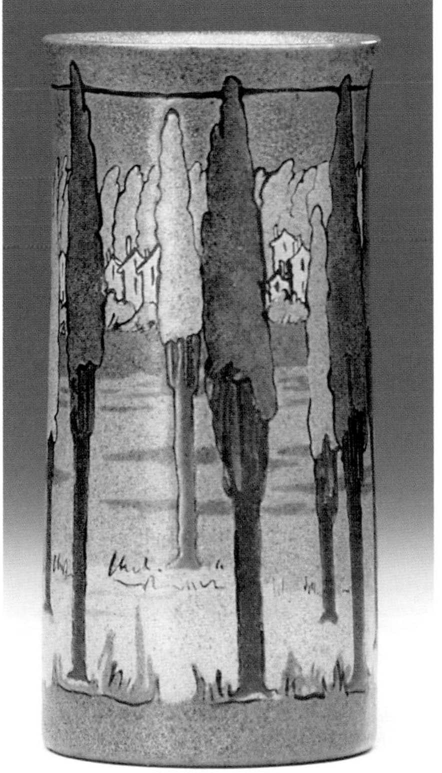

Photo courtesy Rago Arts and Auction Center, Lambertville, N.J.; www.RagoArts.com

Saturday Evening Girls, cylindrical vase decorated in "Cuerda Seca" technique with a village seen through tall trees. Professional restoration to rim chip. Signed 2?8.11.11. SEG IG, 6 3/4" x 3". **$57,000**

Stangl, Magpie Jay and Spotted Owl. Impressed marks on owl, "Stangl USA," oval Stangl pottery birds mark and V.3758 under glaze. Taller, 10 1/2" h. .... **$840 pair**

Teco, vase surrounded with reticulated handles of narrow leaves against a ribbed, flaring neck, covered in matte green glaze. Touch-up to rim tip, stamped Teco. 11 1/2" x 4 1/4". **$12,000**

(American Terra Cotta Tile and Ceramic Co. was founded in 1881 in Terra Cotta, Ill.)

Union Porcelain Works, (Brooklyn, N.Y., established 1848) three shell-shaped oyster plates, each with five wells and raised, colored and gilded decoration of sea life, 19th C. Minor wear. All stamped UNION PORCELAIN WORKS and PAT.JAN.4.1881. 8 1/2" x 6 1/2". .... **$1,200 all**

University City, bud vase covered in matte mustard glaze with fully-formed celadon crystals. Two circular stamps. 8" x 2 1/4". **$3,120**

(Between 1909 and 1914, University City, Mo., was the site of an art academy and porcelain works, divisions of a correspondence school called the Peoples University.)

Van Briggle

Artus Van Briggle, born in 1869, was a talented Ohio artist. He joined Rookwood in 1887 and studied in Paris under Rookwood's sponsorship from 1893 until 1896. In 1899, he moved to Colorado for his health and established his own pottery in Colorado Springs in 1901.

Photo courtesy Rago Arts and Auction Center, Lambertville, N.J.; www.RagoArts.com

Van Briggle early bud vase embossed with trillium and covered in a frothy lime green glaze, the pale clay showing through, 1903. Incised AA VAN BRIGGLE 121 1903. 6 1/2" x 3". **$1,920**

Photo courtesy Belhorn Auction Services LLC, Columbus, Ohio; www.Belhorn.com

Van Briggle, Arts & Crafts vase, early, with hand-tooled leaves and matte-green glaze (circa 1907-1912). Marked Van Briggle with logo, Colo. Spgs., 840 and 18. Mint with a 1/4" factory-grinding flake to the glaze at the base. 4 1/2" h x 3 1/2" w. **$675**

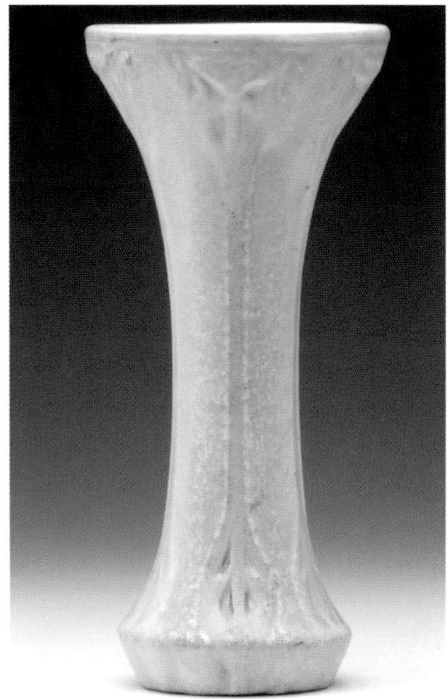

Photo courtesy Rago Arts and Auction Center, Lambertville, N.J.; www.RagoArts.com

Van Briggle, unusual flaring vase embossed with blossoms under a fine yellow and pearl gray frothy glaze, 1906. AA VAN BRIGGLE COLO. SPRINGS 1906 495. 9 1/2" x 4 1/2". **$1,320**

Photo courtesy Rago Arts and Auction Center, Lambertville, N.J.; www.RagoArts.com

Vance/Avon, (Tiltonville, Ohio, early 20th century) large jardinière and pedestal designed by Frederick Rhead, incised and painted in squeeze bag with stylized lotus blossoms and heart-shaped leaves, rare. A few flakes and 1 1/2" chip to pedestal, Y-line to jardinière. 33" x 16". **$9,600**

The Art Nouveau designs he had seen in France heavily influenced Van Briggle's work. He produced a wide variety of matte-glazed wares in this style. Colors varied. Artus died in 1904, but his wife, Anne, continued the pottery until 1912.

The "AA" mark, a date, and "Van Briggle" were incised on all pieces prior to 1907 and on some pieces into the 1920s. After 1920, "Colorado Springs, Colorado" or an abbreviation was added. Dated pieces are the most desirable.

Van Briggle, large vase embossed with daisies under a superior frothy matte green glaze, 1908-11. 2 1/2" chip to base, from manufacturing. Incised AA VAN BRIGGLE COLO SPGS 767. 10 1/4" x 12". **$8,400**

Van Briggle, early vase embossed with poppy pods and covered in robin's-egg-blue glaze, the dark brown clay showing through, 1905. Incised AA 173 VAN BRIGGLE VX 1905. 9 1/2" x 4 3/4". **$4,200**

Van Briggle, early bulbous vase embossed with tobacco leaves under a frothy green and brown matte glaze, 1906. AA VAN BRIGGLE 389 1906. 4 1/2" x 4 3/4". **$1,680**

Van Briggle, flaring vase embossed with morning glories under a fine frothy green glaze, 1908-11. Grinding chips to base, the largest 3/4". AA Van Briggle, Colo Spgs 591. 8" x 6". **$1,440**

Photo courtesy Rago Arts and Auction Center, Lambertville, N.J.; www.RagoArts.com

W.J. Walley, (1852-1917) tall vase covered in curdled semi-matte and lustrous green glaze. Impressed WJW. 16 1/2" x 8". **$5,100**
(Walley was an English immigrant who bought a small pottery in West Sterling, Mass., in about 1890 and operated it until his death.)

Photo courtesy Rago Arts and Auction Center, Lambertville, N.J.; www.RagoArts.com

Walrath, unusual vase with wooded landscape and cabin, 1915. Incised Walrath Pottery. 7 1/4" x 4 1/4". **$14,400**
(Walrath Pottery was operated by Frederick E. Walrath from 1903 to 1918 in Rochester, N.Y.)

Van Briggle, horned toad figural paperweight in amber and green. No visible mark. 1 1/4" x 4 1/2". **$1,140**

Volkmar, tiles (set of three) matte-painted in the Impressionist style with a landscape in tones of green, framed together. (Descended through the Volkmar family). Each signed B. Each tile: 8" sq. .... **$6,600 set**

(Volkmar pottery was made by Charles Volkmar of New York from 1882 to 1911. His designs resemble oil paintings.)

Walrath, vase matte-painted with stylized water lilies. Stilt-pull chip. Incised Walrath Pottery. 7" x 4 1/2". .... **$6,000** (Walrath Pottery was operated by Frederick E. Walrath from 1903 to 1918 in Rochester, N.Y.)

Walrath, vase matte-painted with a landscape, 1" hairline from rim. Signed Walrath Pottery. 6 1/4" x 4 1/2". ....**$3,000** *(Walrath Pottery was operated by Frederick E. Walrath from 1903 to 1918 in Rochester, N.Y.)*

Weller

In 1872, Samuel A. Weller opened a small factory in Fultonham, near Zanesville, Ohio. There he produced utilitarian stoneware, such as milk pans and sewer tile. In 1882, he moved his facilities to Zanesville. In 1890, Weller built a new plant in the Putnam section of Zanesville along the tracks of the Cincinnati and Muskingum Railway. Additions followed in 1892 and 1894.

Weller entered into an agreement with William A. Long in 1894 to purchase the Lonhuda Faience Co., which had developed an art pottery line under the guidance of Laura A. Fry, formerly of Rookwood. Long left in 1895, but Weller continued to produce Lonhuda under the new name "Louwelsa." Replacing Long as art director was Charles Babcock Upjohn. He, along with Jacques Sicard, Frederick H. Rhead and Gazo Fudji, developed Weller's art pottery lines.

Photo courtesy Rago Arts and Auction Center, Lambertville, N.J.; www.RagoArts.com

Weller, Baldin jardinière and pedestal set. Y-line to top of pedestal. Both with kiln stamp. 31 1/2" x 13". **$1,680**

Photo courtesy Belhorn Auction Services LLC, Columbus, Ohio; www.Belhorn.com

Weller, Coppertone lily bowl with frog. Marked with Weller Pottery ink stamp and the numbers 12 and 29. Mint. 11" long x 3 3/4" h. **$300**

Photo courtesy Belhorn Auction Services LLC, Columbus, Ohio; www.Belhorn.com

Weller, Barcelona vase with three vertical handles. Marked Weller with blue ink stamp. Mint. 13 7/8" h x 7 1/2" w. **$525**

Photo courtesy Rago Arts and Auction Center, Lambertville, N.J.; www.RagoArts.com

Weller, Coppertone rare pitcher with fish handle. Unmarked. 7 3/4" x 7 1/2". **$2,520**

Photo courtesy Belhorn Auction Services LLC, Columbus, Ohio; www.Belhorn.com

Weller, Cretone vase with deer, flowers and leaves, decorated in black slip on white x hand. Marked Weller Pottery by hand with incised initials TM. Mint. 6 1/4" w x 5 1/2" h. **$475**

At the end of World War I, many prestige lines were discontinued and Weller concentrated on commercial wares. Rudolph Lorber joined the staff and designed lines such as Roma, Forest and Knifewood. In 1920, Weller purchased the plant of the Zanesville Art Pottery and claimed to produce more pottery than anyone else in the country.

Art pottery enjoyed a revival when the Hudson Line was introduced in the early 1920s. The 1930s saw Coppertone, and Graystone Garden ware was added. However, the Depression forced the closing of the Putnam plant and one on Marietta Street in Zanesville. After World War II, inexpensive Japanese imports took over Weller's market. In 1947, Essex Wire Co. of Detroit bought the controlling stock, but early in 1948, operations ceased.

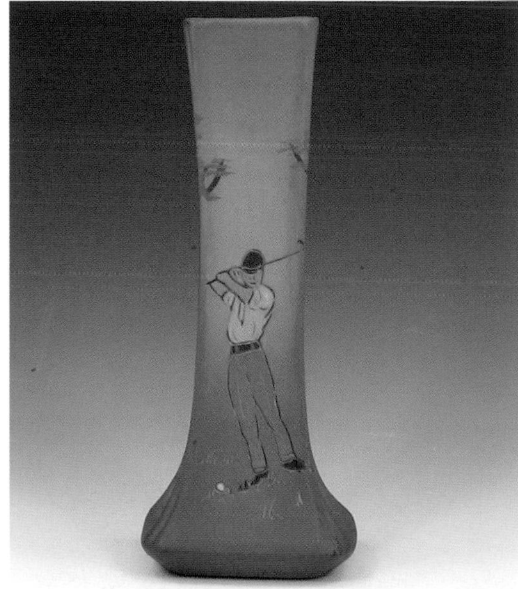

Photo courtesy Belhorn Auction Services LLC, Columbus, Ohio; www.Belhorn.com

Weller, Dickensware II (circa 1900-1905) tapered vase with male golfer in period attire. Golfer is in mid-swing with ball at foot and trees to either side. Marked with Weller Dickensware stamp. Mint and uncrazed. 8 1/2" h x 3 3/8" w. **$1,250**

Photo courtesy Rago Arts and Auction Center, Lambertville, N.J.; www.RagoArts.com

Weller, Dickensware ewer decorated with an American Indian, "Wolf Robe". Dickensware stamp, artist signed ELK or ELH, stamped 176. 11" x 5 1/2". **$840**

Photo courtesy Rago Arts and Auction Center, Lambertville, N.J.; www.RagoArts.com

Weller, Dresden tall cylindrical vase painted by Levi J. Burgess with Dutch scene. 5" line, small glaze miss at rim. Etched Weller Matt L. J. B. 16" x 4 1/2". **$510**

Photo courtesy Rago Arts and Auction Center, Lambertville, N.J.; www.RagoArts.com

Weller, Eocean large vase (1898-1918) painted with purple, yellow, and white irises around the body. Firing flaw to 1/8" area around base (without glaze). Impressed Weller. 17 1/2" x 7 1/4". **$1,920**

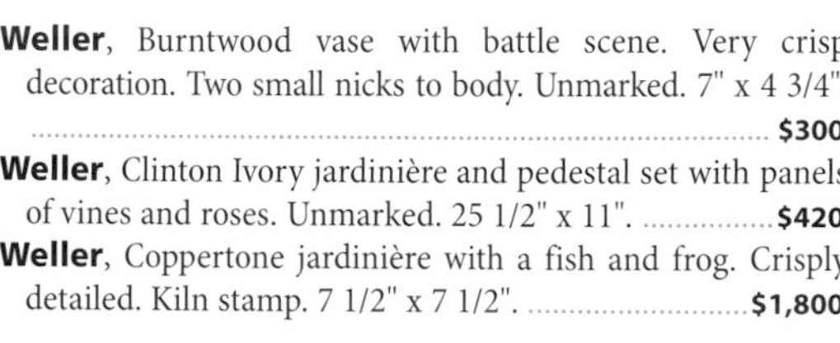

Weller, Burntwood vase with battle scene. Very crisp decoration. Two small nicks to body. Unmarked. 7" x 4 3/4". **$300**

Weller, Clinton Ivory jardinière and pedestal set with panels of vines and roses. Unmarked. 25 1/2" x 11". **$420**

Weller, Coppertone jardinière with a fish and frog. Crisply detailed. Kiln stamp. 7 1/2" x 7 1/2". **$1,800**

Weller, Coppertone double bud vase in the form of two jumping fish, rare. Kiln stamp. 8" x 7". **$3,900**

Weller, Coppertone large frog sprinkler. Includes fittings. Short line, possibly in the firing, to bottom at opening. Unmarked. 10 1/4" x 10 1/4". **$2,760**

Weller, Coppertone jardinière with frog. Kiln stamp. 7 1/2" x 7 1/2". **$1,920**

Weller, Coppertone vase with two frogs at the rim, rare. Kiln stamp. 8" x 8 1/2". **$2,400**

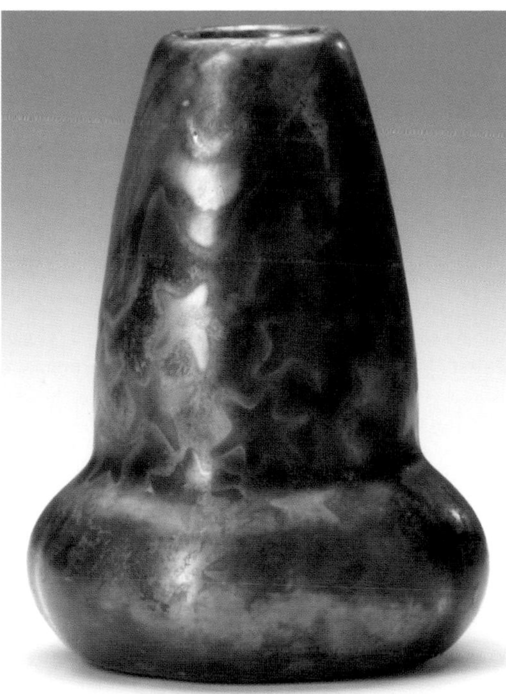

Photo courtesy Rago Arts and Auction Center, Lambertville, N.J.; www.RagoArts.com

Weller, Sicard cabinet vase painted with stars. Stamped 6. 4" x 3". **$540**

Weller, Coppertone flaring vase with two frogs. Restoration to chip on foot. Script mark. 8" x 9 1/2". **$840**

Weller, Etched Matt jardinière incised by Frank Ferrell with pink tulips. 1/4" flake to decoration. Incised Ferrell mark, hand-incised Weller mark on bottom. 8" x 10 1/2". **$1,080**

Weller, Etched Matt ovoid vase decorated with daisies. Overfiring around rim. Impressed mark. 10 1/4" x 3". **$420**

Weller, Hudson vase painted by McLaughlin with irises. Circular ink stamp, Weller, and artist's mark. 9 1/4" x 4". **$900**

Weller, Hudson vase painted by Mae Timberlake with nasturtium blossoms. Stamped kiln mark and signed Timberlake. 12 3/4" x 4 3/4". **$1,080**

Weller, Jewell, rare and tall vase incised with fiddlehead ferns, and embossed with a band of birds against a purple ground. Clean post-factory drill hole through bottom. Impressed Weller. 13" x 7". **$3,600**

Weller, Kenova vase with lizard. Some staining around rim. Impressed Weller. 6 1/4" x 5 1/2". **$480**

Weller, Knifewood ovoid vase with squirrels and oak branches. A few flecks to high points. Impressed mark. 11" x 5 1/4". **$2,280**

Weller, Knifewood corseted vase with colorful peacocks and roses. Impressed mark. 11" x 4 3/4". **$1,200**

Weller, Knifewood vase with owls, squirrels, and birds on oak branches. Stamped Weller. 7". **$720**

Photo courtesy Belhorn Auction Services LLC, Columbus, Ohio; www.Belhorn.com

Weller, Sicard cabinet vase with uncommon wheat or barley decoration in green, purple, gold and blue luster finish. Unmarked. Mint. 3 3/8" h x 2 1/4" w. **$700**

Photo courtesy Rago Arts and Auction Center, Lambertville, N.J.; www.RagoArts.com

Weller, Woodcraft large and rare vase with owl perched on an apple tree branch. Restoration to small area in hole, hairline (possibly from firing) to interior (does not go through). Impressed mark. 15 3/4" x 6 1/2". **$2,040**

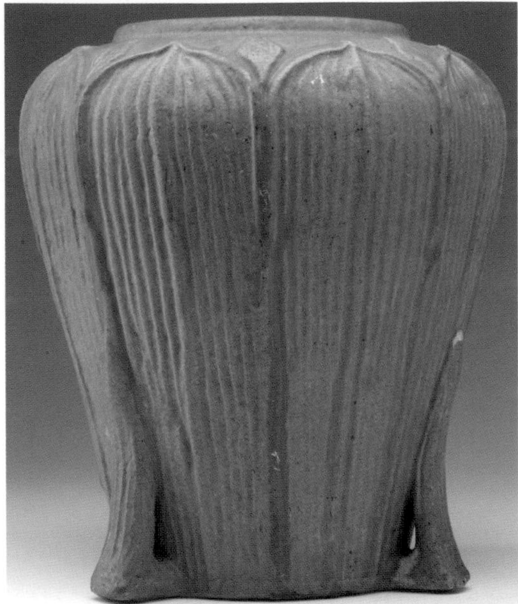

Photo courtesy Rago Arts and Auction Center, Lambertville, N.J.; www.RagoArts.com

Wheatley, lamp base in the Kendrick style with three buttressed feet, full-height leaves, and buds, covered in matte brown glaze. Enlarged factory hole to base, abrasion around rim, some chips to feet. WP 6. 12 1/2" x 10". **$1,560**
(George Prentiss Kendrick was a designer for Grueby Faience Co., Boston.)

Weller, Knifewood ovoid vase with owls in trees under crescent moons. 1/2" glaze miss at base. Impressed mark. 8" x 4 1/4". **$900**

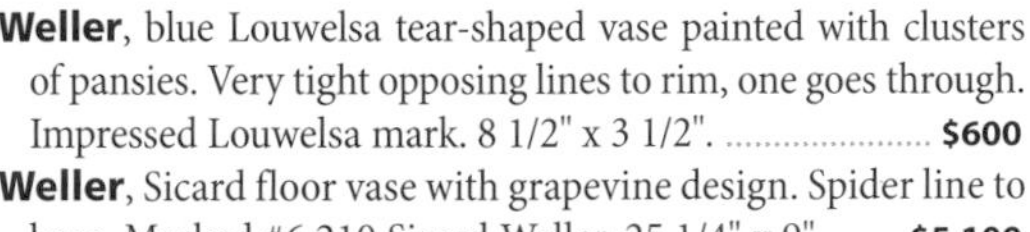

Weller, blue Louwelsa tear-shaped vase painted with clusters of pansies. Very tight opposing lines to rim, one goes through. Impressed Louwelsa mark. 8 1/2" x 3 1/2". **$600**

Weller, Sicard floor vase with grapevine design. Spider line to base. Marked #6 210 Sicard Weller. 25 1/4" x 9". **$5,100**

Weller, Sicard vase with daisies. Nicely fired. Flat glaze chip to bottom, possibly from grinding. Script mark. 5 1/2" x 3". **$720**

Weller, vase decorated by Rudolph Lorber with swimming fish. Tight firing lines and restoration around rim. Impressed mark/artist's initials. 13 1/4" x 4 3/4". **$960**

Weller, Woodcraft tall tree-shaped vase with climbing squirrel and owl. Short, tight line to rim, restoration to another line. Unmarked. 18" x 7 1/2". **$1,080**

Weller, Woodcraft planters (two), one with mushroom (firing separation), the other partitioned with foxes in their den (nick to edge of branch). Both impressed Weller. 5 1/4" each. .... **$660 pair**

Wheatley, lamp base with buttressed feet and leaf and bud decoration under matte green glaze. Incised WP 609. 10" x 8 1/2". **$1,680**

Rick Wisecarver, pillow vase with buffalo. Mint. 7 1/4" w x 7" h. **$190**

REDWARE, STONEWARE

Also see Red Wing Pottery.

Redware

The availability of clay, the same used to make bricks and roof tiles, accounted for the great production of red earthenware pottery in the American colonies. Redware pieces are mainly utilitarian: bowls, crocks, jugs, etc.

Lead-glazed redware retained its reddish color, but a variety of colored glazes were obtained by the addition of metals to the basic glaze. Streaks and mottled splotches in redware items resulted from impurities in the clay and/or uneven firing temperatures.

Photo courtesy Rago Arts and Auction Center, Lambertville, N.J.; www.RagoArts.com

Zark, vase with four buttressed handles, carved with dragonflies in two-tone matte blue. Incised ZARK C.C.B. 4 3/4" x 7 1/4". **$3,900**
(Zark Pottery was produced by the Ozark Pottery Co. of St. Louis from about 1907 to 1910.)

Photo courtesy Skinner Inc., Boston, www.SkinnerInc.com

Plate, "William & Mary" slip-decorated redware, attributed to the Smith Pottery, Norwalk, Conn., 1825-1850, round with coggled rim, yellow slip-trailed inscription, 11 1/8" d, slip is in very good condition, 1/2" d. shallow surface chip, few small rim chips. **$15,405**

Slipware is the term used to describe redware decorated by the application of slip, a semi-liquid paste made of clay. Slipwares were made in England, Germany and elsewhere in Europe for decades before becoming popular in the Pennsylvania German region and other areas in colonial America.

Pitcher, small dark-glazed redware, band of flower heads in relief, flower and paired leaves applied beneath spout, 4" h, slight damage to applied flower. **$46**

Pitcher, Stahl green-glazed redware, inscribed on bottom, "Made/In/Stahl's Pottery/By/Thomas Stahl/April 25/1938"; 6 3/4" h. **$156**
(Three generations of the Stahl family operated a small pottery in Powder Valley, Pa., intermittently from about 1850 to 1956.)

Plate, shallow slipware, three wavy lines, mottled outer border, redware ground, coggled rim, 8 1/2" d. **$517**

Pot, covered, Stahl redware, brownish-green glazed; cover with knop, twin twist handles, two incised green bands, inscribed on bottom, "Made By I.S. Stahl/12-12/1938/S.P."; 6" h, repaired rim. **$57**
(Three generations of the Stahl family operated a small pottery in Powder Valley, Pa., intermittently from about 1850 to 1956.)

Photo courtesy Waasdorp Inc., Clarence, N.Y.; www.antiques-stoneware.com

Cream pot, 3 gallon, ovoid, T. Harrington, Lyons, N.Y., circa 1850, slip blue 3s on either side of a Thomas Harrington folk-art "Star Face" design, some interior Albany glaze loss in the bottom from use, tight hairline at the rim on the left, just touching the "3", 12 1/2" h. **$15,400**

Stoneware

Made from dense kaolin and commonly salt-glazed, stoneware was hand thrown and high fired to produce a simple, bold vitreous pottery. Stoneware crocks, jugs and jars were made to store food products and fill other utilitarian needs. These intended purposes dictated shape and

Photo courtesy Waasdorp Inc., Clarence, N.Y.; www.antiques-stoneware.com

Cream pot, 2 gallon, ovoid, Cowden & Wilcox, Harrisburg, Pa., circa 1870, with bird in a bush design, additional blue at the maker's mark and handles, minor lime staining and a worn chip at the base on the front. Also, a tight hairline up from the bottom on the front just touching the design, 10" h. **$3,190**

Photo courtesy Waasdorp Inc., Clarence, N.Y.; www.antiques-stoneware.com

Crock, approximately 1/2 gallon, cylinder shape, circa 1800, S. Amboy, N. Jersey, deep blue incised swag design below the maker's mark. Further enhanced with reeded shoulder design. There is an old, tight hairline to the left of the name. Stone "ping" at the base on the front, 7 1/2" h. **$3,190**

Photo courtesy Waasdorp Inc., Clarence, N.Y.; www.antiques-stoneware.com

Crock, approximately 1 gallon, unsigned, circa 1850, with original lid, blue vine and leaf decoration all around with matching blue on the lid. Stone ping at the rim of the crock occurred in firing. Chip in the knob handle of the lid, 9" h. **$1,815**

Photo courtesy Waasdorp Inc., Clarence, N.Y.; www.antiques-stoneware.com

Crock, 2 gallon, circa 1880, Fulper Bros., Flemington, N.J., rare with dinosaur design, blue at the maker's mark. There is some minor lime staining, 9" h. **$14,300**

Photo courtesy Waasdorp Inc., Clarence, N.Y.; www.antiques-stoneware.com

Crock, approximate 1 1/2 gallon, ovoid, stamped "LIBERTY FOREV WARNE & LETTS 1807 S. AMBOY N. JERSEY," incised and blue-filled scallop designs above the name, blue accents under the ears. Additionally accented with impressed dental molding around the rim. There is a large "blow out" stack mark just below the name with an additional stack mark on the side. Minor surface wear and staining from use, 10" h. **$26,400** *(Cup not included.)*

Photo courtesy Waasdorp Inc., Clarence, N.Y.; www.antiques-stoneware.com

Crock, 2 gallon, P.H. Webster, North Bay, circa 1870, rare design of standing cat amid groundcover, 9 1/2" h. **$13,750**

design: solid, thick-walled forms with heavy rims, necks and handles and with little or no embellishment. Any decorations were usually simple: brushed cobalt oxide, incised, slip trailed, stamped or tooled.

Stoneware has been made for centuries. Early American settlers imported stoneware items at first. As English and European potters refined their earthenware, colonists began to produce their own wares.

Photo courtesy Waasdorp Inc., Clarence, N.Y.; www.antiques-stoneware.com

Crock, 2 gallon, A.O. Whittemore, Havana, N.Y., circa 1870, with house design, minor surface chip at front rim, 8 1/2" h. **$4,620**

Photo courtesy Waasdorp Inc., Clarence, N.Y.; www.antiques-stoneware.com

Crock, 3 gallon, W.A. MacQuoid Pottery Works, Little 12th St., N.Y., circa 1870, two hearts with "First Love" in blue script, beside cupid holding bow and arrow, minor interior rim chip, 10" h. **$41,800**

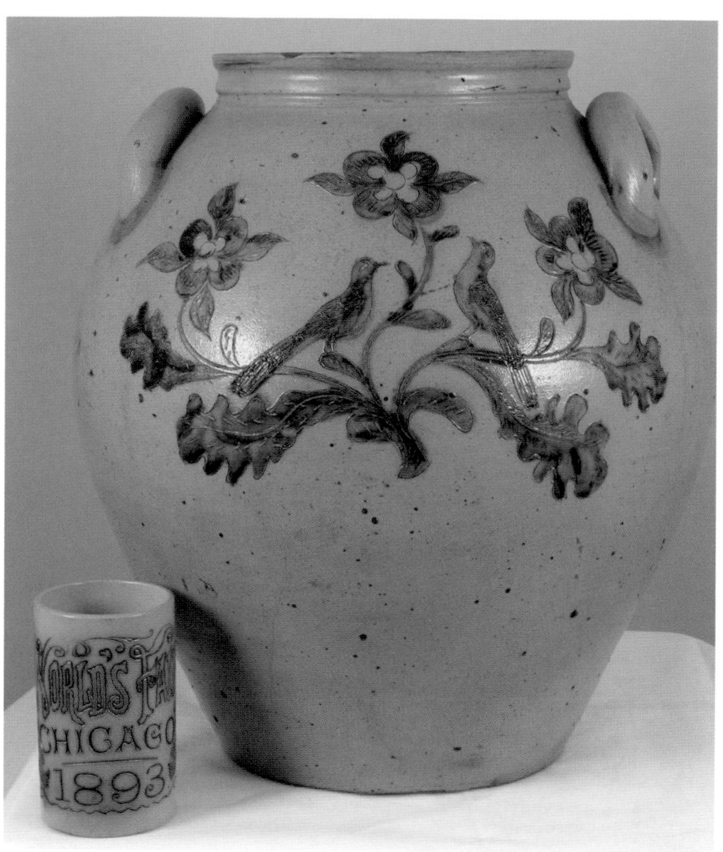

Photo courtesy Waasdorp Inc., Clarence, N.Y.; www.antiques-stoneware.com

Crock, 5 gallon, ovoid, circa 1840, sharply incised design depicts birds in a flower tree, on the back is an equally well-executed design of Germanic-style tulips. The characteristics seen in this decoration are similar to a signed William Farrar (Geddes, N.Y.) jug in the Onondaga County, N.Y., Historical Society collection. There is some old age spidering below the flower design; clay separation that occurred in the making on the bottom, 16" h; cup not included. **$42,900**

Photo courtesy Waasdorp Inc., Clarence, N.Y.; www.antiques-stoneware.com

Crock, 5 gallon, Hubbell & Chesebro, Geddes, N.Y., circa 1870, decorated with a fanciful, folky standing lion, long mane and dot-filled body; professional restoration to glaze loss at and under the rim. Both handles have been replaced, few minor flake spots in the blue have been restored, 12 1/2" h. **$17,050**

Photo courtesy Waasdorp Inc., Clarence, N.Y.; www.antiques-stoneware.com

Flask, salt-glaze stoneware "railroad pig," left side is scribed, "Ohio River/St. Louis the future Great/Railroad and River Guide/With a little Good Old Rye in a Hogs/By/Anna Pottery/1882." Right side has a railroad map which includes the towns of Bloomington, Springfield, Alton/Chester, Grandtourgi, Jonesboro, Cairo, Anna, Gordondale, Duquoin, Tamaroa, Odin. The bottom is scribed "Mounds, Vinggus, Cincinnati the Pork City, Chicago the Corn City," 7" l, 3 1/2" h. **$12,650**

Photo courtesy Waasdorp Inc., Clarence, N.Y.; www.antiques-stoneware.com

Flask, barrel shape, circa 1830, rare, C. Crolius Manufacturer New York, brushed blue accents at the top and bottom. A form not generally found with a maker's mark. Excellent condition, 6 1/4" h. **$7,700**

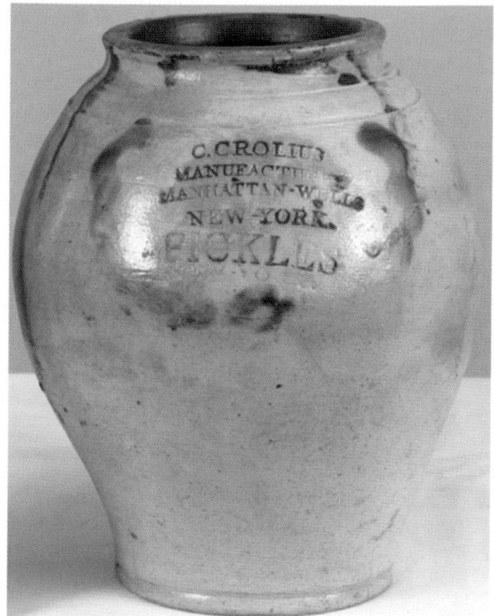

Photo courtesy Waasdorp Inc., Clarence, N.Y.; www.antiques-stoneware.com

Jar, approximately 1/2 gallon, ovoid, marked, "C. Crolius Manufactured Manhattan-Wells – New York Pickles New York," circa 1800, six-line impressed maker's mark is accented in a squiggled blue frame. Blue squiggled drapes accent the back, old hairline down from the rim on the right, old surface chipping at the rim and base with some staining from use, 8" h. **$4,290**

By the late 18th century, stoneware was manufactured in all regions of the country. This industry flourished during the 19th century until glass fruit jars appeared and the use of refrigeration became widespread. By 1910, commercial production of salt-glazed stoneware was phased out.

Batter jug with handle, cobalt blue leaves, wire and wood handle, impressed, "Cowden & Wilcox/ Harrisburg PA"; 7 5/8" h. **$4,887**

Churn, 5 gallon, brushed cobalt and manganese tree-like decoration, additional manganese includes signature – "G N Fulton" (Alleghany County, Va.,) – across base, "5" and feathered wings under handles and across reverse, squared rim with five incised rings below, two double-rib handles; 1867-1885, 18" h, 9" d. Professional restoration to body cracks and losses. **$9,900**

Crock, with Fulper bird, cobalt blue decoration, twin molded handles, 12 3/4" h, cover with chipped edge. **$230**

Crock, 2 gallon with eagle decoration, impress marked "2" with a 6" x 5" spread-winged eagle holding arrows and olive branch. Eagle in deep blue with dot and dash decoration presenting a shield on breast, 9 1/4" h x 10" d without handles. Blue decoration is very good, small chips to base and one to inside of upper rim. **$660**

Jug, 3 gallon salt glazed with blue decoration, Ballard & Brothers, Burlington, Vt., mid-19th century, with applied handle and incised with the "3" above a large stylized blue floral spray, 16" h. Base rim chips, one repaired, an in-painted chip within flower head. **$460**

Photo courtesy Waasdorp Inc., Clarence, N.Y.; www.antiques-stoneware.com

Jug, approximately 2 gallons, David Morgan, New York, circa 1790, with three blue-accented scallop designs at the shoulder, additional blue accents at the handle. Mottled clay color in the making and there is a tight, old hairline up from the bottom on the front. 14 1/2" h. **$17,050**

Photo courtesy Waasdorp Inc., Clarence, N.Y.; www.antiques-stoneware.com

Pitcher, miniature, with Albany slip interior, incised and blue-accented "Clayton/1871," more accents on handle, New York State origin, 3 1/4" h. **$7,150**

Photo courtesy Waasdorp Inc., Clarence, N.Y.; www.antiques-stoneware.com

Preserve jar, approximately 1/2 gallon, unsigned, attributed to M. Woodruff, Cortland, N.Y., rare design of a church and trees filling the front of this small piece, with original lid, 7 1/4" tall. **$7,700**

Photo courtesy Waasdorp Inc., Clarence, N.Y.; www.antiques-stoneware.com

Preserve jar, 2 gallon, Fenton & Hancock, St. Johnsbury, Vt., circa 1852, with design of a lion and trainer, blue at the maker's mark, tight line on bottom that comes up 3" on back, long chip mark on bottom that may have occurred in making, 11" h. **$3,630**

Photo courtesy Waasdorp Inc., Clarence, N.Y.; www.antiques-stoneware.com

Preserve jar, approximately 1 gallon, Cowden & Wilcox, Harrisburg, Pa., circa 1870, with stoneware lid, decorated with variation on "man in the moon" design, additional blue at the maker's mark and under the ears. There is an old surface chip at the rim in front of the left ear, 9 1/2" h. **$8,250**

Photo courtesy Waasdorp Inc., Clarence, N.Y.; www.antiques-stoneware.com

Preserve jar, 2 gallon, L. Marsilliot (one of Ohio's first potters), date "1836" in blue below the deeply impressed and blued pottery mark. Mottled clay color occurred in the making, 12" h. **$6,875**

Capo-di-Monte was copied well into the 20th century by makers in Hungary, Germany, France and Italy.

In 1749, Josiah Spode was apprenticed to Thomas Whieldon and in 1754 worked for William Banks in Stoke-on-Trent, Staffordshire, England. In the early 1760s, Spode started his own pottery, making cream-colored earthenware and blueprinted whiteware. In 1770, he returned to Banks' factory as master, purchasing it in 1776.

Spode pioneered the use of steam-powered, pottery-making machinery and mastered the art of transfer printing from copper plates. Spode opened a London shop in 1778 and sent William Copeland there in about 1784. A number of larger London locations followed. At the turn of the 18th century, Spode introduced bone china. In 1805, Josiah Spode II and William Copeland entered into a partnership for the London business. A series of partnerships between Josiah Spode II, Josiah Spode III and William Taylor Copeland resulted.

In 1833, Copeland acquired Spode's London operations and seven years later, the Stoke plants. William Taylor Copeland managed the business until his death in 1868. The firm remained in the hands of Copeland heirs. In 1923, the plant was electrified; other modernization followed.

In 1976, Spode merged with Worcester Royal Porcelain to become Royal Worcester Spode, Ltd.

Delftware is pottery with a soft, red-clay body and tin-enamel glaze. The white, dense, opaque color came from adding tin ash to lead glaze. The first examples had blue designs on a white ground. Polychrome examples followed.

The name originally applied to pottery made in the region around Delft, Holland, beginning in the 16th century and ending in the late 18th century. The tin used came from the Cornish mines in England. By the 17th and 18th centuries, English potters in London, Bristol and Liverpool were copying the glaze and designs. Some designs unique to English potters also developed.

Augustus II, Elector of Saxony and King of Poland, founded the Royal Saxon Porcelain Manufactory in the Albrechtsburg, Meissen, in 1710. Johann Frederick Boettger, an alchemist, and Tschirnhaus, a nobleman, experimented with kaolin from the Dresden area to produce porcelain. By 1720, the factory produced a whiter, hard-paste porcelain than that from the Far East. The factory experienced its golden age from the 1730s to the 1750s under the leadership of Samuel Stolzel, kiln master, and Johann Gregor Herold, enameler.

The Meissen factory was destroyed and looted by forces of Frederick the Great during the Seven Years' War (1756-1763). It was reopened, but never achieved its former greatness.

In the 19th century, the factory reissued some of its earlier forms. These later wares are called **"Dresden"** to differentiate them from the earlier examples. There were several other porcelain factories in the Dresden region and their products also are grouped under the "Dresden" designation.

Many marks were used by the Meissen factory. The first was a pseudo-Oriental mark in a square. The famous crossed swords mark was adopted in 1724. A small dot between the hilts was used from 1763 to 1774, and a star between the hilts from 1774 to 1814. Two modern marks are swords with a hammer and sickle, and swords with a crown.

Gouda and the surrounding areas of Holland have been principal Dutch pottery centers for centuries. Originally, the potteries produced a simple utilitarian, tin-glazed Delft-type earthenware and the famous clay smoker's pipes.

When pipe making declined in the early 1900s, Gouda turned to art pottery. Influenced by the Art Nouveau and Art Deco movements, artists expressed themselves with freeform and stylized designs in bold colors.

In 1842, American china importer David Haviland moved to Limoges, France, where he began manufacturing and decorating china specifically for the U.S. market. Haviland is synonymous with fine, white, translucent porcelain, although early hand-painted patterns were generally larger and darker colored on heavier whiteware blanks than were later ones.

Haviland revolutionized French china factories by both manufacturing the whiteware blank and decorating it at the same site. In addition, Haviland and Co. pioneered the use of decals in decorating china.

Haviland's sons, Charles Edward and Theodore, split the company in 1892. In 1936, Theodore opened an American division. In 1941, Theodore bought out Charles Edward's heirs and recombined both companies under the original name of H. and Co. The Haviland family sold the firm in 1981.

H&Co
L

H &Co
L
FRANCE

Charles Field Haviland, cousin of Charles Edward and Theodore, worked for and then, after his marriage in 1857, ran the Casseaux Works until 1882. Items continued to carry his name as decorator until 1941.

Thousands of Haviland patterns were made, but not consistently named until after 1926. The similarities in many of the patterns make identification difficult. Numbers assigned by Arlene Schleiger and illustrated in her books have become the identification standard.

The "KPM" mark has been used separately and in conjunction with other symbols by many German porcelain manufacturers, among which are the Königliche Porzellan Manufactur in Meissen, 1720s; Königliche Porzellan Manufactur in Berlin, 1832-1847; and Krister Porzellan Manufactur in Waldenburg, mid-19th century.

Collectors now use the term KPM to refer to the high-quality porcelain produced in the Berlin area in the 18th and 19th centuries.

Creamware is a cream-colored earthenware created about 1750 by the potters of Staffordshire, England, which proved ideal for domestic ware. It was also known as "tortoiseshellware" or "Prattware" depending on the color of glaze used.

The most notable producer of creamware was Josiah Wedgwood. Around 1779, he was able to lighten the cream color to a bluish white and sold this product under the name "pearl ware." Wedgwood supplied his creamware to England's Queen Charlotte (1744-1818) and Russian Empress Catherine the Great (1729-1796), and used the trade name "Queen's ware."

The Leeds Pottery in Yorkshire, England, began production about 1758. Among its products was creamware that was competitive with that of Wedgwood. The original factory closed in 1820, but various subsequent owners continued until 1880. They made exceptional cream-colored ware, either plain, salt glazed or painted with colored enamels, and glazed and unglazed redware.

Early wares are unmarked. Later pieces are marked "Leeds Pottery," sometimes followed by "Hartley-Green and Co." or the letters "LP."

Liverpool is the name given to products made at several potteries in Liverpool, England, between 1750 and 1840. Seth and James Pennington and Richard Chaffers were among the early potters who made tin-enameled earthenware.

By the 1780s, tin-glazed earthenware gave way to cream-colored wares decorated with cobalt blue, enameled colors and blue or black transfers.

Bubbles and frequent clouding under the foot rims characterize the Liverpool glaze. By 1800, about 80 potteries were working in the town producing not only creamware, but soft paste, soapstone and bone porcelain.

The reproduction pieces have a crackled glaze and often age cracks have been artificially produced. When compared to genuine pieces, reproductions are thicker and heavier and have weaker transfers, grayish color (not as crisp and black), ecru or gray body color instead of cream, and crazing that does not spiral upward.

In 1793, Thomas Minton joined other entrepreneurs formed a partnership to build a small pottery at Stoke-on-Trent, Staffordshire, England. Production began in 1798 with blueprinted earthenware, mostly in the Willow pattern. In 1798, cream-colored earthenware and bone china were introduced.

A wide range of styles and wares was produced. Minton introduced porcelain figures in 1826, Parian wares in 1846, encaustic tiles in the late 1840s, and majolica wares in 1850. In 1883, the modern company was formed and called Mintons Limited. The "s" was dropped in 1968.

Many early pieces are unmarked or have a Sevres-type marking. The "ermine" mark was used in the early 19th century. Date codes can be found on tableware and majolica. The mark used between 1873 and 1911 was a small globe with a crown on top and the word "Minton."

Mocha decoration usually is found on utilitarian creamware and stoneware pieces and was produced through a simple chemical action. A color pigment of brown, blue, green or black was made acidic by an infusion of tobacco or hops. When the acidic colorant was applied in blobs to an alkaline ground, it reacted by spreading in feathery designs resembling sea plants. This type of decoration usually was supplemented with bands of light-colored slip.

Types of decoration vary greatly, from those done in a combination of motifs, such as Cat's Eye and Earthworm, to a plain pink mug decorated with green ribbed bands. Most forms of mocha are hollow, e.g., mugs, jugs, bowls and shakers.

English potters made the vast majority of the pieces. Collectors group the wares into three chronological periods: 1780-1820, 1820-1840 and 1840-1880.

William Moorcroft was first employed as a potter by James Macintyre & Co. Ltd. of Burslem, Staffordshire, England, in 1897. He established the Moorcroft pottery in 1913.

The majority of the art pottery wares were hand thrown, resulting in a great variation among similarly styled pieces. Colors and marks are keys to determining age.

Walter Moorcroft, William's son, continued the business upon his father's death and made wares in the same style.

The company initially used an impressed mark, "Moorcroft, Burslem;" a signature mark, "W. Moorcroft" followed. Modern pieces are marked simply "Moorcroft," with export pieces also marked "Made in England."

In 1794, the Royal Bayreuth factory was founded in Tettau, Bavaria. Royal Bayreuth introduced its figural patterns in 1885. Designs of animals, people, fruits and vegetables decorated a wide array of tableware and inexpensive souvenir items.

Tapestry wares, in rose and other patterns, were made in the late 19th century. The surface of the pieces feel and look like woven cloth.

The Royal Bayreuth crest used to mark the wares varied in design and color.

Derby Crown Porcelain Co., established in 1875 in Derby, England, had no connection with earlier Derby factories that operated in the late 18th and early 19th centuries. In 1890, the company was appointed "Manufacturers of Porcelain to Her Majesty" (Queen Victoria) and since that date has been known as "Royal Crown Derby."

Most of these porcelains, both tableware and figural, were hand decorated. A variety of printing processes were used for additional adornment.

Derby porcelains from 1878 to 1890 carry only the standard crown printed mark. After 1891, the mark includes the "Royal Crown Derby" wording. In the 20th century, "Made in England" and "English Bone China" were added to the mark.

Doulton pottery began in 1815 under the direction of John Doulton at the Doulton & Watts pottery in Lambeth, England. Early output was limited to salt-glazed industrial stoneware. After John Watts retired in 1854, the firm became Doulton and Co., and production was expanded to include hand-decorated stoneware such as figurines, vases, dinnerware and flasks.

In 1878, Doulton's son, Sir Henry Doulton, purchased Pinder Bourne & Co. in Burslem, Staffordshire. The companies became Doulton & Co., Ltd. in 1882. Decorated porcelain was added to Doulton's earthenware production in 1884.

Most Doulton figurines were produced at the Burslem plants, where they were made continuously from 1890 until 1978. After a short interruption, a new line of Doulton figurines was introduced in 1979.

Dickensware, in earthenware and porcelain, was introduced in 1908. The pieces were decorated with characters from Dickens' novels. Most of the line was withdrawn in the 1940s, except for plates, which continued to be made until 1974.

Character jugs, a 20th-century revival of early Toby models, were designed by Charles J. Noke for Doulton in the 1930s. Character jugs are limited to bust portraits, while Royal Doulton Toby jugs are full figured. The character jugs come in four sizes and feature fictional characters from Dickens, Shakespeare and other English and American novelists, as well as historical heroes. Marks on both character and Toby jugs must be carefully identified to determine dates and values.

Doulton's Rouge Flambé (Veined Sung) is a high-glazed, strong-colored ware.

Production of stoneware at Lambeth ceased in 1956.

Beginning in 1872, the "Royal Doulton" mark was used on all types of wares produced by the company.

Beginning in 1913, an "HN" number was assigned to each new Doulton figurine design. The "HN" numbers, which referred originally to Harry Nixon, a Doulton artist, were chronological until 1940, after which blocks of numbers were assigned to each modeler. From 1928 until 1954, a small number was placed to the right of the crown mark; this number, when added to 1927, gives the year of manufacture.

ROYAL
DOULTON
FLAMBE

In 1751, the Worcester Porcelain Co., led by Dr. John Wall and William Davis, acquired the Bristol pottery of Benjamin Lund and moved it to Worcester. The first wares were painted blue under the glaze; soon thereafter decorating was accomplished by painting on the glaze in enamel colors. Among the most-famous 18th-century decorators were James Giles and Jeffery Hamet O'Neal. Transfer-print decoration was developed by the 1760s.

A series of partnerships took place after Davis' death in 1783: Flight (1783-1793); Flight & Barr (1793-1807); Barr, Flight & Barr (1807-1813); and Flight, Barr & Barr (1813-1840). In 1840, the factory was moved to Chamberlain & Co. in Diglis, Worcester. Decorative wares were discontinued. In 1852, W.H. Kerr and R.W. Binns formed a new company and revived the production of ornamental wares.

In 1862, the firm became the Royal Worcester Porcelain Co. Among the key modelers of the late 19th century were James Hadley, his three sons, and George Owen, an expert with pierced clay pieces. Royal Worcester absorbed the Grainger factory in 1889 and the James Hadley factory in 1905. Modern designers include Dorothy Doughty and Doris Lindner.

The principal patron of the French porcelain industry in early 18th-century France was Jeanne Antoinette Poisson, Marquise de Pompadour. She supported the Vincennes factory of Gilles and Robert Dubois and their successors in their attempt to make soft-paste porcelain in the 1740s. In 1753, she moved the porcelain operations to Sevres, near her home, Chateau de Bellevue.

The Sevres soft-paste formula used sand from Fontainebleau, salt, saltpeter, soda of Alicante, powdered alabaster, clay and soap.

In 1769, kaolin was discovered in France, and a hard-paste formula was developed. The baroque designs gave way to rococo, a style favored by Jeanne du Barry, Louis XV's next mistress. Louis XVI took little interest in Sevres, and many factories began to turn out counterfeits. In 1876, the factory was moved to St. Cloud and was eventually nationalized.

Louis XV allowed the firm to use the "double L" in its marks.

Spatterware generally was made of common earthenware, although occasionally creamware was used. The earliest English examples were made about 1780. The peak period of production was from 1810 to 1840. Firms known to have made spatterware are Adams, Barlow, and Harvey and Cotton.

The amount of spatter decoration varies from piece to piece. Some objects simply have decorated borders. These often were decorated with a brush, requiring several hundred touches per square inch to achieve the spatter effect. Other pieces have the entire surface covered with spatter. Marked pieces are rare.

Notes: Collectors today focus on the patterns—Cannon, Castle, Fort, Peafowl, Rainbow, Rose, Thistle, Schoolhouse, etc. The decoration on flatware is in the center of the piece; on hollow ware, it occurs on both sides.

Aesthetics and the colors of spatter are key to determining value. Blue and red are the most common colors; green, purple, and brown are in a middle group; black and yellow are scarce.

In 1754, Josiah Wedgwood and Thomas Whieldon of Fenton Vivian, Staffordshire, England, became partners in a pottery enterprise. Their products included marbled, agate, tortoiseshell, green glaze and Egyptian black wares. In 1759, Wedgwood opened his own pottery at the Ivy House works, Burslem, Staffordshire. In 1764, he moved to the Brick House (Bell Works) at Burslem. The pottery concentrated on utilitarian pieces.

Between 1766 and 1769, Wedgwood built the famous works at Etruria. Among the most-renowned products of this plant were the Empress Catherine of Russia dinner service (1774) and the Portland Vase (1790s). The firm also made caneware, unglazed earthenwares (drabwares), piecrust wares, variegated and marbled wares, black basalt (developed in 1768), Queen's or creamware, and Jasperware (perfected in 1774).

Bone china was produced under the direction of Josiah Wedgwood II between 1812 and 1822 and revived in 1878. Moonlight Luster was made from 1805 to 1815. Fairyland Luster began in 1920. All luster production ended in 1932.

A museum was established at the Etruria pottery in 1906. When Wedgwood moved to its modern plant at Barlaston, North Staffordshire, the museum was expanded.

Vilmos Zsolnay (1828-1900) assumed control of his brother's factory in Pécs, Hungary, in the mid-19th century. In 1899, Miklos, Vilmos' son, became manager. The firm still produces ceramic ware.

The early wares are highly ornamental, glazed and have a cream-colored ground. Eosin glaze, a deep, rich play of colors reminiscent of Tiffany's iridescent wares, received a gold medal at the 1900 Paris exhibition.

Originally, no trademark was used, but in 1878 the company began to use a blue mark depicting the five towers of the cathedral at Pécs. The initials "TJM" represent the names of Miklos' three children.

Ceramics Listed by Form or Type

Ceramic styles produced by many makers—including Flow Blue, Majolica and Quimper—are found at the end of this section. *Also see Oriental Objects and Tiffany.*

Bottles (pair), Italian, Cantagalli, of flattened shape, hand-painted with mythological scenes of Hermes and Venus, 20th century, Bottles topped with differing stoppers, marked with Cantagalli rooster symbol. 13 7/8". **$25,200**

Bowl, British pearlware, mochaware, circa 1830. Footed bowl having a wide grayish band with undulating earthworm design. Top rim having a blue border and below decoration, four black lines, 4" h x 7 1/2" d. Discolored with old discolored hairline in base. No chips. **$180**

Bowl and dish, Moorcroft, bowl with fish, and a "Pomegranate" small dish with pewter foot. Dish marked TUDRIC MOORCROFT/H/MADE IN ENGLAND/01339. Dish: 2 3/4" x 4 1/4". .... **$1,320 pair**

Box, china, covered, brown-haired child wearing pink garment cuddles with rabbits; carrots, foliage and two more rabbits below, 4 3/4" h, 5 7/8" w, 3/4" hairline inside at back, not visible from outside. **$402**

Box, coach form, porcelain, young girl in coach shows doll to baby; "11.86" inscribed in black on side of coach and also on bottom of cover, 5 3/4" h, 6" l. **$258**

Box, figural, porcelain, covered, lady holds picture frame around upper body of young girl who sits in a chair, "LL.1" inscribed on each piece, 6 1/4" h, 6 3/4" w. **$480**

Box, French, circular, lidded, china, putti in landscape decoration in bas relief, ormolu mounts, marked "France" on bottom, cobalt blue crowned "N" mark, 5 1/8" h, 4 3/4" d. Hairline to base. **$92**

Box, French, oblong, lidded, china, three putti in landscape, iron red swag border, marked "Made in France" on bottom, cobalt blue crowned "N" mark, 5" w, 3 1/4" d. Separation of metal mount below hinge. **$92**

Box (vanity), Sevres, pink ground, 18th century, reserves with grisaille scenes, interior with painted floral sprays, 3" h, 5 1/2" w. **$1,200**

Butter pat, creamware, marked "And three weeks after the wedding day"; "Happy" and when inverted "Sad", pair of heads, floral border, 3 1/8" d, chips to rim. **$57**

Charger, Delftware, England, mid-18th century, blue and white decorated with central floral landscape, 2 1/2" h, 12 1/4" d; 1" repaired chip, several glaze losses around rim and a few shallow rim chips. **$355**

Charger, Italian, ceramic, painted with a rampant lion against a floral ground. Marked on back C. Novelli Roma 1896, 18 1/2" d. **$1,140**

Charger, Italian, Melandri & Foccaccia, faience painted with a portrait in profile, the wide border with a repeating decorative motif, 20th century, Marked Faenza with an MF monogram and company logo, also large oval spur mark, 16" d. **$480**

Charger, Meissen, porcelain painted with chrysanthemums on a blue ground, 20th century, under-glaze blue mark, impressed numerals, 18" d. **$10,200**

Dinnerware service, (partial), Doulton "Madras" blue and white, circa 1891-1902; consisting of eleven 7 1/2" plates, eight saucers, five demi-saucers, two demi-cups, eighteen 5 3/8" fruit bowls, fifteen 6 1/2" plates, eleven 7 1/2" bowls (one chip), one 9 3/4" oblong vegetable bowl, two 10 1/2" oblong vegetable bowls, eleven 10 1/2" plates, six 9 3/4" plates (one cracked), one 7 3/4" oblong gravy boat liner, two 4 3/4" finger bowls, (one chipped), one 5 1/2" pitcher, one 15 1/2" platter and one covered soup tureen. .... **$1,150 all**

Dinnerware service, (partial), "Iris" pattern, Royal Staffordshire, Burslem; consisting of one 13" platter, one 14 1/2" platter, one 10 1/2" platter, one covered sugar, one gravy boat, ten 8" bowls, eight cups (one chipped), eleven saucers, twelve 8" plates, thirteen 7" plates (3 chipped), eleven 9" plates, one 13 1/2" oval covered vegetable bowl, one 11 1/4" round covered vegetable bowl, one creamer, one

Photo courtesy James D. Julia Auctioneers, Fairfield, Maine; www.JuliaAuctions.com

Bowl, Moorcroft, covered, dark blue shading to light blue glaze with brightly colored floral decoration on front and back of bowl. The matching lid is entirely covered with bright floral decoration. The interior of the bowl is finished in a dark blue glaze. Signed on the underside with impressed "Moorcroft Made in England". 5 1/2" diameter. **$115**

Photo courtesy Sanford Alderfer Auction & Appraisal, Hatfield, Pa.; www.AlderferAuction.com

Bowl, Moorcroft, china with fruit motif, grapevine and leaves in blue, purple and yellow on green ground, 8 3/4" d, 2 3/4" h. **$184**

9 1/4" open vegetable bowl, one 10 1/4" open vegetable bowl, one 5" pitcher, one covered butter with liner, six butter pats, two 6" bowls and five 5 3/8" bowls. .... **$862 all**

Dinner service, (partial), Spode "New Stone" china, Stoke, Staffordshire, England, circa 1825, the floral design in underglaze blue highlighted in gilt, each with impressed maker's mark "Spode New Stone," most with painted iron-red pattern number "3702," comprising two square cut-corner bowls, seven dinner plates, two round serving trays, two covered oval tureens with undertrays, two small oval covered sauce dishes, three oblong platters and a small square covered serving dish, nineteen pieces total, (minor gilt wear). .... **$1,125 set**

Dish, Clews, historical blue china, "Winter View of Pittsfield, Mass.", and spread-wing American Eagle; also an impressed Clews mark with crown, 10 1/2" d. Repair to slight chip on rim. **$218**

Dish (figural), Dresden blue and white, young girl holding nosegay seated on handled baskets; bottom with blue crossed swords mark, impressed "132" or "182"; incised "3024"; 4 3/4" h, 5 1/2" w. **$138**

Envelope, KPM porcelain, crying putto climbs out of envelope, with applied flowers, tasseled blue pillow beneath; marked "1099"; 6 1/8" h. **$195**

Figural groups (pair), Napoleonic, porcelain, possibly Vienna, depicting the defeat of Napoleon by the Russians in 1812, 19th century, one titled, "Bautzen 21 Mai 1813," the other, "La Retraite de Russie 1812." Unmarked, 9" x 10 1/2" x 6 1/2". .... **$840 pair**

Figural stand, European, Chinoiserie porcelain, with a seated Asian elder flanked by stepped cups, possibly for condiments or eggs, late 19th century, iron-red markings on side of cup, likely the maker. 6" x 8 3/4" x 4 1/2". **$480**

Figure, Italian, ceramic, life-sized, poodle, well modeled and finely rendered detail, 20th century, marked on the base Made in Italy. 30" x 20" x 14". **$960**

Figure, Meissen porcelain, Diana retrieving an arrow from a quiver, holding a bow in her left hand, 19th century, underglaze mark and incised numerals on base. Repair to bow. 11". **$1,800**

Figures (pair), French, Chinoiserie porcelain, two gentleman and lady on cushions, painted in Kakiemon style enamels, 18th-19th century, impressed marks D.V., possibly Mennecey. Height: 5". .... **$1,440 pair**

Figures (pair), French porcelain, parrot and ceramic basket, with birds and flowers in high relief, 20th century, losses to both. Parrot marked France. Taller: 17 1/4". .... **$480 pair**

Figures (pair), Venus and Cupid on round bases, KPM porcelain, both with under-glaze and incised marks, 15 1/2". .... **$2,160 pair**

Figures (three), porcelain putti with instruments, each seated on leaf-molded urn, one playing panpipes, second playing two horns, third playing cymbals, approximately 6" h, crowned G mark, Italian, 20th century. .... **$184 set**

Figures (23), Meissen porcelain, monkey band, including the music stand, 20th century, all bear Meissen marks and incised numbers. Conductor: 7". .... **$22,800 set**

Game service, Limoges, Rococo, hand-painted bird and flower decoration on molded ground, gilt trim; consisting of 18 1/4" oval platter, ten 9 1/4" plates and two 5 3/4" shallow bowls. .... **$431 set**

Photo courtesy James D. Julia Auctioneers, Fairfield, Maine; www.JuliaAuctions.com

Ewer, Ernst Wahliss, Art Nouveau. In the form of a young maiden supporting the spout. Art Nouveau decoration with floral flourishes and gilded highlights. Signed "EW Turn Wien" in a crown and "Made in Austria", "4689.237.9." and impressed "Made in Austria 4689". 7 1/2" h. **$2,300**

Photo courtesy Sanford Alderfer Auction & Appraisal, Hatfield, Pa.; www.AlderferAuction.com

Ewer, Austrian pottery, Teplitz, flask form with five spouts at top, stylized yellow flowers on dark blue bands and medallions, cream ground, gilt trim, circa 1910, impressed "1169/7" and red Teplitz mark on bottom, 16 7/8" h. **$460**

Photo courtesy Sanford Alderfer Auction & Appraisal, Hatfield, Pa.; www.AlderferAuction.com

Figures (pair), Capo-di-Monte, classical females, one at desk with compass and scroll, other sculpting helmeted bust on stand, oval base, porcelain, Capo-di-Monte, 19th century, 6 1/2" h. **$510 pair**

Ice cream set, tray and six plates, English majolica, with fan design, maker unknown, 19th century, tray stamped with maker's mark and registration numbers, all illegible. Tray: 1 1/2" x 14 3/4" x 9". .... **$390 set**

Jar (figural), Martin Brothers, stoneware, grotesque bird, a couple of minor flecks. Base inscribed RW Martin & Brothers London + Southall 1893, head inscribed Martin Brothers London + Southall 12-93, 15" x 9". **$54,000**

Jardinière, Fives-Lille (France), organic motif with curled leaf-like handles under a dynamic and flowing white, blue, gold, and pink crystalline glaze. Restoration to small chip on edge of leaf. Die-stamp mark L'ISLE – ADAM, 9" x 12". **$2,040**

Jardinières and pedestals (pair), Doulton Lambeth, stoneware, by Frank A. Butler, the jardinières with a row of carved angels over lotus leaves, the pedestals with complementary leaf designs, 1876. Some losses to angels on jardinières, bottom of one has crude restoration to breaks, which cannot be seen from interior, probably done in factory. Each piece stamped DOULTON LAMBETH 1876, one jardinière inscribed FAB. Jardinières: 14" x 19", pedestals: 38" x 18 1/2" and 37" x 17 3/4". .... **$7,800 pair**

Jug, Liverpool creamware, England, early 19th century, transfer designs of Masonic symbols, signed by the engraver "Kennedy" (probably J. Kennedy of Burslem), under the spout with various Masonic elements with a ribbon inscribed "Mason Form'd out of the Meteirals [sic] of His Lodge," one side with Masonic symbols woven into a wreath surrounding a motto, (imperfections), 11 1/2" h. Old repairs-spout repaired, three repaired cracks on side, handle repaired, brownish discoloration. **$651**

Lamp base, Clement Massier, gourd-shaped with four scalloped buttressed handles, painted with mistletoe in luster glaze. One re-glued handle, a few small glaze chips. Incised MCM 1900 R, 6" x 10 1/2". **$1,020**

Mugs, (three), British creamware, mochaware, two similar with blue background and seaweed stalks. One having wide green band with seaweed stalks and upper blue band. Some discoloring, generally very good. .... **$360 all**

Pitcher, Masonic, commemorative, for the Ancient Landmark Lodge, Portland, Maine. Flow blue pitcher by Royal Doulton, Burslem, to commemorate the Ancient Landmark Lodge

Photo courtesy Sanford Alderfer Auction & Appraisal, Hatfield, Pa.; www.AlderferAuction.com

Figures (pair), Staffordshire, lady and gentleman in Scottish attire, each standing next to sheep, approximately 7 3/4" h, figure of lady with 5/8" hairline running horizontally just above base. **$345 pair**

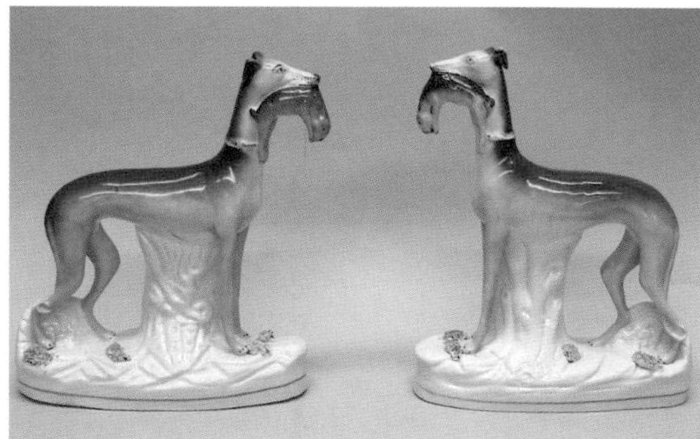

Photo courtesy Sanford Alderfer Auction & Appraisal, Hatfield, Pa.; www.AlderferAuction.com

Figures (pair), Staffordshire, whippets with catch, each with rabbit in mouth, rocky plinth, 11" h. **$330 pair**

No. 17, Portland, Maine Centennial Celebration, 1806-1906, marked in a cartouche and presented at the Centennial celebration June 10th, 1906. Sides with Masonic emblems and writing, "Instituted 5806 A.L.M. Lodge Portland". Decorated overall with foliate sprays and Masonic symbols. Marked on base Royal Doulton England, 8 1/2" h. Small fleck to gold gilding on lip of pitcher. **$172**

Pitcher, Royal Worcester, porcelain, bold lavender flowers on yellow ground, stag horn-form handle side, gilt trim, Reg. No. 37112. **$92**

Pitcher, Royal Worcester, porcelain, gilt bas relief flowers below rim, handle side, gilt trim, Registry No. 117049, 8 3/4" h. **$103**

Plaque, Zsolnay, Art Nouveau, painted with a maiden by a pond with swans, and "framed" with three-dimensional gargoyles, entirely covered in blue and gold luster glaze. A few professional touch-ups to edges. Five churches stamp with ZSOLNAY PECS, 19" x 18". **$31,200**

Plate (cabinet), George Jones & Sons Crescent China, hand-painted with the Three Graces in landscape, and raised gilt decoration. Partially erased puce mark stamped Made In England, signed H. Nosek, 19th century, 10" d. **$5,700**

Plate, (cabinet), porcelain, hand-painted, "Lady Harrington and her two sons," 19th century, signed Wagner, Dec. 314, Deposc, spurious over-glaze blue crest mark, Clairon Germany with green star mark, 9 3/4". **$1,920**

Plate, (cabinet), Royal Vienna, hand-painted with a classical scene, 19th century, signed Fiala, under-glaze blue crest mark, 9 1/4" d. **$660**

Plate, (cabinet), Royal Vienna, hand-painted with classical scene, 19th century, marked Grazien, signed Knoeller, under-glaze blue crest mark, 9 5/8" d. **$960**

Plates, (pair, cabinet), Royal Vienna, hand-painted, one titled "Die Musik," the other "Sehnsucht," 19th century, both signed Riemer, with under-glaze blue crest marks, 9 1/2" d. **$660 pair**

Plates, (pair), historical blue, J. & W. Ridgway, "Beauties of America" and "City Hall/New York"; floral border, 9 3/4" d. **$258 pair**

Plates, (two), Delftware, England, 18th century, polychrome-decorated with bird and floral landscape, (larger plate with repaired crack, crazing, rim chips), 13 1/4" and 8 7/8" d. **$533 both**

Plates, (four) with scenes, Sarreguemines, French faience, interior scenes with Dr. Herr Maire and figures; three signed "Frederic Regainey" and one signed "M. Loux"; 8 5/8" d. **$138 set**

Plates, (eight), Royal Copenhagen, Flora Danica, porcelain painted with various fruit, openwork border with gilding; all marked 'Royal Copenhagen, Denmark', and under-glaze blue stamp; together with two larger plates, one with a moose, the other with a wolf, all 20th century, Flora Danica: 9" d, animal plates: 10" d. **$9,000 all**

Plates, (eight), Sevres porcelain, with portraits of famous women on green enameled ground and stylized gilt decoration, 19th century, some signed Georget, some titled, all stamped M. Imple de Sevres [Manifacture Imperiale de Sevres], 9 1/2" d. **$3,480 set**

Photo courtesy Skinner Inc., Boston, www.SkinnerInc.com

Mug, mochaware, quart, England, early 19th century with thin brown and reeded green bands flanking a wide pumpkin band with brown dendritic decoration, 5 1/2" h. Some segments of brown glaze are missing on the thin bands on rim and base, done in the making, scattered light brownish discoloration. **$1,066**

Photo courtesy Skinner Inc., Boston, www.SkinnerInc.com

Plate, Delftware, England, 18th century, with polychrome decorated floral and bird designs, (rim chips), 11 3/4" d. **$444**

Hand-Painted Pitcher. Back stamp: Set of initials under glaze and second set atop glaze. Date hand painted under glaze of 1893. 5 1/2" t. **$47**

do not go all the way through, 8" d. Oval bowl shows wear, 6 1/2" x 9". .... **$32 both**

Soup Bowls (2), Butter Pats (4) and Creamer. Luray Pattern by Bishop & Stonier. Back stamp: Mark 387. Circa 1899. Butter pats show crazing and two show some discoloration. Soup bowls show slight crazing to one. .... **$59 all**

Open Vegetable Bowl and Plate, Lusitania Pattern by Alfred Colley Ltd. Back stamp: Mark 999. Circa 1910. Bowl shows wear and light staining with small nick to back side of rim, 9 1/4" d. Plate shows wear but not chips or cracks noted, 10" d. .... **$23 both**

Plate and Vegetable Bowl, Lyndhurst Pattern by W.H. Grindley. Back stamp: Mark 1842. Circa 1891. Both pieces show wear. Plate 9" d. Bowl 10" d. .... **$47 both**

Small Oval Platter and Oval Vegetable Bowl, Manhattan Pattern by Henry Alcock & Co. Back stamp: Mark 65. Circa 1891-1900. Vegetable bowl is 7" x 9 3/4". Platter is 8 1/2" x 12 1/2" with crazing and discoloration. .... **$35 both**

Soup Bowl and Small Sauce Dish, Marie Pattern by W.H. Grindley. Back stamp: Mark 1842. Circa 1891. Rd. No. 250387. Small sauce dish has tiny rim spot and bowl has chip under outside rim. Slight crazing in sauce dish. .... **$29 both**

Cup and Saucer, and Small Serving Dish. Cup and Saucer are Medway Pattern by Alfred Meakin Ltd. Back stamp: Mark 2582. Circa 1897. Crazing to cup with tiny chip to foot rim. Small serving dish is Albemarle Pattern (same as Medway) by Alfred Meakin Ltd. Back stamp: Mark 2586. Circa 1891. Small chip to back edge of rim, 7" d. .... **$20 all**

Plate and Platter, Neapolitan Pattern by Johnson Bros. Back stamp: Mark 2177. Circa 1900. Plate shows wear and small chip to back of rim. Platter shows wear and two chips to back rim. Plate 7" d. Platter 10 3/4" x 14". .... **$29 both**

Gravy Boat with Underplate, and Covered Tureen. Oban Pattern by Alfred Meakin. Back stamp: Similar to Mark 2583. Circa 1891. Pieces have some staining and crazing. Small chip to inside lip of tureen. .... **$35 both**

Flat Bowl and Dinner Plate, Osborne Pattern by W.H. Grindley. Back stamp: Mark 1842. Circa 1900. Bowl shows staining and both pieces have crazing. Bowl 7 3/4" d. Plate 10" d. .... **$15 both**

Soup Plate and Sauce Dishes (2), Paris Pattern by Johnson Bros. Back stamp: Mark 2177. Circa 1900. Soup plate shows crazing. Sauce dishes show wear. .... **$18 all**

Shallow Bowl and Small Plate, brush-stroke pattern in the style of Petrus Regout, Dutch. Back stamp: in bowl, impressed "E", "F" and "9.L", in plate, impressed "F" and "AR". Circa 1891-1900. Both pieces have some staining and crazing. Bowl 9 1/4" d. Plate 7 3/4" d. .... **$65 both**

Plate, Bread Plate, Vegetable Bowl and Gravy Boat. Portman Pattern by W.H. Grindley. Back stamp: Mark 1842. Circa 1891. Small chip to back of vegetable bowl, three small chips to back of plate, discoloring and crazing on plate and bread plate. .... **$77 all**

Gravy Boat with Underplate, and Covered Tureen. Princess Pattern by Booths. Back stamp: Mark 451. Circa 1900-1915. Rd. No. 183173. Gravy Boat has crazing with small crack to rim and hairline with chip on bottom foot. Underplate shows some staining. Tureen shows crazing with light staining and hairline to inside lip of dish. Cover shows good repair to handle. .... **$12 both**

Cup and Saucer, Plate and Covered Vegetable Dish. Raleigh Pattern by Burgess & Leigh. Back stamp: Mark 717 & Mark

Milk Pitcher with Gold Trim. Clematis Pattern by Furnivals Ltd. Back stamp: 1653-5 Marks. Circa 1900. Reg. No.: Printed 362684, impressed 356048. **$153**

Chocolate Pot with Lid. Unmarked. Circa Probably 1890-1900. Excellent condition. **$242**

718. Circa 1906-1912. Reg. 393237 on Vegetable dish. Vegetable dish has crazing. Plate is 8 3/4" d with crazing and chip beneath outside of rim as well as a repair mark. Cup and saucer have crazing with a chip to foot of cup, hairline crack and discoloration. .... **$100 all**

Plate and Bone Dish, Richmond Pattern by Johnson Bros. Back stamp: Mark 2177. Circa 1900. Shows wear and crazing, 10" d. .... **$38 both**

Plate and Cup and Saucer, by Sampson Hancock & Son. Back stamp: Mark 1928. Circa 1891. Plate is 8 1/2" d and also marked, "Stoke on Trent" and "England". Saucer has tiny chip beneath outside of rim. Cup has factory flaws. .. **$29 all**

Plate with Cup and Saucer, Splendid Pattern by Societe Ceramique. Back stamp: Maastricht and Made in Holland. Circa 1900. Crazing and discoloration on plate with crazing on back side of saucer and faint hairline on inside of cup. Plate is 9" d. .... **$29 all**

Plate and Cereal Bowl, Somerset Pattern by W.H. Grindley. Back stamp: Mark 1843. Circa 1910-1914. Bowl has one spot of missing glaze, 7" d. Plate shows crazing. .... **$50 both**

Dinner Plate, Small Waste Bowl and Tall Fancy Pitcher. Taylor, Smith & Taylor Co. Back stamp: Mark #B. Circa 1899-1905. Pitcher is 9" tall and has crazing, unmarked. Plate is 9" d and has crazing and discoloration. Waste bowl has some rough edges. .... **$44 all**

Vegetable Bowl and Plate, bowl is Trent I Pattern by Wood & Son. Back stamp: Mark 4285. Circa 1891. Plate is Trent II Patter by Wood & Son. Back stamp: Mark 4285. Circa 1891-1895. Both 9" d. .... **$12 both**

Plate, Pattern is of fruit, flowers and butterfly by Cauldon. Back stamp: Cauldon printed and impressed. Circa 1891. Rgd. No. 183243. Plate shows wear and small chip to rim edge, 10 1/2" d. **$15**

Sugar (no lid) and Creamer, Vista Pattern by G.L. Ashworth & Bros. Ltd. Back stamp: Mark 2530 & Mason's. Circa 1891. Pieces have crazing but no chips or cracks, 4 1/4" t. .... **$12 pair**

Small Platter, Two Plates and Saucer. Waldorf Pattern by New Wharf Pottery. Back stamp: Mark 2886. Circa 1892. Plates are 9" d and show utensil marks. Platter is 9" x 10 3/4" and shows some wear. Saucer is 6" d. .... **$165 all**

Dresser Tray and Sauce Dish, Warwick China Co. with a Wild Rose pattern. Back stamp: Mark 38. Circa 1900. Chip to inside rim of dresser tray, 6" x 10 1/4" and crazing to sauce dish, 3" x 7 3/4". .... **$56 both**

Sauce and Serving Dish, York Pattern by W. & E. Corn. Back stamp: Mark 1113. Circa 1900-1904. Sauce dish shows some wear, 5 1/4" d. Serving dish shows discoloration and crazing along with some missing glaze on rim edges, 10" x 11 1/2". .... **$32 both**

Assorted Flow Blue Pieces Listed by Form

Gravy Boats

Flow Blue and Polychrome Gravy Boat, Derby Pattern by W.H. Grindley. Back stamp: Mark 1842. Circa 1891. **$65**

Gravy Boat and Underplate, Torbay Pattern by Bishop & Stonier. Back stamp: Mark 387. Circa 1900. Three chips on foot of gravy boat with some discoloration. Small spot on underplate rim missing glaze. **$12**

Gravy Boat with Underplate, Grace Pattern by W.H. Grindley. Back stamp: Mark 1842. Circa 1897. Tray has two chips to rim and one chip beneath outside rim. Gravy boat has four chips to base, hairline on handle and light discoloration on spout. **$47**

Teapot. Shapoo Pattern by Thomas Hughes. Back stamp: Printed initials plus pattern name in cartouche, Mark 2121. Circa 1860-1870. Spout lid is either replacement or heavily repaired. Spout has been restored. Small manufacturer's crease in handle. **$354**

Soup Plate. Indian Plant Pattern by Thomas Dimmock. Back stamp: Mark 1298 (Also marked Kaolin Ware and 'D'). Tiny chip on outer rim. 10 1/2" d. **$94**

Gravy Boat with Underplate, Hamilton Pattern by John Maddock & Sons. Back stamp: Mark 2464. Circa 1896. Gravy boat has hairline crack on inside that does go through to the outside with slight discoloration. Platter shows wear with some discolored blemishes on backside. 7 1/4" x 10 1/4". **$29**

Gravy Boat with Underplate, Olga Pattern by Ridgways. Back stamp: Mark 3312 or 3313. Circa 1905-1912. Some staining on both pieces. Gravy boat handle has two cracks, repaired. Crazing on both pieces. **$12**

Gravy Boat, Marguerite Pattern by W.H. Grindley. Back stamp: Mark 1842. Circa 1891. No chips or cracks noted but some crazing. **$23**

Gravy Boat, Verona Pattern by Ridgways. Back stamp: Mark 3313. Circa 1910. Has mended stress line at base of handle. **$29**

Creamers, Pitchers and Pots

Chocolate Pot with Lid, Abbey Pattern by George Jones & Sons. Back stamp: printed pattern name, "1790," potter and "England". Circa 1900. 6" t. **$47**

Creamer, Phoebe Pattern by Wedgwood & Co. Ltd. Back stamp: Mark 4059. Circa 1906. Small hairline on outside bowl as well as small crack that goes through to inside. **$12**

Large Milk Pitcher, Columbia Pattern by Clementson & Young. Unmarked. Circa 1846. Small hairline inside spout, 7 3/4" t. **$106**

Milk Pitcher, Azalia Pattern by J. Kent Ltd. Back stamp: Mark 2267, Except word Fenton instead of Longton. Circa 1913+. 7 1/4" t. **$118**

Milk Pitcher, Decoration includes three poppies. Unmarked. Circa 1900 or earlier. Some staining inside with discoloration and crazing throughout. 7 3/4" t. **$50**

Milk Pitcher, Osborne Pattern by W.H. Grindley. Back stamp: Mark 1842. Circa 1900, 6 3/4" t. **$195**

Milk Pitcher, with top and base trim of gold design and white/yellow enamel dot trim. Pattern not indicated but piece is by Keller & Guerin. Back stamp: K et G, Luneville, France. Circa 1900-1910. No chips or cracks but bit of enamel dots missing around the base design. Crazing. **$91**

Pitcher, decorated with cherubs and gold by Wheeling Pottery, U.S.A. Back stamp: La Belle China. Shows crazing. 8" t. **$124**

Small Cream Ewer, Astoria Pattern by Pitcairns Ltd. Back stamp: Mark 3052. Circa 1895. 3 1/2" t. **$59**

Tall Water Pitcher, Oxford Pattern by William Adderly & Co. Back stamp: Mark 48 and printed trademark #49 with W.A.A. & Co. Circa 1886-1905. 11 1/2" t. **$88**

Teapot with Lid, Lobelia Pattern by G. Phillips. Back stamp: Mark 3012. Circa 1845. Deep crack around base and hairline cracks inside and one outside. Some rough areas to finial. 9" t. **$59**

Plates

Advertising Plates (4), all plates have crazing. No chips or cracks noted. First plate is from the Cleveland Grocery Co., Groceries, Wall Paper, Fancy China, New London, Ohio, and has La Francaise Porcelain printed on back. Second plate is from J. H. Mollenkop, 1913, General Merchandise and also has La Francaise Porcelain printed on back. Third plate is unmarked and is Compliments of H.M. Rule, General Merchandise, Darlington, Ohio. Fourth plate is from Pittsburgh Commandery, 1898. Printed on back is Knowles, Taylor, Knowles, East Liverpool, Ohio, U.S.A. All plates are between 8" and 8 1/2" d. .... **$47 all**

Cake Plate, Gironde Pattern by W.H. Grindley. Back stamp: Mark 1842. Circa 1891. Reg. No. 293169. Some wear and crazing. 9 1/2" x 10 3/4". **$59**

Decorative Plates (2), Birds at Fountain/Exotic Birds Pattern, possibly by Josiah Wedgwood & Sons. Back stamp: imprinted "FN" and "ORD" and "1M". Marks could indicate October 1875. Outer edges of plates have pierced, open borders of vertical bars. Both plates have crazing. 8" d. .... **$23 pair**

Plate. Brush-stroke pattern with bluebells, and grapes and cherry border. Unmarked. Circa 1845-1865. Small nick to rim edge and crazing, 9 1/2" d. **$136**

Oval Platter. Venice Pattern by Upper Hanley Pottery Co. Back stamp: Mark 3929A. Circa 1900-1910. Reg. No. 354458 printed. 11 1/2" x 15 1/2". **$94**

Dessert/Cake Plate, with Molded Handles. Shusan Pattern by F. & R. Pratt & Co. Unmarked but matches Shusan, mark 3144. Circa 1855-65. Small chip to rim, 9" x 10". **$59**

Dinner Plate and Smaller Plate, Excelsior Pattern by Thomas Fell. Back stamp: Mark 1534. Circa 1850. Large plate shows staining and crazing, 9 1/4" d. Small plate shows two tiny nicks to rim edge, 6 1/2" d. .... **$50 both**

Dinner Plate, Agra Pattern by F. Winkle & Co. Back stamp: Mark 4214. Circa 1891. .... **$35**

Dinner Plate, Athens I Pattern by Charles Meigh. Back stamp: Mark 2618 or 2614A. Marked initials "C.M.". Circa 1840. Discoloration and crazing. 10 1/4" d. **$41**

Dinner Plate, Athol Pattern by Burgess & Leigh. Back stamp: Mark 718. Circa 1910. Rd. No. printed 324171, Rd. No. impressed 364190. Plate shows wear, 9 3/4" d. **$12**

Dinner Plate, Canton Pattern by John Maddock. Back stamp: Mark 2461. Circa 1850-1855. Shows wear and crazing, 9 1/2" d. **$18**

Dinner Plate, Coronet Pattern by Sampson Hancock & Sons. Back stamp: Mark 1933. Circa 1912. Reg. No.: 341031. 9" d. **$76**

Dinner Plate, Flora Pattern possibly by Cockson & Chetwynd. Back stamp: Mark 976. Circa 1867. Small chip to under side of rim and to foot rim. Has crazing and shows wear. 9 1/2" d. **$100**

Dinner Plate, Madras Pattern by Doulton & Co., Burslem, England. Back stamp: Mark 1832. Circa 1902. 10" d. **$29**

Dinner Plate, Vinranka, Percy Pattern by Gefle, made in Sweden. Back stamp: marked as stated prior and with circle containing three brick kilns belching smoke. Circa 1967 Modern. 10 1/4" d. **$18**

Flow Blue and Polychrome Plate, Bullfinch Pattern by Wedgwood. Back stamp: printed pattern name, Wedgwood, Etruria, England and impressed Wedgwood, plus others. 10 1/4" d. **$41**

Footed Cake Plate, Napier (Polychrome) Pattern by Wedgwood. Back stamp: FB cartouche containing pattern name and impressed WEDGWOOD and PEARL and gold painted number 2931. .... **$118**

Fourteen-Sided Plate, Arabesque Pattern by T.J. & J. Mayer. Back stamp: Mark 2570 (Also marked "Chinese Porcelain & Longport"). Circa 1850. Large chip to foot ring. 10 1/2" d. **$21**

Heavy Plate, Grandmother's Flowers Pattern by Elsmore & Forster. Back stamp: Unreadable impression in circular pattern. Circa 1850-1860. Plate has some roughness around the edge with heavy discoloration and crazing. 10" d. .. **$12**

Pedestal Cake/Tart Plate, by W.H. Grindley. Back stamp: Mark 1843 printed in green. Circa 1914-1925. 4 1/2" t x 10" w. Crazing around polychrome picture on inside of plate. **$41**

Plate with 10 Smaller Plates, Florida Pattern by Johnson Bros. Back stamp: Mark 2177. Circa 1900. Large plate has discoloration, cracks, chips and crazing, 9 1/2" d. Six of the smaller plates have crazing. The other four have chips and crazing, 7" d. .... **$65 all**

Plate with Six Panels, Nankin Pattern with impressed "Ironstone" on back. Circa 1845. 9 1/2" d with normal wear. **$38**

Plate, Chen-Si Pattern by John Meir. Back stamp: Marked I.M., Mark 2632. Circa 1835. 10 1/2" with hairline cracks, crazing and wear. **$29**

Plate, Chinese Pattern by Wedgwood. Back stamp: Mark 4088 and impressed "Wedgwood". Circa 1908-1910. Plate shows some wear, 8 1/4" d. **$23**

Plate, Chusan Pattern by J. Clementson. Back stamp: Mark 910a. Circa 1839-1864. Piece shows professional repair on rim. 9 1/4" d. **$12**

Plate, Elgar Pattern by Upper Hanley Pottery Co. Back stamp: Mark 3928-29A. Circa 1895-1910. Plate shows some crazing and tiny nick to back side of rim edge. 9" d. **$12**

Covered Tureen. Mongolia Pattern by Johnson Bros. Back stamp: Mark 2177. Circa 1900. Dish has crazing. 9 1/2" x 11". **$366**

Plate, Gladys Pattern by New Wharf Pottery. Back stamp: Mark 2883 (This mark doesn't contain the words "& Co." so may be other than Mark 2883). Circa 1891. Shows some wear, 9" d. **$18**

Plate, Ivanhoe Pattern by Wedgwood. Back stamp: Imprint of IVANHOE, WEDGWOOD and ETRURIA, ENGLAND. Circa 1901-1910. 10 1/4" d. **$35**

Plate, Paneled, 14-sided. Tonquin Pattern by W. Adams & Son. Back stamp: Mark 22. Circa 1845. Shows some wear and crazing, 8 1/2" d. **$100**

Plate, Scinde Pattern by J. & G. Alcock includes some decorative pattern on rear of plate as well. Back stamp: Mark 69, also impressed with "Oriental Stone". Circa 1840. Tiny chip to outside rim and does show crazing. 8 1/2" d. **$41**

Plate, Spanish Festivities Pattern by George Jones. Back stamp: Mark 2218. Circa 1891-1924. 9 1/4" d. **$32**

Plate, Water-Lilly Pattern by Wedgwood/Etruria England. 10" d. **$130**

Plates (2), Avon-Ware Pattern by Booths. Back stamp: Booths impressed. Circa 1880-1890. One plate has crazing. 9" d. .... **$41 pair**

Plates (2), Geisha Pattern by Upper Hanley Potteries Ltd. Back stamp: Mark 3929A. Circa 1901. One plate shows crazing and what looks like a repair. 9" d. **$18**

Plates (2), Hong Pattern by Petrus Regout & Co. Back stamp: P.R. also marked Maastricht. Circa 1900. Crow's foot on bottom of one plate and shows some wear, 8" d. Other plate 8 3/4" d. .... **$23 both**

Plates (2), Manilla Pattern by Podmore Walker & Co. Back stamp: Mark 3075 & Mark 3076. Circa 1845. Both plates are 10" d with crazing and normal wear. .... **$165 pair**

Plates (2), Osborne Pattern by Ridgways. Back stamp: Mark 3312. Circa 1905. Both plates have staining and crazing. 8" and 9" d. .... **$18 both**

Plates (2), Pelew Pattern by E. Challinor. Back stamp: Mark 855A. Circa 1840. Both plates show wear and crazing, 8 3/4" d. **$65**

Plates (2), Sobraon Pattern by Hill Pottery. Back stamp: Cartouche containing pattern name and one plate also has Hill Pottery print. Circa 1870-1880. Plates show wear, with crazing and slight discoloration, 10 1/2" d. .... **$94 pair**

Plates (2), The Temple Pattern by Podmore Walker. Back stamp: Mark 3080. Circa 1850. Both plates show wear and crazing. Large plate has large chip and nick to rim. Also nick to foot rim. 7" and 10 3/4" d. .... **$122 both**

Plates (2), Tokio Pattern by Johnson Bros. Back stamp: Mark 2179. Circa 1913. Plates show crazing. 7" d. .... **$38 pair**

Large Covered Sugar Bowl. Scinde Pattern by Thomas Walker. Unmarked. Circa 1847. Bowl has some discoloration inside and around outside bottom area. Tiny chips to rim of foot. Cover has large chip inside lip with some retouched areas. **$118**

Plates (3), Belport Pattern by John Maddock & Sons Ltd. Back stamp: Mark 2464. Circa 1896 - Two of the three plates also impressed with a crown above the initials "V" and "LX". Tiny chip to rim of third plate. 7" d. .... **$12 all**

Plates (3), Chapoo Pattern by J. Wedgwood. Back stamp: Mark 4276A. Circa 1850. Small plate has two small chips to foot rim, 4 1/4" d. Medium plate shows wear, crazing and small nick to rim edge, 6 1/4" d. Large plate shows wear, crazing and large chip to back of rim, 10 1/2" d. .... **$35 all**

Plates (3), Rock Pattern by E. Challinor or Masons. Back stamp: Cartouche containing pattern name. Circa 1850. Large plate is very worn with crazing, 9 1/2" d. Of the two smaller plates, one shows discoloration and one has staining to back and shows crazing, 6 1/4" d. .... **$59 all**

Plates (3), Somerset Pattern by W.H. Grindley. Back stamp: Mark 1842 & Mark 1843. Circa 1891 & 1910-1914. Medium plate 9" d has chip to rim, hairline crack and crazing. Large plate with Mark 1842. Back stamp shows wear and small chip to back side of plate beneath rim. Other large plate 10" d shows staining and crazing. .... **$23 all**

Plates (4), Pomona Pattern by E. M. Co. (Edge Malkin & Co.). Back stamp: Mark 1445 printed and Mark 1440 impressed. Circa 1880-1891. Plates show some staining and crazing. 8" d. .... **$12 all**

Plates (9), Touraine Pattern by Henry Alcock & Co. Back stamp: Mark 65. Circa 1898. Rd. No. 329815. Of the nine plates, three show staining and crazing and one has small nick to back side of rim, 9" d. .... **$65 all**

Small Plate, in Wire Basket. Decoration includes flowers with buds and leaves. Unmarked. Circa 1890. Plate is 5" and basket measures 8" x 11 1/2". **$53**

Soup Plate, Circassia Pattern by J. & G. Alcock. Back stamp: Mark 69. Circa 1840. Shows crazing and wear. Piece also impressed "ORIENTAL STONE". 10 1/2" d. **$18**

Soup Plate, Countess Pattern by T.R. & Co. Back stamp: Mark 3205. Circa 1912. Hairline on back, small stained area and crazing. **$15**

Soup Plate, Indiana Pattern by Wedgwood & Co. Back stamp: Mark 4055 impressed and Mark 4056 imprinted. Circa 1870. Two tiny chips and one small chip to top of rim, with some staining to back of plate. Shows some wear. 10 1/4" d. **$23**

Soup Plate, Spring Pattern by W.H. Grindley & Co. Back stamp: Mark 1842. Circa 1890-1891. .... **$15**

Soup Plate, Sylvan Pattern by T.C. Brown-Westhead, Moore & Co. Back stamp: Mark 684. Includes initials B.W.M. & Co. with letter "S" and No. "14". Circa 1900. Some crazing. **$23**

Soup Plates (3), Congo Pattern by Dudson Wilcox & Till Ltd. Back stamp: Mark 1412. Circa 1902-1926. One bowl has tiny nick to rim, two bowls have discoloration and all three bowls have crazing. .... **$12 all**

Platters

Deep Platter or Vegetable Dish, Keswick Pattern by Wood & Son. Back stamp: Mark 4285. Circa 1891-1898. 12" x 9". **$20**

Deep Platters or Vegetable Dishes, Keswick Pattern by Wood & Son. Back stamp: Mark 4285. Circa 1891-1898. Both platters/dishes show some wear but no chips or cracks noted. 9 1/2" x 12 1/4". .... **$23 both**

Eight-Sided Platter, Hong Kong Pattern by Charles Meigh. Back stamp: Unmarked with faint pattern name. Should be Mark 2618. Circa 1845. Some discoloration on back. 13 1/2" x 10 1/4". **$242**

Eight-Sided Platter, Kin Shan Pattern by Edward Challinor. Unmarked except for imprinted asterisk "*" on back with a blue "3". Circa 1855. Rim mark to right top corner that looks to have created stained crazing on back of plate. Normal wear. **$206**

Eight-Sided Platter, with a Deep Well. Castle Pattern. Circa 1850. Shows wear. 12 3/4" x 16 1/4". **$82**

Large Oval Platter, Beaufort Pattern by W.H. Grindley. Back stamp: Mark 1842. Reg. No. 408448. Circa 1903. No chips or cracks noted but does have utensil marks. **$141**

Large Platter, Buccleuce Pattern. Back stamp: Cartouche containing pattern name. Circa 1845. Plate shows some staining with two chips and hairline to edge. 14 3/4" x 18 1/4". **$23**

Handleless Cup and Saucer. Chapoo Pattern by J. Wedgwood. Back stamp: Mark 4276A. Circa 1850. Crazing and small nick to cup foot rim. **$82**

Toothbrush Holder with Cover. Cover has three small air holes. Design is a Floral Dogwood Pattern by Copeland/Late Spode. Circa 1847-1867. Crazing with tiny nick to cover rim. **$94**

Large Platter, Chatsworth Pattern by Ford & Sons. Back stamp: Mark 1585/1586. Circa 1893-1900. Plate has crazing. 13 3/4" x 18 3/4". **$29**

Large Platter, Chusan Pattern by J. Clementson. Back stamp: Mark 910A (Ironstone/Phoenix Bird & J. Clementson). Circa 1839-1864. Some discoloration but no chips or cracks. 12" x 16". **$283**

Large Platter, Dresden Pattern by Villeroy & Boch, (German). Back stamp: Mark 40. Circa 1900-1915. Some discoloration and crazing. 14 1/2" x 20 1/4". **$26**

Oval Platter, Clover Pattern by W.H. Grindley. Back stamp: Mark 1843. Circa 1914-1925. Couple small nicks on rim edge, 14 1/2" x 10 3/4". **$23**

Oval Platters (2), Sandringham Pattern by W. Adams & Co. Back stamp: Mark 30 and England. After 1891. Smaller platter has three small nicks to rim edge on back side, 8 1/4" x 11 1/4". Larger platter has two small nicks on rim edge, 9 1/4" x 12 1/4". .... **$41 both**

Platter by Burgess & Leigh, back stamp: Mark 715. Circa 1870, 16" x 13" with crazing, discoloration and a crack. **$15**

Platter, Alaska Pattern by W.H. Grindley. Back stamp: Mark 1842. Circa 1891. Platter shows wear, 7 1/2" x 10 1/4". .. **$47**

Platter, Alaska Pattern by W.H. Grindley. Back stamp: Mark 1842. Circa 1891. Platter shows wear, 10 1/4" x 14 1/4". **$76**

Platter, Alpha Pattern by Knowles, Taylor & Knowles (American). Circa 1890-1900. Piece shows slight wear, 11 3/4" x 15 1/4". **$35**

Platter, Andorra Pattern by Johnson Bros. Back stamp: Mark 2177. Circa 1901. Rd. No. is impressed on back. Shows some wear. 12" x 16". **$35**

Platter, Astral Pattern by W.H. Grindley. Back stamp: Mark 1842. Circa 1891 or a bit later. Reg. No. 426592. Three nicks to rim edge and crazing, 11 1/2" x 16 1/4". **$65**

Platter, Berlin Vase Pattern by I. Ridgway. Back stamp: printed design with pattern name and potter. Circa 1845-1850. Piece shows wear, staining, crazing, hairline crack and chip to rim edge. 10 1/2" x 12 3/4". **$12**

Platter, Clarendon Pattern by Henry Alcock & Co., Ltd. Back stamp: Mark 65. Normal surface wear, some discoloration and crazing. Small chip to rim or edge mark from the kiln rack, 11 3/4" x 16 1/4". **$35**

Platter, Dainty Pattern by John Maddock & Sons. Back stamp: Mark 2464. Circa 1896. Platter has crazing, 11 1/4" x 14 3/4". **$118**

Platter, Derby Pattern by W.H. Grindley. Back stamp: Mark 1842. Circa 1891. Small chip to back rim, 9" x 12". **$15**

Platter, Dorothy Pattern by Johnson Bros. Back stamp: Mark 2177. Circa 1900. Platter shows some wear with tiny chip to back side of rim. 12" x 16 1/4". **$41**

Platter, Dover Pattern by W.H. Grindley. Back stamp: Mark 1842. Circa 1891-1920's. 10 1/4" x 14". **$77**

Platter, Erie Pattern by Bourne & Leigh Ltd. Back stamp: F.B. J F.L. Circa 1900. Discoloration on front and back of platter with a couple tiny chips and some roughness to rim. Also some glazing. 12" x 16 1/4". **$29**

Platter, Flow Blue with Polychrome Chinoiserie with Lustre Chinese Pattern that is impressed "Ashworth". Back stamp: Mark 137. Circa 1862-1880. Shows wear from use with some roughness around outer edge. 11 1/2" x 14 1/4". **$18**

Platter, Gironde Pattern by W.H. Grindley. Back stamp: Mark 1842. Circa 1891. Shows some wear. 10 1/2" x 15". **$77**

Platter, Grace Pattern by W.H. Grindley. Back stamp: Mark 1842. Circa 1897. Some surface wear. 17" x 12". **$188**

Platter, Grosvenor Pattern by Moyatt Son & Co. Back stamp: Mark 2811. Circa 1907. Three small chips to plate edge. 14 3/4" x 18 1/2". **$47**

Platter, Grosvenor Pattern by Moyatt Son & Co. Back stamp: Mark 2811. Circa 1907. Three small chips to plate edge. 14 3/4" x 18 1/2". **$47**

Platter, Haddon Pattern by W.H. Grindley. Back stamp: Mark 1842. Circa 1891. Large chip to back side of end handle and small chips to back side of other end handle with tiny amount visible from the front. 12" x 8 1/2". **$26**

Platter, Kelvin Pattern by Alfred Meakin Ltd. Back stamp: Mark 2586. Circa 1891. 8 3/4" x 12 1/4". **$118**

Platter, Luray Pattern by Bishop & Stonier. Back stamp: Mark 387. Circa 1899. Reg. No. 227450. Two tiny chips to outside of rim. **$23**

Platter, Lyndhurst Pattern by W.H. Grindley. Back stamp: Mark 1842. Circa 1891. Piece shows wear with nick to rim edge. 11 1/2" x 15 3/4". **$82**

Platter, Medina Pattern by Jacob Furnival & Co. Back stamp: Mark 1643. Circa 1845-1870. Shows crazing. 10 1/2" x 13 1/2". **$94**

Platter, Nonpareil Pattern by Burgess & Leigh. Back stamp: Mark 712. Circa 1891. Small nick to inside lip. Shows wear. 10" x 12 1/4". **$35**

Platter, Oregon Pattern by T.J. & J. Mayer. Back stamp: Mark 2570, Longport. Circa 1845. Crazing and repairs to rim and center top surface. 9 1/2" x 12 1/2". **$23**

Platter, Osborne Pattern by W.H. Grindley. Back stamp: Mark 1842. Circa 1900, 10 1/4" x 14 1/4". **$100**

Platter, Peach (Royal) Pattern by Johnson Brothers. Back stamp: Mark 2177. Circa 1891-1900. 9 1/2" x 12 1/4" with wear from use. **$71**

Platter, Princess Pattern by Booths. Back stamp: Mark 451. Circa 1900-1915. Rd. No. 183173. Platter shows crazing. 12 1/2" x 16 1/2". **$41**

Platter, Regent Pattern by S. F. & Co. B. Ltd. Back stamp: Unmarked. Circa 1913-1939 or a bit later. Platter has crazing, 9 1/2" x 12 1/2". **$23**

Platter, Seville Pattern by New Wharf Pottery/Wood & Son. Back stamp: Pattern name and Wood & Son, mark 4285. Circa 1894. Platter is 10" x 14" with stain and crazing. **$94**

Platter, Shapoo Pattern by Thomas Hughes. Back stamp: Printed initials plus pattern name in cartouche, Mark 2121. Circa 1860-1870. 12 1/2" x 9 1/2" with utensil marks on top and crazing underneath. **$165**

Platter, Stafford Pattern by Ridgways. Back stamp: Mark 3313. Circa 1912. Platter shows some wear with tiny nick to rim. 10" x 14 1/2". **$35**

Platter, Torbrex Pattern by Wood & Sons. Back stamp: Wood & Sons. **$12**

Platter, Unknown Pattern Name by George Jones. Back stamp: Similar to Mark 2217 with unreadable impressed mark. Also, pattern name printed in oriental lettering. Circa 1873. Crazing and some staining. 16 1/2" x 20 1/4". **$29**

Platter, Venice Pattern by Johnson Bros. Back stamp: Mark 2177. Circa 1895. Rd. No. 250791 printed, 208597 embossed. Platter shows wear, 11 1/4" x 14 1/2". **$76**

Platter, Verona Pattern by Ridgways. Back stamp: Mark 3313. Circa 1910. 10 1/4" x 13 3/4". **$82**

Platter, Versailles Pattern by Furnivals. Back stamp: Mark 1651 printed and Mark 1650 impressed. Circa 1894. Platter shows some wear with a couple nicks to rim edge. **$35**

Platter, Windsor Pattern by C.H. & H., Tunstall England. Back stamp: shows a crown on top of a circular belt with England underneath, within belt is "Windsor" and in center of belt is C.H.&H. and Tunstall. Shows slight crazing, 10 1/2" x 14 1/2". **$4**

Platter, Yeddo Pattern by Arthur Wilkison. Back stamp: Mark 4170. Circa 1907. Tiny nick to rim. 12" x 16 1/2". **$23**

Tureens

Covered Oval Tureen, Flaxman Pattern by S.H. & S. Back stamp: Mark Similar to 1933. Circa 1912. Rd No. 479163 printed, Rd No. 479164 impressed. Tiny chip to inside lip and some crazing. **$47**

Covered Soup Tureen, Regent Pattern by S. F. & Co. B. Ltd. Back stamp: Unmarked. Circa 1913-1939 or a bit later. Handle on cover has been repaired. Bowl has crazing. 10" w. **$26**

Covered Tureen, Argyle Pattern by Wood & Son. Back stamp: Mark 4285. Circa 1900. Rd. No. 328742. No chips or cracks noted in cover or dish. Dish does have staining and crazing. **$65**

Covered Tureen, Dorothy Pattern by Wedgwood & Co. Back stamp: Mark 4057. Circa 1890-1900. May have repair to one handle. 6 1/2" x 8 1/2". **$29**

Covered Tureen, Lancaster Pattern by New Wharf Pottery. Back stamp: Mark 2886. Circa 1891. Tureen has large chip to rim of foot. **$29**

Covered Tureen, Windflower Pattern by Burgess & Leigh. Back stamp: Mark 717-718. Circa 1895-1896. Rd. No. 249191 printed and No. 236241 impressed. No. 249191 also printed on inside lid. Some crazing to bowl with faint hairline to inside of bowl. **$88**

Covered Tureen, Woodbine Pattern by Wood & Son. Lid has crack underneath with staining coming through to top and a chip to the inside lip. Also has good repair to top handle. **$47**

Deep Eight-Sided Cover for Large Tureen, Amoy Pattern by Davenport. Back stamp: Mark 1181A. Circa 1844. Some blemishes on the surface with crazing on inside, 9 1/4" w. **$153**

Oval Covered Tureen, Louise Pattern by W.H. Grindley. Circa 1891-1910. Rd. No. 269029. Just a tiny nick to inside cover lip. **$29**

Oval Sauce Tureen with Cover, Renown Pattern by Arthur Wilkinson Co. (Royal Staffordshire Pottery). Back stamp: Mark 4170. Circa 1907. Hairline cracks on bottom sides. Tiny hairline on inside of lid by spoon opening. 4 1/2" x 9". **$12**

Tureen with Cover, Loraine Pattern by Leighton Pottery. Back stamp: Mark 487. Circa 1930. Shows a little wear. 8" x 11". **$35**

Other Forms

Bone Dishes (2), Grace Pattern by W.H. Grindley. Back stamp: W.H. Grindley. Circa 1897. One has small discoloration. **$71 pair**

Bone Dishes (2), Rose Pattern by W.H. Grindley. Back stamp: Mark 1842. Circa 1893. Rd. No. 213117. Both pieces have crazing and hairline to rim edge. One piece has nick to rim edge and other piece has chip to rim edge and hairline to foot. **$29 pair**

Bone Dishes (5), LaBelle Pattern by Wheeling Pottery. Back stamp: Mark 28. Circa 1900. Crazing and discoloration. **$200 set**

Cake Plate with pierced handles. Unknown maker. 10 3/4" d. **$212**

Bowl, Cambridge Pattern by New Wharf Pottery. Back stamp: Mark 2886. Circa 1890-1894. 9 1/4" d with small, narrow chip beneath outside rim. **$32**

Bowl, Country Scenes Pattern. Back stamp: Country Scenes England with imprint of No. "214". Circa 1891. Signs of wear. 9" d. **$76**

Bowl, Lahore Pattern. Bowl shows wear. 9 1/4" d. **$71**

Bowl, Trilby Pattern by Wood and Son. Back stamp: Mark 4285. Circa 1907. Shows some wear and tiny chip to outside rim. 9 1/2" d. **$18**

Bowl, Violette Pattern by Keller & Guerin, Luneville, France. Circa 1891. ..... **$12**

Bowl, Warwick China Co. with a Wild Rose pattern. Back stamp: Mark 38. Circa 1900. 8" d. **$41**

Celery Dish, Warwick Pansy Pattern by Warwick China Co., U.S.A. Circa 1900. Shows crazing and small chip to rim, 5 1/4" x 12 1/4". **$23**

Chamber Pot with Lid, Doreen Pattern by W.H. Grindley. Back stamp: Mark 1842. Circa 1891. ..... **$177**

Cheese Keeper, Acme Pattern by Sampson Hancock & Sons. Back stamp: 1929 & 1929A. Circa 1900. Shows crazing and wear. **$71**

Compote, Byzantium Pattern by T.C. Brown-Westhead, Moore & Co., Cauldon, England. Back stamp: Mark 676. Circa 1900. Shows wear and roughness on edge of rim. 10" x 11". **$23**

Covered Chamber Pot, Kelmscott Pattern by F. Winkle & Co. (Colonial Pottery/Stoke England). Back stamp: Mark 4215. Circa 1890-1910. Chip on inside lip of cover and crazing on pot. **$15**

Covered Sardine Dish, Dish is 5" x 6" with a floral pattern. Unmarked. Type and style indicate date about 1880-1895. Chip to inside lip of cover. **$76**

Covered Soap Dish with Liner, Marseilles Pattern by W.H. Grindley & Co., England. Back stamp: like Mark 1842, but with England. Circa 1900-1914. Cover has some rough edges with staining on rim and lip. Some staining to inside of bowl. Liner has holes for draining. **$35**

Covered Sugar Bowl, Iris Pattern by A. Wilkinson/Royal Staffordshire Pottery. Back stamp: Mark 4170. Circa 1907. Cover has chip to inside lip with a crack and does have crazing. Bowl has some staining with a crack to handle and to inside lip. **$18**

Covered Sugar Bowl, Neapolitan Pattern by Johnson Bros. Back stamp: Mark 2177. Circa 1900. Bowl has hairline crack. **$47**

Covered Sugar Bowl, Wentworth Pattern by J. & G. Meakin. Back stamp: Mark 2602. Circa 1907. Bowl has small nick with faint hairline to inside lip. **$35**

Covered Vegetable Dish, Ormonde Pattern by Alfred Meakin. Unmarked. Circa 1891. Cover shows crazing but bowl does not, 9 1/2" x 10 1/4". **$41**

Covered Vegetable Dish, Raleigh Pattern by Burgess & Leigh. Back stamp: Mark 717-718. Circa 1906-1912. Rd. No. 393237. Shows some wear, crazing and hairline on inside corner lip. 7" x 11 1/2". **$65**

Cup and Saucer, Aldine Pattern by W.H. Grindley. Back stamp: Mark 1842. Circa 1891. Rd. No. 325874. Both pieces show some wear. **$12**

Cup and Saucer, Haddon Pattern by Libertas, Prussia. Back stamp: printed Libertas, Prussia. Circa 1891-1900. Short hairline on saucer rim and small nick to rim. Also crazing. **$12**

Large Mug. Brush-stroke decorated with tulips, buds and leaves. Shows some wear and crazing. **$153**

Cup and Saucer, Old Curiosity Shop Pattern by W.R.S. & Co. Back stamp: Mark 3309. Circa 1900. Cup shows wear, hairline from rim, some staining and both pieces show crazing. **$12**

Deep Bowl, Elsa Pattern by W. & E. Corn. Back stamp: Mark 1113. Circa 1891. Shows wear on inside and out. 8" d. **$26**

Deep Bowl, Jenny Lind Pattern by Arthur Wilkinson Ltd. Back stamp: Mark 4170. Circa 1895. This bowl shows some hairlines on bottom and crazing, 7 3/4" d. **$35**

Deep Oval Vegetable Dish, Marie Pattern by W.H. Grindley. Back stamp: Mark 1842. Circa 1891. Rd. No. 250387. Shows wear and tiny nick to outside rim edge, 6 3/4" x 9 1/4". **$29**

Dish, Columbia Pattern by Clementson & Young. Back stamp: Mark 911. Circa 1846. This dish has six pointed sides and a seventh side with embossed handle, 5 1/2" w. **$35**

Fancy Open Bowl, with Pierced Border. Decorated with grapes, leaves and blue roses by C. Tielsch & Co., Germany. Back stamp: "Made in Germany" and "C.T.C." with gold numbers hand written "7206/123". Also imprint of "J" and other mark that looks like "T". Small crack in border. 11 1/4" d. **$71**

Fourteen-Sided Paneled Waste Bowl, Calcutta Pattern by E. Challinor. Back stamp: Mark 835A. Circa 1845. Small chip to foot rim. **$59**

Handleless Cup and Saucer, Lozere Pattern by E. Challinor. Back stamp: Mark 835A. Circa 1850. Cup shows a tiny nick to rim and a couple tiny nicks to foot rim. Saucer shows crazing and staining with small chip to inside rim. **$35**

Large Bowl, Ceicel Pattern by Upper Hanley Pottery. Back stamp: Mark 3929A. Circa 1900-1910. 10" d with crazing and discoloration inside bottom. **$41**

Large Covered Cheese Dish, Unmarked except for large, blue "FB" inside cover. Circa: 1880-1890. ..... **$118**

Large Covered Dish, Lily Pattern by W. Adams & Co. Back stamp: Mark 30. Circa 1891-1900. Cover has two small chips and one large chip to rim. Dish has chip to outside rim and tiny chip to tip of handle. Also has one hairline crack. **$29**

Large Covered Dish, Persian Pattern by Johnson Bros. Back stamp: Mark 2177. Circa 1902. Repair to inside rim of base. Crazing on base and lid. **$75**

Large Covered Vegetable Dish, Nonpareil Pattern by Burgess & Leigh. Back stamp: Mark 712. Circa 1891. Cover and base show crazing with small stain inside cover. 8 1/2" x 12". **$94**

Large Cup and Saucer, imprinted on inside of cup, "Take ye a cuppe o'kindnesse For auldlang syne." Back stamp: The Rowland & Marsellus Co. Staffordshire England. Circa 1905. Cup shows discoloration and crazing. Cup is 5 1/2" w. Saucer is 7 1/4" d. **$44**

Large Open Bowl, Delph Pattern by E. Bourne & J.E. Leigh. Circa 1905-1908. Bowl has some staining, crazing and a hairline crack, 10 1/2" d. **$12**

Large Vegetable Bowl, Fairy Villas Pattern by W. Adams Co. Circa: Printed England, indicates time after 1891. Bowl has 4 cracks, crazing and wear, 10 1/4" d. **$12**

Open Bowl, Beauty Roses Pattern by W.H. Grindley & Co, Back stamp: Mark 61. Circa 1914-1925. Reg. No. 690339. 12" d. **$15**

Oval Covered Vegetable Dish, Milan Pattern by W.H. Grindley. Back stamp: Mark 1842. Circa 1893. .... **$82**

Oval Vegetable Bowl, Navy Pattern by T. Till & Sons. Back stamp: Mark 3858. Circa 1891. Staining, crazing and a couple factory marks on rim, 7" x 9 3/4". **$32**

Oval Vegetable Bowl, Windflower Pattern by Burgess & Leigh. Back stamp: Mark 717-718. Circa 1895-1896. Small chip to glaze on outside rim, some staining and crazing. 7 1/4" x 9 3/4". **$23**

Polychrome Over-Painted Tea Set, this fancy five-piece tea set is thin porcelain, heavily molded and embossed with scrolls and flower forms on all parts. Includes small teapot and sugar bowl, both with covers; creamer and two handled cups. Each cup has a chip to the rim. Unmarked except for cross or plus sign on bottom of all pieces except teapot. .... **$236 set**

Twelve-Sided Deep Vegetable Bowl, Kenworth Pattern by Johnson Bros. Back stamp: Mark 2179. Circa 1900. Slight wear, 9 1/2" d. **$124**

Vase, decorated with fruit and gold trim. 10" with hairline in the base and a small chip to the rim. Unmarked. **$29**

Vase, Floral/Art Nouveau Pattern by Empire China (American). Back stamp: Empire China printed in gilt along with the No. 4138. Circa 1900-1915. 11 1/4" t. **$112**

Vase, Royal Pattern by William Adderly. Back stamp: Possibly Mark 49. Circa 1880. 8 3/4" t with some crazing. **$35**

Vegetable Bowl, Victoria Pattern by Wood & Sons. Back stamp: Mark 4285. Circa 1891. Small nick on rim with wear and some discoloration. 10 1/4" d. **$12**

Vegetable Bowls (3), Conway Pattern by New Wharf Pottery. Back stamp: Mark 2286. Circa 1891. First bowl shows wear and many blemishes on top surface. The second and third bowls have scalloped rims and both also show wear, 9" d. .... **$38 all**

Mulberry Ware

Mulberry, which can vary from almost black to a delicate purple, was a favorite in Victorian homes. Most of the English mulberry was made from the 1830s to the 1850s in Staffordshire. It was made by the same potters who were producing flow blue, often in the same patterns.

Bowl, Potter: Utzchneider & Co., Sarreguemines, France. Circa 19th Century. 6 1/4" bowl with couple stain spots on inside. **$29**

Dish Encased in Wire-ware Basket, Potter: Utzchneider & Co., Sarreguemines, France. Back stamp: Mark 'J'. 19th Century. Dish is 5 3/4" d with slight discoloration. Basket is 9 3/4" with some rust. **$29**

Ewers (2), Jeddo Pattern by W. Adams & Sons. Back stamp: Mark 22. Circa 1845-1850. 5 1/2" ewer has large chip to handle with crack that goes all the way around handle and small nick to top of handle. 6 1/4" ewer shows age wear, staining and crows foot on bottom. .... **$35 both**

Flow Purple Plates (2), Flora Pattern by Hulme & Booth. Back stamp: Hulme & Booth, Burslem (impressed) and pattern name printed. Circa 1840-1845. Small plate has staining and crazing, 6 1/2" d. Large plate 9 1/2" d. .... **$32 both**

Handled Cup, and Sixteen-Side Paneled Saucer. Jardiniere Pattern by Paul Utschneider & Co. Back stamp: U & C Sarraguemines, Mark 6 or Mark 14. Circa 1891. Cup has small chip to pedestal base. .... **$29 both**

Handleless Cup and Saucer, Flora Pattern by Thomas Walker. Back stamp: Unmarked. Circa 1845. Hairline crack in saucer. .... **$23 both**

Handleless Cup and Saucer, Kyber Pattern by John Meir (I. Meir). Back stamp: Mark 2639. Circa 1870. Cup has some discoloration. .... **$47 both**

Three Handleless Cups and Two Saucers, Vincennes Pattern by John Alcock. Back stamp: Mark 67. Circa 1857. One cup has two chips to rim, crack and some discoloration. One cup has crack and some discoloration. One saucer has hairline crack on bottom which does not go through to the top with small area of discoloration just below outside of rim. .... **$41 all**

Plate. Vincennes Pattern by John Alcock. Back stamp: Mark 67. Circa 1857. 10 1/2" d. **$165**

Large Well and Tree Platter, Florentine Pattern by Thomas Dimmock. Back stamp: Mark 1298 with Kaolin Ware printed above. Circa 1844. Platter shows wear, staining, crazing, chips to foot edge, two hairlines on back with one on front that goes around rim to back. 15 3/4" x 19 1/2". **$29**

Miniature Sugar and Creamer, Unknown Pattern and no Back stamp. Bottom is marked with the letter "M". Circa 1845-1855. Creamer has large chip to spout and sugar has no lid. .... **$53 both**

Mulberry and Polychrome Plate, Jeddo Pattern by Beech & Hancock. Back stamp: Mark 312. Circa 1857-1876. Plate has staining and crazing but not chips or cracks noted. 10 3/4". **$59**

Mulberry and Polychrome Platter, Flower Vase Pattern by T. J. & J. Mayer. Back stamp: small impressed "FB". Circa 1843-1855. Crazing and discoloration with chip to outside rim. 14 3/4" x 18 1/4". **$29**

Oval Relish Dish, Albany Pattern by John & Robert Godwin. Back stamp: Unmarked. Circa 1834-1866. Crazing and two chips to foot rim. **$23**

Plate and Saucer, Fern and Tulip Brush-stroke Pattern. Potter unknown. Back stamp: impressed mark. Circa 1840-1855. Plate has a marble design by A. Shaw. Back stamp: Cartouche with potters name (check Mark 3497). Circa 1851-1856. Plate has crazing, 10" d. .... **$35 both**

Plate, Pelew Pattern by E. Challinor. Back stamp: Mark 855 A. Circa 1840. Some staining and crazing. 8 3/4" d. **$23**

Plates (2), Bochara Pattern by John Edwards. Back stamp: Mark 1449. Circa 1850. 9" d plate has tiny chip to rim and rough edges. The other plate is 8 1/2" d. Both have crazing and light discoloration. .... **$20 both**

Plates (2), Pelew Pattern by E. Challinor. Back stamp: Mark 855 A. Circa 1840. Both plates have crazing with slight staining. 9 3/4" d. **$29**

Plates (2), The Temple Pattern by Podmore Walker & Co. Back stamp: Mark 3080. Circa 1850. Both plates show wear, crazing and one plate has some staining, 9 3/4" d. .... **$23 pair**

Plates (3), Foliage Pattern by Edward Walley. Back stamp: All have printed pattern name. Large plate has printed "W" and small plate has impressed "Ironstone China" and "R Walley". Circa 1850. 6 1/4" plate shows wear but not chips or cracks. 7 1/2" plate undamaged. 9 1/4" plate has crazing, some staining and hairline to back. .... **$29 all**

Plates (3), Rhone Scenery by T. J. & J. Mayer. Back stamp: Mark 2570-2571. Circa 1850. 8 1/2" d plate, 7 1/2" d plate and 6" d plate. 6" plate has hairline cracks and discoloration. .... **$23 all**

Platter, Athens Pattern by Charles Meigh. Back stamp: Mark 2618 or 2614A. Circa 1840. Platter has staining, crazing, nick to rim and inside lip, with many spots of glaze loss on backside. 14 1/2" x 18". **$35**

Platter, Killarney Pattern by New Wharf Pottery. Back stamp: Mark 2886. Circa 1891. Piece shows staining, crazing and small chip to rim. **$82**

Platter, Rhone Scenery by T. J. & J. Mayer. Back stamp: Mark 2570-2571. Circa 1850. Platter is 18" x 14" with light discoloration. **$118**

Platters (2), Jeddo Pattern by W. Adams & Sons. Back stamp: Mark 22. Circa 1845-1850. 12" x 15 3/4" platter has some staining, crazing and tiny nick to rim edge. 14" x 18" platter has some staining, two large cracks and some damage and loss of glaze to one rim edge. .... **$53 both**

Three Piece Sauce Set, Corean Pattern by Podmore, Walker & Co. Back stamp: Corean and P.W. & Co. Circa 1840-1850. Chip to inside of lid and some discoloration on all three pieces. No ladle. .... **$100 set**

Three-Piece Soap Dish, Peruvian Pattern by John Wedgwood. Back stamp: Only English date stamp/registry mark. Circa 1849. Repair to cover handle and small flaw on inside corner of base. **$59**

Mulberry (or Black Transfer) Covered Vegetable Bowl. Roses Pattern by Benjamin & Sampson Hancock. Back stamp: Mark 1922. Circa 1876-1881. Crazing, 6 1/4" x 12". **$112**

MAJOLICA

In 1851, California had been the nation's 31st state for only four months, and Millard Fillmore was U.S. president; Elisha Otis was perfecting his brake-equipped elevator, and Robert Bunsen was tinkering with the burner that would one day bear his name. Jenny Lind, the "Swedish Nightingale," toured America in a spectacle organized by P.T. Barnum; Nathaniel Hawthorne's The Scarlet Letter was being hailed by critics.

And an English potter was hoping that his new interpretation of a centuries-old style of ceramics would be well received at the "Great Exhibition of the Industries of All Nations" set to open May 1, 1851, in London's Hyde Park.

Potter Herbert Minton had high hopes for his display. His father, Thomas Minton, founded a pottery works in the mid-1790s in Stoke-on-Trent, Staffordshire. Herbert Minton had designed a "new" line of pottery, and his chemist, Leon Arnoux, had developed a process that resulted in vibrant, colorful glazes that came to be called "majolica."

Joseph Francois Leon Arnoux was born in Toulouse, France, in 1816, the son of a porcelain and earthenware manufacturer. Trained as an engineer, Arnoux also studied the making of encaustic tiles, and had been appointed Art Director at Minton's works in 1848. His job was to introduce and promote new products. Victorian fascination with the natural world prompted Arnoux to reintroduce the work of Bernard Palissy, whose naturalistic, bright-colored "Maiolica" wares had been created in the 16th century. But Arnoux used a thicker body to make pieces sturdier. This body was given a coating of opaque white glaze, which provided a surface for decoration.

Pieces were modeled in high relief, featuring butterflies and other insects, flowers and leaves, fruit, shells, animals and fish. Queen Victoria's endorsement of the new pottery prompted its acceptance by the general public.

Bernard Palissy (1510-1590) was an artist, writer and scientist, yet he is most celebrated for his ceramics, and for the development of enameled earthenware (also called faience, from the Italian city of Faenza), and for the exuberant plant and animal forms his work displayed.

Palissy was born in southwestern France. Around 1540, he moved to Saintes, north of Bordeaux, married and set up shop as a portrait painter. Legend has it that he was once shown an earthenware cup (probably of Italian origin), and was so attracted to its tin-based glaze that he decided to devote his time exclusively to enameling, despite having no previous knowledge of ceramics.

The tradition of tin-glazed and decorated earthenware is believed to have originated in the 9th century, somewhere in Persia. These wares moved along trade routes to the island of Majorca, a regular stop for trading vessels traveling between Spain and Italy. When the ceramics were imported into Italy, they came to be called "Maiolica."

Palissy eventually succeeded in creating brilliant enamel glazes. But after his death in 1590, his work was ignored

George Jones monumental cobalt picket fence, daisy and wheat tall-size cheese keeper with branch handle, outstanding color and detail, professional hairline repair to cover, 12 1/2" h, 12" d. **$7,250**

for centuries. In the 19th century, private collectors and museums started acquiring original Renaissance pieces, and that helped to revive interest in traditional majolica.

When Minton introduced his wares at Philadelphia's 1876 Centennial Exhibition, American potters also began to produce majolica. The Griffen, Smith and Hill pottery of Phoenixville, Pa., produced some of the most collectable American majolica from 1879 to about 1893. The company was best known for the manufacture of "Etruscan Majolica" ware. Most pieces are marked with one of the two versions of their crest. However, some unmarked pottery can also be attributed to Griffen, Smith and Hill.

The Chesapeake Pottery in Baltimore made Clifton, a pattern featuring blackberries and, later, other types of fruit and flowers. This company also made Avalon Faience, a design imitating French faience.

Other Majolica Makers

John Adams & Co., Hanley, Stoke-on-Trent, Staffordshire, England, operated the Victoria Works, producing earthenware, jasperware, Parian, majolica, 1864-1873. (Collector's tip: Jasperware is a fine white stoneware originally produced by Josiah Wedgwood, often colored by metallic oxides with raised classical designs remaining white.)

Another Staffordshire pottery, Samuel Alcock & Co., Cobridge, 1828-1853; Burslem, 1830-1859, produced earthenware, china and Parian.

The W. & J.A. Bailey Alloa Pottery was founded in Alloa, the principal town in Clackmannanshire, located near Edinburgh, Scotland.

The Bevington family of potters worked in Hanley, Staffordshire, England, in the late 19th century.

W. Brownfield & Son, Burslem and Cobridge, Staffordshire, England, 1850-1891.

T.C. Brown-Westhead, Moore & Co., produced earthenware and porcelain at Hanley, Stoke-on-Trent, Staffordshire, from about 1862 to 1904.

The Choisy-le-Roi faience factory of Choisy-le-Roi, France, produced majolica from 1860 until 1910. The firm's wares are not always marked. The common mark is usually a black ink stamp "Choisy-le-Roi" pictured to the right with a large "HBm" which stands for Hippolyte Boulenger, a director at the pottery.

William T. Copeland & Sons pottery of Stoke-on-Trent, Staffordshire, England, began producing porcelain and earthenware in 1847. (Josiah Spode established a pottery at Stoke-on-Trent in 1770. In 1833, the firm was purchased by William Copeland and Thomas Garrett. In 1847, Copeland became the sole owner. W.T. Copeland & Sons continued until a 1976 merger when it became Royal Worcester Spode. Copeland majolica pieces are sometimes marked with an impressed "COPELAND," but many are unmarked.)

Jose A. Cunha, Caldas da Rainha, southern Portugal, also worked in the style of Bernard Palissy, the great French Renaissance potter.

Julius Dressler, Bela Czech Republic, company founded 1888, producing faience, majolica and porcelain. In 1920, the name was changed to EPIAG. The firm closed about 1945.

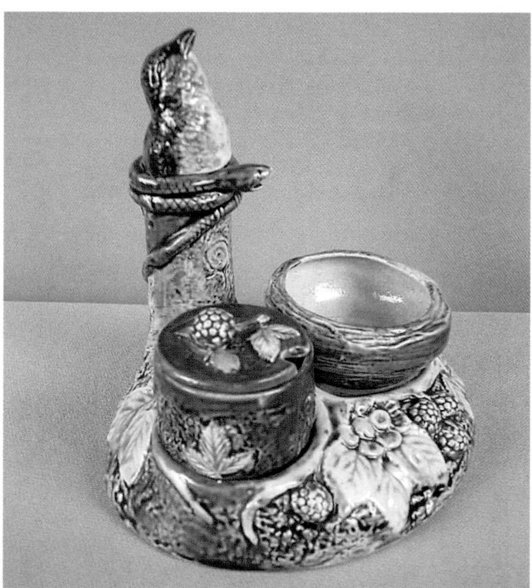

Majolica four-piece condiment set with bird shaker surrounded by snake, bird's-nest salt dip and tree-stump mustard pot and base with berries, rare form, repair to mustard pot and lid, 5 3/4" h. **$250**

George Jones, "Underwater" majolica pitcher, with cobalt top, 9" h, outstanding color, an extremely rare piece. **$5,000**

Eureka Pottery was located in Trenton, N.J., circa 1883-1887.

Railway Pottery, established by S. Fielding & Co., Stoke, Stoke-on-Trent, Staffordshire, England, 1879.

There were two Thomas Forester potteries active in the late 19th century in Staffordshire, England. Some sources list the more famous of the two as Thomas Forester & Sons Ltd. at the Phoenix Works, Longton.

Established in the early 19th century, the Gien pottery works is located on the banks of France's Loire River near Orleans.

Joseph Holdcroft majolica ware was produced at Daisy Bank in Longton, Staffordshire, England, from 1870 to 1885. Items can be found marked with "J HOLDCROFT," but many pieces can only be attributed by the patterns and colors that are documented to have come from the Holdcroft potteries.

George Jones & Sons Ltd., Stoke, Staffordshire, started operation in about 1864 as George Jones and in 1873 became George Jones & Sons Ltd. The firm operated the Trent Potteries in Stoke-on-Trent (renamed "Crescent Potteries" in about 1907).

In about 1877, Samuel Lear erected a small china works in Hanley, Staffordshire. Lear produced domestic china and, in addition, decorated all kinds of earthenware made by other manufacturers, including "spirit kegs." In 1882, the firm expanded to include production of majolica, ivory-body earthenware and Wedgwood-type jasperware. The business closed in 1886.

Robert Charbonnier founded the Longchamp tile works in 1847 to make red clay tiles, but the factory soon started to produce majolica. Longchamp is known for its "barbotine" pieces (a paste of clay used in decorating coarse pottery in relief) made with vivid colors, especially oyster plates.

Hugo Lonitz operated in Haldensleben, Germany, from 1868-1886, and later Hugo Lonitz & Co., 1886-1904, producing household and decorative porcelain, earthenware and metalwares. Look for a mark of two entwined fish.

The Lunéville pottery was founded about 1728 by Jacques Chambrette in the city that bears its name, in the Alsace-Lorraine region of northeastern France. The firm became famous for its blue monochromatic and floral patterns. Around 1750, ceramist Paul-Louis Cyfflé introduced a pattern with animals and historical figures. Lunéville products range from hand-painted faience and majolica to pieces influenced by the Art Deco movement.

The Massier family began producing ceramics in Vallauris, France, in the mid-18th century.

François Maurice, School of Paris, active 1875-1885, also worked in the style of Bernard Palissy.

George Morley & Co., East Liverpool, Ohio, 1884-1891.

Morley & Co. Pottery was founded in 1879, Wellsville, Ohio, making graniteware and majolica.

Orchies, a majolica manufacturer in northern France near Lille, is also known under the mark "Moulin des Loups & Hamage," 1920s.

Faïencerie de Pornic is located near Quimper, France.

Quimper pottery has a long history. Tin-glazed, hand-painted pottery has been made in Quimper, France, since the late 17th century. The earliest firm, founded in 1685 by Jean Baptiste Bousquet, was known as HB Quimper. Another firm, founded in 1772 by Francois Eloury, was known as Porquier. A third firm, founded by Guillaume Dumaine in 1778, was known as HR or Henriot Quimper. All three companies made similar pottery decorated with designs of Breton peasants, and sea and flower motifs.

The Rörstrand factory made the first faience (tin-glazed earthenware) produced in Sweden. It was established in 1725 by Johann Wolff, near Stockholm.

George Jones cobalt pitcher with monkey handle and floral motif, outstanding color and detail, 7", professional repair to spout. **$2,600**

Holdcroft cobalt majolica game tureen with fox and goose atop bed of ferns on cover on basket weave base with holly on branch feet with branch handles, 12 1/2" l, outstanding color and detail, professional rim repair to base. **$5,500**

Monumental Palissy-style 12-piece tea set made in Portugal, set includes coffee pot 10", teapot 8", creamer with lid 7", covered sugar 7" and four cups and saucers, each depicting cabbage leaves with snake handles and spouts, various professional repairs to high points, extremely rare to find a complete set. **$5,750 set**

The earthenware factory of Salins was established in 1857 in Salins-les-Bains, near the French border with Switzerland. Salins was awarded with the gold medal at the International Exhibition of Decorative Arts in Paris in 1912.

Sarreguemines wares are named for the city in the Lorraine region of northeastern France. The pottery was founded in 1790 by Nicholas-Henri Jacobi. For more than 100 years, it flourished under the direction of the Utzschneider family.

Wilhelm Schiller and Sons, Bodenbach, Bohemia, established 1885.

Thomas-Victor Sergent was one of the School of Paris ceramists of the late 19th century who was influenced by the works of Bernard Palissy.

St. Clement: Founded by Jacques Chambrette in Saint-Clément, France, in 1758. Chambrette also established works in Lunéville.

The St. Jean de Bretagne pottery works are located near Quimper, France.

Vallauris is a pottery center in southeastern France, near Cannes. Companies in production there include Massier and Foucard-Jourdan.

Victoria Pottery Co., Hanley, Staffordshire, England, 1895-1927.

Wardle & Co., established 1871 at Hanley, Staffordshire, England.

Josiah Wedgwood was born in Burslem, Staffordshire, England, on July 12, 1730, into a family with a long pottery tradition. At the age of nine, after the death of his father, he joined the family business. In 1759, he set up his own pottery works in Burslem. There he produced cream-colored earthenware that found favor with Queen Charlotte. In 1762, she appointed him royal supplier of dinnerware. From the public sale of "Queen's Ware," as it came to be known, Wedgwood was able to build a production community in 1768, which he named Etruria, near Stoke-on-Trent, and a second factory equipped with tools and ovens of his own design. (Etruria is the ancient land of the Etruscans, in what is now northern Italy.)

Unless otherwise indicated, all majolica listings in this edition come courtesy of Strawser Auction Group, Wolcottville, Ind., *www.strawserauctions.com*, facilitated by Artfact, *www.artfact.com*.

Assorted Serving Pieces

Adams & Bromley, majolica cheese keeper with bull rushes and cow finial, rare form, 13" h, 12 1/2" d, professional rim repair to cover and base rim of base. **$2,100**

Banana leaf and basket-weave, majolica platter, 14". **$140**

Barrel-shaped creamer, with floral motif, 4 1/4". **$40**

Basket-weave and blackberry plate, 8 1/4", good color. **$45**

Basket-weave and floral, rustic cachepot, 7 1/2" h, 7 1/2" d, minor hairline. **$225**

Basket-weave and leaf, syrup pitcher with pewter top, 4 1/2". **$70**

Begonia leaf majolica platter, with basket-weave border, 12 1/2", minor hairline. **$160**

Begonia leaf, on brown ground pitcher, 8", professional spout repair. **$100**

Bird and fan, majolica platter with yellow ground and rope edge, minor wear, 14". **$50**

Bird on branch, syrup pitcher with pewter top, 4 3/4". **$90**

Bird on triple mottled leaf, majolica serving tray, 12" w. **$80**

Brownfield, game tureen in the form of a basket with a cover with rabbit handle and game birds and rabbits on bed of leaves and ferns, 11 1/2", professional hairline repair to cover and base, this is a rare form that came in two sizes and this is the larger of the two. **$1,050**

Brownfield, majolica figural owl pitcher with glass eyes, outstanding detail, rare, 13". **$400**

Cobalt bird on branch, majolica cheese keeper with floral finial, base and rim chips to cover and base, 7" h. **$400**

Cobalt majolica cachepot, with floral and fruit motif and ring handles, hairline to base, 8 1/4" h, 8 1/2" d. **$180**

Cobalt majolica covered butter dish, with bird handle, flowers and leaves. **$350**

Cobalt majolica, bird on branch and bull rush cheese keeper, 10" h, 10" d. **$500**

Cobalt wild rose, cheese keeper with branch handle, great color, 11" d, 12" d, minor nick to stand. **$500**

Copeland, oyster plate, six turquoise wells separated by brown picket fence surrounding cobalt center, 10 1/4", rare form, hairline to one well. **$850**

Copeland, shell jug with lady in shell riding dolphins on one side and lady in clouds on the other, each with lavender ground, ivy and grapes decorate top rim, base is surrounded with shells, professional rim repair, 10 1/2", great color and detail. **$200**

Dragonfly and fan, cobalt majolica pitcher, 7", chip to handle. **$90**

"Eat Thy Bread With Thankfulness", majolica begonia leaf bread tray, 12 3/4", professional rim repair, good color. **$140**

English figural, majolica teapot with Chinaman on melon with vine handle and spout, minor rim chip to teapot, 5" h. **$130**

Etruscan, classical plate with dog, 9". **$50**

Etruscan, cobalt majolica water lily sardine box with swan finial, good color, rim nicks to lid. **$300**

Etruscan, cobalt sunflower syrup pitcher with pewter top, 8". **$200**

Etruscan, daisy compote with brown ground, 9" d, 5" h. **$120**

Etruscan, daisy oval pickle dish, 8 1/2", hairline, crazing. **$75**

Etruscan, majolica cauliflower teapot, good color, minor interior chip to lid, 5 1/2" h. **$80**

Etruscan, majolica cobalt sunflower sauce dish or syrup pitcher tray, excellent color, 5". **$250**

Etruscan, majolica fern pitcher, 8 3/4", hairline, good color. **$120**

Etruscan, majolica fern pitcher, outstanding color and condition, 8 1/2". **$350**

Etruscan, morning glory cake stand with cobalt morning glory flowers, good color, 8 1/4" d, 4" h. **$130**

Etruscan, morning glory cake stand with white ground, good color and condition, 8" d, 4" h. **$90**

Etruscan, oak-leaf bread tray with pink border, 12", minor professional rim repair to back. **$130**

Etruscan, oak-leaf bread tray with pink border, 12". **$120**

Etruscan, pink sunflower majolica syrup pitcher with pewter top, 8", handle reattached. **$130**

Etruscan, shell and seaweed 14" platter, good color, minor rim nicks to back. **$275**

Etruscan, shell and seaweed 14" platter, rim chip and rim glaze nicks. **$110**

Etruscan, shell and seaweed 4" pitcher, good color, professional rim repair. **$85**

Etruscan, shell and seaweed butter pat without seaweed. **$160**

Etruscan, shell and seaweed cup and saucer. **$50**

Etruscan, shell and seaweed plate, good color, 8". **$100**

Etruscan, shell and seaweed shell-shaped sauce dish, good color. **$70**

Etruscan, strawberry and apple basket-weave plate, 9". **$90**

Etruscan, sunflower syrup pitcher with white ground and pewter top, 8", minor wear. **$130**

Eureka, bird and branch low compote, minor hairline, 9" d. **$80**

Fan-shaped majolica tray, with dragonfly on yellow ground, 10". **$150**

George Jones rare form game tureen in the form of a quail with seven chicks on bed of leaves and fern on cover, turquoise base is surrounded with rabbits among ferns and leaves with branch handles decorated with oak leaves and acorns, shape no. 3371, 14" l, professional repair to cover, extremely rare form great color and detail. **$27,500**

Minton monumental garden seat in the form of a monkey with coconut supporting cobalt pillow seat with yellow tassels, shape no. 589, 18" h, rare form, professional surface repair to seat. **$12,000**

Fern and floral plate, with turquoise border, hairline, 9 1/2". **$50**

Fielding, bird and fan turquoise majolica mustache cup and saucer, minor surface wear. **$30**

Fielding, bird and fan turquoise plate, nice color, 9 1/2". **$80**

Fielding, fan and scroll majolica teapot, repair to spout, chip to lid finial, 6". **$45**

Fielding, fan and scroll platter, nice color, 13". **$140**

Fielding, fan and scroll sardine box, lid handle reattached. **$190**

Fielding, fan and scroll with pebble ground majolica pitcher, minor wear to spout, 5". **$100**

Fielding, fish net and shells pitcher with red coral handle, 5 1/2", good color, hairline. **$180**

Fielding, fishnet and shells majolica cream pitcher with coral handle, minor surface wear, good color, 4 1/2". **$160**

Figural fish pitcher, 11", minor rim glaze wear. **$40**

Figural majolica monk pitcher, 6". **$30**

Figural owl pitcher, 10". **$160**

Figural parrot pitcher, with bamboo handle, 10 1/4" hairline. **$120**

Floral and leaf, turquoise majolica three-piece tea set with matching tray, good color, rare to find matching 15" tray. .... **$225 set**

Floral, single-handle majolica bowl with ribbon and bow handle, strong color, rare form, 9" d. **$100**

French face jug, "The Black Bill", shape no. 7891, 5 1/2". **$50**

French face jug, "The Scotsman", professional rim repair, 8 1/2". **$30**

French large majolica figural duck pitcher, with open-wing handle, 17", professional repair to duck's beak, rare size and form. **$300**

French Palissy-style, putto supporting shell compote, 14" h, 10" d, good detail. **$750**

George Jones, calla lily and bird monumental floor jardiniere, 22" w, 18 1/2" h, professional repair to leaves of feet, calla lily rims and rim of jardiniere, great color and detail. **$2,200**

George Jones, cheese keeper with pink ground and cow finial, 9" h, 12" d, great color, professional repair to cow's horns. **$1,600**

George Jones, chestnut leaf on napkin large serving tray with vine handle, 14 1/2" w, minor professional rim repair, rare to find in this size. **$550**

George Jones, chestnut leaf on napkin plate, 9". **$190**

George Jones, cobalt majolica daisy and wheat bowl, 6 1/2" d, great color and detail. **$375**

George Jones, cobalt majolica game tureen with partridge on bed of leaves and ferns on cover, base is decorated with rabbits, oak leaves, acorns, and ferns with branch handles, outstanding color and detail, 13" l. **$6,500**

George Jones, cobalt majolica plate with floral border, 9", excellent color. **$225**

George Jones, cobalt majolica wild rose pitcher, 5", outstanding color and detail. **$500**

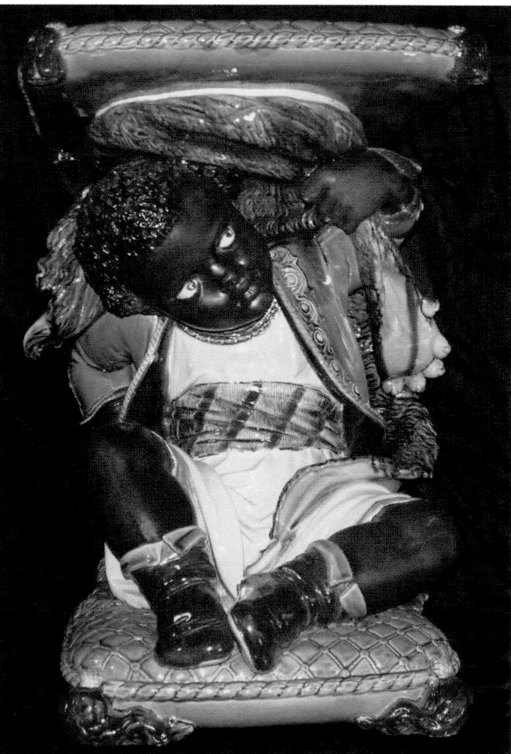

Minton monumental Blackamoor garden seat depicting a Blackamoor boy with lions skin over shoulders seated on green cushion with red/pink tassels supporting a similar cushion on his head with serves as the seat, shape no. 1225. **$7,500**

Majolica large French oval table center with painted portrait of lady and winged dragon handles, good detail, 16" l, 9" h. **$140**

George Jones, cobalt wine jug with putti, wine barrel, grapes and vine in relief, outstanding color and detail, 9", hairlines, rare form. **$1,100**

George Jones, crate sardine boat with three overlapping fish on bed of seaweed on cover, 9" l. **$550**

George Jones, empty-nest turquoise quail game dish, no. 3416, 13 1/2" l, large size, base has rabbits, oak leaves and acorns and ferns in relief, twig handles, great color and detail, professional repair to beak and one handle. ... **$8,000**

George Jones, figural compote with gun dog behind tree looking for quail under cover of leaves, oak tree trunk is supporting turquoise oval bowl with oak leaves and acorns decorating underside of bowl, 8" h, 10" w, professional repair to bowl rim. **$2,200**

George Jones, figural majolica salt with putto atop conch shell supported by dolphin, 7" h, professional rim repair to shell. **$650**

George Jones, figural salt in the form of a dove on a branch supporting a leaf, 3", professional repair to leaf tip and stem of leaf, rare form. **$850**

George Jones, figural salt in the form of green leaf surrounded by flowers and twigs with a branch handle supporting a white dove, rare form, 5" l, 3" h, professional repair to wing of bird. **$1,300**

George Jones, fox and leaf serving tray, good color and detail, 10" w, professional repair to fox ears. **$475**

George Jones, kingfisher bull rush and water lily serving tray, great color and detail, 12" l, hard to find form. . **$2,850**

George Jones, majolica turquoise covered muffin server with butterfly finial handle, professional repair to finial, 11 1/2" d, 7" h, great color and detail, rare form. **$1,500**

George Jones, majolica turquoise oval pate box and tray with cow atop bed of wheat, good color, professional rim repair to cover, 7" w. **$1,000**

George Jones, majolica twin shell two-part server with coral handle, 12 1/2". **$150**

George Jones, platter with overlapping ferns and leaves, 14 1/2", great color and detail, professional repair to handles. **$1,150**

George Jones, set of four turquoise strawberry-pattern majolica plates, 8". .... **$850 set**

George Jones, set of three albino majolica strawberry spoons, 7 3/4" and 4 1/4" l. .... **$275 set**

George Jones, squirrel on chestnut leaf figural serving tray, 10 1/2" w, repair to squirrel's arms, good color and detail. **$425**

George Jones, strawberry server with bird and bird's nest cream and sugar, good color, 11" w. **$700**

George Jones, turquoise majolica apple blossom covered muffin server, 10 1/2" d, 5 1/2" h, great color and detail. **$1,200**

George Jones, turquoise majolica plate with oak leaves and fern border, 9", great color and detail, rare. **$475**

George Jones, turquoise majolica strawberry server without cream and sugar, 14 1/2", hairline. **$275**

George Jones, turquoise napkin strawberry server with pink cream and sugar, 14". **$550**

Holdcroft, basket-weave and dogwood turquoise majolica plate, 8 1/2". **$90**

Holdcroft, honeycomb majolica pitcher, minor rim glaze nick, 5 1/2". **$80**

Holdcroft, lily of the valley oval platter, rare form, 13", professional hairline repair. **$225**

Holdcroft, lily of the valley oval platter, rare form, 13". **$275**

Holdcroft, majolica melon-form, brown-ground cup and saucer with green vine handle, minor nick to base of cup. **$50**

Holdcroft, majolica pond lily pitcher, 4". **$120**

Holdcroft, majolica six-well oyster plate, cobalt ground, white wells with pink accent, great color, 10 3/4", hard form to find. **$500**

Holdcroft, majolica strawberry dish, crested with a bird handle, and decorated in pale green, ochre, white on blue ground and fitted at one end with receptacles for cream jug and sugar, 12", professional rim nick repair. **$325**

Holdcroft, majolica strawberry spoon, 8", minor nick to bowl of spoon, rare. **$225**

Holdcroft, mottled majolica fish and daisy plate, 8 1/2", rare color, surface wear. **$120**

Holdcroft, pond lily deep bowl with lily pad feet, 10 1/2" d. **$55**

Majolica match striker, cigar holder in the form of two pigs eating from trough, minor nick, 4 1/2". **$90**
Majolica match striker, with puppy on leaf, rim nick to leaf, 6" l. **$40**
Majolica military man humidor, 6 1/2". **$35**
Majolica monk figure, with bucket and raised hand, 9" h. **$10**
Majolica monk head humidor, 6". **$25**
Majolica monk, returning from wine cellar figural cigar holder with match striker, 7 1/2". **$60**
Majolica sailor, with beard and pipe humidor, 6". **$15**
Majolica sailor, with rain cap humidor, 4 1/2". **$10**
Majolica smoke set, with match striker in the form of a man playing mandolin, 7", minor nicks. **$10**
Majolica spittoon, with floral motif, 5". **$35**
Majolica, continental frog and floral match striker, frog is playing mandolin, 3" h, minor rim chip. **$120**
Monk head majolica humidor, 4 1/2". **$30**
Monk head majolica humidor, 7", minor nicks. **$10**
Monk head majolica humidor, 9". **$15**
Monk head, majolica wall hanging match striker, 4 1/2". **$50**
Monk majolica humidor, signed BB #8052, 5 1/2". **$45**
Monk with bottle of wine, cigar holder with match striker, 7 3/4", minor hairline. **$10**
Monk with stein, majolica match striker and cigar holder with lid, 8". **$25**
Sarreguemines, majolica tobacco jar with lid in a form of a monkey music lover playing piano, 9 1/2" long, rare to find with lid, circa 1880. .... **$1,550**
Singing man, playing mandolin figural match striker, 4 1/2". **$15**
Stork in marsh, with flying fish majolica spittoon with bamboo base, 6 1/2", minor chip to underside. **$180**
Sultan with pipe and purple cape, majolica humidor, 7 1/2", minor nicks to lid rim. **$60**

Other Forms

Banks and Thorley, basket-weave handled basket, 10" w, 6" h. **$150**
Bird on branch, basket with bamboo handle, 10" l, 6 1/2" h, good color. **$160**
Brownfield, rare figural majolica vase of boy holding on to horn of rearing ram while hiding behind tree, great color and detail, 11". **$1,700**
Brownfield, two-handle majolica vase with grape motif, 10 1/2", handle repair. **$25**
Continental sunflower basket, 4 1/2" h, minor interior rim nick. **$130**
Continental, ewer vase with dragon handle and portrait of lady, 9". **$15**
Continental, figural majolica planter of boy dressed as clown riding pig, 5 1/2". **$70**
Continental, majolica case shelf clock with New Haven clock works, rim nicks to case, 10 1/2". **$40**
Continental, majolica figural vase with lady standing beside tree, 12". **$10**
Continental, majolica figure of man with basket of fish and basket atop his head, 15" h. **$40**

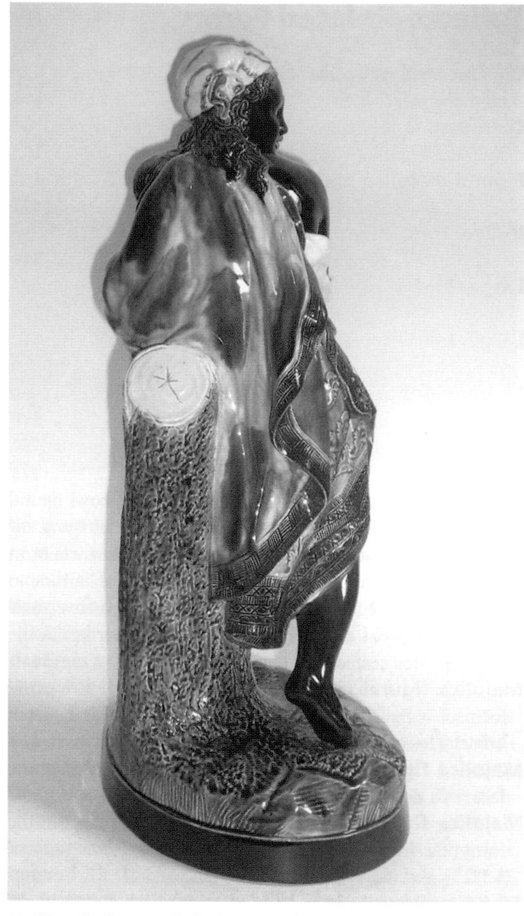

Holdcroft, figure of Blackamoor female slave and baby "Freedom", 14", outstanding detail and an extremely rare form. **$2,700**

Delphin Massier, table center in the form of a wishing well with bucket on chain and seven birds perched on and around wishing well, great color and detail, 13 1/2", professional repair to rim of small barrel, beaks of a couple bird. **$1,000**
English majolica spill vase, in the form of an elephant, 8", professional rim tip repair. **$325**
French figural flower vase, #1637, hairline to base, good color, 9". **$130**
French majolica floral wall pocket, with butterfly, great detail, one leaf reattached, 14". **$200**
George Jones, bull rush and water lily pin tray with turquoise ground, great color and detail, 10", professional hairline repair. **$400**
George Jones, cobalt majolica ball-shaped vase supported by three frogs and decorated with insects and vine, 6", minor base nick. **$900**
George Jones, majolica cobalt dragonfly, swallow, water lily and bull rush garden seat, 19", outstanding color and detail. **$2,500**
George Jones, majolica figural warbler and nest menu holder, 5 1/2" h, great color and detail. **$1,000**

George Jones, Sphinx figural candlestick with cobalt accent on base, 8", professional repair to wing tips. **$600**

George Jones, warbler and nest vase, 9 1/4", professional repair to base and rim, good detail and color. **$950**

Holdcroft, majolica umbrella stand with stork with fish in mouth surrounded by bull rushes, 21". **$800**

Hugo Lonitz, majolica table center with two figures with carriage, great detail and color, 17" l, 15" h, repair to arm of one figure and jacket of the other, unusual form. **$150**

Large majolica monk, figural bell with stein, 10 3/4". **$25**

Mafra Portugal Palissy-style, wall pocket with moth and lizard on nest with heavy green grass, 8 1/4", minor glaze nick. **$275**

Majolica basket, with ribbon and bow on handle and floral motif to side, 7" h, 8 1/2" w. **$160**

Majolica figure, of lion lying on green marble-like base, 14" l, 9" h. **$1,200**

Majolica toothpick holder, with moth and butterfly, 1 1/2". **$120**

Majolica umbrella stand, with cobalt ground and panel with floral motif, good color and detail, 23". **$375**

Majolica wall pocket, with three cornucopias, 5 3/4". **$120**

Massier, iris-form figural vase with stem base, 13", nice color and detail, professional repair to leaf and flower petal rims. **$1,800**

Minton basket, with kitten at base playing with sock, rare form, great detail, 5 1/2" h, shape no. 2049, date code for 1876, professional repair to ear of cat. **$1,800**

Minton pair of spill vases, each in the form of a putto with basket, 10 1/2" h, hairline to basket, good color and detail. **$800 pair**

Minton, covered box in the form of a log with a beetle at each end decorated with ivy and supported by two small logs, shape no. 1604, date code for 1870, professional repair to rim of cover. **$2,300**

Minton, large floor jardiniere with ferns, morning glories, foxglove and leaves in high relief, 13" h, 19" w, shape no. 1056, date code for 1873. **$1,000**

Minton, majolica lavender bamboo garden seat with green ribbon and bow, 19", rare color, base chip to underside of garden seat. **$750**

Minton, majolica matchbox in the form of a crypt with man on cover, chip to hands of man, 4" l, rare form. **$600**

Minton, porcelain dove flower holder, hairline, 6". **$90**

Minton, posy holder in the form of a clamshell atop bed of rocks, shell and seaweed, shape no. 1560, 7", good color and detail. **$1,350**

Minton, table center in the form of a pair of rabbits hiding in ferns supporting turquoise cabbage leaf, shape no. 1451, date code for 1869, 9 1/2" l, 4 1/2" h, great color and detail, professional rim repair to cabbage. **$4,200**

Minton, table center in the form of two cherubs supporting tray with a pair of doves underneath, 10 3/4" l, 7" h, shape no. 930, date code for 1862. **$1,150**

Minton, table center in the form of two vintagers carrying tub on mottled and cobalt base , 11" h, 11" w. **$750**

Minton, table center with two putto carrying shell on mottled and cobalt base, 11" h, 11" w, professional repair to handle of shell. **$750 pair**

Monumental Caldas Palissy-style, plaque decorated with large carp in the center with pike, eel and roach on a profusion of leaves and surrounded by a frog and insects, 15 1/2", circa 1880. **$1,150**

Morley & Co., majolica figural dog doorstop, extremely rare, good color, minor hairline to base, 9 1/2" h. **$3,000**

Pair of bonnet wall pockets, with cobalt ribbon, applied flower and good detail, 13" h. **$600 pair**

Pair of cobalt majolica bull rush and swan, wall pockets, great color and detail, 10". **$1,000 pair**

Pair of continental figures, of man and women seated in chairs, woman playing mandolin with dog on lap and man playing violin with dog on pillow, 7" h, various repairs. **$25 pair**

Holdcroft pair of monumental vases in the form of large swans with cobalt cornucopia vases surrounded by water lilies, great color and detail , 11 1/2" h, 10" w, rare form. **$5,250 pair**

George Jones, "Punch" punch bowl with figure of Punch lying on back supporting large cobalt bowl surrounded by holly and berries, 10 1/2" d, 8 1/2" h, great color and detail. **$10,000**

Pair of French Limoges-style majolica table lamps, with bronze mounted base, top and handles, 21" h to top of vase portion of lamp, 37" overall, complete with matching lamp shades, professional repair to leaf and flower tips. .... **$750 pair**

Pair of French wall pockets, in the form of leaves with purple and yellow flowers and bird on vine, good detail, 10", professional repair to tips. .... **$750 pair**

Pair of majolica monkey figures, with young, 7 1/2" and 8". .... **$200 pair**

Pair of majolica table lamps, with hand-painted portraits of Victorian ladies, good detail, bases 12" h, 22" overall, repair to one. .... **$50 pair**

Rare majolica pipe, with claw-hold pipe bowl with silver cover, unusual form. **$225**

Royal Worcester, egg toothpick holder with two mice, nice detail, 2 1/2". **$600**

Royal Worcester, figure of putto with wine flask and grapes, 3" h, repair to one foot of putto. **$70**

Royal Worcester, majolica toothpick holder with picket-fence motif with snail and butterfly, 2 1/2" h. **$170**

Rustic jardiniere, in the form of tree trunk with floral and leaf motif and acorn handles, 11" h, 14" w. **$450**

Sarreguemines, double dolphin and shell figural majolica vase, 15", shape no. 948. .... **$450**

Sarreguemines, majolica fountain in the form of a turtle, 18 1/2" l, circa 1880, unusual form. **$600**

Table center, with nude lady seated in shells supported by dolphins on sea and rock base, 17" h, unusual form, professional rim repair to shells, creamware with cold painted majolica colors. **$200**

T.C. Brown-Westhead Moore & Co., cobalt majolica vase with bands of leaves tied with pink ribbon, 5 1/2". **$50**

T.C. Brown-Westhead Moore & Co., turquoise and cobalt vase with fruit on one side and leaves on the other with ring handles , 12 1/2" h, great color, professional rim repair. **$850**

Thomas Sergent, bull's head wall pocket, 6". **$90**

Wedgwood, cobalt wicker basket with twig handles, great color, 11". **$400**

Wedgwood, pair of spill vases in the form of boy with wine glass and girl with flower, each seated with baskets, 6 1/2", repair to handle of boy's basket. .... **$550 pair**

Wilhelm Schiller & Son (WS&S), large urn with lady faces and high relief and mask handles on lavender ground, 18" h, chip to rim of one ladies bonnet, good detail. **$150**

Photo courtesy Heritage Auction Galleries, Dallas; www.HA.com

Ulysses S. Grant Majolica Portrait Pitcher. This high relief bust of a more mature Grant in civilian dress probably dates from the period of his 1870s presidency, 9 7/8" in height. **$507**

Quimper

Quimper faience, dating back to the 17th century, is named for Quimper, a French town where numerous potteries were located. Several mergers resulted in the evolution of two major houses—the Jules Henriot and Hubaudière-Bousquet factories.

The peasant design first appeared in the 1860s, and many variations exist. Florals and geometrics, equally popular, also were produced in large quantities. During the 1920s, the Hubaudière-Bousquet factory introduced the Odetta line, which used a stone body and Art Deco decorations.

The two major houses merged in 1968, the products retaining the individual characteristics and marks of the originals. The concern suffered from labor problems in the 1980s and was purchased by an American group.

The "HR" and "HR Quimper" marks are found on Henriot pieces prior to 1922. The "Henriot Quimper" mark was used after 1922. The "HB" mark covers a long time span. Numbers or dots and dashes were added for inventory purposes and are found on later pieces. Most marks are in blue or black. Pieces ordered by department stores, such as Macy's and Carson Pirie Scott, carry the store mark along with the factory mark, making them less desirable to collectors.

Adviser: Al Bagdade.

Additional Terms:

A la touche border decor—single brush stroke to create floral

Breton Broderie decor—stylized blue and gold pattern inspired by a popular embroidery design often used on Breton costumes, dates from the 1920s.

Croisille—criss-cross pattern

Decor Riche border—acanthus leaves in two colors

Fleur-de-lys—the symbol of France.

Basket, 3 1/2" h x 4" d, lobed, female peasant in bowl center with red and green foliage, blue sponged rim and overhead twist handle, exterior with red, green, and yellow centered blue dot flowers, three small feet, "HenRiot Quimper France" mark. **$110**

Beverage Set, pitcher, 9 3/8" h, 4 mugs, 3 3/4" h, band of hanging stylized blue leaves from blue band, gray crackle ground, "P. Fouillen Quimper" marks. **$150**

Bookends, 7" h, stoneware, seated little girl, metallic blue, white, and brown cap, brown vest, metallic skirt, brown shoes, or seated boy, black hat, brown shirt, black vest, gray metallic trousers, lost brown show on base, metallic black bases, Berthe Savigny, "HB Quimper" marks. ...... **$750 pair**

Bowl, 9 1/2" square, with cut corners, female peasant, green foliage, inner border band of red, green, and blue foliage between blue bands, indented sides, pierced for hanging, "R-W Quimper France" mark. **$155**

Butter Tub, covered, 6" d, ribbed body, attached underplate, male peasant on cover, blue floral garlands, yellow and blue butterfly knob, "HR Quimper" mark. **$210**

Crepe Dish, 8" l x 6" w x 3" h, male peasant on interior, band of typical florals separated by four blue dot designs, rolled and ruffled blue sponged borders, molded bows on ends with ermine tails, pierced for hanging, "HR Quimper" mark. **$350**

Cake plate, 11 1/2" handle to handle, Breton Broderie, HB Quimper mark, circa 1925. **$300**

Cup and Saucer, hexagonal form, male peasant, demi fantasie red, blue, and green sprigs, four blue dot designs, blue lined rims, blue striped cup handle, pale blue glaze, "HenRiot Quimper France" mark. **$95**

Cup and Saucer, demitasse, eight lobed design, small red, blue, and green sprig on interior of cup, male peasant on exterior with scattered, red, green, and blue florals, band of same florals on saucer, blue rims, blue dash and gold line wishbone handle, "HenRiot Quimper" mark. **$110**

Doll Dishes, 4" d, iron red, blue, and green star, pinwheel, or geometric patterns, "HenRiot Quimper France" marks, set of four. **$150**

Door Push, 8 1/2" h, standing peasant flanked by usual vertical green, red, and blue florals, yellow and blue striped rim, holes for hanging, "HenRiot Quimper France" mark. **$125**

Dresser Box, covered, 6 3/4" w x 3" h, octagonal, large pink asters, light and dark green foliage in scratched vines, black ground, blue dash and line rim, pink lined base, "HenRiot Quimper France" mark. **$195**

Figure, 6 1/4" h, fisherman holding square box under each arm, overall white glaze, Bouvier, circa 1930. .... **$225**

Figure, 11" h, "St. Barbe," standing female in orange-lined cobalt robe, green cowl and shawl, black dotted white gown, holding orange tower, yellow, green, orange and white striped circular base with "St. Barbe," "HR Quimper" mark. **$525**

Figure, 13" h, dancing couple, male in black hat, med blue jacket, green vest, black trousers, black and white sash, woman in white blouse, green jacket, black skirt with medium blue, white apron, maroon sash, white coif, circular white base with "R. Micheau-Vernez" on top, "HenRiot Quimper" mark. **$960**

Grill Plate, 11" d, blue dash outlined segments with female peasant in large segment, scattered florals in two small segments, blue line rim, "HenRiot Quimper" mark. **$225**

Inkstand, 6" l, double, female peasant in pen well, flanked by red, blue, and green foliage, impressed green outlined red flower head between wells, red netting on sides with green dots, blue borders, cracked inserts, "HenRiot Quimper France" mark. **$450**

Inkwell, 4" h, ball shape on blue sponged ruffled base, seated male peasant with horn, scattered red, blue, and green flowers, blue lined rims, blue sponged ball knob, "HenRiot Quimper France" mark. **$350**

Oyster Plate, 9 1/4" d, 6 yellow wells separated by black arms with white and brown enameled fan highlights, center lemon well, "HB Quimper" mark. **$125**

Match Holder, 4 1/2" h x 4" w, figural envelope, male peasant on front with bunches of red, green, and blue florals, scattered four blue dot designs, blue and gold outlined margins, blue lattice sides, "HR Quimper" mark, hole for hanging. **$325**

Melonniere, 13 1/2" handle to handle, dancing peasant couple in center, dark blue acanthus border between orange lines with crest of Quimper at top, green outlined indented rim, blue acanthus exterior, green handles with molded yellow shells, "HenRiot Quimper" mark. **$450**

Pitcher, 8 5/8" h, standing peasant woman holding basket, scattered clouds, red, blue, and green flowers on reverse, blue dash overhead handle and side handle, orange and blue striped spout and rim, "HB Quimper" mark. **$140**

Plate, 8 5/8" d, large green outlined blue dash central Maltese cross on red net ground, yellow border with band of red single stroke flowers, blue lined rim, unmarked. **$175**

Plate, 9 1/8" d, black or red berries, thorny stems with green and yellow-brown leaves, yellow shaped rim with indentations, Porquier Beau mark. **$1,125**

Plate, 9 1/4" d, standing sailor in blue and white uniform holding maiden wearing blue dress with white apron, orange vest and hem, border band of blue stylized leaves on stems interrupted by circle or Xs and dot designs, orange and blue striped rim, "HB Quimper France" mark. **$225**

Plate, 9 1/2" d, dark blue rooster with blue, red, and yellow tail in center flanked by red, blue, and green fan florals, border of scattered sprigs separated by four blue dot designs, blue lined indented rim, "HenRiot Quimper France" mark. **$125**

Plate, 10" d, full frontal view of standing female peasant holding basket in meadow, cobalt acanthus border between gold-orange stripes, crest of Quimper at top, indented rim, pierced for hanging, "HenRiot Quimper" mark. **$225**

Platter, 13 1/2" l x 9" w, "croisille" pattern, center scene of peasant woman leaning on fence holding distaff, border of alternating blue crosshatching and panels of yellow, red, and green dogwood blossom and orange ferns, scalloped rim, "HenRiot Quimper" mark. **$375**

Porringer, 5 1/2" handle to handle, red dot and green tennis racquet pattern on interior, red, blue, yellow, and red single stroke florals between orange and blue bands yellow and green florals on exterior, blue sponged tab handles, "HB Quimper" mark. **$125**

Quintal, 6 3/8" h, seated male peasant blowing horn on front, large yellow-centered red or blue daisies on reverse, scattered red or blue dot design, black ermine tails, blue, green and orange striped rim on center tube, orange and green striped secondary tubes, "HenRiot Quimper" mark. **$225**

Condiments, 5 1/4" h, HB Quimper marks. **$350 pair**

Snuff Bottle, 3" h, heart shaped, multicolored rooster on front, blue florals on reverse, green-banded sides. **$400**

Sugar Bowl, coverd, 6 1/2" h, hexagonal, paneled, yellow ground, male peasant on front panel, female on reverse, vertical florals, orange outlined wishbone handle with blue striping, blue dash knob, "HenRiot Quimper France" mark. **$150**

Tile, 4 1/2" square, multicolored "Quimper" crest of arms, border band of blue semi-circles with red dots and red V s, "HenRiot Quimper" mark. **$175**

Tray, 10 3/4" l x 6 7/8" w, oval, female peasant in center flanked by green vertical foliage, band of red, green, and yellow centered blue florals on border, blue lined scalloped rim, "HenRiot Quimper France" mark. **$225**

Vase, 4 3/4" h, teardrop shape, bust of female peasant, light blue and white coif with maroon ribbon, orange vest, cream ground, black loop handles, orange-lined spread feet, "HenRiot Quimper" mark. **$135**

Vase, 6 1/2" h, bulbous base and top, narrow collar, stylized yellow dandelions, brown stems, large green leaves, yellow and green ground, "HB Quimper France" mark. **$180**

Vase, 10" h, 13" handle to handle, flat sides with green and orange lined curved rims, peasant man and woman reaching out to children in farm on front, scattered pink and yellow flowers, green foliage on reverse, orange and green outlined panels, green acanthus side panels with green figural gargoyle handles, "entwined PB Quimper" mark, base chips. **$4,800**

Wall pocket, 11 3/4" h, double cone shape, male peasant facing female separated by vertical red, blue, green, and yellow flowers, four black dot designs and ermine tails on bases, blue waves on back plate, "HB Quimper" mark on base. **$230**

COOKIE JARS

Cookie jars, colorful and often whimsical, are popular with collectors. They were made by almost every manufacturer in all types of materials. Figural character cookie jars are the most popular with collectors.

Cookie jars often were redesigned to reflect newer tastes. Hence, the same jar may be found in several different variations and these variations can affect the price.

Many cookie-jar shapes were manufactured by more than one company and, as a result, can be found with different marks. This often happened because of mergers. Molds also were traded and sold among companies.

Drum Major by Shawnee, 10" tall, late 1940s, impressed mark, "U.S.A.," also found marked "#10," and rarely in gold trim. (This example, **$300+; with gold trim, $500+)**

Little Bo Peep by Abingdon, 11 3/4" tall, late 1940s, impressed mark on bottom, "694." **$120+**

Family Circus Billy attributed to Sierra-Vista or Starnes, 12 1/2" tall, late 1950s, unmarked. **$120+**

Dutch Girl by American Bisque, with detail painted decoration under glaze, 12 3/4" tall, 1950s, impressed mark on bottom, "Pat. Design 138577 U.S.A." **$100+**

CLOCKS

The clock is one of the oldest human inventions. The word clock (from the Latin word clocca, "bell"), suggests that it was the sound of bells that also characterized early timepieces.

The first mechanical clocks to be driven by weights and gears were invented by medieval Muslim engineers. The first geared mechanical clock was invented by an 11th century Arab engineer in Islamic Spain. The knowledge of weight-driven mechanical clocks produced by Muslim engineers was transmitted to other parts of Europe through Latin translations of Arabic and Spanish texts.

In the early 14th century, existing clock mechanisms that used water power were being adapted to take their driving power from falling weights. This power was controlled by some form of oscillating mechanism. This controlled release of power—the escapement—marks the beginning of the true mechanical clock.

Also see Modernism, Tiffany.

American brass Chelsea ship's clock, retailed by George B. Carpenter & Co., Chicago, circa first half 20th century. The brass case with brushed steel dial attached to it's original mahogany bracket both with the serial number 76554 and additionally numbered "6008". This model patented December 30, 1901, 7" d. Overall height including bracket 10" x 10 1/4" x 5 1/4". **$862**

Ansonia crystal regulator, Excelsior eight-day clock with overall gilding and elaborate decoration, 19th century. Complete with original pendulum. 20 1/2" x 11". **$1,680**

Ansonia gilt metal clock, with Rococo-style case surmounted by a cherub playing a flute, circa 1900. 19 1/2" x 9" x 8". **$960**

Ansonia Rococo-design mantel clock, cast metal with seated figure (possibly Mercury) to left, case with C-scrolls, S-scrolls and shell work, circular porcelain dial with exposed escapement, gilt egg-and-dart molded bezel, Ansonia Clock Co., New York; 15" h, 16" w. **$517**

Ansonia Royal Bonn mantel clock, Rococo cresting, porcelain dial with exposed escapement, floral painted, brass works marked on back: "Ansonia Clock Co., patented June 14, 81, New York, U.S.A."; pink shaded case, leaf-decorated scroll feet, 13 7/8" h, 10 1/4" w. **$840**

Banjo clock, with reverse painting, white-painted dial, circular glazed brass door, twin pierced brass brackets, reverse-painted throat panel with leaf-scroll, American eagle and shield, reverse-painted pendulum door with ship battle between Americans and British, 32 1/2" h, 10" w. **$1,610**

Banjo clock, Simon Willard, circa 1810, eight-day, weight-driven works, inlaid mahogany case, gilt metal American eagle finial, circular glazed dial door with brass mount, glazed throat panel with reverse-painted gold on white lattice motif and gilt bead border flanked by twin curved brass brackets. Reverse-painted glazed pendulum door with lattice work reserve marker, "S. Willard's/ PATENT", 35" h (including finial), 9 5/8" w, 3 1/2" deep, some reverse paint damage to gilt bead border on pendulum door. **$13,800**

Brass two-day marine chronometer, by Chadwick, Liverpool, late 19th or 20th century. The silver dial with subsidiary seconds dial within a brass gimbal, the dial

Photo courtesy Heritage Auction Galleries, Dallas; www.HA.com

French Tortoiseshell, Brass, And Gilt Bronze Striking Bracket Clock, Late 19th Century, 49 1/2", the case with brass-inlaid tortoiseshell decoration and glazed side panels, the white enameled dial with Roman chapters and metal hands, the glazed door adorned with a gilt plaque depicting the goddess Amphitrite driving a chariot of seahorses. **$5,676**

Photo courtesy Pook & Pook Inc., Downingtown, Pa.; www.pookandpook.com

French black marble mantel clock by Henri Jullien with open escapement, 13" h. (broken glass). **$293**

marked "Chadwick, 69 Lord Street, Liverpool. No. 386". Fitted in a brass-bound mahogany case. Retains original key. Dimensions of box 7 1/2" x 7 1/2" x 7 1/2". The case and exterior of chronometer in very good condition overall. The back plate, once removed, reveals a bent spring. The dial was not removed to inspect interior. **$1,438**

Ephraim Downes, pillar-and-scroll mantel clock, Bristol, Conn., three brass urn and steeple finials, scrolled pediment, white-painted dial with cornucopia spandrels, twin colonnettes, reverse-painting on door with sailboat and house, bracket feet, 27 7/8" to top of central plinth, 16 1/2" w, pediment damaged with some pieces retained. **$575**

Ever-Ready Safety Razor clock, wood face features graphic of lathered gent shaving. Includes original pendulum, 18" w x 28" h. Generally good condition; Roman numerals and dial graphics have had older paint touch-up that extends into black outlines. Original pendulum. **$1,725**

Four-hundred-day clock, exceptionally large, German or French, its porcelain dial painted with musical instruments and champlevé decoration on columns, dome and base, disc pendulum, circa 1900. With wooden base and glass dome, 26". **$8,400**

French bracket clock of baluster form, with a porcelain dial above an elaborate brass coat of arms, circa 1870-1880, 36" x 21". **$1,800**

French bronze and champlevé clock, oval case flanked by two columns with champlevé enamel, painted dial and double vial mercury pendulum, movement marked L. Marti & Co. 1889 Made in France. 14 1/2" x 9 1/2" x 5 1/2". **$2,520**

French champlevé crystal regulator, with painted champlevé panels, dial and pendulum surrounded by rhinestones, circa 1890. 16 1/2". **$9,000**

French country cottage clock, painted metal dial has raised cartouches with Roman numerals, inlaid mother-of-pearl, brass and exotic woods, 19th century. 23" x 20". **$570**

French Marti & Cie, eight-day time and strike crystal regulator shelf clock, circa 1900, the dial inscribed "Bigelow Kennard & Co., Boston", 10 1/2" h. **$305**

Photo courtesy Pook & Pook Inc., Downingtown, Pa.; www.pookandpook.com

French bronze and rouge marble shelf clock, late 19th century, by Lemerle-Charpentier & Cie, the bronze figure of a woman signed "Moreau Mathurin," 22 1/2" h. **$3,042**

Photo courtesy Pook & Pook Inc., Downingtown, Pa.; www.pookandpook.com

French painted mantel clock with ormolu mounts, 16" h. **$439**

Photo courtesy Pook & Pook Inc., Downingtown, Pa.; www.pookandpook.com

French wall clock, late 19th century, inscribed "Georges Chazottes Chateau-Gontier" on the mother of pearl inlaid dial, 24 1/2" h. **$234**

French porcelain mantel clock, 19th century, ormolu-mounted, surmounted by basket of flowers on cobalt blue glazed vase, glazed dial door opening to circular porcelain dial inscribed "1/Hry Marc/A Paris"; festoons of ormolu flowers supported by pair of ram's heads at sides, base having seated child at each side with book, porcelain panel at center with two putto, molded base with leaf-scrolled supports, 25" h, 20" w. **$4,600**

French slate clock, beveled glass on front and back doors, marked H & F Paris 2877, 19th century. 18 1/2" x 12 1/2" x 8". **$840**

French spelter shelf clock, late 19th century, with figure of a knight, 15 1/2" h. **$410**

Gilt bronze mantel clock, blue porcelain urn flanked by cherubs holding a garland of flowers, on a breakfront base with enamel clock dial, 19th century. The top with a floral bouquet and two doves. Restoration to porcelain urn, 18 1/2" x 16" x 5 1/2". **$2,760**

Chauncey Ives pillar-and-scroll mantel clock, Bristol, Conn.; mahogany case, twin scroll pediment, three brass urn finials, white-painted dial, twin colonnettes; reverse-painted

Photo courtesy Pook & Pook Inc., Downingtown, Pa.; www.pookandpook.com

Ithaca No. 3 calendar clock, circa 1875, 38 1/2" h. **$1,404**

Photo courtesy Heritage Auction Galleries, Dallas; www.HA.com

Perfection Leather Oil Baird Advertising Clock. Although repainted some time ago, this Baird clock still has it's original dial and manufacturer's paper on the inside. Complete with pendulum, 18" x 31 1/2". **$2,031**

glass panel with ship and water surrounded by flowers and leafage in earth tones, 28 3/4" h, 16 1/2" w, 4 1/2" deep, reverse-painted glass panel cracked. **$1,035**

Jaeger Le Coultre Atmos clock, square form with glass sides and top, revealing the movement and dial, 20th century. 9" x 8 1/2" x 5 1/2". **$1,200**

Japy Freres, marble and bronze three-piece clock garniture, 19th century, the porcelain dial inscribed "Boursier Jne Paris," the bronze figure of mother and child signed Faillot (Edme-Nicolas Faillot, 1810-1849). 16" h. overall. **$380**

Mantel clock, L. & J.G. Stickley, designed by Peter Hanson with an etched copper face, square wooden details, and a small glass window. Unmarked. 22" x 16" x 8". **$7,200**

McClintock Co. clock, with stained-glass door and face in the style of Purcell and Elmslie. Brass McClintock Co. tag, Minneapolis, 45 3/4" x 17" x 10 3/4". **$2,520**

Sessions clock, with cast iron frog surround, whimsical copper-flashed cast-iron group of frogs playing musical instruments, 9 1/2" w x 11 1/2" h. **$517**

Seth Thomas, faux marble shelf clock, 11 1/2" h. **$176**

Seth Thomas ship's clock, first half 20th century, brass, mounted on custom bracket, the clock now mounted with a brass ship's wheel, the dial marked "Seven jeweled eight day ships bell," 9" x 13" x 3". Appears to be in untouched original condition. Clock has not been disassembled for condition. **$288**

Photo courtesy James D. Julia Auctioneers, Fairfield, Maine; www.JuliaAuctions.com

New England Jeweler's Astronomical Regulator Clock. Mid-19th century. Originating probably in Massachusetts or in central New Hampshire, this example is in a walnut Gothic beehive case, the circular upper door with half-round molding and conforming glass panel hinged and opening upwards, the white enamel painted steel dial with hour and seconds dials within the minutes dial on the outer perimeter, the brass works weight-driven and pendulum regulated with maintaining power and dead-beat escapement, with original brass pendulum and weight behind the rectangular, half-round, molded, glass panel lower door; the case sides with viewing windows to the movement; the case edge with half-round moldings; all raised on a molded plinth. 60 1/2" h x 20 1/2" w. x 6 1/2" d. Case and movement both in fine original condition, showing fine patina; dial with crackle and some early repainting.
$4,600

Photo courtesy Pook & Pook Inc., Downingtown, Pa.; www.pookandpook.com

Swiss Omega square eight-day brass desk clock, #10600650, 5 1/2" h. **$1,404**

Photo courtesy Pook & Pook Inc., Downingtown, Pa.; www.pookandpook.com

Waterbury Sage eight-day repeater carriage clock, 5 1/2" h. **$214**

Sevres shelf clock, decorated with ormolu and rhinestones with painted dial, late 18th century. Porcelain crack upper right of frame. Signed Duryea & Potter, Paris. 14 1/4". **$4,200**

Waterbury, mahogany eight-day mantel clock, patented 1914, with a four-train movement, 16 1/2" h. **$205**

Photo courtesy James D. Julia Auctioneers, Fairfield, Maine; www.JuliaAuctions.com

Seth Thomas Wall Regulator, quartersawn oak cabinet with reeded moldings, and crest with turned finials. Large door in front with glass window allows viewing of large pendulum. Clock face (possible replacement) is marked with Seth Thomas logo and separate second indicator, 66 1/2" h x 19 1/2" w. Appears complete with exception of bottom finials (holes plugged) and small piece that hooks pendulum into mechanism is broken. **$1,610**

Tall-Case Clocks

British tall-case clock, of traditional design in profusely inlaid walnut, early 19th century. Signed "Thomas Heywood, Bangor," probably signature of owner, 90" h. **$2,400**

Cherry tall-case clock, shaped, arched cresting with twin brass hexagonal urn finials, glazed arched door, white painted wood dial, yellow flowers at top, gold spandrels, second hand dial, calendar dial, molded door, molded base, bracket feet, 83" h, 17 1/4" w, 10" deep. **$632**

Dark-stained tall-case clock, quarter-spool-turned cornice, arched glazed door, twin fluted colonnettes flanking, brass dial, painted-moon dial, second hand dial, calendar dial, engraved fruit decoration; glazed beveled pendulum door flanked by fluted quarter-columns, molded base, ogee bracket feet, 92 3/4" h, 20 3/4" w, 12 1/8" deep, hands broken. **$1,092**

Henry Deyken, inlaid mahogany and oak tall-case clock, broken-scroll pediment with two roundels, glazed door, flanked by two reeded colonnettes, opening to brass dial inscribed "Henry Deyken Worcester No. 1172," gilt metal spandrels, second hand dial, molded base with inlaid bird, bracket feet, 82 3/4" h, 17 1/2" w, 9" deep, alteration to back probably to accommodate works. **$900**

Federal inlaid mahogany tall-case clock, probably New Jersey, circa 1815, the arch molded hood below conforming scrolled cresting with brass terminals centering three ball finials, the center with displayed eagle above an astragal glazed door flanked by fluted colonettes and unusual brass stop fluting. Painted enameled moon-phase dial with pink rose spandrels centering an Arabic and Roman numeral chapter ring. Dial centered with a sweep second hand and calendar aperture. Eight-day brass works with iron plate stamped "Wilson", probably Thomas Wilson, London, 1790-1825. Waisted case fitted with rectangular door with molded edges and string inlay flanked by engaged fluted quarter columns with brass capitals and brass stop fluting above a molded box base raised on flared French feet with shaped apron. Clock with two door keys, winder, both weights and pendulum, 90" h x 13 1/2" throat w x 9" deep. Fine condition with original clean surfaces.. **$6,038**

French Morbier tall-case clock, with porcelain dial and articulating pendulum in pine case, 19th century. 90". **$1,920**

(Morbier clocks were made in the Franche-Comté region of eastern France for more than 200 years, beginning in the late 17th century.)

Photo courtesy James D. Julia Auctioneers, Fairfield, Maine; www.JuliaAuctions.com

Philadelphia Sheraton Tall Case Clock, Crowley & Farr. Circa 1823-1825. Figured mahogany example with molded swan's neck pediment terminating in rosettes centering a ball-and-spire brass finial, the astragal-glazed door flanked by free-standing rope-twist colonnettes, opening to the painted dial with moon phase aperture, the dial with paint-decorated and gilt Nautilus spandrels and shells, centering a Roman numeral dial marked with minutes, further centering a calendar aperture and subsidiary seconds dial, marked "Crowley & Farr / PHILAD,a". With winder, door keys, single brass finial, pendulum, and two weights, 8'4" h. x 15" throat w. x 9 1/2" d. **$2,875**

French oak tall-case clock, arched molded cornice, cast-pewter spandrels and dial, arched glazed dial door, twin brackets carved with husk pendants, molded paneled door with carved emblem, bombe form base, 81 3/4" h, 21" w, 11" d. **$4,600**

Jacob Gothart walnut tall-case clock, Lebanon, Pa., twin scroll pediment with pair of urn finials, white-painted dial, moon dial, gilt spandrels, trunk with American Eagle inlay, 99 3/8" h, 18 3/4" w. **$9,000**

Inlaid mahogany tall-case clock, twin scrolled pediment, centering brass ball and steeple finial (replaced), glazed arched door opening to white painted dial inscribed "E. Winftanles/Wigan"; second hand dial, calendar aperture, pointed arch pendulum door with thumb-molded border, two reeded flanking corners, conforming inlaid chamfered base, French bracket feet, 87 3/4" h. **$2,185**

Joseph Krout, (Bucks County, Pa.) cherry tall-case clock, broken-scroll pediment, pair of rosettes, three urn finials, arched glazed door, four slender colonnettes flanking, painted dial and moon dial, sweep second hand, brown painted monograms ("JK" and "BC"); American red, white and blue shield motif; eight-day brass works with strike by "Joseph Krout", 1815; pendulum door with brass plate inside detailing family history of clock; rounded front corners, trunk and base, French bracket feet, 97" h, 17 3/4" w, 10" deep, pendulum door replaced. **$6,600**

Mahogany tall-case clock, twin scrolled pediment with twin brass rosettes (one missing), three brass ball-and-steeple finials, twin colonnettes, arched glazed door opening to painted dial, brass 8-day works, oval gilt reserve with thistles and arch of flowers above, floral painted spandrels, arched pendulum door, twin quarter-columns flanking, serpentine apron, bracket feet, early 19th century, 87 1/4" h, 18 3/8" w, 9" deep. **$1,725**

Oak tall-case clock, pewter eagle on spire (replaced), shaped top, painted leaf scroll, bearing "1776"; square glazed door (flanked by twin columns) opening to steel dial marked "Dav'd Collier Gatley"; works with strike, moon dial, gilt metal mask head and scrollwork spandrels, pendulum door flanked by two rounded corners, molded chamfered base, bracket feet, 85 1/2" h, 19" w, 10" deep. **$2,300**

Secessionist grandfather clock, with brass face and base molding, beveled glass door with added glass shelves where pendulum originally swung, possibly imported by Gustav Stickley. Partial Eastwood label. 78" x 15 1/4" x 9 1/2". **$1,800**

Walnut tall-case clock, cove-molded cornice with large metal inlaid "1776"; steel dial, four gilt metal mask head spandrels; "Franz Iacob/ Braun Eber Bach/ A.M. Kecken"; glazed dial door, low bracket feet, 90 3/4" h, 16 1/4" w, 9" deep, replaced brass H-hinges on right side of dial door. **$1,725**

Walnut tall-case clock, inlaid, twin scroll pediment with twin roundels, inlaid scrolled plinth, brass ball and steeple finial, twin wooden urn finials, arched glazed door flanked by turned spindles, painted dial marked "Blomagerus"; second hand dial, calendar aperture, gilt floral spandrels, inlaid trunk with pendulum door (bird inlay), conforming inlaid base, bracket feet, 83 1/4" h (without finial), 18" w, 8 1/2" deep. **$1,840**

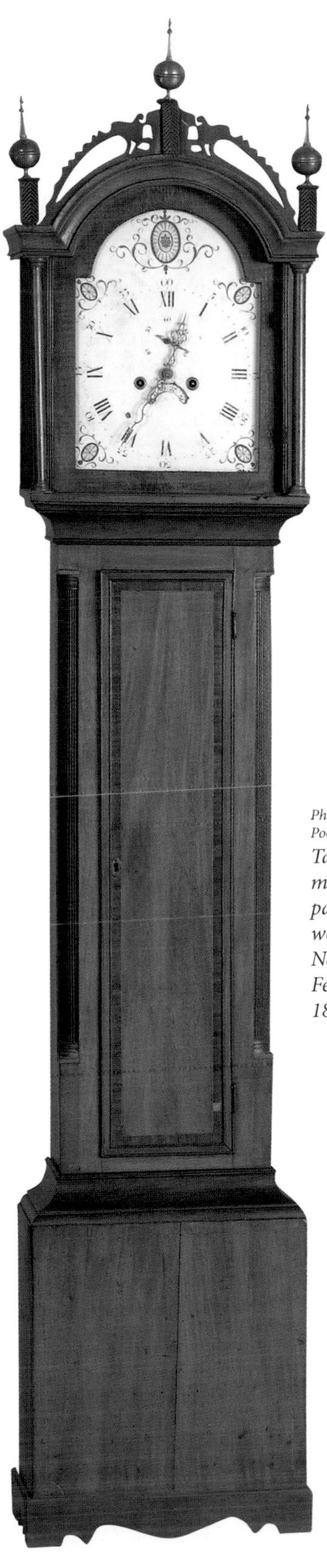

Photo courtesy of Pook & Pook Inc.

Tall case clock, mahogany, painted dial, 8-day works, inlaid case, New England, Federal, circa 1810. **$3,500**

Clothing

FUTURE OF THE MARKET: VINTAGE CLOTHING

Changing buying patterns show importance of client loyalty

By Caroline Ashleigh

Caroline Ashleigh Associates, Birmingham, Mich.

The definition of "vintage clothing" varies from expert to expert. Alison and Melissa Houtte, authors of *Alligators, Old Mink & New Money* (Avon Books, 2006), state that "in the industry, people say that 20 years or older is 'vintage.' However, television programs like Sex and the City have started a whole new trend of buying 'newer' vintage fashion to a generation of sophisticated women who want to stand out from the crowd, like Carrie Bradshaw, to make a true fashion statement."

Valuable vintage does not necessarily have to be expensive to be fresh, carefree and sleek. If you are in the market for tomorrow's vintage fashion today, look for design that breaks the rules, and has classic staying power with a distinctive, singular trademark style. Check out regional designers in your own locale, rather than the off-the-rack regulars.

Photo courtesy Leslie Hindman Auctioneers, Chicago; www.LeslieHindman.com

Dress, Galanos Paisley, 1950s, in a red, orange, green, and black print with tie-back halter, net underskirt, fully lined. Labeled: Galanos. **$457**

Boutiques like Hooti Couture in Brooklyn, N.Y., and Resurrection in New York and California, rummage and estate sales, flea markets, and online auctions are all wonderful sources of vintage fashion if you want to stand out at any party. The "hip" gal of today is not afraid to mix new with vintage, bringing a little whimsy, fun and touch of glam to her wardrobe. She can create miles of look on a minimal budget by adding a vintage beaded or sequined jacket or top, over a smart skirt or slacks and jeans, with a great pair of Manolos, and voila!

Caroline Ashleigh

My longtime friend and colleague, Linda Putman, vintage fashion dealer and owner of When I Was a Kid, of Eton Rapids, Mich., shared these observations:

"Recently I have experienced a significant change in the manner that our clients have determined the purchases that they make. As our clientele is comprised of collectors, fashion design houses, movie costumers and other dealers, their acquisition patterns are extremely varied."

The Collector: Those who are avid collectors of vintage attire and accessories continue to make the purchase, and are not discouraged by the price for rare and incredibly gorgeous items

Fashion Design Houses: These buyers are and always have been looking for the unusual and exceptionally styled item. Although this group has become a bit more selective relative to an item's rarity, fashion houses will make the purchase for sheer glitz and glamour, and pay the fair price

Movie Costumers: Since early 2009, there has been a noticeable up-tick in purchases from this group of buyers. Perhaps as a result of an increase in the number of films scheduled for completion, a "restocking" phenomenon has occurred and an increase in period fashion purchases from this sector

The Dealer: The buying pattern of this segment of the vintage fashion community varies regionally. Dealers on the West Coast, particularly California, continue to be very strong buyers, focusing on the high end of designer pieces. Sales comprised of East Coast and Midwestern dealers tend to be more value oriented.

Putnam astutely observed, "at this point in our economy, the vintage fashion business is no different than any other retail or wholesale business ... client loyalty is crucial, and one must be flexible to retain that loyalty and client base going forward."

Caroline Ashleigh owns Birmingham, Mich.-based Caroline Ashleigh Associates LLC. She is a graduate of New York University in Appraisal Studies in Fine and Decorative Arts and is a board-certified senior member of the Appraisers Association of America. Ashleigh is an internationally known appraiser and regularly appears on the PBS program Antiques Roadshow. Caroline Ashleigh Associates conducts fully catalogued online auctions. Visit www.appraiseyourart.com or www.auctionyourart.com.

Helpful Hints for the Care and Storage of Clothing

Wash your hands thoroughly before handling fine vintage garments. Use white cotton gloves when handling vintage fabric; soiled gloves may transfer dirt.

Before handling textiles, remove any sharp jewelry that could snag or pull delicate threads.

Do not smoke, drink or eat near your garments. Accidents may result in stains on textiles, and food attracts insects.

Avoid prolonged exposure of textiles to direct sunlight as it can weaken fibers.

Roll fabrics—do not fold—as creases can weaken fibers and cause them to become brittle and crack.

Resist cleaning. It is best to clean fabric with a hand vacuum.

Check periodically for mildew and insect damage.

Whenever possible, do not wear makeup when putting on or trying on a valuable vintage garment.

Do not use mothballs or crystals to protect your garment from insects. They are extremely toxic and leave a permanent odor.

Storage

Use acid-free textile storage containers. Do not store textiles in brown cardboard boxes, as they release acids.

Acid-free buffered tissue can be used for cottons, linens, synthetics.

Use acid-free, un-buffered tissue for wool, silk, leather.

Use padded wood hangers to hang garments.

Do not store vintage garments in a damp basement or hot attic.

Do not store fabrics in plastic bags as they hold moisture and can release chemicals. Store in unbleached muslin.

Photo courtesy Leslie Hindman Auctioneers, Chicago; www.LeslieHindman.com

Sweater, Kansai, beige wool, oversized, with waffle knit, faux fur sleeve, Lurex embroidered tiger motif. Labeled: Kansai International. **$183**

Enjoy your vintage piece! With the proper care, you will have it to treasure for many years to come and perhaps pass in on to another family member.

Sources for Archival Materials for Clothing

Gaylord Bros., Syracuse, N.Y.: 800-962-9580; www.gaylordmart.com

Talas, New York, N.Y.: 212-219-0770; www.talas-nyc.com

Light Impressions, Santa Fe Springs, Calif.: 800-828-6216; www.lightimpressionsdirect.com

Textile Terms

Brocade: Rich silk fabric with raised patterns.

Cashmere: Soft twilled fabric made of goat's wool.

Chantilley (pronounced shan-tee-yee): Bobbin lace most commonly found in black.

Chenille: Velvety silk, wool or cotton fabric, with a protruding pile.

Chintz: Glazed printed cotton fabric.

Cutwork: Fabric made "lacy" by cutting away and binding edges with satin or buttonhole stitches. It is not needle lace, but rather cutwork embroidery. Also known as embroidered lace.

Damask: Fine lustrous fabric with flat patterns and a satin weave.

Denim: Firm and durable twilled cotton.

Dresden: Lace that combines a number of embroidery techniques including satin stitch, tambour (chain stitch) and pulled stitches to create a lace-like surface. Also known as white work.

Gabardine: Closely woven cotton or wool twill.

Georgette: Thin silk.

Gingham: Striped cotton cloth.

Grosgrain: Heavy close-woven corded silk.

Hairpin Lace: Lace that is formed over a U-shaped wire frame called a hairpin, with the help of a crochet hook. Also known as Portuguese lace.

Haute Couture: The term "haute couture" is French. *Haute* means "high" or "elegant." *Couture* literally means "sewing" or "tailoring," but has come to indicate the business of creating, designing and selling high-fashion women's clothes. Haute couture originated in the 19th century by Charles Frederick Worth. Made from scratch for each customer, it usually takes from 100 to 400 hours to make one dress.

Jacquard: Name of the mechanism invented by Joseph Marie Jacquard in 1801. A term used to describe coverlets with complex floral and pictorial designs; most typical period from 1830s-1860s.

Moire: Watered silk.

Nylon: First synthetic fiber, invented in 1935.

Organdie: Fine translucent cotton.

Organza: Transparent thin silk or nylon.

Pique: Stiff durable corded fabric or cotton, rayon or silk.

Satin: Closely woven silk with lustrous face.

Shantung: Plain rough silk or cotton.

Stevengraphs: Colorful silk pictures invented by Thomas Stevens, beginning in the 1860s, and also produced by other English makers. Collectors seek examples in original mats with all labels complete.

Taffeta: Thin glossy silk.

Tatting: Tatting is made with a shuttle and is distinguished by rings of knots.

Ticking: Strong cotton or linen fabric used for pillowcases and mattresses.

Tulle: Sheer and delicate silk.

Clothing and Accessories

Photo courtesy Leslie Hindman Auctioneers, Chicago; www.LeslieHindman.com

Blouse, Hermes, orange silk scarf, in an American Indian motif. Labeled: Hermes/Paris. **$671**

Also see Native American, Textiles, Western/Cowboy.

Belt plate, Civil War Confederate, lead-filled brass featuring pelican and young (Louisiana). Plate measure approximately 2 1/8" x 3", with brass hooks on reverse, some bends to edges. **$3,000**

Blouse, Emilio Pucci, cotton, 1960s, in a blue, green and purple geometric print with matching covered buttons. Labeled: Emilio Pucci. Left shoulder needs to be re-stitched about 1". **$156**

Bustier with leggings ensemble, Emilio Pucci, 1970s, in a pink, brown and black geometric print, strapless bustier top. Together with two pairs of leggings. All labeled: Emilio Pucci. .... **$180 all**

Photo courtesy Leslie Hindman Auctioneers, Chicago; www.LeslieHindman.com

Belt, Hermes, navy leather, Constance, 1972, gold hardware, blind stamp B. Stamped: Hermes. **$518**

Photo courtesy Leslie Hindman Auctioneers, Chicago; www.LeslieHindman.com

Belt, Judith Leiber, green alligator, with a jeweled closure. Stamped: Judith Leiber. **$366**

Photo courtesy Leslie Hindman Auctioneers, Chicago; www.LeslieHindman.com

Bolero, Schiaparelli Shocking Pink Velvet with shawl collar, fully lined. Labeled: Schiaparelli. **$231**

Coat, Balenciaga Couture, cream wool, 1955, with cropped sleeves, small collar, cream buttons, fully lined. Labeled: Balenciaga/69262, small tear in lining near the tag, small stain on lining. **$1,020**

Coat, Eisa, cream faux fur, early 1960s, ready-to-wear from the house of Balenciaga, with full length sleeves, straight fit with cream buttons at front, pockets at side, fully lined in silk faille. Labeled: Eisa. Some buttons are loose. **$360**

Coat, Geoffrey Beene, black silk, dress, 1960s, with cropped sleeves, a wrap style, empire waist, full skirt with hidden pockets, fully lined. Labeled: Geoffrey Beene. **$204**

Coat, Givenchy Couture, green, early 1960s, streamlined silhouette, small collar, green round buttons with additional snap closures, center and hem framed in seam lines, two slits at side, fully lined in silk. Labeled: Givenchy/46.178. .... **$420**

Coat, Hattie Carnegie, black silk, evening, 1950s, with two frog closures at front, fully lined. Labeled: Hattie Carnegie. Total length 48". **$240**

Coat, Holly Harp, brown silk chiffon, duster, 1970s, with all-over velvet leaves, three-quartered sleeves with beaded detail, closureless. Labeled: Holly's Harp. **$108**

Coat, dark-brown, three-quarter-length mink, Herbert's Furs, San Francisco label. **$150**

Coat, brown three-quarter-length mink, with shawl collar and floral embroidered lining, I. Magnin, size 10/12. .... **$250**

Coat, dark-brown, three-quarter-length mink, with notch lapel, I. Magnin, size 14/16. .... **$275**

Photo courtesy Leslie Hindman Auctioneers, Chicago; www.LeslieHindman.com

Mesh Shirt,1920s,with long sleeves and a V-neckline. Ex-collection of Atelle L. Chisholm/Elise Meyer. **$1,952**

Photo courtesy Leslie Hindman Auctioneers, Chicago; www.LeslieHindman.com

Coat, Jean-Charles de Castelbajac, printed cotton, trench, 1993, with built-in hood, red and yellow lapels, back "Les Trois Amis" motif, fully lined. Labeled: Jean-Charles de Castelbajac/KC and CO. **$1,037**

Coat, Teal Traina, black velvet, 1950s, double-breasted, full skirt, fully lined. Labeled: Teal Traina. Total length 55". **$96**

Coat, winter fox, full-length, size 10/12. .... **$1,000**

Coat, early 1940s, wool, black and white herringbone with black wool trim, accentuated shoulders, swing fit, slit pockets, fully lined. Total length 41". **$90**

Coat, gray wool, cape, 1960s, with a notched collar, sleeveless with a cape extension at back covering arms, fitted waist, flared skirt, fully lined. **$216**

Cocktail ensemble, 1940s, navy, jacket with cropped sleeves, a sculptured sweetheart neckline, buttoned bodice. Dress with a floral lace bust, fitted bodice, flared skirt. **$120**

Cover up, Emilio Pucci, cotton, 1960s, blue and white floral print with a matching self belt. Labeled: Emilio Pucci/Florence-Italy. Two small stains at the front hem area. **$300**

Dress, Adele Simpson, floral silk, cocktail, 1950s, with a fitted bodice, two bows at waist. No label. **$72**

Dress, Ben Reig, taupe satin, cocktail, 1950s, with thick straps, a fitted bodice with a panel of brown satin and beading at bust, full skirt. Labeled: Ben Reig. **$132**

Dress, Bob Meyer, green wool, 1960s, with cropped sleeves, mock collar, with a cream panel at front and a peach panel at back, fully lined. Labeled: Bob Meyer/Chicago. **$120**

Dress, Chloe, yellow, 1960s, with a round neckline with full length sleeves, rows of clear beading throughout, matching slip underneath. Labeled: Chloe. One area where the beads are loose. **$570**

Dress, Christian Dior, black silk, cocktail, 1956, with three-quarter-length sleeves, a V-neckline, fitted waist with pleated gathering at waist for a full skirt. No label. **$192**

Photo courtesy Leslie Hindman Auctioneers, Chicago; www.LeslieHindman.com

Coat, Koos van den Akker, "Cats", leather with quilted sleeves, smocked cuffs, collar and hem, "Cats" applique on back. Labeled: Koos Couture/Koos Van den Akker New York. **$1,159**

Dress, Claire McCardell, black velvet, 1950s, with elastic band sleeves, "ruched" (a ruffle or pleat of lace, muslin or other fine fabric) front at closures, skirt in a sheer black silk with a cream underlay with glitter dots throughout. Labeled: Claire McCardell Clothes/by Townley. There are missing glitter spots throughout the skirt, the velvet is slightly worn in spots. There is an area where the velvet in the armpit has ripped and been repaired. There is some wear around the closures at front. There is also some wear around the waist to the skirt. **$240**

Dress, Courreges, cream wool, day, 1969, in an A-line fit, with short sleeves, a V-neck and front and back, two patch pockets at front, fully lined. Labeled: Courreges Paris/38139. Slight surface stain at back and two single threads sticking out at the back. **$960**

Dress, Emilio Pucci, cotton, 1960s, strapless in a brown, pink and orange geometric print. Labeled: Emilio Pucci/ Florence-Italy. **$540**

Dress, Emilio Pucci, velvet, 1960s, in a geometric print, full-length sleeves, V-neck, A-line skirt, fully lined. Labeled: Emilio Pucci. **$600**

Dress, Frederick Starke, pink floral, cocktail, 1950s, strapless with a fitted bodice, bow at front, full skirt. Labeled: Frederick Strake. **$450**

Dress, Galanos, floral print with matching shoes, 1958, with cap sleeves, a boat neckline, asymmetrical fitted bodice, decorative buttons at the left side, V back buttoning at right, pleating at waist leading into a full skirt with crinoline underneath, fully lined. No label. Together with matching pumps. Labeled Saks Fifth Avenue/Fenton Last. (This dress was worn to Sammy Davis Jr.'s wedding to Loray White.) .... **$720 ensemble**

Photo courtesy Leslie Hindman Auctioneers, Chicago; www.LeslieHindman.com

Dress, Black Chiffon Beaded, 1920s, in the style of Madeleine Vionnet, straight fit with all-over silver beading, cap sleeves, handkerchief hem, fully lined. No label. **$518**

Dress, Galanos, black lace, cocktail, 1950s, with cape sleeves, round neckline, fitted throughout, fully lined. Labeled: Galanos. **$720**

Dress, Galanos, black silk chiffon, cocktail, 1950s, with flutter sleeves leading into a tier of pleated ruffles at back, banded waist, pleated skirt, fully lined. Labeled: Galanos. **$450**

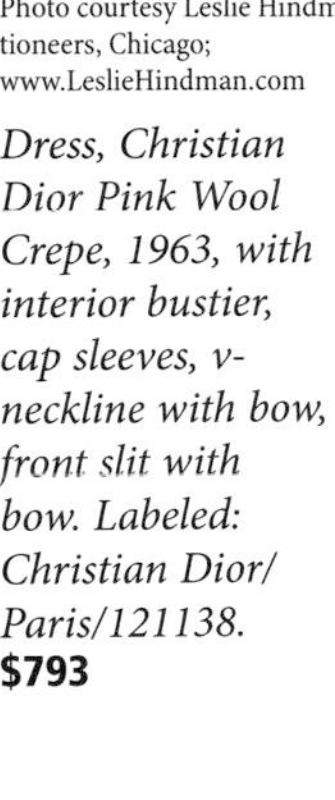

Photo courtesy Leslie Hindman Auctioneers, Chicago; www.LeslieHindman.com

Dress, Christian Dior Pink Wool Crepe, 1963, with interior bustier, cap sleeves, v-neckline with bow, front slit with bow. Labeled: Christian Dior/ Paris/121138.
$793

Photo courtesy Leslie Hindman Auctioneers, Chicago; www.LeslieHindman.com

Dress, Donald Brooks, 1970s, cap sleeves with a round neckline, A-line fit, sequin disc paillettes exaggerating in size at each edge, fully lined. Labeled: Donald Brooks.
$1,586

Dress, Galanos, 1960s, short sleeves, A-line fit, front panel has cream silk pleating, fully lined. Labeled: Galanos. Minor imperfections in pleating. **$330**

Jacket, Geoffrey Beene, floral print, late 1960s, in a flared fit, with round clay buttons, large patch pockets, fully lined. Labeled: Geoffrey Beene. **$60**

Dress, Geoffrey Beene, navy, 1960s, with a button front, breast pocket, oversized belt, pleated skirt. Labeled: Geoffrey Beene. **$120**

Dress, Geoffrey Beene, plaid wool, 1967, with decorative gold-tone buttons at front, fitted waist, flared skirt, fully lined. Labeled: Geoffrey Beene. **$72**

Dress, Leslie Fay, black, 1950s, with a ruffled round-banded neck, with short ruffles in a crisscross pattern. Labeled: Leslie Fay Knits. Hem has been let out. **$120**

Dress, Lilly Pulitzer, tropical print, halter, 1960s, multicolored tropical pattern, inverted pleat at neckline, tie halter. Labeled: The Lilly/Lilly Pulitzer Inc. **$72**

Dress, Marimekko, prototype, pink cotton, 1963, swirl print with full-length sleeves, zipper front, A-line fit, side pockets. Labeled: Marimekko/Suomi-Finland. **$120**

Dress, Mollie Parnis, ivory satin, 1950s, with a scoop neck, empire waist with floral belt, full skirt with hidden pockets, fully lined. Labeled: Mollie Parnis/New York. Possible

Photo courtesy Leslie Hindman Auctioneers, Chicago; www.LeslieHindman.com

Dress, Geoffrey Beene Mod Print Twill, 1960s, with cap sleeves, band collar, full skirt with center box pleat and side knife pleats. Labeled: Geoffrey Beene. **$366**

Photo courtesy Leslie Hindman Auctioneers, Chicago; www.LeslieHindman.com

Dress, Harry Gordon Black and White, Poster, 1968, first edition in a rayon nylon blend, with an image of a cat's head, still in original packaging. Labeled: Poster Dress Ltd. London England. **$231**

zipper replacement, slight overall discoloring at hem line. **$204**

Dress, Mollie Parnis, silk, cocktail, 1950s, one-shoulder taupe bodice gathering at side, fitted waist, full skirt with a cream, grey and orange print, orange taupe and grey panels at side. No label. The printed silk easily rips so there is a lot of ripping throughout. **$540**

Dress, Pauline Trigere, silk chiffon, blue floral print, 1960s, two piece, over blouse with sheer sleeves, cream cuffs, cream collar tying at front, slip with matching floral top and a blue skirt. Labeled: Pauline Trigere. Some slight discoloration at the collar. **$180**

Dress, Suzy Perette, floral brocade, 1950s, with a fitted bodice, sashes at side waist tying at back, full skirt. Labeled: Suzy Perette/New York. Hanger strap on the interior is broken. **$192**

Dress, Tassel, orange, 1960s, with full-length sleeves, rolled collar tying at back, hidden pockets, fully lined. Labeled: Tassel. **$60**

Dress, Traina Norell, floral print, silk, 1950s, original model, with gold metallic yarn throughout, short sleeves, boat neckline, fitted waist, together with a matching fabric and gold leather belt, full skirt. Labeled: Traina Norell/New York/Joan 163. Shoulders are ripping and the cloth belt is in fair condition. **$360**

Ensemble, Christian Dior, pink moire silk, daywear, 1960s, sleeveless dress with a rolled collar, empire waist. Jacket with cropped sleeves, covered buttons. All fully lined. Labeled: Christian Dior New York. **$480**

Ensemble, Courreges, cream, 1965, sleeveless dress with a netted top, mod skirt with faux pockets, fully lined. Jacket in cropped sleeves, closureless ending at waist, fully lined.

Photo courtesy Leslie Hindman Auctioneers, Chicago; www.LeslieHindman.com

Dress, Hattie Carnegie Printed Silk, 1960s, in a green, pink and orange floral print, fitted bodice with high draped neckline, floor length sash at shoulder, attached self belt, long straight skirt, fully lined. Labeled: Hattie Carnegie/Blue Room. **$219**

Photo courtesy Leslie Hindman Auctioneers, Chicago; www.LeslieHindman.com

Mini-dress, Issey Miyake, orange pleated with twisted voluminous paper-lantern sleeves, abstract neckline, sewn using only one seam. Labeled: Issey Miyake. **$2,196**

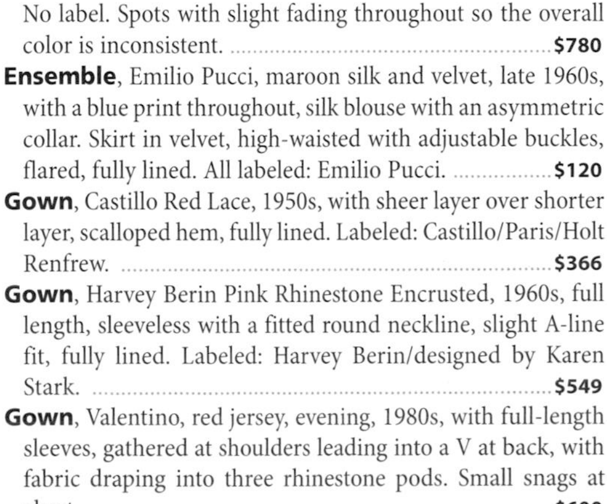

No label. Spots with slight fading throughout so the overall color is inconsistent. **$780**

Ensemble, Emilio Pucci, maroon silk and velvet, late 1960s, with a blue print throughout, silk blouse with an asymmetric collar. Skirt in velvet, high-waisted with adjustable buckles, flared, fully lined. All labeled: Emilio Pucci. **$120**

Gown, Castillo Red Lace, 1950s, with sheer layer over shorter layer, scalloped hem, fully lined. Labeled: Castillo/Paris/Holt Renfrew. **$366**

Gown, Harvey Berin Pink Rhinestone Encrusted, 1960s, full length, sleeveless with a fitted round neckline, slight A-line fit, fully lined. Labeled: Harvey Berin/designed by Karen Stark. **$549**

Gown, Valentino, red jersey, evening, 1980s, with full-length sleeves, gathered at shoulders leading into a V at back, with fabric draping into three rhinestone pods. Small snags at chest. **$600**

Photo courtesy Leslie Hindman Auctioneers, Chicago; www.LeslieHindman.com

Dress, Vicky Tiel, gold sequined, cocktail, 1980s, with a strapless sweetheart neckline, fully lined. Labeled: Vicky Tiel. **$457**

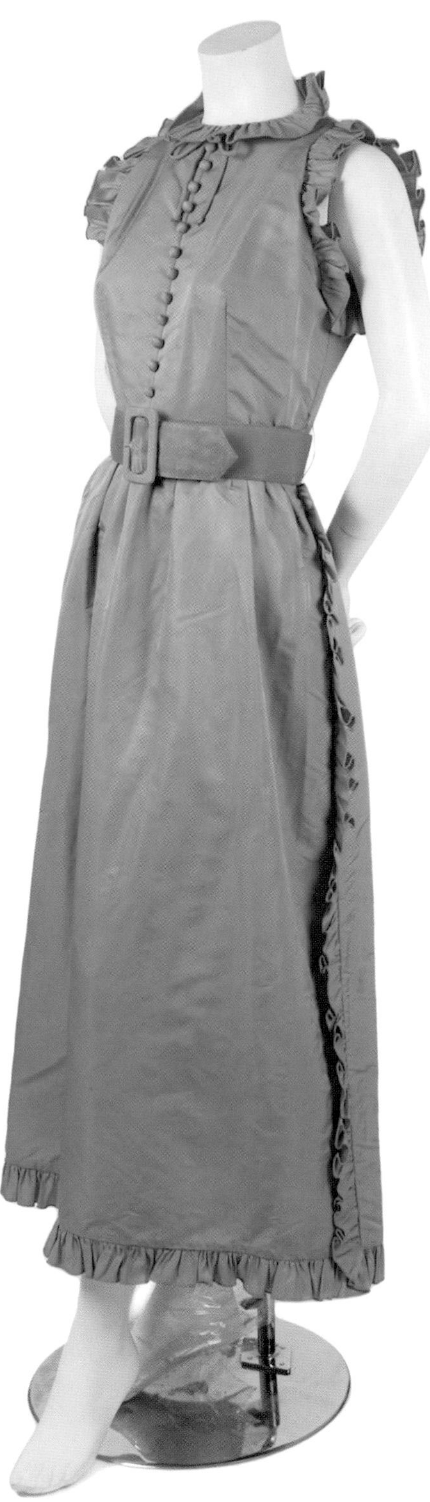

Photo courtesy Leslie Hindman Auctioneers, Chicago; www.LeslieHindman.com

Dress, Oscar De La Renta Green Silk, 1970s, with ruffled armholes, ruffled jewel neckline, bow detail, gathered skirt with side ruffles, matching belt, fully lined. Labeled: Oscar de La Renta Boutique/Saks Fifth Avenue Exclusive. **$549**

Hat, Hattie Carnegie, cream, straw, with patchwork throughout, blue ribbon at brim. Labeled: Miss Carnegie. **$36**

Hat, Yves Saint Laurent, blue, with a petal brim. Labeled: Yves Saint Laurent. **$108**

Jacket, Courreges, brown, bomber, 1960s, with brown wool collar sleeves and hem, leather at both front and back, zipper front. Together with matching brown wool pants. All labeled: Courreges/Paris Made in France. .... **$360 set**

Scarf, Emilio Pucci, in a pink and cream geometric print. Labeled: Emilio Pucci/Firenze. 22" square. **$36**

Scarf, Hermes, cashmere, in a jewel motif at center, signed J. Abadie. Labeled: Hermes, 56" square. **$510**

Scarf, Hermes, silk, white with a circus motif. Labeled: Hermes/Paris, 35" square. **$330**

Shawl, Hermes, black, cashmere, with fringe. Labeled: Hermes/Paris, 54" x 68". **$510**

Skirt, Emilio Pucci, silk, 1960s, in a peach and purple print, flared fit. Labeled: Emilio Pucci. **$60**

Skirt, Moschino, "Art Is Love," black leather, 1990, in a pencil fit, with green and gold leather trim at waist, with the words "Art is love" at the hemline, fully lined. Labeled: Cheap and Chic by Moschino. Slight wear to waistband. **$480**

Skirt, Pierre Cardin, orange wool, 1960s, in a flared fit, with a large patch pocket at hip, white leather lace up side from the hip to the waist, slit at side. Labeled: Pierre Cardin.

Photo courtesy Leslie Hindman Auctioneers, Chicago; www.LeslieHindman.com

Miniskirt, Moschino, Cheap and Chic Leather "Bee" with black and yellow stripes, "bzzz" embroidery, fully lined. Labeled: Cheap and Chic by Moschino. **$183**

Photo courtesy Leslie Hindman Auctioneers, Chicago; www.LeslieHindman.com

Ensemble, Gianfranco Ferre, metallic brocade, coat with beading, sequins and embroidery, three-quarter bell sleeves, hood, scalloped hem, pants with slash pockets, self belt, metallic lace blouse. Labeled: Gianfranco Ferre/Made in Italy/1421. **$1,342**

Photo courtesy Leslie Hindman Auctioneers, Chicago; www.LeslieHindman.com

Ensemble, Courreges Lavender Vinyl Mod jacket with white snap closures and logo at front. Matching mini skirt with white belt. Together with a matching vinyl purse. All labeled: Courreges. **$854**

Photo courtesy Leslie Hindman Auctioneers, Chicago; www.LeslieHindman.com

Ensemble, Larry LeGaspi, Space Age four-piece jumpsuit, 1980s, with a halter style fitted jumpsuit with two unattached arm warmers, with a silver and pink headpiece that has attached ties to wrap around neck, and silver and pink cape. Labeled: LeGaspi. **$1,037**

Photo courtesy Leslie Hindman Auctioneers, Chicago; www.LeslieHindman.com

Hat, Hermes, orange, hardhat with "Hermes Houston" logo at front. This hat was given to clients as a promotion for the construction of the Houston store. **$244**

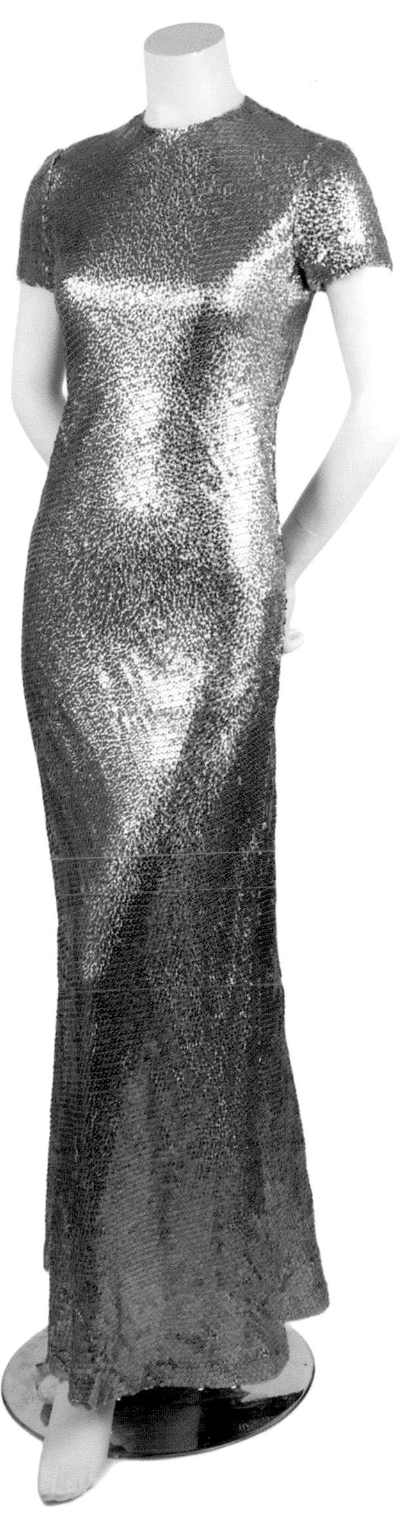

Photo courtesy Leslie Hindman Auctioneers, Chicago; www.LeslieHindman.com

Gown, Bill Blass Pink Sequined Mermaid, 1970s, cap sleeves with a round neckline, fitted, fully lined. Labeled: Bill Blass. **$854**

Photo courtesy Leslie Hindman Auctioneers, Chicago; www.LeslieHindman.com

Jumpsuit, John Anthony, Gold Lace, 1980s, with ruffled cuffs, long sleeves, ruffled collar, sheer top, wide-leg lined pants. Labeled: John Anthony. **$1,098**

Photo courtesy Leslie Hindman Auctioneers, Chicago; www.LeslieHindman.com

Jacket, Hermes, orange silk scarf, Bomber, reversible to navy blue cotton, quilted silk in an American Indian motif. Labeled: Hermes Paris. **$1,464**

Photo courtesy Leslie Hindman Auctioneers, Chicago; www.LeslieHindman.com

Jacket, Moschino Couture! "Playing Card" 1989, with metallic embroidery, fully lined. Labeled: Moschino Couture! **$518**

Photo courtesy Leslie Hindman Auctioneers, Chicago; www.LeslieHindman.com

Jacket, Lanvin Geometric Print, cotton, 1980s, in a multicolor print, fitted waist, fully lined. Labeled: Lanvin. **$219**

Photo courtesy Leslie Hindman Auctioneers, Chicago; www.LeslieHindman.com

Pants, Gianni Versace, leather, with gold-tone grommets and side whip stitching, fully lined. Labeled: Gianni Versace. **$335**

Photo courtesy Leslie Hindman Auctioneers, Chicago; www.LeslieHindman.com

Pants, Missoni Knit Palazzo, 1980s, in black knit with green, pink and red horizontal zigzags, bell-bottom fit, elastic waistband. Labeled: Missoni. **$122**

Photo courtesy Leslie Hindman Auctioneers, Chicago; www.LeslieHindman.com

Robe, Gianni Versace, "Medusa", silk twill, in a black and gold foliate motif, with self belt, Medusa medallions, tassels. Labeled: Gianni Versace. **$1,220**

Photo courtesy Leslie Hindman Auctioneers, Chicago; www.LeslieHindman.com

Suit, Moschino Couture! "Brick Wall", 1997, in all-over red brick motif, jacket with notched lapel, pants with front zip and hook-and-eye closure. Labeled: Moschino Couture!/Made in Italy. **$1,708**

Grommets are slightly tarnished, there is some fading to the leather belt, skirt has one small spot on it. **$300**

Skirt, "Wonder Woman" motif, 1970s, multicolored with a yellow starred waistline, fully lined. No label. Small stain on one of the stars. **$60**

Skirt suit, Balenciaga Couture, black and white wool, 1965, jacket with full-length sleeves, double-breasted, fully lined in silk crepe. Skirt in an A-line fit, fully lined in silk crepe. Labeled: Balenciaga/87786. Small rust stain at left hip lining from hanger. **$720**

Skirt suit, Balenciaga Couture, green wool, 1961, jacket with cropped sleeves, notched collar, three green plastic buttons, fitted, fully lined in silk taffeta. Skirt in a pencil fit, fully lined in silk taffeta. Labeled: Balenciaga/76452. Fading to jacket lining. **$720**

Skirt suit, Balenciaga Couture, green wool, 1960, jacket with a notched collar, full-length sleeves, double-breasted with black buttons, fully lined in silk taffeta. Skirt in an A-line fit, fully lined in silk taffeta. Labeled: Balenciaga/87414. Hem has been let out on skirt, fading to jacket lining, some areas of pilling to wool. **$480**

Skirt suit, Eisa, black wool twill, early 1960s, ready-to-wear from the house of Balenciaga, jacket with full length sleeves, straight fit buttoning at front, fully lined in silk. Skirt in an A-line fit with two buttoning slant pockets, fully lined in silk. Labeled: Eisa. Buttons on the jacket are loose. **$660**

Skirt suit, Eisa, cream wool, 1960s, ready-to-wear from the house of Balenciaga, jacket with a purple velvet collar, gold-tone buttons, fully lined. Skirt in an A-line fit, fully lined. Labeled: Eisa. Missing a button, wear to velvet collar. **$120**

Suit, Bonnie Cashin, yellow tweed, cape, 1960s, flared capelet sleeves, round collar, sides laced up with suede, suede-covered buttons, slant pockets, fully lined. Labeled: Sills/A Bonnie Cashin Design. Together with matching tweed A-line skirt. **$180**

Suit, Ceil Chapman, cream, dress, 1960s, jacket with all-over floral lace, straight fit with covered buttons at front, fully lined. Labeled: Ceil Chapman for Miss Winston. Dress sleeveless with a silk top, ruched waist, lace skirt, fully lined. **$120**

Tunic, Emilio Pucci, brown silk, 1960s, in a brown and grey print, with long sleeves and silk-covered buttons. Labeled: Emilio Pucci. One armpit has slight discolorations and needs reinforcement stitches and the other has been repaired. The buttons were moved; small surface stain. **$144**

Tunic with pants, Geoffrey Beene, navy wool, 1960s, sleeveless with hook-and-eye closures on left shoulder, round neckline, matching belt at waist, hidden pockets, fully lined. Flared pants, fully lined. Labeled: Geoffrey Beene. **$570**

Vest, floral print, full length, 1960s, mandarin neckline, loop closure buttons at bust, ribbon hemline, fully lined. Labeled: Wilson Folmar. **$84**

Photo courtesy Leslie Hindman Auctioneers, Chicago; www.LeslieHindman.com

"Charm" Bag, Louis Vuitton, limited edition, trimmed in brown leather, with gold-tone hardware, chain and leather handles, canvas charm print laminated with plastic, lock at front, fully lined in leather. Stamped: Louis Vuitton/Paris, 12" x 9". **$900**

Bags, Clutches, Purses and Totes

Though these terms are often used interchangeably, the listings here reflect actual auction house catalog entries, divided into subcategories.

Bag, Andrea Pfister, animal print, 1980s, quilted in a boxy shape, gold-tone chain handle, fully lined. Stamped: Andrea Pfister, 13 1/2" x 10". **$72**

Bag, Barry Kieselstein-Cord, evening, 1999, in a bronze satin with floral embroidery, gold-tone handle, gold dragon at front, lined in red satin. Stamped: Barry Kieselstein-Cord, 11" x 5". **$360**

Bag, beaded, early 20th century, in an Asian motif, with a drawstring handle, fringe at base, fully lined in silk, 7" x 8". Small stain to lining and one section of fringe is loose. **$84**

Bag, Christian Dior, leopard print, with tan leather trim, wide shoulder strap, detachable cell-phone compartment, gold-tone hardware, fully lined. Stamped: Christian Dior/Paris, 12" x 6". **$204**

"Birkin" Bag, Hermes Barenia Haut a Courroies, 2000, with palladium hardware, blind stamp D. Stamped: Hermes/Paris, 12 1/2" x 10" x 6 1/4". **$7,200**

"Birkin" Bag, Hermes, black Ardennes leather, 2002, with gold hardware, lock key and sheath, blind stamp D. Stamped: Hermes/Paris, 14" x 9 1/2" x 7". **$8,400**

Bags, beaded, one in a black floral motif, drawstring style with fringe at base. One in cream satin with all-over beads in a floral motif, gold-tone chain handle, with a faux pearl and gold-tone closure, fully lined in cream satin. Stamped: Made in France/Handmade. Black: 6 1/2" x 8 1/2". Cream: 7" x 5". .... **$48 pair**

Bags, beaded, early 20th century, one in a floral motif, a gold-tone frame with rhinestones throughout, fringe at base, fully

Photo courtesy Leslie Hindman Auctioneers, Chicago; www.LeslieHindman.com

Bag, red crocodile, with steel hardware and matching straps. Stamped: Tardini. 15 x 7". **$488**

Photo courtesy Leslie Hindman Auctioneers, Chicago; www.LeslieHindman.com

Bag, Black and White Snake, shoulder, with a hidden shoulder strap. Labeled: Jay Herbert. 16 x 8". **$488**

Photo courtesy Leslie Hindman Auctioneers, Chicago; www.LeslieHindman.com

Handbag, Ann Turk, crocodile with long strap, layered and scalloped flap closure, and crystal embellishments. Labeled: Ann Turk/New Collections. 11 1/2 x 10". **$122**

lined in silk. One in navy silk, with crocheted floral beaded a top, fully lined. Cream: 6" x 6". Navy: 6" x 9". ..... **$390 pair**

Belt purse, Hermes, red leather, 2000, with a thin tie belt strap, and small purse with snap closure, gold hardware. Stamped: Hermes/Paris, 4" x 5 1/2". **$168**

Clutch, burgundy alligator, in an envelope style, fully lined in red leather. Stamped: Saks Fifth Avenue/Made in France, 10" x 6". **$360**

Clutch, gray patent leather, envelope, alligator embossed, V-shaped flap at front. Stamped: Campanile Spatarella, 10" x 7". **$180**

Handbag, Hermes, tan canvas, 1960s, with caramel leather trim and handle, flap closure, multiple interior pockets, fully lined in leather. Stamped: Hermes-Paris/24 fg St Honore, 9 1/2" x 6". **$300**

Handbag, Roberta di Camerino, eagle design, 1960s, in a navy velvet with navy leather trim and handle, with a cream velvet flap with an eagle symbol at front, lifting into a hidden pocket, gold-tone hardware, fully lined in leather. Stamped: Made in Italy by Roberta di Camerino, 10" x 8" x 4". **$240**

Purse, black calfskin and lizard skin, with a chain handle, silver etched closure, fully lined in silk, 8" x 6". **$156**

Purse, black suede, with gold-tone hardware, flap closure, white leather crocodile embossed trim and braided strap, fully lined, 9" x 8". **$96**

Purse, brown crocodile, with a matching handle, gold-tone hardware, 20" x 5". **$132**

Purse, brown eel skin, in a round shape with a matching adjustable shoulder strap, zipper expander at base, zipper closure, fully lined, 16" x 12". Minor wear on bottom of bag. **$168**

Purse, Gucci, nautical motif, 1980s, khaki canvas bag, a rope handle with a leather-wrapped top, white and blue striped lining with a matching nautical wallet. Labeled: Gucci, 9" x 8". **$60**

Purse, Gucci, tan leather, with a long shoulder strap, flap closure with gold-tone logo buckle at front, adjustable buckle at base, fully lined. Stamped: Gucci/Made in Italy, 14" x 11". Several minor scratches from use; four small stains on interior of bag. **$180**

Purse, Pierre Cardin, with blue leather trim and handles, canvas with navy logos at both front and back, fully lined in leather. Labeled: Pierre Cardin/Paris New York, 14 1/2" x 13". **$156**

Purse, Louis Vuitton, in monogram canvas, trimmed in tan leather, long shoulder straps, full zipper closure, fully lined in suede. Stamped: Louis Vuitton Paris, 16" x 12". **$600**

Purse, Louis Vuitton, in monogram canvas, with a long shoulder strap and a flap front opening. Stamped: Louis Vuitton Paris, 14" x 12". **$240**

Purse, Lucille de Paris, crocodile, with two long chain handles, fully lined in leather. Stamped: Lucille de Paris, 9" x 6". **$156**

Purse, Midas, poodle motif, wicker, 1950s, bucket shape with white-painted wicker, painted flowers and a beaded poodle detail, gold-tone hardware with white and gold woven leather handles. Labeled: Midas of Miami, 10" x 8". **$180**

Purse, Midas, roadrunner motif, wicker, 1950s, with gold painted wicker, green roadrunner at front, gold-tone hardware with gold woven leather handles. Labeled: Midas of Miami, 13" x 10". **$84**

Purse, Nancy Gonzalez, black crocodile, in a woven style with a cream canvas bag underneath, matching crocodile handles, toggle closure. Stamped: Nancy Gonzalez/Columbia New York, 8" x 7". **$420**

Purse, Nettie Rosenstein, cream, ostrich, 1970s, with gold-tone hardware, matching handle. Stamped: Nettie Rosenstein, 9 1/2" x 7". **$108**

Purse, Nettie Rosenstein, silver lamé, 1950s, with a silver-tone, metal-detailed handle and knob closure, together with matching compact mirror, fully lined. Labeled: Nettie Rosenstein, 6" x 7". Wear to the edges at back where the fabric and piping has separated slightly. **$120**

Photo courtesy Leslie Hindman Auctioneers, Chicago; www.LeslieHindman.com

Handbag, Kelly, Hermes, tan leather, 1960s, with a key sheath. Stamped: Hermes/Paris. 13" x 9 1/2" x 5". **$2,074**

Photo courtesy Leslie Hindman Auctioneers, Chicago; www.LeslieHindman.com

Minaudiere, Judith Leiber, Pink Pig, with a hidden gold chain shoulder strap, coin purse, fully lined in gold leather. Stamped: Judith Leiber. 4 x 4". **$1,342**

Photo courtesy Leslie Hindman Auctioneers, Chicago; www.LeslieHindman.com

Suitcases, Louis Vuitton, circa 1950s, comprised of two train cases, a cosmetic case and a shoe case, all with a yellow monogram JHW, with keys. All stamped: Louis Vuitton. **$4,148 set**

Photo courtesy Timeless Treasures, Manitowoc, Wis.

Late 1950s – early 1960s Herbert Levine classic pumps, purple suede with butterfly buckle. **$125-$250**

Purse, Rayne, gold silk, with a rhinestone detail at center, two matching straps, fully lined in brown satin. Stamped: Rayne, 9" x 6". **$96**

Purse, yellow Lucite, 1950s, plastic with octagonal shape, flower-top design with gold-tone hardware, 7" x 6". **$60**

Tote, Gucci, canvas shopper, with logo print throughout, red and green handles. Stamped at front: GG, 12" x 14". Slight wear to the corners and Gucci logo is slightly discolored. **$132**

Boots and Shoes

Boots, cowboy, in red leather and lizardskin. Stamped: Rios of Mercedes. **$120**

Shoe tights, silver lamé, 1960s, thigh high, with a round rhinestone decoration. Labeled: Design by Evins. **$180**

Geoffrey Beene, black satin shoes. **$50**

Joseph LaRose, orange rafia shoes. **$80**

Versace, red patent leather thigh-high boots. **$1,100**

Roger Vivier, black satin shoes. **$50**

Roger Vivier, multicolor pumps. **$150**

Vivienne Westwood, white patent leather shoes. ... **$1,300**

Photo courtesy Timeless Treasures, Manitowoc, Wis.

Early 1970s "Cover Girl" red and white Spectator platforms. **$125-$200**

COCA-COLA

Originally intended as a patent medicine when it was invented in the late 19th century by John Pemberton of Columbus, Ga., Coca-Cola was bought out by businessman Asa Griggs Candler, whose marketing tactics led Coke to its dominance of the world soft drink market throughout the 20th century.

The famous Coca-Cola logo was created by Pemberton's bookkeeper, Frank Mason Robinson, in 1885. It was Robinson who came up with the name, and he also chose the logo's distinctive cursive script.

Coca-Cola's advertising has had a significant impact on American culture, and is frequently credited with the "invention" of the modern image of Santa Claus as an old man in red-and-white garments.

Bottles

Coca-Cola Bottling Works, Los Angeles, 8 1/2" tooled crown top, "CCBW" on base. Little wear. **$160**

Coca-Cola San Francisco, Cal., 8" tooled top with slight purplish tint. Some wear. **$240**

Photo courtesy American Bottle Auctions, Sacramento, Calif.; www.AmericanBottle.com

Coca-Cola Denver, 8 3/4" crown top, made between 1905-16, number "30" near the front base. Slight interior stain. **$200**

Photo courtesy American Bottle Auctions, Sacramento, Calif.; www.AmericanBottle.com

The Best By A Dam Site, Boulder Products, Las Vegas, Nev., 7 1/2", automatic bottling machine, wear around the base. **$190**

Photo courtesy American Bottle Auctions, Sacramento, Calif.; www.AmericanBottle.com

The Salt Lake Coca-Cola Bottling Co., Red Seal Brand, automatic bottling machine, 7 1/2" crown top, 1/4" chip off the lip, a little wear and a few scratches. **$40**

Photo courtesy Old Town Auctions LLC, Boonsboro, Md.; www.OldTownAuctions.com

Brunhoff, illuminating countertop display, 1930s, all original except replaced electric cord, round lens has tiny spot of discoloration, minor wear to case finish, 14" h, 12 1/2" w. **$9,350**

Coca-Cola Bottling Co., Las Cruces-Deming New Mexico, 8", automatic bottling machine, slight wear near the base and a couple scratches, scarce. **$120**

Property Of Salt Lake Coca-Cola Bottling Co., Registered (in circle), some wear and a little stain with a tiny ding on the right base of the seam. **$160**

Salt Lake Coca-Cola Bottling Co., Salt Lake City, Utah, 10" with tooled top, brilliant bluish aqua, there is wear around the shoulders and some scratching along with a chip from the bottom front base. **$425**

Assorted Advertising

Photo courtesy Morphy Auctions, Denver, Pa.; www.MorphyAuctions.com

Calendar, 1898, embossed cardboard, with miniscule marks or edge wear. Two missing chips in lower left and right corners, 7 1/4" x 13". **$23,000**

Photo courtesy Heritage Auction Galleries, Dallas; www.HA.com

Coca-Cola 1915 Elaine Calendar. This paper litho is complete with original metal strip and full pad. Condition is strong overall in consideration of the color, and clarity of this example. The calendar has been rolled for some time and, due to rolling, there is a ripple effect from the center to the top. Slight toning of the paper from age and a rip along the area where the calendar is attached, 13" x 33". **$2,390**

Photo courtesy Heritage Auction Galleries, Dallas; www.HA.com

Coca-Cola 1917 Paper Calendar. Complete with original metal strip and a full pad. Two minor ripples are obvious toward the top from the calendar being rolled. Rarely found in excellent condition and complete, 12 3/4" x 31 1/3". **$3,900**

Photo courtesy James D. Julia Auctioneers, Fairfield, Maine; www.JuliaAuctions.com

Glasses, eight, flared, red, of unknown age, purchased in 1960, etched with fill lines. Each 3 3/4" h. Very good to excellent condition. **$120 set**

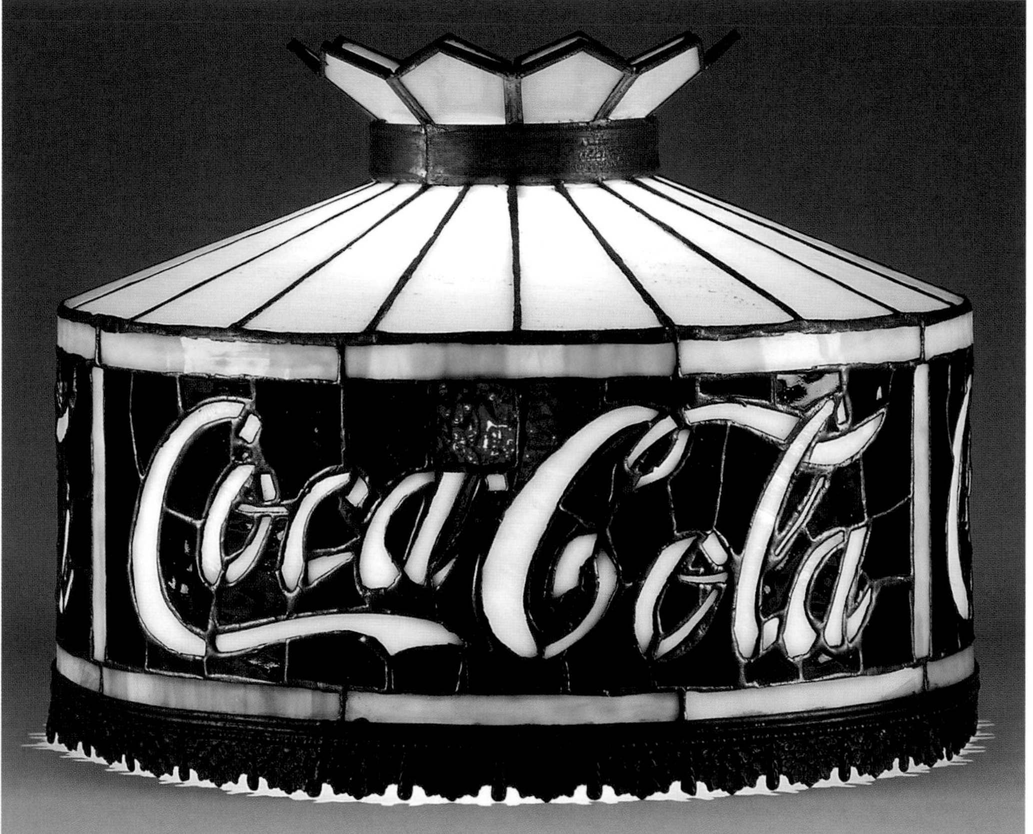

Photo courtesy James D. Julia Auctioneers, Fairfield, Maine; www.JuliaAuctions.com

Leaded Glass Shade. Circa 1920s, Tiffany style shade is one of the most sought after of all Coca-Cola collectibles. This is the somewhat scarcer "leaf edge" version. The top band carries the words "Property of Coca-Cola Co. to be returned on demand" stamped in two locations, 16" diameter. **$5,175**

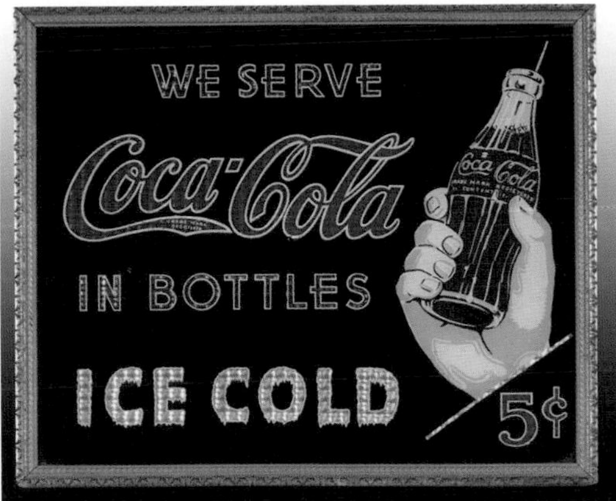

Photo courtesy Morphy Auctions, Denver, Pa.; www.MorphyAuctions.com

"Glo-Glass" easel-back sign, 1930s, retains original cardboard back and attached bent-metal easel and paper label on lower right corner of back, few minor rubs on reverse painted areas from raised bumps, normal for these signs. One tiny nick, quarter inch, in upper right glass edge corner area, nearly concealed by frame. Frame is probably not original, 12 1/2" x 12 3/4". **$15,000**

Photo courtesy James D. Julia Auctioneers, Fairfield, Maine; www.JuliaAuctions.com

Sign, cardboard, produced in 1936 to commemorate Coca-Cola's 50th anniversary while also comparing the evolution of women's bathing fashions. Image 26" w x 46 1/2" h. Some prominent creasing, surface wear and multiple BB sized punctures at the top. **$575**

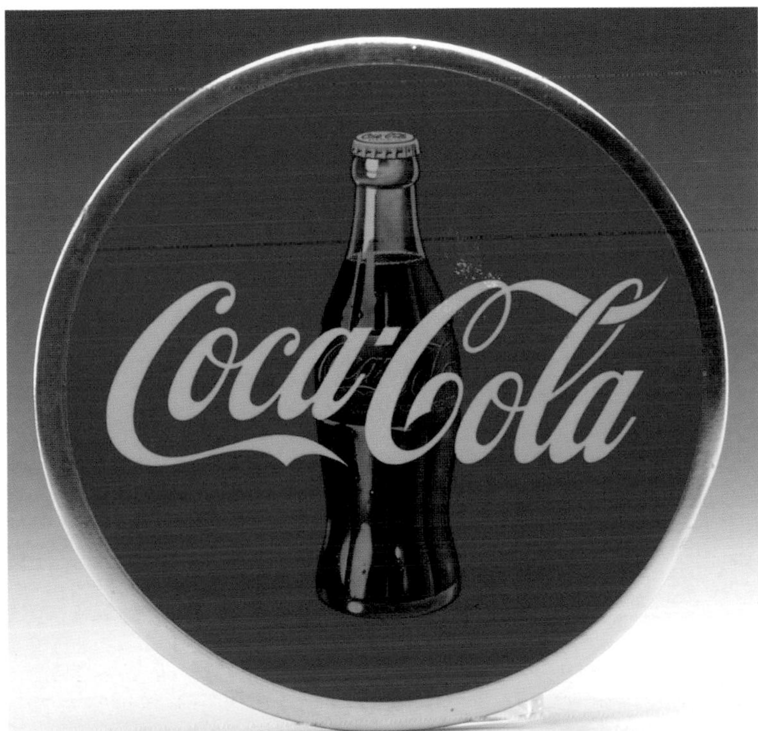

Photo courtesy James D. Julia Auctioneers, Fairfield, Maine; www.JuliaAuctions.com

Sign, button, tin on cardboard, NOS, showing Coke bottle behind "Coca-Cola" in script with gold border. Back of sign has cardboard easel back for display (unopened), red string hanger, and decal reading "Philadelphia Badge Co., Agent J. Paul Cobb, Atlanta, GA". Complete with original unused mailer, 9" d. Like new with light dent to side border and small edge ding. **$287**

Photo courtesy Heritage Auction Galleries, Dallas; www.HA.com

1925 Flapper Girl Coca-Cola Tray. Lithographed by American Art Works Co., this tray has several small surface imperfections. Edge wear to the rim is prevalent but not uncommon in this type of early tray. Fine condition. Size: 10 1/2" x 13 1/4". **$358**

Photo courtesy Heritage Auction Galleries, Dallas; www.HA.com

1941 Skater Girl Coca-Cola Tray, Made by the American Art Works in Coshocton, Ohio, this 10 1/2" x 13 1/4" serving tray pictures a girl seated on a log, relaxing with a bottle of Coke. Only very light wear in general. **$120**

Photo courtesy Old Town Auctions LLC, Boonsboro, Md.; www.OldTownAuctions.com

Vendo machine, on original stand, unrestored, 57 1/2" h.
$2,860

Signs, pair, includes large cardboard advertisement, circa 1940s, in its original gold frame. It pictures two women looking at a globe, pointing to Europe with one stating, "Here's to Our G.I. Joes" while enjoying a Coke. Also, 1930s Canadian paper poster picturing a 36-cent six-pack of Coke with snowy letters stating, "Add Zest to the Holiday." Matted and framed. Sign: 62" w x 34" h. Poster: 23 1/2" w x 9" h. Cardboard sign has scratch in lower left and some scattered touch-up. Poster shows light vertical creases. .... **$1,380 pair**

Photo courtesy James D. Julia Auctioneers, Fairfield, Maine; www.JuliaAuctions.com

Cooler Radio. 1950s tube radio in the shape of a miniature cooler. 12" w x 7 1/2" d x 10" h. Dial lights but no sound. **$402**

Photo courtesy James D. Julia Auctioneers, Fairfield, Maine; www.JuliaAuctions.com

Counter-Top Vending Machine. This 10-cent Coke machine marked "Vendorlator" has original red and white Coca-Cola paint front, "Drink Coca-Cola Delicious and Refreshing". 27" h x 24" w x 18 1/2" d. **$977**

Photo courtesy James D. Julia Auctioneers, Fairfield, Maine; www.JuliaAuctions.com

Vendo Model H81D Vending Machine. Holds 81 bottles and comes with a 10-cent coin mechanism. Shelves are adjustable. Produced mid- to late 1950s. 27" w x 16" d x 58" h. Unrestored working condition. **$1,265**

Photo courtesy James D. Julia Auctioneers, Fairfield, Maine; www.JuliaAuctions.com

1918 Coca-Cola Calendar. Summer beach scene illustration of two ladies enjoying their Coca-Cola refreshment. 13" w x 31 1/4" h. Some horizontal roll creasing. Retains original top metal band and full date pad. **$1,725**

Photo courtesy James D. Julia Auctioneers, Fairfield, Maine; www.JuliaAuctions.com

Smith-Miller Coca-Cola Delivery Truck. aka Smitty Toys. Los Angeles, Calif. Model 1-420. A 1953-54 GMC cab delivery truck with original Coca-Cola decals. Cab is cast aluminum with pressed-steel display bed. Wrapped cases as well as green bottles of probable later manufacture. 13" l. Toy and box in un-played-with condition. Decals are 100%, no chips or loss of paint. **$1,840**

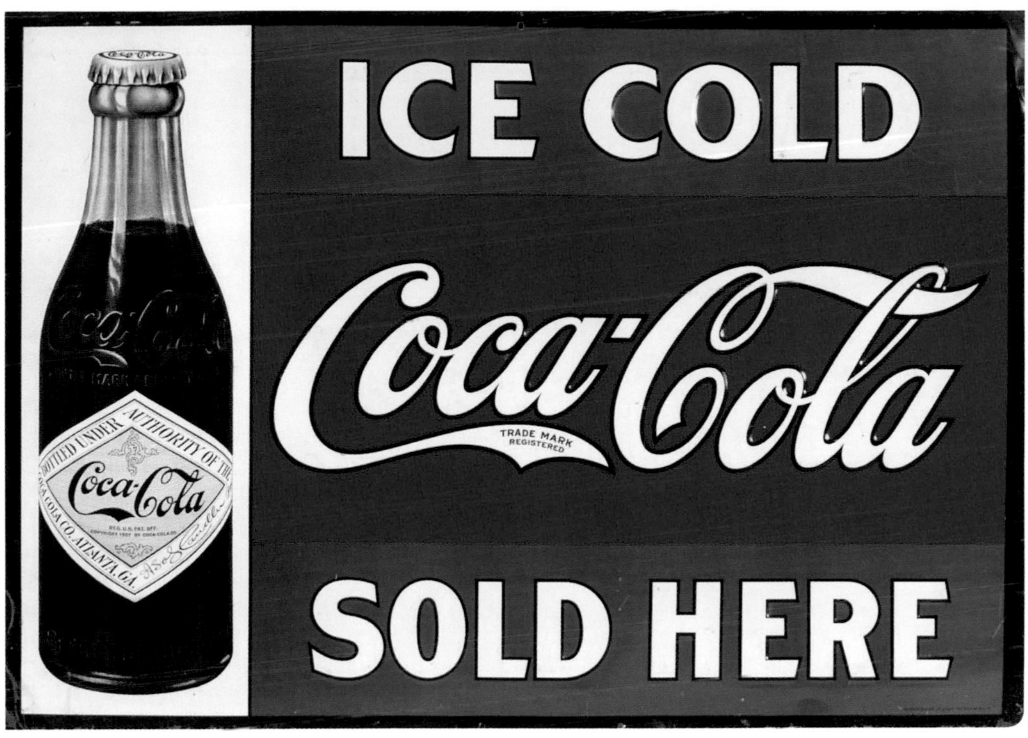

Photo courtesy Morphy Auctions, Denver, Pa.; www.MorphyAuctions.com

Sign, straight-sided with bottle, embossed tin, circa 1910. Few minor crimps and shallow dents. One small hole at top center border for mounting. Minor edge rust and light wear, 20" x 28". **$2,750**

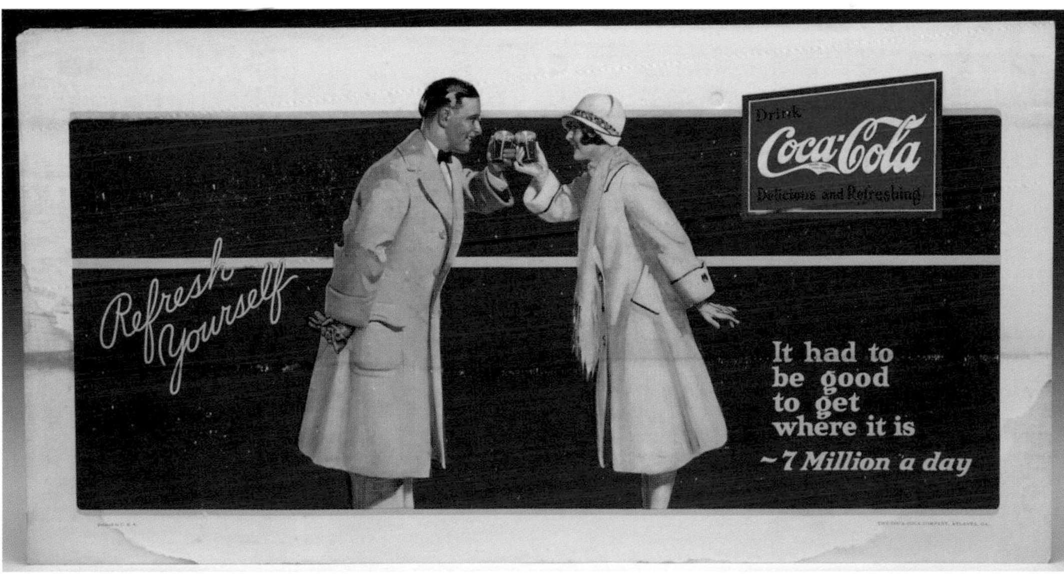

Photo courtesy James D. Julia Auctioneers, Fairfield, Maine; www.JuliaAuctions.com

Sign, trolley, 1926, illustration of young couple toasting one another captioned, "It had to be good to get where it is," 20 3/4" w x 11" h. Some water stains to margins, a horizontal scuff mark through the middle, light scattered pigment loss to green background. **$2,012**

Photo courtesy James D. Julia Auctioneers, Fairfield, Maine; www.JuliaAuctions.com

Sign, trolley, 1905, early cardboard advertisement which reads, "Delicious and Refreshing – Drink Coca-Cola at Fountains in Bottles," 20 3/4" w x 11" h. Paper loss top right corner, nail holes at other corners, right margin tear, several small scattered scuffs. **$1,495**

Photo courtesy James D. Julia Auctioneers, Fairfield, Maine; www.JuliaAuctions.com

Women of the Military die cuts, set of five, WWII-era women from the various military branches have attached cardboard easels for countertop display. Lithographed by Snyder & Black, Inc., N.Y., 1943. Each 17 1/2" h. All appear in near excellent condition, with one or two having slight creases at the necks. **$5,175 set**

COIN-OPERATED DEVICES

Coin-operated devices fall into three main categories: amusement or arcade games, trade stimulators and vending machines.

Also see Music Boxes.

"Advice for Single Men", electrified with one-cent mechanism, tells how to win love, fame and fortune. Wood cabinet with reverse-painted glass front, 11 1/2" w x 25" h x 10" deep. Appears to be working. Some bulbs may need replacement. **$287**

Photo courtesy James D. Julia Auctioneers, Fairfield, Maine; www.JuliaAuctions.com

Arcade crane, tabletop model, manufactured by Buddy Sales of Brooklyn, N.Y., 1920s arcade game in all-original, untouched condition. It features a fanciful cast-aluminum front with a plethora of information and is adorned with two small children similar to those on the Jennings Dutch boy and girl machine. Surrounded by glass on three sides, the rear of the machine depicts an industrial location with a traveling crane. Machine is activated by depositing coin, wheel directs crane to haul up prize, 20" w x 18" deep x 41" h. Crack to glass on right door, lacking keys, machine has not been tested, needs new electrical cord. **$4,600**

Photo courtesy James D. Julia Auctioneers, Fairfield, Maine; www.JuliaAuctions.com

Atlas, baseball countertop penny flip, cast aluminum front on a wood cabinet. Player inserts a penny and bats it into play. Resulting score tracked on bottom abacus. Manufactured by Atlas Indicator Works, Chicago, circa 1931, 12" w x 13" h x 7 1/2" deep. Some staining to baseball lithograph, otherwise good condition, with key. **$2,070**

Photo courtesy James D. Julia Auctioneers, Fairfield, Maine; www.JuliaAuctions.com

Bluebird, gumball machine and trade stimulator, one cent, dispenser mounted atop a wood-cased penny drop that would give your penny back if you deflected it through the opening below, 9 1/4" w x 21 1/2" h x 8 1/4" deep. Lower wood cabinet refinished and metal parts repainted. **$805**

Photo courtesy Old Town Auctions LLC, Boonsboro, Md.; www.OldTownAuctions.com

Digger machine, Esco (Exhibit Supply Co.), Art Deco style, restored, slight use wear, works but cable needs to be adjusted, 71" h. **$9,350**

Photo courtesy James D. Julia Auctioneers, Fairfield, Maine; www.JuliaAuctions.com

Fortuneteller, arcade machine, future predicted based on the color of one's eyes. Wood case rests on four elaborate cast-iron cabriole-type legs. Encased behind glass are a large papier-mâché woman's face and six masks that show different eye colors. Customer chooses their astrological sign, deposits a coin and receives their fortune in the form of a small card, 72" h x 23" w x 14" deep. Older restoration to wood case with some possible replacements to wooden parts. Mechanism appears to be professionally restored. **$4,600**

Photo courtesy Morphy Auctions, Denver, Pa.; www.MorphyAuctions.com

Watling 25-Cent Cherry Rol-a-Top slot machine, 26" t. **$5,500**

Photo courtesy Morphy Auctions, Denver, Pa.; www.MorphyAuctions.com

Dilling's Butter Scotch 1-cent candy dispenser, patented July 25, 1899. Includes key and weights, very rare. **$15,500**

Condom vendor, mid-20th century, wall mount with 25-cent mechanism, in crackled black paint with illegible partial label. Includes key and is filled with more than 20 double packs, various chips and scratches, overall good. **$210**

Fortuneteller, tabletop machine issued by the National Institute for the Blind, featuring a blind man with a cane under a dome that sits atop the machine. Insert a coin and the man spins, pointing his cane to one of several fortunes. The front is emblazoned with directions suggesting to make "A good turn for the blind", 10" h x 10" w x 7" deep. Uniform wear to paint. **$3,105**

Gottlieb, strength tester, insert a penny and squeeze the handles to measure your grip strength. Machine has two side and front decals, 8 1/2" w x 15" h x 10 1/4" deep. Missing rear door and possibly some interior parts; not working. **$230**

International Mutoscope Co., Silver Gloves boxing-theme arcade game from 1962 Seattle World's Fair. **$9,755**

Photo courtesy James D. Julia Auctioneers, Fairfield, Maine; www.JuliaAuctions.com

Peanut vendor, Freeport Dragons, in untouched, as-found, original condition. Made by Goo Goo Gum Co. of Chicago. Retaining its original glass (both front and side viewing windows) with paper on front window detailing how to operate the machine. Decals on the right and left side depict an American eagle clutching the U.S. flag with a banner encompassing the eagle. A small sliver of wood from the right side of the base is missing. The front iron casting is in fair original paint, 17" h. Mechanism not fully tested. Dispensing cup is "frozen" in place. Padlock heavily rusted. One foot on front casting is present but detached. **$10,350**

Photo courtesy of Skinner, Inc.

"Penny-Pack" bandit, 1 cent operation, three cigarette packet reels, gum dispenser lacking button, arched Art Deco metal case, period paintwork, 11" h. **$265.**

Photo courtesy Morphy Auctions, Denver, Pa.; www.MorphyAuctions.com

"Pull the Tiger's Tail and Make Him Roar!", made by Exhibit Supply Co., 1928, wood and painted cast-iron. With original 5-cent coin slide and rope release, the "roar" was originally via an ah-oo-ga horn that was activated as the rope was pulled; the horn sat in the bottom, mounted inside, and flush to the side in a brass screened speaker grille; a replacement electric device has been rebuilt a few times; 64" h x 31" w x 20" deep. **$42,550**

Photo courtesy James D. Julia Auctioneers, Fairfield, Maine; www.JuliaAuctions.com

Postcard dispenser, French, cast iron, circa 1900-1910. One of two known, it depicts a young woman adorned in a sweeping gown, giving a postal card to Cupid himself to mail to her lover. Seated in a garden setting with flowers and vines, a glass window shows a card that is available for purchase. Mechanism is activated by dropping a coin in the slot and pulling lever next to Cupid. Card is then dispensed to holder under machine, 28" h (including marquee) x 13" w x 12" deep. Mechanism and castings appear to be intact. Paint is old, but not original. **$12,650**

Regina, upright 26" disc, elaborate two-part music box with turned columns and large front glass to view disc, with later quarter coin-op mechanism. Rests on detailed, carved base with pull-out door with disc storage in which 10 are stored, 74" h x 36" w x 16 1/4" deep. Replaced back panel, lacking crown molding and small strip of side molding. Uniform wear. Mechanics are good and intact except for broken spring. **$6,900**

"Shake Hands with Uncle Sam", strength tester, circa 1940s-50s by Mechanical Antiques & Amusement Co., reproduction of 1908 original, features cast-iron Uncle Sam bust figure with arm extended. Quarter coin mechanism. Squeeze hand and electrified apparatus reveals strength of contestant's personality. Cast marquee mounted to shoulders, all mounted to wooden base, 76" h. Allover repaint of casting and modern electric wiring. Various small chips and usual wear to paint on Sam's hand. **$2,415**

Stella, upright disc music box, with ample record storage below, egg-and-dart molding in cornice, shelf and base. Two turned and fluted columns on upper doors with pierced panels on the bottom and tops of doors. Gracefully arched

COINS

Collecting Modern U.S. Commemorative Coins

1982-S proof Washington silver half dollar. **$6.50**

For more information, see *The Instant Coin Collector* by Arlyn G. Sieber, 2009, Krause Publications.

Congress has authorized myriad commemorative coin series since 1982. Commemorative coins honor events, people, organizations or other things, and are authorized by law. They are official U.S. government issues and legal tender, but they are not intended to circulate. Instead, the U.S. Mint—at a premium above face value—sells them directly to collectors. Laws authorizing commemorative coins usually mandate that a certain amount of the purchase price benefit a group or event related to the coin's theme.

In terms of cost, collecting modern commemoratives is a step up from collecting coins from circulation at face value or buying them at shops or shows for a few dollars each.

The story behind the coins

The first U.S. commemorative coin was an 1892 half dollar for the Columbian Exposition. The exposition was held May 1-Oct. 30, 1893, in Chicago to commemorate the 400th anniversary of Columbus' arrival in the New World. The U.S. Mint struck 950,000 Columbian half dollars dated 1892 and more than 1.5 million dated 1893.

1997-W proof Franklin Delano Roosevelt five dollar gold. **$565**

The Columbian half dollar opened the door to many other commemorative coins from the 1910s and continuing into the 1950s. Most were silver half dollars, but there was also an 1893 quarter (also for the Columbian Exposition), a number of gold dollars, two gold $2.50 coins and two gold $50 coins.

The coins were sold by the Mint at a premium above face value. Some commemorated state anniversaries or national themes, such as the U.S. Sesquicentennial in 1926.

There were no less than 18 commemorative half dollars issued in 1936 alone. Among them was an issue commemorating the 75th anniversary of the Battle of Gettysburg. Others, however, were of little national importance, such as issues for the Cincinnati Music Center and the centennial of Elgin, Ill.

The first U.S. commemorative coin: 1892 Columbian Exposition half dollar (AU-50). **$18.50**

Congress grew weary of U.S. coinage being used as local fundraisers, and the flow of commemorative coins slowed in the 1940s and '50s. The last issue among what are commonly called "early" commemoratives was a 1954 half dollar honoring Booker T. Washington and George Washington Carver.

A 28-year hiatus on commemorative coinage ensued until Congress authorized a half dollar in the traditional 90-percent-silver composition to honor the 250th anniversary of George Washington's birth in 1982. Thus began the "modern" commemoratives.

The Washington coin was a winner in many respects: First, its theme was of truly national significance and worthy of commemoration. Second, its design by Mint engraver Elizabeth Jones featured a striking depiction of Washington on horseback, a departure from the staid busts used for portraiture on coins since the Lincoln cent of 1909. The reverse, also designed by Jones, features a view of Washington's Mount Vernon home.

These factors, combined with the long break in commemorative coinage, made the coin popular with collectors. The Mint sold more than 2.2 million uncirculated versions ("D" mintmark) and almost 4.9 million proof versions ("S" mintmark).

The proliferation of commemorative coins in the 1930s included a half dollar for the Cincinnati Music Center (AU-50). **$315**

Like the Columbian half dollar 90 years earlier, the George Washington half dollar opened the door to more commemorative coinage, and like the commemorative coinage of the 1930s, an undesirable proliferation resulted. The coins' themes in the 1990s weren't as localized as many of those in the 1930s, but commemorative coinage became an easy mark for senators and U.S. representatives looking to do a favor for a constituency, or for a fellow lawmaker by offering their vote for a commemorative coin program. Commemoratives could raise funds for a pet cause through surcharges on the Mint's sales of the coins, and a vote for a program went largely unnoticed by the general public.

The last of the "early" commemoratives honored Booker T. Washington and George Washington Carver (AU-50). **$40**

The year 1994 alone brought five commemorative coin programs: World Cup soccer, National Prisoner of War Museum, U.S. Capitol Bicentennial, Vietnam Veterans Memorial and Women in Military Service Memorial. Although each theme had its virtues, the market for commemorative coins couldn't keep up with all the issues, and sales plummeted from the highs of the Washington half dollar and other early issues in the modern era.

In response, Congress passed the Commemorative Coin Reform Act of 1996. Among other provisions, it limits the number of commemorative themes to two per year. In addition, congressional proposals for commemorative coins must be reviewed by the Citizens Coinage Advisory Committee, which reports to the Treasury secretary. The 10-person committee consists of members from the general public and those with credentials in American history, sculpture and numismatics.

1994 commemoratives included issues for World Cup soccer, National Prisoner of War Memorial, Bicentennial of the United States Capitol, Vietnam Veterans Memorial and the Women in Military Service Memorial.

1996-P proof Atlanta Olympics silver dollar, high-jumper design. **$60**

1988-W proof Olympiad gold five dollars. **$190**

Where to get them

Current-year commemoratives can be purchased directly from the U.S. Mint (www.usmint.gov). Issues from previous years can be purchased at shows, shops or through advertisements in hobby publications, such as Coins magazine.

Collecting strategies

A complete collection of every commemorative half dollar, silver dollar and gold coin issued since 1982 is a commendable but daunting goal for many collectors, especially beginners. Following are suggestions for getting started in collecting modern commemoratives, which can lead to expanding the collection in the future:

Collect what you like

If you see a modern commemorative coin and you like it, buy it. The coin may appeal to you because of its theme or design. Whatever the reason, if you like the coin and are willing to pay the asking price, it will make a great addition to your collection.

By denomination

A new collector may want to focus on just the commemorative half dollars issued since 1982 or just the silver dollars. With a good value guide in hand and more money to spend, a new collector could also venture into gold coins and select one or more of the many commemorative gold $5 coins.

By theme

Collectors of modern commemoratives can also focus on a particular theme that appeals to them, such as presidents, the Olympics or other sports, women or military themes. Again, collect what you like.

1990-P proof Eisenhower Centennial silver dollar. **$17**

1986-S proof Statue of Liberty Centennial clad half dollar. **$5.50**

1993-S proof Thomas Jefferson silver dollar. **$28**

As a complement to a circulating-coin collection

One or more commemorative coins can complement a collection of circulating coins with similar design themes. For example, a 1993 silver dollar commemorating the 250th anniversary of Thomas Jefferson's birth can complement a collection of Westward Journey nickels. A 1990 silver dollar commemorating the centennial of Dwight Eisenhower's birth can complement a collection of Eisenhower dollars.

By set

When selling a current-year commemorative series, the U.S. Mint often offers various sets containing individual coins in the series in uncirculated and proof versions. For example, the 1986 Statue of Liberty Centennial coin series consisted of a base-metal half dollar, silver dollar and gold $5. Various sets of the series offered by the Mint that year included a two-coin set consisting of an uncirculated silver dollar and clad half dollar; a three-coin set consisting of uncirculated versions of each coin; and a six-coin set consisting of proof and uncirculated versions of each coin.

These and sets of other series can be found in their original Mint packaging from online sellers, at shops and shows, and through advertisements in hobby publications such as Coins magazine.

1986-S proof Statue of Liberty Centennial silver dollar. **$13.50**

How much?

Some of the least popular commemorative coins at the time of their issue are the most expensive on the secondary market today, and some of the most popular commemorative coins at the time of their issue are the most affordable today. Why? The least popular coins didn't sell as well, which resulted in lower mintages. Generally speaking, the scarcer coins are more valued by collectors, which increases demand and drives up their asking prices on the secondary market.

For example, the 1982 George Washington silver commemorative half dollar was popular and sold well at the time of issue. With millions of coins produced, either an uncirculated or proof example can be purchased for under $10.

1986-W proof Statue of Liberty Centennial gold five dollars. **$190**

1993-S proof James Madison clad half dollar. **$16.50**

1996-S proof Atlanta Olympics clad half dollar, swimmer design. **$36**

1991-S proof Mount Rushmore Golden Anniversary clad half dollar. **$20**

In contrast, less than 50,000 uncirculated versions of the 1996 Atlanta Olympics commemorative clad half dollar with the swimmer design were produced. Expect to pay more than $150 for one on the secondary market.

Coin Prices magazine, available on many newsstands, provides a complete list of modern U.S. commemorative coins and a guide to current retail values.

Mintmarks

Modern U.S. commemorative coins have either a "P" mintmark for Philadelphia, "D" for Denver, "S" for San Francisco, or a "W" for West Point, N.Y. Mintmark location varies by coin.

Condition

Commemorative coins are specially handled and packaged at the mints. Thus, grading is less of a factor in purchasing and collecting them.

Still, check each coin before you purchase it or after you receive it in the mail. Make sure its surfaces are clean and free of scratches or other significant blemishes.

The U.S. Mint has a 30-day return policy for coins purchased directly from it. Mail-order dealers, such as those who advertise in Coins magazine, also offer return policies. Check individual ads for specific terms.

1989-S proof Bicentennial of the Congress silver dollar. **$18.50**

1997-S proof Jackie Robinson silver dollar. **$85**

1992-P proof Columbus Quincentenary silver dollar. **$39**

2004-P proof 125th Anniversary of the Light Bulb silver dollar. **$41**

1995-S proof Civil War silver dollar. **$78**

How to store them

Keep commemorative coins in their original U.S. Mint packaging, whether purchased directly from the Mint or on the secondary market. The packaging is suitable for long-term storage and protects the coins from wear and blemishes that occur when handled directly.

Modern commemorative coin specs

Commemorative coins are struck in traditional specifications for the denomination and composition. Future issues may be subject to change from the specs listed.

Clad half dollars

Diameter: 30.6 millimeters.

Weight: 11.34 grams.

Composition: clad layers of 75-percent copper and 25-percent nickel bonded to a pure-copper core.

Silver half dollars

Diameter: 30.6 millimeters.

Weight: 12.5 grams.

Composition: 90-percent silver, 10-percent copper.

Actual silver weight: 0.3618 troy ounces.

Silver dollars

Diameter: 38.1 millimeters.

Weight: 26.73 grams.

Composition: 90-percent silver, 10-percent copper.

Actual silver weight: 0.76 troy ounces.

Gold $5

Diameter: 21.5 millimeters.

Weight: 8.359 grams.

Composition: 90-percent gold, 10-percent alloy.

Actual gold weight: 0.24 troy ounces.

Gold $10

Diameter: 27 millimeters.

Weight: 26.73 grams.

Composition: 90-percent gold, 10-percent alloy.

Actual gold weight: 0.484 troy ounces.

1999-W proof George Washington gold five dollars. **$475**

2006-P proof Benjamin Franklin Tercentenary silver dollar, Franklin portrait design. **$54**

1993-W James Madison gold five dollars. **$265**

2003-P proof First Flight Centennial gold 10 dollars. **$560**

DOORSTOPS

Decorative cast-iron doorstops date from around the turn of the 19th century, and have attracted collectors with their myriad depections of flowers, people and animals. Beware of modern reproductions that simulate aged and worn paint.

Photo courtesy Bertoia Auctions, Vineland, N.J.; www.BertoiaAuctions.com

Accordion Player, cast iron, rare example of black gentleman musician wearing orange and red suit; stands on brown base, pristine, 6 3/4" h. **$977**

Photo courtesy Bertoia Auctions, Vineland, N.J.; www.BertoiaAuctions.com

Ann Hathaway Cottage, Hubley, two-piece cast iron, cottage with a multitude of blooming flowers in foreground, near mint, 6 1/2" x 8 3/8". **$1,380**

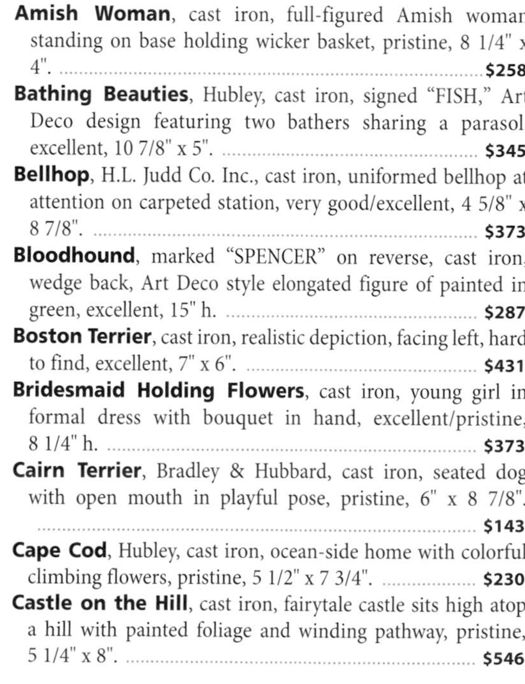

Amish Woman, cast iron, full-figured Amish woman standing on base holding wicker basket, pristine, 8 1/4" x 4". **$258**

Bathing Beauties, Hubley, cast iron, signed "FISH," Art Deco design featuring two bathers sharing a parasol, excellent, 10 7/8" x 5". **$345**

Bellhop, H.L. Judd Co. Inc., cast iron, uniformed bellhop at attention on carpeted station, very good/excellent, 4 5/8" x 8 7/8". **$373**

Bloodhound, marked "SPENCER" on reverse, cast iron, wedge back, Art Deco style elongated figure of painted in green, excellent, 15" h. **$287**

Boston Terrier, cast iron, realistic depiction, facing left, hard to find, excellent, 7" x 6". **$431**

Bridesmaid Holding Flowers, cast iron, young girl in formal dress with bouquet in hand, excellent/pristine, 8 1/4" h. **$373**

Cairn Terrier, Bradley & Hubbard, cast iron, seated dog with open mouth in playful pose, pristine, 6" x 8 7/8". **$143**

Cape Cod, Hubley, cast iron, ocean-side home with colorful climbing flowers, pristine, 5 1/2" x 7 3/4". **$230**

Castle on the Hill, cast iron, fairytale castle sits high atop a hill with painted foliage and winding pathway, pristine, 5 1/4" x 8". **$546**

Photo courtesy Bertoia Auctions, Vineland, N.J.; www.BertoiaAuctions.com

Black Man on Cotton Bale, bale is cast iron, figure is pot metal, figure is preparing to strike a match, excellent, 6 7/8" x 6 7/8". **$1,380**

Photo courtesy Bertoia Auctions, Vineland, N.J.; www.BertoiaAuctions.com

Cat Scratch Girl, H.L. Judd Co. Inc., highly detailed portrayal of little girl examining recent scratch from nearby pet, signed A. Diougy, excellent, 4" x 9". **$373**

Photo courtesy Bertoia Auctions, Vineland, N.J.; www.BertoiaAuctions.com

Crossed Out, cast iron, depicts clown in turmoil, twisted whimsically amidst strewn books and pamphlets, "CROSSED OUT" embossed on base, originally meant to commemorate the N.Y. Times crossword puzzle phenomenon, near mint/pristine, 7 1/8" h. **$4,025**

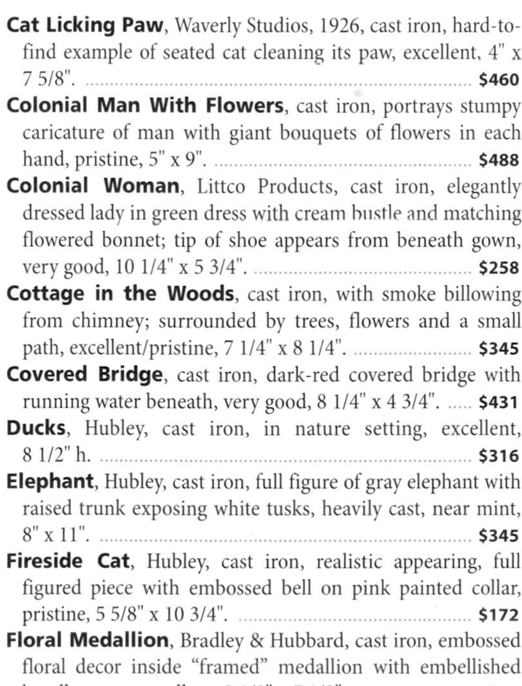

Cat Licking Paw, Waverly Studios, 1926, cast iron, hard-to-find example of seated cat cleaning its paw, excellent, 4" x 7 5/8". **$460**

Colonial Man With Flowers, cast iron, portrays stumpy caricature of man with giant bouquets of flowers in each hand, pristine, 5" x 9". **$488**

Colonial Woman, Littco Products, cast iron, elegantly dressed lady in green dress with cream bustle and matching flowered bonnet; tip of shoe appears from beneath gown, very good, 10 1/4" x 5 3/4". **$258**

Cottage in the Woods, cast iron, with smoke billowing from chimney; surrounded by trees, flowers and a small path, excellent/pristine, 7 1/4" x 8 1/4". **$345**

Covered Bridge, cast iron, dark-red covered bridge with running water beneath, very good, 8 1/4" x 4 3/4". **$431**

Ducks, Hubley, cast iron, in nature setting, excellent, 8 1/2" h. **$316**

Elephant, Hubley, cast iron, full figure of gray elephant with raised trunk exposing white tusks, heavily cast, near mint, 8" x 11". **$345**

Fireside Cat, Hubley, cast iron, realistic appearing, full figured piece with embossed bell on pink painted collar, pristine, 5 5/8" x 10 3/4". **$172**

Floral Medallion, Bradley & Hubbard, cast iron, embossed floral decor inside "framed" medallion with embellished handle at top, excellent, 3 1/2" x 7 1/2". **$57**

Photo courtesy Bertoia Auctions, Vineland, N.J.; www.BertoiaAuctions.com

Flapper Girl, cast iron, marked "8", fashionably attired flapper in layered dress, umbrella in hand, detailed casting, very good/excellent, 9 1/2" h. **$690**

Photo courtesy Bertoia Auctions, Vineland, N.J.; www.BertoiaAuctions.com

Flower Basket, Hubley, cast iron, marked "471", tulips and starflowers in basket with pink base, near mint, 5 1/2" x 9 3/4". **$316**

Photo courtesy Bertoia Auctions, Vineland, N.J.; www.BertoiaAuctions.com

Jungle Boy, cast iron, boy in leopard skin pelt, on one knee with arm out stretched, pristine, 12" h. **$1,092**

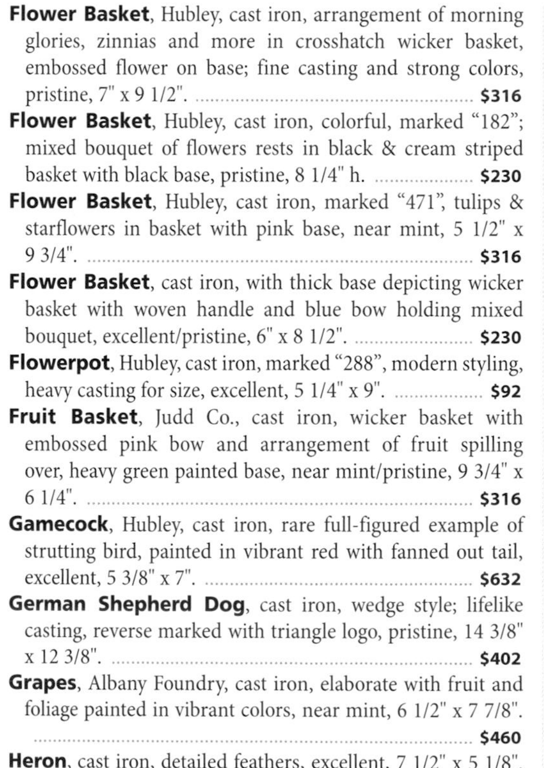

Flower Basket, Hubley, cast iron, arrangement of morning glories, zinnias and more in crosshatch wicker basket, embossed flower on base; fine casting and strong colors, pristine, 7" x 9 1/2". **$316**

Flower Basket, Hubley, cast iron, colorful, marked "182"; mixed bouquet of flowers rests in black & cream striped basket with black base, pristine, 8 1/4" h. **$230**

Flower Basket, Hubley, cast iron, marked "471", tulips & starflowers in basket with pink base, near mint, 5 1/2" x 9 3/4". **$316**

Flower Basket, cast iron, with thick base depicting wicker basket with woven handle and blue bow holding mixed bouquet, excellent/pristine, 6" x 8 1/2". **$230**

Flowerpot, Hubley, cast iron, marked "288", modern styling, heavy casting for size, excellent, 5 1/4" x 9". **$92**

Fruit Basket, Judd Co., cast iron, wicker basket with embossed pink bow and arrangement of fruit spilling over, heavy green painted base, near mint/pristine, 9 3/4" x 6 1/4". **$316**

Gamecock, Hubley, cast iron, rare full-figured example of strutting bird, painted in vibrant red with fanned out tail, excellent, 5 3/8" x 7". **$632**

German Shepherd Dog, cast iron, wedge style; lifelike casting, reverse marked with triangle logo, pristine, 14 3/8" x 12 3/8". **$402**

Grapes, Albany Foundry, cast iron, elaborate with fruit and foliage painted in vibrant colors, near mint, 6 1/2" x 7 7/8". **$460**

Heron, cast iron, detailed feathers, excellent, 7 1/2" x 5 1/8". **$345**

Photo courtesy Bertoia Auctions, Vineland, N.J.; www.BertoiaAuctions.com

King Tut, cast iron, rare, elaborately cast and colorfully painted, pristine, 10 5/8" h. **$2,300**

Photo courtesy Bertoia Auctions, Vineland, N.J.; www.BertoiaAuctions.com

Little Red Riding Hood and the Wolf, cast iron, embossed "NUYDEA" and "LITTLE RED RIDING HOOD" on reverse, crisp overall casting details, pristine, 7 1/2" x 9 1/2". **$1,840**

Jonquils, Hubley, cast iron, colorfully painted depiction of jonquil blooms bending in the breeze, pristine, 7 1/2" x 8". **$230**

Lighthouse, cast iron, with keeper's house, depicted on landscaped yard with recessed shoreline, excellent, 6 1/4" x 8". **$287**

Little Red Riding Hood and the Wolf, Albany Foundry, cast iron, forward-facing example with ominous wolf peering from behind, near mint, 7 1/4" h. **$862**

Mad Hatter, cast iron, full-figured character stands with nose in air, sporting a top hat and red jacket, excellent/pristine, 2 7/8" x 6 5/8". **$172**

Mammy, Hubley, cast iron, with hands on hips; expressive facial features, wears blue dress and polka-dot head wrap. Minor touch-up, otherwise pristine, 8 3/4" h. **$345**

Nathanael Green House, cast iron, Colonial-era house embossed on back "NATHANAEL GREEN", old repaint, 4 3/4" x 7 7/8". **$460**
(His last name was actually spelled Greene (1742-1786). He was a major general of the Continental Army in the American Revolutionary War. When the war began, Greene was a militia private, the lowest rank possible. He emerged from the war with a reputation as George Washington's most gifted and dependable officer.)

Old Salt, cast iron, full-figure example depicting bearded fisherman, vibrant colors, pristine, 4 1/8" x 11". **$402**

Old Woman, Bradley & Hubbard, cast iron, woman walking in profile on Art Deco "carpeted" base; wearing a ruffled Victorian dress and shawl, she holds a basket of flowers and parasol, pristine, 11" x 7". **$1,380**

Oriental Boy, Hubley, "TOKO", cast iron, colorful, three-piece casting, boy seated on tufted pillow, near mint, 5 1/4" x 6". **$172**

Oriental Girl, cast iron, full-figured girl on base, hand painted in colorful attire, pristine, 7 3/4" h. **$316**

Parlor Maid, Hubley, cast iron, Art Deco design, features maid serving cocktails; signed "FISH" on base, very good/excellent, 3 1/2" x 9 1/2". **$258**

Penguin in Top Hat, Hubley, cast iron, Art Deco style depiction, dressed in tuxedo, standing in proud pose, excellent/pristine, 3 3/4" x 10". **$632**

Pheasant, Hubley, designed by Fred Everett, cast iron, finely detailed, hand-painted depiction in underbrush, near mint, 1 1/4" x 8 1/2". **$488**

Poppies, Hubley, cast iron, marked "440", vibrant colors, features red poppies in classic-style vase; black base, excellent/pristine, 10 5/8" x 7 1/8". **$172**

Quails, Hubley, cast iron, marked with copyright symbol and "Everett" fine painted details, near mint, 7 1/4" h. **$575**

Rabbit in Top Hat, Albany Foundry, cast iron, vivid overall coloring with blue top hat and coattails, excellent, 4 3/4" x 9 7/8". **$632**

Photo courtesy Bertoia Auctions, Vineland, N.J.; www.BertoiaAuctions.com

Popeye, Hubley, cast iron, rare full-figured example of United Features Syndicate cartoon figure; vibrant colors overall, near mint, 9" h. **$17,250**

Photo courtesy Bertoia Auctions, Vineland, N.J.; www.BertoiaAuctions.com

Sitting Black Cat, marked, "Copyright 1927 A.M. Greenblatt Studios #20," wedge-back design, animated side-glancing expression on face, excellent, 9" h. **$402**

Photo courtesy Bertoia Auctions, Vineland, N.J.; www.BertoiaAuctions.com

Rabbit, Bradley & Hubbard, cast iron; one of the largest animal doorstops, jackrabbit on hind legs, embossed base, excellent/pristine, 8" x 15". **$4,025**

Rose Vase, Hubley, cast iron, one-sided piece depicts pastel roses in pierced handle, urn-shaped vase, pristine, 6 1/8" x 10 3/8". **$402**

Senorita, Hubley, cast iron, young woman in dress and shawl with fan in hand, near mint, 9" x 5". **$1,495**

Sitting Cat, cast iron, unusual flat-back example, seated facing forward with mischievous painted eyes and finely detailed fur on chest, pristine, 6 3/8" h. **$316**

Terrier, Creations Co., cast iron, attentive pose, painted in white with tan markings and brown collar, excellent, 6 3/4" x 7". **$86**

Terrier, Hubley, cast iron, dog seated on green base, excellent/pristine, 6" x 7 1/8". **$287**

Twin Cats, Hubley, Drayton design, cast iron, marked "73" on reverse side; colorful depiction of two side-glancing, arm-in-arm felines, one in a dress and the other in a jumper, excellent, 5 1/4" x 7". **$546**

Wine Merchant, cast iron, full-figured merchant grasping multiple wine bottles in each hand; white wines in right hand, red wines in left, pristine, 9 3/4" x 7". **$1,265**

Zinnias, Hubley, cast iron, in various colors, hand-painted pot done in blue & cream color scheme with embossed design, pristine, 9 3/4" x 8 1/2". **$230**

Zinnias (Basket of), cast iron, depicting pastel-colored flowers overflowing from basket, crisp casting details, pristine, 10 1/2" x 8". **$287**

FIREARMS

Laws regarding the sale of firearms, especially modern-era weapons, continue to evolve. Be sure to buy and sell firearms through auction houses and dealers properly licensed to transact business in this highly regulated area.

Machine gun, A.O.S.A American Historical Foundation, semiautomatic, "50th Anniversary of the Thompson Machine Gun," serial no. 26982, 19" barrel including the muzzle break, complete with 50-round drum magazine, checked walnut stocks. New and unfired. **$862**

Pistol, A.A. Arms Inc. Model AP9, 9mm, 5" barrel, military-type sights and black composition grip. **$172**

Pistol, Accu-Tek Model AT-380, semiautomatic, serial no. 014558, .380 caliber, 2 3/4" barrel, satin-gray finish with polished sides, black plastic grips. **$86**

Pistol, Advantage Arms Model 422, breech loading, serial no. 2107, .22 caliber, 2 3/8" four-barrel cluster. **$143**

Pistol, Advantage Arms Model 422 Pocket, serial no. 3024, .22 magnum caliber, 2 1/2" four-barrel tip-over breech **$230**

Pistol (air), Benjamin Franklin, no visible serial number, .22 caliber. 8 5/8" barrel. Primarily brass, silver-plated, with unfinished gray cast-metal frame. **$115**

Pistol, American Arms Co. P98, semiautomatic, serial no. 006246, .22 caliber, 5" barrel. Contained in factory box with literature. **$230**

Pistol, AMT "Back Up" Model, semiautomatic, serial no. A76153, 9mm, 2 3/4" barrel. Sold together with factory box, manual and extra magazine **$258.75**

Pistol, AMT "Lightning," semiautomatic, serial no. G12287, .22 caliber, 5" barrel with target sights. Contained in original factory box with magazine. **$201**

Pistol, AMT Automag II, semiautomatic, serial no. H41859, .22 rim-fire magnum, 4 3/4" barrel. **$431.25**

Pistol, Argentinian Bersa Model 83, semiautomatic, serial no. 262301, .380 caliber, 3 5/8" barrel. Contained in original factory box with factory literature. **$172**

Pistol, Auto Ordnance 1927 A-5 Thompson, semiautomatic, serial no. 392, .45 caliber, 13 1/2" ventilated barrel and top-bolt toggle. **$920**

Pistol, Beretta Model 92F, semiautomatic, serial no. BER045077Z, 9mm, 5.9" barrel. Black Bruniton finish. **$345**

Pistol (pocket), Beretta Model 950 "Minx," semiautomatic, with extra magazine, serial no. 71503CC, .22 caliber, 2 1/2" barrel. **$230**

Photo courtesy Greg Martin Auctions, San Francisco; www.GregMartinAuctions.com

Gatling Gun, U.S. Model 1883, with U.S. inspector markings "D.F.C." for David F. Clark on field carriage, with accompanying limber marked "F. Bannerman, New York". **$172,500**

Pistol, Bersa Model 23, semiautomatic, serial no. 183858, .22 long-rifle caliber, 3 1/2" barrel. Frost nickel-plated finish. Made in Argentina. **$201**

Pistol, Bersa Model 85, semiautomatic, serial no. 167673, .380 caliber, 3 1/2" barrel. Made in Argentina. **$230**

Pistol (derringer), American Derringer Corp. Model M-1, serial no. 120630, .45 caliber, 3 1/8" over-and-under barrels, stainless steel. **$143**

Pistol (derringer), BJT Model DA, serial no. 006617, .38 caliber, 3" barrels. **$287**

Pistol (pocket), Belgian Bayard, semiautomatic, serial no. 76244, .380 caliber, 3 1/2" barrel. **$201**

Pistol, "protector," semiautomatic, serial no. 31330, 6.35mm, 2" barrel. **$69**

Photo courtesy Greg Martin Auctions, San Francisco; www.GregMartinAuctions.com

Pistol (revolver), J.H. Dance & Brothers, Confederate Dragoon, with history of original ownership by Private Mile C. Bell, Co. F, 23rd Brigade of Texas Cavalry. **$57,500**

AFFADAVIT

19 March,1959

The following described firearm was acquired by the undersigned as follows:

In the spring of 1933 one John Dillinger and gang was captured as the result of a fire which destroyed the Congress Hotel on Congress Street in Tucson,Arizona. He was taken into custody at the time by John Belton,Sheriff of Pima County,Jimmy Herron ,and Joe Rice of the Tucson Police force. The firearm below described was removed from the person of John Dillinger by Sheriff Belton and later presented to my mother,Evelyn Jenney Fields,who was then Secretary to Superior Court Judge Fred Fickett and also A'sst Probation Officer.
The firearm described below was presented to me in 1949 by Evelyn Jenney Fields.

Firearm:
Make: Remington Arms Co.,UMC,Utica,New York
Model: Derringer Pattern
Caliber: 41 Rimfire Derringer
Serial No. L 97255

The above is to the best of my knowledge a true and correct statement.

William LeB.Jenney

Subscribed and sworn to before me this 19th day of March,1959

Marjorie I. Berridge
Notary Public

My Commission Expires April 11, 1961

Photo Courtesy Heritage Auction Galleries, Dallas; www.HA.com

Remington .41 Caliber Rimfire "Double Derringer" Taken from the Person of one John Herbert Dillinger when arrested in Tucson, Arizona, Jan. 25, 1934. Dillinger, using the alias "Frank Sullivan," along with gang members Henry Pierpoint, Russel Clark and Charles Makley, and their "molls," including Billie Frechette, were all arrested over a three-day period from Jan. 22-25, through a series of coordinated police raids, without a shot being fired. Upon being arrested, Dillinger was quoted as saying, "My God, how did you know I was in town? I'll be the laughing stock of the country! How could a hick-town police force ever suspect us." In reality, and unbeknownst to Dillinger, a local fireman, called to a fire in the hotel where some of the gang members were staying, recognized Russel Clark from his "wanted" picture in True Detective magazine, and alerted the local police. After their uneventful arrest, the gang members were all booked by the County Sheriff, John Belton, on fugitive warrants and held in the county jail. The next day the gang members were "put on display" to the curious public, and some 2,000 people trooped past their cells exchanging disparaging remarks. On Jan. 28, Arizona Governor B.B. Moeur signed extradition papers, and Dillinger was secretly flown to Indiana to face trial for murder. The rest of the gang was sent back to Ohio by train. Five weeks later, using a carved wooden pistol, Dillinger escaped from jail in Crown Point, Ind. Just four months later, on July 22, 1934, Dillinger was gunned down by FBI agents at the Biograph Theater in Chicago. 2009 was the 75th anniversary of Dillinger's death. The gun bears serial #L97255 and retains most of the original blue on screws, hammer and trigger, the balance with the original blue-gray matte finish mixing with gray patina. Perfect grips, mint bore, mechanically fine. The tip of the barrel-release lever is broken/missing. The hammer exhibits the late-circa-1930 detail of being grooved rather than knurled. The gun is accompanied by copies of the Tucson arrest reports on each of the fugitives (with the exception of Dillinger's which vanished many years ago). The property slips that accompany the reports list money, jewelry and vehicles with absolutely no mention of weapons. Apparently the Sheriff's Department already had plans for those, as two of the women were charged with possessing machine guns. This gun was concealed in Dillinger's sock when he was arrested by Sheriff John Belton, who presented the pistol to Evelyn B. Jenney, an attractive young widow, who was Deputy County Probation Officer and Secretary to Superior Court Judge Fred W. Fickett. Mrs. Jenney was the widow of William LeBaron Jenney Jr., who was the grandson of famed Chicago "Sky Scraper" architect William LeBaron Jenney. In 1949 she gave the gun to her son, William LeBaron Jenney III. Included with the gun are two notarized affidavits from Mr. Jenney, dated March 19, 1959, describing the gun, with serial number, and attesting to receiving the pistol from Sheriff Belton. The gun is accompanied by much additional research from the consignor, who was the purchaser of the gun from William LeBaron Jenney III on March 19, 1959. **$95,600**

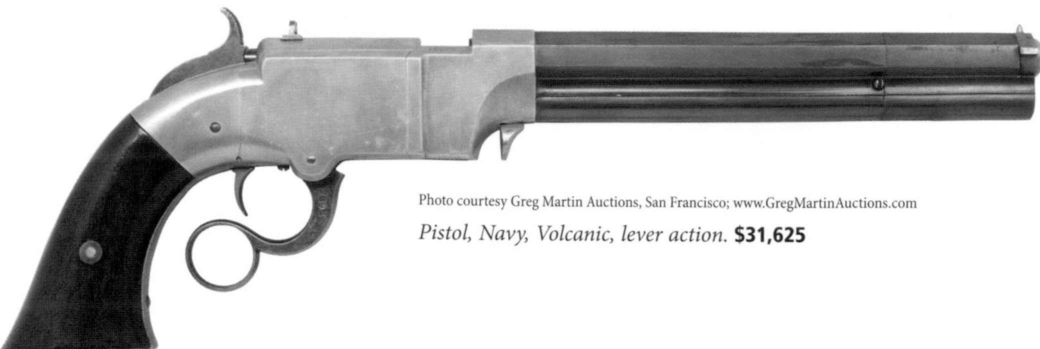

Photo courtesy Greg Martin Auctions, San Francisco; www.GregMartinAuctions.com

Pistol, Navy, Volcanic, lever action. **$31,625**

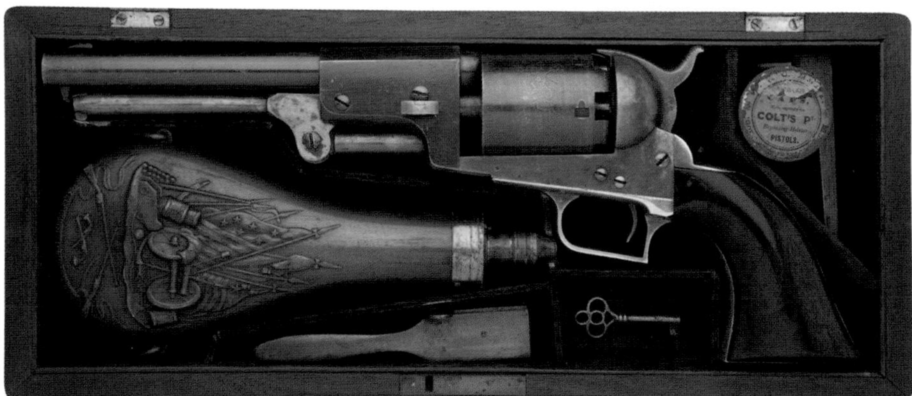

Photo courtesy Greg Martin Auctions, San Francisco; www.GregMartinAuctions.com

Pistol (revolver), Colt Second Model Dragoon with accessories, U.S. martially marked, cased. **$97,750**

Photo courtesy Greg Martin Auctions, San Francisco; www.GregMartinAuctions.com

Pistol (revolver), Colt Texas Paterson No. 5, holster model, rare 9". **$97,750**

Photo courtesy Greg Martin Auctions, San Francisco; www.GregMartinAuctions.com

Pistol (revolver), Colt Texas Paterson, U.S. martially marked, accompanied by leather-flap holster. **$69,000**

Pistol (revolver), Beretta Model 950B "Minx" Long Barrel, serial no. H02129, .22 caliber, 3 1/2" barrel. **$287**

Pistol (revolver), Charter Arms "Off Duty" Double Action, serial no. 1018679, .38 special caliber, 1 7/8" barrel with florescent front sight. **$115**

Pistol (revolver), Dolne, Apache folding knife with steel knuckles, serial no. 1641, 6.35mm pin-fire caliber, six-shot blued fluted cylinder, case-hardened frame and steel knuckle, with double-action folding trigger and spurless hammer; engine-turned finish to dagger. Light patina on dagger blade. **$4,887**

Pistol (revolver), L. Dolne, Apache "knuckleduster" with dagger, serial no. 5770, 7mm, six-shot cylinder with long flutes, folding steel knuckleduster grips. Frame marked: L. Dolne Invor. Folding trigger and dagger blade. (Named for the infamous "Apache" Parisian gang known to use them.) Metal with gray age patina. **$2,875**

Pistol, (revolver, composite), Colt Bisley, single action, serial no. 292547, .45 caliber, 3 3/4" barrel, marked, "COLT'S PT F.A. CO. HARTFORD CT. U.S.A." **$488**

Pistol (revolver), Colt "Viper" Double Action, serial no. 61894R, .38 caliber, 4" barrel. Contained in original factory box with factory literature. **$431**

Pistol (revolver), Colt Detective Special Double Action, serial no. 540662, .38 caliber, 2" barrel. Contained in original brown factory box with cleaning rod and instruction sheet. **$862**

Pistol (revolver), Colt Diamondback 22 Magnum Double Action, serial no. D90630, .22 long-rifle caliber, 4" barrel with vented rib and target sights. **$1,725**

Pistol (revolver), Colt Lawman Mark V Trooper Double Action, serial no. 21521V, .357 magnum caliber, 2" barrel. Contained in original factory box with literature. **$632**

Pistol, Colt Mark IV/Series 70 Gold Cup National Match, semiautomatic, with special customizing, serial no. 19553N70, .45 caliber, 5" barrel with target sights. Contained with extra slide spring in original factory box. **$1,092**

Pistol, Colt Mark IV Series 80 "El Jefe," semiautomatic, serial no. EL JEFE 376, .38 Super caliber, 5" barrel. Nickel-plated finish. Pearl grips. **$920**

Pistol, Colt Mark IV/Series 70 Government Model 1911, semiautomatic, serial no. 70L01267, 9mm. Contained in original factory box. **$862**

Pistol (revolver), Colt Model Python Double Action, serial no. VO5958, .357 magnum caliber, 2 1/2" barrel with elevated rib and target sights. Contained in factory carton with factory literature. **$1,150**

Pistol, Colt M1911A1, "World War II American Legion" commemorative, semiautomatic, serial no. FR11615, .45 ACP caliber, 5" barrel, cased, left side of slide marked, "1941 THE AMERICAN LEGION WORLD WAR II VICTORY M1911A1 'FOR GOD AND COUNTRY' 1945." **$805**

Pistol, Colt Mark IV, Series 80, Gold Cup National Match commemorative, semiautomatic, serial no. FN06278E, .45 ACP caliber, 5" barrel, cased, slide marked, "GOLD CUP SERIES' 80 COLT MARK IV GOLD CUP NATIONAL MATCH LIMITED EDITION." **$747**

Photo courtesy Greg Martin Auctions, San Francisco; www.GregMartinAuctions.com

Pistols (revolvers, pair), Colt Baby Dragoon transition, book-cased with consecutive serial numbers and accessories. **$28,750 pair**

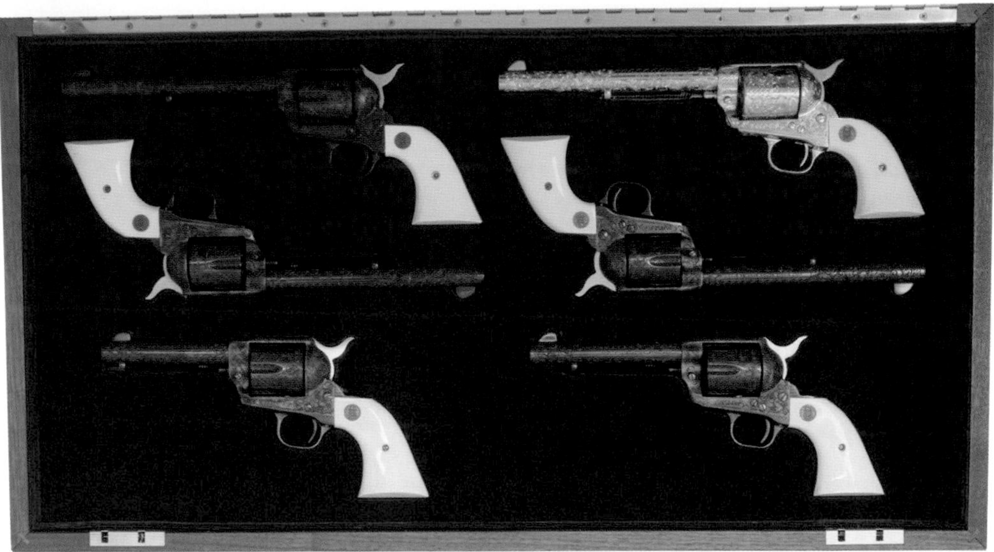

Photo courtesy Greg Martin Auctions, San Francisco; www.GregMartinAuctions.com

Pistol (revolver) ensemble, Colt Custom Shop, single-action, each is Type D, factory engraved, individually designed and sold as a factory-cased group, with Colt factory letters for the six revolvers. **$23,000 set**

Photo courtesy Greg Martin Auctions, San Francisco; www.GregMartinAuctions.com

Pistol (revolver), Smith & Wesson, hand ejector, engraved and inscribed to Sheriff Buck Garrett (1871-1929), with documentation, photographs and memorabilia. **$25,875**

Pistol, Hungarian Model 37M, semiautomatic, serial no. 155056, 9mm Kurz caliber, 4" barrel. **$230**

Pistol, Ruger, standard semiautomatic, with rare serial no. 444444, .22 long-rifle caliber, 6" barrel, blued, standard markings. **$690**

Pistol (revolver), Smith & Wesson Model 25-2 Double Action, serial no. N301067, .45 long Colt caliber, 6 1/2" barrel with target sights. Case-hardened hammer and trigger. Contained in original shipping carton. **$632**

Pistol (revolver), Smith & Wesson Model 10 (.38 military and police), serial no. C 60207 on butt, .38 S&W Special, 2" barrel, customary trademark and maker/address markings on right side of frame, circa 1951. .... **$345**

Pistol (revolver), Smith & Wesson Model 640 Centennial, hammerless, double action, serial no. BFV8288, .38 Smith & Wesson caliber, 2" barrel, varnished Smith & Wesson medallion, boxed. **$345**

Pistol, Sturm-Ruger KP-85 Mark IIC, semiautomatic, serial no. 303-00001, 9mm x 19, 4 3/8" barrel, satin stainless steel finished slide. Round hammer spur. Case contained in original brown cardboard shipping box. **$345**

Photo courtesy Greg Martin Auctions, San Francisco; www.GregMartinAuctions.com

Pistol, Walther MP hammerless model, semiautomatic in .45 ACP caliber, Pre-World War II Prototype, circa 1935-36. **$126,500**

Pistol, "Titan," semiautomatic, by F.I.E. Corp., serial no. 156904, .25 caliber, 2 3/8" barrel, chrome-finished barrel, slide, hammer and trigger, gray-alloy metal frame. **$86**

Pistol, Walther ac43 Code P-38, semiautomatic, serial no. 7749, 9mm, 5" barrel, Waffenamt markings. **$345**

Pistol, Carl Walther engraved P 38, semiautomatic, serial no. 351006, 9mm caliber, 5" barrel. Oak leaf and border engraved, with front of grip strap with crosshatched pattern. Silver-plated finish. Appears to be unfired. **$1,955**

Pistol, Carl Walther P 38/II, semiautomatic, with extra magazine, serial no. 322122, 9mm caliber, 5" barrel. Brown box with manual, extra magazine and cleaning rod. Made at Ulm factory for Interarms, Alexandria, Va. **$460**

Rifle, Adler-Jager Model AT74, with telescopic sight, serial no. 101029, .22 caliber, 21" barrel including flash hider, military-type sights. **$258**

Rifle, (air), .20 Caliber Beeman Model R1, with Leupold telescopic sight, serial no. 1517378, 20 1/2" barrel. **$517**

Rifle, (air), Beeman Model HW 50S, serial no. 715999, Marked "Kal. 4.5," 18 3/8" round barrel. Wear, patina (more pronounced at muzzle), storage marks. **$86**

Rifle, (air), .177 Daisy/Feinwerkbau 300, serial no. 189917, 19" barrel, side-lever cocking, hooded front sight, adjustable aperture sight. **$488**

Rifle, (air, target), BAIKAL (Russia) Model 1ZH-61, serial no. 9817677, 4.5mm caliber, 17 1/2" round barrel. **$57**

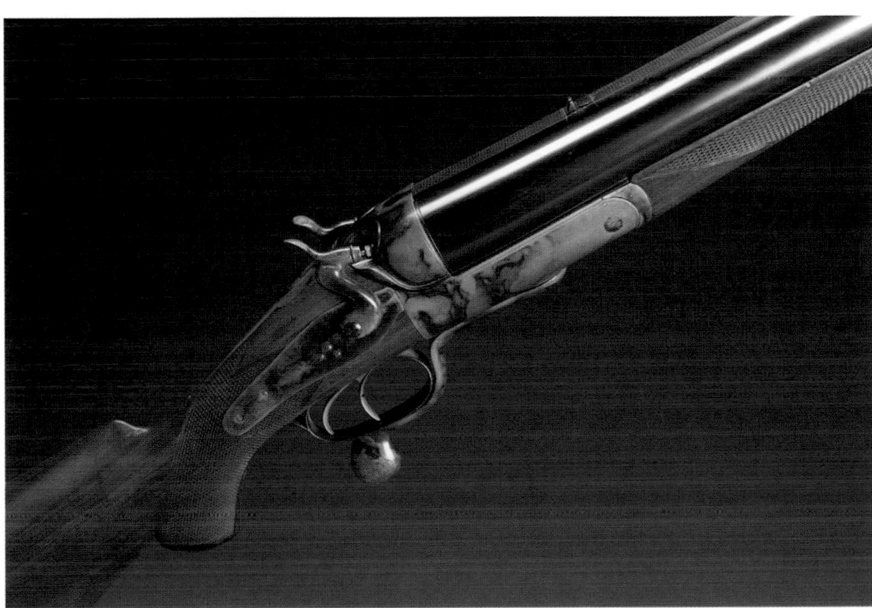

Photo courtesy Greg Martin Auctions, San Francisco; www.GregMartinAuctions.com

Rifle (double), massive four-bore, British, black powder. **$86,250**

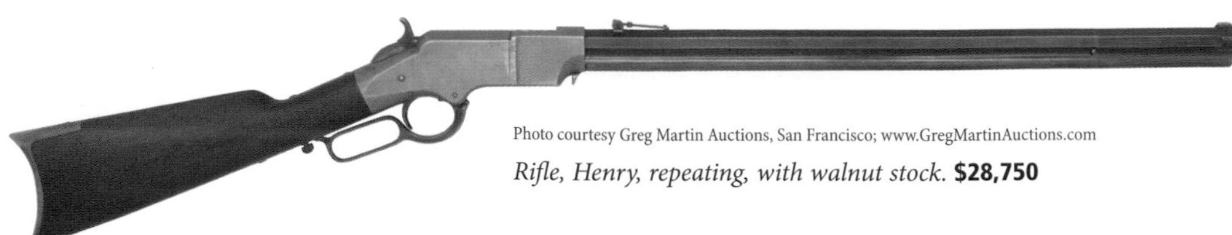

Photo courtesy Greg Martin Auctions, San Francisco; www.GregMartinAuctions.com

Rifle, Henry, repeating, with walnut stock. **$28,750**

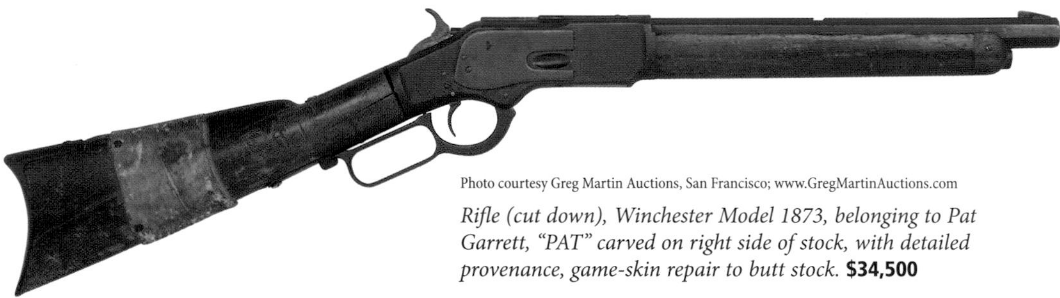

Photo courtesy Greg Martin Auctions, San Francisco; www.GregMartinAuctions.com

Rifle (cut down), Winchester Model 1873, belonging to Pat Garrett, "PAT" carved on right side of stock, with detailed provenance, game-skin repair to butt stock. **$34,500**

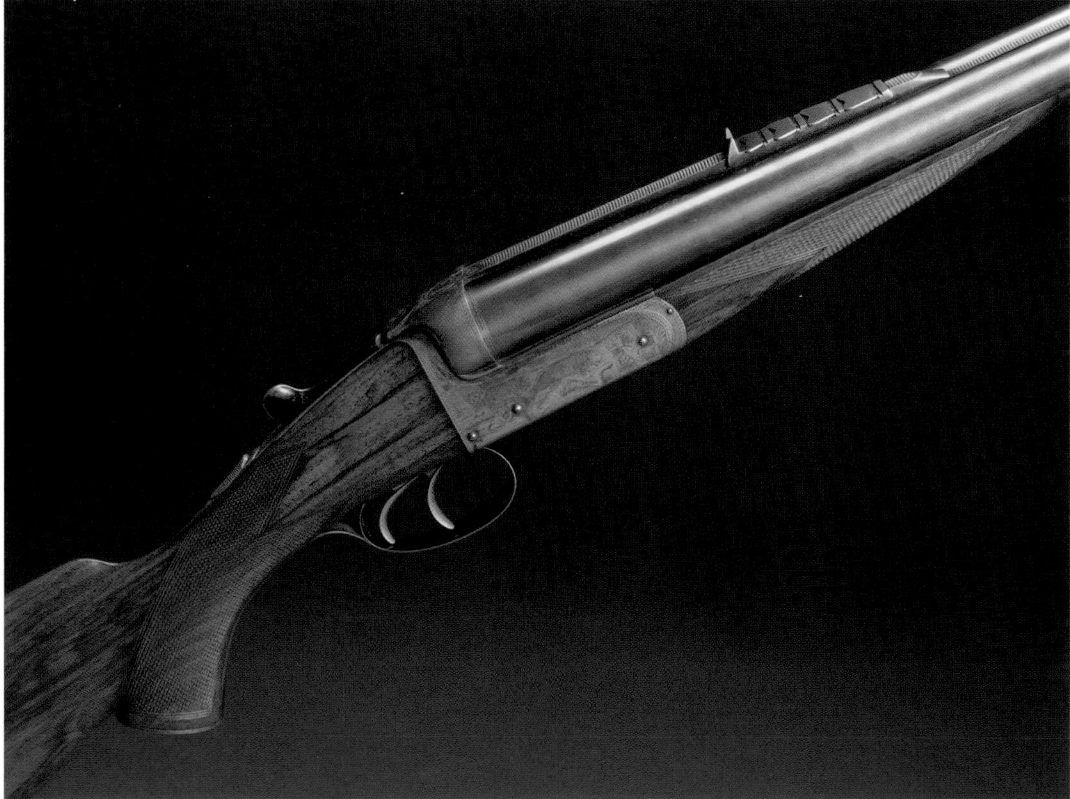

Photo courtesy Greg Martin Auctions, San Francisco; www.GregMartinAuctions.com

Rifle, W.J. Jeffery, double barrel, cased .475 Number 2 Nitro, box-lock ejector. **$25,875**

Photo courtesy Greg Martin Auctions, San Francisco; www.GregMartinAuctions.com

Rifle (sporting), Winchester Model 1873, lever action, deluxe gold and silver inlaid and engraved, with custom sights and relief-carved and checkered walnut stocks. **$54,625**

Rifle, Armalite AR-10T, semiautomatic, serial no. US50040, 308 caliber, 24" round barrel with fiberglass free-floating armguard tube, together with four 20-round and four 10-round magazines and canvas pouch. **$920 all**

Rifle, American Historical Foundation Commemorative, Winchester M-1 Garand, "1 of 100," serial no. 2355102, barrel date 5-44, this is the showcase edition, 30/06 caliber, 24" barrel, military front and rear sights. **$1,035**

Rifle, Armi Jaeger Model AP80, serial no. 019408, .22 long-rifle caliber, 17" barrel. **$230**

Rifle, Armscorp of America M14, semiautomatic, serial no. A004741, 7.62mm, 22" barrel, adjustable military sights. Frame marked Armscorp of America, Baltimore, MD. Rifle is unassembled. **$920**

Rifle, .303 British No. 3 (Pattern 1914), bolt action, .30 caliber, serial no. ERA7211, 26" barrel, standard markings, and British proof marks, War Department broad arrow, with olive-drab canvas sling. **$488**

Rifle, Birmingham Small Arms, Martini action, single shot, serial no. 16577, 25" barrel, marked "Commonwealth of Australia." **$402**

Rifle, Camo U.S. Springfield Model M1-A, semiautomatic, with telescopic sight, serial no. 147618, .30-06 caliber, 24" barrel with recoil compensator. Box with scuffs and wear. **$1,265**

Rifle (carbine), A.O.S.A. American Historical Foundation U.S. Marine Corps Commemorative, serial no. 27515, 45ACP caliber, 19" barrel including muzzle brake, walnut stock complete with sling and sling swivels. **$805**

Rifle (carbine), Winchester Model 94, lever action, serial no. 1836624, .32 Winchester Special, 19 1/2" barrel. **$402**

Rifle, German, Mauser-action magazine, .30 caliber, unmarked, serial no. 3225, 24" replacement barrel, spear front sight on a matted ramped base, action with Redfield aperture sight, wood shows a few nicks and handling marks. **$575**

Rifle, Mossberg Targo 42TR, bolt action, serial no. M336, 20" barrel. **$230**

Rifle, percussion, with octagonal barrel, including ramrod, tiger maple stock, brass mounts, 51 3/4" l (overall); crazed surface on one side. **$632**

Rifle, Siamese Model 1903 Mauser, bolt action, military, produced in Japan, serial no. not visible. Appears to be 7.92 x 57mm caliber, 29" barrel, Thai Chakra stamped on top of breech. **$316**

Rifle, .22 Winchester Magazine RF 61, slide action, serial no. 326996, 24" barrel, standard iron sights. **$1,495**

Rifle, Winchester pre-64 Model 70 National Match, bolt action, serial no. 159460, .30/06, 24" standard-weight barrel, marked Winchester. **$1,725**

Rifle, (sporting), Barrett Model 99, bolt action, high power, single shot, serial no. 0262, .50 caliber, approximately 32" heavyweight barrel, with folding bipod; matte-blue finish, with olive-drab breech. Fitted with IOR 10 x 56 scope for extremely long distance shooting. **$3,162**

Rifle, (sporting), "1 of 1000" Winchester Model 70 Featherweight, gold inlaid and engraved, serial no. UG 485; .270 Winchester caliber, 22" barrel; Big Horn sheep head panel scene engraved on floor plate; two gold-inlaid barrel bands at muzzle; "1 of 1000" flush gold-inlaid on right side of barrel at breech. **$1,840**

Rife, unmarked .30 caliber custom Springfield 1903, bolt-action magazine, no visible serial number, possibly .30-06, 24" barrel. **$287**

Shotgun, .410 Browning Citori Lightning Grade 6, over and under, serial no. 240477PN983, 26" barrels with ventilated rib, marked Made in Japan, boxed. **$2,875**

Shotgun, Browning A-5, light semiautomatic, 12 gauge, serial no. 73G 32290, 27 1/2" barrel with ventilated rib. **$862**

Shotgun, .410 Iver Johnson Skeeter, double barrel, hammerless, serial no. 25148, 28" barrels, automatic safety. **$3,162**

Shotgun, Frank Malin .410 side lock, "The Royal Presentation," gold inlaid, engraved and cased, commemorating the wedding of Prince Charles and Lady Diana Spencer, serial no. 81003, .410 gauge, 27 3/4" side-by-side barrels, British scroll-engraved, solid rib gold inlaid: "F.E. Malin, London, Ont." **$6,900**

Shotgun, Remington Model 11-48, slide action, serial no. 4033682, 28 gauge, 25" ventilated-rib barrel. **$460**

Shotgun, Remington Model 1100 LW, slide action, serial no. L335956H, 24 1/2" barrel. **$402**

Shotgun, Ruger Red Label, 20 gauge, over and under, serial no. 400-12054, 26" barrels with ventilated rib. **$1,495**

Shotgun, L.C. Smith Grade 3, double barrel, hammerless, by Hunter Arms Co., serial no. 202801, 12 gauge, 30" blued barrels with textured rib. **$1,840**

Shotgun, Winchester, 12 gauge, slide action, serial no. 1918194, 28" barrel, wood shows marks and three 1" long scratches on right side. **$258**

Shotgun, Winchester Model 12, pump action, skeet, serial no. 1586740, 20 gauge, 24" ventilated-rib barrel with Cutts compensator. **$546**

Shotgun, Winchester Model 97, slide action, serial no. 380017, 12 gauge, 28" barrel. **$517**

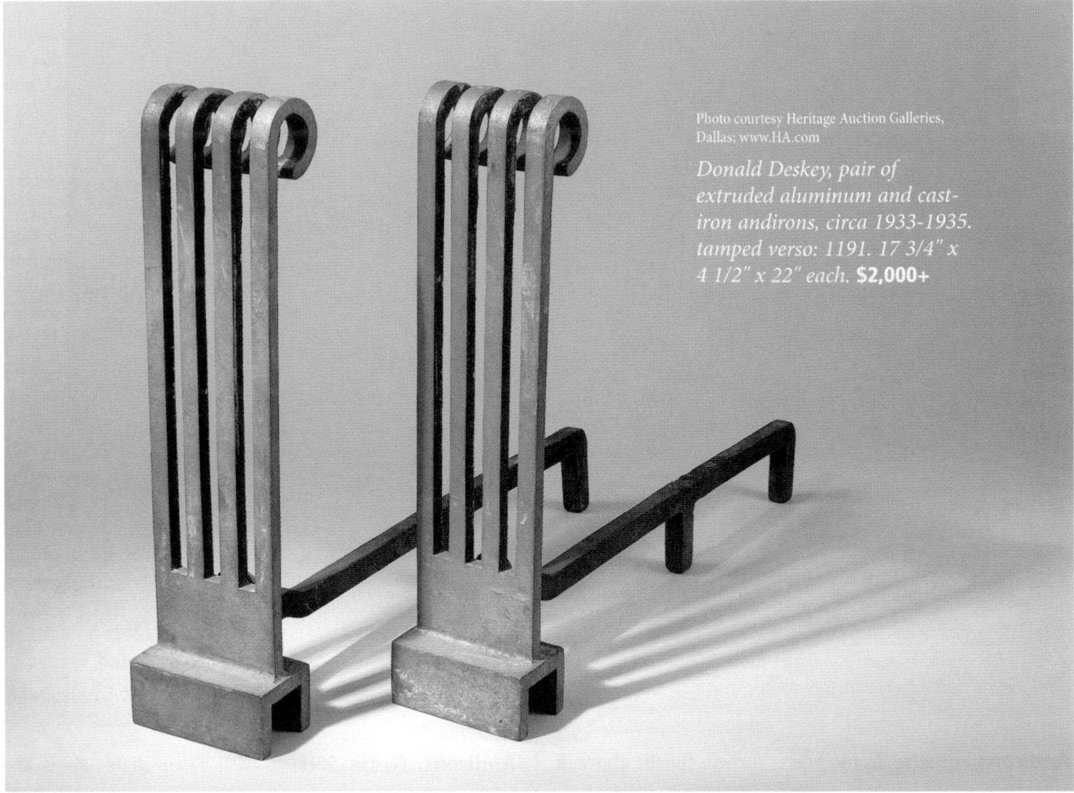
Photo courtesy Heritage Auction Galleries, Dallas; www.HA.com

Donald Deskey, pair of extruded aluminum and cast-iron andirons, circa 1933-1935. tamped verso: 1191. 17 3/4" x 4 1/2" x 22" each. **$2,000+**

Andirons, wrought iron, knife-blade, brass urn-form finials, small in-curved feet, 15 3/4" h. **$143**

Screen, carved mahogany, needlepoint and petit point insert, two arched trestles with leaf carving, 37 1/2" h, 26 1/4" w. **$143**

Screen, pole, George III, mahogany, fluted bun-form finial on round shaft (with fluted knops) supported by four cabriole legs with acanthus-carved knees, adjustable molded screen with ovolo corners, having beaded image of angel and child on light brown woven cloth background, 59" h overall, screen 19 1/2" h, 15" w. **$460**

Screens, pair, George III, mahogany; panel fitted with light brown pleated silk, two ring-turned horizontal stretchers, twin trestle base with four saber legs, bun feet, small folding shelf with two brass supports, circa 1820, 38" h, 17" w, 14 1/4" deep (at base). Repairs to bases of some stiles. .... **$977 pair**

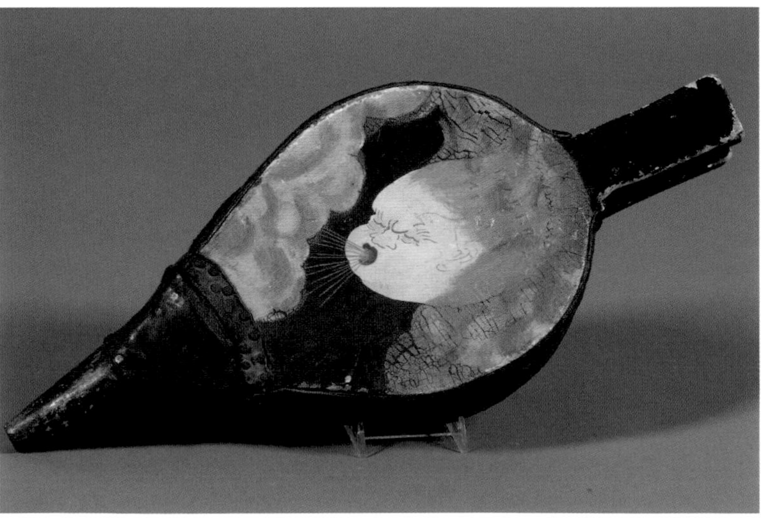
Photo courtesy Skinner Inc., Boston; www.SkinnerInc.com

Bellows, polychrome painted "North Wind" decorated, wood and leather, American, early 19th century, with indistinct impressed maker's mark, "WM DO-----MAKER," bellows torn but still works, 19" l. **$325**

FISHING, HUNTING EQUIPMENT

Bird Decoys

Carved wooden decoys, used to lure waterfowl to the hunter, have become widely recognized as an indigenous American folk-art form. Many decoys are from 1880 to 1930, when commercial gunners commonly hunted and used rigs of several hundred decoys. Fine carvers also worked through the 1930s and 1940s. Individuals and commercial decoy makers also carved fish decoys.

The skill of the carver, rarity, type of bird, condition and age all affect the value.

Black-bellied plover by Obediah Verity. **$94,875**

Black duck by Jess Heisler. **$28,175**

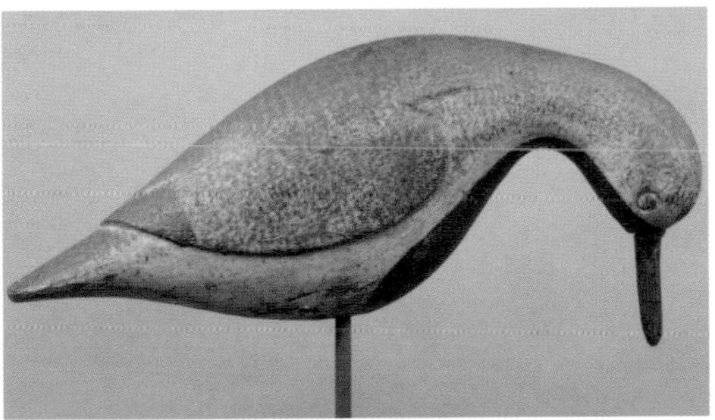

Black-bellied plover, feeding, by Obediah Verity. **$86,250**

Bluebill, "fat jaw," by Charles Perdew. **$15,525**

Black duck by John Blair Sr. **$97,750**

All photos courtesy Guyette & Schmidt Inc., St. Michaels, Md.; www.GuyetteandSchmidt.com

Bluebill hen by Wilfred Benham. **$1,610**

Brant duck by Joseph Lincoln. **$106,375**

Bufflehead drake by the Mason Decoy Factory. **$35,650**

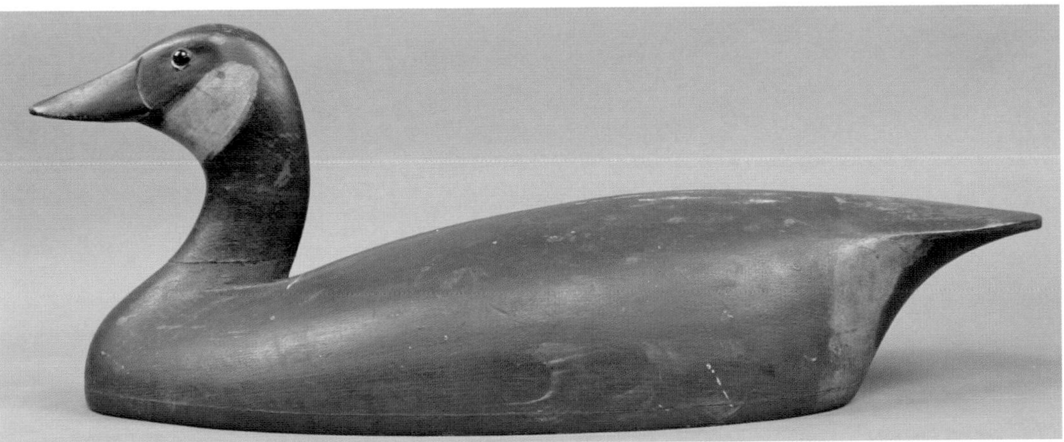

Canada goose by Tom Chambers. **$46,000**

Canvasback by the Ward Brothers. **$43,700**

Curlew by the Mason Decoy Factory. **$24,725**

Mallards (pair) by Heck Winnington. **$8,913**

Merganser hen by Joseph Lincoln. **$83,375**

Mergansers (pair) by Harry V. Shourds. **$46,000**

Peep, running, by Obediah Verity.
$36,800

Pintail by Ivar Fernlund.
$126,000

Pintail hen by John English.
$225,000

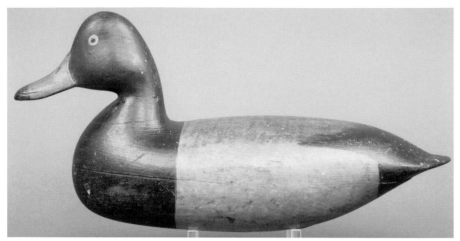

Redhead by Harry V. Shourds. **$28,175**

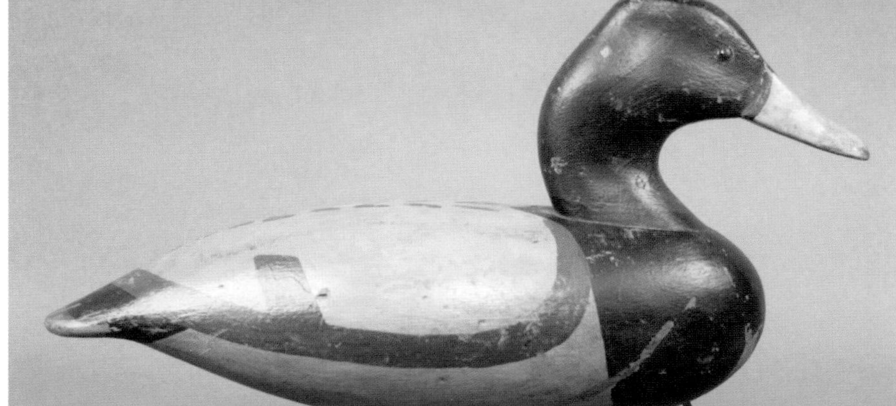

Redhead drake by Mark Whipple. **$11,500**

Ruddy duck by Ben Dye. **$12,650**

Ruddy duck by Lee Dudley. **$269,000**

Sanderling by Daniel Lake Leeds. **$25,300**

Swan, 19th century, from Oregon. **$54,625**

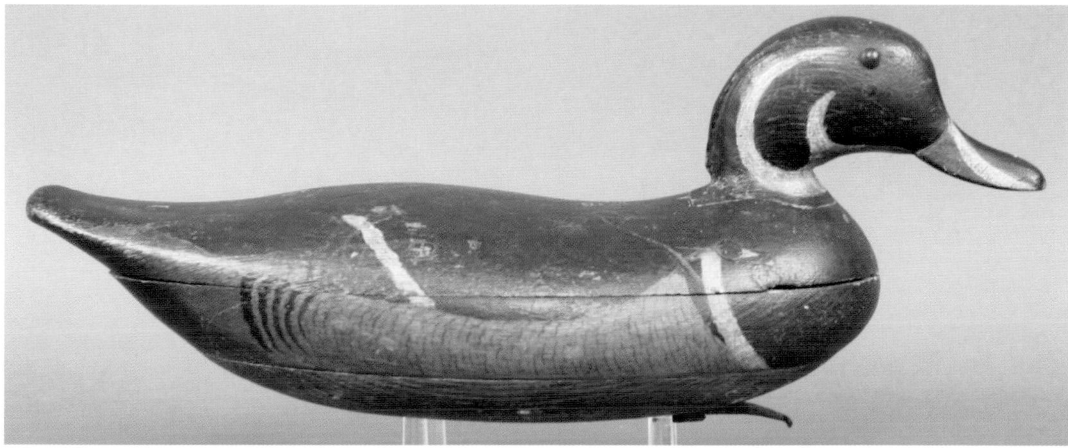

Wood duck drake by John Blair, Sr. **$54,625**

FISHING EQUIPMENT

Lures and Fish Decoys

Chapman # 3 minnow propeller. **$240**

Carl Christiansen whitefish decoy. **$280**

Creek Chub baby jigger. **$398**

Creek Chub Deluxe wagtail. **$673**

All photos courtesy Lang's Sporting Collectibles, Waterville, N.Y.; www.LangsAuction.com

Creek Chub gar minnow. **$354**

DAM Ever Ready "Punkinseed" minnow. **$240**

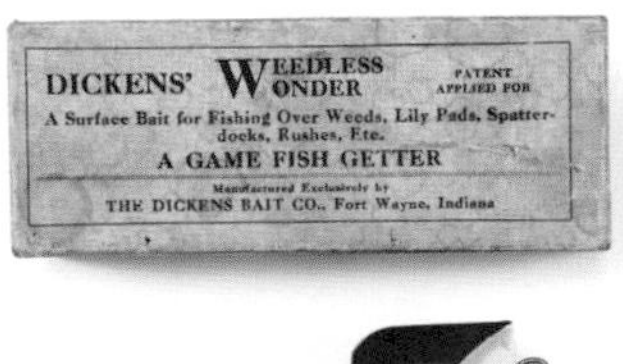

Dicken's Weedless Wonder in box. **$287**

Froglegs Mechanical Fishing Lure in box. **$230**

Heddon Crackleback # 100 minnow. **$172**

Heddon near-surface wiggler. **$360**

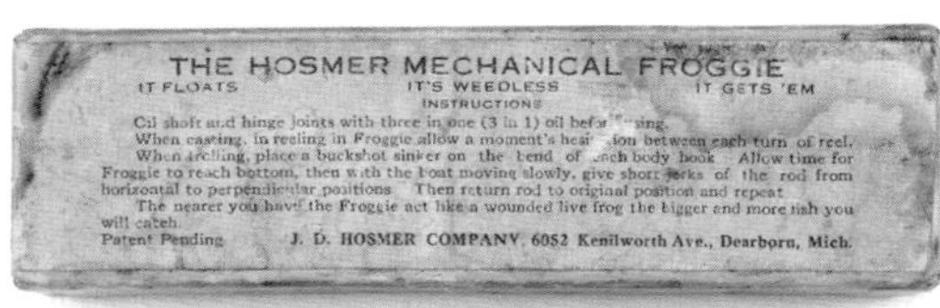

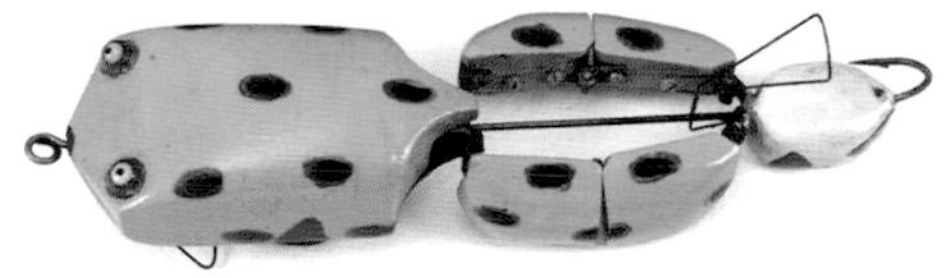

Hosmer Mechanical Froggie in box. **$13,437**

Immell Bait Co. Chippewa minnow. **$918**

Lovelace breathing minnow. **$168**

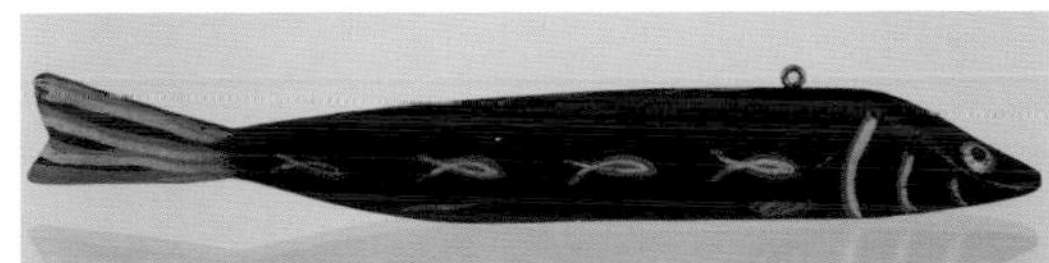

Frank Mizra 9" fish decoy. **$1,163**

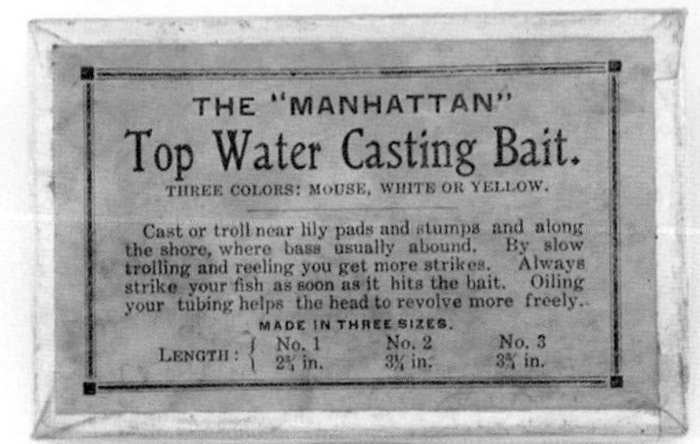

Manhattan top-water casting bait in box. **$306**

Paw Paw pike caster minnow. **$245**

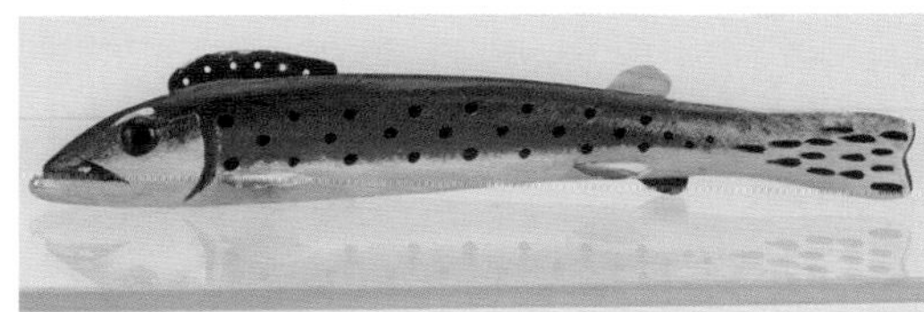

Oscar Peterson trout fish decoy. **$6,944**

Pflueger Crackleback Surprise minnow. **$316**

Pflueger Ketch-Em wooden minnow. **$776**

Pflueger Neverfail underwater minnow. **$316**

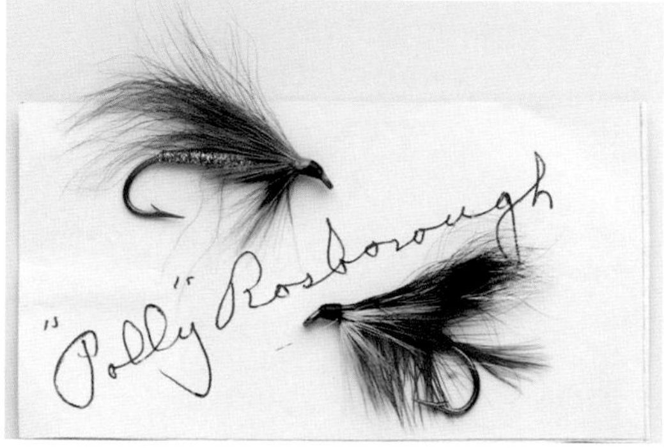

Polly Rosborough flies (two). **$90 pair**

Shakespeare Midget minnow. **$120**

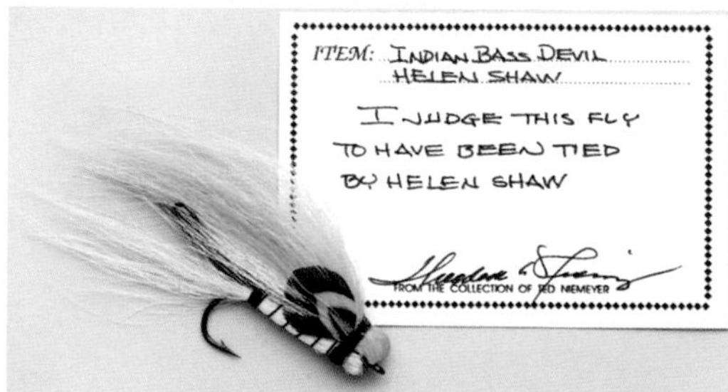

Helen Shaw Indian Bass Devil fly. **$300**

South Bend King-Oreno in box. **$460**

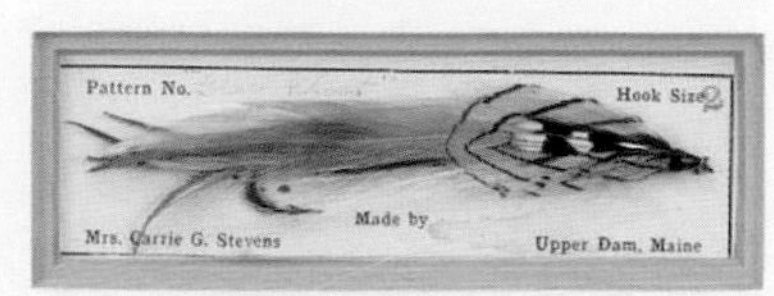

Carrie Stevens streamer fly. **$1,715**

9" Bud Stewart sucker fish decoy. **$300**

Wilson fluted wobbler in box. **$252**

Winchester five-hook underwater minnow. **$460**

Lee Wulff dry fly. **$280**

Reels

Abel Super 11 fly reel. **$431**

Alcedo Omnia Minor ultra-light reel. **$198**

Acme First Click trout reel. **$488**

Ambassadeur 2500C Deluxe reel. **$252**

Billinghurst birdcage fly reel in box (record price for an American reel at auction). **$40,320**

Kopf raised-pillar casting reel. **$2,587**

Leonard-Mills grilse reel. **$896**

Kovalovsky 14/0 big-game reel. **$9,520**

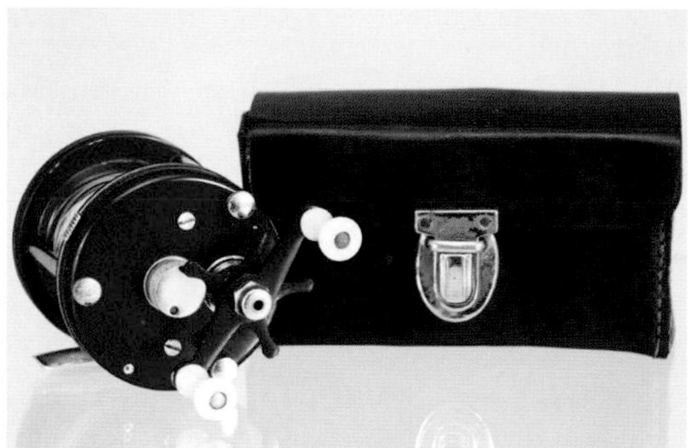

Record Ambassadeur 5000 casting reel. **$258**

H.L. Leonard marbelized fly reel. **$29,120**

Redington large arbor fly reel. **$172**

Saracione Monarch fly reel. **$546**

Silas Terry fly reel. **$252**

Seamaster Mark III fly reel with bag. **$1,150**

A.B. Shipley & Son ball-handle reel. **$501**

Wm. Shakespeare Style B reel. **$240**

Edward Vom Hofe Restigouche salmon reel. **$1,495**

Edward Vom Hofe tournament casting reel. **$3,307**

Yawman & Erbe Automatic reel. **$214**

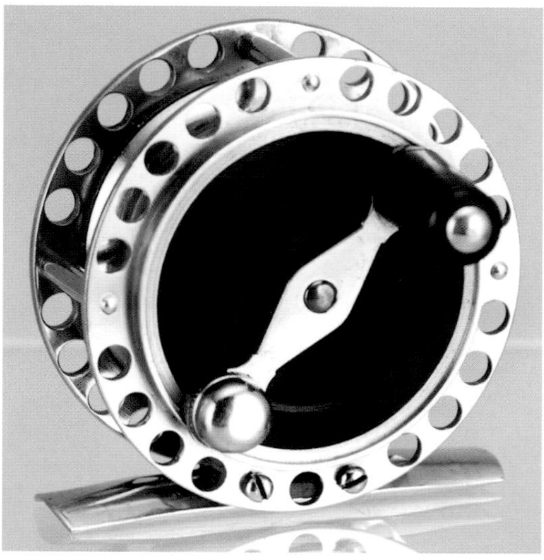

Julius Vom Hofe perforated fly reel. **$14,375**

Zwarg 1/0 salmon fly reel. **$2,082**

Arthur Walker Model TR-2 fly reel. **$2,180**

Rods

6' Airex-Uslan spinning rod. **$224**

8' L.L. Bean trout rod. **$367**

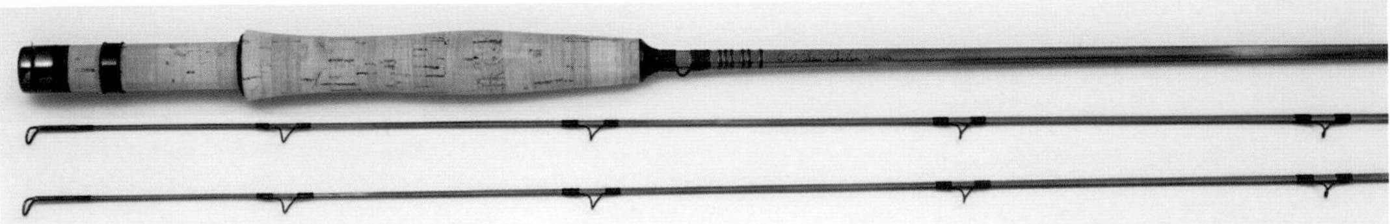

7 1/2' Sam Carlson "Four" trout rod. **$7,043**

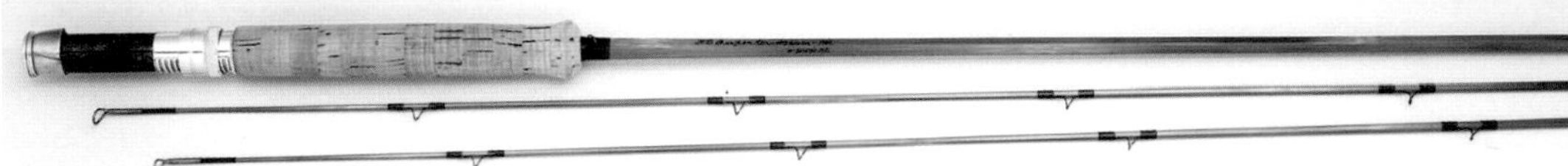

8 1/2' Walt Carpenter fly rod. **$3,480**

11 1/2' Conroy Bissett salmon rod. **$1,200**

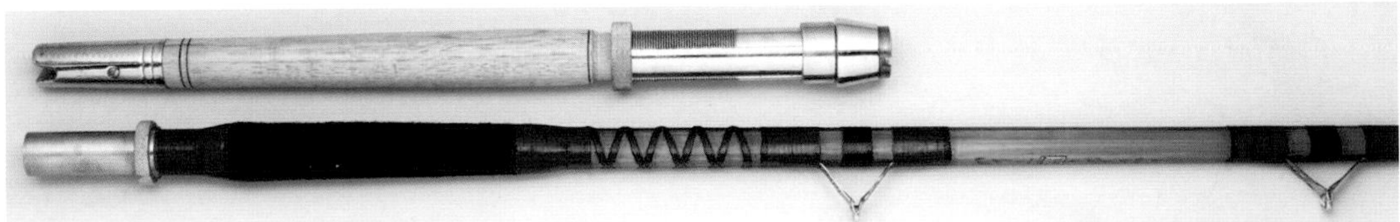

6' 10" Custom Tycoon rod. **$805**

9' Edwards Quadrate trout rod. **$857**

8' Gene Edwards DeLuxe fly rod. **$532**

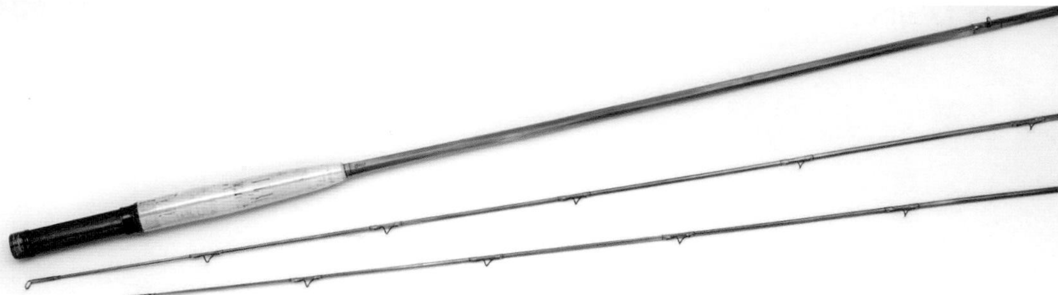

7 1/2' Leonard Ausable 39-5 fly rod. **$2,072**

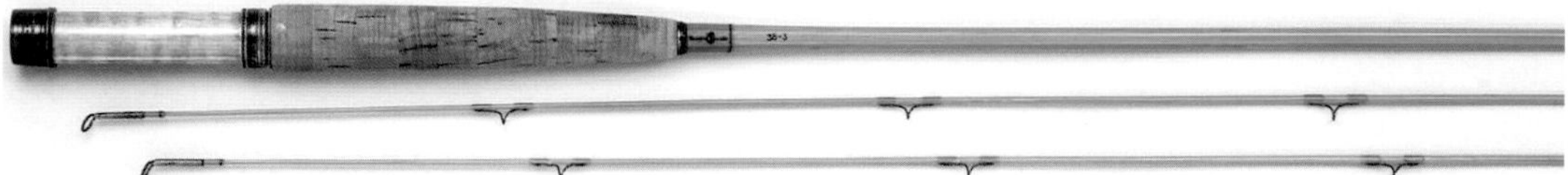

7' Leonard Model # 38 fly rod. **$2,200**

9' Orvis antique fly rod. **$1,041**

8' Orvis Battenkill fly rod. **$420**

6' Orvis Superfine fly rod. **$918**

9 1/2' Payne salmon rod. **$517**

7' 9" Spring Creek Series fly rod. **$390**

8' Thomas & Thomas Hendrickson rod. **$977**

Other Objects

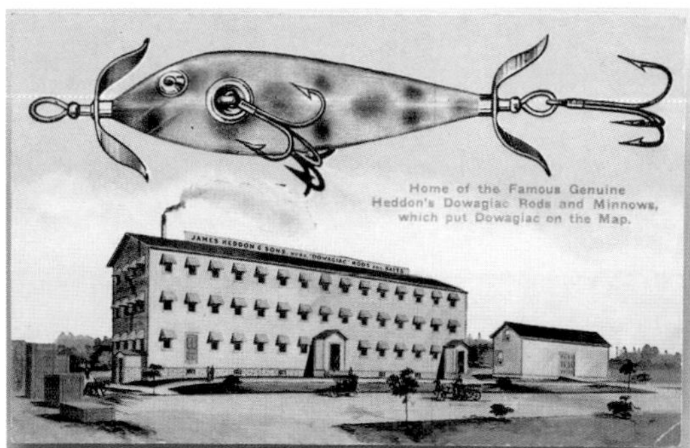

1912 Heddon postcard. **$560**

Antique slide-top wooden fly box. **$510**

1880s Chubb Rod Co. catalog. **$402**

Davis ice fishing tip-up. **$448**

Copper minnow bucket. **$390**

"The Fisherman" ship pennant, ex-Zane Grey collection. **$21,450**

Fighting chair, ex-Zane Grey collection. **$24,640**

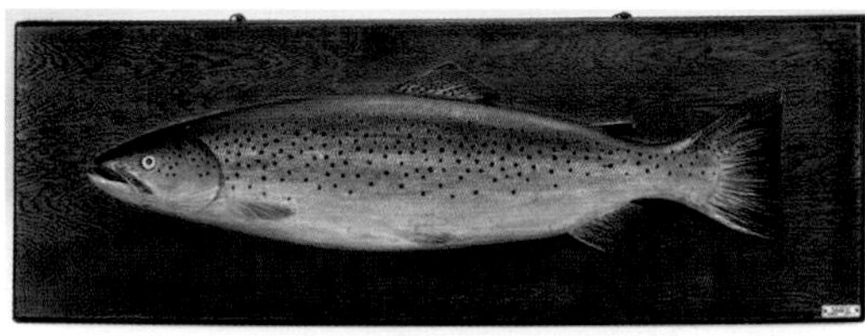

W.B. Griggs carved trout plaque. **$9,890**

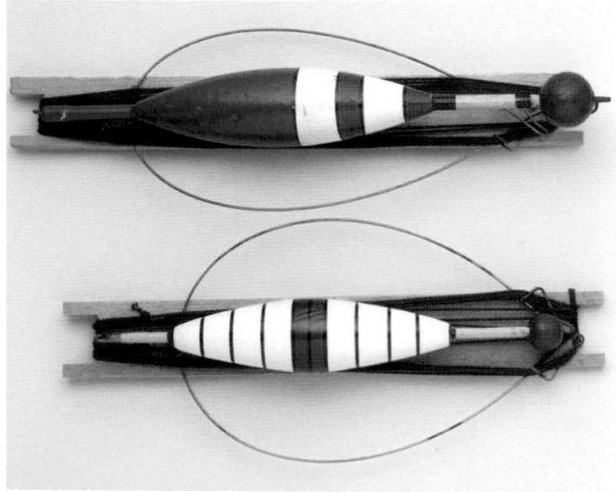

Ideal bobbers (two). **$210 pair**

George Lawrence creel. **$1,792**

Leather-covered tackle box. **$390**

Leather-bound turtle creel. **$1,020**

Native American Salish creel. **$4,255**

Tackle shop fish sign, metal. **$2,990**

OCT 20 '11

SEASON OF 1912

CATALOGUE

...OF...

JULIUS VOM HOFE

351 SOUTH FIFTH STREET

BROOKLYN BOROUGH

NEW YORK CITY

Julius Vom Hofe 1912 catalog. **$690**

Walnut and brass fly chest. **$3,024**

Zane Grey record broadbill photograph, 1926. **$4,287**

Folk Art

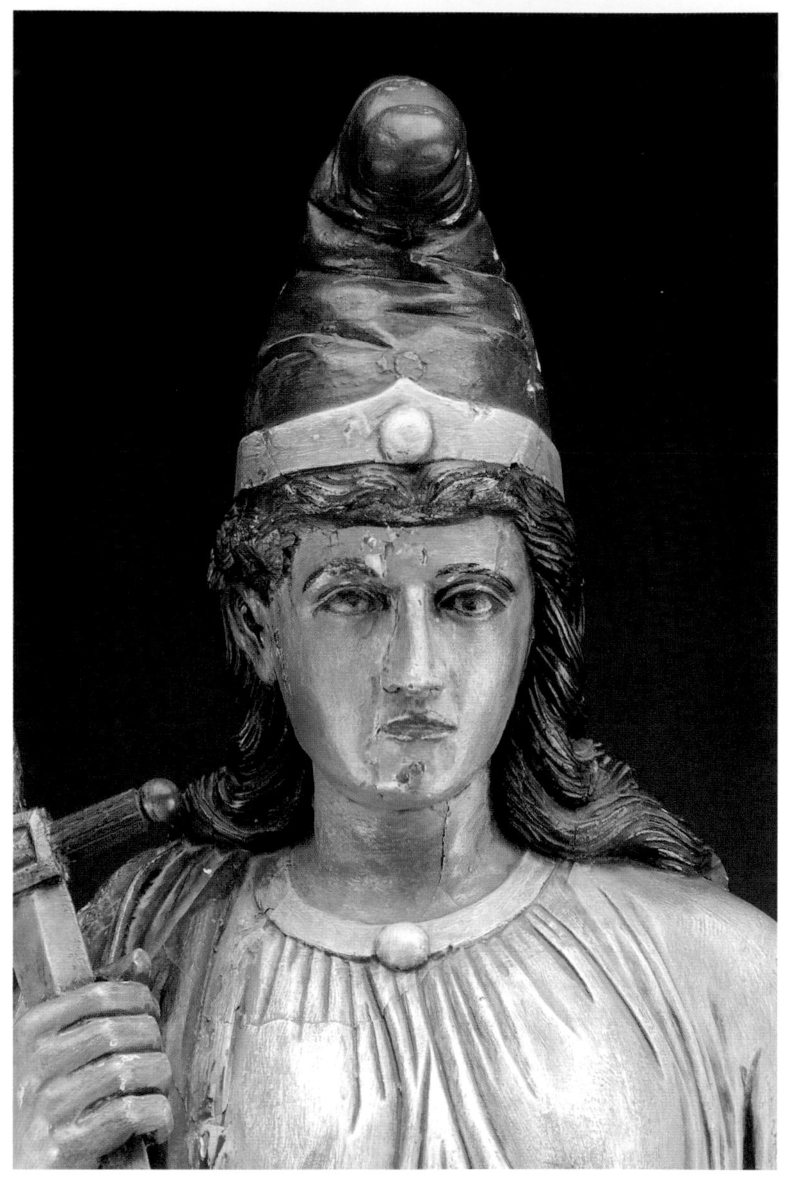

FUTURE OF THE MARKET: FOLK ART

Folk art captivates, but what is it?

By Tim Chambers
Missouri Plain Folk, Sikeston, Mo.

Folk art? What in the world is it? Where can I find it? How do I know what it is worth when I do find it? This is, in fact, what I deal with every day in my line of work. Work? Yes, Mother. After almost 20 years I still have close friends who can't figure out what it is I do when I get up in the morning! By accident or choice, I've become a dealer in early and vintage folk art, almost exclusively American.

This seemingly ambiguous material in the world of antiques captivated my wife and me early on in my dawning desire to become an antiques dealer in the late 1980s. My wife, Charline, is equally attracted to folk art. She shares many of the duties of the business with me, but she will also be the first to tell you it's "Tim's business," and a business it is. So, as in any other business, a working knowledge is needed to perform to the best of one's ability. Whether in the business of buying and selling folk art, which I am, or in the "business" of collecting folk art, the rules remain the same. We should gather as much information about our interests in order to be more educated. The more knowledge and understanding of the task at hand, the greater the confidence we have in our pursuits. The satisfaction we derive from a job well done only adds to our enjoyment in doing what we like!

Folk art as a classification of antiques very likely offers more opportunity to express our individuality based on the pieces we purchase. The almost endless variety of material that falls under the category of folk art makes this possible. Experts have a difficult time agreeing on a conclusive definition of what constitutes folk art, but can agree on the attraction to be found in its many forms. For example, two items commonly referred to as folk art today are early manufactured weathervanes, as well as handmade weathervanes, which were created in more humble circumstances. What is important to note are the similarities in such diverse objects and not their obvious differences. Consider a horse weathervane of finely molded copper by one of America's commercial makers around the turn of the 20th century. The other a simpler but well conceived silhouette of a horse made of sheet iron or wood by a capable farmer. In either case the objects were intended for a utilitarian purpose, but a sense of beauty is found in both. It is that beauty which they have in common. An awareness of this link between two such dissimilar objects is of utmost importance when it comes to an understanding of folk art. It is an appreciation of this innate beauty that must be achieved by collectors and dealers to develop the skills needed to recognize a great piece of folk art.

"Beauty is in the eye of the beholder." Regarding folk art, this old cliché is probably as accurate and to the point as anything I could write. Simply put, we are most inclined

to pursue an object we're drawn to. That beauty we're beholding in any piece of folk art must resonate on a personal level. This is one of the great attractions folk art offers for the dealer and the collector: the freedom to follow one's own interests. If we're going to acquire folk art that pleases us, this is perhaps one of the most important aspects to be understood. Even as a dealer, it is my experience that when it comes to folk art, my customers expect me to be passionate about the piece. If I'm not passionate, then the chances are my customer won't be either. At that point it becomes very difficult to make a sale! Likewise, if you're buying for your collection, isn't it logical to surround yourself with pieces for which you have great affection? Buy what you like!

Don't know what you like? Let's see if we can work on that! Due to the vast array of categories that fall under the heading of folk art, perhaps the most important first step is to simply look at some. This may sound incredibly naïve, but it really is the best way to begin forming your own opinions, likes, and dislikes. When you've looked at enough, trust me, you will know what I mean.

There are any number of ways this can be accomplished. Without a doubt the very best approach is to see and touch pieces firsthand. Go to an antiques show. These venues offer the chance to see a broad selection of pieces from a wide variety of dealers. My wife and I participate in about 15 antiques shows a year, from California to Connecticut. I can tell you plainly that nothing makes us happier than to have someone interested in learning about a piece we have in our display. The majority of dealers I know enjoy sharing information concerning the material they have for sale. It is this constant dialogue that provides the ongoing education in folk art for collectors and dealers alike. The point is, if you have real interest in something, engage the dealer in conversation regarding your interests. What you learn can become groundwork for the future. From a dealer's perspective I can tell you it is time well spent for both my customer and myself. Such conversations may not result in a sale at that time, but every effort is made to see that the customer leaves my space knowing more about the item of interest than when they entered. Even if it ultimately turns out to be something that would never interested them to the point of purchase, they leave with a greater insight and more information to add to a growing knowledge of folk art.

Single-owner shops also offer excellent opportunities. Besides the same hands on shopping that a show provides, a single-owner shop can be especially helpful from a regional stand point. Often the inventory found in a local shop is just that, local. The shop owner may be able to provide more details as to the maker and origin of a given piece. It is always a bonus to get the history along with the object. This may also increase the object's value.

Group shops and antiques centers are also helpful in terms of looking at and comparing different items. Although some are not equipped to field a lot of questions concerning the goods they have for sale, they do allow the methodical shopper ample time to peruse the aisles at their own speed. Undoubtedly, museums as well as reference books offer a wealth of information that can be turned to on a regular basis. Collectors themselves can be one of the best sources for information due to their experience over a period of time. Virtual shopping can also be helpful. With the information available on the Internet, anyone with access to a computer has a world of knowledge at their fingertips. Web sites specializing in antiques and folk art are increasing daily.

Photo courtesy Heritage Auction Galleries, Dallas; www.HA.com

Patriotic Folk Art Carte de Visite Frame. 19 1/2" x 11 1/4", carved of walnut with CDV frame at the center, at top surrounded by scroll work, leaves. The central panel depicts a scroll suspended from an arrow and chain with the carved date "Jan. 1st 1863". The lower section composed of an American shield with 13 stars flanked by furled flags. One crack. **$1,912**

We are now to the point where I tell you what folk art is. I wish I could. Actually that's not entirely true. There are many accepted areas of collecting when it comes to folk art. Most of these categories by definition refer to goods made by hand. Countless objects were made down on the farm, up in the city, or somewhere in between. Whether driven by necessity or a desire to create, folks hooked rugs, sewed quilts, painted game boards or constructed a whirligig just to see which way the wind was blowing. Maybe a sign was needed to show the way to the apple orchard. A means was needed to hold an ashtray, so a cut-out painted butler extending his arm was created for the job. The list goes on. Children made things at church or school, soldiers made things while in training or on the frontlines. And who can forget the tramps? Look at all the tramp art that exists. (Actually there's no proof that tramps were that prolific when it came to chip carving.) Frankly, it is human nature to create and most of those objects created fall somewhere in the definition of folk art. What is considered the most desirable in this abundance of choices? That, of course, varies from person to person. However, it is safe to say the best example of anything in its field becomes the standard by which all other examples are judged.

The central questions remains: Why the attraction and what gives folk art value? As I've tried to point out, the attraction is and should be personal. It may simply come from an appreciation of the object and the maker's ability to create it. Folk art often represents a slower, less complicated time, which resonates with many of us. Then there's just plain old American ingenuity, which can be intriguing. Something was needed and something was made. Just because it was a necessity didn't mean it couldn't be artfully accomplished.

Value: If you think it's hard to completely understand what folk art is, let me tell you, value can be even harder to define. Consider the fact that, by definition, nearly all examples of folk art are essentially one of a kind. Value, on the other hand, is generally determined by comparing two similar objects. One is deemed better than the other and is thus given a higher value. That's tough to do when there's only one exactly like this one. That being said, comparison is still the closest means of assigning a value to a piece. This is another example of the importance of looking at as much material as you can to create your own database regarding prices. Like any other field of collecting, there are the basics of age, condition and desirability that come into play. As a dealer, I'm often asked why a piece is priced higher than another piece. I always try to give the simplest answer: "More people want this one. It was that way when I bought it and will be that way when I sell it."

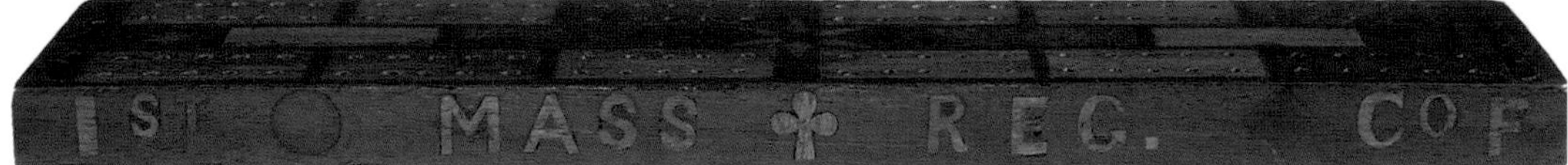

Photo courtesy Heritage Auction Galleries, Dallas; www.HA.com

Folk Art Cribbage Board with Inlaid ID to John Noyes, 1st Mass. Inf Measures 2 1/4" x 9 3/4" x 1/2". Playing surface inlaid with squares for pegs and decorated with stars. The side of the board is inlaid all the way around with "J. N. 1st Mass Reg. Co. F 1864 Feb Brandy Station Va." with Corps badges inlaid between each of the words. Small compartment with sliding lid on the bottom to store the pegs (missing). Overall in perfect condition with an old coat of varnish. Noyes enlisted on May 24, 1861, and served with the regiment until muster out on May 25, 1864. **$4,780**

If you have read this far then you are well aware that you have learned everything there is to know about folk art. Just kidding! I do hope you have a better understanding of the subject. We have discussed what it is and places to look for it. Now let's get to the fun part and talk about buying some! Let's say we have $10,000 available to purchase folk art. Where should we spend it? Well, let's understand a basic principal first. Folk art, and antiques in general for that matter, are very much a "fashion" business. Things rise and fall in popularity/desirability. It's not quite Seventh Avenue, but there are trends. What's hot now? Most things of a visual, colorful nature seem to be right at the top of the list. I'm known for painted game boards, having written a book on the subject. I can tell you firsthand the more colorful a game board the more desirable, hence the more expensive, as I explained earlier. To put it another way, I would take some of that $10,000 and purchase one great colorful game board, not four mediocre brown ones (sorry, brown!). A great weathervane is always desirable. Again, the wise buy is the one in the budget in the best condition with wonderful form. Hand-painted trade signs remain at the top of the list. Here are a couple of pointers in making a choice: consider the subject matter and the graphics. A colorful sign advertising strawberries will generally be more desirable than a more colorful sign advertising funerals.

The truth of the matter is, with $10,000 you could absolutely fill a house and have money left over with some types of folk art. On the other hand, $10,000 would not even be a decent down payment on some single pieces. To me this is the beauty of this area of collecting. No matter how deep your pockets, I can promise you one thing. It's not what it costs you that will bring satisfaction in folk art. It's what living with it does for you. So far, no one has been able to put a price on that!

I would like to close with some encouraging words. First, for those of us attracted to folk art, it is an endless source of pleasure and we welcome those new to this area of collecting. It is truly an adventure. This material, in all its forms, has been produced all over the world since man's arrival. Even as this country was being formed some 400 years ago, folk artists were among the colonists. As the population spread west, so did they. Folk art in one form or another can be found almost anywhere we are. I haven't really talked about age, but folk art is generally accepted from its earliest origins up to the mid-20th century. That's a large body of work. Ultimately there is plenty to go around. Now, get out there and find it! And remember, buy what you like!

Tim Chambers and his wife, Charline, are active dealers in folk art and Americana, doing business at shows across the country as Missouri Plain Folk. In 2001, Tim authored the book, The Art of the Game, showcasing the game-board collection of Selby Shaver. As a result, Chambers works extensively with collectors in this field. Besides game boards, Missouri Plain Folk is known for vintage Americana with an emphasis on surface, form, color and graphic impact. An ever-changing selection of game boards and Americana may be found on their Web site: www.missouriplainfolk.com.

Also see Advertising, Art, Quilts.

Photo courtesy Heritage Auction Galleries, Dallas; www.HA.com

Leach Signed Folk Carving Bull Head Wall Plaque, circa 1870s. Detailed bull's head with glass eyes. Often used by butchers as a trade sign, examples by this artist have become increasingly difficult to find. The back is marked "H LEACH WOBURN MASS". Approximately 13 3/4" x 16 1/4". Leach's works can be found at such museums as the Shelburne and the Smithsonian. **$5,228**

Carousel chariot boards, set of two, red-painted wood, possibly by Gustav Dentzel, circa 1900, 46" x 78". .... **$300 both**

Carousel horse, Karl Muller (attributed), prancer with original paint and detailed overall carvings, late 19th/early 20th century, 64" x 62". **$3,600**

Carousel horse, Parker, 19th-20th century, outside row "Flying Horse" is shown with all legs up, turned head and intricately carved mane, head and tail. The old park paint surface shows a light brown horse with white mane and tail, with a green, blue and orange blanket with brown and orange-trimmed saddle. There is a large grape cluster carving on hindquarters. Glass jewel decoration on bridle, blanket and front. Marked on bottom of all four hooves "Parker, Leavenworth, Kansas". With display stand, approx. 51" h x 60" l, minor defects. **$4,830**

Eagle, American, late 19th century, with yellow beak, carved with spread wings clutching three arrows and green-painted branch in talons, 17" l, repair to left wing and small losses to both wingtips, good patina. **$575**

Eagle, American, carved and paint-decorated wall plaque in the manner of John Haley Bellamy, late 19th century, depicted with shield, 47" w. Retains all original surfaces, with repairs to upper and lower beak and old repair to right upper wing facing. Head retains original dowel fastener. **$3,335**

Eagle, carved and gilded, depicted in full flight with good details to the wings. Carved from pine, 34" x 15", modern replaced gilding, chip to upper beak and seam repairs

Photo courtesy Skinner Inc., Boston; www.SkinnerInc.com

Fire bucket, painted leather, American, early 19th century, with leather handle painted dark blue with polychrome scrolled foliage and lettering "No. 1, Semper Fidelis," and "Thomas Carter 1815," paint losses, 12 1/4" h to top of collar. **$1,185**

Photo courtesy Skinner Inc., Boston; www.SkinnerInc.com

Fencepost whimsy, green-painted, carved, wooden with birds, American, late 19th/early 20th century, including stand, minor wear, overall 15 1/4" h, 15 3/4" d. **$1,070**

Photo courtesy Morphy Auctions, Denver, Pa.; www.MorphyAuctions.com

Folk art Victrola in carved-wood cabinet with floral and reptilian decoration. **$5,750.**

Photos courtesy Heritage Auction Galleries, Dallas; www.HA.com

Carved Civil War Pipe. Massive size and weight carved entirely by hand of burl wood. The front of the pipe is deeply carved with a full-spread-wing eagle with shield, holding a riband in its beak, "The Union Now And Forever". One side of the pipe is carved with an artillery piece with "64" on the barrel, doubtless referring to the date the pipe was made. The other side of the pipe depicts a mounted soldier. The back of the pipe is carved with the nude figure of a woman holding a riband inscribed "Liberty", the whole surrounded by a laurel wreath. The flat bottom of the pipe bears the incised carved legend, "Made In Camp Near Falmouth, Va. By Benj. G. Chapman 146 NYSV". The pipe is in perfect untouched condition, with no indication of having been smoked. Chapman enlisted in the 146th on Oct. 10, 1862, and served with the regiment until May 3, 1863, when he transferred to the Veteran Reserve Corps. The 146th, known as Garrard's Tigers, were, for a period, uniformed as Zouaves. The regiment was heavily engaged at Chancellorsville and Gettysburg during Chapman's term of service. Accompanied by a complete set of records. **$5,377** along the body extending into the right wing facing. **$345**

Paperweight, carved in form of an ear of corn, bone or horn, realistically depicting a partially husked ear of corn with graduated kernels and tipped with silk, 11 1/4" l, original patina, corn-silk tips showing dark patina, overall mellow ivory color. **$1,610**

Sculpture, carved wood and burl, three-dimensional scene showing building landscape and train with locomotive, tender and two cars. Carved wooden portrait surmounts frame, exhibits some minor wood loss and crazing to some varnish, 28" x 39". **$1,035**

Sign, carved and painted wood, "Post Office," American, 19th century, arched pine panel with applied molding, the lettering painted mustard yellow on a cream-colored ground, (minor molding losses), 16 1/2" h, 31 3/4" w. **$2,962**

Whimsy bottle, rack with birds, flower pots, etc., signed "Adam Selig" and dated "1891"; fan-like form below signature; painted blue, brick red on wood, large bottle, 11 1/8" h. **$316**

Whimsy bottle with animals by Daniel Rose, two squirrels on pedestals and three stylized trees below, fan-form upper section, 7 3/4" h. **$1,380**
(Daniel Rose [1871-1926] was a master whittler and bottle-whimsy maker living in Johnstown, Pa. He created elaborate and delicate folk art despite suffering with debilitating rheumatism from an early age.)

Whimsy bottle, with Christ on cross, interior with meticulous wood construction, 10" h. **$316**

Whimsy bottle, red and white yarn, wood stopper, 6 3/4" h, inscribed on paper on bottom: "Made by/H. H. Hutchins Feb. 14, 1914". **$420**

Photo courtesy Heritage Auction Galleries, Dallas; www.HA.com

Devil's Island Handmade Miniature Wood and Metal Guillotine, "Prisoner's Art." An inscription under the lid of the coffin which lies beside the machine of death reads "Ile du Diable / H de H 1928." An accompanying handwritten letter from collector Robert White states that it was purchased from a doctor's collection of prison art. Devil's Island was the French prison off the northern coast of South America. It was abandoned in 1938. This highly detailed model is in excellent condition and stands 14" tall. **$600**

Photo courtesy James D. Julia Auctioneers, Fairfield, Maine; www.JuliaAuctions.com

Grotesque Carved Folk Art Pine Center Table. Last quarter of the 19th Century. The rectangular tray top with serpentine and scalloped edging projecting above the heavily carved rectangular frieze, the corners carved with theatrical masks, one end carved with a fanciful crouching cat flanked by leaf tips, the opposing end carved with a fanciful leaping horse above a stag's head. One long side carved with a wide-eyed, winged, fanciful full moon mask among C and S scrolling volutes, the opposing long side with similar scrollwork centering a tornado-like funnel. The whole raised on exaggerated, tapering, cabriole legs with shell-carved knees and claw feet with knuckled toes. 28 1/2" h. x 39 1/2" l. x 26 1/2" d. With weathered and worn original white paint. Loss to tail of horse, some losses to toes, small knothole at end of top at edge. **$26,450**

Photo courtesy James D. Julia Auctioneers, Fairfield, Maine; www.JuliaAuctions.com

Grotesque Carved Folk Art Pine Console Table. Last quarter of the 19th Century. The rectangular tray top with wavy-molded edges above the conforming wide frieze fancifully carved with grotesque theatrical masks on the corners, the ends each carved with the face of a bearded gentleman. The front apron carved with a displayed eagle in high relief, flanked by two seated gentlemen wearing long coats and brimmed hats, further flanked by flags. The legs in the form of carved leaf-tip and scrolled corbels, raised on S-scrolled, knuckled, and acanthus-carved feet. 28 1/2" h. x 41" w. x 21 1/4" d. The top with heavily weathered surface and shrinkage crack through center. Original white paint, scrubbed on top, discolored on table base. Structural damages as follows: one leg missing on seated gentleman, half of one eagle foot missing, damages to two feet on table.
$25,300

Photos courtesy James D. Julia Auctioneers, Fairfield, Maine; www.JuliaAuctions.com

Patriotic Carved Wood Figure of the "Goddess of Liberty". Last quarter 19th century. Carved and polychrome painted, she is depicted standing erect wearing a soft peaked "Liberty" cap, dressed in a full-length white tunic with rolled sleeves, draped in a red robe trimmed in gold. In her right hand she holds a sword, in her left a laurel wreath and federal shield, her sandaled feet showing beneath her robe. Carved standing on a square stepped plinth, further raised on a larger box plinth with canted sides, carved with swag draperies and mounted with carrying handles. 53" h. of statue. 71" overall h. 25" sq. base. This figure was originally discovered by Helena Penrose of New York City, who was a friend and colleague of Abby Aldridge Rockefeller in the pursuit of folk art during the 1930s and '40s. Penrose was an acknowledged authority and dealer on American folk art carvings, assisting in research with A.W. Pendergast in the compilation for Cigar Store Figures in American Folk Art, 1953 and also in Tuttle's et al Drawing on America's Past: Folk Art, Modernism and the Index of American Design. When Penrose sold the figure to a wealthy, avid antique collector, in the late 1940s/early '50s for a "significant" amount of money, she informed him that this figure originally resided in Tammany Hall in New York City before 1920. It was removed and was then present at the inauguration of President Harry Truman. Around the period of 1850 to 1900 there were likely a considerable number of similar patriotic goddess figures in use throughout the country, unlike cigar store figures which were manufactured in large numbers for purposes of business, these were likely far fewer in number and today only a handful survive. The entire surface was repainted some time ago, possibly done by Penrose in the 1940s when she acquired and sold this. Prior to repainting, the checks, cracks and separations were plastered, the largest of which were on the backside draped figure, however there were various other separations scattered over the figure, most nearly all of which have been re-gessoed prior to repaint. The cross-guard of the sword was also probably repainted at that time. The carvings on the base are original and the base appears to be original to the figure and has some old modifications on the interior. There are no modern restorations or repaint on any part of the figure. Note: This and other carved figures of their type were designed to be transported in parades and/or displayed in public or semi-public places, hence the installation of carrying handles on the primary plinth. This use also subjected these figures to stresses and torque from repeated moving and to extreme and frequent weather changes while out of doors. Any damages and subsequent restorations, including any areas of in-painting or repainting, whether of 19th- or 20th-century origin, were done for cosmetic reasons and not with the intent of disguising any element of this figure. **$143,750**

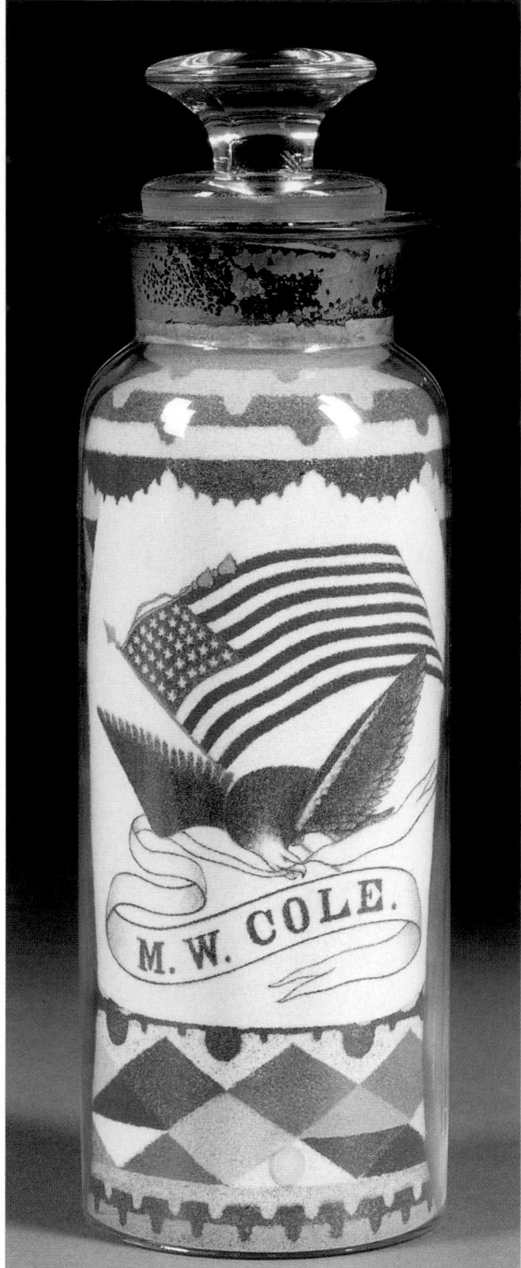

Photo courtesy Skinner Inc., Boston; www.SkinnerInc.com

Sand Picture in a Glass Bottle with American Eagle, Flag, and Urn of Flowers, Andrew Clemens, McGregor, Iowa, circa 1885, multicolored sand arranged in a glass bottle, one side of the bottle portraying an American eagle in flight, an American flag, and a banner reading "M.W. COLE," the reverse depicting a flower-filled urn, both designs flanked by several multicolored and shaped borders, 9 3/4" h. Note: Andrew Clemens was born in Dubuque, Iowa, in 1857. At the age of five he became deaf and mute after an illness. He earned his livelihood by painstakingly arranging colored sand to make pictures in glass bottles. The sand came from the naturally colored sandstone in the Pictured Rocks area of Iowa. He worked in McGregor, and for a short time he made and exhibited his work at South Side Museum, a dime museum in Chicago, Ill. He died in 1894 at the age of 37. **$7,110**

Photo courtesy Skinner Inc., Boston; www.SkinnerInc.com

Sand Picture in a Glass Bottle with Ship, Andrew Clemens, McGregor, Iowa, 1889, the multicolored sand arranged to show a foreshortened ship and distant vessels in a reserve on one side and the name and date "H.A. BAILEY 1889" flanked by multicolored geometric and marbled borders, (some sand shifting on upper border), 6 5/8" h. The cover is loose. Some substance was applied to the top sand surface prevent further shifting of sand. Note: Andrew Clemens was born in Dubuque, Iowa, in 1857. At the age of five he became deaf and mute after an illness. He earned his livelihood by painstakingly arranging colored sand to make pictures in glass bottles. The sand came from the naturally colored sandstone in the Pictured Rocks area of Iowa. He worked in McGregor, and for a short time he made and exhibited his work at South Side Museum, a dime museum in Chicago, Ill. He died in 1894 at the age of 37. **$1,896**

SCRIMSHAW

Scrimshaw is the name given to handiwork created by whalers made from the byproducts of harvesting marine mammals. It is most commonly made out of the bones and teeth of sperm whales, the baleen of other whales, and the tusks of walruses. It takes the form of elaborate carvings of pictures and lettering on the surface of the bone or tooth, with the engravings highlighted using a pigment.

Warning: To avoid illegal ivory, contemporary collectors and dealers check provenance and deal only with other established and reputable sellers. Scrimshaw that is found to have an illegal source may be seized by customs officials worldwide.

Reproduction Alert: The biggest problem in the field is fakes, although there are some clues to spotting them. A hot needle will penetrate the plastics and resins used in reproductions, but not the authentic material. Ivory will not generate static electricity when rubbed, plastic will. Patina is not a good indicator; it has been faked by applying tea or tobacco juice.

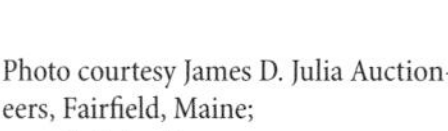

Photo courtesy James D. Julia Auctioneers, Fairfield, Maine; www.JuliaAuctions.com

Scrimshaw Whale's Tooth. Second half 19th century. Depicting an imperial robed figure standing above a coat of arms with crown, flanked by laurel leaves. 6" h. **$1,610**

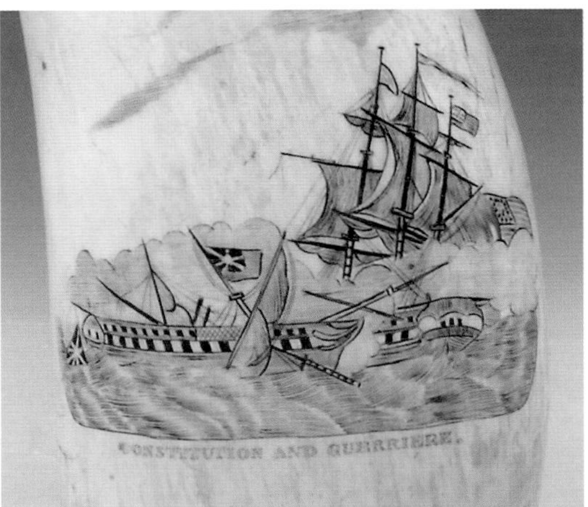

Photo courtesy James D. Julia Auctioneers, Fairfield, Maine; www.JuliaAuctions.com

Scrimshaw Whale's Tooth. Second half 19th century. With a depiction of the battle between the U.S.S. Constitution and the Guerriere, the opposing side depicting a woman in period dress, holding a book. 6" h. **$2,990**

Weathervanes

Photo courtesy James D. Julia Auctioneers, Fairfield, Maine; www.JuliaAuctions.com

American Mule Copper Weathervane. Late 19th, early 20th century. The full-bodied standing mule with sheet-copper ears and detailed mane, with dark mottled patina over original gilded surface, mounted on original tubular support. Rare. Overall 35" l. x 33" h. With minor dents and creases to ears. No repairs or restorations noted. **$117,300**

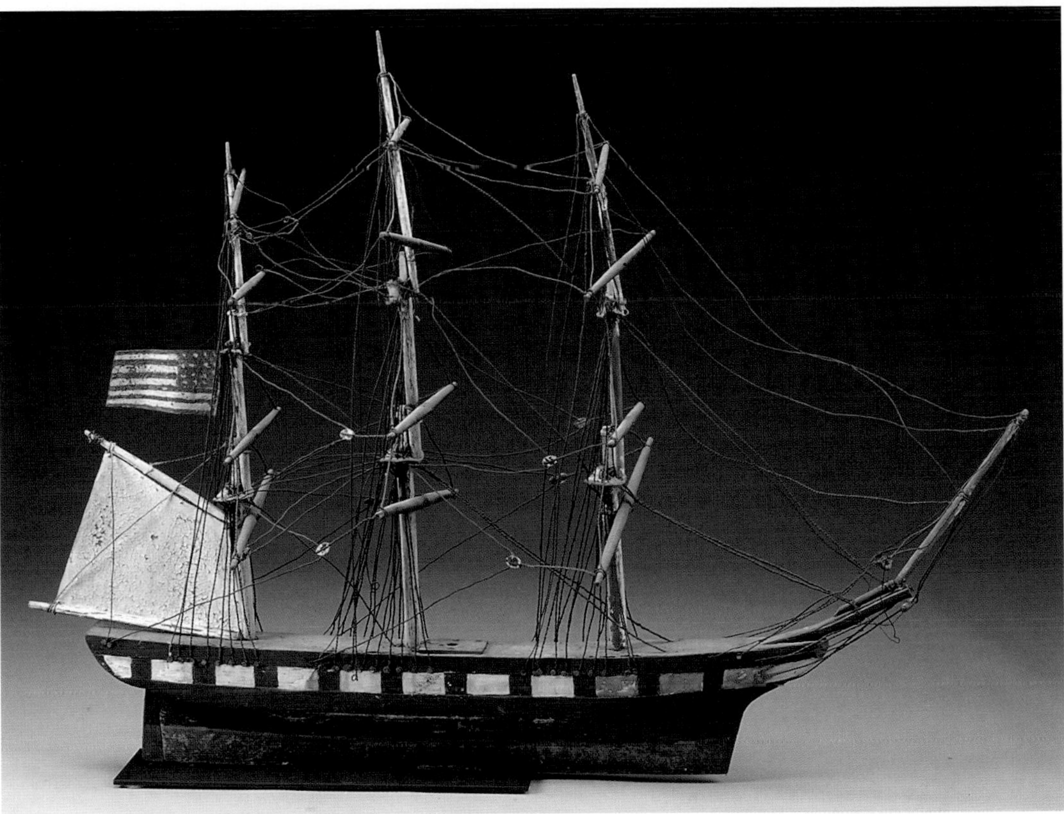

Photo courtesy James D. Julia Auctioneers, Fairfield, Maine; www.JuliaAuctions.com

Primitive New England Wooden Weathervane of the U.S.S. Constitution. Late 19th, early 20th century. The three-masted carved wooden ship with sheet-metal back staysail and sheet-metal American flag, the whole outfitted with wire rigging, the hull painted black and white, green beneath the water line. Overall 16" d, 37" h. x 50" l. Overall weathered surfaces, the painted surfaces dry and flaking, structurally sound with the exception of a split bowsprit, in need of cosmetic restoration. **$5,175**

Photo courtesy James D. Julia Auctioneers, Fairfield, Maine; www.JuliaAuctions.com

Rochester, N.H., Cast-Iron Sheet Metal Rooster Weathervane. Circa 1880. The full-bodied rooster with strongly detailed image, cast in two parts, the sheet-iron tail pierced to depict feathers. 31" h. x 34 1/2" l. Original painted surfaces absent, iron body and tail well rusted with brown patina, one foot with damaged and missing talons, both feet with extensive rust. Original mounting pole is absent. **$6,900**

Photo courtesy Skinner Inc., Boston, www.SkinnerInc.com

Leaping stag, gilt copper, attributed to the E.G. Washburne & Co., New York, and Danvers, Mass., late 19th century, flattened full-body molded copper figure, mounted on a copper rod and small copper sphere, including stand, minor dents, overall 24" h, 29" l, surface regilded some time ago with traces of verdigris, one hind quarter area dented inward, few small bullet dents on rod. **$7,702**

Photo courtesy Skinner Inc., Boston, www.SkinnerInc.com

Running horse, yellow-painted molded copper, American, late 19th/early 20th century, full-body figure mounted on a copper rod, no stand, dents, 16 1/4" h, 28 1/2" l. **$1,422**

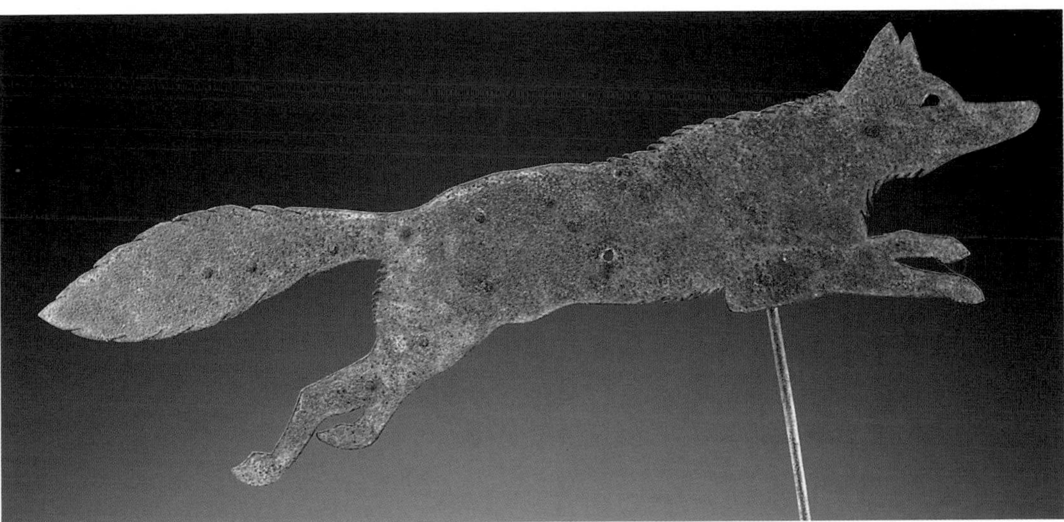

Photo courtesy James D. Julia Auctioneers, Fairfield, Maine; www.JuliaAuctions.com

Running Fox Weathervane. Second half 19th century. Depicting a fox in full stride with pierced eye and serrated outline simulating fur, mounted to a steel rod and reinforced with original decorative wrought-iron supports. Fox: 10 1/2" x 38". Overall h. with rod: 21 1/2". Structurally very good overall, with old rusted and pitted surfaces, one old bullet hole in mid-section. **$1,150**

Photo courtesy James D. Julia Auctioneers, Fairfield, Maine; www.JuliaAuctions.com

Trotting Horse Full-Body Copper Weathervane. Late 19th century. With good verdigris surface over original gilding with zinc head. 19 1/2" h x 39 1/2" l. Supporting bar has been removed, original tail lost and replaced with sheet-copper section (8" in length). One sheet copper ear with damage, second ear absent. **$2,300**

Photo courtesy James D. Julia Auctioneers, Fairfield, Maine; www.JuliaAuctions.com

American Leaping Stag Copper Weathervane. The full-bodied leaping copper stag with hammered surfaces, similar in form and style to those by J.W. Fiske, depicted with forward-angled antlers and upright curled tail, mounted on an L-shaped pipe extending to top of head. Stag: 31" h. x 41" l. Retains old brown patina and black-painted hoofs over original gilding, seam splits beneath forelegs and back at tail. Top of head has suffered substantial damage from pipe being forced through it, tearing top of head and damaging antlers at juncture to head. Sheet metal ears also damaged as is tail at juncture to body. **$25,300**

Furniture

FURNITURE AND ACCESSORIES

Furniture styles

Furniture styles can be determined by careful study and remembering what design elements each one embraces. To help understand what defines each period, here are some of the major design elements for each period.

William and Mary, 1690-1730: The style is named for the English King William of Orange and his consort, Mary. New colonists in America brought their English furniture traditions with them and tried to translate these styles using native woods. Their furniture was practical and sturdy. Lines of this furniture style tend to be crisp, while facades might be decorated with bold grains of walnut or maple veneers, framed by inlaid bands. Moldings and turnings are exaggerated in size. Turnings are baluster-shaped and the use of C-scrolls was quite common. Feet found in this period generally are round or oval. One exception to this is known as the Spanish foot, which flares to a scroll. Woods tend to be maple, walnut, white pine or southern yellow pine. One type of decoration that begins in the William and Mary period and extends through to Queen Anne and Chippendale styles is known as "japanning," referring to a lacquering process that combines ashes and varnish.

Photo courtesy Sanford Alderfer Auction & Appraisal, Hatfield, Pa.; www.AlderferAuction.com

Cabinet on stand, continental, walnut, top section with molded cornice with sides extended, panel below, carved cartouche and scrolling stems with flowers; intricately carved paneled door below flanked by two tapered round columns, door with border of bas relief leafage, twin vertical panels with conforming cartouche and leafage; lower section with molded mid-band, single drawer with conforming leaf scroll and flowers, two free-standing front columns with drapery swags, stretcher shelf; twin vertical panels with neo-classic portrait heads, leafage with rosettes; urns with birds below, bun feet, late 19th century; tin plate reinforces top of right front corner; left column with repaired split at top; damage to left top corner of cornice, 68 5/8" h, 31" w, 18" deep. **$1,035**

Queen Anne, 1720-1760: Evolution of this design style is from Queen Anne's court, 1702 to 1714, and lasted until the Revolution. This style of furniture is much more delicate than its predecessor. It was one way for the young Colonists to show their own unique style, with each regional area initiating special design elements. Forms tend to be attenuated in New England. Chair rails were more often mortised through the back legs when made in Philadelphia. New England furniture makers preferred pad feet, while the makers in Philadelphia used triffid feet. Makers in Connecticut and New York often preferred slipper and claw and ball feet. The most popular woods were walnut, poplar, cherry, and maple. Japanned decoration tends to be in red, green and gilt, often on a blue-green field. A new furniture form of this period was the tilting tea table.

Chippendale, 1755-1790: This period is named for the famous English cabinetmaker, Thomas Chippendale, who wrote a book of furniture designs, *Gentlemen and Cabinet-Maker's Director*, published in 1754, 1755 and 1762. This book gave cabinetmakers real direction and they soon eagerly copied the styles presented. Chippendale was influenced by ancient cultures, such as the Romans, and Gothic influences. Look for Gothic arches, Chinese fretwork, columns, capitals, C-scrolls, S-scrolls, ribbons, flowers, leaves, scallop shells, gadrooning and acanthus leaves. The most popular wood used in this period was mahogany, with walnut, maple and cherry also present. Legs become straight and regional differences still existed in design elements, such as feet. Claw and ball feet become even larger and more decorative. Pennsylvania cabinetmakers used Marlborough feet, while other regions favored ogee bracket feet. One of the most popular forms of this period was a card table that sported five legs instead of the four of Queen Anne designs.

Federal (Hepplewhite), 1790-1815: This period reflects the growing patriotism felt in the young American states. Their desire to develop their own distinctive furniture style was apparent. Stylistically it also reflects the architectural style known as Federal, where balance and symmetry were extremely important. Woods used during this period were mahogany and mahogany veneer, but other native woods, such as maple, birch or satinwood, were used. Reflecting the architectural ornamentation of the period, inlays were popular, as was carving and even painted highlights. The motifs used for inlay included bellflowers, urns, festoons, acanthus leaves and pilasters, to name but a few. Inlaid bands and lines were also popular and often used in combination with other inlay. Legs of this period tend to be straight or tapered to the foot. The foot might be a simple extension of the leg, or bulbous or spade shaped. Two new furniture forms were created in this period. They are the sideboard and the worktable. Expect to find a little more comfort in chairs and sofas, but not very thick cushions or seats.

When a piece of furniture is made in England, or styled after an English example, it may be known as Hepplewhite. The time frame is the same. Robert

Adam is credited with creating the style known as Hepplewhite during the 1760s and leading the form. Another English book heavily influenced the designers of the day. This one was by Alice Hepplewhite, and titled *The Cabinet Maker and Upholsterer's Guide,* published in 1788, 1789 and 1794.

Sheraton, 1790-1810: The style known as Sheraton closely resembles Federal. The lines are somewhat straighter and the designs plainer than Federal. Sheraton pieces are more closely associated with rural cabinetmakers. Woods would include mahogany, mahogany veneer, maple and pine, as well as other native woods. This period was heavily influenced by the work of Thomas Sheraton and his series of books, *The Cabinet Maker and Upholsterer's Drawing Book*, from 1791-1794, and his *The Cabinet Directory,* 1803, and *The Cabinet-Maker, Upholsterer, and General Artist's Encyclopedia* of 1804.

Empire (Classical), 1805-1830: By the beginning of the 19th century, a new design style was emerging. Known as Empire, it had an emphasis on the classical world of Greece, Egypt and other ancient European influences. The American craftsmen began to incorporate more flowing patriotic motifs, such as eagles with spread wings. The basic wood used in the Empire period was mahogany. However, during this period, dark woods were so favored that often mahogany was painted black. Inlays were popular when made of ebony or maple veneer. The dark woods offset gilt highlights, as were the brass ormolu mountings often found in this period. The legs of this period are substantial and more flowing than those found in the Federal or Sheraton periods. Feet can be highly ornamental, as when they are carved to look like lion's paws, or plain when they extend to the floor with a swept leg. Regional differences in this style are very apparent, with New York City being the center of the design style, as it was also the center of fashion at the time.

New furniture forms of this period include the sleigh bed, with the headboard and footboard forming a graceful arch. Several new forms of tables also came into being, especially the sofa table. Because the architectural style of the Empire period used big, open rooms, the sofa was now allowed to be in the center of the room, with a table behind it. Former architectural periods found most furniture placed against the outside perimeter of the walls and brought forward to be used.

Victorian, 1830-1890: The Victorian period as it relates to furniture styles can be divided into several distinct styles. However, not every piece of furniture can be dated or definitely identified, so the generic term "Victorian" will apply to those pieces. Queen Victoria's reign affected the design styles of furniture, clothing and all sorts of items used in daily living. Her love of ornate styles is well known. When thinking of the general term, think of a cluttered environment, full of heavy furniture, and surrounded by plants, heavy fabrics and lots of china and glassware.

French Restoration, 1830-1850: This is the first sub-category of the Victoria era. This style is best simplified as the plainest of the Victorian styles. Lines tend to be sweeping, undulating curves. It is named for the style that was popular in France as the Bourbons tried to restore their claim to the French throne, from 1814 to 1848. The Empire (Classical) period influence is felt, but French Restoration lacks some of the ornamentation and fussiness of that period. Design motifs continue to reflect an interest in the classics of Greece and Egypt. Chair backs are styled with curved and concave crest rails, making them a little more comfortable than earlier straight-back chairs. The use of bolster pillows and more upholstery is starting to emerge. The style was only popular in clusters, but did entice makers from larger metropolitan areas, such as Boston and New Orleans, to embrace the style.

The Gothic Revival period, 1840-1860: This is relatively easy to identify for collectors. It is one of the few styles that celebrates elements found in the corresponding architectural themes: turrets, pointed arches and quatrefoils—designs found in 12th through 16th centuries that were adapted to this mid-century furniture style. The furniture shelving form known as an étagère was born in this period, allowing Victorians to have more room to display their treasured collections. Furniture that had mechanical parts was also embraced by the Victorians of this era. The woods preferred by makers of this period were walnut and oak, with some use of mahogany and rosewood. The scale used ranged from large and grand to small and petite. Carved details gave dimension and interest.

Rococo Revival, 1845-1870: This design style features the use of scrolls, either in a "C" shape or the more fluid "S" shape. Carved decoration in the form of scallop shells, leaves and flowers, particularly roses, and acanthus further add to the ornamentation of this style of furniture. Legs and feet of this form are cabriole or scrolling. Other than what might be needed structurally, it is often difficult to find a straight element in Rococo Revival furniture. The use of marble for tabletops was quite popular, but expect to find the corners shaped to conform to the overall scrolling form. To accomplish all this carving, walnut, rosewood, and mahogany were common choices. When lesser woods were used, they were often painted to

Photo courtesy Rago Arts and Auction Center, Lambertville, N.J.; www.RagoArts.com

Chair, Egyptian Revival, with carved winged figure, pierced skirt and light rose upholstery, 19th/20th century, 39" x 24" x 21".
$1,680

Photo courtesy Sanford Alderfer Auction & Appraisal, Hatfield, Pa.; www.AlderferAuction.com

Highboy, William and Mary, maple and ebonized in two sections; upper section with two small drawers over three wide graduated drawers, brass drop handles; lower section with frieze drawer flanked by two deep drawers, trumpet-turned legs joined by flat shaped stretcher, short turned feet, 60" h, 37 3/4" w, 17 1/2" deep. **$3,450**

reflect these more expensive woods. Some cast-iron elements can be found on furniture from this period, especially if it was cast as scrolls. The style began in France and England, but eventually migrated to America where it evolved into two other furniture styles, Naturalistic and Renaissance Revival.

Elizabethan, 1850-1915: This sub-category of the Victorian era is probably the most feminine-influenced style. It also makes use of the new machine-turned spools and spiral profiles that were fast becoming popular with furniture makers. New technology advancements allowed more machined parts to be generated. By adding flowers, either carved or painted, the furniture pieces of this era had a softness to them. Chair backs tend to be high and narrow, having a slight back tilt. Legs vary from straight to baluster-turned forms to spindle turned. This period of furniture design saw more usage of needlework upholstery and decoratively painted surfaces.

Louis XVI, 1850-1914: One period of the Victorian era that flies away with straight lines is Louis XVI. However, this furniture style is not austere; it is adorned with ovals, arches, applied medallions, wreaths, garlands, urns and other Victorian flourishes. As the period aged, more ornamentation became present on the finished furniture styles. Furniture of this time was made from more expensive woods, such as ebony or rosewood. Walnut was popular around the 1890s. Other dark woods were featured, often to contrast the lighter ornaments. Expect to find straight legs or fluted and slightly tapered legs.

Naturalistic, 1850-1914: This furniture period takes the scrolling effects of the Rococo Revival designs and adds more flowers and fruits to the styles. More detail is spent on the leaves—so much that one can tell if they are to represent grape, rose or oak leaves. Technology advances enhanced this design style, as manufacturers developed a way of laminating woods together. This layered effect was achieved by gluing thin layers together, with the grains running at right angles on each new layer. The thick panels created were then steamed in molds to create the illusion of carving. The woods used as a basis for the heavy ornamentation were mahogany, walnut and some rosewood. Upholstery of this period is often tufted, eliminating any large flat surface. The name of John Henry Belter is often connected with this period, for it was when he did some of his best design work. John and Joseph W. Meeks also enjoyed success with laminated furniture. Original labels bearing these names are sometimes found on furniture pieces from this period, giving further provenance.

Renaissance Revival, 1850-1880: Furniture made in this style period reflects how cabinetmakers interpreted 16th- and 17th-century designs. Their motifs range from curvilinear and florid early in the period to angular and almost severe by the end of the period. Dark woods, such as mahogany and walnut, were primary with some use of rosewood and ebony. Walnut veneer panels were a real favorite in the 1870s designs. Upholstery, usually of a more generous nature, was also often incorporated into this design style. Ornamentation and high relief carving included flowers, fruits, game, classical busts, acanthus scrolls, strapwork, tassels and masks. Architectural motifs, such as pilasters, columns, pediments, balusters and brackets, are another prominent design feature. Legs are usually cabriole or have substantial turned profiles.

Néo-Greek, 1855-1885: This design style easily merges with both the Louis XVI and Renaissance Revival. It is characterized by elements reminiscent of Greek architecture, such as pilasters, flutes, column, acanthus, foliate scrolls, Greek key motifs and anthemion high-relief carving. This style originated with the French, but was embraced by American furniture manufacturers. Woods are dark and often ebonized. Ornamentation may be gilded or bronzed. Legs tend to be curved to scrolled or cloven hoof feet.

Eastlake, 1870-1890: This design style is named for Charles Locke Eastlake, who wrote a popular book in 1872 called *Hints on Household Taste*. It was originally published in London. One of his principles was the relationship between function, form and craftsmanship. Shapes of furniture from this style tend to be more rectangular. Ornamentation was created through the use of brackets, grooves, chamfers and geometric designs. American furniture manufacturers were enthusiastic about this style, since it was so easy to adapt for mass production. Woods used were again dark, but more native woods, such as oak, maple and pine, were incorporated. Legs and chair backs are straighter, often with incised decoration.

Feet

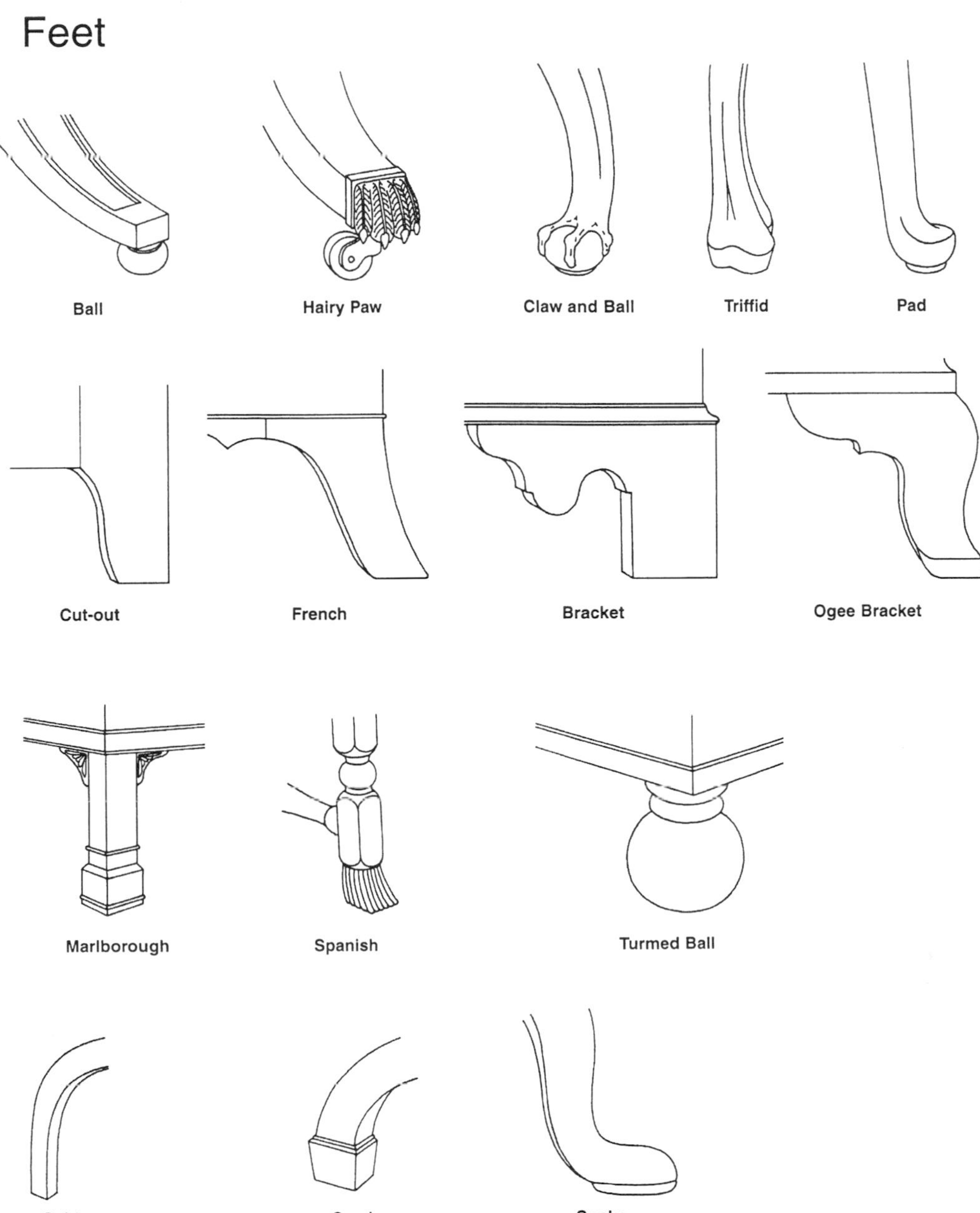

Art Furniture, 1880-1914: This period represents furniture designs gone mad, almost an "anything goes" school of thought. The style embraces both straight and angular with some pieces that are much more fluid, reflecting several earlier design periods. This era saw the wide usage of turned moldings and dark woods, but this time stained to imitate ebony and lacquer. The growing Oriental influence is seen in furniture from this period, including the use of bamboo, which was imported and included in the designs. Legs tend to be straight; feet tend to be small.

Arts & Crafts, 1895-1915: The Arts & Crafts period of furniture represents one of the strongest trends for current collectors. Quality period Arts & Crafts furniture is available through most of the major auction houses. And, for those desiring the look, good quality modern furniture is also made in this style. The Arts & Crafts period furniture is generally rectilinear and a definite correlation is seen between form and function. The primary influences of this period were the Stickley brothers (especially Gustav, Leopold and John George), Elbert Hubbard, Frank Lloyd Wright and Harvey Ellis. Their furniture designs often overlapped into architectural and interior design, including rugs, textiles and other accessories. Wood used for Arts & Crafts furniture is primarily oak. Finishes were natural, fumed or painted. Hardware was often made in

Legs

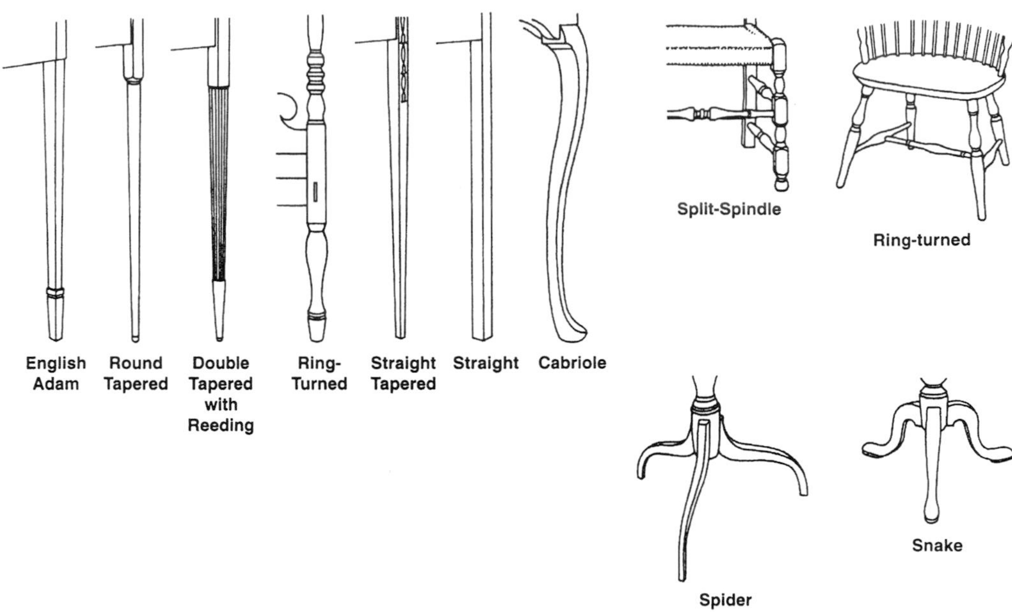

Hardware

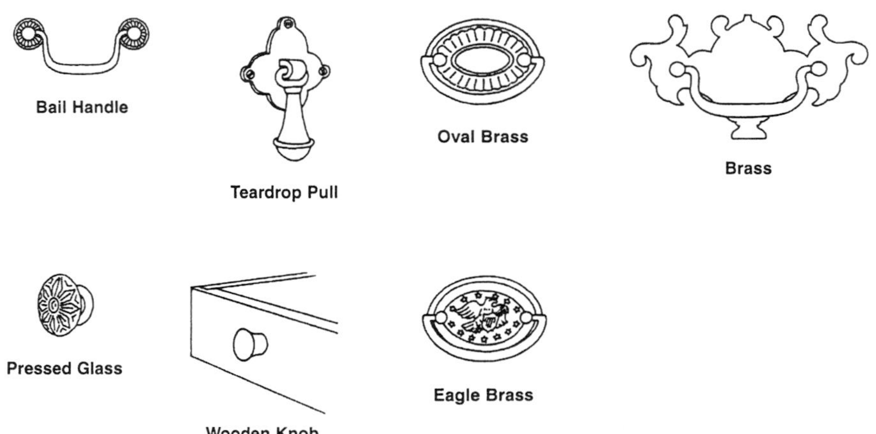

copper. Legs are straight and feet are small, if present at all, as they were often a simple extension of the leg. Some inlay of natural materials was used, such as silver, copper and abalone shells.

Art Nouveau, 1896-1914: Just as the Art Nouveau period is known for women with long hair, flowers and curves, so is Art Nouveau furniture. The Paris Exposition of 1900 introduced furniture styles reflecting what was happening in the rest of the design world, such as jewelry and silver. This style of furniture was not warmly embraced, as the sweeping lines were not very conducive to mass production. The few manufacturers that did interpret it for their factories found interest to be slight in America. The French held it in higher esteem. Legs tend to be sweeping or cabriole. Upholstery becomes slimmer.

Art Deco, 1920-1945: The Paris *"L'Exposition International des Arts Décorative et Industriels Modernes"* became the mantra for designs of everything in this period. Lines are crisp, with some use of controlled curves. The Chrysler Building in New York City remains among the finest

Construction Details

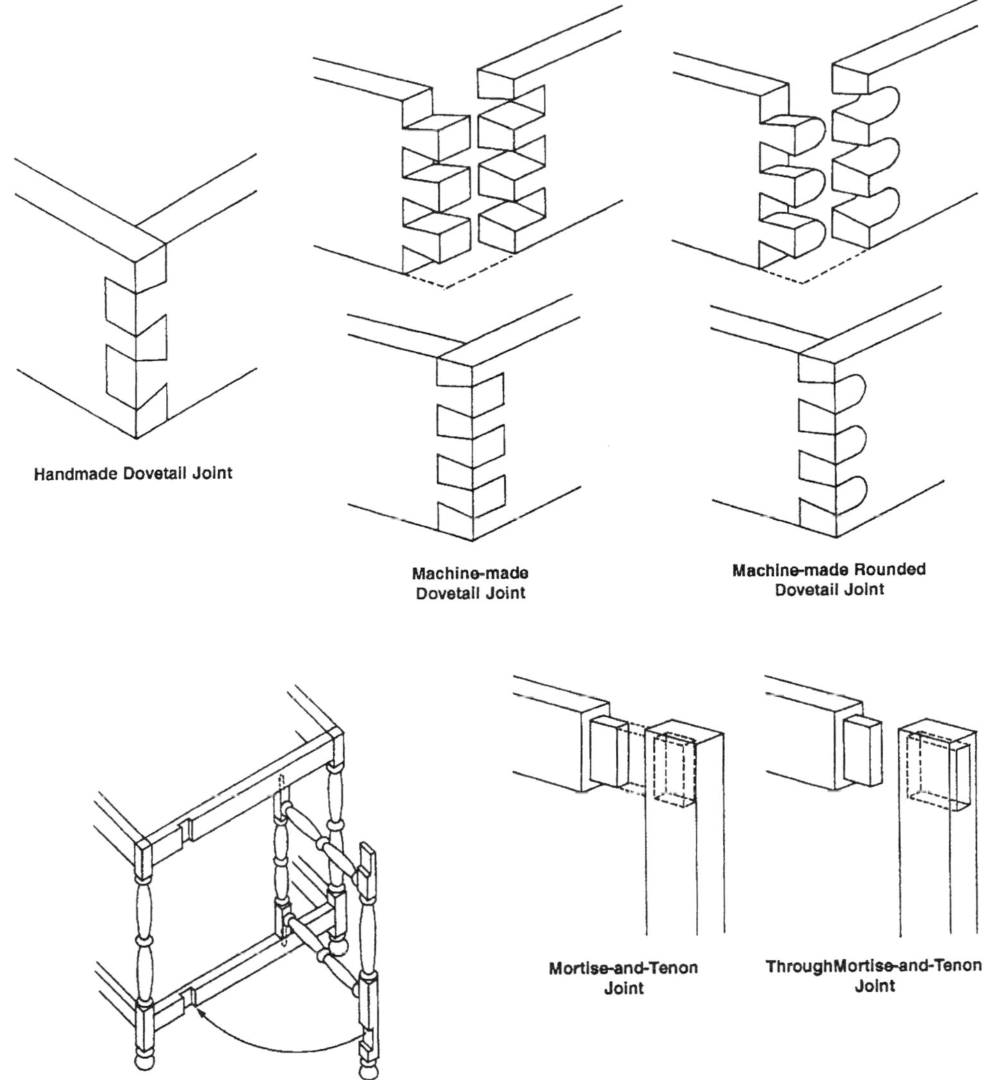

Handmade Dovetail Joint

Machine-made Dovetail Joint

Machine-made Rounded Dovetail Joint

Typical Gateleg Construction

Mortise-and-Tenon Joint

ThroughMortise-and-Tenon Joint

example of Art Deco architecture and those same straight lines and gentle curves are found in furniture. Makers used expensive materials, such as veneers, lacquered woods, glass and steel. The cocktail table first enters the furniture scene during this period. Upholstery can be vinyl or smooth fabrics. Legs are straight or slightly tapered; chair backs tend to be either low or extremely high.

Modernism, 1940-present: Furniture designed and produced during this period is distinctive, as it represents the usage of some new materials, like plastic, aluminum and molded laminates. The Bauhaus and also the Museum of Modern Art heavily influenced some designers. In 1940, the museum organized competitions for domestic furnishings. Designers Eero Saarien and Charles Eames won first prize for their designs. A new chair design combined the back, seat and arms together as one unit. Tables were designed that incorporated the top, pedestal and base as one. Shelf units were also designed in this manner.

Also see Folk Art, Modernism, Oriental Objects.

Beds

Bed, Art Deco, France, single curvilinear bed frame with hanging shelf compartments, price for pair, circa 1930, 82" l. **$1,410**

Bed, Limbert, #651, daybed, angled headrest with spade cut-out, original finish, recovered cushions, branded, numbered, 74" w, 25" d, 23" h. **$650**

Bed, Stickley Bros, attributed to, headboard with narrow vertical slats and panels, tapered feet, original side rails, original finish, minor scratches, stenciled "9001-1/2," 80 1/2" l, 56 1/2" w, 30" h. **$1,355**

Bed, Biedermeier, figured mahogany veneer, octagonal posts, turned feet and finials, paneled head and footboards, original rails, veneer damage, 38" w, 72" l, 45" h, pair. **$750**

Bed, Chippendale, tall post, curly maple, turned posts, scrolled headboard with poplar panel, original side rails, old mellow refinishing, minor repairs to posts, 60" w, 72" l, 80" h. **$3,000**

Bed, country, American, rope, high post, curly maple, areas of tight curl, evidence of old red wash, turned and tapered legs, boldly turned posts taper toward the top, paneled headboard with scrolled crest, turned top finial, pierced restorations, 53 1/2" w, 70" l rails with original bolts. **$1,890**

Bed, Renaissance Revival, walnut, double, high headboard topped by rounded pediment, pointed finial **$1,700**

Bed, Gustav Stickley, a custom order variation of No.924, Prairie School influence, well-proportioned low form with double horizontal rail above 12 vertical spindles, fine original finish, branded signature, 58" w x 79" l x 37" h, excellent condition. **$3,500**

Bed, Sheraton, tester, straight headboard, carved baluster-turned posts, turned legs and feet, 88 1/2" h, tester incomplete. **$373**

Daybed, No.292, L. & J.G. Stickley, flared legs with through tenon construction and four vertical slats at sides, original spring cushion recovered in leather, includes two back bolsters, original finish, signed with Handcraft decal, 80" w x 30" d x 28" h, excellent condition. **$3,500**

Bookcases

Bookcase, American Renaissance Revival, carved cherry, circa 1890. The center cabinet with acorn and oak-leaf carved frieze, the bowed cornice surmounted by brass gallery, fitted with a bowed glass door opening to an interior of four adjustable shelves, flanked by bookcase sections, the pilasters rope-twist and acanthus-carved, on a conforming base fitted with three aligned drawers on a molded plinth, 78 1/2" overall h x 71" w x 20 1/2" deep. All original, including cast-brass hardware; various scuffs and mars overall. Bowed glass door with L-shaped crack in glass lower right facing. **$2,588**

Bookcase, American Victorian, carved walnut, circa 1875. In three parts; the arched molded cornice with incised scrolled crest fitted to the upper case having a step-molded cornice fitted with a pair of astragal-glazed doors opening to an interior of adjustable shelves, stepped back on the lower case fitted with two aligned short drawers on a molded plinth, 8' 6 1/2" h x 53" overall w x 17" overall deep. Professionally cleaned and repolished, otherwise original. **$1,898**

Bookcase, (no. 357), Limbert, single door with three adjustable shelves, branded mark, 57" x 29 1/2" x 14". **$5,700**

Bookcase, (no. 358), Limbert, double door with six adjustable shelves, branded mark, 57" x 48" x 14". **$4,200**

Bookcase/secretary, Governor Winthrop, American carved mahogany, 20th century. In two parts; the upper bookcase section with molded swans' neck pediment and carved floral terminals centering a turned finial above a pair of astragal glazed doors fitted to the lower section with sloping writing surface opening to an interior of cubby holes, drawers and prospect door above four serpentine drawers on a molded base. Raised on short cabriole legs with scalloped returns terminating in ball and claw feet, 82" h x 36" case w x

Photo courtesy Rago Arts and Auction Center, Lambertville, N.J.; www.RagoArts.com

Bookcase (no. 359), Limbert, triple door with nine adjustable shelves, branded mark, 58 3/4" x 66 1/2" x 14". **$5,400**

Photo courtesy Rago Arts and Auction Center, Lambertville, N.J.; www.RagoArts.com

Bookcase, Victorian, oak with carved vine detail, three leaded-glass doors over three drawers and turned columns, 19th century, 65 3/4" x 68 1/2" x 16 1/4". **$2,160**

20 1/2" deep. Original finish and hardware. There is some damage to the left and right lower moldings and one chip of veneer off the right side of case between the second and third drawer. **$288**

Boxes

Pipe box, cherry, American, early 19th century, two-section box with pierced backboard, lower drawer, shrinkage crack on right side, 20 1/4" h, 6" w, 4 3/4" deep. **$237**

Pipe box, red-painted pine, American, early 19th century, shaped box with pierced backboard, lower drawer, shrinkage cracks, loss of drawer back causing loose drawer joinery, probable later paint, 20 1/4" h, 6" w, 4 3/4" deep. **$829**

Cabinets

Vitrine, gilt "vernis Martin" design, raised molded top, shaped swell-front glazed door, molded glass side panels, mirror back, ormolu border and mounts; base of door with painted garden scene with musician and lady, signed "Ch Olivier" lower left; painted side panels, flaring cabriole legs, 65 1/4" h, 24 1/2" w, 14 5/8" overall depth. .... **$1,610** *(In interior design, "vernis Martin" is a type of lacquer named for the French brothers Guillaume and Etienne-Simon Martin. It is an imitation of Chinese lacquer and was applied to a wide variety of items, from furniture to coaches.)*

Photo courtesy Sanford Alderfer Auction & Appraisal, Hatfield, Pa.; www.AlderferAuction.com

Knife boxes (pair), Hepplewhite, inlaid mahogany with sloping lid having shell-inlaid patera, geometric inlaid edges, serpentine front with four "stop fluted" inlaid pilasters, small ring handle with back-plate, reverse of lid inlaid with compass star, sloping fitted interior with numerous slots framed by line inlay, circa 1790, 14 1/2" h, 8 1/2" w, 11" deep. **$8,050 pair**
(A patera is a circular ornament, resembling a dish, often worked in relief on friezes.)

Photo courtesy of Treadway Toomey Galleries, Cincinnati and Oak Park, Ill.; www.treadwaygallery.com

Cabinet, Arts & Crafts style, single door with strap hinges and original hardware, interior contains one shelf, refinished, 20" w x 20" d x 29" h, very good condition. **$450**

Chairs

Armchair, Chippendale style, mahogany, strapwork splat, flame needlework-covered slip seat, shell-carved serpentine apron and knees, cabriole legs, claw and ball feet, 40 3/4" h. **$258**

Armchair, Empire, mahogany, with inverted C-scroll armrests and later tufted brown leather upholstery, 19th century, 39 1/2" x 32" x 26 1/2". **$1,020**

Armchair, Gothic Revival, walnut, crest with center spire and twin acorn finials, crockets on pointed arch; earth-toned oriental design fabric on back, arm-pads and seat, tapered round legs, 71" h, 27 1/2" w, 25 1/2" deep. **$1,840**

Photo courtesy of Treadway Toomey Galleries, Cincinnati and Oak Park, Ill.; www.treadwaygallery.com

Map cabinet, circa 1910, manufactured for Rand McNally and Co., tambour front with two adjustable shelves, original label, cleaned original finish, 21" w x 14 1/2" d x 28" h, very good condition. **$700**

Photo courtesy Sanford Alderfer Auction & Appraisal, Hatfield, Pa.; www.AlderferAuction.com

Vitrine, Hepplewhite-style, mahogany, lift lid top, four glazed sides, all glass beveled, line-inlaid apron and tapered square legs, casters, 35 1/2" h, 22" w, 30" l. **$1,440**

Photo courtesy Skinner Inc., Boston; www.SkinnerInc.com

Armchair, polychrome, Sweden, late 18th century, scrolled cresting with a beaded paneled back with shaped arms on block, vase, and ring-turned legs and square stretchers, old surface, worn paint, back is dated "1790," 40" h, seat height 16". **$1,540**

(A crocket is an architectural ornament of curved foliage used at the edge of a spire or gable.)

Photo courtesy Leslie Hindman Auctioneers, Chicago; www.LeslieHindman.com

Renaissance Revival Hall Chair, heavily carved with cherubs, scrolls and masks, 46 1/4" t. **$427**

Photo courtesy Sanford Alderfer Auction & Appraisal, Hatfield, Pa.; www.AlderferAuction.com

Armchair, Battleship Maine, oak, back with battleship carved in relief, "Maine" below; cresting of crossed flags with "1898" between paired C-scrolls, saddle seat, cabriole legs, tapered feet, baluster-and-ball turned H-stretcher, 40" h, 26" across arms. (The sinking of the Maine on Feb. 15, 1898, precipitated the Spanish-American War.) **$720**

Armchair, griffon carved, Victorian, Gothic carved pediment, paneled back, scrolled arm, conforming carving on frieze. **$780**

Armchair, Shop of the Crafters, tall back, inlaid with tacked-on red leather seat. Unmarked. 47 3/4" x 27 1/2" x 23". **$1,800**

Armchair, Windsor, branded under saddle seat "J.B. Ackley" (John Brientnall Ackley, Philadelphia, working 1791-1802); old black surface, arched back, nine bamboo-turned spindles, down-scrolled arms, turned legs with stretchers, 38 3/4" h. Replaced arm support. **$1,380**

Armchairs (pair), No. 318, Gustav Stickley, five vertical slats to back over a recovered leather drop-in spring cushion, corbel supports to sides, original finish, branded signature, 27 1/2" w x 24 1/2" d x 37" h, excellent condition. .... **$1,500 pair**

Chairs, (six), painted balloon backs, shell and fruit cresting, floral splat, green-bordered plank seat, conforming splayed legs and stretchers, circa 1870. .... **$330 set**

Dining chairs (eight), Chippendale-style, carved mahogany with shaped crest rail with centering shell, strapwork splat, upholstered slip seat, apron with shell, cabriole legs, claw and ball feet; including open armchair and seven side chairs, 42" h, 21 1/4" w. .... **$4,800 set**

Dining chairs, (12), upholstered, possibly by R.J. Horner; mahogany; consisting of two armchairs and 10 side chairs; armchairs with acanthus leafage near back, acanthus hand rests, tapered square legs headed by scrolled, undercut carving above husk pendants; garden upholstery on backs, arm-pads and over-upholstered seats, 50 3/8" h. .... **$3,105 set**

Photo courtesy Rago Arts and Auction Center, Lambertville, N.J.; www.RagoArts.com

Armchair, Roycroft, rare, with tooled leather, carved Orb and Cross mark, 36 1/2" x 24" x 25". **$7,200**

Photo courtesy of Treadway Toomey Galleries, Cincinnati and Oak Park, Ill.; www.treadwaygallery.com

Arm rocker, No.715, Stickley Brothers, massive form with five vertical slats to back and three under each arm, through tenon construction, recovered leather cushion, back cushion included, refinished, unsigned, some chips to edges, 28 1/2" w x 39" d x 35" h, very good condition. **$950**

Photo courtesy Sanford Alderfer Auction & Appraisal, Hatfield, Pa.; www.AlderferAuction.com

Armchair, Windsor, continuous arm, eight spindles, saddle seat, baluster and tapered round legs, H-stretcher, 35" h, early 19th century, split from back left leg to front of seat. **$270**

Photo courtesy James D. Julia Auctioneers, Fairfield, Maine; www.JuliaAuctions.com

Chairs (six), Southern Chippendale, carved fruitwood, possibly Virginia, second half 18th century. Each with serpentine crest rail with flared backswept ears above the upswept pierced five-ribbed splat with urn-form base set in a cove-molded cleated shoe, joined to the trapezoidal molded rail fitted with slip seat raised on frontal square legs, with shaped returns, the rear legs backswept joined by a recessed box stretcher, 38 1/2" h. Chairs retain original cleaned finish and framing, no visible restoration or repairs, ears with old losses. **$7,475 set**

Photo courtesy of Treadway Toomey Galleries, Cincinnati and Oak Park, Ill.; www.TreadwayGallery.com

Chalet chair, No. 2578, Gustav Stickley, single broad slat at back over a recovered leather seat, original finish, signed with box mark, 16" w x 16" d x 29" h, very good condition. **$350**

Photo courtesy Sanford Alderfer Auction & Appraisal, Hatfield, Pa.; www.AlderferAuction.com

Corner chair, maple, three ring-turned tapered round supports, conforming turned legs with X-stretcher, needlework seat with musical trophies, early 19th century, 33 3/4" h, 27 3/8" w. **$230**

Dining chairs, (four), Gustav Stickley, early U-back style with rush seats, circa 1901, unmarked, 34 3/4" x 19" x 17". .... **$6,600 set**

Dining chairs, (six), Gustav Stickley, V-Back, one armchair (no. 354) and five side chairs, circa 1905, small red decals.

Armchair 36" x 26" x 22", side chairs 35 1/2" x 19" x 19". **$7,200 set**

Dining chairs, (six), Victorian, walnut, carved with barley-twist columns, circa 1900, 39 1/2" x 16 1/2" x 19". **$1,140 set**

Morris chair, No. 332, Gustav Stickley, classic flat-arm form with five vertical slats under each arm and original leatherette cushions, complete with original pegs and washers, branded signature, lightly re-coated original finish, 31" w x 38" d x 41" h, very good condition. **$6,000**

Morris chair, (no. 410), L. and J.G. Stickley, drop-arm with slats to the floor and original drop-in spring seat, branded mark, 38" x 32 1/2" x 38". **$8,400**

Side chair, No. 354, Gustav Stickley, "V"-back form with five vertical slats over a replaced seat, refinished, unsigned, 19" w x 19" d x 36" h, very good condition. **$375**

Side chair, No. 394, Gustav Stickley, "H"-back form with recovered drop-in seat, original finish, unsigned, some looseness, 17" w x 16" d x 40" h, very good condition. **$225**

Photo courtesy Rago Arts and Auction Center, Lambertville, N.J.; www.RagoArts.com

Hall chairs (pair), Charles Rohlfs, with tall cutout backs and saddle seats, 1901, carved R 1901, 54 3/4" x 18" x 17". **$19,200 pair**

Photo courtesy of Treadway Toomey Galleries, Cincinnati and Oak Park, Ill.; www.treadwaygallery.com

Hall chair, Stickley Brothers, Prairie School influence, three vertical slats at back over a replaced leather drop-in seat, original finish, signed with Quaint tag, 17" w x 17" d x 42" h, very good condition. **$400**

Photo courtesy Rago Arts and Auction Center, Lambertville, N.J.; www.RagoArts.com

Rocker (no. 393), Gustav Stickley, rare, high back with inverted V arm supports, drop-in spring seat with new leather cover, red decal, 44" x 27 3/4" x 24". **$7,200**

Photo courtesy of Treadway Toomey Galleries, Cincinnati and Oak Park, Ill.; www.treadwaygallery.com

Rocker, L. and J.G. Stickley, similar to No. 1321, large high-back form with 13 spindles at back over a replaced leather sling seat, original finish, 31" w x 32" d x 42" h, unsigned, very good condition. **$900**

Photo courtesy Sanford Alderfer Auction & Appraisal, Hatfield, Pa.; www.Alderfer-Auction.com

Side chair, Windsor, fan-back, deeply bowed crest rail, seven spindles, saddle seat, splayed bamboo-turned legs with stretcher, circa 1790, 35" h. **$575**

Side chair, banister-back, rush seat, bun-form finials, four flat spindles, turned round legs with stretchers, circa 1720, 45 3/8" h. **$92**

Side chair, William & Mary, circa 1730, shaped crest rail over vase splat, turned and blocked front legs with ball-turned front stretcher. **$240**

Side chairs, (eight), Chippendale style, carved crest rail over strapwork splat back, serpentine apron with carved shell, cabriole legs with acanthus knees, claw and ball feet; mahogany. **$1,150**

Side chairs, (four), Old Hickory, with woven seats. Old Hickory metal tag on one, 39" x 20" x 16 1/2". .... **$1,800 all**

Side chairs, (eight), upholstered, carved oak, possibly by R.J. Horner, crest rail with oval cartouche flanked by twin lion figures, fluted round stiles with banded ball finials; urn-turned round front legs with casters, twin leaf-scroll apron, upholstered back rest and over-upholstered seat, 44 1/8" h; missing some casters, loss to finial .... **$1,265 set**

Chests

Blanket chest, English, Victorian, oak, with carved decoration of geometric shapes, 19th century, 29" x 50" x 20 3/4". **$780**

Chest, English, 17th century, walnut, three carved reserves with interlaced scroll forms, raised supports at ends, front

Photo courtesy Sanford Alderfer Auction & Appraisal, Hatfield, Pa.; www.AlderferAuction.com

Wing chair, upholstered, carved walnut, carved leaf-scrolled crest rail; upholstered small wings, back support, arm-pads and seat, all in pastel-shaded flame stitch; scrolled acanthus hand-rests, ring-turned and blocked legs with carved stretchers, 53 3/4" h, 29 1/2" w, 27" deep. **$345**

Photo courtesy James D. Julia Auctioneers, Fairfield, Maine; www.JuliaAuctions.com

Blanket chest in old blue paint, American, pine, bootjack legs, circa 1820. Rectangular molded top hinged on the conforming case fitted with till, case ends arched, wear to painted surfaces, top with normal shrinkage split, 19 1/2" h x 42 1/2" l x 14" deep. **$1,035**

hinged at bottom and drops down, 29 1/2" h, 43" w, 18 3/4" deep. **$575**

Chest, green painted pine, inscribed "Peter Michel Anno 1785"; two oblong reserves with brown sponge decoration; interior with till to left; wrought-iron strap hinges, two skid supports, 21 1/2", 48 7/8" l, 22 3/4" deep. **$1,495**

Chests of drawers

Chest of drawers, blonde mahogany, molded oblong top, four graduated cock-beaded drawers, oval brasses (replaced), straight bracket feet, split near right front top corner, 37 3/8" h, 37 3/8" w, 20 5/8" deep. **$805**

Photo courtesy James D. Julia Auctioneers, Fairfield, Maine; www.JuliaAuctions.com

Sea chest, New England, paint-decorated pine, circa 1850. The rectangular hinged lid with applied molding painted with a fully rigged ship above the conforming case, the interior fitted with till, the sides with beckets, the front decorated with opposing dolphins centering a ship's wheel. The whole painted on a blue-green ground on a plinth base, 16" h x 46" l x 17 1/2" deep. **$1,150** *(Beckets are short lines with an eye at one end and a knot at the other; used to secure loose items on a ship.)*

Photo courtesy of Treadway Toomey Galleries, Cincinnati and Oak Park, Ill.; www.treadwaygallery.com

Chest, Arts & Crafts style, paneled top and sides, original finish, 40" w x 21" d x 20" h, very good condition. **$800**

(A cock bead is a narrow half-round trim detail that surrounds a drawer front or door.)

Chest of drawers, Bucks County, Pa., walnut, cove-molded cornice above band of dentil molding, three small drawers over two small drawers over five graduated drawers, all thumb-molded and with oval sickle and sheaf brasses (replaced), twin fluted quarter-columns flanking, ogee bracket feet, 64" h, 43 5/8" w, 23" deep. **$2,875**

Chest of drawers, Chippendale, cherry, molded top, four graduated thumb-molded drawers, brass bail handles (replaced), fluted quarter-columns flanking, ogee bracket feet, Pennsylvania, circa 1780, 36 1/2" h, 37 3/8" w, 20 1/2" deep. **$3,450**

Chest of drawers, Chippendale, cherry, top section with three small over four wide graduated thumb-molded drawers, flanking fluted chamfered corners with lamb's tongues; lower section with four graduated wide drawers, flanking fluted chamfered corners with lamb's tongues, brass bail handles (replaced), bracket feet, 74 1/2" h, 43 1/2" w, 22" deep. **$4,025**

Chest of drawers, Chippendale, mahogany, molded top, four graduated cock-beaded drawers, brass bail handles, flanked by twin fluted quarter-columns, ogee bracket feet, circa 1780, 32 7/8" h, 37 1/2" w, 22 1/8" deep. **$2,070**

(A cock bead is a narrow half-round trim detail that surrounds a drawer front or door.)

Chest of drawers, Hepplewhite, mahogany, two small drawers over three wide graduated cock-beaded drawers, oval brasses (replaced), French bracket feet, 40 1/4" h, 37" w, 18 3/8" deep; interiors of two small drawers refinished. **$660**

(A cock bead is a narrow half-round trim detail that surrounds a drawer front or door.)

Chest of drawers, inlaid, cherry, four graduated thumb-molded drawers, brass bail handles and escutcheons, line-inlaid vertical bands, twin fluted quarter columns, ogee bracket feet, circa 1800, 41 5/8" h, 39 1/2" w, 20 1/2" deep. **$2,300**

Cupboards

Corner cupboard, cherry, two sections, glazed 12-light door, hinges on right, painted shelved interior, chamfered corners, 86" h, 42" w. **$2,990**

Cupboard, walnut, single door, top thumb-molded on three sides, door with two wrought-iron H-hinges, shelved interior, bracket feet, early 19th century, 43 1/4" h, 30 1/4" w, 16 1/2" deep. **$1,440**

Wall cupboard, Rococo Revival, oak, upper section with bowed cresting with fruit and scrollwork above, beveled mirror, oblong beveled mirrors at sides, twin mirror-back glazed cabinets at sides with two beveled mirrors flanking below and twin acanthus-carved supports; lower section with lower leaf-scroll-carved center frieze drawer flanked

Photo courtesy Sanford Alderfer Auction & Appraisal, Hatfield, Pa.; www.AlderferAuction.com

Chest of drawers, Chippendale, cherry, molded top, four graduated scratch-molded drawers, brass bail handles and escutcheons, ogee bracket feet, 37 5/8" h, 38 3/4" w, 18 1/4" deep, replaced glue blocks on feet. **$920**

Photo courtesy Sanford Alderfer Auction & Appraisal, Hatfield, Pa.; www.AlderferAuction.com

Corner cupboard, cherry, two section, cove-molded cornice, glazed 12-light door, hinges on right, off-white painted butterfly shelves, twin cabinet doors, chamfered corners, bracket feet, 87 1/2" h, 43" w. **$2,587**

Photo courtesy James D. Julia Auctioneers, Fairfield, Maine; www.JuliaAuctions.com

Corner cupboard, New England Sheraton, birch and maple, upper case with molded cornice and canted sides centering a pair of glass paneled doors opening to two fixed shelves, fitted to the lower case having a pair of cupboard doors opening to a shelf. Base with shaped and arched apron, 79" h, 46 1/2" w, 23 1/2" deep. Early refinished medium-brown surface. Retains original backboards with hand-cut nails, original feet. **$2,300**

Photo courtesy Sanford Alderfer Auction & Appraisal, Hatfield, Pa.; www.Alderfer-Auction.com

Hanging cupboard, Pennsylvania, walnut, cove-molded cornice, six-light glazed door with brass H-hinges, pale green painted interior, thumb-molded drawer below, oval molded brasses, flanking fluted quarter-columns, early 19th century, 38" h, 39 1/2" w (overall), 9 7/8" deep (overall). **$3,162**

by two drawers with large carved mask-head pulls, opening below above conforming drawer; four fluted tapered round columns flanking twin leaf-carved cabinet doors, bun feet, circa 1880s; 82" h, 82" w, 25 1/2" deep. **$2,875**

Cupboard section, Chippendale, walnut, circa 1780, cove-molded cornice, twin doors, each with two raised panels, twin flanking quarter columns, front molding with conforming right molding. Shelved interior, 44 3/4" h, 39" w, 11 1/2" deep. Left side molding missing; repair at lower hinge on right door. **$1,150**

Desks

Desk, English, Victorian, oak, slant front with four graduated drawers, 19th century, 42" x 37" x 19 1/2" (when closed). **$480**

Desk, George III, mahogany, slant-front, fitted interior with five open pigeonholes, two banks of six small drawers to each side; case with four graduated cock-beaded drawers, brass bail handles and back plates, pair of lopers, bracket feet, 41" h, 42 5/8" w, 21" deep; writing board broken out; splits and damage to outer edge of writing board. **$575**

(A cock bead is a narrow half-round trim detail that surrounds a drawer front or door.)

Desk, inlaid, mahogany slant-front, English, early 19th century, prospect door with satinwood border, twin half-column document drawers, six arched pigeonholes over six small drawers and two wide drawers, lightwood band on slant lid, four graduated ebonized drawers, oval brasses with

Photo courtesy James D. Julia Auctioneers, Fairfield, Maine; www.JuliaAuctions.com

Desk, American Chippendale, maple and curly maple, slant lid, last half of the 18th century, rectangular dovetailed case fitted with a sloping lid opening to an interior of six valanced cubby holes over five aligned drawers above four long graduated and thumb molded drawers. Raised on a molded plinth with shaped bracket feet, 41 1/2" h x 32 1/2" h writing surface x 36" case w x 18 1/2" deep, fully restored and refinished with replaced hardware. **$4,485**

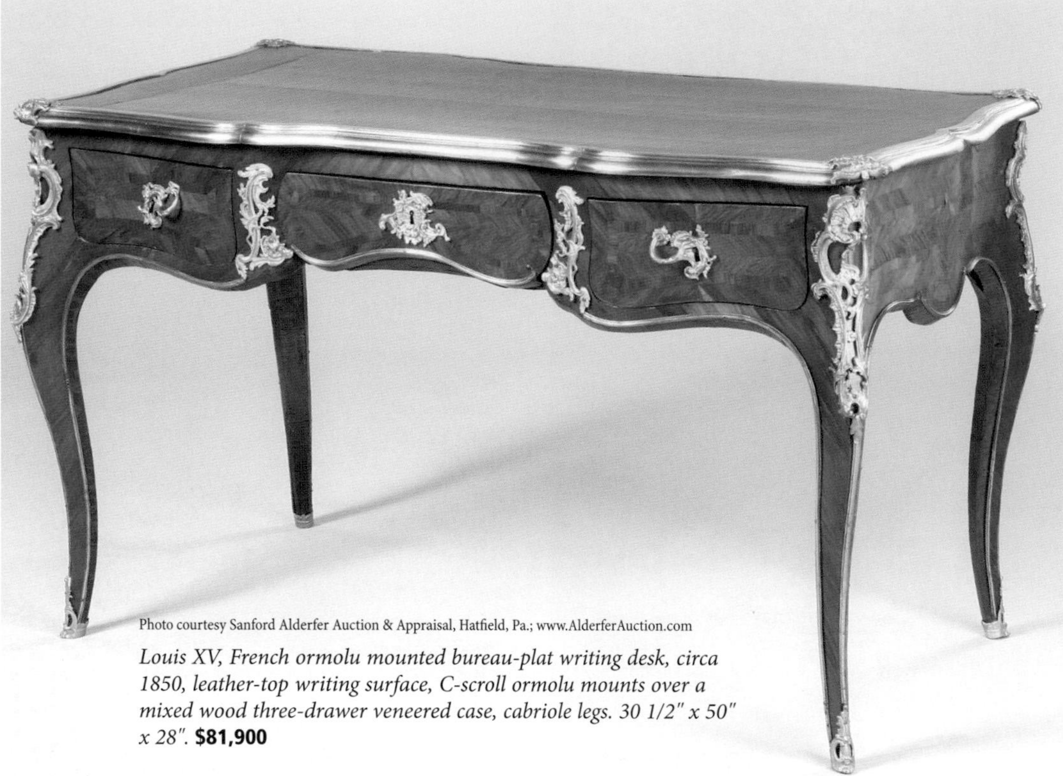

Photo courtesy Sanford Alderfer Auction & Appraisal, Hatfield, Pa.; www.AlderferAuction.com

Louis XV, French ormolu mounted bureau-plat writing desk, circa 1850, leather-top writing surface, C-scroll ormolu mounts over a mixed wood three-drawer veneered case, cabriole legs. 30 1/2" x 50" x 28". **$81,900**

thistles (replaced), bracket feet, 42 1/4" h, 39 1/4" w, 19 1/4" deep. **$517**

Desk, Lancaster County, Pa., inlaid cherry, slant front; writing board opening to fitted interior with inlaid arched prospect door with five small drawers behind, twin flanking document drawers, four arched pigeonholes, six small drawers; case with four cock-beaded graduated drawers, oval brasses, two lopers, French bracket feet, 44 7/8" h, 38" w, 20 1/2" deep. **$5,462**

Drop-front desk, (no. 91), Roycroft, with gallery interior, carved Orb and Cross mark, 44 1/4" x 38 1/2" x 19 1/2". **$6,600**

Drop-front desk and cabinet, Gustav Stickley, rare, with strap hinges, chamfered back, interior gallery, early red decal, 56" x 38" x 15". **$18,000**

Slant-front desk, carved oak, possibly by R.J. Horner, circa 1880; oblong top, mask head and patera-carved shallow map drawer, scroll-carved writing board; fitted interior with three convex-front drawers and pigeonholes, serpentine-front case with three conforming frieze drawers and small drawers beneath, supported by carved griffons, resting on stretcher shelf, molded set-back for feet, conforming carved side paneling, low square molded feet, 45 1/2" h, 42 1/2" w, 22" deep. **$8,625**

Traveler's desk, Hepplewhite, inlaid, oblong lift lid with centering blonde wood patera, four quarter-fans at corners, dark figured exotic wood with blonde wood borders, dovetailed drawer in base with brass bail handle, when open, sloping surface revealed with dark blue felt, glass ink bottle and pen tray, circa 1790, 6" h, 16 3/8" w, 10" deep. **$747**

Photo courtesy Sanford Alderfer Auction & Appraisal, Hatfield, Pa.; www.AlderferAuction.com

Sea captain's travel desk, line-inlaid mahogany with centering foil inlay marked "JH"; folding writing surface, green felt lined, including wood inkwell and wood sand shaker, three small interior drawers, twin brass handles, turned feet, 8 1/2" h, 19 5/8" w, 12" deep (closed). **$1,610**

Settees, Settles and Sofas

Settle, No. 220, L. & J.G. Stickley, paneled Prairie School form with wide arms supported by corbels, nicely recovered leather cushions, branded signature, cleaned

Photo courtesy Rago Arts and Auction Center, Lambertville, N.J.; www.RagoArts.com

Drop-arm settee (no. 219), Gustav Stickley, with slatted back and original drop-in spring seat recovered in black leather, unmarked, 37 1/2" x 71 1/2" x 26". **$2,160**

Photo courtesy Rago Arts and Auction Center, Lambertville, N.J.; www.RagoArts.com

Cube settle, Gustav Stickley, spindle sides with drop-in spring seat recovered in brown leather, red decal, 30 3/4" x 68 1/2" x 30". **$21,600**

Photo courtesy of Treadway Toomey Galleries, Cincinnati and Oak Park, Ill.; www.treadwaygallery.com

Settle, No. 775, L. and J.G. Stickley, even-arm paneled form with recovered cushion, original finish, signed with Handcraft decal, re-pegged, 84" w x 32" d x 40" h, very good condition. **$6,500**

Photo courtesy Sanford Alderfer Auction & Appraisal, Hatfield, Pa.; www.AlderferAuction.com

Sofa, William & Mary style, oak, high-back, double-arched top, outward scrolled arms, center ball-turned support flanked by molded scrollwork, domical foot; two conforming supports at front corners, turned and blocked stretchers; covered in pink, red and ivory flame-stitch patterned upholstery; 56 1/2" h, 64" w, 37" deep. **$2,400**

Photo courtesy Sanford Alderfer Auction & Appraisal, Hatfield, Pa.; www.AlderferAuction.com

Sideboard, Baroque Revival, mahogany, three "Atlas" figures providing support, three protruding mask head frieze drawers, two cabinet doors carved with women figural drawers, carved feet with mask heads, sides carved with shells, scrolls and flowers, 50" h, 73" w, 26 1/2" deep, top section missing. **$6,325**

original finish, rarely comes to market, 84" w x 37" d x 29" h, very good condition. **$18,000**

Settle, Arts & Crafts style, even-arm form with an upholstered seat and back, refinished, reupholstered, 72" w x 27 1/2" d x 39 1/2" h, very good condition. **$800**

Sideboards

Sideboard, Jacobean style, oak, oblong molded top, three drawers, each with recessed molded X-forms, brass drop handles, three vase-form and ring-turned front legs, bun feet, 35 1/4" h, 74 3/8" w, 20" deep. **$1,725**

Photo courtesy Rago Arts and Auction Center, Lambertville, N.J.; www.RagoArts.com

Sideboard (no. 814), Gustav Stickley, with plate rack and strap hardware, branded mark, 48" x 66" x 24". **$8,400**

Photo courtesy Sanford Alderfer Auction & Appraisal, Hatfield, Pa.; www.AlderferAuction.com

Sideboard, Sheraton, mahogany, two small cock-beaded drawers with brass ring handles, over arched opening, tapered round legs with vase-turned feet, 33 3/4" h, 37 1/8" w, 19 1/4" deep. **$2,587**
(A cock bead is a narrow half-round trim detail that surrounds a drawer front or door.)

(Jacobean style is the name given to the second phase of Renaissance design in England, following the Elizabethan style. It is associated with King James I, reign 1603–1625.)

Sideboards, (pair), marble tops, mahogany, beige marble tops, early 20th century, with dentil molding, canted corners, each with paw foot below and lion head above, 35" h, 72" w, 25 3/4" deep. .... **$920 pair**

Photo courtesy Clars Auction Gallery, Oakland, Calif.; www.Clars.com

Marshall Laird, Los Angeles, Elizabethan-style carved oak server, circa 1920, the hand-planed top having a hinged left side above double doors featuring portrait panels over a frieze carved with grapes and acanthus leaves, on carved supports and box stretcher base, retaining maker's plaque, 37" h x 41" x 20" d. **$450**

Photo courtesy Clars Auction Gallery, Oakland, Calif.; www.Clars.com

Marshall Laird, Los Angeles, Elizabethan-style carved oak sideboard, circa 1920, with hand-planed and carved surface over conforming base with linen-fold side panels, three drawers with grape and vine carved motif, flanked by relief carved doors, the whole rising on turned legs with beaded stretchers, retaining Marshall Laird plaque, 36" h x 71" w x 21" d. **$475**

American Late Classical-style three cushion sofa, circa 1940, with cornucopia crest rail and arms ending in rosettes, above plume knees and claw feet, upholstered in floral tapestry fabric, 34 1/2" h x 84" w x 34" d. **$150**

American Late Classical-style, flame mahogany two-door bookcase, mid- to late 19th century, rectangular top with outset corners above pilasters with carved capitols, double mullioned glazed glass doors, the whole rising on paw feet with acanthus leaf knees, 49 1/2" h x 50" w x 15 1/2" d, lacking one 8" section of mullion molding. **$950**

Berkey & Gay Federal-style chest of drawers having a shield-form mirror and turned, ebonized wood accents, with reverse serpentine front, enhanced with beading and oval brasses, rising on tapered legs, retaining maker's label, 70" h x 48" w x 19" d. **$250**

Carved oak Jacobean-style, blind-door china cupboard, circa 1890, with pegged joinery, molded, paneled double doors with floral carving opening to reveal four adjustable shelves, above double short drawers with brass drops, the whole rising on turned stretcher base, 61" h x 41 1/2" w x 18" d. **$700**

Century Furniture Co., Grand Rapids, Cromwellian walnut china cabinet, with molded cornice above double doors centered with shell carved relief, with ebonized and turned split spindle panels having geometric inlay, above a molded long drawer flanked with acanthus leaves, the whole rising on turned stretcher, beaded base, ending in Spanish feet, 59" h x 46" w x 21" d. **$250**

China Trade Regency-style cane sofa, early 19th century, hardwood in lacquer layers, the back rail centered in a large concave shell carving flanked with scroll molding with rosettes joined by rolled arms with floral carving, rosettes and quarter-fan, the seat rail with central and flanked reserves, the whole rising on lyre legs ending in urn feet, 35" h x 81 1/2" w x 24 1/2" d. Seat upholstered in Classical motif fabric with bolsters. **$4,500**

Mayhew Furniture Co., Milwaukee, custom mahogany Chippendale-style side chairs (six) and an armchair, having oxbow crest rail, pierced splats, slip seats, on ball and claw feet, the side chairs with latticework frieze panels, armchair 38" h x 24" w x 18" d. .... **$300 set**

Oval marble top, Victorian lantern parlor table with open-work walnut base, 28 1/2" h x 29" w x 21" d, hairline crack to marble. **$150**

Walnut open armchair attributed to Maison Jansen, Paris, mid-20th century, acanthus leaf crest rail above interlaces loop splat, serpentine shaped arms the whole rising on carved cabriole legs ending in pad feet, seat upholstered in chinoiserie motif damask, 38" h x 28" w x 23" d. **$750**

White marble Victorian pedestal with rope-carved column with black veining, having ringed collars, ending in a circular and octagonal stepped base, 44" h. **$400**

Tables

Banquet table, Sheraton, mahogany, two sections, each with rounded corners, single leaf, five reeded tapered round legs (one support leg swings out), ball feet, circa 1820, 28 1/2" h, 48" w, 84 1/2" l, additional bracing underneath. **$920**

Boulle table, ormolu-mounted, shield-form top, center with chariot driver holding spear, conforming serpentine front drawer, mask heads at corners, cabriole legs, ormolu paw feet, 30 1/4" h, 35 1/4" l, 21" w, inlay damage at one rounded end. **$977**
(André-Charles Boulle [1642–1732], was a French cabinetmaker generally considered the preeminent artist in the field of marquetry.)

Center table, marquetry inlaid, center reserve with profusion of flowers, stems, leafage and birds, heavily leaf-scrolled border, single frieze drawer, marquetry drawer front, apron, tapering square legs and shaped stretcher, bun feet, 28" h, 42 3/4" w, 33" deep, refinished. **$1,955**

Center table, oval, late 19th century, mahogany, conforming inner top band of low relief scroll- and latticework; conforming acanthus leaf apron, four acanthus-carved vase and ball supports on oval platform base with narrow acanthus apron and four bold paw feet with casters, 29 1/2" h, 53 3/4" x 35 3/4" (top). **$2,300**

Dining table, massive mahogany, circular, possibly by R.J. Horner, late 19th century, molded extension top, paneled octagonal pedestal supported by carved S-scrolled braces, resting on shaped stretchers, square paneled legs headed by scrolled, undercut carving above husk pendants, molded square feet, casters, 29 1/2" h, 65 1/2" d. With additional leaves. **$5,750**

Dining table, mahogany, made by Baker, extension top with rounded ends and corners, cross-banded blonde mahogany, twin tapered round ringed pedestals, each on four splayed reeded saber legs with brass caps and casters, including three 18" leaves, 28 1/2" h, 72" l (no leaves in place), 46" w. **$6,000**

Dining table, mahogany, early 19th century, deep drop leaves, tapered square legs; two legs swing out for support, 29" h, 42" w, 58" l (leaves up). **$201**

Dining table and five side chairs, Shop of the Crafters, with one leaf. Unmarked. Table, 28" x 54", 11" leaf, chairs 43 1/2" x 19" x 18". .... **$9,600 set**

Dining table and eight chairs, Federal style, extension-top dining table with cross-banded border and rounded corners, twin pedestals, each with fluted urn, four down-swept reeded legs with acanthus decoration, brass paw feet with casters; 29 1/8" h, 42" w (leaves down), 60" l including five 12" leaves in case and set of pads; together with eight mahogany square-back chairs (2 armchairs and 6 side chairs); strapwork urn splat with drapery swags; over-upholstered gold and pale green seat; molded tapered square legs with spade front feet, 36 5/8" h, 23" w. .... **$2,875 set**

Drop-leaf table, birch, deep overhang at ends, slender tapered square legs, 28 3/8" h, 31 1/2" w (leaves up). **$126**

Drop-leaf table, Sheraton, mahogany, reeded round legs (two swing out to support leaves), circa 1820, 29 1/8" h, 68 3/8" l (leaves up). **$270**

Drop-leaf table, Victorian, mahogany, with D-end flaps and ball-and-claw feet, 19th century, 28" x 43" x 20". **$480**

Gaming table, inlaid, exotic mixed-wood circular top with checkerboard, faceted apron, small drawer, three legs with carved zigzag motif. **$632**

Library table, Arts & Crafts style, rectangular top with four vertical slats to each side over a lower shelf, through tenon construction, original brass hardware, worn original finish, some damage to side, 36" w x 24" d x 30" h, good condition. **$275**

Library table, Arts & Crafts style, possibly Harden, rectangular top over two drawers with original hardware, slatted sides with through tenon construction, refinished, 49" w x 29" d x 30" h, good condition. **$450**

Photo courtesy Sanford Alderfer Auction & Appraisal, Hatfield, Pa.; www.AlderferAuction.com

Card table, Hepplewhite, inlaid, mahogany; folding top, "ovolo" corners, oval blonde wood reserve, geometric border inlay, tapered square legs with line inlay; diamond-form inlay above legs, 30" h, 35 3/4" w, 16 7/8" deep (closed). **$1,380**
(Ovolo refers to a convex molding having a cross section in the form of a quarter of a circle or of an ellipse.)

Photo courtesy Sanford Alderfer Auction & Appraisal, Hatfield, Pa.; www.AlderferAuction.com

Dining table, oak, circa 1900, extension top, circular top with gadrooned border, four carved lion heads with acanthus, short curved legs, massive paw feet; including five 12" leaves in case and turned central support, 28 3/4" h, 59 1/4" d. **$5,750**

Photo courtesy James D. Julia Auctioneers, Fairfield, Maine; www.JuliaAuctions.com

Dressing table, State of Maine, Sheraton faux-grained paint-decorated pine, circa 1825, shaped splash guard with paint-decorated cluster of fruit and ochre striping fitted to the rectangular top above the conforming frieze with long drawer raised on cylindrical swelled and ring-turned legs on ball feet, 31 1/2" h, 32 1/2" w, 17" deep. Retains good original surface and patina. Paint mostly intact showing nominal and normal wear. **$1,380**

Photo courtesy Sanford Alderfer Auction & Appraisal, Hatfield, Pa.; www.AlderferAuction.com

Library table, Elizabethan style, oak, molded apron with two drawers with brass drop handles, twin leaf-carved bulbous supports resting on trestles connected by carved stretcher, 34" h, 60" w, 22" deep. **$517**

Occasional table, Samuel Yellin, wrought iron, tripod with hammered copper tray, normal cleaning to tray, authenticated by Samuel Yellin Metalworkers, unmarked, 33" x 21". **$4,200**

Pembroke table, English, mahogany, molded drop-leaf top with rounded corners, cock-beaded end drawer with two brass pulls, conforming opposite mock drawer, tapered square legs, casters; circa 1840, 28" h, 36" w, 45 1/4" l. (leaves up). **$316**

(A cock bead is a narrow half-round trim detail that surrounds a drawer front or door. The characteristic that gives a table the name of Pembroke involves the drop leaves, which are held up, when the table is open, by brackets that turn under the top.)

Photo courtesy Rago Arts and Auction Center, Lambertville, N.J.; www.RagoArts.com

Luncheon table (no. 647), Gustav Stickley, with stretcher on edge, mortised with keyed-through tenons, unmarked, 29 1/2" x 40" x 28". **$2,160**

Photo courtesy Rago Arts and Auction Center, Lambertville, N.J.; www.RagoArts.com

Pembroke table, mahogany, with reeded legs and shaped corner flaps, 19th century, 29" x 36" x 21 1/2". **$420**

Photo courtesy Rago Arts and Auction Center, Lambertville, N.J.; www.RagoArts.com

Refectory table, English, oak, with single drawer on frieze, barley-twist legs and stretchers, 19th century, 32" x 45 1/2" x 22". **$780**

Photo courtesy Rago Arts and Auction Center, Lambertville, N.J.; www.RagoArts.com

"Rocket" occasional table, Bradley & Hubbard / Longwy, embossed brass, top and shaft inlaid with Longwy tiles, circa 1880-1885, 33 1/4" x 14" sq. **$6,600**

Photo courtesy James D. Julia Auctioneers, Fairfield, Maine; www.JuliaAuctions.com

Sewing table, Massachusetts, Sheraton, circa 1810, figured mahogany inlaid three-drawer, rectangular top with canted corners and figured birch cross banding above the conforming case, fitted with three long string-inlaid drawers, two with ivory escutcheons and the third fitted for a bag. Raised on cylindrical reeded and ring-turned slender legs with multiple ring cuffs. Old dry finish with minor losses to cross banding on top; top two drawers with original escutcheons and hardware. Bag slide has original front and slide but has been reconstructed into a drawer. Old repairs rejoining the four legs to the table top, professionally done. Other minor veneer chips, 30" h x 20 1/2" w x 14 3/4" deep. **$690**

Side table, Chippendale, walnut, top with invected front corners, thumb-molded frieze drawer, two brass bail handles, straight legs with molded outer corners, chamfered inner corners, 28 3/4" h, 35" w, 19 1/8" deep. **$1,265**

(Invected means having a border or outline composed of semicircles with the convexity outward; the opposite of engrailed.)

Side table, gilt wood, white alabaster top, apron with acorn and oak leaf decoration, conforming out-set fluted tapered round legs with ball feet, 19th century, 29 1/4" h, 28 1/4" w, 19 1/2" deep. **$480**

Side table, tiger maple, single drawer with pressed glass pull, tapered round legs with vase-form feet, 28 3/4" h, 25" w, 15" deep. **$920**

Side table, walnut, oblong top, single drawer with two brasses (replaced), ring-turned round legs, ball feet, 19th century. **$201**

Table, Bucks County, Pa., red painted, molded top, drawer with brass pull, splayed tapered square legs, 19th century, 29" h, 16 1/4" w, 17" deep. **$1,150**

Table with lift top, cherry, three small compartments to rear, single drawer with figured cherry facing and brass pull, twin half-spindle sides flanking, ring-turned tapered round legs, circa 1840, 28 3/4" h, 22" w, 21 7/8" deep. **$575**

Table, marble top, walnut, octagonal black marble top with white striations, walnut tripod base with three partially disrobed women at corners, low relief images of birds, musicians and other figures; bold paw feet, 30 1/4" h. (not including marble top), vertical shrinkage splits in base. **$3,900**

Taboret (no. 46), Gustav Stickley, rare, with hexagonal top over six angled legs and corbels, circa 1901, unmarked, 21" x 19" sq. **$7,200**

Photo courtesy Rago Arts and Auction Center, Lambertville, N.J.; www.RagoArts.com

Table, attributed to Old Hickory, with quarter-sawn oak veneered oval top over five legs. Unmarked, 30" x 66" x 36". **$1,560**

Work table, pine, drawer with wood pull, tapered square legs with splay, 19th century, 29 1/2" h, top 19" x 18 7/8". **$184**

Other Forms

Bench, Arts & Crafts style, spindle form with 18 vertical spindles to back over a recovered leather seat, cleaned original finish, 44 1/2" w x 22" d x 39" h, very good condition. **$600**

Bookstand, wrought iron, slanting scrolled rests for two books, "spear" point at center, pair of swiveling candleholders, twist standard with tripod scrolled base, 61 1/2" h. **$1,150**

Cradle, red finish, heart-form cutout in headboard and footboard, twin rocker base, 19th century, 22 1/2" h, 40" l. **$86**

Footstool, No. 300, Gustav Stickley, original leather and tacks over a base with original finish, signed with red decal and partial paper label, 20 1/2" w x 16 1/2" d x 16" h, excellent condition. **$1,800**

Footstool, Victorian, American, carved mahogany with floral bouquets on the skirt, Spanish feet and needlepoint

Photo courtesy of Treadway Toomey Galleries, Cincinnati and Oak Park, Ill.; www.treadwaygallery.com

Bench, circa 1910, rectangular top with pyrographic cattail design, original finish, 38 1/2" w x 15" d x 19" h, very good condition. **$550**

Photo courtesy Sanford Alderfer Auction & Appraisal, Hatfield, Pa.; www.AlderferAuction.com

Butler's tray on stand, mahogany, 19th century, oblong with shaped gallery and pierced hand-holds, dovetailed corners, folding stand; tray, 27 1/2" x 17 1/4". **$570**

Photo courtesy of Treadway Toomey Galleries, Cincinnati and Oak Park, Ill.; www.treadwaygallery.com

Footstool, Arts & Crafts style, contemporary, in mahogany, similar to Gustav Stickley No. 395, seven vertical spindles to each side, 20" w x 16" d x 16" h, very good condition. **$150**

Photo courtesy Sanford Alderfer Auction & Appraisal, Hatfield, Pa.; www.AlderferAuction.com

Footstool, Berks County, Pa., made by Marks DeTurk, Jan. 5, 1920; oblong with splayed tenoned legs, finely detailed bird and tree decoration, 6" h, 12" l, 5 5/8" w. **$1,560**

Photo courtesy Rago Arts and Auction Center, Lambertville, N.J.; www.RagoArts.com

Hanging wall shelf, Charles Rohlfs, with scrolled sides, 1905, carved R 1905, 44" x 27" x 7 1/2". **$5,100**

Photo courtesy Rago Arts and Auction Center, Lambertville, N.J.; www.RagoArts.com

Magazine stand (no. 80), Roycroft, tall trapezoidal, carved Orb and Cross mark, 64" x 17 3/4" sq. **$18,000**

upholstery of a reclining dachshund, 17" x 23" x 16". **$360**

Parlor suite, Victorian, mahogany, 19th century: armchair with carved rams heads and paw feet on metal casters; fire screen with needlework panel and applied glass beads; and Chippendale-style side table. Tallest: 43". .... **$1,800 set**

Screen, Arts & Crafts style, in mahogany, peaked top over leaded amber glass panels, original strap hardware, original finish, each panel: 24" w x 63" h, very good condition. **$325**

Stand, Arts & Crafts style, rectangular top over a drop-front cabinet door with original strap hinges, slatted sides with

Photo courtesy Rago Arts and Auction Center, Lambertville, N.J. www.RagoArts.com

Picnic set, Old Hickory, with table and two benches. Branded marks. Table 30" x 60" x 30", benches 18" x 48" x 14". **$3,600 set**

through tenon construction, original finish, 25" w x 14" d x 30" h, very good condition. **$500**

Tabouret, circa 1915, Moorish influence, octagonal top with deeply carved and inlaid designs in mother-of-pearl, some wear and separation, 16 1/2" w x 16 1/2" d x 20" h, good condition. **$250**

Wardrobe, Gustave Serrurier-Bovy, with mirrored door next to five-drawer cabinet, wrought-iron hardware. Branded Serrurier Liege, 82 1/2" x 58 1/4" x 23 1/2". **$10,200**

(Gustave Serrurier-Bovy [1858-1910] was a Belgian architect and furniture designer.)

Barometers

Mahogany-cased barometer, C-scroll cresting over mercury thermometer, barometer with steel dial marked "Royal Hotel," 47 3/8" h, 15" w. **$632**

Mahogany-cased barometer, unsigned, 19th century, having a single dial with thermometer and mirror. In an older refinish, 38" l. **$345**

Stick barometer, walnut, baluster form, with mercury tube covered with a turned half-column along most of its length, with a turned rosette at the base. Printed dial marked "S. Bennett" across the bottom, with different weather conditions along the sides. Mounted to the face and flanking the dial is a thermometer and indicator; retains old varnish, 42" l. **$287**

Stick barometer, telescope form, in walnut and ebonized walnut with tombstone top, silvered dial with barometer vertical through center and thermometer mounted along right margin, marked "The Standard" at top and "Storm King/Barometer/Warranted Correct/Manufactured/And Sold by/C. Spooner/Boston," with original cover glass, in original finish, 42" l. **$287**

Photo courtesy James D. Julia Auctioneers, Fairfield, Maine; www.JuliaAuctions.com

Shaving stand, Federal, mahogany and boxwood, inlaid, circa 1810. Oval mirror suspended on cyma-curved arms resting on a rectangular box with serpentine front fitted with three aligned drawers each with a brass knob pull, the whole raised on ogee bracket feet, minor staining on surface of glove box probably due to perfume or cologne bottles leaving ring outlines. Brackets for mirror appear original as do the feet, 22 1/2" h x 17" w x 8" deep. **$402**

Photo courtesy Rago Arts and Auction Center, Lambertville, N.J.; www.RagoArts.com

Vanity and mirror (no. 110), Roycroft, with single drawer, carved Orb and Cross mark, 56" x 39" x 17 1/2". **$3,900**

Photo courtesy Sanford Alderfer Auction & Appraisal, Hatfield, Pa.; www.AlderferAuction.com

Washstand, mahogany, lift top revealing circular basin opening and openings for two glasses, cabinet door below flanked by twin spiral molded pilasters, spiral turned round legs, ball feet, circa 1840, 32 3/4" h, 18" w, 16 1/4" deep; split at right rear corner of lid. **$805**

Mirrors

Convex mirror, classical gilt gesso and wood, England or America, circa 1800, re-gilded, (imperfections), 43" d, may lack candle sconces; most of the frame is repainted; chips to gesso. **$2,370**

Dressing table mirror, Hepplewhite, mahogany veneer, early 19th century, shield-shaped mirror, bowed base with three drawers on ogee bracket feet, cross-banded borders, 23" h, 16 1/2" w, 8" deep, one drawer pull replaced, unobtrusive crack to top surface, missing one circular ivory disk decoration, crack across on side. **$207**

Chippendale-style mirror, with carved and gilded bird's eye maple frame, circa 1900, 47" x 25". **$900**

Classical gilt and black-painted mirror, split-baluster, Massachusetts, circa 1825, tablet with a fruit-filled cornucopia, (minor imperfections), 44" h, 20 3/4" w. **$2,962**

Federal parcel-gilt mirror, American, with reverse-painted panel, circa 1820, stepped cornice with 12 spherules above the rectangular painted panel depicting a basket of fruit within stylized green and red spandrels over the rectangular mirror plate. Flanked by engaged concave balusters, housing rope twist columns on a concave plinth, 33" h x 17" w, panel is original with some paint loss above the basket of fruit and at the foot rim of basket. Minor rubbing to gilding. **$1,265**

Federal gilt-wood mirror, circa 1840, oval mirror plate within opposing cornucopia surmounted by a displayed eagle perched on leafy boughs, 23" x 26". **$2,300**

Federal carved gilt wood over-mantel mirror, American, circa 1830, stepped cornice above the rectangular frame, frieze with carved draperies flanked by fluted columns with anthemion leaves and oval reeded patera centering three rectangular mirror plates. Surrounds with attached floral garlands. Lower molded apron with acorn leaf carvings, 27" h x 60" l, retains original glasses and backboards. Original surfaces are somewhat chipped with losses to gesso and some of the gilt work throughout the entire mirror frame, overall probably 3-4 percent. **$2,990**

Fret-scrolled mahogany mirror, gilt molded bezel, original beveled glass, 29 3/4" h. **$488**

Fret-scrolled mahogany frame mirror, molded bezel, circa 1800, 41 1/4" h, 22" w, replaced glass; shrinkage splits to cresting. **$690**

Hall mirror, No. 65, L. & J.G. Stickley, arched top over original glass and hammered iron hooks, signed with Handcraft decal, original finish, some restoration, 40" w x 26 1/2" h, very good condition. **$700**

Hall Mirror, L. & J.G. Stickley, long rectangular form with original dark finish, signed "The Work of ...," original glass, 56" w x 17" h, excellent condition. **$650**

Over-mantel mirror, classical gilt gesso and wood, probably New England, circa 1825, (minor imperfections), 25" h, 56" l, gesso loss and some gilding loss, minor clouding in mirrors. **$948**

Glass

GLASS

Listed by Form, Style or Type

For glass grouped by specific makers, see end of this section. *Also see Perfume Containers, Tiffany.*

Art Glass

Art Deco, Decorated Rib Optic Cylindrical Vase, colorless with polychrome enameled flower decoration, pink enameled background signed "Leg." near base. Possibly Legras. First quarter 20th century. 4 3/4" h, 1 5/8" d. **$96**

Art Deco, Tinted Crystal Vase, colorless to green with spaced blue and green spirals, random embedded mica flakes to upper half, polished bottom with ground pontil mark. Possibly French. First half 20th century. 12" h, 5" d rim. Several bruises to edge of base. **$108**

Cluthra-Type Vase, mottled green, polished pontil mark. Possibly Steuben or Kimball. First half 20th century. 4 3/4" h, 3 5/8" d rim. **$172**

Daum Nancy, Art Deco Vase, smoky topaz with some amethyst, flattened hexagonal rim with cut and polished edges, polished base, signed "Daum (cross) Nancy, France" at the edge of base. Second quarter 20th century. 6 7/8" h, 10" d overall. Minute nick to the edge of rim. **$270**

Dorflinger Honesdale, Cameo Pinch Vase, green cut to clear Art Nouveau pattern with textured background, gilt decoration, polished pontil with gilt signature. Early 20th century. 7 1/4" h. Some wear to gilt and an open bubble to rim interior. **$460**

Etling, art glass figural vase with nude, opalescent glass, circa 1930. Marked Etling France, 7 7/8" h. **$1,800**

Photo courtesy Green Valley Auctions, Mt. Crawford, Va.; www.GreenValleyAuctions.com

Durand, Lustre Ware Vase, gold iridescent, polished pontil mark signed "Durand / V / 1982-14". Vineland Flint Glass Works. First quarter 20th century. 14" h.
$920

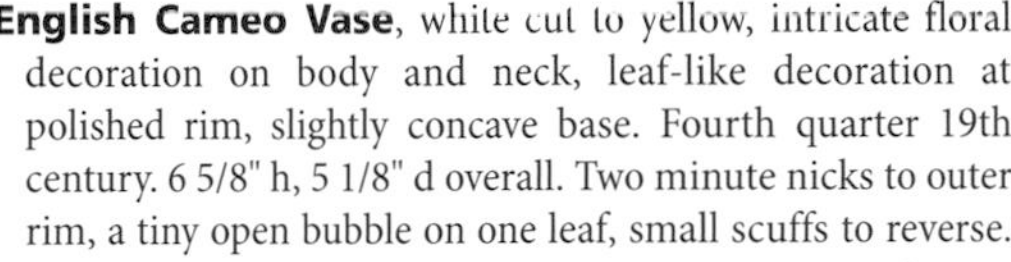

English Cameo Vase, white cut to yellow, intricate floral decoration on body and neck, leaf-like decoration at polished rim, slightly concave base. Fourth quarter 19th century. 6 5/8" h, 5 1/8" d overall. Two minute nicks to outer rim, a tiny open bubble on one leaf, small scuffs to reverse. **$2,070**

Gallé, Cameo Vase, brown cut to yellow green cut to peach, landscape decoration full round, signed, polished slightly concave base. First quarter 20th century. 6 1/2" h, 4" d overall. **$1,320**

Gallé, Enameled and Etched Vase, ice green with polychrome and gilt decoration, icicle-like decoration at rim and all-over roughed background, signed "GaLLé / Nancy, Paris / Depose / g.g" in gold under base. Emile Gallé. Late 19th/early 20th century. 8" h, 4 3/4" d overall. Flake to edge of foot, loss of majority of gilding. **$1,092**

Gilt-Decorated, Spangle and Crackle Basket, heavy olive green glass with red, white and blue mottling, embedded gold foil, crackled interior, and gilt floral decoration, polished table ring and slightly concave base. Late 19th/early 20th century. 9 3/4" h, 6 1/2" d overall. Wear to handle and rim gilding. **$360**

Gold Iridescent Vase, tooled rim, scratched "3689" under base, polished pontil mark. Shape number not identified although similar shapes were produced by Durand and Steuben, among others. First half 20th century. 8" h, 7 3/4" d overall. **$517**

Photo courtesy Green Valley Auctions, Mt. Crawford, Va.; www.GreenValleyAuctions.com

English Cameo Footed Vase, white cut to yellow, intricate floral decoration on body, stylized scrollwork on neck, polished rim, slightly concave base. Probably Thomas Webb & Sons. Fourth quarter 19th century. 9" h, 3 1/4" d overall.
$3,737

Photo courtesy Green Valley Auctions, Mt. Crawford, Va.; www.GreenValleyAuctions.com

Loetz, Giant Clam-Like Fan Vase, red to yellow green swirling mottled iridescent, unmarked, partially polished pontil mark. Late 19th/early 20th century. 12" h, 5 1/2" x 12 1/4" rim, 6" d base. **$488**

Imperial, Lead Lustre Vase, swirling blue and opal mosaic exterior with blue luster interior, shape no. 623, decoration 11, polished pontil mark. Imperial Glass Co. Circa 1925. 9 3/4" h, 3 1/4" d rim. **$517**

Kew-Blas, Water Pitcher, shaded gold iridescent, applied handle, polished pontil mark with engraved signature. Union Glass Co., Somerville, Mass. Late 19th/early 20th century. 7 1/2" h overall. **$373**

Libbey-Nash, Threaded Jug, colorless with blue decoration, shape K-540, colorless applied handle and foot, polished pontil mark signed with Libbey trademark. Libbey Glass Manufacturing Co. Second quarter 20th century. 9" h, 3 3/4" d foot. **$287**

Libbey-Nash-Type, Hat-Form Vase, colorless with green wavy thread decoration, not signed, polished pontil mark. Possibly Libbey Glass Manufacturing Co. Second quarter 20th century. 2" h, 5 1/8" d. **$57**

Locke Art-Style, Buster Brown and Tige Mug, colorless, the front featuring Buster Brown holding a jumping jack toy with his dog by his side, back with floral decoration. First quarter 20th century. 3 1/4" h. **$805**

Loetz, Karneol Pair of Pinch Vases, marbled red with opal interior, gilt decoration on neck and shoulder with tiny white enamel dots. Fourth quarter 19th century. 11" h. Some wear to gilt. .... **$575 pair**

Collector's Note: Loetz is a type of iridescent art glass that was made in Austria by J. Loetz Witwe in the late 1890s. The Loetz factory at Klostermule produced items with fine cameos on cased glass, as well as the iridescent glassware commonly associated with the Loetz name.

Loetz, Neptune Vase, green iridescent, three-point rim, polished pontil mark. Early 20th century. 6 5/8" h. **$517**

Loetz, Papillon Decorated Covered Jar, deep cobalt blue with mottled iridescent, hexagonal form with polished rim. First quarter 20th century. 5 1/4" h overall, 4 3/4" d overall. Minute flake to cover rim. **$460**

Loetz-Type, Diamond Quilted Bowl, opal cased beige iridescent, raised on three green scrolled feet, polished rim. First quarter 20th century. 4 1/8" h, 5 3/4" d rim, 8 1/4" d overall. **$126**

Loetz-Type, Marmorierte-Style Vase, cased red and deep green with tiny mica flecks, gilt decoration, square pinched-side form with four small applied handles on shoulder, polished rim. First quarter 20th century. 12 1/4" h, 5 3/4" sq base. Wear to gilt on handles and rim. **$480**

Loetz-Type, Phanomen-Style Decorated Vase, opaque black with purple iridescence, slightly swirled pinched-side form, polished rim, kick-up to base. First quarter 20th century. 12 1/4" h, 5 1/4" d overall. **$149**

Loetz-Type, Ribbed Waisted-Form Vase, amethyst iridescent, crimped rim and pinched base, rough pontil mark. First quarter 20th century. 12" h, 4 1/2" d rim. Small shear mark to one lower rib. **$144**

Loetz-Type, Thread-Decorated Vase, amethyst iridescent, applied random threading, polished rim. Late 19th/early 20th century. 6 1/4" h. Losses to threading, flake to base, possibly reduced in height. **$84**

Moser, Cameo-Frieze Decorated Vaseline Low Vase, Amazon warrior frieze above cut panels, polished base signed, "Made in Czechoslovakia, Moser, Karlsbad" in script. First quarter 20th century. 3 3/4" h, 3 3/8" d rim. Inner rim with two minute flakes and a small polished area. **$330**

Collector's Note: Ludwig Moser (1833-1916) founded his polishing and engraving workshop in 1857 in Karlsbad, Czechoslovakia. In 1900, Moser and his sons, Rudolf and Gustav, incorporated Ludwig Moser & Söhne. Moser art glass included clear pieces with inserted blobs of colored glass, cut colored glass with classical scenes, cameo glass and intaglio-cut items. Many inexpensive enameled pieces also were made.

Moser-Style, Cobalt Blue to Colorless Nut Cup, gilt dogwood decoration, unusual cut and tooled "finger" rim and single applied hook-like handle, polished table ring. Fourth quarter 19th century. 3 1/4" h overall, 2 1/4" h rim, 3" d rim. **$69**

Moser-Style, Footed Mug, colorless, six panels each with finely detailed gilt filigree and amber-stained cabochon, two panels and reserve with applied handle, base with cut rays and polished pontil mark. First quarter 20th century. 5 3/4" h, 2 3/4" d rim, 3 3/4" d base. Minute nick to end of one ray, slight wear to gilt at rim. **$92**

Moser-Type, Persian-Style Urn, smoky amethyst with bright polychrome enamel decoration, two gold applied handles, polished table ring. Late 19th/early 20th century. 12" h. Some light residue in base. **$2,185**

Photo courtesy James D. Julia Auctioneers, Fairfield, Maine; www.JuliaAuctions.com

Loetz Jack In The Pulpit Vase. Gold iridescent with stretched glass face with pink and green highlights. 12" t x 7 1/4" diameter of face. **$1,140**

Photo courtesy James D. Julia Auctioneers, Fairfield, Maine; www.JuliaAuctions.com

Loetz Decorated Vase. With platinum iridescent wave design against an amber background. The cylindrical body gives way to a slightly flaring lip. Unsigned. 6 1/8" t. **$517**

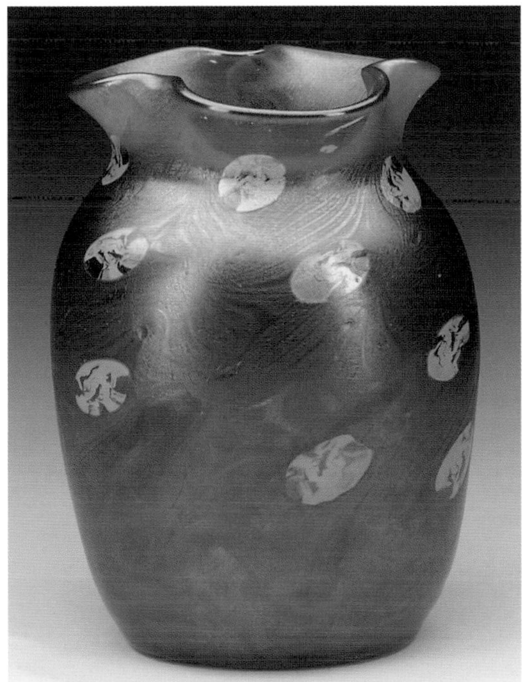

Photo courtesy James D. Julia Auctioneers, Fairfield, Maine; www.JuliaAuctions.com

Loetz Decorated Vase. With body of salmon at the lip shading to orange with a lightly iridescent wave pattern throughout the body. Vase is further highlighted with platinum and blue iridescent oval spots. Unsigned. 5 1/4" t. **$966**

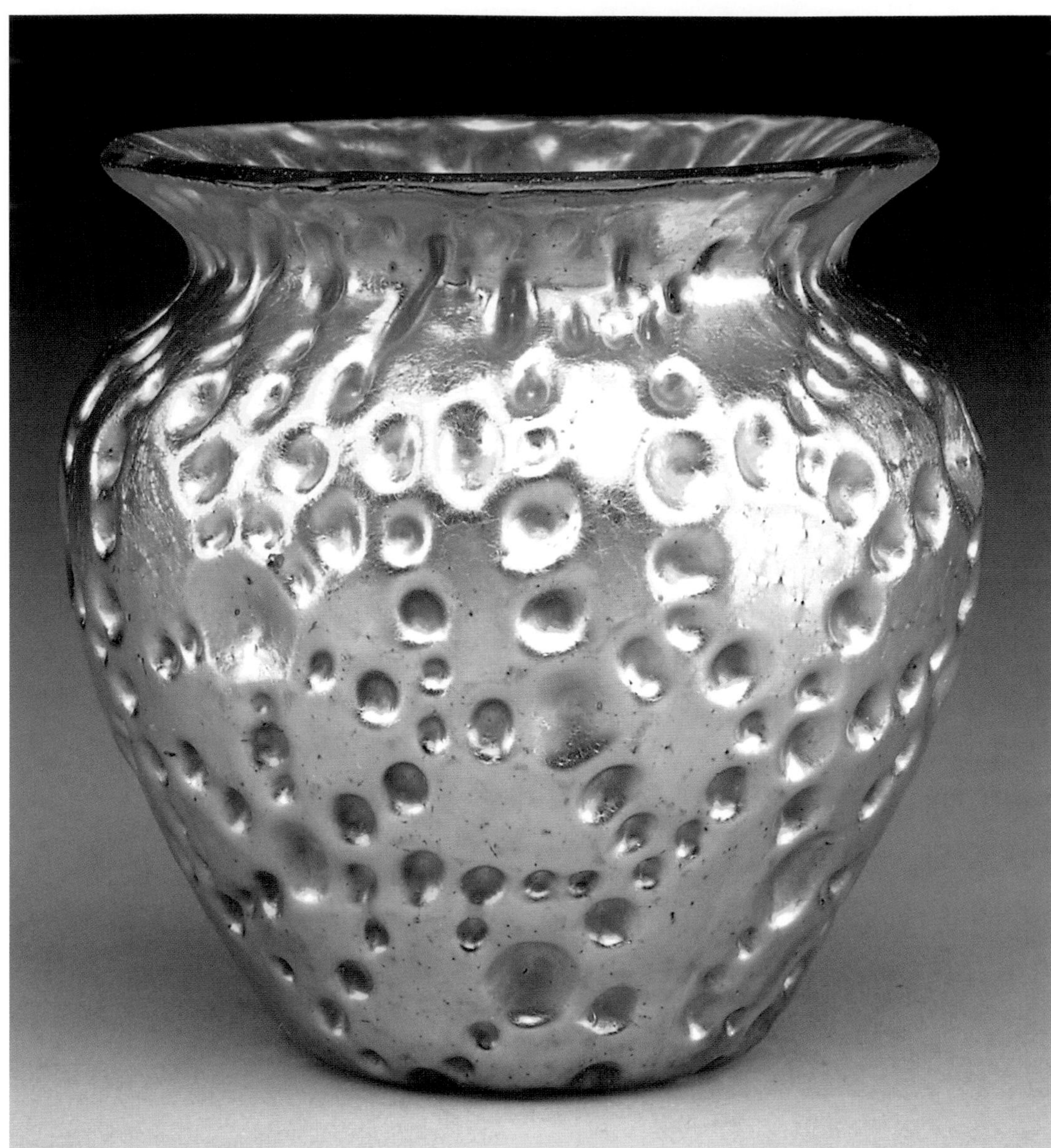

Photo courtesy James D. Julia Auctioneers, Fairfield, Maine; www.JuliaAuctions.com

Loetz Gold Crater Vase. With deeply impressed moon crater design with rich gold iridescent finish showing pink and blue highlights. Unsigned. 3 1/4" t. **$180**

Photo courtesy James D. Julia Auctioneers, Fairfield, Maine; www.JuliaAuctions.com

Bohemian Art Glass Bowl. Probably produced by Von Poschinger, features lightly iridized frosted glass body with purple threading and lightly stretched ruffled rim. 11" diameter. **$115**

Photo courtesy James D. Julia Auctioneers, Fairfield, Maine; www.JuliaAuctions.com

Kew Blas Decorated Vase. Cabinet vase has squat body with yellow to gold iridescent pulled-feather design against a creamy white background. The interior of the vase is finished with a bright gold iridescence. Signed on the underside within the polished pontil "Kew Blas". 3" t. **$115**

Photo courtesy James D. Julia Auctioneers, Fairfield, Maine; www.JuliaAuctions.com

Steuben Blue Jade Vase. Large bulbous form with flaring rim, shape no. 6500. 6 1/2" t x 7 1/2" w. **$4,025**

Photo courtesy James D. Julia Auctioneers, Fairfield, Maine; www.JuliaAuctions.com

Steuben Acid Cut-Back Vase. Rose quartz vase has deep acid cut-back design in the Acanthus pattern with pink color and crackling. The vase is signed on the side with acid cut-back fleur de lis mark. 10 1/2" t. **$2,587**

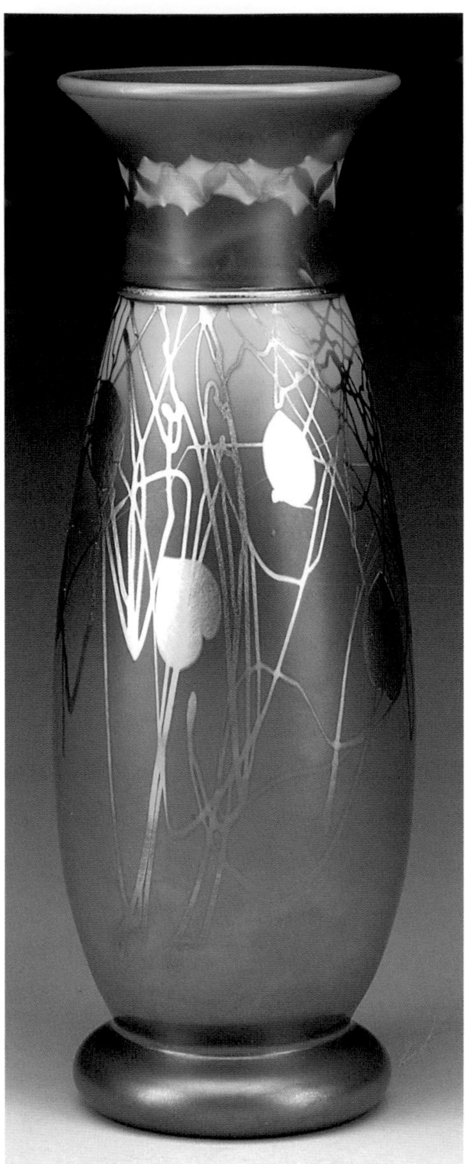

Photo courtesy James D. Julia Auctioneers, Fairfield, Maine; www.JuliaAuctions.com

Steuben Tyrian Vase. With gold iridescent leaf and vine design against a body shading from sea-foam green to rich bluish purple. The vase is finished with an applied neck with intarsia design and slightly flaring rim. Signed on the underside "Tyrian". 10" t. **$25,000**

Photo courtesy James D. Julia Auctioneers, Fairfield, Maine; www.JuliaAuctions.com

Steuben Acid Cut-Back Vase. Green jade cut to alabaster in a Japanese pattern. Unsigned. 7" t x 7 1/2" diameter. **$920**

Photo courtesy James D. Julia Auctioneers, Fairfield, Maine; www.JuliaAuctions.com

Steuben Green Jade Vase. With slightly flaring neck and rolled rim. The vase is finished with two applied alabaster "M" handles. Signed in center of polished pontil with acid etched script signature "Steuben". 10 1/4" t. **$1,380**

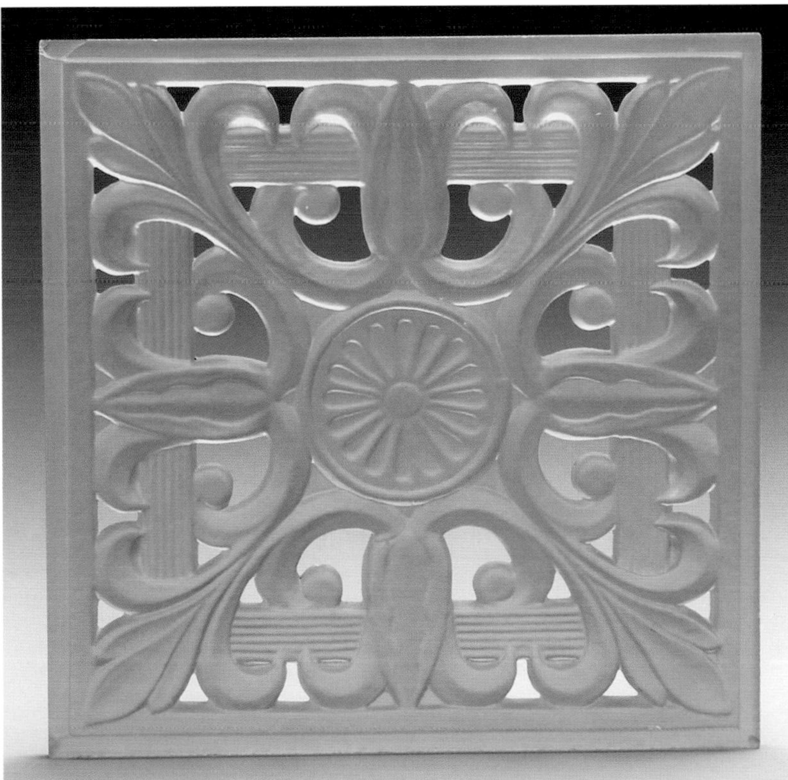

Photo courtesy James D. Julia Auctioneers, Fairfield, Maine; www.JuliaAuctions.com

Steuben Cast Glass Grill. Made as a ventilation grate for a cruise liner. Bristol yellow and features a fleur de lis design in each corner with a spoked wheel in the center. 9 7/8" sq. Some minor fleabites and a bruise to the design with some slightly larger chips on the outside edge, which would be concealed if the grill was mounted. **$1,610**

Photo courtesy James D. Julia Auctioneers, Fairfield, Maine; www.JuliaAuctions.com

Steuben Figural Flower Frog. Clear glass frog mounted with original Gorham sterling silver foot. Frog is finished with a figural insert of a kneeling nude woman with head raised. Overall 8" t. **$920**

Photo courtesy James D. Julia Auctioneers, Fairfield, Maine; www.JuliaAuctions.com

Steuben Figural Flower Frog. Moonstone double-tier flower frog with clear glass figural insert. Insert depicts a standing Oriental woman with long gown and bouquet of flowers. Overall 9" h. Some chips to peg of insert. **$862**

Photo courtesy James D. Julia Auctioneers, Fairfield, Maine; www.JuliaAuctions.com

Steuben Green Figural Flower Frog. Emerald green glass with a double row frog and figural insert of an Oriental woman with flowing gown and bouquet of flowers. Overall 9" h. Large flake to top of frog and some minor grinding to bottom of woman's gown. **$517**

Photo courtesy James D. Julia Auctioneers, Fairfield, Maine; www.JuliaAuctions.com

Durand Ginger Jar. Decorated with bright white hearts and vines on a shaded platinum-blue to deep mirror-blue iridescent ground. Jar is topped with transparent maize-colored fluted knop resting on a matching lid. Unsigned. Overall 9" t. **$3,600**

Photo courtesy James D. Julia Auctioneers, Fairfield, Maine; www.JuliaAuctions.com

Durand Cocktail Shaker. Green cut to clear Art Deco design on a large cocktail shaker with nickel-plated top. The shaker comes with a note on Farber's Antiques paper stating that the green cocktail shaker was the personal property of Victor Durand. The note is signed by Samuel Farber. 12 1/4" t. **$1,437**

Photo courtesy James D. Julia Auctioneers, Fairfield, Maine; www.JuliaAuctions.com

Steuben Figural Insert. Pomona green glass with an acid-textured finish featuring a nude maiden kneeling within a circle. Insert is signed on the back with acid-etched signature "CGW 1929". CGW stands for Corning Glass Works and the style number for this insert is 7039. 8" h. Some minor roughness to the back edges as well as a 1/2" chip to backside of woman's shoulder. **$690**

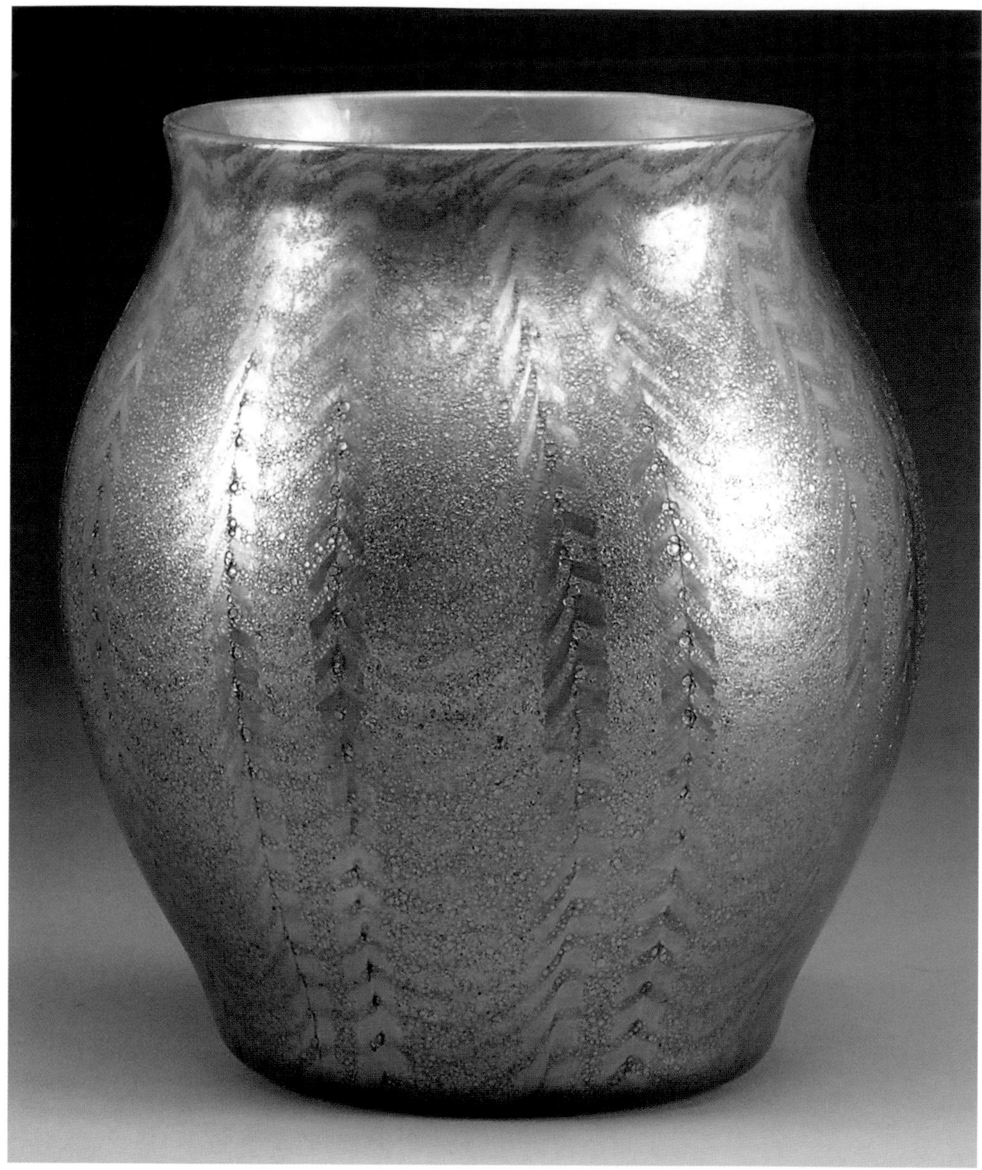

Photo courtesy James D. Julia Auctioneers, Fairfield, Maine; www.JuliaAuctions.com

Nash Art Glass Vase. Chintz decorated with fine Cypriot texture to the decoration. Engraved "GD 72 NASH" on the foot rim. 7 1/4" t. **$805**

Photo courtesy James D. Julia Auctioneers, Fairfield, Maine; www.JuliaAuctions.com

Daum Nancy Cameo and Enamel Floral Vase. With delicate blue enameled flowers and green foliage that rest against a mottled background of blue, purple and green. Signed on the underside "Daum Nancy" with the Cross of Lorraine in gold. 5" h. Minor enamel loss to stems. **$2,400**

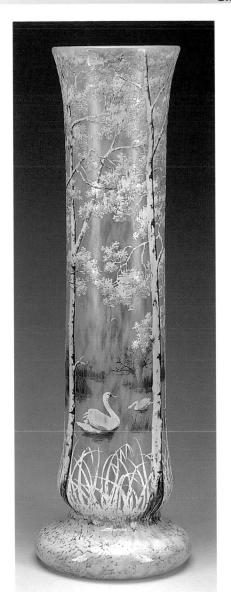

Photo courtesy James D. Julia Auctioneers, Fairfield, Maine; www.JuliaAuctions.com

Monumental Daum Nancy Cameo Vase. With decoration of swans and birch trees. Decoration adorns both from and back of the vase and is finished with enameled scene of islands and trees in the background. A superior example. Signed in enamel on the foot rim "Daum Nancy". 25 1/4" t. **$18,400**

Photo courtesy James D. Julia Auctioneers, Fairfield, Maine; www.JuliaAuctions.com

Daum Nancy Art Deco Vase. With deep acid cut-back Art Deco design against a smoky gray glass. The design has a textured finish in contrast with the polished glass highlights. Signed on the underside with engraved "Daum Nancy France" with Cross of Lorraine. 4" t. **$460**

Photo courtesy James D. Julia Auctioneers, Fairfield, Maine; www.JuliaAuctions.com

Daum Nancy Cameo and Enameled Vase. Square vase is decorated on each side with a cameo poppy, stem and leaves against a mottled yellow shading to orange background. Each poppy, in various stages of bloom, is enameled with bright orange flowers and subtle green and brown stems and leaves. The foot of the vase is trimmed with a simple gold gilt line. Signed on the side in cameo "Daum Nancy" with the Cross of Lorraine. 4 3/4" t. **$4,200**

Photo courtesy James D. Julia Auctioneers, Fairfield, Maine; www.JuliaAuctions.com

Daum Nancy Cameo Cruet. Winter scene in rare shape. Signed in enamel on the underside "Daum Nancy" with Cross of Lorraine. 3" t. **$3,220**

Photo courtesy James D. Julia Auctioneers, Fairfield, Maine; www.JuliaAuctions.com

Daum Nancy Cameo Vase. Acid etched and enameled winter scene. Signed in enamel on the underside "Daum Nancy" with the Cross of Lorraine. 4" t. **$6,325**

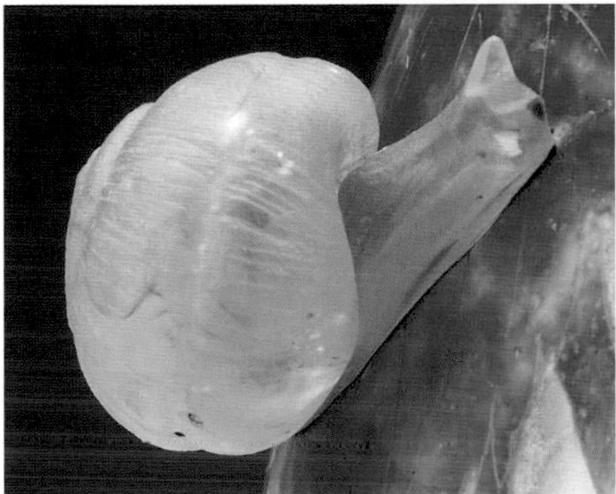

Photo courtesy James D. Julia Auctioneers, Fairfield, Maine; www.JuliaAuctions.com

Daum Nancy Snail Vase. Design of grapes, leaves and vines in autumn-colored vitreous glass against a mottled yellow, orange and brown background. The unusually large egg-shaped vase is finished with two applied glass snails (second view). Vase is signed on the side in cameo "Daum Nancy" with the Cross of Lorraine. 8 3/4" t. **$10,925**

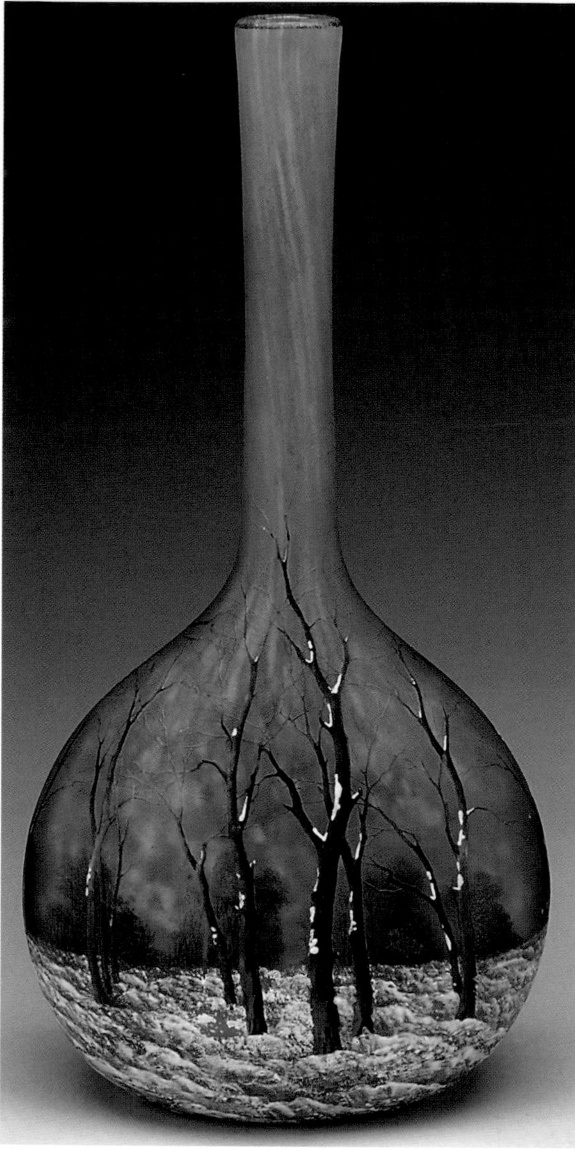

Photo courtesy James D. Julia Auctioneers, Fairfield, Maine; www.JuliaAuctions.com

Daum Nancy Cameo Vase. Winter scenic banjo vase. Unusual shape. Signed in enamel on the underside "Daum Nancy" with Cross of Lorraine. 12" t. **$10,350**

Photo courtesy James D. Julia Auctioneers, Fairfield, Maine; www.JuliaAuctions.com

Daum Nancy Cameo Rose Bowl. Winter scenic decoration, strongly colored and detailed. Engraved signature "Daum Nancy" with Cross of Lorraine on underside. 3 3/4" t x 5" diameter. **$8,625**

Photo courtesy James D. Julia Auctioneers, Fairfield, Maine; www.JuliaAuctions.com

Daum Nancy Cameo Vase. Canoe shape with acid-etched and enameled winter scene. Enameled signature on the underside "Daum Nancy" with the Cross of Lorraine. 6 3/4" w. **$6,325**

Photo courtesy James D. Julia Auctioneers, Fairfield, Maine; www.JuliaAuctions.com

Daum Nancy Rain Scene Vase. Extremely rare, square form is enameled with earthen-hued trees with green grass and foliage in the background. This design is set against a gray, rose and green ground. The "rain" effect is created by scoring the glass down to its transparency. Signed "Daum Nancy" with the Cross of Lorraine. 4 1/4" h. **$8,625**

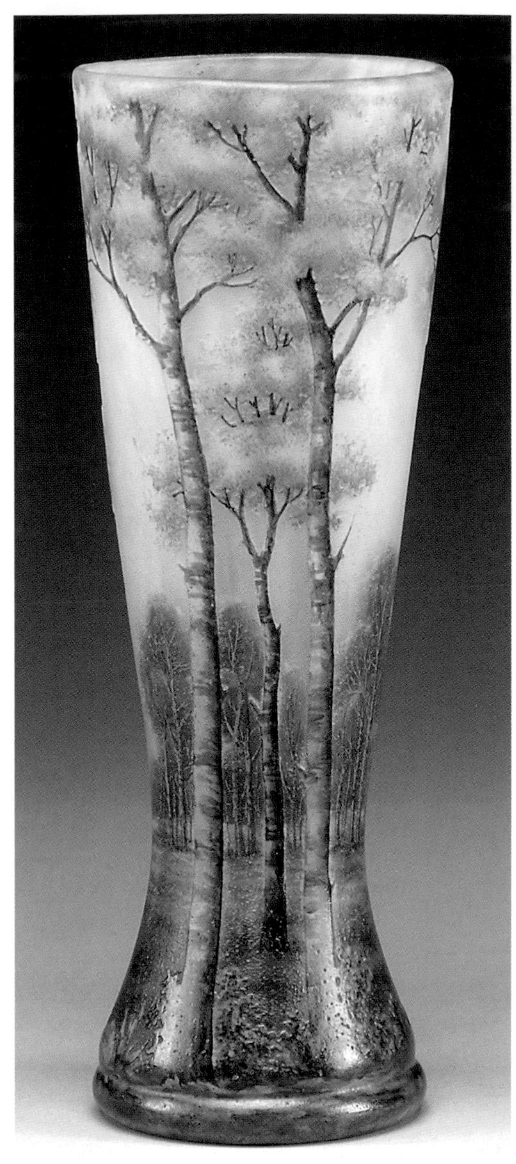

Photo courtesy James D. Julia Auctioneers, Fairfield, Maine; www.JuliaAuctions.com

Daum Nancy Cameo Vase. Spring scenic vase with acid-etched and enameled trees. Signed in enamel on the side "Daum Nancy" with the Cross of Lorraine. 10 1/2" h. **$6,325**

Photo courtesy James D. Julia Auctioneers, Fairfield, Maine; www.JuliaAuctions.com

Early Daum Cameo and Enameled Vase. Decorated with a large, central heavily enameled thistle and flower with gold highlights. The flower is set against an acid-etched background of creamy yellow shading to clear. The back and sides of the vase are decorated with all-over cameo thistle design with black enamel highlighting the stems and leaves with gold gilt thistle flowers and red enamel highlights. The vase is finished with an enameled floral band at the lip. Signed on the underside in red enamel "Daum Nancy" with the Cross of Lorraine. 8" h. Some minor wear to gilt trim on lip. **$5,750**

Photo courtesy James D. Julia Auctioneers, Fairfield, Maine; www.JuliaAuctions.com

Daum Nancy Cameo Vase. Acid etched and enameled pillow vase with red berries and green leaves on a yellow to brown mottled background. Vividly colored. Signed on the side in enamel "Daum Nancy France" with the Cross of Lorraine. 4 3/4" h. **$5,175**

Photo courtesy James D. Julia Auctioneers, Fairfield, Maine; www.JuliaAuctions.com

Daum Nancy Floral French Cameo Vase. Pillow-shaped vase has a frosted mottled ground which flows into a golden yellow hue. Accenting this is a pattern of violets enameled in purple with green foliage front and back. Signed "Daum Nancy" with Cross of Lorraine. 4 1/2" x 4 1/2". **$4,312**

Photo courtesy James D. Julia Auctioneers, Fairfield, Maine; www.JuliaAuctions.com

Daum Nancy Cameo and Applied Covered Jar. Rare example with one green-gold applied cabochon, one green applied insect and one red applied leaf on body with acid-etched maple leaves. The lid with applied and wheel-carved handle with red applied insect on top (second view). Signed on the underside with engraved and gilded "Daum Nancy" with the Cross of Lorraine. 4 1/2" h. **$9,200**

Photo courtesy James D. Julia Auctioneers, Fairfield, Maine; www.JuliaAuctions.com

Daum Nancy Cameo Vase. Padded and wheel-carved lavender and brown iris flowers and buds on a frosted to chartreuse background together with acid-etched, deep purple leaves. Acid etched signature on the side "Daum Nancy" with the Cross of Lorraine. 12" h. **$7,200**

Photo courtesy James D. Julia Auctioneers, Fairfield, Maine; www.JuliaAuctions.com

Daum Nancy Cameo Vase. Acid-etched green daffodils on wheel-carved green to frosted to green background with simulated hammered texture and foot with opalescent interior. Signed on the underside with engraved "Daum Nancy" with the Cross of Lorraine. 7 3/4" h. **$6,000**

Photo courtesy James D. Julia Auctioneers, Fairfield, Maine; www.JuliaAuctions.com

Daum Nancy Cameo Vase. Single wheel-carved parrot tulip in shades of purple with wheel-carved leaves on a shaded clear to purple background with simulated hammered texture. Signed on the underside with engraved "Daum Nancy" with the Cross of Lorraine. 6" h. **$6,000**

Photo courtesy James D. Julia Auctioneers, Fairfield, Maine; www.JuliaAuctions.com

Gallé Cameo Bowl. Red roses on yellow ground. Cameo signature on the side "Gallé". 8 1/2" w. Polishing on several of the pulled tips. **$2,040**

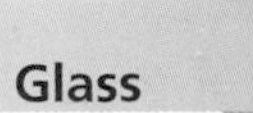

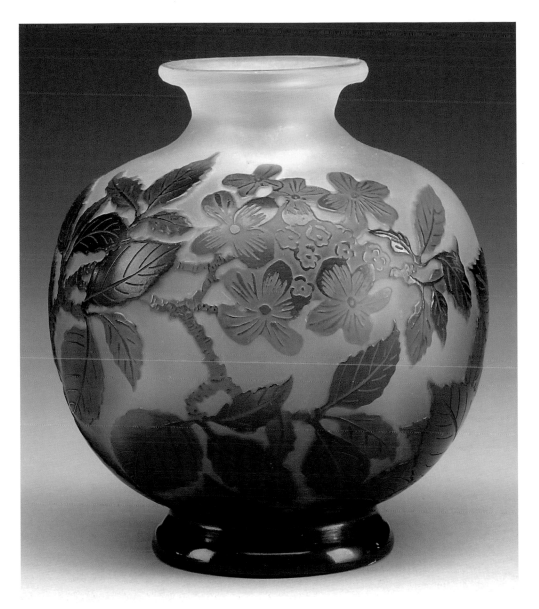

Photo courtesy James D. Julia Auctioneers, Fairfield, Maine; www.JuliaAuctions.com

Gallé Cameo Vase. Blue acid-etched Japanese peach blossoms with purple leaves and branches on a yellow ground. Windowpane technique behind the blue flowers. Acid-etched signature on the side "Gallé". 5" h. **$4,800**

Photo courtesy James D. Julia Auctioneers, Fairfield, Maine; www.JuliaAuctions.com

Gallé Cameo Vase. Burnt orange flowers and leaves on a shaded apricot and frosted ground. The entire vase is fire polished. Fancy engraved "Gallé" within a stylized flower on the underside. 7" h. **$2,880**

Photo courtesy James D. Julia Auctioneers, Fairfield, Maine; www.JuliaAuctions.com

Gallé Cameo Vase. Salmon red windowpane floral decoration on a yellow ground. Teardrop form. Cameo signature on the side "Gallé". 9 3/4" h. **$3,600**

Photo courtesy James D. Julia Auctioneers, Fairfield, Maine; www.JuliaAuctions.com

Gallé Cameo Vase. Red windowpane floral decoration on a yellow ground. Cameo signature on the side "Gallé". 8 1/1" h. **$6,000**

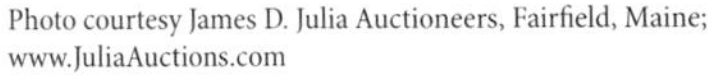

Photo courtesy James D. Julia Auctioneers, Fairfield, Maine; www.JuliaAuctions.com

Gallé Fire-Polished French Cameo Vase. Background of frosted white shading to a soft blue/purple. The design is a cameo cutback of clematis flowers in various stages of bloom created in vibrant purple with hints of blue. This vase is completely fire-polished. Signed "Gallé" in cameo on side. 4 1/2" h. **$1,955**

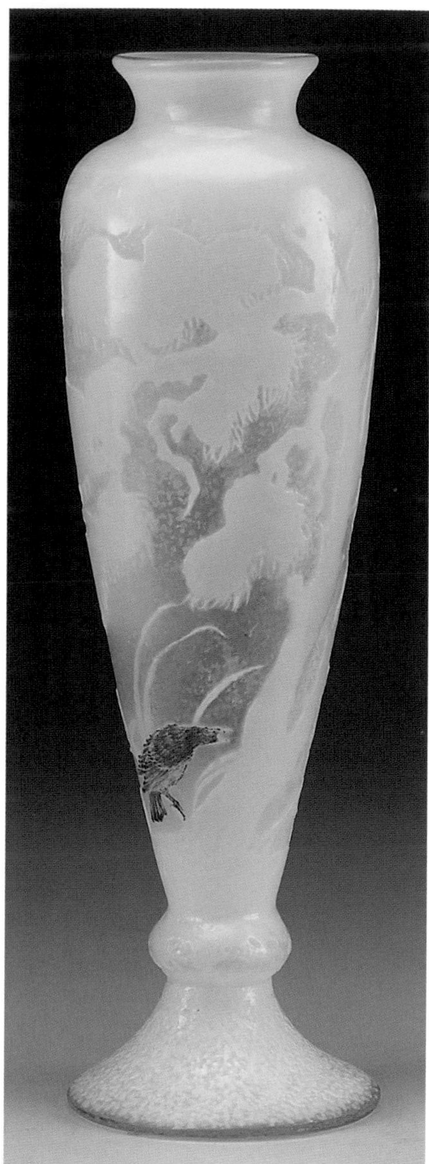

Photo courtesy James D. Julia Auctioneers, Fairfield, Maine; www.JuliaAuctions.com

Gallé Cameo Verrerie Parlant Vase. Decoration of an enameled reddish-brown and dark brown bird in a snowy landscape with acid-etched trees and snow and inscription "Dans les neiges en fleur le jeune an souriait" ("In the snows in flower the young year smiled") towards the top of the vase. Acid-etched signature on the side of the vase "Gallé". 13" h. **$11,400**

Photo courtesy James D. Julia Auctioneers, Fairfield, Maine; www.JuliaAuctions.com

Gallé Rio De Genaro Cameo Vase. Highly detailed tropical scenic vase with mountains and lake in russet tones on buff colored background. Acid-etched signature on the side "Gallé". 14 1/4" h. **$9,600**

Photo courtesy James D. Julia Auctioneers, Fairfield, Maine; www.JuliaAuctions.com

Gallé Cameo Covered Box. Rare and fine decoration of two brown and blue dragonflies on the lid with blue water lilies and brown foliage on the body. Cameo signature on the lid (second view) and the side of the box "Gallé". 6 1/2" diameter. Two nicks to one leaf on the side of the box. **$7,475**

Photo courtesy James D. Julia Auctioneers, Fairfield, Maine; www.JuliaAuctions.com

Gallé Cameo Vase. Early Crystallerie vase with acid-etched and heavily enameled gold and brown floral decoration on transparent green background with snowflake etching. Gilded highlights. Cameo signature on the side "Gallé" with gilded highlights to signature. 7" h. **$6,600**

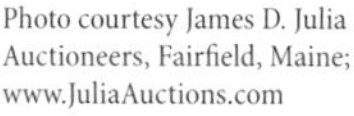

Photo courtesy James D. Julia Auctioneers, Fairfield, Maine; www.JuliaAuctions.com

Gallé Blown Out Cameo Vase. Blue gooseberries and purple leaves on strong yellow, shading to deep purple ground. Cameo signature on the side "Gallé". 9 1/2" h. **$9,775**

Photo courtesy James D. Julia Auctioneers, Fairfield, Maine; www.JuliaAuctions.com

Gallé Cameo Vase. Large windowpane blue clematis flowers with lavender leaves and vines on an irregular yellow ground. 12 1/2" h. **$6,600**

Photo courtesy James D. Julia Auctioneers, Fairfield, Maine; www.JuliaAuctions.com

Gallé Cameo Vase. Banjo form with lavender flowers and olive-colored leaves and branches on a shaded frosted to peach background. Acid-etched signature on the side "Gallé". 5 1/2" h. **$720**

Photo courtesy James D. Julia Auctioneers, Fairfield, Maine; www.JuliaAuctions.com

Gallé Lily Pond Vase. Cameo-cut lily pond design with lily pads floating in a pond with tall iris flowers extending up the length of the vase with brown stems and light blue flowers. Hovering beside the iris is a large, detailed dragonfly with brown body and blue wings. The pond scene gives way to subtle, almost indistinct trees in the background. The cameo decoration is all set against a background of subtle yellow shading to cream. The vase is finished with three seashells lightly acid cut into the foot. Signed within a lily pad with engraved signature "Gallé". 16 1/4" h. **$9,200**

Photo courtesy James D. Julia Auctioneers, Fairfield, Maine; www.JuliaAuctions.com

Gallé French Cameo Fern Vase. Lemon-yellow ground, complemented by ferns and blossoms overall in a deep purple hue. The vase is of simple tapering form. Signed in cameo "Gallé". 7" h. **$840**

Photo courtesy James D. Julia Auctioneers, Fairfield, Maine; www.JuliaAuctions.com

Gallé French Cameo Art Glass Vase. Classic form and flared upper rim. Background is frost to mottled green with a purple leaf and berry design prominent on the front of vase. Signed in cameo "Gallé". 6 1/4" h. **$690**

Photo courtesy James D. Julia Auctioneers, Fairfield, Maine; www.JuliaAuctions.com

Gallé French Cameo Vase. Multi-layered design depicts water lilies in various stages of bloom with pads and foliage set in water. This design is a deep purple hue and it is set against a yellow mottled to blue to purple ground. Signed "Gallé" in cameo. 7" h. **$1,680**

Photo courtesy James D. Julia Auctioneers, Fairfield, Maine; www.JuliaAuctions.com

D'Argental French Cameo Vase. Soft yellow background and decorated with an all-over floral pattern in red. The red is carried down to the padded foot. Signed in cameo "D'Argental". 12" h. **$920**

Photo courtesy James D. Julia Auctioneers, Fairfield, Maine; www.JuliaAuctions.com

Decorchemont Pate De Verre Figure. Art Deco stylized fish in waves decoration in sienna shading on deep blue water. Marked on the side with impressed Decorchemont seal. 7 1/2" h. **$2,280**

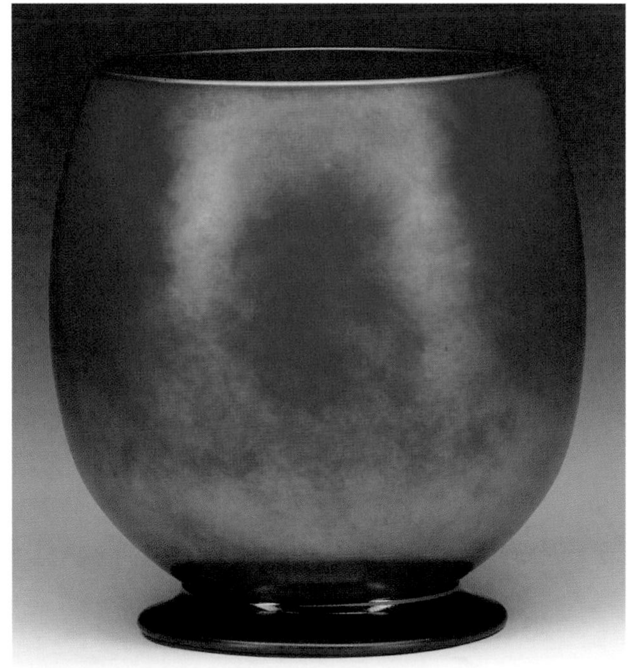

Photo courtesy James D. Julia Auctioneers, Fairfield, Maine; www.JuliaAuctions.com

Fenton Red Karnak Vase. Rich red, slightly iridescent body with an applied cobalt blue foot. The iridescence on the vase shows flashes of gold and blue. 5 3/4" t. **$1,150**

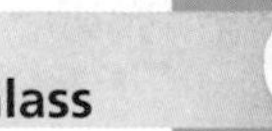

Photo courtesy James D. Julia Auctioneers, Fairfield, Maine; www.JuliaAuctions.com

Le Verre Francais Monumental Cameo Vase. In the Cerises pattern with burnt orange cherries and leaves on a mauve background. Engraved signature "Le Verre Francis" on the foot rim as well as a candy cane on the foot rim. 17" h. **$4,200**

Photo courtesy James D. Julia Auctioneers, Fairfield, Maine; www.JuliaAuctions.com

Schneider Glass and Wrought Iron Vases. Large orange mottled glass vases are supported by dark purple glass saucer feet. Each vase rests in a wrought iron support of leaves and berries. Each is signed on the underside "France" in block letters. 16" h. **$690 pair**

Photo courtesy James D. Julia Auctioneers, Fairfield, Maine; www.JuliaAuctions.com

Harrach Guba Duck Jar. Done in the style of Royal Flemish with raised gold enameling separating geometric shapes of lightly frosted yellow and clear glass. Decorated with Guba-style ducks and finished with a decorated dome lid with a single Guba duck against gold filigree background. Signed on the underside with Harrach red propeller mark and "5233". 3 1/2" h. **$1,725**

Photo courtesy James D. Julia Auctioneers, Fairfield, Maine; www.JuliaAuctions.com

Wheeling Peach Blow Morgan Vase. Maroon-red shading to a creamy amber with interior white lining. The vase is supported by its original glass Griffon holder. 10" h. Holder has chips to two of the feet. **$2,012**

Photo courtesy James D. Julia Auctioneers, Fairfield, Maine; www.JuliaAuctions.com

Royal Flemish Covered Jar. With gold gilt decoration of cherubs fighting mythological beasts on front and back. The neck of the jar is decorated with a swirling leaf design outlined in gold with a mauve background and the wide outer lip is decorated with stylized spread eagles in gold against a dark mauve background. The jar is further embellished with two delicate applied glass handles with gold gilt decoration. Topping the jar is its original glass stopper with gold vertically ribbed finial and swirling leaves against a dark mauve background. 15 1/2" h. Minor wear to gilt trim on lip. **$11,500**

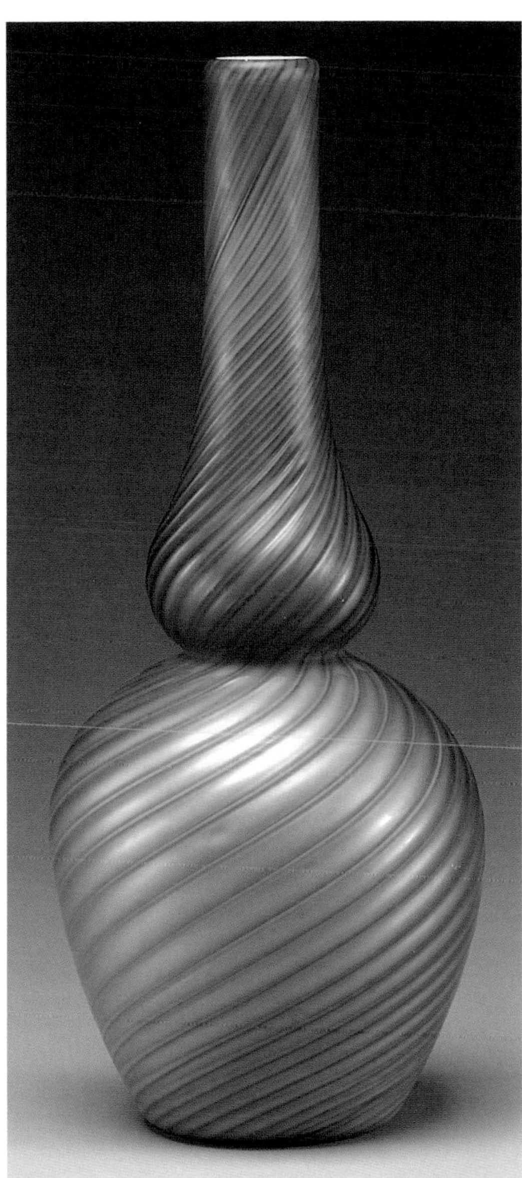

Photo courtesy James D. Julia Auctioneers, Fairfield, Maine; www.JuliaAuctions.com

Stevens & Williams Pompeian Swirl Vase. Bulbous body with pinched waist with amber and dark red ribbing. Vase is cased with a bluish-white interior. 15 1/2" h. **$1,782**

Photo courtesy James D. Julia Auctioneers, Fairfield, Maine; www.JuliaAuctions.com

Northwood Pull-Up Vase. Creamy tan colored body with purple pull-up design extending upward from the foot. The vase is finished with a cased blue interior and is marked on the underside "Patent". 7 1/4" h. **$1,725**

Photo courtesy James D. Julia Auctioneers, Fairfield, Maine; www.JuliaAuctions.com

Moser Applied Decorated Vase. "Underwater" vase has three applied and decorated fish with enameled vegetation encircling the vase. Decoration is done against a smoky gray glass and the foot and lip are gilt. Unsigned. 8 1/4" h. Minor wear to gilt. **$920**

Photo courtesy James D. Julia Auctioneers, Fairfield, Maine; www.JuliaAuctions.com

Webb Cameo Sweet Meat. Six white wheel-carved butterflies on rose-red ground with applied metal rim, handle and lid. Unsigned. 5" diameter. **$1,200**

Photo courtesy James D. Julia Auctioneers, Fairfield, Maine; www.JuliaAuctions.com

Webb Cameo Vase. White wheel-carved morning glories on cerulean blue ground with matching butterfly (second view) on the reverse. 9" h. Minor nicks to foot rim. **$2,040**

Photo courtesy James D. Julia Auctioneers, Fairfield, Maine; www.JuliaAuctions.com

Moser Pitcher. Padded and wheel-carved golden grapes, green leaves and charcoal gray stem. The other leaves and vines are intricately wheel carved on a clear background. Pitcher is finished with a silver-plated stem, spout and lid. Engraved "B178" on underside. 8" h. **$1,610**

Photo courtesy Green Valley Auctions, Mt. Crawford, Va.; www.GreenValleyAuctions.com

Mt. Washington, Bowl, shaded blue to white with polychrome pansy decoration, satin finish, ground pontil mark. Mt. Washington Glass Co. Fourth quarter 19th century. 2 3/8" h, 3 3/8" d rim. **$115**

Collector's Note: The Mt. Washington Glass Works began operating in 1837 in the Mount Washington area of South Boston. The factory was relocated to New Bedford, Mass., in 1870. From 1880 until 1894, Mt. Washington supplied glass to the Pairpoint Manufacturing Corp. Pairpoint purchased Mt. Washington in 1894. Production of reverse-painted and "puffy" lampshades continued until about 1915.

Mt. Washington, Burmese No. 60 1/2 Toothpick Holder, satin or plush finish, bulbous base with square top, undecorated, polished pontil mark. Mt. Washington Glass Co. Fourth quarter 19th century. 2 3/4" h, 2" sq rim. **$195**

Mt. Washington, Burmese No. 146 Gourd Vase, satin or plush finish, undecorated, partially ground pontil mark. Mt. Washington Glass Co. Fourth quarter 19th century. 7 3/4" h, 4 1/8" d overall. Minute burst surface bubble and a small scuffs to body. **$168**

Mt. Washington, Burmese No. 146 Gourd Vase, satin or plush finish, undecorated, ground pontil mark. Mt. Washington Glass Co. Fourth quarter 19th century. 7 7/8" h, 4 1/8" d overall. **$345**

Mt. Washington, Burmese No. 151 Toothpick Holder/ Whiskey Tumbler, satin or plush finish, cylindrical, undecorated, polished pontil mark. Mt. Washington Glass Co. Fourth quarter 19th century. 2 3/4" h, 2 1/4" d. **$115**

Mt. Washington, Burmese No. 181 Vase, satin or plush finish, undecorated, ground pontil mark. Mt. Washington Glass Co. Fourth quarter 19th century. 9 3/4" h, 5 1/2" d overall. **$373**

Mt. Washington, Burmese Vase, satin or plush finish, applied low collared foot with rough pontil mark. Probably Mt. Washington Glass Co. Fourth quarter 19th century. 6 3/8" h, 2 1/8" d foot. With a 3/4" x 1/2" area and several nearby small spots of crizzling to body. **$115**

Mt. Washington, Colonial Ware Square Tray, free-hand polychrome floral decoration, turned-up sides, worn gold on rim, ground pontil mark inscribed "100". Mt. Washington Glass Co. Fourth quarter 19th century. 1 1/2" h, 5 1/2" x 5 3/4". **$80**

Mt. Washington, Creamer, shaded pink to white with polychrome violet decoration, applied reeded handle, satin finish, gilt rim, ground pontil mark inscribed 401. Mt. Washington Glass Co. Fourth quarter 19th century. 3 5/8" h, 3 1/4" d overall. **$138**

Mt. Washington, Crown Milano Covered Jar, with two reeded curled handles and a steeple top, delicate polychrome floral decoration, polished pontil mark, unsigned. Mt. Washington Glass Co. Fourth quarter 19th century. 5 3/4" h overall, 4 1/4" d overall. One handle has a faint hairline and spot of professional restoration. **$316**

Mt. Washington, Crown Milano Cracker Jar, leaves, flowers and berries decoration, silver-plated repoussé decorated lid which fits over the decorated and gilded rim, base inscribed with "537". Mt. Washington Glass Co. Fourth quarter 19th century. 6 3/4" h overall. Several flakes and roughness to jar rim. **$240**

Mt. Washington, Crown Milano Cracker Jar, with two glossy reserves, the front depicting two colonial-dressed

Photo courtesy Green Valley Auctions, Mt. Crawford, Va.; www.GreenValleyAuctions.com

Mt. Washington, Crown Milano Mushroom Sugar Sifter / Flower Holder, shape No. 535, polychrome daisy-like decoration on a shaded ground, "Albertine / Mt. W. G. Co." paper label under base of undetermined association. Mt. Washington Glass Co. Fourth quarter 19th century. 2 3/4" h, 5 1/4" d overall. **$862**

children, the boy blowing bubbles, the back with simple gilt floral decoration, original plated-silver rim, bail handle and lid marked "M W / 4419", jar inscribed "520," only under base. Mt. Washington Glass Co. Fourth quarter 19th century. 5" h rim, 7" d overall. **$460**

Mt. Washington, Crown Milano Diamond Quilted Spoon Holder, opal with heavy gilt and enamel floral decoration on a mottled ground, ten-petal rim, polished pontil mark. Mt. Washington Glass Co. Fourth quarter 19th century. 4 1/4" h, 3" d rim. Some high-spot wear to decoration, wear to rim gilt. **$240**

Mt. Washington, Crown Milano Large Rose Bowl, fired-on Burmese with polychrome floral decoration, satin finish, ground pontil mark. Mt. Washington Glass Co. Fourth quarter 19th century. 5" h, 6 1/4" d overall. Light wear and scuffs, worn rim gilt. **$168**

Mt. Washington, Crown Milano Pickle Jar, blue and white with polychrome floral decoration, unusual molded design at top and bottom, marked "M W" plated-silver lid with embossed flowers and twig finial. Mt. Washington Glass Co. Fourth quarter 19th century. 4 3/4" h overall, 4 1/2" d overall, 2 1/2" d base. Minor bruise and flake to inner rim, light wear to decoration, wear to edge of lid. **$316**

Mt. Washington, Decorated Peach Blow No. 145 Vase, rich decoration No. 30, "Lace Embroidery, Queen's patt.," original dark red painted top rim, ground pontil mark. Mt. Washington Glass Co. 1886-1890. 7 3/4" h, 4 1/2" d overall. **$6,325**

Collector's Note: Peach Blow derives its name from a fine Chinese glazed porcelain, resembling a peach or crushed strawberries in color. Three American glass manufacturers and two English firms produced Peach Blow glass in the late 1800s.

Mt. Washington/Pairpoint, Burmese Vase, satin finish, eight-crimp rim, applied button stem and circular foot with polished pontil mark. Pairpoint Corp. at the Mt. Washington factory. Late 1920s/early 1930s. 10 1/2" h, 6 3/4" d rim, 4 1/2" d foot. **$207**

Nakara, Portrait Dresser Box, shaded pink ground, top featuring the bust of a lady with flowing hair, brass mounts, lid interior with original mirror, signed under base. C.F. Monroe Co. Late 19th/early 20th century. 2 1/2" h, 4 1/2" d overall. Loss of some white enamel dots on top and lacking rim clasp. **$230**

Nash, Chintz Footed Tumbler, colorless with blue and green vertical decoration, polished pontil mark engraved "Nash 178L". A. Douglas Nash Corp. 1928-1931. 4" h, 2 7/8" d rim. **$156**

Nash-Attributed, Chintz Vase, colorless with vertical decoration, unsigned, polished pontil mark. Probably A. Douglas Nash Corp. 1928-1931. 5 5/8" h, 5 1/2" d overall. **$192**

Nash-Attributed, Chintz Vase, shaded blue green with vertical decoration, unsigned, rough pontil mark. Probably A. Douglas Nash Corp. 1928-1931. 4 3/4" h, 3 5/8" d base. **$84**

New England Glass Co., bride's bowl, pink overlay Mount Washington cameo on Pairpoint quadruple silver-plated stand, 19th century, marked on the base Pairpoint Mfg. Co. 10" h (with stand) x 7 5/8" d. **$1,320**

Pairpoint, Burmese Footed Cup, glossy finish, applied handle, rough pontil mark. Mid 20th century. 3 1/2" h overall, 3 1/4" h rim, 3 1/2" d rim. **$96**

Pairpoint, Burmese Goblet, satin finish, applied stem and slightly domed foot, rough pontil mark, paper label. Pairpoint Glass Co. Second half 20th century. 7" h. **$120**

Photo courtesy Green Valley Auctions, Mt. Crawford, Va.; www.GreenValleyAuctions.com

Mt. Washington, Lava/Sicilian Glass Vase, virtually opaque black amethyst with multi-color inclusions, square rim, polished pontil mark. Produced for a short period of time. Mt. Washington Glass Co. 1878-1880. 3 3/8" h, 3" sq.
$4,887

Pairpoint, Melon Rib Presentation Cracker Jar, shaded green opal with gilt and green floral decoration, original plated-silver rim, bail handle and lid marked with P in Diamond and "3914", jar inscribed "3914/1112" under base, lid engraved "From Myrtle Chapter, No. 6, O.E.S. for Luella W. Stearns, G.M., June 18th, 1903" around edge. Pairpoint Mfg. Co. Late 19th/early 20th century. 4 3/4" h rim, 6 3/4" d overall. Normal wear to plating. **$316**

Schneider, "Le Verre Francais" Cameo-Etched Ewer, mottled mauve overlaid with plum, stylized floral design, boldly applied handle with the lower terminal trailing across the lower body, engraved signature, polished pontil mark. Retains a partial Maude B. Feld paper label. Second quarter 20th century. 12 1/2" h. Annealing crack to handle tail between lower terminal and first peak, open bubble near end of tail. **$1,150**

Steuben, Aurene Centerpiece Bowl, blue iridescent, shape #5061, polished base signed "Aurene / 5061". First quarter 20th century. 2 1/2" h, 10 3/8" d. Some wear to interior. **$373**

Collector's Note: Frederick Carder, an Englishman, and Thomas G. Hawkes of Corning, N.Y., established the Steuben Glass Works in 1904. In 1918, the Corning Glass Co. purchased Steuben. Carder remained with the firm and designed many of the pieces bearing the Steuben mark. Probably the most widely recognized wares are Aurene, Verre De Soie and Rosaline.

Photo courtesy Green Valley Auctions, Mt. Crawford, Va.; www.GreenValleyAuctions.com

Smith Brothers, Decorated Ball Vase, delicate daisy decoration on soft beige ground, gilt and white enamel dot rim, marked with lion shield trademark under base. Fourth quarter 19th century. 4" h, 4 1/8" d overall. Undamaged except for the loss of one rim dot, no wear to decoration. **$103**

Photo courtesy Green Valley Auctions, Mt. Crawford, Va.; www.GreenValleyAuctions.com

Steuben, Grotesque Vase, amethyst to crystal, shape #7091, polished base. First half 20th century. 6" h, 7 3/4" x 8 1/4". **$316**

Steuben, Aurene Footed Bowl, gold iridescent, signed "Aurene" and "3067", rough pontil mark. First quarter 20th century. 3" h, 6" d. With a 3/8" embedded annealing crack in lower shoulder, does not break the surface. **$180**

Steuben, Aurene Low Bowl, gold iridescent, applied disk-like foot, signed "Aurene" and what appears to be "5061", rough pontil mark. First quarter 20th century. 2 1/4" h, 10" d. Part of signature obscured by scratches. **$230**

Steuben, Crystal Covered Dish, colorless, cover with applied bold ram's head finial, signed under base. Designed by Irene Butler. 20th century. 7 1/4" h overall, 5" d rim. **$172**

Steuben, Footed Shallow Bowl, Sea Green and Amber, shape #3379, short swirled-rib stem, polished pontil mark. Second quarter 20th century. 5 1/2" h, 10" d overall. **$330**

Steuben, Ivrene Rib Optic Three-Piece Console Set, iridized, consisting of a shape #7563 footed center bowl with polished pontil mark and a pair of shape #7564 footed candleholders, both with a rough pontil mark and factory engraved signature. Second quarter 20th century. 7" h, 9 1/4" x 14 1/8", and 3 1/4" h. .... **$540 set**

Steuben, Ivrene Rib Optic Footed Vase, iridized, shape #7564, rough pontil mark and factory engraved signature. Second quarter 20th century. 9 1/2" h, 7 1/4" x 10". **$420**

Steuben, Rib Optic Footed Vase, Pomona Green, probably shape #938 or #6629, polished pontil mark with block letter acid-stamped signature. Second quarter 20th century. 13" h, 9 3/8" d rim, 6 1/8" d foot. **$345**

Steuben-Type, Footed Bowl, gold calcite lead glass, small rough pontil mark. Possibly Steuben or Quezal. First quarter 20th century. 3 5/8" h, 4 7/8" d. **$149**

Steuben-Type, Low Bowl, Rosaline, rolled-over rim, polished pontil mark. First half 20th century. 1 1/2" h, 10 1/4" d overall, open bubble and light wear to interior. **$144**

Stevens & Williams, Cameo Inkwell, white cut to peach shading to yellow, overlapping leaf decoration, silver hinged lid hallmarked for London, 1902, slightly concave base signed "Stevens & Williams / Art / Glass / Stourbridge". Early 20th century. 2 3/4" h, 3 1/2" d overall. Minute nicks to body and a small dent to edge of lid. **$1,840**

Wave Crest, Atomizer, puffy egg-crate mold, pink luster scrolls with dainty daisy decoration, original gilt-metal mount lacking bulb, not marked. C.F. Monroe Co. Late 19th/early 20th century. 4 1/4" h overall, 2 3/4" sq. **$207**

Collector's Note: The C.F. Monroe Co. of Meriden, Conn., produced the opal glassware known as Wave Crest from 1898 until World War I. The company bought the opaque, blown-molded glass blanks from the Pairpoint Manufacturing Co. of New Bedford, Mass., and other glassmakers, including European factories. The Monroe company then decorated the blanks, usually with floral patterns. Trade names used were "Wave Crest Ware," "Kelva" and "Nakara."

Wave Crest, Cherub Decorated Dresser Box, scroll and acanthus leaf mold, top decorated with hand painted daisies and a transfer of two cherub artists, two-line mark under base. C.F. Monroe Co. Late 19th/early 20th century. 3 1/4" h, 5 1/2" d overall. Light wear to transfer, lacking interior fabric. **$218**

Wave Crest, Cracker Jar, Helmschmied Swirl mold, two-tone ground with floral decoration, silver-plated mount and lid, unmarked. C.F. Monroe Co. Late 19th/early 20th century. 6 1/2" h rim, 5" d jar. Light marking to jar, plating worn off handle, some wear to lid. **$168**

Wave Crest, Cracker Jar, Helmschmied Swirl mold, polychrome floral decoration, silver-plated mount and lid, unmarked. C.F. Monroe Co. Late 19th/early 20th century. 6 1/2" h rim, 5 1/4" d jar. Plating worn off handle, some wear to lid. **$180**

Wave Crest, Cracker Jar, panel mold, two-tone ground with transfer floral decoration, silver-plated mount and lid, unmarked. C.F. Monroe Co. Late 19th/early 20th century. 6" h rim, 5 3/4" d jar overall. Light wear and marking, handle with loss of decorative crest, some wear to lid. **$126**

Wave Crest, Creamer and Sugar, matching polychrome floral decoration, plated-silver mounts, sugar cover not original, unmarked. C.F. Monroe Co. Late 19th/early 20th century. 3" h overall. Creamer undamaged, sugar with crack in base, normal wear and minor marring to mounts. **$103**

Wave Crest, Dresser Box, painted cherub decoration with floral sprays on each side, 3 3/4" h, 6 1/8" w, 5 1/4" deep. **$402**

Collector's Note: Thomas Webb & Sons was established in 1837 in Stourbridge, England. The company is best known for its English cameo glass. However, many other types of colored art glass were produced, including enameled, iridescent, heavily ornamented and cased.

Photo courtesy Green Valley Auctions, Mt. Crawford, Va.; www.GreenValleyAuctions.com

Wave Crest, Dresser Box, Helmschmied Swirl mold, polychrome rosebud decoration, gilt-brass mounts, with interior lining which is probably later, unmarked. C.F. Monroe Co. Late 19th/early 20th century. 4 3/4" h, 6 1/4" d overall. **$258**

Photo courtesy Green Valley Auctions, Mt. Crawford, Va.; www.GreenValleyAuctions.com

Webb, Burmese Footed Vase, satin or plush finish, seven-point flared and ruffled rim, undecorated, polished pontil mark with circular etched signature. Thos. Webb & Sons. Fourth quarter 19th century. 4 3/4" h, 2 7/8" d rim. **$287**

Webb, Burmese Vase, glossy finish, five-point infolded and crimped rim, undecorated, polished pontil mark with circular etched medallion signature. Thos. Webb & Sons. Fourth quarter 19th century. 3 1/2" h, 2 3/4" d rim. Minor inner-rim flake at one crimp. **$156**

Webb, Burmese Vase, satin or plush finish with polychrome floral decoration, seven-point flared and ruffled rim, polished pontil mark with circular etched medallion signature. Thos. Webb & Sons. Fourth quarter 19th century. 2 3/4" h, 3" d rim. **$258**

Webb, Burmese Vase, satin or plush finish, seven-point flared and ruffled rim, undecorated, polished pontil mark. Thos. Webb & Sons. Fourth quarter 19th century. 3 1/2" h, 3" d rim. **$149**

Webb, Burmese Trumpet Vase, satin or plush finish, five-point infolded and crimped rim, undecorated, applied foot. Thos. Webb & Sons. Fourth quarter 19th century. 4 1/2" h, 2 7/8" d rim. **$228**

Webb, Ivory Cameo Bowl, single color with stained highlights, floral and foliage decoration, signed "Thomas Webb & Sons" under base. Late 19th/early 20th century. 3" h, 2 7/8" d. rim. Light wear to staining. **$510**

Wheeling, Coral No. 22 Morgan Vase, glossy, polished pontil mark. Hobbs, Brockunier & Co. Fourth quarter 19th century. 8" h. **$600**

Wheeling, Peach Blow glass vase with burgundy fading to golden yellow, 19th century, 8" h. **$510**

Bottles, Assorted

Also see Coca-Cola.

Alta Crest Farms, Spencer Mass. Quart with embossed cow head in a brilliant green. Some scratches and light wear on the high points. Most of the wear is toward the base and around the lip. **$1,100**

Borden's, Quart Milk Jar. U.S. Pat No. 2,177,396 60 NY Royal Ruby Anchor Glass, Automatic bottle machine. This is a bottle that was made by Anchor Hocking as an experiment for the Borden's Milk Co. in the 1950s. Less than a dozen were made. The color was named "Royal Ruby." **$1,800**

Boughton & Chase, graphite pontil. 10 sided, 7 1/2" Backwards "N". Crudeness, rarity, and excellent condition. **$3,000**

Buffum & Co., Pittsburgh Sarsaparilla and Mineral Water, 8 1/4" with open pontil. In the form of a 10-pin. Deep cobalt blue that gets lighter towards the top. Significant whittle. **$1,900**

California Natural Seltzer Water, H&G on reverse with walking bear (1875-85). Regarding the grass under the walking bear, these come in aqua and rarely blue or green. This example is light green. **$4,600**

S.I. Comp, Cottage Ink, milk glass. Crudely applied lip. "S.I. Comp" on the roof, which stands for "Senate Ink Company." Unusual to see an example of a cottage ink in milk glass. A little natural wear around the mouth. **$550**

Cottle Post & Co., Portland OGN. These have a tooled top and also come in a teal coloration. There is an area on the top front lip, which under extreme close examination looks like an open bubble. No high-point wear and minor imperfections. Rare bottle in amber. **$1,800**

Photo courtesy American Bottle Auctions, Sacramento, Calif.; www.AmericanBottle.com

Brown's Celebrated Indian Herb Bitters, in golden amber, 12". **$3,000**

Photo courtesy American Bottle Auctions, Sacramento, Calif.; www.AmericanBottle.com

California Fig Bitters, California Extract of Fig Co., San Francisco, Cal., 9 3⁄4". Tooled top. The company that was responsible for these bottles also made an aqua variant. These were made for an Angel's Camp, Calif., company. There are two variants; the later variant has the word "herb" in the name. With a scratch. **$120**

Photo courtesy American Bottle Auctions, Sacramento, Calif.; www.AmericanBottle.com

Chalmer's Catawba Wine Bitters, 12". slight interior stain and a couple tiny areas of wear. Only about a dozen of these are known. There's also a variant without the "Sutter's Old Mill" embossing. **$22,000**

Photo courtesy American Bottle Auctions, Sacramento, Calif.; www.AmericanBottle.com

Dr. Wonser's USA Indian Root Bitters, 11 1/2". Applied top. Amber variant. **$10,500**

Photo courtesy American Bottle Auctions, Sacramento, Calif.; www.AmericanBottle.com

Geo. Eagle, graphite pontil with applied tapered collar and ribbing, all of its original graphite intact. **$4,600**

Covert's/Balm of Life, 6 1/4". Applied top, open pontil. Emerald green, crudely applied double tapered collar. **$6,000**

Crystal S.W. Co., S.F. Cider. A rare bottle from San Francisco. There is an iridescent area inside the lip. In addition, there are a couple of open bubbles on the front. This has a sloppy applied top with a minor flaw. **$1,300**

James Dewar, Elko Nevada, 1892-95. James Dewar began his soda business in 1892, only to close shop three years later. This example is the variant that reads "Nevada" and is clear glass and considered much more rare than its aqua counterpart. Has the original clay marble and rubber seal. Minor scratches and tiny areas of wear. **$900**

Dr. Kilmer's Cough Cure, Consumption Oil Catarrh Specific, 9" with embossed lungs. Tooled top. Brilliant aqua. The embossing within the lungs is somewhat double struck, and all the embossing is strong. **$850**

Elk Pool Hall, Elko Nev. With Brass Token. In Palmer green. This comes with both a pewter and cork stopper, which is then covered with a metal shot glass. Brass token is applied to the front of the flask. **$1,100**

Photo courtesy American Bottle Auctions, Sacramento, Calif.; www.AmericanBottle.com

Embossed Owl, whiskey top. 8 1/4". This is arguably the rarest Owl bottle made. An extremely hard to find bottle. **$3,000**

Photo courtesy American Bottle Auctions, Sacramento, Calif.; www.AmericanBottle.com

Fancy Cologne, 5 3/4". Rolled lip, pontil. Highly decorative, sapphire blue. It is described as palmette and scrolled acanthus. **$1,200**

Photo courtesy American Bottle Auctions, Sacramento, Calif.; www.AmericanBottle.com

R.L. Higgins, Virginia City, 6 1/2" h. With applied mouth and pour spout, circa 1875. One of the most important and rare master inks ever made. Significant whittle (marks caused by a reaction of the hot glass hitting the surface of a colder mold) with an extremely crude top. Museum quality. **$12,000**

Gun Wa's, Chinese Herb and Vegetable Remedy Dose Glass, 2". Could have come packaged with the bottle. Minor amount of stain. **$425**

R.L. Higgins, Virginia City, Cone Ink, 2" h. This Higgins cone ink is the only known embossed inkwell from Nevada. Made around 1875, Higgins' store was located on South C Street. There is a repaired neck on this bottle, with approximately two-thirds of the neck redone, though hard to discern. **$1,100**

IXL Valley Whiskey, E&B Bevan Pittston PA, with a series of embossed stars. Pontil. 8". Rare early whiskey. The IXL initials were used quite extensively by a gentleman named Dr. Henley. Significant whittle and slightly weak embossing on the shoulder. **$2,800**

Lacquor's Bitters Sarsapariphere, Applied top (replaced), 9 1/4". There are a couple small annealing checks just below the top. **$1,500**

Photo courtesy American Bottle Auctions, Sacramento, Calif.; www.AmericanBottle.com

Igloo Inkwell, 2", ground lip. With vertical lines running down the side, in amethyst. **$1,100**

Photo courtesy American Bottle Auctions, Sacramento, Calif.; www.AmericanBottle.com

Loomis's Cream Liniment, 5". Early flared mouth, tooled lip, pontiled. Six-sided, corset waisted. Rare. **$3,400**

Photo courtesy American Bottle Auctions, Sacramento, Calif.; www.AmericanBottle.com

H.P. Herb Wild Cherry Bitters, tooled top, 9". There are a couple variants of the Herb Wild Cherry Bitters, including this pure green example, also comes in amber. Minor scratches and a tiny flake off the bottom. **$4,600**

Photo courtesy American Bottle Auctions, Sacramento, Calif.; www.AmericanBottle.com

Keach Balt, torpedo-type soda, 9 1/2" with applied top. These unusual soda bottles came in various colors. This example is an apricot-puce. Medium tone with significant "whittle" (marks caused by a reaction of the hot glass hitting the surface of a colder mold) and overall crudity. Minor scratches, possibly from taking it in and out of the holder. Comes with holder. **$16,000**

Photo courtesy American Bottle Auctions, Sacramento, Calif.; www.AmericanBottle.com

A Merry Christmas and Happy New Year, Label Under Glass with Santa, 6", with the ground lip and original screw cap. With crisscross design on reverse and label under glass is perfect. **$1,300**

Photo courtesy American Bottle Auctions, Sacramento, Calif.; www.AmericanBottle.com

Pacific Congress Water Springs, Saratoga California, with Running Deer. A pint olive-amber example. Often seen in lime green, overall crudity and bubbles. **$8,000**

Masonic Eagle, Pint, sheared lip. Pontil. Variation in color, going from deep olive amber to a light green, back to an almost black color in the base. There is some highpoint wear on both sides. Unusual crimped lip. **$9,000**

M. McCormack's Celebrated Ginger Ale, Nashville Tenn. Applied top, 8 1/4". Light to medium blue with embossing and the large blob top. There are a few minor imperfections including the tiniest of pings on the base and one letter disturbed. **$550**

McKeon & McGrann, Washington DC. These torpedoes come in two variants, both being equally rare. This example has the two names and is a light to medium sapphire blue. Significant whittle, minor wear and probably been cleaned at some point. **$4,000**

Molded Chestnut-Shaped Cologne, or Pocket Flask, 4". With tooled mouth and pontil. Possibly the beginning of the 1700s or older. Near mint. **$1,900**

National Bitters, Patent 1867 on base. Applied top. Yellow-olive variant. There is an open bubble on the left side. Significant whittle on the label area. **$3,000**

Photo courtesy American Bottle Auctions, Sacramento, Calif.; www.AmericanBottle.com

Mohawk Whiskey, Pure Rye Patented Feb. 11, 1868. With much of the original paint. It is a light amber and varies in hue throughout the arms and head area. The top has a chip, which was most likely done during the making. There is a tiny nick on the base. **$1,500**

Photo courtesy American Bottle Auctions, Sacramento, Calif.; www.AmericanBottle.com

Palmer's Perfumes, Tea Rose, 9" with stopper. The gold lettering is backed by a rose-colored background. In addition, this has a 2-cent revenue stamp on the base, featuring George Washington. **$3,200**

Photo courtesy American Bottle Auctions, Sacramento, Calif.; www.AmericanBottle.com

Poison, in Shape of Skull, 2 7/8". Small amount of crudity throughout the piece. A hard-to-find poison. **$5,000**

Photo courtesy American Bottle Auctions, Sacramento, Calif.; www.AmericanBottle.com

Teakettle Inkwell, with fancy design. Turquoise with the original brass lid and gold paint. Unusual to find the original paint and lid intact, especially in this color. It has little gold painted stars on the top and gold painting around the middle and stem of the ink. **$1,400**

Pacific Congress Springs, blob-style top. For many years, this variant of the Pacific Congress Springs bottle was largely unknown by Western collectors and virtually unheard of in the East. Light blue, made in the mid to late 1860s. **$2,200**

Pacific Congress Water Springs, Saratoga California/ Pacific Congress Springs. Pint with smooth base. These have variants and a number of different colors. The most prominent color is a bright green. Teal coloration with strong strike. **$3,400**

Poison, with Diamond Design, 8" tooled top. One of the larger, amber, diamond cornered poisons. Light to medium amber and pristine. **$350**

Poison, Triangular with original contents and label, 5". An example with the entire original label and contents. The label says it contains mercury bichloride. **$750**

Poison, Quilted with stopper, 11" without stopper. This is the second-largest of the 12 sizes known for the quilted, round poisons. This example has no embossing on the base. These are considered extremely rare. **$650**

Pold & Co., Barnums Building Balto. Applied top, smooth base. Sapphire-blue color, heavy whittle (marks caused by a reaction of the hot glass hitting the surface of a colder mold) and overall crudity, extremely rare. Some light wear. Comes with holder. **$4,000**

Race & Sheldon's, Magic Waterproof Boot Polish, 5 1/2", applied top with open pontil. The embossing is crude. Lockport green color with significant whittle. **$3,200**

Return to Joe Gribble, Old Crow Saloon Douglas, A.T., 6" screw cap with ground lip. Close to a half-pint. An Arizona Territory flask. In 1903, Joe Gribble opened a saloon called "The Whitehouse" and another called "The Old Crow". Rare. **$4,600**

Rowlers Rheumatism Medicine, Prepared by Dr. J.R. Boyce Sacramento, 7 1/2". Applied top and smooth base. These Western medicines come with and without a pontil mark. Probably made in the mid-1860s. This has an unusual and smaller than normal applied top and the overall odd shape. **$1,200**

Star Whiskey, W.B. Crowel Jr. New York, 8 1/4" with applied handle and mouth. Pontil. A yellowish amber with bubbles and overall crudity. **$1,200**

Thos. Taylor & Co., Sold, Agents P. Vollmer's Old Bourbon Louisville KY. Virginia, Nev. Tooled top, pint coffin flask.

Photo courtesy American Bottle Auctions, Sacramento, Calif.; www.AmericanBottle.com

Umbrella Inkwell, Rolled lip, 2 1/2" h, in a brilliant blue. The pontil is quite a bit off center, which gives the base an unusual look. **$1,300**

Mid-1880s. Thomas Taylor is a colorful and intriguing name in the history of the Nevada wholesale liquor business. **$1,800**

U.S.A. Hosp Dept., applied top and smooth base. Orange-puce with some strawberry. Significant whittle (marks caused by a reaction of the hot glass hitting the surface of a colder mold) and overall crudity. Possibly an earlier variant. Areas of dullness where the glass may have touched the surface of another bottle during manufacture, minor. **$1,400**

Victorian Inkwell, 2" h. Circa 1870s into the 1890s. Embossed design. This was an inkwell used by a person of substance. Its blue color is accented by ornate flower design. **$1,000**

Warner's Safe Nervine, London. 9 1/2". Applied top. This example does not have the slug plate, and has quotes around the word "safe." A crude bottle, yellowish olive, light scratches on the reverse. **$475**

The Wellington Saloon, the F.G. McCoy Co Inc. Prescott Ariz. 6 1/2" half-pint. The Wellington Saloon was located on Montezuma Street in 1902 and it is believed that it closed in 1906. The bottom also reads, "Design Pat. Aug 9 1898." Considered a rare bottle. Some light stain. **$900**

WFJ, Socorro, N.M. Applied top. The embossing is quite bold. **$600**

Photo courtesy American Bottle Auctions, Sacramento, Calif.; www.AmericanBottle.com

W.B. Co. S.F. Trademark, with sun design in center. It is believed these odd-looking bottles were made for beer, but little is known about the company. Significant whittle (marks caused by a reaction of the hot glass hitting the surface of a colder mold) and bubbles. Brilliant bluish-aqua. **$2,200**

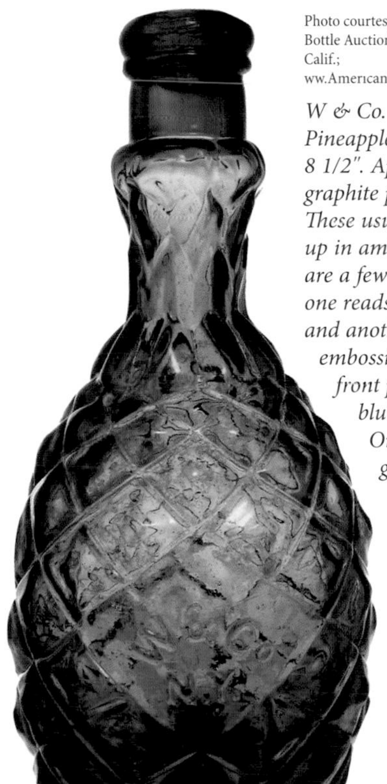

Photo courtesy American Bottle Auctions, Sacramento, Calif.; ww.AmericanBottle.com

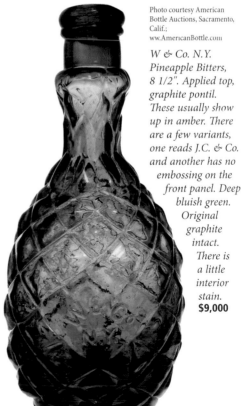

W & Co. N.Y. Pineapple Bitters, 8 1/2". Applied top, graphite pontil. These usually show up in amber. There are a few variants, one reads J.C. & Co. and another has no embossing on the front panel. Deep bluish green. Original graphite intact. There is a little interior stain. **$9,000**

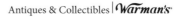

Photo courtesy American Bottle Auctions, Sacramento, Calif.; www.AmericanBottle.com

Wheeler's Berlin Bitters Baltimore, variant, also comes in aqua, amber and olive colorations. It is a little fatter and about a half an inch wider at the base. It has the graphite pontil and is yellowish amber with some green. It appears it may have been cleaned at some point and is crude. Minor scratches. **$7,000**

Bottles, Barber

In the 19th century, barbers filled their own bottles with hair tonic and oil, bay rum, shampoo and rosewater. The bottles came in distinctive colors/shapes so the barber could identify what was in each one of them. Barber bottles stopped being made after the 1906 Pure Food and Drug Act made it illegal to refill non-labeled bottles.

Hobbs, No, 323 Dew Drop / Hobnail Barber's Bottle, blue opalescent, ceramic pourer, polished pontil mark. Hobbs, Brockunier & Co. Fourth quarter 19th century. 6 3/4" h, 3 3/4" d overall. Loss of one hob and chip to two others, lowest row of hobs with multiple flakes. **$120**

Hobnail Barber's Bottle, cranberry opalescent, rough pontil mark. Late 19th/early 20th century. 8 1/4" h, 4 1/4" d overall. One flake to a hob and several with manufacturing roughness. **$144**

Inverted Thumbprint Barber's Bottle, amber, polished pontil mark. Fourth quarter 19th century. 7" h, 3 1/4" d overall. **$34**

L.G. Wright, Swirl Barber's Bottle, cranberry opalescent. L.G. Wright Glass Co. Second half 20th century. 7" h, 3 1/2" d overall. **$120**

L.G. Wright, Opal Rib Barber's Bottle, opalescent. L.G. Wright Glass Co. Second half 20th century. 7" h, 3 1/2" d overall. **$115**

Seaweed/Coral Barber's Bottle, blue opalescent, polished pontil mark. Late 19th/early 20th century. 7" h, 3 1/2" d overall. Pattern flake. **$345**

Photo courtesy Green Valley Auctions, Mt. Crawford, Va.; www.GreenValleyAuctions.com

Seaweed/Coral Barber's Bottle, cranberry opalescent, polished pontil mark. Late 19th/early 20th century. 7" h, 3 1/2" d overall. **$452**

Stars and Stripes Barber's Bottle, opalescent, polished pontil mark. Late 19th/early 20th century. 6 7/8" h, 3 1/2" d overall. **$373**

Swirl Barber's Bottle, blue opalescent, polished pontil mark. Late 19th/early 20th century. 7" h, 3 1/2" d overall. **$195**

Swirl Barber's Bottle, cranberry opalescent. Late 19th/early 20th century. 7" h, 3 1/4" d overall. **$184**

Vesta/Hobnail in Square, Barber's Bottle and Tumbler, colorless opalescent, bottle slightly tinted. Aetna Glass & Mfg. Co. Fourth quarter 19th century. 6 3/4" and 4" h. Bottle with the partial loss of one hob and a flake to another, also some interior dirt/residue. .... **$92 both**

Victorian, Enamel Decorated Barber's Bottle, cobalt blue with white enamel stylized floral decoration, rough pontil mark. Late 19th/early 20th century. 7 1/2" h, 3 3/4" d overall. **$46**

Photo courtesy Green Valley Auctions, Mt. Crawford, Va.; www.GreenValleyAuctions.com

Victorian, Enamel Decorated Rib Optic Barber's Bottle, green with polychrome floral decoration, rough pontil mark. Late 19th/early 20th century. 7 1/8" h, 3 1/2" d overall. **$56**

Carnival Glass

Carnival glass is colored, pressed glass with a fired-on iridescent finish. It was first manufactured about 1905 to imitate the more expensive art glass made by Tiffany and other firms. More than 1,000 different patterns have been identified. Production of old carnival glass ended in the 1920s. Most of the popular patterns of carnival glass were produced by five companies: Dugan, Fenton, Imperial, Millersburg and Northwood. The term "carnival glass" did not arise until the 1960s.

Acorn Bowl, red/Amberina, scalloped edge. Fenton Art Glass Co. First quarter 20th century. 2" h, 7 1/2" d. **$460**

Collector's Note: Joseph Locke developed Amberina glass in 1883 for the New England Glass Works. "Amberina," a trade name, describes a transparent glass that shades from deep ruby to amber. It was made by adding powdered gold to the ingredients for an amber-glass batch. A portion of the glass was reheated later to produce the shading effect. Usually it was the bottom that was reheated to form the deep red; however, reverse examples have been found.

The New England Glass Co., Cambridge, Mass., first made plated Amberina in 1886; Edward Libbey patented the process for the company in 1889. Plated Amberina was made by taking a gather of chartreuse or cream opalescent glass, dipping it in Amberina, and combining the two, often using a mold. The finished product had a deep-amber to deep-ruby-red shading, a fiery opalescent lining and often vertical ribbing for enhancement.

Acorn Bowl, red, scalloped rim with points. Fenton Art Glass Co. First quarter 20th century. 2 3/8" h, 7 1/2" d. Minor nicks on two points. **$316**

Big Basket-weave Vase, amethyst. Dugan Glass Co. First quarter 20th century. 10" h, 3 1/4" d base. **$204**

Blackberry Spray Whimsical Hat, red, scalloped rim. Fenton Art Glass Co. First quarter 20th century. 3" h, 6 1/2" d. **$138**

Blackberry Spray Whimsical Hat, red/Amberina, scalloped rim. Fenton Art Glass Co. First quarter 20th century. 3" h, 6 1/2" d. Annealing fissure on side. **$184**

Bushel Basket Dish, amethyst, four-footed novelty basket with round rim, "N" in circle in base. Northwood Glass Co. First quarter 20th century. 4 5/8" h, 4 1/4" d. **$80**

Bushel Basket Dish, blue opalescent, four-footed novelty basket with round rim, "N" in circle in base. Northwood Glass Co. First quarter 20th century. 4 5/8" h, 4 1/4" d. **$120**

Bushel Basket Dish, aqua opalescent, four-footed novelty basket with round rim, "N" in circle in base. Northwood Glass Co. First quarter 20th century. 4 5/8" h, 4 1/4" d. Annealing fissure to rim. **$230**

Marigold carnival glass loving cup in Orange Tree, Fenton, with interior ribbing similar to Peacock Tail, 6" h. **$150+**

Cobalt Blue carnival glass bowl in Peter Rabbit, Fenton, with Bearded Berry back, 8" diameter. **$4,000+**

Bushel Basket Dish, white, four-footed novelty basket with eight sided rim, "N" in circle in base. Northwood Glass Co. First quarter 20th century. 4" h, 4 7/8" d. Tiny nick to rim. **$115**

Corn Vases, Pair, ice green, "N" in circle in base. Northwood Glass Co. 6 1/2" h, 3 1/8" d base. One with significant crack at rim. ..... **$345 pair**

Drapery Rose Bowl, aqua opalescent, crimped top. Northwood Glass Co. First quarter 20th century. 3 7/8" h, 5 1/4" d. Several small manufacturing flaws. **$184**

Photo courtesy Green Valley Auctions, Mt. Crawford, Va.; www.GreenValleyAuctions.com

Grape and Cable, Cologne Bottle with Stopper, amethyst. Northwood Glass Co. First quarter 20th century. 8 3/4" h overall. Minor flake to stopper tip. **$192**

Embroidered Mums Bowl, ice blue, scalloped rim with beaded edge. Northwood Glass Co. First quarter 20th century. 2 1/2" h, 8 3/4" d. **$575**

Fine Cut Roses Rose Bowl, green, crimped rim, plain interior. Northwood Glass Co. First quarter 20th century. 4" h. **$161**

Fine Rib Vase, red/Amberina, scalloped rim. Fenton Art Glass Co. First quarter 20th century. 10 1/2" h, 2 7/8" d base. **$230**

Fisherman Mug, amethyst. Dugan Glass Co. First quarter 20th century. 4" h. Annealing fissure on rim. **$72**

Fruits and Flowers Bon-Bon, aqua opalescent, footed bowl with two handles, beaded rim. Northwood Glass Co. First quarter 20th century. 3 3/4" h, 5" d. Minute flake to handle and minor interior scratches. **$431**

Good Luck Bowl, blue, crimped rim, ribbed exterior. Northwood Glass Co. First quarter 20th century. 2" h, 9" d. **$517**

Grape ruffled bowl, Imperial, purple with electric blue iridescence. **$150**

Grape & Cable, footed 9" plate, Northwood, ice green. **$250**

Grape & Cable, Fenton, fruit bowl with Persian Medallion interior, green. **$215**

Grape and Cable, Sweetmeat Compote with Lid, amethyst. Northwood Glass Co. First quarter 20th century. 8 3/4" h overall. **$168**

Hearts and Flowers Bowl, amethyst, scalloped rim with beaded edge. Northwood Glass Co. First quarter 20th century. 2 1/2" h, 9" d. **$258**

Green carnival glass table set in Butterfly and Berry, Fenton, including creamer, covered sugar, covered butter dish and spooner; butter, 6" h; creamer, 5" h; spooner, 4 1/4" h; sugar, 6 1/2" h. **$2,500+ set**

Hearts and Flowers Bowl, ice blue, scalloped rim with beaded edge. Northwood Glass Co. First quarter 20th century. 8 1/4" d. Expected wear to base. **$258**

Hearts and Flowers, Footed Compote, ice green. Northwood Glass Co. First quarter 20th century. 5 7/8" h, 6 3/4" d. **$690**

Heron Mug, amethyst. Dugan Glass Co. First quarter 20th century. 4" h. Annealing fissure to rim, does not sit level. .. **$69**

Inverted Feather, Cracker Jar with Lid, green, Hobstar and Feather design. Cambridge Glass Co. First quarter 20th century. 6 1/2" h overall, 6 3/4" d. Lid rim with 1 1/4" x 3/16" filled-in chip. **$72**

Lined Lattice Vase, amethyst. Dugan Glass Co. First quarter 20th century. 10" h, 3 1/4" d overall base. **$180**

Mikado Compote, blue, Cherry pattern on exterior, scalloped rim with beaded edge. Fenton Art Glass Co. First quarter 20th century. 7 7/8" h, 9 1/2" d. Wear to base. **$575**

Nippon Bowl, ice blue, ruffled rim with beaded edge. Northwood Glass Co. First quarter 20th century. 8 7/8" d. **$228**

Open-Edge Basket-weave, Whimsy Hat with Jack-in-the-Pulpit Rim, red, reticulated rim. Fenton Art Glass Co. First quarter 20th century. 2 3/4" h, 5 3/4" x 4 1/4". Annealing lines to rim. **$184**

Orange Tree Mug, red/Amberina. Fenton Art Glass Co. First quarter 20th century. 3 1/2" h. Undamaged except for a minute flake on handle, expected wear to base. **$184**

Panther Small Footed Bowls, two, blue, Butterfly and Berry exterior, one example with scalloped rim, the other with plain rim. Fenton Art Glass Co. First quarter 20th century. 2 1/4" h, 5" to 5 1/4" d. .... **$144 pair**

Peacocks, 9" plate with ribbed back, ice green. **$265**

Peacock at Urn, 9" plate, Fenton, blue. **$325**

Peacock at the Fountain, water pitcher, Northwood, purple. **$325**

Peacocks, 9" plate with ribbed back, pastel marigold. **$225**

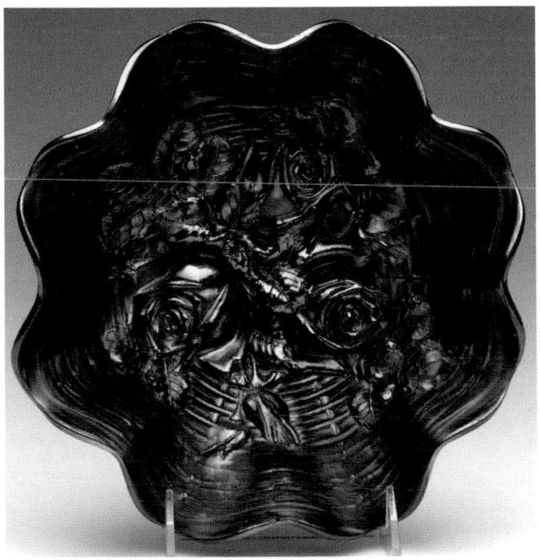

Photo courtesy Green Valley Auctions, Mt. Crawford, Va.; www.GreenValleyAuctions.com

Rose Show Bowl, amethyst, scalloped. Northwood Glass Co. First quarter 20th century. 2 3/4" h, 8 5/8" d. Minute pattern flake. **$734**

Peacocks, 9" plate with ribbed back, marigold. **$250**

Pony Bowl, amethyst, scalloped rim. Dugan Glass Co. First quarter 20th century. 2 3/4" h, 8 3/4" d. Minute wear to iridescence on pattern. **$287**

Poppy Pickle Dish, amethyst, scalloped, crimped rim. Northwood Glass Co. First quarter 20th century. 2" h, 5 1/4" x 8". **$172**

Poppy Show Plate, amethyst, scalloped rim. Northwood Glass Co. First quarter 20th century. 1 3/4" h, 9 3/8" d. **$1,035**

Rose Show, 9" plate, lime green, extremely rare color, couple small chips on roses. **$600**

Photo courtesy Green Valley Auctions, Mt. Crawford, Va.; www.GreenValleyAuctions.com

Rose Show Bowl, aqua opalescent, scalloped rim. Northwood Glass Co. First quarter 20th century. 3" h, 8 3/4" d. **$678**

Rustic Vase, amethyst. Fenton Art Glass Co. First quarter 20th century. 10 1/2" h, 3 1/4" d base. **$48**

Rustic Vase, marigold. Fenton Art Glass Co. First quarter 20th century. 16 1/2" h, 4 1/8" d base. **$126**

Singing Birds Mug, amethyst, plain background, "N" in circle in base. Northwood Glass Co. First quarter 20th century. 3 1/2" h. **$46**

Singing Birds Mug, marigold, stippled background, "N" in circle in base. Northwood Glass Co. First quarter 20th century. 3 1/2" h. Minute nick on handle. **$23**

Photo courtesy Green Valley Auctions, Mt. Crawford, Va.; www.GreenValleyAuctions.com

Tornado Vase, amethyst, ribbed, "N" in circle in base. Northwood Glass Co. First quarter 20th century. 6 1/4" h, 2 3/4" d base; 3/8" chip in spot of exfoliation on foot, flake to rim. **$300**

Thin Rib Vases, Pair, blue. Fenton Art Glass Co. First quarter 20th century. 14" h, 3 3/4" d base. Minute rim nick to one. .... **$69 pair**

Three Fruits Bowl, amethyst, stippled interior, ribbed exterior. Northwood Glass Co. First quarter 20th century. 1 7/8" h, 8 3/4" d. Minute wear to iridescence on pattern. **$228**

Three Fruits Medallion, Spatula Footed Bowl, aqua opalescent, Meander pattern on exterior of bowl, scalloped rim with beaded edge, stippled background. Northwood Glass Co. First quarter 20th century. 3 1/4" h, 8 3/4" d. A few minute scuffs to interior of bowl. **$373**

Tree Trunk Vase, green. Northwood Glass Co. First quarter 20th century. 10" h, 3 3/4" d base. **$57**

Trout and Fly Bowl, green, scalloped rim. Millersburg Glass Co. First quarter 20th century. 2 3/4" h, 8 3/4" d. Annealing line and some light interior scratches. **$360**

Victorian Bowl, amethyst, ruffled rim. Dugan Glass Co. First quarter 20th century. 3" h, 11 3/4" d. Pattern nick. **$161**

Wishbone and Spades Plate, amethyst. Northwood Glass Co. First quarter 20th century. 6 1/2" d. **$230**

Children's Glass, including Mugs

Castle, Boat and Church Medallion Mug, vaseline, stippled handle. Fourth quarter 19th century. 3 1/8" h, 2 3/4" d rim. Faint annealing line at top of handle. **$69**

Children's ABC Plates, two, amber, consisting of Clock with Scalloped Edge and an unidentified example with stippled background, beaded swag and fine-cut center, each with numbers as well as ABCs. Fourth quarter 19th century. 7" d. Unidentified example with minor mold roughness to interior rim and a flake to a heavy fin, clock undamaged. .... **$30 pair**

Children's ABC Plates, two, amber, consisting of Emma and Rover. New Martinsville Glass Co. Fourth quarter 19th century. 6 3/8" d. Each with normal mold roughness to interior rim. .... **$57 pair**

Child's Fish Platter, colorless with frosted center, polished table ring. Late 19th/early 20th century. 7/8" h, 3 1/8" x 5 1/4". **$180**

Garfield Memorial Toy Mug, colorless, bust on front and dates on reverse, 1880 to top of handle, beaded under base. Fourth quarter 19th century. 2 1/4" h, 1 7/8" d. Minute bruise under base. **$34**

Menagerie Fish, Child's Spooner, blue. Bryce, Higbee & Co. Fourth quarter 19th century. 3 1/2" h, 2 5/8" d base. **$126**

Mephistopheles Mug, opaque white/milk glass, plain handle. Fourth quarter 19th century. 3 1/8" h, 3 3/4" d rim. Small open bubble to base. **$60**

Ribbon Candy, Child's Cake Stand, green. Fourth quarter 19th century. 3 1/2" h, 6" d. Minor mold roughness to foot. **$92**

Seesaw/Children at Play Plate, colorless with frosted center, detailed scene also features dogs and chickens, 24-scallop rim. Fourth quarter 19th century. 10 1/8" d. Light wear. **$144**

Depression Glass

Depression glass is clear or colored translucent glassware that was distributed free, or at low cost, around the time of the Great Depression. Some food manufacturers and distributors put a piece of glassware in boxes of food, as an incentive to purchase. Movie theaters and businesses would hand out a piece simply for coming in the door.

Dozens of manufacturers made scores of patterns. In addition to clear or crystal, common colors include pink, pale blue, green and amber. Depression glass has been highly collectible since the 1960s. Some manufacturers continued to make popular patterns after World War II, or introduced similar patterns, which are also collectible. Popular and expensive patterns and pieces have been reproduced, and reproductions are still being made.

For more information, see *Warman's Depression Glass Identification and Price Guide 5th Edition* by Ellen T. Schroy.

Avocado, No. 601

Manufactured by Indiana Glass Co., Dunkirk, Ind., from 1923 to 1933. Pieces were made in crystal, green, pink, and white.

Reproductions: † Creamer, 8" pickle, 64-ounce pitcher, plates, sherbet, sugar, and tumblers. Reproductions can be found in amethyst, blue, dark green, frosted green, frosted pink, pink, red, and yellow, representing several colors not made originally.

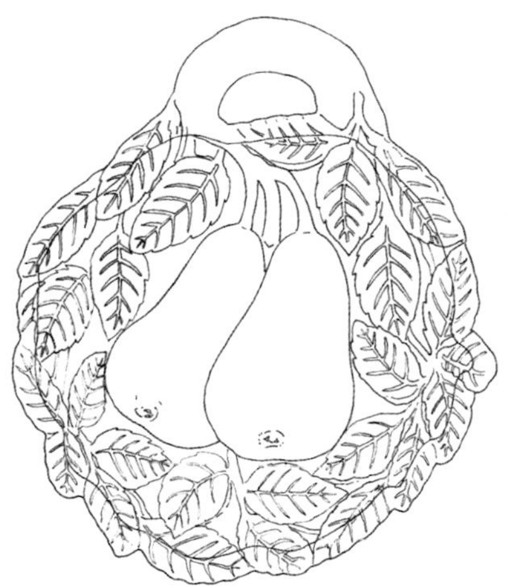

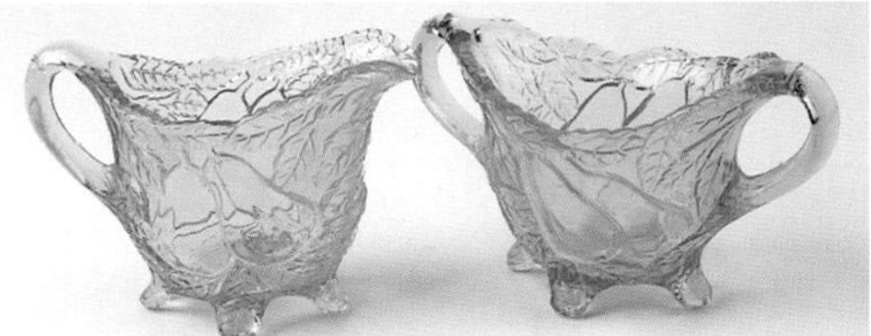

Avocado, green sugar, creamer, **$40 each**

Item	Crystal	Green	Pink	White
❒ Bowl, 5-1/4" d, 2 handles	12.00	38.00	27.50	—
❒ Bowl, 8" d, two handles, oval	17.50	30.00	25.00	—
❒ Bowl, 8-1/2" d	20.00	60.00	50.00	—
❒ Bowl, 9-1/2" d, 3-1/4" deep	35.00	175.00	150.00	—
❒ Cake plate, 10-1/4" d, two handles	17.50	60.00	40.00	—
❒ Creamer, ftd †	17.50	40.00	35.00	—
❒ Cup, ftd	—	36.00	30.00	—
❒ Pickle bowl, 8" d, two handles, oval †	17.50	30.00	25.00	—
❒ Pitcher, 64 oz †	385.00	1,100.00	900.00	425.00
❒ Plate, 6-3/8" d, sherbet †	6.00	18.00	15.00	—
❒ Plate, 8-1/4" d, luncheon †	7.50	22.00	20.00	—
❒ Preserve bowl, 7" l, handle	10.00	32.00	28.00	—
❒ Relish, 6" d, ftd	10.00	30.00	25.00	—
❒ Salad bowl, 7-1/2" d	9.00	55.00	37.50	—
❒ Saucer	6.00	24.00	15.00	—
❒ Sherbet, ftd †	—	75.00	55.00	—
❒ Sugar, ftd †	17.50	40.00	35.00	—
❒ Tumbler †	25.00	250.00	150.00	35.00

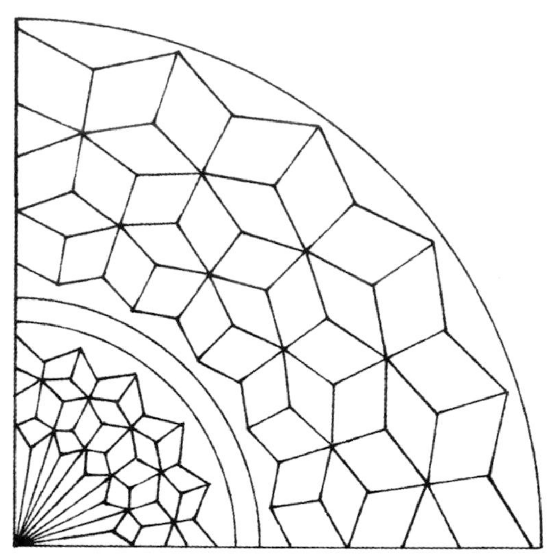

Cube, Cubist

Manufactured by Jeannette Glass Co., Jeannette, Pa., from 1929 to 1933. Pieces were made in amber, crystal, green, pink, ultramarine, and white. Production in white is limited in both the number of items made as well as collector interest.

Cube pink cup, **$8**

❐ Bowl, 4-1/2" d, deep	—	7.00	9.50	35.00
❐ Bowl, 7-1/4" d		20.00		
❐ Butter dish, cov	—	60.00	65.00	—
❐ Candy jar, cov, 6-1/2" h	—	35.00	30.00	—
❐ Coaster, 3-1/4" d	—	10.00	10.00	—
❐ Creamer, 2-5/8" h	5.00	10.00	10.00	70.00
❐ Creamer, 3-9/16" h	—	9.00	9.00	—
❐ Cup	—	7.00	8.00	—
❐ Dessert bowl, 4-1/2" d, pointed rim	4.00	8.50	9.50	—
❐ Pitcher, 8-3/4" h, 45 oz	—	235.00	215.00	—
❐ Plate, 6" d, sherbet	—	11.00	3.50	—
❐ Plate, 8" d, luncheon	—	8.50	9.50	—
❐ Powder jar, cov, three legs	—	30.00	35.00	—
❐ Salad bowl, 6-1/2" d	6.00	15.00	15.00	—
❐ Salt and pepper shakers, pr	—	35.00	36.00	—
❐ Saucer	1.50	3.00	3.50	—
❐ Sherbet, ftd	—	8.50	12.00	—
❐ Sugar, cov, 2-3/8" h	4.00	22.00	6.00	—
❐ Sugar, cov, 3" h	—	25.00	25.00	—
❐ Sugar, open, 3"	5.00	8.00	7.00	—
❐ Tray, 7-1/2" l	9.00	—	5.00	—
❐ Tumbler, 9 oz, 4" h	—	70.00	65.00	—

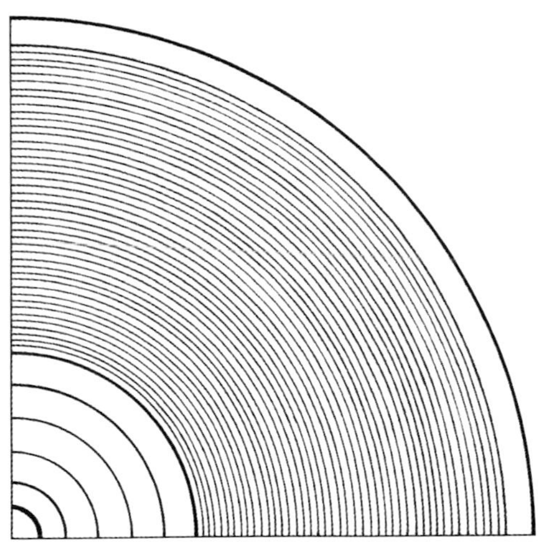

Old English, Threading

Manufactured by Indiana Glass Co., Dunkirk, Ind., in the late 1920s. Pieces were made in amber, crystal, green, and pink.

Old English, green compote, **$24**

Item				
❒ Bowl, 4" d, flat	20.00	18.00	22.00	20.00
❒ Bowl, 9-1/2" d, flat	35.00	25.00	35.00	35.00
❒ Candlesticks, pr, 4" h	35.00	25.00	35.00	35.00
❒ Candy dish, cov, flat	50.00	40.00	50.00	50.00
❒ Candy jar, cov	55.00	45.00	55.00	55.00
❒ Cheese compote, 3-1/2" h	17.50	12.00	17.50	17.50
❒ Cheese plate, indent	20.00	10.00	20.00	20.00
❒ Compote, 3-1/2" h, 6-3/8" w, two handles	24.00	12.00	24.00	24.00
❒ Compote, 3-1/2" h, 7" w	24.00	12.00	24.00	24.00
❒ Creamer	18.00	10.00	18.00	18.00
❒ Egg cup	—	10.00	—	—
❒ Fruit bowl, 9" d, ftd	30.00	20.00	30.00	30.00
❒ Fruit stand, 11" h, ftd	40.00	18.00	40.00	40.00
❒ Goblet, 8 oz, 5-3/4" h	30.00	15.00	30.00	30.00
❒ Pitcher	70.00	35.00	70.00	70.00
❒ Pitcher, cov	125.00	55.00	125.00	125.00
❒ Sandwich server, center handle	60.00	—	60.00	60.00
❒ Sherbet	20.00	10.00	20.00	20.00
❒ Sugar, cov	38.00	14.00	38.00	38.00
❒ Tumbler, 4-1/2" h, ftd	24.00	12.00	28.00	24.00
❒ Tumbler, 5-1/2" h, ftd	40.00	20.00	40.00	40.00
❒ Vase, 5-3/8" h, 7" w, fan-shape	48.00	24.00	48.00	48.00
❒ Vase, 8" h, 4-1/2" w, ftd	45.00	20.00	45.00	45.00
❒ Vase, 8-1/4" h, 4-1/4" w, ftd	45.00	20.00	45.00	45.00
❒ Vase, 12" h, ftd	72.00	35.00	72.00	72.00

Early American Pattern Glass, Flint, Etc.

Early pattern glass (flint) was made with a lead formula, giving many items a ringing sound when tapped. Lead became too valuable to be used in glass manufacturing during the Civil War, and in 1864, Hobbs, Brockunier & Co., Wheeling, W.V., developed a soda lime (non-flint) formula. Pattern glass also was produced in transparent colors, milk glass, opalescent glass, slag glass and custard glass.

Collector's Note: Fostoria Glass Co. began operations at Fostoria, Ohio, in 1887, and moved to Moundsville, W.V., in 1891. By 1925, Fostoria had five furnaces and a variety of special shops. In 1924, a line of colored tableware was introduced. Fostoria was purchased by Lancaster Colony in 1983. See more Fostoria beginning on page 465.

Artichoke – Frosted, Finger Bowl with Under Plate, colorless, each with polished table ring. Fostoria Glass Co. Fourth quarter 19th century. 3" h overall, 6" d overall. Bowl with a flake to the table ring and light wear above pattern, plate with flake/roughness and manufacturing frosted-over chip to table ring. **$92**

Artichoke – Frosted, Open Compote, colorless, pillared stem and circular foot, wafer construction. Fostoria Glass Co. Fourth quarter 19th century. 8 3/4" h, 8" d. Molding flaw to stem. **$103**

Ashburton, Large Flip Glass, colorless flint, polished pontil mark. Third quarter 19th century. 6 7/8" h, 5 5/8" d rim. **$115**

Barred Ovals Water Pitcher, colorless and frosted, applied handle. George Duncan & Sons. Fourth quarter 19th century. 9 3/4" h overall, 5" d. Minor high point wear. **$80**

Collector's Note: George Duncan, his sons, Harry and James, and Augustus Heisey, his son-in-law, formed George Duncan & Sons in Pittsburgh in 1872. After a devastating fire in 1892, James Duncan relocated the firm to Washington, Pa. Designer John E. Miller was responsible for creating many fine patterns, the most famous being Three Face. Miller became a partner in 1900 and the firm used the name Duncan and Miller Glass Co. until the plant closed in 1955.

Bowtie Salt Shaker, colorless with a slight tint, period lid. Fourth quarter 19th century. 3" h overall. Lid with small spots of rust and light denting. **$57**

Brilliant – Amber Stained, Salt Shaker, colorless, period lid. Riverside Glass Works. Fourth quarter 19th century. 3" h overall. Minor pattern flakes/roughness, lid with denting and short splits. **$138**

California / Beaded Grape, Tankard Water Pitcher, green with gilt decoration. Fourth quarter 19th century. 10 1/8" h overall, 4 5/8" d. Wear to gilt decoration. **$80**

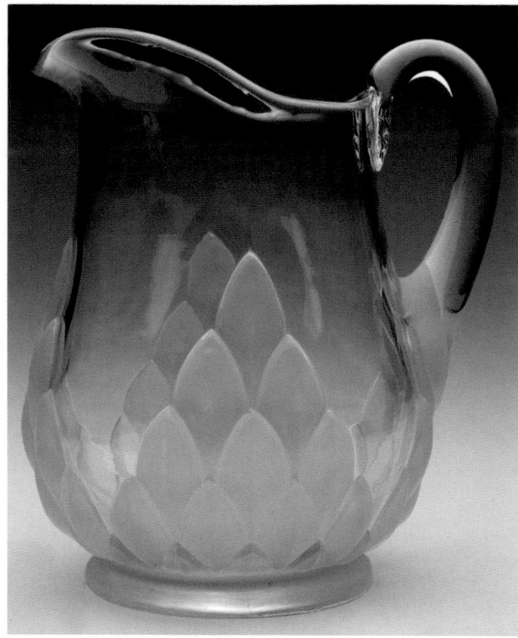

Photo courtesy Green Valley Auctions, Mt. Crawford, Va.; www.GreenValleyAuctions.com

Artichoke – Frosted, Bulbous Water Pitcher, colorless, applied handle with pressed fan design to upper terminal. Fostoria Glass Co. Fourth quarter 19th century. 8 1/2" h overall, 5 3/4" d overall. Two flat chips, area of roughness and manufacturing frosted-over chips to table ring. **$192**

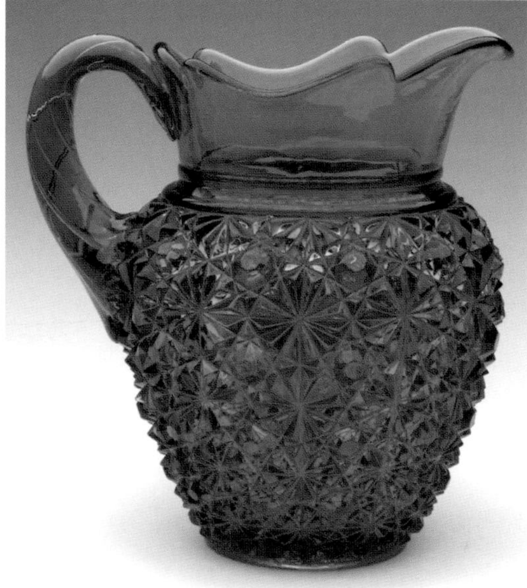

Photo courtesy Green Valley Auctions, Mt. Crawford, Va.; www.GreenValleyAuctions.com

Belmont, No. 100 / Daisy and Button – Scalloped Edge, Water Pitcher, amber, applied air-twist handle with pressed fan design to upper terminal. Belmont Glass Co. Fourth quarter 19th century. 8 3/4" h overall. Two pattern chips. **$192**

Photo courtesy Green Valley Auctions, Mt. Crawford, Va.; www.GreenValleyAuctions.com

Colorado, Four-Piece Table Set, green with very good gilt decoration, consisting of a butter dish, covered sugar bowl, creamer and spooner. U.S. Glass Co. Late 19th/early 20th century. 4 1/4" to 7" h overall, 4" to 6 7/8" d overall. **$218 set**

California / Beaded Grape, Nine-Piece Berry Set, green, consisting of a master berry bowl and eight berry dishes. Fourth quarter 19th century. 2 3/4" h, 8 1/4" sq and 1 1/4" h, 3 1/2" sq. Light interior wear to master berry bowl. .... **$46 set**

Cambridge Peacock, Seven-Piece Water Set, colorless, consisting of a tankard water pitcher and six tumblers. First quarter 20th century. Pitcher 11 1/2" h overall, 4 1/2" d base, tumblers 4 1/4" h, 3" d rim. One tumbler with small bruise to rim, one with a base flake and another with a 3/8" bruise under base, all tumblers with normal expected wear. .... **$360 set**

Central, No. 796 / Rope and Thumbprint Water Pitcher, vaseline, applied reeded handle. Central Glass Co. Fourth quarter 19th century. 8 1/2" h overall, 5 1/2" d overall. **$184**

Champion, Butter Dish, colorless with gilt decoration. McKee & Brothers. Late 19th/early 20th century. 5 1/4" h overall. Wear to gilding. **$36**

Collector's Note: McKee & Brothers Glass Works was established in 1853 in Pittsburgh. In 1888, the factory was relocated to Jeannette, Pa., and began to produce many types of glass kitchenware. Production continued until 1951, when McKee-Jeannette Co. was sold to the Thatcher Manufacturing Co.

Chandelier, Salt Shaker, colorless, period lid. Fourth quarter 19th century. 3 1/2" h overall. Some flakes/roughness, lid with small spots of rust. **$34**

Classic Butter Dish, colorless and frosted, log feet. Gillinder & Sons. Fourth quarter 19th century. 6 3/4" h overall, 6 1/2" d overall. Single flake to interior rim of base, one foot with annealing crack, and another with a flake. **$192**

Coach Bowl, amber, three wheels with front tongue. Fourth quarter 19th century. 4 1/2" h, 5 1/4" x 9" overall. **$120**

Colorado, Five-Piece Beverage Set, green with good gilt decoration, consisting of footed pitcher with applied handle, and four tumblers with polished bases. U.S. Glass Co. Late 19th/early 20th century. 8" h overall, 5 1/2" d overall. Two tumblers with minute roughness to edge of base. **$230**

Photo courtesy Green Valley Auctions, Mt. Crawford, Va.; www.GreenValleyAuctions.com

Colorado, Celery Vase, green with gilt decoration, on three feet. U.S. Glass Co. Late 19th/early 20th century. 6" h, 4" d rim. Nick on one foot. **$270**

Photo courtesy Green Valley Auctions, Mt. Crawford, Va.; www.GreenValleyAuctions.com

Daisy and Button with Ornament, Celery Vase, vaseline. Fourth quarter 19th century. 6 3/4" h, 4 7/8" d overall. **$108**

Colorado, Pair of Footed Salt and Pepper Shakers, green with gilt decoration, period lids. U.S. Glass Co. Late 19th/early 20th century. 2 3/4" h. One with chip to exterior of foot, both with minor flakes on rim. **$120**

Colorado-Maiden's Blush, Footed Toothpick Holder, gilt decoration, beaded rim. U.S. Glass Co. Late 19th/early 20th century. 2 1/2" h, 2 1/2" d rim. **$115**

Colorado Vase, colorless, on three feet. U.S. Glass Co. Late 19th/early 20th century. 14 3/4" h, 5 1/4" d rim. Minute nick to one foot. **$120**

Columbian Coin, Pair of Salt and Pepper Shakers, colorless with frosted coins, matching period lids. Central Glass Co. Fourth quarter 19th century. 3" h overall. Both with moderate to heavy wear, lids with minor imperfections. **$115**

Daisy and Button, Inkwell, vaseline, original glass cover. Fourth quarter 19th century. 2 1/4" h, 2" sq. Minor flake and hint of mold roughness to cover rim. **$172**

Daisy in Oval Panels, Seven-Piece Beverage Set, green with gilt decoration, consisting of a tankard pitcher and six tumblers. Fourth quarter 19th century. 9 3/4" h overall, 4 3/4" d and 3 3/4" h, 2 7/8" d. Pitcher with one chip and polished area to a lower rib. **$84**

Deer and Pine Tree, Bread Tray, vaseline. Fourth quarter 19th century. 1 1/4" h, 7 3/4" x 12 7/8". Minor mold roughness to inner rim. **$80**

Dewdrop with Flowers, N.S. Starflower Water Pitcher, colorless. Fourth quarter 19th century. 8 1/4" h overall, 5" d. Interior crizzeling/stretching, minor mold roughness. **$48**

Diamond Quilted Tray, vaseline, leaf shape. Fourth quarter 19th century. 1" h, 10" d overall. Some surface wear. **$46**

Early Thumbprint, Open Compote, colorless flint glass, rim with 32 even scallops, double step hollow stem with 12 flutes, circular foot with 24 scallops, single band of 24 thumbprints under foot, wafer construction. Bakewell, Pears & Co. Third quarter 19th century. 10 3/4" h, 12 3/4" d, 6 7/8" d foot. Single chip under the rim and an open bubble to one scallop. **$632**

Ellrose - Amber Stained, Goblet, colorless. George Duncan & Sons. Fourth quarter 19th century. 6 3/8" h. **$126**

Ellrose - Amber Stained, Butter Pats, Set of Four, colorless. George Duncan & Sons. Fourth quarter 19th century. 2 3/4" sq. Two with a single corner flake, two with flake/roughness to two or more corners. .... **$132 all**

Eye-Winker Salt Shaker, colorless, period lid. Dalzell, Gilmore & Leighton Co. Late 19th century. 3" h overall. Normal manufacturing roughness under lid, lid with scratches and light corrosion. **$57**

Feather, Pair of Salt and Pepper Shakers, colorless, period lids. Late 19th century. 2 3/4" h overall. Several minor flakes to shoulder rib and a small spot of roughness to one, one lid with corrosion and minor denting. **$72**

Fine Cut and Block - Amber Stained, Sugar Bowl, colorless, domed lid. Fourth quarter 19th century. 8 3/8" h overall, 5 1/2" d. **$115**

Fine Cut and Block, Marmalade / Pickle Jar, amber. Fourth quarter 19th century. 7" h overall, 3 3/4" d rim. Minute mold roughness to interior of lid. **$36**

Photo courtesy Green Valley Auctions, Mt. Crawford, Va.; www.GreenValleyAuctions.com

Early Thumbprint, Salver/Cake Stand, colorless flint glass, curved rim with 32 even scallops, double-step hollow stem with 12 flutes, circular foot with 24 scallops, single band of 24 thumbprints under foot, wafer construction. Bakewell, Pears & Co. Third quarter 19th century. 6" h, 11 1/2" d rim, 5 3/8" d foot. Small area of pattern roughness under the plate and a flake on one point of the stem. **$1,073**

Photo courtesy Green Valley Auctions, Mt. Crawford, Va.; www.GreenValleyAuctions.com

Fine Cut and Block – Amber Stained, Goblet, colorless. Fourth quarter 19th century. 6 1/4" h. **$96**

Florida / Emerald Green, Herringbone Water Pitcher. Fourth quarter 19th century. 9 3/4" h overall, 4 1/2" d. Minute open bubble to one herringbone panel. **$34**

Fostoria, No. 183 / Victoria Boat-Shaped Relish, colorless. Fostoria Glass Co. Fourth quarter 19th century. 3 1/2" h overall, 2 3/4" x 8". **$48**

Frosted Dolphin, Creamer, colorless. Hobbs, Brockunier & Co. Fourth quarter 19th century. 6 3/4" h overall, 3 1/2" d rim. Lightly tinted. **$57**

Heart with Thumbprint, Ruby Stained Goblet, colorless. Fourth quarter 19th century. 5 7/8" h. **$1,610**

Hexagon Block, Ruby Stained, Tumbler, colorless, with leaf engraving. Fourth quarter 19th century. 3 7/8" h. Minute wear to stain on rim. **$57**

Hobbs, No. 339 / Leaf and Flower – Amber Stained Four-Piece Table Set, colorless, consisting of a butter dish, covered sugar bowl, creamer with applied handle and spooner, later three with polished pontil mark. Hobbs, Brockunier & Co. Late 19th/early 20th century. 3 1/2" to 5" h overall, 3 1/2" to 8" d overall. Butter with chip to lid rim and base flange, and other minor nicks and roughness, sugar lid with flake to rim, each example with minor to moderate roughness to scalloped line above pattern. .... **$96 set**

Photo courtesy Green Valley Auctions, Mt. Crawford, Va.; www.GreenValleyAuctions.com

Flying Birds Goblet, colorless. Fourth quarter 19th century. 5 5/8" h. Flake to line above pattern. **$147**

Photo courtesy Green Valley Auctions, Mt. Crawford, Va.; www.GreenValleyAuctions.com

Frosted Flower Band, Water Pitcher, colorless, collared foot. Fourth quarter 19th century. 9 3/8" h overall, 5" d. **$96**

Photo courtesy Green Valley Auctions, Mt. Crawford, Va.; www.GreenValleyAuctions.com

Stippled Fleur-De-Lys, Seven-Piece Water Set, green with traces of gilt decoration, consisting of a water pitcher and six tumblers. Fourth quarter 19th century. Pitcher 8" h overall, 5" d, tumblers 3 3/4" h, 2 3/4" d. Pitcher with a single foot flake. **$72**

creamer and spooner. Riverside Glass Works. Late 19th/early 20th century. 4 3/4" to 5 1/2" h overall. Creamer with crack to upper handle terminal. .... **$115 set**

Riverside, No. 484 / Croesus Breakfast Covered Sugar and Creamer, green with above-average gilt decoration. Riverside Glass Works. Late 19th/early 20th century. 4 1/8" and 5 3/4" h overall. Creamer with ghost-like crack to right side of upper terminal of handle, sugar with several minute nicks to edge of lid. .... **$84 both**

Riverside, No. 484 / Croesus Three-Piece Beverage Set, green with good gilt decoration, consisting of a water pitcher with an applied handle with impressed feather at upper terminal, and two tumblers with polished table rings. Riverside Glass Works. Fourth quarter 19th century. 11 1/4" h overall, 5 1/4" d overall, and 3 7/8" h, 2 3/4" d. .... **$132 set**

Rose in Snow, Water Pitcher, amber, applied amber handle. Bryce Bros. Fourth quarter 19th century. 8 1/2" h overall, 5" d overall. **$103**

Rose Sprig, Cake Stand, amber. Fourth quarter 19th century. 6 1/4" h, 9 1/8" sq. Mold roughness to interior of base. **$84**

Royal Oak, Three-Piece Table Set, colorless and frosted, consisting of a covered sugar bowl, creamer with applied handle and spooner. Northwood Glass Co. Late 19th/early 20th century. 3 3/4" to 6" h overall, 3 1/2" to 4" sq. Chip to rim of sugar base. .... **$108 set**

Shoshone/Victor, Cake Stand, green. U.S. Glass Co. Fourth quarter 19th century. 4 1/4" h, 9" d. **$57**

Snail, Covered Sugar Bowl, colorless, engraved foliate decoration. George Duncan & Sons. Fourth quarter 19th century. 7 1/4" h overall, 4 1/8" d. Minor high-point wear to base. **$57**

Sunken Primrose/Florida, Ruby and Amber Stained Tumbler, colorless, polished table ring. Greensburg Glass Co. Fourth quarter 19th century. 3 3/4" h. **$115**

Swan, Four-Piece Table Set, opaque white/milk glass, consisting of a butter base, covered sugar bowl, creamer and spooner. Fourth quarter 19th century. Sugar 7 1/8" h, 4 1/2" d rim. Creamer with rim roughness and annealing fissure to foot, butter base with annealing crack to rim, spooner with flaking/roughness and annealing fissure to rim, with graphite speckles. .... **$108 set**

Photo courtesy Green Valley Auctions, Mt. Crawford, Va.; www.GreenValleyAuctions.com

Swirled Feather and Diamond Point, Covered Nappy / Butter, fiery opalescent flint, cover with acorn-like finial, base with alternating large and medium scallop rim, eight-petal rosette in base. Possibly Boston & Sandwich Glass Co. Mid 19th century. 6 1/8" d overall. Some light mold roughness. **$226**

Collector's Note: In 1818, Deming Jarves was listed in the Boston directory as a glassmaker. That same year, he was appointed general manager of the newly formed New England Glass Co. In 1824, Jarves toured the glassmaking factories in Pittsburgh, left New England Glass and founded a glass factory in Sandwich, Mass.

Originally called the Sandwich Manufacturing Co., it was incorporated in April 1826 as the Boston & Sandwich Glass Co. The firm closed on Jan. 1, 1888.

Texas - Maiden's Blush, Cruet, colorless, original colorless stopper. Late 19th/early 20th century. 6 1/2" h overall, 4" d base. Several spots of manufacturing roughness to shoulder ribs and light to moderate wear to lower ribs and stain. **$450**

Thousand Eye, Three-Piece Water Set, amber, consisting of a water pitcher, goblet and oval tray. Adams & Co. Fourth quarter 19th century. Pitcher 9 5/8" h overall, tray 12" x 13 7/8". Pitcher with chip to end of one support under bowl. **$57**

Tulip, Covered Sweetmeat, opaque white flint with fiery opalescence, on a simple six-panel standard, wafer construction. Third quarter 19th century. 7 1/4" h overall, 6" d rim. Minor chip under bowl rim. **$450**

Wildflower, Five-Piece Water Set, amber, consisting of a water pitcher, three tumblers and an oval tray. Adams & Co. Fourth quarter 19th century. Pitcher 8 1/2" h, tumblers 3 7/8" h, tray 11" x 13". Flake on the base of the water tray. ..... **$72 set**

Willow Oak, Four-Piece Table Set, amber, consisting of a butter dish, creamer, sugar base and a spooner. Bryce Bros. Fourth quarter 19th century. 5" to 5 1/2" h overall. Minor mold roughness to rim of butter cover. ..... **$149 set**

Early Cut and Engraved Glass

Bowl, Free-Blown and Engraved, Footed, colorless, deep U-shape bowl with cross-hatched swag and tassel decoration below rim, small crude applied foot with rough pontil mark. Probably continental. 19th century. 4 3/4" h, 4" d rim, 2 3/8" d foot. **$67**

Celery Glass, Cut Laurel Wreath and Roundels, colorless, plain rim, cut lined panel base, applied button stem and plain circular foot with polished pontil mark. Probably Bakewell, Page & Bakewell. 1820-1830. 7 7/8" h, 5 1/4" d rim, 4 1/8" d foot. **$282**

Celery Glass, Cut Strawberry Diamonds and Rayed Roundels, colorless, cut laurel wreath below the delicately notched rim, panel cut base, applied knop stem and star-cut circular foot. Probably Bakewell, Page & Bakewell. 1820-1830. 8" h, 5 1/4" d rim, 4 1/8" d foot. Light 1/2" scratch below rim. **$270**

Compote, Cut Strawberry Diamonds and Fans, colorless, delicately notched rim, band of short panels cut below diamonds, applied knop stem and star-cut circular foot. Bowl is somewhat tilted. Probably Bakewell, Page & Bakewell. 1820-1830. 6 1/2" to 6 3/4" h, 9" d rim, 4 1/4" d foot. Several short scratches under bowl and some light wear to interior. **$282**

Chalice, Free-Blown, Cut and Engraved, colorless soda-lime glass, conical bowl elaborately engraved with birds, daisies, grapes and floral wreaths, along with cut punties, applied inverted baluster stem and wide sloping foot with light rough pontil mark. Probably continental. First half 19th century. 7 1/4" h, 4 3/4" d rim, 5" d foot. Light wear to interior base. **$450**

Celery Glass, Heavy Cut, colorless, bowl cut with 10 panels and pointed arches, raised on a panel-cut stem and star-cut foot. American or English. Mid-19th century. 7" h, 4 5/8" d rim, 3 5/8" d foot. Light interior wear. **$45**

Photo courtesy Green Valley Auctions, Mt. Crawford, Va.; www.GreenValleyAuctions.com

Wildflower, Water Pitcher, blue. Adams & Co. Fourth quarter 19th century. 8 3/4" h overall, 5 1/4" d rim. **$69**

Decanter (quart), Cut Strawberry Diamonds, Fans and Rayed Roundels, colorless, three applied neck rings above shoulder flutes, applied circular foot with large polished pontil mark, hollow roundel and star-cut stopper. Probably Pittsburgh, possibly Bakewell, Page & Bakewell. 1820-1830. 10 1/4" h overall, 8" h bottle, 3 3/4" d foot. Two minute flakes to cuttings and a small chip to the lower ring of stopper. **$214**

Decanter, colorless cut glass with white sulfide bust of Washington, American, late 19th century, the decanter throat and shoulder cut with concentric circles, the sides with ribs, one section inset with a white sulfide bust of George Washington, with an acorn-form cut-glass stopper, (small chips), overall 12 1/4" h, roughness to two ribs below right of bust about 1/2" and 1/4" long, several small unobtrusive chips on the ribbed cuts, some cloudy, grimy residue around lip and interior and some darkish residue on the interior bottom, loss on bottom of stopper. **$5,925**

Photo courtesy Green Valley Auctions, Mt. Crawford, Va.; www.GreenValleyAuctions.com

Celery Glass, Free-Blown, Pattern-Molded and Engraved, colorless with a light gray tint, superimposed 20-rib gadrooning around lower body, applied compressed knop stem and slightly sloping foot with rough pontil mark. Decoration consists of a flower basket and two floral plumes within intricate floral swags with tassels. Probably Pittsburgh region, possibly Bakewell, Page & Bakewell. 1815-1830. 8 1/2" h, 5 3/8" d rim, 4" d foot. **$1,243**

Photo courtesy Green Valley Auctions, Mt. Crawford, Va.; www.GreenValleyAuctions.com

Flip Glasses (two), Free-Blown and Engraved, colorless, each decorated with a similar bird within a circular sunburst frame, additional simple flower on reverse, each with a rough pontil mark. Probably continental. 19th century. 3 3/4" h, 3" d rim, and 4 3/8" h, 3 5/8" d rim. Smaller with unusually heavy wear under base and some wear to interior. **$390 both**

Decanter (pint) and Tumbler, Cut Strawberry Diamonds and Fans, colorless, decanter with three applied neck rings above shoulder flutes, applied circular foot with large cut star, and hollow matching stopper, tumbler with basal flutes and star-cut base. Probably Pittsburgh. 1820-1840. Decanter 9 1/2" h overall, 7 1/4" h bottle, 3 1/8" d foot; tumbler 3 1/2" h. Decanter with minute pattern nicks, polishing to edge of foot, stopper is a different tint, tumbler with minor base flakes. .... **$390 both**

Flip Glass, Free-Blown and Engraved, colorless, stylized tulip decoration, rough pontil mark. Probably continental. 19th century. 5 3/4" h, 4 3/8" d rim. **$330**

Flip Glasses (two), Free-Blown and Engraved, colorless, first with basket of flowers decoration, second with stylized daisy and tulip decoration, ground and rough pontil marks. Probably continental. 19th century. 3 1/8" h, 2 5/8" d rim, and 5 3/8" h, 4" d rim. One with a ring of interior wear above base. .... **$300 both**

Goblet, Free-Blown, Cut and Engraved, colorless soda-lime glass, conical six-panel bowl, three panels elaborately engraved with a different landscape reserve surrounded by foliage, separated by single roughed panels each with a cut daisy and quatrefoil, applied panel-cut stem and wide sloping foot with light rough pontil mark. Probably continental. 19th century. 6" h, 3" d rim, 3 5/8" d foot. Minute flake to rim. **$192**

Jars (pair), sweetmeat, colorless cut glass, American, late 19th century, each with oval body with floral and flute cuts, domed lid with oval faceted finial on a flute cut shaft and stepped square base, 12" h, lids each with a couple of minute nicks, some base corners and edges ground slightly, one base edge has a small clamshell chip. .... **$770 pair**

Jug (panel), Cut Diamond, colorless, body features six diamond panels with plain panels above and rays below, step-cut neck and partially serrated rim, applied solid handle with cut and polished lower terminal, wide polished pontil mark. Probably Irish. 1815-1830. 6 1/8" h, 4 1/4" d rim. Minute nicks to numerous points, light interior wear. **$156**

Jug (quart), Panel Cut and Engraved, colorless, eight neck flutes and 12 basal flutes, medial engraved Vintage decoration, applied handle, factory-polished sides of rim and handle terminal, polished pontil mark. Probably New England or New York. Third quarter 19th century. 8 3/4" h overall, 4 1/4" d rim, 4 1/4" d base. Two minute nicks to one base flute. **$113**

Mug, Free-Blown and Engraved, lead glass, short cylindrical form with thick base and applied solid handle, simple leaf and spray decoration, rough pontil mark. American or European. 19th century. 3" h, 2 1/2" d. **$158**

Mug, Free-Blown and Engraved Barrel-Form, colorless, stylized tulip decoration, applied strap handle, rough pontil mark. Probably continental. 19th century. 6 1/4" h, 3 7/8" d rim. **$254**

Wine Glasses, Cut Plumes and Roundels, Set of Six, colorless, each with an applied bladed-button stem and plain foot, one with rough pontil mark and others with polished pontil mark. Probably Pittsburgh. 1820-1840. 4" to 4 1/4" h. One with a foot flake and under-fill, one with a stem flake. **$228**

Early Pressed and Lacy Glass

Covered Sugar Bowl, California, canary, octagonal with circular foot, an unusually crude and thick example with a very slight cover seat causing a poor fit. New England Glass Co. or Curling, Robertson & Co. 1850-1870. 6" h overall, 5" d rim overall, 3" d foot. One large and two moderate chips to base rim, chip and two flakes to foot, several moderate chips to cover. **$84**

Photo courtesy Green Valley Auctions, Mt. Crawford, Va.; www.GreenValleyAuctions.com

Covered Rectangular Dish, Extremely Rare, Midwestern, Lacy, colorless, dish with lancet and ellipse design on sides, bold scroll and fan rim, and 28 bull's-eye scallops around the base, stepped cover with Gothic arches and a bold fan-form finial. Probably Pittsburgh. 1830-1840. 5 5/8" h overall, 3 1/4" h rim, 4" x 6 1/4" overall. Dish rim with the partial loss of one corner scroll and a few small chips to fan tips, cover with light chip to one corner and minor flaking under the rim. This casket is one of only three or four recorded examples. **$11,300**

Creamer, Heart and Scale, colorless, molded handle and plain circular foot. Boston & Sandwich Glass Co. 1835-1850. 4 1/2" h overall, 3" d rim, 2 3/4" d foot. Shallow 3/4" spall to upper edge of spout, minor mold roughness. **$67**

Nappy on Foot, Heart and Sheaf of Wheat, colorless, double-scallop alternating with single-scallop rim, four overlapping hearts in center, attached by a sloping wafer to a medial-knop stem and sloping foot, rough pontil mark. New England. 1828-1835. 3 3/8" h, 4 7/8" d rim, 3 1/8" d foot. Three shallow chips to rim edge and two spalls (one 1" long) to upper rim. **$367**

Plate, Heart and Fleur-De-Lis central star and scrolls surrounded by a wide band of strawberry diamonds, broad scroll and scallop rim. Probably French. 1840-1860. 7 3/4" d. Some under-rim mold roughness. **$22**

Window Pane, Heavy Pressed Glass, Square, colorless, quatrefoil acanthus leaf and scroll design with a central bull's eye, lightly pebbled background, upper edge molded with a "J" initial and a bobbin and disk chain. While the design of this pane parallels those of the Lacy period, its soda-lime content indicates a later production date. Probably American. Fourth quarter 19th to first quarter 20th century. 1 1/4" thick, 8 1/4" sq. Large bruise and numerous chips to outer edge. **$30**

Photo courtesy Green Valley Auctions, Mt. Crawford, Va.; www.GreenValleyAuctions.com

Window Pane, Marked "J.&C. Ritchie," Lacy, colorless, central reserve depicting a side-wheel steamboat below the lettering and a draped tassel, surrounded by neo-classical style urns and flowers with a thistle centered below. A previously unrecorded example. Wheeling Flint Glass Works, Wheeling, W.V., John and Craig Ritchie, proprietors. 1833-1836. 7" x 5". Minute flake and hint of mold roughness to reverse edge. **$11,300**

Free-Blown Glass

Bowl (deep), Free-Blown, slightly cloudy aquamarine bottle glass, slightly tapered sides with folded rim, domed base with rough pontil mark. Probably Midwestern. First half 19th century. 7 1/4" h, 11" d. Minor wear, numerous light open bubbles. **$339**

Bowl (deep), Free-Blown, bottle green, slightly tapered sides with a boldly folded rim, domed base with rough pontil mark. Probably Midwestern. First half 19th century. 5 1/2" h, 8 1/2" d. Light wear, primarily on rim, small open bubble on outer edge of rim. **$367**

Bowl (deep), Free-Blown, swirling cobalt blue, somewhat crudely formed, slightly flaring rolled and folded rim, slightly domed base with rough pontil mark. First half 19th century. 4 1/8" h, 6 3/4" d rim. Areas of light wear. **$480**

Bowl (deep), Free-Blown, bottle green, nearly straight-sided with a narrow rolled rim, slightly domed base with rough pontil mark. Probably South Jersey. First half 19th century. 5 1/2" h, 7 1/8" d rim. Rim with a small open bubble and wear, interior with several open bubbles, scattered light wear. **$240**

Bowl (deep), Free-Blown, light bottle green, tapered sides with a boldly folded rim, domed base with rough pontil mark. Probably Midwestern. First half 19th century. 6 3/4" h, 9 1/4" d. Crack in side from below rim to near base. **$56**

Cracker Bowl, Free-Blown, colorless, applied lower knop stem and thick foot with partially polished pontil mark, original tin hinged cover with Britannia knob held in place by a tin band around rim. Probably Pittsburgh. Mid-19th century. 6" h rim, 7" d rim, 4 3/4" d foot. Light flake to inner rim, expected wear to cover. (The 1859 McKee & Brothers catalog illustrates this unusual form in a pressed-panel pattern, which they called a cracker bowl. The form continued to appear in their subsequent catalogs through 1871.) **$791**

Dome, Free-Blown, green bottle glass, elongated cylindrical form rough cut at one end. Probably 19th century. 20 3/4" h, 7" d. Several scratches and scuffs. **$56**

Egg Cup or Pedestal Salt, Free-Blown, deep cobalt blue with applied opal galleried rim, applied button stem and plain foot with rough pontil mark, high lead content. Probably English. Mid-19th century. 3 3/8" h, 2 1/4" d rim. **$101**

Ewer, Free-Blown, cobalt blue, pear-shape body with threaded neck, wide folded rim with long drawn spout, and applied hollow handle, kick-up base with rough pontil mark. 19th century. 7 1/2" h overall, 4 1/8" d overall. Loss to the lower end of threading, expected wear to rim and body, light interior residue. **$156**

Fish Globe on Foot, Free-Blown, colorless, tooled flattened rim and flared foot, rough pontil mark. American. 19th century. 14 1/2" h, 6 3/4" d rim, 8 1/4" d foot. Minor flake to rim. **$621**

Fish Globe on Foot, Free-Blown, colorless, tooled flattened rim and flared foot, rough pontil mark. American. 19th century. 11 1/4" h, 6 1/8" d rim, 7 1/8" d foot. Scratches and wear to bowl. **$423**

Inkwell, Free-Blown and Decorated, Teakettle-Form, strong aquamarine, bell-form body molded with faint ribs and fitted with two applied spouts, topped with a tooled triangular-shaped ornament mounted with a swan, additional applied prunts and threading on body, base with light four-point pontil mark. Possibly South Jersey. 19th or 20th century. 6 1/4" h, 3 1/4" d base. A 1" and 1/2" loss to threading at base and a light crack to another piece of threading. **$214**

Photo courtesy Green Valley Auctions, Mt. Crawford, Va.; www.GreenValleyAuctions.com

Inkwell, Free-Blown Bird-Form, light green, globular body with applied head, wings and tail, raised on a short drawn stem and applied wide irregular sloping foot with light rough pontil mark. Possibly South Jersey. Probably 20th century. 4 3/4" h overall, 4 1/2" d foot. Chip and short crack to one tail feather, minor flake to beak. **$158**

Jar and Ball Cover, Free-Blown, pale aquamarine, crude jar with slight shoulder and faint rough pontil mark, well-formed ball with a 2 1/2" open rough pontil. Possibly Connecticut. 19th century. 5 1/4" h overall, jar 3" h x 2" d rim, ball 2 1/2" d overall. Two small pieces of rough extra glass near jar base. **$45**

Jug (cream), Free-Blown, medium violet, squat low-shoulder body with pulled spout, applied solid delicate handle, rough pontil mark. 19th century. 3" h, 2 1/8" d rim. **$791**

Jug (cream), Free-Blown, Footed, aquamarine, pear-shaped body with delicate applied three-rib handle, short drawn stem, applied oversized domed foot with boldly folded rim and rough pontil mark. Undetermined origin. 19th or 20th century. 5 5/8" h, 2 5/8" d rim, 4" d foot. Lacking handle curl and tip is polished, cloudy interior. **$734**

Jug (quart), Cains-Attributed, Double-Chain-Decorated, colorless with light gray tint, applied strap handle, kick-up base with rough pontil mark. Probably Thomas Cains, South Boston Flint Glass Works or Phoenix Glass Works. First quarter 19th century. 6 5/8" h overall, 4 3/4" d rim. **$2,147**

Jug (quart), Free-Blown, colorless, low shoulder, three tooled rings below rim, bold applied hollow handle, kick-up base with rough pontil mark. Probably Pittsburgh. First half 19th century. 7 3/4" h overall, 4 3/4" d rim, 3 3/4" d base. **$367**

Pan, Free-Blown, slightly cloudy medium amber, slightly flared boldly folded rim, slightly domed base with light rough pontil mark. Probably Midwestern. First half 19th century. 4 1/4" h, 10" d. Expected wear, heavier on rim, small spot of extra glass on exterior. **$1,469**

Pan, Free-Blown, colorless soda-lime, folded pale blue rim, slightly domed base with rough pontil mark having traces of olive green. Possibly Midwestern. Probably 19th century. 2" h, 6" d. Small rough area under the rim fold. **$124**

Ring Jar, Free-Blown, colorless, tall cylindrical form with two applied rings, domed cover with pinched flange and hollow button-top finial, domed base with rough pontil mark. American. Second half 19th century. 12 1/2" h overall, 5 7/8" d. **$144**

Salver, Free-Blown, colorless lead glass, plate with a slight upper and lower rim, raised on an applied multi-knop, tiered stem and domed foot with folded rim and rough pontil mark. English. 19th century. 4 1/2" h, 6 1/4" d rim, 3 3/4" d foot. Two short, light scratches under the plate. **$621**

Salver, Free-Blown, colorless soda-lime glass, plate with galleried rim, raised on a wafer-joined hollow Silesian stem with lower rings and a domed foot with tooled edge and rough pontil mark. 19th or 20th century. 6 1/4" h, 10 3/8" d rim, 6 1/2" d foot. Light usage wear to plate. **$360**

Specie Jar, Free-Blown, colorless, tall cylindrical form with sharp shoulder and tin cover, domed base with rough pontil mark. American. Mid-19th century. 14 1/2" h overall, 4 1/2" d rim, 7" d base. Minor scattered wear, two light dents and wear to cover. **$146**

Photo courtesy Green Valley Auctions, Mt. Crawford, Va.; www.GreenValleyAuctions.com

Jug (cream), Free-Blown, Cains-Attributed, Chain-Decorated, colorless with light gray tint, tooled rim, applied handle, thick drawn foot with rough pontil mark. No other examples this size known. Probably Thomas Cains, South Boston Flint Glass Works or Phoenix Glass Works. First quarter 19th century. 3 7/8" h overall, 3 3/8" d rim, 2 3/8" d foot. **$4,237**

Photo courtesy Green Valley Auctions, Mt. Crawford, Va.; www.GreenValleyAuctions.com

Specie Jar, Free-Blown, light bottle green, tall cylindrical form with sharp shoulder and tin cover, domed base with rough pontil mark. American. First half 19th century. 10" h overall, 3 1/2" d rim, 4 3/4" d base. Scattered light scratches/wear, wear to cover. **$203**

Specie Jar, Free-Blown, colorless, tall cylindrical form with domed cover featuring an applied hollow prunt-top finial, domed base with rough pontil mark. American. Mid-19th century. 13" h overall, 5" d. **$101**

Specie Jars, Free-Blown, Graduated Set of Four, colorless, one with a faint green tint, each of squat cylindrical form with sharp shoulder, tin cover, and domed base with rough pontil mark. American. Mid 19th century. 5 1/4" to 8" h overall, 3 1/2" to 6 1/8" d bases. Flake to rim of the largest and holes and corrosion to cover of the smallest, minor scattered wear to jars and expected wear to covers. .... **$339 set**

Storage Jar, Free-Blown, colorless, squat cylindrical form with wide folded rim and rough pontil mark, well-fitting stained composition cover of unknown association.

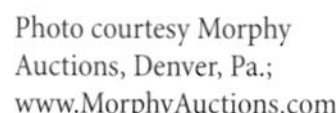

Photo courtesy Morphy Auctions, Denver, Pa.; www.MorphyAuctions.com

Soda fountain straw holder, circa 1880, with applied glass "jewels," rare to find with original glass top, 14" h. **$6,900**

Photo courtesy Green Valley Auctions, Mt. Crawford, Va.; www.GreenValleyAuctions.com

Sugar Bowl, Free-Blown, Footed, fiery opalescent, cup-shape bowl raised on an applied compressed baluster stem and circular folded foot with rough pontil mark. First half 19th century. 5" h, 4 1/2" d rim, 3 5/8" d foot. **$124**

American. 19th century. 8" h, 9 1/2" d. Scattered light scratches and wear. **$180**

Storage Jar, Free-Blown, colorless, somewhat crude globular form with folded rim and kick-up base with thick rough pontil mark. Probably 19th century. 12" h, 7" d rim, 13" d overall. Scattered scratches and wear. **$79**

Sugar Bowl, Free-Blown Footed, medium yellowish-green bottle glass, somewhat crude deep U-shape bowl raised on a compressed-funnel foot with folded rim and faint rough pontil mark. Midwestern, probably Gallatin-Kramer or a nearby glasshouse. Late 18th or early 19th century. 4 1/4" h, 4 5/8" d rim, 3 3/8" d foot. Interior wear and scratching, some cloudiness, ring of wear under bowl. **$1,808**

Sugar Bowl With Cover, Free-Blown, Footed, cobalt blue, U-shape bowl with an applied sloping foot and polished pontil mark, cover with an applied solid spire finial, which is factory polished at the top, rough pontil mark under cover. American or English. Late 18th or early 19th century. 6 5/8" h overall, 4" d rim, 2 7/8" d foot. Some wear to lower exterior of bowl. **$423**

Sugar Bowl With Ball Cover, Free-Blown, aquamarine, bowl with galleried rim, pronounced shoulder, and a

Photo courtesy Green Valley Auctions, Mt. Crawford, Va.; www.GreenValleyAuctions.com

Sugar Bowl With Cover, Heavy Free-Blown Footed, colorless, applied short solid stem and thick foot with rough pontil mark, flattened cover with applied button finial and interior rough pontil mark. Probably Pittsburgh. First half 19th century. 7 1/4" h overall, 5 1/4" h bowl, 4 3/4" d rim, 4 1/2" d foot. Moderate wear to interior and exterior of bowl. **$1,130**

Photo courtesy Green Valley Auctions, Mt. Crawford, Va.; www.GreenValleyAuctions.com

Vase or Chalice, Free-Blown Marbrie Decorated, colorless flared bowl with opaque white loops, blown into a pale yellow-green cup supported on a heavy solid stem and circular foot with rough pontil mark. Probably Midwestern or South Jersey. Mid-19th century. 8 1/2" h, 4 7/8" d rim, 4 3/4" d foot. Wear under foot. **$1,073**

slightly domed base with rough pontil mark, ball is a slightly bluer color and features an open 1" rough pontil. Probably New York State. Mid-19th century. 8" h overall, 4 1/8" h bowl, 4 1/8" d rim, 5" d ball. Slight wear at shoulder. **$734**

Twine Holder, Free-Blown, colorless with applied cobalt top ring and lower rim, top of ring factory polished. Probably Midwestern. Second half 19th century. 4 1/4" h, 4 3/4" d rim. Minute flake to ring hole. **$169**

Vase, Free-Blown, trumpet form, amethyst, plain rim, applied inverted baluster solid stem and sloping foot with polished pontil mark. Probably New England, possibly New England Glass Co. Third quarter 19th century. 11 7/8" h, 4 1/2" d rim, 4" d foot. **$847**

Whimsy Powder Horn, Free-Blown, Marbrie Decorated, deep amber with internal opaque white loops, tooled mouth, applied bottle green ring, amber applied end cap with rough pontil mark. Probably Pittsburgh or South Jersey. Mid-19th century. 14" long. Small surface bruise, which displays two 1/8" refractions under strong light, light wear. **$101**

Whimsy Powder Horn, Free-Blown, opaque white, applied mouth and neck ring, rough pontil mark. Second half 19th century. 13" long. Several areas of light wear. **$67**

Flint Glass, Colored

Bowl (footed low), O'Hara/Loop, deep fiery opalescent teal blue, made from the large sugar bowl base which was flattened and expanded outward and the rim turned up, six large scallops, short hexagonal stem and circular single step foot, one-piece construction. Probably Jas. B. Lyon & Co., Pittsburgh (as identified in company catalogs). 1860-1870. 3 1/4" h, 9" to 9 1/4" d rim, 3 7/8" d foot. Interior with scattered small areas of wear, numerous impurities and striations to glass. **$847**

Photo courtesy Green Valley Auctions, Mt. Crawford, Va.; www.GreenValleyAuctions.com

Bowl (footed low), O'Hara/Loop, deep fiery opalescent teal blue, made from the large sugar bowl base which was flattened and expanded outward and the rim turned up, six large scallops, short hexagonal stem and circular single step foot, one-piece construction. Probably Jas. B. Lyon & Co., Pittsburgh (as identified in company catalogs). 1860-1870. 2 3/8" to 2 5/8" h, 8 3/4" d rim, 3 7/8" d foot. Minute flake to foot, interior with light to moderate wear. **$452**

Photo courtesy Green Valley Auctions, Mt. Crawford, Va.; ww.GreenValleyAuctions.com

Covered Dish and Under Plate, melon form, translucent starch blue, dish of oval form, the base with 11 ribs, the cover with nine ribs, bent-stem finial, and rough pontil mark to interior, both with factory polished rims, the plate of leaf form with an oval seat to accept the melon, factory rough ground under base. Boston & Sandwich Glass Co. 1850-1870. 5 3/4" h overall, 4" x 5 3/8" cover, 6 1/4" x 7 3/8" plate. Cover with a minor flake to finial, and a shallow chip and two flakes to outer rim edge, plate with two small potstones and associated light bruises, a chip under one leaf point and a flake to several others. **$3,672**

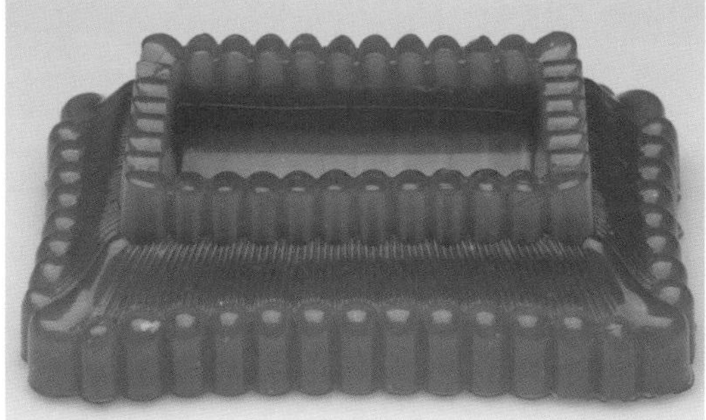

Photo courtesy Green Valley Auctions, Mt. Crawford, Va.; www.GreenValleyAuctions.com

Match Tray, Onion/Eaton, translucent soft blue with a slight lavender tint, rectangular form with a ribbed gallery, deep concave well, striker sides and a ribbed base. Boston & Sandwich Glass Co. 1860-1880. 1 1/2" h, 3 1/2" x 5" base. Two shallow chips and several flakes to rim scallops, base with flakes and roughness to a moderate fin at one end. **$1,073**

Goblet, Fedora Loop, unrecorded brilliant deep amethyst, deep polished pontil mark. Probably New England or Pittsburgh. 1840-1860. 5 7/8" h. Foot exhibits a uniform polished bevel to the top edge, which most likely was executed at the factory since it shows the expected wear. **$791**

Toothpick Holder, Pressed Covered Basket, alabaster/clam broth, base with decorative handles, cover with ribbed finial. Boston & Sandwich Glass Co. 1850-1870. 3 7/8" h overall, 2 1/4" d. Cover with shallow sliver chip to finial side and light inner-rim flaking. **$101**

Tumbler, Eight-Flute, brilliant fiery opalescent with strong pooling, faint pontil ring. Probably Midwestern. 1850-1870. 3 1/4" h, 3 1/4" d rim. Minute roughness to base points. **$254**

Tumbler, Loop and Arch, unusual slightly translucent soft blue, no resonance. Probably Pittsburgh. 1850-1870. 3 1/2" h, 3 1/8" d rim. Minor flake under base. **$180**

Tumbler, Loop and Arch, brilliant cobalt blue, faint pontil ring. Probably Pittsburgh. 1850-1870. 3 3/8" h, 3 3/8" d rim. Minute roughness to base points. **$79**

Tumbler, Six-Flute, medium golden amber, faint pontil ring, no resonance. Probably Pittsburgh. 1850-1870. 3 3/8" h, 3 1/4" d rim. Minute flake to one base point. **$192**

Tumbler (footed), Excelsior, brilliant fiery opalescent with strong pooling of color, short hexagonal stem, polished pontil mark. New England or Pittsburgh. Third quarter 19th century. 4 1/4" h, 3 5/8" d rim, 2 3/4" d foot. **$960**

Tumbler (footed), Excelsior Variant, deep fiery opalescent, short hexagonal stem, rough pontil mark. Probably Pittsburgh. Third quarter 19th century. 4 1/2" h, 3 3/8" d rim, 2 7/8" d foot. Small shallow chip under foot, numerous flakes and roughness to pattern, small rim under-fill. **$84**

Vase, Blown-Molded, Five-Petal Rosette, translucent jade green, trumpet top, polished base. Boston & Sandwich Glass Co. 1850-1870. 6 1/4" h, 2 1/2" d rim. Minute rim flake. **$508**

Vase, Loop, canary, gauffered six-flute rim, single-piece construction, factory polished under base. New England. 1850-1870. 9 1/2" h, 3 7/8" d rim. Two base edges reduced by polishing, which may have been done at the factory. **$282**

Vase, Three-Printie Block, deep violet blue, gauffered six-flute rim, single-piece construction. New England. 1850-1870. 9 3/4" h, 4 1/4" d rim. Minute flakes/roughness to base mold lines, light residue to lower bowl. **$960**

Vase, Three-Printie Block, medium amethyst, gauffered six-flute rim, single-piece construction. New England. 1850-1870. 9 1/4" h, 4 1/8" d rim. Moderate chip to three base corners, manufacturing separation below stem knop. **$330**

Vases (pair), Circle and Ellipse, canary, each with gauffered six-petal rim, hexagonal base, one-piece construction, factory polished lower mold lines and under base. New England. 1850-1870. 7 1/2" h, 3 1/4" d rims, 3 3/4" d bases overall. .... **$536 pair**

Vases (pair), tulip form, brilliant medium amethyst, panels continue to peg extension, octagonal base, wafer construction. Boston & Sandwich Glass Co. 1845-1865. 10" h, 5 1/8" and 5 3/8" d rims, 4 3/4" d foot overall. One with a minor flake to one lower panel and two shallow chips and minor mold roughness to base. .... **$6,780 pair**

Photo courtesy Green Valley Auctions, Mt. Crawford, Va.; www.GreenValleyAuctions.com

Tumbler, Ringed Framed Ovals, bright yellow green, polished table ring. 1850-1870. 3 1/4" h, 2 3/4" d rim. **$270**

FRUIT JARS

Fruit and canning jars used to preserve food. Thomas W. Dyott, one of Philadelphia's earliest and most innovative glassmakers, was promoting his glass canning jars in 1829. John Landis Mason patented his screw-type canning jar on Nov. 30, 1858. (This date refers to the granting of the patent, not the age of the jar.) There are thousands of different jars and a variety of colors, types of closures, sizes and embossings.

Collectors often refer to fruit jars by the numbering system "RB," which was established by Douglas M. Leybourne Jr. in *The Collector's Guide to Old Fruit Jars, Red Book No. 10.*

Photo courtesy American Bottle Auctions, Sacramento, Calif.; www.AmericanBottle.com

Airtight, barrel-shaped quart, solid wax sealer groove. Iron pontil instead of the sticky ball. All of its original graphite intact. Includes metal cap; may not be original. **$1,000**

Photo courtesy American Bottle Auctions, Sacramento, Calif.; www.AmericanBottle.com

Masons Improved Butter Jar. Half-gallon with original lid. This example is one of three different sizes. In addition to this half-gallon, there is even a taller three-quart size. This has the ground lip and original rubber seal. The glass lid reads, "MASONS IMPROVED MAY 10 1870." (There are reproductions of these being passed off as original.) **$325**

Photo courtesy American Bottle Auctions, Sacramento, Calif.; www.AmericanBottle.com

Masons Improved Butter Jar. Pint with original lid. Redbook-1688. With the original glass lid and metal screw cap. This one has some light whittle. **$275**

Photo courtesy American Bottle Auctions, Sacramento, Calif.; www.AmericanBottle.com

Knowlton Vacuum Fruit Jar with original lid, quart. Redbook-1432. The Knowlton jar is listed in Redbook in a number of different colors, although this ice blue is not one of them. This example has the original glass lid, which reads, "KNOWLTON PAT'D MAY 1903." A couple scratches. **$50**

Photo courtesy American Bottle Auctions, Sacramento, Calif.; www.AmericanBottle.com

Beaver Jar, quart, made in several colors with amber and olive amber variations being most desirable. With the original amber lid with a small button in the center, and with the typical ground lip. There is a number "10" on the base, RB 424. **$1,100**

Photo courtesy American Bottle Auctions, Sacramento, Calif.; www.AmericanBottle.com

Mason's Patent Nov 30th 1858, A62 on base, quart with embossed Tudor Rose. Lid is milk glass and also has an embossed Tudor Rose. Not the original zinc screw band with original porcelain liner. It reads "FOR MASON FRUIT JARS PORCELAIN LINED CAP." Has a series of bubbles throughout the neck area, RB 1875. **$5,500**

Photo courtesy American Bottle Auctions, Sacramento, Calif.; www.AmericanBottle.com

Millville Atmospheric Fruit Jar, Whitehall's Patent June 18, 1861, with original closure, pint. Small nick off the lid and a radiating potstone on the base. RB 2181. **$80**

Photo courtesy American Bottle Auctions, Sacramento, Calif.; www.AmericanBottle.com

Food jar with applied mouth and iron pontil. Fluting on shoulders and base area, 12". Circa 1850s. Early pickle jar, it is described there as a round berry jar with draped and arched panels. With most of its graphite intact. **$750**

Photo courtesy American Bottle Auctions, Sacramento, Calif.; www.AmericanBottle.com

Helme's Railroad Mills, 24 oz with original closure, no embossing on base. Redbook-1235. A jar that is a little bit newer, these are not particularly rare. **$110**

Photo courtesy American Bottle Auctions, Sacramento, Calif.; www.AmericanBottle.com

P.D. Code & Co S.F. Applied top and smooth base, 11 1/4". These tall green bottles were known as berry jars. Possibly made around 1871. These are desired for a number of reasons, the least of which is the spectacular shades of green they come in. This one is a vivid bright green. Just a few scratches, typical of a food bottle. **$500**

Photo courtesy American Bottle Auctions, Sacramento, Calif.; www.AmericanBottle.com

Pickle jar with star on shoulder. Applied lip and smooth base. 8 1/2" Pint. This is a pickle jar that we have seen in two sizes and was made at Pacific Glass Works in San Francisco. These come with embossing on the base stating the glassmaker. However this example has no writing on the base and is considered even more rare. It is believed this smaller size is also harder to come by. **$300**

Photo courtesy American Bottle Auctions, Sacramento, Calif.; www.AmericanBottle.com

CAL A Bonzest, 8 1/2", applied top and smooth base. These are early San Francisco bottles and come in two sizes, this being the larger of the two. Circa 1850. Small scrapes on the back base area. **$500**

Photo courtesy American Bottle Auctions, Sacramento, Calif.; www.AmericanBottle.com

Barrel Shaped Unembossed Mustard Jar. 5". San Francisco glass houses began using a snap case versus a pontil rod, here is one that might have been pontiled if blown elsewhere. With immense amount of crudity and color, minor damage to a ring or two. **$275**

Historical and Novelty Glass

Admiral Dewey, Five-Piece Water Set, colorless, consisting of a water pitcher and four tumblers. Fourth quarter 19th century. Pitcher 9" h overall, 4 7/8" d, tumblers 3 7/8" h, 2 3/4" d. Pitcher with three annealing fissures at rim, tumblers with nicks/roughness to line above pattern. **$138**

Bricks and Horse Heads, Covered Mustard, apple green, original cover with spoon slot. Fourth quarter 19th century. 3 5/8" h overall, 2 3/4" d base. One horse head with chip to one ear, two shallow chips under base. **$57**

Dog House, Two-Part Box, blue, the top being the entire house which sits on the base featuring an interior well. Fourth quarter 19th century. 3" h, 2 1/2" x 4 1/4". Top with a chip to lower front edge which does not affect the rim and a tiny potstone with light bruise to interior, base with light flake to one corner and an 1/8" annealing crack to inner rim. **$103**

English Castle-Form, Cigar Holder, opalescent, embossed "Rd 29780" in base, ribbed under base, polished table ring. Fourth quarter 19th century. 3 1/4" h, 3 1/8" sq. minor mold roughness and short annealing separations to base. **$57**

Fish Covered Dish, pale green with all-over satin finish, fully patterned on cover and base, protruding tail and one fin on base and two fins on cover. Late 19th/early 20th century. 2 1/4" h overall, 4 3/4" x 8 1/2" overall. Hint of interior mold roughness. **$36**

Jenny Lind/Columbia Statue, colorless and frosted, on a circular domed base molded with a floral wreath underneath. This is the standard illustrated in Lindsey's American Historical Glass, p. 434, fig. 424, which is wafer attached to a Beaded Panels bowl. The statue features fully molded hair on top of her head and was never attached to another unit. Probably Crystal Glass Co. Fourth quarter 19th century. 4 1/4" h, 4 3/4" d base. **$108**

Photo courtesy Green Valley Auctions, Mt. Crawford, Va.; www.GreenValleyAuctions.com

Canary, Covered Dish, vaseline, round basket-weave base, signed under cover. McKee & Brothers. Late 19th/early 20th century. 3 3/4" h overall, 4 1/2" d. Two minute flakes to base rim. **$310**

Photo courtesy Green Valley Auctions, Mt. Crawford, Va.; www.GreenValleyAuctions.com

Daisy and Button Umbrella, amber, on foot, with metal handle. George Duncan & Sons. Fourth quarter 19th century. 6 5/8" h overall, 3 3/8" d rim, 2 7/8" d foot. Chip to the point of the umbrella probably done when it was ground to sit flat on the foot. **$546**

Liberty Bell, Miniature Mug, opaque white/milk glass, embossed "1776 1876" between the bells. Fourth quarter 19th century. 2" h, 1 3/4" d rim. Minute rim flake, normal short annealing lines. **$103**

Recumbent Dog, Covered Pomade Jar, colorless, unpatterned panel on jar, presumably for a product label, remainder of jar and under cover patterned with diamonds, beaded-edge foot with rosette underneath. Fourth quarter 19th century. 4" h overall, 2" x 2 5/8" overall. Cover with a shallow chip to rear outer edge and flaking/mold roughness under rim. **$103**

Vaseline, Pressed Glass Smoking Stand, cigarette cup and horizontal-ribbed cup for matches, each on two rows of brick, on base with interior ribbing. Fourth quarter 19th century. 3" and 4" h, 3" x 5 3/4". Several flakes to the rim of each cup, a short annealing line to the rim of the match cup and another to the base. **$69**

Victorian, Gilt Brass and Glass Door Bell, exterior knotted rope-form frame with two facet-cut amber glass mounts, brass bell on interior. Fourth quarter 19th century. 6 1/4" h, 3 1/2" wide. Minor wear to gilt. **$138**

1893 World's Fair, Boat-Form Dish, colorless, embossed "Santa Maria" on sides, and "World's Fair 1893" and "Libbey Glass Co., Toledo, Ohio" under base. Libbey Glass Co. Fourth quarter 19th century. 2 1/4" h, 2 5/8" x 6 1/2". Chip to lower edge of rudder. **$300**

Milk Glass

Milk glass is a relatively recent name for opaque, milky white or colored glass that is blown or pressed into a wide variety of shapes, including animal-form covered dishes. First made in Venice in the 16th century, the white color is achieved through the addition of tin dioxide. Nineteenth-century glassmakers called milky white opaque glass "opal glass."

Alligator, Toothpick/Match Holder, opaque white/milk glass, curled tail forms handle. Fourth quarter 19th century, 2 7/8" h. **$287**

Big Owl, Salt Shaker, opaque white/milk glass, period lid. Possibly Atterbury & Co., fourth quarter 19th century, 5 3/4" h overall. Minor mold roughness, legs with manufacturing roughness/flakes. **$138**

Black Clown, Match Holder, opaque white/milk glass, ribbed circular base, remnants of original paint decoration. Fourth quarter 19th century, 3 1/4" h. **$120**

Boar's Head, Covered Dish, opaque white/milk glass, on a ribbed base, non-original applied eyes, patent date on lid interior and under base. Atterbury & Co., fourth quarter 19th century, 5 1/2" h overall, 6 1/8" x 9 3/8" rim overall. Shallow vertical chip to the rear mold line on cover and two minute flakes to base rim. **$1,150**

Canary, Covered Dish, opaque white/milk glass, round basket-weave base, signed under cover. McKee & Brothers, late 19th/early 20th century, 3 3/4" h overall, 4 1/2" d. Two minute flakes to base rim. **$780**

Duck, Covered Dish, opaque blue with light mottling, applied eyes, patent date under base. Atterbury & Co., fourth quarter 19th century, 5" h overall, 11" long overall. Hint of mold roughness and short annealing lines. **$156**

Eaglet with Eggs and Snake, Covered Dish, opaque white/milk glass with original paint decoration, interior of cover embossed "SV/2", underside of base embossed "SV/9". Late 19th/early 20th century, 5 1/4" h overall, 5 5/8" d overall. Cover with a chip under edge, base with a significant crack and glued section of rim. **$204**

Fish Pitcher, opaque white/milk glass, three-pint, molded handle, ground table ring. Atterbury & Co., fourth quarter 19th century, 7 1/4" h, 4 1/2" d rim. Trace of mold roughness to handle and table ring. **$120**

Frog Covered Dish, opaque white/milk glass, split-rib base, not signed. McKee & Brothers, late 19th/early 20th century, 3 5/8" h, 4 1/8" x 5 3/8" base. Base with rim chip and interior annealing line. **$345**

General Electric, Refrigerator-Form Covered Jar, opaque white/milk glass, name lightly embossed above doors. First quarter 20th century, 5" h overall, 2 1/8" x 3 1/2". Two minor flakes under feet. **$103**

Horse, Covered Dish, opaque white/milk glass, split-rib base, not signed. McKee & Brothers, late 19th/early 20th century, 4 1/2" h, 4 1/4" x 5 1/2" base. **$258**

Horseshoe-Form, Covered Box, opaque white/milk glass, embossed horse's head on cover, horseshoes, horn and riding crop on sides of box, somewhat worn original decoration. Probably Alton Mfg. Co., Sandwich, Mass., first quarter 20th century, 1 7/8" h overall, 3 1/4" x 3 5/8 overall. Minute flakes under cover. **$80**

Photo courtesy Green Valley Auctions, Mt. Crawford, Va.; www.GreenValleyAuctions.com

1988 NMGCS, Commemorative Rabbit Covered Dish, green slag, a reproduction of the Greentown rabbit on a split-rib base, National Milk Glass Collector's Society logo and "NMGCS / 88 MN" embossed in base, 4 1/4" h overall. **$339**

Lion, Covered Dish, opaque white/milk glass, split-rib base possibly later, signed under cover. McKee & Brothers, late 19th/early 20th century, 4 1/4" h, 4 1/4" x 5 1/2" base. **$126**

Lion, Covered Dish, opaque white/milk glass with traces of paint decoration, split-rib base probably later, signed under cover. McKee & Brothers, late 19th/early 20th century, 4 1/4" h, 4 1/4" x 5 1/2" base. **$69**

McKinley-Roosevelt, Campaign Plate, opaque white/milk glass, intricate foliate rim. Early 20th century, 8 1/4" d. Shallow chip to the front of one rim point. **$115**

Moses in the Bulrushes, Covered Dish, opaque white/milk glass, traces of paint decoration on cover. Late 19th/early 20th century, 3" h overall, 4" x 5 3/8" base. A few light flakes. **$69**

Owl Head, Covered Dish, opaque white/milk glass, split-rib base possibly later, signed under cover. McKee & Brothers, late 19th/early 20th century, 4 1/4" h, 4 1/4" x 5 1/2" base. Chip to base table ring. **$149**

Pig, Covered Dish, opaque white/milk glass, split-rib base signed in bottom. McKee & Brothers, late 19th/early 20th century, 3 1/2" h, 4 1/8" x 5 3/8" base. Small chip and minute flake to tips of ears. **$600**

Pope Leo XIII, Covered Dish, opaque white/milk glass, round base with paneled sides. Late 19th/early 20th century, 5 1/4" h overall, 4 7/8" d. **$149**

Spaniel, Covered Dish, opaque white/milk glass showing slight opalescence, lattice on two long sides of base, stippled ends and beaded rim. Boston & Sandwich Glass Co., or one of the short-lived succeeding companies, late 19th/early 20th century, 4" h overall, 4 3/4" x 3 3/8". Cover with minute flake, base rim with two minor flakes and light mold roughness. **$149**

Photo courtesy Green Valley Auctions, Mt. Crawford, Va.; www.GreenValleyAuctions.com

Steer's Head, Covered Dish, opaque white/milk glass, on a swirled rib base, non-original applied eyes. Challinor, Taylor & Co., fourth quarter 19th century, 5" h overall, 5 3/8" x 7 3/4" rim. Minor flake to inner rim of base, normal short annealing lines. **$3,955**

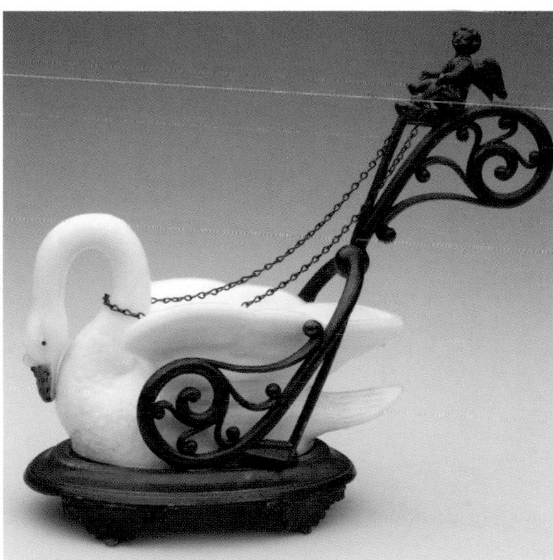

Photo courtesy Green Valley Auctions, Mt. Crawford, Va.; www.GreenValleyAuctions.com

Swan, Chariot Master Salt, opaque white/milk glass, original unmarked plated-silver stand with cherub holding chain reins. Gillinder & Sons, fourth quarter 19th century, 6 3/4" h overall. **$339**

"Trilby" Foot Match Holder, opaque white/milk glass, embossed lettering on side of base, patent date under base. Fourth quarter 19th century, 2 3/4" h, 1 7/8" x 4 1/8" base. Normal short annealing lines. **$80**

Turkey, Covered Dish, opaque white/milk glass with slight pink tint, split-rib base, signed under cover. McKee & Brothers, late 19th/early 20th century, 4 1/2" h, 4 1/8" x 5 3/8" base. Several light flakes. **$258**

1989 NMGCS, Commemorative Horse Covered Dish, opaque white/milk glass, a reproduction of the McKee Horse on split-rib base, National Milk Glass Collector's Society logo and "NMGCS / ILL.89" embossed in base. With original ID card, which indicates that Summit Art Glass Co. produced slightly over 200 pieces for Society members, 4 1/4" h overall. **$126**

1999 NMGCS, Commemorative Dog Covered Dish, chocolate slag, a reproduction of the L.G. Wright spaniel dog on a split-rib base, National Milk Glass Collector's Society logo and "NMGCS / IN 99" embossed in base, also embossed under cover, 4" h overall. **$69**

Opalescent Glass

Opalescent glass, a clear or colored glass with milky white decorations, looks fiery or opalescent when held to light. This effect was achieved by applying bone ash chemicals to designated areas while a piece was still hot and then refiring it at extremely high temperatures. There are three basic categories of opalescent glass: (1) blown (or mold blown) patterns, e.g., Daisy & Fern and Spanish Lace; (2) novelties, pressed glass patterns made in limited quantity and often in unusual shapes such as corn or a trough; and (3) traditional pattern (pressed) glass forms. Opalescent glass was produced in England in the 1870s. Northwood began the American production in 1897 at its Indiana, Pa., plant. Jefferson, National Glass, Hobbs and Fenton soon followed.

Buttons and Braids, Water Pitcher, cranberry opalescent, triangular crimped rim, colorless applied handle. Jefferson Glass Co. / Fenton Art Glass Co. Late 19th/early 20th century. 9 3/4" h overall. Two open bubbles to the interior base, small impurity at shoulder. **$920**

Collector's Note: The Fenton Art Glass Co., the oldest continuously running American glass firm, was founded in 1905 by Frank L. Fenton and his brother, John W. Fenton, in an old glass factory building in Martins Ferry, Ohio. They began by painting decorations on glass blanks made by other glass manufacturers. Soon, being unable to get the glass they needed, they decided to produce their own glass. The first glass from the new Fenton factory in Williamstown, W.V., was made on Jan. 2, 1907. After a century in business, the firm announced it would close in the fall of 2007. But a surge of customer orders allowed it to remain open. See more Fenton beginning on page 486.

Carnelian/Everglades, Six-Piece Water Set, blue opalescent with bright gilt decoration, consisting of a water pitcher and five tumblers. H. Northwood Co. Early 20th century. 7 3/4" and 4" h. Light wear to rim gilt, pitcher with two small manufacturing chips to foot, which are gilded over. **$316**

Chrysanthemum Swirl, Celery Vase, blue opalescent with frosted finish, traces of gilt decoration. Late 19th/early 20th century. 6 1/2" h. Minor mold roughness and interior residue. **$80**

Photo courtesy Green Valley Auctions, Mt. Crawford, Va.; www.GreenValleyAuctions.com

Chrysanthemum Swirl, Bar Bottle, cranberry opalescent, very rare. Late 19th/ early 20th century. 12" h, 3 1/2" d overall. **$2,300**

Chrysanthemum Swirl, Celery Vase, blue opalescent with satin finish. Late 19th/early 20th century. 6 1/2" h, 4 1/4" d overall. Minute nicks to rim. **$92**

Coin Spot-Star Crimp, Water Pitcher, blue opalescent, transparent blue applied handle, polished pontil mark. Northwood Glass Co. Late 19th/early 20th century. 8" h overall. Manufacturing flaw to lower portion of body, and a spall to pontil. **$149**
(A spall is a fragment broken off from the edge or face of a surface, and having at least one thin edge.)

Coin Spot-Star Crimp, Water Pitcher, colorless opalescent, colorless applied handle. Northwood Glass Co. and others. Late 19th/early 20th century. 8 3/4" h. Light wear and 1/4" scratch to body. **$80**

Coin Spot-Star Crimp, Water Pitcher cranberry opalescent, colorless applied handle with pressed fan design to upper terminal. Northwood Glass Co. Late 19th/early 20th century. 8 1/2" h. Light wear to shoulder, minute irregularities to rim. **$161**

Coin Spot-Star Crimp, Water Pitcher, green opalescent, transparent green applied handle. Jefferson Glass Co. Late 19th/early 20th century. 9 3/4" h overall. Light wear to exterior of body. **$115**

Daffodils, Water Pitcher, green opalescent, round crimped and ruffled rim, transparent green applied handle with pressed fan design to upper terminal. H. Northwood Co. Late 19th/early 20th century. 10 1/4" h overall. Small area of wear and scratches to shoulder. **$510**

Daisy and Fern, Water Pitcher and Six Tumblers, blue opalescent, square crimped rim, transparent blue applied handle. Northwood Glass Co. Late 19th/early 20th century. Pitcher 8 1/2" h, tumblers 3 3/4" h. Light wear and scratches to body, tumblers each with normal rim flakes/roughness and polishing. .... **$218 set**

Drapery tiebacks, four pairs, white opalescent glass floral rosettes, American, mid- to late 19th century, with white metal shanks and iron screw ends, 4 1/2" d, all have some minor chips, three have larger chips (losses) on the tri-lobed sections between the larger petals. .... **$474 all**

Double Greek Key, Three-Piece Table Set, colorless opalescent, consisting of a butter dish, covered sugar bowl and spooner. Nickel Plate Glass Co. Late 19th/early 20th century. 5 1/4" to 7" h overall, 3 1/4" to 7 1/4" d overall. Slight roughness to rims of covers and interior rim of butter base. .... **$287 set**

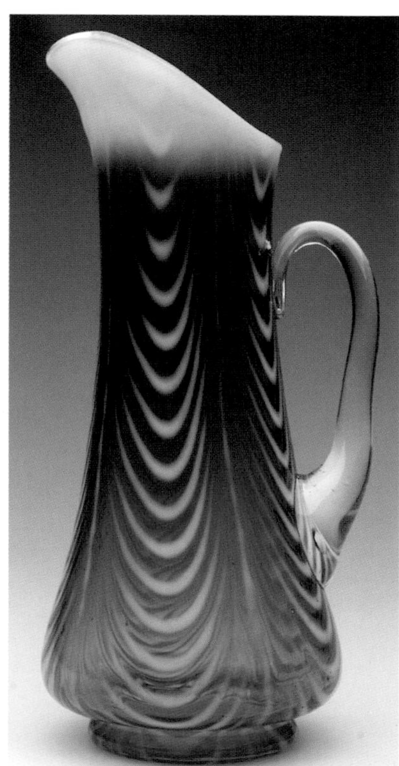

Photo courtesy Green Valley Auctions, Mt. Crawford, Va.; www.GreenValleyAuctions.com

Drapery-Blown, Tankard Water Pitcher, cranberry opalescent, colorless applied handle. Late 19th/early 20th century. 13" h overall. Manufacturing flaws to body and base, short annealing lines to spout and spots of manufacturing exfoliation around rim. **$1,035**

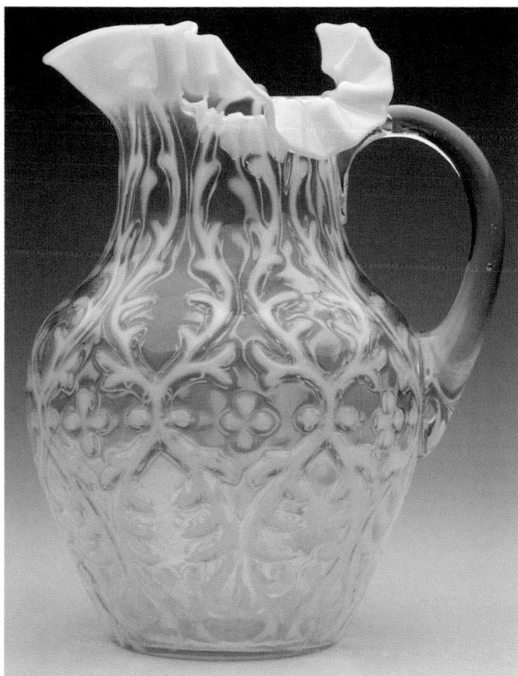

Photo courtesy Green Valley Auctions, Mt. Crawford, Va.; www.GreenValleyAuctions.com

Opaline Brocade / Spanish Lace, Water Pitcher, vaseline opalescent, tri-corner crimped rim, vaseline applied handle. Late 19th/early 20th century. 9 1/2" h overall. Two small surface irregularities. **$450**

Hobbs, No. 323 Dew Drop / Hobnail Jug No. 5, Ruby opalescent/cranberry opalescent, square rim, colorless applied handle, polished pontil mark. Hobbs Brockunier & Co. Late 19th/early 20th century. 7 3/4" h overall. Flake to one hob and several others with light wear. **$184**

Hobbs, No. 325 / Swirl Water Pitcher, Ruby opalescent/cranberry opalescent, square rim, colorless applied handle with pressed fan design to upper terminal, polished pontil mark. Hobbs, Brockunier & Co. Late 19th/early 20th century. 8 3/4" h. Several impurities at neck, several minute areas of polishing to rim. **$316**

Hobbs, No 326 / Windows Swirl Water Pitcher, Sapphire opalescent/blue opalescent, translucent blue applied handle with pressed fan design to upper terminal. Hobbs, Brockunier & Co. Late 19th/early 20th century. 7" h overall. Flakes and polishing to exterior and minute nicks to interior of rim, all probably done in the manufacturing process. **$1,610**

Hobbs, No. 333 / Windows Water Pitcher, Ruby opalescent/cranberry opalescent, square rim, colorless applied handle with pressed fan at upper terminal, polished pontil mark, heavy opalescence. Hobbs, Brockunier & Co. Late 19th/early 20th century. 8 1/2" h overall. **$431**

Lattice, Water Pitcher, cranberry opalescent, colorless applied handle. Late 19th/early 20th century. 9 1/4" h. Several light scratches to body and handle and a tiny spot of roughness to rim. **$1,092**

Northwood, Drapery Three-Piece Table Set, colorless opalescent, consisting of a butter dish, covered sugar bowl and creamer, butter and creamer marked with an "N" in circle on base. H. Northwood Co. First quarter 20th century. 4 1/2" to 7" h overall, 3 3/4" to 7 3/4" d overall. Sugar cover with slight interior roughness, butter cover having a single rim flake. .... **$126 set**

Opaline Brocade / Spanish Lace, Rose Bowl, vaseline, crimped rim. First quarter 20th century. 3 7/8" h, 4 1/4" d overall. **$84**

Poinsettia, Tankard Water Pitcher, opalescent, colorless applied handle with pressed fan design at upper terminal. H. Northwood Co. Late 19th/early 20th century. 13" h overall. Light scratches to lower portion of body and one side of handle, and two open bubbles to interior. **$1,955**

Poinsettia, Bride's Bowl, rubina opalescent, crimped and ruffled rim. Late 19th/early 20th century. 3 1/4" h overall, 10" d. Light interior residue. **$144**

Poinsettia, Tankard Water Pitcher, blue opalescent, blue applied handle with pressed fan design to upper terminal. H. Northwood Co. Late 19th/early 20th century. 13" h overall. Upper terminal with two cracks and 1/4" crack at body, manufacturing flaw to interior base. **$69**

Queen's Crown, Cake Stand, vaseline opalescent. English. Late 19th/early 20th century. 5 3/4" h, 10" d. Minute roughness to pattern and slight wear to plate. **$204**

Reverse Swirl, Set of Six Sauce Dishes, cranberry opalescent. Buckeye Glass Co. / Model Flint Glass Co. Late 19th/early 20th century. 1 3/4" h, 4 3/8" d. Each with rim flakes/roughness and one with a base crack. .... **$138 set**

Reverse Swirl, Water Bottle, blue opalescent. Late 19th/early 20th century. 8 1/4" h, 5" d overall. Minute nicks to rim. **$115**

Photo courtesy Green Valley Auctions, Mt. Crawford, Va.; www.GreenValleyAuctions.com

Stars and Stripes, Tumbler, cranberry opalescent. Late 19th/early 20th century. 3 3/4" h, 2 3/4" d. **$287**

Ribbed Opal Lattice, Creamer, cranberry opalescent, colorless applied handle. Late 19th/early 20th century. 4 3/4" h. Numerous glass impurities. **$600**

Seaweed, Water Pitcher, cranberry opalescent, triangular crimped rim, colorless applied handle with lightly pressed fan design to upper terminal, polished pontil mark. Hobbs, Brockunier & Co./Beaumont Glass Co. Late 19th/early 20th century. 9" h overall. Light wear/scratches to body, interior with two open bubbles. **$805**

Stars and Stripes, Water Pitcher, blue opalescent, translucent blue applied handle with pressed fan design to upper terminal, polished pontil mark. Hobbs, Brockunier & Co. Late 19th/early 20th century. 8" h. **$2,990**

Stripe, Bottle-Form Vase, blue opalescent, tooled rim. Late 19th/ early 20th century. 9" h, 5 1/4" d overall. **$115**

Swirl, Water Pitcher, cranberry opalescent, triangular crimped rim, colorless applied handle with pressed fan design to upper terminal, polished pontil mark. Late 19th/early 20th century. 9" h overall. Short scratch to body. **$488**

Swirl, Seven-Piece Water Set, pale cranberry opalescent, consisting of a bulbous base water pitcher with high neck, applied colorless angular handle and polished pontil mark, along with six matching tumblers with polished rims. First half 20th century. 8 3/4" and 5 3/4" h. Minor flake to one tumbler rim. .... **$488 set**

Swirl, Water Pitcher, cranberry opalescent, star-crimped rim, colorless applied handle. Late 19th/early 20th century. 8 1/2" h. Single rim flake, some impurities to interior rim, irregular shading to opalescence. **$172**

Swirl, Water Pitcher, rubina opalescent, ball form, square crimped rim, colorless applied handle. Late 19th/early 20th century. 8 1/2" h. Polishing to handle, possibly done during manufacturing. **$156**

Victor/Jeweled Heart, Water Pitcher, blue opalescent. Dugan Glass Co. Late 19th/early 20th century. 8 3/4" h overall, 5 1/4" d. Light interior haze. **$149**

Zigzag Optic/Herringbone, Water Pitcher, vaseline opalescent, colorless applied handle, polished pontil mark. Phoenix Glass Co. Late 19th/early 20th century. 7 3/4" h. **$1,610**

Salts

Beaded Scroll and Basket of Flowers, Pressed Salt (BS-2), light opalescent, on four scroll feet. Scarce. Boston & Sandwich Glass Co. 1835-1845. 1 7/8" h, 1 7/8" x 3 1/4". Minor inner-rim flake. **$113**

Blow-Over and Crack Off, Salt, deep cobalt blue, oblong octagonal form with diamond-diaper sides and ends divided by corner ribs, 30-ray base, plain ground and polished rim. Extremely rare, possibly unique. Probably New England Glass Works or South Boston Flint Glass Works. 1813-1830. 1 1/2" h, 2 1/8" x 3 1/4". Slightly disfiguring rim chip at one end, shallow chip to outer edge of opposite end, light high-point wear. **$480**

Blow-Over and Crack Off, Salt, colorless, oblong octagonal form with diamond-diaper sides and ends divided by corner ribs, 30-ray base, plain ground and polished rim. Probably New England Glass Works or South Boston Flint Glass Works. 1813-1830. 1 1/2" h, 2 1/4" x 3 1/4". Rim with one shallow chip and light mold roughness, exterior high-spot wear. **$24**

Photo courtesy Green Valley Auctions, Mt. Crawford, Va.; www.GreenValleyAuctions.com

Basket of Flowers, Pressed Salt (BF-1B), strong fiery opalescent, on four feet. Rare. Boston & Sandwich Glass Co. 1830-1840. 2" h, 1 3/4" x 3 1/8". Light chipping/mold roughness to two upper corners and feet. **$203**

Photo courtesy Green Valley Auctions, Mt. Crawford, Va.; www.GreenValleyAuctions.com

Blow-Over and Crack Off, Pedestal Salt, colorless, rectangular form with vertically ribbed sides, plain ground and polished rim, applied pressed square three-step "lemon-squeezer" pedestal with polished edges. American or Irish. 1813-1830. 2 3/4" h, 2" x 3 1/8". Minute flake to outer rim, some polishing, possibly post production. **$90**

Blow-Over and Crack Off, Pedestal Salt, colorless, rectangular form with diamond-diaper sides, notch ground and polished rim, applied pressed rectangular three-step pedestal. Possibly New England Glass Works or South Boston Flint Glass Works. 1813-1830. 3" h, 1 7/8" x 2 7/8". Rim with four small chips and flakes, foot with shallow flake to one end and two corners. **$79**

Blow-Over and Crack Off, Salts (three), colorless, each of oblong form with diamond diapering on sides, one with split ribs on ends and two with fan on ends, serrated and plain ground and polished rims, one with plain base

Photo courtesy Green Valley Auctions, Mt. Crawford, Va.; www.GreenValleyAuctions.com

Checkered Diamond, Pattern-Molded Salt, Footed, unusual swirled purple blue, double ogee bowl with four horizontal rows of seven four-section diamonds, drawn short stem and applied sloping slightly irregular circular foot with rough pontil mark. Probably the New Bremen Glass Manufactory of John Frederick Amelung, Frederick Co., Md. Fourth quarter 18th century. 2 3/4" h, 2 1/4" d rim, 2" d foot. **$10,170**

Photo courtesy Green Valley Auctions, Mt. Crawford, Va.; www.GreenValleyAuctions.com

Covered Lyre, Pressed Salt (CD-3), colorless, on four scrolled feet, variant cover with pinecone finial and beads on rim interior arranged 10 x 20 x 10 x 20. Extremely rare. Boston & Sandwich Glass Co. 1835-1845. 2 7/8" h overall, 2" x 3 1/8" base, 1 7/8" h. Cover with a small chip under one corner and a few light flakes, base with a rim flake at one end and slight mold roughness to interior of feet. **$2,147**

and two with rayed base. Possibly South Boston Flint Glass Works or New England Glass Works. 1813-1830. 1 3/4" h, 2" x 3" to 2 1/4" x 3 1/2". Minor chipping to rims. .... **$113 all**

Blown and Pressed, Pedestal Salt, colorless, unusual boat-shape bowl molded with 18 vertical ribs extending to the rolled-over rim, stuck to a pressed standard featuring a single-knop stem and an oblong quatrefoil base with triple-scallop extensions and a rosette underneath. 1820-1830. 2 3/4" h, 2 3/4" x 4 1/4" rim, 2 1/4" x 3" base. **$135**

Expanded Diamond, Pattern-Molded Footed Salt, colorless, two complete rows of 11 diamonds above elongated pointed flutes, short ribbed stem, applied circular foot tooled into five irregular petals, rough graphite pontil mark. Late 18th or early 19th century. 3" h, 2 1/4" d rim, 2 1/8" d foot. **$144**

Expanded Diamond, Pattern-Molded Footed Salts (two), colorless, first with two complete rows of 11 diamonds swirled slightly right above elongated pointed flutes, second with one complete row of 12 diamonds above elongated pointed flutes, both with short ribbed stem and applied circular foot tooled into five and six irregular petals, rough pontil marks. Late 18th or early 19th century. 2 7/8" and 3" h. First with lightly polished rim, both with light interior residue. .... **$124 both**

Free-Blown, Pedestal Salt, slightly translucent powder blue, lead content, plain slightly flared rim, short stem and circular foot with rough pontil mark. 1840-1860. 2" h, 2 3/4" d rim, 2 1/4" d foot. **$101**

"Lafayet" Steamboat, Pressed Salt (BT-5), unlisted, soft pale blue with opalescent bloom, marked "B. &. S. / Glass. / Co" on stern and "Sandwich" on interior and under base. Very rare. Boston & Sandwich Glass Co. 1830-1845. 1 5/8" h, 2" x 3 5/8". Rim with a shallow chip to one paddlewheel and a chip and several flakes to interior, minor flake to table ring, light wear to some highpoints, light interior residue. **$1,320**

"Lafayet" Steamboat, Pressed Salt (BT-5), unlisted, colorless, marked "B. &. S. / Glass. / Co" on stern and "Sandwich" on interior and under base. Boston & Sandwich Glass Co. 1830-1845. 1 5/8" h, 2" x 3 5/8". Rim with three V-shape chips at stern, minor mold roughness, numerous annealing lines and impurities. **$79**

Swirled Rib, Pattern-Molded Footed Salt, colorless with a gray tint, ogee bowl with 10 ribs swirled to the right, short lightly ribbed stem, applied circular foot with rough pontil mark. Late 18th or early 19th century. 2 3/4" h, 2" d rim, 2 1/8" d foot. **$158**

Glass Listed by Maker

The Sainte-Anne glassworks at Baccarat in Voges, France, was founded in 1764 and produced utilitarian soda glass. Baccarat began the production of paperweights in 1846. In the late 19th century the firm achieved an international reputation for cut-glass table services, chandeliers, display vases, centerpieces and sculptures. Products eventually included all forms of glassware.

Baccarat, cardholders (12), shell form, each signed with frosted Baccarat mark, 2 1/4" h; together with 12 individual boxes and large matching box. .... **$138 all**

Baccarat, paperweight, scattered millefiori and Gridel silhouette canes on ruffled upset muslin, with signature date cane, 1848, 2 7/8" d. **$2,040**
("Gridel" refers to Emile Gridel, nephew of Jean-Baptiste Toussaint, general manager of the Baccarat factory in about 1846.)

Baccarat, paperweight, scattered millefiori and Gridel silhouette canes on ruffled upset muslin, with signature date cane, B 1848. 3 1/6" d. **$1,920**
("Gridel" refers to Emile Gridel, nephew of Jean-Baptiste Toussaint, general manager of the Baccarat factory in about 1846.)

Baccarat, crystal red-wine glasses (12), signed, 7 1/2" h. .... **$632 set**

Baccarat, crystal white-wine glasses (12), signed, 6 1/2" h. .... **$805 set**

Baccarat, cut-glass vase and cover with ormolu fittings, its handles inset with cut beads, 20th century, 19" h. ... **$1,920**

Fenton Art Glass

The Fenton Art Glass Co. was founded in 1905 by Frank L. Fenton and his brother, John W., in an old glass factory in Martins Ferry, Ohio. They initially sold hand-painted glass made by other manufacturers, but it wasn't long before they decided to produce their own glass. The new Fenton factory in Williamstown, W.V., opened on Jan. 2, 1907. Despite economic difficulties in their 100th-anniversary year, the firm remains in business and in family hands.

Also see Carnival Glass.

Fenton Iridescent Burmese Poppy Show Vase using an old Imperial mold, 2003, custom-made for Singleton Bailey, 13 3/4". **$100+**

Fenton Wheat vases, early 1980s, each 7 1/2", in overlay colors of, from left, Honey Amber, Wild Roase, Apple Green and Glacial Blue. **$30+ each**

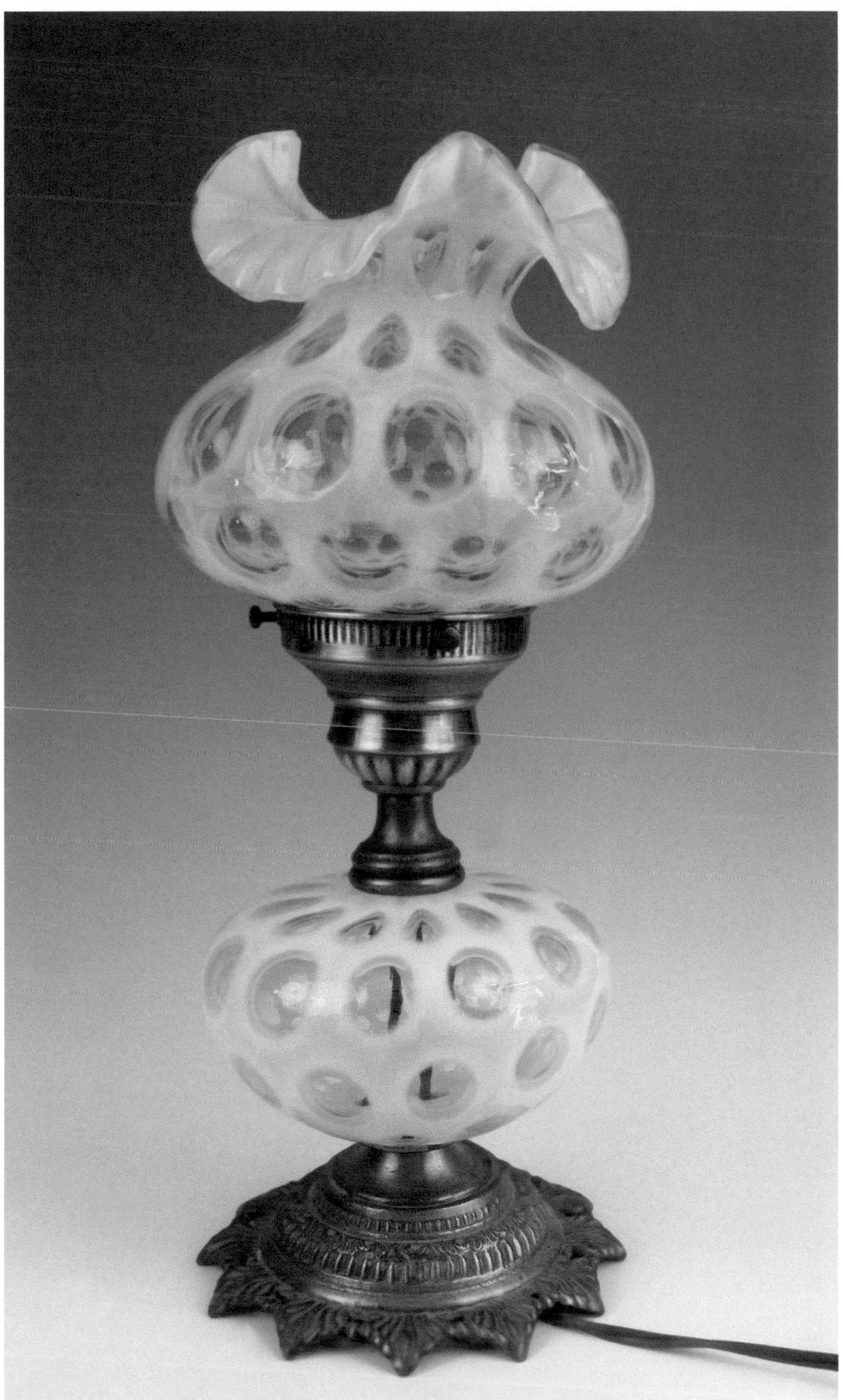

Fenton Honeysuckle Opalescent lamp in Coin Dot, late 1940s, 16". **$125+**

Fenton French Opalescent three-horn epergne in Emerald Crest/Diamond Lace, 1949-55, 11". **$125+**

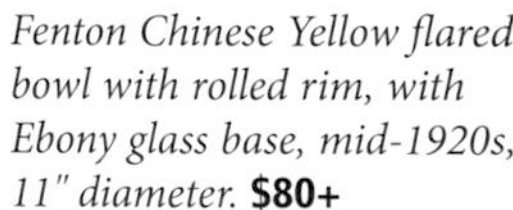

Fenton Chinese Yellow flared bowl with rolled rim, with Ebony glass base, mid-1920s, 11" diameter. **$80+**

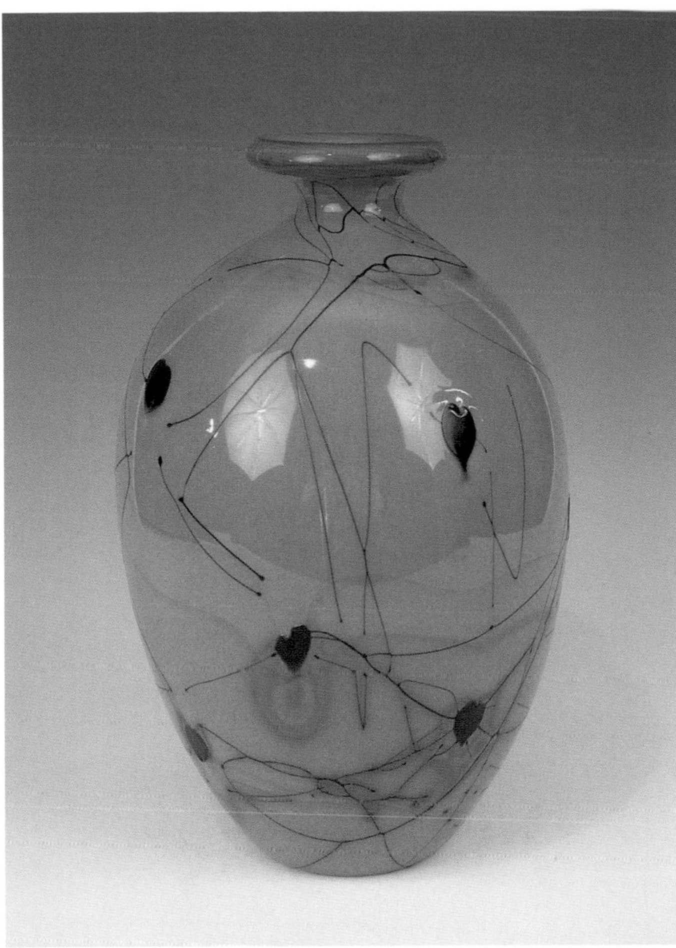

Fenton, Robert Barber experimental off-hand vase in Hanging Hearts and Bittersweet glass, 1975-76, 10". **$250+**

Fenton Original Formula Carnival Glass pieces, amethyst base. Left: Persian Medallion chalice, 1972-73, 7" h, **$25+**
Right: Grape and Cable tobacco jar, 1969, 7 1/4" h, marked, "Preznick's Carnival Glass Museum–Lodi, Ohio 1969," **$80+**

Photo courtesy Green Valley Auctions, Mt. Crawford, Va.; www.GreenValleyAuctions.com

Greentown, No. 200 / Austrian Child's Covered Sugar and Creamer, chocolate. Indiana Tumbler and Goblet Co. Early 20th century. 3 3/4" x 3 1/4" h overall. Sugar base with mold roughness to a slight inner rim fin, creamer with normal minor annealing lines. **$536**

Greentown Glass

The Indiana Tumbler and Goblet Co. of Greentown, Ind., operated from 1894 to 1903. The company's wares in chocolate glass and "Holly Amber" are highly prized. The factory was destroyed by fire in 1903. Collectors use the term "Greentown glass" when referring to their products.

Greentown, No. 98 / Brazen Shield Covered Sugar Bowl, cobalt blue. Indiana Tumbler and Goblet Co. Fourth quarter 19th century. 6 3/4" h overall, 4" d. 5/8" chip under the edge of the base rim. **$138**

Greentown, No. 102 / Teardrop and Tassel Cordial, colorless. Indiana Tumbler and Goblet Co. Late 19th/early 20th century. 3" h. Normal annealing lines below rim. **$287**

Greentown, No. 102 / Teardrop and Tassel Bowl, cobalt blue, beaded rim. Indiana Tumbler and Goblet Co. Late 19th/early 20th century. 2 5/8" h, 7 3/8" d rim. Minor mold roughness to rim. **$287**

Greentown, No. 102 / Teardrop and Tassel Sauce, Nile Green, beaded rim. Indiana Tumbler and Goblet Co. Early 20th century. 1 5/8" h, 4 5/8" d. Bruise to one bead. ... **$373**

Greentown, No. 140 Columbia / Herringbone Buttress Cruet, emerald green, with an appropriate stopper of a slightly different shade. Indiana Tumbler and Goblet Co. Late 19th/early 20th century. 6 1/2" h overall. Two shallow chips and roughness to tops of ribs. **$156**

Greentown, No. 200 / Austrian Child's Sugar Bowl Base, canary. Indiana Tumbler and Goblet Co. Fourth quarter 19th century. 2 3/4" h, 2 3/8" d. **$149**

Greentown, No. 350 / Cord Drapery Syrup, period lid. Indiana Tumbler and Goblet Co. Early 20th century 6 1/2" h overall. Corrosion/rust to lid. **$126**

Greentown, No. 350 / Cord Drapery Syrup, chocolate, period lid. Indiana Tumbler and Goblet Co. Early 20th century. 6 1/2" h overall. Wear to several small beads, color separation line to handle. **$138**

Greentown, No. 350 / Cord Drapery Syrup, colorless, non-period lid. Indiana Tumbler and Goblet Co. Fourth quarter 19th century. 6 1/4" h overall, 3 5/8" d overall. **$195**

Greentown, No. 375 / Cactus Mustard Pot, chocolate, plated-silver screw-on rim with hinged lid, twisted bail handle and spoon slot. Indiana Tumbler and Goblet Co. Early 20th century. 3 5/8" h overall. Shallow chip to top of foot. **$402**

Greentown, No. 375 / Cactus Water Pitcher, chocolate. Indiana Tumbler and Goblet Co. Early 20th century. 8" h overall, 5 1/2" d. Flake to the spout and minor mold roughness to the feet. **$192**

Greentown, No. 375 / Cactus Iced Tea Tumblers, Lot of Four, chocolate. Indiana Tumbler and Goblet Co. Early 20th century. 5" h. One with several pattern flakes, others with several minor to moderate annealing lines. **$92 set**

Greentown, No. 375 / Cactus Cruet, chocolate, appropriate well-fitting stopper of a slightly differing color. Indiana Tumbler and Goblet Co. Early 20th century. 6 5/8" h overall. Minute nicks to ribs. **$69**

Greentown, No. 375 / Cactus Sauce Dish, Golden Agate, footed. Indiana Tumbler and Goblet Co. Early 20th century. 1 7/8" h, 4 1/8" d. **$60**

Greentown, No. 400 / Leaf Bracket Cruet, chocolate, appropriate but off-color Dewey stopper. Indiana Tumbler and Goblet Co. Early 20th century. 5 1/2" h overall. Slight mold roughness. **$69**

Greentown, No. 400 / Leaf Bracket Butter Dish, chocolate. Indiana Tumbler and Goblet Co. Early 20th century. 5" h overall, 7 3/8" d overall. Shallow chip under the base rim. **$46**

Greentown, No. 400 / Leaf Bracket Salt Shaker, chocolate, period lid. Indiana Tumbler and Goblet Co. Early 20th century. 3" h overall. Undamaged, normal overall annealing lines. **$92**

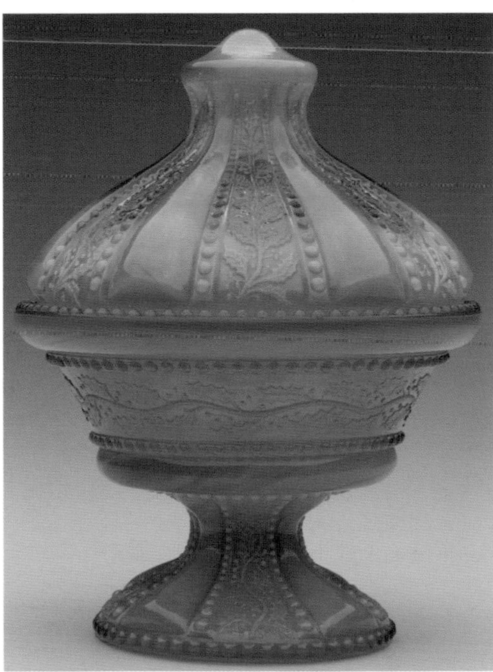

Photo courtesy Green Valley Auctions, Mt. Crawford, Va.; www.GreenValleyAuctions.com

Greentown, No. 450 / Holly Low Pedestal Covered Comport, Golden Agate, beaded base rim. Indiana Tumbler and Goblet Co. Early 20th century. 6" h overall, 3 3/8" h base, 4 5/8" d base. Cover with a chip to inner flange, base with a chip to edge of foot removing one bead. **$791**

Greentown, No. 450 / Holly Bowl, Golden Agate, beaded rim. Indiana Tumbler and Goblet Co. Early 20th century. 3 1/8" h, 8 1/2" d. Minute flakes/nicks to inner rim. **$450**

Greentown, No. 450 / Holly Tumbler, Agate, plain rim. Indiana Tumbler and Goblet Co. Fourth quarter 19th century. 4" h, 3" d. Minute abrasion to rim. **$510**

Greentown, No. 450 / Holly Nappy, Golden Agate, single handle, beaded rim. Indiana Tumbler and Goblet Co. Early 20th century. 2" h, 4 5/8" d rim. Rim with partial loss of one bead and some minute interior flakes, light wear to handle edge. **$270**

Greentown, No. 450 / Holly Sauce Dishes, Lot of Four, Golden Agate, each with beaded rim. Indiana Tumbler and Goblet Co. Early 20th century. 1 5/8" h, 4 1/4" d. Slight inner-rim mold roughness, one with interior wear. **$431 all**

Greentown, No. 450 / Holly Oval Bowl, Golden Agate. Indiana Tumbler and Goblet Co. Fourth quarter 19th century. 1 7/8" h, 4 1/2" x 7 3/8". Minor roughness to interior rim. **$258**

Greentown, Bird with Berry Covered Dish, on basket-weave base. Indiana Tumbler and Goblet Co. Late 19th/early 20th century. 4 1/2" h overall, 4 1/8" x 5 3/8". **$480**

Greentown, Buffalo Paperweight, Nile Green, without date, beaded table ring. Indiana Tumbler and Goblet Co. Early 20th century. 3 1/8" h, 4" d overall. Partial loss of one ear. **$747**

Greentown, Cat on Hamper Covered Dish, chocolate, tall version. Indiana Tumbler and Goblet Co. Early 20th century. 4 3/4" h overall, 3 1/2" sq overall. Cover with a small chip under one corner and manufacturing roughness to one ear, base with several shallow chips to rim exterior, none of which disfigure the rim profile. **$132**

Greentown, Cat on Hamper Covered Dish, chocolate, tall version. Indiana Tumbler and Goblet Co. Early 20th century. 4 3/4" h overall, 3 1/2" sq overall. Minor flake under one base corner. **$172**

Greentown, Cat on Hamper Covered Dish, emerald green, tall version. Indiana Tumbler and Goblet Co. Late 19th/early 20th century. 4 3/4" h overall, 3 1/2" sq overall. Chip to one ear. **$192**

Greentown, Cat on Hamper Covered Dish, teal blue, tall version. Indiana Tumbler and Goblet Co. Late 19th/early 20th century. 4 3/4" h overall, 3 1/2" sq overall. Light flake to one vertical edge and a small chip under one base corner. **$218**

Greentown, Hen Covered Dish, chocolate, basket-weave pattern base. Indiana Tumbler and Goblet Co. Early 20th century. 4 1/4" h overall, 4 1/8" x 5 3/8" d base. Minor flake to one base rim bead. **$373**

Greentown, Dewey Three-Piece Table Set, amber, consisting of a covered sugar bowl, creamer and spooner. Indiana Tumbler and Goblet Co. Fourth quarter 19th century. 4 1/2" to 6 3/4" h overall. Foot flakes/roughness. **$92 set**

Greentown, Dewey Four-Piece Water Set, emerald green, consisting of a water pitcher and three tumblers. Indiana Tumbler and Goblet Co. Fourth quarter 19th century. Pitcher 8" h, 5 1/4" d, tumblers 3 7/8" h, 3" d. Pitcher having a chip to one foot and several open bubbles to ribbing, two tumblers with high-point wear to medallions. **$345 set**

Greentown, Dolphin Covered Dish, Red Agate, beaded rim. Indiana Tumbler and Goblet Co. Early 20th century. 4 1/4" h overall. Minute flake to one front fin. **$300**

Photo courtesy Green Valley Auctions, Mt. Crawford, Va.; www.GreenValleyAuctions.com

Greentown, Cat on Hamper Low Covered Nappy, chocolate, base with scalloped tab handle. Indiana Tumbler and Goblet Co. Early 20th century. 3 1/2" h overall, 5 1/8" x 6 1/4" overall. Cover with what appears to be light factory grinding to the back of one ear, which does not affect the profile of the ear, base with several flakes to front edge. **$840**

Greentown, Dolphin Covered Dish, Golden Agate, beaded rim. Indiana Tumbler and Goblet Co. Early 20th century. 4 1/4" h overall. Minor flake to the tip of the front fin on cover. **$431**

Greentown, Hen Covered Dish, blue, on basket-weave base. Indiana Tumbler and Goblet Co. Late 19th/early 20th century. 4 1/2" h overall, 4 3/8" x 5 1/2". Shallow chip to base rim. **$207**

Greentown, Hen Covered Dish, chocolate, basket-weave pattern base. Indiana Tumbler and Goblet Co. Early 20th century. 4 1/4" h overall, 4 1/8" x 5 3/8" d base. Cover rim with two shallow chips to upper edge, base rim with loss of two beads. **$92**

Greentown, Indian Head Creamer, Nile Green, lacking cover. Indiana Tumbler and Goblet Co. Early 20th century. 5 3/4" h overall. With a 1/2" loss and adjacent 1" glued section at spout. **$108**

Greentown, Picture Frame Toothpick / Match Holder, pale blue, embossed "R. &. M." under base. Indiana Tumbler and Goblet Co. Late 19th/early 20th century. 3 1/2" h. **$575**

Greentown, Rabbit Covered Dish, amber, on basket-weave base. Indiana Tumbler and Goblet Co. Late 19th/early 20th century. 4 1/4" h overall, 4 1/4" x 5 1/2". Minute bruise to top mold line, base rim with several flakes and normal minor roughness to interior seat. **$144**

Greentown, Rabbit Covered Dish, chocolate, on basket-weave base. Indiana Tumbler and Goblet Co. Early 20th century. 4 1/8" h overall, 4 1/8" x 5 3/8". Chip to one rim bead, normal annealing lines to cover. **$228**

Greentown, Rabbit Covered Dish, emerald green, on basket-weave base. Indiana Tumbler and Goblet Co. Late 19th/early 20th century. 4 1/8" h overall, 4 1/2" x 5 1/2". Base with a small rim chip and flake as well as a bruise to outside of rim. **$69**

Greentown, Trunk Covered Box, opaque white/milk glass, embossed "Pan American 1901" and "Put Me Off at Buffalo" on ends, slightly worn original gold decoration. Indiana Tumbler and Goblet Co. Early 20th century. 2 1/4" h, 2 1/4" x 3 3/8". Two shallow chips to base rim. **$218**

Greentown, Trunk Covered Box, white/milk glass, no lettering on ends, worn original gold decoration. Indiana Tumbler and Goblet Co. Early 20th century. 2 1/4" h, 2 1/4" x 3 3/8". Small manufacturing chip to one upper corner of cover, which has traces of decoration, otherwise a flake to inner rim of base and short annealing lines. **$92**

Photo courtesy Green Valley Auctions, Mt. Crawford, Va.; www.GreenValleyAuctions.com

Greentown, Rabbit Covered Dish, teal blue, basket-weave pattern base. Indiana Tumbler and Goblet Co. Late 19th/early 20th century. 4 1/8" h overall, 4 1/4" x 5 1/2" base. Cover with light polishing under rim, base rim with an under-fill to one outer-rim scallop and several inner-rim flakes. **$226**

Photo courtesy Green Valley Auctions, Mt. Crawford, Va.; www.GreenValleyAuctions.com

Greentown / McKee, Daisy Covered Butter, chocolate, on three feet. Indiana Tumbler and Goblet Co. and/or McKee & Brothers. Early 20th century. 4 1/8" h overall, 4 5/8" d overall. Two minute flakes to cover rim, normal short annealing lines. **$84**

Lalique

René Lalique (1860-1945) first gained prominence as a jewelry designer. Around 1900, he began experimenting with molded-glass brooches and pendants, often embellishing them with semiprecious stones. By 1905, he was devoting himself exclusively to the manufacture of glass articles. He produced many objects, especially vases, bowls and figurines, in the Art Nouveau and Art Deco styles.

Also see Perfume Containers.

Photo courtesy James D. Julia Auctioneers, Fairfield, Maine; www.JuliaAuctions.com

R. Lalique Archers Vase. With a design of nude male archers shooting arrows at flocks of birds. The vase is finished in a satiny blue patination ending in a clear rim. Signed on the underside with etched script signature "R. Lalique France". 10 3/4" h. **$5,175**

Photo courtesy Rago Arts and Auction Center, Lambertville, N.J.; www.RagoArts.com

R. Lalique, "Ronces" vase, red, molded R. LALIQUE, engraved R. Lalique, France, circa 1921, 9" h. **$5,400**

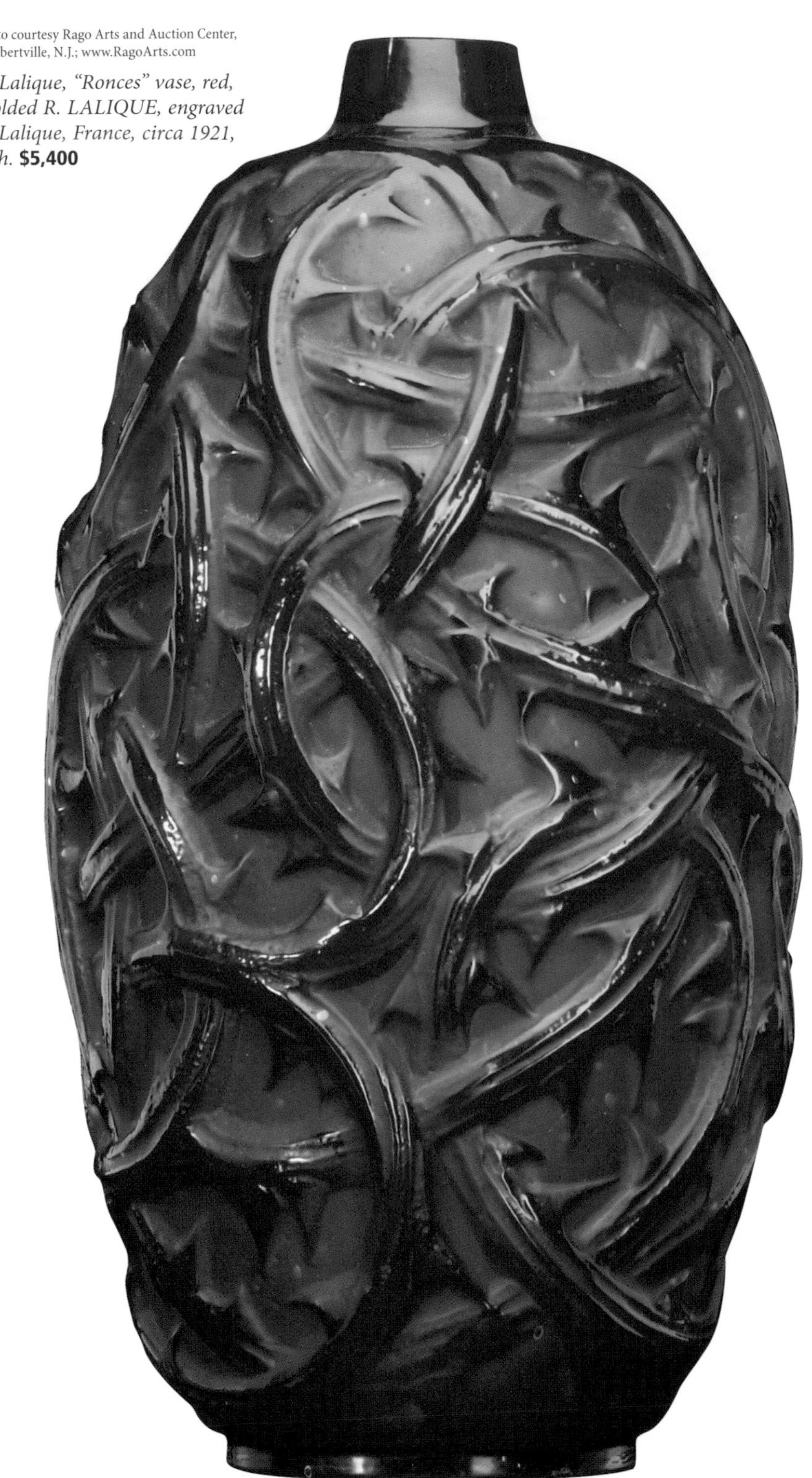

Photo courtesy James D. Julia Auctioneers, Fairfield, Maine; www.JuliaAuctions.com

R. Lalique Gros Scarabees Vase. All-over design of large scarabs against a gray patinated background. The vase is signed on the underside with engraved block letters "R. Lalique France". 11 1/2" h. **$7,200**

Photo courtesy James D. Julia Auctioneers, Fairfield, Maine; www.JuliaAuctions.com

R. Lalique Bacchus Vase. Decorated with a wide horizontal panel with deeply impressed design of satyrs sitting amongst heavy vegetation. The heavily decorated central band is finished in a gray patination and is bordered top and bottom by clear glass. Signed on the underside with etched block letters "R. Lalique France". 6 3/4" h. **$2,300**

Photo courtesy James D. Julia Auctioneers, Fairfield, Maine; www.JuliaAuctions.com

R. Lalique Grignon Vase. Impressed all over with stylized wheat stalks and finished with a beautiful green patination. Vase is signed on the underside with lightly etched block letters "R. Lalique France". 7" h. **$1,840**

Photo courtesy James D. Julia Auctioneers, Fairfield, Maine; www.JuliaAuctions.com

Lalique Coquilles Vase. Decorated with pressed design of overlapping seashells and finished with a light blue patination. Vase is signed on the underside with lightly etched script letters "Lalique". 7" h. **$1,610**

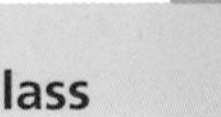

Photo courtesy James D. Julia Auctioneers, Fairfield, Maine; www.JuliaAuctions.com

R. Lalique Bouchardon Vase. Simple bulbous body with applied pressed glass handles depicting a nude maiden holding a spray of flowers. The vase is done in smoky gray glass and is double signed on the underside with impressed block letters "R. Lalique" and engraved script signature "R. Lalique France". 4 3/4" h. One fleabite on edge of rim. **$4,025**

Photo courtesy James D. Julia Auctioneers, Fairfield, Maine; www.JuliaAuctions.com

Lalique Bacchantes Vase. Decorated with Art Deco maidens surrounding the entire vase. Frosted with original sepia patina in the recesses. This model was produced from the 1920s to the present day, but this example dates from just after WWII. Signed "LALIQUE FRANCE" on the underside. 9 1/2" h. **$3,737**

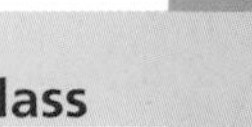

Photo courtesy James D. Julia Auctioneers, Fairfield, Maine; www.JuliaAuctions.com

R. Lalique Gobelet Six Figurines Vase. Deep olive green impressed with six vertical panels, each showing a different maiden in flowing gowns holding bouquets of flowers. Vase is signed on the underside with engraved block letters "R. Lalique". 7 1/2" h. Minor staining to bottom interior. **$3,795**

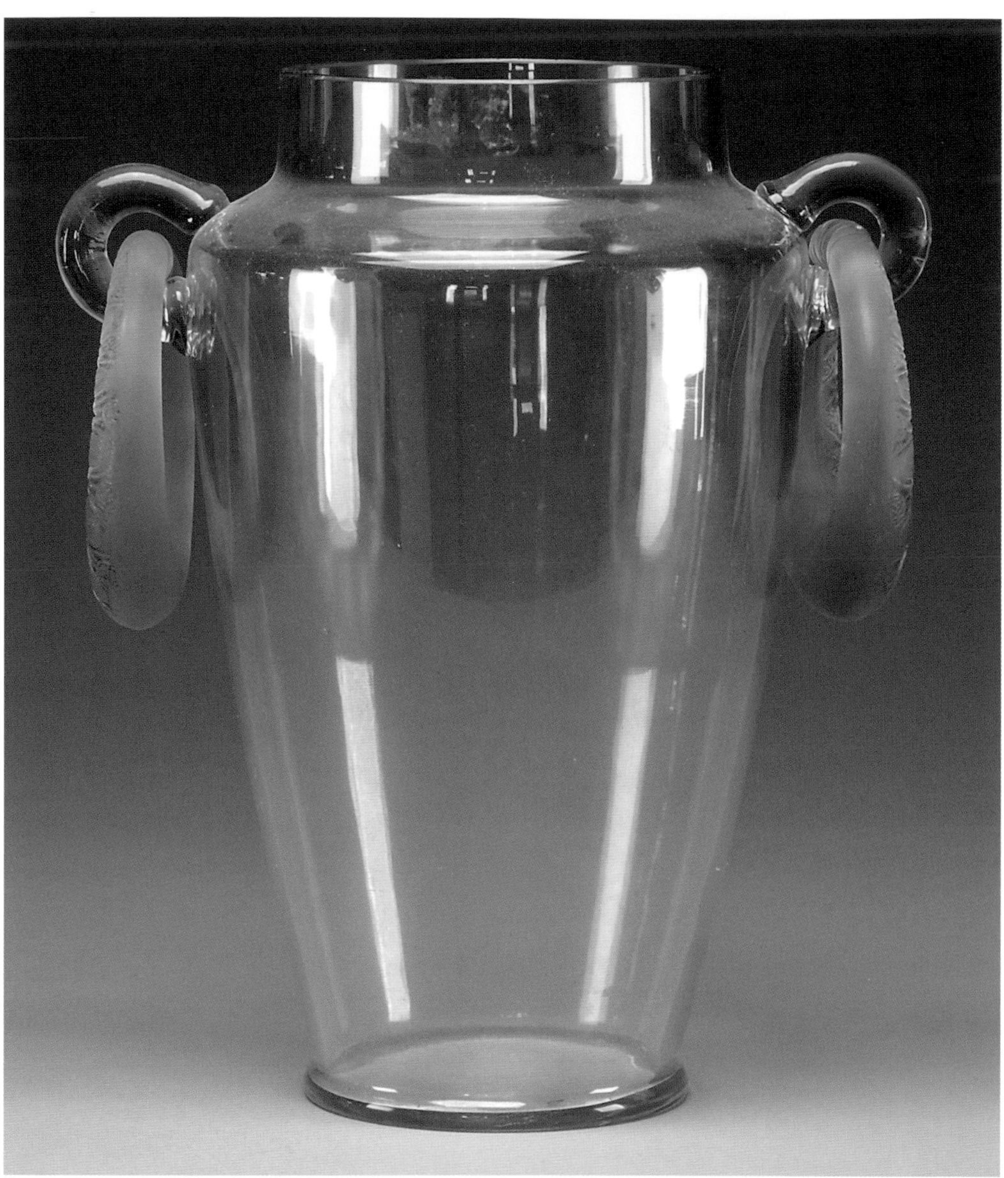

Photo courtesy James D. Julia Auctioneers, Fairfield, Maine; www.JuliaAuctions.com

Lalique Scarabees Vase. Clear classic form vase has two small ear handles that support two rings with molded scarab design that carries a gray patination. 13" h. Heat check at one handle. **$3,162**

Photo courtesy James D. Julia Auctioneers, Fairfield, Maine; www.JuliaAuctions.com

R. Lalique Saint Francois Vase. Decorated with high-relief birds resting on leafy branches against a frosted background. The design is further enhanced with green patination and the vase is signed on the underside with etched block letters "R. Lalique France". 7" h. **$1,725**

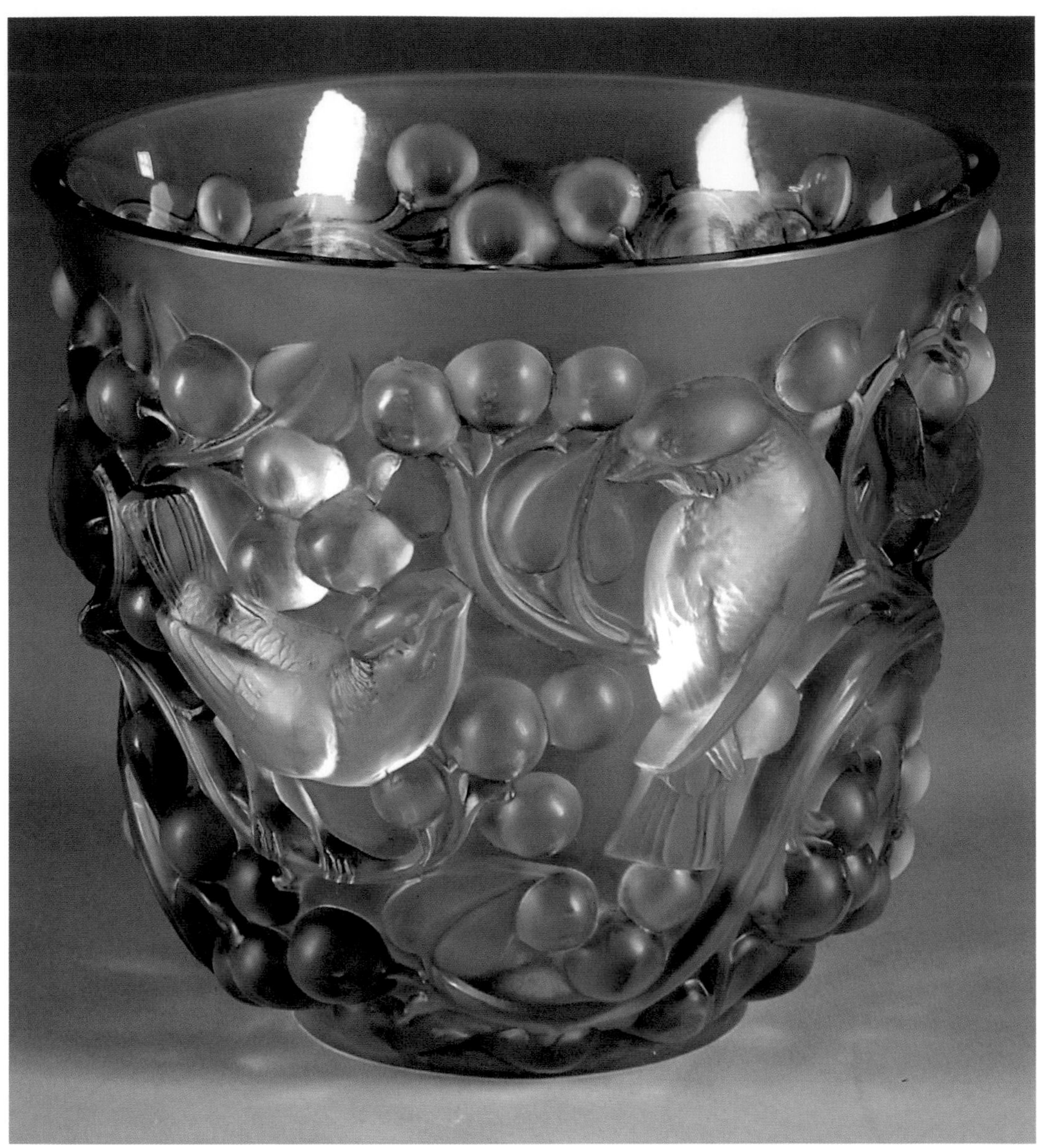

Photo courtesy James D. Julia Auctioneers, Fairfield, Maine; www.JuliaAuctions.com

R. Lalique Avallon Vase. Deeply impressed design of birds resting amongst cherry branches laden with fruit. The vase is finished with blue patination. Signed on the underside with acid-etched block signature "R. Lalique". 5 3/4" h. **$1,955**

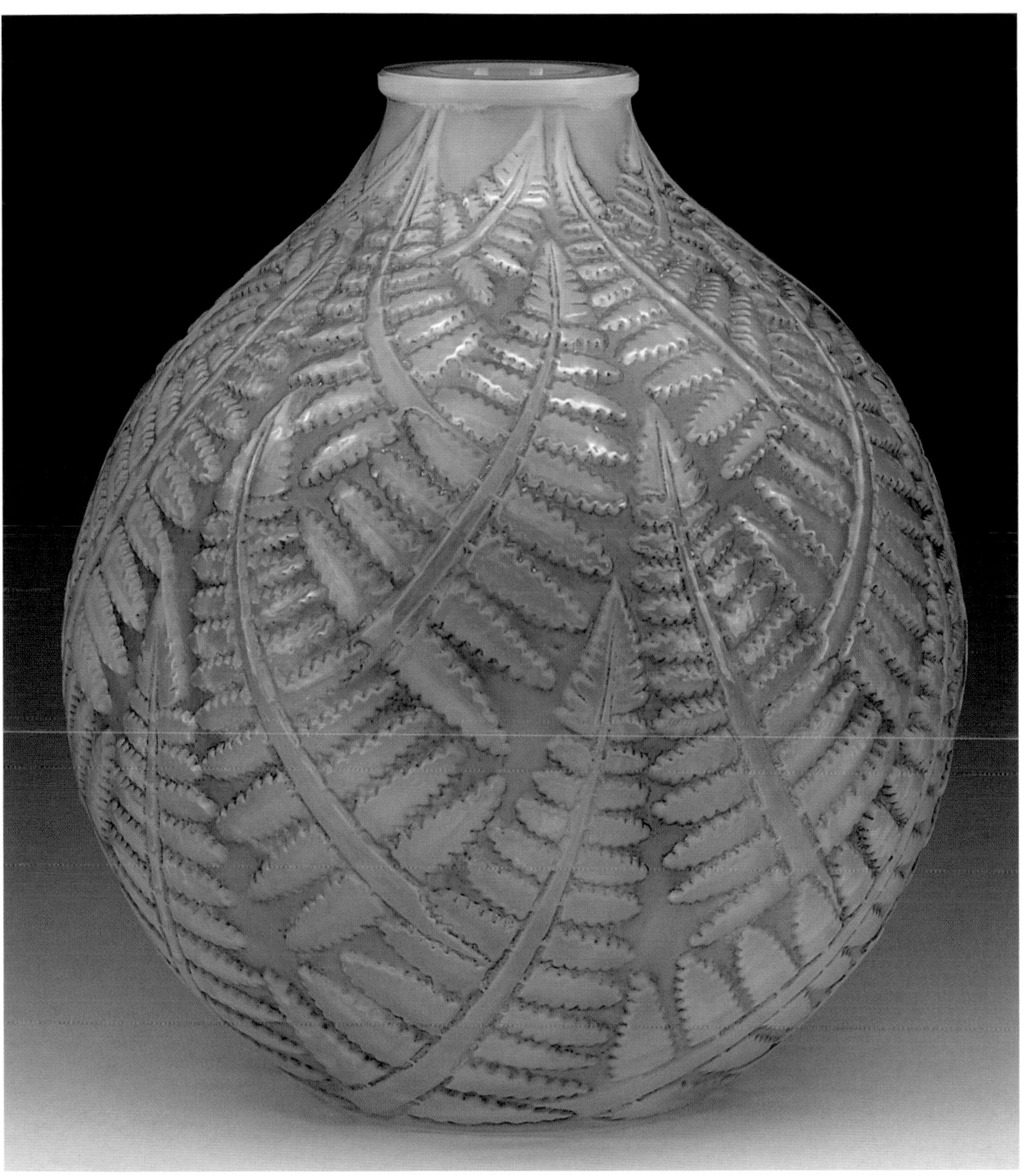

Photo courtesy James D. Julia Auctioneers, Fairfield, Maine; www.JuliaAuctions.com

R. Lalique Espalion Vase. With overlapping fern design covering the entire body of the vase. The vase is done in opalescent glass and is finished with a rich green patination. Signed on the underside with engraved script signature "R. Lalique France". 7 1/4" h. **$1,955**

Photo courtesy Rago Arts and Auction Center, Lambertville, N.J.; www.RagoArts.com

R. Lalique hood ornament, "Libellule Grande," clear and frosted glass, gray patina, lucite stand, engraved R. Lalique France, circa 1928, 8 1/8" h. **$7,200**

Photo courtesy Rago Arts and Auction Center, Lambertville, N.J.; www.RagoArts.com

R. Lalique hood ornament, "Tete De Coq," clear and frosted glass, molded LALIQUE, FRANCE, circa 1928, 7" h. **$960**

Photo courtesy Rago Arts and Auction Center, Lambertville, N.J.; www.RagoArts.com

R. Lalique hood ornament, "Cinq Chevaux," amethyst tint glass, restorations, molded R. LALIQUE, engraved France, circa 1925, 6" h. **$2,520**

QUEZAL

The Quezal Art Glass Decorating Co., named for the quetzal—a bird with brilliantly colored feathers found in tropical regions of the Americas—was organized in 1901 in Brooklyn, N.Y., by Martin Bach and Thomas Johnson, two disgruntled Tiffany workers. They soon hired Percy Britton and William Wiedebine, two more former Tiffany employees.

The first products, unmarked, were exact Tiffany imitations. Quezal pieces differ from Tiffany pieces in that they are more defined and the decorations are more visible and brighter. No new techniques were developed by Quezal.

Johnson left in 1905. T. Conrad Vahlsing, Bach's son-in-law, joined the firm in 1918, but left with Paul Frank in 1920 to form Lustre Art Glass Co., which in turn copied Quezal pieces. Martin Bach died in 1924, and by 1925, Quezal had ceased operations.

The "Quezal" trademark was first used in 1902 and placed on the base of vases and bowls and the rims of shades. The acid-etched or engraved letters vary in size and may be found in amber, black or gold. A printed label that includes an illustration of a quetzal was used briefly in 1907.

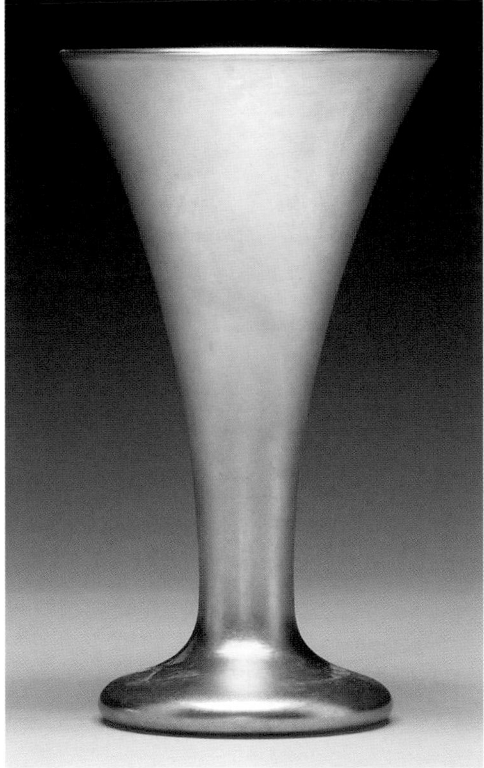

Photo courtesy James D. Julia Auctioneers, Fairfield, Maine; www.JuliaAuctions.com

Quezal Trumpet Vase. With bright gold iridescent finish with a band of platinum iridescence at the foot. Vase is signed in the polished pontil "Quezal". 8 1/2" t. **$230**

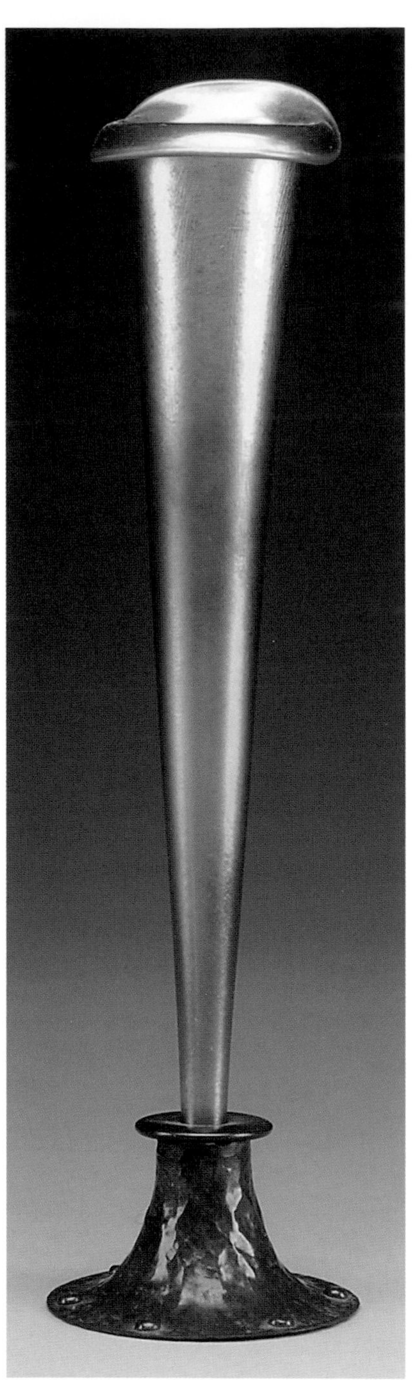

Photo courtesy James D. Julia Auctioneers, Fairfield, Maine; www.JuliaAuctions.com

Quezal Flower-Form Vase. Flaring cylindrical shape with Jack in the Pulpit folded mouth resting in an Arts & Crafts hammered and patinated copper foot. Early engraved "Quezal" signature on the tip of the glass. 10 3/4" t. **$1,552**

Photo courtesy James D. Julia Auctioneers, Fairfield, Maine; www.JuliaAuctions.com

Quezal Pulled Art Glass Vase. Simplistic Art Nouveau design consists of three pulled handles to top of bulbous shaped vase. Deep gold coloration has a soft magenta iridescence. Signed "Quezal" in script on pontil. 8" h. **$660**

Photo courtesy James D. Julia Auctioneers, Fairfield, Maine; www.JuliaAuctions.com

Quezal Silver Overlay Vase. Decorated with King Tut design with gold iridescence showing pink and blue iridescence. The vase is overlaid with an Art Nouveau floral design in sterling silver. The silver carries the Alvin Silver Co hallmark, "999/1000 Fine" and "Patented 49". Vase is signed on the underside in the polished pontil "Quezal" with a scroll beneath. 9 3/4" t. **$3,680**

Photo courtesy James D. Julia Auctioneers, Fairfield, Maine; www.JuliaAuctions.com

Quezal Decorated Vase. With bulbous body leading to long slender neck and flaring rim. The cream-colored background gives way to the gold iridescent neck, which is finished with a hooked-feather design at the shoulder. The gold iridescence on the neck has a strong green overtone with flashes of pink. Signed on the underside in the polished pontil "Quezal B952". 11" t. **$8,050**

GUITARS, BANJOS, MANDOLINS

The guitar has ancient roots and is used in a wide variety of musical styles. It typically has six strings, but four-, seven-, eight-, 10-, 11-, 12-, 13- and 18-string guitars also exist. The size and shape of the neck and the base of the guitar also vary. There are two main types of guitars, the electric guitar and the acoustic guitar. The banjo is a stringed instrument developed by enslaved Africans in the United States, adapted from several African instruments. The mandolin is part of the lute family (plucked, or strummed). It is descended from the mandore, a soprano lute. It usually has a body with a teardrop-shaped soundboard, or one which is essentially oval in shape, with a soundhole, or soundholes, of varying shapes which are open.

The instruments featured in this year's edition of the Warman's guide all come from the May 3, 2009, auction conducted by Skinner Inc., Boston and Marlborough, Mass.; *www.SkinnerInc.com.*

Mandolin, Gibson Mandolin-Guitar Co., Kalamazoo, circa 1923, Model F4, labeled GIBSON MANDOLIN STYLE F4, ..., etc., length of back 12 7/8", with case. Missing pick guard. surface scratches and abrasions. 1 cm chip in face of headstock. Fracture near upper treble body point, approx. 3 cm, fracture below body scroll, approx. 3 cm. Wear to upper edge, back of headstock. **$3,081**

American Guitar, Gibson Mandolin-Guitar Co., Kalamazoo, circa 1924, Model L-2, labeled GIBSON STYLE, NUMBER 160403 IS HEREBY, GUARANTEED..., etc., length of back 18 15/16", width of lower bout 13 9/16", with case. Surface scratches and abrasions. **$948**

American Ukulele, C.F. Martin & Company, Nazareth, Pa., circa 1920, Style 1, stamped internally CF MARTIN & CO, NAZARETH PA, and on the back of the peghead, length of back 9 3/8", with case. Surface scratches and abrasions. **$563**

American Tiple, C.F. Martin & Co., Nazareth, Pa., circa 1931, stamped CF MARTIN & CO, NAZARETH PA on the center strip and on the back of the peghead, and T-17 and 46751 at the upper block, length of back 11 1/16", with case. Surface scratches and abrasions. **$830**

American Harp Guitar, Gibson Mandolin-Guitar Co., Kalamazoo, circa 1920, Style U, labeled GIBSON STYLE U, NUMBER 78381 IS HEREBY, GUARANTEED..., etc., GIBSON MANDOLIN GUITAR CO, MANUFACTURERS, KALAMAZOO MICH, USA, length of back 26 1/2", width of lower bout 18 1/2", with case. Surface scratches and abrasions, wear to back of neck. Fracture to peg head of sympathetic tenth string.
$3,081

American Guitar, Gibson Mandolin-Guitar Co., Kalamazoo, circa 1920, Style O, labeled GIBSON STYLE O, NUMBER 60358? IS HEREBY, GUARANTEED... etc..., GIBSON MANDOLIN-GUITAR CO, MANUFACTURERS, KALAMAZOO, MICH USA, length of back 17 3/4", width of lower bout 16 1/16", with case. Body clear coated. Surface scratches and abrasions.
$2,607

American Electric Guitar, Gibson Inc., Kalamazoo, circa 1953, Model ES-175-D, labeled STYLE ES 175 D, GIBSON GUITAR, NUMBER A 15390 IS HEREBY, GUARANTEED..., etc., length of back 20 1/8", width of lower bout 16 1/16", with case. Later strap-hook at heel of neck, slight surface check, re-fretted. Surface scratches and abrasions. **$3,081**

American Electric Guitar, John D'Angelico, New York, 1955, Model Excel, stamped 1980, JOHN DANGELICO at the upper block, the bound peghead with D'ANGELICO NEW YORK and EXCEL pearl inlay, length of back 20 1/2", width of lower bout 16 7/8", with case. Replaced pickups, finish or hairline cracks near pickup switch, finish check, finish wear to back of neck, pickguard a replacement. Refretted with zero fret added. Two face cracks under tailpiece, one repaired. **$8,295**

American Electric Guitar, Fender Electric Instruments, Fullerton, Calif., 1954, Model Stratocaster, labeled FENDER STRATOCASTER, WITH SYNCHRONIZED TREMOLO..., etc., and ORIGINAL CONTOUR BODY, PAT PEND on the headstock decals and stamped 1099 on the neck plate, (factory refinished in 1962 in "Lake Placid Blue"), length of back 15 3/4", with later 1962 case. Factory refinished in 1962, neck refinished with decals, body refinished in Lake Placid blue, pickguard replaced in 1962 with contemporary style. With original strap and polish cloth. Pot codes 250K, 304429. **$8,295**

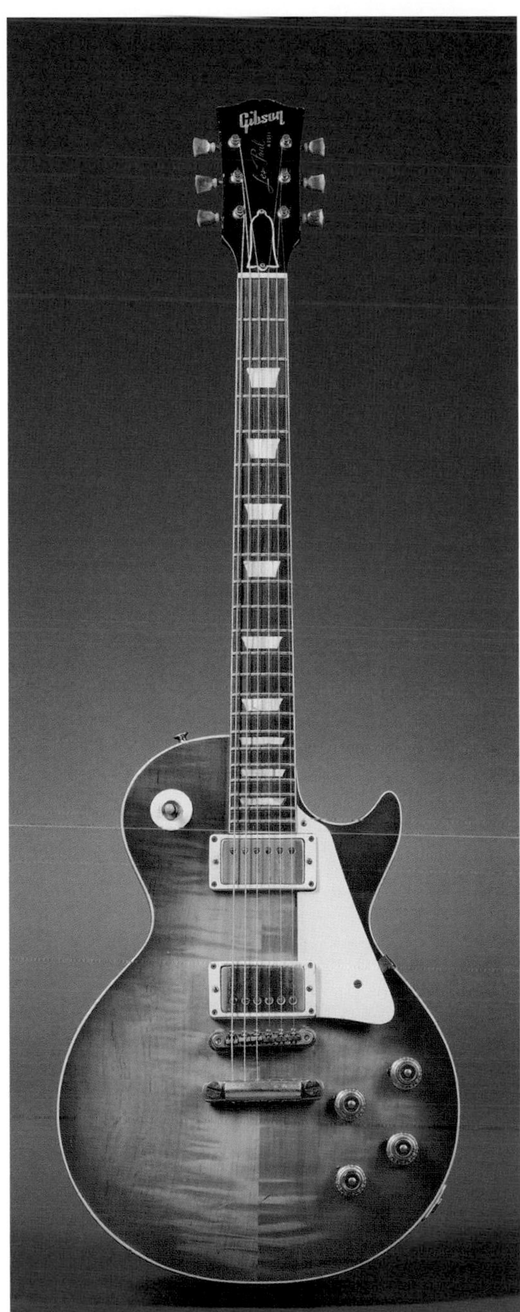

American Electric Guitar, Gibson Inc., Kalamazoo, 1959, Model Les Paul Standard, Serial Number 9 1950, the mahogany back and neck, the painted headstock with GIBSON pearl inlay and LES PAUL MODEL silkscreen logo, the bound rosewood fingerboard with trapezoid pearl inlay, the carved two-piece maple top of irregular curl, the tune-o-matic bridge, stop tailpiece and all hardware original, the original "PAF" design double-coil humbucking pickups, the cherry sunburst finish, length of back 17 3/8", with original Les Paul Custom case. All hardware original. All electronics original and unmolested. **$237,000**

American Electric Guitar, Gibson Inc., Kalamazoo, circa 1969, Model ES-335TD, labeled STYLE GUITAR, GIBSON ES335TD, NUMBER 118204, IS HEREBY GUARANTEED..., etc., UNION MADE GIBSON INC, KALAMAZOO MICHIGAN, USA, and stamped 118204 at the back of the headstock, length of back 18 3/8", width of lower bout 15 7/8", with case. **$3,851**

American Banjo, Vega Co., Boston, circa 1921, Model Tubaphone #9, stamped on the dowel stick TUBAPHONE 45097, FAIRBANKS BANJO, MADE BY, THE VEGA COMPANY, BOSTON MASS, NO 9..., etc., and stamped 45097 on the inside rim, diameter of head 10 15/16", with later case. Very good condition. Later gold Grover tuners, Wear to fingerboard at first and second position. **$4,444**

Pair of American Mandolins, Gibson Mandolin-Guitar Co., Kalamazoo, 1926, Master Model F5, labeled THE GIBSON MASTER MODEL, STYLE F5 NUMBER 84264, IS HEREBY GUARANTEED...etc., the bound quartersawn back of strong narrow curl, the bound top of fine to medium grain, the sides of medium curl, the neck of strong medium curl, the bound peghead with THE GIBSON and "fern" pearl inlay, the bound ebony fingerboard with pearl dot inlay, the tailpiece and pickguard original, length of back 13 3/8". Master Model F5, labeled THE GIBSON MASTER MODEL F5 NUMBER 84265, IS HEREBY GUARANTEED...etc., the bound slab-cut back of irregular curl, the bound top of fine to medium grain, the sides of medium curl, the neck of strong medium curl, the bound peghead with THE GIBSON and "fern" pearl inlay, the bound ebony fingerboard with pearl dot inlay, the tailpiece and pickguard original, length of back 13 3/8". The original custom-built Artist double case with green velvet lining. Provenance: Robert L. Sharp. From the Sharp family archives; "As an agent for the Gibson Mandolin-Guitar Company in 1926, Robert L. Sharp ordered and purchased these twin F5 mandolins. He enjoyed playing these instruments in front of audiences in Memphis and Little Rock. If a mandolin string broke, he could reach down and pick up the twin without missing a note. These instruments became a part of the Sharp family, joining a guitar, mandocello, mandola, and ukulele all from Gibson in the late 20's and early 30's." Number 84265: minor chips to surface of top. Slightly distressed varnish surface on back, Medium fret ware, top five positions. Lost to gold plateing of tailpiece cover. Number 84264: replaced top bridge section, original in case, slightly distressed varnish surface on back, surface check to top, slight loss to gold plating on tailpiece cover. Case in good condition, distressed on edges. **$136,275 pair**

HALLOWEEN

The commercialization of Halloween in the United States did not start until the 20th century, beginning perhaps with Halloween postcards (featuring hundreds of designs) which were most popular between 1905 and 1915. Dennison Manufacturing Co., which published its first Hallowe'en catalog in 1909, and the Beistle Co. were pioneers in commercially made Halloween decorations, particularly die-cut paper items. German manufacturers specialized in Halloween figurines that were exported to the United States in the period between the two world wars.

Mass-produced Halloween costumes did not appear in stores until the 1930s, and trick-or-treating did not become a fixture of the holiday until the 1940s.

For more information, see *Vintage Halloween Collectibles,* by Mark Ledenbach, 2007. *Also see Postcards.*

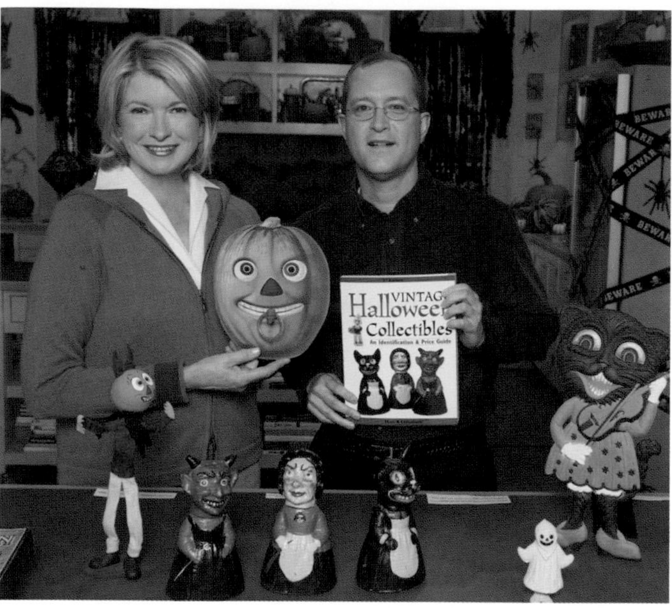

Mark Ledenback appeared on the Martha Stewart Show in the fall of 2008.

Halloween witch hanging decoration, USA, Beistle, (no mark), late 1930s-early 1940s, 43 1/2" h x 11 1/2" w. **$175**

Owl Tell Your Fortune game, USA, Beistle, (no mark), mid-1950s, 9 1/4" h x 6" w. **$110**

Large witch-head transparency, a candle would be placed on the attached holder behind, USA, Beistle, (HE Luhrs mark), early 1940s, 14" h x 8 1/2" w. **$285**
This is one of a set of three similarly sized. The others are a cat and a JOL-head.

Photo courtesy Morphy Auctions, Denver, Pa.; www.MorphyAuctions.com

None Such Mince Meat advertising lantern, 16" t, includes four decorative glass panels. **$5,200**

Tongue Twister novelty game with glassine envelope, USA, Gibson Art Co of Cincinnati, 1928-1932, 5 1/2" h x 6 3/4" w, non-embossed. **$50**
Sample tongue twister: Forty flagrant fighters flayed fifty ferocious fanatics who finally fled.

Metal parade lantern, USA, 1905-1910, 7" diameter. **$1,100**
It opens at the center and is designed for an interior candle The paper insert has almost always been burned away. This example has the original internal hardware and wooden finial.

Watermelon candy container (opens at bottom), Germany, 1920s, 4" h. **$425**

Set of 4 light cardboard interlocking sides that form a Veggie-people centerpiece, USA, pre-1920s. From left: 6" h x 5 3/4" w; 6 1/4" h x 5 1/4" w; 6 1/4" h x 5 1/4" w; 6" h x 4 3/4" w. **$150 set**

Jewelry

THE FUTURE OF THE MARKET: JEWELRY

By Kathy Flood

Musician Joni Mitchell once observed how differently we interact with the arts. "People shout at me from the audience, 'Sing Chelsea Morning again, Joni!,' but no one ever yelled at van Gogh, 'Hey, Vinnie, paint The Starry Night again.'" Similarly, we might prefer reading literature silently, alone in bed, but gather with gallery goers to get a glimpse of new paintings – and judge them loudly, to make our brilliant insights heard.

We respond to and interact with collectible objects, and they engage us, in their own unique ways, too, one category so different from another. Art collectors don't wear canvases around their necks, Civil War buffs don't match uniforms to their décor, doll devotees don't take their Dresden china out to dinner – but jewelry is another matter entirely. It's "out there," everywhere, highly visible in the public domain, for all to respond to immediately.

Predicting the future of the jewelry market is clear on one hand, but some of the forecast is far cloudier because it depends on … so many things. It often depends on what happens in the world.

For instance, who could have guessed in 2007 that in 2009, diamonds would be disparaged as a girl's past friend, or know the extent to which diamonds would fall out of favor and fashion? In light of the economic meltdown, these gems were suddenly deemed déclassé for their political incorrectness. Who imagined DeBeers would close two of its African mines to prevent even more ice melting all over a market flooded both by new diamonds – and old ones sold off by people suddenly strapped? Diamond values were forecast to drop by 20 to 60 percent. Yet was there any doubt the diamond would eventually rebound?

Who could have guessed pirates would cause panic on the open seas and at the same time spark a small passion for pirate pins?

The Scottish Terrier dog brooch became a huge bestseller because of FDR's best friend, Fala, but would Obama's Bo engender the same fad?

And here's one for you: why on earth would silver jewelry from Peru suddenly heat up in 2009?

Some things are unknowable and unpredictable.

The wearing (and not wearing) of the bling seriously affects jewelry's power in the present tense and alters its future. So, for instance, when best-actress nominee Helen Hunt took minimalism to the extreme in 1998, on the Oscar red carpet, wearing a severe up-do and plain-Jane strapless sheath adorned with … nothing, she plunged a stiletto into the heart of the jewelry market. What Gable did to undershirts and JFK to hats, Hunt did to jewelry that year, for nary a Harry Winston bauble nor Swarovski bib chilled her collarbone. (And if that wasn't bad enough, the costume-jewelry industry was already reeling, both from Chinese imports, and the American woman's sudden passion for beading jewelry – herself.) It was a far cry from the Eighties, when being heavily jeweled in either rhinestones or the real thing was pretty much de riguer. Resale prices then were stratospheric, with visitors from Germany and Japan only too happy to shell out boatloads of marks and yen from coast to coast. That was pre-Internet, so eager buyers were live and in person.

Kathy Flood

Compare the Hunt red-carpet incident with the more verdant pasture of 2009, when best-actress nominee Angelina Jolie arrived on the red carpet not only adorned with Brad Pitt, but the most sensational 65-carat Colombian emerald cocktail ring and 115-carat emerald earrings anyone had ever seen. Wealthy women might have lusted after the real thing, but the gorgeous greenery was also wanted by the Everywoman, so faceted glass was just fine.

Or, take the 20-million-plus viewers who tuned in to American Idol twice each week: they saw not only the brutal Brit's trademark T-shirt, but also judge Paula Abdul, drenched in jewels under an intense and loving spotlight. All that glitter was mesmerizing … and memorable. So we wanted some of it.

The tenor of the times affects jewelry trends, too, and sometimes those trends then evolve and harden. A preference on the part of collectors for signed jewelry (or at least jewelry with rock-solid, unimpeachable provenance if unsigned), might have started out as "signature snobbery" in the Eighties, but evolved to a form of self-protection by the end of the first decade of the 21st century. Collectors reasoned (or rationalized, if they felt guilt over their expenditures) that to recoup their money, or to know they were leaving something of real value as an inheritance, jewelry had to be connected to a name, and preferably a hot one. Jewelry lovers increasingly set out with rigorous determination to avoid anything merely beautiful or interesting. The economic downturn of 2009 made pure aesthetics seem an unaffordable luxury. Generally, goods had to be liquid to be any "good," and resaleability was in a name. For example, one expert in Mexican silver mentioned even the most exquisitely made vintage pieces were almost impossible to sell if unmarked.

As recovery restores faith in investing, the final effect of the "panic" will be fascinating to study. Will Americans behave as our Depression-deflated ancestors did, socking money away and spending conservatively, or – after the deep and dismal recession, when all that virtual money was there one day and gone the next – will we crave more personal control over our earnings and even set out to enjoy what we have? If the latter, then Americans may catch up with Europeans, who are more likely with intention to include collectibles in their personal portfolios than we are. Obama of America spends his extracurricular energies on basketball; Sarkozy of France collects stamps. As noted in the London Evening Times, antiques and collectibles are part of the investment portfolio of many young British professionals: "One in six said they collected just as an investment. Eleven percent thought collections were as good an investment as stocks and bonds …" They said even if they didn't know how much they'd make, they felt confident they wouldn't lose money. Digging up antique gold and gemstones is a lot more fun than purchase orders for pharmaceuticals.

Jewelry is desirable for three reasons, and that won't change.

1. We buy for style's sake, to accessorize our fashions. When you're wearing something wonderful but want punctuation, a brilliantly designed $9.99 Deco ring at T.J. Maxx that resembles a Raymond Templier masterpiece is impossible to pass up.

2. Or we buy to wear and also purchase with an eye toward investment or resale. Before we plunk down $900 on an Iradj Moini moth brooch to make everyone envious at an elegant soiree, we want to be certain it will be worth more in a decade or hold its value (= forced savings) in the nearer future.

3. Or we buy purely as investment. Maybe you never wear necklaces, but recognize the value of a Sixties KJL creation that's dripping emerald pendants and just happens to close around the throat.

Jewelry also has some inherent qualities that assure an eternal sunshine of the golden kind, making it a reliable collecting destination where no one need be afraid of protracted darkness. An anagram is handy to help jewelry lovers remember why it's always OK to love and continue looking for more lariats and lavalieres:

(With a nod to Emeril): BAM!

B is for beauty. Jewelry is one of a limited group of collecting categories that has a two-way aesthetic. It, itself, is beautiful, yes, but also adds to the beauty and status of the wearer. Compare that with, say, guns and dolls. No one's toting his Derringers to a party to impress girls, and if you bring your baby Bru to brunch at the café, the stares won't be in admiration. Shimmering crystals glinting on a wrist or dangling from an earlobe, however, transfix and distract the gazes of onlookers and make them imagine you're even more beautiful than you are. Never underestimate the power of anything so pretty. Jewelry's got it, so jewelry's not going away.

A is for availability. (Ubiquity might be a better word, but it makes a bad anagram.) A character in Larry McMurtry's novel Cadillac Jack says, "Anything can be anywhere." That's true, but it's truest for costume jewelry. It's literally all over the place. Stop at any roadside retail dive connected to a filling station along a country highway … and you'll not only find vintage bracelets or brooches, but it's possible to discover a treasure – anywhere. A related "A" might be ad infinitum: there appears to be no end to the variety of this widely available commodity. About what other collectible object can you say: If you look for it on any given day, you'll find something you've never seen before? That allure is almost electrifying.

Courtesy Janet Romanchik collection; photograph by Ann M. Pitman

Brooch, polychrome rhinestones, 1960s, unmarked DeLizza and Elster "Juliana" jewelry (verified), 2" x 2".
$150-$200

M is for money. Costume jewelry can be acquired cheaply and some of it sold bullishly. It may take longer to turn a $1,000 profit on a $100 investment than it is to turn $3 into $30, but profit's definitely part of the picture, and that's useful for many more people than take advantage of it. Adolescents to octogenarians should develop a working knowledge of costume jewelry because it absolutely can help pay their bills, whether collegiate or pharmaceutical. The rap on costume jewelry is, unlike gold or precious gems, it has no inherent value. Detractors consider costume nothing short of fool's gold, and many view it as throwing money away on faddish junk. While they admit some costume jewelry possesses tremendous artistry and design integrity, they say it's in the eye of the beholder, so any given piece's appeal is less broad and its investment value less liquid. But very little money is required for entrée into the market for a new collector, and since costume jewelry sells regularly for hundreds and thousands of dollars, it's quite clear people consider it much more than base metal and glass.

S is for size. (Make that anagram "BAMS".) Jewelry's size is a huge factor in its appeal. Consider guns and dolls again. How much space does it take to house a hundred Winchester rifles … or Madame Alexanders? Collectors require major storage space for many categories. But 1,000 pieces of jewelry fit perfectly into a chest of drawers, manageable even for apartment dwellers. The psychological well-being of a collector is something else that should never be under-considered, so the feeling of not being burdened or over-crowded gives a lift to tender psyches rather than bringing on major depression in the face of cramped space.

For its beauty and value, jewelry bestows a great measure of joy on its wearers and bearers. Or, as I put it on T-shirts for a bijou bunch, "Life is cruel; buy jewels."

JEWELRY STYLES

Jewelry has been a part of every culture throughout time. It is often reflective of the times, as well as social and aesthetic movements, with each piece telling its own story through hidden clues that, when interpreted, will help solve the mysteries surrounding them.

Jewelry is generally divided into periods and styles. Each period may have several styles, with some of the same styles and types of jewelry being made in both precious and non-precious materials. Additionally, there are recurring style revivals, which are interpretations of an earlier period. For example, the Egyptian Revival that took place in the early and late 1800s, and then again in the 1920s.

Georgian, 1760-1837. Fine jewelry from this period is quite desirable, but few good-quality pieces have found their way to auction in recent years. Sadly, much jewelry from this period has been lost.

Victorian, 1837-1901. Queen Victoria of England ascended the throne in 1837 and remained queen until her death in 1901. The Victorian period is a long and prolific one; abundant with many styles of jewelry. It warrants being divided into three sub-periods: Early or Romantic period dating from 1837-1860; Mid or Grand period dating from 1860-1880; and Late or Aesthetic period dating from 1880-1901.

Sentiment and romance were significant factors in Victorian jewelry. Often, jewelry and clothing represented love and affection, with symbolic motifs such as hearts, crosses, hands, flowers, anchors, doves, crowns, knots, stars, thistles, wheat, garlands, horseshoes and moons. The materials of the time were also abundant and varied. They included silver, gold, diamonds, onyx, glass, cameo, paste, carnelian, agate, coral, amber, garnet, emeralds, opals, pearls, peridot (a green gemstone), rubies, sapphires, marcasites, cut steel, enameling, tortoise shell, topaz, turquoise, bog oak, ivory, jet, hair, gutta percha and vulcanite.

Sentiments of love were often expressed in miniatures. Sometimes they were representative of deceased loved ones, but often the miniatures were of the living. Occasionally, the miniatures depicted landscapes, cherubs or religious themes.

Hair jewelry was a popular expression of love and sentiment. The hair of a loved one was placed in a special compartment in a brooch or a locket, or used to form a picture under a glass compartment. Later in the mid-19th century, pieces of jewelry were made completely of woven hair. Individual strands of hair would be woven together to create necklaces, watch chains, brooches, earrings and rings.

In 1861, Queen Victoria's husband, Prince Albert, died. The queen went into mourning for the rest of her life, and Victoria required that the royal court wear black. This atmosphere spread to the populace and created a demand for mourning jewelry.

Mourning jewelry is typically black. When it first came into fashion, it was made from jet, fossilized wood. By 1850, there were dozens of English workshops making jet brooches, lockets, bracelets and necklaces. As the supply of jet dwindled, other materials were used such as vulcanite, gutta percha, bog oak and French jet.

By the 1880s, the somber mourning jewelry was losing popularity. Fashions had changed and the clothing was simpler and had an air of delicacy. The Industrial Revolution, which had begun in the early part of the century, was now in full swing and machine-manufactured jewelry was affordable to the working class.

Edwardian, 1890-1920. The Edwardian period takes its name England's King Edward VII. Though he ascended the throne in 1901, he and his wife, Alexandria of Denmark, exerted influence over the period before and after his ascension. The 1890s was known as La Belle Epoque. This was a time known for ostentation and extravagance. As the years passed, jewelry became simpler and smaller. Instead of wearing one large brooch, women were often found wearing several small lapel pins.

Brooch, gem-set 18k gold, Arts and Crafts style, the delicate openwork lacy gold mount in a winged design, set in the center top with a ring of circular-cut amethysts enclosing a large oval-cut amethyst, surrounded by various bands of gems including blue, purple and yellow sapphires, peridots, amethysts, rubies, green tourmalines, aquamarines and seed pearls, three gem-set pendant drops at the bottom, designed and signed by Frank Gardiner Hale (1876-1945), early 20th century, 2 x 2 1/2". **$10,575**

In the early 1900s, platinum, diamonds and pearls were prevalent in the jewelry of the wealthy, while paste was being used by the masses to imitate the real thing. The styles were reminiscent of the neo-classical and rococo motifs. The jewelry was lacy and ornate, feminine and delicate.

Arts & Crafts, 1890-1920. The Arts & Crafts movement was focused on artisans and craftsmanship. There was a simplification of form where the material was secondary to the design. Guilds of artisans banded together. Some jewelry was mass-produced, but the most highly prized examples of this period are handmade and signed by their makers. The pieces were simple and at times abstract. They could be hammered, patinated and acid etched. Common materials were brass, bronze, copper, silver, blister pearls, freshwater pearls, turquoise, agate, opals, moonstones, coral, horn, ivory, base metals, amber, cabachon-cut garnets and amethysts.

Art Nouveau, 1895-1910. In 1895, Samuel Bing opened a shop called "Maison de lArt Nouveau" at 22 Rue de Provence in Paris. Art Nouveau designs in the jewelry were characterized by a sensuality that took on the forms of the female figure, butterflies, dragonflies, peacocks, snakes, wasps, swans, bats, orchids, irises and other exotic flowers. The lines used whiplash curves to create a feeling of lushness and opulence.

1920s-1930s. Costume jewelry began its steady ascent to popularity in the 1920s. Since it was relatively inexpensive to produce, there was mass production. The sizes and designs of the jewelry varied. Often, it was worn a few times, disposed of and then replaced with a new piece. It was thought of as expendable, a cheap throwaway to dress up an outfit. Costume jewelry became so popular that it was sold in both the upscale stores and the "five and dime."

During the 1920s, fashions were often accompanied by jewelry that drew on the Art Deco movement, which got its beginning in Paris at the "Exposition Internationale des Arts Décoratifs et Industriels Modernes" held in 1925. The idea behind this movement was that form follows function. The style was characterized by simple, straight, clean lines, stylized motifs and geometric shapes. Favored materials included chrome, rhodium, pot metal, glass, rhinestones, Bakelite and celluloid.

One designer who played an important role was Coco Chanel. Though previously reserved for evening wear, Chanel wore it during the day, making it fashionable for millions of other women to do so, too.

With the 1930s came the Depression and the advent of World War II. Perhaps in response to the gloom, designers began using enameling and brightly colored rhinestones to create whimsical birds, flowers, circus animals, bows, dogs and just about every other figural form imaginable.

Retro Modern, 1939-1950. Other jewelry designs of the 1940s were big and bold. Retro Modern had a more substantial feel to it and designers began using larger stones to enhance the dramatic pieces. The jewelry was stylized and exaggerated. Common motifs included flowing scrolls, bows, ribbons, birds, animals, snakes, flowers and knots.

Sterling silver now became the metal of choice, often dipped in a gold wash known as vermeil.

Designers often incorporated patriotic themes of American flags, the V-sign, Uncle Sam's hat, airplanes, anchors and eagles.

Post-War Modern, 1945-1965. This was a movement that emphasized the artistic approach to jewelry making. It is also referred to as Mid-Century Modern. This approach was occurring at a time when the Beat Generation was prevalent. These avant-garde designers created jewelry that was handcrafted to illustrate the artist's own concepts and ideas. The materials often used were sterling, gold, copper, brass, enamel, cabochons, wood, quartz and amber.

1950s-1960s. The 1950s saw the rise of jewelry that was made purely of rhinestones: necklaces, bracelets, earrings and pins.

The focus of the early 1960s was on clean lines: pillbox hats and A-line dresses with short jackets were a mainstay for the conservative woman. The large, bold rhinestone pieces were no longer the must-have accessory. They were now replaced with smaller, more delicate gold-tone metal and faux pearls with only a hint of rhinestones.

At the other end of the spectrum was psychedelic-colored clothing, Nehru jackets, thigh-high miniskirts and go-go boots. These clothes were accessorized with beads, large metal pendants and occasionally big, bold rhinestones. By the late 1960s, there was a movement back to mother nature and the "hippie" look was born. Ethnic clothing, tie dye, long skirts, fringe and jeans were the prevalent style and the rhinestone had, for the most part, been left behind.

Mexican Silver, 1930-1970. Mexican silversmiths first made jewelry for tourists. The jewelry had pre-Hispanic and traditional Mexican motifs as well as some abstract modern designs. Artisans used silver, a combination of silver with brass or copper, alpaca, amethysts, malachite, obsidian, sodalite, tiger eye, turquoise, abalone, ebony, rosewood and enameling to create their original designs. While hundreds of artists set up their shops in the town of Taxco, Mexico, in the 30s and 40s creating a silversmith guild, there are only a relatively small number of well-known artisans who gained their reputation for their designs and craftsmanship.

OPENING PAGE:

Photo courtesy Leslie Hindman Auctioneers, Chicago; www.LeslieHindman.com

Brooch, 14k white gold and shell cameo, filigree depicting a lady in profile wearing a diamond-set pendant. Stamp: 14K. 7.90 dwts. **$146**

Bracelets

Bracelet, 18k yellow gold, wide mesh, 62.00 dwts. Length 7". **$1,952**

Bracelet, 14k yellow gold double-link charm, with various gold and gold-filled vintage and antique charms including two compasses, an agate arrowhead, two lockets, a tiny magnifying glass and others. 77.35 dwts. **$976**

Bracelet, Miriam Haskell Faux Pearl and Coral, Stamped: Miriam Haskell. **$231**

Bracelet, 18k yellow gold, Italian, in a textured mesh design. 62.67 dwts. **$2,684**

Bracelet, Hermes, silver with wheat enameling at side. Stamped: Hermes. **$366**

Bracelet, 18k yellow gold, platinum and diamond, Chaavae, containing numerous round brilliant-cut diamonds weighing approximately 2.50 carats total. Stamp: TGD 18K PLAT. 78.20 dwts. **$4,636**

Bracelet, Hermes, black leather cord and silver. Stamped: Hermes. **$274**

Bracelet, Victorian gold-filled in the style of a belt. **$61**

Bracelet, Victorian gold-filled with floral engravings. **$61**

Bracelet, enameled 18k gold and jadeite, Art Moderne style, composed of four wide arched gold links each centered by a carved blossom of green jadeite surrounded by black champlevé enamel and joined by triple-bar small links with further black enamel trim, French guarantee stamps and mark of Gross et Cie, Paris, 8" l. **$4,818**

Bracelet, Yves Saint Laurent Couture gilded wood, in a carved-leaf motif. **$976**

Bracelet, clamper, signed HAR, 1960, base metal with "French Provincial" (antiqued cream) enamel finish, floral glass motif, graduated aurora borealis diamante stones. Floral motif likely a replacement for simulated Baroque pearl cabochon. **$250+**

Bracelet, 18k yellow gold, lapis lazuli and diamond, containing numerous round brilliant-cut and single-cut diamonds weighing approximately 3.00 carats total and five large fluted fine blue lapis lazuli. 109.00 dwts. **$6,100**

Bracelet, white leather, silver plated metal and Plexiglas, cuff-style, a semi-rectangular metal cuff lined on the exterior with a wide band of white leather, inset near the top with a large rectangular block of Plexiglas, attributed to Courrèges, France, 1965-68, unsigned, inside length 5 3/4". **$717**

Bracelet, sapphire, emerald and 18k gold, cuff-type, the wide hinged gold band with a textured surface decorated with a repeating design of a large oval emerald cabochon encircled by sapphire cabochons alternating with pairs of sapphire cabochons. **$12,338**

Bracelet, 18k yellow gold, diamond and emerald bangle, Chaavae, containing one oval cabochon cut emerald weighing approximately 4.45 carats and numerous round brilliant-cut diamonds weighing approximately 2.70 carats total. 59.10 dwts. **$5,124**

Bracelet, 18k yellow gold, diamond and ruby bangle, Chaavae, containing one oval cabochon ruby weighing approximately 4.50 carats and numerous round brilliant-cut diamonds weighing approximately 1.10 carats total. Stamp: TGD 18K PLAT. 49.60 dwts. **$3,660**

Bracelet, 18k yellow gold, red coral and diamond hinged bangle containing 60 round brilliant-cut diamonds weighing approximately 1.70 carats total and a large curved coral measuring approximately 60 mm x 15 mm. 39.80 dwts. **$3,904**

Bracelet, chrysoberyl, enamel, diamond and gold, cuff-style, Renaissance Revival style, the wide band set with cat's-eye quatrefoil designs punctuated by rose-cut diamond florettes joined by applied wirework on a pale blue enameled ground, white and black enamel accents, gadrooned edge, hallmark of Falize Freres, France, and French guarantee stamps, enamel loss, one diamond and cat's-eye missing, 19th century, inside circumference 6 1/2". **$56,400**

Bracelet, diamond and 14k gold, bangle-type, the back half a solid band and the front half a delicate flaring openwork design of leaves centered by a flower bead- and bezel-set overall with old European- and mine-cut diamonds, diamonds weighing about 1.99 carats, platinum-topped 14k gold mount, interior circumference 6 1/2". **$2,585**

The abbreviation "dwts" stands for pennyweights. For example, 100 pennyweights equal 155.5 grams, or about five Troy ounces. By comparison, 100 carats equal about .64 Troy ounce.

Photo courtesy Kathy Flood

Bracelet, 1960s, "Asian Princess" figural links with simulated jade spirals, amethyst crystals and faux pearls, unmarked Selini, 7 1/2" x 1 7/8". **$175-$300**

Photo courtesy Leslie Hindman Auctioneers, Chicago; www.LeslieHindman.com

Bracelet, 18k yellow gold and diamond, containing numerous round brilliant-cut diamonds weighing approximately 3.75 carats total. 53.20 dwts. Length 7". **$3,416**

Bracelet, diamond, enamel and yellow gold, bangle-type, the wide tapering foliate- engraved bangle mounted with a large engraved oval plaque fitted with a large stylized daisy-like flower and leaves trimmed with opalescent pink and green enamel and rose-cut diamond accents, Tiffany and Co., New York, in original box with an inscription dated 1866, interior diameter 5 3/8". **$2,468**

Bracelet, emerald, diamond and 14k gold, the wide snake chain centered by a crossed wide ribbon design set with emerald-cut emeralds and 12 small mine-cut diamonds, inscribed 1863, later safety, minor solder, 7 1/2" l. **$2,938**

Bracelet, gem-set enamel, composed of large figure-eight openings, each enameled in various colors and centering a small blossom with seed pearls surrounding a turquoise center, the large squared central openwork plaque composed of ornate leafy scrolls enameled in various colors and centered by a large oval-cut aquamarine framed by a band of alternating seed pearls and turquoise beads, 18k gold and silver mount, made in Switzerland with European and French import stamps, 6 3/8" l. **$3,055**

Bracelet, "Vauxhall Glass," pearl and 15k gold, centered by a large dark blue glass oval plaque centered by a small sprig with a baroque pearl and an old single-cut diamond mélée flower, a simple gold frame and a bracelet composed of small, square hinged gold plaques each with flower and leaf engraving, with later safety chain, England, mid-19th century, 7 1/4" l. **$353**

Bracelet, platinum and diamond, composed of articulated geometric-form plaques set with three marquise, four half-moon, ninety baguette, and 394 full- and single-cut diamonds, approx. total weight 11 carats, 7 1/4" l. **$22,913**

Bracelet, earrings, ring, brooch, gold (18k), diamond and ruby, "Bat" pattern, the flexible links each designed as a stylized bat set with princess-cut diamonds and circular-cut rubies, diamonds weighing about 1.74 carats, signed. .... **$5,523 set**

Bracelet, silver, composed of wide, concave links, No. ZZ 571, mark of maker Antonio, Taxco, 6" l. **$1,116**

Bracelet, silver and wood, cuff-style, wide band composed of alternating silver and wood scallops with bead accents, maker's mark of Spratling, Taxco. **$999**

Bracelet, citrine, diamond and 14k white gold, bangle-type, the tapering wide band prong-set at the top by a large rectangular fancy-cut citrine flanked by tapering panels of fancy pierced leafy scrolls set with full-cut diamond mélée, diamonds weighing about 4.57 carats, two diamonds missing, interior circumference 6 1/2". **$4,994**

Bracelet, platinum and diamond, composed of three large openwork rectangular links centered by a row of three large marquise-cut diamonds surrounded by stepped openwork designs and border bands set with further baguette and full-cut diamonds, each long link joined by wide bars and narrow oblong diamond-set open links, diamonds weighing about 20.70 carats, millegrain accents, 7 1/4" l. **$38,775**

Bracelet, platinum, diamond, emerald and onyx, composed of three long flexible plaques spaced by pairs of oblong links, set throughout with 318 old European- and single-cut diamonds, approx. 8.40 carats, highlighted by carved emerald leaves and cabochon onyx, millegrain accents and open gallery, a few nicks and abrasions to emeralds, 7" l. **$14,100**

Bracelet, platinum, sapphire and diamond, a wide flat band composed of sections with rows of bezel- and bead-set old European- and single-cut diamonds alternating with openwork sections with a geometric arrangement of further diamonds and calibré-cut sapphire highlights all centered

Photo courtesy Alderfer Auction & Appraisal, Hatfield, Pa.; www.AlderferAuction.com

Bracelet, Diamond and Ruby Bangle, 18KY, six round old mine-cut diamonds (3.00 ct.), twelve 4.00 mm x 3.00 mm oval rubies, 63.2 grams. **$5,148**

by a large round diamond, diamonds weighing about 8.65 carats, millegrain accents, engraved sides, 6 3/4" l. .**$17,625**

Bracelet, sapphire, emerald, diamond, platinum and 14k yellow gold, designed as graduating lines of prong-set cabochon blue sapphires and emeralds joined by curving yellow gold links, two links with bead-set diamond mélée, with original box, 7 1/4" l. **$18,800**

Bracelet, Salvador Teran, sterling silver, 7" long, hallmarked, link style, 2" diameter inside, 83.6 grams. **$643**

Bracelet, gem-set and enameled 18k gold, bangle-type, the wide hinged bangle decorated at the top with an abstract design with six scattered prong-set, step-cut citrines surrounded by scattered full-cut diamonds against a ground with black enameled geometric blocks with the black enamel continuing around the gold band, by Ugo Bellini, Florence, Italy, contemporary, boxed, interior circumference 6 1/2". **$1,880**

Bracelet, gold (20k and 18k), cuff-style, designed as a 20k gold human hand with four fingers opposing the thumb, completed by an 18k white gold cuff, designed by Bruno Martinazzi, signed "Martinazzi X/XII". **$16,450**

Bracelet, silver and rhinestone, the flat side straps set down the sides with three rows of circular-cut rhinestones flanked by outer rows of baguette rhinestones, the swelled central section composed of arched links set overall with small circular-cut and larger baguette rhinestones with a large circular-cut rhinestone in the center, France, circa 1930, mark of maker and French assay mark for silver, 7" l. **$1,016**

Bracelet, gold tone and enamel, "H" style bangle-type, the hinged wide band enameled in bright red, swiveling H-form closure, signed. **$470**

Bracelet, diamond and 18k gold, cuff-style, the wide flexible band composed of long rectangular links each set with a long oval ring of full-cut diamonds, the top cast with a large stylized scarab, diamonds weighing about 12.32 carats, French guarantee stamps and mark of the maker, signed Cartier, Paris, expands from 5 3/4 x 6 1/4". **$12,925**

Bracelet, diamond and gem-set 18k gold, bypass bangle-type, the sides textured and trimmed with bead-set single-cut diamonds and ending in a figural lion heads with collars also trimmed with diamonds and set with ruby eyes, Greek hallmarks. **$1,645**

Brooches

Brooch, enameled and gem-set gold, designed as a comical octopus decorated with basse taille enamel in shades of dark and light blue, the ends of the tentacles set with full-cut diamonds, ruby eyes, 18k bicolor gold mount, 1 3/4 x 2". **$940**

Photo courtesy Leslie Hindman Auctioneers, Chicago; www.LeslieHindman.com

Bracelet, Chanel Ivory Plastic, Chunky Bangle, 1985, with a faux pearl inset, ruby, and emerald cabochon stones. Stamped: Chanel. **$610**

Brooch, emerald, diamond and 18k gold, designed as a tight spiral with two tiers prong- and bead-set with 98 single-cut diamond mélée, highlighted with an inner band of 21 circular-cut emeralds, diamonds weighing about 1.00 carat, 1 1/2" l. **$2,703**

Brooch, gem-set 18k bicolor gold, designed as a round grotesque mask with flame-like beard and hair, bead-set with 26 circular-cut rubies and 125 full-cut diamonds, two circular-cut emeralds in the eyes, signed "R.W.," 2" d. **$4,113**

Brooch, gem-set gold, carved rock crystal and emerald, designed as a flower on a leafy stem, the large blossom with the five petals carved from frosted clear rock crystal centered by small diamonds surrounded by small round emeralds, the long curved gold stem with one gold leaf and two other oblong leaves carved from emeralds, the stem also with a tiny flower with blue sapphire petals around a diamond center, 14k gold mount, 2" h. **$764**

Brooch, 18k yellow gold, Tiffany & Co., in a twisted rope and tassel design. Stamped: Tiffany & Co. 18K Italy. 18.70 dwts. **$2,074**

Brooch, gold-backed silver, diamond and ruby in the form of an eagle with turtle in clenched claws, containing numerous round rubies weighing approximately 6.50 carats total and numerous old European-cut diamonds, single-cut and rose-

Photo courtesy Leslie Hindman Auctioneers, Chicago; www.LeslieHindman.com

Bracelet, Hermes, hinged and gold-plated with enameled decoration at front. Stamped: Hermes. **$274**

cut diamonds weighing approximately 3.00 carats total. 27.80 dwts. **$1,708**

Brooch and earrings, seed pearls, Late Georgian, in an openwork floral design. **$305**

Brooch, gold-plated brass and glass stone, design inspired by Josef Hoffmann (1870-1956), an open rectangular bar frame enclosing vertical bars topped by dark glass cabochons flanking an openwork design composed of blue, red, purple and green glass cabochons, marked "Ugo Correani Per Chloe," designed by Karl Lagerfeld and Ugo Correani for Chloe, France, 1984, 4 1/4" sq. **$538**

Brooch, jadeite, diamond and 14k gold, an oval pierced and carved jadeite plaque flanked by gold bow designs highlighted by full-cut diamond mélée, maker's mark of Wordley, Allsopp and Bliss (Newark, N.J.), retailed by Tiffany and Co., boxed, 2" l. **$2,938**

Brooch, ruby, diamond and platinum, an angled round bar wrapped by three ribbon and buckle-style devices, channel- and bead-set with 64 full-cut and 48 baguette diamonds and channel-set with step- and calibré-cut rubies, diamonds weighing about 12.05 carats, 2 1/2" l. **$24,675**

Brooch, 14k white and yellow gold, red coral and diamond, the large oval red coral cabochon measuring approximately 42.00 mm x 30.00 mm with numerous single-cut diamonds weighing approximately 0.60 carat total. 19.50 dwts. **$1,464**

Brooch, silver and bronze, designed as two curled silver ribbons suspended from a bronze disk, mark of Spratling, Taxco, 3 1/8" l. **$470**

Brooch, chalcedony, citrine and 18k gold, chalcedony piece carved as a stylized scrolling shell design with an inlaid center band of gold below a row of four inset circular-cut citrines and with an arched band of citrines set across the top, signed, 2" l. **$3,525**

Brooch, reverse-painted crystal and 14k gold, a large rectangular mount with slightly bowed top and bottom, set with a reverse-painted crystal depicting two hound heads, 5/8 x 1 3/8". **$1,880**

Brooch, Chanel Byzantine Red and Green Pate de Verre Maltese Cross, 1994, in the style of Robert Goossens, with a pendant hook, baroque pearls. Stamped: Chanel. **$732**

Photo courtesy Leslie Hindman Auctioneers, Chicago; www.LeslieHindman.com

Brooch, Chanel Byzantine Red and Green Pate de Verre Maltese Cross, 1994, in the style of Robert Goossens, with a pendant hook, baroque pearls. Stamped: Chanel. **$732**

Photo courtesy Leslie Hindman Auctioneers, Chicago; www.LeslieHindman.com

Brooch, 18k yellow gold, lapis lazuli and diamond, in a floral motif, containing numerous round brilliant-cut diamonds weighing approximately 7.00 carats total, a large square fluted lapis lazuli cabochon and 14 lapis lazuli petals. 37.20 dwts. **$4,392**

Brooch, Chanel Gripoix Frameless Blue Camellia Flower, circa 1970s, with a pendant hook. Stamped: Chanel. **$488**

Brooch, Chanel Gripoix Red, Amber, Blue and Clear Maltese Cross, circa 1980s, with a pendant hook. Stamped: Chanel. **$610**

Brooch, Chanel Gripoix Lavender and Purple frameless, 1998, with a rhinestone center. Stamped: Chanel. **$610**

Brooches, painted wood heads, unmarked Elzac, 1940s, 2 3/4". .... **$50-$100 each**

Brooch, 18k yellow gold, diamond, amethyst and green tourmaline, Italian, containing four pear-shape amethysts weighing approximately 15.60 carat total, nine round brilliant-cut diamonds weighing approximately 0.28 carat total and 12 marquise-cut green tourmalines weighing approximately 5.70 carats total, with double pin back and pendant bale. Stamp: 750 1021 AL. 28.98 dwts. **$1,830**

Brooch, silver and shell cameo depicting Apollo and Aphrodite, set in a silver prong mounting. 15.60 dwts. **$396**

Brooch, 18k yellow gold and shell cameo, depicting a double eagle with cross topped crown and shield. 10.71 dwts. **$457**

Brooch, 14k yellow gold and coral cameo, depicting a woman in profile, in a ornate yellow gold and seed pearl frame. 8.70 dwts. **$335**

Brooch, silver and shell cameo, depicting an outdoor scene with Grecian women and cherubs. 10.70 dwts. **$305**

Brooch and earrings, mourning set, 9k black onyx and seed pearls in a buckle motif. .... **$305 set**

Photo by Kathy Flood, courtesy the book, Collecting Costume Jewelry Christmas Tree Pins.

Brooches, Christmas trees, vintage 1930s, Art Deco, French galalith with Swarovski crystal square-cuts in base, unsigned, by Woloch, 4 5/8". **$150-$200**

Brooch, yellow gold and carved coral, depicting the bust of a Grecian woman. 4.10 dwts. **$85**

Brooch, yellow gold and shell cameo, depicting the Greek goddess Artemis. 7.10 dwts. **$61**

Brooch, gem-set tricolor 18k gold, designed as a large beetle-like winged insect, the back centered by a large cabochon emerald surrounded by a ring of small cabochon blue sapphires, two of the wings and the lower body set with small single- and full-cut diamonds, the neck set with two pear-shaped rubies flanking a pear-shaped andalusite (a stone named after Andalusia, the province of Spain where it was first discovered), the head mounted with large circular-cut diamond eyes flanking a cabochon blue sapphire, signed by Cazzaniga, Rome, 2 1/8" l. **$3,055**

Brooch, gold (14k), an abstract rounded outer frame enclosing three openwork panels, one framing a fish, one framing a row of standing figures and the third framing a running unicorn, designed by Eric de Kolb (1916-2001), signed, circa 1960s-1970s, 1 1/2 x 1 3/4". **$353**

Brooch, ruby, cultured pearl and 18k gold, designed as large smiling lips bead-set with about 212 circular-cut rubies, the mouth set with ten white pearl teeth, designed by Dali, unsigned but made by Henryk Kaston (violinist and bow maker, born 1910). **$16,450**

Brooch, sterling silver, moonstone and sapphire, designed as a flower with five long oval moonstone petals centered by a circular-cut sapphire, long thin silver stem and leaves, signed by the Parenti Sisters, Boston, first half 20th century, 3 1/4" l. **$441**

Brooch, sunstone feldspar and 18k gold, designed as the head of a blackamoor wearing turban with a curved petal-form necklace, signed by Luis Sanz, Madrid, Spain, 1 1/2" l. **$705**

Brooch and earrings, 18k yellow gold in original box. 9.30 dwts. .... **$518 set**

Brooch, 14k yellow gold and shell cameo, depicting two women, in a foliate frame. 13.20 dwts. **$488**

Brooch, yellow gold and lava stone cameo, depicting a Victorian woman in profile, in a yellow gold rope-style frame. 15.30 dwts. **$122**

Brooch and earrings, yellow gold and hardstone cameo, each white on black onyx carving depicting a lady in profile. 18.50 dwts. .... **$1,220 set**

Brooch, 18k yellow gold, 14k white gold and diamond, in a floral motif, containing numerous round brilliant-cut diamonds measuring approximately 1.00 mm each and weighing approximately 2.65 carats total. 23.70 dwts. **$2,684**

Brooch, 18k yellow gold, turquoise, lapis lazuli, ruby and diamond, containing four oval turquoise cabochons, one oval lapis lazuli cabochon, 15 round ruby cabochons and 16 round brilliant-cut diamonds weighing approximately 1.00 carat total. 24.00 dwts. **$1,586**

Brooch, silver and shell cameo, depicting the Madonna and child. 800 silver. 4.90 dwts. **$122**

Brooch, amethyst and diamond, oblong quatrefoil design centered by a clipped-corner amethyst within a pierced frame, bead- and bezel-set overall with old mine-, single- and European-cut diamonds, platinum and 18k gold mount, in a fitted box marked "Jays of London," Edwardian, missing brooch attachment. **$5,405**

Brooch, diamond and gold, a large starburst design, pavé-set with 81 old European-cut diamonds weighing about .926 carat, platinum-topped 14k gold mount with removable pin stem, Edwardian, England, early 20th century. **$22,325**

Brooch, diamond and gold, bow-form, the top four-loop fancy openwork gold bow set with table- and rose-cut diamonds, suspending a small bow pendant topped with scrolls also set with diamonds and suspending another cross-form pendant with scrolling details further set with diamonds, gold mount, diamonds possibly foiled, later pin stem, evidence of solder, 1 3/4 x 3 7/8". **$3,819**

Brooch, enameled 14k gold and freshwater pearl, Art Nouveau style, an openwork design of a swimming mermaid with swirling hair and red basse-taille enameled tail, a freshwater pearl mounted below her extended arm, diamond accents. **$411**

Brooch, sapphire, diamond and 14k gold, designed as a dancing ballerina with her hands above her head, a cabochon sapphire face with three diamonds forming a tiara, the flaring ruffled tutu set with scattered small prong-set sapphires. **$881**

Brooch, enameled 14k gold and seed pearls, Art Nouveau style, designed with the profile bust of an Art Nouveau maiden with a butterfly-wing-like headdress enameled in shaded green to yellow with red dots, against an openwork vining, mount set with seed pearls, unsigned, 1 1/4" l. **$2,820**

Brooch, gem-set 14k gold, in the shape of a gold salamander, pavé-set down the body with opal cabochons, step-cut peridot accent on the head, circa 1920, 2" l. **$529**

Brooch, gold (18k) and diamond, Art Nouveau style, a large square gold plaque chased with a design of three angels with a censer and casket amid swirling incense, edged with a narrow border of rose-cut diamonds, French guarantee stamp, late 19th - early 20th century, pin stem closure replaced. **$940**

Brooch, gold and hand-painted, mourning-type, a thin gold mount and frame enclosing a long oval hand-painted scene of a memorial obelisk centered by a covered urn above initials against a landscape of hair work poplar trees and ink work details, the back inscribed and dated 1782, Georgian era, England, 1 1/4" l. **$2,468**

Brooch, green tourmaline, seed pearls and 14k gold, Arts and Crafts style, centered by a long rectangular fancy-cut green tourmaline flanked by scroll and floret gold ends accented with seed pearls, unsigned piece by Edward Oakes (1891-1960), early 20th century, 5/8 x 1 1/2" l. **$5,581**

Brooch, Limoges enamel and 15k gold, the round enameled center decorated with a white cherub with palette and canvas against a black ground, the scalloped gold frame applied with bead and wirework designs, first half 19th century, 1" d. **$676**

Brooch, micro-mosaic and 14k gold, the round center in polychrome tesserae depicting a recumbent lamb with banner on a red platform representing the Agnus Dei, within a wide gold frame ornately decorated with rope-twist and grape leaves, 19th century, 1 1/4" d. **$411**

Brooch, platinum, emerald and sapphire, Mughal-style, designed as a large diamond- form floral-carved emerald tablet within a scrolling narrow frame channel-set with calibré-cut emeralds and sapphires, cabochon sapphire highlights, with pendant hook, signed "Cartier N.Y.," evidence of solder at pin stem. **$270,000**

Brooch, platinum, jadeite and diamond, composed of three green jadeite cylinders each capped at both ends with diamond-set pointed arches, convertible into three pins, designed and signed by Raymond Yard (firm established 1922). **$6,756**

Brooch, lapis lazuli and 18k gold, model of a stylized snail with a gold body and the shell carved from lapis, signed, Paris, 1 1/2" l. **$999**

Brooch, moonstone and 14k gold, Arts and Crafts style, the oblong gold mount decorated with leaves and delicate scrolls, centered by an oval moonstone flanked by round cabochon moonstones, unsigned work of Edward Oakes (1891-1960), 1 1/2" l. **$5,875**

Brooch, pietra dura, a large oval plaque depicting a floral bouquet with a rose, lily-of-the-valley and forget-me-nots on a black ground, mounted in a ribbon and floret gilt wirework frame, mid-19th century, 2 x 2 1/2". **$646**

Brooch, Shakudo, enamel and 18k gold, the large round central disk depicting a raised design of a Japanese samurai with sword and fan, within a polychrome blue and white enamel frame with red stone accents, the reverse with a locket compartment, minor enamel loss, 19th century, 1 1/2" d. **$1,175**

Brooch, sterling silver, Art Nouveau style, designed as a bar of overlapping graduated medallions each molded in relief with a bust portrait of an Art Nouveau maiden or a man, No. 598, mark of Geo. W. Shiebler and Co., New York, early 20th century, 2 5/8" l. **$235**

Brooch, gem-set 14k gold, Egyptian Revival style, designed as a winged scarab with the body formed by an oval amazonite cabochon enclosed by thin diamond-set bands and flanked by small S-scroll snakes and tall curved feathered gold wings bezel-set with old European-cut diamonds and step-cut rubies, European assay marks, possibly Austrian. **$4,230**

Brooch, green chalcedony, enamel and 14k gold, an oblong open ring of chalcedony carved with stylized floral designs, each end mounted with an openwork pierced gold tapering bar highlighted with orange and black enamel, mark of Carter, Howe and Gough, Newark, N.J., 3" l. **$1,880**

Brooch, jadeite, onyx, diamond and gold, rectangular openwork plaque centered by a design of overlapping circles each set with an old European-cut diamond and trimmed with rose-cut diamonds all flanked by green jadeite panels, within a rectangular border of calibré-cut onyx and an outer border band of small rose-cut diamonds, French guarantee stamps, 7/8 x 1 7/8". **$9,988**

Brooch, platinum, coral and diamond, centered by a long oval floral and scroll pierce- carved coral plaque framed by baguette and single-cut diamond mélée, onyx highlights. **$2,233**

Brooch, platinum, rock crystal and diamond, a large open diamond composed of rock crystal sections capped by a geometric band set with three large old European-cut diamonds and small full- and single-cut diamonds, the bottom tip set with a floret device further set with diamonds, originally a dress clip, diamonds weighing about 3.50 carats. **$3,525**

Brooch-pendant, jadeite, a large pierce-carved oval green jadeite plaque with overall vines, flowers and a bird, platinum fittings, 7/8 x 1 3/4". **$2,115**

Brooch and earrings, pink coral, the brooch of squared shape carved in the center with the head of a classical lady framed by leafy roses and carved at each side with another classical profile, suspending three carved coral teardrops, the longest central one carved with a classical head, the matching earrings with the small top carved as a classical head suspending a larger tapering carved plaque carved with another classical head and suspending three carved coral teardrops, 14k yellow gold mounts, Victorian. .... **$2,350 set**

Brooch-pendant, enameled 18k gold and diamond, a flat round disk centering a small hand-painted image of a maiden with a flower garland framed by light green guilloché enamel and delicate platinum overlay bead-set with rose-cut diamonds, a seed pearl border frame, Edwardian era, early 20th century, No. 3443. .... **$940**

Brooch-pendant, reverse-painted crystal and 18k gold, the large round domed crystal reverse-painted with a scene of chickadee on a pine bough, mounted in a gold twig and leaf frame, American made, 1 1/4" d. **$2,703**

Ear clips and Earrings

Ear clips, Billy Boy, 1989, silver tone in a skull-and-bones design with rhinestone eyes. Stamped: Billy Boy. **$457**

Photo courtesy Leslie Hindman Auctioneers, Chicago; www.LeslieHindman.com

Earrings, 18k yellow, white gold and diamond, Modele Sterle Paris, each earring containing 36 round brilliant-cut diamonds measuring approximately 2.50 mm and weighing approximately 4.35 carats total. Signed: Modele Sterle Paris. 14.20 dwts. **$5,368**

Photo courtesy Leslie Hindman Auctioneers, Chicago; www.LeslieHindman.com

Earrings, yellow gold, turquoise and seed pearls, circa 1880, containing numerous graduated round white seed pearls and graduated turquoise cabochons, in a fitted leather box. 10.20 dwts. **$2,928**

Ear clips, Chanel, 1980s, with large cone-like drops with Chanel stamped at center, logo at front. **$305**

Ear clips, Chanel Gripoix Pink and Blue, 1997, with rhinestones at center, multiple exaggerated tassels. Stamped: Chanel. **$1,220**

Ear clips, Chanel Gripoix Pink, Green Blue and Pearl, circa 1980s, with an exaggerated drop pendant with baroque pearl fringe. Stamped: Chanel. **$1,220**

Ear clips, Chanel Gripoix Ornate Purple, 1984, with purple and pearl poured-glass tassels. Stamped: Chanel. **$610**

Ear clips, Chanel Gripoix Blue, circa 1980s, with baroque poured-glass pearls. Stamped: Chanel. **$732**

Ear clips, Chanel Gripoix Turquoise Cluster, mid-century, with rhinestones throughout. No stamping. **$976**

Ear clips, Chanel Gripoix Green Camellia Flower, circa 1970s, with drop pendants. Stamped Chanel. **$1,220**

Ear clips, Christian Lacroix, with bows and rhinestones. Stamped: Christian Lacroix. **$48**

Ear clips, 18k yellow gold and turquoise in a floral motif. 9.10 dwts. **$732**

Earrings, opal and diamond, with multicolor precious opal briolettes measuring approximately 16 mm each in length and two old European-cut diamonds weighing approximately 0.30 carat total and numerous small rose-cut diamonds. 3.69 dwts. **$1,708**

Earrings, grisaille enamel and 18k gold, pendant-type, the wide gold oval mount centered by a grisaille enameled scene of a dancing cherub, the border and upper loop finely detailed with C-scrolls and applied bead and wirework, in a fitted box, 1 3/4" l. **$5,581**

Earrings, pearl and 18k gold, Art Nouveau style, pendant-type, the top designed as an open flower and leaves centered

Photo courtesy Leslie Hindman Auctioneers, Chicago; www.LeslieHindman.com

Earrings. Art Deco Silver and Enamel, screw back. **$61**

by a small European-cut diamond and suspending a foliate-designed gold framework enclosing a rounded blister pearl, European hallmarks, late 19th - early 20th century, 2 5/8" l. **$4,994**

Earrings, yellow gold, lapis lazuli and pearl, in a fringe design, with drop-shape lapis lazuli measuring approximately 30.00 mm in length. **$457**

Earrings, Yves Saint Laurent Couture Rose Quartz, with three drop-down stones. **$122**

Earrings, 14k yellow gold and ruby cabochon and ancient coin, 15.14 dwts. **$488**

Earrings, 18k yellow and white gold, diamond and lapis lazuli, containing numerous round brilliant-cut diamonds weighing approximately 1.50 carats total and six fine blue lapis lazuli carved flutes, with 14 karat yellow gold backs. 22.50 dwts. **$1,464**

Earrings, aquamarine, diamond and platinum, pendant-type, a three-leaf top suspending angular open loops set overall with single- and old European-cut diamonds and baguettes and centered by a rectangular step-cut aquamarine, millegrain accents, diamonds weighing about 3.10 carats. **$3,408**

Earrings, chalcedony, coral, marcasite and onyx, each designed as a shaped blue chalcedony tablet suspended from a marcasite pagoda form with coral bead accents, cabochon onyx tops, silver mounts, hallmark of Theodor Fahrner (Pforzheim, Germany, in business 1855-1979), circa 1930. .... **$2,938**

Necklaces

Necklace, Robert Goossens, Vermeil and Amethyst Bead, with a graduating band of double bullhead links surmounting amethyst beads, mounted in vermeil. **$1,220**

Necklace, Alexis Kirk Gold-tone Breastplate, 1980s. Stamped: Alexis Kirk. **$146**

Necklace, 18k yellow gold and diamond, Wander, France, containing numerous round brilliant-cut diamonds weighing approximately 3.10 carats total. Stamp: WANDER FRANCE. 62.10 dwts. Length 17". **$4,636**

Necklace and Ear clips Set, Chanel Gripoix Dark Red and Pearl Multi-strand, 1984, necklace with a red cabochon spacers, pendant with rhinestone trim and pearl tassel fringe. Stamped: Chanel. Ear clips in an ornate setting with pearl briolettes. Stamped: Chanel. .... **$5,124 set**

Necklace, Chanel Gripoix Large Green, Amber, Red and Purple, 1980s, with all-over poured glass cabochons, multiple circle links with drop pendants. Stamped: Chanel. **$4,636**

Necklace, Chanel Pearl Pate de Verre Byzantine, 1999, in the style of Robert Goossens. Stamped: Chanel. **$915**

Necklace, Chanel Gripoix Pink, Purple and Green, circa 1970s, with carved poured glass in a floral motif, with rhinestones throughout. Stamped: Chanel. **$4,880**

Necklace, Chanel Gripoix Red Byzantine with Disk Pendant, circa 1970s. Stamped: Chanel. **$1,220**

Necklace, Coro, in gold hardware, with multiple layers of mini-chain links and gold beads. Stamped: Coro. **$85**

Necklace, Gerda Lynggarde Blue Crystal Torsade, 1980s, with a horn wood clasp. **$732**

Necklace, Miriam Haskell Faux Pearl with four strands and a gold-tone clasp. Stamped: Miriam Haskell. **$219**

Necklace, Hobe Rhinestone with multiple dropped-feathered details. Stamped: Hobe. **$231**

Necklace, Hobe Diamond Rhinestone, 1950s, in a collar style with a floating floral pendant. Faint stamp at interior clasp: Hobe. **$915**

Necklace, Kenneth Jay Lane for Avon Seashells Charm, 1970s. Stamped: KJL for Avon. **$122**

Necklace with Matching Ear clips, Kenneth Jay Lane Duchess of Windsor, 1980s. Stamped: Kenneth Lane. **$305**

Necklace, Kenneth Jay Lane, Flower, 1980s, with pearl leaves, rhinestone centers. Stamped: Kenneth Lane. **$518**

Photo courtesy Leslie Hindman Auctioneers, Chicago; www.LeslieHindman.com

Necklace, 14k yellow gold, diamond and red coral multi-strand, containing numerous single-cut diamonds weighing approximately 2.35 carats and nine strands of red coral beads measuring approximately 5.00 mm 6.00 mm. **$1,952**

Photo courtesy Leslie Hindman Auctioneers, Chicago; www.LeslieHindman.com

Necklace, Schiaparelli Gold-tone, with blue rhinestones, fish hook clasp. Stamped: Schiaparelli. **$396**

Necklace, Trifari, a four-strand pearl choker, with rhinestone pendant and rhinestone encrusted clasp. Stamped: Trifari. **$610**

Necklace, Yves Saint Laurent Red, Green, and Purple Glass Beads, 1970s. Stamped: YSL. **$244**

Necklace, Yves Saint Laurent chain link, gold-tone chunky link choker with hook clasp. **$457**

Necklace, agate and 15k yellow gold, composed of hinged narrow rectangular engraved gold plaques each set with two agate, jasper or bloodstone panels flanking a foil-backed cabochon, Scotland, 19th century, 16" l. **$8,519**

Necklace, carved nephrite, the long green serpentine sides each carved as a dragon joined at the front with small links and a carved fruit-form cabochon, in a silver mount. **$2,115**

Necklace, carved ruby, diamond and platinum, composed of ornate openwork platinum links with geometric, feather-style and ribbon designs set overall with old European-, mine- and single-cut diamond mélée, the openwork links joining 12 graduating oval carved rubies with stylized floral and geometric designs all centered by a large oval cameo-carved ruby featuring the bust profile of a lady, seed pearl accents, gemstones weighing about 9.27 carats, circa 1920, 15 1/2" l. **$22,325**

Necklace, garnet, graduated wide form set overall with faceted garnets in a graduating florette design, gilt-metal mount, Victorian, one stone missing, 14 1/2" l. **$1,763**

Necklace, gold (18k), composed of large graduating quatrefoil links each with a domed center with a sunburst design of alternating solid and filigree panels, the same sunburst design continues on the flat sides of each link with bead highlights, late 19th century, 16" l. **$2,233**

Necklace, onyx and enameled gold, composed of graduating open carved onyx rings each suspending a bulbous onyx drop and joined by small diamond-shaped, floral-engraved and black-enameled links, the three central links enclosing a second smaller link, 19th century, 14" l. **$2,350**

Necklace, gem-set platinum and diamond, the wide front section composed of leaf- carved, disk-form and cabochon rubies, sapphires and emerald leaves attached to a diamond-set band and with geometric diamond-set links, finished with a narrow link chain of diamonds, diamonds weighing about 8.96 carats, signed "Mauboussin - France," No. X1024, 16 1/2" l. **$149,000**

Necklace, jadeite, onyx and 10k gold, composed of bezel-set oval jadeite cabochon links joined by onyx-set flat bars and

Photo courtesy Leslie Hindman Auctioneers, Chicago; www.LeslieHindman.com

Necklace, Kenneth Jay Lane, star in gold-tone chain links, hanging stars with rhinestones. **$61**

wire-wrapped links, suspending a green jadeite pi ring, 16" l. $823

Necklace, carnelian and enamel, five graduating floral-carved and pierced carnelian plaques joined by bow-form celadon green and black enamel links, seed pearl accents, 14k gold mount, partially obliterated hallmark for Carter Howe and Gough, Newark, N.J., 16 1/2" l. $4,700

Necklace plaques, gold (18k), diamond and turquoise "Placque de Cou," Art Nouveau design, largest 2 x 7" rectangular curved openwork plaque centered with carved turquoise woman's head with chased flowing gold hair highlighted by old European-cut diamond blossoms, signed "Lalique," similar 2" square plaque also with carved turquoise head and signed "Lalique," also a pair of smaller openwork plaques set with diamond blossoms, accompanied by 18k gold flattened baton-link chain, 20 1/2" l., two gold satin ribbons, one gold satin cord, and two screwdrivers, may be worn as chokers or necklaces, one plaque with brooch fitting. $49,938 all

Necklet, platinum and diamond, designed as a long hinged bow with upward curling ends and a circular center with swirled leaves, bead- and bezel-set overall with old European- and single-cut diamonds, diamonds weighing about 6.65 carats, millegrain accents, suspended from a 10k white gold chain, 17" l. $5,875

Pendants

Pendant, Argy Rousseau Crane. Amethyst-colored crane is supported by blue scrollwork over the entire pendant. Pendant is suspended from a pink tasseled cord. Pendent is 2 1/2" diameter. $1,840

Pendant, Argy Rousseau Ballerina In amber glass set against a clear background with yellow scrollwork around framed ballerina. Pendant is suspended from a russet colored tasseled cord. 2" diameter. $2,530

Pendant, 18k yellow gold with pale blue glass cabochons and a pale pink glass cabochon. 6.80 dwts. $195

Photo courtesy Leslie Hindman Auctioneers, Chicago; www.LeslieHindman.com

Pendant, Judith Leiber, floral with blue and red resin with a snake chain. Stamped: Judith Leiber. **$158**

Photo courtesy Alderfer Auction & Appraisal, Hatfield, Pa.; www.AlderferAuction.com

Pendant, Swan Pearl and Enamel, W. Bauscher, 14K, handmade mabe pearl and enamel pendant, 3" x 1 3/4", gold weight: 11.3 grams. **$380**

Pendant-brooch, gold (18k), designed as a large octopus with wide curled arms and engraved body and bezel-set cabochon opal eyes, by Ugo Bellini, Florence, Italy, circa 1973, unsigned, 3 1/4 x 3 1/2". $3,055

Pendant, 14k yellow gold and gemstone in a filigree style. 9.10 dwts. $231

Pendant, carved jadeite, emerald, diamond and 14k gold, a long rectangular orange jadeite plaque carved with exotic foliage, mounted in a serpentine gold frame decorated with leaf-like designs accented with single-cut diamonds and four small emeralds, 3 1/2" l. $881

Pendant, emerald, diamond and enamel, Art Nouveau style, a large central cabochon emerald and a tear-shaped emerald drop, the cabochon within a gold scroll mount framed by 47 old European-cut diamonds, platinum-topped 18k gold mount, chased and engraved on the reverse, by Marcus and Co., later pin stem, some enamel loss. $17,625

Pendant, gold (18k), Art Nouveau style, round disk stamped in relief with the head of an Art Nouveau maiden with flower-filled flowing hair, early 20th century, 1 1/8" d. $264

Pendant, moonstone and 14k gold, Art Nouveau style, a long oval openwork gold mount with scrolling cattails suspending a long, narrow oval cabochon moonstone, mark of Gorham Mfg. Co., Providence, R.I., late 19th - early 20th century. **$588**

Pendant-brooch, enamel, seed pearls and gold, an oval narrow frame set with tiny seed pearls enclosing an openwork leaf and blossom wreath surround a rectangular plaque painted en grisaille with a scene of two cherubs, suspended from three flattened open-link chains attached to the upper pin mount bordered by seed pearls and decorated with a flower, 18k gold and silver-gilt mount, 19th century. **$1,528**

Pendant-brooch, enameled 14k gold, diamond and seed pearl, Art Nouveau style, designed as an enameled dark purple and white pansy blossom centered by a diamond and edged with a thin band of seed pearls. **$1,528**

Pendant, Hand-Carved, Bauscher Signed, 14K, amethyst, garnet and pearl pendant, 1" x 3/4" amethyst face, pendant measures 2" x 1 1/4", gold weight: 11.5 grams. **$321**

Pendant-brooch, moonstone, diamond and gold, the central oval flat-topped moonstone intaglio-carved with a bust figure of Diana, flanked by four old mine-cut diamonds, 14k gold mount, 3/4 x 7/8". **$1,410**

Pendant-locket, chalcedony and 14k gold, "Lover's Eye" type, designed as a Maltese cross of carved chalcedony tablets centered by a gold square enclosing a portrait of a blue eye, framed by ornate gold "cannetille" (similar to filigree) work, circa 1830, small chips. **$2,350**

Pendant-locket, micro-mosaic and 14k gold, a scroll-engraved rectangular plaque with gold scroll and bead trim, centered by an oval panel with polychrome tesserae depicting a pair of white doves among leafy branches on a deep red ground, 19th century. **$764**

Pendant-necklace, diamond, pearl and platinum, the filigree pendant designed as a ribbon bow atop a long triangular banded drop, set overall with bands of old European- and mine-cut diamonds accented by pearls, suspended from a baton-link chain punctuated by bezel-set diamonds alternating with pearls, millegrain accents, Edwardian era, early 20th century, missing pin, necklace extended by later 14k white gold trace-link chain, 17 1/4" l. **$6,756**

Pendant-necklace, black opal, diamond and 14k gold, Arts and Crafts style, the delicate fancy-link gold chain fitted with an oblong gold slide decorated with tiny pine cones and leaves and enclosing an oblong black opal, suspending an ornate, long gold-frame pendant with open leafy scrolls with tiny pine cones flanking a large almond-shaped black opal above an openwork spear-point frame set with five old European-cut diamonds suspending a black opal teardrop, mark of William Bramley, Montreal, and "14B," 15" l. **$17,625**

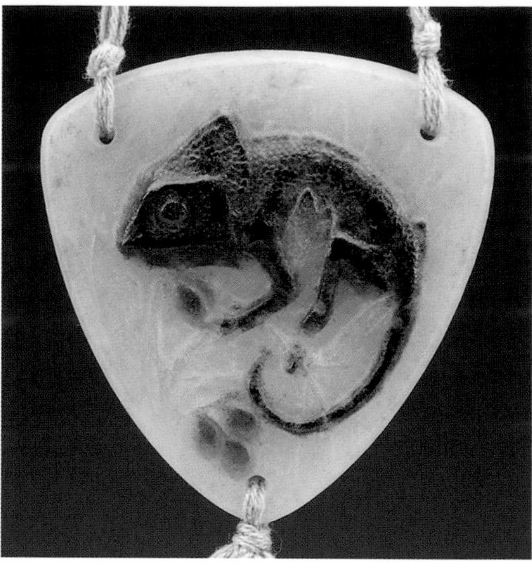

Photo courtesy James D. Julia Auctioneers, Fairfield, Maine; www.JuliaAuctions.com

Pendant, A. Walter Pate De Verre Iguana. Triangular-shaped butterscotch pendant features an iguana with green spots perched on a berry branch. Signed "AW" above its head. Pendant is suspended from a soft orange tasseled cord. Pendant is 2 1/2" w. **$1,150**

Pendant-locket, gold (18k), Etruscan Revival style, flattened oval form decorated with a central diamond and a border of diamond devices against a background finely decorated with bead and wirework, 19th century, 2 1/2" l. **$1,528**

Pendant-necklace, enamel, pearl and 14k yellow gold, Art Nouveau style, the bottom pendant in the form of stylized freshwater pearl blossoms on scrolling leafy stems enameled in shaded orange and pale green and trimmed with tiny seed pearls, suspended on delicate trace-link chains below a necklace composed of three leafy scroll enamel and pearl blossoms along double delicate trace-link chains accented with seed pearls, Bippart Griscom & Osborn (Newark, N.J., circa 1885 - 1920s), 15 1/2" l. **$4,406**

Pendant-necklace, plique-a-jour enamel, 18k gold and diamond, Art Nouveau style, designed as the gold dancing figure of an Art Nouveau maiden wearing a swirled long gown enameled in turquoise and gold, the figure flanked by heavy gold vines curling up to suspend a pair of three-petal blossoms with blue and lavender plique-a-jour enamel and accented with old European- and rose-cut diamonds, the base suspending a long freshwater pearl drop, the whole suspended by a pair of trace links joined to another three-petal blossom suspending a diamond drop, later trace-link chain, overall 18" l. **$7,931**

Pendant watch, lady's, enameled sterling silver, Art Deco style, the domed and paneled case decorated with alternating panels of black and green enamel, the small top with alternating yellow and black enameled panels, the metal dial with abstract numerals, suspended from a tapering enameled baton-link chain, dial replaced, overall 19" l. **$353**

Pins

Bar pin, diamond, seed pearl and platinum, composed of openwork arched and oblong side panels centered by a narrow bar, all centered by a wheel-like ring, mounted overall with bead- and bezel-set old European-cut diamond mélée and seed pearls, platinum-topped 14k gold mount, Edwardian, England, early 20th century. **$1,528**

Bar pin, garnet, amethyst and 14k gold, Arts and Crafts style, long oblong form centered by a cabochon amethyst flanked by rose-cut garnets bezel-set among leaves and berries, signed, early 20th century. **$646**

Bar pin, moonstone, diamond and seed pearl, the thin 14k gold bar with seed pearl tips centered by a large sugarloaf-shaped moonstone framed by a band of old European-cut diamonds and seed pearls, 19th century. **$1,645**

Pin, 22K Gold Angel, handmade pin with hand-painted angel, 2 1/4" x 1 1/4", 18.4 grams. **$1,404**

Pin, Shell Cameo, silver, with red stones and pearls, handmade frame with hand-engraved back, 2" x 1 1/2". **$360**

Figural pin, pirate, carved wood head, Lucite knife, leather kerchief, suede eye patch, metal hoop earring, unsigned Elzac, 3 1/2" l, 1943. ..... **$75**

Pin with ear clips, Miriam Haskell Gold-tone Bar with three large faux pearls and multi-sized rhinestones. Gold-tone ear clips in a circular floral motif, faux pearls at center. All stamped: Miriam Haskell. ..... **$195 set**

Pin, 18k yellow gold, turquoise and ruby crab, Italian, containing an oval turquoise cabochon and small ruby eyes. Stamp: 18K 750 ITALY, obscured maker's mark. 6.80 dwts. **$244**

Pin, Multicolor Flower, 14KY, two pear-shaped opals, two-pear shaped diamonds (0.50 ct.), two pink stones, one green stone, 2 1/4" x 2", gold flower is set on crystal. **$585**

Pin, 18k yellow gold, blue sapphire and ruby lion cub, with ruby cabochon nose and blue sapphire cabochon eyes. 17.30 dwts. **$488**

Pin courtesy FiguralPins.com — Photo by Kathy Flood

Figural pin, Peruvian art icon, mythical feline deity, fertility symbol, enamel on silver, hallmarked 925, signed Peru, artist-signed CMC, 2 3/8" l, 19??. **$150+**

Photo courtesy Leslie Hindman Auctioneers, Chicago; www.LeslieHindman.com

Pin, yellow gold, ruby, diamond, and demantoid garnet dragonfly, containing 19 round rubies weighing approximately 1.50 carats total and 28 round single-cut and full-cut diamonds weighing approximately 0.50 carat total. 4.60 dwts. **$793**

Pin, 14k yellow gold, turquoise and cultured pearl. 10.00 dwts. **$274**

Pin, 18k yellow gold bear, with oval-shape ruby cabochon eyes and black enamel nose. 17.00 dwts. **$518**

Pin, 18k yellow gold and multicolor enamel, Italian, depicting a circus elephant balancing on a ball. Stamp: ITALY 18K. 6.90 dwts. **$244**

Pin, an ancient Egyptian alabaster and obsidian eye from an anthropoid coffin, mounted in modern 18k gold with a 14k gold pin stem, eye circa 700 B.C., 2 5/8" l. **$3,173**

Pin, carved carnelian and 14k gold, carved as the head of a racing horse, gold mount, mark of Enos Richardson and Co. (Newark, N.J., 1841-1969), 1 1/4" l. **$470**

Pin, diamond, enamel and 18k gold, Art Nouveau style, designed as a pair of large scrolled leaves enameled in bluish green and framed by looping leaves and arching blossoms and buds, bead-set with single-cut diamond, suspending a freshwater pearl drop, early 20th century. **$2,233**

Pin, enameled 14k gold, Art Nouveau style, designed as a three-petal blossom enameled in peach and yellow and attached to a green-enameled bud stem and a gold curled stem with two green-enameled leaves, small freshwater pearl accents, small enamel chip, late 19th - early 20th century. **$764**

Pin, enameled and gem-set 14k gold, the top enameled in color with two cherubs with a torch and letter above a wide fan-shaped lower panel with two gold spear-point drops, accented with seed pearls and red and green stone accents, enamel losses. **$1,058**

Pin, gold and seed pearls, "Lover's Eye" design, a double oval row of seed pearls set in gold enclosing a small oval picture of a painted blue eye, late 18th - early 19th century, 1" l. **$3,819**

Pin and earrings, rhinestone, ice blue baguettes, ovals in snowflake motif, pin 2" d., screw-on earrings, 3/4" h. .... **$70 set**

Pin, Scottish agate, in the form of a butterfly with the body and wings composed of various pieces of patterned agate, silver mount, Scotland, mid-19th century, 2 3/8" w. **$1,998**

Pin, 18k yellow gold, blue sapphire and diamond, in a hand-woven hat motif, containing numerous small round dark blue sapphires and four small round diamonds. Stamp: K 18 ITALY. 11.32 dwts. **$579**

Pin, Lovebird, 1940s, gold tone, with emerald and ruby rhinestones. **$158**

Rings

Ring, Emporio Armani, in sterling silver, with snake-chain fringe. **$48**

Ring, 18k yellow gold, diamond, black onyx and mabe pearl, containing one mabe pearl measuring approximately 14 mm and numerous round brilliant-cut diamonds weighing approximately 1.00 carat total. 13.40 dwts. **$1,098**

Ring, 18k yellow gold, diamond, orange coral and black enamel, David Webb, containing a sugar-loaf-shape coral flanked by black enamel and numerous small round brilliant-cut diamonds weighing approximately 0.42 carat total. Stamp: WEBB 18 Karat PLAT. 11.70 dwts. **$2,684**

Ring, natural pearl, diamond and platinum, centering a grey natural pearl measuring 12.80 mm, the shoulders with channel-set baguette diamonds and bead-set full-cut diamond mélée, signed, France. **$18,800**

Ring, 18k yellow gold and orange coral, David Webb, the square hammered form with a carved coral frog set on top. Stamp: 18K WEBB. 20.20 dwts. **$2,684**

Ring, 18k yellow gold and blue and green enamel. Stamp: 750. 10.60 dwts. **$396**

Ring, 18k yellow gold, lapis lazuli and green enamel, David Webb, the fluted design decorated with green enamel with a carved lapis lazuli frog set on top. Stamp: DAVID WEBB 18K. 15.10 dwts. **$2,928**

Ring, 18k yellow gold, platinum, diamond and azurite-malachite, David Webb, containing a fluted domed azurite-malachite and 18 round brilliant-cut diamonds weighing approximately 0.66 carat total. Stamp: WEBB 18K PLAT. 10.90 dwts. **$2,684**

Ring, 18k yellow gold, platinum, diamond, ruby and white and brown enamel, David Webb, giraffe with two round ruby cabochon eyes and nine round brilliant-cut diamonds weighing approximately 0.09 carat total. Stamp: WEBB PLAT 18K. 11.00 dwts. **$2,684**

Photo courtesy Alderfer Auction & Appraisal, Hatfield, Pa.; www.AlderferAuction.com

Ring, Aquamarine and Diamond, 18K, two fancy-cut aquamarines, one single-cut diamond (0.02 ct.), size 7, 3.9 grams. **$204**

Courtesy Sandi Moore

Pin, Art Deco, frosted glass and turquoise (damaged), marked "Germany Sterling," 3 1/2" l. **$75**

Ring, Emerald-Cut Diamond, platinum, one 8.00 mm x 5.80 mm x 3.30 mm diamond, six baguette side diamonds, fancy-cut diamond (0.40 ctw.), one emerald-cut diamond (1.30 ct.), size 7 with ring guard. **$4,972**

Ring, 18k yellow gold, ruby and green enamel, dolphin containing 10 small round ruby cabochons decorating the back, with green enamel eyes rimmed in orange enamel. Stamp: 750, maker's mark obscured. 4.70 dwts. **$158**

Ring, 18k yellow gold, diamond and emerald frog, containing two emerald cabochon eyes and numerous small round brilliant-cut diamonds weighing approximately 0.24 carat total. Stamp: 18 K KN 1970 21209. 9.70 dwts. **$671**

Ring, 18k yellow gold, platinum and diamond in an octagonal design, containing numerous round brilliant-cut diamonds weighing approximately 3.00 carats total. 15.10 dwts. **$1,464**

Ring, gold (18k), diamond and platinum, two old European-cut and six single-cut diamonds vertically set in platinum tiered shoulders, size 6. .... **$294**

Ring, platinum and diamond, the wide band with a scroll device at the top prong-set with a marquise-cut diamond weighing about 1.40 carats, surrounded by baguette and old single-cut diamonds, size 3 3/4. .... **$4,230**

Ring, Rose Gold Wedding Band, 14KY, with 11 red round stones, some chipped, bezel set, size 6, gold weight: 11.5 grams. **$175**

Ring, Carnelian, 14K rose gold, one 20 x 17mm carved carnelian face, size 6 3/4, 7.4 grams. **$438**

Ring, diamond and platinum, eternity band- style, the wide band composed of 18 prong-set marquise-cut diamonds weighing about 5.85 carats, size 5 1/2. .... **$4,113**

Ring, diamond and platinum, prong-set with a large emerald-cut diamond weighing about 7.90 carats flanked by tapered baguette diamonds, size 7 1/2. .... **$56,400**

Ring, enameled 18k gold and diamond, designed as a snarling tiger head with black and white enameled stripes and a red and black-enameled nose and a red tongue, the upper lips

Photo courtesy Leslie Hindman Auctioneers, Chicago; www.LeslieHindman.com

Ring, 18k yellow gold, platinum, diamond, emerald and black enamel, David Webb, containing one leaf-shape carved emerald measuring approximately 18.00 mm x 15.50 mm, eight small round emerald cabochons and numerous round brilliant-cut and single-cut diamonds weighing approximately 1.50 carats total. Stamp: WEBB 18K. 13.40 dwts. **$5,612**

and side of the head set with single-cut diamonds, the black and white-striped tail curls up at one side, size 5. .... **$499**

Ring, green tourmaline, diamond and 18k white gold, the top prong-set with a long rectangular step-cut tourmaline flanked by curved clusters of full-cut diamonds, diamonds weighing about 3.30 carats, size 7 1/2. .... **$5,581**

Ring, 14k yellow gold, coral and diamond, containing one coral cabochon measuring approximately 18.15 mm and numerous small round brilliant-cut diamonds weighing approximately 0.15 carat total. 10.34 dwts. **$549**

Ring, 18k yellow gold and turquoise, containing numerous round turquoise cabochons measuring approximately 2.55 mm each. 6.60 dwts. **$396**

Ring, 14k yellow and white gold, red coral and diamond, vintage style, containing one oval coral cabochon measuring approximately 24 x 14 mm and numerous round brilliant-cut diamonds weighing approximately 1.15 carats total. 15.20 dwts. **$1,708**

Ring, gem-set 18k gold, a wide gold band mounted with alternating heavy square and round frames each set with a fancy-cut amethyst, green beryl, citrine, pyrope and spessartine garnet, No. 9C335, French guarantee mark, size 7 1/4. .... **$1,058**

Ring, gem-set 18k white gold, the large squared top centered by a large cushion-shape faceted amethyst framed by fancy-cut iolites (blue stones) and pink tourmalines, size 7. .... **$3,525**

Ring, Tiger's Eye and Diamond, 14KY, features gold head with diamond eye, size 10 1/2, 30 x 21mm oval flat tiger's eye, 28.7 grams. **$409**

Ring, amethyst, seed pearl and 14k gold, the top set with a faceted oval amethyst decorated with a gold and diamond floral design, the wide rectangular gold mount accented with seed pearls and decorated with flower and leaf engraving, 19th century, size 7 1/2. .... **$411**

Ring, diamond and amethyst, the top set with a ring of eight pear- and cushion-shaped rose-cut diamonds surrounding a later amethyst cabochon, silver-topped 14k gold mount, size 6. .... **$1,528**

Ring, diamond and gold, the openwork top decorated with scrolls flanking a row of three large old mine-cut diamonds, the sides bead-set overall with small diamonds, silver-topped gold mount, diamonds weighing about 1.20 carats, size 8 3/4. .... **$1,058**

Ring, diamond, ruby and gold, the long top centered by a round cluster of old European-cut diamonds flanked with double curves further set with diamonds with a teardrop cabochon ruby accent, foliate shoulder and pierced scrolling gallery, silver-topped 18k gold mount, size 7 1/2. .... **$705**

Ring, diamond, sapphire and 14k gold, the long navette-shaped (in the form of a shuttle) top centered by a prong-set, oval-cut blue sapphire surrounded by old mine-cut diamond mélée, 19th century, one diamond replaced with single-cut, bend to band, size 8 1/4. .... **$705**

Ring, emerald, diamond and 18k gold, a three-stone top with a central old mine-cut diamond weighing about 1.11 carats flanked by pear-cut emeralds, in an open scrolling mount, emeralds with minor nicks, size 6 1/4. .... **$7,050**

Ring, garnet, diamond and 14k gold, the rectangular gold top with serpentine ends and a textured ground accented by a row of three circular-cut garnets and two small old mine-cut diamonds, open shoulders, inscribed and dated 1871, size 6. .... **$499**

Ring, gem-set high-carat gold, a double gold band with each claw-set at the top with two differently hued tumbled pink sapphire beads, together with invoice from Spinks, London

Photo courtesy Alderfer Auction & Appraisal, Hatfield, Pa.; www.AlderferAuction.com

Ring, Rose Gold Ruby and Diamond Wedding Band, 14K rose and white gold, hand-carved stones and diamonds, 24 round diamonds (.30 ct.), size 6 1/2, red stones quite worn, gold weight: 7.2 grams. **$570**

Photo courtesy Leslie Hindman Auctioneers, Chicago; www.LeslieHindman.com

Ring, yellow gold and carnelian intaglio, depicting a soldier in profile. 4.50 dwts. **$134**

stating it dates from the 10th-11th centuries in what is now Vietnam, size 4 1/4. .... **$2,938**

Ring, Enamel and Diamond, 18K, green and blue enamel, 19 round diamonds (0.76 ct.), size 6 1/2, enamel is worn, 22.6 grams. **$702**

Ring, ruby and diamond, the round top centered by a cushion-cut ruby surrounded by a ring of rose-cut diamonds within a ring of circular-cut rubies, silver-topped 18k gold mount, size 3 3/4. .... **$1,500**

Ring, sapphire and 14k gold, designed as a curled alligator with engraved scales and the top of the head set with a cabochon sapphire, size 7 1/4. .... **$470**

Ring with locket, gold (14k), fraternal-order-type, the oval top cast in the shape of a Bacchus mask, opening to reveal a compartment, shoulders inscribed "sous le ... la verité," (roughly, "under the truth") 19th century, size 7 3/4. .... **$1,058**

Ring, diamond and platinum, the long rectangular top centered by a large bead-set old European-cut diamond weighing about 1.12 carats, surrounded by other old mine- and European-cut diamonds weighing about 3.82 carats, open gallery, size 5. .... **$2,350**

Ring, diamond and sapphire, the square top with beveled corners, centered by a square-cut diamond surrounded by narrow bands of French-cut sapphires and full-cut diamond mélée, open gallery, size 6. .... **$3,525**

Ring, emerald, diamond and platinum, centering a large step-cut emerald flanked by graduating diamond baguettes, size 7. .... **$3,819**

Ring, Snake, 14K, with two 2.50mm diamonds, one diamond chip, size 6, gold weight: 8.0 grams. **$163**

Ring, turquoise, diamond and platinum, the oval top set with a gadrooned and domed turquoise plaque centered by a bezel-set, transitional-cut round diamond, foliate shoulders with diamond, black enamel and cabochon jadeite highlights, millegrain accents, signed by Black, Starr & Frost, New York (established 1810), size 5 1/4. .... **$4,113**

Watches

Chatelaine watch, lady's, a silver-gilt waist clasp centered by a crystal orb and suspending gold bar links suspending the 18k gold round watch with domed crystal over the white enamel dial with Roman numerals, lever escapement movement, signed pin-set, display back, by Henry Capt, French import stamp on waist clasp, in original fitted box. **$940**

Watch pin, glass and 18k gold, designed as a tiny hourglass, the silver-tone metal dial with abstract numerals, hourglass with running sands within a rope-work frame, crystal with slight bloom, pin stem detachable, Gubelin, Switzerland, 1 1/2" l. **$1,410**

Lapel watch, open-faced, lady's, Marcus and Co., 14k gold, the rose-tone metal dial with Arabic numerals, the watch within a cage of openwork C-scrolls and tendrils and suspended from a matching bar-form lapel pin, the cage engraved front and back, watch replaced, 2 1/8" l. **$2,468**

Pocket watch, hunting case, man's, Elgin, white enamel dial with Arabic numerals and a subsidiary seconds dial, enclosing an engraved 15-jewel movement, front of the 14k gold case centered by an oval reserve enameled with blue forget-me-nots divided by a band set with old mine-cut diamonds, a tiny red ribbon at the top, inscribed and dated 1897. .... **$499**

Pocket watch, open-faced, man's, enamel and gold, the enamel and gold-tone dial with Arabic numerals within

Wristwatch, lady's, Cartier, 18k gold, platinum, enamel and diamond, the round dial framed by bezel-set full-cut diamonds, the blue enamel dial with baton numerals, diamonds weighing about 1.00 carat, completed by a band composed of ring-shaped blue enamel links, French guarantee stamps, circa 1960-70, 7 3/4" l. **$7,050**

Photo courtesy Leslie Hindman Auctioneers, Chicago; www.LeslieHindman.com

Collar, Chanel Gripoix Red Flower, circa 1970s, with all-over floral clusters, rhinestones throughout. Stamped: Chanel. **$6,710**

arches centering an en grisaille painted scene of a classical kneeling woman greeting a sailing ship, quarter-hour repeating fusee movement, plain polished 18k gold case, with watch key, early 19th century. **$1,645**

Pocket watch, open-faced, man's, P. Jerrot, Paris, the white enamel dial with Roman numerals, cylinder fusee two-bell quarter hour repeating movement, engraved 18k gold case decorated with a colorful enamel scene of a lady paying homage to Amistad with rose-cut diamond accents, a frame of tiny seed pearls, late 18th century. **$3,290**

Assorted Jewelry

Choker, Chanel Gripoix Pearl Camellia, circa 1970s, with eight strands of pearls with an off-center camellia flower. Stamped: Chanel. **$1,830**

Choker, gem-set 14k yellow gold, Art Nouveau style, composed of openwork looped and serpentine links highlighted with seed pearls, diamonds, rubies, sapphires or turquoise, joined by trace link chains, American hallmark, late 19th - early 20th century, 13" l. **$3,819**

Photo courtesy Leslie Hindman Auctioneers, Chicago; www.LeslieHindman.com

Comb, Amber Resin in a fan motif, with blue crystals. 9 x 7 1/2". **$61**

Photo courtesy Leslie Hindman Auctioneers, Chicago; www.LeslieHindman.com

Headband, gold-tone with attached leaves around entire band. **$170**

Choker, silver plated metal, rhinestone and glass bead, composed of two graduated wide flat bands with multiple strands of black alternating with brown beads, decorated at the front with a large beaded spear-point device with clusters of yellow, orange, green, dark blue and light blue glass beads, the clasp accented with clear rhinestones, Italy, 1962, 15" l. **$1,195**

Clip, gem-set 14k gold, a large stylized blossom with five deep petals with rolled and pointed tips, centered by a pyramidal double cabochon green tourmaline set en tremblant, long flexible stem with three long slender gold leaves, signed by Cartier, No. 3497, 4" l. **$4,113**

Clip, gem-set 18k gold, designed as a stylized flower and leaf, the tall curved feather-like leaf set with circular-cut emeralds and enclosing a stylized blossom composed of oval cabochon sapphires, engraved mount, 1 x 1 1/2". **$8,250**

Clip-brooch, aquamarine, ruby, diamond and 18k gold, an ornate design centering a large emerald-cut aquamarine above a domed base section set with old European- and full-cut diamonds and a band of small baguette rubies, the top issuing multiple arched and curled leaves in gold and gold set with old European- and full-cut diamonds, interspersed with slender stems with circular-cut ruby blossoms, 2" l. **$1,410**

Collar, glass bead, faux pearl and leather, the wide graduating wreath-like band with a wide pointed front, set overall with a mixture of greenish blue and orange beads imitating coral and turquoise and small faux pearls, accented with sewn-on large gilt leather leaves, Ken Scott, Italy, 1965, 15" l. **$1,793**

Cross pendant-brooch, diamond and 18k gold, the gold mount set with ten old European- and mine-cut diamonds weighing about 3.75 carats, each arm with a pointed and forked tip accented with black enamel, 2 1/8" l. **$3,525**

Cuff with Matching Pin, Kenneth Jay Lane, in silver tone with an attached tiger at center. Pin is gold-tone tiger with rhinestone collar. No stamp. .... **$109 set**

Cuff, Louis Vuitton Purple Patent Leather with embossed monogram. Stamped: Louis Vuitton/Paris/Made in France. **$122**

Slide locket, silver, Art Nouveau style, a flattened, waisted rectangular shape, the top embossed with sinuous vine and abstract leaf designs highlighted by green cabochons, gilt interior, European assay marks, early 20th century, 1 3/8 x 2". **$529**

Stickpin, enameled 14k gold, the top designed as the head of an Egyptian woman wearing a diamond and blue stone headdress topped by a seed pearl, some enamel loss, late 19th - early 20th century. **$353**

Stickpin, moonstone and 18k gold, the top of moonstone carved in the shape of the head of a jockey wearing a gold cap and collar, later 14k gold pin stem, 19th century. **$1,528**

Tiara, diamond and platinum, designed as three intersecting floral garlands set throughout with old European- and single- cut diamonds, with a white metal tiara mount and later brooch attachment, evidence of solder, Edwardian, England, early 20th century, diamonds 7 1/4 carats. **$15,275**

Tiara, rhinestone, green glass beads and Russian gold-plated metal, the round metal wire frame mounted with a wreath of repeating rhinestone-set leaves accented with faceted green glass leaves, unsigned Miriam Haskell, 1950s, 12 5/8" l. **$956**

Photo courtesy Leslie Hindman Auctioneers, Chicago; www.LeslieHindman.com

Cuff, Chanel, 1980, in azure-purple Lucite, with Maltese cross design in red and greens stones. Stamped: Chanel. 4". **$1,464**

JUDAICA

Judaica is any object or text used to practice and observe Jewish commandments or traditions, or celebrate and portray its customs, philosophy and way of life.

Advertising, Y. Weisberg, mid-20th century, poster for the Orient Dryer, which promises to be the "best and least expensive" solution for women concerned with the health of their family. **$207**

Antiquities Judaicae Pragenses, Prague, printed by M. Schultz, S.A., (no date) early 20th century, soft-cover booklet of twenty-five duotone photographic reproductions on card depicting scenes from Jewish Prague, (worn). .. **$59**

Beith Tephilah (prayers), Livorno, 1866 According to Sephardic rite, original calf, spine gilt-tooled in Hebrew, with printed presentation label in front: "A Present to Mordecai Fonseca in Memory of Judith, Lady Montefiore, From Sir Moses Montefiore, Bart. At Purim, 5625 [sic]." **$355**

Etrog Container, Polish silver-mounted coconut, 19th century, marked "12," coconut resting on a realistically cast leaf, hinged lid, 6 1/2" l. **$3,851**

Haggadah Shel Pessach, Passover Haggadah with Commentary of Don Yitzhak Abarbanel and others, Amsterdam, Shlomo Proops, 1712, with copper plate engravings, fold-out map, wear, rebound. **$7,702**
(The Haggadah is the Jewish religious text that sets out the order of the Passover Seder.)

Hanukkah Lamp, carved stone with candle arms and facade to verso, 8" h, restoration. **$533**

Ivory Figure of a Fiddler, German, late 19th century, poised with a violin, 4" h, mounted on a carved wood base. **$1,777**

Kiddush Cup, Bohemian engraved glass, late 19th/early 20th century, beaker-form with ruby flashing and engraved Hebrew text, 5 1/4" h. **$711**

Photo courtesy Skinner Inc., Boston; www.SkinnerInc.com

Hanukkah Lamp, Italian bronze, 17th/18th century, arched form with Cohan, flanked by columns enclosing a palm tree and lions about a tray of oil wells, lacking shamus, damages, repairs, 11" h. **$3,555**

Photo courtesy Heritage Auction Galleries, Dallas; www.HA.com

Silver traveling worship set, various makers, various locations. Comprised of 10 separate pieces that combine to form a standing lidded cup, with inset gems, hallmarks from Europe and Baltic states as well as early 19th century American, this was probably assembled by several generations, 11.2" t assembled. **$657**

Photo courtesy Skinner Inc., Boston; www.SkinnerInc.com

Photography, Berenice Abbott (American, 1898-1991), East Side Portrait, signed "Berenice Abbott" on mat lower right, numbered "25/40" on mat lower left, gelatin silver print, sheet size 23 1/8" x 18 3/4", not examined out of frame. **$1,422**

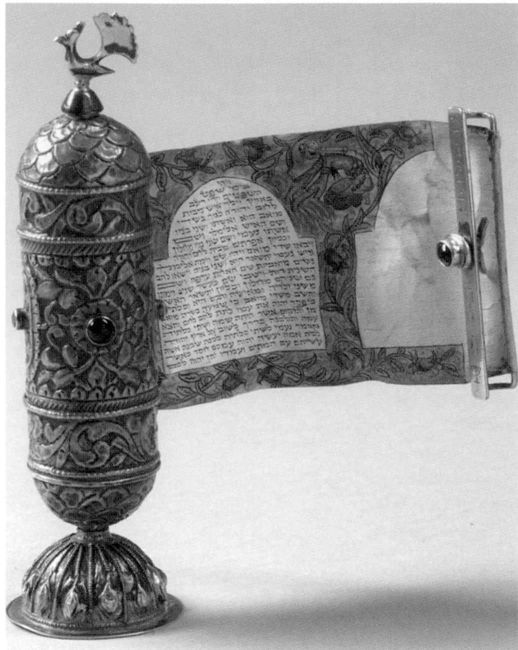

Photo courtesy Skinner Inc., Boston; www.SkinnerInc.com

Scroll, Ruth (Megillah), Persian silver-cased, 19th century, with finely hand-lettered black ink on parchment text with later illumination, in a standing scroll case with bird finial and colored stone embellishments, adapted, overall 6" h. **$2,607**

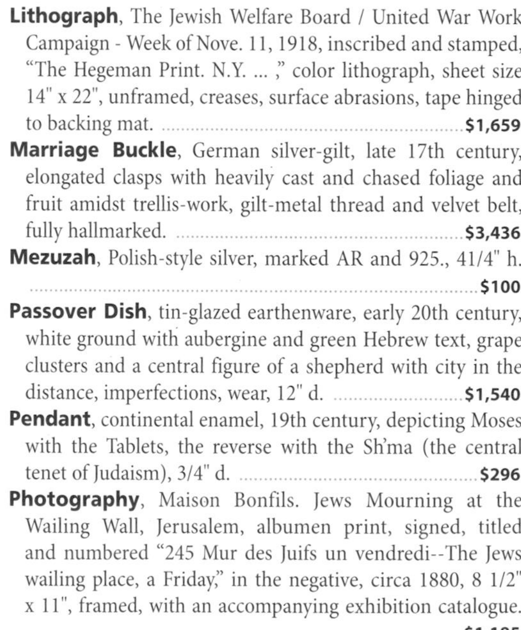

Lithograph, The Jewish Welfare Board / United War Work Campaign - Week of Nove. 11, 1918, inscribed and stamped, "The Hegeman Print. N.Y. ... ," color lithograph, sheet size 14" x 22", unframed, creases, surface abrasions, tape hinged to backing mat. **$1,659**

Marriage Buckle, German silver-gilt, late 17th century, elongated clasps with heavily cast and chased foliage and fruit amidst trellis-work, gilt-metal thread and velvet belt, fully hallmarked. **$3,436**

Mezuzah, Polish-style silver, marked AR and 925., 41/4" h. **$100**

Passover Dish, tin-glazed earthenware, early 20th century, white ground with aubergine and green Hebrew text, grape clusters and a central figure of a shepherd with city in the distance, imperfections, wear, 12" d. **$1,540**

Pendant, continental enamel, 19th century, depicting Moses with the Tablets, the reverse with the Sh'ma (the central tenet of Judaism), 3/4" d. **$296**

Photography, Maison Bonfils. Jews Mourning at the Wailing Wall, Jerusalem, albumen print, signed, titled and numbered "245 Mur des Juifs un vendredi--The Jews wailing place, a Friday," in the negative, circa 1880, 8 1/2" x 11", framed, with an accompanying exhibition catalogue. **$1,185**

Scroll, Esther (Megillah), possibly Italian, 19th century, hand-lettered in black ink on parchment, in four membranes, with additional text, on ivory rollers, overall 9" l. **$1,066**

Seder saltwater egg-shaped container, transfer-decorated porcelain, late 19th/early 20th century, with polychrome decoration pertaining to the dipping of herbs in saltwater, on scrolled feet, the base marked "3H-4667/HB-NS," 6" h. **$385**

Spice Container, Italian silver, late 18th century, cylindrical form with piercing throughout, set on a stepped circular foot, surmounted by a spire and urn-form knop, 7" h. **$3,081**

Spice Tower, Polish silver, 19th century, possibly struck with maker IW in an oval, three cylindrical tiers with pierced and engraved foliage, the lower section with a door, on a domed base ending in a square foot, surmounted by a knop and pennant flag, 8 1/2" h. **$2,488**

Timepiece, Judaic bronze, probably Germany or Austria, early 20th century, the housing formed as rampant lions holding the dial with Star of David and Hebrew numerals aloft, on an oval base, the works signed Georg Jacob Luz, Forzbein, of an earlier date, overall 6 1/2" h. **$474**

Torah Breast Plate, silver, 20th century, cartouche form with lions flanking a crown about columns and the tablet, 7 3/4" h, with suspension chain. **$562**

Torah Curtain, Hungarian, embroidered velvet and silk, 19th century, with crown and Hebrew text, some staining, loss, 64" x 44" h. **$177**

Torah Pointer, continental silver and silver gilt, mid-19th century, hallmarked, tapered form with heavily cast and chased leaves, terminating in a pointed hand, finial formed as a lion's head, 10 1/4" l, with suspension loop and chain. **$2,725**

LIGHTING

Also see Modernism, Oriental, Tiffany.

Bandstand light, Art Deco, miniature, four-piece band on green-finished, cast-metal bandstand, leaded glass backdrop, pair of orange, black and yellow striated glass "candles," 9 1/8" h (overall), 12 1/2" w, 6" deep. **$660**

Candelabra (pair), brass and cut glass, electrified, four branches, center support ornamented with button and pad-and-spear prisms, cut-glass drip pans with button prisms cascades below, 26 1/2" h, with small cloth shades. .... **$3,450 pair**

Candelabra (pair), silver-plated, three-light, twin branches, gadrooned borders, tapered round shaft, 16" h; convertible to pair of candlesticks. .... **$287 pair**

Candelabra (pair), J. Pradier, seven lights, bronze, each with a different figure supporting seven ornate bobeches, on a black marble base. Signed J. Pradier, height to topmost bobeche, 25 1/4". .... **$1,800 pair**

(Jean-Jacques Pradier, French/Swiss, 1790-1852.)

Candleholder, Indian silver, inlaid of double bell form with a waisted center and decorated to the exterior with a dense pattern of leafy blossoms within floral bands, further foliate-patterned details on the interior rim (silver oxidized, wear), 6 1/4" h. **$100**

Candleholder, Stahl redware, brown glazed half-vase form, handle at back, 8 1/4" h; inscribed on bottom, "Made By/J.S. Stahl/May 12th-1941/The weather/clear and very/cool." **$120**

(Three generations of the Stahl family operated a small pottery in Powder Valley, Pa., intermittently from about 1850 to 1956.)

Candleholder, Weller, Woodcraft with owls perched atop an apple tree. Impressed mark. 14 3/4". **$960**

Candle lantern, colorless free-blown cut glass and brass, hanging hall-style, France, early 19th century, with folded base rim, overall 21 1/4" h. **$503**

Candlestick, Midwestern, Free-Blown, colorless, galleried bulbous socket with pewter insert, hollow pyriform stem, and circular foot with polished pontil mark. Probably Pittsburgh. 1810-1830. 9 1/4" h, 2 1/2" d rim, 4 3/4" d foot. Undamaged with heavy usage wear under foot. **$791**

Photo courtesy Rago Arts and Auction Center, Lambertville, N.J.; www.RagoArts.com

Candelabra, bronze, designed for candles or flame-shaped electric bulbs, by Jessie Preston, in a thistle pattern. (Exhibited at "Women Designers in the USA 1900-2000," and accompanied by a copy of the catalog.) Original patina. Stamped J PRESTON CHICAGO, 13 1/2" x 10". **$9,600**

(Jessie Preston, early 20th century, Chicago.)

Photo courtesy Heritage Auction Galleries, Dallas; www.HA.com

Russian silver figural candlestick, with classically draped female figure holding snake, four lions paws on plinth support raised canopy base. L. Wapinski, Minsk, Russia, 1890. Marks: L. WAPINSKI, o.c. (over) 1890, 84, (radiating triangle), 7 3/8" x 4", 10.07 troy ounces. **$1,195**

Photo courtesy Rago Arts and Auction Center, Lambertville, N.J.; www.RagoArts.com

Candlestick, bronze, Jarvie, complete with bobeche. Exceptional, in a original patina. Unmarked, 10 1/4" x 5 1/4". **$10,200**
(Robert Riddle Jarvie, active 1904-1920, Chicago.)

Candlestick, double, brass, Jarvie, missing bobeches. Unmarked, 11" x 8". **$2,160**
(Robert Riddle Jarvie, active 1904-1920, Chicago.)

Candlestick, Steuben Diamond Optic, blue with yellow reeding, probably shape #6593, block letter acid-stamped signature. Second quarter 20th century. 4 1/2" h, 4 3/4" d foot. **$103**

Candlestick, Steuben Gold Calcite shape #3581, polished table ring, original Kaufmann's paper label inscribed "#3581 / 2J / 7 ea" under base. Second quarter 20th century. 6" h, 5 1/2" d overall. **$517**

Candlesticks, (pair), Grape and Cable carnival glass, marigold, single light. Northwood Glass Co. First quarter 20th century. 5 1/2" h. One with ground top socket. .... **$23 pair**

Candlesticks (pair), brass petal-base push-up, England, first half 18th century, (imperfections), 6 1/2" h, one with a small crack on the candle cup edge, both stem bases filled with solder reinforcement. .... **$237 pair**

Photo courtesy Green Valley Auctions, Mt. Crawford, Va.; www.GreenValleyAuctions.com

Candlesticks (pair), small dolphin scallop base, unrecorded deep purple blue and opaque white, each featuring a 12-petal socket and 16-scallop circular base with two pairs of concentric rings underneath, wafer construction. Probably Boston & Sandwich Glass Co., possibly Cape Cod Glass Co. or Mt. Washington Glass Co. 1860-1880. 6 3/8" and 6 5/8" h, 4" d base. Single shallow chip to one socket petal and one under-base, snap-ring flake, both standards with the usual annealing fissures and lines associated with opaque white glass. **$4,802 pair**

Photo courtesy Green Valley Auctions, Mt. Crawford, Va.; www.GreenValleyAuctions.com

Candlesticks (pair), pillar-molded, colorless, each featuring a plain socket with wide flanged rim and pewter insert, applied to a mushroom-cap knop topping a hollow baluster stem with eight pronounced ribs, applied to a short standard and a wide slightly sloping foot with rough pontil mark. Probably Pittsburgh. Second quarter 19th century. 10 1/2" h, 2 5/8" d socket rim, 5" d foot. **$5,560 pair**

Photo courtesy Heritage Auction Galleries, Dallas; www.HA.com

Gustav Gurschner (Austrian, 1873-1971) Bronze Art Nouveau Candlesticks, circa 1895, 7 1/4". **$2,390**

Candlesticks with bells (pair), brass, tavern, England, mid- to late 19th century, with dish base, 11 1/4" h, some spots of corrosion. .... **$207 pair**

Candlesticks (two pairs), dolphin form, Boston & Sandwich Glass Co., Sandwich, Mass., circa 1845-70, in yellow and colorless glass with petal sockets over dolphin standards with large heads on square bases, 10 1/2" h; yellow candlesticks: one socket with unobtrusive crack, minor petal chip, the other stick with petal chip fairly shallow about 1/2" l, both with minor lower base edge chips; colorless candlesticks: one with a small petal chip, mold under-fill on tail tip, the other stick with a 1/2" clamshell chip to underside of one petal, both with minor base edge roughness. .... **$503 pairs**

Candle sconces (pair), glazed pottery, Henry Mercer (1856-1930), Doylestown, Pa., decorated with four birds, scrolls in beige, green ground, 11" h, 4 5/8" w, minor chips. .... **$862 pair**

Candle stand, paint-decorated, adjustable, wooden, American, late 18th/early 19th century, double-arm stand adjusts on a threaded shaft, tripod feet, with gilt linear decoration, 35 1/2" h. **$3,673**

Photo courtesy Heritage Auction Galleries, Dallas; www.HA.com

Pair of Royal Minton Bone China Candlesticks, Commemorating Silver Jubilee of Queen Elizabeth II, 1977, with maker's stamp on base and inscribed: 1952 The Queen's Silver Jubilee 1977; no. 76 of a limited edition of 250. **$597**

Photo courtesy James D. Julia Auctioneers, Fairfield, Maine; www.JuliaAuctions.com

Daum Nancy Cameo Glass Night Light. Cameo cut-back shade of grapes and grape leaves in earthen hues on an orange to yellow mottled ground. The shade is supported by a wrought-iron base with complimentary berries and leaves. Shade is signed on the side in cameo "Daum Nancy" with Cross of Lorraine. 6 1/2" h. **$1,560**

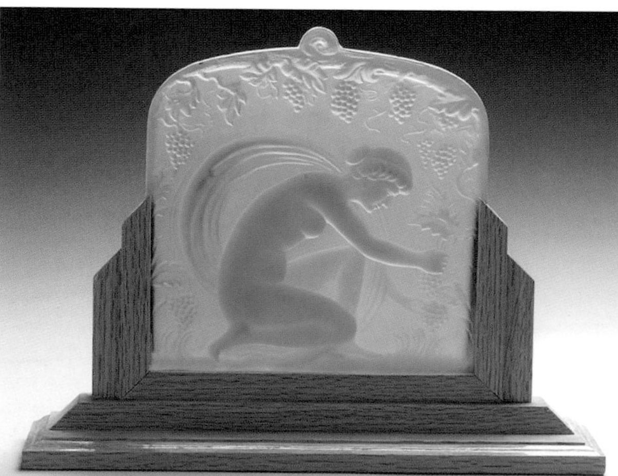

Photo courtesy James D. Julia Auctioneers, Fairfield, Maine; www.JuliaAuctions.com

Steuben Deco Luminaire Panel. Deeply impressed with figure of nude woman picking grapes. The grapevine and grapes extend around the outside edge of the panel. The panel is done in a rich green glass. The panel is housed in a contemporary oak table frame for display. Unsigned. Panel is 9" x 9 1/4". Overall in frame 11 1/2" h. Minor roughness to back edge. **$1,150**

Photo courtesy Rago Arts and Auction Center, Lambertville, N.J.; www.RagoArts.com

Ceiling sconce, Roycroft, designed by Dard Hunter (1883-1966) with cylindrical shade of leaded glass in bright green and purple, complete with cap. Unmarked, 18" x 5". **$7,800**

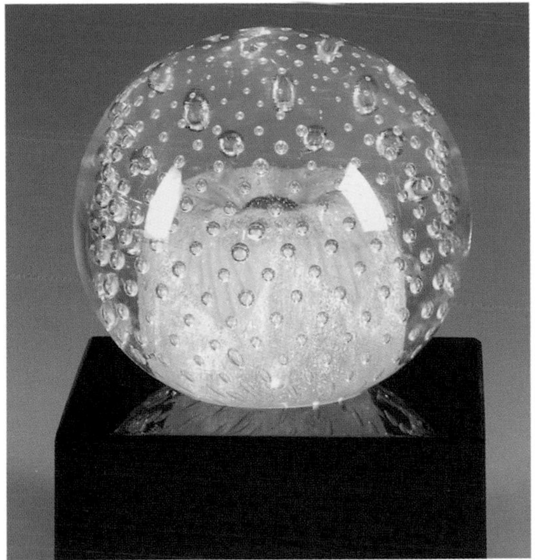

Photo courtesy James D. Julia Auctioneers, Fairfield, Maine; www.JuliaAuctions.com

Steuben Florentia Luminor. Paperweight design with green Florentia floral pattern on the interior with clear glass paperweight exterior with controlled-bubble decoration. The Florentia ball rests upon original Luminor base of black glass with round opening at the top exposing the bulb. 4 3/4" sq. Overall 7" t. **$2,645**

Ceiling sconce, Roycroft, designed by Dard Hunter (1883-1966) with cylindrical shade of leaded glass in bright green and purple, complete with ceiling hook. Missing chain, break to two pieces. Unmarked, 10" x 5". **$9,000**

Chandelier, Arts & Crafts style, caramel slag glass in hammered bronze frame. Complete with ceiling cap and chain. Unmarked, 60" x 20". **$960**

Photo courtesy Rago Arts and Auction Center, Lambertville, N.J.; www.RagoArts.com

Chandelier, Arts & Crafts style, iron, with six candle fixtures, complete with chain and ceiling cap, 55" x 30". **$660**

Chandelier, four-tiered, brass, octagonal "drip pans" on scrolled branches, electrified, 40 lights, center pedestal with paneled urn and vase forms, 20th century, 66" h, approximately 70" (greatest diameter). **$4,887**

Chandelier, brass and chrome, three-tiered, six octagonal "drip pans" over six, over 12 "drip pans"; all on S-scrolled branches, electrified, three-tiered center column, 30" to top of ring, approximately 46" outside diameter overall. **$575**

Chandelier, gilt metal, six-light, leaf scroll and swag bracket supports, fluted center shaft, pad prism swags at base of main body, six smaller lights, approximately 30" w around fitting at base. **$632**

Chandelier, Gothic Revival, brass, octagonal section, each side with pointed arch backed by frosted glass panel, six twin scrolled "spears" pointing upward, 53 1/8" h (overall), 24 3/8" w (overall). **$230**

Chandelier, Handel, hollyhock motif, four-sided with pink and yellow leaded slag glass blossoms against a green geometric ground. Complete with four sockets, original chain, and floriform ceiling cap. Breaks to a few small glass pieces. Unmarked, 23 3/4" sq. x 34". **$32,400**

Chandelier, Handel, with five leaded-glass shades hanging from individual arms, fastened to a square brass ceiling plate. Total: 33" x 14" sq.; shades: 4 1/2" x 5 1/2". **$9,000**

Chandelier, Lalique, Champs-Élysées, in clear and frosted glass with chrome mounting. Engraved Lalique France. **$2,400**

Chandelier, Prairie School, with three hanging copper lantern drops lined in caramel slag glass. Unmarked, 36" x 30" x 13 3/4". **$1,920**

Photo courtesy Rago Arts and Auction Center, Lambertville, N.J.; www.RagoArts.com

Lamp, boudoir, Handel, hammered copper conical shade suspended from hooks by chain links, pierced with stylized tulips and lined in caramel slag glass. Its single-socket base has two shafts and is lined in glass. Original dark patina. Shade stamped HANDEL. 14" x 8 1/4". **$9,000**

Photo courtesy Green Valley Auctions, Mt. Crawford, Va.; www.GreenValleyAuctions.com

Lamp, banquet, cut double-overlay Moorish Windows, kerosene period, cobalt blue cut to white cut to colorless font and matching stem, cast and stamped brass mounts retaining a good percentage of original gilding, double-step marble base, #2 fine line collar. Boston & Sandwich Glass Co. 1860-1880. 17" h, 5 3/8" sq base. Exceptional undamaged condition except for a few scattered flakes to edges of marble. **$6,780**

Chandelier, Roycroft, hammered copper, from the Roycroft Inn, with three reflective sockets, complete with original chains and ceiling cap. Fine original dark patina. Orb & Cross mark, 31" x 17". **$7,200**

Chandelier, wrought iron, circular, each of 16 lights with stylized horse's head, electrified, ring with lower border of pendants, small ring suspended by bars; late 19th century. **$1,150**

Font, unlisted footed hanging or bracket, kerosene period, deep cobalt blue, wafer attached undersized standard with short eight-panel stem and plain circular foot, #2 fine-line collar, period burner and chimney, 5 1/4" h, 5 3/4" d overall, 3 1/2" d foot, minor mold roughness to a shoulder fin. **$4,675**

Lamp, astral, patinated brass with cut-glass shade, American, early 19th century, electrified, overall 18 1/8" h, wheel-cut shade in very good condition, the old font is a little rusty with several small cracks, there is an electric bulb socket in the center of the top with a cord attached but it was severed at one point; the ring holding the shade is affixed to the top of the font and there is a similar one attached below. **$1,777**

Lamp, boudoir, Handel, its "chipped ice" glass shade obverse- and reverse-painted with a Nordic landscape of evergreens, over a rare single-socket tree-trunk base in bronze patina. Light spots to interior. Signed Handel with illegible number, 15" x 7". **$6,000**

Lamp, desk, Roycroft, hammered copper with helmet shade. Cleaned patina. Orb & Cross mark, 17" x 7". **$960**

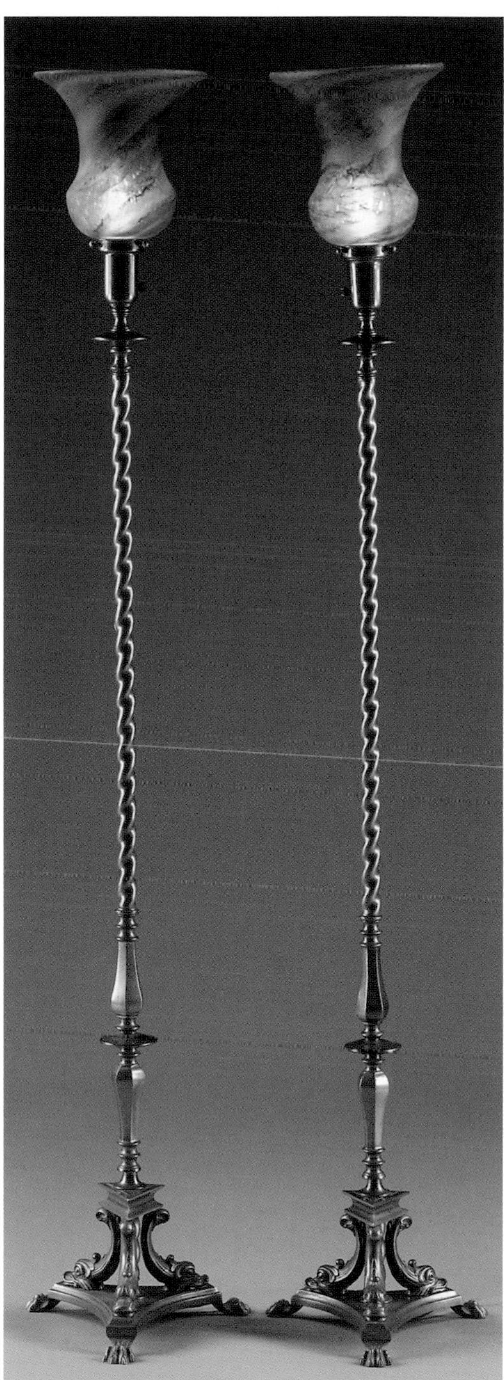

Photos courtesy James D. Julia Auctioneers, Fairfield, Maine; www.JuliaAuctions.com

Pair of Steuben Moss Agate Torchieres. Acid-finished Moss Agate shades resting in a brass floor stand with lion paw feet, cast dolphin supports and twisted riser. The shades have a rich Moss Agate design in shades of green, red, brown and amber. The exterior of each shade is acid etched to give a frosted finish. Shades are 9" diameter x 9" t x 2 1/4" fitter. Overall 65 1/2" t. **$12,650 pair**

Photo courtesy Rago Arts and Auction Center, Lambertville, N.J.; www.RagoArts.com

Lamp, figural, monumental bronze and ormolu, with gilt "socle" (a plain plinth that supports a wall) and five-arm candelabra on black painted wooden base, fitted for electricity, 19th century, 66" h. **$5,400**

Lamp, floor, Handel, its two faceted frosted-glass shades obverse-painted with a geometrical band on a plain T-base in bronze patina. Minute fleabite to lower edge of one shade. Both shades stamped HANDEL No. 2702, base has cloth label. Base: 55 1/2" x 33", shades: 4 3/4" x 6". **$3,600**

Lamp, fluid, cut overlay glass, brass and marble with glass prisms, American, circa 1870, brass font over white cut to red glass shaft in a star and grid design, on a square double-step marble base with brass mounts, 17 3/8" h, solder repair on font, dent on font, missing one long prism, old minor edge chips on marble, overlay good. **$207**

Lamp, piano, Arts & Crafts style, hammered copper with a riveted hanging lantern, lined in raspberry and amber slag glass. Normal cleaning to original patina. Unmarked, 8 1/2" x 10" x 17". **$1,020**

Lamp, stand, New York Lamp Co. "Dewdrop," kerosene period, cased red to off-white font, opaque black base, font with applied glass peg which is plastered into top of the hollow stem, #3 collar, 11" h, 5 5/8" d base, minute flake under base, two minute open bubbles to top of foot. **$2,860**

Lamp, student's, brass, acorn-shaped font, green overlay milk glass shade, two knobs marked "Duplex PA.", 21 1/4" h. **$690**

Lamp, table, art glass vase, pulled blue feather motif, applied threading on off-white iridescent ground, possibly Durand, gold finished hexagonal base, 9" h vase. **$862**

Photo courtesy Green Valley Auctions, Mt. Crawford, Va.; www.GreenValleyAuctions.com

Lamp, stand, cut double-overlay Punty, kerosene period, deep rose cut to white cut to colorless font, opaque black square base with gilt decoration, brass connector, #1 brass collar. Boston & Sandwich Glass Co. Second half 19th century. 9 3/4" h, 4" sq base. Minute flake to edge of one punty and a few minute flakes to lower base, several cut-through open bubbles on lower punties, some wear to gilt. **$2,599**

Photo courtesy Rago Arts and Auction Center, Lambertville, N.J.; www.RagoArts.com

Lamp, table, Albert Berry, its four-panel shade of pierced and hammered copper with sylvan scenes lined in green and white slag glass, and garland chain suspending bone drops, over a single-socket mahogany base. Dark original patina, 3" break to one glass pane, two small corner chips to another. Unmarked, 20" x 8 3/4". **$6,600**

Lamp, table, Arts & Crafts style, eight bent-glass panels with metal overlay, supported by a column base, 19" d x 21" h, very good condition. **$425**

Lamp, table, Arts & Crafts style, domed leaded-glass shade with a multi-colored border supported by a metal base, some cracked segments, 16" d x 21" h, very good condition. **$425**

Lamp, table, Arts & Crafts style, its leaded glass shade over a two-socket oak base. Original finish. Unmarked, 25" x 19" sq. **$480**

Lamp, table, Arts & Crafts style, its helmet-shaped shade with hammered metal bands lined in curved caramel slag glass, over a two-socket faceted base, in bronze patina. Unmarked, 22 1/4" x 15 1/2". **$1,440**

Lamp, table, Arts & Crafts style, its faceted shade lined in green slag glass over a cut-out and riveted single-socket oak base. Unmarked, 24" x 18". **$1,680**

Lamp, table, Dirk Van Erp, hammered copper and mica, its four-panel shade over a two-socket bulbous base. Fine original patina. Windmill stamp with remnant of D'Arcy Gaw. 16 1/2" x 15 1/2". **$8,400**
(Designer D'Arcy Gaw worked with Dirk Van Erp in his San Francisco studio in 1910-11.)

Photo courtesy Rago Arts and Auction Center, Lambertville, N.J.; www.RagoArts.com

Lamp, table, Dirk Van Erp, hammered copper and mica, its four-panel conical shade atop a two-socket trumpet-shaped base. Original patina and mica. Open box windmill mark, 18" x 17". **$14,400**

Photo courtesy James D. Julia Auctioneers, Fairfield, Maine; www.JuliaAuctions.com

Duffner & Kimberly Peony Table Lamp. With red peony blossoms surrounding the entire bottom two-thirds of the shade. The upper third is done with a cream, yellow and tan background glass and the peony leaves are done in a bluish-green mottled glass (second view). The shade rests on a large bronze base with stylized leaves surrounding the foot and adorning the stem. The lamp is finished with a four-socket cluster and original Duffner heat cap with heart cutouts. The base is finished with a brown patina with strong green overtones. Shade is 24 1/2" diameter. Overall 32" h. A few tight hairlines. Base has some replacement socket parts. **$57,500**

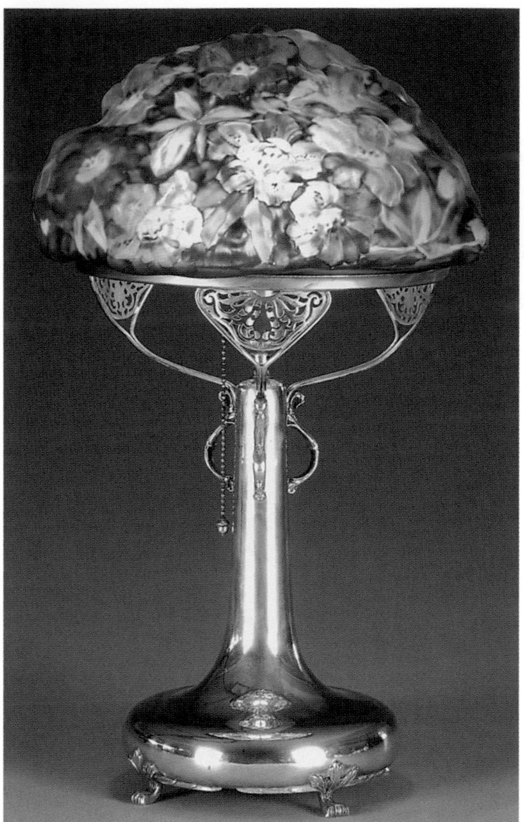

Photo courtesy James D. Julia Auctioneers, Fairfield, Maine; www.JuliaAuctions.com

Pairpoint Puffy Azalea Table Lamp. The stamens are an earthen color against the yellow centers (second view). The background is painted in a variety of greens. The shade is supported by a silver-plated base having three Art Nouveau stylized arms that support the ring, a single socket and a simple center shaft flowing into a padded bulbous base with four applied feet. Shade is signed on the exterior rim "The Pairpoint Corp July 9 1907". Base is signed "Pairpoint Mfg Co", a "P" in a diamond and "3033". Shade is 10" diameter. Overall 21" h. Minor wear to silver plate on base. **$17,250**

Lamp, table, Handel, its lobed, acid-etched shade reverse-painted with a lakeside landscape at dusk, over a rare three-socket Teroma base, obverse-painted with a river landscape. Flecks to edge of shade. Shade stamped HANDEL Lamps with patent, base signed F. Gubisch, 23 1/2" x 18". **$10,200**

Lamp, table, Handel, its acid-etched shade reverse- and obverse-painted with an autumnal landscape, over a three-socket, orb-shaped base. Strong base and excellent original patina. Shade signed HANDEL 5209, artist signed R. Lockrow, stamped Handel Pat, stamped HANDEL on base, 24 1/2" x 18". **$21,600**

Lamp, table, Handel, its hemispherical acid-etched shade reverse-painted by F. Gubisch with daffodils on a three-socket, bulbous bronzed base; 3/8" chip inside rim. Shade signed with HANDEL LAMPS, patent number, and HANDEL 7122 Gubisch, base stamped HANDEL, 24" x 18". **$8,400**

Photo courtesy James D. Julia Auctioneers, Fairfield, Maine; www.JuliaAuctions.com

Duffner & Kimberly Thistle Table Lamp. Shade begins with striated earthen-hued geometric panels accented by green teardrops in the upper portion of the shade with purple textured glass accented in yellow, turquoise and blue glass on the apron. Irregular bordered shade is supported by a three-socket thistle base in high relief. Shade is 19" diameter. Overall 24" h. A few tight hairlines. **$10,350**

Lamp, table, Handel, its ribbed "chipped ice" glass shade reverse-painted with a landscape at dusk, over a matching three-socket base in bronze patina. Soft white spots inside shade do not show through the outside, restored patina, two small, flat flakes to side of shade. Base and shade stamped HANDEL, 22 1/2" x 15 1/2". **$4,200**

Lamp, table, Handel, its "chipped ice" glass shade obverse-painted with a landscape, reverse-painted with shading, over a two-socket fluted base in bronze patina. Shade stamped HANDEL with patent number, 22" x 16". ... **$4,560**

Lamp, table, Handel, its faceted shade overlaid with Queen Anne's lace on green and caramel slag glass, over a bronzed two-socket tree trunk base. Two splits to bottom of shade, replaced cap soldered onto shade, some replaced glass panels. Base stamped HANDEL 5339, 24 1/2" x 18". **$3,120**

Lamp, table, Jefferson/Handel, Jefferson shade of acid-etched glass reverse-painted with a bucolic landscape, over a smaller Handel two-socket base with bronzed patina. Small nicks to edge of shade, remnants of glue from tape, replaced sockets. Shade marked 1897 and stamped Jefferson, base unmarked, 20 1/2" x 18". **$2,040**

Lamp, table, Jefferson, its "chipped ice" glass shade reverse-painted with a sepia tone landscape, over a two-socket bulbous chipped-ice glass base with copper finish. Shade signed 1885 Jefferson and rare artist signature M.G., 22 1/2" x 18". **$2,400**
(Jefferson Lamp Co., Steubenville, Ohio, and Follansbee, W.V., 1900-1933.)

Lamp, table, leaded glass, mushroom-shaped shade in a tulip design on a three-light quatrefoil base with bronze patina, 19th century, couple of short breaks on glass. Unmarked, 25" x 19". **$2,760**

Lamp, table, with slag-glass shade, hexagonal paneled brown and white slag-glass shade, three sockets, bronze base with slender baluster standard, leaf-and-berry motif, circular base, 22 3/4" h (including finial), 17" w shade. **$747**

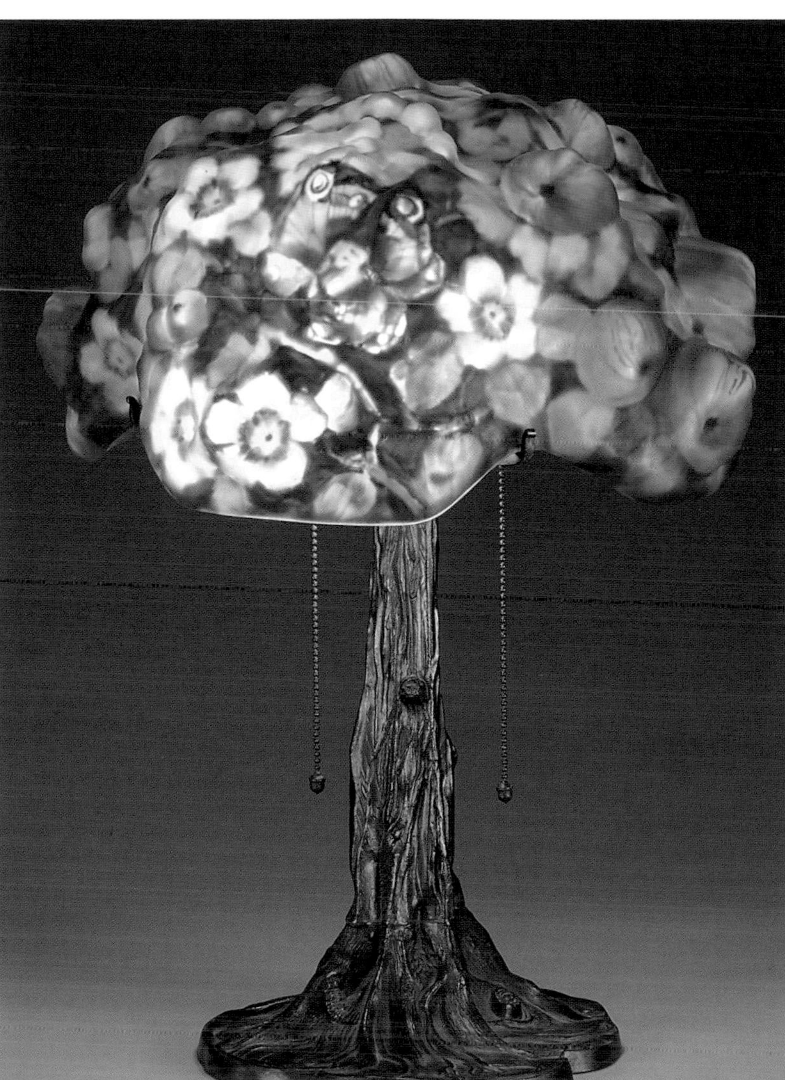

Photo courtesy James D. Julia Auctioneers, Fairfield, Maine; www.JuliaAuctions.com

Pairpoint Puffy Apple Tree Lamp. Background of rich green leaves with bluish highlights with pink apple blossoms surrounding green and red apples. The shade is further highlighted with a cluster of three bumblebees on one side and two butterflies on the opposing side. The shade rests on a Pairpoint tree-trunk base with four-arm spider and double-socket cluster. Shade is unsigned. Base is signed on underside "Pairpoint Mfg. Co." with a "P" inside a diamond and "3091". Shade is 16" diameter at the widest. Overall 21" t.
$32,200

Photo courtesy James D. Julia Auctioneers, Fairfield, Maine; www.JuliaAuctions.com

Handel Cattail Table Lamp. With eight textured caramel-glass panels that are decorated with metal overlay design of cattails and foliage in green and brown. Shade is supported by a simple three-socket Handel Art Nouveau base. Overall chocolate brown patina finish. Shade is signed "Handel" on the ring and base is signed with a Handel cloth tag. Shade is 20" diameter. Overall 22" h. **$8,775**

Photo courtesy James D. Julia Auctioneers, Fairfield, Maine; www.JuliaAuctions.com

Handel Treasure Island Table Lamp. Dome-shaped shade reverse painted with a decoration of palm trees, ocean and sailing ships against a moon-lit bay. The colors used are predominantly blues, greens and subtle earthen hues. Shade is signed "Handel 6391" on interior as well as "Handel Lamps" on the ring. Shade rests on a bronzed inverted trumpet-style, three-socket base complete with three acorn pull chains having brown patina. Shade is 18" diameter. **$14,400**

Photo courtesy James D. Julia Auctioneers, Fairfield, Maine; www.JuliaAuctions.com

Handel Blue Chinese Pheasant Table Lamp. Shade has two Chinese pheasants painted in vibrant oranges, yellows, mauve, green and gray with minute detailing given to every aspect of the bird. The birds are set against a royal-blue background with green vertical stripes that represent the stylized foliage. Also decorating the shade are flowers painted in various shades of pink with yellow foliage and buds. The shade is completed with areas of gray and white to give it a three-dimensional effect. The shade is supported by a three-socket base with two gargoyle heads supporting rings. The shade rests atop an original Handel three-legged base with stylized leaf design at the termination of each leg. Base is finished with an original Handel heat cap with square cutout design and three-socket cluster. Shade is signed "Handel Lamps" on the aperture ring and is signed "Handel 2175 PAL" on the interior rim. Base is unsigned. Shade is 18" diameter. Overall 24" h. Minor blistering to finish on base. **$27,600**

Photo courtesy James D. Julia Auctioneers, Fairfield, Maine; www.JuliaAuctions.com

G. Argy Rousseau Luminaire. Depicts eel heads impressed into the luminaire panel on both front and back giving a three-dimensional feel to the luminaire. The glass panel has wispy colors of purple, pink and maroon against a clear background. The panel rests in original hammered metal stand with lighted interior. Panel is signed on the front "G. Argy-Rousseau France". Overall 9 1/4" w x 7" h. **$9,660**

Photo courtesy James D. Julia Auctioneers, Fairfield, Maine; www.JuliaAuctions.com

Wilkinson Swirling Daffodil Table Lamp. Fully leaded table lamp has a border of realistic daffodils created in lemon yellow with green foliage and border glass of tan. This decoration is set against a swirl-effect leaded background in amethyst glass that was a favorite of the Wilkinson Company. This irregular-bordered shade is supported by a four-socket base with four acorn pulls. Base has an antique brass finish and appears to be all original. Shade is 20" diameter. Overall 26" h. Some tight hairlines. Base has minor wear to patina. **$11,500**

Photo courtesy James D. Julia Auctioneers, Fairfield, Maine; www.JuliaAuctions.com

Gorham Leaded Table Lamp. Leaded shade has rich red poppies extending around the entire shade (second view). Butterflies in flight surround the shoulder of the massive shade. The shade rests on a bronze base with raised poppy design in high relief at the four feet. The bulging stem is also decorated with high-relief poppies on two sides and butterflies on the other two sides. The riser supports a large six-socket cluster. The base is finished in a green patina. Shade is 25" diameter. Overall 30" h. minor wear to patina on base. **$47,150**

Lamps (pair), floor, brass, electrified, two circular tiers with six lights and brass flame finial, larger tier below with 12 lights, ringed round shaft on domical base with three cast brass lion supports, 72" h (top of flame finial). .... **$488 pair**

Lamps (pair), mantel, bronze, Argand style, mid-19th century, bell-form top with anthemion cresting supporting pod-and-spear prisms, cast curved arm supporting light fixture, short fluted columnar support on square base, 17 3/4" h. .... **$3,450 pair**
(Named for Ami Argand [1755-1803], a Swiss inventor.)

Lamps (pair), Murano Glass, fluted glass with controlled bubbles, "spruzzata" (spattered) gold and metal fittings, 20th century, height without socket: 23". .... **$1,080 pair**

Lamps (hand), pair, pewter, Roswell Gleason (1799-1887), Dorchester, Mass., active 1822-71, the lamps with camphene burners on acorn-shaped fonts, dish base with ring handles, impressed maker's marks, (wear), 6 1/2" h, uneven surface, fine pitting on the dish bases. .... **$444 pair**

Lamps (stand), pair, blown-molded overshot fonts, kerosene period, cranberry fonts with medial gilt rings, each on an opaque white square base with worn gilt and American flag decoration, differing #1 fine-line collars, matching Miller burners and flattened petal-top chimneys. Probably Boston & Sandwich Glass Co., 9 3/4" h, 4" sq base. One with wear to font gilt, both with minor annealing lines to lower edge of base, one with open bubbles to base and shallow chips/roughness under base. .... **$1,870 pair**

Lamps (pair), table, porcelain, figural, girl in 18th-century costume holding basket of flowers, rocky, gilt metal base; lady wearing bonnet and flowered dress, small purse on arm, 8 1/2" h (figures), index finger of left hand of one figure broken off. .... **$230 pair**

Lamps (two), table, Bradley & Hubbard, their "chipped ice" glass shades obverse-painted with a band of stylized ivy, and reverse-painted with a mossy ground, over three-socket Arts & Crafts bases. Different bronze patinas, both caps and finials replaced. Bases marked B304, 25 1/2" x 18". .... **$6,000 both**

Lantern, Arts & Crafts style, geometric design in metal, and mottled green and white leaded glass, unmarked, 7" w x 20" h. **$1,500**

Lantern, Arts & Crafts style, cylindrical shape in hammered copper with oval cutouts and a mica liner, original patina, unmarked, 9 1/2" w x 13" h. **$550**

Lantern, pierced tin and glass, kerosene, marked "S. Sargent's Patent Sept. 17, 1861," with ring handle, tin font with kerosene burner, embossed brass patent label, 18 1/2" h. **$296**

Lantern, Gustav Stickley, unusual oversized wrought copper with pyramidal shade, heart cut-outs, original ceiling plate and chain, and fine original amber glass, under a rich original dark brown patina. Unmarked. Lantern to tip of hook: 15" x 9 1/2", chain to ceiling mount: 10". **$19,200**

Lanterns (pair), Gustav Stickley, wrought iron rectangular with pyramidal tops, with original pyramidal wall mounts. Complete with original hammered amber glass and pyramidal mounting screws. Sanded finish, replaced inner tabs. Lanterns: 5 1/2" x 6" sq. Back plate: 6" sq. .... **$3,360 pair**

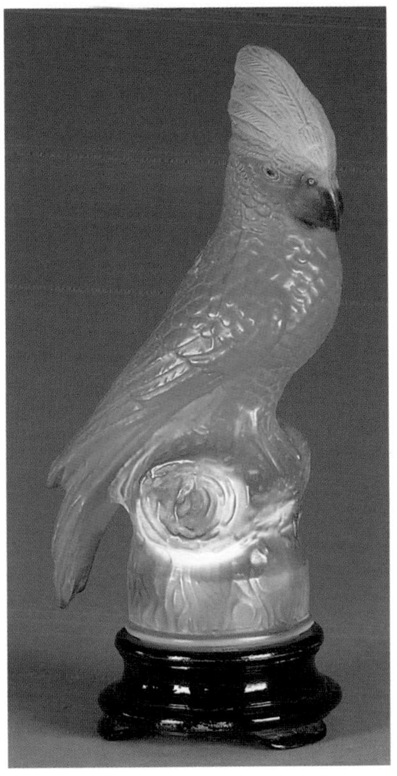

Photo courtesy James D. Julia Auctioneers, Fairfield, Maine; www.JuliaAuctions.com

Consolidated Parrot Lamp. Pressed-glass shade in the shape of a parrot perched atop a brown log. The parrot is painted in bright orange with green topknot. Shade screws on to a black glass footed base. 13" h. One tiny chip to bottom rim of shade. **$300**

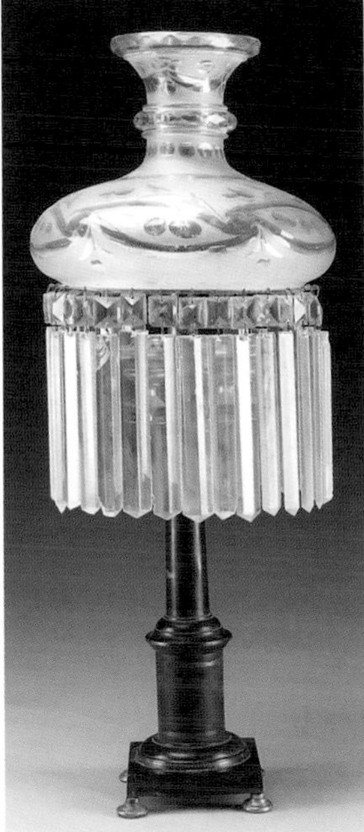

Photo courtesy James D. Julia Auctioneers, Fairfield, Maine; www.JuliaAuctions.com

Early Sinumbra Lamp. With four brass turned feet supporting a square base with pillar-type stem leading to the Sinumbra font. The lamp is finished with a frosted cut to clear shade with stylized floral design and large prisms. Lamp is signed with a square tag on the font "Stoutenburg & Morgan New York". 29" h. Lamp has been electrified and three prisms are missing. A few of the other prisms have chips. **$1,725**

Photo courtesy James D. Julia Auctioneers, Fairfield, Maine; www.JuliaAuctions.com

Decorated Webb Burmese Miniature Lamp. Peach-pink shading to yellow with enamel decoration including a branch with a bird. The base with peach to pink shading to yellow having an enamel decoration of flowering branches. Base is marked on the underside "Thos. Webb & Sons Queens Burmese Ware Patent". Foreign burner. 8 1/2" h. **$2,300**

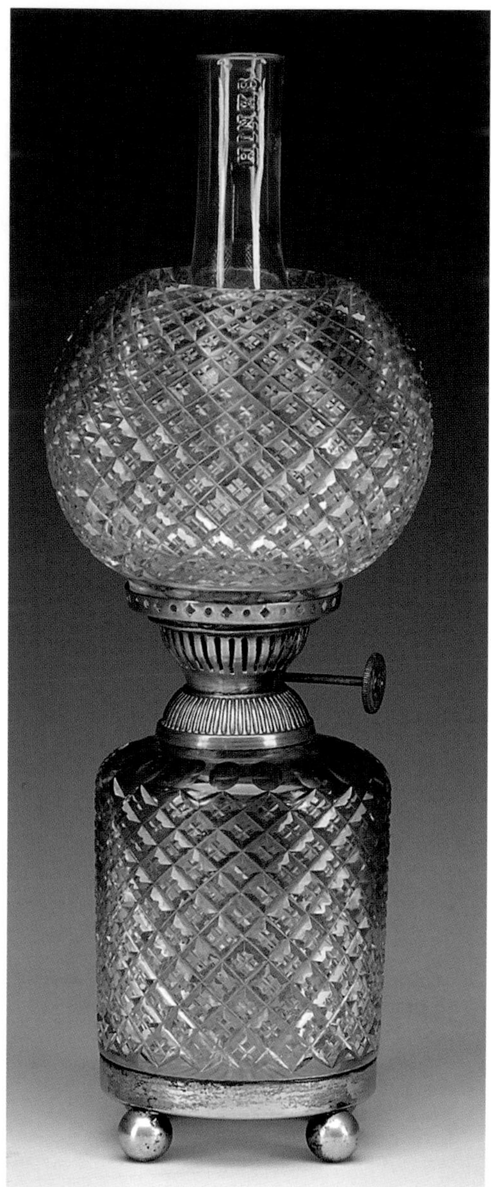

Photo courtesy James D. Julia Auctioneers, Fairfield, Maine; www.JuliaAuctions.com

Rainbow Cut-Glass Mini Lamp. SII-547. Strawberry pattern, yellow and pink coloring. Applied silver band with four ball feet around the base of the lamp. Hinks burner with signed "Hinks" chimney. 9 1/2" h. There are two minor imperfections in the cut design on the base, also one small imperfection in the cut on the shade. **$9,775**

Lanterns (two), Roycroft, copper, one with clear glass panes and smooth ceiling cap, the other with amber bubble glass and hammered cap. (From Elbert Hubbard's son's residence in East Aurora, N.Y.) Unmarked. With plate: 18" x 8" and 20" x 7". .... **$2,400 both**

Sconce, hanging, Gustav Stickley, hammered copper with four hammered amber glass hanging panels, complete with chain and ceiling cap. Stamped Als-ik-kan, 42" x 7" sq. **$22,800**

Sconce, wall, Roycroft, designed by Dard Hunter (1883-1966) with cylindrical shade of leaded glass in bright green and purple, complete with wall cap. Unmarked, 8 1/2" x 5" x 6 1/4". **$9,600**

Sconces (four), wall, Roycroft, hammered brass, three with candle fixture. Original patina and switch. (From Elbert Hubbard's son's residence in East Aurora, N.Y.) Unmarked, 10" x 3 1/2". .... **$1,680 all**

Shade, cased glass ring-top cone, kerosene period, pale blue with opal interior, 5 1/2" h, 10 3/8" d. **$357**

Shade, flaring, Roycroft, designed by Dard Hunter (1883-1966) of bright green and purple leaded slag glass. Unmarked, 6" x 18". **$11,400**

Shade, Handel, domed leaded glass with overall dogwood design. Marked Handel on the inside, 6 3/4" x 15 5/8". **$2,760**

Shade, Oregon, kerosene period, cut overlay foliate, ruby rough cut to colorless, crimped and tooled rim, 6 1/2" h, 3" fitter, two shallow chips and flake to fitter. **$825**

Photo courtesy James D. Julia Auctioneers, Fairfield, Maine; www.JuliaAuctions.com

Miniature Hanging Lamp. SII-381. Brass frame and chain with side arms depicting birds sitting on tree branches. Removable font marked "LP Lamp Co Sample" and "83" in the center. Green transparent prisms. Cosmos pattern clear glass shade flashed green. Acorn burner. Overall 12" l. **$1,840**

Photo courtesy Rago Arts and Auction Center, Lambertville, N.J.; www.RagoArts.com

Shade, Handel, leaded glass with dogwood design and a graded checkered design on top. Marked Handel on inside of shade, 9" x 18 1/2" d. **$2,520**

Photo courtesy James D. Julia Auctioneers, Fairfield, Maine; www.JuliaAuctions.com

Quezal Art Glass Shade. Snake skin dark green decorated shade with platinum iridescence. Unlined interior. Signed on the fitter rim with early engraved "Quezal" signature. 6 3/4" diameter. Minor wear to gold iridescence. **$3,600**

Photo courtesy James D. Julia Auctioneers, Fairfield, Maine; www.JuliaAuctions.com

Steuben Art Glass Shade. Gold iridescent hearts and vines decoration on indigo blue iridescent background, with applied gold iridescent border. The shade has metal fitter. Unsigned. 10" diameter. **$4,600**

Photo courtesy James D. Julia Auctioneers, Fairfield, Maine; www.JuliaAuctions.com

Quezal Art Glass Shade. Platinum pulled-feather decoration on dark green striped ground, gold iridescent interior. Early engraved signature "Quezal" on the fitter rim. 5" t x 2 1/4" fitter. **$1,610**

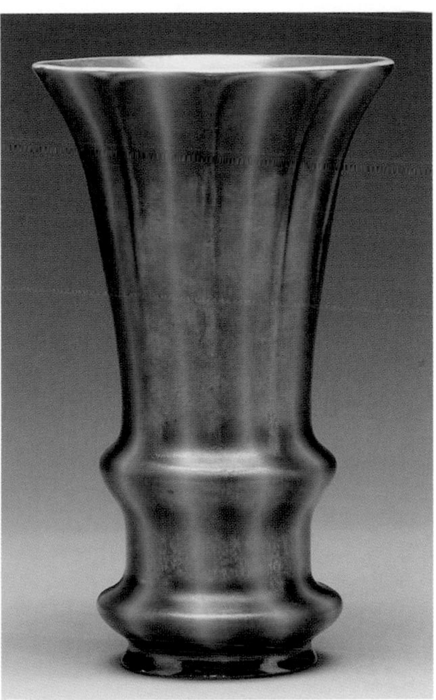

Photo courtesy James D. Julia Auctioneers, Fairfield, Maine; www.JuliaAuctions.com

Durand Art Glass Shade. Oversized green optic ribbed art glass shade has unusual shape of elongated trumpet form decorated with gold interior and exterior having blue and pink highlights. 10" t with 3" fitter. **$1,092**

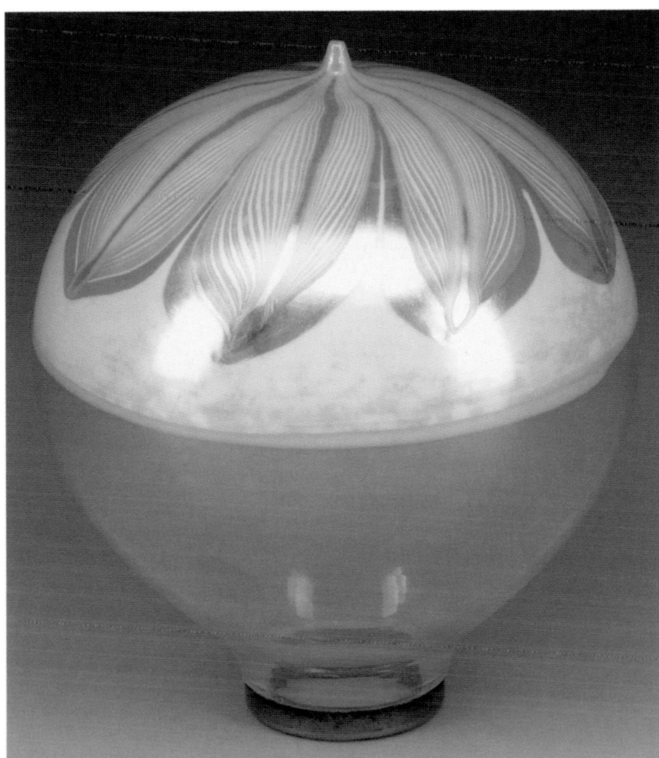

Photo courtesy James D. Julia Auctioneers, Fairfield, Maine; www.JuliaAuctions.com

Decorated Bulb Shade. Clear glass form bulbs out to the end where it is decorated with a green pulled-feather pattern with gold trim on an ivory ground. The shade is completed with a metal collar. This style of shade is considered to be from the transitional period and is a rarity to still find. 6" t x 1 1/2" fitter. **$402**

Modernism

FUTURE OF THE MARKET: MODERNISM

The deep roots and far reach of Modern

By Noah Fleisher

Noah Fleisher

There is more than a little irony in the fact that, in the world of collecting, "Modern" has a retro connotation.

It is the stuff of the 1933 Chicago World's Fair "Century of Progress," the boundless optimism of post-World War II America, the sleek comic lines and manic music of Tex Avery's MGM 1949 "House of Tomorrow" cartoons, and the ever-present acres of the suburban ranch house that subsequently spread endlessly across the nation.

The fact is that "Modernism" has never gone out of style. Its reach into the present day is as deep as its roots in the past. Just as it can be seen and felt ubiquitously in the mass media of today – on film, television, in magazines and department stores – it can be traced to the mid-1800s post-Empire non-conformity of the Biedermeier Movement, the turn of the 20th century anti-Victorianism of the Vienna Secessionists, the radical reductionism of Frank Lloyd Wright and the revolutionary post-Depression thinking of Walter Gropius and the Bauhaus school in Germany. There is no end to the ways in which the movement of Modernism, its evolution and continuing influence, can be parsed.

Photo courtesy Heritage Auction Galleries, Dallas; www.HA.com

Gilbert Rohde, Brazilian rosewood table clock, model no. 4738, manufactured by Herman Miller Modern Electric Clocks, circa 1939. 6 1/8" x 5 1/2" x 2". **$1,500+**

Photo courtesy Rago Arts and Auction Center, Lambertville, N.J.; www.RagoArts.com

LA II (Angel Ortiz, American, born 1967), untitled, acrylic on plaster bust of Tutankhamen. Signed and tagged throughout, 21 1/2" h. **$840**

Klaus Ihlenfeld, (German/American, 20th century), untitled sculpture, phosphorous bronze, signed, 14" h. **$3,600**

Klaus Ihlenfeld, (German/American, 20th century), Espalier, circa 2000, phosphorous bronze, signed, 13 1/2" h. **$2,520**

Klaus Ihlenfeld, (German/American, 20th century), Tonal, phosphorous bronze, signed, 14 1/2" h. **$4,500**

Ilonka Karasz, (American, 1886-1981), cover Illustration for The New Yorker, July 19, 1941, gouache on paper (framed), signed, 16 7/8" x 12 1/4" (sight). **$9,600**

Philip and Kelvin Laverne, wall-hanging plaque in patinated metal with two women gazing from a window in sculptural relief, 1993. Engraved PHILIP KELVIN LAVERNE 93, 21 1/2" x 13 1/4". **$1,560**

Philip and Kelvin Laverne, acid-etched and patinated bronze plaque, "Making Love," within integrated frame. Signed Philip Kelvin Laverne, with original artist label and title on verso, 39 1/2" x 25". **$1,800**

Robert Loughlin, (American, born 1949), Rome IIIX, 2007, acrylic on canvas. Signed, dated and titled, 48" x 48"; accompanied by a Brillo Box painted by the artist. .... **$1,320 both**

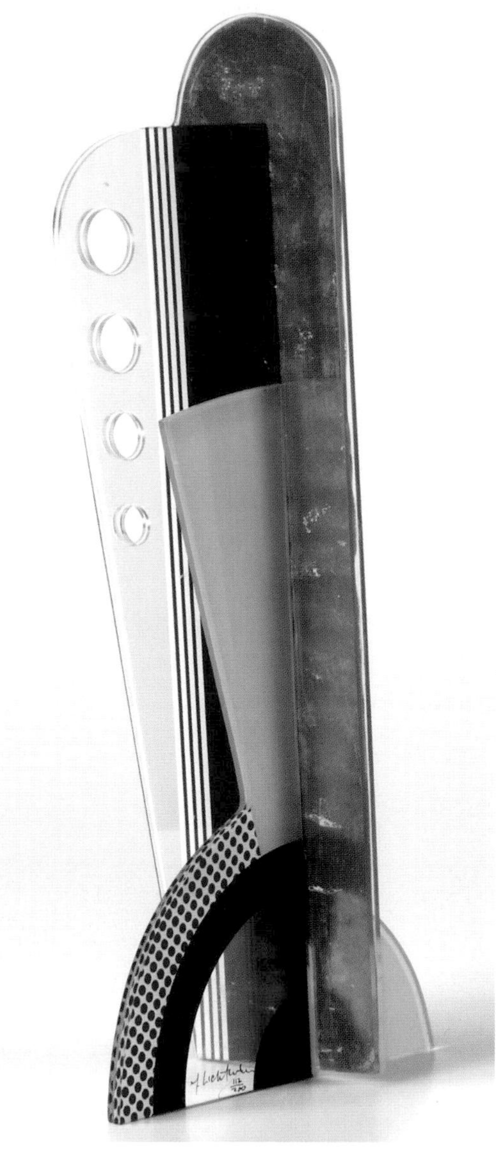

Photo courtesy Rago Arts and Auction Center, Lambertville, N.J.; www.RagoArts.com

Roy Lichtenstein (American, 1923-1997), Modern Sculpture with Apertures, 1967; Plexiglas with enamel screen print and silver Mylar; signed and numbered 112/200, 16 5/8" high. **$5,400**

Graham Marx, massive glazed terra-cotta ribbed sculpture with "torn" rim, approx. 23 1/2" x 34" x 23 1/2". **$4,200**

Graham Marx, massive glazed terra cotta gourd-shaped sculpture, approx. 30" x 29" x 23". **$16,800**

Isamu Noguchi / Gemini G.E.L., Neolithic, hot-dipped galvanized steel sculpture, 1983. Welded initials and date (i.n. 82.) Edition of 18, 72" x 26 1/2" x 16 1/2". **$90,000**

Albert Paley, sculpture of forged and fabricated steel, 1990. Signed PALEY with copyright, also inscribed 4/15 1990, 40" x 8" d. **$9,600**

Emile-Jacques Ruhlmann, Art Deco gilded plaster ceiling sculpture with stylized flowers from the Bon Marche department store. Approx. 47" x 29". **$3,900**

Silas Seandel, ribbon wall sculpture of forged steel. Script signature, 13 1/4" x 61 1/4". **$1,680**

Paul Soldner, slab-built, Raku-fired abstract sculpture, 1981, 14 1/2" x 35". **$22,800**

Paul Soldner, Raku fired sculpture from the Winged Series, 27" x 40" x 17". **$2,400**

Akio Takamori, ceramic sculpture, "Man with Faces," 1982, signed Akio, 11" x 16". **$7,800**

Jack Thompson, ceramic sculpture, "Dog Moses' Transition," 1981, 25" x 13" x 12". **$3,240**

Abraham Joel Tobias, (American, 1913-1996), untitled, pastel on paper, signed, 24 3/4" x 19". **$1,440**

Paul Wunderlich, (German, born 1927), Torse De Femme and Torse De L'Homme, 1983, bronze, each signed and numbered 139/250, 17 1/2" h (male figure, including base), 14" high (female figure, including base); Foundry: Albrecht, Altrandsberg, Germany, 1984. .... **$3,120 pair**

Edward Zucca, wall sculpture, "A Victorian Time Machine," with tintype photographs mounted in a tiger maple frame, 1993. Signed, dated, titled, with personal inscription, verso, 7" x 53 1/2". **$1,440**

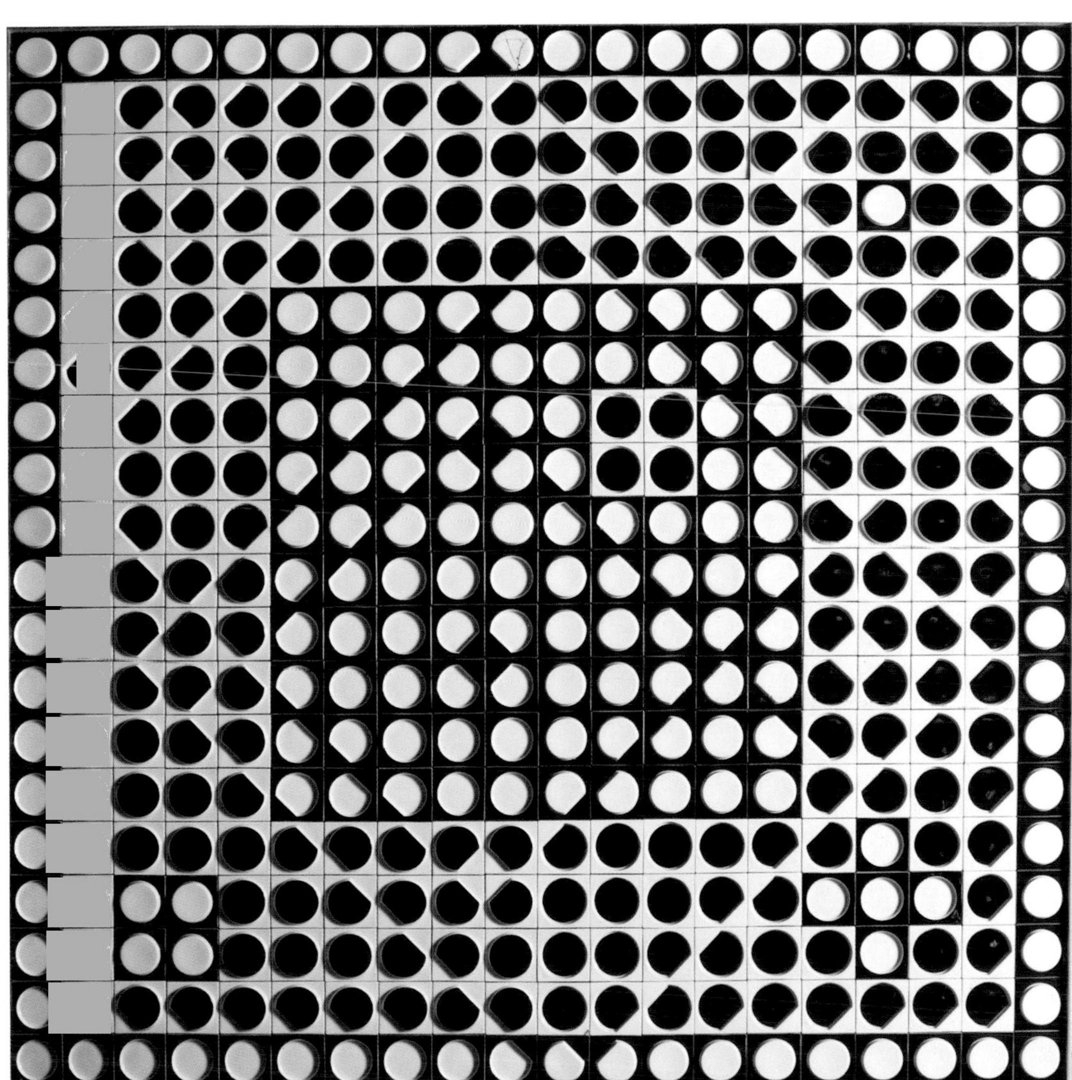

Photo courtesy Rago Arts and Auction Center, Lambertville, N.J.; www.RagoArts.com

Victor Vasarely / Rosenthal NB 22, Caope, wall-hanging sculptural relief panel composed of raised and inset black and white porcelain tiles, in metal frame. (Illustrated: Sixties Design by Philippe Garne, page 179), 78" sq. **$51,000**

Ceramics, Functional

Wesley Anderegg, Raku-fired figural earthenware cup and saucer, 1995. Signed and dated. Cup and saucer together: 5 3/4" x 6" x 3 1/4". **$900**

Wesley Anderegg, Raku-fired figural cup and saucer on human sandwich base, 1996. Signed and dated. Cup and saucer together: 6 1/2" x 5 1/2" x 7 1/2". **$2,040**

Claude Conover, stoneware vessel, "Acalac." Signed and titled, 20 1/2" x 16 1/2". **$5,400**

Richard Devore, flaring stoneware vessel, "Untitled no. 1024," with a dead-matte gray interior with small shelf, 12" x 12 3/4". **$7,200**

Richard Hirsch, large tripod ceramic vessel, 1992. Signed and dated, approx: 37 1/2" x 29" x 29". **$2,160**

Karen Karnes, stoneware winged tureen covered in deep-green matte mottled glaze. Chop mark KK., 8" x 21". **$5,100**

Michael Lucero, faience sculptural double-vessel glazed in bright polychrome. Signed Michael Lucero with oversized barcode, 25-40 ML, 8 1/4" x 11 1/2" x 3 1/2". **$2,400**

Warren MacKenzie, stoneware platter with random white pattern on mirrored brown ground, along with porcelain covered jar in celadon glaze. Jar signed with chop mark, 2 1/2" x 12 3/4" and 3 1/2" x 4 1/2". .... **$900 both**

Marc Newsom / Cor Unum, sci-fi ceramic vase in white glaze. Decal with Cor Unum Ceramics and Art the Netherlands, stamped cipher, 13 1/2" x 12". **$720**

Picasso / Madoura, faience pitcher with abstract animal design. Signed EDITION PICASSO MADOURA, and numbered 165/200, 8" x 11 1/2" x 4 1/2". **$5,400**

Picasso / Madoura, faience pitcher with abstract bird design. Signed EDITION PICASSO MADOURA, 11 1/2" x 8 1/2" x 6". **$5,700**

Picasso / Madoura, figural faience vessel depicting a woman in black and white glaze. Signed EDITION PICASSO MADOURA, 11 1/2" x 8 1/2" x 5 1/2". **$7,200**

Picasso / Madoura, faience pitcher with abstract faces design. Signed EDITION PICASSO MADOURA, and numbered 84/300, 9 1/4" x 7 1/2" x 4 1/2". **$7,200**

Pillin, oval charger with circus performers on horses, signed, 10 1/2" x 16 3/4". **$1,800**

Pillin, jardinere painted with horses and ladies, signed, 8 1/2" x 9 1/2". **$2,520**

Photo courtesy Rago Arts and Auction Center, Lambertville, N.J.; www.RagoArts.com

Picasso / Madoura, faience pitcher with abstract animal design. Signed EDITION PICASSO MADOURA, 10" x 6" x 4". **$4,200**

Photo courtesy Rago Arts and Auction Center, Lambertville, N.J.; www.RagoArts.com

Pillin, vase painted with ladies holding fish-laden nets, signed, 14 1/2" x 6 1/4". **$2,400**

Mary Roehm, flaring wood-fired porcelain bowl covered in celadon semi-matte glaze. Script signature, 9" x 21 1/2" d. **$1,200**

Paul Schreckengost, glazed earthenware Art Deco teapot and cup, 7" x 11 1/2" x 4" and 2 1/2" x 5" x 3 3/4". .... **$6,000 both**

Paul Soldner, Raku-fired spherical footed vessel, circa 1965-72, 9 3/4" x 11". **$1,800**

Paul Soldner, slab-built, Raku-fired vessel, "Voco," 1981, 14 3/4" x 11 1/4". **$1,560**

Paul Soldner, Raku-fired vessel with applied and painted floral motifs, 1981, 19" x 14" x 9". **$2,400**

Rudolph Staffel, flaring porcelain cup, circa 1980, 3" x 3 1/2". **$720**

Henry Takemoto, stoneware charger with abstract brush strokes in indigo and gunmetal brown, 1959. Signed and dated, 2 1/2" x 16 1/2". **$4,200**

Peter Voulkos, wood-fired stoneware charger with three small "prunts" (ornaments) covered in ivory glaze, 1981. Signed V.O.U.L.K.O.S., 5 1/2" x 21". **$14,400**

Peter Voulkos, Shigaraki stoneware charger inscribed to the kiln in which it was fired, "FOR BIG 'AUTASH' KEEP PUFFIN AND BE GOOD Voulkos 91," 1997. Signed V.O.U.L.K.O.S. 97, U.C.F., 5 1/2" x 23". **$4,800**

Peter Voulkos, Raku-fired plate with torn chunks, 1995. Signed and dated, 5" x 21". **$10,800**

Peter Voulkos, stoneware plate, gas-fired, 1978. Signed V.O.U.L.K.O.S. 78, 4" x 22". **$14,400**

Betty Woodman, stoneware footed jardinere with ribbon decoration. Stamped WOODMAN, 7 1/2" x 12". **$3,120**

Photo courtesy of Treadway Toomey Galleries, Cincinnati and Oak Park, Ill.; www.TreadwayGallery.com

Ben Seibel Modern Stoneware dinnerware, by Roseville for Raymor, USA, ceramic, 12 cups, 12 saucers, 12 dinner plates, seven bread plates, three salad plates, three serving dishes, three large covered casseroles, one small covered casserole, one creamer, one covered ramekin, one pitcher, one bowl, one small handled covered dish with lid, and one bean pot, one extra lid (not shown), all in terra-cotta, signed "Raymor by Roseville", dinner plate 12" d, creamer 4 1/4" h, excellent condition. **$700 all**

Photo courtesy Rago Arts and Auction Center, Lambertville, N.J.; www.RagoArts.com

George Nakashima, eight-drawer walnut wall-hanging cabinet with burl-wood pulls. (An exceptional and unusual early Nakashima cabinet, the piece was originally designed as part of the interior of a residence on King's Point, Long Island, for his early patrons, the Hammer family. Nakashima served as both the architect and interior designer, and the home was heralded as a new style of modern design influenced by handmade materials.) 11 3/4" x 96 1/4" x 19 1/4". **$78,000**

Philip and Kelvin Laverne, coffee table, its scalloped top etched with Asian vignettes, 17" x 47" x 23 1/4". **$5,700**

Thorald Madsens / Tove and Edvard Kindt-Larsen, rosewood dining chairs (eight) with black leather upholstery. Thorald Madsens metal tags, 32" x 19 1/2" x 17". .... **$21,600 set**

Bruna Mathsson / Karl Mathsson, teak and beech expandable dining table, 28 1/2" x 60" x 43 1/2". **$540**

George Nakashima, walnut wall-hanging bar with glass shelves and illuminated base, 18" x 60" x 6". **$4,200**

George Nakashima, Kornblut cabinet with burl-wood handle, 22" x 19" x 19 3/4". **$44,400**

George Nakashima, conoid cushion chair, in walnut with hickory spindles and black fabric cushions, 33 1/2" x 34" x 30". **$14,400**

George Nakashima, conoid cushion chair, in Burmese laurel with hickory spindles, 33 1/2" x 34" x 30". **$22,800**

George Nakashima, walnut conoid chairs (pair) with hickory spindles, marked with client's name, 35 1/2" x 21" x 19 1/2". .... **$19,200 pair**

George Nakashima, walnut Conoid chairs (six) with hickory spindles, marked with client's name, 35 1/2" x 21" x 20". .... **$51,000 set**

George Nakashima, lounge chair with free-edge writing arm in English walnut, 1987. Signed George Nakashima April 15, 1987, and marked with client's name, 33 1/4" x 31" x 25". **$13,200**

Photo courtesy Rago Arts and Auction Center, Lambertville, N.J.; www.RagoArts.com

George Nakashima, English walnut single-pedestal desk with freeform, free-edge top incorporating four rosewood butterfly keys, over a bank of three drawers with finished back, and a rosewood cross-plank support, 29" x 78" x 40 1/2". **$132,000**

George Nakashima, "New Chair with Arms," walnut, 1970, marked SHOWROOM and signed George Nakashima 1970, 39" x 25" x 21". **$7,800**

George Nakashima, "New Chairs with Arms" (pair), walnut, marked with client's name. 38 1/2" x 25" x 21". .... **$10,800 pair**

George Nakashima, walnut lounge rocker with free-shaped arm. Signed STUDIO-ROCKER, 34" x 33" x 35". **$10,200**

George Nakashima, walnut credenza with four interior drawers and two shelves, and finished back, 32" x 60" x 24". **$19,200**

George Nakashima, double-pedestal desk in walnut, its free-edge top with single rosewood butterfly key, marked with client's name, 27 3/4" x 80 1/2" x 30 1/2". **$43,200**

George Nakashima, single-drawer desk in walnut on trestle base with free-edge top, 30" x 70" x 29 1/2". **$96,000**

George Nakashima, walnut four-drawer dresser with free-edge top, marked with client's name, 32" x 36" x 22". **$14,400**

George Nakashima, free-edge headboard in English walnut with five rosewood butterfly keys, 42" x 104 1/2". **$48,000**

George Nakashima, walnut two-drawer nightstands (pair), one marked with client's name, 25 1/2" x 15 1/2" x 19 1/4". .... **$24,000 pair**

George Nakashima, coffee table with free-edge walnut top, marked with client's name, 13" x 82 1/2" x 21 1/4". **$30,000**

George Nakashima, Minguren I walnut coffee table with free-form, free-edge top incorporating two rosewood butterfly keys, 1977. (Accompanied by original drawing and sales receipt.) Marked with client's name, 15 1/2" x 98 1/2" x 34 1/2". **$144,000**

George Nakashima, slab coffee table in walnut with freeform top and single butterfly key, 13 1/4" x 44" x 20". **$43,200**

George Nakashima, sled-base coffee table with free-edge Persian walnut top, 1980. Marked with client's name; also reads, "Sled-type/Persian walnut/George Nakashima 1980," 14 1/2" x 81 1/2" x 28 1/2". **$54,000**

George Nakashima, walnut Frenchman's Cove table, marked with client's name, 28" x 49 1/2" x 50". **$16,800**

George Nakashima, round pedestal table in walnut, 28" x 42" d. **$9,000**

George Nakashima, walnut trestle table, its top with three rosewood butterfly keys, 28" x 60" x 24". **$26,400**

George Nakashima,Wohl table with free-edge top, 1988, signed George Nakashima, June 24, 1988, 12 1/2" x 23 1/4" x 15 1/2". **$5,700**

George Nakashima / Widdicomb, high-back lounge chair upholstered with ecru fabric, 41 1/2" x 31 1/2" x 33 3/4". **$10,200**
(John Widdicomb Co., Grand Rapids, Mich.)

George Nakashima / Widdicomb, lounge chair and ottoman upholstered with ecru fabric, 33" x 32 1/4" x 33" and 16" x 25" sq. .... **$11,400 both**
(John Widdicomb Co., Grand Rapids, Mich.)

George Nakashima / Widdicomb, walnut six-drawer dresser. Branded George Nakashima inside drawer, 32" x 76" x 22". **$5,700**
(John Widdicomb Co., Grand Rapids, Mich.)

George Nakashima / Widdicomb, 12-drawer dresser with recessed brass pulls in Sundra finish. Widdicomb fabric label, 32" x 105 1/2" x 22". **$6,600**
(John Widdicomb Co., Grand Rapids, Mich.)

George Nakashima / Widdicomb, king-size headboard with Sundra finish, and pair of single-drawer nightstands. Headboard: 38" x 109", nightstands: 21" x 22" x 21". **$7,200 all**
(John Widdicomb Co., Grand Rapids, Mich.)

Photo courtesy Rago Arts and Auction Center, Lambertville, N.J.; www.RagoArts.com

George Nakashima, round Minguren coffee table, in walnut with three rosewood butterfly keys, 1979, inscribed "To Alene, Abe, Merry Christmas 1979 George Nakashima," 15" x 48".
$33,600

Photo courtesy Rago Arts and Auction Center, Lambertville, N.J.; www.RagoArts.com

George Nelson / Herman Miller, CSS unit in rosewood veneer and brushed metal, with eight vertical supports, four black enameled metal light fixtures and numerous drawers, cupboards and shelves, 95" x 226" x 18 1/2". **$24,000**

George Nakashima / Widdicomb, single-arm sofa and settee with slatted side panels, upholstered in ecru fabric, 25 1/2" x 103" x 34" and 25 1/2" x 62" x 34". **$32,400**
(John Widdicomb Co., Grand Rapids, Mich.)

George Nakashima / Widdicomb, long coffee table in Sundra finish with burl-wood veneer panel to free-form top. Widdicomb factory number, 13 1/2" x 84" x 30 1/2". **$5,700**
(John Widdicomb Co., Grand Rapids, Mich.)

George Nakashima / Widdicomb, side tables (two) in Sundra finish, one with spindled lower shelf. Marked George Nakashima 9/59 Sundra, with Widdicomb decal, 21 1/4" x 30" x 20" and 16 1/2" x 30" sq. ....**$1,920 both**
(John Widdicomb Co., Grand Rapids, Mich.)

George Nelson, home office desk with tan leather covering to sliding doors and to writing surface, a lift-top storage compartment, and mesh Pendaflex file, 40 1/2" x 54 1/4" x 28". **$7,800**

George Nelson / Charles Deaton, CSS unit designed by George Nelson, consisting of 4 vertical supports with multiple drawers, cabinet and shelves, along with clock, barometer and radio unit, accompanied by L-shaped desk designed by Charles Deaton. CSS unit: 87" x 97" x 20", desk: 26" x 70" x 78". ....**$6,000 both**

George Nelson / Herman Miller, Thin Edge two-door rosewood cabinet with porcelain pulls and single interior shelf. Herman Miller foil label, 30" x 33" x 19 1/2". ...**$3,900**

George Nelson / Herman Miller, Thin Edge four-drawer rosewood chest with porcelain pulls. Herman Miller foil label, 30" x 33" x 19 1/2". **$4,200**

George Nelson / Herman Miller, Thin Edge five-drawer walnut chest with porcelain hourglass pulls, 41" x 40" x 19 1/2". **$2,400**

George Nelson / Herman Miller, swag-leg desk with two shallow drawers, 34 1/2" x 39" x 28 3/4". **$4,500**

George Nelson / Herman Miller, "Marshmallow" sofa upholstered in burnt orange velvet on brushed and enameled steel frame, 31 1/2" x 51 1/2" x 31 1/2". **$10,800**

George Nelson / Herman Miller, Catenary coffee table with plate glass top on polished steel base, 15 1/4" 36" sq. **$1,500**

Norwegian, curvilinear sofa with dark-green wool upholstery and paisley fabric seat cushions, 29" x 130" x 31". **$2,640**

Ottoman, 1950s, maker unknown, ebonized wood frame with sculptural curved legs placed on the center of each side, cushion reupholstered in beige mohair with a rectangular tufted button, refinished, 40" w x 40" d x 15" h, very good condition. **$1,300**

Albert Paley, plant stand of formed and fabricated steel with marble top, 1992. Signed Albert Paley 1992, 56" x 16" x 20". **$21,600**

Tommi Parzinger, "American Modern" sectional sofa, by Salterini, circa 1950, two middle and two end pieces, black metal frames with circle motif to backrests, removable cushions in original leopard print fabric, (back cushions and two round bolsters included but not shown), unsigned but documented, as shown: 109" w x 30 1/2" d x 28" h, frames repainted, very good condition. **$5,000**

Tommi Parzinger, occasional tables (pair), for Charak Modern, 1950s, two triangular forms can be used together to form a square, mahogany bases with lower shelf, leather tops with tooled edge and green/gold finish treatment, each signed with Charak label, original finish to tops, bases refinished, each is 54 1/2" w x 28" d x 18" h, used together: 40 1/4" square, very good condition. .... **$5,500 pair**

Phillip Lloyd Powell, walnut bench with woven ecru fabric cushions, and integrated marble-top table, 34 1/4" x 100 1/2" x 27". **$20,400**

Phillip Lloyd Powell, two-seat walnut bench with integrated table, and woven ecru fabric cushions, 30" x 65" x 29". **$20,400**

Phillip Lloyd Powell, two-door walnut cabinet with sculpted bi-fold doors concealing an enameled and silver-leafed interior with drawers, cabinets, shelves, and slate shelf, 92 1/2" x 48 1/2" x 21 1/4". **$60,000**

Phillip Lloyd Powell, interchangeable three-seat settee in mahogany with integrated travertine-top tables, 30" x 120" x 29". **$9,600**

Phillip Lloyd Powell, elliptical coffee table with slate top on mahogany base, 15 1/2" x 29 3/4" x 22 1/4". **$4,800**

Phillip Lloyd Powell, walnut coffee table with free-edge top, single butterfly key, and legs mortised through the top, 13 1/2" x 79" x 18 1/2". **$16,800**

Phillip Lloyd Powell / Paul Evans, walnut wall-hung vertical cabinet with sculpted bi-fold doors and bronze loop panel backed with beige linen, circa 1962, 54" x 30" x 19 1/4". **$60,000**

Plymouth, chest, 1940s, cherry-stained mahogany case has four recessed drawers with carved wood handles and square cutout detail, branded mark on back and metal tag in drawer, refinished, 30" w x 19 3/4" d x 33 1/2" h, very good condition. **$250**

John Risley, figural black wire lounge chair and ottoman. Chair: 40 1/2" x 26 1/2" x 29 3/4", ottoman: 17" x 20" x 40". .... **$6,000 pair**

John Risley, figural black wire chairs (two), one with arms, 49 1/2" x 28 3/4" x 19" and 47" x 18 3/4" x 17 1/2". .... **$4,800 both**

T.H. Robsjohn-Gibbings cabinet, for Widdicomb, bleached mahogany, five drawers with beveled edges and original brass ring pulls atop a curved platform base on hidden casters, refinished, Widdicomb Modern Originals tag in drawer, 54" w x 20 1/2" d x 32 3/4" h, very good condition. **$1,400**

Photo courtesy Heritage Auction Galleries, Dallas; www.HA.com

Charles And Ray Eames, set of five PKW side chairs, manufactured by Herman Miller USA, circa 1951, 31 1/2" x 18 1/2" x 16 1/2" each. Minor scratches and abrasions to the dowel legs. Surface wear throughout appropriate to age.
$1,800 set

Photo courtesy of Treadway Toomey Galleries, Cincinnati and Oak Park, Ill.; www.TreadwayGallery.com

T.H. Robsjohn-Gibbings dining set, for Widdicomb, table and six chairs, mahogany, table with round top and sunburst veneer pattern, 3 1/2" apron over curved reverse-tapered legs, lower curved stretchers, three 12" leaves, original finish, signed with cloth "Widdicomb Modern Originals" label, 48 1/4" d x 29" h, chairs with exaggerated curved backrests over oval front legs and splayed square back legs, original upholstery, original finish, 21" w x 21" d x 37 3/4" h, all in very good original condition. **$6,000 set**

Photo courtesy Rago Arts and Auction Center, Lambertville, N.J.; www.RagoArts.com

Eero Saarinen / Knoll, Grasshopper chair with corduroy upholstery, 34 1/2" x 27" x 32 1/2". **$2,160**

T.H. Robsjohn-Gibbings dining table, for Widdicomb, rectangular bleached mahogany top with thick apron over four legs with curved stretcher to base, two 14" leaves (not shown), original finish, signed with Widdicomb Modern Original tag, 40" w x 76" d x 29" h, very good condition. **$1,800**

Gilbert Rohde / Herman Miller, seven-piece bedroom suite, consisting of a vanity and stool, two four-drawer chests with Bakelite handles (one replaced), and a king-sized headboard. Marked with metal tag and stenciled numbers. Chests: 36 1/4" x 43" x 18", headboard: 35" x 77 1/4". .... **$1,500 all**

Gilbert Rohde / Herman Miller, East Indian laurel cabinet with two doors and two drawers. Herman Miller foil label, 41" x 48" x 15". **$3,600**

Gilbert Rohde, two-piece sectional sofa with single arm and tufted white fabric upholstery on tapering wood legs, 30" x 90 1/2" x 34 1/2" and 30" x 66 1/2" x 33". **$6,000**

Gilbert Rohde, custom-designed mahogany coffee table with scallop-edged marble top, 18" x 56" x 22". **$1,800**

Gilbert Rohde / Herman Miller, "Cloud" coffee table with exotic wood veneer top, and leatherette-covered supports, 15 1/2" x 41" x 31". **$1,920**

Rustic, cast-aluminum faux antler sofa with green and white fabric upholstery, 40 1/2" x 67" x 29 1/4". **$9,600**

Sabena (Mexico), pine log bar with three matching stools, on iron frames. Branded mark. Bar: 34" x 98" x 21 1/2". .... **$3,120 all**

Sabena (Mexico), pine log magazine rack in iron frame. Branded mark, 21" x 28" x 18". **$720**

Screen, maker unknown, three mahogany panels with geometric fretwork design, unsigned, original finish, 71 1/4" w x 71 3/4" h, each panel: 23 3/4" w, very good condition. **$225**

Photo courtesy Rago Arts and Auction Center, Lambertville, N.J.; www.RagoArts.com

Ludwig Mies van der Rohe / Knoll, Barcelona chairs (pair) with black leather cushions on polished steel frames. (Provenance: Seagram Building.) One with Seagram label, 30" x 31" x 28". **$5,700 pair**

Silas Seandel, primitive coffee table of cast bronze with polychrome patina, and plate glass top. Script signature, 15" x 38" x 17 1/4". **$1,560**

Silas Seandel Ironworks, dining table of fabricated and welded steel with plate glass top, 1975. Signed Silas Seandel '75 with copyright, 29" x 64" x 38 1/4". **$2,160**

Selig, Danish Modern high-back lounge chairs (pair), walnut frames with sculptural sides and flared arms, reupholstered in light tan leather, signed with round metal Selig tag, 34" w x 32" d x 39 1/2" h, very good condition. .... **$1,600 pair**

Jay Stanger, king-size polychrome bed in mixed wood veneers with metal accents, and two integrated nightstands. Approx. 77" x 122 3/4" x 103". **$4,500**

Photo courtesy Rago Arts and Auction Center, Lambertville, N.J.; www.RagoArts.com

Hans Wegner / A.P. Stolen, ox chair with "horns" covered in striped fabric over original slate-gray fabric. Circular Danish Furniture control tag, 35" x 38" x 32". **$13,200**

Storage unit, 1970s, Italy, possibly by Giotto Stoppino for Heller, white molded plastic unit designed to be configured as desired, 49 pieces and 4 metal brackets for attaching to wall, overall measurement as shown: 100" w x 102" d x 73" h, large opening at left is 46 1/2" x 30 1/2" x 12" d, height of right side section is 49 1/2", also includes a letter sorter at center, which is marked "Giotto Stoppino Heller Made in Italy", six other pieces are also included: two "T" sections, one 32" straight section, one 16" straight section, and two 9" straight sections, some discoloration and yellowing, good condition. .... **$1,900 all**

Wall unit, 1960s, four black wood vertical supports with open framework support five cabinets and five shelves in rosewood, three cabinets with two doors, one cabinet with three drawers, one cabinet with a locking drop-front lined in mahogany, five shelves with spring-loaded wood pegs, includes original assembly instructions, necessary hardware and key, back is finished, unsigned, original finish, 87" w x 16 1/2" d x 73" h, very good original condition. **$1,400**

Ole Wanscher, colonial chair and ottoman in rosewood with caned seat supports and dark brown leather cushions. Danish Furniture Control Tag. Chair: 33 1/4" x 25 1/2" x 23 1/2", ottoman: 16" x 23 1/2" x 16". .... **$3,900 both**

Hans Wegner, Papa Bear armchair and ottoman upholstered in dark charcoal wool. Chair Stamped Hans J. Wegner Made in Denmark, with Danish Furniture Control tag. Chair: 39" x 31 1/2" x 29". .... **$14,400 pair**

Hans Wegner / Fritz Hansen, oak dining chairs (four) with black vinyl seats. Stamped FH Denmark, 29" x 22 1/2" x 17 1/2". .... **$1,800 set**

Hans Wegner / Fritz Hansen, Etc., teak dining chairs (four), along with one oak armchair with black leather upholstery. Set marked with metal tag, Crafted in Denmark for Raymor, with two also marked FH Made in Denmark, 29" x 20" x 17" and 29 3/4" x 25 1/2" x 13". .... **$2,040 all**

Photo courtesy Heritage Auction Galleries, Dallas; www.HA.com

Gilbert Rohde (American, 1894-1944), chrome plated steel and ebony laminated wood side table, model no. 100-A, manufactured by Troy Streamline Metal, circa 1935 18 1/4" x 28 1/4" x 16". With the original aluminum band. Surface wear and scratches throughout. Some splitting and rippling of the wood veneer on the underside, with minor losses on one side. **$1,075**

Hans Wegner / Johannes Hansen, teak valet chair with hinged seat. Branded mark, 37 1/2" x 20" x 18". **$15,600**

Hans Wegner / Johannes Hansen, armless settee upholstered in Jack Lenor Larsen fabric. (Accompanied by original sales receipt), 32" x 58" x 34". **$4,800**

Hans Wegner / Ry Mobler, two-piece rosewood sideboard with interior drawers and shelves, mid-late 1950s. Stamped Made in Denmark, 67 3/4" x 79" x 19 1/4". **$6,600**

Hans Wegner / A.P. Stolen, ox chair with striped fabric over original slate-gray fabric. Circular Danish Furniture control tag, 35" x 36" x 30". **$4,800**

Hans Wegner / A.P. Stolen, Papa Bear teak armchair upholstered in beige wool. Stamped mark, 39" x 35" x 28". **$8,400**

Hans Wegner / Andreas Tuck, cross-legged dining table with teak top. Branded mark, 28 1/4" x 62 1/2" x 33 1/2". **$6,600**

Hans Wegner / Andreas Tuck, teak extension dining table with two 21 3/4" leaves. Branded mark. Closed: 27 1/2" x 55" x 43". **$1,440**

Werner West / Kerava Woodworks, (Finland), lounge chairs (pair) with birch frames upholstered in mauve cotton. Stamped Made in Finland, 32 1/2" x 23" x 20". ...... **$720 pair**

Edward Wormley, dining chairs, by Dunbar, set of eight, mahogany frames with original caned backrests, original upholstery, seven signed with "Dunbar for Modern" labels, original finish, 21 1/4" w x 21 1/2" d x 32 3/4" h, very good original condition. ...... **$3,500 set**

Edward Wormley, mirror, by Dunbar, model 5544, square form with solid brass frame, signed with green metal "Dunbar for Modern" tag and paper label, 32" w x 32" h, excellent condition. **$600**

Frank Lloyd Wright / Henredon, Taliesin ten-drawer sideboard with recessed handles, 33" x 65 1/2" x 20 1/2". **$2,040**

Russel Wright, American Modern bookshelves (pair), by Conant Ball, solid maple, each signed with a burned mark, refinished, 39" w x 10" d x 31" h, very good condition. **$850**

Jewelry

Harry Bertoia, (American, 1915-1978), untitled, circa 1945, bronze bracelet, 3 1/4" d. **$3,600**

Claire Falkenstein, five abstract sculptural buttons in sterling silver. Stamped with artist's cipher. Each: 1 1/4" x 1". .... **$2,520 all**

Claire Falkenstein, abstract serpentine earrings in hammered copper. Each: 4". .... **$900 pair**

Ed Weiner, abstract spiral box brooch and earrings in sterling silver. Brooch stamped ED. Wiener, all stamped sterling. Brooch: 2 1/2", earrings: 1 1/8". .... **$1,080 all**

Photo courtesy Rago Arts and Auction Center, Lambertville, N.J.; www.RagoArts.com

Claire Falkenstein, abstract spiral brooch and earrings in hammered copper. Stamped signature to brooch. Brooch: 1 3/4" x 4 3/4", earrings each: 2 1/4". **$3,600 all**

Lighting

Ron Arad / One Off, tree-form floor lamp with concrete base and two flexible arms. Marked MADE IN ENGLAND MALLEABLE CH 8 BS4668, 71" h. **$14,400**

Clayton Bailey, glazed earthenware figural lamp on stand, in luster pink. (Provenance: Brooklyn Museum "Masters of American Craft," 1970.) Lamp only: 13" x 8 1/4". **$900**

Jonathan Bonner, patinated copper billfish candlestick. Signed Bonner with copyright, 11 3/4" x 5 1/2" x 3". ... **$660**

Mark Burns, ceramic sculptural lamp, "Mad Hatters Tea Party." Signed Burns, 22 1/2" x 17". **$3,900**

Photo courtesy Rago Arts and Auction Center, Lambertville, N.J.; www.RagoArts.com

Tommaso Barbi, floor lamp with leaf-shaped hammered brass reflector on coiled base, 1970s, 47 1/2" x 20". **$2,160**

Pierre Cardin, brushed steel table lamps (pair) with stamped logo to lower corner. Base: 19 1/2" x 7" x 4". .... **$2,880 pair**

Wendell Castle, candlestick in carved and gilded walnut with patinated metal. Signed W.C. 90, 16 3/4" x 3 1/4". **$1,800**

Wilhelm Hunt Diederich, (style of), iron floor lamp patterned with hunting dogs, 63" x 16" x 13". **$1,800**

Wharton Esherick, flame table lamp in carved walnut, 1933. Carved WE 1933, 19 1/4" x 4". **$21,600**

Richard Etts, plaster lamps (pair) with enameled ivory finish, modeled with lifelike hands, 1972. Signed, dated RICHARD ETTS with copyright, 17 1/2" x 10". .... **$3,000 pair**

A.W. and Marion Geller / Heifetz, brass and enameled metal lamp with single socket on tripod base, 36 1/2" x 20 1/2". **$5,400**

Curtis Jere, flashlight floor lamp/sculpture, 1981. Signed C. Jere 1981 with paper tag from Artisan House Inc., 67 1/2" x 26 1/4". **$4,800**

Modern Primitive, totemic candleholders (pair) in forged and fabricated iron. Both marked GRS 88, smaller also marked A.P., 24" and 18 1/2". .... **$2,520 pair**

George Kovacs Inc., black metal floor lamps (pair) with red neon tubes, 72 3/4" x 14" sq. .... **$1,200 pair**

Wendy Maruyama, mixed media wall sconce, 1981. Signed Maruyama '81, 19 1/2" x 10" x 4 3/4". **$780**

Herman Miller, E-6310 modern table lamps (pair), molded tiered shades in gray plastic with maroon bottom over black enameled bases, each: 15 1/4" d x 26 1/2" h, very good condition. .... **$300 pair**

Photo courtesy of Treadway Toomey Galleries, Cincinnati and Oak Park, Ill.; www.TreadwayGallery.com

Floor lamps, pair, metal tubular base supporting a broad painted paper shade with a white glass inner shade, #E1713, 25 1/2" d x 56" h. **$475 pair**

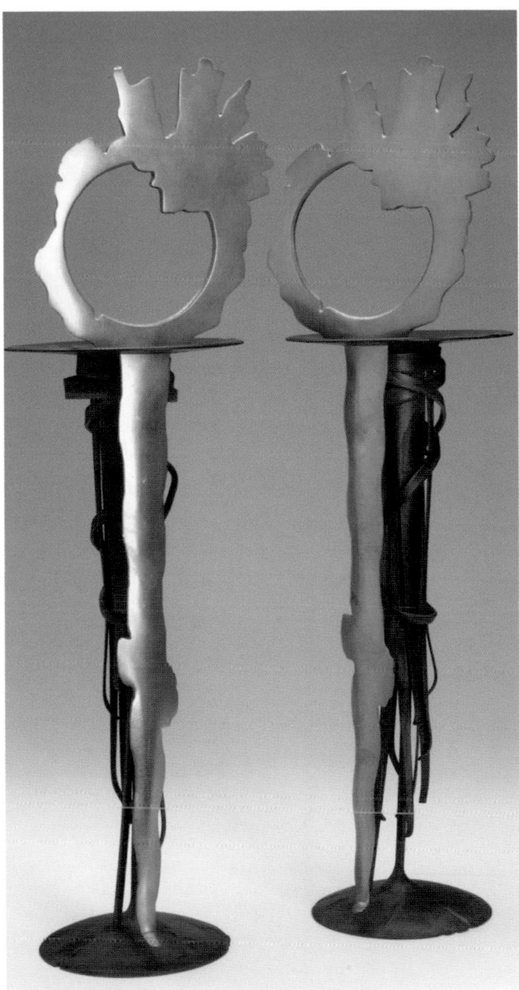

Photo courtesy Rago Arts and Auction Center, Lambertville, N.J.; www.RagoArts.com

Albert Paley, Eclipse candlesticks (pair) of forged, milled steel with brass inserts, 1994. Stamped Albert Paley 1994, also numbered 36 and 27 of 50, 23 1/2" x 7" x 6 1/4". **$2,640**

Albert Paley, floor-standing candlestick of forged steel, 1970. Stamped Paley 1970, 60 1/4" x 28 1/2". **$25,200**

Albert Paley, forged steel table lamp, 1993. Stamped Albert Paley 1993 with copyright, also marked C114 and numbered 11/25, 30" x 9" d. **$14,400**

Gino Sarfatti / Arredoluce, Triennale floor lamp with enameled metal shades and handles, 69 1/2" x 42 1/2". **$7,200**

Richard Sextone, hand-forged iron candleholder sconces (pair), 1978. Stamped R. SEXSTONE 1978, 37". ... **$1,560 pair**

Table lamp, 1950s, rectangular black metal frame with four legs, supports a coated linen shade, unsigned, 6" w x 6" d x 14" h, very good condition. **$275**

Edward Zucca, Mystery Science Lamp #8 in white oak, ebony, copper and brass with Plexiglas shades, 2003. Signed and dated, 8" x 16 1/2" x 5". **$1,800**

Edward Zucca, Mystery Science Lamp #10 in white oak, ebony, copper and brass with Plexiglas shades, 2003. Signed and dated, 13" x 15" x 9". **$2,280**

Photo courtesy of Treadway Toomey Galleries, Cincinnati and Oak Park, Ill.; www.TreadwayGallery.com

Roland Smith "Victor" floor lamp, circa 1948, collapsible metal base supports an adjustable boom arm with metal ball counterweight, includes catalog of the Detroit Institute of Arts An Exhibition in Modern Living from 1949 illustrating this lamp, arm as shown: 48 1/2" h x 44" w, very good original condition. **$750**

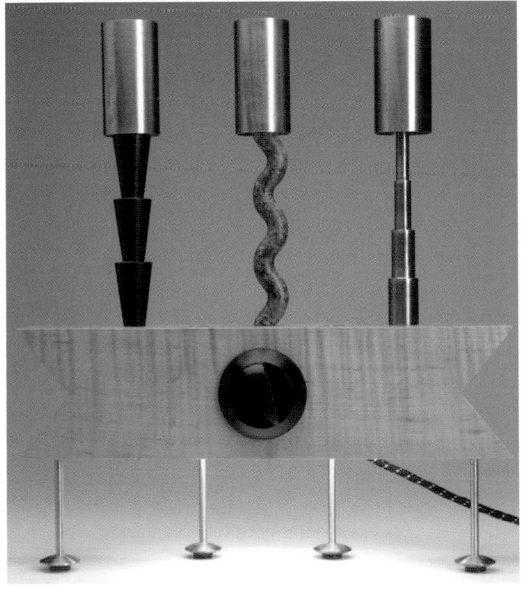

Photo courtesy Rago Arts and Auction Center, Lambertville, N.J.; www.RagoArts.com

Edward Zucca, Mystery Science Lamp #4 in curly maple, ebony, copper and brass, 2003. Signed and dated, 20" x 18" x 5". **$3,120**

Edward Zucca, television lamp in painted wood and glass, 2005. Signed and dated, also marked Third Edition and numbered one of six, 14 1/2" x 11" x 10". **$1,320**

Metal, Functional

Jonathan Bonner, zoomorphic wood holder in stainless steel with brushed finish, 1987. Signed and dated with copyright, 16 1/2" x 18" x 9". **$2,520**

Morgan Colt, wrought-iron fireplace trivet with revolving hanging hook, 28 1/2" x 16" x 16". **$1,020**

Wilhelm Hunt Diederich, (American, 1884-1953), adjustable wrought-iron fireplace crane supporting a figural hunt scene in cast bronze, circa 1930, 38" x 44". **$15,600**

Irving Harper / George Nelson / Charles D. Briddell, Carvel Hall stainless steel flatware service for eight, complete with original case signed by Irving Harper. Stamped CARVEL HALL STAINLESS U.S.A. **$1,020**

Albert Paley, steel door handles (pair) covered in rust patina, 11" x 6 1/2". **$2,400**

Albert Paley, four-piece fireplace tool set of forged and fabricated steel, 2005. Stamped Albert Paley 2005, 43 1/2" x 14". **$12,000**

Albert Paley, steel paperweights (pair), 1994. Stamped Paley 1994, 8 1/2" x 4 3/4". **$660**

Russel Wright, set of silver-plated flatware for eight, with dinner and salad forks, dinner knives, dinner and soup spoons, designed 1933, produced 1987. Missing one salad fork. Stamped MMA 1987 Korea. **$4,500**

Photo courtesy Rago Arts and Auction Center, Lambertville, N.J.; www.RagoArts.com

Wilhelm Hunt Diederich, (American, 1884-1953), figural sheet-iron weathervane depicting leaping polo players, mounted on an enameled metal stand. Overall height: 87", weathervane only: 39" x 46". **$48,000**

Photo courtesy Rago Arts and Auction Center, Lambertville, N.J.; www.RagoArts.com

Albert Paley, bookends, 1993. Stamped Albert Paley 1993, numbered 4/10. Each: 9" x 13" x 3". **$2,760**

Textiles

Amacani, modern circular hooked wool rug with abstract design in oatmeal and black on mottled orange ground. Tagged Amacani, S.A, 84" d. **$1,140**

Alexander Calder, tapestry, "Balloons," in maguey fiber with abstract design in navy, yellow, red, peach and black, 1974. Bon Art tag, signed with embroidered copyright, CA 74 57/100, 6' x 8'. **$7,200**

Alexander Calder, tapestry, "Turquoise," in maguey fiber with abstract design in yellow, red, black and turquoise, 1975. Bon Art tag, signed with embroidered copyright, CA 75 1/100, 6' x 8'. **$5,700**

Sonia Delaunay / Articurial, assortment of five limited-edition fabrics. Each signed Sonia Delaunay and marked with an edition number. All approximately 108" long. Four cotton with 55" selvages. One cotton velvet with 45" selvage. .... **$6,600 all**

Edward Fields, rectangular wool rug with minimalist design in blue, gray and black, 1988. Signed and dated on selvage, 107" x 81 1/2". **$720**

Rug/tapestry, 1960s, hand-knotted wool, abstract design in yellow, brown and orange, light wear, 51" x 79", very good condition. **$250**

Elsa Rush, rectangular hooked wool rug with abstract flowers and insects in shades of brown and beige. Signed Elsa Rush, 117 1/2" x 81 1/2". **$1,140**

Photo courtesy Rago Arts and Auction Center, Lambertville, N.J.; www.RagoArts.com

Alexander Calder, tapestry, "Turquoise," in maguey fiber with abstract design in yellow, red, black and turquoise, 1975. Signed with embroidered copyright, CA 75 92/100, 5' x 7'. **$4,500**

Other Objects

Harry Bertoia, (American, 1915-1978), double-sided gong, silicone bronze, 47" diameter. **$54,000**

Michael Coffey, Perceptions II laminated and carved serpentine wall-hanging mirror in African Mozambique. Signed M. Coffey, 27" x 54 1/2". **$5,400**

Danish Modern bucket, round form in teak veneer with copper fasteners and swiveling handle of solid teak, unsigned, original finish, 17 1/2" d x 16" h, very good condition. **$125**

Wharton Esherick, sculptural carved walnut bowl, 1962. Marked WE 1962, 2 1/2" x 11 1/2" x 6 1/4". **$9,000**

Wharton Esherick, mahogany tray, signed WE 1967, 1" x 23 3/4" x 13 1/2". **$4,800**

Paul Evans, patchwork steel ice bucket, 11" x 10" x 10". **$1,920**

Paul T. Frankl / Warren Telechron, Modernique electric clock in burnished and lacquered brass-tone metal, Bakelite and glass with detachable cord, 7 3/4" x 5 3/4" x 4". **$1,200**

Hans Hansen, hinged rosewood box with sterling silver insets. Stamped Hans Hansen Sterling Denmark 925 8, 1 3/4" x 8 3/4" x 5 3/4". **$1,920**

George Nelson / Herman Miller, Thin Edge jewelry chest with nine drawers and hourglass pulls. Circular Herman Miller tag, 23 1/2" x 10 1/2" x 13". **$8,400**

Isamu Noguchi / Knoll, collection of nine large pencil and ink blueprint drawings for Knoll. Each signed Isamu Noguchi in pencil, 27" x 36" and 32" x 40". ....**$16,800 all**

Reference literature, 1950s, including Herman Miller Illustrated Price list, 1958; *The Dunbar Book of Modern Furniture*, 1953; Chairs by Bertoia, an illustrated fold-out pamphlet; two Nessen lamp catalogs, 1959-60 and 1966; and a vintage Herman Miller postcard; plus various Herman Miller brochures, all in very good condition. ....**$300 all**

Andy Warhol books (two), and puzzle; Andy Warhol's Index (Book), First printing, 1967, Random House, with hologram cover; Andy Warhol, publication for exhibition at Moderna Museet, Stockholm, Sweden, third ed., 1970, printed in Sweden; with Andy Warhol "Red Marilyn" puzzle, 550 pieces, unopened, 12" x 12". ....**$400 all**

Russel Wright / Klise Woodworking USA, Oceana salad bowl, "Wave". Branded signature, 3 3/4" x 15" x 9 3/4". **$1,440**

Photo courtesy Rago Arts and Auction Center, Lambertville, N.J.; www.RagoArts.com

Wendell Castle, sculptural anthropomorphic clock in maple and walnut with enameled and patinated metals, 1989. Signed and dated, 21" x 15 1/2" x 9 1/4". **$9,000**

Photo courtesy Rago Arts and Auction Center, Lambertville, N.J.; www.RagoArts.com

Isamu Noguchi / Zenith, Bakelite Radio Nurse, embossed marks, 8" x 6 1/4" x 6". **$7,200**

Oriental

ORIENTAL OBJECTS

Now and Zen: Japanese woodblock prints

By Mary P. Manion

Acting director, Landmarks Gallery and Restoration Studio, Milwaukee

Reprinted from *Antique Trader* magazine

The art of Japan was unknown until Commodore Perry and his U.S. Navy flotilla sailed into Tokyo Bay in 1853. Art was probably the least of Perry's considerations behind his show of force and diplomacy, which convinced Japan's rulers to open their country to the outside world after centuries of self-imposed isolation. Perry's mission exposed Japan to the West, triggering the country's industrialization and modernization, and its rapid rise as a world power. Perry's voyage also had an unanticipated impact on Western artists, who found inspiration in the simplified lines and white space of Japanese woodblock prints. James Abbott McNeill Whistler introduced the prints to London's Pre-Raphaelites as early as 1859. Before long, Japan's influence could be seen in the work of artists across Europe and America.

The art of Japan, which found distinct expression in the medium of woodblock prints called ukiyo-e, was profoundly indebted to the contemplative spirit of Zen Buddhism. It was a meditative art that sought to strip away human complexity in exchange for glimpsing the essence of scenes. It was also a democratic art, reproduced in large numbers and reaching into every corner of the country. When Japan became a trading partner with the West, its prints were prolifically produced for export. Soon enough, Japanese artists went abroad, rendering sites familiar to Western audiences in the style of the home islands.

Perhaps the bulk of pre-World War II prints, and the legion of largely anonymous artisans who made them, accounts for their startling availability. Many antique Japanese woodblock prints can be found on eBay for under $100. However, as in any genre of visual art, the recognized masters command higher prices.

Creating a woodblock print is a three-step process involving an artist, an engraver and a printer. The artist creates the sketch on thin paper. The engraver traces the sketch onto a block of wood and carves the impression. The completed carved block is given to the printer who applies ink on the block and prints the image on a paper support. Multiple colors are achieved by repeating the ink application one color at a time within the same printed image. All steps require skilled artisans with knowledge of the process and deft handling of paper, ink and wood.

Japanese woodblock art has a long history, originating with the propagation of Buddhist teachings and evolving into commercial production in the early 17th century. The production continued into the early 20th century. The tradition is divided between two distinct eras in Japanese history, during which the finest works of the art form were produced. The Edo period began in the 1620s, characterized by feudal military dictators known as shoguns. Their regime ended in 1867 with the restoration of imperial rule under Emperor Meiji. The Meiji period closed with the death of the emperor in 1912.

Throughout the Edo period, artists focused on Japan's insular life with depictions of the four seasons of the islands, sometimes featuring animal and plant life; iconic representations of sacred temples and landmarks; studies of women; portraits of children, shogun warriors and Sumo wrestlers; and the depiction of Japan's other popular art form, the Kabuki Theater. The Kabuki prints (called Yakusha-e) were woodblock images of elaborately costumed actors on stage and in performance. They were received in much the same way as movie and theater posters are collected today.

The Meiji period saw a great change in art as the focus turned to the western market. Japanese artists began to travel abroad for the first time in centuries and depicted Western scenes in Japanese style.

Many masters emerged from the Edo period, and among the most prolific were Katsushika Hokusai (1760-1849), Gototei Kunisada (1786-1865), Ando Hiroshige (1797-1858) and the last great master of the period, Ichiyusai Kuniyoshi (1797-1861).

Hokusai's reputation was established as a landscape painter. His masterwork, Thirty-Six Views of Mount Fuji, included a 10-print supplement featuring additional views of Mount Fuji from the interior, or 46 prints in all. Sotheby's in London sold The Great Wave Off Kanagawa, a signed print from the set, for $60,000 including buyer's premium.

Kunisada (who later signed his work as Toyokuni III) shared no equal in commercial success, There was a time

The Great Wave Off Kanagawa, an image from Thirty-six Views of Mount Fuji, created by Katsushika Hokusai between 1826 and 1833.

when the word ukiyo-e meant only one thing: Kunisada, or so it was noted during his lifetime. His series, Selection of Actors, with Scenes of the Fifty-three Stations on the Tokaido Highway, was praised in a popular song of the time. Auction prices for his prints generally range from $1,000 to $4,500.

Hiroshige (also known as Hiroshige I) produced more than 5,400 prints, many with up to several hundred impressions per image. One Hundred Views of Famous Places in Edo was one of his last, great journeys in art. His son-in-law, who became known as Hiroshige II (1826-69), was fascinated by the landscape of Japan and traveled the length of the nation for inspiration. At auction Hiroshige prices range from $500 up to the thousands, with a rare, 70-print set Views of the Province selling at Sotheby's Amsterdam for $76,692 including buyer's premium.

Many ukiyo-e prints were produced in sets, and a landscape series could bear the same title by different artists. Both Hiroshige and Hokusai produced 53 stations on the Tokaido as well as 36 views of Mt. Fuji. Additionally, Hiroshige produced two versions of the 36 views. Titles were often descriptive if not lengthy. Kuniyoshi's Pictures of All Sorts of Places in the Eastern Capital gets to the point in a rather meandering pace. Three Great Bridges of the Eastern Capital, signed by Kuniyoshi, sold at Christie's New York for $3,000, including buyer's premium.

The Meiji period nurtured at least three great masters, Yoshitoshi Tsukioka (1839-92), Yoshiiku Ochiai (1833-1904) and Kunichika Toyohara (1835-1900). The early years expressed dark emotion and gloom with depictions of bloodthirsty battles and military heroes. Japan's war with Russia (1905) was depicted in traditional style. Afterward artists returned to more pastoral images.

Prints by some of the masters of ukiyo-e continue to be struck nowadays and are often available at modest prices. Many fine works by older woodblock artists can be found for under $1,000. Ukiyo-e remains a field of art accessible to collectors with modest budgets.

Woodblock Prints

Ikeda Eisen, (1790-1848), indigo blue (aizuri-e), a large format (oban tate-e) from the series "Modern Music Like Clusters of Pine Needles" of a maiden rendered in shades of blue, with a hint of red on her lips, signed Keisai Eisen ga, circa 1830s, (late impression, somewhat toned, rough edges), 14 1/2" h x 10" w. **$200**

Takahashi Hiroaki, (Shotei) (1871-1944), two views, each featuring Mount Fuji, one with the peak wreathed in bands of mist, the other with fishing boats pulled up on a beach, each signed "Hiroaki" and sealed "Shotei," (slightly toned, good color, slight soiling, some staining to second), 10 1/4" h x 15 1/4" w. .... **$1,200 pair**

Utagawa Hiroshige, (1797-1858), a mid-size horizontal sheet (aiban-yokoe) from the so-called Gyosho Tokaido Road series, depicting "Akasaka," published by Ezaki-ya/Yamada-ya, with a single censor seal (circa 1841-42), signed TL (late impression, faded, trimmed, foxed), 7 3/4" h x 12 1/2" w. **$200**

Kawano Kaoru, (1916-1965), portraying a girl holding a fan to the front, with mica-printed accents, sealed (minor tape residue to reverse, otherwise very good condition) 16 3/4" h x 11 1/4" w. **$120**

Kawano Kaoru, (1916-1965), Japanese, modern, two views, the first of a landscape with a pagoda tower silhouetted in the distance, pencil signed LL, with one seal "Kaoru," the second of a young girl seated with a small blue bird in her hands, pencil signed LR, with one seal (second with tape residue to top reverse corners), 16 3/4" h x 11 1/4" w. .... **$50 pair**

Kawano Kaoru, (1916-1965), Japanese, modern, two views, the first depicting a young girl in a pose of veneration, sealed "Kaoru," the second an abstract rendering of a seated maiden in red, grey and black, pencil signed LR, with one seal, 16 3/4" h x 11 1/4" w. .... **$50 pair**

Kiyochika Kobayashi, (1847-1915), titled "Honcho dori yasetsu" (Night snow, in Honcho Street), signed Kobayashi Kiyochika hitsu, right margin with date Meiji 13? (1880, unclear) and publisher cartouche of Fukuda Kumajiro (slightly toned and minor staining, crease to right margin), 10" h x 14 1/2" w. **$250**

Photo courtesy Heritage Auction Galleries, Dallas; www.HA.com

Ando Hiroshige (Japanese, 1797-1858), Canyon Scene, color woodblock on paper, minor foxing. Matted and framed, not examined out of frame, 20" x 6 1/2". **$143**

Tsukioka Kogyo, (1869-1927), two views, the first depicting a female demon in a Noh drama, the second of two figures in the kyogen play "Obake-zaki," each signed and sealed, shaped seal of the publisher (first toned and torn, second with minor matt mark), 15" h x 10" w and 10" h x 15" w. .... **$60 pair**

Odake Kunikazu, (1868-1931), set of 12, from the series "Tokyo junigatsu no uchi" (The Twelve Months of Tokyo), eight with publisher notation "Shimizu-do" and date Meiji 34 (1901) on the left margin, most signed "Kunikazu-hitsu," each featuring a contemporary beauty (one in Western dress) and landscape inset of a famous place in Tokyo (center crease, some with tears along the crease, two sides with remnants of the original paper backing, otherwise relatively good condition), each sheet: 9" x 12 1/4". .... **$750 set**

Utagawa Kuniyoshi, (1797-1861), a large format sheet (oban tate-e) of Shoki, the Demon Queller, pursuing a pair of oni floating above, signed "Ichiyusai Igusa Kuniyoshi," with aratame censer, date (1854) and publisher notation of Tsujioka-ya (losses, some staining, rough edges), 14" h x 9 3/4" w. **$110**

Koichi Okumura, (Japanese, 1904-1974), six prints, signed; together with Toshi Yoshida, "From the Star, Night," 1957, with printed title, date, and signature, 2/20. Largest: 36" x 24". .... **$720 all**

Kiyoshi Saito, (1907-1997), titled "Haniwa," with the clay figure in red, grey, black and mica accents, signed LR in white ink, with one seal reading "Kiyoshi," (pencil notation to reverse, otherwise excellent condition), 17" h x 11 1/4" w. **$175**

Ohara Shoson (Koson), 1877-1945, featuring a pair of bar-tailed godwits feeding in shallow waters next to reeds, signed and sealed "Shoson," 1926, circular publisher seal of Watanabe, (toned, paper tape to reverse top), 15 1/4" h x 10 1/4" w. **$80**

Hiroaki Takahashi, (Japanese, 1871-1944), two color views of Mt. Fuji with lake and Torii in the foreground, signed lower right and sealed Shotei; man and child in silhouette, signed and sealed lower right Hiroaki. Both 14 5/8" x 6 1/4". .... **$480 pair**

Ito Takashi, (1894-1982), a night scene of boats on a lake, signed and sealed "Takashi," circular publisher seal of Watanabe in the lower right corner (very slightly toned, otherwise very good condition), 10 1/4" h x 15 1/2" w. **$550**

Hiroyuki Tajima, (1911-1984), titled "Tradition" in English and Japanese, signed in pencil LR and dated '69, edition 50-8, 36 1/2" h x 27 1/2" w. **$200**

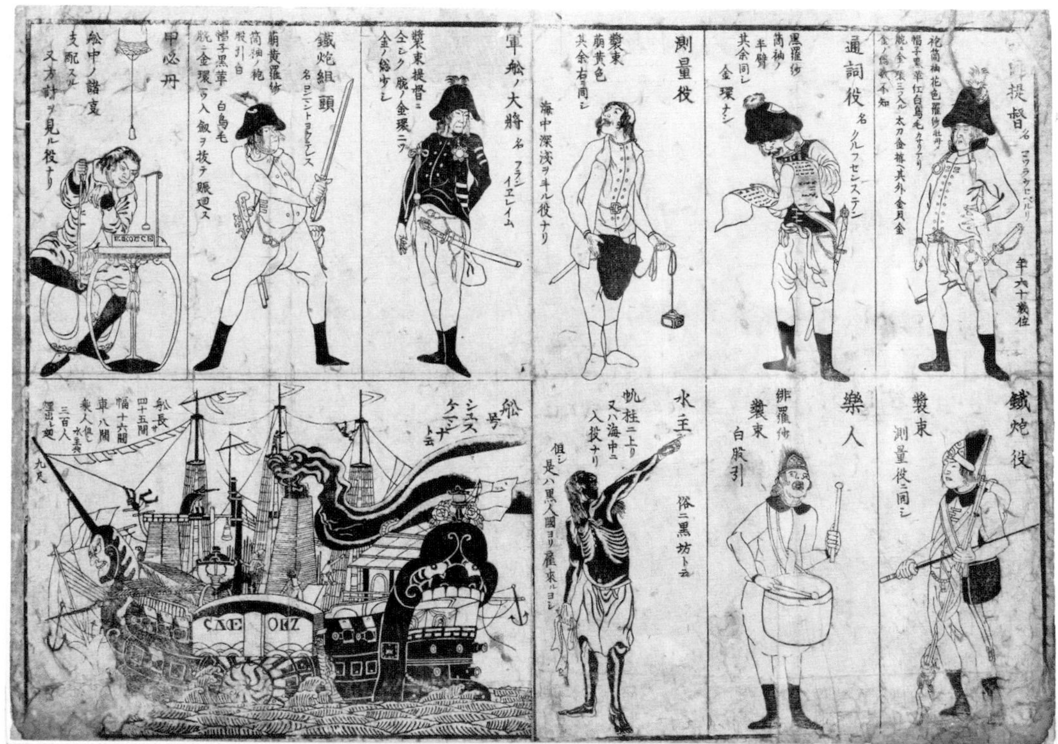

Photo courtesy Heritage Auction Galleries, Dallas; www.HA.com

1800s Japanese Woodblock Print illustrating the Japanese stylized concept of the appearance of Western European people. A 19" x 13 1/2" print showing a steam-powered ship, several officers, sailors and a black man. These images are remarkably similar to drawings the Japanese made of Admiral Perry on his opening U.S. visit to Japan; this print possibly pre-dates that period. Generally very good condition with old file folds, some light soiling, and edge wear. **$1,015**

Photo courtesy Heritage Auction Galleries, Dallas; www.HA.com

Kiyoshi Saito (Japanese, 1907-1992), Nanzen-Ji Kyoto (B), 1963, color woodblock, 20 3/4" x 15", ed. 34/100. Signed in the plate lower right: Kiyoshi Saito. Watermark along left margin: Kiyoshi Saito. Titled, numbered and dated in the lower margin. Labeled on verso: Self-Carved Self Printed / Kiyoshi Saito. **$239**

Ceramics

The history of Asian pottery spans thousands of years. By the 16th century, Chinese ceramic wares were being exported to India, Persia and Egypt. During the Ming Dynasty (1368-1643), earthenware became more highly developed. The Ch'ien Lung period (1736-1795) of the Ch'ing Dynasty marked the golden age of trade with the West.

In 1557, the Portuguese established a permanent settlement in Macau. The Dutch entered the trade early in the 17th century. With the establishment of the English East India Company, all of Europe sought Oriental-influenced pottery and porcelain. Styles, shapes, and colors were developed to suit Western tastes, a tradition that continued until the late 19th century.

Canton is a term given to porcelain made in the Canton region of China from the late 18th century to the present. It was produced largely for export. Canton china has a hand-decorated, light- to dark-blue under glaze on white ground. Design motifs include houses, mountains, trees, boats, and bridges. A design similar to willow pattern is the most common.

Borders on early Canton feature a rain-and-cloud motif (a thick band of diagonal lines with a scalloped bottom). Later pieces usually have a straight-line border.

Early plates – dating from about 1790-1840 – are often heavy and may have an unfinished bottom, while serving pieces have an overall "orange peel" bottom. Early covered pieces, such as tureens, vegetable dishes and sugars, have berry finials (also called knops) and twisted handles. Later ones have round finials and a straight, single handle. The markings "Made in China" and "China" indicate wares made after 1891.

Celadon refers to a pale, grayish-green glaze color. It is derived from the theatrical character Celadon, who wore costumes of varying shades of grayish green in Honore d'Urfe's 17th-century pastoral romance, L'Astree. French Jesuits living in China used the name to refer to a specific type of Chinese porcelain.

Celadon is divided into two types. Northern celadon, made during the Sung Dynasty up to the 1120s, has a gray-to-brownish body, with relief decoration and monochromatic olive-green glaze. Southern (Lung-ch'uan) celadon, made during the Sung Dynasty and much later, is paint-decorated with floral and other scenic designs and is found in forms that appeal to the European- and American-export market. Many of the southern pieces date from 1825 to 1885. A blue square with Chinese or pseudo-Chinese characters sometimes appear on pieces after 1850. Later pieces also have a larger and sparser decorative patterning.

Famille Rose is Chinese Export enameled porcelain on which the pink color predominates. It was made primarily in the 18th and 19th centuries. Other porcelains in the same group are Famille Jaune (yellow), Famille Noire (black), and Famille Verte (green).

Decorations include courtyard and home scenes, birds and insects. Secondary colors are yellow, green, blue, aubergine (dark purple) and black.

Imari porcelain is the collector name for Japanese wares made in the town of Arita, in the former Hizen Province, northwestern Kyūshū, and exported from the port city of Imari for the European trade. Although Imari ware was manufactured in the 17th century, the pieces most commonly encountered are those made between 1770 and 1900.

Early Imari was decorated simply, quite unlike the later heavily decorated brocade pattern commonly associated with Imari. Most of the decorative patterns are an under-glaze blue and over-glaze "seal wax" red complimented by turquoise and yellow.

The Chinese copied Imari ware. The Japanese examples can be identified by grayer clay, thicker glaze, runny and darker blue and red opaque hues.

The patterns and colors of Imari inspired many English and European potteries, such as Derby and Meissen, to adopt a similar style of decoration for their wares.

Photo courtesy Clars Auction Gallery, Oakland, Calif.; www.Clars.com

Bowl, Japanese blue-glazed porcelain, square, Meiji period, thickly molded from fine white paste of Hirado type with rounded corners, its canted interior walls each displaying a raised cloud scroll and its flat floor centered with a raised kirin in white silhouette against a deep cobalt wash, all beneath a celadon-tinged glaze (minor glaze flaws), 8" sq. **$225**

Rose Mandarin, Rose Medallion and Rose Canton are mid- to late-19th-century Chinese-export wares similar to Famille Rose.

Rose Mandarin, produced from the late 18th century to approximately 1840, derives its name from the Mandarin figures found in garden scenes with women and children. The women often have gold decorations in their hair. Polychrome enamels and birds separate the scenes.

Rose Medallion, which originated in the early 19th century and was made through the early 20th century, has alternating panels of figures, birds and flowers. The elements are four in number, separated evenly around the center medallion. Peonies and foliage fill voids.

Rose Canton, introduced somewhat later than Rose Mandarin and produced through the first half of the 19th century, is similar to Rose Medallion except the figural panels are replaced by flowers. People are present only if the medallion partitions are absent. Some patterns have been named "Butterfly and Cabbage" and "Rooster." Rose Canton actually is a catchall term for any pink enamelware not fitting into the first two groups.

Nippon, Japanese hand-painted porcelain, was made for export between 1891 and 1921. In 1891, when the McKinley Tariff Act dictated that all items of foreign manufacture be stamped with their country of origin, Japan chose to use "Nippon." In 1921, the United States decided the word "Nippon" was no longer acceptable and required all Japanese wares to be marked "Japan," ending the Nippon era.

There are more than 220 recorded Nippon back stamps or marks; the three most popular are the wreath, maple leaf and rising sun. Wares with variations of all three marks have been widely reproduced.

The majority of the marks are found in three different colors: green, blue or magenta. Colors indicate the quality of the porcelain used: green for first-grade porcelain, blue for second-grade, and magenta for third-grade. Marks were applied by two methods: decal stickers under glaze and imprinting directly on the porcelain.

Satsuma, named for a warlord who brought skilled Korean potters to Japan in the early 1600s, is a handcrafted Japanese faience (tin-glazed) pottery. It is finely crackled, has a cream, yellow-cream or gray-cream color, and is decorated with raised enamels in floral, geometric and figural motifs.

Figural Satsuma was made specifically for export in the 19th century. Later Satsuma, referred to as Satsuma-style ware, is a Japanese porcelain also hand decorated in raised enamels. From 1912 to the present, Satsuma-style ware has been mass-produced. Much of the ware on today's market is of this later period.

For details on Noritake China, see end of the ceramics section. Also see Oriental rugs in the Textiles section.

Photo courtesy Clars Auction Gallery, Oakland, Calif.; www.Clars.com

Amphora, Chinese Tang-style white glazed, the ovoid body with a tall waisted neck surmounted by a dished mouth bracketed by a pair of arching dragon-head handles extending down to the shoulder, the slightly green-tinged glaze stopping short to reveal the buff body (crazing, minor losses), 9" h. **$30**

Photo courtesy Clars Auction Gallery, Oakland, Calif.; www.Clars.com

Bowl, Japanese Imari, the interior well painted in polychrome enamels, gilt and under-glaze blue with a landscape medallion encircled on the side with further landscape panels alternating with floral reserves repeated on the exterior, 12 1/4" d. **$90**

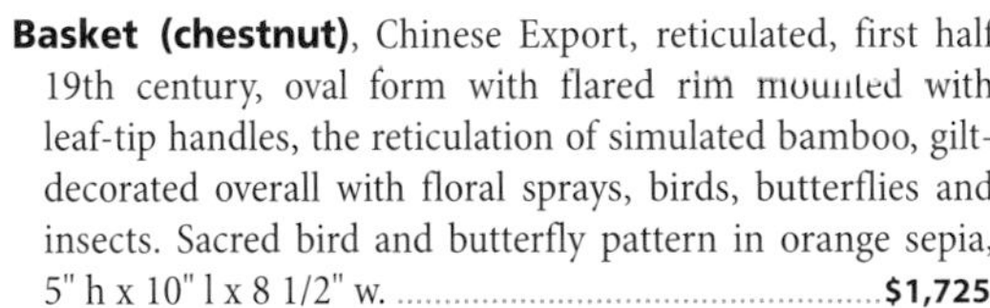

Basket (chestnut), Chinese Export, reticulated, first half 19th century, oval form with flared rim mounted with leaf-tip handles, the reticulation of simulated bamboo, gilt-decorated overall with floral sprays, birds, butterflies and insects. Sacred bird and butterfly pattern in orange sepia, 5" h x 10" l x 8 1/2" w. **$1,725**

Bottle, Korean Punch'ong (Chosôn Dynasty, 1392-1910), sgraffito pear form with inlaid slip on a celadon ground, Yi Dynasty, 12" h. **$1,200**

Bowl, Korean Punch'ong (Chosôn Dynasty, 1392-1910), incised and stamped decoration filled with slip, the well with five spur marks, on a celadon glaze. Together with a small celadon plate stamped with flower head and leaf designs, Yi Dynasty. Larger: 7 5/8" d. .... **$1,080 pair**

Bowl (center, oval), Satsuma style, Makuzu Kozan, with four phoenix, their open wings forming the rim of the bowl, the interior with radiating petals in gosu blue centered by a dragon, on original carved base, Meiji Period. Marked in seal form Makuzu Kozan. 10 3/4" x 15 1/4" x 12". **$6,600**

Bowl, Chinese Export, blue Canton, mid-19th century, square bowl with notched corners and wavy edges, decorated overall in blue and white oriental landscapes, 4 3/4" h x 9 3/4" d. **$690**

Bowl on stand, Rose Medallion, decorated with Chinese domestic scenes; enclosures decorated with flowers, birds and fruit. Bowl is 6 1/2" h x 15 1/2" d. Stand is 6 1/2" h x 11 1/4" d. **$1,035**

Bowl (sugar), blue and white Canton, footed bowl having strap handles, medium blue decoration with a slightly domed lid and crab finial, 5" h x 4" d (without handles), small chip to edge of cover. **$150**

Brush box, Chinese Export Famille Rose, mid-19th century, rectangular lidded box fitted with an interior divider, decorated overall in Famille Rose design with fanciful birds and butterflies, 2 3/4" h x 7 1/4" l x 3 3/4" w. **$518**

Candlesticks (pair), Chinese Export, inverted trumpet form, cobalt blue decorated landscape with boats, figures, trees and pagodas, flaring drip pan, 10 1/4" h. ..... **$540 pair**

Photo courtesy Clars Auction Gallery, Oakland, Calif.; www.Clars.com

Bowls (pair), Chinese polychrome enamel glazed, covered, Tongzhi mark and period (1861-1875), each decorated with shaped bird-and-flower reserves on a turquoise ground with a dense pattern of flowers amid leafy tendrils, the covers decorated en suite (minor rim chip), 4 1/4" d. **$120 pair**

Candlesticks (pair), Chinese Export elephant figural porcelain, China, late 18th/early 19th century, 4 1/2" h, 5 1/4" w, one with unobtrusive hairline across base at mid-belly, the other stick with glue repair where candle cup meets figure, and a chip on ear edge and saddle. ....**$3,555 pair**

Candlesticks (pair), Chinese Export Rose Medallion, mid-19th century, decorated overall in Famille Rose figural, floral and bird decoration, 7 3/4" h. ....**$1,380 pair**

Charger, Imari decorated porcelain, Japanese, late 19th century, scallop-rim charger decorated in under-glaze blue with polychrome enamel and gilt decoration, 16" d, unobtrusive 1/2" rim chip. **$325**

Charger, Japanese, blue and white, three asymmetrical reserves with bamboo, flowering branches and tree with Mount Fuji in background, 18" d. **$149**

Container, (circular, covered), Chinese Imari-inspired, Qing Dynasty, the circular exterior with a pair of short handles and painted in gilt, under-glaze blue and shades of red enamel with a sparse design of butterflies amid flowering sprays repeated on the low convex lid with a knob finial (minor rim chips), 4 1/2" d. **$90**

Dinnerware, Imari porcelain, iron red and cobalt blue decoration, gilt trim; some variations in patterns; six- and four-character signatures; consisting of 12 large 12" dinner plates, 19 punch cups, three cordial cups, four 3 1/2" cordial cups, four 3 1/2" sauce plates, three 9 1/2" plates, four 8" plates, twelve 5" bowls (3 chipped), four 6 1/2" bowls, six teacups and saucers, six 7 1/2" plates, nine 5" miscellaneous sauce plates, eight 4" sauce plates, 13" punch bowl, 9" bowl and 7 1/2" bowl. ....**$1,560 set**

Dish, (vegetable) with cover, Canton, rectangular dish with typical scenic decoration and notched corners, the lid with a berry knop, 5 1/2" h x 11" l x 9 1/2" w. **$518**

Dish, (vegetable), Chinese Export Canton, covered, rectangular bowl with notched corner fitted with a domed lid and knopped berry finial. Decorated overall with blue and white Oriental scenic decoration of typical form, 6 3/4" h x 11 1/2" l x 10" w. **$518**

Dish, (warming), Rose Medallion, four alternating floral and figural reserves, hot water well beneath, 10 1/4" d, slight chip near one spout, slight rim chip. **$460**

Dishes, (two), Chinese blue-and-white porcelain, Qing Dynasty, 19th century, the first a small plate painted with a figure on a garden terrace, the edges with fruiting scrolling vines, brown rim (rough foot), the second with the interior well painted with rocks and flowering plants, a wide floral band on the everted rim (minor chips to foot rim), 6" x 8 1/2" d. ....**$80 pair**

Photo courtesy Clars Auction Gallery, Oakland, Calif.; www.Clars.com

Charger, Japanese-style Imari, scallop edged, the interior well painted in gilt, under-glaze blue and shades of red enamel with a flower vase medallion bordered by a floral band and surrounded on the curving sides with alternating shaped floral and dragon reserves separated by vertical bands of cash-emblems, all set against a dense brocade-patterned ground, 17" d. **$425**

Photo courtesy Clars Auction Gallery, Oakland, Calif.; www.Clars.com

Cup (stem), Chinese wucai, the exterior of the circular bowl painted in under-glaze blue and bright enamels with three mythical animals flying amid cloud scrolls above stylized waves, the squared stem flaring towards the base and decorated en suite with a Lishui River border, the interior with a spurious Wanli inscription, 3 1/4" h, 2 3/4" d. **$200**

Photo courtesy Clars Auction Gallery, Oakland, Calif.; www.Clars.com

Jar (covered), Chinese Export porcelain for the Thai market, the exterior painted overall in gilt and polychrome enamels with a dense Thai-inspired floral pattern repeated on the tiered lid (hairline crack to lid), 6" h. **$500**

Figure, (nodder), Asian porcelain, seated lady in blue and white dress, nodding head, movable hands extended, 6" h, small counterbalance missing from right hand. **$632**

Jar, Japanese porcelain, blue and white painted jar with domed cover, possibly Seto, mounted as a lamp and fitted with a gilded bronze base depicting a tree trunk and flowers, Meiji Period. With base: 20" h. **$540**

Mug, Chinese Export porcelain, late 18th century, decorated with a three masted sailing vessel carrying a British flag, 4 1/4" h, minor 1/2" hairline on rim edge, no chips or repairs. **$1,540**

Mug, Chinese Export porcelain, with American eagle and shield, late 18th/early 19th century, 3 3/8" h, spreading hairline on base, one line going up side near handle about 2 1/2". **$1,007**

Planter, Chinese Export Rose Medallion, first half 19th century, hexagonal form with flat flared edges, each side decorated in panels depicting views of daily life alternating with floral decorated panels with birds and butterflies on shaped bracket feet, 5" h x 7" d. **$690**

Platter, Chinese Export Canton, blue, mid-19th century, rectangular with canted corners decorated overall in a blue and white Oriental landscape, 16" x 12 1/2". **$575**

Platter, Canton porcelain, China, late 19th century, 14 1/4" x 17". **$503**

Platter, Chinese Export Famille Rose, oval form with canted corners, bold floral sprays, conforming border, 12 7/8" l, 9 3/4" w. **$402**

Platter, (meat), Chinese Export porcelain, blue and white, 19th century, round platter decorated with floral designs, (lacking drainer), 2 1/2" h, 17 3/8" d, 1/2" shallow rim chip. **$385**

Platter, (oval), Chinese Export porcelain, Rose Mandarin decoration with three flower, bird and butterfly reserves alternating with three figural reserves, 17 5/8" l. **$373**

Platter, (oval), Chinese Export porcelain, blue and white landscape with water, pagodas and bridge, reticulated border, 11" l, 9 5/8" w. **$258**

Platter, (oval), Famille Rose palette Chinese Export porcelain, circa 1800, decorated with flower sprigs with gilt spearhead borders, 17 5/8" d, 1/2" rim chip, scattered enamel losses. **$266**

Platters, (pair), Chinese Export Canton, cut-corner, mid-19th century, each of typical form decorated with oriental landscapes in blue and white. Both 12" l x 9 1/2" w. .... **$575 pair**

Pillow, Chinese Export porcelain, oblong with multicolored vases and assorted trophies, pierced ends, 2 1/2" h., 5 3/4" l, 4 3/4" w, chips to corners and edges. **$126**

Pot, (brush), Korean, with openwork decoration of two large roundels with Buddhistic swastika, bamboo and pomegranates in under-glaze blue enamels, 19th/20th century, 5 1/2" x 4" d. **$480**

Pot, (bough), Chinese Export porcelain, twin-handled flaring form, five-hole cover, landscape reserve with figures, interior reserve with figures, green N or Z mark on bottom, 8 1/4" h, 6 3/8" w (overall), 4 3/4" d, cover repaired. **$805**

Punchbowl, Tobacco Leaf decorated, Chinese Export, 19th century, inside and out decorated with tall green tobacco leaves, Famille Rose border, butterflies among the leaves, 6 1/4" h x 14 3/4" d, some roughness to rim. **$1,725**

Punchbowl, Chinese Export, Rose Mandarin, mid-19th century, rim borders profusely decorated in floral vinery

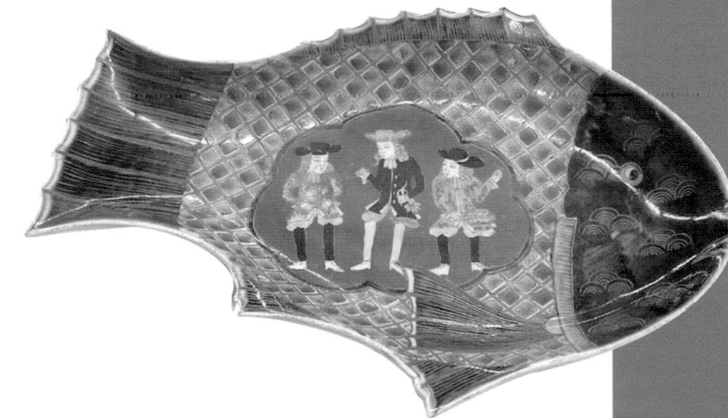

Photo courtesy Clars Auction Gallery, Oakland, Calif.; www.Clars.com

Plate, Japanese-style Imari fish form, the interior painted with a ruyi-head-shaped figural reserve of three Dutchmen on a red ground silhouetted against a geometric pattern of purple and green squares, the cobalt painted head and fins with additional gilt and red accents, 13" l. **$375**

with fanciful butterflies and birds. Center showing panels of domestic Oriental life outlined in Greek key borders alternating with panels of floral and butterfly decoration. Center panel decorated with a scene of scholarly learning, 5 3/4" h x 12 1/2" d, nominal wear to interior painting in bowl. **$2,242**

Punchbowl, ormolu-mounted, Rose Medallion, exterior with four multicolored painted reserves with flowers, birds and butterflies; floral band just under twin handles, four cabriole legs with scroll feet; interior with four conformingly decorated reserves and centering round reserve, 12 1/2" h., 12 1/2" d. **$1,800**

Sauceboat, Chinese Export Famille Rose, and a Rose Mandarin teapot, mid-19th century, sauceboat with applied strap handle and floral butterfly and bird decorated panel opposing a landscape-decorated panel. The drum-form teapot with polychrome-decorated lid, with panels depicting Oriental life alternating with panels of floral sprays and exotic animals. Sauceboat 3" h x 7 1/4" l. Teapot 6 1/2" h. Sauceboat with minor flakes to edge of spout. .... **$201 pair**

Tableware items, (three), Fitzhugh Pattern (blue) porcelain, China, 19th century, including a covered oval dish and two oval platters; dish 4 1/4" h, 11 d, platters 11 1/4" and 14 1/2" d. .... **$711 all**

Stoneware items, (four), Korean, Yi Dynasty: gray stoneware pedestal bowl and cover; gray water dropper with stamped designs; small vase with stamped design, and a black glaze stoneware vase. Tallest: 9 1/2". .... **$480 all**

Tableware items, (three), Chinese Export Canton, blue, cut-corner platter, 15 3/4" x 13", and two similar-shaped sauce or gravy boats, having handles and scalloped edges, each 8" l. .... **$402 all**

Teapot and trivet, Chinese Export Canton, mid-19th century, teapot with berry knopped finial and applied strap handle. Trivet of hexagonal form. Both decorated in blue and white bucolic scenes. Teapot 7" h. Trivet 5 1/4" d, teapot with very minor roughness on spout. Trivet with tiny flakes on edge. .... **$575 pair**

Tureen with cover, Chinese Export Canton, mid-19th century, cover with pointed finial fitted to the deep oval tureen with boar's head handles raised on conforming footed base, decorated overall in typical blue and white pastoral scenes, 6" h overall x 9 1/2" l x 8" w, probable small repair with missing glaze on finial, some discoloration in glaze on lid interior. **$345**

Tureen with cover, Chinese Export Canton, rectangular form, with canted corners and boar's head handles, 9 1/4" h x 12 1/2" l x 8 3/4" w, two pitting spots in lid. **$1,035**

Vase, Chinese mirror black glazed ovoid, possibly Qing, the high shoulder body surmounted by a wide everted rim and tapering sharply to a flared foot, the base with a spurious Kangxi mark, 9" h. **$90**

Vase (garniture), Chinese Export polychrome decorated, mid-19th century, covered vase with Foo Dog finial decorated overall with stylistic raised grapevines and mice, centering polychrome painted court scenes, 12 1/2" h, finial with tiny chip on ear of dog. **$978**

Vase, Celadon, late 19th century, with dark blue dragon, bird and flowers, stylized opposing Foo Dog handles and large

Photo courtesy Clars Auction Gallery, Oakland, Calif.; www.Clars.com

Vase, Chinese, ox-blood glazed, 19th century, the ovoid exterior covered in a rich red glaze ground down on the foot (chipped foot rim, neck ground down), 15" h. **$60**

Photo courtesy Clars Auction Gallery, Oakland, Calif.; www.Clars.com

Vase, Chinese, tea dust glazed, ovoid with a long neck and low slung body (bingdu) raised on a high flaring ring foot, covered overall in the characteristic mottled olive-green glaze, the base with a spurious Qianlong cartouche, 12 1/2" h. **$1,300**

upturned flaring rim: 23 1/4" h x 8 1/2" d top, some old hairlines to rim. **$172**

Vase, Japanese Hirado porcelain, painted with asters in under-glaze blue and yellow, some in moriage, Meiji period. Signed with Mikawachi Kiln marks, 13" x 5 1/4" d. **$5,100**

Vase, Kinkozan Satsuma, painted with a gilt dragon and sea spray on a mottled green glaze, Meiji period. Signed and sealed, 8 1/2" x 5". **$1,920**

Vase, Korean porcelain, squat baluster form with raised and slightly tapering neck painted with birds perched on a tree, the obverse with a bamboo stalk, Yi Dynasty, 6 3/4" h. **$8,400**

Vase, Nippon, decorated with a crane among lotus in moriage relief. Marked on the base Hand-painted Nippon, 10 1/8" h. **$2,400**

Vase, Nippon, ornate porcelain with coralene flowers and gilding on cobalt blue ground, 20th century, small losses to coralene and wear to gilding. Marked 'Patent Applied For, 38257' with three-column stamp, 8" x 5". **$1,440**

Photo courtesy Clars Auction Gallery, Oakland, Calif.; www.Clars.com

Vases (bottle, pair), Japanese-style Kutani, each of tapering square section and painted in bright enamels with figural panels alternating with flowering chrysanthemums along a fence, the angular shoulder with further flowering chrysanthemums below linked key frets, the circular neck accented with flaming jewels, the base with a recessed "fuku" cartouche, 9 3/4" h. **$450 pair** *(A cartouche is an ornate panel in the form of a tablet or shield, usually framed by foliage and scrollwork, and usually bearing an inscription or maker's name and date.)*

Photo courtesy Clars Auction Gallery, Oakland, Calif.; www.Clars.com

Vases (pair), Chinese Famille Verte-decorated phoenix-tail, the wide trumpet mouth and high-shouldered body each painted in bright enamels with a frieze of mythical birds in a lush flowering landscape within geometric patterned borders, the base with a spurious Kangxi mark (some surface wear), 16 3/4" h. **$425 pair**

Photo courtesy Clars Auction Gallery, Oakland, Calif.; www.Clars.com

Vases (pair), Chinese polychrome enamel decorated porcelain, each pear-form body painted with Chinese immortals, one with a long colophon with a cyclical date "bingxu" and signed (unread) mark to base, 6 1/2" h. **$800 pair**

Photo courtesy Clars Auction Gallery, Oakland, Calif.; www.Clars.com

Teapot, Chinese, "chicken blood" stone, faux bamboo, the rectangular body carved and incised as a bundle of bamboo secured by a twisted rope, a few stalks with leafy twigs, with a faux-bamboo curved spout and opposing loop handle, the fitted lid carved en suite, the bright red matrix with mushroom-colored inclusions, 5" h. **$450**

Photo courtesy Clars Auction Gallery, Oakland, Calif.; www.Clars.com

Center: Figure, Chinese, ivory carving, early 20th century, depicting a scholar standing in long robes secured by an ornate sash, his right hand suspending a large brush, the right holding a qin to one side of his youthful face framed by an official's cap, with stained accents and together with a tall wood stand carved as cresting waves, 11" h excluding stand. **$500**

Right: Figure, Chinese, ivory carving, Qing Dynasty (1644–1911), well carved and incised as "Fu" of the three star immortals standing in long robes with a smiling child holding a peach cradled in his hands to the front, the bearded face with a gentle smile and framed by a soft cloth cap secured by ribbons suspended down the back, together with a carved wooden stand, 9 3/4" h excluding stand. **$1,100**

Left: Figure, Chinese, ivory carving, Guanyin, Qing Dynasty (1644–1911), portrayed as a beauty clothed in long robed with black-lacquered accents and holding an up-turned amphora to the front, further lacquer accents applied to the elaborate coiffure framing the smiling face (age cracks), with a footed wood stand, 6 1/2" h excluding stand. **$650**

Ivory

Brush pot, probably late 18th century, depicting a mountainous landscape with birds in flight, the reverse with Chinese characters, the base segmented and detachable, 3 3/4" h, 3 3/4" d, base rim has an old 1/2" elliptic chip. **$1,438**

Container, of cylindrical form and finely carved to the exterior with diminutive figures in a landscape scattered with pavilions (no bottom), fixed to a wooden stand (wear), 4 1/2" h (overall). **$150**

Container, Meiji/Taisho period, the sections of the tusk carved and incised to the exterior with two felines, one of a lion approaching an elephant walking with trunk raised, pigment accents, 4" l. **$100**

Figure, Budai, the "Laughing Buddha," well carved and incised, seated on a brocade-patterned treasure sack, a group of five Chinese children frolicking to the top and back of the deity, 5 3/4" h. **$225**

Figure, Budai, the "Laughing Buddha," seated in a pose of royal ease with his left knee raised and left hand holding prayer beads, with finely defined facial features, 4" h. .. **$200**

Figure, bearded fisherman in an animated pose, a small dog to the side of the rocky outcropping (lacking pole), with a wooden stand, 7" h (figure only). **$60**

Figure, fisherman, mid-19th century, with inked highlights depicting a fisherman with bandana and floral tunic, with creel and bamboo spear perched on a rock plinth with a captured fish, height minus spear, 7 3/4", spear present, needs reattaching. **$575**

Figure, flowering peony bush issuing from a rectangular container, a spray of ripe millet to one side, 6 1/2" h. .. **$150**

Vase, (miniature), with inlaid accents, carved and incised as an archaic vessel with a trumpet mouth, the ovoid body with archaic motifs with occasional inlay of turquoise and coral, with loose ring handles (possible restorations), 2 3/4" h. **$120**

Jade

Bracelet, the convex sides well carved and pierced with leafy peony blossoms, the pale sea-green translucent matrix of even tone, 2 7/8" d. **$150**

Brush washer, carved and pierced as an open Buddha hand citron flanked by leafy stems to either side, the translucent olive green matrix with white striations and flecked with black, 8" l. **$700**

Clasp, archaic, well carved and incised as a dragon with a snake-form body tapering to a hooked tail, with its curving body turning back to form a narrow slot, the mottled translucent green stone with brown and white inclusions, 2" l. **$325**

Figure, elephant, carved and incised standing with its head turned to one side and trunk swaying upwards, of pale-green color mottled with white and brown fissures and inclusions, some incorporated into the design, 6 1/2" l. **$425**

Figure, Foo Lion, 20th century, in a recumbent pose with forelegs outstretched and resting on a large cash emblem, the translucent grayish-white matrix with opaque white inclusions, 3" l. **$50**

Figure (jadeite), God of Wealth, Wen Cai Shen (Bi Gan), as a bearded official holding an ingot and ruyi-head scepter in his hands, the corpulent deity surrounded by laughing children, auspicious animals, birds and symbols amid cloud scrolls, all supported on an oversize metal ingot, portions

Photo courtesy Sloans & Kenyon Auctioneers and Appraisers, Chevy Chase, Md.; www.SloansandKenyon.com

Figure of deity, Chinese, carved, multi-armed, holding attributes, seated on double lotus throne, high chignon, figure of Buddha, attendants, 20th century, 11" h x 13" l x 7" w. **$945**

Photo courtesy Sloans & Kenyon Auctioneers and Appraisers, Chevy Chase, Md.; www.SloansandKenyon.com

Okimono of fisherman, holding bamboo-form stick, wearing hat, signed, late Meiji period, Japanese, 6 1/2" h. **$355**

of the design picked out from the apple green and russet inclusions in the translucent mottled pale green stone, 5 3/4" h. **$650**

Figure, recumbent horse with its legs tucked close to its emaciated torso and head turned back, the greyish white translucent matrix with occasional inclusions, 2 1/4" l. **$325**

Figure, recumbent ram in a frontal pose with its legs tucked close to the body, the pale green matrix with occasional white inclusions, 2 1/4" l. **$550**

Figure, tree, with multiple blossoms fashioned from nephrite jade, agate, rose quartz and rock crystal on stems with dark green jade leaves, the rectangular container of mottled green jade (losses), 12 1/4" h. **$60**

Photo courtesy Clars Auction Gallery, Oakland, Calif.; www.Clars.com

Vessel, Chinese, fine spinach jade archaic-style, 19th century, well carved and incised as a jia (family), a tripod wine vessel with a wide trumpet mouth surmounted by a pair of tall cap-form knobs, a single animal-head handle attached to the body decorated with taotie masks centered on pierced flanges, all resting on three splayed leaf-form supports with further archaic motifs, the translucent muted green stone with occasional dark flecks, together with a conforming hardwood stand with silver wire inlay, 8" h excluding stand. **$2,250**

Photo courtesy Sloans & Kenyon Auctioneers and Appraisers, Chevy Chase, Md.; www.SloansandKenyon.com

Celedon jade vase and cover, tao tie masks, Chinese, 19th century, 5" h. **$1,770**

Figure, water buffalo, carved in a recumbent posture with its head raised and turning to one side, its right foreleg held to the front, the olive-green matrix mottled with white and brown striations, incised details, 10" l. **$275**

Figures, birds, 20th century, carved and pierced as a long-tailed crested bird and its mate cavorting near a fruiting pomegranate tree, the translucent pale green stone suffused with russet in one fruit and the head of the main bird, with wooden stand, 6 1/4" h. **$120**

Figures, elephants, 20th century, realistically rendered as an African elephant attempting to comfort a calf standing to one side, the muted green stone with overall white inclusions, 7 1/2" l. **$400**

Pebble, the interior carved and undercut with a laughing figure of Shou-lao (god of longevity and luck) seated in a pose of royal ease, a youthful attendant holding a spray of peach standing to the left, the tableau picked out from the milky white interior of a red-skinned pebble, 6 3/4" l. **$225**

Pebble, 20th century, the top featuring a celestial maiden in flight with her long robes fluttering in the wind, her left hand holding a floral spray, the high-relief figure crafted from the milky white interior of a red-skinned pebble, 9" l. **$50**

Photo courtesy Sloans & Kenyon Auctioneers and Appraisers, Chevy Chase, Md.; www.SloansandKenyon.com

Apple jade vase, Rouleau form, flowering lotus decoration, elephant head loose-ring handles, Chinese, 19th century. **$945.**

Pendant, Qing Dynasty, of oval shape and carved to the front with a pair of Chinese children chasing a butterfly while playing in a fruiting melon patch, the upper portion finely carved with linked cloud scrolls, the pale green translucent matrix of even tone, 2 1/4" l. **$425**

Pendants (pair), the first of circular mutton-fat jade carved to either side with shou medallions (symbols of long life) bracketed by bats interspersed with wan-li symbols (strength), the second of rectangular shape, either side carved to the top with a pair of Mandarin ducks above a reserve of a carp in a lotus pond, reversed by an auspicious four-character seal-script inscription, the stone of even greenish-white hue, 2" d and 2 1/4" l. .... **$350 pair**

Table screens (pair), each large rectangular dark-green panel carved and incised with figures in a landscape, some traveling on horseback, working in the field or conversing in a pavilion, both reversed by two five-character poetic couplet, one with a spurious Qianlong mark, each set within a reticulated frame of foliate repeated on the separately fashioned stand, 26 1/2" h. .... **$4,250 pair**

Vase, carved as two joined lengths of bamboo fronted by a pair of recumbent rams, the reverse with a bat amid scrolling clouds above further bamboo and a rocky outcropping, the translucent green stone with russet fissures and striations, occasional white inclusions and black flecks, 3 3/4" h. **$200**

Netsuke and Okimono

The traditional Japanese kimono has no pockets. Daily necessities, such as money and tobacco supplies, were carried in leather pouches, or inros, which hung from a cord with a netsuke toggle. The word netsuke comes from "ne"—to root—and "tsuke"— to fasten.

Netsuke originated in the 14th century and initially were favored by the middle class. By the mid-18th century, all levels of Japanese society used them. Some of the most famous Japanese artists, including Shuzan and Yamada Hojitsu, worked in the netsuke form.

Netsuke average from 1 to 2" in length and are made from wood, ivory, bone, ceramics, metal, horn, nutshells, etc. The subject matter is broad based, but almost always portrayed in a lighthearted, humorous manner. A netsuke must have smooth edges and balance in order to hang correctly on the sash.

Value depends on artist, region, material and the skill of the maker. Western collectors favor "katabori," pieces that represent an identifiable object.

An okimono is a Japanese carving, often small, similar to but larger than a netsuke. Unlike netsuke, which had a specific purpose, okimono were purely decorative and were displayed in the "tokonoma," a small, raised alcove. During the Meiji Period (1868-1912) many okimono were made for export to the West.

Recent reproductions are common. Some are molded resin. Newly made netsuke are carved from vegetable ivory, also known as corozo, a name used for the tagua nut in the South American rainforest.

Photo courtesy Rago Arts and Auction Center, Lambertville, N.J.; www.RagoArts.com

Netsuke, carved wood, Shishi (stylized figure of a snarling lion) crouched over a ball, natural himotoshi, 19th century, unsigned, 1 3/4" h. **$720**

(The channel or hole carved into the netsuke for the passage of the cord is called the himotoshi. Such holes also occur naturally.)

Photo courtesy Rago Arts and Auction Center, Lambertville, N.J.; www.RagoArts.com

Netsuke, by Masanao Shinzan, carved wood, of a curled-up rat with inlaid eyes, natural himotoshi and well-rendered details. Signed Shinzan (Masanao Shinzan, born 1904), 1 1/4" h. **$2,400**

Netsuke, (three) by Nanryu, of Oni, 20th century: one carrying Hotei's sack over his shoulder; one with Benkei's bell; and one with a large jar, all with inlaid eyes. Signed Nanryu (Keizo Kurata, born 1935). Tallest: 1 3/8" h. .... **$900 all**

(Oni are creatures from Japanese folklore, variously translated as demons, devils, ogres or trolls.)

Netsuke, three pieces, 19th/20th century: wood netsuke of a puppy, natural himotoshi, signed Toko-To, 1 1/2" h; ivory Oni emerging from lotus leaf, unsigned, 2 1/4" h; two fish with scales carved in openwork, with inlaid eyes, signed Koetsu, 1 1/2" h. .... **$720 all**

(The channel or hole carved into the netsuke for the passage of the cord is called the himotoshi. Such holes also occur naturally.)

Netsuke, three pieces, 20th century: two Shishi (stylized figure of a snarling lion) with openwork ball in negoro lacquer with traces of gilding, unsigned, 1 1/4" h; wood Shishi with openwork ball, signed on the base Minkoku, 1 1/4" h; ivory horse with inlaid eyes, unsigned, 1 7/8" h. .... **$540 all**

Netsuke, three carved pieces, 20th century: wood baboon holding a peach, well-rendered details, signed Yukimasa; ivory monkey and fish with inlaid eyes, signed Ippo(?); and a wood Daruma doll, signed Mitsunobu. Tallest: 1 3/4". .... **$600 all**

Netsuke, ivory, six pieces, 19th-20th century: Ebisu and Daikoku riding a fish, signed; Ashinaga and Tenaga playing with children; two chicks emerging from egg, signed and sealed; group of people under a pine tree; man playing a drum with a monkey, signed; and man playing a drum. Tallest: 2". .... **$780 all**

Photo courtesy Rago Arts and Auction Center, Lambertville, N.J.; www.RagoArts.com

Netsuke and okimono, four pieces, carved ivory and wood; okimono: Pekinese dog holding a pierced ball; man sitting in a palanquin, being carried by two others, signed; man holding a stick; man with two children and a dog; together with four netsuke: carved wood Okame; horse, signed; water buffalo, signed, 19th/20th C. Tallest: 12". **$1,200 all**

Photo courtesy Rago Arts and Auction Center, Lambertville, N.J.; www.RagoArts.com

Netsuke and tonkotsu (tobacco box), four pieces, 19th-20th century: wood netsuke of a monk piercing his chest with an ivory needle, inlaid part of himotoshi, signed on ivory tablet Ryugyoku; wood netsuke of a Sambaso dancer (part of a Kabuki theater performance) holding a fan, with metal and mother-of-pearl inlay, ivory details, signed on the box; and wood Daruma tonkotsu inlaid with mother-of-pearl eyes and ivory himotoshi, together with a wood fish pipe-holder, both unsigned. Tallest: 4 1/4". **$1,560 all**

(The channel or hole carved into the netsuke for the passage of the cord is called the himotoshi. Such holes also occur naturally.)

Photo courtesy Rago Arts and Auction Center, Lambertville, N.J.; www.RagoArts.com

Okimono, ivory and lacquered wood, Geisha with a parasol in wood with applied lacquer and carved ivory, Meiji period. Signed, 16 1/2" h. **$3,900**

Photo courtesy Rago Arts and Auction Center, Lambertville, N.J.; www.RagoArts.com

Okimono, ivory, large sectional figure of an egg tester, with an egg-filled basket strapped over his shoulder and eggs at his feet, Meiji period. Stained detail, some losses. Signed, 14 1/2" h. **$1,080**

Netsuke, ivory, six pieces, Meiji period: horse emerging from a gourd, held by a bearded elder; carved horn octopus hiding in a wooden tub; scholar holding a scroll; Daruma waking from sleep; man with children at his side; and a bent figure holding a drum. All but octopus signed. Tallest: 2 1/4". .... **$540 all**

Netsuke, ivory, six pieces, Meiji period: riverboat with passengers and rower sitting underneath a canopy, signed; tiger sitting on a large bamboo trunk; badger wrapped in a robe holding a fly whisk; group of five people standing under a pine tree; Okame; and swordsmith forging a blade, signed. Tallest: 1 3/8". .... **$720 all**

Netsuke, ivory, six pieces, Meiji period: horse and boar; coiled snake on skull; man with gourds; monkey, signed; hunter with rabbit; and rat with purple inlaid eyes, signed. Tallest: 2". .... **$600 all**

Netsuke and okimono, four pieces, mostly ivory, 19th century: Mokugyo bell with loose interior ball, seal-type characters on sides and swivel handle; Okimono of a monk splitting wood, signed on red tablet; man weaving a basket with a Sagemono hanging from his belt, signed; and wood turtle with its young, well-rendered detail. Tallest: 1 1/2". .... **$960 all**

Okimono, carved ivory and wood, man sitting on a bundle of branches, his head, hands, feet and logs carved from ivory, Meiji period. Missing accessories from hands, possibly an ax from side of bundle and signature tablet from base, 8 1/4" x 9". **$1,560**

Okimono, ivory, two pieces, 19th-20th century: three rats climbing on a mask, stained and inlaid details, 1 3/4" h; skull, 2" x 1 1/2". Both unsigned. **$960**

Okimono (three), ivory, Meiji period: rooster with hen and chicks, eyes inlaid with mother-of-pearl, one talon missing from rooster's and chick's foot, signed on base, 3" x 3 1/2"

x 2 1/2"; chick emerging from broken egg, eyes inlaid with mother-of-pearl, signed on base, 2" x 4" x 2"; smaller similar to previous, one eye missing pupil, unsigned, 1 1/2" x 2 1/2" x 1 1/4". .... **$1,920 all**

Statuary

Figure of a bodhisattva, (one who leads an enlightened existence), Chinese, black-pigmented copper, seated on a double lotus base in long flowing robes, her hands held to the front and clutching prayer beads, the smiling face framed by an elaborate coiffure partially hidden by a cowl (some wear to finish), 13 1/2" h. **$140**

Figure of a female bodhisattva, (one who leads an enlightened existence), Nepalese, bronze, the lithe figure in a dance pose with one leg raised, the right hand holding a ghanta (ritual bell), the other with another attribute (losses), the meditative expression framed by large ear hoops and a coiffure drawn up into a tall chignon (loose), all supported on an oval double-lotus pedestal, incised details, 15 1/4" h. **$175**

Figure of Budai, (Hotei), the "Laughing Buddha," Chinese, white marble, seated with his robes partially open and holding prayer beads, his joyful face with crisply rendered features, 7" l. **$60**

Figure of a Buddha, Chinese, gilt-painted wood, seated in dhyanasana (profound meditation) with his hands to the front, the serene face with-red painted lips and crisply defined features framed by a coiffure of conical curls, 20" h. **$600**

Figure of a Buddha, Japanese, gilt lacquer, wood, 19th century, standing in monastic robe with his hands in the "fear not" and "boon granting" gestures, backed by an almond-shaped mandorla (two circles coming together) and supported on a high galleried pedestal, 10 3/4" h. **$80**

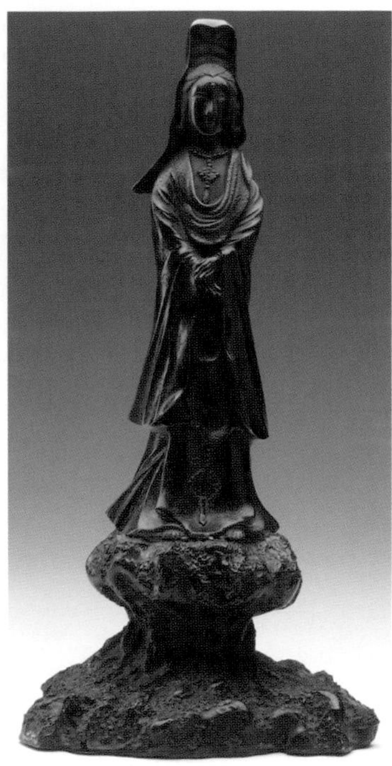

Photo courtesy Rago Arts and Auction Center, Lambertville, N.J.; www.RagoArts.com

Figure of Kwannon, Japanese bronze, her robes finely chased with flowers and cloud designs, standing on a rockwork base, 19th century, 15 3/4" h. **$660**

Figure of the Buddha, Southeast Asian, gilt bronze, probably Thailand, 19th century, seated in meditation on a triangular plinth with the hands joined together, the smiling face framed by a gilt diadem (restoration, wear), 6" h. **$90**

Figure of a donor, Chinese, gilt lacquered, wooden, Qing Dynasty, the chaste maiden standing in long flowing robes and holding a sacred jewel (cintamani) to the front, her face with pigment accents, all supported on a high facetted plinth (extensive wear, wormage), 15 1/2" h. **$90**

Photo courtesy Sloans & Kenyon Auctioneers and Appraisers, Chevy Chase, Md.; www.SloansandKenyon.com

Snuff bottle, Chinese, rose glass, depicts qilin on brocade ground. **$445**

Photo courtesy Sloans & Kenyon Auctioneers and Appraisers, Chevy Chase, Md.; www.SloansandKenyon.com

Snuff bottle, Chinese, dark brown overlay glass, flattened ovoid form, carved, depicts flowering lotus branch above bird. **$475**

Figure of Guanyin, Chinese, celadon glazed, the deity seated with prayer beads in her right hand, the serene face framed by an elaborate diadem fronted by a small seated Buddha, the translucent bluish-green glaze pooling in the recesses, 6 1/2" h. **$80**

Figures (two), Chinese, polychrome painted wood, Qing Dynasty, the first of Guanyin seated in a pose of royal ease with and holding prayer beads, a small figure of Amitabha Buddha to the front of his diadem; the second of a bodhisattva seated in meditation with his hands to the front and cradling a scroll (extensive wear, wormage), 9 1/2" and 8" h. .... **$50 both**

Figures (two), of deities, Indian, carved wood, the first a sandalwood image of the elephant-headed Ganesha in his four-arm manifestation, the second a larger sculpture of Vishnu in princely raiment and standing on a tiered lotus base, two of his four arms with couch and disk attributes and all backed by a foliate mandorla, 6 3/4" and 16" h. .... **$110 both**

Robe, Chinese, woman's yellow ground silk, the silk damask woven with dragon roundels framed by patterned cream and green ribbons and a wide edge band embroidered in blue silk thread with flowering lotus scattered with brightly colored butterflies repeated to the inside of the wide sleeves (staining), 52" l. **$250**

Skirt, Chinese, woman's two-section, yellow silk, each with a damask ground woven with auspicious emblems amid scrolling tendrils, the corner panel densely embroidered with fluttering moths, the right with multiple small panels of blossoming flowers framed by a black satin ground border with blue foliates, 37 3/4" l. **$350**

Jacket, Chinese, Han, woman's silk, the damask blue ground woven with various flowers all framed by a black satin trim embroidered with butterflies and prunus, further with a pink foliate border forming a ruyi head to the front and back, (fading, stains, and wear), 27 1/2" l. **$200**

Clothing

Photo courtesy Clars Auction Gallery, Oakland, Calif.; www.Clars.com

Robe, Chinese, Manchu-style embroidered red satin ground, child's, displaying eight dragons couched in metallic threads chasing sacred jewels amid scrolling clouds and auspicious emblems executed with Peking knots, all above a modified lishui (standing water) border, the collar and sleeve band decorated en suite with dragons meandering above waves on a black satin ground, (loose couching, wear, staining to exterior and lining), 30 1/2" l. **$1,700**

Photo courtesy Clars Auction Gallery, Oakland, Calif.; www.Clars.com

Jacket, Chinese, Han, woman's silk, finely embroidered with bird roundels surrounded by scattered butterflies and flowers on a purple satin ground, framed by a white satin ground neck band and border featuring shou medallions further by auspicious animals and florals, bracketing a blue ground trim woven with stylized white birds, all forming a large ruyi head pattern to the front and back, (some fading and staining to the exterior, further staining to the lining), 30 1/2" l. **$800**

PERFUME CONTAINERS

The earliest known perfume containers date back more than 4,000 years. Knowledge of perfumery came to Europe as early as the 14th century, due partially to the spread of Islam. The Hungarians introduced the first modern perfume. Made of scented oils blended in an alcohol solution, it was made in 1370 at the command of Queen Elizabeth of Hungary and was known throughout Europe as "Hungary Water."

Also see Tiffany.

Ancient glass, late Roman Empire, neck chip, body crack and cloudiness, 3" h. **$28**

Atomizer, green opalescent glass with gilt metal fittings and original bulb, 5 3/4" h. **$57**

Atomizer (travel), continental, silver and Venetian glass, circa 1900, with original bulb (loose) and carrying purse; purse 4" l. **$30**

Aventurine, donut shape, silver mounts with monkey stopper, black glass with copper mica flake, 3" h. **$84**

Baccarat, cobalt blue and clear cut-glass atomizer with original silvered metal pump fitting, stenciled mark, 3 1/2" h. **$72**

Photo courtesy Rago Arts and Auction Center, Lambertville, N.J.; www.RagoArts.com

Baccarat, for Delettrez "XII," pink crystal, with label, in hand-painted box, circa 1927, Marked Baccarat, 4 1/2" h. **$20,000**

Photo courtesy Rago Arts and Auction Center, Lambertville, N.J.; www.RagoArts.com

Baccarat, for Guerlain, "A Travers Champs," crystal, cord sealed, with label, in faux marble box, circa 1924, Marked Baccarat, 5" h. **$900**

Photo courtesy Rago Arts and Auction Center, Lambertville, N.J.; www.RagoArts.com

Baccarat, for J. Viard, Madhva "Ta Wao," gilded and enameled crystal, with original beaded tassel, circa 1923, marked Baccarat, 2 1/2" h. **$5,000**

Photo courtesy Rago Arts and Auction Center, Lambertville, N.J.; www.RagoArts.com

Brosse Jovoy, "Hallo! Coco!", enameled glass, cord sealed, in rare cage display, with box, circa 1924, bottle 4" h. **$13,000**

Baccarat, Toujours Fidle, 3" h. **$230**

Bohemian glass, atomizer and perfume bottle, the amber atomizer with original bulb, the bottle with sterling silver screw cap and original stopper; taller 3 1/2" h. .... **$84 pair**

Bottle and matching atomizer, Art Deco, green flash glass with original gilt metal fittings and bulbs, bottle with dauber and stopper, 4" h. .... **$144 pair**

Bourjois, Evening in Paris, presentation in blue Bakelite box modeled as an owl, 3 1/2" h. **$60**

Bourjois, Evening in Paris, presentation in blue Bakelite box modeled as a tall-case clock, 4 1/2" h. **$115**

Bouton, Piano, presentation, circa 1930s, 4 3/4" l. **$57**

Ciro, Bouquet Antique, circa 1932, finished in blue, black, and yellow enamel, 3 1/4" h. **$517**

Ciro, Bouquet Antique, with original tassel and packaging, 3" h. **$330**

Continental porcelain, circa 1930s, modeled as a seated cat, gilt metal replacement stopper, 3 3/4" h. **$240**

Corday, Rue de la Paix, figural with ashtray base, 8" h. **$103**

De Vigny, Golli Wogg, circa 1930s, with original label (worn), 5 1/2" h. **$120**

De Vigny, Golli Wogg, 1950s, with original box, 3 1/2" h. **$360**

Diviblis, topaz glass atomizer with original bulb and metal fitting, 6" h. **$72**

Dresden porcelain, circa 1900, in 18th-century Meissen style with figures in landscape and flowers, signed Carl Theime, 3 1/2" h. **$258**

Photo courtesy Rago Arts and Auction Center, Lambertville, N.J.; www.RagoArts.com

Czech, Art Deco, blue crystal with dauber, in unusual jeweled metalwork holder, circa 1920s, 5" h. **$1,500**

Photo courtesy Rago Arts and Auction Center, Lambertville, N.J.; www.RagoArts.com

Lalique, "Parfum Lalique," clear and frosted crystal, circa 1992, script Lalique, 10 1/2" h.
$550

English, Victorian, opalescent glass, with brass cap and original internal stopper, horn shaped, 6" l. **$149**

English, Victorian, satin glass, with Japanese-style gilt decoration, with silver top (frozen), 3 1/4" h. **$144**

Fenton, frosted glass, 1930s with floral design, 5 1/2" h. **$92**

Guerlain, Liu, circa 1930, in original black and gilt Art Deco box, bottle 2 1/2" h. **$230**

Hovenvansoeg box, Danish, circa 1770, with eagle surmount, base with Latin engraving, gold wash interior, 3" h. **$240**

Kerr, American, silver pendant vial, modeled as a Renaissance baton, with cherub faces and XXX touchmark, signed Kerr, 4" h. **$195**

Collector's Note: The William B. Kerr Co. was established in Newark, N.J., in 1855. The firm was purchased by Gorham in 1906.

Kerr, American, silver pendant vial, with dolphin-shape design in Renaissance style, sprinkler form with XXX touchmark, Kerr, 3 1/4" h. **$287**

Kewpies, assembled set of five with varied hand positions, each with different pose, each with sprinkler tops, average 3" h. ....**$230 all**

Lalique, Coeur Joie for Ninna Ricci, 1950s, stenciled "BOTTLE MADE BY LALIQUE", 4 3/4" h. **$161**

Lalique, Enfants, 1980s, engraved Lalique France, 4 1/4" h. **$270**

Lalique Perfume, Limited Edition, 1996 with original packing and contents, bottle: 4" h. **$345**

Lalique Pour Homme, "Les Mascotes," three miniature bottles, presentation set in original box, average 2" h. **$161**

Lalique Society of America, Clairfontaine, 1991, in original box, stenciled marks, 4 1/2" h. **$230**

Lalique Society of America, Degas box, 1989, in original box, stenciled marks, 2 1/2" h. **$126**

Photo courtesy Rago Arts and Auction Center, Lambertville, N.J.; www.RagoArts.com

R. Lalique, "Amphitrite," green glass, circa 1920, engraved R. Lalique France No. 514, 3 1/2" h.
$4,350

Photo courtesy Rago Arts and Auction Center, Lambertville, N.J.; www.RagoArts.com

R. Lalique, for Molinard, "Le Baiser Du Faune," clear and frosted glass, circa 1928, molded R. LALIQUE, engraved Molinard Paris France, 5 3/4" h. **$4,000**

Lalique Society of America, Hestia Medallion, 1990, in original box, stencil marks, 5 1/2" h. **$103**

Lalique-style, Ambre Antique, presentation for Coty, 1990 reissue, with original box, bottle 6 1/4" h. **$172**

R. Lalique, Dans La Nuit, for Worth, with original contents and packaging, unsigned, bottle: 3" h, box worn. **$180**

R. Lalique, figural atomizer for Marcas et Bardel, with green patina and original gilt metal fitting, molded 'R. Lalique' on bottle, 2 3/4" h. **$460**

R. Lalique, Jasmine, for Worth, molded "R. Lalique", 2 1/2" h. **$168**

R. Lalique, Sans Adieu, for Worth, molded "R. Lalique", 2 1/2" h. **$204**

Photo courtesy Rago Arts and Auction Center, Lambertville, N.J.; www RagoArts.com

R. Lalique, for Roger et Gallet, "Flausa," clear and frosted glass with sepia patina, circa 1914, molded LALIQUE on stopper, matching engraved control numbers, slight cloudiness to interior, 4 3/4" h. **$3,500**

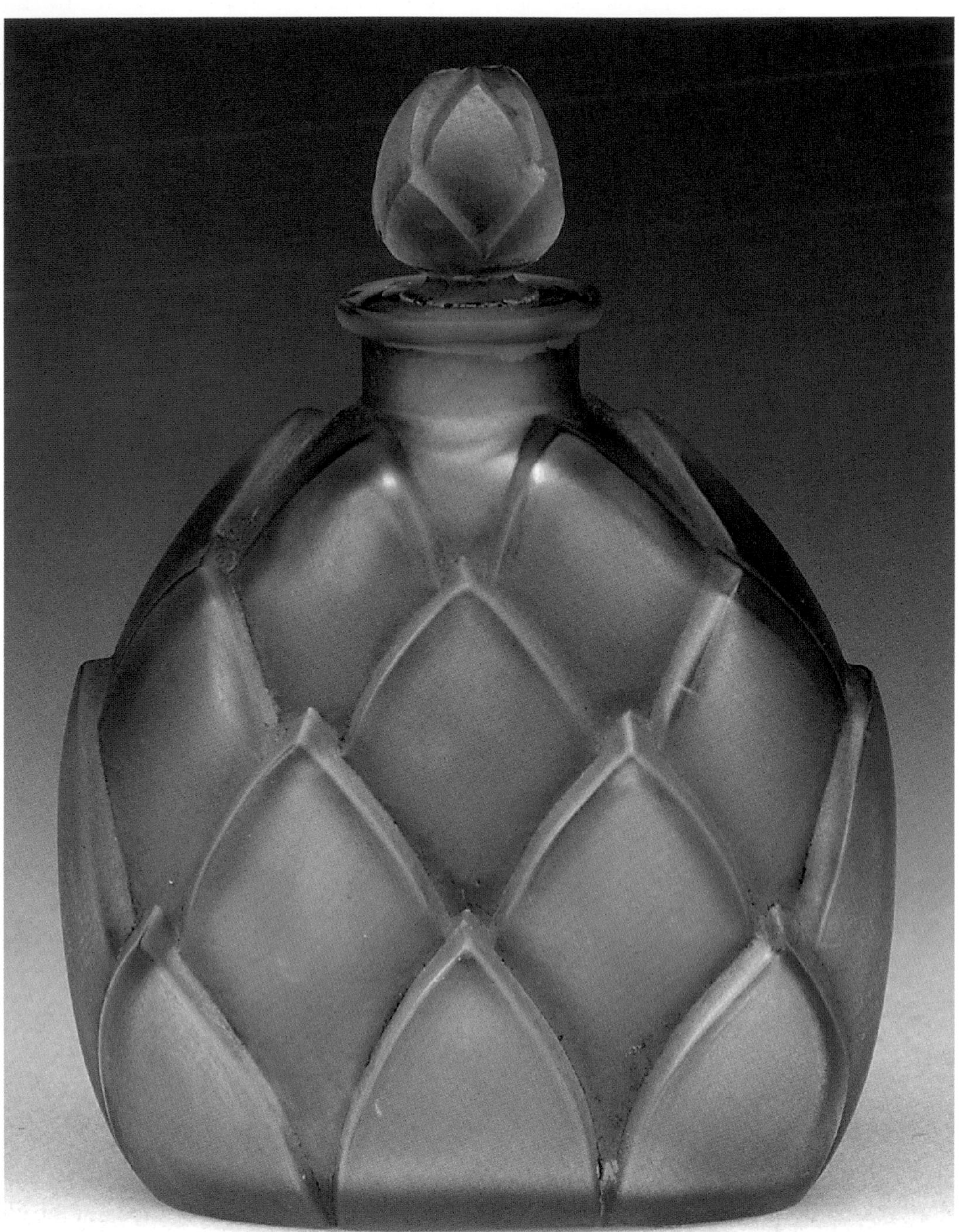

Photo courtesy James D. Julia Auctioneers, Fairfield, Maine; www.JuliaAuctions.com

R. Lalique Perfume Bottle. Artichoke design impressed around entire body of the bottle with a matching pressed floral stopper. The bottle is finished in a rich green patination and is double signed on the underside with impressed block letters "R. Lalique France" and engraved script signature "R. Lalique France 515". 3 1/4" h. **$1,140**

Lili of Bermuda, "Easter Lily," circa 1940, in original wooden box, perfume 3 1/2" h. **$168**

James McIntyre, vial, porcelain egg, circa 1885, Burslem, England, modeled as a bird's egg, with figural silver shape of baby-chicken-head screw cap, registered number 20772, 2 1/2" h. **$862**

Collector's Note: James MacIntyre & Co., founded circa 1860, Burslem, Staffordshire, England.

James McIntyre, vials (three), porcelain, modeled as a walnut, acorn and hazelnut, circa 1860, two with plated screw caps (one frozen, one lacking stopper), one with silver cap (also lacking stopper), tallest 2 1/4" h. .... **$570 all**

Lanvin, display tester set, modern bottles on plastic stand, 6" h, including "My Sin" (1923), "Scandal" (1931), "Pretext" (1937), "Rumeur" (1934) and "Arpege" (1927). **$132**

Latticino, swirl pattern, with dauber stopper, missing handles, 6 1/2" h. **$92**

L'Air du Temps, in silk box, 8 oz. bottle, by Nina Ricci, doves in flight. **$510**

Lenox, porcelain for Devilbiss, with cat stopper, 3 3/4" h. **$218**

Lute form, continental, silver, lacks internal stopper, 4 1/2" l. **$373**

Mickey Mouse (pair), pottery, circa 1930, 2 1/2" h. .... **$195 pair**

Norwegian, enamel, silver gilt and guilloché, circa 1920s, signed Anderson (Norway), 5" h. **$402**
(Guilloché refers to a process of engine-turned design on metal.)

Paris Charme, a modern presentation of 13 French perfume miniatures, in original packaging. Box: 7" x 7". **$60**

Pouncet box, continental, silver, circa 1840, heart-shaped with crown surmount, gold-wash interior, 3" h. **$168**
(A pouncet box is a small perfume container with perforated top.)

Pouncet box, continental, silver, heart-shaped with floral surmount, late 19th century, silver marks on interior of cover, 2 1/2" h. **$195**
(A pouncet box is a small perfume container with perforated top.)

Pouncet box, silver, with fleur de lis touch-mark, circa 1850, heart-shaped with crown surmount, 2" h. **$149**
(A pouncet box is a small perfume container with perforated top.)

Royal Worchester, porcelain, Victoria Silver Jubilee Commemorative, dated 1887, chip and restoration to stopper and neck of bottle, 3" h. **$96**

Salvador Dali (two), black glass and plastic, taller: 2 3/4" h. .... **$184 both**

Schiaparelli, "Zut," torso of a woman in felt bag, 3 1/2". **$480**

Schuco bear, yellow mohair, jointed body, 5" h. **$373**

Schuco gnome, green hat and orange shirt, wear to face, loss to hair on top. **$402**

Steuben, Rosaline, with calcite stopper, 4 1/2" h. **$390**

Schuco monkey, brown mohair, worn material, replaced foot, jointed body, 5" h. **$69**

Schuco monkey (bellboy), jointed body with red jacket and blue pants, 5" h. **$72**

Seven Dwarfs, with Cyrillic (Russian) labels, average 4 1/2" h. .... **$180 set**

Silver pendant perfume bottle case, continental, circa 1890, with micro mosaic, Italian silver plate, 3" h. **$207**

Steuben, Blue Aurene, 4 1/2" h. **$460**

Steuben, Blue Aurene, engraved Aurene J 414, 8" h. **$780**

Steuben, Blue Aurene, engraved Aurene L 835, 3" h. **$977**

Steuben, Blue Wisteria, with dauber stopper, 4 1/2" h. **$1,020**

Steuben, Crystal Yellow Cologne, with black threading and stopper, 5 1/2" h. **$570**

Steuben, glass bottle, with Alvin sterling silver overlay, 4 1/2" h. **$345**

Steuben, Gold Aurene on calcite, with engraved floral decoration, 5 1/4" h. **$1,121**

Steuben, Gold Aurene, with dauber stopper, engraved Stueben Aurene, 6 1/2" h. **$960**

Photo courtesy Rago Arts and Auction Center, Lambertville, N.J.; www.RagoArts.com

Paul Poiret, Rosine "Maharadjah," clear and black glass with label, on green glass stand, circa 1926, 4" h. **$3,750**

Photo courtesy Rago Arts and Auction Center, Lambertville, N.J.; www.RagoArts.com

Schiaparelli, "Sans Souci," clear glass with interior blown windmill, sealed with lace cap and hang tag, with animated figural box and outer box, circa 1943, 3 1/2" h.
$6,500

Steuben, Rosalie, with red and calcite stopper, 4 1/4" h. **$570**

Steuben, Verre de Soie, engraved with monogram C, stopper married, 8" h. **$172**

Steuben, Verre de Soie, with blue glass dauber stopper, 4 1/2" h. **$316**

Steuben, Verre de Soie, with blue jade dauber stopper, 4 1/2" h. **$373**

Steuben, Verre de Soie, with green jade stopper, 4 1/4" h. **$510**

Steuben, Verre de Soie, with green threading and green dauber stopper, 4 3/4" h. **$660**

Steuben, Yellow Jade, 4 1/2" h. **$1,725**

Stevens and Williams, vial, English, Victorian, with diamond quilted pattern, brass cap and internal stopper, 5 3/4" h. **$632**

Collector's Note: Stevens and Williams, 1880s, Stourbridge, Worcestershire, England.

Stevens and Williams, (attributed) vial, English, Victorian, Lithalyn glass with chased silver top with original internal stopper, 4 1/4" h. **$402**
(Stevens and Williams, 1880s, Stourbridge, Worcestershire, England.)

Stevens and Williams, (attributed) vial, English, Victorian, with wave pattern (Northrup Loop) in blue and white, silver screw cap lacking internal stopper, 5" h. **$480**

Stuart Manufacturing Co., Dionne Quintuplets, presentation, circa 1936, with original stand and fabric, lacking box cover, overall length: 5 1/2". **$84**

Thomas Webb, cameo glass, signed, floral design white on green, silver stopper engraved and monogrammed, internal stopper, 3" h. **$2,415**

Thomas Webb-style, cameo glass spear-shaped vinaigrette, white floral design on ruby ground, silver top is engraved and monogrammed, 4" l. **$2,300**

Thomas Webb-style, cameo glass, "Palms and Bamboo" pattern, white on pale blue, silver cap chased with Japanese floral, has original internal stopper, 3 3/4" h. **$2,587**

Collector's Note: Thomas Webb and Sons, founded 1837, Stourbridge, Worcestershire, England.

Thomas Webb, duckbill form, white over red cameo glass, flakes to bill, silver mounts, Percy Edwards and Company, Piccadilly, 5 3/4" h. **$9,200**

Thomas Webb-style, cameo glass, rare three-color, floral design in white, mauve on pale blue, silver screw cap engraved with monogram and date 1919. Lacks internal stopper. Hallmark: London 1887, 2" h. **$1,955**

Thomas Webb-style, cameo glass, floral design in white on ruby with butterfly, silver gilt stopper in Moorish taste, has original internal stopper, 3 1/4" h. **$1,920**

Thomas Webb-style, vial, cameo glass, with floral design on lemon ground, silver screw cap with monogram, lacks internal stopper, 6" l. **$960**

Thomas Webb-style vial, Victorian, gooseberry shape, with silver-chased screw top, 1 1/2" long. **$546**

Torquay, porcelain, Devon, England, with Japanese-style silver screw top, tan, turquoise, gold colors, lacks internal stopper, Registration # 74858, circa 1887-1888, 2 1/2" h. **$575**

Travel bottle, continental, silver, circa 1900, with enamel floral panel, 2 1/4" h. **$92**

Vial, Bohemian, double-ended, circa 1880, with engraved hunting scenes, brass tops, lacking internal stoppers, 5 1/2" l. **$300**

Photo courtesy Rago Arts and Auction Center, Lambertville, N.J.; www.RagoArts.com

Viard, Depinoix Boissard "Madelon," figural clear and frosted glass with enamel and multi-hued patina, circa 1919, 4" h. **$2,000**

Photo courtesy Rago Arts and Auction Center, Lambertville, N.J.; www.RagoArts.com

Viard, Depinoix, Monna Vanna "Bouquet Cavalieri," clear and frosted glass with enameled raised detail, metal pendant label, in box, circa 1900, 5" h. **$2,000**

Vial, continental, opalescent glass, 19th century, with gilt metal top, 2 1/2" h. **$149**

Vial, continental porcelain, hand painted with flowers and with silver filigree overlay, modeled as a knife handle, lacks internal stopper, 4" h. **$218**

Vial, continental, silver, circa 1850, with engraved and reticulated design, in fitted wood case (not original), 4 1/4" h. **$517**

Vial, continental, silver, modeled as an owl head with glass eyes on fob chain, stopper frozen, 1 1/4" h. **$192**

Vial, English, Victorian, blue opalescent glass with silver screw top, lacks internal stopper, in original leather case, 4 1/2" l. **$373**

Vial, English, Victorian, double-ended, both silver tops and hinged center, green glass lacks internal stoppers, 5 1/4" l. **$373**

Vial, English, Victorian, double-ended, both silver gilt tops and hinged center, ruby glass, lacks internal stoppers, 5 1/4" l. **$345**

Vial, English, Victorian, double-ended, silver gilt tops engraved with monograms, dated 1876. .... **$345**

Vial, English, Victorian, porcelain, in the form of two blue willow pattern plates, with English silver screw cap, circa 1850, lacks internal stopper, marked with registered number 29260, 2 1/4" h. **$546**

Vial, English, Victorian, ruby flash cut glass with silver stopper and silver screw cap, lack internal stopper, 6" l. **$402**

Vial, French enamel, painted with a cherub and flora on deep-red ground, hinged silver gilt top, has internal stopper, gold wash interior, 3" h. **$1,035**

Vial, French enamel, painted with a couple in natural landscape, loss to hinge, silver gilt top, 2" h. **$300**

Vial, French enamel, painted with figure in natural landscape, hinged silver gilt top, has internal stopper, 2" h. **$460**

Vial, French enamel, painted with nesting birds, deep-blue ground, hinged silver gilt top, has internal stopper, 2 1/4" h. **$540**

Vial, German porcelain, goat herder, circa 1900, in 18th-century Meissen style with silver-metal screw top, modeled by Vogelmann. 3" h. **$240**

Vial (scent), Victorian, cut glass and 14K gold top set with topaz and diamond jewels, has original internal stopper, 3 1/4" h. **$402**

Vial (scent), Victorian, cut glass, acorn form, in original conforming leather box, height of box: 2 1/4". **$345**

Vial (scent), Victorian, glass with silver top and internal stopper, 2" h. **$132**

Vial (scent), English, Victorian, with silver screw top, registered 72627, 2 1/4" h. **$84**

Viard, 1920s, brass top, gilt decorated with birds, molded mark, lacks internal stopper, 3" h. **$600**

Viard, Chypre Celtic, clear with grey patina, 4 3/4" h. **$632**

Vinaigrette, Asian silver, modeled as an articulated fish, and fitted as a brooch, 3 1/2" l. **$161**

Vinaigrette, continental, silver, modeled as an articulated fish, with ruby glass eyes, 19th century, 6 1/2" l. **$1,035**

Ybry, Desir du Couer, In pink glass with original enamel cap and internal stopper (frozen), in original red Morocco leather case, bottle 4" h. **$510**

PHONOGRAPHS

Thomas Alva Edison conceived the principle of recording and reproducing sound between May and July 1877 as a byproduct of his efforts to play back recorded telegraph messages and to automate speech sounds for transmission by telephone. He announced his invention of the first phonograph, a device for recording and replaying sound, on Nov. 21, 1877. Edison's early phonographs recorded onto a tinfoil sheet cylinder using an up-down motion of the stylus.

Also see Folk Art.

Baby Grand Piano-form Phonograph, by Fern-O-Grand Co., Cincinnati, Ohio, with H.J. Ellis Melodius Music Master sound box, in mahogany case with square tapering legs, 32" l x 35" h, (surface craquelure). **$652**

Berliner Lever-Wind Gramophone, circa 1897, with 7" turntable, clamp, Clark-Johnson reproducer, No. J 1159 on oak traveling arm, oak case with winding lever and speed control lever on the side, transfer Berliner Gramophone, National Gramophone Co., 874 Broadway, New York City and patent dates to February 1895, underside with part of maker's operating label, and straight-flared black horn with gilt line decoration, case 9 1/2" square, (period elbow and felt, modern elbow included). Note: The lever-wound motor was designed by Eldridge Johnson and Levi Montross, and first appeared in 1896 enclosed in a circular metal case (on a rectangular baseboard like that of the hand-cranked model). **$11,850**

Columbia Model AB Graphophone, with nickel-plated, open-works mechanism, removable 5" aluminum concert mandrel, reproducer, carved oak base and matching lid with The Graphophone banner transfer and patent dates to 1897, 14 1/2" w, and aluminum witch's-hat horn. **$2,370**

Columbia Type AJ Disc Graphophone, by Columbia Phonograph Co., New York, early style, with horizontal top-wind motor, four-ball governor with threaded speed control, 7" turntable, replica sound box and arm on original bracket (repaired), oak case with corner pilasters, egg-and-dart plinth, carrying handle, banner transfer with patent dates to 1897, and brass-belled horn, case 11" square, (missing turntable clamp and brake). **$1,304**

Columbia Type AQ Graphophone, with nickel-plated, open-works mechanism, three-ball governor, floating reproducer connected to replacement horn with adapted mount, feed-screw, and shaped black enameled base with gilt line decoration, 12" l. **$415**

Columbia Type BC "Twentieth Century Premier" Graphophone, circa 1905, with Higham amplifying reproducer, 6" mandrel and massive triple-spring motor, in oak case with hinged front flap, 19" w, (case refinished), associated brass witch's-hat horn and floor stand, 57" x 23". Note: The BC took the newly introduced 6" long cylinders, and played through a mechanically amplified reproducer with a 4" diaphragm connected to the stylus via a friction wheel. **$1,778**

Columbia Type BF Graphophone, with nickel-plated bedplate, black japanned chassis (decoration worn), 6" l mandrel, reproducer, and paneled oak case with banner and exposition transfers, rounded plinth and lid, 16" w, with small nickel-plated witch's-hat horn. **$830**

Columbia Type N Coin-Operated Graphophone, No. 43889, by American Graphophone Co., Washington, D.C., with single-spring motor, replacement aluminum reproducer, curved oak case with The Graphophone banner transfer, lift-off lid, coin slot, coin drawer and marquee with modern print, 14" w. **$5,333**

Photo courtesy Skinner Inc., Boston, www.SkinnerInc.com

Berliner Improved Gramophone, with top-wind motor, speed control, sound box No. J13243 and patent date Feb. 19, 1895, turntable brake (disc and screws replaced), oak traveling arm, armrest, record clamp, oak case with replacement Berliner transfer, leather elbow and later brass horn, 9 3/4" w, (case refinished, winder replaced, arm possibly replaced). **$2,015**

Edison Concert Phonograph, No. C5623, circa 1899-1900, with Model D reproducer (cut down), 5" mandrel, Triton motor, patent dates to May 1898, plaque, Licensed by the Edison-Bell Consolidated Phonograph Co. Ltd. Not to be Used in Connection with an Automatic or Slot Device. In oak case with drawer and all-enveloping cover, 14" w, (case refinished, cover in original finish, bedplate finish restored), with brass witch's-hat horn, 31" l, two cranes and three 5" brown wax cylinders in cartons. **$2,844**

Edison Gem Phonograph, No. G87305, with key-wind motor, Model C reproducer, black japanned case with gilt line decoration, patent dates to 1908, oak base and domed lid, 10" w, with black octagonal horn (partly repainted) and crane. **$533**

Edison Home Phonograph, Model A, with Model C reproducer, brush, plaque with patent dates to 1893, and green oak case with banner transfer, 18" w, with crane and shaded tin flower horn with painted border. **$1,067**

Edison Opera Phonograph, Type SM, Model A, No. 981, with Model L reproducer, brown-painted bedplate, oxidized bronze finish on mandrel and reproducer, double-spring motor, oak case with corner columns, Edison transfer, domed lid, plaque with patent dates to 1910, 18" w, and oak Music Master horn with transfer and patent date 1908, (bedplate repainted, case and horn refinished but retaining original transfers). **$4,148**

Photo courtesy Heritage Auction Galleries, Dallas; www.HA.com

Victor phonograph, type M 20007, owned by gospel singer J. D. Sumner (1924-1998). It was given to him as a birthday present in 1977 by his family to celebrate his participation on "Way Down", Elvis Presley's last chart hit prior to his death the same year. The paper license sticker is still attached to the bottom of the phonograph, and lists a date of 1902. **$896**

Edison Speaking Phonograph Co. "Parlor" Tinfoil Phonograph, No. 1588, the black japanned iron base with gilt line decoration and central gilt legend, Edison's Speaking Phonograph Patented Feb 19th 1878, No. 1588, Manufactured by Brehmer Bros. Philadelphia, the mandrel with groove for foil ends (originally with rubber wedge), on threaded shaft in fixed supports with balanced crank, and the speaker in arm with adjustment for aligning the stylus with the mandrel grooves, 13" l, on mahogany base and a later glass cabinet. The Parlor model was the Edison Speaking Phonograph Co.'s attempt to catch a wider market for the new invention, beyond the elaborate Exhibition and Drawing Room models made by Sigmund Bergman in 1878. The first Parlor phonographs were also made by Bergmann early in 1879, but even at $15, sales were slow. The Brehmer version, slightly modified, was in production at the end of 1879, though Edison's slowness to approve the first models, followed by a fire at Brehmer's factory in April 1880, prevented rapid sales development, even though the price was now $10. .... **$22,515**

Edison Standard Phonograph, Model A, No. 40216, with H 4-minute reproducer, oak case with "suitcase" clips and rectangular lid, and brass witch's-hat horn, 12" w. **$563**

Edison Standard Phonograph, Model B, No. S 303078, with Model C reproducer, in refinished oak case, 13" w, (bedplate repainted). **$296**

Edison Standard Phonograph, Model B, No. 507638, with Model K reproducer, combination gearing, oak tall case in original finish with Edison transfer, 13" w, with horn, crane and a large quantity of cylinders. **$1,126**

Edison Triumph Phonograph, Model E, No. 85500, with triple-spring motor, Model O reproducer, plaque with patent dates to 1906, oak case with domed lid, 18" w, two-piece crane, and black No. 11 cygnet horn, (bedplate and horn repainted, case refinished). **$1,067**

Oak Phonograph Cylinder Cabinet and Contents, with six pegged drawers containing approx. 190 Edison 2-minute cylinders (untested) in a variety of genres, including opera, band, comedy and Southern titles, 37" h x 23" w. **$1,422**

Thorens Excelda Portable Gramophone, with sound box, crank and tone arm stowing in brown crackle-finish camera-form metal case with strap, 11" l, (some paint loss) and maker's instruction manual. **$119**

Victor Type B Talking Machine, No. 8979, circa 1901, with 7" turntable, clamp, bolt brake, top-wind motor, Concert sound box No. 5622, oak traveling arm, oak case with applied fleur-de-lis motif and bead-and-reel carved baseboard molding, plaque on the front, Victor Made by Eldridge R. Johnson, Type B 8979, Patented U.S. and Foreign Countries. Camden, New Jersey, and black horn with gold pin-striping, base 9 1/2" square, (old split in baseboard, replacement felt and elbow). **$5,629**

Victor Type C Talking Machine, No. 6175, circa 1901-02, with Concert sound box No. 41420, oak traveling arm, 7" turntable with original felt and clamp, nickeled bedplate (some corrosion), side-wind motor, brass-belled black horn stamped Pat. Apl'd For, original leather elbow, oak case with fluted pilasters and metal Victor plaque. Made by Eldridge R. Johnson, Type C 6175, 11" w, horn 14 1/2" l x 9 1/2" d. Note: The first side-wind Victor, which could be wound while playing, and could also accommodate 10" records. **$2,844**

Victor Monarch Special Talking Machine, Type MS, No. 1004, with triple-spring bevel-drive motor, 10" turntable, Exhibition sound box, curved back bracket, oak traveling arm, oak case with paneled sides, rope-twist top, corner pilasters, honeysuckle plinth molding, plaque, Victor Made by Victor Talking Machine Co., Type MS 1004, Patented in U.S. and Foreign Countries, Camden, New Jersey, U.S.A., and flared brass horn, case 12 3/4" w, horn 22" l, (old splits in top, case finish rubbed down). **$2,252**

Victor Monarch Talking Machine, Type M, No. 2406, circa 1901, with single-spring bevel-drive motor, 10" turntable, Eldridge Johnson sound box on oak traveling arm, oak case with stepped plinth molding and engaged baluster corner columns, plaque, Victor Made by Eldridge R. Johnson, Type M 2406, Patented in U.S. and Foreign Countries. Camden, New Jersey, U.S.A., and brass-belled black horn, horn 21 1/2" l. Note: The first Monarch, with 10" turntable. **$2,015**

Victor Type VI Talking Machine, No. 3138, with triple-spring motor, Exhibition sound box No. 32870B, gilt fittings, transfer decorated back bracket, mahogany case with carved corner columns and gilt capitals, plaque and fluted mahogany horn, 21 1/2" d, (arm dented, missing strip of molding from front, repairs to horn). **$3,555**

Victor VV-IV Phonograph, No. 181740 F, with Exhibition sound box No. 427029A, in oak case with double-doors enclosing louvers, 13" w, (dent and pitting on tone arm). **$148**

Victor Style VV-VI Hornless Phonograph, No. 121656 F, with Exhibition sound box No. 65557 3A, in oak case with double doors enclosing louvers, 15" w. **$71**

Victrola Type VV-IX, with Exhibition sound box, in mahogany cabinet with ogee lid and double-doors enclosing louvers, 15" w, (tone arm and sound box defective). **$95**

Victrola VV-XVI Talking Machine, No. 61169, with triple-spring motor, Exhibition sound box No. 43823G, gilt fittings, Circassian walnut cabinet with ogee lid and apron, two sets of double doors, and foliate-carved supports, 50" h. Note: Accompanied by instruction manual and record index in original envelope, and a framed letter from the Victor Talking Machine Co., to the original owner. **$4,148**

Victrola, Cabinet Model VV XVI, No. 121895H, with Exhibition sound box, gilt fittings, and mahogany case with two sets of double doors enclosing horn and record-storage compartment, 51" h. **$237**

Victor Electrola Type VE-XVIII, No. 555, with electric motor, Exhibition sound box, gilt fittings, retailer's transfer of Percy & Foster Piano Co., 1330 G St., Washington, D.C., and bow-fronted serpentine mahogany case with scroll-carved corners, two sets of double doors and maker's transfer, 49" h, and a box of 78 rpm records. **$1,778**

Victrola VTLA Talking Machine, No. 788, early model, with triple-spring motor, Exhibition sound box No. 88056, gilt fittings, internal mahogany horn and upright mahogany cabinet with flat lid with transfer, ogee-form top section and apron, and straight-sided mahogany cabinet with "L" doors enclosing drawer and ten original albums with gilt ring handles, 47" h, with maker's booklet, needle tin, needle packet and record cleaner. **$4,740**

Zon-O-Phone Type C Talking Machine, No. 6043, with 7" turntable, enclosed sound box on nickel-plated arm and bracket, papier-mâché horn, oak case with stepped plinth and celluloid plaque, Zon-O-Phone. Made Expressly for the National Gram-O-Phone Corporation, 874 Broadway, New York, by the Universal Talking Machine Co., N.Y. and pattent date Dec. 13, 1898, 9" w, horn 15" l. **$2,844**

Zon-O-Phone Concert Talking Machine, No. 1330, circa 1903, with V-Concert sound box, steel traveling arm, 7" turntable with original felt, brass horn and rectangular oak case with Concert and Zon-O-Phone, Universal Talking Machine Mfg. Co., New York, 14 1/2" w, horn 16" l x 9" d, (attractive patina on horn, some corrosion on bedplate). **$2,133**

Zon-O-Phone Home Talking Machine, No. 40025, circa 1901-02, with V-Concert sound box, ornate extension arm, 27" turntable with original felt, large brass horn and oak base with celluloid plaque, Manufactured by Universal Talking Machine Mfg. Co., New York, 11" w, horn 24" l x 11" d. **$2,489**

Photo courtesy Skinner Inc., Boston, www.SkinnerInc.com

Zon-O-Phone Type A Talking Machine, by Universal Talking Machine Co., New York, with steel traveling arm, enclosed sound box, 7" turntable, brake, brass horn and oak case with glazed panels showing motor, recessed baluster corner columns and celluloid plaque, Zon-O-Phone, Made Expressly For the (Nati)onal Gram-O-Phone Corporation, 674 Broadway, New York, by the Universal Talking Machine Co., New York; base 9" x 10", horn 14 1/2" l; with three Zon-O-Phone records and a framed facsimile advertisement. **$9,480**

PHOTOGRAPHY

Modern photographic images date back to the 1820s with the development of chemical photography. The first permanent photograph was an image produced in 1826 by the French inventor Nicéphore Niépce. However, the picture took eight hours to expose, so he went about trying to find a new process. Working in conjunction with Louis Daguerre, they experimented with silver compounds based on a Johann Heinrich Schultz discovery in 1724 that a silver and chalk mixture darkens when exposed to light. Niépce died in 1833, but Daguerre continued the work, eventually culminating with the development of the daguerreotype in 1837.

Many advances in photographic glass plates and printing were made all through the 19th century. In 1884, American George Eastman developed the technology to replace photographic plates, leading to the technology used by film cameras today.

Eastman patented a photographic medium that used a photo-emulsion coated on paper rolls. The invention of roll film greatly sped up the process of recording multiple images.

Also see Autographs, Judaica.

Berenice Abbott, (American, 1898-1991) Stone and William Streets, 1936, From Berenice Abbott, Retrospective, 1982; gelatin silver print (printed later); Signed and numbered 13/40; 23 3/8" x 18 3/8" (sheet). **$3,600**

Berenice Abbott, (American, 1898-1991) Portrait of John Sloan, 1940s; gelatin silver print (printed 1960s); Signed; 14 7/8" x 13 5/8" (sheet). **$1,680**

Berenice Abbott, (American, 1898-1991) Princess Eugene Murat, circa 1928, from Berenice Abbott; gelatin silver print (printed 1976); Signed and numbered 25/50; 13 1/2" x 10 1/2" (sheet). **$360**

Berenice Abbott, (American, 1898-1991) Eugene Atget, 1927, from Berenice Abbott; gelatin silver print (printed later); Signed and numbered 25/50; 13 1/4" x 10 3/8" (sheet). **$3,120**

Ansel Easton Adams, (American, 1902-1984) Gottardo Piazzoni in His Studio, San Francisco (image 10), circa 1932, from Portfolio VI; gelatin silver print (printed 1974); Signed, dated, titled and numbered 81/110; 15 3/4" x 19 1/2" (sheet). **$2,280**

Ansel Easton Adams, (American, 1902-1984) White Post and Spandrel, Columbia, California (image 7), 1953, From Portfolio VI; gelatin silver print (printed 1974); Signed, dated, titled and numbered 81/110; 19 1/2" x 15 3/4" (sheet). **$2,520**

Ansel Easton Adams, (American, 1902-1984) Nasturtiums, Big Sur, Calif., 1951; gelatin silver print (printed 1970s); Signed, titled and with studio stamp; 13 3/4" x 10 3/4" (sheet). **$4,800**

Ansel Easton Adams, (American, 1902-1984) Half Dome, Merced River, Winter, circa 1938, From Photographs of Yosemite; gelatin silver print (printed circa 1970); Signed, titled and with studio stamp; 7 5/8" x 9 5/8" (sheet). **$4,500**

Edward K. Alenius, (Finnish/American, 1892-1950) Manhattan, circa 1930; gelatin silver print (printed circa 1930); 13 1/2" x 10 3/8" (sheet). **$480**

Eugene Atget, (French, 1857-1927) Lampshade Seller, circa 1900; gelatin silver print (printed 1956 by Berenice Abbott); Titled, dated and inscribed; 8 1/4" x 6 1/2" (sheet). **$1,320**

Eduard Baldus, (French, 1813-1889) Untitled (View of the Seine, Paris), circa 1800s; Albumen print; Stamped; 8 3/8" x 11 1/4" (sheet). **$360**

Photo courtesy Rago Arts and Auction Center, Lambertville, N.J.; www.RagoArts.com

Berenice Abbott (American, 1898-1991) James Joyce (image 2), circa 1920, from Berenice Abbott; gelatin silver print (printed 1976); Signed and numbered 29/50; 10 3/8" x 13 3/4" (sheet). **$2,280**

Ruth Bernhard, (German/American, 1905-2006) Doll's Head, 1936; gelatin silver print (printed later); Signed, titled and dated; 7 1/4" x 9 1/2" (sheet). **$2,160**

Felix Bonfils, (French, 1831-1885) Place du Marche a Jaffa (Marketplace at Jaffa), circa 1870s; Albumen print; 8 1/2" x 10 7/8" (sheet). **$120**

Edouard Boubat, (French, 1923-1999) Inde, 1964; gelatin silver print; Signed, titled and dated; 11 7/8" x 15 3/8" (sheet). **$1,560**

Margaret Bourke-White, (American, 1904-1971) Shaking Down Slag, 1930; gelatin silver print (printed 1930); Titled with studio stamps; 13 3/8" x 9 1/4" (sheet). **$3,120**

Margaret Bourke-White, (American, 1904-1971) Italy - Details of Locking Bridge in Place, circa 1944; gelatin silver print (printed circa 1944); Signed; 10 3/8" x 10 3/8" (sheet). **$1,560**

Brassai, (Romanian/French, 1899-1984) Brassai: A Portfolio of Ten Photographs, 1973; Portfolio of 10 gelatin silver prints; Signed, dated and numbered Artist Proof 3/5 from an edition of 50; Various sizes, 21" x 17" x 1 1/4" (portfolio). **$48,000**

Adolphe Braun, (French, 1812-1877) Panorama from Murreu, circa 1860s; Albumen print; Titled; 8 3/4" x 19" (sheet). **$240**

Manuel Alvarez Bravo, (Mexican, 1902-2002) Montana Negra, Nube Blanca (Black Mountain, White Cloud) (image 10), 1974, from The Manuel Alvarez Bravo Platinum Portfolio, 1980; Platinum print (printed 1980); Signed; 10" x 12" (sheet). **$1,800**

Manuel Alvarez Bravo, (Mexican, 1902-2002) Calabaza y Caracol (Squash and Snail) (image 2), 1929, from The Manuel Alvarez Bravo Platinum Portfolio, 1980; Platinum print (printed 1980); Signed; 10" x 7 3/4" (sheet) **$2,520**

Frederic Brenner, (French, b. 1959) Dans le quartier hongrois de Mea Shearim, 1979; gelatin silver print (printed later); Signed; 12" x 16" (sheet). **$360**

Paul Auguste Briol, (American, 1889-1969) Untitled, 1930s; gelatin silver print (printed 1930s); Signed; 7 1/2" x 9 1/2" (sheet). **$540**

Esther Bubley, (American, 1921-1998) Brazilian Street Scene, Ouro Preto, 1957; gelatin silver print (printed 1957); Signed, dated and titled; 11" x 13 7/8" (sheet). **$1,800**

Harry Callahan, (American, 1912-1999) Siena, 1968; gelatin silver print (printed circa 1968); Signed; 6" x 6" (sheet). **$3,600**

Harry Callahan, (American, 1912-1999) Detroit, 1942; gelatin silver print (printed circa 1970); Signed; 5" x 7" (sheet). **$4,800**

Camera Work Issue No. 3, July 1903; Magazine with photogravures (incomplete); Including 8 images by Clarence H. White (5), John Francis Strauss (1), Joseph T. Keiley (1) and Alvin Langdon Coburn (1); 11 3/4" x 8 1/2" x 1/2"; Publisher: Alfred Steiglitz, New York. **$960**

Camera Work Issue No. 5, Jan. 1904; Magazine with photogravures (complete); Including 8 images by Robert Demachy (6), Prescott Adamson (1) and Frank Eugene (1); 11 3/4" x 8 1/2" x 1/2"; Publisher: Alfred Steiglitz, New York. **$570**

Camera Work Issue No. 19, July 1907; Magazine with photogravures (complete); Including 6 images by J. Craig Annan (5) and Eduard J. Steichen (1); 11 3/4" x 8 1/2" x 1/2"; Publisher: Alfred Steiglitz, New York. **$720**

Camera Work Issue No. 20, Oct. 1907; Magazine with photogravures (incomplete); Including 9 images by George H. Seeley (6) and Alfred Stieglitz (3); 11 3/4" x 8 1/2" x 1/2"; Publisher: Alfred Steiglitz, New York. **$2,280**

Camera Work Issue No. 25, Jan. 1909; Magazine with photogravures (incomplete); Including 9 images by Annie W. Brigman (5), Ema Spencer (1), Yarnall Abbott (1) and Frank Eugene (2); 11 3/4" x 8 1/2" x 1/2"; Publisher: Alfred Steiglitz, New York. **$1,020**

Camera Work Issue No. 28, October 1909; Magazine with photogravures (complete); Including 10 images by David Octavius Hill (6), George Davison (1), Paul B. Haviland (1), Marshall R. Kernochan (1) and Alvin Langdon Coburn (1); 11 3/4" x 8 1/2" x 1/2"; Publisher: Alfred Steiglitz, New York. **$600**

Paul Caponigro, (American, b. 1932) Nahant, MA, 1958; gelatin silver print; Signed; 6 3/8" x 5 1/2" (sheet). ... **$1,080**

Keith Carter, (American, b. 1948) Megan, Jefferson County, 1988; gelatin silver print; Signed, dated and titled; 20" x 16" (sheet). **$570**

Henri Cartier-Bresson, (French, 1908-2004) Mexico, 1963; gelatin silver exhibition print (printed circa 1963); 9 1/4" x 13 1/2" (sheet). **$6,000**

William Clift, (American, b. 1944) Reflection: Old St. Louis County Courthouse, St. Louis, MO, 1976, from County Courthouses: A Portfolio of 6 Prints; gelatin silver print; Signed; 13" x 15 3/4" (sheet). **$1,560**

Alvin Langdon Coburn, (American/British, 1882-1966) Untitled (Landscape), 1910s; Photogravure; Signed; 15 3/8" x 11 1/4" (sheet). **$2,280**

Gordon Coster, (American, 1906-1988) Untitled, 1930s; gelatin silver print (printed circa 1930s); Titled illegibly with studio stamp; 14" x 11" (sheet). **$480**

Bruce Cratsley, (American, 1944-1998) Louvre Window, Paris, 1980; gelatin silver print (printed circa 1980); Signed, dated and titled; 9 1/2" x 9 1/2" (sheet). **$300**

Photo courtesy Rago Arts and Auction Center, Lambertville, N.J.; www.RagoArts.com

Wolf von dem Bussche (German, b. 1934) Totem: The Papago Legend of the Creation of the Giant Cactus, Called Saguardo, 1993; Portfolio of 12 gelatin silver prints; each signed, dated, titled and numbered 6/44; 22" x 17 7/8" (sheet) each; Publisher: Three Plowshares, 1993.
$4,800 all

Photo courtesy Rago Arts and Auction Center, Lambertville, N.J.; www.RagoArts.com

Imogen Cunningham (American, 1883-1976) Triangles, 1928; gelatin silver print (printed later); Signed and dated with photographer's label; 3 3/4" x 2 3/4" (sheet). **$9,000**

Ralston Crawford, (American, 1906-1978) Interior View of Station, Newark, 1942; gelatin silver print (printed circa 1942); with estate stamp; 3 1/4" x 4 1/2" (sheet); Exhibition: "Ralston Crawford," Whitney Museum of American Art, New York, 1985. .... **$3,000**

Edward S. Curtis, (American, 1868-1952) Volume 8: The Nez, Wallawalla, Umatilla, Cayuse, and the Chinookan Tribes, 1911, From The North American Indian; Unbound volume including 67 of the original 77 photogravures; 12 3/4" x 9 5/8" (sheet) each; Printer: The Plimpton Press, Norwood, MA; Publisher: Edward Sheriff Curtis, Seattle; Engraver: John Andrew & Son, Boston, MA. **$3,000**

Edward S. Curtis, (American, 1868-1952) Untitled (Wood Carrier), circa 1908; Platinum print (printed circa 1908); Signed with blind stamp; 5 7/8" x 7 7/8" (sheet). **$2,400**

Edward S. Curtis, (American, 1868-1952) Modern Designs in Washo Basketry (Plate 542), 1924; Photogravure on vellum; 17 3/4" x 21 3/4" (sheet). **$1,020**

Louise Dahl-Wolfe, (American, 1895-1989) Untitled (Nude), circa 1937; gelatin silver print (printed circa 1937); Dated with studio stamp; 12 3/4" x 10 3/8" (sheet). .. **$2,520**

Judy Dater, (American, b. 1941) Imogen and Twinka at Yosemite, 1974; gelatin silver print (printed 1974); Signed, titled and dated with studio stamp; 9 5/8" x 7 5/8" (sheet). **$4,800**

Liliane De Cock, (American, b. 1939) Evening, Taos, New Mexico, 1970; gelatin silver print; Signed; 20" x 24" (sheet). **$570**

Jed Devine, (American, b. 1944) Untitled; Palladium print; Signed; 10 3/4" x 9" (sheet). **$660**

Robert Doisneau, (French, 1912-1994) Jacques Tati et Sa Bicyclette, 1949; gelatin silver print (printed 1980); Signed, dated, titled and numbered 3/3; 24" x 20" (sheet). **$1,560**

Robert Doisneau, (French, 1912-1994) Portraits, 1943-1971; Portfolio of 15 gelatin silver prints (printed 1984); Signed and numbered 5/50; 16" x 20" (sheet) each. .... **$12,000 all**

Frantisek Drtikol, (Czechoslovakian, 1883-1961) Untitled, 1923; gelatin silver print (printed circa 1923); with blind stamp; 10" x 7 1/2" (sheet). **$1,800**

Walker Evans, (American, 1903-1975) Untitled, 1970s; SX-70 Polaroid print; 4 1/4" x 3 3/8" (sheet). **$3,120**

Walker Evans, (American, 1903-1975) Doorway, 204 West 13th Street, New York City (image 10 of 15), circa 1931, from Walker Evans: Selected Photographs, 1974; gelatin silver print (printed 1974); Signed and numbered 71/75; 11 1/8" x 8 3/4" (sheet); Publisher: Double Elephant Press, New York, 1974. .... **$1,800**

Adolf Fassbender, (American, 1884-1980) Today, World's Fair, 1938; Silver bromide print (printed circa 1938); Signed and titled; 17" x 14" (sheet). **$2,280**

Louis Faurer, (American, 1916-2001) Freudian Handclasp, New York City, 1948; gelatin silver print (printed 1980); Signed, dated and titled; 14" x 11" (sheet). **$2,160**

Nat Fein, (American, 1914-2000) Aqueduct Race Track, 1940s; gelatin silver print (additional gelatin silver print adhered to verso); Signed, dated and titled; 10 3/4" x 12 1/2" (sheet). **$1,560**

Andreas Feininger, (French/American, 1907-1999) Jewish Shop on the Lower East Side, Manhattan, circa 1940; gelatin silver print (printed later); Signed; 14" x 10 3/4" (sheet). **$1,800**

Photo courtesy Rago Arts and Auction Center, Lambertville, N.J.; www.RagoArts.com

Elliott Erwitt (American, b. 1928) Venice (image 7 of 10), 1965, From A Portfolio of Ten Photographs; gelatin silver print (printed 1974); Signed; 13 1/2" x 9 1/8" (sheet). **$1,080**

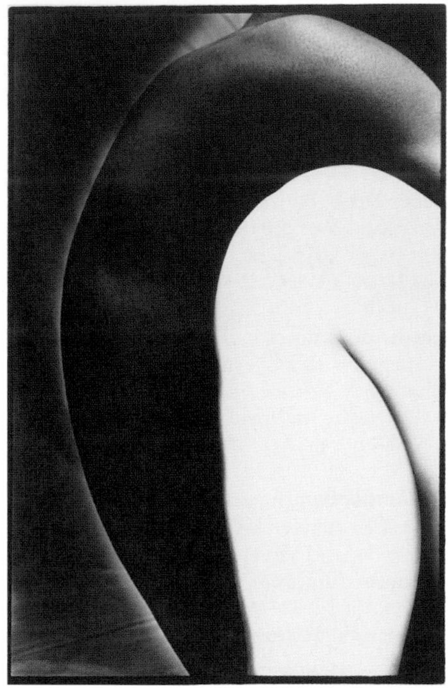

Photo courtesy Rago Arts and Auction Center, Lambertville, N.J.; www.RagoArts.com

Eikoh Hosoe (Japanese, b. 1933) Embrace #15, 1970; gelatin silver print (printed circa 1970); Signed and titled with blind stamp; 8" x 10" (sheet). **$2,640**

Larry Fink, (American, b. 1941) Graduation - Bangor High School, Pa., June 1977; gelatin silver print (printed 1983); Signed, dated and titled; 16" x 20" (sheet). **$1,080**

Larry Fink, (American, b. 1941) English Speaking Union N.Y.C., December 1975; gelatin silver print (printed 1983); Signed, dated and titled; 14" x 14" (sheet). **$1,140**

Neil H. Folberg, (American, b. 1950) Zalman Kleinman Painting in His Studio, Brooklyn, 1975; gelatin silver print; Signed, dated and titled; 11" x 14" (sheet). **$480**

Francis Frith, (British, 1822-1898) Athens, circa 1870; Albumen print; Titled; 6 1/4" x 8 1/4" (sheet). **$510**

Allen Ginsberg, (American, 1926-1997) View out my Kitchen Window, 1987; gelatin silver print (printed circa 1987); Signed, dated and titled; 14" x 11" (sheet). **$3,900**

Allen Ginsberg, (American, 1926-1997) Paul Bowles Preparing Tea at Christopher Wanklyn's House, Marrakesh, Morocco, July 20, 1961; gelatin silver print (printed later); Signed, dated and inscribed; 16" x 20" (sheet). **$1,200**

William Paul Gottlieb, (American, 1917-2006) Duke Ellington, circa 1948; gelatin silver print (printed later); Signed and titled; 14" x 11" (sheet). **$360**

Lois Greenfield, (American, b. 1949) Daniel Ezralow and Ashley Roland, 1988; gelatin silver print; Signed, titled and numbered 5/50; 20" x 16" (sheet). **$1,080**

F. Bedrich Grunzweig, (American, b. 1910) Washington Square Arch, New York, 1965; gelatin silver print (printed later); Signed; 20" x 16" (sheet). **$1,200**

F. Bedrich Grunzweig, (American, b. 1910) The Midtown Elevated, New York, 1954-55; gelatin silver print (printed later); Signed, dated and inscribed; 19 7/8" x 15 7/8" (sheet). **$3,240**

Philippe Halsman, (American, 1906-1979) Two works of art: Edward Albee, 1961; gelatin silver print; Dated and titled with studio stamp; 13 7/8" x 10 7/8" (sheet); Woody Allen; gelatin silver print; Titled with studio stamp; 10 1/2" x 10 5/8" (sheet). .... **$1,200 both**

Philippe Halsman, (American, 1906-1979) Untitled; Four gelatin silver prints; Each with studio stamp; 10" x 8" (sheet) each. .... **$1,800 all**

Eugene V. Harris, (American, 20th Century) Peruvian Flute Player, 1955; gelatin silver print (printed circa 1955); with Collier's Encyclopedia Art Department stamp; 9 1/4" x 7 1/4" (sheet); Note: From the cover of "Family of Man" by Edward Steichen, Museum of Modern Art, 1955. .... **$4,500**

George E. Hurrell, (American, 1904-1992) Raymond Navarro, 1930s; gelatin silver print (printed circa 1930s); Signed and titled with studio, Sid Avery copyright and The Avery Collection stamps; 13 3/8" x 10 5/8" (sheet). ... **$2,640**

Izis (Izis Bidermanas), (French, 1911-1980) Paris - quai de l' Horloge, 1946; gelatin silver print (printed 1970s); Signed, titled, dated and inscribed with studio stamp; 11 5/8" x 9" (sheet). **$960**

William Henry Jackson, attributed (American, 1843-1942) Untitled, circa 1870s; Process unknown; 16 5/8" x 21" (sheet). **$1,200**

Japanese (19th-20th Century) Two albums, including 72 hand-colored albumen prints; Many titled in negative; 10 1/2" x 13 3/4" x 1" and 9 3/4" x 12 1/4" x 1 1/4" (overall). .... **$2,040 both**

Photo courtesy Rago Arts and Auction Center, Lambertville, N.J.; www.RagoArts.com

Photographer Unknown (possibly Alvin Langdon Coburn, 1882-1966) George Bernard Shaw, circa 1905; gelatin silver print; Inscribed (possibly titled); 9 3/4" x 8" (sheet). **$300**

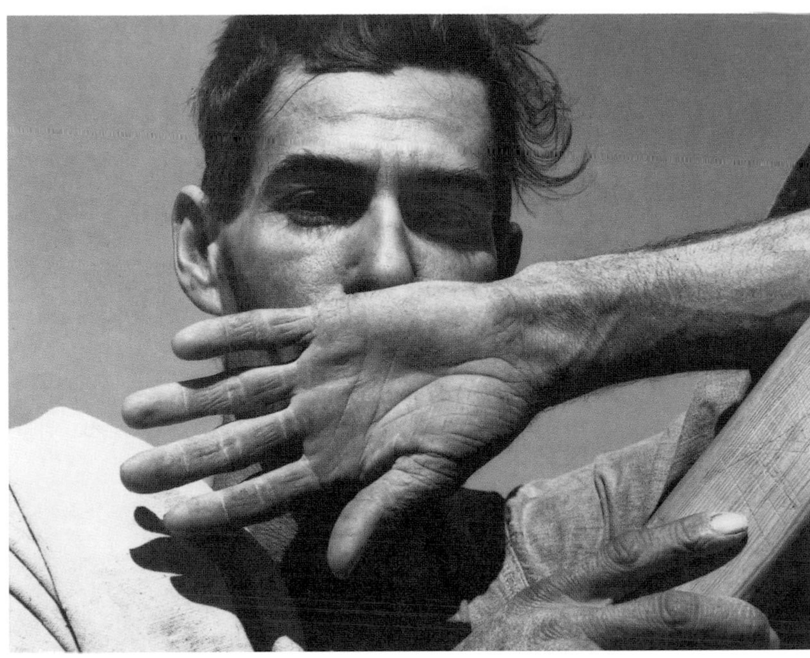

Photo courtesy Rago Arts and Auction Center, Lambertville, N.J.; www.RagoArts.com

Dorothea Lange (American, 1895-1965) Migratory Cotton Picker, Eloy, Arizona, 1940; gelatin silver print (printed later); 13" x 16" (sheet). **$9,000**

Constantin Joffe (20th Century) Untitled, 1947; gelatin silver print (printed circa 1947); with artist's Vogue studio stamp and Conde Nast publication stamp; 14" x 11" (sheet). **$840**

Yousuf Karsh, (Canadian, 1908-2002) Georgia O'Keeffe, 1950s; gelatin silver print; Signed and titled; 23 3/4" x 20" (sheet). **$6,000**

Clarence Kennedy, (American, 1892-1972) Untitled (XXXIV); gelatin silver print; 6 1/2" x 10 3/8" (sheet). **$180**

Andre Kertesz, (Hungarian/American, 1894-1985) Melancholic Tulip, February 10, 1939; gelatin silver print (printed later); Signed, dated, titled and numbered 26/150; 13 7/8" x 10 7/8" (sheet). **$4,200**

Andre Kertesz, (Hungarian/American, 1894-1985) Untitled, 1959; gelatin silver print (printed circa 1959); Dated and with studio stamp; 10" x 8" (sheet). **$1,440**

Andre Kertesz, (Hungarian/American, 1894-1985) Swimming, Duna Haraszti (image 3), Sept. 14, 1919, From Portfolio: Andre Kertesz, Volume I, 1913-1929; gelatin silver print (printed 1973); Signed and dated; Number 9 from an edition of 50; 9 3/4" x 7 3/4" (sheet); Publisher: Light, New York, NY. **$3,000**

Manuel Komroff, (American, 1890-1974) E.E. Cummings; Vintage gelatin silver print; Titled and inscribed with studio stamp; 8 1/2" x 6 1/2" (sheet). **$420**

Dorothea Lange, (American, 1895-1965) Road Leading to Small Farm in Northern Oregon, Irrison, Morrow County, Oregon, October 1939; gelatin silver print (printed circa 1939); Titled and dated with Farm Security Administration credit stamp; 8" x 10" (sheet). **$3,900**

Dorothea Lange, (American, 1895-1965) Ditched, Stalled and Stranded, San Joaquin Valley, California, 1936; gelatin silver print (printed later); 16" x 13 3/4" (sheet) irregular. **$4,200**

Jacques Henri Lartigue, (French, 1894-1986) Woman with Fox Fur, Avenue des Acacias, 1911; gelatin silver print (printed before 1973); Signed, dated and inscribed to Dan Berley; 11 3/4" x 15 3/4" (sheet). **$6,600**

Danny Lyon, (American, b. 1942) Untitled, circa 1969, from Conversations With the Dead; gelatin silver print (printed 1970s); Signed; 11" x 14" (sheet). **$2,040**

Wendell MacRae, (American, 1896-1980) Builder's Dream, circa 1935; gelatin silver print (printed circa 1935); Signed and titled with studio stamp; 17 7/8" x 13 7/8" (sheet). **$600**

Reginald Marsh, (British, 20th Century) The Steps of St. Paul's, 1926; gelatin silver print (printed circa 1926); Signed, dated, titled and inscribed; 8 1/2" x 11 1/2" (sheet). **$540**

Ray K. Metzker, (American, b. 1931) Untitled, 1983; gelatin silver print (printed 1983); Signed, and numbered 4/30; 13 7/8" x 10 7/8" (sheet). **$7,200**

Ray K. Metzker, (American, b. 1931) Philadelphia, From City Whispers, 1982; gelatin silver print (printed circa 1982); Signed and numbered 6/30; 10 7/8" x 14" (sheet). **$4,800**

Joel Meyerowitz, (American, b. 1938) House Without Walls: Blue Sky, 1991; C-print; Signed, dated, titled and numbered 58/100; 11" x 14" (sheet). **$1,560**

Lisette Model, (American, 1901-1983) Fashion Show, Hotel Pierre, New York, 1940-46; gelatin silver print (printed later); Signed and numbered 61/75; 15 3/4" x 19 1/2" (sheet). **$5,400**

Denny Moers, (American, b. 1953) Hallway #2, 1979; Toned gelatin silver print; Signed, dated and titled; 17" x 15" (sheet). **$240**

Inge Morath, (Austrian, 1923-2002) Saul Steinberg with Nose Mask, Manhattan, 1966; gelatin silver print (printed circa 1966); Signed, dated and titled; 14" x 11" (sheet). **$5,700**

Barbara Morgan, (American, 1900-1992) Merce Cunningham, "Root of the Unfocus," 1944; gelatin silver print (printed circa 1970); Signed, dated and titled with artist's copyright stamp; 7 7/8" x 9 5/8" (sheet). **$660**

Arnold Newman, (American, 1918-2006) Untitled, 1941; gelatin silver print (printed circa 1948); Signed, dated and inscribed; 5 7/8" x 9 5/8" (sheet). **$2,640**

Beaumont Newhall, (American, 1908-1993) Edward Weston, Carmel, California, 1940; gelatin silver print (printed 1993); Signed, dated and titled with studio stamp; 11 3/8" x 8 7/8" (sheet). **$600**

Janine Niepce, (French, b. 1921) Le chat de la concierge, Rue de Tournon, Paris, 1956; gelatin silver print (printed 1970s); Signed, dated and titled; 15 3/4" x 11 3/4" (sheet). **$1,020**

Ferdinando Ongania, (Italian, 1842-1911) Streets and Canals of Venice and in the Islands of the Lagoons, circa 1896-1899; Album including 85 gravures and 15 engravings; Haverhill Public Library blind stamp and stamp; 23 1/4" x 16" x 1 3/4" (album); Publisher: Ferdinando Ongania, Venice. .... **$1,680 all**

Photographer Unknown, (Late 19th Century) Two works of art: Gargoyle, Paris, Notre Dame, 1870s; Albumen print; 10 5/8" x 8" (sheet); Gargoyle, Paris, Notre Dame, 1870s; Albumen print; 10 5/8" x 8" (sheet). .... **$660 pair**

Photographer Unknown, (19th-20th Century) Views of Italy; Album of 84 albumen prints; Many titled in the negative; Album measures 11 1/2" x 14 1/4" x 1 3/4", print sizes vary. .... **$480 all**

Photographer Unknown, (19th-20th Century) Two Photography Albums (New York City and Environs), circa 1900; gelatin silver prints; Inscribed and dated; Each print approximately 3 1/2" x 4 1/2" (sight), each album approximately 11" x 14 1/2" x 2". .... **$480 both**

Eliot Porter, (American, 1901-1990) River Edge at Sunset, Below Piute Rapids, San Juan, Colorado, May 24, 1962; Dye-transfer print; Signed; 13 5/8" x 10 3/4" (sheet). **$3,900**

Edward Quigley, (American, 1898-1977) Untitled (Philadelphia), 1938; gelatin silver print (printed circa 1938); with studio stamp; 3 5/8" x 3 1/4" (sheet). **$1,680**

John Rawlings, (American, 1912-1970) Nude Study, circa 1966; gelatin silver print (printed circa 1966); with studio stamp; 12 3/4" x 9 1/2" (sheet). **$600**

Albert Renger-Patzsch, (German, 1897-1966) Hainbuchen-Kruppelwuches, Holstein, circa 1950; gelatin silver print (printed 1950s); Dated and titled with studio stamps and Galerie Wilde Koln stamp; 15 1/8" x 11 1/8" (sheet). **$1,200**

Wynn Richards, (American, 1888-1960) Dotted Glassware, circa 1930; gelatin silver print (printed circa 1930); 7 5/8" x 9 1/2" (sheet). **$480**

Walter Rosenblum, (American, 1919-2000) Women with Carriage, Pitt Street, New York, 1938; gelatin silver print (printed later); Signed, dated and titled; 10 7/8" x 13 7/8" (sheet). **$1,800**

Sanford Roth, (American, 1906-1962) Untitled, circa 1950; Vintage gelatin silver print; 8" x 10" (sheet). **$480**

Arthur Rothstein, (American, 1915-1985) Three works of art: Agate, Nebraska, 1939; gelatin silver print (printed 1981); Signed, titled and with publisher's blind stamp; Edition 16/50; 11" x 14" (sheet); John Dudeck, Dalton, New York, 1937; gelatin silver print (printed 1981); Signed and with publisher's blind stamp; Edition 16/50; 11" x 14" (sheet); Young Coal Miner, Wales, 1947; gelatin silver print (printed 1981); Signed and with publisher's blind stamp; Edition 16/50; 14" x 11" (sheet); Publisher: Hyperion Press, New York. .... **$1,200 all**

Eva Rubinstein, (American, b. 1933) Italy, 1973; gelatin silver print; Signed, dated and titled; 8 1/2" x 6 1/4" (sheet). **$330**

George Segal, (American, 1924-2000) Sequence: New York/ New Jersey: Window display, St. Marks Place, New York, 1990-1990, 1991; gelatin silver print (printed later); Signed and numbered with copyright stamp; 16" x 20" (sheet). **$540**

Photo courtesy Rago Arts and Auction Center, Lambertville, N.J.; www.RagoArts.com

Sebastiao Salgado (Brazilian, b. 1944) Three Coal Miners, India, 1989; gelatin silver print; Signed, dated, titled and numbered; 19 1/8" x 23 1/8" (sheet).
$3,900

Photo courtesy Rago Arts and Auction Center, Lambertville, N.J.; www.RagoArts.com

August Sander (German, 1876-1964) Pastry Cook, 1928; Oversized gelatin silver print (printed circa 1980 by Gunther Sander); with "Aug. Sander, Lindenthal, Koln" blindstamp; 16 1/2" x 12" (sheet). **$9,000**

Tomio Seike, (Japanese, b. 1943) Rue Saint Honore, 1992; Toned gelatin silver print (printed 1997); Signed, dated, titled, numbered 22/30 with studio stamp; 13 1/2" x 10 1/2" (sheet). **$1,440**

Stephen Shore, (American, b. 1947) U.S.1, Arundel, Maine, July 17, 1974; C-print (printed circa 1974); Signed, dated, titled and inscribed; 10" x 12" (sheet). **$5,700**

Jeanloup Sieff, (French, 1933-2000) Cabines de Gair, 1972, Gelatin silver print (printed circa 1972); Signed, dated and titled; 12" x 16" (sheet). **$1,800**

Clara Estelle Sipprell, (Canadian/American, 1885-1975) Along the Gaspe Peninsula, 1920; Silver bromide print (printed circa 1920); Signed, dated and titled; 7 1/4" x 9 1/4" (sheet). **$420**

Clara Estelle Sipprell, (Canadian/American, 1885-1975) Street in Sarajevo, Yugoslavia, 1924; Silver bromide print (printed circa 1924); Signed, dated and titled; 7 3/8" x 9 1/2" (sheet). **$330**

Aaron Siskind, (American, 1903-1991) North Carolina 30, 1951; gelatin silver print (printed later); Signed, titled and dated; 14" x 11" (sheet). **$3,600**

Aaron Siskind, (American, 1903-1991) Chicago 224, 1953; gelatin silver print (printed circa 1955); Signed and dated with Art Institute of Chicago curatorial stamp; 11 3/4" x 10 7/8" (sheet). **$3,900**

Aaron Siskind, (American, 1903-1991) Chicago, 1952; gelatin silver print (printed circa 1955); Signed and dated with Art Institute of Chicago curatorial stamp; 10 1/2" x 13 1/8" (sheet). **$4,200**

W. Eugene Smith, (American, 1918-1978) Untitled; gelatin silver print; Signed; 8 1/2" x 10 7/8" (sheet). **$3,000**

Frederick Sommer, (Italian/American, 1905-1999) Virgin and Child with Saint Anne and the Infant St. John, 1966; gelatin silver print; Signed, dated and titled; 14" x 11" (sheet). **$4,800**

Edward Steichen, (American, 1879-1973) In Memoriam, New York, 1904; gelatin silver print (printed 1950s); Inscribed; 8 7/8" x 7" (sheet). **$7,200**

Edward Steichen, (American, 1879-1973) The George Washington Bridge, New York, 1931; gelatin silver print (printed circa 1931); Signed and titled; 9 3/8" x 7 1/2" (sheet). **$10,800**

Ralph Steiner, (American, 1899-1986) Three works of art: Lollipop, circa 1924; gelatin silver print; 4 3/4" x 3 5/8" (sheet); Typewriter Keys, 1921-22; gelatin silver print; 7 7/8" x 6" (sheet); Carnovsky and Lee Strasberg, 1936; gelatin silver print; 9 3/8" x 7 1/2" (sheet). .... **$1,920 all**

Ralph Steiner, (American, 1899-1986) Untitled, circa 1930; gelatin silver print; Signed; 4 3/8" x 10 3/8" (sheet). **$1,440**

Alfred Stieglitz, (American, 1864-1946) Portrait of John Marin, circa 1913; waxed platinum print; 9 1/2" x 7 1/2" (sheet). **$16,800**

William James Stillman, (American, 1828-1901) Greece, circa 1870; Carbon print; 9 1/2" x 7 1/4" (sheet). **$1,020**

Paul Strand, (American, 1890-1976) Photograph - New York, 1917, from Camera Work, June 1917; Photogravure (printed circa 1917); 9" x 6 1/2" (image). **$3,120**

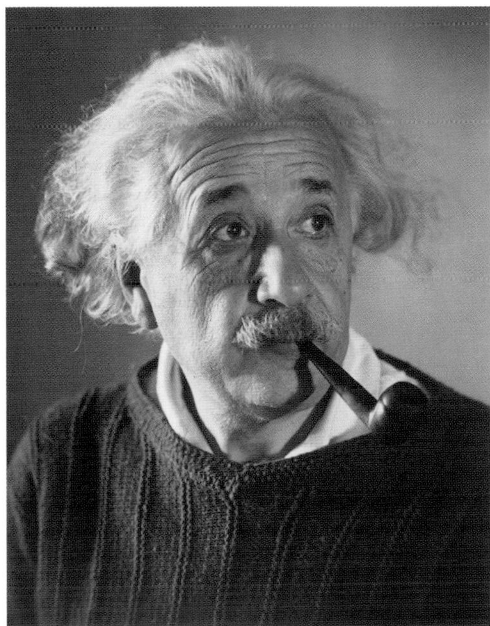

Photo courtesy Rago Arts and Auction Center, Lambertville, N.J.; www.RagoArts.com

Roman Vishniac (Russian, 1897-1990) Albert Einstein in Princeton, circa 1941; gelatin silver print; Signed, titled and inscribed; 13 1/2" x 10 3/4" (sheet). **$1,200**

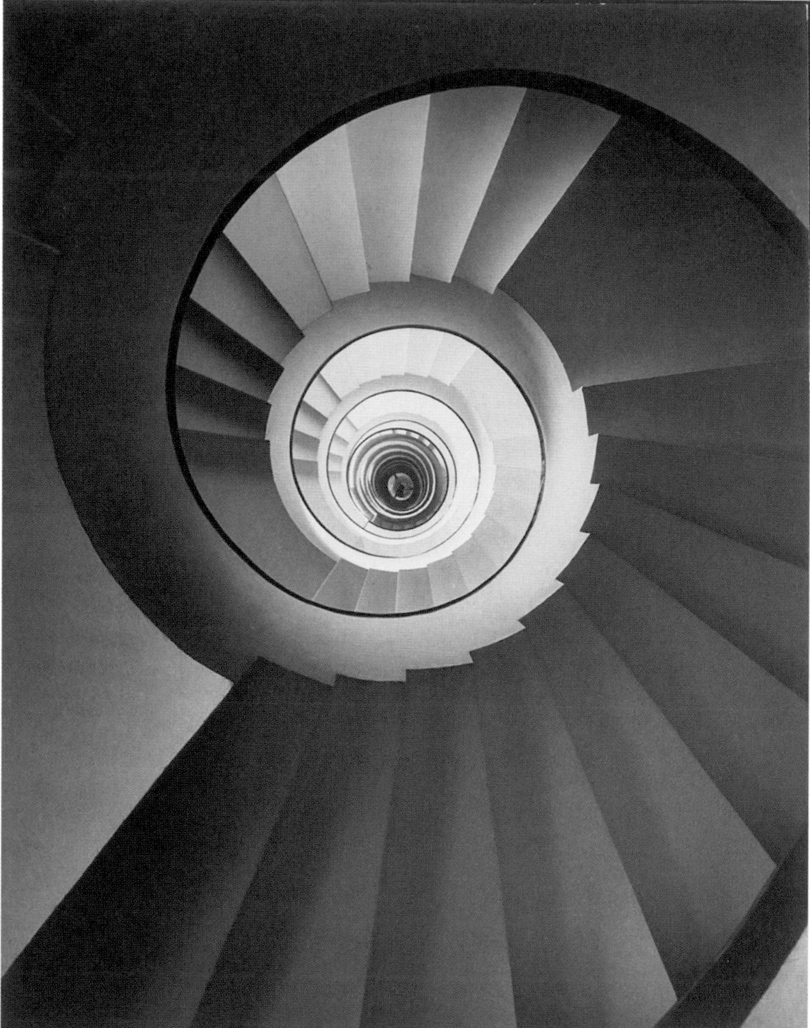

Photo courtesy Rago Arts and Auction Center, Lambertville, N.J.; www.RagoArts.com

F.S. Lincoln (1894-1976) Upshot of Stairway, Paris Apartment House, Architect: Mallet-Stevens, circa 1930; gelatin silver print (printed circa 1930); Signed and titled with studio stamp; 13 1/4" x 10 3/8" (sheet). **$3,360**

Paul Strand, (American, 1890-1976) The Mexican Portfolio, 1932-33; Portfolio of 20 photogravures (printed 1967); Signed and numbered 233/1000; 15 3/4" x 12 3/4" (sheet) each, 17" x 13 1/4" x 1 1/4" (overall); Publisher: Da Capo Press, New York, 1967. .... **$2,040**

Karl Struss, (American, 1886-1981) Flatiron Building, Twilight, 1912; gelatin silver print (printed circa 1912); 4 1/2" x 3 5/8" (sheet). **$2,880**

Josef Sudek, (Czechoslovakian, 1896-1976) St. Guy's Cathedral, Prague, circa 1948; gelatin silver print (printed circa 1948); with studio stamp; 9 1/4" x 6 1/4" (sheet). **$3,480**

Frank Meadow Sutcliffe, after (British, 1853-1941) Water Rats, 1886; gelatin silver print (printed later); Stamped; 12" x 15" (sheet). **$1,080**

Edmund Teske, (American, 1911-1996) Image of Young Man and Brooklyn Bridge Combined, 1973; gelatin silver print; Signed, dated and titled; 9 3/4" x 9 3/8" (sheet). **$900**

George Andrew Tice, (American, b. 1938) Oak Tree, Holmdel, N.J., 1970; Selenium-toned gelatin silver print (printed 1970); Signed, dated and titled; 15 3/8" x 19 1/2" (sheet). **$3,600**

Karen Truax, (American, b. 1946) Painted Woman, 1970s; Hand-colored and painted gelatin silver print; Signed and titled; 13 1/8" x 8 7/8" (sheet). **$240**

Jerry N. Uelsmann, (American, b. 1934) Portfolio, 1959-1971; Portfolio of 9 gelatin silver prints (print 1 missing); Signed, titled, dated and numbered Artist Proof 1/5 from an edition of 25; Various size prints, 21" x 17" x 1 3/4" (portfolio). .... **$12,000 all**

Doris Ullman, (American, 1884-1934) Standing Woman with Basket, from Roll Jordan Roll (Deluxe Edition); Photogravure; 8 3/8" x 6 1/2" (image). **$900**

Irving Underhill, (American, 1872-1960) 60 Wall Tower, 1932; gelatin silver print (printed circa 1932); Signed, titled, and dated in negative; 13 3/8" x 10 1/2" (sheet). **$360**

Burk Uzzle, (American, b. 1938) Untitled, 1969; gelatin silver print; with studio stamp; 11" x 14" (sheet). **$540**

John Vachon, (American, 1914-1975) Cincinnati, Ohio, circa 1940; gelatin silver print (printed circa 1940); Titled with Farm Security Administration stamp; 10" x 8" (sheet). **$480**

Various Photographers, Group of five Woodbury types from Galerie Contemporaine, Paris, circa 1870. Including portraits of: Zola, Sylvestre, Dumas, Delacroix and Garnier; Various sizes, largest: 9 3/8" x 7 1/2" (image). .... **$600 all**

Roman Vishniac, (Russian, 1897-1990) A Rabbi Carrying His Books, 1938; gelatin silver print (printed circa 1977); Signed; 12 1/2" x 10 3/8" (sheet). **$2,160**

Brett Weston, (American, 1911-1993) Nine photographs from the portfolio "New York: Twelve Photographs": Forty-Seventh Street (image 2), Brownstone in the Fifties (image 3), Church Door, Bowery (image 4), Brooklyn Bridge (image 6), Church- Brooklyn Outskirts (image 8), Washington Square (image 9), Sutton Place (image 10), End of Forty-Second Street (image 11), Manhattan Courtyard (image 12); gelatin silver prints (printed circa 1951) with folio; Each signed and stamped; From an edition of 50; 9 1/2" x 7 5/8" (sheet) each; Printer: Adrian Wilson, San Francisco (cases by Perry Davis, San Francisco). .... **$12,000 all**

Edward Weston, (American, 1886-1958) Cyprus, Point Lobos (image 5), 1929, From Edward Weston Portfolio, 1971; gelatin silver print (printed 1971 by Cole Weston); Signed, titled and dated by Cole Weston, numbered 44/50 with Edward Weston signature stamp; 7 1/2" x 9 3/8" (sheet); Publisher: Witkin-Berley, New York, NY, 1971. .... **$1,320**

Edward Weston, (American, 1886-1958) Dante's View, 1938; gelatin silver print (printed later by Cole Weston); Signed by Cole Weston; 7 1/2" x 9 3/8" (sheet). **$1,560**

Geoff Winningham, (American, b. 1943) Houston Wrestler, 1971, from A Texas Dozen; gelatin silver print (printed circa 1971); Signed, dated and titled; 16" x 20" (sheet). **$510**

Garry Winogrand, (American, 1928-1984) Untitled, circa 1969; gelatin silver print; 11" x 14" (sheet). **$3,120**

Marion Post Wolcott, (American, 1910-1990) Car Attempting to go up Creek Bed, 1940; gelatin silver print (printed circa 1970 from original negative); Titled and dated with Library of Congress stamp; 8" x 10" (sheet). **$180**

Paul J. Woolf, (American, 1899-1985) Museum of Natural History Park, circa 1935; gelatin silver print (printed circa 1935); Titled with studio stamp, copyright stamp and Frederic Lewis Agency stamp; 8" x 10" (sheet). **$720**

Don Worth, (American, b. 1924) Tree and Fog, San Francisco, 1962; gelatin silver print (printed circa 1962); Signed, dated and titled; 9 5/8" x 7 5/8" (sheet). **$1,440**

Photo courtesy Skinner Inc., Boston, www.SkinnerInc.com

Canon S-II Camera 15326, engraved Seiki-Kogaku, Tokyo, chrome, shutter speeds 20-500, slow speeds dial, with a Nippon Kogaku Nikkor Q.C f/3.5 5cm lens no. 570999. Normal use and wear; apparently working; optics cloudy or require professional cleaning and servicing; body covering replaced. **$533**

CAMERAS

Exakta B Camera No. 517969, Ihagee, Dresden, chrome, leather-covered body, with a Carl Zeiss, Jena Tessar f/2.8 7.5cm lens no. 2149849, in maker's everready case. Light-normal wear; not working; lens is clean and clear, minor handling marks. **$148**

Golden Ricoh "16" Subminiature Camera No. 10717, Riken Optical Industries Ltd., Japan, 16mm, gilt body, with a Riken Ricoh f/3.5 2.5cm lens, a matching Ricoh 16-Tele f/5.6 40mm lens in maker's case and embossed wood box, ever-ready case, strap, boxed and unboxed cassettes, and manual. Light signs of wear; apparently working; lens is clean and clear, minor handling marks. Note: Inspired by the spy cameras of the 1950s and '60s. **$296**

Heidoscope Stereo Camera No. 8403, Franke & Heidecke, Germany, leather-covered body, nickel magazine back, with a pair of Carl Zeiss, Jena Tessar f/4.5 5.5cm taking lenses no. 638884 and 838888, color filters and cable-release, in maker's leather case. Light-normal wear and use. **$415**

Hektor f/1.9 7.3cm Lens No. 437237, screw-fit, with caps and hood, in leather case. Light signs of wear; lens is clean and clear, minor handling marks. **$948**

Kodak Aero-Ektar f/2.5 7 in. (178mm) 5 x 5 Lens No. EE16351, engraved Delta on barrel, in wood case. **$148**

Kodak Bantam Special Camera, black and chrome Art Deco-styled body, with a Kodak Anastigmat Ektar f/2 45mm lens no. 18243 in Compur-Rapid shutter, in maker's ever-ready case, in maker's box with original packaging, manual and tags. Light signs of wear; apparently working; lens is clean and clear, minor handling marks. Note: The Bantam Special was part of Kodak's ongoing attempt to challenge the prominent German makers by producing 35mm cameras that were functional as well as sophisticated and stylish. Produced from 1936-40 with this shutter combination. **$356**

Leica I(c) Calf-skin No. 67655, black, nickel fittings, dark-red leather body covering, with a Leitz Elmar f/3.5 50mm lens (unnumbered) in standard mount, in maker's ever-ready case. Normal use and wear; apparently working; optics cloudy or require professional cleaning and servicing. **$4,740**

Leica IIIc Luftwaffen Camera No. 375858, chrome, engraved Luftwaffen-Eigentum on back and Fl. No. 38079 on top plate, red shutter blind, with a Leitz Summitar f/2 5cm lens no. 585806, in maker's ever-ready case. Normal use and wear; apparently working; lens is clean and clear, minor handling marks. Note: 1941-42. Accompanied by an USFET (United States Forces European Theater) certificate dated Aug. 12, 1945, stating that Alfred S. Resendes has been authorized to retain Leica Camera No. 375858, Summitar lens No. 585806, and three other lenses (not present). **$1,896**

Leica LHSA 25th Anniversary Summicron-M f2 90mm Lens No. 25-063, M-fit, Canada, silver chrome, with caps, warranty and plastic wrapper, in maker's soft case and box. New factory condition, apparently unused. **$1,185**

Leica IIIf Camera No. 713996, chrome, red-scale, delayed timer, with a Leitz Summarit f/1.5 5cm lens No. 1120854. .... **$652**

Leica IIIf No. 606534, chrome, black-scale. Light wear, apparently working. **$178**

Leica M4 50th Anniversary No. 1412936, black, with white paint filled engravings, the front with 50 Jahre laurel leaf motif, the back numbered 136-E, in maker's box with manual and registration certificate from Leitz, New York. New factory condition, apparently unused. Note: According to Leitz records, 1,730 units were made, 350 each with the letters L, E, I, and C, and 330 with the letter A. **$3,555**

Cameras for LHSA 25th Anniversary, grained leather body covering, with maker's case, manual and strap, in maker's box and wood presentation box. New factory condition, apparently unused. **$2,844**

Leicaflex SL Camera Outfit No. 1280021, black paint body, with a Leitz Elmarit-R f/2.8 35mm lens no. 2430683, a Summicron-R f/2 50mm lens no. 2432606, a (Canada) Elmarit-R f/2.8 135mm lens no. 2405035, and an Elmarit-R f/2.8 180mm lens no. 2456636, in maker's ever-ready case with manual. Good condition, minimal marks to camera body; apparently working; lens is clean and clear, minor handling marks. **$830**

Leitz Elmar f/4 9cm Lens No. 960783, screw-fit, chrome, with caps, in maker's keeper. Normal use and wear; lens is clean and clear, minor handling marks. **$47**

Leitz Hektor f/25 5cm Lens, no number visible, screw-fit, nickel. Normal use and wear; fine scratches on outer element. **$356**

Leitz Hektor f/2.5 12.5cm Lens No. 1223399, Midland, Ontario, Viso-fit, with caps and hood. Light signs of wear; optics cloudy or require professional cleaning and servicing. **$444**

Leitz Summarex f/1.5 8.5cm Lens No. 940241, screw-fit, with caps and hood, in maker's leather case. Good condition, minimal marks to camera body; lens with defects, may include scratches, fungal growth, separation or problems with focusing and aperture. **$1,126**

Photo courtesy Skinner Inc., Boston, www.SkinnerInc.com

Leica M6 Platinum 150th Anniversary Camera No. 2490145, commemorative no. 1994, the top-plate engraved 150 Jahre Optik 1849-1999, Summilux-M f/1.4 35 ASPH, diced green/gray leather body covering, with a Leitz Summilux-M f/1.4 35mm, a spherical lens engraved around the rim 15 Jahre Optik 1994, in matching silk-lined polished walnut case, with warranty, manual, commemorative booklet, receipt, hood, caps, and strap, in maker's box. New factory condition, apparently unused. Note: Produced in limited edition of 30 to commemorate 150 years of the Wetzlar Optisches Institute. **$7,110**

Leitz Telyt f/5 40cm Lens No. 1486413, Viso-fit, with caps, cable-release, Visoflex and two magnifiers, in maker's fitted leather case. Good condition, minimal marks to camera body; apparently working; optics cloudy or require professional cleaning and servicing. **$948**

Makinette Camera, Plaubel A.G., Germany, 127-roll film, black, folding-strut construction, with a Plaubel Anticomar f/2.7 5cm lens no. 87707; and a Plaubel & Co. Tele Makinar lens and five supplementary lenses, in fitted leather case. Normal use and wear; apparently working; lens with defects, may include scratches, fungal growth, separation or problems with focusing and aperture. **$652**

Minox B Subminiature Camera No. 744737, 16mm, chrome, with a Complan f/3.5 15mm lens, in maker's leather case with chain. Light signs of wear; apparently working; lens is clean and clear, minor handling marks. **$59**

Nikkormat FT Camera No. 4510537, chrome, with a Nikon Nikkor-H.C Auto f/2 50mm lens no. 2254909, in maker's ever-ready case. Good condition, minimal marks to camera body; apparently working; lens is clean and clear, minor handling marks. **$119**

Nikon MIOJ Variframe Finder No. 363919, chrome, engraved on the shoe Made in Occupied Japan. Normal use and wear. **$474**

Nikon Motor Drive F-36, black, with power pack, pistol grip, cables, cable-release, manuals, and guarantee dated 1968. Light signs of wear, untested. **$444**

Nikon Reflex Housing Type II No. 471292, black crackle finish, white paint-filled engravings Nippon Kogaku, Tokyo, with caps, 45 prism no. 67103, three cable-release attachments, printed instruction sheets (one annotated), and N-F adapter. Good condition, minimal marks to camera body (ding on release-housing). **$5,629**

Nippon Kogaku W-Nikkor f/4 2.5cm Lens No. 402579, Nikon rangefinder-fit, chrome, with body cap and hood, in maker's case; with promotional booklet. Good condition, minimal marks to camera body; lens is clean and clear, minor handling marks. **$1,304**

Nippon Kogaku W-Nikkor C f/4 2.5cm Lens No. 402579, Nikon rangefinder-fit, with body cap and hood, and promotional booklet. Good condition, minimal marks to camera body; lens is clean and clear, minor handling marks. **$1,422**

Nippon Kogaku Nikkor-Q.C f/4 25cm Lens No. 272114, Nikon rangefinder-fit, black, with caps, hood, leather pouch, and guarantee from Nikon Inc., New York, dated 1958. Good condition, minimal marks to camera body; lens is clean and clear, minor handling marks; small scratch and a couple of tiny edge chips on inner element. **$830**

Rollei 35 Camera No. 3020206, Germany, chrome, with a Carl Zeiss Tessar f/3.5 40mm lens no. 4529970, in maker's slipcase, manual and filters. **$207**

Rolleiflex "Baby" TLR Camera, 4 x 4 cm on 127-roll film, gray body covering, with a Heidosmat f/2.8 60mm viewing lens and a Schneider Xenar f/3.5 60mm taking lens no. 5311877, in matching ever-ready case, with shade and manual. Good condition, minimal marks to camera body; apparently working; lens is clean and clear, minor handling marks. **$148**

Rolleiflex 3.5 TLR Camera No. 1767412, 120-roll film, with meter, a Heidosmat f/2.8 75mm viewing lens no. 2436008, and a Carl Zeiss Planar f/3.5 75mm taking lens no. 1780943, ever-ready case, strap, manual and leather reflex hood. Good condition, minimal marks to camera body; apparently working; lens is clean and clear, minor handling marks. **$504**

Photo courtesy Skinner Inc., Boston, www.SkinnerInc.com

Nikon SP Camera No. 6201995, chrome, with a Nippon Kogaku Nikkor-S.C f/1.4 5cm lens no. 352600, in maker's ever-ready case with strap and manual. Good condition, minimal marks to camera body; apparently working; lens is clean and clear, minor handling marks. **$2,252**

Schneider Symmar f/5.6 300-f/12 500mm Lens No. 4933716, in rim-set Compur shutter, with custom adaptor rings, shade and caps, in maker's box. Good condition, minimal marks to camera body; lens is clean and clear, minor handling marks. **$296**

Stecky Model III Camera No. 2210, 16mm, with a Stekinar Anastigmat f/3.5 25mm lens, in maker's ever-ready case, a Stecky f/5.6 40mm Sun-Tele # 40 lens in leather case, part of the manual, and other items. **$83**

Tessina Automatic 35mm Camera No. 463001, Concava S.A., Switzerland, chrome, with a f/2.8 25mm lens, finder and meter, in maker's ever-ready case; chain, manuals, film loader, and three film canisters. Light signs of wear; apparently working; optics cloudy or require professional cleaning and servicing. **$326**

Veriwide 100 Camera No. 60/684, Brooks-Plaubel, 120-roll film, with popup finder, frame finder, and a Schneider Super-Angulon f/8 47mm lens no. 6661243, ever-ready case (front only), and manual. Light-normal wear and use; not working, lens is clean and clear, minor handling marks. **$1,007**

Carl Zeiss (Jena) Biotar f/2 8cm Lens No. 2245038, Leica screw-fit, chrome, with meter scale. Normal use and wear; optics cloudy or require professional cleaning and servicing. **$563**

Carl Zeiss (Jena) Brass-bound Protar 690mm Lens No. 89610, with adaptor. Normal use and wear; optics cloudy or require professional cleaning and servicing (diaphragm jammed). Note: Custom conversion for use in medical photography. Handwritten notes gives directions for using the lens with Novoflex and Visoflex Leica attachments. Untested. **$830**

Carl Zeiss (Jena) Sonnar f/2.8 18cm Lens No. 2119896, Flektoscop-fit, chrome, with Zeiss Ikon shade; and a custom Leica M-fit mount. Normal use and wear; lens is clean and clear, minor handling marks. **$474**

Carl Zeiss (Jena) Tele-Tessar K f/8 30cm Lens No. 1622674, screw-fit, black, with yellow filter, shade and custom filter. Light signs of wear; optics cloudy or require professional cleaning and servicing. **$593**

Zeiss Bobette II Camera 548, roll film, leather-covered body, with an Ernostar Anastigmat f/2 4.2cm lens no. 224674. Light, normal wear. **$415**

Zeiss Contax II No. G.7313, chrome, numbered internally and on rewind knob. Light signs of wear, apparently working. **$148**

POLITICAL ITEMS

Initially, American political-campaign souvenirs were created to celebrate victories. Items issued during a campaign to show support for a candidate were actively being distributed in the William Henry Harrison election of 1840.

For more information, consult *Warman's Political Collectibles* by Dr. Enoch L. Nappen, 2008.

POLITICAL CONVENTION BADGES

A major responsibility at national party conventions was checking delegate credentials to insure valid voting rights. This could be crucial as in the 1912 Republican Convention when different sets of delegates claimed they represented several of the same states, resulting in the Republican Party split and Woodrow Wilson's election.

Delegates, alternates and a host of other functionaries usually wore official badges identifying their status. The great variety of badge designs is revealed in the following examples, which are in the **$35-$60** range, except where noted.

Republican badges from 1901, 1908,1912 and1920, Democratic badges from years 1908 and 1916, and a suffrage badge from 1920. **$75-$125 each**

Republican badges from 1924 and 1932, and Democratic badges from years 1928 and 1932. **$40-$75 each**

Democrat Convention badge and two Republican badges, 1936.

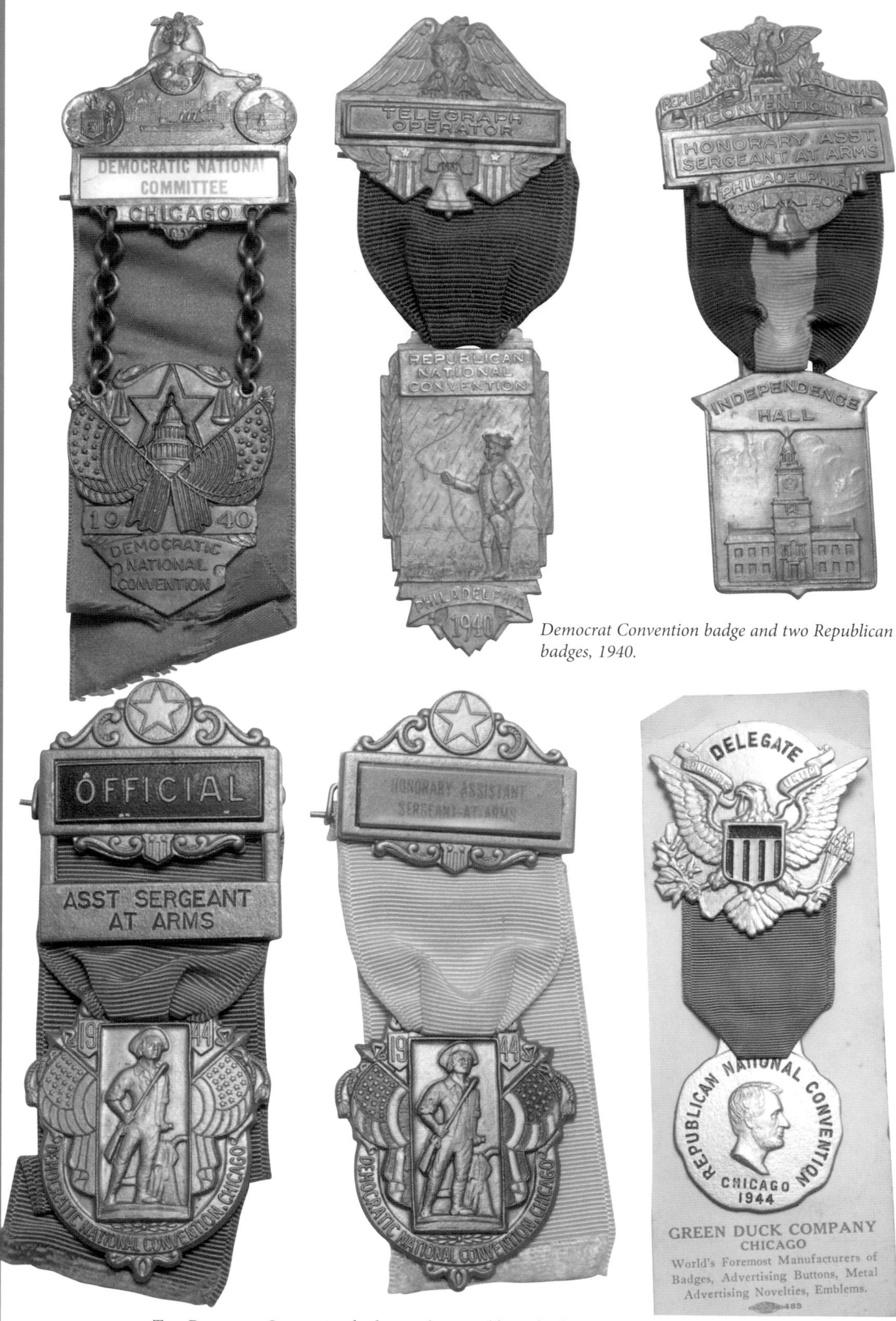

Democrat Convention badge and two Republican badges, 1940.

Two Democrat Convention badges and a Republican badge, 1944.

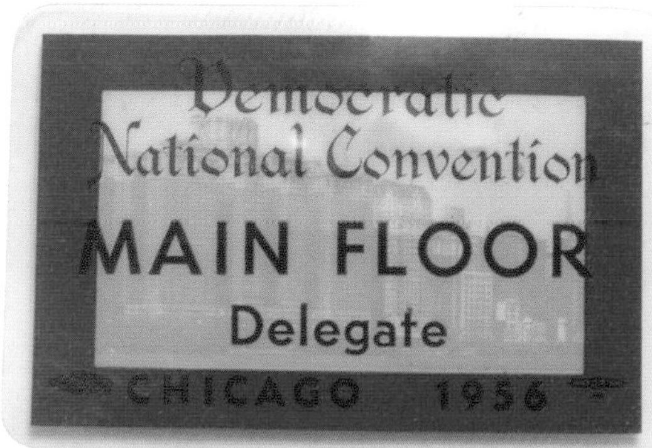

Democrat Convention badges 1956, 1960 and 1964, and a 1964 Republican badge.

POSTCARDS

John P. Charlton of Philadelphia patented the postcard in 1861, selling the rights to H.L. Lipman, whose postcards, complete with a decorated border, were labeled "Lipman's postal card." Within a decade, European countries were also producing postcards.

The United States Postal Service began issuing pre-stamped postal cards in 1873. The postal cards came about because the public was looking for an easier way to send quick notes. The USPS was the only establishment allowed to print postcards, and it held its monopoly until May 19, 1898, when Congress passed the Private Mailing Card Act.

Initially, the United States government prohibited private companies from calling their products "postcards," so they were known as "souvenir cards." Although this prohibition was rescinded in 1901, it was not until 1908 that people were permitted to write on the address side of a postcard.

Photos courtesy Haritage Auction Galleries, Dallas; www.HA.com

Metropolis (UFA, 1927). German Postcards. Science Fiction. These postcards, printed in Berlin, show scenes from Fritz Lang's futuristic masterpiece. Unrestored postcards with clean overall appearances. Film title and director's name is written lightly in pencil on the back. **$104 pair**

Photo courtesy Heritage Auction Galleries, Dallas; www.HA.com

Orville Wright Kitty Hawk Signed Postcard Photo image of the "First Man-Flight", 6 1/4" x 4 1/4", Dayton, Ohio, Jan. 25, 1929. Black and white image of the Wright brothers' first flight at Kitty Hawk, NC, on December 17, 1903. This photocard and the accompanying transmittal envelope were both apparently custom designed and produced for use in responding to autograph requests. Following the death of his brother Wilbur in 1912, Orville built an aeronautics laboratory and dedicated himself to developing and inventing aeronautical devices and equipment. He also stayed active in the public eye, promoting aeronautics, inventing, and using such marketing tools as the image here, which has been signed by Wright at lower left. A small tear at upper center and creases along the lower edge affect only the white borders of the image. Paper clip crease at upper left of border. Very good condition. Accompanied by Orville Wright's imprinted transmittal envelope, which features a 5-cent air mail stamp. Envelope shows occasional wear along edges; small tear at upper center edge. The image has been attached to the envelope, and the envelope is attached to a 7 3/4" square backing board. **$2,151**

Photo courtesy Heritage Auction Galleries, Dallas; www.HA.com

Woman's Suffrage: The Pankhursts in Prison Dress Real Photo Postcard. Mrs. Pankhurst, one of the co-founders of the W.S.P.U., in prison dress along with her daughter, Christabel. Note the arrow image on their dresses that another daughter, Sylvia, incorporated into suffrage iconography. An unused card in excellent condition. **$1,673**

Photo courtesy Heritage Auction Galleries, Dallas; www.HA.com

Woman's Suffrage: Three Postcards Featuring Suffrage Headquarters. All examples approximately 3 1/2" x 5 1/2"and in very good condition. Offices in the Metropolitan Life Insurance building in New York, another in New York on Fifth Avenue, and the National Headquarters of the National American Woman Suffrage Association in Warren, Ohio. **$180 all**

Photo courtesy Heritage Auction Galleries, Dallas; www.HA.com

Jimi Hendrix Experience Concert Postcard Group (Russ Gibb, 1968). Two colorful postcards from Jimi's tour with the Soft Machine; the February 23, 1968 show at Detroit's Masonic Temple (with the MC5 and the Rationals), and the next day's show in Toronto's CNE Coliseum Arena (with the Paupers). Both cards feature designs by Gary Grimshaw, excellent condition. **$360 all**

Photo courtesy Heritage Auction Galleries, Dallas; www.HA.com

Elvis Signed Postcard, 3 1/2" x 6" postcard featuring a B&W image of a young Elvis in the broadcast studio with TV and radio personality George Klein, inscribed and signed on the reverse in blue ink. Klein was a close friend of Elvis' in high school and throughout his career. Accompanied by a letter of provenance from Klein. **$1,732**

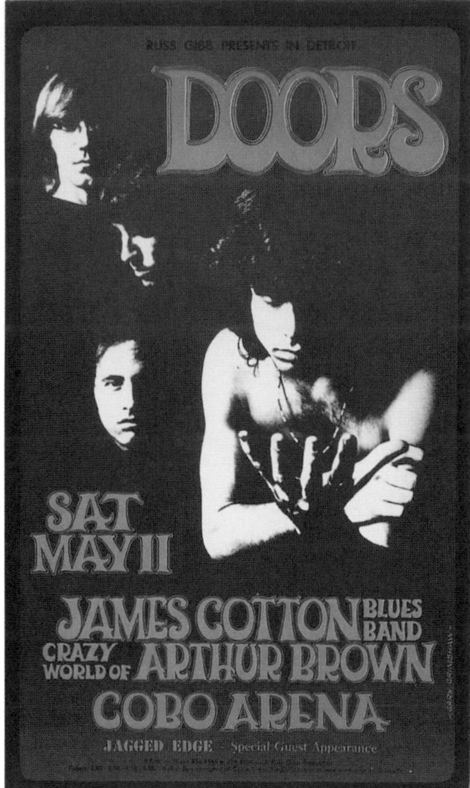

Photo courtesy Heritage Auction Galleries, Dallas; www.HA.com

Three postcards from "Uncle" Russ Gibb's Detroit shows: December 1967 Vanilla Fudge, Grande Ballroom; April '68 Cream, Grande Ballroom, and May '68 Doors (with the Crazy World of Arthur Brown), Cobo Arena. All three are in excellent condition. **$300 all**

POSTERS

The advancement of printing techniques in the 18th century —including lithography, which was invented in 1796 by the German Alois Senefelder—allowed for cheap mass production and printing of posters. The invention of lithography was soon followed by chromolithography, which allowed for mass editions of posters illustrated in vibrant colors.

By the 1890s, chromolithography had spread throughout Europe. A number of noted artists created poster art in this period, foremost amongst them Henri de Toulouse-Lautrec and Jules Chéret. Chéret is considered to be the "father" of advertisement placards. He was a pencil artist and a scene decorator, who founded a small lithography office in Paris in 1866. He used striking characters, contrast and bright colors, and created more than 1,000 advertisements, primarily for exhibitions, theatres and products. The industry soon attracted the service of many aspiring painters who needed a source of revenue to support themselves.

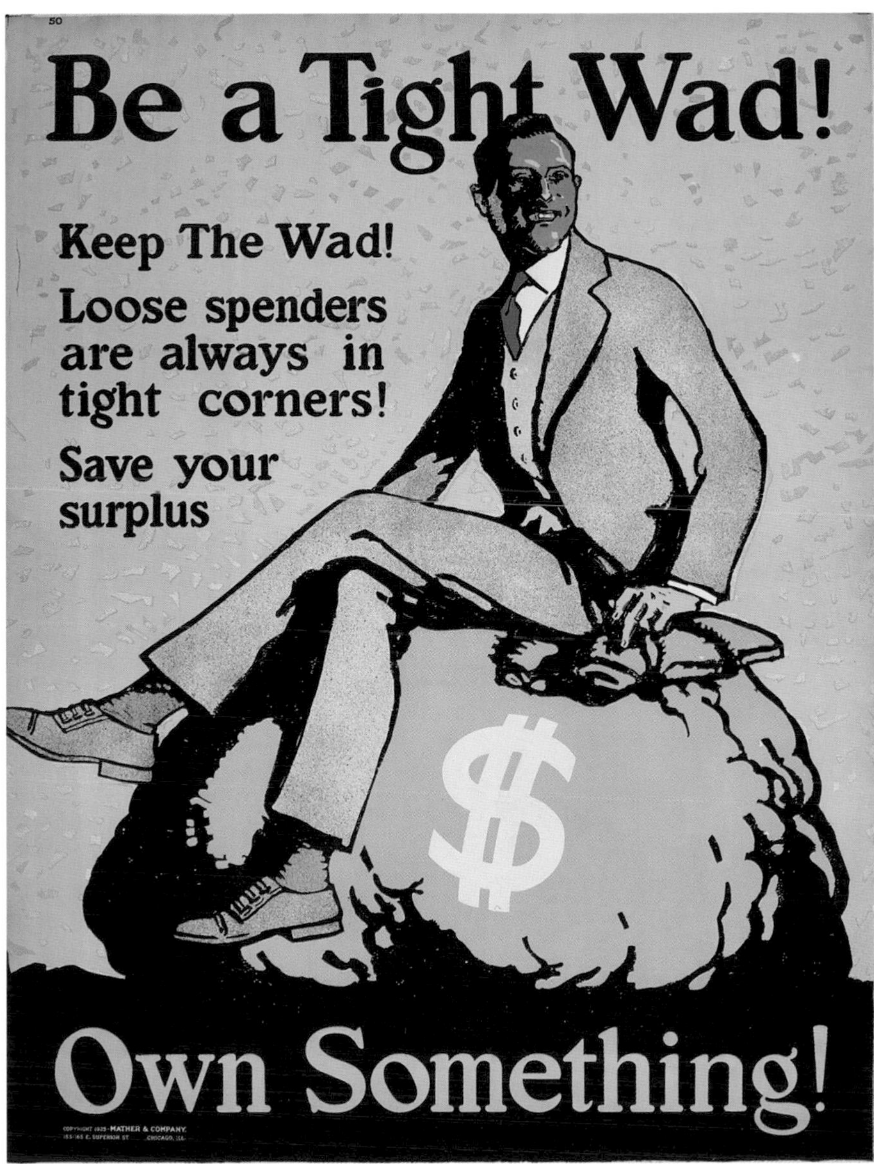

Photo courtesy Swann Auction Galleries, New York; www.SwannGalleries.com

Be a Tight Wad!, 1925, Mather & Co., Chicago, restored punch holes in top and bottom of image; repaired tears and restoration in margins, 48" x 36". **$3,400**

Canadian Pacific, with art by Kenneth Shoesmith, showing the liner Empress of Britain. Text reads, "Canadian Pacific – To Canada or USA." Published by Sander Phillips & Co., The Bayard Press. Poster measures 40" x 25" and is framed, has been laid down and exhibits light repairs and restoration. **$1,035**

Cunard Line, with art by Odin Rosenvinge showing the liner Berengaria. Text reads, "Cunard-Europe-America." Published by Turner & Dunnett. Poster measures 40" x 24" and is framed, has been laid down and exhibits repairs, restoration and in-painting. **$1,035**

Dartmouth / Winter Carnival, 1947, by D.B. Leigh, Winthrop Printing & Offset Co., Boston, repaired tears and creases in margins and image; restored loss in top left corner; restored pinholes in top corners, 34" x 22 1/4". **$2,000**

Don't Lose Your Head, 1924, Mather & Co., Chicago, minor losses and repaired tears along lower left edge and upper left corner; restored punch holes in bottom and top of image, 48" x 36". **$900**

French Line/French Railways, with art by Albert Sebille showing passenger train at dock with ocean liner to right. Text reads, "Paris-Havre-New York – Chemins de fer de L'etat Cie Gle TransAtlantique." Published by Novia, Paris, and printed in Paris. Poster measures 40 1/2" x 26" and is framed, exhibits repair, restoration and some in-painting. **$1,150**

Photo courtesy Swann Auction Galleries, New York; www.SwannGalleries.com

(The) Century For Xmas, 1895, by Louis John Rhead, tears and losses in margins and corners; staining in text at bottom. 21 1/2" x 14 1/2". **$500**

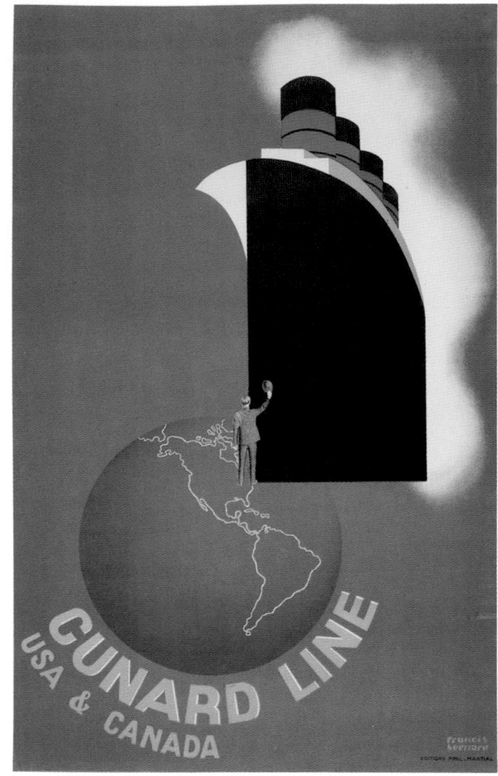

Photo courtesy Swann Auction Galleries, New York; www.SwannGalleries.com

Cunard Line, circa 1935, by Francis Bernard (1900-1979), Paul Martial, repaired tears and creases in margins and image; pinholes in corners. Bernard's contribution to the world of French graphic design was considerable. In addition to the posters he designed, he was Art Director of the Paul Martial studio and in charge of advertising for the Arts Menagers exhibitions as well as for the Office Technique pour l'Utilisation de l'Acier. After World War II he became the director of communication for the French State Radio and Television. During the 1930s he was a member of the Union des Artistes Moderne. During the 1930s, Bernard was the only artist within the impressive group to use photomontage. The Cunard Line was one of the largest and most prestigious companies running ships between Europe and the United States. This exceedingly rare poster combines an impeccable stylization of an ocean liner, with a sophisticated airbrush background of white smoke, a globe, with the Americas outlined in white, and a photomontage of a man waving the vessel off. A daring and modernist image, it qualifies as one of the best travel posters of the 1930s, 39 1/4" x 24 3/4".
$24,000

Photo courtesy Robert Edward Auctions, Watchung, N.J.; www.RobertEdwardAuctions.com

Burke Ale, lithograph, featuring Cap Anson and Buck Ewing, 1889, represents the first documented paid endorsement of a product of any kind by baseball players. It is also certainly the first advertising piece featuring players in promotion of an alcoholic beverage, which is ironic, in that the use of alcohol at games in the 1880s and 1890s was such a serious problem that there was concern for the future success of the game as a pastime suitable for attendance by the entire family. The Anson-Ewing Beer poster is exceedingly rare. Only three examples are known. All of the colors are bold, flawless and vibrant; and the poster exhibits none of the tears, creases or stains so common to similar displays of this vintage. The poster (18" x 24") has been professionally cleaned for preservation purposes (no restoration) and has been mounted and framed to total dimensions of 26" x 32". **$188,000**

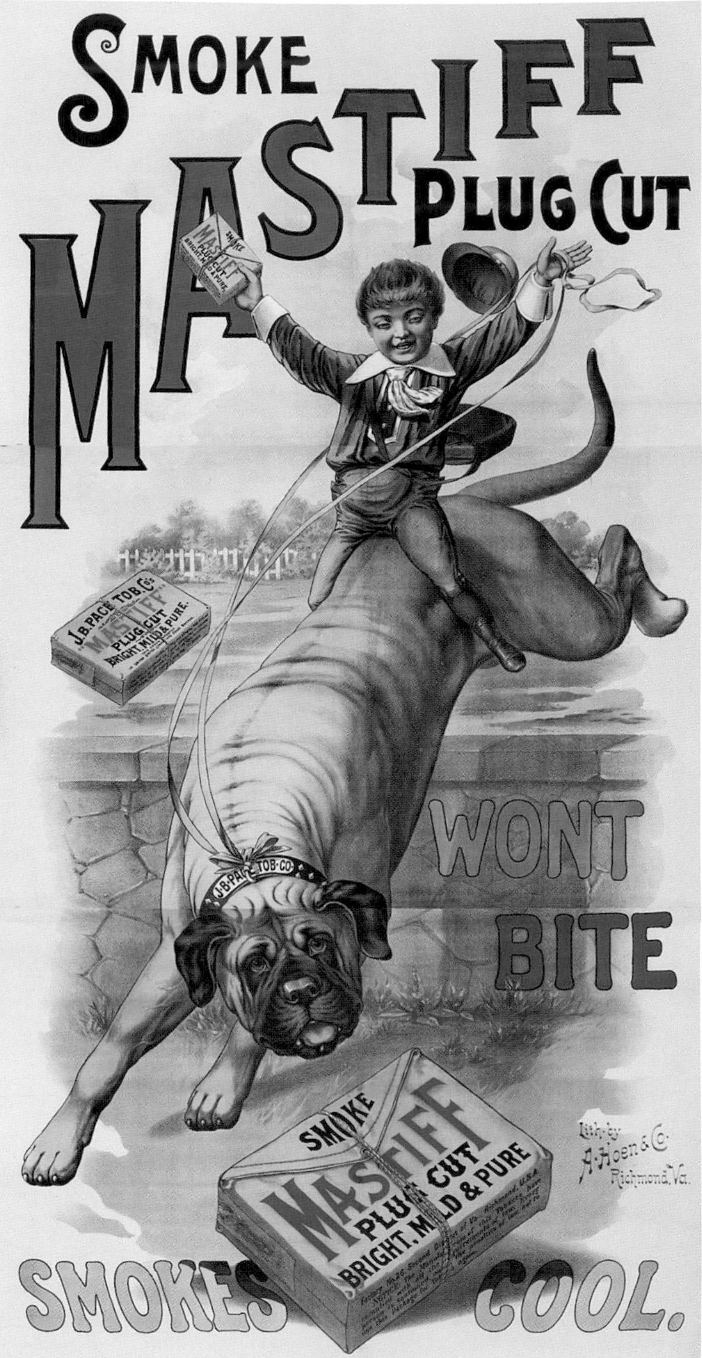

Photo courtesy Swann Auction Galleries, New York; www.SwannGalleries.com

Smoke Mastiff, A. Hoen & Co., Richmond, Va., repaired tears and creases in margins and image. Three sheets, 81 3/4" x 41 3/4". **$3,600**

Goal, by Joseph Leyendecker, Close Graham & Scully Inc. N.Y., light discoloration and foxing in image and margins; minor tears and creases in corners and at edges. Printed on thick stock, 26 1/2" x 20". **$1,800**

Inkograph, 1915, Collioud & Cie, Berne, trimmed left and right margins; creases and abrasions in image; pin holes in top and bottom margin; minor foxing in margins, 48" x 31 1/2". **$250**

Kar-Mi Magic, one sheet of stone lithograph, titled "Kar-Mi Swallows a Loaded Gun Barrel and Shoots a Cracker from a Man's Head." Copyright 1914 by Joseph B. Hallworth, 40" w x 28" h. Vertical fold at middle; some paper loss around perimeter border. **$1,200**

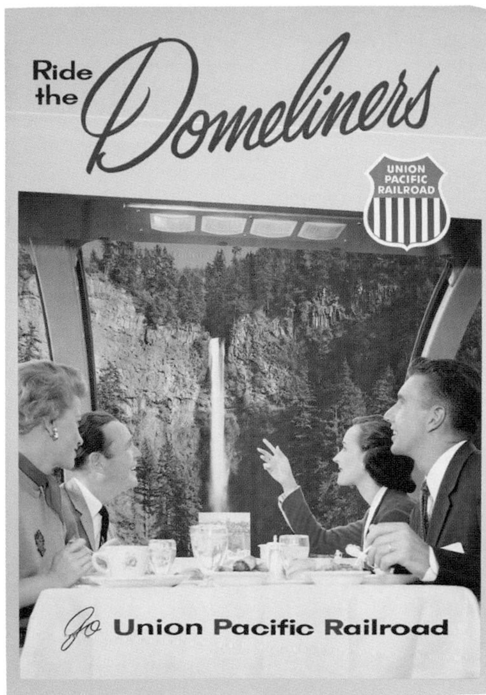

Photo courtesy Swann Auction Galleries, New York; www.SwannGalleries.com

Domeliners / Union Pacific Railroad, creases in margin and image; minor loss in upper right corner; minor tears in right margin, 35 1/2" x 25". **$400**

Photo courtesy Swann Auction Galleries, New York; www.SwannGalleries.com

Grafton Gallery, 1893, by Eugene Grasset, Verdoux, Durcourtioux & Huillard, SC., minor restoration and repaired tears in margins; abrasions in image. Matted and framed, 27" x 18 1/2". **$2,000**

Photo courtesy Swann Auction Galleries, New York; www.SwannGalleries.com

German Spas, by Jupp Wiertz, Reichsbahnzentrale fur den Deutschen Reiseverkehr, Berlin, tears in margins; losses in top corners, 39 3/8" x 24 3/4". **$850**

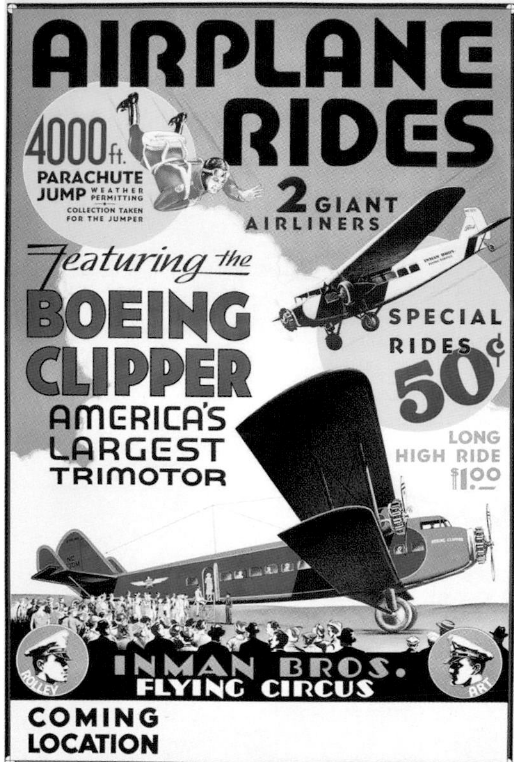

Photo courtesy Swann Auction Galleries, New York; www.SwannGalleries.com

Inman Brothers Flying Circus, circa 1929, expertly replaced bottom and right margins; minor repaired tears in margins and image. The Inman Brothers' flying circus operated a 20-passenger Boeing 80-A and a smaller Ford tri-motor. These models were used by airline companies on their airmail and passenger routes. The Inman Brothers offered novelty flights to the American public for just 50 cents. Their show also delighted visitors with a parachute jump. They called their 80-A a "Boeing Clipper." The Clipper trademark was registered by Pan American Airways in 1931 for their aircraft. The huge B-314 flying boats were the planes most remembered as Boeing Clippers. Inman had to sue to retain the rights to the Clipper name, 37 3/8" x 27 7/8". **$2,400**

Photo courtesy Swann Auction Galleries, New York; www.SwannGalleries.com

Job, 1894, by Georges Meunier, Chaix, Paris, minor repaired tears at edges. Two sheets. Meunier's design in this poster is one of the best utilizing the elongated format that was current in Paris in the mid-1890s, 95" x 34 1/4". **$8,000**

Photo courtesy Swann Auction Galleries, New York; www.SwannGalleries.com

Jeux Olympiques / Paris, 1924, by Orsi, Phogor 92, Paris, vertical and horizontal folds; minor creases and abrasions in image; repaired tears and restoration in image. A taut, poised and powerful image set against the Parisian skyline. One of two posters chosen by the French Olympic Committee to advertise the 8th Olympiad. French version, 46 7/8" x 31 1/4". **$4,400**

Les Coulisses de L'Opera, 1891, by Jules Chéret, Chaix, Paris, text trimmed at bottom; tears and losses at edges and in image, 82 1/4" x 34". **$650**

Lorenzaccio, 1896, by Alphonse Mucha, F. Champenois, Paris, losses, wrinkles, creases and repaired tears along

Photo courtesy Lang's Sporting Collectibles, Waterville, N.Y.; www.LangsAuction.com

Original Kingfisher poster. **$6,727**

Photo courtesy Swann Auction Galleries, New York; www.SwannGalleries.com

Omega, circa 1910, by Leonetto Cappiello (1875-1942), Vercasson, Paris, restored tears, creases and abrasions in margins and image; restored pin holes in margins; restoration and minor losses along vertical and horizontal folds, 42 1/2" x 29". **$1,800**

Photo courtesy Swann Auction Galleries, New York; www.SwannGalleries.com

Mobil Oil, 1952, by Blaise Bron (1918-?), horizontal folds, creases and abrasions in image. It is impossible to look at this image without seeing a resemblance to Roy Lichtenstein's early graphic work. However, this poster precedes Lichtenstein's first Pop Art creations by nearly 10 years. The influence of "hyper-real" Swiss posters from the late 1930s until 1960 on many Pop artists is a given, but no poster relates so closely to specific Pop Art as this one for the design-conscious Mobil Corp. Little biographical information exists on this artist. Another poster of his for Mobiloil appears in the 1952 International Poster Annual. Also in the late 1960s and early 1970s, he designed a few posters for fairs around Switzerland. This poster is a proto-Pop masterpiece that stands as an exceptional vanguard to the Pop movement of the 1960s, 50 1/8" x 35 1/2". **$28,800**

Photo courtesy Swann Auction Galleries, New York; www.SwannGalleries.com

Le Petit Dauphinois. 1933, by Leonetto Cappiello (1875-1942), Devambez, Paris, vertical and horizontal folds; repaired tears at edges. Cappiello was the most influential poster artist of the first quarter of the 20th Century, and also the most prolific. Although executed towards the end of his career, this is one of Cappiello's most spectacular and rare posters, 35 1/2" x 62". **$38,400**

vertical and horizontal folds and in image. Wooden dowels affixed to top and bottom margins. Two sheets, 80" x 29". **$2,800**

Newcomb College, exhibition posters (two), one for Jean Bragg Gallery, New Orleans, 1998, the other "An Enterprise for Southern Women, 1895-1940, Tulane University." Both framed. Sight: 24" x 16", and 33" x 17 1/2". .... **$360 both**

Pneu Michelin, M. de Brunoff et Cie., Paris, repaired tears and creases in margins and image; restored losses in right margin; repaired tears and restoration along vertical and horizontal folds; discoloration in margins and image, 42 1/2" x 58 3/4". **$1,700**

Red Star Line, featuring liner Westerland at sea. Poster measures 24 1/2" x 19 1/2" and is framed, exhibits repairs, restoration. **$540**

Remington Union Metallic Cartridge, Edmund Osthaus illustration of a returning hunter being greeted at the gate. Poster retains both top and bottom metal bands, 17" w x 25" h. One horizontal roll crease near bottom edge. **$900**

Rice's Seeds, humorous stone-lithographed image of jovial gardener harvesting a colossal cabbage. Sign is captioned, "True Early Winningstadt - The Best Cabbage In The World". Lithographed by Cosack & Co., Buffalo, for the Cambridge Valley Seed Gardens, Cambridge, N.Y., circa 1890, 21 3/4 w x 27 1/2" h. Minor moisture stain on bottom left margin. **$1,093**

Savage-Stevens, with metal bands at top and bottom, this unusual poster has a central panel titled, "Nature's Rogues Gallery" with information regarding a variety of predators. The bottom center has the image of a desert wolf with a Stevens single-barrel shotgun and a Savage Sporter rifle. The outer edges have eight panels of various predators and varmints, 18" w x 26" h. Colors are vivid and bright with a few minor creases and a small gouge in the top right center, not affecting the images. Also a small tear on the right edge, again, not affecting the image. The white background is slightly yellowed with a couple water stains on left edge. **$120**

Sportsmen's Exposition, 1896, Liebler & Maass Litho., N.Y., repaired tears and restored minor losses in margins and along vertical and horizontal folds, 45 7/8" x 29". **$2,600**

Straight As An Arrow, 1929, by Willard Frederic Elmes, Mather & Co., Chicago, restored loss in lower left margin and in image; restored punch holes in top margin; abrasions in image, 43" x 35 1/2". **$2,000**

White Star Line/Red Star Line, featuring liner Majestic at dock with woman sitting on trunks. Text reads, "White Star Line/Red Star Line – Winter Cruises DeLuxe Around the World." Poster measures 33" x 23" and is framed, has been laid down and exhibits repairs, restoration and in-painting. **$1,150**

Movie Posters, Lobby Cards and Stills

American Graffiti, (Universal, 1973) One Sheet (27" x 41"). Vintage, theater-used poster for this comedy-drama that was directed by George Lucas and stars Richard Dreyfuss, Ron Howard, Cindy Williams and Mackenzie Phillips. **$138**

Angels With Dirty Faces, (Warner Brothers, 1938). French Grande (47" x 63"). One of the cornerstone films of the gangster genre, starring James Cagney, Humphrey Bogart, Pat O'Brien and the Dead End Kids. Professional restoration on linen. **$1,434**

Apocalypse Now, (United Artists, 1979). One Sheet (27" x 41"). War. Starring Marlon Brando, Martin Sheen and Robert Duvall. Un-restored poster with fresh, saturated colors. Rolled. **$167**

Dracula (Universal, 1931). Lobby Card (11" x 14"). This card features Bela Lugosi seducing the innocent Helen Chandler by feeding upon her blood. Extremely rare. **$44,812**

Photo courtesy Heritage Auction Galleries, Dallas; www.HA.com

Magnum Force (Warner Brothers, 1973). Promotional Poster (20" x 28"). Warner Brothers followed up the success of Dirty Harry (1971) with this action-packed sequel, for which they released this rare portrait poster. This particular copy has some slight edge wear. Rolled, near mint. **$310**

Photo courtesy Heritage Auction Galleries, Dallas; www.HA.com

The Lady Vanishes (Gaumont, 1938). Insert (14" x 36"). British travelers Margaret Lockwood and Michael Redgrave unwittingly become entangled in espionage, kidnapping, and murder, after Miss Froy (Dame May Whitty) disappears. Insert has been restored to address two corner chips, small tears in the bottom border, and fold and edge wear. There was a chip, a tape lift and a tear in the left border. There are smudges in the center, and two creases that occurred after the restoration; on Linen. **$4,780**

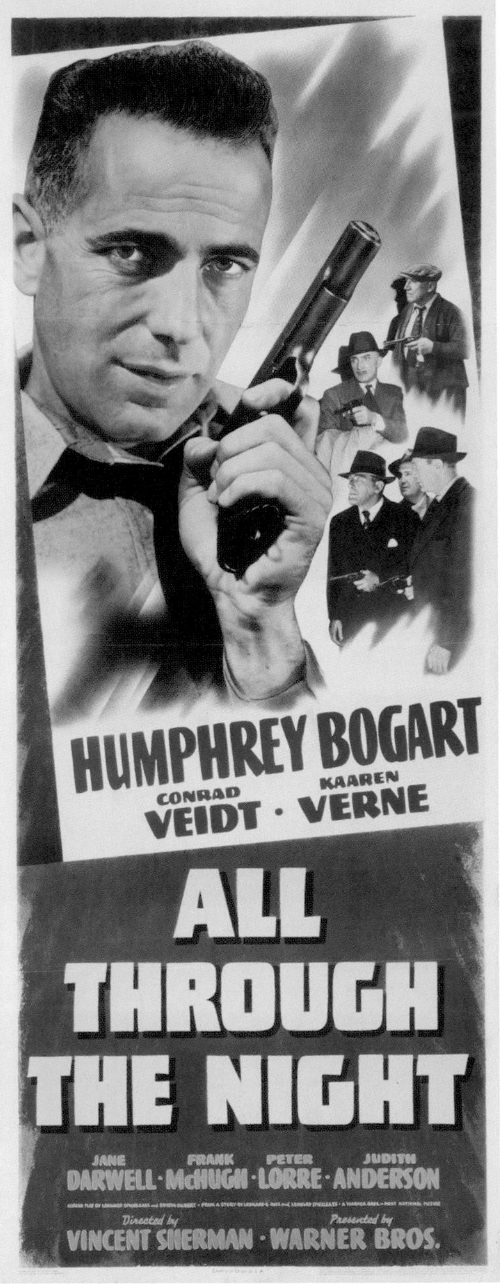

Photo courtesy Heritage Auction Galleries, Dallas; www.HA.com

All Through the Night (Warner Brothers, 1942). Insert (14" x 36"). This Warner Brothers classic may look like a typical gangster picture of the era, but in reality, it was a comedy that proved Bogart had more depth and range than the studio suspected. This insert has had the fold lines reinforced with paper tape on the back, has a few tiny tears in the edges and a light abrasion in the lower right corner. **$657**

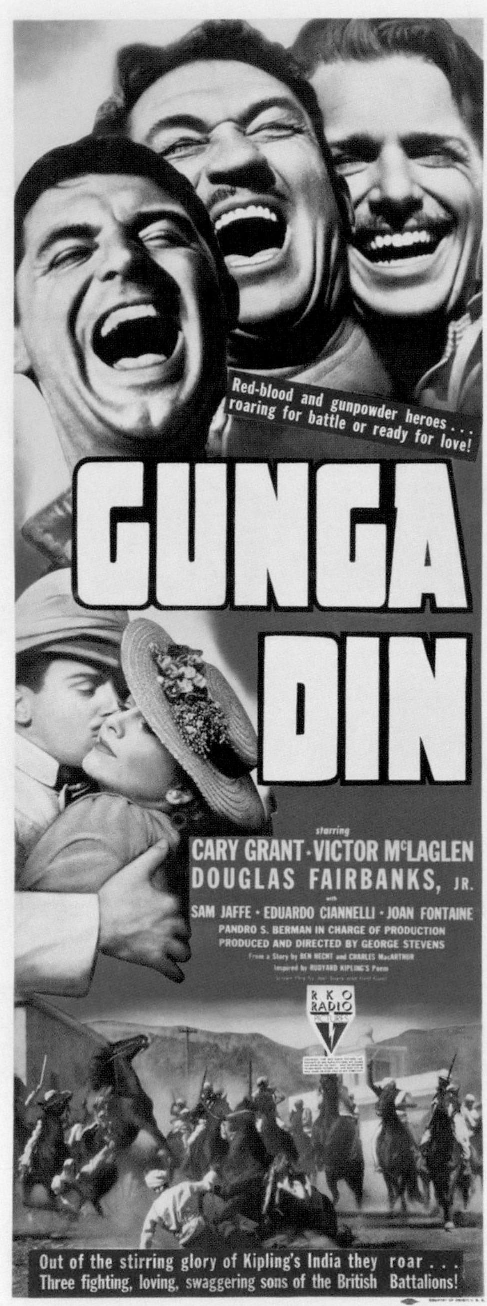

Photo courtesy Heritage Auction Galleries, Dallas; www.HA.com

Gunga Din (RKO, 1939). Insert (14" x 36"). The insert has been professionally restored to address fold wear with small paper losses at the center fold, a tear in the top left border and a tear at the bottom border. There were also two small chips in the top right corner and one in the top left corner. Mounted on paper. **$597**

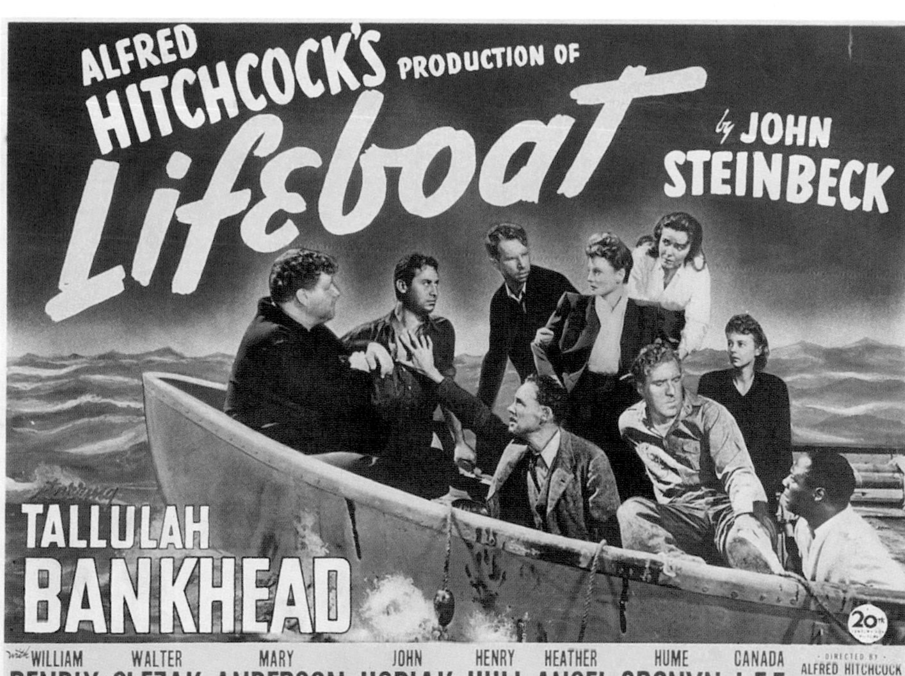

Photo courtesy Heritage Auction Galleries, Dallas; www.HA.com

Lifeboat (20th Century Fox, 1944). Title Lobby Card (11" x 14"). Some smudging in the borders, corner bends in the bottom and top left, creasing in the right side, and a small tear in the right border. **$776**

Fargo, (Polygram, 1996). One Sheet (27" x 40") DS. Crime. Starring Frances McDormand, William H. Macy and Steve Buscemi. Directed by Joel Coen, Ethan Coen. An unused, un-restored poster. Rolled. **$65**

The Godfather, (Paramount, 1972). One Sheet (27" x 41"). Crime. Starring Marlon Brando, Al Pacino, James Caan and Robert Duvall. Directed by Francis Ford Coppola. An un-restored poster that appears virtually unused. Folded. **$131**

The Great Dictator, (United Artists, 1940). One Sheet (27" x 41"). Directed by and starring Charlie Chaplin. One of Chaplin's last films, this was also his biggest box office success. The film garnered five Academy Award nominations. On linen. **$1,792**

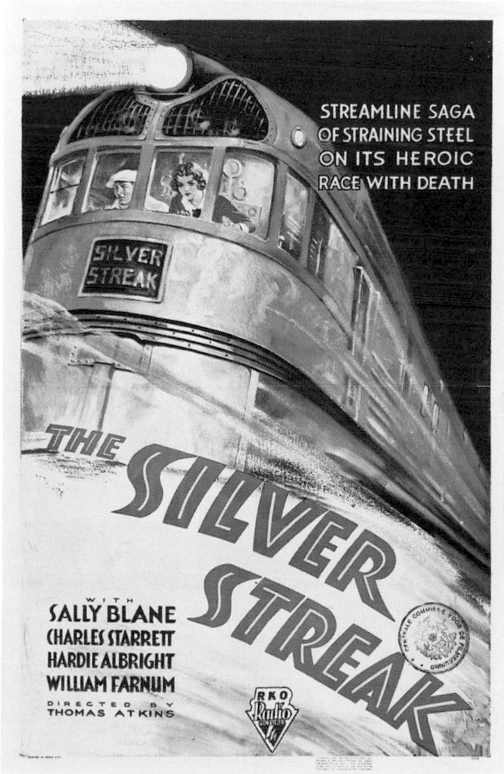

Photo courtesy Heritage Auction Galleries, Dallas; www.HA.com

The Silver Streak (RKO, 1934). One Sheet (27" x 41"). Not to be confused with the Gene Wilder version, this film featured future B Western star Charles Starrett designing a revolutionary new passenger train capable of speeds over 100 miles per hour. Excitement mounts as he has to prove his train's worth by delivering emergency medical supplies across the country. This poster has pinholes in the corners, tears at the edges, tape on the reverse, a Dutch censor stamp in the bottom right corner, and creases to the right border and top right and bottom left corners. **$717**

Photo courtesy Heritage Auction Galleries, Dallas; www.HA.com

The She-Devil (Fox, 1918). Three Sheet (41" x 81"). Between 1914 and 1926, Theda Bara made more than 40 films, nearly all of which are now considered lost following a fire at Fox Studios' New Jersey-based nitrate film storage vault in 1937. Only three complete pictures remain, as well as a handful of brief fragments. The She-Devil, one of Bara's lost films, was reportedly a solid effort, featuring Bara as the fiery Spanish girl Lolette. professional restoration, on Linen. **$3,883**

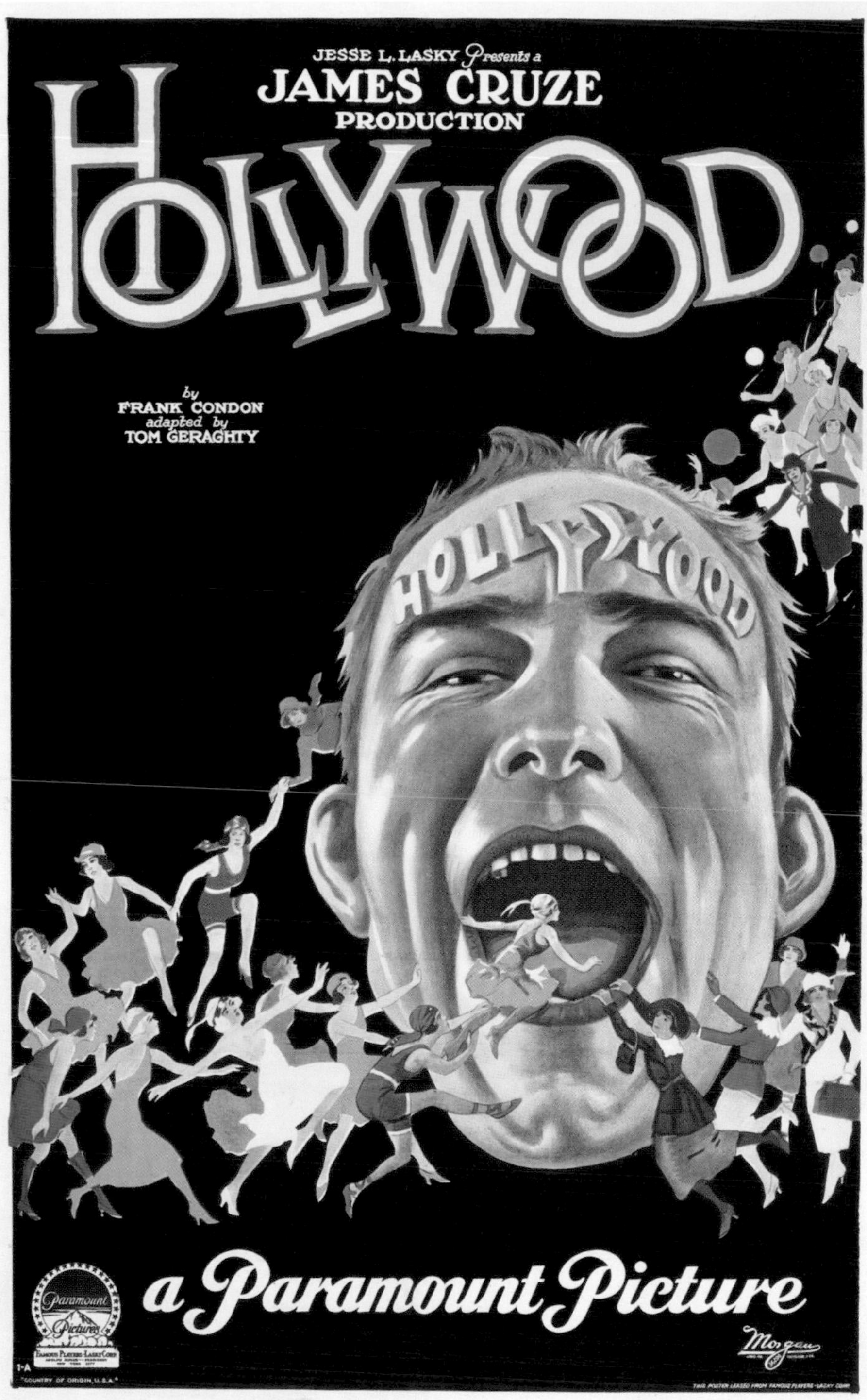

Photo courtesy Heritage Auction Galleries, Dallas; www.HA.com

Hollywood (Paramount, 1923). One Sheet (27" x 41") Style A.Star cameos in this silent film include Mary Astor, William Boyd, Charles Chaplin, Bebe Daniels, Cecil B. DeMille, Douglas Fairbanks, Sid Grauman, Alan Hale, William S. Hart, Jack Holt, Pola Negri, Anna Q. Nilsson, Charles Ogle, Mary Pickford, Zasu Pitts, Will Rogers, Gloria Swanson, and Ben Turpin. In perhaps the most poignant cameo of all, Roscoe "Fatty" Arbuckle appears briefly as an unemployed actor, standing forlornly in a casting line, unable to get work. Professional restoration on Linen. **$89,625**

Photo courtesy Heritage Auction Galleries, Dallas; www.HA.com

Bride of the Monster (Filmmakers Releasing, 1956). Half Sheet (22" x 28"). Director Edward D. Wood's biggest budget film, and the only one that proved financially successful in its original release, this picture also marked Lugosi's last starring role in a feature film. As with all of Wood's films, paper advertising is scarce and highly collectible. This half-sheet had a vertical crease in the right side, tears in the top border, wrinkling overall, a small area of surface paper loss in the bottom, pinholes in the corners, a missing top left corner, edge wear, and a bottom right corner bend. Professional restoration. **$776**

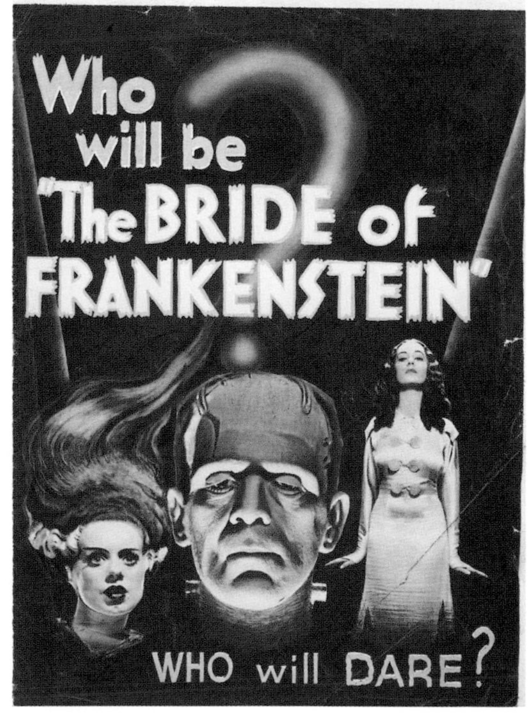

Photo courtesy Heritage Auction Galleries, Dallas; www.HA.com

The Bride of Frankenstein (Universal, 1935). Herald (7" x 9 1/2"). This small single-fold handout has a couple of tiny edge tears and a crease on the front cover. There is a small date inked on the backside. **$1,195**

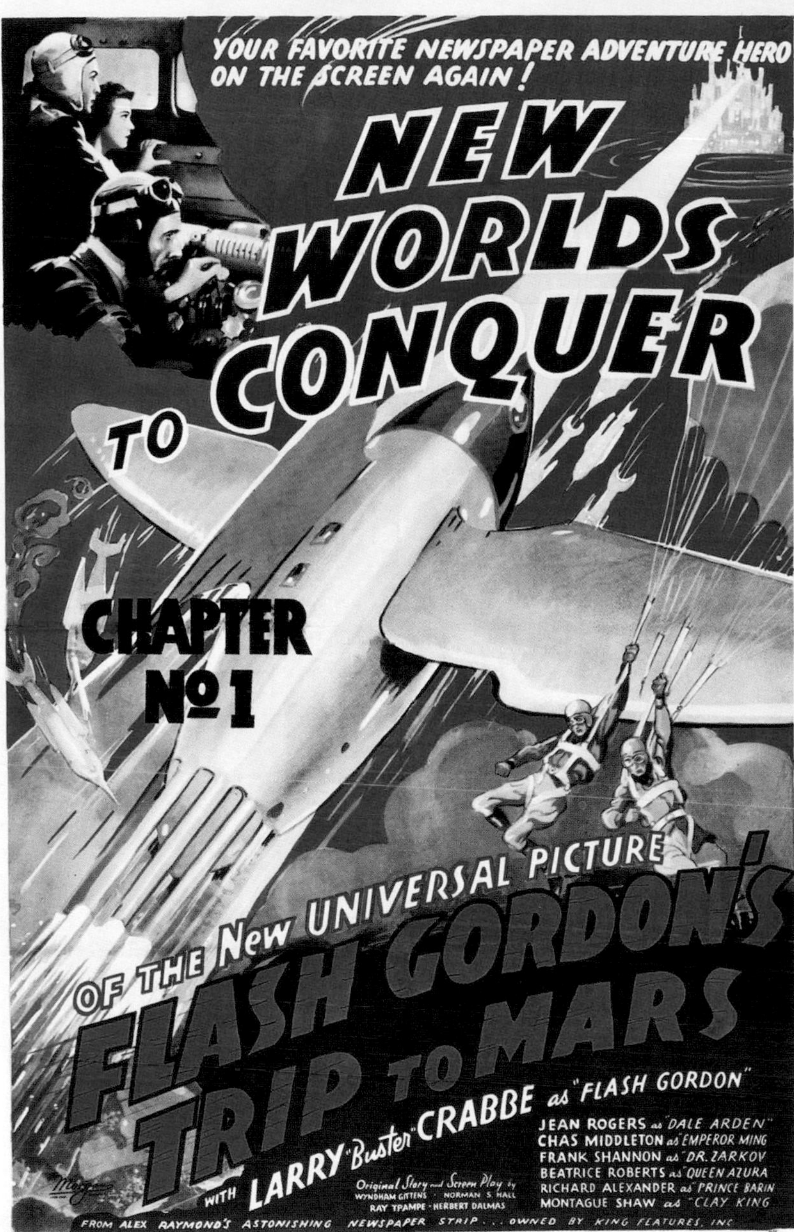

Photo courtesy Heritage Auction Galleries, Dallas; www.HA.com

Flash Gordon's Trip to Mars (Universal, 1938). One Sheet (27" x 41") Chapter 1 -- "New Worlds to Conquer." After the success of the first Flash Gordon serial in 1936, Universal knew they had a winner on their hands, and went ahead with production on this sequel, with the action switched to Mars (rather than Mongo), to take advantage of the Red Planet hysteria caused by Orson Welles' infamous radio broadcast. Buster Crabbe is back as Flash, as is Charles Middleton as the evil dictator, Ming the Merciless, and Jean Rogers as Dale Arden. Professional restoration, on Linen.
$1,434

King Kong, (Paramount, 1976). One Sheet (27" x 41"). Horror. Starring Jeff Bridges, Charles Grodin and Jessica Lange. Directed by John Guillermin. An un-restored poster with bright color. Folded. **$57**

The Manchurian Candidate, (United Artists, 1962). One Sheet (27" x 41"). Thriller. Starring Frank Sinatra, Laurence Harvey and Janet Leigh. Directed by John Frankenheimer. An un-restored poster with bright color. Folded. **$71**

Raiders of the Lost Ark, (Paramount, 1981). One Sheet (27" x 41"). Adventure. Starring Harrison Ford and Karen Allen. Lightly used, un-restored poster with fresh, saturated colors. Folded. **$358**

The Searchers, (Warner Brothers, 1956). One Sheet (27" x 41"). Director John Ford's film of a war weary ex-Confederate soldier, John Wayne, who becomes obsessed with hunting down the Comanche tribe that has massacred his family and kidnapped his young niece, played by Natalie Wood. Restored on linen. **$4,780**

Singin' in the Rain, (MGM, 1952). One Sheet (27" x 41"). Musical. Starring Gene Kelly, Donald O'Connor, Debbie Reynolds and Jean Hagen. It received two Academy Award nominations, including Best Supporting Actress for Hagen, and Best Music. **$3,585**

The Sound of Music, (20th Century Fox, 1965). TODD-AO Six Sheet (81" x 81"). Professional restoration on linen. **$896**

Spartacus, (Universal International, 1960). One Sheet (27" x 41") Academy Awards Style. Adventure. Starring Kirk Douglas and Laurence Olivier. Directed by Stanley Kubrick. An un-restored poster with good color. Folded. **$51**

Superman the Movie, (Warner Brothers, 1978). One Sheet (27" x 41"). Action. Starring Christopher Reeve, Marlon Brando and Gene Hackman. Directed by Richard Donner. An un-restored poster with bright color. Folded. **$45**

The Treasure of the Sierra Madre, (Warner Brothers, 1948). One Sheet (27" x 41"). John Huston's epic saga of treasure and man's greed, starring Humphrey Bogart, Walter Huston and Tim Holt. John Huston won an Oscar for Best Direction and Screenplay. **$5,078**

Photo courtesy Heritage Auction Galleries, Dallas; www.HA.com

Fighting Death (Box Office Attractions, 1914). One Sheet (27" x 41"). In the early years of the 20th century, professional daredevils were all the rage. It wasn't long before Hollywood noticed these daring young men, and signed the best of them to lucrative film contracts. One of the very best was Rodman "Daredevil" Law, a pioneering parachut e performer. Law made four films between 1912 and 1914, with this marking his last silver screen appearance. The stone litho poster has missing paper along all four borders, fold wear with cross-fold separation, tears in the image area, and a tear on the right side. Professional restoration on linen. **$836**

RECORDS

With the advent of the more sophisticated recording materials, earlier phonograph records became collectors' items. Condition is critical.

As with many types of collectibles, a grading scale has been developed.

Mint (M): Perfect condition, no flaws, scratches or scuffs in the grooves. The cardboard jacket will be crisp.

Near Mint (NM) or Mint-Minus (M-): The record will be close to perfect, with no marks in the grooves. The label will be clean, not marked, or scuffed. There will be no ring wear on the record or album cover.

Very Good Plus (VG+): Used for a record that has been played, but well taken care of. Slight scuffle or warps to the grooves is acceptable as long as it does not affect the sound. A faint ring wear discoloration is acceptable. The jacket may appear slightly worn, especially on the edges.

Very Good (VG): Used to describe a record that has some pronounced defects, as does the cover. The record will still play well. This usually is the lowest grade acceptable to a serious collector. Most records listed in price guides are of this grade.

Good (G): This category of record will be playable, but probably will have loss to the sound quality. The cover might be marked or torn.

Poor or Fair (P, F): Record is damaged, may be difficult to play. The cover will be damaged, usually marked, dirty or torn.

Note: Most records, especially popular recordings, have a value of less than $3. Picture sleeves will generally increase values, and often have an independent value.

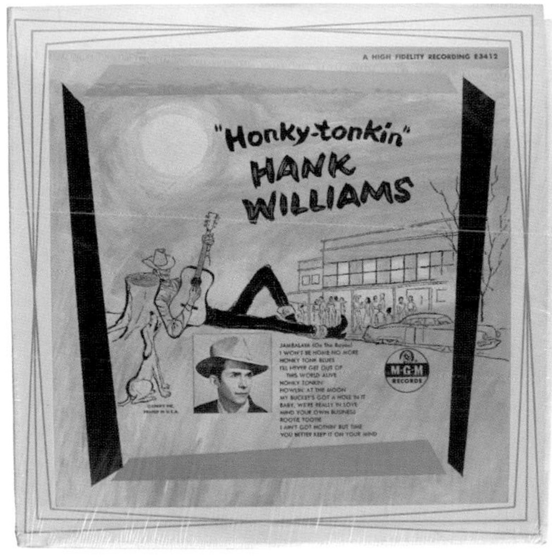

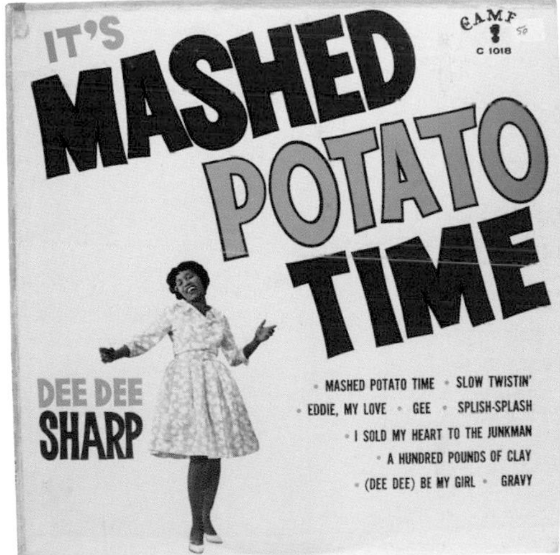

Hank Williams, Honky-tonkin', MGM E-3412, 1957.
$100

Dee Dee Sharp, It's Mashed Potato Time, Cameo C-1018, 1962. **$60**

Jerry Lee Lewis, Jerry Lee Lewis, Sun SLP-1230, 1958.
$200

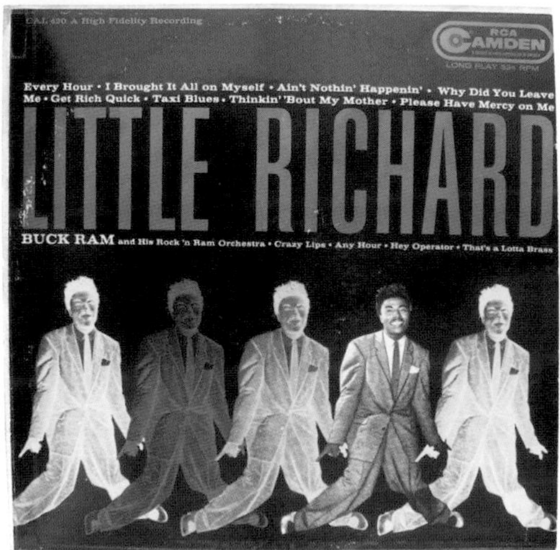

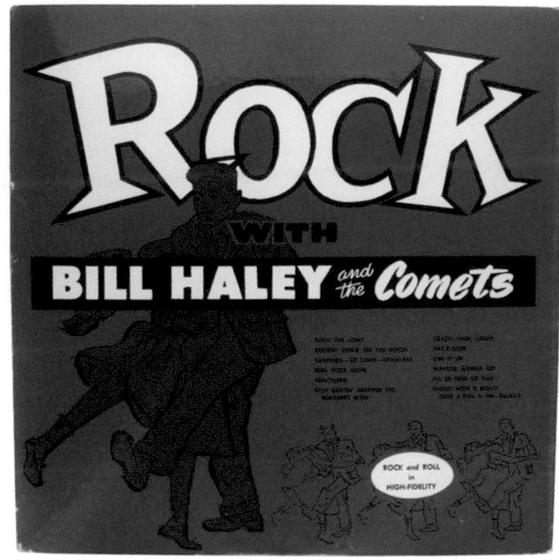

Little Richard, Little Richard, RCA Camden CAL-420, 1956. **$200**

Bill Haley and the Comets, Rock with, Somerset P-4600, 1958. **$150**

Buddy Holly, Buddy Holly, Coral CRL 57210, 1964. **$100**

Ray Charles, Country and Western meets Rhythm and Blues, ABC-Paramount ABC-520, 1965. **$20**

James Brown, Mighty Instrumentals, King 961, 1966. **$100**

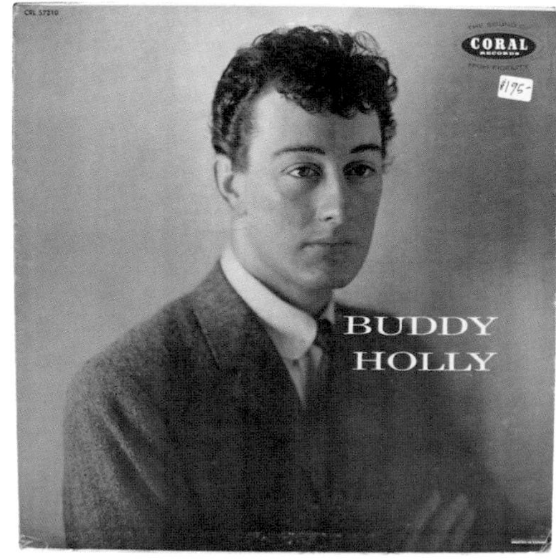

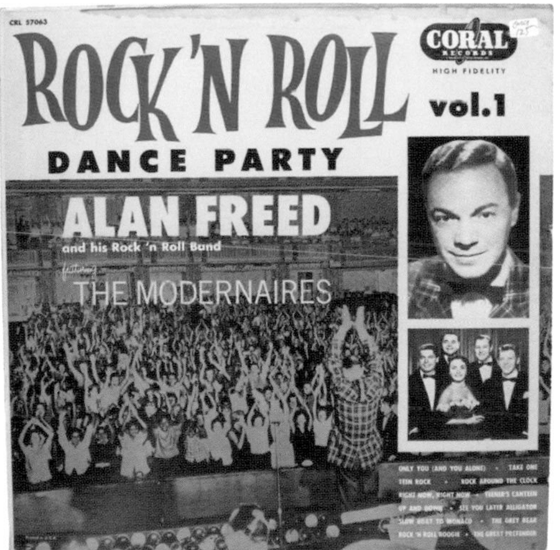

Dion, Alone With, Laurie LLP 2004, 1960. **$200**

Bo Diddley/Chuck Berry, Two Great Guitars, Checker LP 2991, 1964. **$60**

Alan Freed, Rock 'n Roll Dance Party, Coral CRL 57063, 1956. **$150**

Frank Zappa, Sleep Dirt, Discreet/Warner DSK 2292, 1978. **$15**

Atomic Rooster, In Hearing of, Elektra EKS-74109, 1971. **$20**

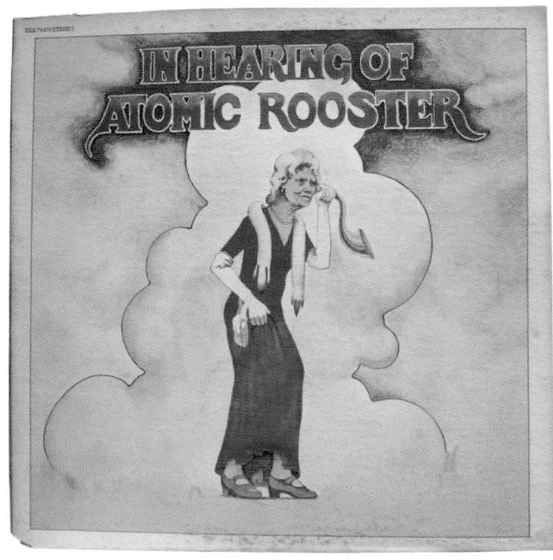

Roger Daltrey, Daltrey, Track 328, 1973. **$12**

Molly Hatchet, Molly Hatchet, Epic JE 35347, 1978. **$6**

The Moody Blues, Every Good Boy Deserves Favour, Threshold THS 5, 1971. **$15**

Peter Gabriel, So, Geffen GHS 24088, 1986. **$10**

Jethro Tull, Thick as a Brick, Chrysalis CHR 1003, 1973. **$12**

SALT AND PEPPERSHAKERS

Rare, unique and decorative salt and peppershakers have become such popular collector's items over the years that many shaker sets are produced for the sole purpose of being a collectible and are rarely used to hold seasonings

Salt and peppershakers can be found in nearly every conceivable shape and size and are made in a variety of materials including wood, metal, ceramics, glass, and plastics. They are abundant, colorful, fun, span almost every theme, and best of all, they're often inexpensive.

This year's edition of the Warman's guide features "nodding" shakers. Before there were bobble-heads, there were "nodders." In this case, little figural shakers that sit in a holder and pivot in a nodding motion. As you might expect, they are fragile and easily damaged, so they often have a premium price.

For more information, see *Antique Trader Salt and Pepper Shaker Price Guide* by Mark F. Moran, 2008.

Bass, late 1940s, made in Japan, 3" h overall. **$65-$75**

Mr. and Mrs. Cat, contemporary, marked "Clay Art – Made in China," car 5" long. **$25-$35**

Ribbon cats, 1940s, souvenir of Chillicothe, Ohio, made in Japan, 3 3/4" h. **$65-$75**

Ducks, late 1940s, made in Japan, 3 1/4" h overall. **$65-$75**

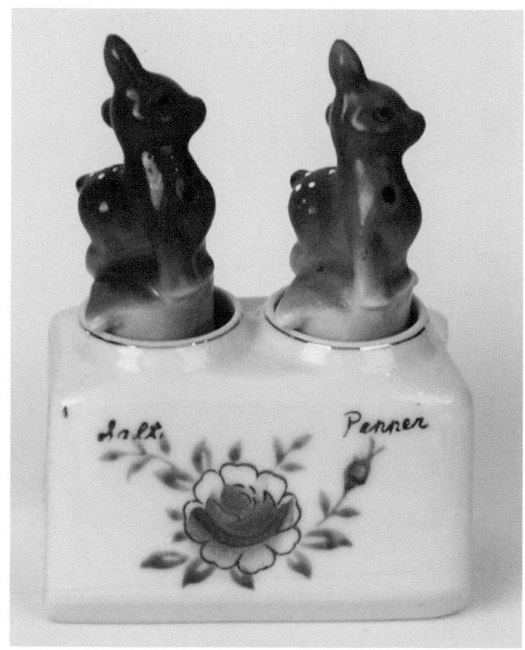

Fawns, 1950s, made in Japan, 4" h. **$55-$65**

Game birds, 1950s, made in Japan, 3 1/2" h. **$55-$65**

Hen and rooster with condiment holder, 1940s, Occupied Japan, 5" wide. **$125-$150**

Hen and rooster, 1950s, souvenir of Grand Coulee Dam, made in Japan, 3 1/2" h. **$55-$65**

Indians in a drum, 1950s, made in Japan, 3 1/2" h. **$65-$75**

Kangaroo and joey, 1950s, made in Japan, 4 1/4" h. **$65**

Pheasants, 1950s, made in Japan, 3 1/8" h. **$55-$65**

Pretentious pigs, late 1940s, made in Japan, 4" h. **$200-$225**

Pretentious pigs, with gold trim, late 1940s, made in Japan, 4" h. **$200-$225**

Snake charmer and cobra, 1950s, made in Japan, 3 1/4" and 4" h. **$125-$150**

Turkeys, late 1940s, made in Japan, 3 1/4" h overall. **$65-$75**

Skulls with rhinestone eyes, souvenir of Louisville, Ky., 1950s, made in Japan, 3 1/2" h overall. **$55-$65**

STERLING SILVER

Silver has been known since ancient times and has long been valued as a precious metal, used to make ornaments, jewelry, tableware and utensils, and coins. Following are select objects from *Warman's Sterling Silver Flatware, 2nd Edition*, by Phil Dreis.

Also see Lighting.

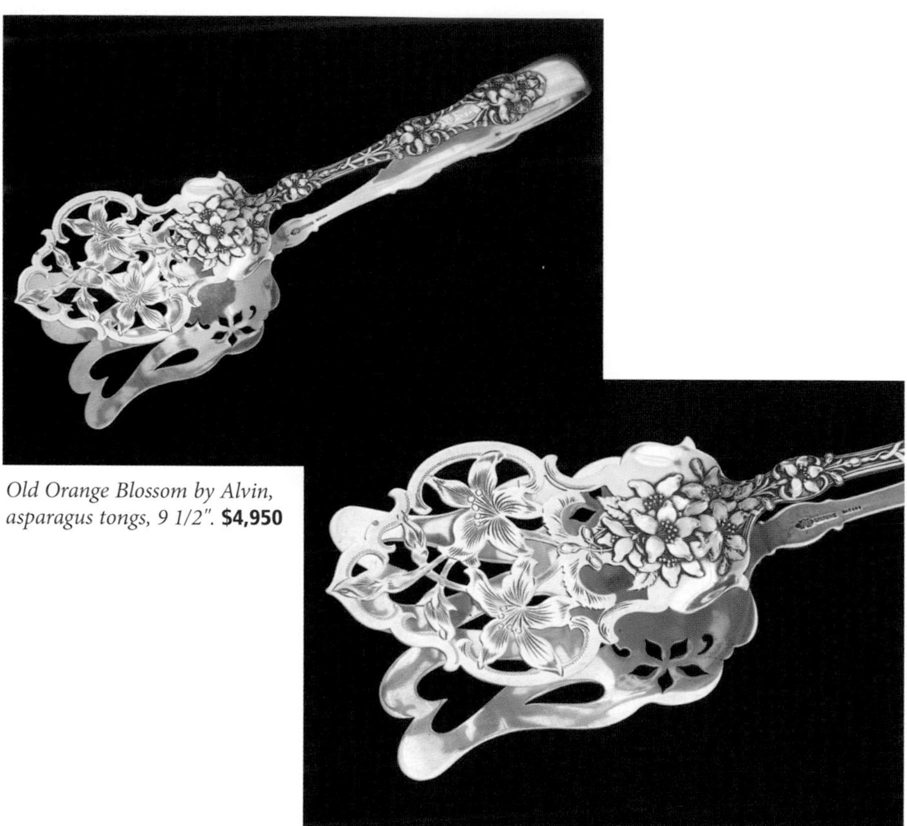

Old Orange Blossom by Alvin, asparagus tongs, 9 1/2". **$4,950**

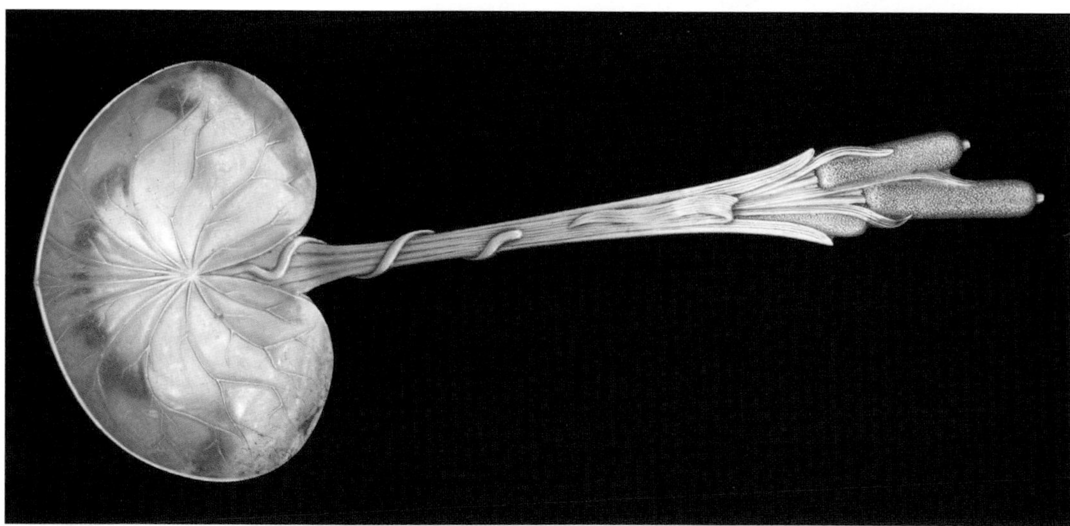

Cattails by Durgin, sauce ladle, 5 1/2". **$695**

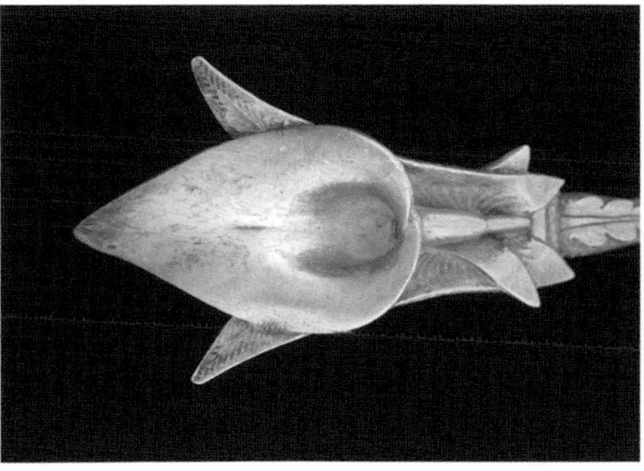

Calla Lily by Whiting, ice cream server, 10 1/2". **$1,295**

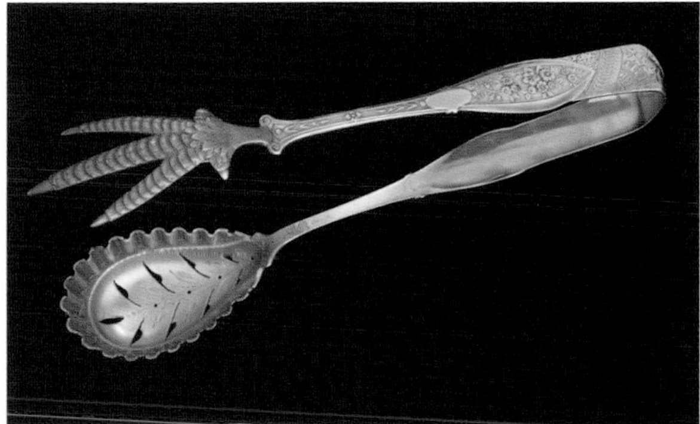

Montezuma by George W. Shiebler & Co., ice tongs, 9 1/2". **$695**

Lily by Whiting, cucumber server. **$495**

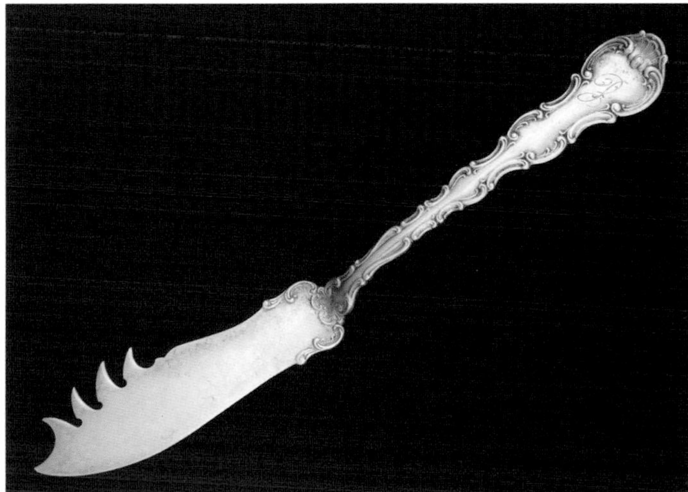

Strasbourg by Gorham, cheese knife with pick, 7 7/8". **$279**

Lady's by Gorham, sauce ladle with bucket bowl, 6 1/2". **$795**

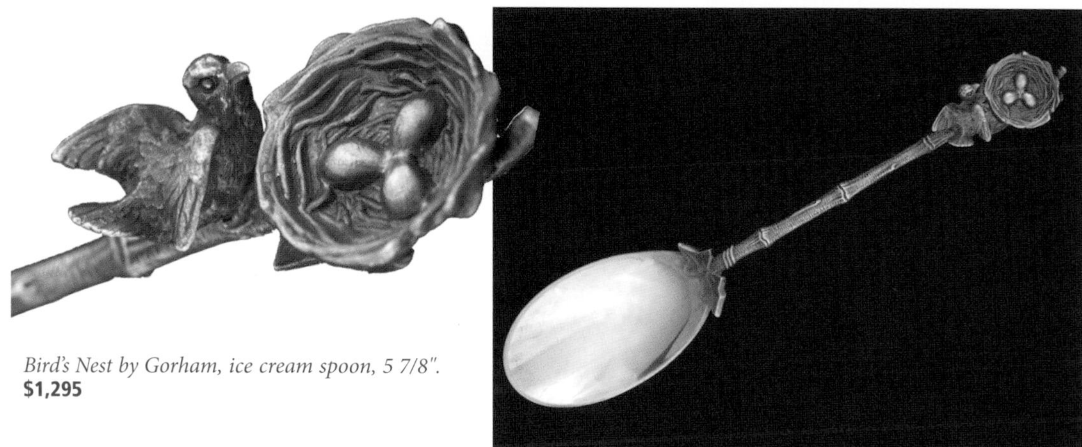

Bird's Nest by Gorham, ice cream spoon, 5 7/8". **$1,295**

Fuchsia by Whiting, sugar sifter, 8 1/4". **$1,295**

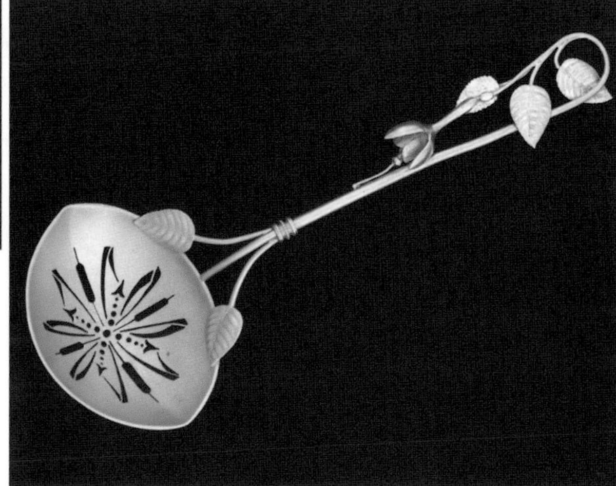

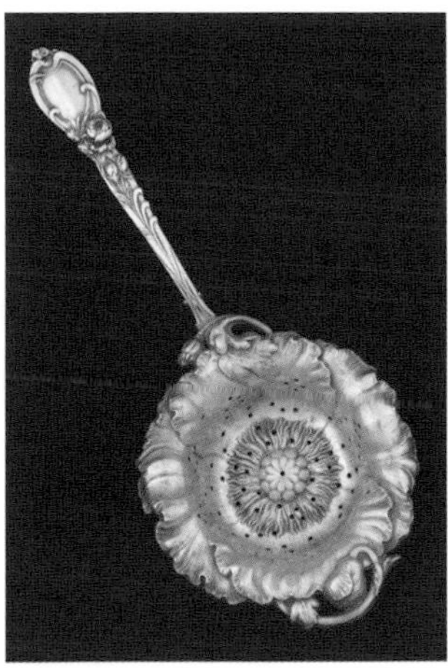
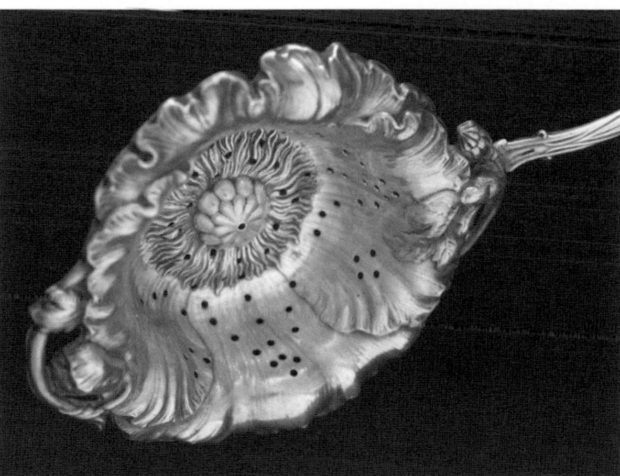

La Parisienne by Reed & Barton, tea strainer. **$495**

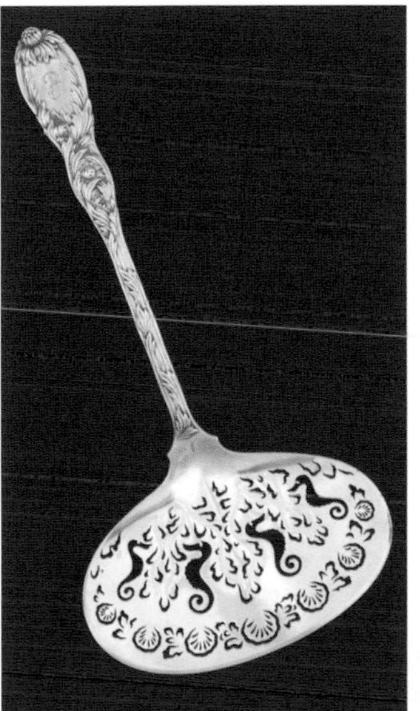

Chrysanthemum by Tiffany & Co., fish server, pierced with seahorses, French style. **$17,500**

Les Cinq Fleurs by Reed & Barton, pierced asparagus server. **$495**

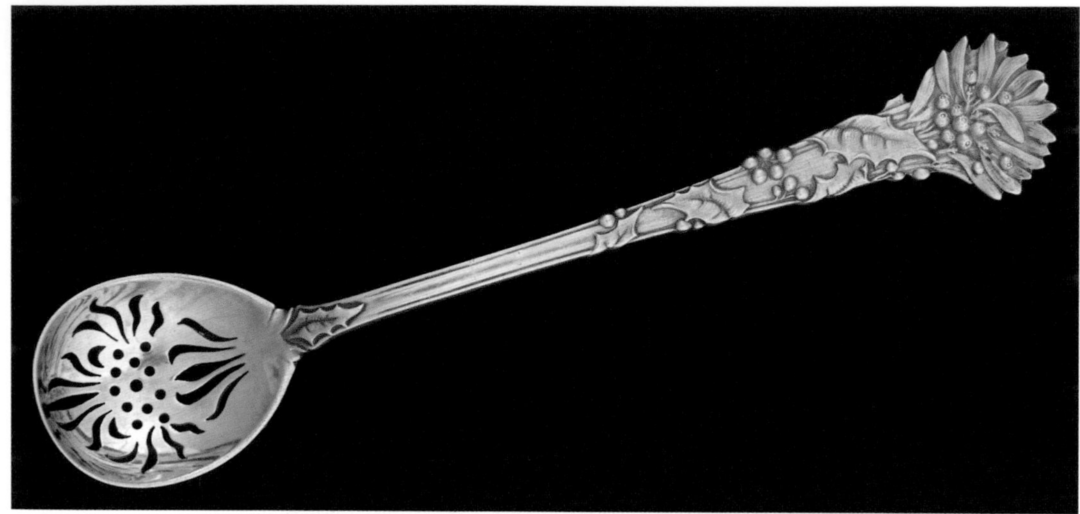

Holly by Tiffany & Co., pierced olive spoon. **$650**

Japanese by Tiffany & Co., fish server, bright cut with fishermen, 12″. **$6,900**

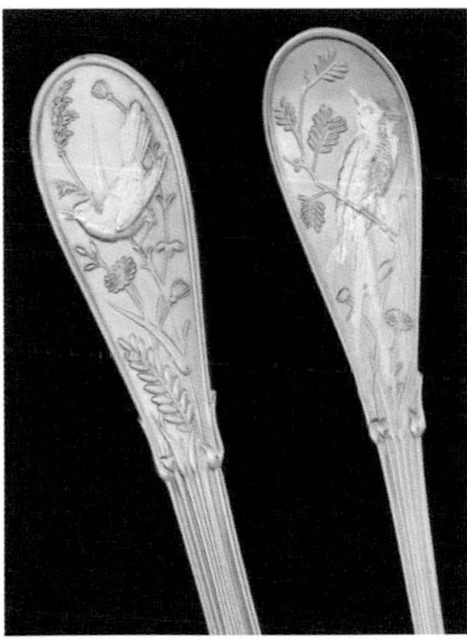

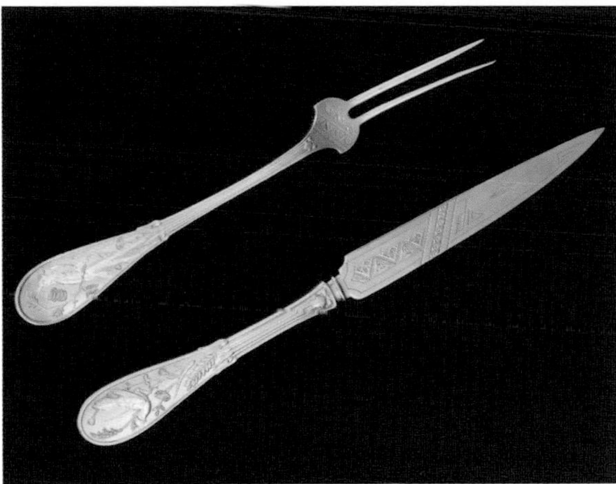

Japanese by Tiffany & Co., gilt fruit knife and fruit fork, bright cut. **$2,650**

Lap Over Edge, acid-etched by Tiffany & Co., sorbet set in fitted box. **$8,900**

SPACE: COLLECTING'S FINAL FRONTIER?

By Noah Fleisher

Human conquest of the cosmos has the ability to inspire humans like little else and, in the brief time we've been slipping these surly bonds, we've done remarkably well, all things considered. In the cosmic sense this span but a blink of blink. We've walked on the moon, sent craft to mars to explore the surface, sent satellites hurtling headlong into the unknown of the Milky Way beyond our system and we've taken pictures of the beginning of time. These are but baby steps for which future generations will be grateful because they will enjoy the fruits of this early labor.

Noah Fleisher

Little wonder then that the pieces, parts, ephemera and personal memorabilia associated with America's space program – the men and women who, in large part, made science fiction a reality – have made collectors of all sorts sit up and take notice.

"The supply of the really important items is certainly finite," said Howard Weinberger, Senior Space Consultant for Heritage Auction Galleries in Dallas, and CEO of Asset Alternatives. "The old saying is that if you collected all the personal items from the six missions that landed on the moon, all of it would fit in a small suitcase."

Weinberger is talking about the cream of the crop, the things that the Apollo astronauts took special pains with to make sure they were on the lunar surface and spent time in the vacuum of space. The rest of the field – from souvenir patches, parts and models, autographs and well beyond – has as much room for variance of budget as a collector could wish and a plethora of material that – like the very subject it covers – can sometimes seem infinite.

Unlike so many categories of collecting, the market for Space is still being established. The subject has long been popular, but the ability to get the very best of The Right Stuff was not there until recently, as many of the astronauts themselves – or their families, if they've passed on – have realized the value, both historic and financial, of their accomplishments. The more that the remaining original astronauts release key pieces of their extra-terrestrial lives, the more established the market will become.

One of the most important things Space collecting has going for it is its appeal, said Weinberger. The steady increase in prices at auction in the three years he's been working with Heritage shows just how broad this appeal is.

"I think it's a function of the fact that people are now aware that these items can be bought," said Weinberger, who is among the few with the connections to bring the choicest pieces to auction. "The genre is unique because the demographic, in my opinion, is among the top three to five potential demographics for collecting."

Meaning there's almost no soul on this planet that doesn't know about, and isn't at least peripherally fascinated by, space travel.

"Show a baseball card, a comic book or a regional American quilt to a woman in Asia," Weinberger said, "and it won't translate. If you go back to 1969, to Apollo 11 and the first moon landing, you have the entire planet watching. Everybody remembers where they were when Neil Armstrong walked on the moon, or when Allan Sheppard went up with Mercury."

The broad scope of potential buyers is indeed as varied as the material, as a few minutes with the following pages will show. As the field sorts itself out, it is tough to break down into categories. The astronauts, and all the workers at NASA – from the men who walked on the moon to the guys that swept up at the end of the day – were all aware from the beginning of the historic nature of their pursuit – and it potential value.

This prospective worth, then, necessitates at least an attempt at breaking the hobby into categories. According to Weinberger, this is not something that should be done by item type, but rather by mission type and purpose.

"There's not a lot of the very best stuff, so there is a hierarchy of sorts that has evolved," he said. "The highest rung is for items that actually landed on moon and went on the surface. Then it's something that landed on the moon but didn't leave capsule. After that it's memorabilia that

Buzz Aldrin's 1923-S Peace Silver Dollar Flown on the Moon Mission Aboard Apollo 11. This was part of his Personal Preference Kit (PPK). Accompanied by a signed letter of authenticity from him. **$31,070**

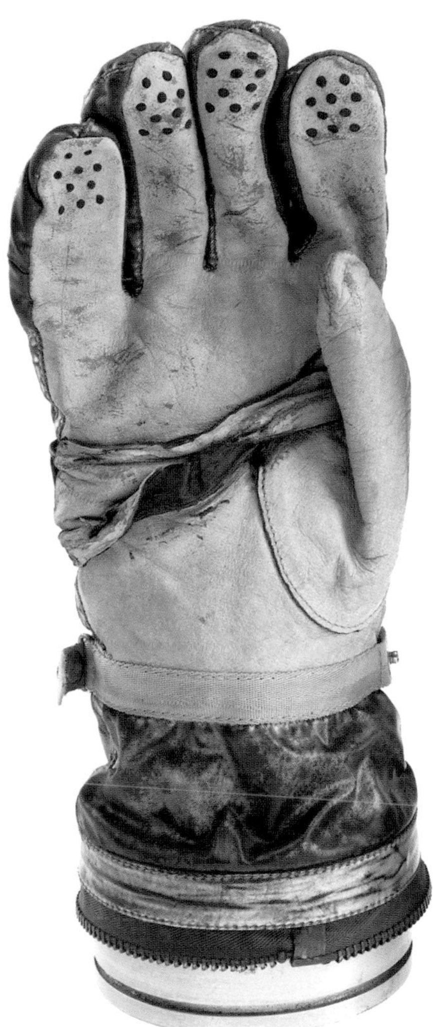

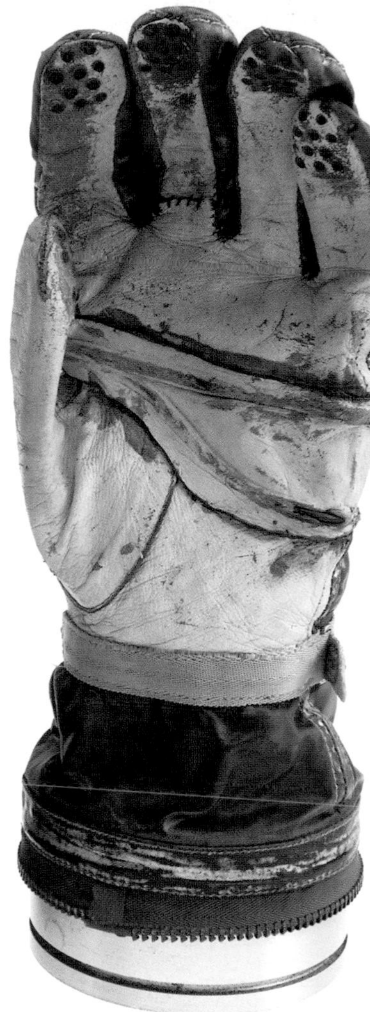

Mercury 7 Type M Astronaut's Test Gloves worn by John Glenn and Wally Schirra. Two 11" x 4" aluminized nylon gloves manufactured by the B.F. Goodrich Co. for NASA during the agency's testing of the Mercury Astronauts' spacesuits. Both gloves include an internal cloth Project Mercury label. One glove has the name "Glenn" and one "Shirra" (sic) written in black marker inside the aluminum fittings. **$7,170 both**

flew to the moon but only stayed in orbit. From there it's about things that flew in space, things that were strictly in earth orbit and things that didn't fly in space but are of a personal nature belonging to the astronauts, or having their autographs."

Within these several categories, however, again there can be a striking difference in price depending on the name and the program it's associated with.

Whatever level a collector is looking at to get into the market for Space memorabilia, the most important thing is authenticity, especially at the high end. In fact, Weinberger said, if it comes from an astronaut's personal collection, a signature and/or a letter of authentication is of paramount importance.

"No matter what it is, even if it's purchased personally from an astronaut, it has to be certified," he said. "The most desirable certification is having the signature on the item itself. If it has that, and a letter as well, then so much the better."

The most important thing to get started is not a broad general knowledge of what's out there, but to simply have a passion for it no matter how much cash you can put in. You can buy autographs, first-day covers or specially minted Robbins medals that flew on every Apollo mission. You can spend a few hundred or a few hundred thousand; either way, it's an accessible market.

"You can start with something basic," Weinberger said. "The overall amount of memorabilia related to space is endless."

It's a good thing, then, that the enthusiasm of collectors, especially for something as inspiring as space travel, seems to be equally as endless.

Noah Fleisher is a media and public relations liaison for Heritage Auction Galleries in Dallas, and former editor of Antique Trader magazine.

All listings and images courtesy Heritage Auction Galleries, Dallas; *www.HA.com*

BUZZ ALDRIN, HANDWRITTEN NOTES AND SCRIPTURES FLOWN TO THE SURFACE OF THE MOON

Front and verso of a 3" x 5" buff-colored lightweight card, one horizontal fold affecting some text. The astronauts of the Apollo 8 mission were so inspired by their view of the earth from moon orbit the previous Christmas Eve that they read the biblical account of the creation story from Genesis. Noted atheist Madalyn Murray O'Hair brought suit against NASA over this Bible reading, asking the courts to ban any further such activity.

Though the courts eventually rejected the suit, NASA was quite nervous about further religious activities throughout the rest of the Apollo program. Buzz Aldrin, a Christian and an elder at the Webster, Texas, Presbyterian Church, wished to express his personal faith and give thanks to God by the taking of the Holy Communion on the moon. His church furnished him with the wine and wafer, which he stowed secretly in his kit. He described the activity in his book Return to Earth (Bantam Books, 1973): "During the first idle moment in the LM before eating our snack, I reached into my personal preference kit and pulled out two small packages which had been specially prepared at my request. One contained a small amount of wine, the other a small wafer. With them and a small chalice from the kit, I took communion on the moon, reading to myself from a small card I carried on which I had written the portion of the Book of John used in the traditional communion ceremony."

He had wanted to read the scripture back to earth, but NASA requested that he not do so. Instead, he read from this card, on which is written: "Houston This is Eagle The LM Pilot speaking. I would like to request a few moments of silence. Over. I would like to invite each person listening in, wherever and whomever he may be, to contemplate for a moment the events of the past few hours and to give thanks in his own individual way - - My way shall be by partaking of the elements of Holy Communion." His fellow astronaut, Neil Armstrong, watched but did not partake.

The verses he would have liked to have read are found at the top of the other side of this handwritten card: "An [sic] Jesus said, 'I am the vine, you are the branches. Whoever remains in me, and I in him, will bear much fruit; for you can do nothing without me.' [John 15:5]". There are additional, and appropriate, verses beneath in a different ink that Aldrin did actually quote three days later during a TV broadcast by the astronauts aboard Columbia the evening before they splashed down safely in the Pacific. He writes: "Psalm 8: v. 3,4 'When I consider thy heavens, the work of thy fingers, the moon and the stars, which thou has ordained; What is man that thou art mindful of him? And the Son of Man, that thou visitest Him?'"

From the personal collection of Dr. Buzz Aldrin and also accompanied by a signed letter of authenticity from him. **$179,250**

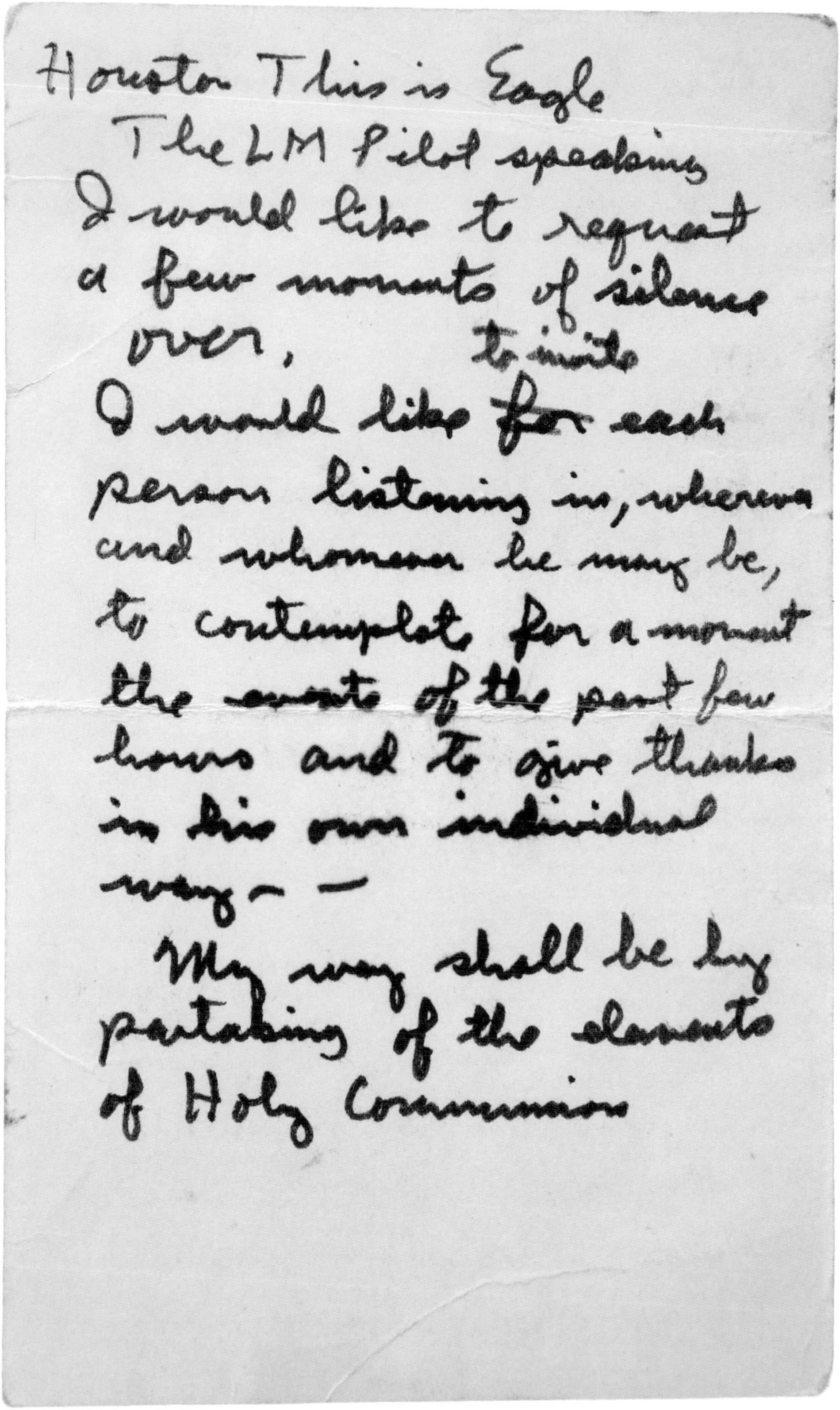

Houston This is Eagle
The LM Pilot speaking
I would like to request
a few moments of silence
over. to invite
I would like ~~for~~ each
person listening in, wherever
and whomever he may be,
to contemplate for a moment
the events of the past few
hours and to give thanks
in his own individual
way — —
My way shall be by
partaking of the elements
of Holy Communion

U.S. Flag Carried on the Moon by Neil Armstrong, affixed to a 12" x 14" wooden shield plaque, flag is 6" x 3 3/4" and an Apollo 11 patch, covered in clear plastic. The 5" x 3" metallic plaque affixed certifies that "This flag was carried on the moon by/ astronaut Neil Armstrong/ on July 20, 1969/ and presented to/ Joe D. Garino Jr./ by/ The Apollo 11 Astronauts." As Armstrong set foot on the lunar surface, he carried this flag. Accompanied by a signed certificate of authentication from Garino verifying its provenance.
$56,763

Buzz Aldrin's Apollo 11 Slide Rule, Flown to the Moon. A Pickett Model N600-ES (Eye Saver) Log Speed Rule, 6" with 22 five-inch scales. Flown to the moon aboard Apollo 11 by Aldrin. Very fine condition. Accompanied by a signed letter of authenticity from him. **$77,675**

Space Shuttle Columbia Commander John Young's Flight Suit Patches, Worn on the First Shuttle Mission, directly from his Personal Collection, Certified and Signed on the Display Frame. On the paper backing of the frame, Young has written: "Patches From My Suit Flown Aboard STS-1. John Young". **$56,762**

Apollo 8 Flown CMP Checklist, Directly from the Personal Collection of Mission Command Module Pilot James Lovell, Certified and Signed. Lovell has certified and signed the front: "James Lovell Flown". With normal wear and light soiling. **$47,800**

Apollo 13-Flown, Lunar Module Spacecraft Identification Plate Display Directly from the Personal Collection of Mission Commander James Lovell, certified and signed. A metal plate 5 1/4" x 1 3/4" mounted to a 10" x 11" wooden display plaque beneath a metal die-cut representation of the lunar module and an engraved brass plate with the words: APOLLO XIII LUNAR MODULE – 7, "FAREWELL AQUARIUS, AND WE THANK YOU" – Capt. J. Lovell - F. Haise - J. Swigert Jr. At the top left of this wooden plaque, Lovell has written in silver: "From the personal collection of James Lovell". On the back, he has written: "Apollo 13 Lunar Module/ name plate -- removed/ prior to jettison LM./ James Lovell." **$47,800**

Apollo 10, Complete Lunar Module-Flown Rendezvous Checklist with Original Signed Snoopy Sketch by Charles Schulz. Twenty-nine numbered card stock pages of 8 1/4" x 10 1/2", three-hole punched, and bound with rings inside heavier boards. Just inside is an additional card stock leaf containing a full-page black-felt-tip drawing of Snoopy. Drawn and signed by Schulz, Snoopy is shown in his "flying ace" goggles and scarf (along with a space helmet); sitting atop his "Sopwith Camel" (doghouse). Snoopy was the semi-official nickname given to the lunar module (the command module was called Charlie Brown). From the personal collection of Captain Gene Cernan accompanied by written authentication by Cernan. **$41,825**

1969 Omega Speedmaster, Professional Apollo XI Commemorative Watch, Serial No. 9. 18K Gold Presented to Him by the Omega Watch Co, Signed on Case and Box. Inscribed on the back: "ASTRONAUT JOHN W. YOUNG- to mark man's conquest of space with time, through time, on time GEMINI 3 & 10 - APOLLO 10 No 9". The Omega Speedmaster chronograph, often known as the "Moonwatch," was first manufactured in 1957 and has a long history with NASA. There are numerous photos available showing astronauts wearing their NASA-issue Omega Speedmasters during various spaceflights and moon landings. **$38,837**

Apollo Bracelet, Containing All 11 Flown Silver Robbins Medallions from the personal collection of astronaut Paul J. Weitz. Individual serial numbers as follows: Apollo 7 (#197); Apollo 8 (#254); Apollo 9 (#320); Apollo 10 (#225); Apollo 11 (#139); Apollo 12 (#243); Apollo 13 (# 371, made from flown metal); Apollo 14 (#118); Apollo 15 (#116); Apollo 16 (#55); and Apollo 17 (#F42). A handwritten and signed letter of authenticity from Paul Weitz is included. **$37,344**

Apollo 16, Lunar Module Flown Needle-Nose Pliers from the collection of Lunar Module Pilot Charles M. Duke Jr., overall length 5". These pliers were flown to the moon aboard the Lunar Module Orion and used on the lunar surface during April 16-27, 1972. From the collection of Charles M. Duke, Jr., who has included a handwritten and signed letter of certification verifying its provenance. **$33,460**

Apollo 17, Command Module Flown Flight Plan, Volumes I and II, Both signed by and from the personal collection of Mission Commander Gene Cernan. Two separate books, each one is 8 1/2" x 10 1/2", printed on cardstock, and bound between two heavier boards with three binder rings. Cernan has certified and signed each: Volume I- "Flown to the Moon Apollo XVII Gene Cernan" and Volume II- "Flown on Apollo XVII Gene Cernan." **$33,460**

Apollo 8, Flown Update Book Signed by and from the Personal Collection of Mission Command Module Pilot James Lovell. This 5 1/2" x 8", 200+-page book, printed on cardstock and bound between stiff covers with two binder rings, is titled "APOLLO 8 UPDATES". Certified and signed on the cover by Lovell: "James Lovell Flown on Apollo 8". **$33,460**

Apollo 16, Lunar Module Flown Spacecraft Identification Plate Display Directly from the Personal Collection of Mission Commander John Young, Certified and Signed. A metal plaque of 5 1/4" x 1 3/4" mounted to a 10" x 11" wooden display plaque beneath a metal die-cut representation of the lunar module and an engraved brass plate. At the bottom of this wooden plaque, Young has written in silver: "Plaque Flown on Apollo XVI John Young". **$33,460**

Buzz Aldrin's Space Flown Cutting Tool, Used on the Apollo 11 Mission, with original Velcro still attached. Measuring 8" in length, this stainless steel hand tool was used on the lunar module by Buzz Aldrin on Apollo 11. From the personal collection of Dr. Buzz Aldrin and accompanied by a signed letter of authenticity from him. **$31,070**

Buzz Aldrin, Apollo 11 Space Flown Book by Robert Goddard. The small leather-bound book, The Autobiography of Robert Hutchings Goddard: Father of the Space Age, Early Years to 1927 (Worchester, Mass.: Achille J. St. Onge, 1966), is 2" x 3" and has 85 gilt-edged pages. The book is inscribed in pencil, "Flown on Apollo 11 July 16-24-'69 E.E. Aldrin Jr. (signed) Buzz Aldrin." The book was published to commemorate the 40th anniversary of Goddard's first liquid propellant rocket. There were 1,926 copies printed, of which this is number 659. The book was carried on Apollo 11 by Buzz Aldrin as a favor to his father and as a token of respect for Goddard, the "Father of Modern Rocketry." Accompanied by a signed letter of authenticity from Aldrin. **$29,875**

Buzz Aldrin's Original Gemini 12 Space Suit Patches, originally presented to his parents for Christmas in 1966. Framed 16 1/2" x 13 1/2" with printed text, "These articles were worn on the space suit of Astronaut Edwin E. Aldrin, Jr. during the historic flight of Gemini XII in November, 1966." To the left of that is a handwritten inscription, "To Mother & Dad With a grateful son's love, Buzz Christmas 1966." **$29,875**

Apollo 11 Flown Robbins Silver Medallion, Serial Number 188, from the collection of astronaut Charles M. Duke Jr., 25mm, with the mission dates engraved on the reverse. From the collection of Charles M. Duke, Jr., with a handwritten and signed letter of certification verifying its provenance. **$28,680**

Apollo 17, Lunar Module Flown Lunar Rover Malfunction Procedures Checklist Card, signed by and from the personal collection of Mission Commander Gene Cernan, with smudges of lunar dust. **$28,680**

Apollo 13-Flown CSM Systems Data Checklist, from the personal collection of Mission Commander James Lovell, certified and signed. An 8 1/2" x 10 1/2" book of approximately 100 pages including dozens of multi-page pull-out schematic diagrams, bound with three binder rings between two heavyweight covers. Rare in complete form. **$28,680**

Apollo 14, Lunar Module Antares Flown American Flag, signed by Edgar Mitchell. The Apollo 14 Lunar Module (LM) Antares was the third crewed vehicle to land on the

Apollo 10 Command Module Pilot John Young's Flown Space Suit Patches (four) Directly from his Personal Collection, certified and signed on the display frame. A 10" x 17" framed display containing all four pressure suit patches from the May 18-26, 1969, Apollo 10 mission, a dress rehearsal for the first manned lunar landing. On the paper backing of the frame, Young has written: "I certify that these 4 patches were on my Apollo 10 Pressure Suit when I went to the MOON. John Young". **$31,070**

Apollo 11 Signed and Flown Commemorative Cover with Notation. Neil Armstrong, Michael Collins and Buzz Aldrin have all signed in blue felt-tip this NASA Manned Spacecraft Center Stamp Club Official Commemorative Cover of the First Manned Lunar Exploration with a colorful cachet of two astronauts on the lunar surface. From the personal collection of Dr. Buzz Aldrin and accompanied by a signed letter of authenticity from him. **$26,290**

moon. The flag was carried by LM Pilot Edgar Mitchell during the Apollo 14 mission. Inscribed and signed: "Flown to the Lunar surface aboard Antares - Feb. 5, 1971. Edgar Mitchell, Apollo 14 LMP". The flag is accompanied by two certificates of authenticity - one handwritten and one typed - by Ed Mitchell on his personal Apollo 14 letterhead. **$26,290**

Apollo 17-Flown, Robbins Sterling Silver Medallion, obtained by Astronaut Joseph P. Kerwin as a member of the Astronaut Flight Office. The 35mm medal, with the serial number 38, was flown aboard Apollo 17, the 11th manned space mission in the NASA Apollo program. There were only 80 Apollo 17-flown silver Robbins medals. From the collection of Joseph P. Kerwin M.D., who has included a signed letter of certification verifying its provenance. **$26,290**

Gene Cernan's Apollo 17 Lunar Module-Flown Fisher AG-7 Space Pen, used during the flight and actually carried by Cernan in a spacesuit pocket onto the surface of the moon. From the personal collection of Captain Gene Cernan accompanied by written authentication by Cernan. **$23,900**

Gemini 10, Mission Commander John Young's Flown Space Suit Patches (three) directly from his personal collection, certified and signed on the display frame. On the paper backing of the frame, Young has written: "I certify that these patches flew on my pressure suit on Gemini 10. John Young". **$23,900**

Apollo 17-Flown, Omega Stainless Steel Speedmaster Professional Watch and Flown-Metal Attachment directly from the personal collection of Mission Command Module Pilot Ron Evans, certified and signed. Included is a signed letter of certification from Jan Evans (Mrs. Ron Evans). **$23,900**

Apollo 15, Lunar Module-Flown Miniature Lunar Rover License Plate certified by Mission Commander Dave Scott. A 1 1/4" x 3/4" mini Moon 1971 license plate numbered "LRV 001." Novaspace Galleries Certificate of Authenticity signed by Dave Scott included. **$21,510**

Gene Cernan's Apollo 17 Lunar Module-Flown Sunglasses, and Beta Cloth Case. Manufactured by American Optical, 5 1/2" size, 1-10 12K GF, with a NASA part number of "SEB12100033-201" and serial number of "60" printed on the right earpiece. These sunglasses were worn by Cernan during the final mission to the moon in December 1972. From the personal collection of Captain Gene Cernan accompanied by written authentication by Cernan. **$20,315**

Apollo 14, Lunar Module-Flown Portable Utility Light as presented by Mission Commander Alan Shepard to Support Crew Member William Pogue. Portable light of approximately 2 1/4" x 2 1/4" x 1 1/2" plus mounting bracket and attached coiled electrical cord. The light is accompanied by a signed ASF Certificate of Authenticity from Edgar Mitchell. **$20,315**

Original Russian Sokol Spacesuit, Sokol (Falcon) Type KV-1 or KV-2 as manufactured by the Zvezda company. **$17,925**

Apollo 8-Flown, Unopened Bottle of Coronet Brandy from the personal collection of Mission Command Module Pilot James Lovell. A two-ounce, still-sealed bottle of Coronet VSQ California Grape Brandy, 100 proof, that was included in Lovell's holiday dinner aboard the Apollo 8 spacecraft during its historic journey on Christmas 1968. The second signed letter of authenticity from Lovell on his letterhead states: "I hereby certify that this bottle of brandy was part of the Christmas Day dinner on board the Apollo 8 spacecraft. Apollo 8 circled the moon on December 25, 1968. This bottle of brandy is from my personal collection of space artifacts and has been in my possession since the mission." **$17,925**

Apollo 13-Flown, Pair of "Booties" from the personal collection of Mission Commander James Lovell. This lot includes a signed letter of authenticity from Lovell stating, "[These] Internal flight suit beta cloth booties - worn during flight of Apollo 13 [were] flown on board the Apollo 13 Command Module Odyssey during its perilous flight around the moon April 11-17, 1970." **$17,925**

Apollo 17, Lunar Module-Flown Commander's Armrest signed by and from the personal collection of Mission Commander Gene Cernan. This metal, right-side armrest has overall dimensions of 7 1/4" x 10 3/4" x 7" including brackets. There is a label on the top, "Pull Down Armrest to Release From Stowed Position", around which Cernan has certified and signed: "LM CDR Arm Rest - LM/ Flown as part of Apollo XVII Lunar Module Challenger Gene Cernan." $14,340

Apollo 17, Lunar Module-Flown LM Water Gun and Filter from the personal collection of Mission Commander Gene Cernan. This was used aboard the Lunar Module Challenger during three days on the surface of the moon, allowing astronauts Gene Cernan and Harrison Schmitt to drink clean water and to prepare their meals. Certified and signed by Cernan: "Flown to the Lunar Surface on Apollo XVII Gene Cernan." $14,340

Apollo 11, Lunar Landing Astronauts signed photograph. Official NASA photograph of the Apollo 11 lunar landing signed "Buzz Aldrin" and "Neil Armstrong", 9 3/4" x 8", April 22, 1983. $13,145

Apollo 17-Flown, Beta Cloth Lunar Module Astronaut Preference Kit belonging to Apollo 17 Commander Gene Cernan. An off-white bag of approximately 4" x 8" x 1 1/2" with a drawstring top and original red wax seal. From the personal collection of Captain Gene Cernan accompanied by written authentication by Cernan. $11,950

Apollo 8-Flown, Flashlight from the personal collection of Mission Command Module Pilot James Lovell. A heavy, brass-milled two-cell flashlight, 5" in length and with a maximum diameter of 1". The original batteries are still inside. Includes a signed letter of authenticity from Lovell on his letterhead. $10,157

Apollo 16, Lunar Module-Flown Mechanical Pencil directly from the personal collection of Mission Commander John Young. Includes a signed letter of certification from John Young. $10,157

Apollo 16, Lunar Module-Flown Engraved Spoon, directly from the personal collection of Mission Commander John Young. Engraved on the handle. Letter of certification from John Young included. $10,157

Apollo 12, Lunar Module-Flown Paperweight with Lunar Surface Experiments Package Emblem. The Apollo Lunar Surface Experiments Package (ALSEP) comprised a set of scientific instruments placed by the astronauts at the landing site of each of the five Apollo Moon missions following Apollo 11 (Apollos 12, 14, 15, 16, and 17). Designed and built by Bendix Aerospace of Ann Arbor, Mich., the instruments were designed to run autonomously after the astronauts left and to make long-term studies of the lunar environment. Bendix designed a number of small silver emblems, depicting an astronaut carrying the ALSEP, to be carried into space and returned for use as mementos. From the collection of Richard Gordon. $9,560

Large Section of Apollo 11-Flown "Kapton Foil", from Buzz Aldrin's personal collection. Measures approximately 8 1/4" x 2". Accompanied by a signed letter of authenticity from him. $8,962

Apollo 16-Flown, Hand Tools (three) directly from the personal collection of Mission Commander John Young. All three of these items flew on Apollo 16 to the moon and back during its 11-day mission, April 16-27, 1972. Includes letter of certification from John Young. $8,962 all

Apollo 17, Command Module-Flown Pan Camera Spring Pin directly from the personal collection of Mission Command Module Pilot Ron Evans, certified. A steel pin 3 3/4" long overall including a 1 1/2" round ring at top, still with its spring action, and engraved "AVDEL PUSH PULL/ MS17990C310". Letter of certification from Jan Evans (Mrs. Ron Evans) included. $8,365

Neil Armstrong, Michael Collins, and Edwin E. Aldrin, Jr. First on the Moon. A Voyage with Neil Armstrong, Michael Collins, Edwin E. Aldrin Jr. Written with Gene Farmer and Dora Jane Hamblin. Epilogue by Arthur C. Clarke. Boston: Little, Brown and Co., (1970). First edition. Inscribed and signed on the half-title page: "To Joseph Sakmyster- With Best Wishes Neil Armstrong", and signed "Buzz Aldrin" and "Michael Collins". Octavo. xiii, 434 pages. Black and white illustrations. Signed certificate of authenticity from Space Coast Cover Service included. $7,767

Apollo 10, Lunar Module-Flown Spotlight and Power Cord. From the personal collection of Captain Gene Cernan accompanied by written authentication by Cernan. $7,767

Apollo 13-Flown, Spacesuit Repair Kit signed by and from the personal collection of Mission Commander James Lovell. This Beta cloth kit with Velcro closures is 6" x 4 3/4" x 1" when folded and 13" x 14" overall when opened out. Lovell has certified and signed the outside front. $7,767

Apollo 17, Command Module-Flown Lunar Orbit Chart "A" signed by and from the personal collection of Mission Commander Gene Cernan. $7,767

Apollo 8-Flown, Mismatched Pair of Cufflinks directly from the personal collection of Mission Command Module Pilot James Lovell. $7,170

Neil Armstrong Color Spacesuit Photo signed but not inscribed, the "smiling" pose. An 8" x 10" NASA lithographed print showing the Apollo 11 Commander, helmet off, in front of a large image of the moon. He has signed boldly in blue felt-tip on his white spacesuit beneath the American flag patch. **$8,365**

Apollo 14, Command Module-Flown Optics Handhold. Once owned by astronaut Stuart Roosa, this piece of the Apollo 14 Command Module Kitty Hawk was presented to a friend as a gift. **$7,170**

Neil Armstrong Autograph Letter, signed "Neil," on right half of photocopy of article, one page, 8 1/2" x 11". From the collection of former physical trainer of the astronauts, Joe Garino. Accompanied by a signed certificate of authentication from Garino verifying its provenance. **$6,573**

Gemini 4-Flown, 1902 U.S. $2.50 Gold Coin originally from the collection of Mission Command Pilot Jim McDivitt, NGC Certified. This gold quarter-eagle was carried along on the Gemini 4 mission, the first U.S. multi-day flight, and the one in which Ed White performed the first American EVA (extra-vehicular activity). **$5,377**

Apollo 16, Lunar and Command Module-Flown Metal Comb used by Charles Duke. It remained on the surface of the moon for almost 72 hours and was exposed to the vacuum of space on each of the three EVAs. From the collection of Charles M. Duke Jr., who has included a handwritten and signed Letter of certification verifying its provenance. **$5,138**

Yuri Gagarin, Inscribed and Signed Photograph. Printed black and white and is inscribed and signed by him in purple ink. **$5,078**

Apollo 16-Flown, Toothbrush with Original Pouch directly from the personal collection of Mission Commander John Young. This was Young's personal toothbrush on man's fifth moon-landing mission, April 16-27, 1972. With signed letter of certification from John Young. **$5,078**

Apollo 14, Command Module Flown American Flag directly from the personal Collection of Mission Lunar Module Pilot Edgar Mitchell, certified and signed. Includes signed letter of certification from Dr. Mitchell on his personal letterhead. **$4,780**

Skylab I (SL-2), Robbins Gold Medallion with Skylab-Flown Emerald directly from the collection of Astronaut Paul Weitz. **$4,780**

Two Apollo 16, Command Module-Flown Freeze Dried Food Packets from the collection of Lunar Module Pilot Charles M. Duke Jr. One packet of four sugar cookie cubes, and one packet of six strawberry cubes. From the collection of Charles M. Duke Jr., with a handwritten letter of certification. **$4,780**

Buzz Aldrin, Signed Lunar Plastic Relief Map Showing the Apollo 11 Landing Site. Dr. Aldrin has signed at the top in the Mare Tranquillatis (Sea of Tranquility): "Apollo XI Landing Site/ Buzz Aldrin." **$4,481**

Roll of 70mm Images from the Apollo 11 Mission, containing dozens of full-color images taken prior to landing on the Moon. This first-generation duplicate was owned by Buzz Aldrin and includes numerous views of the Earth from space, photos of the astronauts, the command module, the lunar module and close-ups of the lunar surface. **$5,676**

Apollo 11, Command Module-Flown Heat Shield Ablater Plugs (14) in Acrylic. Included is a collectSPACE.com statement of provenance. **$4,481**

Neil Armstrong, Buzz Aldrin, Wernher von Braun, and others: Signed 1970 Banquet Program. Approximately 20 signatures total including several of major aeronautic executives. **$4,183**

Apollo 7 Flown Turtle Flag Signed By Wally Schirra, the Imperial Potentate of the Interstellar Association of Turtles. Membership in this group has been sought by other astronauts since the Apollo years. Signed by Wally Schirra. **$3,585**

Apollo 8-Flown, Heat Shield Ablative Plug in Plastic. Likely removed by a technician working on the command module after its return to Earth. **$3,884**

Apollo 11, The First Moon Landing - Group of 33 Original NASA Photographs. From the collection of the former physical trainer of the astronauts, Joe Garino, accompanied by a signed certificate of authentication. **$3,884**

Invitation to attend a Space Shuttle Launch, with STS-1 Pilot Bob Crippen. **$3,585**

Space Shuttle Columbia (STS-3)-Flown Ascent Checklist, with added notations, used by crew members Jack Lousma and Charles G. Fullerton during the March 22-30, 1982, mission. From the collection of Jack Lousma, with handwritten letter of certification. **$3,586**

Neil Armstrong, First Step on the Moon Photo, signed. A 10" x 8" officeal NASA B&W photo, with caption on verso. **$3,346**

Apollo 13-Flown, Custom Communication Ear Plugs from the personal collection of Mission Commander James Lovell. Includes a signed letter of authenticity from Lovell on his letterhead. **$3,107**

Colonel Buzz Aldrin, United States Air Force, Flyer's Summer Coveralls. Worn by Aldrin at a reunion of the 22nd Fighter Squadron, a unit where he flew F-100 Super Sabres as a flight commander. From the personal collection of Dr. Buzz Aldrin and accompanied by a signed letter of authenticity from him. **$3,107**

Apollo 14, Command Module Kittyhawk-Flown Stitched Cloth Mission Emblem. From the collection of Edgar D.

Mitchell, Sc.D., with signed typed letter of certification and a handwritten letter. **$2,987**

Gemini Foldout Desktop Cockpit Control Training Aide, directly from the personal collection of Gemini 3 and 10 Astronaut John Young, certified and signed. **$2,988**

Gemini Program Reentry Control System Thruster, Rocketdyne SE-6. Neil Armstrong fired the RCS thrusters to regain enough command of the spacecraft to make an emergency landing only 10 hours into the mission. **$2,032**

Neil Armstrong Signed Moon Globe, with special notations of all landing sites made by man. **$1,256**

Lunar Receiving Lab Squeegee, he squeegee is accompanied by 2" spring that appears to fit into the hollowed squeegee handle. The spring package bears a NASA tag indicating that it was last "Cleaned for Service" on July 30, 1971, five months after the last astronauts were quarantined in the LRL. **$1,195**

Headset, Pacific Plantronics Spencomm, as used by Apollo and Skylab astronauts. **$1,195**

Neil Armstrong, Signed Baseball, very rare. **$856**

Apollo 17, Crew-Signed Large Color Challenger Photo directly from the collection of Mission Command Module Pilot Ron Evans. Evans took this photo as he inspected the lunar module during the rendezvous before docking. **$837**

Apollo 17, Crew-Signed Large Color "Tracy's Rock" Photo directly from the collection of Mission Command Module Pilot Ron Evans. This rock formation, also known as Split Rock or the Station Six Boulder, was visited and studied by Schmitt and Cernan on their third lunar EVA. Tracy is the name of Gene Cernan's daughter. **$777**

Neil Armstrong "First Man on the Moon" Stamp Sheet, Signed. A full sheet of thirty-two 10-cent U.S. airmail stamps (Scott #C76) signed "Neil Armstrong" at the very edge of the right selvage, just above "Mr. Zip." **$628**

Large Assortment of Astronaut-Signed Christmas Cards, various sizes on card stock. From the collection of former physical trainer of the astronauts, Joe Garino, accompanied by a signed certificate of authentication. **$478**

Gemini Titan-6 First Day Cover, Signed by Schirra and Stafford. Postmarked Dec. 15, 1965, Cape Canaveral, Fla. **$448**

NASA Camera Control Unit, metallic, rectangular cube-shaped device, 4" x 4" x 2 1/2", manufactured by the Mitchell Camera Corp. Two small NASA "Property of U.S. Government" metallic plates affixed. **$287**

Apollo "Snoopy", 1969 Moon Landing Commemorative Medallion. From the collection of former physical trainer of the astronauts, Joe Garino, with a signed certificate of authentication. **$287**

John Young's Personal ID Badge, for the Space Shuttle External Tanks Assembly Plant. Directly from his personal collection, certified and signed. **$287**

Gemini 8 Mission Report, from the estate of Dr. D. Owen Coons, Chief of NASA's Manned Spacecraft Center Medical Office. **$263**

Skylab Oxygen Tank Art, Glass Paperweight by Correia, 3" in diameter, in fitted walnut box. The paperweight is signed on the bottom "Correia" and "1985 Limited Edition WCLSYB 337/1000". **$263**

Sally Ride and Richard Truly, signed photographs. .... **$168 both**

Space-Worn International Space Station Underwear and Socks, made for U.S. astronaut C. Michael Foale. **$155**

1963 Popsicle Space Card #7, The Seven Astronauts. Slabbed by PA Sports and graded EX - MT 6. .... **$96**

Framed Display, of 27 NASA and Space Exploration souvenir patches. .... **$72 set**

First Day Cover, and Color Litho of First Space Shuttle Crew. .... **$72 both**

Alan Shepard and Deke Slayton, Moon Shot: The Inside Story of America's Race to the Moon. Introduction by Neil Armstrong. Atlanta: Turner Publishing, Inc., 1994. First edition. Inscribed and signed by Alan Shepard in black marker on the title page. Octavo. 383 pages. **$54**

Nine Astronaut Signatures, including Charles D. Gemar, Jim Wetherbee, Steve Oswald, Carl Meade, Michael Baker, and Brian Duffy. Each signature is on or near a space related stamp mounted on a 5" x 3" card. **$42**

Apollo 8-Flown, Rotational Controller Handle signed by and from the personal collection of Mission Command Module Pilot James Lovell. A milled aluminum handle, approximately 4 1/2" tall with a black "trigger" and indented finger grips, custom mounted. Includes a signed letter of authenticity from Lovell on his letterhead.
$21,510

SPORTS MEMORABILIA

Baseball

The grading of sports memorabilia, especially baseball cards, has reached such a level of detail that space does not allow for an in-depth discussion of it here. For more information, visit the Web sites of any of the professional grading services.

Also see Autographs, Posters, Toys.

Chicago Americans Giants, circa 1914 panoramic photo including Rube Foster, by Stuart Thompson, a successful commercial photographer in Vancouver, B.C., during the early 1900s. The photograph displays a few insignificant border tears, and a small corner chip in the lower right. Negro League photos dating from the early 1900s are exceedingly rare, especially those picturing prominent clubs and/or players, 16 1/2" x 6 1/2". **$35,250**

Ty Cobb, 1909-1911 T206 card, with "Ty Cobb" back, one of only about 12 known examples. With evenly rounded corners, bright colors and perfect registry. Graded fair, a couple small surface chips of paper loss do not affect Cobb's portrait. On the back is printed: "'Ty Cobb' King of the Smoking Tobacco World/Factory No. 33-4, Dist. of N.C." **$64,625**

Ty Cobb, 1911 M110 Sporting Life cabinet card, pastel artwork of Cobb in a classic batting stance on the front and an advertisement for Sporting Life on the reverse. Bright and clean, both front and back, with bold blue text on the reverse, 5 5/8" x 7 1/2". **$41,125**

Cracker Jack, #144 Series, 1914 E145, complete card set, recognized as one of the most significant of all prewar baseball card issues. Total 145 cards. **$88,125**

George Davis, 1894 N142 Duke cabinet card, advertising Duke's Honest Tobacco brand in the lower left. There are only four ballplayers in this set. Hall of Famer Davis was one of the premier shortstops of his day, and at the time this card was issued he was a member of the New York Giants. The card has some light staining along the right border (common with Dukes), and virtually no wear to the edges and corners. Some light shading on the blank reverse. **$7,050**

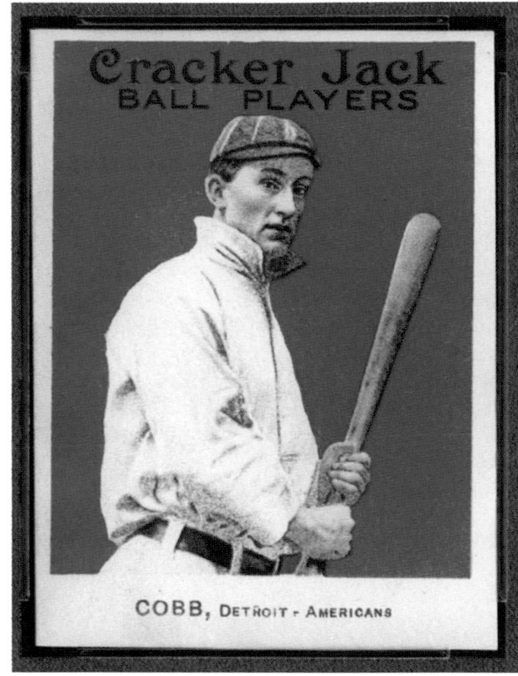

Photo courtesy Robert Edward Auctions, Watchung, N.J.; www.RobertEdwardAuctions.com

Ty Cobb, 1915 E145 Cracker Jack card, #30, pristine, crisp, with flawless registration, sharp corners, no stains. The red color of the background is particularly deep and bold. The reverse is flawless with bold black text. **$15,275**

Photo courtesy Robert Edward Auctions, Watchung, N.J.; www.RobertEdwardAuctions.com

American Tobacco Trust, 1909-1911 T206 White Border cards, near complete, a set assembled with an eye for centering and the overall visual appeal of each card. Extremely high grades, 520 cards. **$176,250**

Bob Feller, 1938 Goudey "Heads-Up" card, #288. Crisp and clean, with virtually perfect registration, a slightly imperfect cut along the top border (detectable only when examined closely from the reverse), four sharp corners with just the slightest hint of wear, bright colors, and a flawless reverse. **$8,225**

Goudey Gum, 1934 near complete set (89 of 96 cards), high grade, including no. 37 and no. 61 Lou Gehrig, and no. 1 Jimmy Foxx. **$64,625**

Walter Johnson, 1909 T204 Ramly Tobacco card, one of the most popular of all 1910-era tobacco issues. The card displays light rounding to the corners, and a hint of minor wear to a few spots on the edges. With 30/70 left to right centering and minor crease in the lower left corner, and a couple of very small areas of toning on the back. **$9,987**

Addie Joss, 1910 D380 Clement Bros. Bakery card, extremely rare. Joss died from meningitis on April 14, 1911, cutting short one of baseball's greatest careers. Clement Bros. cards were issued only in Rochester, N.Y. With rounded corners, no major creases, some light staining, and pencil notations on the reverse. The back of the card features advertising for Clement Bros. bread and pies. **$11,750**

Mike "King" Kelly, 1888 N162 Goodwin Champions, one the key cards from the colorful set of 50, issued by Old Judge and Gypsy Queen Cigarettes. Bright and clean, with flawless colors and perfect registration **$9,400**

Mickey Mantle/Roger Maris, "61 in '61 or Bust" pinback. Several different pin styles were sold by vendors in 1961 commemorating, and cheering on, Mantle's and Maris' race for Ruth's record of 60 home runs in a single season. This style pin is the rarest of all. Excellent to mint condition, 3 1/2" diameter. **$3,525**

Christy Mathewson, 1904 Allegheny Card Co., extremely rare sample card from the Allegheny Card Co. set, featuring New York Giants' young star pitcher, one of Mathewson's earliest cards. Near mint appearance. **$10,575**

Christy Mathewson, 1915 E145 Cracker Jack #88, ultra high-grade example, perfectly centered, with flawless color, a perfect red background, perfect registration, an ideal "rough" Cracker Jack card surface under magnification, bright and clean, both front and back, with sharp corners. **$16,450**

Milligan and Larkin, 1887 N690 Kalamazoo Bats, Athletics, high-grade double-player pose Kalamazoo Bats tobacco card featuring catcher Jocko Milligan tagging out left fielder Henry Larkin. With misplaced canopy that covers only 70 percent of the background, accidentally exposing the wood slats that support the canopy and the cinder blocks of the building in the immediate background. The result is one of the most amusing and ridiculous photographs to appear on a 19th-century baseball card. **$17,625**

Stan Musial, 1953 St. Louis Cardinals game-used road jersey, gray zipper-front features the team name "Cardinals" embroidered on the front, above which is displayed the club's distinctive logo of two cardinals perched upon a bat. The number "6" is appliquéed on the reverse in red on navy felt. Both the name, "Musial," and the year, "53," are chain-stitched in red along the left front tail. Situated in the collar are a "Rawlings" label and an adjacent "44" size tag. Musial has inscribed the jersey, "Stan 'The Man' Musial" on

Photo courtesy Robert Edward Auctions, Watchung, N.J.; www.RobertEdwardAuctions.com

Mickey Mantle, 1952 Topps card, #311, ultra high-grade example, pack-fresh example with brilliant colors. The deep blue background, which is so prone to wear, is exceptionally strong. The white interlocking "NY" on the front of Mickey's cap contrasts sharply against the dark navy blue of his cap. The corners are strong and sharp. Centered 70/30 left to right and 50/50 top and bottom. Mantle's most celebrated card. **$35,250**

Photo courtesy Grey Flannel Auctions, Westhampton Beach, N.Y.; www.greyflannelauctions.com

From 1952, the earliest known Mickey Mantle game used New York Yankees home jersey. **$188,318**

Photo courtesy Robert Edward Auctions, Watchung, N.J.; www.RobertEdwardAuctions.com

Babe Ruth, 1933 R306 Butter Cream Confectionery card, only one other example known to exist, but its whereabouts is a mystery. **$111,625**

the front, below which he has added his batting statistics for 1953, "Avg 337 30 HRs 113 RB's." The jersey is completely original, with no alterations, and displays moderate wear throughout. **$44,062**

Jackie Robinson, 1951 Brooklyn Dodgers game-used home jersey. **$341,779**

Alex Rodriguez, autographed 1994 Seattle Mariners rookie alternate jersey. **$29,881**

Babe Ruth, 1915 M101-5 Sporting News #151 Rookie card. Ruth had only pitched in four games with Boston in 1915 but impressed the card manufacturer enough to warrant inclusion in this issue. Near mint example. **$44,062**

Babe Ruth, 1939-1943 signed sepia Hall of Fame postcard, the first such plaque postcard set issued. Inscribed "Sincerely Babe Ruth" in black fountain pen. Sepia Hall of Fame postcards were issued in two types. The first, designated "Type-1," was issued just prior to the opening of the Hall of Fame in 1939, while "Type-2" cards (this example) were issued shortly after the dedication. The card displays a small amount of paper residue in the corners of the reverse from having once been mounted in a scrapbook album. **$44,062**

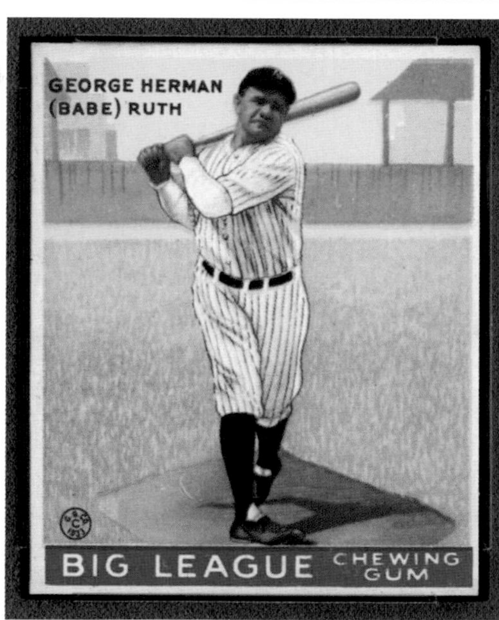

Photo courtesy Robert Edward Auctions, Watchung, N.J.; www.RobertEdwardAuctions.com

Babe Ruth, 1933 R319 Goudey #144, featuring the Babe in his classic follow-through batting pose. Four square corners with white borders and flawless colors; Ruth's image is centered slightly towards the bottom right. Crisp and clean, both front and back, with a boldly printed reverse. **$23,500**

Photo courtesy Robert Edward Auctions, Watchung, N.J.; www.RobertEdwardAuctions.com

Babe Ruth, 1914 Baltimore News rookie card. Ruth just happened to be with the Baltimore Orioles in 1914, as a complete unknown, when the Baltimore News issued the card set that included him. **$517,250**

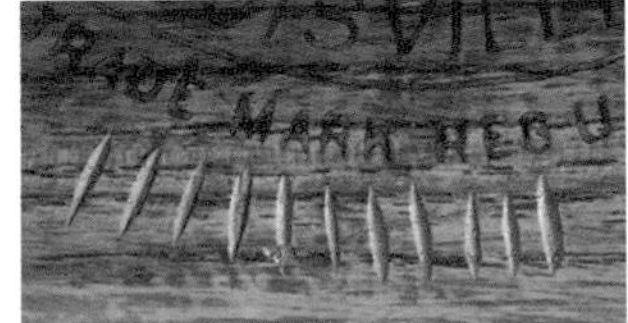

Photo courtesy Grey Flannel Auctions, Westhampton Beach, N.Y.; www.greyflannelauctions.com

Babe Ruth's bat from the 1926-1929 period, into which he carved 11 notches to represent 11 home runs. **$155,628**

Photo courtesy Robert Edward Auctions, Watchung, N.J.; www.RobertEdwardAuctions.com

Honus Wagner, 1904 "Our Protection Against Loss" pinback, issued by a Pittsburgh insurance firm, the Commercial Oldest Accident Co. Only three known. The back paper is missing, there is rust on the reverse, and some foxing along the perimeter, 1 1/4" diameter. **$4,406**

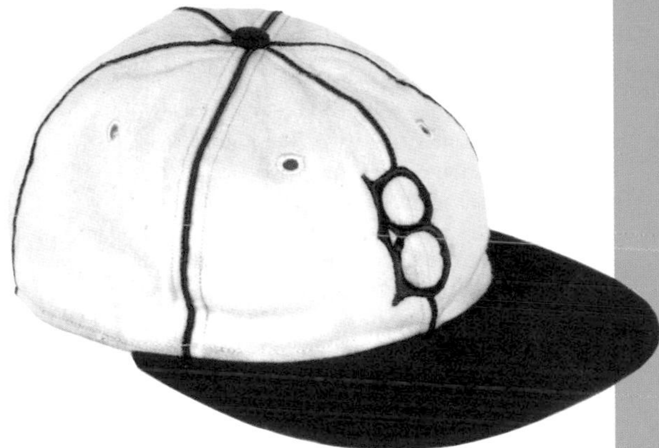

Photo courtesy Robert Edward Auctions, Watchung, N.J.; www.RobertEdwardAuctions.com

Babe Ruth, 1938 Brooklyn Dodgers game-used cap, accompanied by two non-vintage black-and-white photos (each 10" x 8") of Ruth as a coach with the Dodgers in which he is shown wearing an identical-style cap (possibly this very one). The first of these photos pictures Ruth sitting in the dugout with Larry MacPhail, while the second captures him standing next to the grandstand as he poses with his wife and daughter. **$70,500**

Casey Stengel, 1910 T210 Red Border Old Mill Tobacco, shows Stengel as an outfielder with Maysville of the Blue Grass League at the beginning of his career. Bright and clean, with consistent, even wear on the corners (predominately the upper and lower left), fairly well centered (approximately 60/40 left to right), and with virtually no chipping to the fragile red borders. The front of the card has a hairline surface crease to Stengel's right (running from his shoulder to the upper left corner), and a similar surface crease in the lower right edge. The reverse has a few scattered spots. **$41,125**

Jim Thorpe, 1916 M101-5 Sporting News #176. M101-5 cards have a glossy coated surface, susceptible to creasing. This card has no creases. The front is bright and clean. The image is crisp and has perfect contrast. The corners are sharp. The card is centered approximately 70/30 left to right. The blank back is clean with a hint of toning and two tiny pinpoint chips of paper loss on the extreme edge of the top and left borders. **$41,125**

TEXTILES

Including coverlets, embroidery, needlework, quilts, samplers, tapestries, rugs and carpets.

Coverlets

Beiderwand, William Ney, Meyerstown, Lebanon County, Pa., mid-19th century, woven red, white, green and blue wool, and cotton, one-piece coverlet with central sunburst medallion with eight-point star surrounded by eagles and stars, and borders with bird, scroll, leaf, lyre and cornucopia motifs, fringed on three edges, the bottom border with inscriptions "MADE BY WM. NEY MEYERSTOWN LEBANON CO. PA.," 86 x 90", about a 2" x 1/2" irregular shaped area of fairly unobtrusive light brown stain in center field area, fringe is good. **$1,007**

Blue and white checked, some loose seams where panels are sewn together, 79" x 82". **$57**

Brown square and geometric decoration, on off-white ground; 96" x 72", slight tear on one edge. **$172**

Jacquard, blue and white woven wool and cotton, American, 1839, two-piece double cloth weave coverlet, the center field with rows of vase and flower designs and medallions with hearts bordered on three sides with spread-wing eagles with shields and arrows, the corner blocks inscribed "SUSAN THOMPKINS WOVE IN 1839," 92" x 78", approx. 1" x 1" loss on top right corner (not corner block), one side is longer (stretched, sagged, or woven looser) than the other. **$385**

Jacquard, Bucks County, Pa., at one corner: "M. K./ Springfi/ eld: To/ Bucks: co./1843", field with eagles, flowers and geometric decoration in salmon, dark blue, and mustard, 82" x 92". **$360**

Jacquard, Fayette County, Ind., circa 1841, double lily and medallion form coverlet with cutters, oak tree and quail border, two corner panels signed "Woven in Fayette Co Indiana 1841", 7' 1" x 5' 9", minimal discoloration to fringe and outer edges. **$1,150**

Jacquard, marked "Woven by/Henry O./Overholt/1841/For_ __", stylized flowers, acorns and leafage in dark blue and red on white ground, 87" x 70". **$690**

Jacquard, Pennsylvania, at one corner, "This/Coverlet/ Belongs/To/ Catherine?Diehl/1844"; field with stylized rosettes, tulips and roosters, at another corner: "S. B. Mus/ selman/ Coverlet/Weaver/Milford./ Bucks. Co/ No 473". All in red, green, and black; repetition of "Pennsylvania" in border, 80" x 88". **$600**

Embroidery, Needlework

Crewelwork panel, by Mary Balentine, western Massachusetts, 18th century, the panel with shaped hem probably a valance from a set of bed hangings, worked in polychrome wool yarns in a curvilinear floral and fruit design on a natural-colored linen ground, accompanied by an old typed exhibition card reading, "Sheffield 1733-1933/ Loaned by Mary A. Durlack/Piece of valence embroidered

Photos courtesy Heritage Auction Galleries, Dallas; www.HA.com

Pair of Framed Silk Needlework Pictures, unknown artist, French, late 18th century, colored silk, 13 1/2" x 14 1/2" each (sight). Woven with gold background featuring a maiden playing the flute and the other a maiden carrying a basket amongst landscape. Normal signs of wear as appropriate with age, framed. **$657 pair**

Abraham Lincoln Memorial Sampler in the Original Frame. The printed pattern was sold commercially. The quote "Malice Toward None, Charity for All" is from Lincoln's second inaugural address. Undated, this sampler could have been produced as early as the mourning period following his 1865 assassination, but the style suggests dating more in the range of the 1876 Centennial. Excellent condition, 23 1/4" x 11". **$388**

Photo courtesy Heritage Auction Galleries, Dallas; www.HA.com

by Mary Balentine who married General John Ashley," toning, minor spots, 11 1/2" x 81". **$5,036**

Floral, blue vase of flowers, signed beneath "Hannah R. Knight 1837"; encircling leafy vine with tulips and other flowers, off-white ground, 23 1/4" x 23 1/4" (sight), some discoloration, maple frame. **$1,725**

Newcomb College, square table scarf (very rare) embroidered with stylized trees in amber and green, excellent original condition, unmarked, 15" x 15 1/4". **$7,200**

Picture, needlework with watercolor, two women holding lower branches of tree, third woman sitting at base of tree with lamb, house in left middle distance, 17 1/4" x 20 1/2", some damage to face of middle woman and damage to leafage near her; some rippling to paper, gilt frame. **$360**

Show towel, framed, Bucks County, Pa., needlework with spread-wing American eagle with stylized emblems in red, white and blue above "Mary Fretz/1847"; other birds, trees and flowers below; tassels at bottom, 49" x 16" (sight); bird's eye maple frame. **$1,955**

Show towel, framed Ott Family tree, Bucks County, Pa., headed by "MO"; "Elias Ott" with "1840" below; "Fredercik/ Ott born/Nov. 10-1782/Eve Ott born March 26-1781" with other Otts following; asymmetrical group of stylized flowering trees in multicolors; at bottom: "Mary Ott of Bedminster Made/This Needlework Anno Domini/1844"; 47" x 13 3/4" (sight), bird's eye maple frame. **$5,750**

Silk embroidery, of three figures under tree, two women and man nearby, 8" h, 6 1/8" w (sight). **$149**

Samplers

Hannah Bainbridge, alphabet at top, Tree of Knowledge with Adam and Eve at base; inscribed "Be/thou fait/h full unto death/and I will give thee a/crown of life"; stylized flowers and urns of flowers flanking, 10 3/4" x 8 1/4" (sight); signed lower left and right; bird's-eye maple and rosewood frame. **$1,265**

Keziah Jeffs, Mrs. Wetherells School, Byfield (Mass.), dated 1821, executed in a variety of green, blue, pink, and brown stitching on a cream linen ground with a central panel of floral-filled urns, stylized pine trees, perched birds and dogs beneath lines of alphabet and pious verse, all above the third panel wrought with pious verses centering a tree flanked by floral-filled baskets within a border of scrolling floral vinery. Signed at bottom, "Keziah Jeffs aged 12 years November 16 1820 Wrought this sampler at Mrs Wetherells School Byfield May 21 1821." Sight: 13 1/2" x 12", some staining and minor weakness in edges, some small holes in ground. Mounted in a later frame. **$2,300**

Susan Magill, silk needlework with an invocation to Jesus, framed by a running border of flowers, mounted on gold foil and in wooden frame, 19th century, signed at the bottom "Susan Magill Newtown 1819," 11 1/2" x 9 1/2". **$1,140**

Ann Catherine Streeper, seven-line passage begins: "Jesus permit thy sacred name to stand ...", green and yellow flowering trees, birds flanking tree; "Ann Catherine Streeper the daughter/Of Leanord Streeper & Sarah his Whife/Was born September the Ninth in the/Year One thousand eight hundred & 25"; birds in reeds below, followed by: "Ann Catherine Streper her work/In the 13 year of her age in the year 1838"; flowering vine border on three sides, 16 5/8" x 15 1/2" (sight). **$1,150**

Sophia Swartz, alphabet sampler, the bottom centered by a vase with flowers and a bird on a tree branch, the number 4 and ducks on either side, unframed, 19th century, signed and dated "Sophia 83 Swartz," 16 1/2" x 16 1/2". **$510**

Elizabeth Ulrick, alphabet and numerals, prose passage and "Elizabeth Ulrick 1806"; pair of birds at basket; "A rural walk in Statehouse yard"; stylized green and white flowering vine border, 20 5/8" x 15 5/8" (sight), brown letters in passage faded. **$1,610**

Tapestries

Louis Phillipe scenic tapestry, circa 1850-1860, depicting a formal garden landscape within a cartouche bordered by columns and urns beneath a foliate arch on a salmon ground. Various animals and a shepherd incorporated in scene. Whole within a border of flower heads and S-scrolls, 5' 5" x 4' 5", showing minimal and acceptable wear and fading. **$1,725**

Five tapestry seat coverings, 19th Century, one having a fox in landscape, another a deer in landscape, two with a shepherdess, another with a boy walking to school, varying from 17" x 15" to 25" x 27", some discoloration, tears and uneven edges. **$460 all**

Quilts

Album, pieced and appliquéd cotton, American, circa 1865, composed of 42 blocks appliquéd with flower, basket, leaf, heart, sun and moon, bird and geometric designs in solid and printed cotton fabrics on a white cotton ground, many blocks signed or stitched with the initials of the maker, one square indistinctly dated 1861 or 1867, edged and backed in white cotton, 79" x 67", several areas of light brownish stains, one square has some wool fabric with a few moth holes. **$1,125**

Album (top), pieced and appliquéd cotton, America, circa 1871, composed of 25 diamond and 21 triangle segments decorated with appliquéd and embroidered solid and printed cotton motifs including flowers, leaves fruit, Masonic emblem, shield and paisley, many squares signed by the makers, one dated 1871, edged in red cotton, 80 1/2" x 81", some of the ink signatures have run, the center diamond has a needlepoint floral design done in wool yarns and some of the stitches are missing. **$592**

American eagle, mid-19th century, appliquéd and patchwork, eagle within an oval bellflower and egg floral cartouche within a rectangular border, the whole within scrolled flowering vines. Quilted in tomato red, green and yellow calico on a cream ground, 7' 10" x 6' 7", minimal small stains in outer border. **$460**

Amish, broad open blue field with green border, 80" x 80". **$115**

Amish, repeating pink tree emblems, purple border, green ground, 81" x 81". **$258**

Cotton chintz, American, early to mid-19th century, five-piece whole cloth quilt, the bottom corners removed to fit a four-poster bed, one side of the quilt is a polychrome roller-printed woven cotton fabric in a pheasant and palm tree design, the other side is roller-printed in a red and white flower and leaf design, woven braid binding, 107" x 124". **$888**

Friendship, 30 patchwork squares with small red and yellow patterned squares, centering off-white square in each center with signature and date: "Abraham Rohn/1861," "Susan

Photo courtesy James D. Julia Auctioneers, Fairfield, Maine; www.JuliaAuctions.com

Baltimore album, Captain Hosea C. Wyman, Civil War motif, decorated with fourteen border square panels, a large central panel with two squares below. Central large panel having a five-pointed blue star with inner white and red star. Between the upper two points is a red, white and blue American shield with owner's name "Capt. HC Wyman" and "Baltimore M.D 1863". Right side with an American flag having star-shaped field, four stars in corners. Left of American flag having crossed cannons with cannon balls. Below star on left is a displayed red eagle with blue banner in beak. Right side with a large red anchor with blue chain. Below this panel are two square panels, one with orange pot of flowers and cornucopias, the other red and yellow tulips with green leaves. Outside panels include four wreaths of red and yellow tulips; panel with rust-colored house, birds on fence and flowers signed "A.B.H."; another panel with spread wing eagle holding flowering branch with decorative banner above; another panel with colorful cornucopia of fruit and flowers; panel with red flowers and birds; panel with golden urn with flower vine; another with a green leaf heart with red dots; panel with stylized sheaf of wheat in green, yellow and red; panel with opposing green and red leaves; panel with a fruit tree with red fruit and yellow birds; and a panel with a spray of red green stemmed flowers. Appliqué work on white linen with no quilting, bound at edges with a center stitched linen backing. Colors are bright and vivid, 81" h x 64" w. Light stains to front, some minor imperfections and some additional water stains on reverse. **$13,800**

Photo courtesy James D. Julia Auctioneers, Fairfield, Maine; www.JuliaAuctions.com

Lone Star Quilt With Dark Blue Background, Lancaster County, Pa. Circa 1875. Maker unknown. With eight satellite stars. The large star is pieced from 17 rows of diamonds (each point has 81 diamonds). All fabrics are solid cottons in cheddar, light yellow, red, light pink, medium blue and indigo blue. The background is a dark blue. The large red border has inner border of triangles in light yellow, light pink, cheddar and red. Hand quilted with eight stitches per inch, outlined 1/8" from seams of diamonds. Background is quilted in a hanging grid; large border has a triple cable. Quilt has a thin cotton batting, a hand-sewn light pink binding, and a large turkey-red paisley cotton print back. 82" x 84". **$3,162**

Photo courtesy James D. Julia Auctioneers, Fairfield, Maine; www.JuliaAuctions.com

Four-Block Appliqué Quilt With Eagles And Roses Border, Southeast Pennsylvania. Dated 1856. Maker unknown. Construction of quilt is four 33" appliquéd blocks in center with 13 1/2" border. Appliqué blocks have intertwined stems with flowers and pomegranates. Each block has three tiny birds appliquéd on the vines. In the center is a star surrounded by four butterflies. Border has eight (displayed) eagles with shields above crossed (laurel) leaves. Center of each border has quarter-moon shape appliqué, with bouquets of roses in the corners. Quilted in white thread at 12 stitches per inch. All appliqué shapes are outlined in the background, veins quilted on large leaves. Background quilted with various small motifs including pineapples, scissors, flowers, stars, leaves, crossed spoons, pitchers and many hearts. One border with the initials "LH" and "SAH" quilted on either side of the moon shape, with the date "1856" above the moon and intertwined hearts below it. Two houses are quilted in the center near the star. Fabric is all solid cottons in green, turkey red, yellow, cheddar and blue (in the shields). Batting is thin cotton, white matching front. Edge finish is a separate 1/4" green binding, hand applied. 94" x 94 1/2". Faded. Stains throughout. **$2,587**

Charles/1861," "Cordelia Charles/1861," etc., 83" x 94". **$632**

Hawaiian, "The Comb of Kaiulana," circa 1850, wrought with a combination of eight-rayed combs and crowns within a stylized lei of leaves, with waffle quilting, 6' 1 1/2" x 6', with staining. **$2,300**

Oak Leaf and Flower, pieced and appliquéd cotton, American, late 19th century, with nine squares composed of four oak leaves alternating with fan-shaped flower blossoms, both surrounding a flower blossom, enclosed in an undulating flower bud and leaf vine, the motifs in red and green printed cotton on a white ground, edged and backed in white cotton, with outline and diagonal line quilting, 86" x 71", light stains, toning. **$385**

Pieced wool, American, early 20th century, with 35 squares set on point with four two-color stylized tulip blossoms on an off-white ground alternating with light blue squares, edged in red silk binding, off-white woven wool backing, with outline, grid, grape cluster and stylized flower blossom quilting stitches, 92" x 70", losses to edging and wool fabric around edges. **$592**

Thistle and Oak Leaf, Augusta County, Va., third quarter 19th century, the pattern repeated nine times with a diamond quilted border separating the blocks, dramatic swag and tulip border, green printed edging, each block with vine and leaf quilting, 77 1/2" x 84 1/2", small spots of fabric deterioration and some light spotting. **$2,090**

Urn of Flowers, pieced and appliquéd cotton, American, late 19th century, composed of four large squares with an urn issuing several flower stalks bordered by carnation blossoms and leaves in solid red and green cotton fabric, some motifs embroidered with blanket stitching, the quilt edged and backed with white cotton and quilted in outline and chevron stitches, 82" x 79", some light moisture stains showing mainly on the reverse. **$2,370**

Carpets and Rugs

Hooked

Though many have a folk-art flavor, hooked rugs were also created from popular patterns in the late 19th and early 20th centuries.

Hooked rug, wool and cotton, American, early 20th century, depicting a man and woman in the pursuit of romance, with the hooked inscription: "Take Oh! Take Those Lips Away!", mounted on a wooden frame, 33" x 50", fading, toning, scattered edge losses. **$1,303**

Hooked rug, wool and cotton, with a squirrel, American, early 20th century, mounted on a wooden frame, 20 3/4" x 41", minor wear, fading. **$503**

Hooked rug, wool and cotton, geometric, American, early 20th century, centered with a diamond pattern with square/triangle borders, bound with cotton twill tape, toning, 69" x 43". **$1,125**

Hooked rug, wool, geometric, American, early 20th century, with square/diamond optical illusion field with striped border, 30" x 61". **$770**

Hooked rug, wool yarn, with houses in a landscape, American, early 20th century, mounted on a wood frame, 23 1/2" x 40 1/4", couple small dark stains, small yarn loss within orange yarn-repaired area on foreground house. **$770**

Hooked rug, Pied Piper, colorful and graphic, mounted on wood stretcher, 43 1/2" w x 25 1/2" h. **$575**

Hooked rug, with vignettes of birds and plants, all in earth tone colors with black border, 51" x approx. 60", overall scattered damage and deterioration. **$172**

Penny rug, wool, American, late 19th/early 20th century, composed of concentric discs of multicolored wool fabric edged with blanket stitching, arranged and sewn in a diamond pattern, on a woven wool backing, mounted on a wood frame, 24 1/2" x 42 1/2". **$711**

Photo courtesy James D. Julia Auctioneers, Fairfield, Maine; www.JuliaAuctions.com

Hooked rug, 19th century, yarn on burlap in a period frame, heart within a heart with anchor and cross with either side being decorated with a flowering vine. Initialed at the top "HH" and signed "Mary" and dated below "1880". The small heart in a deep blood-red coloration with the larger heart on the exterior a lighter red, the overall rug in various earth tones. Rug only, 24 1/2" w x 20" h. **$3,335**

Photo courtesy James D. Julia Auctioneers, Fairfield, Maine; www.JuliaAuctions.com

Hooked rug, starfish, first quarter of the 20th Century, woven with rows of polychrome striped squares alternating with squares depicting starfish/five petal flowers, mounted on a museum frame, 74" x 71". **$1,380**

Oriental Rugs

An authentic oriental rug or carpet is handmade, either knotted with pile or woven without pile. These rugs normally come from a broad geographical region extending from China and Vietnam in the east, to Turkey and Iran in the west, and from the Caucasus in the north to India in the south.

Bokhara, Afghanistan, with four rows of six indigo and madder red gulls on a madder red field within a lattice work and dog tooth border, 9'3" x 8'3", overall wear. **$632**

Caucasian carpet, with geometric design and alternating panels of people and animals; blue ground with yellow, green and gray, 19th/20th century, Low pile with small losses on end borders, 61" x 41 1/2". **$1,560**

Heriz, Northwest Persia, dense geometric lattice work vinery on a rose pink ground with saw tooth edge within a deep indigo guard border of stylized polychrome flower heads, 10' 1" x 7' 6", fading and discoloration throughout one quarter of end. **$1,150**

Heriz, North Persia, circa 1900, polychrome stylistic geometric latticework on a madder red field within a deep indigo main border of geometric flower heads, 10' 3" x 7', nearly full pile, ends and edges intact, some moth damage evident in corners and edges. **$1,840**

Heriz, Northwest Persia, first quarter 20th century, indigo angular central medallion within the madder red field filled with polychrome devices centered by ivory spandrels, within the midnight-blue main border of geometric latticework, 11' 7" x 8' 6", overall general wear, losses to ends (selvage). **$345**

Isfahan prayer rug, Persia, two trees with birds centered by a vase with emerging flowers underneath a blue niche and two reserves with calligraphy, 19th/20th century, 6' 2" x 4' 5". **$1,800**

Kilim, runner, Iran, first half 20th century, typical form, comprised of a series of joined rectangular panels, each of differing geometric design. Woven in shades of red, brown, blue and cream, 9' 3" x 2' 2", minor separation of panels, minor rolling at one end. **$230**

Kuba Caucasian rug, in Lesghi star design in reds, blues, and ivory. Some wear, 3' 4" x 5' 3". **$600**

Runner, Northwest Persia, central ivory scarab medallion on a midnight-blue field with dense polychrome flower heads and vinery within an ivory border of geometric designs, 10' x 3' 1". **$460**

Sarouk, Central Persia, first quarter 20th century, indigo floral polled medallion within a wine field with scrolling polychrome floral vinery centered by turquoise spandrels, the whole within a deep indigo main border of profusely scrolling vinery and flower heads, 17' 8" x 12'. **$8,338**

Sarouk carpet, with a floral field on a rose ground and various borders, 20th century, 12' x 8' 10". **$1,140**

Photo courtesy James D. Julia Auctioneers, Fairfield, Maine; www.JuliaAuctions.com

Angelis, Central Persia, circa 1910-1920, central oversized stepped medallion on a blue-black field with a grouping of nine polychrome herati design set on a madder red field with similar herati, all within a triple-stripe border, 6' 6" x 4' 5", normal wear. **$1,150**

Savonnerie carpet, with diagonal quatrefoil in ivory and caramel tones, framed by a red band and shell and leaf motif on each corner, 20th century, 18' 5" x 7' 5". **$1,140**

Collector's Note: Savonnerie is a French pile floor covering, usually large, whether made at the Savonnerie workshop or made in that manner and style. The Savonnerie factory (on the site of a former soap factory, hence the name) was established in Paris in 1627 at the Hospice de la Savonnerie at Chaillot by royal order, to provide pile carpets for use in the king's palaces and as royal gifts. The patterns are floral and architectural Renaissance conceptions, many based upon paintings and cartoons.

Tabriz, area rug with ruby red medallion and ivory spandrels, circa 1970, 6' 7" x 9' 10". **$360**

Tabriz, Persian Azerbaijan, early 20th Century, central palmette rose and pale indigo medallion within a deep indigo field of profuse floral vinery centered by pale indigo and rose spandrels, pale indigo dark border with palmettes and latticework vinery, 13' x 8' 3", minimal even wear. **$1,495**

Photo courtesy James D. Julia Auctioneers, Fairfield, Maine; www.JuliaAuctions.com

Dagestan, Northeast Caucasus, five differently colored octagons on a dark blue ground surrounded by a modified Kufic border, dated repeatedly "1313" in the Moslem calendar (1894). Images include saddled horses, birds, running beasts, peacocks, women in tribal dress, strange human figures, a clock telling time, combs signifying cleanliness for prayer, and other wild and diverse symbols, 12' 7" x 5'. **$6,900**

Photo courtesy James D. Julia Auctioneers, Fairfield, Maine; www.JuliaAuctions.com

Lavar Kirman, Southeast Persia, circa 1900, dense polychrome floral vinery interspersed with stylized cypress trees and alternating flowering vases, the central panel forming opposing half medallions within a conforming main border of pink, beige and pale indigo flower heads, all four sides with a burnt orange cartouche in Arabic of poetic couplets, 11' 4" x 8' 1". **$14,375**

Tabriz, Northwest Persia, second quarter of the 20th Century, circular center poled medallion defined by turquoise lotus blossoms centering a floral medallion flanked by lesser urn medallions on a beige ground densely filled with vinery within a scrolling polychrome arabesque border, 18' 11" x 10' 7 1/2", staining on edge, approximately 5 1/2' from end. **$920**

Photo courtesy James D. Julia Auctioneers, Fairfield, Maine; www.JuliaAuctions.com

Serapi, Northwest Persia, first half of the 20th century, large center red medallion with ivory and red field. Wide and thin border. Colors of brown, red, ivory with some blues and greens, 11' 10" x 9' 3", shows wear, some repairs and some small evidence of insect damage, which has been stabilized. **$920**

Tabriz, room-size carpet with a geometric floral pattern on deep red field and indigo medallion, circa 1970, 9' 7" x 12' 10". **$660**

Turkoman prayer rug, Turkmenistan, circa 1900, mihrab center containing four panels of candlestick design, the field with saw-tooth and tarantula latticework within a key and fret border, 4' 8" x 3' 10", minimal wear. **$1,610**

William Morris

William Morris (1834-1896) is the most famous of the Arts & Crafts pioneers and probably the most influential figure involved in 19th-century textile production. Key elements in Morris' designs were inspired by historic textiles that incorporated flowers found in Elizabethan gardens, and in 16th-century embroideries.

William Morris-style carpet, with floral pattern on olive green ground, 10' x 13' 9". **$1,560**

William Morris-style area rug ,with floral pattern on jade green ground, 6' x 9' 3". **$960**

William Morris-style carpet, with a floral pattern and cream border on midnight blue ground, 8' x 10'. **$510**

William Morris-style carpet, with floral and vine pattern in deep jewel tones, 8' 2" x 10". **$840**

William Morris-style carpet, with a floral pattern in rich jewel tones, 8' 10" x 11' 9". **$1,560**

William Morris-style runners, with floral pattern, one on indigo field, the other in greens and sand, 2' 6" x 8' and 2' 6" x 11' 5". .... **$1,200 both**

Photo courtesy Rago Arts and Auction Center, Lambertville, N.J.; www.RagoArts.com

William Morris-style carpet with a floral pattern in amber and dark plum on a black field, 9' 1" x 12' 1". **$660**

Photo courtesy Rago Arts and Auction Center, Lambertville, N.J.; www.RagoArts.com

William Morris-style area rug with floral pattern in jewel tones on a pale celadon field, 5' x 6' 10". **$480**

Tiffany

FUTURE OF THE MARKET: TIFFANY

Collecting Tiffany: Less is more

By Reyne Haines

Unfortunately, there is no crystal ball to see into the future of collecting. Collectors can be fickle and the economy can play a role in what price point people buy, and when. With that said, we can look for trends in any collecting category to help determine what markets have been stable, or volatile.

Stable markets are those that have small, but consistent, increases in value over numerous years. Volatile markets are those that have extreme highs and extreme lows. Something may enter the market at a strong price, only to cool as collecting interests wane.

Since the late 1960s, we can find a "trend" in collecting all things Tiffany. Over the last 40+ years, there has been a continued increase in value, be it 5-10 percent a year. Some types of Tiffany have increased in value in a shorter period of time. Most of these areas had little initial interest from Tiffany enthusiasts. However, as the price to obtain a piece of work by Tiffany increased, the lower-end Tiffany markets became more desirable.

Reyne Haines

My two biggest recommendations for collecting anything are 1) only buy what you like, you can never go wrong. If you buy something on speculation, and the market for such an item fades, not only does everyone else not want it, but neither do you. 2) When you find an area of collecting you do like, buy the best you can buy within your budget. In simpler terms, less is more. Buy one higher-end piece, instead of three lower-ends that equal the same price as the more expensive one. In a bad economy, the higher-end things will always sell. That market is rarely affected by economic woes. The lower to middle-of-the-road collectors tend to hold on to their money during tough times.

For many years, fine art and antiques have been a place for investors to "park" their money. A solid collection – or even a single quality piece – has often shown to increase in value at a stronger rate than that of the stock market. With that said, here are my recommendations for what to buy in the wonderful world of Louis Comfort Tiffany:

Leaded Windows: One of the more sizable and pricier categories of Tiffany collecting. While many Tiffany leaded windows sell for six figures or higher, some can still be bought on the more limited budget. Windows with religious fig-

Photo courtesy James D. Julia Auctioneers, Fairfield, Maine; www.JuliaAuctions.com

Tiffany Studios Abalone Frame. Calendar-style bronze frame in the Abalone pattern with gold finish. Tiffany originally created this design to represent a grape pattern and used the abalone disc to form the design. Signed on the underside "Tiffany Studios New York 1166". 6 1/2" x 5 3/4". Opening: 3 1/4" x 2 1/4" h. One abalone disc missing. **$1,680**

Photo courtesy James D. Julia Auctioneers, Fairfield, Maine; www.JuliaAuctions.com

Tiffany Studios Blown-Glass Candelabra. Six-arm candelabra is made of bronze and has patina finish of brown with hints of green and red. From the oval-shaped platform base arises a single center stem with three candle cups on either side. Each of these candle cups has green blown-glass ornamentation and a bobeche. In the center stem of the candlestick rests a Tiffany snuffer that is concealed when in place. Signed on the underside "Tiffany Studios New York 1648". 15" x 21". One tight hairline to blown glass and one blown glass insert is slightly different color. **$6,900**

ures or dedications were often used in churches and seem to have been all but forgotten in the Tiffany community. Perhaps an untapped market?

Lighting: Lamps, stalactites and sconces have long been a staple with Tiffany enthusiasts. The values range from the low end of a few thousand dollars to top-of-the-line at a few million. Beginning collectors should start with a desk lamp, but pursue a more rare, colored shade, or more unique base. Gold damascenes, while attractive, are the more common in the color shades. Watch for a blue or green damascene shades instead.

With leaded lamps, there are numerous factors that determine value and desirability. The first is the size and design of the shade. Is the shade common or not? Floral designs tend to be more desirable than geometric shades. The color and type of glass is another factor. You can have two identical patterned lamps, one being monochromatic, while the other is vibrant with color. This would create a dramatic difference in value. Usually (but not always), the more colorful the shade, the pricier it is.

When buyers went to Tiffany Studios to purchase a lamp for their homes, not only could they choose the style of shade they wanted and the colors, but also the type of base they wanted it to go on. Some bases were simple in design; some were more ornate. They also came in a few different patinas.

One of the more important aspects to consider when buying a Tiffany lamp is condition. If you are eyeing a great floral lamp with strong colors and a great base, but it has replacement glass, numerous loose cracks or the patina has been polished, take a moment to reconsider. With these factors in mind, make sure you pay accordingly, and know that they will make the lamp a little tough to sell down the road.

Pottery: A medium many people don't recognize as one made at Tiffany Studios. Tiffany had an interest in pottery, and this should come as no surprise considering the success of other American artists like George Ohr, or that of Newcomb College and Rookwood. While Tiffany had a passion for pottery, it was not one of his more successful ventures. Tiffany pottery was made from 1904 until 1914. It is estimated that around 2,000 pieces were made during that time.

Tiffany's pottery was quite organic in nature. The shapes, designs and glazes often imitate leaves and floral motifs. Numerous pieces can still be found today unglazed. It has been said the pieces were thrown and then left unglazed until purchased so the customer could determine the look they wanted.

This market, while still a little untapped, is gaining interest among Tiffany collectors and art-pottery enthusiasts. When acquiring a piece of Tiffany pottery, the best examples are often glazed in more than one color, or are heavily carved.

Bronze: Collecting Tiffany bronze offers something for everyone, from simple bronze figural paperweights to complete desk sets, cigar stands to planters. The sheer volume of things made in bronze by Tiffany Studios is staggering.

While the paperweights are interesting, they are not an investment-level collectible. There are also a multitude of bronze bowls, plates and compotes readily available for a few hundred dollars each. These will also stay fairly inexpensive in price due to the volume available on the market.

If you like investment-level items that have function, I would recommend collecting one of the desk sets. There are a number of different designs available, but collecting one of the more rare patterns will make finding pieces challenging, and also offer desirability with collectors when the time comes to sell. A few patterns that fall into the "rare"

Photo courtesy James D. Julia Auctioneers, Fairfield, Maine; www.JuliaAuctions.com

Tiffany Studios Grapevine Carriage Clock. Signed "Tiffany & Co." on the face and "Tiffany Studios New York 877" on underside as well as "Made in France" on the mechanism. 5" h. Some crazing lines to the clock face. **$6,900**

category would be Nautilus, Spanish or Enameled.

Tiffany also made a short run of bronze mirrors. They were very Art Nouveau in design, functional and are not often seen on the market.

Finally, there were a variety of inkwells made over the years that were not part of any desk-set series. They sometimes took form as sea life, or were a combination of two media, like glass and bronze. Finding an example can take time, and will often cost considerably more than a desk-set inkwell.

Glass: One of the most diverse categories you can collect. You can build a collection based on shape, color, decoration or period. Collecting glass can be affordable for any budget, starting with tiles selling for as low as $50 each, or a museum-quality aquamarine vase for as much as $500,000.

As with many creations, there are uncommon shapes, colors that are more desirable than others, rare techniques, and exhibition pieces that can greatly increase the value of one piece over another.

Simple gold and blue pieces, while attractive, are readily available on the market and will never increase that substantially in your lifetime. I have heard the argument many times: How one cannot afford a $10,000 piece of glass, but they have 10 pieces valued at $1,000 each in their collection. When collecting for investment, less is more. It is better to have the one highly desirable piece in your collection than a dozen common pieces. When the time comes to sell the collection, the higher-end piece will most often have increased in value faster, and will be easier to sell.

Some of the shapes and techniques recommended when collecting Tiffany glass are:

Floriforms – decorated, not plain, tall with strong color. Weak color can lower the value on what might normally be considered a desirable piece.

Tel el Amarna vases – especially in unusual colors

Engraved and Cameo vases – Cameo glass is often thought of as being a product designed by French artisans, however it was also a technique used in Tiffany glass for several years. Most cameo vases are heavily carved with padded flowers, leaves and grapes.

Agate – These vases came in colors such as blue, olive, tan/brown and were sometimes faceted.

Paperweights - Paperweight vases are quite desirable among collectors. The term "paperweight" essentially means a vase that is cased in an outer layer of clear glass. They are often internally decorated with a variety of colorful flowers and leaves. Some vases offer an iridescent interior, while others do not. Also, you may find some made with reactive glass, which seemingly changes color depending on the light.

Cypriote – Cypriote glass offers an unusual surface made to emulate that of early Roman glass.

Lava – The term best describes the outward appearance of Tiffany lava vases: Dark-colored vessels with a gold "molten lava" overflowing from the mouth of the piece.

One of the most important caveats to remember when collecting Tiffany: There are many reproductions on the market and new ones surface every year. Some are better

Photo courtesy James D. Julia Auctioneers, Fairfield, Maine; www.JuliaAuctions.com

Tiffany Blue Favrile Cabinet Vase. Blue iridescence at the foot shading to platinum iridescence at the shoulder and neck. Signed on the bottom "L.C.T. D3473". 2 1/2" h. minor scratches to iridescence. **$805**

Photo courtesy James D. Julia Auctioneers, Fairfield, Maine; www.JuliaAuctions.com

Tiffany Studios Fireball Lamp. One of two known examples. Exceptional early Tiffany Studios leaded orb shade has flame design in mottled red and orange glass against a textured green and brown swirled background. The flames are made up of numerous types of glass, including heavily rippled to lightly textured, giving the effect of dancing flames when lit. The shade rests atop a bronze saucer base with single socket. Base is finished with rich brown patina with green highlights. Shade and base are unsigned. Shade is 12" diameter. Overall 15" h. Few tight hairlines. **$48,875**

than others. Until you have spent a good deal of time learning the difference between what is new and what is old, my strongest recommendation is to buy from a dealer you know and trust.

Reyne Haines, co-owner and founder of www.JustGlass.com, is a regular appraiser on PBS' *Antiques Roadshow*. She is the author of *The Art of Glass: The Collection from the Dayton Art Institute* and has contributed to numerous books and articles on collecting.

Louis Comfort Tiffany (1849-1934) established a glass house in 1878 primarily to make stained-glass windows. In 1890, in order to utilize surplus materials at the plant, Tiffany began to design and produce "small glass," such as iridescent glass lampshades, vases, stemware and tableware in the Art Nouveau manner. Commercial production began in 1896. Tiffany developed a unique type of colored iridescent glass called Favrile, which differs from other art glass in that it was a composition of colored glass worked together while hot. The essential characteristic is that the ornamentation is found within the glass; Favrile was never further decorated. Different effects were achieved by varying the amount and position of colors. Tiffany and the artists in his studio also are well known for their fine work in other areas: bronzes, pottery, jewelry, silver and enamels. *Also see Jewelry.*

Opening page:

Photo courtesy James D. Julia Auctioneers, Fairfield, Maine; www.JuliaAuctions.com

Tiffany Studios Chinese Tyler Table Lamp. Massive leaded glass shade in the Tyler family. The shade is comprised of true "dichroic" Tiffany glass (containing multiple micro-layers of metal oxides), which changes from heavily mottled green and yellow unlit to vibrant green and fiery orange when lit. The shade itself begins with small rectangular tiles, which gradually increase in size until a band of horizontal tiles are introduced. Horizontal bands extend from this pattern that repeat 48 times with each pattern having two long vertical tiles of glass along with two small geometric tiles. The apron is comprised of five rows of horizontal tiles with the underskirt having a half-moon pattern atop the final geometric band. The shape of the shade is commonly referred to as a Chinese Tyler shade and is signed with an early small tag "Tiffany Studios New York". The base begins with four sockets and swan-shaped necks and extends down into a decorated canister form with large applied bronze beadwork. From there, three slender curving legs are finished with cat's-paw feet, all of this set on a raised platform with circular plate and completed with a final band of beadwork. The lamp is finished with the original top cap. The entire lamp carries a green-brown patina finish. Base is signed twice on the underside, "Tiffany Studios New York". Shade is 18" diameter. Overall 34" h. The shade has a few tight hairlines with no missing glass or damage cracks. Two sockets are modern replacements. **$41,400**

Photo courtesy James D. Julia Auctioneers, Fairfield, Maine; www.JuliaAuctions.com

Tiffany Studios Lemon Leaf Table Lamp. Heavily mottled apple-green background glass with heavily mottled maize-colored lemon-leaf band. Shade is signed "Tiffany Studios New York 1470". Base is signed "Tiffany Studios New York 531". Original patina on base and shade. Shade is 18" diameter. Overall 25 1/2" h. Some tight hairlines primarily in lower border with no missing glass. Slight lead separation in one small area where lemon-leaf band meets lower geometric bands. Slight dent in heat cap. **$17,250**

Photo courtesy James D. Julia Auctioneers, Fairfield, Maine; www.JuliaAuctions.com

Tiffany Studios Ruffled Bowl. Deep gold iridescent finish with magenta, blue and pink highlights. Signed on the underside "L.C.T.". 4 1/2" diameter. **$287**

Photo courtesy James D. Julia Auctioneers, Fairfield, Maine; www.JuliaAuctions.com

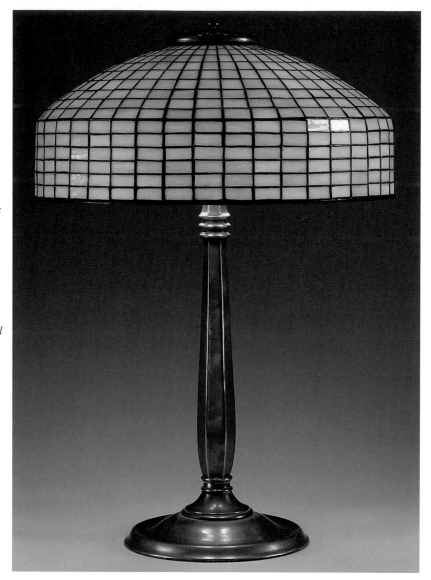

Tiffany Studios Geometric Table Lamp. Colors of butterscotch and caramel striated with white. Shade is supported by a Colonial-style, four-socket base with inverted saucer foot. Shade is signed "Tiffany Studios NY 1469". Base is marked "Tiffany Studios New York 532". Shade is 18" diameter. Overall 25" h. Base has replaced pull chains and has been cleaned down to copper finish. **$8,050**

Photo courtesy James D. Julia Auctioneers, Fairfield, Maine; www.JuliaAuctions.com

Tiffany Studios Footed Candy Dish. With applied gold iridescent border on opaque blue body and foot. Scratched in "59" on the underside. 6" diameter. Multiple chips to foot rim, some scratches on interior. **$60**

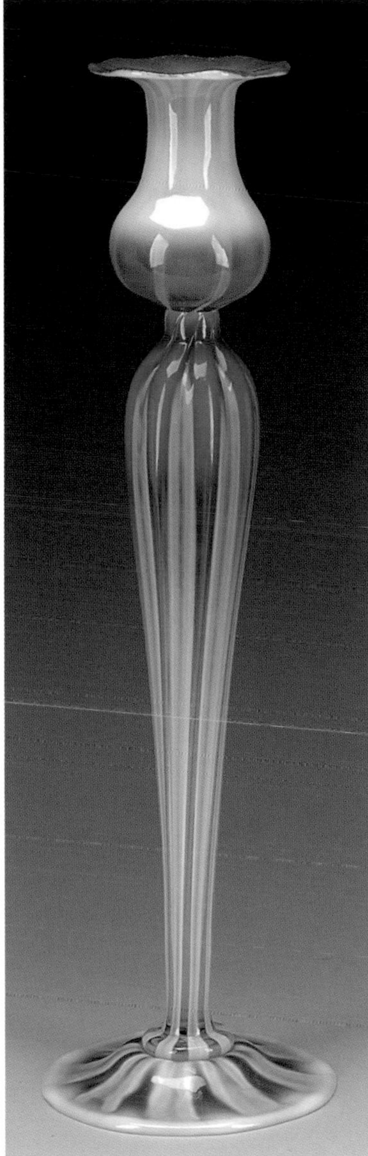

Photo courtesy James D. Julia Auctioneers, Fairfield, Maine; www.JuliaAuctions.com

Tiffany Pastel Tulip Candlestick. With raspberry opalescent cup applied to blue-to-green opalescent stem with white pulled striping and applied raspberry foot with opalescent ribbing. Signed on the underside "1845 L.C. Tiffany-Favrile". 16" t. **$6,612**

Photo courtesy James D. Julia Auctioneers, Fairfield, Maine; www.JuliaAuctions.com

Tiffany Studios Nautilus Lamp. Natural shell shade on a patina harp base with additional hook on the underside for possible wall hanging as well as five ball feet. Impressed on underside "403 Tiffany Studios New York". 12 1/2" h. Minor wear to patina. **$6,900**

Photo courtesy James D. Julia Auctioneers, Fairfield, Maine; www.JuliaAuctions.com

Tiffany Studios Mini Flower-Form Vase. Blue iridescent with vertical ribbing and applied foot. Irregular iridescence to top quarter of the vase shading down to deep purple mirror iridescence on the foot. Engraved signature "7311N 1522 L.C. Tiffany-Inc Favrile" on the underside. 6 1/4" t. **$2,400**

Photo courtesy James D. Julia Auctioneers, Fairfield, Maine; www.JuliaAuctions.com

Tiffany Reactive Glass Shade. Green and orange flame design extending from the foot to near the rim. The smokey gray body of the shade has a slightly swirling rib running vertically. When shade is lit in a darkened room, it appears like a dancing flame. Shade is unsigned. 5" t x 2 1/4" fitter. **$4,025**

Photo courtesy James D. Julia Auctioneers, Fairfield, Maine; www.JuliaAuctions.com

Tiffany Studios Art Glass Shade. Vertical ribbing and deep gold with purple and blue iridescence. Shade is finished with a gently scalloped border. Signed "L.C.T. Favrile" in rim. 2 1/4" fitter x 4 3/4" h. **$862**

Photo courtesy James D. Julia Auctioneers, Fairfield, Maine; www.JuliaAuctions.com

Tiffany Studios Flower-Form Vase. Pulled-feather vase on opalescent ground with everted rim and decorated foot. Engraved signature "L.C. Tiffany Favrile 539A". 11 1/4" h. Some staining to the interior. **$3,680**

Photo courtesy James D. Julia Auctioneers, Fairfield, Maine; www.JuliaAuctions.com

Tiffany Studios Lily & Prism Chandelier. With six gold lily shades and 19 prisms in colors of oyster, gold, amber and green with a deep iridescence over the lilies and complimentary prisms. All of this Tiffany glass surrounds a decorated stalactite Tiffany shade with deep vertical ribbing and a hooked-feather pattern. The shade is supported by a bronze collar, three chains and hooks. The shades are supported by a Moorish-style bronze hanging fixture with openwork at the top, medallions of roping above six lily shade holders, nineteen prism hooks and a single stem for the stalactite shade. Further accenting this lamp, alternating between the prisms, are 19 beaded chains that end in bronze balls. This entire lamp is supported by a bronze decorated ceiling cap, chain and S hook. Stalactite shade is signed "S323" and one lily shade is signed "L.C.T. Favrile" and another is signed "L.C.T." and the remainder are unsigned. Overall 42" l. Some parts are authentic while other parts are exact replications of Tiffany Studios hardware. Three lily shades have broken fitter rims, one has roughness to fitter rim. Stalactite shade has chips to fitter rim that are concealed when in place. All prisms either have chips or are cracked. **$32,775**

Photo courtesy James D. Julia Auctioneers, Fairfield, Maine; www.JuliaAuctions.com

Tiffany Studios Favrile Desk Lamp. Gold Favrile shade with rainbow iridescent finish with stretched edge. The cased white-lined shade is supported by a three-arm, leaf-decorated base with a statuary finish. The lamp is completed with a top cap in a patina finish. Shade is signed on the fitter "L.C.T. Favrile" and base is signed on the underside "Tiffany Studios New York 426". Shade is 7" diameter. Overall 14" t. **$4,200**

Photo courtesy James D. Julia Auctioneers, Fairfield, Maine; www.JuliaAuctions.com

Tiffany Stalactite Hanger. Shade has gold iridescent hooked-feather design extending from the bottom of the shade. There is an additional hooked-feather design descending from the fitter. Design is set against a lighter gold iridescent background of the vertically ribbed body of the shade. Interior of the shade has a light chartreuse color. Shade is unsigned and numbered "L2400". It is suspended from three chains attached to hooks on a center light post which terminates to a ceiling cap having beaded rim. The bronze replacement hardware is finished in a rich brown patina with strong red and green highlights. Shade is 8" l x 6" diameter x 4 3/4" fitter. Overall 24" h. **$7,187**

Photo courtesy James D. Julia Auctioneers, Fairfield, Maine; www.JuliaAuctions.com

Tiffany Studios Mosaic Pentray. Inlaid blue decorated Favrile glass. Impressed on the underside "TIFFANY STUDIOS NEW YORK 24336" together with the monogram of the Tiffany Glass & Decorating Co. 7 3/4" l. Patina may be enhanced. **$8,000**

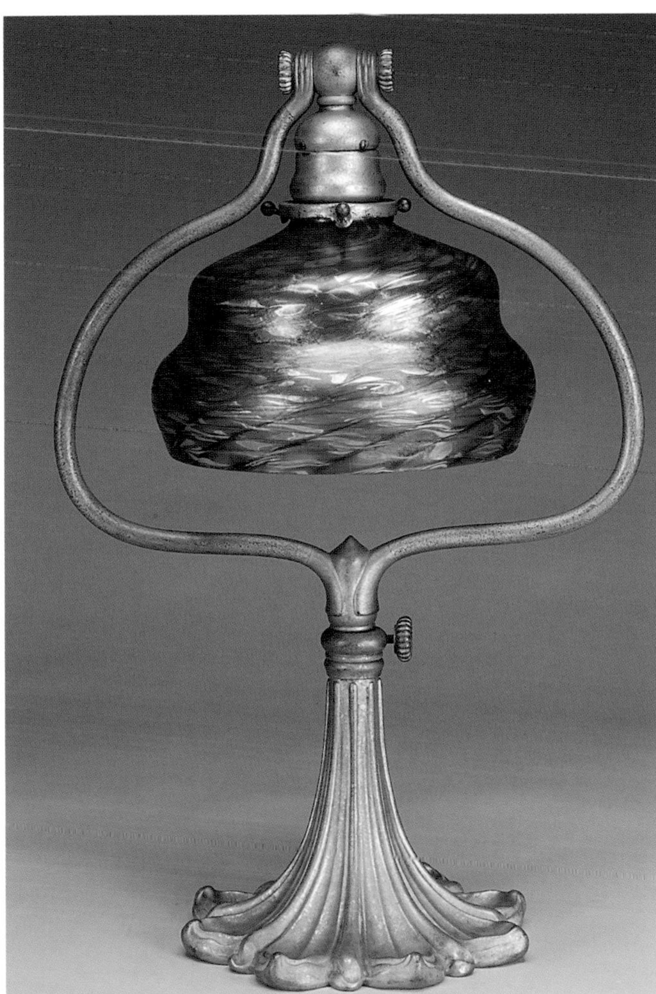

Photo courtesy James D. Julia Auctioneers, Fairfield, Maine; www.JuliaAuctions.com

Tiffany Studios Desk Lamp. Bronze harp adjustable table base with ornate foot having gold doré finish. Base is signed on underside "Tiffany Studios New York 569". Base supports an unsigned art glass shade with a damascene-type decoration of gold with platinum accents on a green transparent ground. Interior of shade has full-blown magenta iridescent finish. Shade is 7" diameter. Overall 18" h. Shade has minor chips to fitter rim. Base has minor oxidation to gold doré finish. **$4,200**

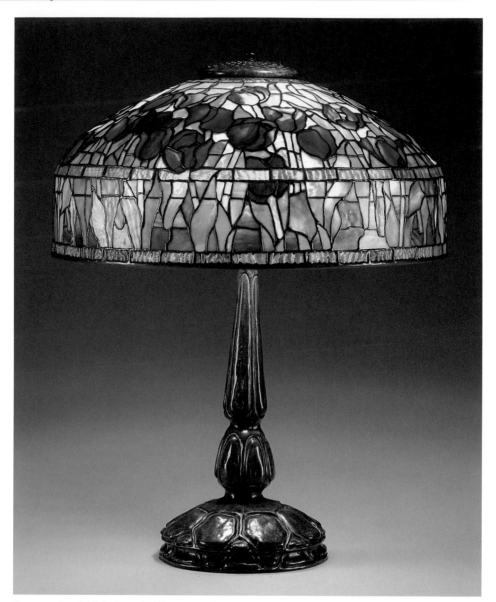

Photo courtesy James D. Julia Auctioneers, Fairfield, Maine; www.JuliaAuctions.com

Tiffany Studios Red Tulip Table Lamp. The shade depicts the tulip flower in every stage of bloom (second view). The colors used encompass the entire range of the red family from pink to purple. Some blossoms are entirely constructed of the softer colors, while others use striations of light, medium and dark to give a three-dimensional effect. There are other blossoms that used only the deepest colors and represent the flower in its later stage of bloom. This tulip pattern also shows the foliage in most every color of green. Glass used in this shade is also of a wide variety from striated to cat's paw to rippled and finally granular. The shade is completed with three geometric bands of rippled glass in earthen hues of fiery orange with hints of green. The shade is supported by a mock-turtleback base. This three-socket base is complete with riser, wheel and top cap all in a rich patina finish. Shade is signed "Tiffany Studios New York 1596". Base is signed "Tiffany Studios New York 587". Shade is 18" diameter. Overall 22 1/2" h. A few tight hairlines in shade. Patina has been enhanced on shade and base. **$109,250**

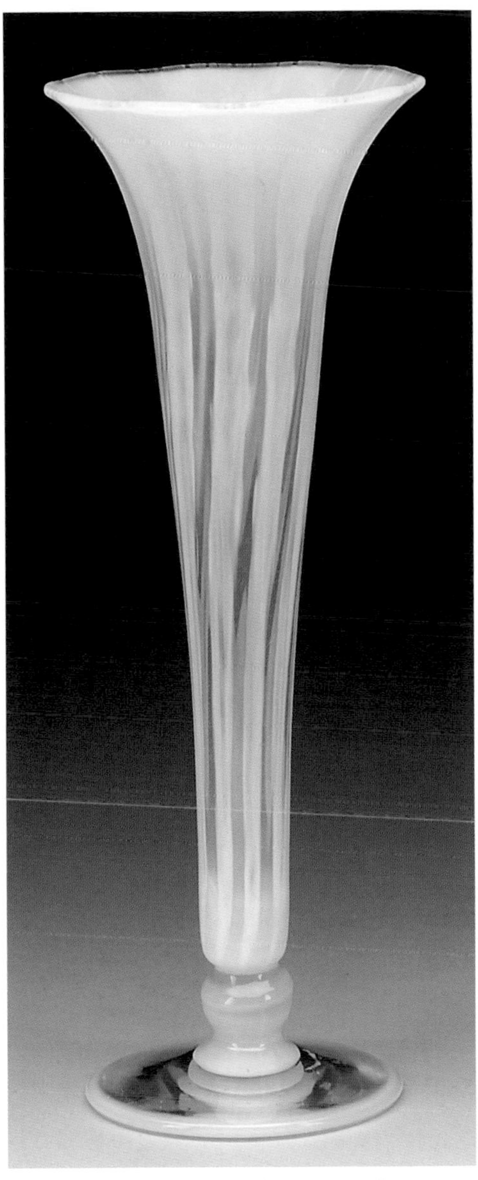

Photo courtesy James D. Julia Auctioneers, Fairfield, Maine; www.JuliaAuctions.com

Tiffany Studios Pastel Vase. Clear foot with white opalescent rim. Foot gives way to a white opalescent stem with white opalescent ribs vertically extending to the slightly flaring lip. Interior of the mouth is finished with a rich pastel yellow. Signed on the underside "L.C. Tiffany Favrile 1886". 9 3/4" t. **$1,380**

Photo courtesy James D. Julia Auctioneers, Fairfield, Maine; www.JuliaAuctions.com

Tiffany Studios Damascene Table Lamp. Green Favrile shade with a damascene-wave pattern decoration in gold shading to platinum having eight vertical ribs, which give it highlights of blue. The cased lined shade is supported by a patinated single-socket, three-arm bronze base with elongated rib decoration over an ornate root-style foot resting on four ball feet. Lamp is completed with a bronze heat cap. Shade is signed on the fitter rim "L.C.T.". Base is signed "Tiffany Studios New York 431". Shade is 9 1/2" diameter x 3 3/4" fitter. Overall 19 1/2" t. **$6,612**

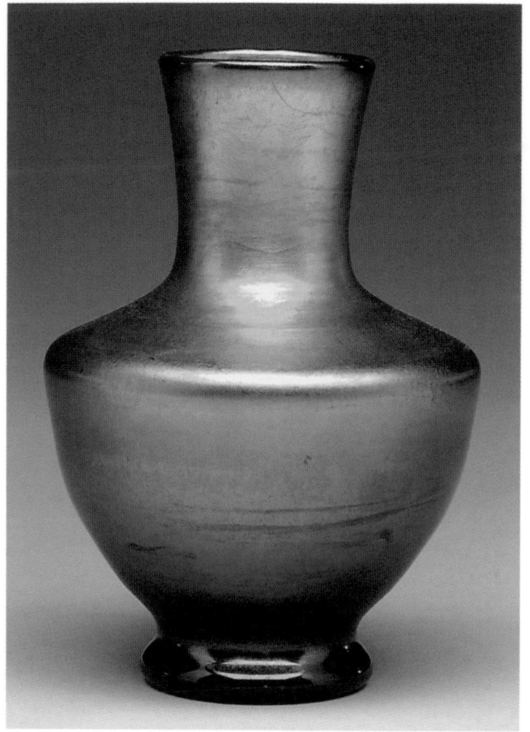

Photo courtesy James D. Julia Auctioneers, Fairfield, Maine; www.JuliaAuctions.com

Tiffany Studios Blue Favrile Vase. Classic Egyptian form with elongated neck and squared shoulder. Vase begins with a platinum iridescence over the neck area that recedes into a medium blue and a cobalt blue at the foot. Signed "L.C. Tiffany Inc. Favrile X1421024". 5 3/4" h. Tiny spot of missing iridescence on shoulder. **$920**

Photo courtesy James D. Julia Auctioneers, Fairfield, Maine; www.JuliaAuctions.com

Tiffany Studios Pine Needle Card Case. Constructed of green slag panels with darker striations. These panels are set in a bronze frame with decorative pine-needle decoration overall. Exceptional patina finish. Signed on underside "Tiffany Studios New York 875". 4" x 3" x 1". **$1,495**

Photo courtesy James D. Julia Auctioneers, Fairfield, Maine; www.JuliaAuctions.com

Tiffany Studios Favrile Cabinet Vase. Round squat body with pulled handles on each side and a slightly flaring mouth. The gold Favrile finish shows purple and blue highlights at foot and lip. Signed on the underside "L.C. Tiffany-Favrile 4014L". 2" t. **$540**

Photo courtesy James D. Julia Auctioneers, Fairfield, Maine; www.JuliaAuctions.com

Tiffany Studios Tel El Amarna Vase. With applied and decorated collar. Engraved "Exhibition Piece" and "6340N L.C. Tiffany - Favrile" on the underside. 5 3/4" h. Hairline crack to applied rim. **$5,750**

Photo courtesy James D. Julia Auctioneers, Fairfield, Maine; www.JuliaAuctions.com

Tiffany Studios Favrile Lily Vase. Slender body, slightly flaring at the lip with saucer foot. Gold iridescence shows flashes of pink and blue at the foot. Signed on the underside "L.C. Tiffany Inc. Favrile 1504-7408M". 6" t. **$660**

Photos courtesy James D. Julia Auctioneers, Fairfield, Maine; www.JuliaAuctions.com

Tiffany Studios Bronze Pottery Vase. Decorated with an organic overlapping leaf pattern. The finish is basically silver with copper showing through in some areas. Signed on the underside "L.C. Tiffany Favrile Bronze Pottery" as well as "B.P. 249529" as well as "LCT" logo. 4 3/4" h. Minor wear to exterior and tight hairlines to interior glaze that do not penetrate the surface. **$3,910**

Photo courtesy James D. Julia Auctioneers, Fairfield, Maine; www.JuliaAuctions.com

Tiffany Studios Counterbalance Desk Lamp. With pendulous turtleback tile counterweight. Artichoke design stand and blue decorated damascene shade. Shade is signed "L.C.T. Favrile". Base is marked "Tiffany Studios New York". Shade is 8" diameter. Overall 14 1/2" h. Minor chips to three turtleback tiles in the counterweight, one tile with tight hairline, some minor wear to patina. **$32,775**

Photo courtesy James D. Julia Auctioneers, Fairfield, Maine; www.JuliaAuctions.com

Tiffany Studios Bell Shade. Decorated with a translucent green pulled-feather motif with gold trim on an oyster ground. Signed "L.C.T.". 2 1/4" fitter rim x 4 1/2" h. Minor grinding to fitter rim. **$2,530**

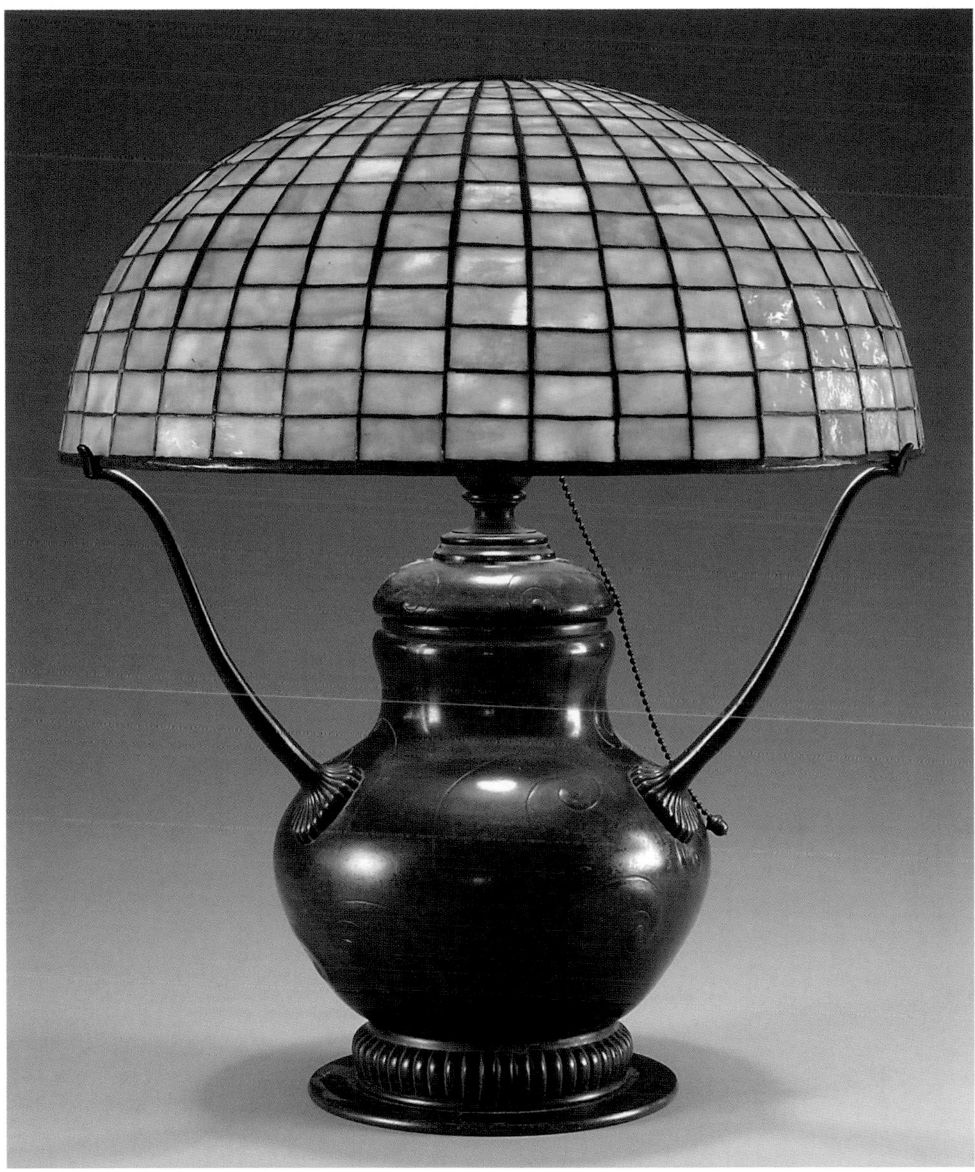

Photo courtesy James D. Julia Auctioneers, Fairfield, Maine; www.JuliaAuctions.com

Tiffany Studios Geometric Table Lamp. With leaded "dichroic" glass shade glass (containing multiple micro-layers of metal oxides) that shows colors of green, tan and mauve when unlit. When lit, the glass turns a rich orange. Shade is signed "Tiffany Studios New York 1436" and rests atop an early Tiffany Studios base with an incised and slightly raised wave design. Base is finished with three attached arms to support the shade. Marked on the underside "25778". Shade is 16" diameter. Overall 20" h. A few tight hairlines in the shade. Bottom of font has been drilled. **$15,525**

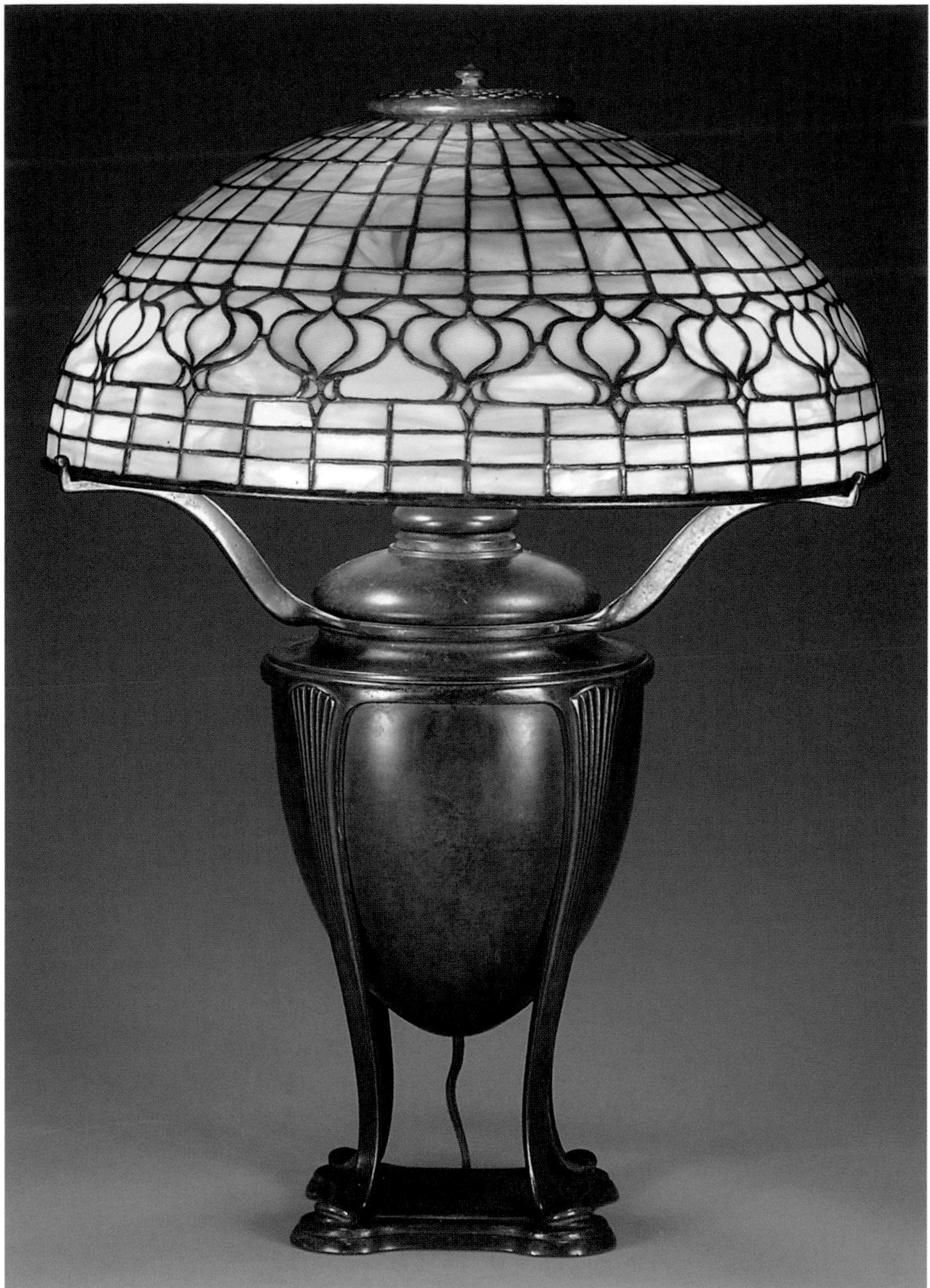

Photo courtesy James D. Julia Auctioneers, Fairfield, Maine; www.JuliaAuctions.com

Tiffany Studios Pomegranate Table Lamp. Shade has an allover geometric background of green striated glass with hints of blue, yellow and white. The shade is decorated with a single band of pomegranates in fiery mottled yellow and orange glass. Shade is supported by a three-socket, three-armed Grecian urn that is supported by four flaring feet on a pedestal stand. Shade is signed on "Tiffany Studios New York" with a small early tag. Shade is 16" diameter. Overall 20" h. Several spider cracks. **$16,100**

Toys

FUTURE OF THE MARKET: ANTIQUE TOYS

By Catherine Saunders-Watson

How can you accurately gauge the direction of a marketplace sector as vast and heterogeneous as that of antique toys, especially within an economic landscape as topsy-turvy as the one we've been experiencing? Ordinarily I would say it can't be done in an entirely conclusive way, but 2009 proved to be the year in which trends in toy buying would be revealed across the board because of one stellar auction event. Investment-minded toy buyers were able to dip into a golden treasure chest of toys they never dreamed would be sold: the 59-year collection amassed by K-B Toys' co-founder Donald Kaufman.

The Kaufman collection's magnitude, depth and maturity positioned it above all others. It contained no duplicates, many one-offs, and every known color variation. In an auction series that debuted March 19-21, 2009, at Bertoia's in Vineland, N.J., its out-of-the-gate performance provided market-watchers with a unique and unprecedented litmus test. It declared in big, round dollar figures exactly which examples savvy collectors seek and how deeply they'd empty their wallets in order to own them.

This breathtaking assemblage of several thousand toys – even Kaufman himself doesn't know how many there are – was extraordinary in its breadth and quality. It took a crew of 10 Bertoia staff member a full week to pack and load the first of the auction goods into three trucks – two of them 26-footers allocated solely to Don's mind-boggling pedal cars and pressed-steel toys.

"To keep it organized, we tried to separate the toys into affinity groupings, and there simply wasn't a weak category anywhere in the collection," recalled Bertoia Auctions associate Rich Bertoia. "Everything Don owns is just incredible. It's the ultimate-upgrade collection."

Because it contained superlative, extremely rare examples from virtually every major toy classification – cast-iron, European and American clockwork, pressed-steel, comic character, et al. – the collection was pure catnip to many investors bitten by Wall Street and seeking the comfort of high-grade tangible assets.

The collection will require two to three years of semiannual auction events in order to be dispersed in its entirety, so the full story won't be known till the last toy is sold, but the March 2009 Kaufman sale spoke volumes about toy-market trends.

I feel quite comfortable in going on record with these predictions, based on the Kaufman Part I results. These are five categories I like for investment purposes:

Hubley's Royal Circus series – My no. 1 pick for American cast iron is Hubley's series of Royal Circus vans, which depict old-fashioned, wheeled cages used for transporting circus animals. This charming series of toys is a perennial favorite with collectors. En masse, the toys display beautifully in any collection, and I believe their values are going to hold strong in the marketplace, especially for those examples exhibiting fine, original paint. Kaufman owned the most elusive of the Royal Circus vans – a Monkey Cage, complete with figures of impish monkeys and an ingeniously designed mesh interior housing that revolves as the toy is pulled along. Estimated at $30,000-$40,000, it sold for a staggering $97,750.

Marklin tin – The premier brand in European tin toys and trains is Marklin. I see no turning back for this brand. There will always be buyers worldwide for this German maker's beautifully crafted designs. It's not unusual for Marklin toys to top the prices realized in major toy sales, and that's precisely what happened at the Kaufman sale. A rare, hand-painted circa-1909 "Fidelitas" clown-car caravan measuring 37 1/2 inches long lured not only collectors of European clockwork toys but also collectors of clown toys. (Anytime you have crossover interest from two or more categories, that's like having back-up insurance on your investment.). Estimated at $30,000-$40,000, the Fidelitas handily exceeded expectations to reach top-lot status at $103,500. The buyer was a private collector from Europe.

Catherine Saunders-Watson

Early European tin cars – The fascination many of us have for full-size classic cars was grounded in childhood play. Some collectors reclaim their youth by chasing examples of the very toys they actually played with, but serious investment-oriented collectors know the money is in early German, French and Spanish autos. Seven of the top 10 lots sold in Kaufman Part I fell into this category. An extraordinary production by the little-known Barcelona firm Hispania proved to be the connoisseurs' choice. Believed to be the largest of all manufactured toy limousines at 22 1/2 inches in length, the circa-1907 luxury car was as finely detailed as its full-size counterpart of a century ago. The toy was purchased for $80,500 – probably 80,000 times its original price!

Here are some other prices achieved by European tin cars in the sale: circa 1906-1909 Marklin two-seat open roadster, $57,500; circa-1914 Marklin roadster with spare tire on toolbox trunk, $57,500; circa-1912 Bing luxury taxi, $46,000; and Fischer Father Christmas in open car, $39,100. Other brands we favor for investment are Carette and Gunthermann.

Racers – In more than 20 years of writing about toys, I've never seen a dip in the market for antique tin racers such as the Gordon Bennet cars in the Kaufman sale. With the rule usually being "the larger the racer, the higher the price," this auction made a strong statement when a possibly unique 6 3/4-inch example zoomed past its $6,000-$7,500 estimate to cross the finish line at $25,300.

Figural biscuit tins – Here's a wild-card category. Unless you've spent time in the U.K., you may not know what biscuit tins are, but they left quite a few people slack-jawed in the auction room at Bertoia's when they hammered incredible prices. In latter 19th- and early 20th-century Europe, biscuits – or cookies, as we call them in the United States – were packaged in novelty tins that had a second life after the contents were consumed. Quite often the tins were crafted as toys, and with bakeries in ferocious competition for market share, the tins were sometimes nicer than toys available in retail shops. The most desirable biscuit tins are those depicting vehicles, including cars, delivery vans, airplanes, motorcycles, racers and boats. They can run well into the thousands of dollars.

Kaufman's collection held some beauties. An Alfa-Romeo biscuit tin for the Italian company Biscotti Delser was especially rare in that it was outfitted with a clockwork motor. Estimated at $10,000-$12,000, it produced a sweet payday for when it sold for $25,300.

Caution: Sometimes tin toys are represented as biscuit tins when in actuality they are standard manufactured toys of lesser value. I've never seen a case of intentional deceit; it's just that these tins require a particular expertise in order to be properly identified. When buying biscuit tins, it pays to work with a specialty dealer.

Since I've now brought up the subject, I'd like to emphasize that any investor with an inclination to sink their money into old toys should not spend a cent till they've tapped into the toy network and know who the reputable dealers are. Trust is everything when you're buying antique toys.

Nowadays, auctions are the dominant source for investment-grade toys. There are several outstanding auction houses that specialize in toys, including Bertoia's, Morphy Auctions and Noel Barrett Auctions. When you buy from toy auctioneers of this caliber, you know your purchases have been vetted and described by people who really know the toy field.

There's an added bonus to buying at auction that you don't read about very often, if at all: preview scrutiny. At any auction preview, the toys are carefully examined by dealers and collectors who've been at it for many years. If something isn't "right," if it looks like there's a touch of repaint or a replaced part, you may be sure it will be pointed out by someone at the preview and duly noted on the catalog addendum. This can only help in your quest to purchase authentic, original toys, and it's why I recommend buying from auction houses that specialize in toys.

There's another avenue one can take in purchasing toys for investment, and I touched on it earlier. These are the nostalgia toys you may remember from childhood. Because so many of these later toys were mass-produced – even overproduced – during an era in which the collecting phenomenon had already become well entrenched, it takes skill and exceptional market expertise to buy wisely. In this category I would say proceed with caution, as the market is much more fickle than that of antique toys, whose numbers and availability are already well established – there are no more factory finds with the potential of flooding the market when it comes to the antiques, but I wouldn't count out that possibility vis a vis newer toys.

The toys to which I refer when I say "nostalgia" toys are: Star Wars, Star Trek, Transformers, G.I. Joe and other action figures, Barbies and Superheroes. Be sure that if you buy these types of toys for investment, you choose only items you really love because then it won't hurt quite as badly if their values drop.

Personally, my recommendation for boomer-era investment toys would be tin robots of the 1950s and 1960s, preferably mint/boxed; Nightmare Before Christmas rarities, early (Gold and Silver Age) Superhero comics acquired only from experienced, reputable dealers and auction houses, and monster collectibles, which are hotter than ever. Kids loved to be creeped out, and those Saturday matinees with Wolfman and Frankenstein seem to have made a lasting impression on our generation of collectors.

Visit *www.bertoiaauctions.com* or information on future auction sessions featuring the Donald Kaufman Antique Toy Collection.

Photo courtesy Bertoia Auctions, Vineland, N.J.; www.BertoiaAuctions.com

Made around 1911 by the German manufacturer Carette, this hand-painted tin luxury limo has beveled glass windows, nickel lamps, fully opening doors, embossed upholstered seating, roof rack, and full running boards. Measuring 16" long, the clockwork toy sold at Bertoia's inaugural auction of the Donald Kaufman collection for **$39,100.**

TOYS

Barbie

Barbie the fashion doll was launched in 1959. The doll is produced by Mattel Inc., founded in 1945 by Harold "Matt" Matson and Elliot Handler. Handler's wife, Ruth, is regarded as the creator of Barbie.

In the early 1950s, Ruth Handler watched her daughter, Barbara, at play with paper dolls, and noticed that she often gave them adult roles. At the time, most children's toy dolls were representations of infants.

During a trip to Europe in 1956 with her children, Barbara and Kenneth, Ruth Handler came across a German doll called Bild Lilli. She purchased three of the adult-figured dolls, gave one to her daughter and took the others back to Mattel.

Ruth Handler redesigned the doll (with help from engineer Jack Ryan) and named her Barbie, after Handler's daughter. The doll made its debut at the American International Toy Fair in New York on March 9, 1959. This date is also used as Barbie's official birthday. Mattel acquired the rights to the Bild Lilli doll in 1964 and production of Lilli was halted.

Barbie's full name is Barbara Millicent Roberts. In a series of novels published by Random House in the 1960s, her parents' names are given as George and Margaret Roberts from the fictional town of Willows, Wis. Her beau, Ken Carson, first appeared in 1961.

Photo courtesy McMasters Harris Auction Co., Cambridge, Ohio; www.McMastersHarris.com

#1 Ponytail Barbie, with stand, blonde hair, black/white eyes, red lips, straight legs. Gold hoop earrings. Hair has replaced rubber band in ponytail. Torso slightly stained. One metal reinforcement missing from hole in foot. Pedestal stand prongs slightly bent. **$3,450**

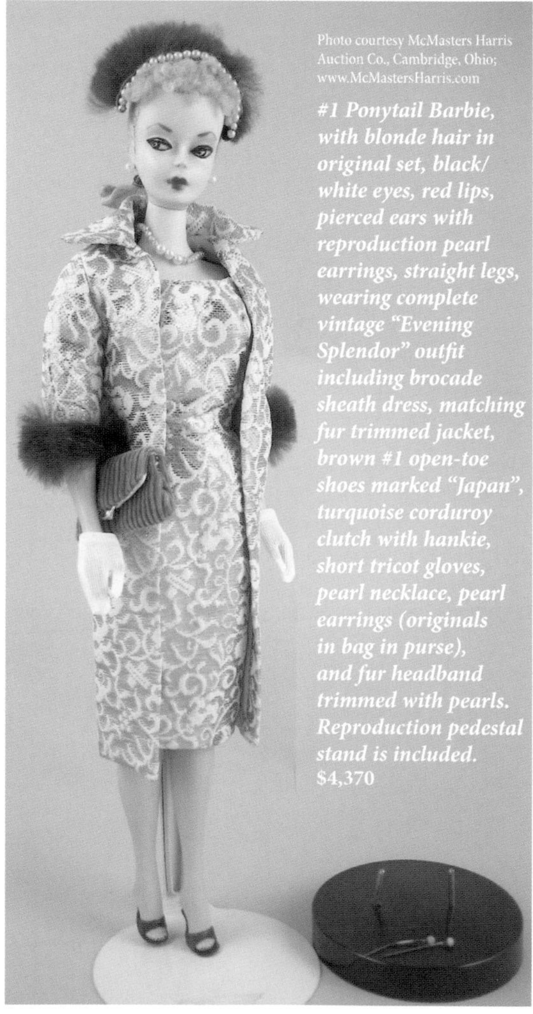

Photo courtesy McMasters Harris Auction Co., Cambridge, Ohio; www.McMastersHarris.com

#1 Ponytail Barbie, with blonde hair in original set, black/white eyes, red lips, pierced ears with reproduction pearl earrings, straight legs, wearing complete vintage "Evening Splendor" outfit including brocade sheath dress, matching fur trimmed jacket, brown #1 open-toe shoes marked "Japan", turquoise corduroy clutch with hankie, short tricot gloves, pearl necklace, pearl earrings (originals in bag in purse), and fur headband trimmed with pearls. Reproduction pedestal stand is included. $4,370

#1 Ponytail Barbie, brunette hair, black/white eyes, red lips, cheek blush, pierced ears with hoop earrings, straight legs, wearing black/white striped swimsuit and black "Japan" marked open-toe shoes, in box with black pedestal stand and booklet. Ponytail is loose and rubber band is replaced, left leg does not move and appears to be "welded" to body. Stand is slightly scuffed and has a couple of tiny scratches, prongs are rusted. Box insert is replaced; box is creased and worn and corners are split, two have been repaired with tape. 11 1/4" doll. **$8,050**

#2 Ponytail Barbie, in original box with pedestal stand. Blonde hair, black/white eyes, red lips, faint cheek blush, pierced ears, wearing original black/white striped swimsuit and black "Japan" marked #1 open-toe shoes, in box with black wire and pedestal stand. Feet stained from shoes, hair appears to be in original set, bottom rubber band replaced in ponytail. Black wire stand is discolored, pedestal is slightly scuffed. Box insert is replaced, box not mint, writing on box bottom. **$6,900**

Photo courtesy McMasters Harris Auction Co., Cambridge, Ohio; www.McMastersHarris.com

#3 Brunette Ponytail Barbie. Brunette hair, blue eyes, red lips, pierced ears, straight legs. Wearing Commuter Set, navy jacket with matching skirt, white satin body blouse, blue/white checked body blouse, floral silk hat, "Japan" marked open-toe shoes, crystal necklace with matching bracelet, short white nylon gloves; red cardboard hatbox. One shoe is navy, the other is black. **$1,035**

#4 Blond Ponytail Barbie, blonde hair, blue eyes, red lips, pierced ears, straight legs. Wearing original black/white striped swimsuit and black open-toe shoes (both marked "Japan"). Feet are stained from shoes. **$201**

#4 Ponytail Barbie, wearing "Theatre Date". Straight legs, blonde hair in original top knot (bottom rubber band replaced), pierced ears, blue eyes, light cheek blush. Wearing complete outfit of green satin skirt and jacket with matching hat, white satin blouse and green "Japan" marked open toe shoes. Skirt has small amount of dark discoloration on front. **$172**

#5 Ponytail Barbie, in original swimsuit. Titian hair, blue eyes, red lips, pierced ears, faded eyebrows. Wearing original one-piece black/white striped swimsuit and black "Japan" marked open-toe shoes. Discoloration on back of right leg. **$201**

#5 Ponytail Barbie, with black wire stand, blonde hair, blue eyes, red lips with some color loss, pierced ears, straight legs. Wearing homemade dress with blue corduroy purse, unmarked black o/t shoes (one strap split). Black wire stand included. **$115**

American Girl Barbie, wearing "Swingin' Easy", blonde hair, blue eyes, yellow lips, bendable legs. Wearing green floral print dress. **$258**

Photo courtesy McMasters Harris Auction Co., Cambridge, Ohio; www.McMastersHarris.com

Blonde American Girl Barbie. Blonde hair, blue eyes, cream lips, pierced ears, bendable legs. Wearing "Music Center Matinee", two-piece outfit of red chiffon over taffeta with diamond look pin, rose colored picture hat, and red closed toe spikes marked "Japan". Sides of head are dark. **$460**

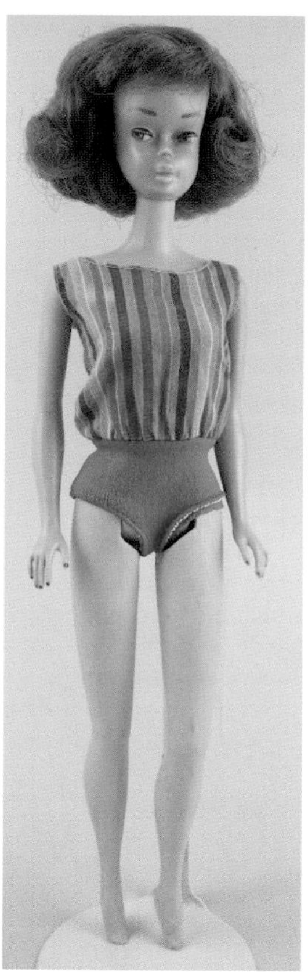

Photo courtesy McMasters Harris Auction Co., Cambridge, Ohio; www.McMastersHarris.com

American Girl Barbie, brunette side-part hair, blue eyes, beige lips, wearing original multicolored stripe swimsuit. Head is dark, legs are very loose, several small pin-sized holes in feet and left toe chip. Scratch on back. Swimsuit has small section of stitching missing at seam. **$805**

Photo courtesy McMasters Harris Auction Co., Cambridge, Ohio; www.McMastersHarris.com

American Girl Barbie, wearing "Fashion Luncheon". Bendable legs, brunette hair, blue eyes, pale yellow lips. Wearing pink knit and satin dress with matching jacket, pink satin hat with floral decoration, white long sleeved gloves. Pink "Japan" marked closed toe shoes. Left leg extremely loose and joint broken, face slightly dark; outfit age discolored with stain on collar of jacket. **$258**

Photo courtesy McMasters Harris Auction Co., Cambridge, Ohio; www.McMastersHarris.com

Bubblecut Barbie wearing "After Five" with vinyl case. Barbie has golden blonde hair, pierced ears, blue eyes, pink lips, straight legs. Wearing black dress with white organdy collar, matching organdy hat with black velvet hat band, and replaced black open toe shoes. Case has Bubblecut Barbie graphic, circa 1963. Case is scuffed, but with no tears in vinyl. **$92**

Photo courtesy McMasters Harris Auction Co., Cambridge, Ohio; www.McMastersHarris.com

Bubblecut Barbie, wearing "Friday Night Date", Barbie has straight legs, titian hair, blue eyes, light red lips and pierced ears. Face is slightly dark. Wearing white cotton underdress with blue corduroy jumper decorated with felt appliques and black "Japan" marked open-toe shoes. Included are her serving tray and one glass (has crack) and two straws. **$143**

Photo courtesy McMasters Harris Auction Co., Cambridge, Ohio; www.McMastersHarris.com

Fashion Queen Barbie, wearing "Let's Dance". Doll has molded brown hair with blue vinyl headband, blue eyes, red lips, pierced ears, straight legs. Wearing blue floral print dress. In black vinyl Fashion Queen Barbie case. Circa 1963. Case is scuffed and worn with no noted tears in vinyl. Plastic inside has several cracks and holes. **$69**

Bubblecut Barbie, boxed, in original swimsuit. Black bubble cut hair, red lips. Includes original box, stand and brochure. **$103**

Color Magic Barbie, yellow hair with blue clip, blue eyes, dark pink lips, bendable legs. **$287**

Color Magic Barbie, yellow hair with blue clip and multi-colored scarf, blue eyes, red lips, cheek blush, bendable legs, wearing print skirt and blouse. Left leg is slightly loose, small split in left toes. **$345**

Hair Fair Brunette Barbie, Brunette bob cut, blue eyes, real lashes, a few nicks and marks. Wearing original green dress tagged "Barbie". **$46**

Swirl Ponytail Barbie, wearing orange nylon swimsuit, brunette hair, blue eyes, dark pink lips, pierced ears, and straight legs. Wearing orange one-piece nylon swimsuit. Small scratches on backs of legs. Swimsuit is missing some stitching and has small "runs". **$115**

Talking Barbie, in original outfit. Brunette hair in original set with pink bow, blue eyes, real lashes, pink lips. String does not work, a few nicks and marks. Wearing original swimsuit tagged "Barbie", 1968. **$103**

Talking Barbie, NRFB. Brunette hair, blue eyes, coral lips, rooted eyelashes, bendable legs, wearing original swimsuit with net cover-up, wrist tag, in box with clear plastic stand. Vinyl attachments for arms in box are split, box has a few small creases. **$258**

Talking Barbie head on Twist 'N' Turn Body, blonde hair, blue eyes, coral lips, cheek blush, rooted eyelashes, bendable legs, wearing black nylon swimsuit. Head has slight yellow tone. **$46**

Twist 'N' Turn Barbie, wearing original outfit. Brunette hair with bright orange hair tie, pierced ears, blue eyes, sparse rooted eyelashes, pink lips, faded cheek blush, bendable legs. Wearing original bright orange two-piece swimsuit with net cover. Head has slight yellow tone and left ear is discolored. **$92**

Twist 'N' Turn Barbie, in original outfit. Brunette hair with orange ribbon tie, blue eyes, red/orange lips, cheek blush, rooted eyelashes, bendable legs, wearing orange vinyl two-piece swimsuit with net cover-up. Face and hands are slightly yellowed. Swimsuit waist is stretched and back discolored. **$143**

Twist 'N' Turn Barbie, Wearing original swimsuit with mesh cover (no bikini top), matching hair ribbon. Swimsuit bottom is stained. 1966. **$69**

Twist 'N' Turn Barbie and Hair Happenin's Francie, Twist 'n turn Barbie has Living Barbie head with shoulder length hair, real lashes (several lashes missing), wearing off the shoulder body suit. Hair Happenin's Francie wearing original dress tagged "Francie", brown eyes framed by real lashes, pink lips. 1969. **$69 pair**

Walking Miss America & Drum Major Ken, Barbie includes original gown, bouquet of flowers, wand, cloak, crown, and sash. Hair is in original set and she walks gracefully. Ken includes uniform, hat, shoes marked "Japan" and baton. **$46 pair**

Barbie: Family, Friends

Allan, in original box, red painted hair, brown eyes, straight legs, wearing multicolored striped jacket and blue swim trunks. **$46**

Twist 'N' Turn Casey, Blonde hair, wearing tagged one-piece outfit with belt. Open mouth, real lashes. Some wear to outfit. Uneven skin tone. **$57**

Talking Christie, in original box, oxidized red hair, brown eyes, pink lips, wearing orange vinyl two-piece swimsuit and multi-colored cover-up, wrist tag, in box with clear plastic stand. Doll is loose in box, box not mint. **$287**

Twist 'N' Turn Christie, in original box, brunette hair, brown eyes, rooted eyelashes, bright pink lips, wrist tag. Wearing yellow, pink and orange one-piece swimsuit, in box with clear plastic stand. Original cellophane on box. **$345**

Francie, with "Growin' Pretty Hair", in orig. outfit. Bendable legs, blonde hair, brown eyes, rooted eyelashes, hot pink lips, cheek blush. Wearing pink lame and satin dress with pink netting overskirt and attached panty. Original rubber band in hair is in fragments, head is slightly dark and has yellow tone. Color is faded on back of lame. **$46**

Francie, in original box, blonde hair with plastic cover, brown eyes, cheek blush, bright pink lips, straight legs. Wearing original red/white two-piece swimsuit in box with gold wire stand, booklet, comb and red closed toe shoes. Face is slightly yellow and arms are light. **$402**

Black Francie, with real lashes wearing tagged dress. 1965. ..... **$460**

Black Francie, in original swimsuit. Brunette hair, brown eyes, rooted eyelashes, bright pink lips, twist 'n turn waist, bendable legs, attached wrist tag. Wearing original swimsuit and has booklet. Nose is slightly light. **$1,610**

Growin' Pretty Hair Francie, wearing original dress tagged "Francie". Brown eyes framed by real lashes, pink lips. Hair does not retract. 1970. ..... **$34**

Twist 'N' Turn Francie, in original outfit, blonde hair with hot pink hair ribbon, brown eyes, rooted eyelashes, cheek blush, dark pink lips, and bendable legs. Wearing floral print with lace trim top and hot pink panties. Nose is light, small blue discoloration on right ankle. **$345**

Walking Jamie, in original outfit, light brown hair and brown eyes framed by real lashes. Wearing original outfit. Walking mechanism in working order. A few nicks on back of legs. **$69**

T'NT Julia, in original outfit, oxidized red hair, brown eyes, rooted eyelashes, pink lips, bendable legs, wearing two-piece white nurse's uniform and cap, white pilgrim shoes, wrist tag. Tag is creased and has tear at wrist, cap is discolored. **$143**

T'NT Julia, wearing "Apple Print Sheath", oxidized red hair, brown eyes, rooted eyelashes, cheek blush, pink lips, bendable legs, wearing apple print Barbie dress and black "Japan" marked open-toe shoes (split straps). **$57**

Ken, in original box. Brunette painted hair Ken wearing original red/white striped jacket and red trunks in box with booklet. Box not mint; replaced insert. **$46**

Ken, in original box. Brunette painted hair, straight legs, wearing white knit shirt and red shorts with white polka dots, cork sandals with red straps. Box not mint. **$69**

Ken, in original box. Painted hair, blue eyes, wearing "Tuxedo Ken" outfit including white shirt, black slacks with matching jacket, maroon cummerbund and bow tie, black socks and

Photo courtesy McMasters Harris Auction Co., Cambridge, Ohio; www.McMastersHarris.com

Francie, with bendable legs, wearing "Gad-Abouts", Brunette hair, brown eyes, rooted eyelashes, cheek blush, plum lips. Wearing blue and green printed knit shirt with matching hose, green knit skirt with matching hat, soft green ankle boots, and rare white plastic glasses with green stripe. Francie's nose and ears are slightly light. Right arm is light and light spots on left arm. Hair is stiff. **$172**

Photo courtesy McMasters Harris Auction Co., Cambridge, Ohio; www.McMastersHarris.com

Julia, wearing one-piece white nurse uniform. Julia has brown eyes, dark red hair, rooted eyelashes, twist 'n' turn waist, bendable legs, cheek blush, pink lips. Wearing white cotton dress with matching nurse cap and white pilgrim shoes. A few small blue marks on back of right leg. **$92** *(Not part of the Barbie line. Based on the 1968 TV character, Julia, played by Diahann Carroll.)*

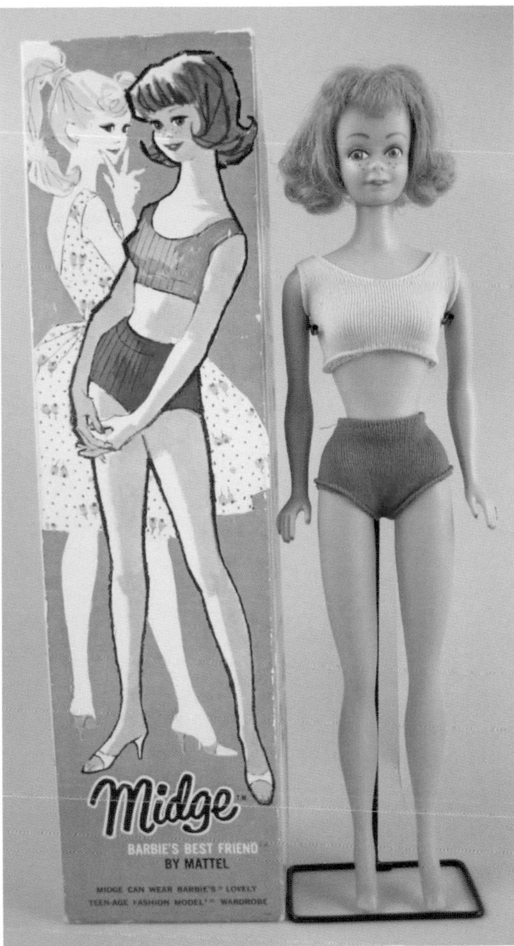

Photo courtesy McMasters Harris Auction Co., Cambridge, Ohio; www.McMastersHarris.com

Midge, in original box, blonde hair, blue eyes, plum lips with painted teeth, pierced ears, straight legs, wearing two piece turquoise and blue swimsuit, in box with black wire stand. Box insert replaced. **$115**

shoes, and corsage. Booklet included. Box not mint, insert missing. **$80**

Flocked Hair Ken, in original box. Flocked blonde hair, blue eyes, straight legs, wearing red swim trunks and cork sandals with red vinyl straps. Yellow terry cloth towel also included. Box insert replaced, box not mint. **$80**

MOD Hair Ken, NRFB, brunette hair Ken wearing brown/white checked jacket over white turtleneck, brown slacks and shoes. In box with white plastic stand. Box edges are worn. **$57**

Midge, in original box, straight legs. Midge has straight legs, titian hair, blue eyes, dark plum lips. Wearing two-piece swimsuit with pale aqua top and orange bottom. She comes with box marked "Blonde" in good condition. Also included are a gold wire stand and booklet. **$57**

Midge, in original swimsuit and box with stand, titian hair, blue eyes, dark pink lips, straight legs. Wearing original two-piece yellow and orange swimsuit and red "Japan" marked open toe shoes. Black wire stand included. Box not mint. **$69**

Bendable Leg Midge, in original swimsuit. Brunette hair in original set with headband. Deep coral lips with light brown freckles. Both bendable legs work smoothly. 1964. .... **$230**

Brunette Midge, in original box. Brunette hair, blue eyes, pierced ears, straight legs, wearing two-piece pink and red swimsuit, red open-toe shoes, in box with booklet and black wire stand. Box not mint, three split corners repaired with tape, replaced box insert. **$57**

Titian Midge, in original box, titian hair, blue eyes, pink lips, straight legs, wearing yellow and orange two-piece swimsuit. Replaced box insert, box not mint. **$46**

Titian Bendable Leg Midge, in original swimsuit. Titian hair with faded blue ribbon headband, blue eyes, plum lips, pierced ears. Wearing original multicolored stripe one-piece knit swimsuit. Legs are loose and right leg has pin-sized hole. Both feet and ankles have several pin-sized holes. **$143**

Midge and Ken, Midge has titian hair, blue eyes, straight legs, and is wearing original orange and yellow two-piece swimsuit. Ken has blonde painted hair, blue eyes, and is wearing original red/white striped swimsuit and red swim trunks. .... **$46 pair**

Straight Leg Midge & Blonde Bubblecut Barbie, Brunette straight-leg Midge wearing pink and red two-piece swimsuit. Minor wear to swim top and small stain on bottom. Coral lips, coral fingernails and toenails, light brown freckles. Blonde bubble cut Barbie wearing original red swimsuit. Red lips and fingernails. Pierced ears with no green ear. .... **$115 pair**

P.J., in original outfit. Blonde hair with bead ties, brown eyes, rooted eyelashes, bright pink lips, cheek blush, twist 'n' turn waist and bendable legs. Wearing hot pink one-piece nylon swimsuit with crocheted skirt and orange vinyl waistband. **$46**

Live Action P.J., with microphone, wearing orange dress, sheer blouse and tights, silver knee-high boots, "suede" vest with long tassels. Also includes microphone. **$80**

Skipper, in original box. Boxed Skipper with original swimsuit, shoes marked Japan, sandals, headband, comb, brush, wrist tag, pamphlet and stand. 1964. .... **$172**

Skipper, in original swimsuit with 3 extra outfits. Blonde hair, rooted eyelashes, blue eyes, pink lips, cheek blush, a twist 'n' turn waist and bendable legs. "Pink Princess" outfit includes pink crepe dress with three gold buttons and lace trim, green crepe coat with gold buttons trimmed with pink velvet, and pink nylon panty hose. Hat and shoes not included; items are slightly age discolored; "Budding Beauty" includes hot pink/white taffeta with floral print dress only; "Daisy Crazy" is complete with hot pink knit dress and yellow floral print tricot, matching socks and yellow "Japan" marked flats. **$103**

Blonde Skipper, in original box. Blonde hair, blue eyes, pink lips, straight legs, wearing original red/white one-piece swimsuit and red "Japan" marked flats, in box with booklet. Box bottom has small tear. **$103**

Quick Curl Skipper, NRFB, circa 1962. Age discolored but in excellent condition. **$70**

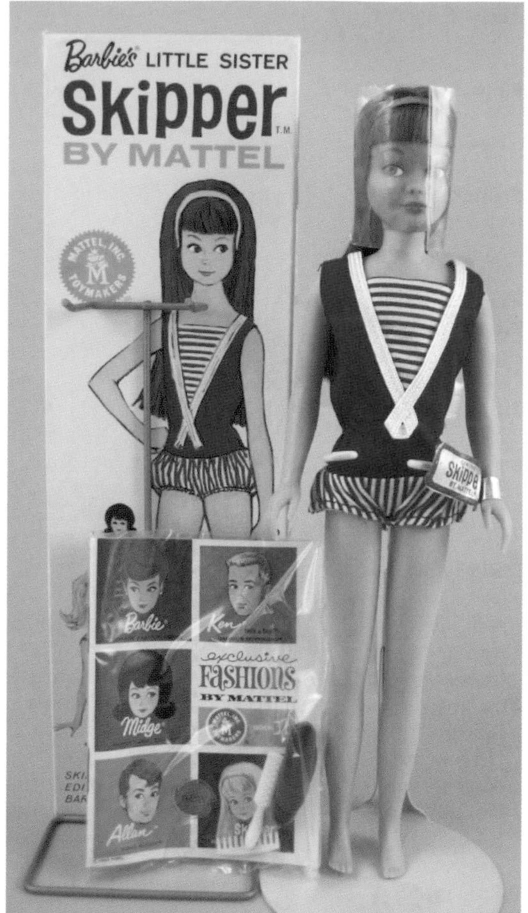

Photo courtesy McMasters Harris Auction Co., Cambridge, Ohio; www.McMastersHarris.com

Brunette Skipper, MIB. Brunette hair with metal headband and plastic wrap, blue eyes, pink lips, straight legs, wearing original red/white one-piece swimsuit, wrist tag. Gold wire stand and cellophane packet containing booklet, white comb and brush, and red "Japan" marked flats included in box. Box insert has small tears. Box label has creased edge. **$201**

Photo courtesy McMasters Harris Auction Co., Cambridge, Ohio; www.McMastersHarris.com

Skooter, in "Hearts 'n' Flowers", two versions. Straight legs, blonde hair, brown eyes, wearing green cotton print skirt with yellow knit bodice and matching jacket and cap, yellow knit knee socks, and yellow "Japan" marked boots. Skooter has her "Arithmetic" and "English" books in black vinyl book strap and a yellow vinyl purse with shoulder strap. Also included is the "blue" version of this outfit, dress with jacket only. Small discoloration on lower front of skirt. This outfit is hard to find. One rubberband in hair is broken. **$172 all**

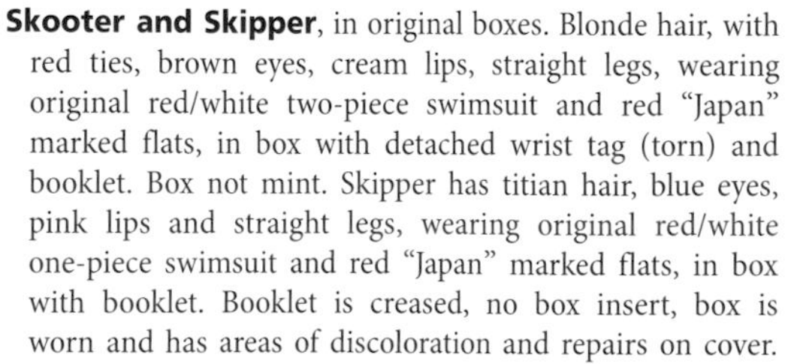

Skooter and Skipper, in original boxes. Blonde hair, with red ties, brown eyes, cream lips, straight legs, wearing original red/white two-piece swimsuit and red "Japan" marked flats, in box with detached wrist tag (torn) and booklet. Box not mint. Skipper has titian hair, blue eyes, pink lips and straight legs, wearing original red/white one-piece swimsuit and red "Japan" marked flats, in box with booklet. Booklet is creased, no box insert, box is worn and has areas of discoloration and repairs on cover. .... **$103 pair**

Twist 'N' Turn Stacey, blonde hair with ribbon tie, blue eyes, rooted eyelashes, dark pink lips with teeth, cheek blush, bendable legs. Wearing two-piece multicolored swimsuit. Head is slightly yellow. **$201**

Twist 'N' Turn Stacey, in original box. Box labeled "Copper Penny," blue eyes, dark pink lips with teeth, cheek blush, rooted eyelashes, bendable legs. Wearing multi-colored one-piece swimsuit, in box with clear plastic stand. Circa 1967. Original cellophane on box. **$575**

Talking Stacey & TNT Casey, Talking Stacey wearing original swimsuit, blonde hair, blue eyes and real lashes; string does not work. Twist 'N' Turn Casey wearing swimsuit tagged "Francie", brunette bob cut, blue eyes and real lashes. .... **$80 pair**

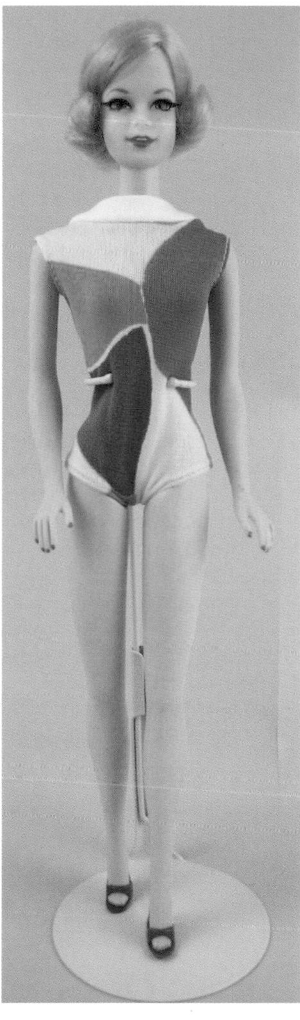

Photo courtesy McMasters Harris Auction Co., Cambridge, Ohio; www.McMastersHarris.com

Twist 'n' Turn Stacey, hair with attached string, blue eyes, rooted eyelashes, dark pink lips, cheek blush, and bendable legs. Wearing multicolored one-piece nylon swimsuit and unmarked blue open-toe shoes. Head is yellowed. **$172**

Photo courtesy McMasters Harris Auction Co., Cambridge, Ohio; www.McMastersHarris.com

Brunette "Walk Lively" Steffie, in original outfit. Dark brunette hair, brown eyes, bright orange lips, cheek blush, bendable legs, and attached wrist tag. Wearing original multicolored print nylon outfit, red chiffon scarf, and red pilgrim shoes. She also has her stand and instructions sheet. **$201**

Barbie: Accessories

Barbie shoes (24 pairs), includes 13 pairs of closed-toe and 11 pairs of open-toe shoes marked "Japan". Variety of colors. .... **$230 all**

"Bouncy Flouncy", "Tenterrific" Outfits. "Bouncy Flouncy" Barbie outfit: Multicolored floral print dress with matching purse and orange closed-toe shoes on card with label. Complete. "Tenterrific" Francie outfit: Multicolored floral print dress with matching hat, white vinyl purse with green ribbon straps, and green low heel shoes to complete the outfit on card with label. .... **$230 pair**

"Commuter Set" Barbie Outfit, white silk body blouse, blue/white checked body blouse, navy knit suit, black #1 open-toe shoes (both marked "Japan"), crystal necklace and bracelet, red floral hat, short white nylon gloves, and red hat box. White blouse has discolored spots. **$230**

Formal Occasion Barbie Fashion, #1697. Complete with dress, regal hooded cape, closed-toe pumps marked "Japan". 1967. .... **$115**

Furry Go Round, Sears Exclusive Barbie Fashion, orange suede cloth coat with rows of brown fur, hood, matching lace stockings, orange boots marked "Japan", 1967. .... **$125**

"Gay Parisienne" Barbie Outfit, blue "bubble" dress, white fur stole, blue net hat, gold velvet clutch, pearl earrings, pearl necklace, long white nylon gloves, blue #1 "Japan" marked open-toe shoes. **$977**

Picnic Set #967 and After Five #934, Complete Fashions, Picnic Set is complete and includes shirt, jeans, hat, wedge shoes, woven picnic basket, bamboo fishing pole with fish, 1959. After Five fashion is also complete with dress, hat and shoes marked "Japan", 1962. .... **$115 both**

Roman Holiday Barbie Fashion, #968. Includes dress, coat and high-heeled shoes marked "Japan", 1959. .... **$172**

"Student Teacher" Outfit, for Barbie and Midge, NRFB. Box is in very good condition. **$373**

Vintage Barbie Stands, four black pedestal bases (three marked TM, one marked R), three black wire attachments, one black wire base. One base is chipped, all are scuffed. .... **$316 all**

Dolls, General

Photo courtesy James D. Julia Auctioneers, Fairfield, Maine; www.JuliaAuctions.com

Bebe Mothereau. Most commonly found on composition bodies, this particular example appears to be all original and on a straight-wristed metal body, marked "B4M" on rear of head. She is jointed at shoulders, elbows, knees and hips, but the body has hollow metal construction and strung accordingly. Fine pale bisque with threaded blue paperweight eyes, slight mauve shadow and skin wig. 15 1/2" h. Some wear and flaking of paint to metal body. **$12,650**

A.M. Fany, All original, largest size ever made, character doll contained on the proper chunky composition body with original finish and straight wrists. Marked on rear of the head "231 FANY A. 5 M." he has pale bisque with well defined features such as large ears, arched eyebrows, blue glass sleep eyes and a pouting mouth. 18" h. Some minor wear at fingertips and minute chip at neck socket. **$9,200**

Size 1 Tete Jumeau, Blue paperweight eyes, this cabinet-sized young lady is on a marked straight-wristed Jumeau body. Finely painted features such as eyebrows, eyelashes and mouth. **$5,750**

Cabinet-Sized Bru Jne 4, Brown-eyed bebe on a chevrot body with the hint of a tongue, this young lady features perfect bisque hands, antique aqua outfit and appropriate antique Bru-style shoes. Doll is marked "BRU Jne 4" on head and "BRU Jne 2" on shoulder plate, which is appropriate. Darker brown eyes accented by blonde mohair wig. 13" h. Some minor wear to outfit, kid body slightly soiled. **$12,650**

JDK 206 Character Child, The firm of Kestner made a series of character dolls known as the 200 series. This particular example, a #206, is on a pink ball-jointed composition body with blue glass sleep eyes, flyaway eyebrows and crooked smile. She is wearing a white cotton lace-like dress, antique pink leather shoes, and retains her original mohair wig with right and left braids forming buns over her ears. 12" h. Paint touch-up to right hand, left composition thigh has had extensive repair. **$8,625**

Photo courtesy James D. Julia Auctioneers, Fairfield, Maine; www.JuliaAuctions.com

BSW "Wendy" With Original Box. She appears to be all original from head to toe on a pink composition body and contained within a marked BSW box labeled, "Mon Petit Coeur". Peaches-and-cream bisque, pale blue glass sleep eyes, and a fine mohair wig with coiled braids. 14 1/2" h. Near mint original condition. **$17,250**

French Fashion, Contained Within Presentation Box. Swivel neck French fashion on gusseted kid body adorned in a stylish wool outfit and accompanied by a second outfit. Pale bisque with lined blue paperweight eyes and finely detailed facial painting. Outfits appear to be all original with possible exception of shoes. 14 1/2" h. **$1,150**

French Fashion Doll, Cabinet-sized, most likely by the firm of F.G., she is on a straight-legged kid body and dressed in a velvet costume of newer vintage. Finely feathered eyebrows, blue paperweight eyes, and a pursed mouth. 11" h. **$920**

Simon & Halbig, 1294 Character Child With Clockwork Eyes. Most commonly used for store displays, these dolls with side-glancing clockwork eyes were used to draw attention to goods being sold. This particular example has a lifelike expression with an open mouth, mohair wig and when wound, eyes that would move from left to right for several hours before needing to be rewound. Usually found on composition baby bodies, this bisque-headed example is on a ball-jointed composition child body. 31" t. With normal wear and some old repairs at joints. Bisque head appears free of damage. Clockwork mechanism in working order. **$1,265**

Conta & Boehme, China Head Doll. Unusual china head doll from the 1860s-70s. Her hair is drawn into two curls, twirled and made into a bun on the back of her head. Wearing an antique flower print dress affixed to a leather and cloth body. 14" h. Some wear to eyebrows and braids on rear of head. **$540**

Alt Beck & Gottschalk, Victoria Parian Doll. With golden blonde hair, well-defined comb marks and black beaded band in front, pierced ears, circa 1870. She is on an old cloth body with leather upper arms and bisque lower arms. Although old, this body is slightly newer than the head. She is dressed in black taffeta floor-length dress with white lace overlay panels on the front of the skirt and also wears a black beaded necklace and blue enamel drop earrings. 31". Faint hairline on back shoulder plate, small inherent firing flaw on front right shoulder edge. **$747**

Simon-Halbig, "Little Women" Doll. Larger than normally found, glass-eyed shoulder doll, she is incised "S&H 1160-2/0". She has a solid dome head with closed mouth and is on her original cotton-stuffed body with bisque forearms. Costumed in a vertical-striped silk dress with black taffeta cape and antique black leather shoes. Light brown mohair wig is original and is pulled back into four long curls at the neck. 11 1/2". Two finger tips repaired on right hand. **$240**

Shirley Temple Doll, with Original Box. Composition doll portraying the child star with original dress, wig, button and shoes. 19" h. Considerable crazing to face, slightly loose in the joints, otherwise generally good. Box is fair to good with water staining and settling. **$287**

Volland, Beloved Belindy Doll. Stereotype black mammy would accompany Raggedy Ann & Andy on their adventures. In all-original condition with watermelon smile and button eyes. 15" h. Some distress/holes/tear to dress, foot, and right arm area. Minute chip to underside of right eye button. Left side of torso is re-stitched on seam under dress. **$1,035**

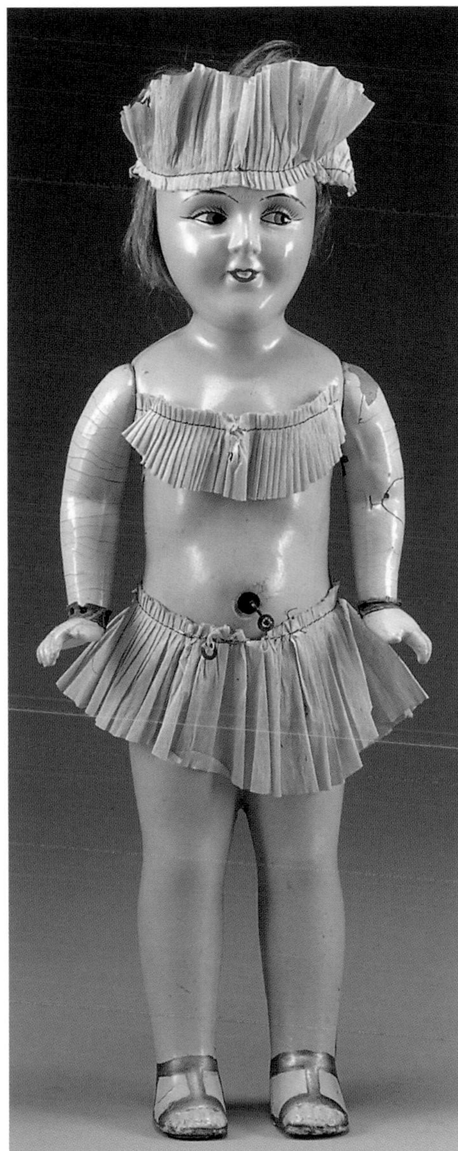

Photo courtesy James D. Julia Auctioneers, Fairfield, Maine; www.JuliaAuctions.com

Composition Automated Novelty Doll. Flapper girl dressed in crepe skirt and swimsuit top with matching headpiece. She has painted facial features and sandals. When wound, clockwork mechanism in chest makes her bosom shake. 18" t. Crazing to arms and some scattered chips to body finish, fully functional. **$460**

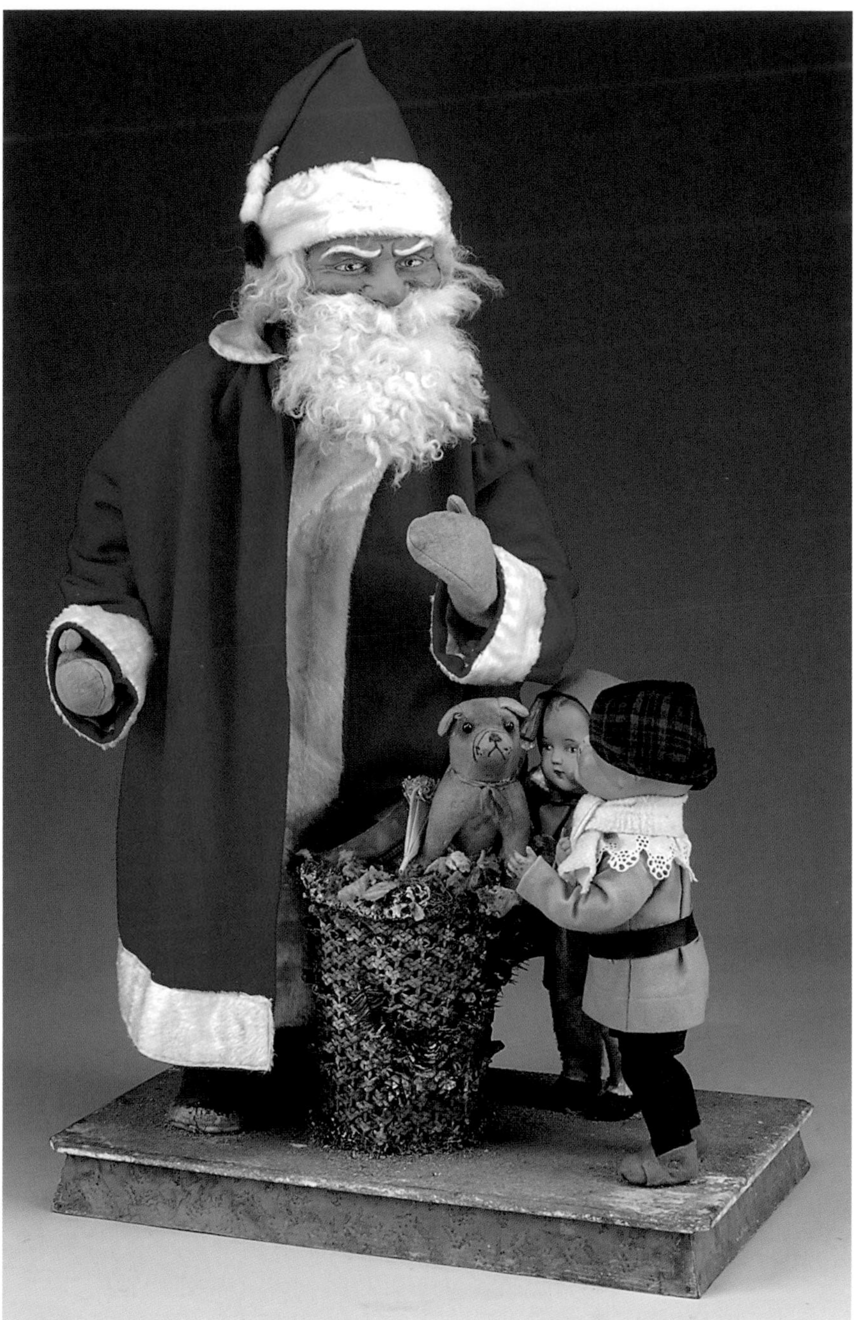

Photo courtesy James D. Julia Auctioneers, Fairfield, Maine; www.JuliaAuctions.com

Clockwork Nodding Santa With Children. Originally on display in the Mary Merritt Doll Museum since the early 1960s, Santa is standing with his basketful of toy treasures and at his feet are two little tots beseeching Santa to remember them on Christmas Eve. Clockwork mechanism within Santa's body is operational, and the children as well as Santa are mounted upon a snow-covered (mica) base with holiday paper trimming on sides. 32" overall h. Some old redressing to figures possible. **$2,300**

Photo courtesy James D. Julia Auctioneers, Fairfield, Maine; www.JuliaAuctions.com

Exposition Doll & Toy Co. Raggedy Ann. In as-found, untouched condition, with original and lightly soiled clothing. Exposition Toy Co. produced these dolls beginning in 1934. Perhaps only 20 or so have survived over the last 75 years. 20" h. Thigh joint has some re-enforced stitching. **$4,600**

Photo courtesy James D. Julia Auctioneers, Fairfield, Maine; www.JuliaAuctions.com

Circle Dot Bru. Cabinet sized French bebe with amber paperweight eyes, original skin wig (not fully removed) and an original French bebe dress. On a kid body (minor wear) with bisque lower arms, her mouth slightly parted with hint of a tongue, typical of a Circle Dot Bru. 14" h. Hint of whiteness to nose. As typical with early dolls, sometimes some light "dustiness" to bisque is present. Minute chip to bisque at earring hole on underside of right ear and a small patch to kid at shoulderplate on arm. **$11,500**

Dollhouses, Dolls, Accessories

Photo courtesy James D. Julia Auctioneers, Fairfield, Maine; www.JuliaAuctions.com

Ten-Room Mystery Dollhouse. Circa 1890. Sold by F.A.O. Schwartz of New York City, this was one of the largest in a series of Mystery Dollhouses sold in the 1890s. The term "Mystery Dollhouse" was given by Flora Jacobs (1918-2006) as the maker has never been identified. This particular house has the gambrel roof and has the carved shingles on the main roof as well as the wing on the right side. Painted a soft cream color with black chamfered wood. There are two entrances; one going into the main part of the house and the other going into the wing. The house has four sections that open to reveal eight rooms. All the rooms have wallpaper, baseboards and raised-panel interconnecting doors. The floors are often referred to as parquet, but are actually scored and hand painted to look like parquet. An elaborate staircase with an alcove is found under the staircase. Additional attic rooms are in the openings on the roof, there is a dormer on the front that opens, a window that opens on the side of the gambrel roof and a window that opens in the back; all having small rooms. Overall house is 39 1/2" t x 59" w x 24 3/4" d. Replaced scalloped trim work at ceiling level of each room, wallpapers in both hallways seem to be original and other rooms appear to have replacement paper. Exterior cream facades are repainted and some trim on interior appears repainted. The small raised-panel door entering the wing is unhinged. **$8,625**

Christian Hacker, Dollhouse With Elevator. German dollhouse with many architectural features, a large front porch and side porch with carved columns, a large front balcony and an elaborate side balcony. The house is painted a cream color with brown timbering decorating the facade of the second story. Although there is repaint on most of the house, it still retains the original design and details. The basement has windows and does open outward to allow storage for a transformer for wiring of electricity. There are painted brackets under the roof and a larger center dormer and balcony on the roof. The roof has lithograph paper that appears to be replaced and also supports a chimney. The house opens from the front and has four large rooms and two hallways for the elevator that moves up and down by a clockwork mechanism. The floors and walls have been re-papered with appropriate papers. All the rooms have their original electrical outlets in the ceiling with beaded chandeliers that do work and provide lighting in the house. 45" t x 44" w x 24" d. The creamy yellow facade may have some touch-up but the brown timbering has been repainted. The blue outlines on the porches and brackets under the roof have been repainted. Gold paint has recently been used on the turned posts and knobs on top of the railings. The doors appear original. The base to the house has been repainted, the back of the house has original brick paper. **$6,900**

Gottschalk, Red-Roof Dollhouse. Circa 1910. Stationary front with both sides and back that are open. The front facade has many architectural features such as curved porches with elaborate railings and columns on both levels, bay windows on both corners, extending from the ground level to the roof, double-door entrances with glass transoms over them at both levels and a set of front steps. On the rooftop is a large dormer with flower boxes and a Dutch gable to accent the house. The exterior of the house is painted a light tan with darker tan trim, cream-colored railings and posts, outline decoration in gray/green. Each side of the house is open, exposing three levels. The rooms have inter-connecting doors and the walls are papered and are angular in shape. One side of the house has an elaborate mahogany staircase that extends all three levels. (There is a small room on the bottom floor that is open.) The back of the house has all three levels open with the addition of railings and posts that enclose the corners of the house. 36" t x 28" w x 28" d. Exterior is repainted, interior repapered but professionally done. **$4,025**

Christian Hacker, Dollhouse With Bay Windows. Two-story house with unusual front, two bays and large dormer on roof and over hanging front porch. House is painted a soft tan with white trim and it has the original lithographed papered roof. Sides of the house have brick paper and the back is painted white. The house opens from the front and has four rooms with interconnecting doors. House is partially furnished with Schneegas furniture. 31" t x 28" w x 19" d. Wallpaper appears to be original; trim work, side brick work and floor papers are possible replacements. One door missing. Front of house has had some restoration. **$2,875**

Homemade, Brown Brick Dollhouse. Circa 1880. Original brown brick facade of double windows, an entrance with a door and skylights and a single window above the doorway. The slanting framed roof is painted black having two chimneys. There are four rooms and two halls with a staircase. There are windows on the front and sides of the house as well as an etched glass window at the top of the stair landing which is on the back of the house. There are also interconnecting doors with porcelain knobs and there is a fireplace in each room. 37" t x 33" w x 16 3/4" d. The floors and the walls have been repapered. **$2,300**

Photo courtesy James D. Julia Auctioneers, Fairfield, Maine; www.JuliaAuctions.com

Homemade Dollhouse, With Stained Glass. Exterior of house has been repainted to resemble stucco with a painted dark-red roof having two chimneys. The house opens from the front, a large center hall opens in two parts with a staircase and stained glass windows on the landing of the staircase. There are four large rooms, two large halls with a staircase. The house has a gray stone foundation with matching front steps. The front windows of the house are trimmed with flower boxes. The house has been electrified and a lock and key are found on the front entrance to lock up the entire house. 49" t x 48" w x 21 1/2" d. The interior of the house has been repapered and repainted recently.
$1,150

Photo courtesy James D. Julia Auctioneers, Fairfield, Maine; www.JuliaAuctions.com

Gottschalk, Red Roof Dollhouse. Exterior of the house has been repainted, but the original structure remains intact. It has a light olive-green facade with dark aqua and cream paint. There are cardboard mullions in the windows and doors. The front of the house has three balconies with fancy columns and railing. The house opens from the front to expose six rooms. The wallpapers and floor papers are not original to the house. The house also features side windows, outdoor steps and has been electrified. The roof has been repainted maroon and has two chimneys. 38" t x 31" w x 19" d. **$3,565**

Photo courtesy James D. Julia Auctioneers, Fairfield, Maine; www.JuliaAuctions.com

Silber & Fleming Dollhouse, Three-story house, considered a flat-box type; the roof is flat with the front facade rising above the roof, has been over-painted with similar colors to the original surface. The first level has bay windows with paint resembling stone. The two upper levels are painted in a red-orange brick with darker red brick over the windows. The house opens from the front to show six rooms; all wallpapered and three halls with staircases. Each room has a built-in fireplace and each window in the front of the house has lace curtains. There are balconies located on the second floor. 45" t x 34" w x 18 1/2" d. The wallpaper on the back of the large doors that open to the house are original and extends to all levels. The floor papers in all six rooms appear original as they are all the same, the wallpapers in all six rooms may have been replaced. **$2,300**

Photo courtesy James D. Julia Auctioneers, Fairfield, Maine; www.JuliaAuctions.com

Doll House Furniture and Accessories. Circa 19th Century. Walterhausen (Boulle) furniture includes six Gothic chairs upholstered in blue cut velvet with gold background, a rectangular marble top dining room table, an upright piano with gold transfer work and depressible keys, a china cabinet with drawers on legs with its original blue interior paper and a fancy wall clock with pendulum and porcelain face. There is a matching pair of ormolu prints made by Erhardt & Sohne, an ornate ormolu mantle clock and a crumber set in ormolu. Largest is 7 3/4" t. **$2,415 all**

Dollhouse Furniture and Accessories, Waltershausen (Boulle) furniture consisting of four-drawer chest with marble top having backsp lash, a drop-front desk with carved white front columns and beautiful gold transfer work on the front with the interior having original blue paper and a round marble top table with pedestal base. Accessories include an ormolu cutlery tray with soft metal utensils, vase in ormolu base, soft-metal painted gold metal holder, an ormolu birdcage with wax bird, an Art Nouveau soft-metal clock with paper face, two mantle clocks with one in soft metal painted gold and paper face and the other is ormolu with pendulum and black face, an ormolu coo-coo clock, an amber glass chandelier with soft-metal decoration on the side suspended by a chain, a soft metal compote holder with fishbowl and fish attached, an ormolu holder missing green bowl, an ormolu framed mirror, filigree framed print, a tin painted gold framed print and an ormolu framed print. Desk is 6 3/4" t. Some silver loss to mirror, ormolu clock with pendulum is missing one hand and coo-coo clock is missing string that pulls bird as well as the clock weights. .... **$2,875 all**

Dollhouse Ormolu Revolving Picture Frame, Circa 19th Century. Each photo is set in a separate ormolu frame, which is attached to a stand. Back of each photo has a foil lining. SIZE: 2 1/4" t. **$3,737**

Two Dollhouse Ormolu Accessories, Circa 19th Century. 1) Fancy ormolu telephone with two cranks on the side of the box with receiver mounted on top. 2) Ormolu floor lamp with white Bristol shade and chimney. Both items were made by Erhard & Sohne; 2 1/4" t and 4 1/2" t. .... **$2,300 pair**

Artisan Dollhouse Furniture, Eight pieces, seven of which were made by craftsman Renee Isabelle consisting of a flat top highboy, bonnet top highboy, armoire, drop-front desk (signed by Judith Dunger), corner cabinet, chair, two-drawer chest and small oval table. All are made with scenes in lacquered Japanned designs. Fine detailed pulls, hinges and trim work. In addition there are three original paintings; two larger ones are signed "Whitford"; 2 1/8" to 7 3/4" t. .... **$2,875 all**

Artisan Dollhouse Furniture, Accessories. Six pieces were made by craftsman Renee Isabelle including a linen press, drop front desk, armoire, four-drawer chest, Japanned tall cabinet and round candle stand. These pieces are intricately painted with scenes on back of cupboard doors; doors open to interiors having fine detail and hand painted scenes on backs of doors. Other items include inlaid sideboard, display stand, framed piece of needlework, small boxes with covers by other artists as well as hand-painted portraits framed in gold frames with one being signed "Whitford" and an enameled covered box with jeweled birds on lid; 2 1/2" to 8 1/4" t. .... **$2,185 all**

Artisan Dollhouse Furniture, Consisting of 10 pieces by craftsman Renee Isabelle including two armoires; one on legs with interior scenes on doors and other with hand painted interior drawer, an oval pedestal base with finely painted Japanese motif, two pedestal tables; one topped with a hinged-lid box, a settee upholstered with silk taffeta fabric printed by the artisan, two side chairs upholstered in cream silk with hand-painted flowers and the backs of the chairs have exquisite hand-painted flowers and a demilune cabinet on legs painted in pale gold with swags, scrolls and medallions of various scenes. Includes a sewing table intricately made with a medallion of a country scene hand painted on the lid that opens and a smaller lid of hand-painted scenes that also open with intricate interior space for housing sewing implements which includes a small box with cover. The last piece in the lot is a drop-front secretary with the exterior hand painted in Japan scenes with flower decoration on the front and sides as well as the interior. All edges are painted in gold with serpentine drawers. Included in the lot are four Russian covered boxes all with hand painted decoration, one painting of an 18th Century woman by Whitford housed in a gold frame, a framed black and white image of ballerinas and a large image of a woman in the countryside in gold frame as well as a miniature perfume bottle with lovebirds on lid; 2" to 7 1/4" t. .... **$3,105 all**

Handmade Dollhouse Carpets, 10 rugs from Eastern Europe or India. Copied from original Oriental rugs, these contemporary silk rugs have fine detail. Range from 8 1/2" to 15 1/2" l. .... **$1,495 all**

Dollhouse Furniture And Accessories, Circa 1920s.Set of parlor furniture by Paul Leonhardt made in the 1920's-1930's including a sofa and four side chairs with upholstered seats and backs with gold paint accompanied by a matching marble-top table with four turned legs and a display cabinet with glass on three sides and glass shelves having porcelain dishes. Three additional pieces in cream, including a round table and two side chairs. All are original pieces. Accessories include an ormolu birdcage on legs, two soft-metal framed prints, an Art Nouveau mantle clock painted green with gold decoration and a miniature book with printed pages. Tallest is approx. 8". Parlor set shows slight wear to upholstery, one chair has small piece of decoration missing. .... **$2,875 all**

Antique Dollhouse Dolls, 13 dollhouse dolls; three ladies, one boy and nine men from sizes 5" to 6 3/4" t. Most are redressed and all have painted eyes and molded hair. Remaining dolls are six all bisque children having glass eyes and original dress with a 7 1/2" glass-eyed maid; two sets of twins and the maid appear to be redressed with old fabric. One man has feet broken off, another man has chipped feet. .... **$2,415 all**

Antique Dollhouse Kitchen Accessories, Including a tin Marklin water basin painted white with blue trim with water tank storage on top and a faucet, a blue and white tin onion holder, a six-drawer tin spice holder painted white with blue decoration, two tin brush holders painted blue and white, a large blue and white tin dust pan, early tin kerosene lamp, a blue and white tin cutlery tray, a good tin picnic basket with blue and white Delft photos on each side of the base as well as top with two openings on spring and handle, hanging spice rack with small handled drawers painted white with blue lettering, a tin box that hangs on the wall for brushes and shoe polish painted white with blue lettering, two porcelain-covered boxes with Herring and Asparagus written in German on the lids, a hanging tin shelf with three porcelain canisters with lids and a tin kitchen stove with two open burners with pots and lids that rest inside the burners and a tin plate door on the front. Water basin is 5 1/4" t. .... **$3,565 all**

Antique Dollhouse Accessories, Including a filigree plant stand in soft metal having an asphaltum finish (brown wash) with large circular top holding flower pots and birdcage suspended in center with soft metal flowering tree supporting it and base has fancy scroll design. Marklin tin fireplace having painted brick in soft yellow lined in blue with a grate and fender around it with the trim at the top being tin painted gold, tin birdcage with red roof and bird hanging on a suspended ring, a fancy circular ormolu birdcage on a stand with a wax bird on a swing made by Erhard & Sohne, an ormolu compote with impressed floral design in center, large Art Nouveau hanging mirror with lilies and bellflower in center, an Art Nouveau console mirror which hangs from the wall, a square ormolu birdcage with parrot, an ormolu hanger, an ormolu mantle clock with pendulum and porcelain face, a soft-metal, double-covered inkwell desk set with marble and two ormolu framed prints. Birdcage on stand is approx. 5 1/4" t. Red-roof birdcage having poor repaint and both Art Nouveau mirrors have some dark discoloration. .... **$3,105 all**

Ormolu Dollhouse Miniatures, large-scale chandelier with bulbs and shades, console mirror, three-part folding mirror with lithograph scenes on the reverse, a gilt metal three-part picture frame, cruet set, round birdcage as well as

Photo courtesy James D. Julia Auctioneers, Fairfield, Maine; www.JuliaAuctions.com

Nine Antique Dollhouse Dolls. Four glass-eyed Simon & Halbig ladies wearing evening gowns; two having original dresses and all having original wigs. Five gentlemen with mustaches with four in suits and the other wearing a tuxedo. All men have painted eyes and original limbs. Tallest woman is 8" and the tallest man is 7". Three of the doll's gowns are fragile and are melting, there are no broken or missing limbs. The men's clothing shows wear. **$2,520 all**

Photo courtesy James D. Julia Auctioneers, Fairfield, Maine; www.JuliaAuctions.com

Antique Dollhouse Kitchen Furniture and Accessories. Includes two kitchen furniture sets; one set is cream trimmed in blue consisting of a 9 1/2" tall cupboard with matching table and two chairs, a work table and hanging shelf. The second set is mustard trimmed in red consisting of a 9" tall cupboard with matching table and chair as well as a hanging shelf and a workbench having two doors below. A large tin cupboard painted beige and blue in original paint as well as an odd table and two chairs in cream are included. Accessories include a tin egg container with eggs which hangs on the wall, a water basin in mustard trimmed in red with faucet, heavy metal dishes with platters, tureens in tan trimmed in blue. A white tin hanging shelf with canisters labeled with spices having drawers below all trimmed in blue, a tin canister set with four large and four small canisters having lids with four hanging tin containers in tan and blue decoration and a similar wall clock. Two tin hanging utensil racks. Metal clock with movable hands and some treenware plates, bowl, compote and vase in two different patterns. Tallest is 9 1/2". All tin pieces have wear and flaking to paint and some wooden kitchen pieces show minor wear to paint. **$3,737 all**

three framed prints. Tallest is 7 3/4". Chandelier is missing one bulb. Console mirror is missing tabletop cover. Three-part folding mirror is missing some silvering with slight discoloration at weld points and small amount of lithograph image missing. Cruet set and birdcage show some dark discoloration. .... **$2,185 all**

Four Dollhouse Dolls, 1) Soldier with a red jacket having gold Dresden paper decoration wearing black felt pants and high leather boots. Soldier has rare brown eyes and fine black mustache and hair. 2) Gentleman dressed in a black felt tuxedo with shirt, bow tie and vest. He has painted blue eyes and molded brown hair. 3) Black butler in black felt tuxedo carrying a white towel on his arm with a white shirt, bow tie and vest. He has finely painted eyes, eyebrows and mouth with smooth black hair. 4) Soldier with a red jacket, gold Dresden paper decoration and matching hat as well as a dark velvet jacket on his shoulder complete with a sword at his side and tall leather boots. 7" t each. Black-haired solder has a tiny moth hole in the arm of his jacket. .... **$3,600 all**

Dollhouse Fireplace And Dolls, Circa 19th Century. Large gilt tin fireplace with over-mantel mirror, with hearth area being black tin with a grate and red foil paper to represent a fire. The fireplace has impressed designs around the hearth and on the columns as well as under the mantel. The mantel has a scalloped edge and the over-mantel mirror is divided into three parts with scalloped designs on the outer mirrors and a sunburst in the pediment at the top. Also included are two soldiers with original uniforms; one with red and navy blue having a sword at his side, high black boots, a decorative helmet with gold eagle on the front and tassel on the side. Other soldier has royal blue coat with red decoration, gold buttons with epaulets and he has a sword at his side. Both soldiers have molded hair and mustaches; the soldier in the royal blue jacket has molded black hair and mustache. Fireplace is 8 5/8" t x 6" w. Both soldiers are 7 1/4" t. .... **$3,565 all**

Toys, General

Althoff Bergman, camel on platform, American, tin, circa 1880, in original yellow paint with red mouth, mounted on a green base with small cast-iron wheels, 9" l x 7 1/4" h. Scattered paint flaking all over the surface of the camel and base. A piece of the tin on one side of the leg missing. **$1,035**

Arcade, Andy Gump Car, elaborate version features a crank, license plates, painted comic figure and additional highlighting to wheels and trim, 7 1/2" l, some damage to rear license plate. **$840**

Arcade, Buick sedan, enameled in blue and black with white rubber tires, circa 1930s, 8 3/4" l. Overall paint is very fine with some restoration to hood. **$1,552**

Arcade, Chevy sedan, black with silver grille and gold headlights. Nickel-plated wheels with black hubs, 8 1/4" l. Replaced spare tire. **$2,520**

Arcade, gas pumps (pair), one is yellow with red trim, with moveable gas indicator on front and stenciled "Arcade Gas" at top; second is red with gold highlights and has its original hose, 6 1/4" and 6 1/2" h, respectively. Yellow pump has minor chipping. Red pump with some rusting to front. .... **$805 pair**

Arcade, Mack coal dump truck, painted red with "coal" stenciled on back dump. Has cast-iron wheels painted white with red hubs. Also has an original Arcade decal on bed of dump, 10 1/4" l, most of its wear to wheels and sides of bed and hood of truck. Figure is a replacement. **$1,150**

Arcade, Mack tank truck, with Mack decal on grille. This version has a cast-iron tank, it also came with a tin tank and has dual wheels on the back of truck. Painted red with spoke steel wheels and a nickel-plated driver, 13" l. Overall paint chipping and wear to truck especially on the grille. **$920**

Arcade, Plymouth (?) coupe, one of the largest toy coupes made by Arcade, it features a removable spare tire mounted to the trunk, 8 1/2" l. Old paint restoration and probable replaced spare. **$747**

Arcade, "Red Baby" dump truck, with original stencil on front doors, "International Harvester Trucks". Contains original nickel-plated driver, four cast-iron, nickel-plated wheels with red hubs, and a working nickel-plated wrench used to lift the dump body, 10 3/4" l. **$1,200**

Arcade, red-top cab, usually found in black and orange. Enameled in black with a white center section and red windows and roof, it sports white hubs and gray tires, 5" l. Overall very good, heavier paint loss due to flaking on roof. **$805**

Arcade, T-Bar Mack dump truck, painted gray with nickel-plated spoke wheels and nickel-plated driver. Also has

Photo courtesy Morphy Auctions, Denver, Pa.; www.MorphyAuctions.com

Buddy L, 26" Tank Line truck with original decals. **$5,500.**

Photo courtesy Bertoia Auctions, Vineland, N.J.; www.BertoiaAuctions.com

Britains, 17" toy of painted metal features a whimsical hand-painted figure with a striking resemblance to the puppet show character "Punch." The cloth-dressed figure rides in a circle on a two-wheel bicycle attached by a wire support to a heavy base. **$21,850**

"Mack" embossed on driver door, 12" l. Heavy wear throughout. **$360**

Bandai, Ford Custom Ranch Wagon with original box, wagon is lithographed yellow with dark blue roof, chromed bumpers and headlights, rubber tires and celluloid windshield and hubcaps that read "Ford". Box is brightly lithographed, 11 1/2" l. Car has a few rub marks. Friction motor inoperative. Box lid with minor soiling and creases. **$517**

Battleship, scale model, tin, ram front with many gun turrets, ventilators, railings, lifeboats, riggings, etc. Meant to be operational with an electric motor, it was powered in the water with three propellers. Of unknown vintage, but most likely made in the 1920s, primarily out of tin with some wood, and painted in proper colors. At the stern of the ship, the name "Liberte" is applied, suggesting that this was a French vessel, 53" l. In need of re-rigging, partial front mast, no motor present. Bottom shows some damage with replacement keel. **$6,000**

Photo courtesy Bertoia Auctions, Vineland, N.J.; www.BertoiaAuctions.com

Yonezawa Space Man, 1950s Japanese skirted robot, with box 9 1/2". **$9,200**

Bing, touring car, tin, lithographed red with white and peach wheels. Marked "GBN" on back of car. Also has a lithographed driver/chauffeur with goggles, 9 1/4" l. Considerable amount of rust to fenders and floor of car. **$747**

British, limousine, lithographed olive green with tan running boards, black and green lithographed wheels and cream bumpers. Stamped on side, "MADE IN GT. BRITAIN", 13 1/2" l. Some scratching to roof, hood and fenders and some minor denting to roof. **$345**

British, town car, late 1920s, with chauffeur, having wind-up motor and is stamped on back, "MADE IN GB, MADE IN ENGLAND", 9 1/4" l. Some rusting to roof, back of one fender detached. **$300**

Buddy L, aerial ladder truck, electric headlights, separate steel grille and pressed-disk simulated spoke tires. With a pull-along wire handle. Overall painted red with original "Buddy L" decals, 29" l. Some discoloration and some areas lacking paint. Minor rust. **$1,380**

Buddy L, cement mixer, and heavy steam shovel painted red and black. Shovel has two pistons that help move it up and down. Cement mixer is painted gray and is on steel wheels. Larger is 18" l. Shovel appears to be intact, heavy wear throughout. Cement mixer is lacking door on boiler. Having partial original decals with heavy overall wear. .... **$977 both**

Buddy L, coal truck, with opening doors and headlamps, simulated pressed tires. Painted black and has original Buddy L decals and original coal chute, 11" h x 25" l. Some rusting and wear to fenders. **$6,325**

Buddy L, express line truck, 1920s, some paint loss to roof area, where either a child sat or pushed on the truck with hands. Still retains original tailgate and opening/closing doors on rear, 24 1/2" l. Also with wear to internal bed and dashboard decal. **$2,185**

Buddy L, railway express truck, green removable roof and sides, two back opening doors. Cab painted black and has red disk steel wheels, 24" l. Decals are of more recent vintage. Bed and cab of truck over-painted. **$805**

Buddy L, road roller, as toy is pulled, the pistons go back and forth and the roller smooths the ground in front of it. Painted green and retains all original decals, 18" l. Some rusting to the roller and wheels, uniform wear to roof, and wear to decals. **$1,840**

Buddy L, sand and gravel truck with opening doors. Deluxe version has headlights, two opening doors and pressed-disk simulated spoke tires, 26" l. Black body of truck has been repainted. **$3,450**

Buddy L, tank truck, cab is painted black with green tank. Also has original spout and cap on tanker. With original decals, "Buddy L Tank Line" on both sides, 23 1/2" l. Some minor flaking to tank. Front fenders are slightly. **$2,587**

Buddy L, fire trucks (two), aerial ladder truck painted red with nickel-plated extension ladders. With original decals and brass bell. Hook and ladder truck also painted red with original decals, ladder racks, reel and ladders. Longer is 30". Aerial ladder appears all original with original decals and bell, with most of its wear on fenders and high points. The hook and ladder is all original with original ladders, even wear throughout. ..... **$1,150 both**

Buddy L, flivvers (two), a flivver truck painted black with steel spoke tires. Also has the earlier Buddy L decal on bottom. Along with a Buddy L dump flivver. Longer is 12". Truck is all original in poor to fair condition with significant paint wear and rusting. Dump (rarer) over-painted. ..... **$840 both**

Cap gun, monkey with coconut, animated, when coconut in monkey's hand is raised, cap is placed on top of gun and trigger is pulled. Coconut slams down and explodes cap, 4" h x 4" l. Retains more than half of its original japanned finish and is in working condition. **$230**

Carette, limousine, rubber-tired wheels, four original headlights, and beveled glass windows. Lithographed in dark green with opening doors to passenger compartment, with chauffeur, 16" l. Minor flaking to lithograph sides and driver and typical chipping around the doors. **$6,325**

Carette, limousine, lithographed red with a blue roof, white spoke tires. Has a brake and a reverse, also has two original head lamps and a hand-painted chauffeur, 13" l. With some minor discoloration to hood and some wear around the doors and on one fender. **$2,587**

Carette, ocean liner, with four funnels, three crow's nests, search light, 12 ventilators. Painted cream, tan, black and white, 15" h x 27" l. The boat has been over-painted and has replaced string. **$4,200**

Carousel, European, tin clockwork, circa 1900, Turn of the Century, horses with riders and gondolas with passengers. With dual flags (replacements) atop a cloth canopy protecting the passengers from the elements. When wound, the carousel propels in a counterclockwise fashion, 14" h. Some significant flaking to various horses and riders. Clockwork mechanism appears to have been repaired. **$2,300**

Photo courtesy Mosby & Co. Auctions, Frederick, Md.; www.MosbyAuctions.com

Betty Boop, 9" prewar Japanese celluloid with fur stole.
$2,805

Carousel, German, hand-painted tin, circa 1910, likely by Mueller & Kaderer, containing four pressed-cardboard horses and riders. The toy is activated by either a hand crank or is attached to a live steam engine. When activated, the carousel goes around in a counterclockwise motion while emitting "plink plank" music (inoperative). Three glass and tin lights suspended from an internal canopy would illuminate the platform for nighttime rides. Still retains original flag at top, 17" h. Significant flaking to tin. One lamp missing, but tin shade is present. **$690**

Charlie Chaplin, wind-up walker, lithographed German tin features a blue coat, black pants and black trademark derby with cane in his right hand. Charlie stands on cast-iron feet, and when he is wound, he does his famous penguin shuffle, 9" h. Left arm appears to be a replacement. Wear on high spots with some minor scratches, and Charlie's face has some discoloration. **$540**

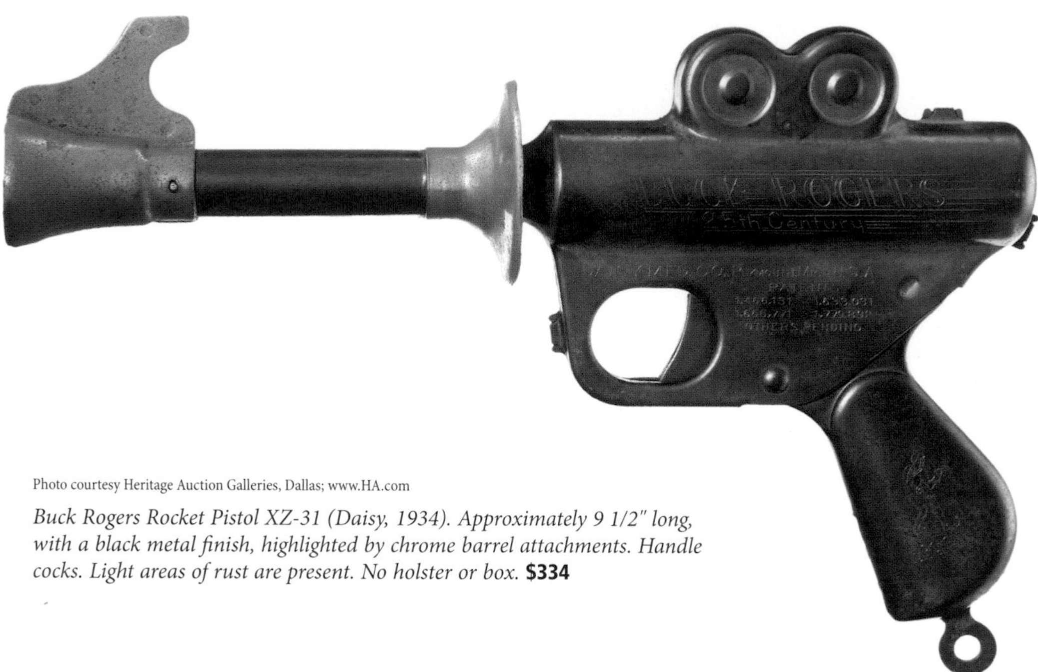

Photo courtesy Heritage Auction Galleries, Dallas; www.HA.com

Buck Rogers Rocket Pistol XZ-31 (Daisy, 1934). Approximately 9 1/2" long, with a black metal finish, highlighted by chrome barrel attachments. Handle cocks. Light areas of rust are present. No holster or box. **$334**

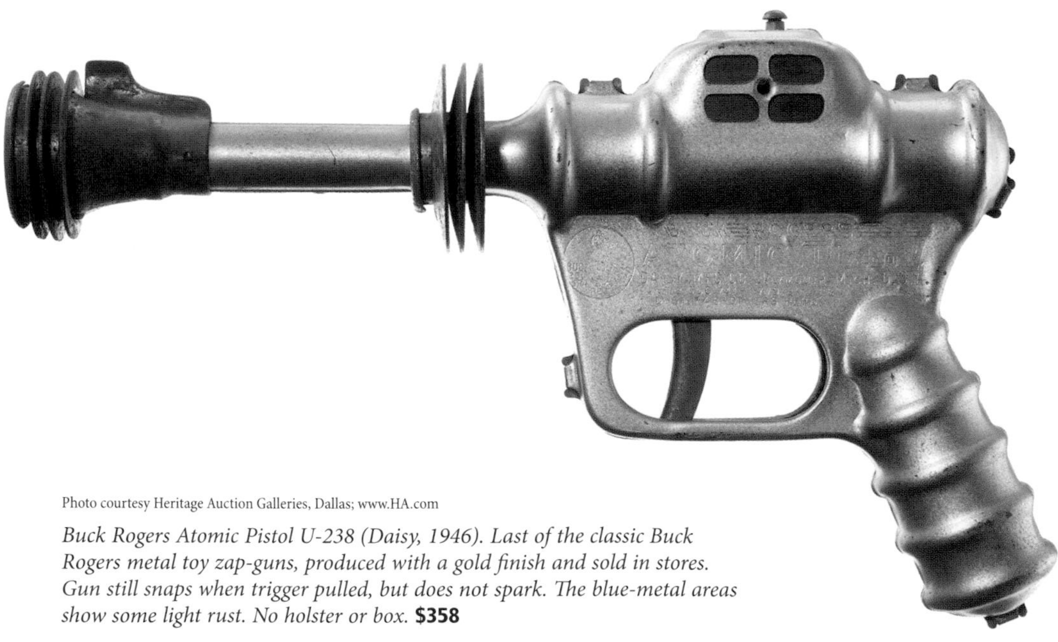

Photo courtesy Heritage Auction Galleries, Dallas; www.HA.com

Buck Rogers Atomic Pistol U-238 (Daisy, 1946). Last of the classic Buck Rogers metal toy zap-guns, produced with a gold finish and sold in stores. Gun still snaps when trigger pulled, but does not spark. The blue-metal areas show some light rust. No holster or box. **$358**

Photo courtesy Bertoia Auctions, Vineland, N.J.; www.BertoiaAuctions.com

Marklin, Circa-1909 Fidelitas clown car caravan. The German hand-painted tinplate toy measures 37 1/2" long and is rarely seen. **$103,500**

Photo courtesy Morphy Auctions, Denver, Pa.; www.MorphyAuctions.com

Harley-Davidson, cast-iron 8 1/2" toy motorcycle replicating a 1930 factory DAH Hill Climber. **$57,500**

Photo courtesy Morphy Auctions, Denver, Pa.; www.MorphyAuctions.com

U.S. Hardware Co., 14" painted cast-iron scull with oarsmen and coxswain. **$11,500**

Photo courtesy Morphy Auctions, Denver, Pa.; www.MorphyAuctions.com

Fisher-Price, "Push-Cart Pete," #740, wood, hand-painted face and legs. Head moves as he is pushed. Only known example, 9" l. **$14,400**

Chess set, cased, Bakelite, set in red and ochre in green felt-lined case. King is 4" h. **$840**

Dent, police patrol truck, painted blue with black roof and embossed "police patrol" on side panel of truck. Has four steel wheels and fifth wheel side-mounted to driver's side of truck, 8 3/4" l. Assembled in the 1970s. Wear to roof and some light oxidation to tires. **$1,320**

Doepke, Rossmoyne aerial ladder fire truck, authentic recreation of the American La France truck, in the original box. The paint is vibrant, the aluminum painted ladders are shiny and bright. With original brochure featuring many other Doepke toys, 33" l. Like new in box, some minor soiling. Box condition overall is very fine with some staining and minor tearing to flaps on one end. **$1,265**

Doepke, Rossmoyne ladder truck, with extension ladder and extra ladders and spare tire, wind up working siren, steerable front wheels, 33 1/2" l. Significant overall chipping, possibly clear coated. **$120**

Fallows, horse-drawn trolley, with original painted and stenciled decoration, red trolley with green roof stenciled "Central Transportation". Has four delicate cast-iron wheels and pulled by two brown horses with white manes and red saddles, 16" l. Roof still retains its gold-decorated stencil design. Paint flaked and pitted in places and scattered flaking and pitting over the trolley and horses. **$2,587**

Fallows, horse-drawn trolley, car painted green, red and yellow with four cast-iron wheels being pulled by two black horses, 19" l. With rusting and paint loss to the horses and some fading to the back of trolley. **$1,265**

Fallows, tin bell toy with Cupid astride a butterfly's body, as the toy is propelled along the floor, the butterfly's wings flap, Cupid rises and falls, and the bell rings. Luminescent, large multicolored embossed wings, Cupid is in flesh-tone paint with gilt wings and sash about his midsection and highlighted with brown hair, on an embossed orange-red painted tin base with iron wheels. Period catalog cut from Conway Brothers of Philadelphia refers to this toy as #1032 "Mechanical Cupid Butterfly with Gong Attachment", 8" l x 8 1/2" h. Untouched condition. **$6,325**

Fisher-Price, Donald Duck Cart, #544, with car and base painted blue. Lithographed Donald on wood and when toy is pulled, Donald's arms swing up and down and toy clicks, 10" l. Minor discoloration to paper. **$143**

Football players, hollow lead, unknown origin and manufacture, probably from 1920s, 11 opposing figures on two teams, one in red, the other in blue. Finely cast and lightweight. Each team consists of six crouched players, four standing, and one crouched player with ball. Range from 1 3/4" to 3 1/4" h. Heavy damage to one red player and one blue player. .... **$575 set**

George Brown, double ox cart, tin toy features original painted and stenciled design on the cream cart being

Photo courtesy Noel Barrett, Carversville, Pa.; www.NoelBarrett.com

General Grant Smoker clockwork toy (left), Ives, 14" h, cloth uniformed with cast-metal head and hands and cast-iron feet. **$18,700**; *Banjo Player, Jerome Secor, clockwork, cloth-dressed wood and metal figure with painted-tin banjo on cast-iron stool.* **$22,000**

drawn by two cream-colored oxen. The cart rides on original cast-iron wheels. Approximately 9 1/2" l. Scattered paint flaking over the entire surface of the cart and oxen. **$2,645**

George Brown, toy carts (two), red cart with mustard interior being drawn by a small white-painted horse; with its original delicate cast-iron wheels. The second, a covered green cart being pulled by a brown horse with red saddle having its original delicate cast-iron wheels. Red cart approximately 7 3/4" l, the green colored cart approximately 8" l. Much scattered paint loss and scratches on the red cart. The green cart with some flaking to the roof. ..... **$287 both**

Giraffe, wooden, circa 1950s-60s, multi-ball joints in crackled black and yellow paint. Partial decal on bottom of foot reads "Oakland", 14" h. Various paint chips, predominantly to head. **$150**

Gunthermann, clockwork trolley, lithographed, embossed doors and windows, 8 1/2" l. Some staining and/or corrosion to roof. Mechanism intact, but does not appear to catch. **$575**

Gunthermann, Foxy Grampa, tin, depicting a young man astride Foxy Grampa, who is on all fours and is propelled forward by the boy raising and lowering his legs, pushing his feet against the floor, 8" l. Mechanism functioning, paint is poor, lacking one leg and one arm. **$1,552**

Haji, Japanese, car with boat, trailer and original box, friction, 1950s, red lithographed car with orange trailer and bright

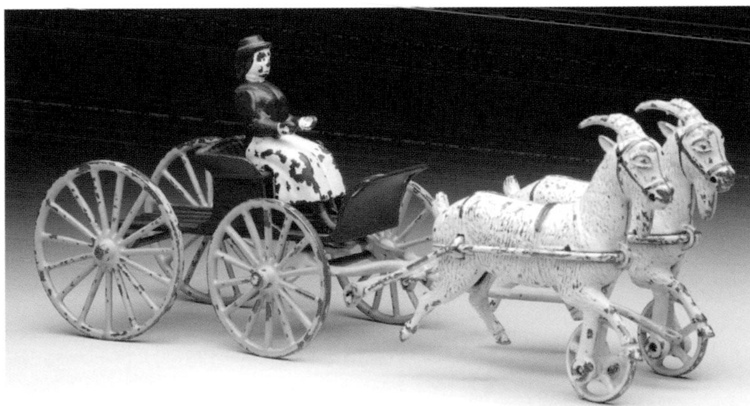

Photo courtesy James D. Julia Auctioneers, Fairfield, Maine; www.JuliaAuctions.com

Harris, goat cart, two white goats with black and red trappings pulling a blue buckboard with bright yellow wheels, being driven by a woman in a white and blue dress, 5" h x 13" l. Minor chipping and general wear, replaced driver. **$2,070**

Photo courtesy Morphy Auctions, Denver, Pa.; www.MorphyAuctions.com

Buddy L Jr., circa 1930 pressed-steel dairy truck, 24" long with opening doors, nickel-plated bumper with headlights, accompanied by six original accessory milk cans. **$11,500**

multicolored boat has an outboard motor, 16" l (total). **$460**

Harris, buckboard, two black prancing horses on wheels pulling a red buckboard with yellow enamel wheels and a polychrome driver in gray and flesh tones, 5" h x 13 1/2" l. Some overall wear. **$1,495**

Horseless carriage, cast iron and wood, simulating a turn-of-the-century vehicle with a large friction weight that would propel it forward. Finely detailed cast-iron canopy and kickboard with a female driver and her Buster Brown-type passenger atop a wooden chassis enameled in red with pinstripes. Of unknown manufacture, perhaps by Scheibel or Dayton Friction, 6 1/4" l. **$1,035**

Hubley, general digger, with green and red body, with nickel shovel on swivel rear. White rubber tires with wooden hubs, 10" l. CONDITION: Some minor flattening to tires. **$1,035**

Hubley, Lindy airplane, in gray paint with "Lindy" emblazoned in red across the wings. Celebrating Lindbergh's flight from the U.S. to France, 13 1/4" wingspan. Overall paint chips with pitting to nickel-plated nose and propeller. Underside shows some rust and replaced pulley string. **$977**

Hubley, phaeton, white carriage being pulled by a prancing black horse, with yellow wheels and a blue-painted woman driver. 5" h x 16 3/4" l. Color of back wheels does not match the front wheels. The figure is old but is not original to this toy. The white cart has heavy wear. The black horse is in excellent condition. **$632**

Hubley, #5 racer, large steel wheels that simulate the look of balloon tires, hunched-over driver, and hoods emblazoned with the number 5 that lift to reveal the engine, 9 1/2" l. Left and right hoods have been replaced. **$840**

Hubley, racer with moveable flames, rubber tires. When racer is rolled, twelve flames shoot from engine, 11" l. Colors on racer are bright with four original wheels and hubs. Paint is above average. **$3,600**

Hubley, crash car and Harley Davidson cycle, crash car painted red with gold highlights and nickel plated iron wheels; together with a green civilian Harley Davidson cycle with nickel-plated wheels. Crash car 5" h x 9" l, Harley is 4" h x 6" l. Crash car is very good to excellent, still has a partial Hubley decal on back step; replaced hose reel. Harley is in near excellent condition. .... **$2,415 pair**

Ideal, three-horse pumper, with two silver horses and one brown, all three in full gallop pulling a nickel-plated boiler and an electroplated airbag with four red enameled wheels, one original driver, 9" h x 22" l. **$2,760**

Ives, clockwork runabout, rare to find cast-iron toys with clockwork motors, with steerable front wheels, 7" h x 7 1/2" l. Repainted, with a reproduction driver. **$747**

Japanese, wooden boat with dragon, battery power, boat with two head lamps, two horns and life preserver. Painted white and brown with a large dragon painted on either side, 17 1/2" l. Some minor cracking on the deck boards and wear at the high points. **$360**

JEP, Citroen roadster, painted green with black running boards, electric head lamps, spare tire with license plate, 15 1/2" l. Minor flaking and distress on bottom of car. **$977**

JEP, Hispana Suiza open-air car, big clockwork motor and original JEP tag on side. Painted yellow with red running boards, electric headlights and two original composition figures, 7" h x 20" l. Some paint loss to seats and minor rusting to windshield and some chipping to fenders and car body. One rubber tire split in half. **$4,600**

Karl Bubb, limousine, has slip-on headlamps, side brake, side lever for forward and reverse, glass windshield and side windows, and a lithographed chauffeur. Lithographed brown with black roof and brown fenders, 13 3/4" l. Has been exposed to elements, light oxidation and rust throughout. One of the side windows has a crack. **$1,610**

Photo courtesy James D. Julia Auctioneers, Fairfield, Maine; www.JuliaAuctions.com

Hubley, Packard, intricate detailing including opening doors and hoods, nickel-plated chauffeur is poised upon a simulated tufted leather seat, 12-cylinder nickel-plated engine, nickel-plated radiator with attached lights projecting over the front bumper with the license plate marked "Iowa 1927". Spare is fastened to the rear of car, the tires being of iron simulating balloon tires with blue hubs, 11" l. Overall paint is very fine plus, passenger door has had paint touch-up and is a possible replacement. Appears to have had a small repair to chassis under spare tire. **$12,650**

Photo courtesy James D. Julia Auctioneers, Fairfield, Maine; www.JuliaAuctions.com

JEP, Rolls Royce Open Phaeton, circa 1930, detailed radiator grille with rare custom Flying Lady sterling hood ornament, spring bumpers, forward and reverse gears, brake mechanism, electric headlamps, powerful motor, propeller shaft and rear axle and differential. Also included is a composition driver/chauffeur with articulated arms, 20" l. Older professional restoration. **$3,600**

Karl Bubb, limousine, lithographed red with black roof and fenders with white and brown lithographed tires, 11" l. With bright litho, a superior example. **$2,012**

Kelmet, White crane truck, painted black and red with a nickel-plated crane that moves up and down. Also comes with rubber tires over cast-iron spoke wheels. Marked "WHITE" on radiator and side fenders, 27" l. Some wear and light oxidation and some separation to the red paint. **$5,175**

Kenton, horse-drawn farm wagon with black driver wearing simulated straw hat, detachable cart, being pulled by a black and white horse, 6 3/4" h x 14" l. Bright enameling. **$1,150**

Kenton, Overland circus bandwagon, with six musicians, driver and a red-painted rider on each horse. Wagon is red with gold highlights, yellow and silver wheels. It has white horses with gold trappings, 7" h x 14" l. **$632**

Kenton, Overland circus wagon and circus truck, truck painted yellow with a white bear and silver driver. The circus wagon with a white bear and a blue driver with gold cap. Truck is 5 3/4" h x 9" l and wagon 6 3/4" h x 13" l. Truck appears all original with overall wear especially to the tires. Wagon is in very good condition. .... **$862 both**

Keystone, fire vehicles (two), water tower with original ladders, side horn and bell. Also has original decals. With a Mack City Fire Department fire truck, 31" l. Both appear to be all original. Water tower has its ladders, tank, cap, bell and horn. Fire Department truck has its original ladders and reels. .... **$1,800 both**

Keystone, water tower, water could be put in the tank and it could be pumped out through the water tower nozzle. Has original tank, painted red with original decals, 31" l. Some parts of more recent vintage. Paint is faded. **$660**

Kingsbury, coupe, painted blue with a tan roof and black and silver running boards. With moveable front wheels, taillights and headlights and luggage box on rear bumper. Also has a lift-out rumble seat, 12 7/8" l. Noticeable flaking to the passenger side of car, but with bright enameled paint. **$1,667**

Kingsbury, hook and ladder with original wooden box, with a molded tin seat, nickel-plated ladders, white rubber tires, red enameling with black and silver fenders. Turn crank for a full range of movement, 31" l. Toy with moderate wear throughout. Box has some staining. **$1,380**

Kingsbury, motor-driven stake truck, with rubber tires, orange and green polychrome paint with gilt and silver trimming, it is driven by a clockwork motor cranked from the front bumper, 24" l. Exposed to the elements, retains some orange on the bed, but most other original paint is lacking. **$1,610**

Kingsbury, motor-driven stake truck, with rubber tires, orange and green polychrome paint with gilt and silver trimming, it is driven by a clockwork motor cranked from the front bumper, 24" l. Professionally restored. **$3,450**

Kingsbury, motor-driven stake truck, with rubber tires, orange and green polychrome paint with gilt and silver trimmings, driven by clockwork motor cranked from the front bumper. In original paint, also features a decal of the American Flag on top of the cab roof, which is probably original or added at the point of sale, 24" l. **$5,175**

Kingsbury, panel truck, painted blue with black running boards. Has electric headlights and swivel front wheels, white rubber tires with orange hubs, 13" l. With minor rusting and paint flaking throughout. **$1,150**

Kingsbury, Sunbeam Racers (pair), one in original box, 1930s, both in red. Both with original figure and Dunlop

Photo courtesy Heritage Auction Galleries, Dallas; www.HA.com

Arcade Mack Wrecker Truck. Cast iron with nickel driver figure, dual rear wheels, 12 1/2" x 5" x 4". Retains original paint. **$717**

Cord racing tires. One comes with highly lithographed original box, 19" l. Both with some paint loss and soiling. One missing steering wheel. Box with professional restoration. .... **$3,000 pair**

Kyser & Rex, Philadelphia, Miss Liberty bell toy, painted cast-iron, 8" l. **$29,700**

Lehmann, autobus, colorful lithograph in reds and yellows with a white roof. Has Lehmann logo on front grill, 8 1/4" l. Minor discoloration to sides and some wear at the high points. **$1,552**

Lehmann, "Naughty Boy," car in which mischievous boy tries to take tiller from the driver, 4 1/2" l. The litho on the toy is bright with some minor scratches and slight oxidation on wheels. **$230**

Lehmann, Oho Car, lithographed green with brown lithographed driver and has white and red spoke wheels, 4" l. Some minor flaking on back of car. **$690**

Lehmann, Titania limousine, red and blue lithographed tin limo has electric head lamps, coil-spring clockwork drive, adjustable and lockable wheels, chauffeur, detailed graphics and lithography, 11" l. Slight oxidation and some minor wear to wheels. **$3,680**

Marklin, large brougham with original horse, enameled in dark blue and black with a multitude of trim colors and carried by the trademark Marklin red undercarriage, large lanterns (possible replacements) adorn the exterior, 44" l. Glass possibly replaced, and the horse lacking some trappings (some detached but included). **$24,150**

Photo courtesy Hake's Americana & Collectibles, York, Pa; www.Hakes.com

Little Nemo bisque comic character figurines (five), early 20th century, German made, with movable arms. **$22,412 all**

Photo courtesy Heritage Auction Galleries, Dallas; www.HA.com

Donald Duck Mechanical Tricycle Wind-up Toy and Box (Line Mar, 1950s). Box shows some minor wear, including a chip missing from the top edge, toy is in NM. **$215**

Milton Bradley, Motor Cycle Game, lithographed box lid depicting a cyclist on a 1905 cycle, 9" square. Lithograph is bright and shiny. **$425**

Modern Toys, Japanese Super Buick in original box, lithographed red with blue stripes. With chrome-plated bumpers, headlights and hood ornament and rubber tires. When friction motor is engaged, a siren sound is emitted, 11" l. Slight oxidation on chrome. Box is in near excellent condition. **$517**

Moxie, "Horsemobile," rare blue version, double-sided color lithographed toy from the Moxie Co., patented Feb. 27, 1917. Depicting a man on horseback alongside an early roadster, 8 1/2" l x 6 1/2" h. A few soft bends to the driver and front of car, with a few scattered paint chips and scuffs. **$1,495**

Mustang Fastback, 1967, in original box, blue plastic car with rubber tires and a metal undercarriage. Toy is complete with assembly instructions, manual, decals and extra parts, 16" l. Box is soiled and missing one end flap. **$210**

P & L/Wilkins, Deluxe Pumper, brown and white horse sitting on erratic wheels so when the toy is pulled, the horses seem to gallop pulling a pumper with red wheels. When the toy is pulled, a bell rings under carriage, 6 3/4" h x 18" l. Overall chipping and wear to toy, wheels may be replacements. **$1,265**

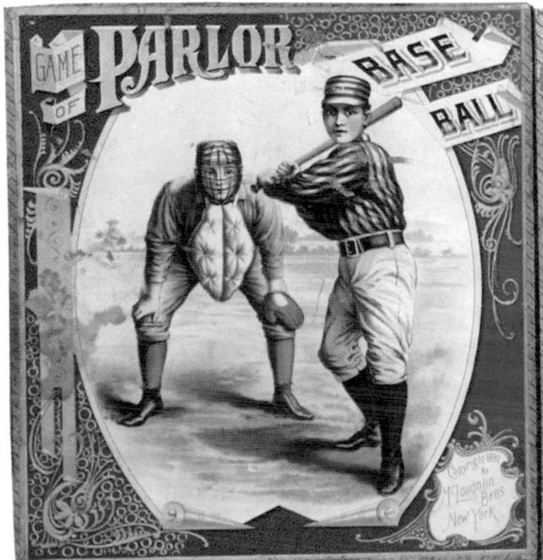

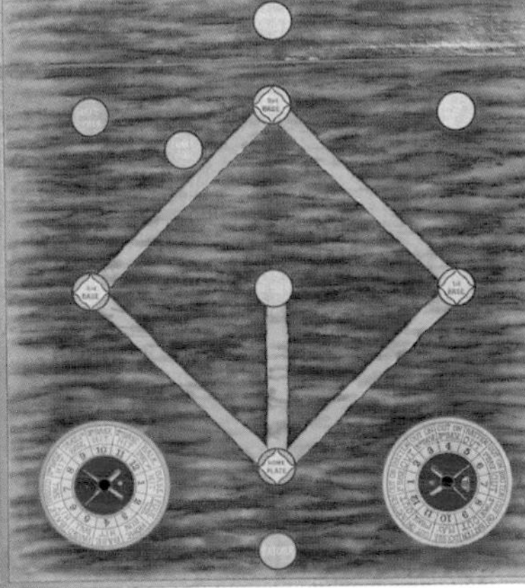

Photo courtesy Morphy Auctions, Denver, Pa.; www.MorphyAuctions.com

McLoughlin Bros., Parlor Base Ball Game, 1897, two spinners, nine yellow, nine blue game pieces. Only known example. Scratching and water stains on front cover, edge wear. Box: 17 1/2" x 18 1/2". **$13,800**

Photo courtesy Noel Barrett Antiques & Auctions Ltd., Carversville, Pa.; www.NoelBarrett.com

Gunthermann tinplate clockwork toy depicting a lady with her baby in a spoke-wheeled pram. **$5,175**

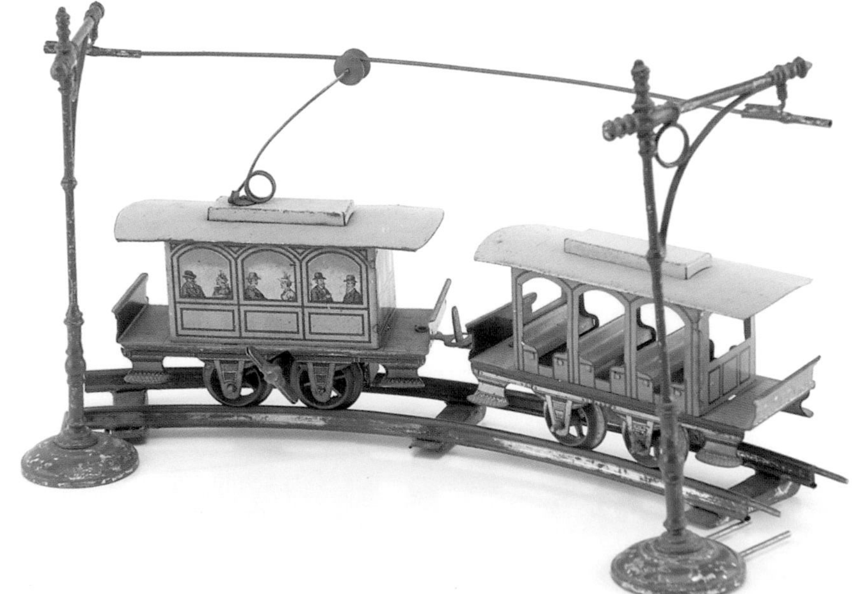

Photo courtesy Noel Barrett Antiques & Auctions Ltd., Carversville, Pa.; www.NoelBarrett.com

Issmayer clockwork tin trolleys, made in Germany for the U.S. market. **$9,200**

Photo courtesy Noel Barrett Antiques & Auctions Ltd., Carversville, Pa.; www.NoelBarrett.com

Tinplate crank-operated Vielmetter Clown Artist, with four changeable cams enabling the clown to "draw" portraits. **$10,350**

Photo courtesy Noel Barrett Antiques & Auctions Ltd., Carversville, Pa.; www.NoelBarrett.com

Britains sci-fi figures set, in fine original condition, includes Buck, Wilma, Mekkano Man Robot and three other characters from the Buck Rogers comic strip. **$4,600**

Photo courtesy Heritage Auction Galleries, Dallas; www.HA.com

Battery-Operated Mod Monster Blushing Frankenstein in the Original Box, 12 1/2" tall. Operated by two D-size batteries. Made in Japan. Activate a button and Frankenstein's arms move, his pants fall down revealing his red-striped underwear and his face blushes. Monster is in fine condition, no batteries have been stored in the toy. The pictorial box is complete, a bit pushed in on the top panel. **$60**

Schoenhut, carnival tent, with side banner depicting period attractions (1900s-1930s) featuring the Wild Man, the Bearded Lady, Siamese Twins. Inside, the bleachers are packed with spectators who gawk at the show below. Tent, 42" w x 26" h x 18" d. Banner, 49" w x 18" h. Wood on sideshow banner has been expertly redone. Tent lacking some flags and banners on top. **$2,875**

Schoenhut, farmer and wife, original clothing on the wife. Farmer has replaced pants, belt and hat, 7 1/2" and 8" h, respectively. Heads appear to have paint restoration. .. **$270**

Schoenhut, glass-eye polar bear and brown bear; polar bear with open mouth is in fine original condition, the brown bear features an open/closed mouth, 8" and 7 1/2" h. respectively. Brown bear lacking one ear. .... **$862 both**

Schoenhut, kangaroo and bison, original-condition, painted-eye kangaroo with open mouth, and a glass-eye, carved-hair bison, 7 1/2" and 5 1/2" h, respectively. Overall kangaroo is excellent. Bison with some wear to high spots. .... **$690 both**

Photo courtesy Morphy Auctions, Denver, Pa.; www.MorphyAuctions.com

Marklin 2-gauge F&E live steam train, 22" loco and tender with 15" long selection of cars. **$32,200**

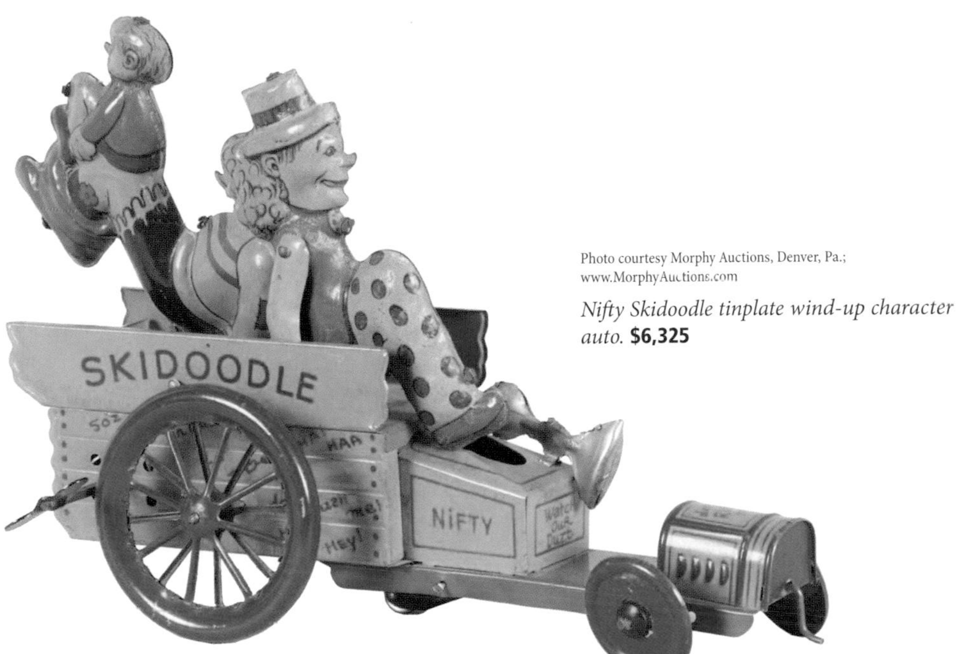

Photo courtesy Morphy Auctions, Denver, Pa.; www.MorphyAuctions.com

Nifty Skidoodle tinplate wind-up character auto. **$6,325**

Schuco, wind-up dancers, Bavarian boy with green felt hat lifts his partner (made of celluloid) over his head, 5" h. Some wear to the paint on the top of the girl's head. Lacking key. **$172**

Sled, painted wooden "CHIEF" Child's, America, early 20th century, with iron runners, the underside inscribed, "EAC DEC 25 1910," paint wear, 4 1/4" h, 10 1/2" w, 36 1/2". **$118**

Smith-Miller, Mack Army truck, green cab with wooden body, 19" l. Minor flaking to decals on cab. **$402**

Smith-Miller, Mack Bell Telephone truck, two-tone green Mack cab with a wooden body and canvas top, 19" l. Minor corrosion to aluminum parts. **$1,955**

Smith-Miller, Mack West Coast Fast Freight truck, all original box freight truck. Tin back end labeled, "West Coast Fast Freight", 20" l. **$1,265**

Smith-Miller, Mobiloil tractor-trailer, all-original oil tanker in red with Mobiloil decals, 22" l. **$517**

Smith-Miller, Pie Mack tractor-trailer, all original truck with red cab and aluminum back end, 28" l. Overall box wear, some flaking to decals on side of trailer. **$1,265**

Smith-Miller, MIC dump truck, yellow with lever inside to activate dumping mechanism, 17 1/2" l. Minor corrosion to aluminum parts. **$1,380**

Smith-Miller, MIC flatbed with lumber, yellow cab with green frame with a chained load of lumber and lever to activate lift bed, 19 1/2" l. Minor corrosion to aluminum parts, some soiling to cab of truck. **$1,440**

Smith-Miller, MIC L.A.F.D. aerial ladder fire truck, with working ladders that extend through a series of gears, 26" l. Minor corrosion to aluminum parts. **$747**

Photo courtesy James D. Julia Auctioneers, Fairfield, Maine; www.JuliaAuctions.com

Steiff, Felix the Cat on Irish Mail, Felix sitting upon his bellows seat will propel the Irish Mail forward, pumping and leaning back as the bellows (non-functional) make a squeaking sound. Believed to be of 1920s vintage, retaining its original script Steiff button with remnants of paper tag, 9 1/2" h. Near mint, tail is intact but appears wire within is broken. **$10,350**

Smith-Miller, MIC stake body truck, all original with power tailgate lift, 18" l. Minor corrosion to aluminum parts. **$1,020**

Smith-Miller, MIC tractor-trailer, red tractor with Fruehauf trailer in polished aluminum, 28" l. Minor corrosion to aluminum parts. **$920**

Smith-Miller, MIC wrecker, white with boom, marked, "Official tow car–24 hour service", 16" l. Minor corrosion to aluminum parts, some corrosion to tow boom. **$1,200**

Collector's Note: Margarete Steiff (1847-1909) was born in Giengen, Germany. She was a seamstress and confined to a wheelchair due to polio she contracted as a baby. She started making stuffed animals as a hobby in 1880.

These toys began as elephants, based on a design Steiff found in a magazine, and were originally sold as pincushions to her friends. However, children began playing with them, and in the years following she went on to design many other successful animal-themed toys for children, such as dogs, cats and pigs. She designed and made most of the prototypes herself.

By 1903, the firm she established with her brother, Fritz, was producing a jointed mohair teddy bear, whose production dramatically increased to more than 970,000 units in 1907. The famed "button in ear" was devised by Margarete's nephew, Franz, in 1904, to keep counterfeits from being passed off as authentic Steiff toys.

Steiff, Bear, blond mohair, ear button, shoe-button eyes, vertically stitched nose, embroidered mouth and claws, long arms and body, large feet, non-functioning growler, 16" h, one paw pad recovered, stuffing compressed, minor fur loss, soiled. **$4,200**

Steiff, Bear, blond mohair, rattle, no button, black shoe-button eyes, fully jointed, embroidered nose and mouth, overall wear, stains, rip on arm, working rattle, excelsior stuffing, no pad style, circa 1910, 5" h. **$410**

Steiff, Bear, blond mohair, script ear button, glass eyes, embroidered nose, mouth, claws excelsior stuffed, fully jointed, felt feet pads have scattered moth holes, break at sides, mid-19th century, 30" h. **$1,955**

Steiff, Bear, blond mohair, shoe-button eyes, fully jointed, embroidered nose and claws, excelsior stuffing, loss to fur, stuffing and fiber, circa 1905, 9 1/2" h. **$710**

Steiff, Bear, white mohair, fully jointed, long curly fur, embroidered brown nose, mouth, and claws, glass eyes, felt pads, excelsior stuffing, circa 1910, 20" h, slight fur loss on snout. **$7,100**

Steiff, Bear, cinnamon mohair, swivel head, black shoe-button eyes, cotton floss stitched nose with vertical stitching, stitched mouth, center seam body and head, no button in ear, original felt pads on paws, 20" h. **$9,500**

Steiff, Bear, golden mohair, 100th anniversary, ear button, fully jointed, plastic eyes, black embroidered nose, mouth, and claws, peach felt pads, excelsior stuffing, certificate no. 3934, original box, 17" h. **$210**

Steiff, Bear, golden mohair, ear button, black embroidered nose and claws, mouth missing, black shoe button eyes, squeaker, fully jointed body, excelsior stuffing, original felt pads, 1" fabric tear right front arm joint, minor fur loss, overall soiling, circa 1905, 14" h. **$1,955**

Steiff, Bear, golden mohair, shoe-button eyes, embroidered nose, mouth and claws, fully jointed, excelsior stuffing, no

Photo courtesy James D. Julia Auctioneers, Fairfield, Maine; www.JuliaAuctions.com

Early Steiff Officer And His Wife. Officer has shoe-button eyes and woman has glass eyes, both retain original Steiff button and are in all original, untouched condition with only minor soiling and/or staining to outfits. 22" and 17". Lady has small moth hole below right eye, lacking left arm and slight soiling to face. Officer has slight fading to outfit, lacking three buttons and left arm under white sash needs to be reattached at shoulder. **$6,900 pair**

Photo courtesy James D. Julia Auctioneers, Fairfield, Maine; www.JuliaAuctions.com

Early Steiff Black Coachman's Attendant. With side-glancing glass eyes, he retains his original Steiff button and is in all original, untouched condition with only minor soiling and/or staining to his outfit. 16" t. **$6,900**

Photo courtesy James D. Julia Auctioneers, Fairfield, Maine; www.JuliaAuctions.com

Early Steiff Coachman. He has glass eyes, retains his original Steiff button and is in all original, untouched condition with only minor soiling and or staining to his outfit. Some soiling to face, lacking two buttons on vest, sleeves of overcoat torn at seam. **$6,325**

Photo courtesy James D. Julia Auctioneers, Fairfield, Maine; www.JuliaAuctions.com

Early Steiff Blacksmith. He shoe button eyes, retains his original Steiff button and is in all original, untouched condition with only minor soiling and or staining to his outfit. 20" h. With soiling and minor staining to face and minor hair loss at top of head. **$4,025**

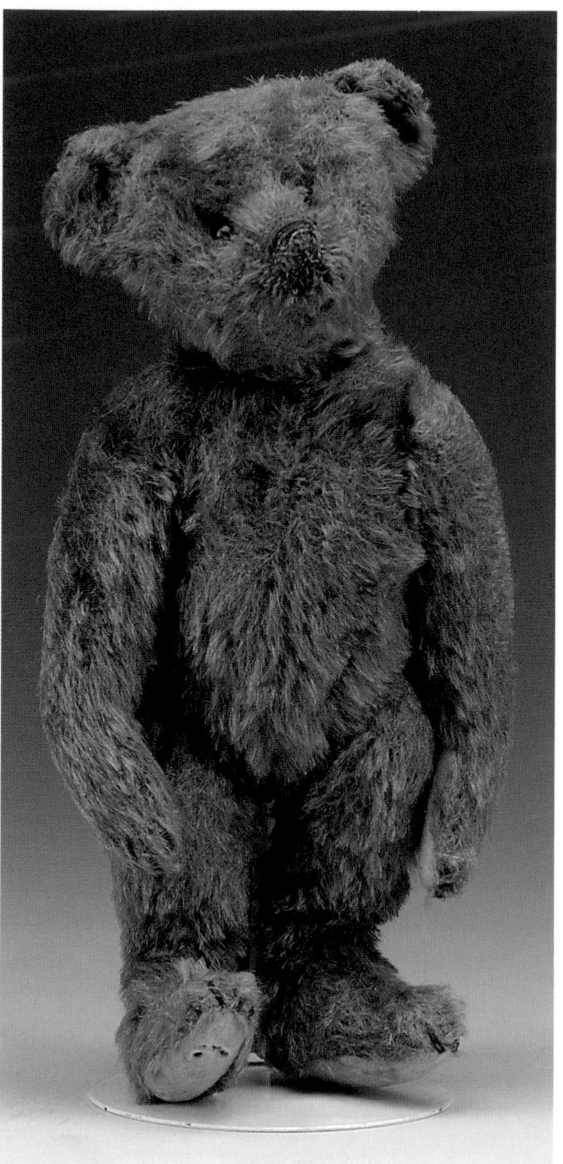

Photo courtesy James D. Julia Auctioneers, Fairfield, Maine; www.JuliaAuctions.com

Early Chocolate 9" Steiff Bear. In as-found, untouched condition, bear retains his button as well as a large amount of his chocolate/cinnamon (?) fur and his felt pads are intact other than a few small moth holes. Shoe button eyes, hump on back, black-stitched nose and a cocked head. Right leg has had amateur old repair at hip by original owner and is stitched back into place. **$1,560** pad arms, moth damage to foot pads, circa 1915, 8 1/2" h. **$1,380**

Steiff, Bear, light apricot mohair, ear button, fully jointed, shoe-button eyes, embroidered nose, mouth, and claws, excelsior stuffing, felt pads, fur loss to lower back and back of legs, slight moth damage on pads, circa 1905, 12 1/2" h. **$1,610**

Steiff, Bear, light golden mohair, underscored ear button, black shoe-button eyes, center seam, black embroidered nose, mouth and claws, fully jointed, tan felt pads, holes in pads, circa 1905, 14" h. **$4,890**

Steiff, Bison, mohair, ear button, chest tag, post WWII, 9 1/2" l. **$200**

Steiff, Boxer, beige mohair coat, black trim, glass eyes, leather collar marked "Steiff," head turns, minor wear, straw stuffing, 16 1/2" l, 15 1/2" h. **$165**

Steiff, Boxer puppy, paper label "Daly," 4 1/4" h. **$130**

Steiff, Cat, pull toy, white mohair coat, gray stripes, glass eyes, worn pink ribbon with bell, pink felt ear linings, button, cast iron wheels, 14" l. **$1,980**

Steiff, Cocker spaniel, sitting, glass eyes, ear button, chest tag, post WWII, 5 3/4" h. **$125**

Steiff, Cocker spaniel puppy, button, 4 3/4" h. **$90**

Steiff, Dalmatian puppy, paper label "Sarras," 4 1/4" h. ... **$145**

Steiff, Dog, pull toy, orange and white mohair coat, glass eyes, steel frame, cast iron wheels, one ear missing, button in remaining ear, voice box does not work, 15 1/2" l, 14" h. **$280**

Steiff, Frog, velveteen, glass eyes, green, sitting, button and chest tag, 3 3/4" l. **$125**

Steiff, Goat, ear button, 6 1/2" h. **$150**

Steiff, Horse on wheels, ear button, glass eyes, white and brown, wear and breaks to fabric, on solid metal wheels, non-functioning pull-ring, circa 1930, 21" l, 17" h. **$215**

Steiff, Kanga and Roo, shaded mohair, glass eyes, swivel neck and arms, 21" h kangaroo, 4" h velveteen joey in pouch. **$450**

Steiff, Kitten, Gussy, white and black, glass eyes, ear button, chest tag, post WWII, 6 1/2" l. **$125**

Steiff, Koala, glass eyes, ear button, chest tag, post WWII, 7 1/2" h. **$135**

Steiff, Lion, pull toy, worn gold mohair coat, glass eyes, worn streaked mane incomplete, no tail, ring-pull voice box, steel frame, sheet metal wheels with white rubber treads marked "Steiff," 21" l, 18" h. **$500**

Steiff, Owl, Wittie, glass eyes, ear button, chest tag, post WWII, 4 1/2" h. **$95**

Steiff, Parakeet, Hansi, bright lime green and yellow, airbrushed black details, plastic eyes, button tag, chest tag, plastic beak and feet, 6 1/2" h. **$115**

Steiff, Rabbit, unmarked, wear, 9 1/2" h. **$220**

Steiff, Soldier, slight moth damage, hat and equipment missing, circa 1913, 14" h. **$460**

Steiff, Turtle, Slo, plastic shell, glass eyes, ear button, chest tag, post WWII, 7" l. **$85**

Steiff, Walrus, Paddy, plastic tusk, glass eyes, ear button, chest tag, post WWII, 6 1/2" l. **$145**

Strauss, Ham & Sam "The Minstrel Team", when wound, Sam plays the piano while Ham dances and plays the banjo, 6 1/2" l. Overall fading with rust spots on the piano and figures. **$480**

Photo courtesy Noel Barrett Antiques & Auctions Ltd., Carversville, Pa.; www.NoelBarrett.com

French-made Fernand Martin tin wind-up Black Waiter. **$16,100**

Thimble Drome, Prop Rod Racer, futuristic, circa 1960s, with a red plastic body on a die-cast metal chassis, black rubber tires, and a propeller in the back, 12 3/4" l. Stress cracks to plastic where propeller is attached. **$57**

Tricycle, Victorian, cast iron with two large spoke wheels and one smaller wheel in front to which tiller is attached. Oilcloth-covered seat with backrest, 45" l x 26" w x 27" h. Rubber that wraps iron wheels shows some hardening and flattening. Front wheel is missing rubber. Black-painted finish shows age-appropriate wear. Seat has some slight tears. **$540**

Vindex, Bates 40 bulldozer, painted gray throughout and embossed on side, "The Bates 40". Also has a nickel-plated driver, 6 1/4" l. Overall wear and has a replaced driver. **$3,162**

Vindex, case plow, red with swivel guiding front wheel in embossed case with green wheels, 4" h x 9 1/2" l. Most of its wear to wheels. **$1,092**

Vis-a-Vis, German, clockwork, early horseless carriage, automobile had a driver and woman passenger (now missing). Lead headlights are still intact as well as the rubber tires on the cast-lead wheels, 7" l. Overall paint condition is poor. **$4,800**

Wilkins, dump cart, horse enameled in black pulling a red dump cart with yellow wheels. The driver is polychrome in

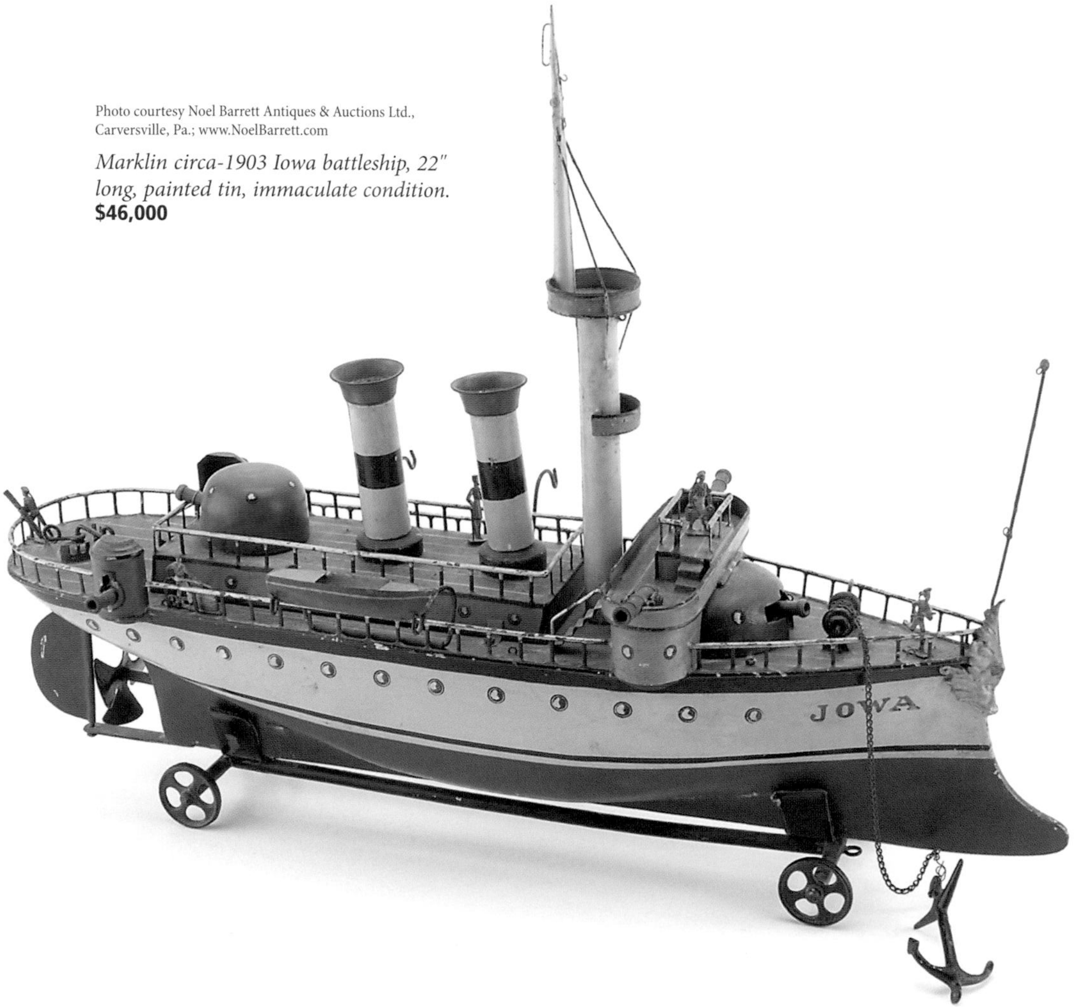

Photo courtesy Noel Barrett Antiques & Auctions Ltd., Carversville, Pa.; www.NoelBarrett.com

Marklin circa-1903 Iowa battleship, 22" long, painted tin, immaculate condition.
$46,000

blue and flesh tones. Also comes with a cartful of cast-iron shovels, rakes, picks etc. Also has its original back gate, 5" h x 13" l. Some paint loss to horse, wheels and figure. **$2,760**

Wilkins, hay rake, tin and bent-wire back with a handle. Also has a black cast-iron horse, red frame and yellow wheels. The driver is painted brown/black and has flesh-tone face and hands, 5" h x 9" l. Wear to wheels and horse. The figure is old but not original to this toy. **$2,012**

Wilkins, hay tedder (only about five or six known), black horse, yellow cast-iron frame with red wheels. When toy is pulled, the tedder arms turn. 5 1/2" h x 9 1/4" l. Even wear throughout. **$6,325**

Wilkins, horse-drawn fire chief wagon, single horse pulling robust fireman, 5" h x 12" l. Considerable paint loss, but no breaks or repairs. **$1,092**

Wilkins, horse-drawn plow, black horse with gold and red highlights and a red frame with yellow wheels and an original figure. When lever is pressed, plow blade drops, 4 3/4" h x 10" l, plow blade appears to be an old recast. **$5,175**

Willkins, horse-drawn wagon, two horses painted black, wagon and wheels are yellow. 6" h x 13" l. Professionally restored. **$287**

Wilkins, mower, cast iron with moveable tin and iron mowing blades. Two black horses pulling mower with yellow and black wheels driven by a farmer with a derby cap, 5 1/2" h x 9 3/4" l. Even wear throughout. Driver is repainted. **$2,070**

Wilkins, two-horse pumper, two big black horses (detachable) in full prance pulling the pumper with a robust fireman

Photo courtesy Noel Barrett Antiques & Auctions Ltd., Carversville, Pa.; www.NoelBarrett.com

George Brown Excelsior locomotive of painted and stenciled tin, with cast-iron wheels. **$6,300**

Photo courtesy Noel Barrett Antiques & Auctions Ltd., Carversville, Pa.; www.NoelBarrett.com

Ernst Plank hot-air-powered Praxinoscope optical toy with 12 full-color animation strips, extremely rare. **$8,050**

Photo courtesy Morphy Auctions, Denver, Pa.; www.MorphyAuctions.com

Papier-mache frog ball-toss game on wheeled platform, with original painted-wood balls.
$6,300

Photo courtesy Morphy Auctions, Denver, Pa.; www.MorphyAuctions.com

Rare circa-1850s boxed set of paper dolls known as "The Boy & His Horse." **$4,600**

HOT WHEELS

Hot Wheels is a brand of die-cast toy car, introduced by Mattel on Sept. 7, 1968. It was the primary competitor of Johnny Lightning and Matchbox until 1996, when Mattel acquired rights to the Matchbox brand from Tyco.

Of the first 16 cars (sometimes called the "Sweet 16" by collectors), 10 were based upon customized versions of regular production automobiles of the era, and six were based upon real show cars and cars designed and built for track racing. All of the cars featured "Spectraflame" paintwork, bearings, redline wheels and working suspensions.

Beatnik Bandit, based on Ed "Big Daddy" Roth's show car of the same name. **$50 NM**

Custom Corvette. **$90-$125 NM**

Custom Eldorado. **$65-$100 NM**

Custom Barracuda. **$350 NM**

Custom Camaro. **$125 NM**

Custom Cougar. **$150-$200 NM**

Custom Firebird. **$75-$450 NM**

Silhouette. **$30-$50 NM**

Custom Mustang. **$150-$450 NM**

Hot Heap. **$50-$175 NM**

Custom Fleetside. **$75 NM**

Python. **$30-$175 NM**

Ford J-Car. **$40-$250 NM**

Custom T-Bird. **$150-$700 NM**

Deora. **$65-$85 NM**

Custom Volkswagen. **$55-$275 NM**

Marbles

Glass marbles were invented around 1848 in Germany and went into mass production in the early 20th century, but World War I cut off their importation from Europe. American makers introduced mechanized glass-marble production, which became the most common manufacturing method in the world.

Aqua Blue Mica Marble, 2 1/8". Extremely rare large size and color. Loaded with mica. **$6,325**

Aqua Tornado Latticino Swirl Marble, 1 1/16". Unusual aqua tornado latticino swirl with outer white latticino cage. **$1,150**

Blue Glass Swirl Marble, 7/8". Blue glass with latticino swirl in center and four bands of red edged by white. **$460**

Caramel Swirl with Mica, 1 1/16". Caramel colored with mica. **$258**

Cobalt Ribbon Core Marble, 11/16". Dark cobalt-blue ribbon core with outer white latticino bands. **$316**

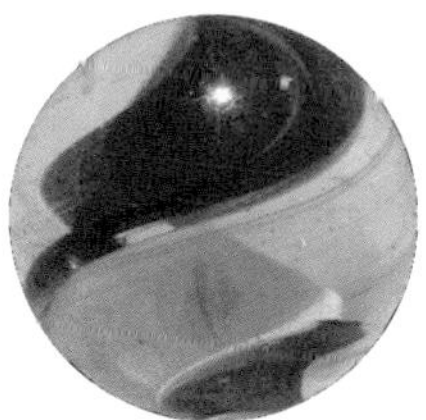

Double Ribbon Marble, 7/8". Nude double ribbon. White ribbon with transparent red ribbon. **$1,035**

Double Ribbon Marble, 1 5/8". Unusual double ribbon with white tightly corkscrewed ribbons. Transparent red that flows in twists give it a pink appearance. Two sets of yellow latticino lines. **$8,050**

Double Ribbon Swirl Marble, 13/16". Double ribbon with one white latticino and one yellow latticino ribbon. Two wide transparent red bands alternating with two wide bands of white latticino. **$517**

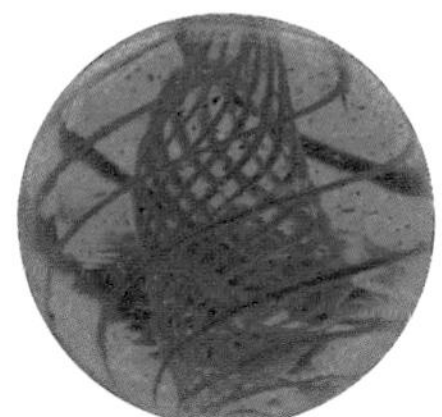

Emerald Green Glass Swirl Marble, 7/8". Unusual emerald green glass. White latticino center with outer white lines. **$460**

End of Cane Swirl Marble, 22/32". With multicolored bands and a layer of latticino. **$402**

Four-Lobed Solid Core Marble, 1 15/16". Four lobes with a red/orange solid core. Four white lines on outer edge of peaks. Two outer lines of blue and green. Four outer lines of orange. **$1,035**

Four-Stage Yellow Lobe Core Marble, 2 7/16". Yellow lobe core with white valleys. Four sets of three latticino lines in the next stage. Five red, white, blue and white bands in the next stage. Four bands of yellow, white, yellow latticino strands on the surface. **$3,162**

Indian Mag Lite Marble, 1 9/16". Deep cobalt blue with strong outer bands of yellow, white, blue, purple, green and orange lines. Rare. **$9,200**

Indian Marble, 1 25/32". Wide bands of blue, orange, yellow and green. Rare. **$7,475**

Latticino Cased Core Marble, 29/32". Unusual white latticino core cased in aqua blue with red and white outer lines. **$575**

Multi-lobed Solid Core Marble, 2 3/16". Multi-lobed solid-core valleys alternating blue and turquoise. Red highlights on each. Outer yellow lines. **$6,900**

Naked Corkscrew Ribbon Swirl Marble, pontil to pontil center with white bands and red running through the middle. Flanked on both sides by pink line, followed by blue, turquoise, yellow, and burnt orange. Opposing side of ribbon has a pink line running down the center band, 1 5/8" d. **$14,950**

All marble images courtesy Morphy Auctions, Denver, Pa.; www.MorphyAuctions.com

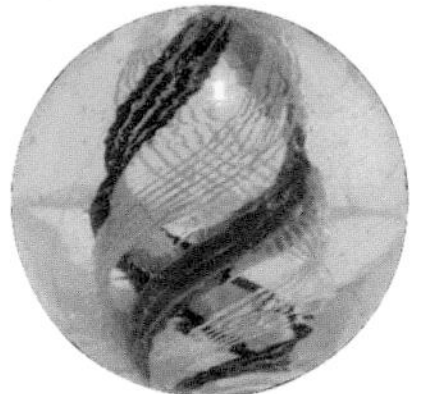

Naked Divided Core Marble, 1 3/4". With two ribbons of latticino and two ribbons of opaque. Unusual pattern. **$517**

Naked Swirl Marble, 15/16". Unusual naked clear glass swirl with latticino core. **$517**

Onionskin with Mica Marble, 2 1/4". Unusual in that the one end of the marble has tighter twisting than the other. **$402**

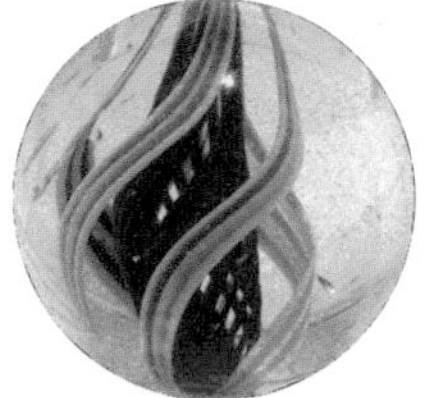

Red Latticino Core Marble, 1 1/16". Bright red latticino core with four mid-layer bands of orange/white, olive/white, blue/white, and grey/white. **$632**

Ribbon Core Marble, 11/16". Unusual ribbon core with four distinct panels. **$258**

MOR-Ribbon Core Marble, 11/16". Alternating bands of blue/white and red/white. Outer layer of yellow latticino. **$115**

Ribbon Core Marble, 11/16". Two sets of red/white and blue/white ribbons with outer yellow latticino bands. **$115**

Ribbon Core Marble, 11/16". Red and green single ribbon with outer pink/white bands. **$172**

Ribbon Core Swirl Marble, 21/32". Tight ribbon core with multicolored bands. **$230**

Ribbon Core Swirl Marble, 2". Unusual thick white ribbon core capped with yellow outer decoration. Outer red/white, green/white and blue/white bands. **$805**

Ribbon Marble, 23/32". Unusual red-ribbed yellow ribbon with green jelly core. **$805**

Single Ribbon Marble, 25/32". Three-stage single ribbon. White ribbon with four latticino lines above the face. Four outer red lines. **$316**

Single Ribbon Marble, 7/8". Single ribbon of yellow latticino capped by white bands. Two outer sets of three yellow latticino and four transparent red lines. **$287**

Single Ribbon Swirl Marble, 15/16". Single ribbon with alternating blue, red, green and white. Outer layer latticino panel of white and yellow. Both edges of the ribbon have alternating blue and red lines. **$201**

Photo courtesy Rago Arts and Auction Center, Lambertville, N.J.; www.RagoArts.com

Rare Chilkat Dance Blanket, Northwest Coast: Classic ceremonial garb of hand-woven mountain goat hair, dye with natural pigments, decorated with highly stylized clan symbols and animal forms, mid-19th century. Top edge reinforced with animal hide, woven mountain goat hair and cedar bark. Such blankets were prestigious items for the elite. Fair overall condition, a few small areas of wear and tribal repair. With fringe: 64" x 50". **$22,800**

TRIBAL ARTS

Native American Cultures

Haida Mask, Northwest Coast: Carved wooden face with traditional features, painted in red, black, and green, late 19th-early 20th century. It has been suggested that this mask may have originally been part of a totem pole or house facade. Miniature masks are known to exist, but are very rare. One stress fracture possibly reattached, likely retouched on lips. Mounted on custom display stand. 5 1/4" x 4 3/4". **$2,280**

Otter Potlatch Bowl, Northwest Coast: Elegantly carved wooden bowl with prominently curved tail, inlaid with abalone discs and eyes, 1977. Excellent condition. Indecipherable signature, dated. 4 1/2" x 16". **$1,800**

Athabaskan Shot Pouch With Accoutrements, Alaska: Beaded leather bag and strap on trade cloth with incised powder horn, early 19th century. Fair condition with minor bead loss. 6" x 6 1/2" fold bag, 38" x 3" strap, 8" horn. **$7,800**

Feather Cape, Great Lakes: Exquisite collar of concentric feathers rings sewn together, including peahen, prairie chicken, and guinea fowl, backed and bound in pink woven cloth, mid-19th century. Good condition and color, intact, mounted in a display frame under glass. 12" radius; framed mount 26" x 31". **$1,080**

Chippewa Beaded Shot Pouch, Great Lakes: Overall floral design on black cotton, wool backing, geometric glass bead border, late 19th century. Fair condition, a few minor holes. Including strap, 30 1/4" x 6". **$1,800**

Apache Strike-A-Light, Midwest: Beaded leather pouch fringed with tin cones and four drops, circa 1880. Excellent original condition. 12 1/4" x 4 1/2". **$1,560**

Sioux Tobacco Bag, Midwest: Spider Woman design in quillwork, above quill drops and long leather fringe, accented with tin cones, late 19th century. Remarkably good condition, very minor losses to quill work. With fringe: 38" x 6". **$3,000**

Anasazi Tularosa Vessel, Arizona: Pre-historic black and white jug with zoomorphic lug handle, painted in typical step and swirl designs, AD 1125-1300. Intact with no restoration. 5" x 5 3/4". **$1,080**

Anasazi Tularosa Olla, Arizona: Black and white vessel, AD 1125-1300. Approximately 15-20% restored. 8 3/4" x 12" dia. **$1,800**

Hopi Salako Mana Kachina Doll, Southwest: Painted cottonwood with colorful tabletta, accented with feathers, early 20th century. Good condition, some loss to pigment, overall intact. Mounted on Lucite base. 10" x 6". **$840**

Photo courtesy Rago Arts and Auction Center, Lambertville, N.J.; www.RagoArts.com

Iroquois/Seneca False Face, New York: Exceptional carved wood mask with strong downward mouth, bulging cylindrical eyes, bold red paint, and black horse hair, early 20th century. Worn in healing ceremonies. Interior shows wear and handling consistent with ritual use, several layers of paint evident. 12" x 7 1/2". **$3,360**

Photo courtesy Rago Arts and Auction Center, Lambertville, N.J.; www.RagoArts.com

Hopi Corn Kachina Doll, Southwest: Stout cottonwood figure painted in brilliant polychrome, with attached ears and snout, mid-20th century. Good condition, some loss to pigment. 7" x 3". **$240**

Large Kachina Doll, Southwest: Cottonwood figure topped with a tall tabletta headdress accented with feathers and sweetgrass necklace, its eyes representing profiled faces, frog motif on reverse, early to mid-20th century. Fair condition with reattached legs, loss to foot and repair to other, some decay to pigment. 20 1/2" x 6 1/2". **$720**

Soyal Kachina Doll, Southwest: Carved cottonwood figure accented with feather regalia and long bird-like beak, painted with a pouch and jewelry. The Soyal Kachina, also known as the Return Kachina, is associated with the Third Mesa. His reappearance in late December signals the beginning of a new Kachina season. He tours the village placing prayer feathers at each kiva. These prayer offerings open the way for other Kachinas to return to the village from the spirit world. Good condition. 9" x 2 3/4". **$360**

Hopi Kachina Doll, Southwest: Carved cottonwood with polychrome colors in traditional wrapped shirt and mask, early to mid-20th century. Fair condition with light fading to pigments. 7" x 3 1/4". **$450**

Hopi Flower Kachina, Southwest: Painted cottonwood sculpture with facial tattoos, textile design, and applied comb and beak, early 20th century. Citoto takes part in the Ayavanu water serpent ceremony and in mixed kachina dances. Excellent condition, minimal loss to pigment, original feather regalia removed previously. Mounted on custom metal base. 12 3/4". **$3,000**

Pueblo Clown Mask, Southwest: Painted canvas and textile construction with attached corn husk regalia and applied mouth, early to mid-20th century. Well worn with signs of use, overall intact, mounted on custom wood display stand. 14 1/2" x 8 1/2". **$3,360**

Mela Youngblood, Blackware Vase , New Mexico: Carved vessel from Santa Clara pueblo with cloud, rainbow, and kiva step motif, 1970. Excellent condition. Signed and dated. 3 1/2" x 2 3/4". **$900**

Mound Builder, Feline Effigy Pipe, Ohio: Fort Ancient Culture, carved stone with image of a shaman transforming into a cat, AD 1000-1650. Overall good condition. Custom-mounted on display stand. 2 1/2" x 3 1/2" dia.. .... **$1,200**

Caddo Vessel, Arkansas: Terra cotta bottle form with incised sunflower design, AD 1200-1400. (Provenance: Private collection, Pennsylvania). Completely intact, with no restoration. 7 1/2" x 5 1/4". **$480**

Mississippian, Bell Plain Vessel, Arkansas: Grayware bulbous vessel with four applied faces representing the four directions, AD 800-1200. Restoration to spout, some wear to high points. 8" x 8 1/2". **$720**

Large Caddo Vessel, Arkansas: Terra cotta bottle form, Friendship style, AD 1200-1400. Reassembled from fragments, with approx. 95% original materials. 9 3/4" x 8". **$420**

Crow Parfleche, Fringed Envelope, Montana: Rawhide bag painted with red, yellow, white and indigo pigments in geometric pattern, with red woven wool border and long fringe, early to mid-20th century. Excellent condition. With fringe: 31" x 14". **$420**

Crow Parfleche Envelope, Montana: Rawhide bag painted with red, yellow, white and indigo pigments in geometric pattern, fastened with a leather tie, early 20th century. Fair condition with slight staining and signs of use. 26" x 12". **$780**

Small Ute Beaded Pouch, Midwest: Leather bag with tin cone fringe and tin button, lazy-stitched bead work, early 20th century. Good condition, minor rust on cones. 7" x 3 1/8". **$480**

Blackfoot, Beaded Knife Sheath And Knife, Montana: Floral design on leather, wood handle on steel blade by Silney R. Baxter & Co., Boston, decorated with brass tack, early 20th century. Excellent original condition, 1/4" loss to bead work. Sheath: 15 1/4" x 3 1/4"; knife: 10 3/4". **$900**

Plains Horse Effigy Mirror, Iowa: Carved wood frame with brass tacks around original mirror, late 19th century. Used as trade goods circa 1890. Overall intact with signs of age. 13" x 7 1/4". **$900**

Iroquois, Beaded Cloth Purse And Hat: Both fully embroidered with polychrome beads in floral patterns: bag, mid-19th century. Fair condition, minor losses consistent with use. Bag: 6 1/2" x 5", hat: 4" x 10 1/2". .... **$780 both**

Ojibwa Bandolier Bag, Great Lakes: Beaded on trade cloth, silk, and red wool, with large glass beads and wool tassels, late 19th century. Fair condition, some losses to silk. 41 1/2" x 10". **$1,200**

Cree, Silk-Embroidered Elk Hide Wall Pocket: Exceptional tulip-shaped pouch of delicate leather, stitched with blossoms in polychrome, lined in silk, 19th century. Overall good condition with light staining from use. 10" x 9 1/4". **$900**

Athabaskan Beaded Medicine Bag, Alaska: Intricately beaded leather pouch with a floral vine on each side, bordered in leather fringe and topped with a leather cord handle, late 19th century. Overall fair condition, with some bead loss and minor stains. 15" x 10 1/2". **$480**

Sioux Doll, Midwest: Cloth body with pressed and stitched leather face accented with glass bead eyes, earrings and necklace and attached human hair, clothed in elk hide garments, late 19th-early 20th century. Fair condition overall with light stains and lost to hair. 12". **$600**

Eastern Woodlands Quilled Leather Case, Northeast: Finely crafted box with intricate porcupine quillwork in floral patterns, embossed design on the bottom and stitched construction, late 19th-early 20th century. An exceptional example. Overall good condition. 3 1/2" x 10 3/4" x 6 1/4". **$2,160**

Tunxis/Wangunk Lidded Splint Basket, Northeast: Woven black ash rectangular container with separate lid, stained with natural dyes, mid-19th century. Fair condition with signs of use, minor breaks. 12" x 19" x 13". **$2,040**

Inuit Ivory Bracelet, Alaska: Made of carved medallions depicting two polar bears, a seal, and a walrus, joined by contrasting bone tablets, on elastic, 1940s. Perfect condition. 3" x 1 1/8". **$1,560**

Horse Hair Bosal Bridle, Montana: Braided multicolor horse hair reins with bosal nose band decorated with wool in shades of red and brown, and horse hair tassels, circa 1915. Prison made, likely at a Montana correction facility. Good condition with signs of use, minor split to lining of browband. 18" with 144" reins. **$480**

Sioux Quilled Hair Drop, Midwest: Fully quilled hair extension on leather, in red, purple, and green geometric designs, attached with red dyed hair and feathers capped in tin cones, late 19th century. Excellent condition with minor loss to quill work. 21" x 3". **$960**

Latin American Cultures

Aztec Stone Metate With Carved Relief, Mexico: Ceremonial stone depicting supplicant figure before a seated lord, AD 1200-1500. Excellent condition with no restoration, reverse of stone worn by use. Custom metal display stand. Total: 13" x 15". **$3,240**

Mayan Orangeware Vessel, Mexico: Traditional Mayan pot with painted insect motif, AD 500-700. Excellent condition, intact with root marks and dendrite deposits. 5" x 4 3/4". **$960**

Large Mayan Copador Ceramic Vessel, Honduras: Tall cylinder painted with twin bands of glyphs and images of lords in full regalia, divided by bands of trophy heads, AD 600-900. Minor chipping to rim, a few stabilized hairlines, light wear to surface in some areas consistent with age, in otherwise remarkable state of preservation. 8 1/4" x 6 3/8". **$1,680**

Exceptional Colima Redware Dog, Mexico: Large terra cotta figure with classic plump body and tail spout, incised eyes, mouth and nose, and negative-resist design, 200 BC-AD 250. Intact condition with heavy dendrite deposits and root marks visible. 10 1/2" x 14". **$8,400**

Colima Dwarf Figural Vessel, Mexico: Burnished terra cotta figure with diminutive arms, ear spools and conch shell trumpet, 200 BC-AD 250. Possible professional restoration to the neck, heavy dendrite deposits throughout. 11 1/2" x 7 1/2". **$1,080**

Nayarit Chinesco Painted Female Figure, Mexico: Burnished ceramic idol kneeling with one arm to her abdomen, the other under her breast, 200 BC-AD 250. Adorned with incised plated hair, a nose ring, painted and negative-resist designs, most notably a red hand on her breast. Head has been re-attached and the knees have been restored. 10 1/2" x 6". **$7,800**

Photo courtesy Rago Arts and Auction Center, Lambertville, N.J.; www.RagoArts.com

Sioux Child's Vest, Plains: Lazy-stitched with polychrome beads in geometric design, on animal hide, early 20th century. Excellent condition. 5 3/4" x 8 1/2". **$570**

Photo courtesy Rago Arts and Auction Center, Lambertville, N.J.; www.RagoArts.com

Monumental Colima Shaman Figural Vessel, Mexico: Burnished terra cotta in classic "Admiral" form with stylized shell necklace, traditional top knot, horn hat and spout, 200 BC-AD 250. The shaman tomb guardian protected the deceased in the afterlife. Rare Pre-Columbian indigenous repair evident by two holes to the front and back of the neck, through which sinew or twine would have been wound; such restoration shows particular care for the piece, or for the deceased; heavy dendrite deposits throughout. 16 1/2" x 9". **$10,200**

Nayarit Bichrome Painted Male Warrior, Mexico: Classic image shown with helmet and staff regalia, painted with linear and spot designs, 200 BC-AD 250. Restoration to arm and tip of staff; heavy dendrite deposits throughout. 6 3/4" x 3 1/2". **$360**

Jalisco Mother And Child, Mexico: Early figural ceramic rattle depicting a nursing mother, with remnants of a negative-resist design, adorned with arm bands, nose ring, and necklaces suggesting a person of status, 200 BC-AD 200. Re-assembled from several pieces, appears to be all original. 11" x 7". **$720**

Veracruz Soriente Head Fragment, Mexico: Terra cotta sculpture with serene smiling face related to the Pulque cult, accented with a rare monkey glyph on the headdress, AD 300-600. Stable condition, minor chipping to nose and decay around neck break. Custom metal display stand. 5" x 5". **$840**

Large Mixtec Carved Stone Female Idol, Mexico: Volcanic stone figure wearing a headdress, shown with hand to breast, archaic face with heart-shaped brow and ear spools, AD 800-1500. Some weathering and chipping to finial. In custom display stand. 24 3/4" x 8 1/4". **$5,100**

Veracruz Stone Hacha, Mexico: Unusual carved volcanic stone image of sacrificial victim relating to the Mesoamerican ball game, featuring a large nose ring and ornate head gear, AD 550-800. Intact with some original pigment remaining. On custom display stand. 8 1/4" x 4". **$3,360**

Veracruz Stone Head, Mexico: Unusually expressive carved head of elongated form, possibily depicting a man with deformity, AD 550-800. Overall good condition. Custom metal display stand. 4 1/2" x 4 1/2". **$660**

Nicoya Jaguar Metate, Atlantic Watershed Culture, Costa Rica: Carved volcanic stone ceremonial implement in feline form, AD 1000-1500. Overall good condition, tail reattached. 4 1/2" x 11" x 5". **$960**

Usulutan Ceramic Flying Shaman, Costa Rica: Burnished terra cotta figural vessel in full reclining posture, holding an owl amphora, AD 300-500. Often referred to as "swimmers", these traditional forms are believed to represent shamans in ritual trance, in flight to the heavens with offerings for the gods. This particular example features an owl vase, relating to the underworld spirits and the night. Restoration to some areas, two well-worn holes suggest loss of original finials long ago. 7 1/4" x 14 1/2". **$1,800**

Quimbaya Terra Cotta Idol, Columbia: Figurine with negative-resist designs and highly stylized facial features, AD 300-1500. Heavy dentrite deposits and small areas of loss, overall intact with no restoration. Custom-mounted to wood base. 8 1/2" x 6 1/2". **$2,400**

Photo courtesy Rago Arts and Auction Center, Lambertville, N.J.; www.RagoArts.com

Nicoya Jaguar Mace Head, Atlantic Watershed Culture, Costa Rica: Carved dense green stone featuring the transformation of a shaman into a jaguar, AD 1000-1500. Good condition. Mounted on custom metal stand. Total: 3" x 2 1/4". **$960**

Marajo Terra Cotta Vessel, Brazil: Spherical black and white vessel painted with stylized animal form, AD 800-1400. Intact condition with light erosion. 6" x 5 3/4". ..**$900**

Chancay Mummy Mask, Peru: Carved wooden mask with red mineral pigment, accented with woven cotton textile and remains of human hair, AD 1200-1450. Fair condition, with remains of textile imprints on mask, eyes retouched. On display stand. 22 1/2" x 11". **$600**

Inca Terra Cotta Frog Vessel, Peru: Highly stylized zoomorphic vessel with spiraling eyes suggesting a hallucinogenic trance, accented with snake motifs, AD 1450-1550. Overall intact condition with no restoration. 8 1/2" x 6 3/4". **$1,200**

Moche Phase I Stirrup Vessel, Peru: Traditional form vessel painted in a checkerboard pattern in terra cotta on cream slip ground, with a burnished spout, AD 100-300. Completely intact with no restoration, heavy dentrite deposits and root marks present, professionally cleaned and conserved. 8" x 5 1/4". **$900**

Moche Corn God Vessel, Peru: Mold-made ceramic with deity faces and embossed corn motif with cream slip decoration, AD 500-750. Possible restoration to spout and shallow fracture on back of form. 9" x 6". **$300**

Tiwanaku (Tiahuanaco) Ceramic Vessel, Bolivia: Terra cotta jug with painted geometric designs resembling period textiles, AD 300-900. Intact condition with possible restoration to handle. 6 1/2" x 8". **$660**

Taino Ritual Vessel, Caribbean: Carved wood anthropomorphic receptacle with stylized ancestor and traditional geometric motifs, AD 1200-1500. Crystallized residue on interior evidences ceremonial use. 3" x 6 1/2". **$6,000**

Other World Cultures

Bamana Medicine Container, Mali: Carved figural vessel, its lid featuring a classic female ancestor with elaborate headdress and elongated facial features, early 20th century. The incised vessel sits on a star-shaped base. Good condition with slight erosion and signs of ritual use. 23" x 6". ..**$1,800**

Senufo Kpelie Janus Mask, Ivory Coast: Carved wood with elaborate facial regalia and stylized finial, early to mid-20th century. Images of duality among the tribes of this region often refer to the link between the world of the living and the spirit realm, the moral portrayed is that humans are inextricably connected to the souls of their forebears. Overall good condition. Mounted on custom display stand. 12" x 6 1/2". **$1,920**

Baule Rifle Stock Comb, Ivory Coast: Elegant carved with stylized handle and simple incised linear designs, early 20th century. Fine honey-colored patina, well-worn, loss to three tines. On custom display stand. 10 1/2" x 2 1/2". **$360**

Baule Gong With Carved Handle, Ivory Coast: Hand-forged iron gong with attached wooden handle possibly carved as a cupped hand, early to mid-20th century. A classic percussion instrument used in ceremony and dance. Well-worn handle suggests years of use, some rust and pitting to gong, overall good condition, clear tone. 22 1/4" x 5 1/4". **$360**

Akan Colonial Figural Comb, Ghana: Carved wood sculptural comb topped by a colonialist wearing coat and

Photo courtesy Rago Arts and Auction Center, Lambertville, N.J.; www.RagoArts.com

Dan Zakpai Runner Mask, Ivory Coast: Carved wood accented with animal teeth and remains of red textile, early to mid-20th century. Traditionally used in annual races. Well-worn interior showing obvious use. Mounted on custom metal base. 9" x 6". **$2,280**

hat, linear pattern to base, early to mid-20th century. A rare and superior example, featuring a statuette almost as tall as its tines. Mint condition with lustrous patina. On custom display stand. 6 3/4" x 2". **$1,680**

Ashanti Figural Comb, Ghana: Elegant carved wood example featuring an akuaba fertility doll with traditional facial features accented with kaolin clay, ringed neck with adornment, linear designs to reverse, early 20th century. Excellent condition with signs of use. On custom lucite display stand. 10 1/2" x 2 1/2". **$720**

Kwahu Akan Terra Cotta Memorial Head, Ghana: Ceramic human effigy with abstract and enlarged head on ringed neck, late 19th-early 20th century. Fair condition, some chips around top edge, otherwise intact and stable, permanent display post inserted in base. Mounted on wood block. 7 1/2" x 5 1/8". **$660**

Ashanti Queen Mother Memorial Idol, Ghana: Carved wooden shrine idol adorned with various textiles and strings of glass beads, early 20th century. Complete with infant Akua'ba on her back(daughter of Akua). Intact condition, heavy erosion to bottom of original base, signs of ritual use. Mounted on custom metal display stand. 19" x 5". ...**$1,140**

Fante Female Shrine Idol, Ghana: Well-handled honey-colored wooden figure accented with red glass beads, mid-20th century. Good condition with losses to feet. Custom-mounted on metal base. 13 1/4" x 3". **$300**

Dan Passport Mask, Ivory Coast: Elegant and classic example, with excised geometric design around the eyes accented with kaolin, early 20th century. Excellent condition with deep, well-handled patina. On custom display stand. 6" x 3 1/2". **$1,680**

Mende Sowei Mask, Sierra Leone: Carved wooden helmet with stylized coiffure featuring female genetalia finial, early

Photo courtesy Rago Arts and Auction Center, Lambertville, N.J.; www.RagoArts.com

Large Bedu Plank Mask, Togo: Carved wood with abstracted face and stylized bush cow horns, with paint and kaolin on surface, early to mid-20th century. Well-handled surface consistent with field use. 52" x 21 1/2".
$1,140

20th century. Worn exclusively by the women of the Sande society during initiation ceremonies. Good condition with signs of obvious use. 13 3/4" x 8". **$360**

Vai or Gola Helmet Mask, Liberia: Carved wood Borwu (Long-Neck) accented with aluminum elements, early 20th century. Representing female spirit, these masks were used in dance masquerades. Fair condition, heavy use and tribal repairs. 27 1/4" x 9". **$900**

Three Mossi Bigga Dolls, Burkina Faso: Three carved wood dolls, early 20th century. These are used in teaching young girls to care for children, and carried by them until they have children of their own. Overall good condition, signs of handling and use. All mounted on bases. Tallest 15". .... **$420 all**

Jimini Heddle Pulley, Ivory Coast: Uncommon example of a weaving loom implement decorated with a stylized antelope head and incised linear design, early to mid-20th century. Overall good condition, well-handled, area around pulley shows heavy wear. Mounted on custom display stand. 6 1/2" x 2 1/2". **$330**

Two Lobi Bateba Shrine Figures, Burkina Faso: Two carved wood slender female idols, the smaller having unusual treatment of base, early 20th century. Overall good condition with smooth patinas showing years of use. Mounted on custom display stands. 7 1/2" and 5 1/2". .... **$300 both**

Dogon Toguna House Post, Mali: Carved architectural element with stylized female breasts, early 20th century. Used exclusively for men's meeting houses. Obvious erosion to base, wood strong and stable. Mounted on custom metal base. 55" x 17 3/4". **$1,560**

Dogon Sirige Mask, Mali: Classic carved wood mask with superstructure painted in various designs, mid-20th century. Meaning "storied house," the name refers to the family house, and by extension, the lineage of the human family. A dancer would swing the giant superstructure in a circular motion, representing the perceived revolution of the sun around the earth. Fair condition with obvious signs of use. 10' 2 1/2" x 8". **$1,200**

Dagara Phallic Shrine Fetish, Burkina Faso: Tall carved figural ritual object with male and female attributes, early to mid-20th century. Obvious weathering and minor stress fractures, intact and stable. Mounted on custom metal display stand. 26" x 12". **$840**

Nupe Granary Door, Nigeria: Carved wooden panel with geometric designs and spiral motifs. (Provenance: Private collection, New York) Well-worn surface, otherwise intact. Custom metal display stand. 43" x 15". **$420**

Baga Parade Staff, Guinea: Carved wooden female figure shown riding a fish, adorned with a fish finial, mid-20th century. Wear consistent with use, one rattan-wrap tribal repair to fishtail, minor stress fractures throughout. Custom mounted on wood base. 27" x 20". **$1,920**

Chiwara Antelope Headdress, Mali: Carved horizontal wooden finial of crouching animal, its head attached with original leather straps, mid-20th century. Translating to "heart of a lion," chiwara were typically used in agricultural dances honoring hard-working farmers. Excellent condition with signs of use. 11" x 28". **$1,200**

Mossi Terra Cotta Vessel, Burkina Faso: With applied anthropomorphic design under a burnished surface, mid-20th century. Overall good condition, signs of use. 18 1/2" x 17". **$1,080**

Dogon Terra Cotta Vessel, Mali: Highly decorated with incised designs and three spouts around shoulder, mid- to late 20th century. Overall good condition, some minor chipping. 23" x 15". **$360**

Yoruba Ibeji Twin Figures, Nigeria: Carved honey-colored wood male and female shrine objects with elaborate coiffure, classic facial features, adorned with several strands of glass beads, early 20th century. Complete with cowrie shell double garb. Traditionally carved after the death of a twin, these were meant to house the spirit of the deceased, and ritually fed for the remaining lifetime of its owner. The Yoruba have the highest twin birth rate in the world, leading to the creation of a twin cult. Overall good condition with minor stress fractures and signs of use. With robe: 9" x 12". **$480**

Yoruba Osanyin Ritual Staff, Nigeria: Wrought-iron post topped with an elegant avian finial and surrounded with a ring of smaller stylized birds, early to mid-20th century. Used in healing ceremonies. Some rust, overall good condition. On custom metal stand. 30" x 11". **$1,320**

Yoruba Beaded Diviner's Bag, Nigeria: Textile bag adorned with the face of Eshu, various glass beads and large natural seeds, on a long neck strap, early 20th century. Worn during ritual divination as part of the priest's regalia. Overall fair condition with signs of ritual use, mounted on a display board. 35" x 5". **$360**

Yoruba Beaded Coronet, Nigeria: Four-cornered hat with floral designs and avian finial, accented with a band of green and white bias design, early 20th century. Fair condition with signs of heavy use, possible losses to bottom edge. Mounted on custom metal display stand. 13 1/2" x 13 1/2". **$360**

Bini Horned Face Mask, Nigeria: Ekpo society mask carved from a single piece of wood, wearing a serene expression, accented with indigo and white kaolin pigments, early 20th century. Reputed to cleanse the society of disease and protect the village from witchcraft. Overall good condition with signs of handling and use. 11" x 5 3/4". **$960**

Ogoni Articulated Mask, Nigeria: Carved wood with raised scarification, stylized coiffure, attached lower jaw supported with wrapped rattan, painted black and accented with kaolin clay, early to mid-20th century. Overall fair condition with signs of use. On custom display stand. 8 1/2" x 5 1/2". **$480**

Ogoni Antelope Mask, Nigeria: Carved wood accented with red and black paint, and kaolin clay, early to mid-20th century. Well worn condition, several broken attachement holes consistent with years of field use. Mounted on custom display stand. 12 1/2" x 6". **$600**

Ogoni Articulated Mask, Nigeria: Carved wood mask featuring an avian beak, its lower jaw attached with wrapped rattan which, when open, reveals a full set of spindled teeth, the face painted black and red, and accented with kaolin clay, early to mid-20th century. Complete with raised scarification and stylized coiffure. Overall good condition with signs of use. On custom display stand. 8 1/4" x 5". **$600**

Tiv Imborivungu Cult Fetish, Nigeria: Ritual staff with carved wood male head featuring inlaid glass eyes, scarification of tears, and human hair woven in braids, over a femur bone wrapped with beads, early 20th century. The traditional use of these objects from the only documented cannibal cult in Africa relates to the legend of a Tiv ancestor known as Poor. According to local legend, his original thigh bone was removed so that his memory would be perpetuated. Over time, the original artifact was lost, and was substituted with relics (Imborivungu). Fair condition with some loss to bead work and light decay to hair. Mounted on custom metal display stand. 7" x 2 3/4". **$2,400**

Ibibio Female Marionette, Nigeria: Carved wooden figurine with articulated arms, painted designs, accented with kaolin clay, early to mid-20th century. Fair condition with losses to feet, nose, and hair. 24" x 8". **$480**

Bini Polychrome Mask, Nigeria: Carved wooden mask with stylized coiffure and collar, painted with white and green geometric pattern on a bold burnt-orange ground, early to mid-20th century. Fair condition, loss to collar, obvious handling and wear. Mounted on a custom display stand. 10 1/2" x 6". **$360**

Ibibio Dance Mask, Nigeria: Carved wooden abstract male face with brilliant yellow natural pigment, traditional scarification and tribal repair, early 20th century. Fair condition with obvious signs of use. On custom display stand. 10 1/2" x 6". **$360**

Photo courtesy Rago Arts and Auction Center, Lambertville, N.J.; www.RagoArts.com

Mumuye Horizontal Mask, Nigeria: Abstract form accented with red clay, featuring oversized eyes and flat snout, early 20th century. Well-weathered with signs of heavy use. Mounted on custom display stand. 6" x 7" x 14 1/2". **$4,800**

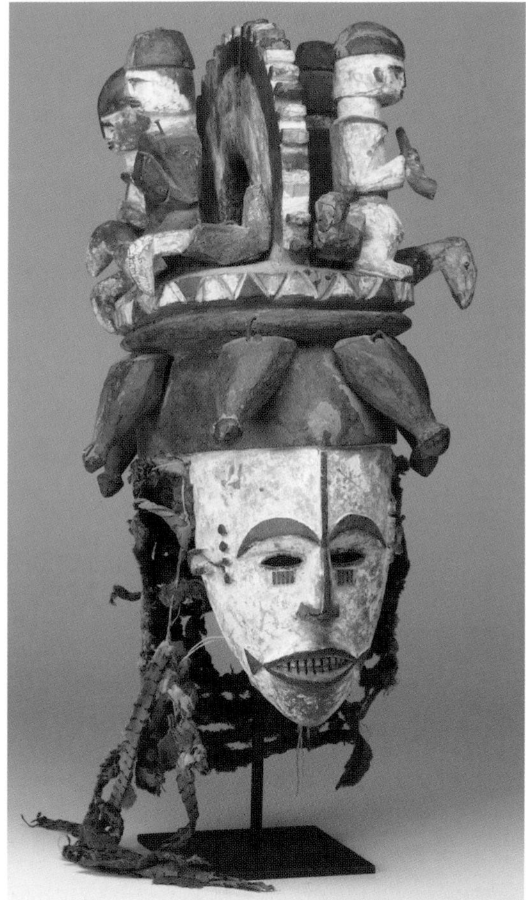

Photo courtesy Rago Arts and Auction Center, Lambertville, N.J.; www.RagoArts.com

Ibo Helmet Mask, Nigeria: Carved wood with elaborate superstructure featuring ancestors and avian images, early to mid-20th century. With raised scarification on kaolin-covered face and remnants of traditional costume, these represent the spirit of a young deceased maiden, thought of as a protective entity. Fair condition with losses to finial and figures. Mounted on metal display stand. Without costume: 22" x 14". **$1,800**

Ijebu Yoruba Water Spirit Mask, Nigeria: Carved wood fantastical mask with ornate spiral finials, adorned with avian images and archaic human face, mid-20th century. The mirror fragment suggests the reflection of water, domain of the water spirit. Fair condition with several repairs to the finial, and well-weathered surface. 40" x 10 1/2". **$600**

Bamoun Kola Nut Offering Bowl, Cameroon: Highly stylized zoomorphic form, with incised geometric designs, and deeply carved bowl, late 19th-early 20th century. Signs of heavy use, overall intact, with light chipping. 10" x 11 1/2". **$360**

Mboum Headdress, Cameroon: Carved wooden plank mask with stylized cowrie shell images, accented with kaolin and other natural pigments, and adorned with kola nuts, late 19th century. Overall good condition, some minor losses to top of finial. Mounted on custom wood and metal display stand. 34 1/2" x 7". **$1,800**

Ibo Parade Bust, Nigeria: Carved wood ancestor, his fierce features including stylized tattoos and ritual scars, mid-20th century. Fair condition, loss to rear top finial and base. 34" x 12". **$1,200**

Mbundu Mask, Angola: Carved wood with incised linear and geometric design, classic coffee bean eyes, and well-defined cheeks, early to mid-20th century. Such masks are worn during the initiation of young men into adulthood. Fair condition with obvious weathering and minor areas of loss, some restoration to stress fractures. 15 1/2" x 11 1/2". **$1,560**

Bembe Female Mukuya Fetish, Democratic Republic Of The Congo: Shown offering a small bird, with classic body scarification and features, her eyes inlaid with ivory, early 20th century. Traditionally thought of as a household protective statue. Overall glossy, well-handled surface; both arms re-attached, loss to part of one arm and both feet. Mounted on custom metal base. 6" x 2 1/2". **$2,280**

Punu Maiden Spirit Mask, Gabon: Classic female face with incised coiffure, accented with red pigment on forehead band, and several layers of kaolin clay, early 20th century. Fair condition, some weathering to one side and signs of handling. Mounted on custom metal display stand. 11 1/2" x 6". **$2,760**

Luba Janus Comb, Democratic Republic Of The Congo: Carved wood with two archaic ancestor heads above incised geometric design, late 19th-early 20th century. Overall good condition with lustrous patina. On custom display stand. 6 1/2" x 3". **$1,920**

Songye Kifwebe Society Mask, Zaire: Carved wood with incised linear designs and tall central crest designating a male mask, painted in bold black and white kaolin pigments, mid-20th century. Attached raffia grass regalia includes sleeves for the wearer. Fair condition with signs of field use. 33" x 12". **$1,020**

Songye Kifwebe Society Mask, Zaire: Boldly carved example with precise linear design, raised finial, protruding four-sided mouth, complete with nose hairs, early to mid-20th century. Very well worn interior, light staining to kaolin, small chip to eye, all consistent with field use. 18" x 7 1/2". **$480**

Kuba Ceremonial Dance Sword, Democratic Republic Of The Congo: Classic painted prestige object incised with design on stylized blade, white and red earthen pigments, early 20th century. Includes original wooden scabbard with woven rattan supports. Custom-mounted on display stand. 25" x 9". **$480**

Fang Figural Comb, Gabon: Small carved wooden comb with ancestral image carved in relief and some linear designs, early 20th century. Excellent condition with well-handled patina. On custom display stand. 6" x 1". **$1,680**

Pende Figural Comb, Democratic Republic Of The Congo: Carved female ancestor adorning hair implement with geometric designs accented in kaolin, early 20th century. Excellent condition with well-handled patina. On custom display stand. 8" x 2". **$1,440**

Yaka Figural Comb, Democratic Republic Of The Congo: Carved wood sculptural comb with classic ancestor face with up-turned nose and large flared ears, adorned with a stylized cap and linear design, early 20th century. Excellent condition with signs of use and wear. On custom display stand. 5 1/2" x 1". **$540**

Luena Mask, Angola: Carved wood with various layers of paint and natural pigment, adorned with a ring of feathers, early 20th century. Used as a dance mask, likely representing the ideal woman. Fair condition with obvious field use. On custom display stand. Total: 9" x 6 1/2". **$480**

Pende Munyangi Mask, Zaire: Carved wood Munyangi with strong geometric features, early to mid-20th century. Used in performances associated with youthful energy. Fair condition, some loss to back, showing heavy use. Custom mounted. On base: 13 1/2" x 5 1/2". **$480**

Suku Helmet Mask, Zaire: Carved wooden mask with serene expression, topped by a whimsical animal finial, accented with kaolin clay and natural blue pigment, glass-bead earrings, and grass collar, early to mid-20th century. Stress fracture on forehead, minor chipping, signs of use. 14 1/2" x 11" x 12". **$1,920**

Lega Bwami Society Maskette, Zaire: Carved wood bearing delicate features, the eyes highlighted with kaolin and exposed wood with fine patina, early to mid-20th century. Maskettes were typically worn as armband regalia, or hung around the village as clan totems. Overall good condition with signs of use. Includes a custom metal display stand. 7 3/4" x 3 3/4". **$1,560**

Lwalwa Mask, Democratic Republic Of The Congo: Highly stylized concave human face with large open eyes, and diminutive ears and mouth, the head with remnants of kaolin, mid-20th century. Overall good condition with well-handled surface, minor scrapes, shallow stress fracture on chin. 13" x 9". **$900**

Tabwa Terra Cotta Vessel, Zaire: Shaped as a vessel over a brazier on four feet, decorated with roped medallions, one with an elegant European face, with painted copper details, early to mid- 20th century. Overall good condition, some restoration to rim, one foot re-attached. 15" x 13". **$1,080**

Terra Cotta Vessel, Rwanda: With raised waves accented in red and white pigment, mid-20th century. Overall good condition, with a few minor flecks to high points, consistent with use. 15" x 10 1/2". **$1,560**

Large Shona Terra Cotta Beer Vessel, Zimbabwe: Spherical pot accented with orange and black paint, mid-20th century. Typically used to store millet beer. Some restoration to rim, otherwise intact with signs of use. 14" x 17". **$1,320**

Chewa Animal Mask, Malawi: Carved wood zoomorphic mask with stylized facial features, deep scarification, two bands of glass beads, and evidence of former animal skin regalia, early 20th century. Fair condition with loss to two cowrie shell teeth, signs of heavy ritual use. On custom display stand. 11" x 6 1/2". **$660**

Turkana Male and Female Dolls, Tanzania: Mated pair of carved wood dolls with classic facial features, the female adorned with glass beads and a leather skirt, early 20th century. Overall good condition, chip to back of female's arm. On custom display stands. 16" and 15". .... **$240 pair**

East African Figural Staff: Carved wood with elegant female image, minial incised design and stylized coiffure, early to mid 20th century. Overall good condition with stable stress fractures, custom metal display stand. 35". **$1,200**

Painted Hide Shield, Nigeria: Geometric red and white designs with animal motifs. Wear consistent with use. 23" dia. **$360**

Rapa Nui Moai Kava Kava, Easter Island: Carved wood male ancestor figure, eyes accented with shell and obsidian, mid-19th century. Deified ancestral beings, bearers of knowledge, and dispensers of wisdom, the Kava Kava were worn around the neck of the men who took part in ritual dances. Overall good condition. 24 3/4" x 4 1/2". **$7,800**

Photo courtesy Rago Arts and Auction Center, Lambertville, N.J.; www.RagoArts.com

Feather Currency Roll, Santa Cruz, Solomon Islands: Traditional band of wound plant fiber adorned with Myzomela cardinal feathers and strands of shell beads, attached to two bark frames, mid-19th century. Overall good condition, some wear to feathers commensurate with age and use. On custom display stand. Total: 28 1/2" x 29 1/2". **$3,360**

Ceremonial Chalice, Trobriand Islands: Highly stylized carved wooden vessel with incised geometric designs accented with kaolin clay, late 19th - early 20th century. Overall good and stable condition, well handled patina with signs of use and two stress fractures. 15" x 5 1/2". **$480**

Wooden Paddle, Austral Island: Elaborately carved with stylized faces and precise geometric design, 19th century. (A very refined example, of a quality seldom found.) Overall excellent condition. On custom stand. Remains of a pre-WWI label. 40" x 6". **$4,200**

Grade Society Fern Figures, Vanuatu: Carved tree fungus with original tree-trunk still evident, early 20th century. Fair condition with heavy erosion to wood, otherwise stable. Male: 80" x 16" x 18", female: 75" x 16" x 17". .... **$3,360 pair**

Marionette Figure, S. Malekula, Vanuatu: Painted tree fern and wood Temes Nevinbur figure, accented with boar's tusks and feathers, early 20th century. Fair condition with losses to natural materials, overall stable. On custom mount. 42 1/2" x 18 1/2". **$1,020**

Baining Fire Dance Mask, New Britain, Papua New Guinea: Light fig tree bark and rattan-frame mask accented with red and black natural pigments, mid-20th century. Excellent overall condition, a few minor holes. On custom display stand. 30 1/2" x 12". **$840**

Root Club, Gilbert Island, Micronesia: Naturally formed spiral staff with woven cane handle, reddish patina of unknown origin, 19th century. Good condition, minor loss to wrap. Mounted on custom metal display. 28" x 4 1/4". **$1,920**

Limestone Memorial Sculpture, Sumba Island, Indonesia: Carved anthropomorphic figure, late 19th - early 20th century. Used locally as markers for sacred sites. Fair condition, erosion consistent with tribal use. Mounted on custom metal stand. 21 1/2" x 7". **$1,560**

Kantu Dayak Hampatong, Borneo: Carved wooden female Padi with stylized top knot and long slender spike carved from a single piece of wood, early 20th century. Used as a protective fetish in fields and granary storage. Fair condition with some erosion. On custom display stand. 18 1/2" x 2". **$480**

Dayak Ancestor Hampatong, Borneo: Carved wood female figure of elongated neck and form, with archaic features, 19th century. Traditionally used as protective idols for villages and ceremonial sites. Heavily eroded surface suggesting generations of use. Mounted on custom metal display stand. 21 1/2" x 3 1/2". **$420**

Kayan/Kenyah Dayak Hudoq Mask, Borneo: Classic mask with attached ears and horn-like appendages, bone fangs, and rattan basketry helmet, eyes accented with small mirrors, early to mid-20th century. Typically used in agricultural dances, the painted red, black, and white designs mimic rainforest vines. Fair condition with repairs to ears, horn appendages reglued. Mounted on custom display stand. 20" x 17". **$1,020**

Batak Keris Sword, Sumatra, Indonesia: Iron sword of stylized form topped by an elegant silver-inlaid wood handle, late 19th century. Fits in a carved wooden sheath with scrolled finial. Excellent original condition, slight pitting to blade. Total: 21 3/4". **$480**

Dayak Modang Head-Hunter Mandau Sword, Borneo: Classic iron sword with deer antler handle carved with a stylized head and incised design, 19th century. The unusually decorative blade features an intricately forged edge and is inlaid with copper stars and brass roundels. Fits in a highly ornate carved wooden sheath featuring the dragon Aso among vines. Complete with attached Piso Raout featuring a finely carved antler, missing its small blade. Minor wear to bottom of scabbard, excellent condition. Total: 24". **$840**

Photo courtesy Rago Arts and Auction Center, Lambertville, N.J.; www.RagoArts.com

Dayak Bronze Gong Handle, Borneo/Indonesia: Stylized Aso dragon, early 20th century. Excellent condition. Hanging from custom mount. Handle: 4 3/4" x 3 1/2".
$960

Keris Dagger, Sumatra, Indonesia: Fine traditional weapon with ivory handle carved with an abstract form of Garuda, over an iron blade in the Damascus technique, early 20th century. Fits in its original burlwood sheath with repousse metal collar. The confluences of Islam and Hinduism are shown in the depiction of the god Garuda, treated here in its simplest of forms. Small chip and restoration to handle, missing a collar to sheath. Total: 20 1/2" x 6". **$540**

Dragon-Head Sword, Sumatra, Indonesia: Klewang with carved horn handle banded in ivory, above an iron blade chiseled with Islamic script, late 19th century. Complete with contemporary rosewood scabbard. Excellent condition, minor pitting to blade. Sword: 26". **$780**

Dayak Shield, Borneo: Carved wooden shield painted with unusual stylized eyes and mouth, along with traditional tribal motifs in black, ochre and red pigments, two Aso dragons on the reverse, accented with woven rattan bands, early 20th century. Fair condition with minor areas of loss and one fracture. 50" x 14". **$1,920**

Dayak Mualang Iban Altarpiece, Borneo: Carved dark wood figure of ancestor rising from aristocratic burial urn, early 20th century. Overall good condition. 16". **$600**

Tangkhul Naga Architectural Panel, India: Carved wooden facade from a morung (men's meeting house) featuring three archaic mask faces, the central image with feathered headdress, early 20th century. Fair condition with obvious weathering. 46" x 22". **$1,200**

Gunwinggu Bark Painting, Oenpelli, Australia: Traditional painting by George D. Jayngurrnga depicting Mimi spirits, mid-20th century. Good condition. 53 1/2" x 21". **$1,020**

Waksuk Female Idol, Papua New Guinea: Carved wood elongated figure with abstract facial features and incised scarification, red pigment accenting the face, mid-20th century. Good condition with signs of use, custom metal display stand. 54". **$3,120**

Canoe Prow Ornament, Trobriand Islands: Carved wooden finial with classic geometric designs, early 20th century. Intact with signs of use. 19" x 9". **$480**

Skull Rack, Papua New Guinea: Carved wood incised with tribal motifs, accented with two avian images and three trophy heads, with cowrie shell eyes, pierced for hanging, early to mid-20th century. Fair condition with some repairs to finials. 9 1/2" x 43 1/2". **$480**

Hook Mask, Hunstein Mountain, Papua New Guinea: Yam-shaped carved wood with classic curved finials, early to mid-20th century. Kept in the men's cult houses, the hooks or curved beaks relate to the sacred hornbill bird. Overall good condition, one minor chip. 24" x 4 3/8". **$600**

Dani Jade Adze, Papua New Guinea: Braided plant fiber wrap and cassowary bird feathers around a fine speckled jade blade, early 20th century. Most likely used in the preparation of sago, a local food staple. Fair condition with signs of heavy use. On custom display stand. 23" x 12". **$1,320**

Karawari Hook Figure, Papua New Guinea: Carved wooden Yipwon, mid-20th century. Charm used to promote successful hunting. Fair condition with minor loss and short break. On painted wooden base. 23" x 3". **$540**

Basket Hook, Sepik River, Papua New Guinea: Carved wood in figural form, mid-20th century. 22" x 6 1/2". **$420**

Large Abelam Male Figure, Papua New Guinea: Ancestor carved from a single piece of wood, likely an architectural element from a men's meeting house, with headdress and carved arm bands, geometric designs painted in earthen red, yellow, black and white pigment, early to mid-20th century. Fair with obvious erosion, reattached element. 55" x 10". **$600**

Asmat Canoe Prow, Papua New Guinea: Carved openwork finial featuring two ancestors, adorned with cassowary bird feathers and shells, accented in orange and white kaolin clay, mid-20th century. Overall good condition, loss to small piece on edge. 43" x 10". **$780**

Bena Bena Fofona Breast Plate, Eastern Islands, Papua New Guinea: Woven grass adornment accented with various sea shells including two large cowrie shell finials, dyed with natural red and blue pigments with attached neck strap, early to mid-20th century. Overall good condition. 13 1/2" x 13 1/2". **$240**

Conch-Shell Trumpet With Carving, Hawaii: Classic shell instrument with unusual fish hook emblem carved on top, possibly an early signature, 19th century. Well-handled and smooth example, showing much use. 9" x 6 1/2". **$1,200**

Palm Leaf Fan, Hawaii: Classic form in traditional Lauhala weave, late 19th century. In remarkable state of preservation. Professionally conserved in museum wall mounting. Total: 28" x 21 3/4". **$900**

Lava Whetstone, Hawaii: Rare utilitarian object, showing generations of use as a adze stone sharpener, 18th-19th century. Overall good condition with signs of use. 3 3/4" x 16" x 7". **$960**

Maori Raptor Claw Fish Hook, New Zealand: Unusual natural avian claw implement, mid- to late 19th century. Used by native fishermen before the introduction of European fish hooks. Overall fair condition with signs of use. On custom display stand. 3" x 2 1/2". **$240**

Photo courtesy Rago Arts and Auction Center, Lambertville, N.J.; www.RagoArts.com

Dayak Bidayuh Clan Mask, Borneo: Carved wood face of a shaman, early 20th century. Used in ritual dances. (Seldom comes to market). Excellent condition with signs of use. On custom display stand. 11" x 7 1/2". **$1,200**

VIETNAM WAR COLLECTIBLES

The Vietnam War is a unique part of the American experience. Because of the controversy surrounding U.S. involvement in the conflict, it is not surprising that many returning veterans discarded their uniforms and gear, or stowed them away in footlockers in dusty attics or damp basements. New generations are now asking about the Vietnam War and the objects associated with it.

The values given are for new or excellent-condition, unissued items in most instances. Items known to have been used in Vietnam, with documented provenance, command premium prices, but that provenance is essential.

For more information, consult *Warman's Vietnam War Collectibles* by David Doyle, 2008.

Quartermaster Corps

The U.S. military is organized so that it is almost self-contained. The objective is to be able to keep an army of thousands of men in the field operating independently of local supplies of any type of material. Much of this material—food, clothing, petroleum products among them—are the responsibility of the Quartermaster Corps.

The Second Continental Congress established the position of Quartermaster General on June 16, 1775. The Quartermaster Corps proper was created by Congress in 1912 by merging the Subsistence, Pay and Quartermaster departments. The responsibility of the Quartermaster Corps in Vietnam was to provide supplies needed by the individual combat soldier in the field.

In this section of the book are grouped the items typically supplied by the Quartermaster Corps for use by Army personnel in the field. Specialized items used by MP, Medics, etc., are found in their respective sections. Within the Quartermaster section of this book, the collectibles are further broken down

Boots

During the Vietnam War a variety of footwear was distributed and worn by U.S. forces. The "classic" footwear was the jungle boot. Development of what was to become the jungle boot began in 1955, with the intent to eliminate a long-standing problem with U.S. combat boots.

At least as far back as WWII, the army had experienced problems with the stitching in conventional boots deteriorating rapidly when worn in tropical environments.

www.vietnamgear.com

Tropical Combat Boots

The earliest of the U.S. jungle boots featured canvas uppers, and two buckle fasteners held the boot to the leg. These fasteners were among the shortcomings of this boot style, as they became entangled in the dense undergrowth found in Southeast Asia. **$150-200**

www.vietnamgear.com

Jungle Boots DMS

The Tropical Combat Boot was a considerable improvement over its predecessors, but was far from ideal. The extremely moist and hot conditions of the tropics brought about stitching failure at the sole. Sometimes these failures could occur after only one month of service. Hence, the Direct Molded Sole (DMS) began to be used. In this manufacturing technique, the sole was vulcanized to the upper rather than stitched to it. The uppers of these boots were made from nylon duck and leather, and laced all the way up, rather than using a combination of laces and buckles. Both the top stay as well as the backstay were leather-reinforced. On the inside arch of each boot were a pair of screened brass drainage eyelets countersunk into the boot. **$125-175**

Headgear

The primary purpose of military headgear is to protect the soldier's head from sun, rain, and of course, from wounds. A secondary function is to provide distinctive identification to friend and foe. Despite regulations, troops in the field have long tended to personalize their headgear by shaping their caps, and making other subtle changes. In Vietnam, such trends reached record highs. Straps on helmets and hats were often festooned with cigarettes, repellents and other lightweight items that needed to be kept dry and easily accessible. Helmet covers and "boonie" hats became canvases for trench art—with decorations drawn or sewn on—often to the dismay of officers.

Such customized items warrant a premium—sometimes substantial—over pristine as-issued items. However, fraudulent items are frequently encountered. Was a helmet cover decorated with a ballpoint pen in the Central Highlands four decades ago, or was it decorated in a basement in Cleveland four days ago? Provenance is critical in establishing that a premium is warranted.

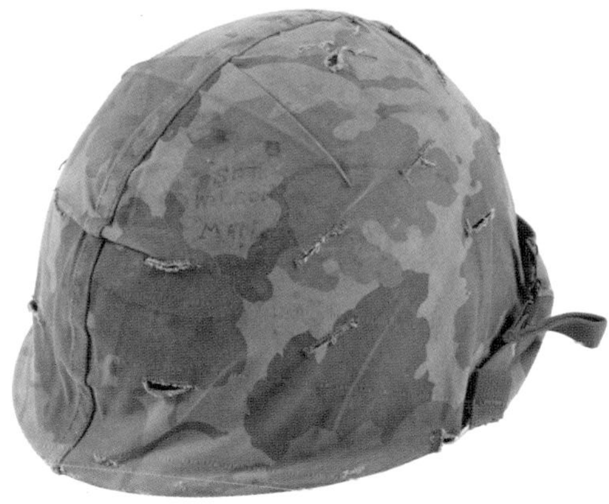

M1 Helmet

The classic M1 Helmet, which dated to WWII, remained the primary headgear for U.S. troops in combat areas during the Vietnam War. However, the Vietnam-era "steel pots" differed from the ones their fathers wore. An aggregate had long been added to the paint applied to the steel cover to decrease luster. During WWII, this aggregate was ground cork; during the Vietnam era it was sand. Through 1967, helmets were painted OD 319; after 1967 the helmets were painted Munsell 10Y 3/3.

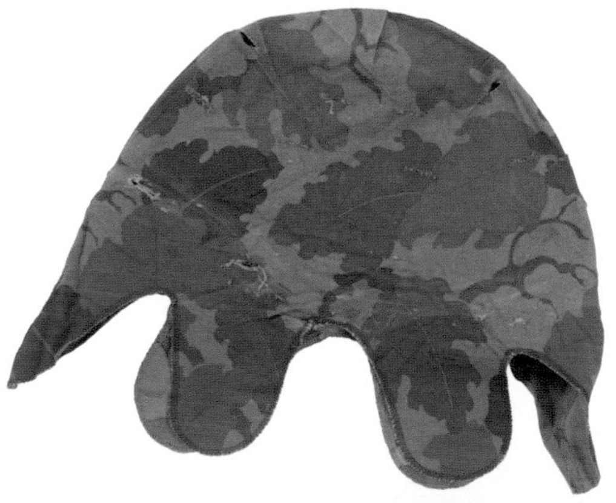

Camouflage covers, which the Marine Corps had begun to use during WWII, became standard with the army as well in Vietnam. The M1 shown here is covered with the Camouflage Helmet Cover, Leaf Pattern, which was introduced in 1959 and was used until 1977. Local foliage was to be inserted in the buttonholes visible in the cover to aid in camouflage.

Helmet, with liner, chinstrap, and band. **$30-70**

Also visible in the photo is the 23-inch circumference camouflage helmet band. Though intended to secure additional concealment items, it most frequently was used to secure personal items such as insect repellent, matches, etc.

Chinstraps were issued with helmets, but were not always used.

Resin-impregnated cotton duck was used to form the M1 Helmet Liner until 1969. However, in 1962, experiments began with laminated nylon liners that offered improved protection with only a moderate increase in weight. The nylon units, known as Combat Helmet Liners, were tested in the field in Vietnam, and by 1964 the new liners were being mass produced. Production of liners with removable suspensions did not begin until late 1972, and production of liners with permanent suspensions did not end until 1974.

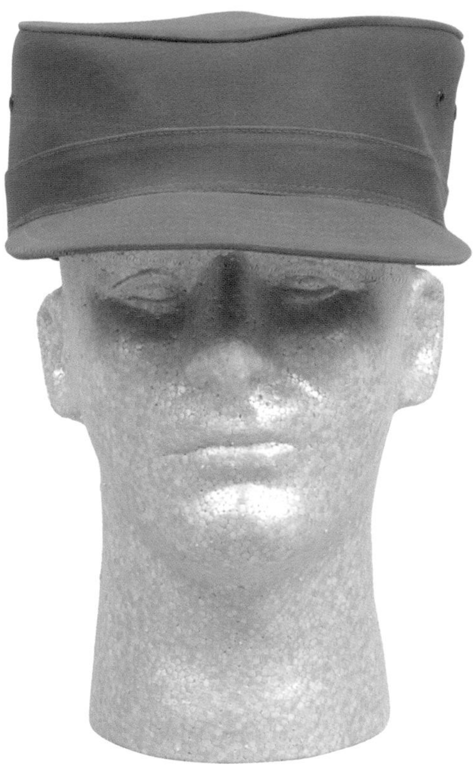

Combat Vehicle Crewman Helmet

This bullet-resistant helmet is made of ballistic nylon. The wide-open frontal area allowed the wearer to use vision and sighting systems installed in armored vehicles without having to remove the helmet. The helmet included microphone and headset. The integral cable plugged directly into the vehicle's communication system. **$30-60**

Ridgeway Cap

In 1953, Army Chief of Staff Matthew Bunker Ridgeway directed that troops have a neat appearance, which often involved inserting cardboard stiffeners in their M1951 cotton field caps. A commercially available substitute with spring reinforcements became popular with the troops, who were willing to spend the few dollars to buy this rather than deal with stiffening their issue M1951. This commercial replacement is commonly known as the "Ridgeway Cap". This hat was used in Vietnam until July 1, 1964. **$20-30**

SPH-4 Flyer's Helmet

The SPH-4 began replacing the earlier APH-5 flying helmet in July 1969. Both acrylic and polycarbonate visors have been used on these helmets; however, the latter were not available until late in 1972. These helmets included an M87 microphone as well as headset, and were used by both helicopter and scout aircraft pilots. **$75-200**

Tropical Hat, aka "Boonie Hat"

Perhaps the quintessential piece of Vietnam war head gear is the Tropical Hat, sometimes referred to as a hot-weather hat or jungle hat—but known universally to GIs and collectors as the boonie hat. Field-testing of this hat began in Vietnam during 1966, with mass production beginning the next year. However, in July 1968, General Creighton Abrams took command of MACV, and he strongly disliked the boonie hat, largely because it lent itself to individualization and because of its non-rigid shape. By late 1971, Abrams and his staff had, for all intents and purposes, eliminated the boonie hat. The boonie hat was most commonly found in olive drab. **$20-30**

Camouflaged Tropical Hat

A limited number of the boonie hats were produced with the ERDL camouflage pattern. These hats were not widely used in Vietnam, in part because they were not produced in this pattern until immediately before Abram's virtual ban on this style of cover. **$40-60**

Bush Hat

Vietnamese-made "bush" hats were popular with advisors from 1962-66. The advent of the tropical "boonie" hat contributed to the demise of the bush hat, which typically had only local authorization. The example shown here has the tiger-stripe camouflage pattern. **$75-125**

Black Beret

Black berets were worn by a host of units in Vietnam. Among these were advisors to ARVN tank and mechanized units, National Police Force, Mobile Advisory Teams, as well as U.S. scout dog and combat tracker teams and certain Ranger units. **$40-60**

Green Beret

Made famous by the Army Special Forces, the Rifle Green Army shade 297 wool beret is arguably the most famous piece of headgear to come out of the war. It is also the only beret officially approved for wear by men in the Army during the Vietnam War. **$250-350**

Shirts/Jackets

This is what is commonly referred to as a second-pattern Jungle Fatigue Coat. It differed from the first-pattern jacket by having hidden rather than exposed buttons, and did not have a gas flap. The official nomenclature is Jungle Fatigue Coat, Man's, Combat, Tropical DSA100-1387. **$30-60**

Maybe 1952-pattern utility jacket

The third pattern of the Jungle Fatigue Coat was made of wind-resistant cotton poplin dyed OG-107. Unlike its predecessors, it did not have shoulder tabs. These were introduced in 1967 and were from the 8405-935-4702 series. **$30-60**

Coat, Bush, Hot-Wet, T-54-4, Experimental

Lightweight green coat with four flapped pockets on front. Dark brown plastic buttons. Cotton belt with gold gilt sliding buckle. Experimental hot-weather bush jacket that was not adopted. ***Too rarely traded to establish accurate value.***

Coat, Man's, Combat, Temperate, Cotton Sateen, OG-107 Jungle Fatigue coat, same weight as cotton fatigues. Has four bellows pockets with hidden buttons, sewn-down epaulets and three belt loops. **$30-60**

Shirt, man's cotton, OG-107, special warfare. Epaulets added in the field. **$15-25**

Insignia and Medals

Some collectors focus on patches and insignia, others entirely on medals and awards of valor. Still others view both to be only "accessories" for the uniforms they collect. Listed here are some of the most popularly examples of both insignia and medals. Because these categories of collectibles are so popular, there are many excellent books – larger than this one – that deal exclusively with each category.

Medals, awards and insignia are often reproduced. It is strongly recommended that novices considering making a significant purchase in these areas seek the advice of one or more experienced collectors, and buy only from a reputable dealer with a clearly stated guarantee and return policy. Because the trading of the Medal of Honor is illegal, it is not listed here.

VIETNAM CAMPAIGN MEDAL

The Vietnam Campaign Medal was awarded to any member of the U.S. or allied military forces who completed at least six months of duty in the Republic of Vietnam between March 1, 1961, and March 28, 1973. It was also awarded to any service member who, while serving outside the geographical limits of South Vietnam, provided direct combat support to the Republic of Vietnam Armed Forces for a period exceeding six months. The Vietnam Campaign Medal is considered a foreign award by the U.S. government. **$10-15**

VIETNAM SERVICE MEDAL

The Vietnam Service Medal was awarded to all members of the armed forces who served in Vietnam and contiguous waters and airspace between July 3, 1965, and March 28, 1973. **$10-15**

DISTINGUISHED SERVICE CROSS

The Distinguished Service Cross (DSC) is the second-highest military decoration of the U.S. Army. It is awarded to a person who, while serving in any capacity with the Army, distinguished himself or herself by extraordinary heroism not justifying the award of a Medal of Honor; while engaged in an action against an enemy of the United States; while engaged in military operations involving conflict with an opposing or foreign force; or while serving with friendly foreign forces engaged in an armed conflict against an opposing armed force in which the United States is not a belligerent party. The act or acts of heroism must have been so notable and have involved risk of life so extraordinary as to set the individual apart from his or her comrades. **$125-175**

Insignia

Virtually every unit in Vietnam had a distinctive insignia or patch, whether authorized or not. Some were plain and utilitarian; others were brightly colored. Shown here are but a few of the hundreds of different insignia to have been worn during the course of the war. For a comprehensive list of army units deployed to Vietnam and their histories, consult Shelby Stanton's *Vietnam Order of Battle.*

MILITARY ASSISTANCE COMMAND, VIETNAM
Military Assistance Command, Vietnam was established Feb. 8, 1962. It was reorganized on May 15, 1964, and departed Vietnam March 29, 1973. **$5-10**

UNITED STATES ARMY, VIETNAM
The United States Army, Vietnam was created July 20, 1965, and disbanded May 15, 1972. **$5-10**

I FIELD FORCE VIETNAM
I Field Force Vietnam was created March 19, 1966, and was absorbed into the Second Regional Assistance Command on April 30, 1971. **$2-8**

4TH INFANTRY DIVISION
The Fourth Infantry Division arrived in Vietnam Sept. 25, 1966 and departed Dec. 7, 1970. **$5-10**

9TH INFANTRY DIVISION
The Ninth Infantry Division arrived in Vietnam on Dec. 16, 1966, and departed Aug. 27, 1969. **$6-12**

25TH INFANTRY DIVISION
The 25th Infantry Division arrived in Vietnam on March 28, 1966, and departed Dec. 8, 1970. **$5-10**

FUTURE OF THE MARKET: WESTERN MEMORABILIA

Rockmount still sets standard for cowboy couture

By Caroline Ashleigh

From the minute I slipped into my miniature cowgirl ensemble and sashayed onto the playground as a little tyke, I felt, instantly, like a larger-than-life character. Such an outfit has the power to transform you: It was a two-piece bright turquoise gabardine riding outfit, accented with gold leather and rhinestones. It came with a hat, split-fringed skirt, holster, play pistol, belt, bandana, boots, and spurs that went jingle, jangle, jingle. When I wore it, I exuded attitude and style. It seemed to create an aura that made all of the other little buckarettes and buckaroos feel like they were in the presence of the newly crowned Queen of Cowgirl Couture.

Caroline Ashleigh

That's when I fell in love with fancy Western clothes. It turned into a life-long love affair.

Fast forward to the summer of 2009 in Denver, an Antiques Roadshow event drew an unexpected surprise, one that stirred up the cowgirl in me. On a hot, sultry, summer evening in late July, I was invited to attend a private party by Steven E. Weil, president of Rockmount Ranch Wear Manufacturing Co. at his three-generation-owned family business, located in a red brick warehouse in the LoDo district of Denver for over 62 years.

It was there that I had the privilege of meeting Steve, the grandson of the legendary "Papa Jack" Weil, maker of iconic western wear worn around the world, who held the title of the oldest living CEO until his death in 2008, at 107 years of age.

Not unlike my own experience wearing Western wear as a little tyke, Steve began modeling Western wear as an infant in fashion shows. His love for vintage Western wear began in high school when he raided his grandfather's closet for shirts from the 1940s. And that's probably when he fell, cowboy-hat-over-heels, for Western wear, which turned into a lifelong love affair. Today, as president of the company, he is responsible for all design lines and operations, and could easily lay claim to the title as the current King of Cowboy Couture.

As Steve points out in his book titled, *Ask Papa Jack*, "We live and learn from stories in a way far more deeply than any other way short of actual experience." In an era when storytelling is becoming a vanishing art, I was mesmerized listening to Steve talk about his family business that started in the West, and how this original regional market would one day span the globe.

I was fascinated to learn that during the Great Depression in 1935, Papa Jack went into the business of Western wear, and the strategy worked, even in the worst of economic times. Rockmount prospered during the 1940s, as the rural West fared better than large urban areas.

Colleen Long of the Associated Press wrote in a syndicated news story appearing in the Los Angeles Times in 2001, "Rockmount Ranch Wear Ropes in Clients by Bucking Retail Trendiness." Rockmount today is still roping in clients and bucking trends in the second-worst economic downturn since the Great Depression.

Rockmount is the quintessential American success story. Papa Jack proudly stated in an interview with CNN in March 2001, at the age of 100, "We take pride in making it in this country. We would like very much to make it all in this country. It's a philosophy of self-preservation in this country, our way of life. If the people in this country earn their money here, and live here, there's a pretty good chance they will buy some of our products."

Steve adds, "Holding on to our roots at Rockmount became our salvation. Now we are virtually the last guys standing." They are not only the last guys standing, but they are continuing to prosper.

Steve reminisces, "Back in the early '80s, I was browsing through a Los Angeles vintage store on Melrose, and found a brown gabardine shirt that was so old at first I didn't recognize it as Rockmount. It dated from the 1940s and was marked $75, which was twice the price of Rockmount shirts then. I told the retailer it was one of the first Western shirts my grandfather had made. Touched, he told me to take the shirt and send him a couple of new ones for it. Excited by the find, I didn't wait until returning home to tell my grandfather. In those pre-cell-phone days, I found a phone booth and called the office. 'WHAT?' Papa exclaimed, 'you traded two perfectly good new shirts for an old one we sold for $3 forty years ago?'" Fast forward to February 2006. Rockmount shirts that were worn in the movie Brokeback Mountain sell for $101,000 on eBay.

Even though I do not fit the celebrity status as some of Rockmount's clients — such as Elvis Presley, Robert Redford, David Bowie, Bob Dylan and Eric Clapton — after visiting Steve's shop in Denver, there was only one thing I could do. Before sliding up to the bar with my fellow appraisers on Antiques Roadshow in Denver, I got decked out in full Western regalia: my fringed black and silver studded cape, sterling silver snaffle-buckled belt, my rhinestone-encrusted spurred stilettos, and my boldly colored Rockmount shirt with smile pockets, embroidered arrows, piping, enamel snaps, and tiered fringe. And just like that, I was transported back to the playground with all my little buckaroo buddies. I'm still in love with fancy cowboy clothes and spurs that go jingle, jangle, jingle.

Steve Weil points out in his book, *Western Shirts – A Classic American Fashion*, there is no consistent standard for pricing vintage clothes. Factors such as demand, condi-

Above, three generations of the Weil family proudly pose in front of the Rockmount Ranch Wear Manufacturing Co. in Denver. From left, Steve, "Papa Jack" and Jack B.

At left is an Art Deco-inspired Rockmount shirt designed by Jack B. Weil in the 1950s. It is highly stylized with chenille embroidery, saddle stitching, special cuff treatment.

Above: Fancy custom red and white parade boots.
$150+

Left: Western shirt designed by Fay Ward Co., cowboy tailors for "The Sundowners," circa 1970.
$300-$400

Below: John Wayne off-white Stetson hat, imprinted "McLintock No.1 — Especially Made for John Wayne".

Elvis Presley studio-stressed Stetson hat imprinted "Charro — Made by Nudies of North California Especially for Elvis Presley."

Gene Autry white Stetson hat imprinted "Made by Stetson for Gene Autry."

tion, rarity, as well as original packaging affect the price. "New/old" is a rarified category highly sought after by collectors. This is the "dead stock" that has escaped the ravages of time. Sometimes it is found in wholesale quantities — forgotten in storage — or it surfaces as a single piece that was put away new and never worn.

The modern-day master tailor who brought mass-media attention and razzle-dazzle to the Western-wear scene was a Russian immigrant by the name of Nuta Kotlyarenko, better known as Nudie Cohn (1902-1984), a.k.a. "Dior of the Sagebrush," and "The Original Rhinestone Cowboy." Cohn influenced the Western-wear industry for nearly 40 years, whipping up costumes for Hank Williams, Hopalong Cassidy, Clayton Moore, Ronald Reagan, Liberace, Elton John, the Rolling Stones and Elvis Presley, among others.

In 1957, he was commissioned to create the most expensive suit he had ever made: a 14k gold lame outfit bejeweled with 10,000 rhinestones. Over the years, Nudie is said to have sold Elvis $100,000 worth of clothes, today worth $400,000-$500,000.

Another immigrant who created a market niche was Nathan Turk from Minsk, Poland. Beginning in the 1930s, movie studios began commissioning Turk to design costumes for Westerns. By the 1940s, Western musicians began frequenting Turk's shop in Van Nuys, Calif. He created the blueprint for most of the successful country bands: a unique ensemble for group leaders to set them apart, with the advertising slogan, "With real western wear from the movies."

The original cost of a Western garment is in direct proportion to the volume produced. Tailor-made shirts by Rodeo Ben and Nudie Cohn were quite expensive and out of the reach of the public when new. These early designs were "one-off" custom makes for celebrities like Roy Rogers and Gene Autry. Later they went to limited production runs but remained much more expensive than production-made garments. By the same token, the more expensive the ready-to-wear garment, the lower the volume in which it was produced. It is not uncommon to find only a single surviving example of the best highly stylized designs.

Generally, today's pricing seems to fall into four ranges:

$300+: extremely fine, rare, ornate shirts.

$100-$300: highly ornate embroideries, pre-1960.

$25-$100: nicely detailed basic shirts in good vintage fabrics, pre-1970.

Less than $25: generic, mass-produced commodity styles, including imports, since 1970s.

Note: Pricing changes along with trends, so these figures have a limited window of accuracy.

Caroline Ashleigh owns Birmingham, Mich.-based Caroline Ashleigh Associates LLC. She is a graduate of New York University in Appraisal Studies in Fine and Decorative Arts and is a board-certified senior member of the Appraisers Association of America. Ashleigh is an internationally known appraiser and regularly appears on the PBS program Antiques Roadshow. Caroline Ashleigh Associates conducts fully catalogued online auctions. Visit www.appraiseyourart.com or www.auctionyourart.com.

Collection of Western ties, circa 1950/1960. **$15-$30 each**

A

B

C

I

J

K

L

M

N

O

P

Q

R

S